BENSON and HEDGES
CRICKET YEAR
ELEVENTH EDITION

Editor's note

The aim of *Benson and Hedges Cricket Year* is that the cricket enthusiast shall be able to read through the happenings in world cricket, from each October until the following September (the end of the English season). Form charts are printed and a player's every appearance will be given on these charts, and date and place allow these appearances to be readily found in the text.

The symbol * indicates 'not out' or 'wicket-keeper' according to the context, and the symbol † indicates 'captain'.

The editor wishes to express his deepest thanks to Brian Croudy, Les Hatton, Victor Isaacs, Anthony Lalley, Qamar Ahmed, Ian Smith, Philip Bailey and Robin Isherwood.

First published in 1992
by HEADLINE BOOK PUBLISHING PLC

10 9 8 7 6 5 4 3 2 1

A CIP catalogue record for this book is available from the British Library

ISBN 0-7472-0682-1

Designed and produced by The Pen & Ink Book Co. Ltd,
Huntingdon, Cambridgeshire

Printed and bound in Great Britain by
Butler and Tanner Limited, Frome, Somerset

HEADLINE BOOK PUBLISHING PLC
Headline House
79 Great Titchfield Street
London W1P 7FN

OPPOSITE: *England v. Pakistan, 4th Test at Leeds, July 1992. (Allsport)*

CRICKET YEAR

ELEVENTH EDITION

SEPTEMBER 1991 to SEPTEMBER 1992

EDITOR–DAVID LEMMON

FOREWORD by ALEC STEWART

HEADLINE

CONTENTS

Sponsor's message

Why is it that formidable fast bowlers come in pairs? Trueman and Statham, Hall and Griffith, Lillee and Thomson, Waqar Younis and Wasim Akram. The latter brace hit the headlines in a 1992 Test series that confirmed Pakistan's position of dominance in international cricket. England's batsmen faced a fusillade of fire and guile from Pakistan's pace men. Not all fared well. But there were exceptions. The doughty Captain Gooch led from the front, as ever. While Alec Stewart – who I'm delighted to say writes the foreword to this yearbook – was top scorer for England in the series. His 190 in the first Test at Edgbaston was a stirring high spot of the summer. David Gower returned to the national team, scored 150 characteristically elegant runs in three Tests, overtook Geoff Boycott as the highest run-maker for England in history – and was then omitted from the squad chosen to tour India.

No series would seem complete without 'The voice of cricket', Brian Johnston. In his 80th year, Johnners amused, informed, entertained and chomped chocolate cake from the commentary box to the pleasure radio of listeners everywhere.

South Africa returned to international competition, acquitting themselves with distinction in the World Cup. Also back from the cold came formerly banned players such as Gatting, Foster, Broad, Emburey and Jarvis. In the County Championship Essex took the title for the second consecutive year. And Durham enjoyed its debut season with first-class status.

Ominous clouds loomed over Lord's on Saturday, 11 July when Hampshire and Kent squared up for the 22nd Benson and Hedges Cup final (cricket's longest-running sponsorship incidentally). Rain and gloaming sent the players padding pavilion-wards in the early afternoon. So it was not until the following day that Hampshire acquired the trophy, scoring 253 for 5 in 55 overs to win by 41 runs. Robin Smith took the Gold Award, cracking 90 typically hard-punched runs. But perhaps the most enduring memory is of Malcolm Marshall – who took 3 wickets and scored 29 runs in the game – holding aloft the Benson and Hedges Cup. Beaming with pride, the veteran campaigner's dream of being on the winning side in a one-day final at Lord's at last came true.

You now hold the Eleventh Edition of the *Benson and Hedges Cricket Year*. There's much to enjoy. It is packed with fine photography, compelling cricket statistics, meaty reading . . . but I fear even this weighty and authoritative tome leaves unanswered the question about why formidable fast bowlers come in pairs. Any ideas?

DEREK STOTHARD
Marketing Manager
Benson and Hedges

Benson and Hedges World XI, 1992

The eleven is chosen on consistency of form shown in first-class cricket throughout the world in the period covered by this annual.

1	G.A. Gooch	(1)
2	D.C. Boon	(5)
3	A.J. Stewart	(14)
4	Salim Malik	(3)
5	D.M. Jones	(13)
6	M.D. Crowe	(9)
7	Wasim Akram	(5)
8*	I.A. Healy	(–)
9	C.E.L. Ambrose	(2)
10	Waqar Younis	(1)
11	C.A. Walsh	(8)

The Coopers & Lybrand ratings are given in brackets.

Comment

Those who love cricket absorb the history of the game, and events which happened years before they were born are embraced as if part of their lives. So it was with the opening partnership of 172 between Hobbs and Sutcliffe against Australia at The Oval in 1926. It was, of course, shot with romance, as all cricket should be, for it was batting of the highest order on a wicket affected by rain, against two of the greatest leg-break bowlers the game has seen, Grimmett and Mailey. It gave England the chance of victory and the regaining of the Ashes for the first time since before the First World War. It was a partnership that passed into cricket folklore, and it is true to say that we shall not see its like again.

That is not to disparage Gooch, Gower, Atherton and the rest. It is true simply because such conditions as occurred at The Oval in August 1926 would not be able to occur today. They would not be allowed to occur because cricket is now based on a fallacy.

Ben Travers, who brought joy to millions through his work in the theatre, and who gained joy himself from a lifetime of watching cricket, expressed it most succinctly in his reminiscences on the game which were published just after his death.

'The administration of the game has, of recent years, been based on a cardinal fallacy, namely that the greatest attraction cricket has to offer is easy run-getting under conditions favouring the same. This has not only resulted in the discouragement of the spin bowler; it goes deeper than that. It means that the younger generation never, or very seldom, has the chance of seeing the most enthralling spectacle cricket has to offer, the absorbing, anguishing fascination of watching great batsmanship on a ruined wicket.'

This is not the first time that I have quoted this passage, but I make no excuses, for in 1992, the administrators missed the opportunity to invigorate the three-day game by returning to uncovered wickets. Instead, they chose to introduce a solely four-day programme, to kill the three-day game and to offer people less cricket. As Derek Pringle wrote, one sensed 'a bit of conspiracy here', for only two years ago a huge majority had voted against a solely four-day game. In fact, many of its opponents, though by no means all, were beaten into submission by the insistence on benign pitches on which results in three days, and often in four, could only be achieved through arranged declarations and run-chases. There was almost a dread that if three or four wickets fell before lunch on the first day, the men from the ministry would arrive and fine you 25 points.

The reason offered for not reverting to uncovered wickets was that Test matches are not played on such pitches. And there's the rub. All that has been decided has been decided on the presumption that there is a 19th county more important than the rest – England – that cricket, in effect, is five days in August or July, and that all must be subservient to the desires of this 19th county. The belief is that all income will be generated from the centre.

It was admitted that every county will lose at least £25,000 a year in its own revenue, but that this will be offset by income from the other areas. At the time of deepest recession, one is stunned by the introduction of a system that guarantees a loss of income in one area, but hopes to increase it from other sources. The attendances at the Old Trafford Test and at the NatWest Trophy final, coupled with the fact that three exciting Test matches ended after little more than three days, cricket, would suggest that the economic reasoning could be false. Or is cricket simply to become a television game?

The introduction of coloured clothing would suggest that it is. But how far are you prepared to surrender a sport's integrity? And how long will it survive if you do? Even those in the media who have been ardent supporters of the new format for next season freely admit that some four or five counties will cease to exist within the next few years. Ironically, some of the first to go may well be those who have most fervently supported the four-day game.

The decision to place all emphasis on the England side and on its presumed needs can only have a depressing effect upon the county game. To play for England should ever be an ambition, a sparkling pinnacle for a cricketer. The format now adopted seems doomed to encourage the pedestrian, to relegate county cricket totally to a position where it becomes merely practice for the big occasion. With its diminishment, traditions are to be violated, a heritage has been forsworn.

It is false to claim that the new format is revolutionary in concept. Far from it, it is a charter for the pedestrian and the mundane. At a time when all are being asked to work harder and produce more, cricketers are being encouraged to do less. They will bowl fewer overs, play fewer matches and bat less. The constant argument is that the game has changed. It is more demanding. There is not a profession that has not changed and is not more demanding. The actor who once used to have to be able to wear a dinner jacket and smoke a cigarette like Noel Coward must now sing, dance, do cartwheels and speak his lines while suspended on a rope. The teacher works longer hours, has numerous forms to complete and is required to attend a plethora of courses in order to learn of new demands and changes in syllabus and technique. Alec Bedser is one who believes that cricketers should be playing more, not less.

There is a real fear that the pedestrian will triumph. The system of physical training which has become part of the England programme, and of some counties, produces fitter men – although some may ask why we have more injuries today than ever before – but it does not necessarily make better cricketers or encourage players of flair. Since the selection of the side to tour India early in 1993 there has been an increasing worry that players of flair are no longer welcome in the England set-up. The decision to omit David Gower has caused a public outcry.

It should not be seen simply as a protest against the omission of a man who has scored more runs for England than any other batsman. It is also a protest against the dismissal of individuality and the joy of uncertainty. Gower represents the beauty that flirts with danger. He is the music of the game, and, as Anthony Trollope has told us in another context, when you take away the music you take away the mystery. When you take the mystery from cricket you deprive it of its charm.

The proffered excuse for Gower's non-selection as being due to his age is so fatuous an excuse as to not merit discussion. He is two months younger than Gatting who was selected for the tour, as were Emburey and Jarvis. These three, it will be remembered, were members of the rebel party that went to South Africa and whose ban for that action was lifted by the ICC in 1992. One must accept this decision even if one does not agree with it, but one must still be allowed to mourn for the Baileys, the Bicknells, the Crofts and those who declined the money because they wanted to play for England. They know now that they could have had both. Graham Greene was right. If the price they ask is loyalty, be a double agent.

There is one more worrying aspect of cricket at present, and that is the seeming unwillingness of those in authority to accept any criticism or, indeed, to allow any view that is different from theirs. There is an unhealthiness in this which is disturbing.

During the Texaco Trophy match at The Oval, I spoke to a county chairman and discussed the format under which cricket in this country will played in 1993 and for at least another two years after that. He claimed that there had been some sort of victory in that they had managed to reduce the trial period from the TCCB's original request for a five-year period to three years. I asked 'What about the paying customer who is so opposed, in the main, to four-day cricket and who will now get less for his money?' His reply was simple and instant – 'They were not considered. They don't bring in enough money.'

This, surely, is the saddest and most short-sighted of policies. If you alienate the spectator, what is there left?

It has given me no pleasure to write these words. I hope that my pessimism proves to be totally unfounded, that within the next 18 months I am eating my words, that Leicestershire, Gloucestershire and all other counties will still be in operation long after I am gone. I hope that county cricket will flourish and that Test cricket will become more of an entertainment and less of a round of political in-fighting and accusation. There will be no joy in me should my worst fears prove to be correct.

DAVID LEMMON

Foreword
by Alec Stewart

Where shall I begin? With Waqar Younis, Wasim Akram and the ball-tampering allegations? With Jack Russell and the continuing debate over the England wicket-keeping position? With David Gower and the public outcry over his treatment by the selectors?

There has been so much controversy off the field during the past year that it has tended to obscure some of the excellent cricket played on it – not least by England in beating New Zealand in both the Test and one-day international series, reaching the World Cup final and engaging in a fascinating summer-long struggle with Pakistan which brought victory in the one-dayers but defeat in the Tests.

The biggest disappointments, of course, were losing the final in Melbourne, where we just did not do ourselves justice, and the last Test at the Foster's Oval, where, frankly, we were completely outplayed. And no one can have failed to notice that Pakistan's match-winners were Wasim and Waqar who are simply the best fast bowlers in the world today. Waqar missed the World Cup because of his back injury, which made Pakistan's success all the more creditable, though people should not forget that if it had not been for the rain rule we would have beaten them in Adelaide and almost certainly put them out of the competition. As it was, they got better as the tournament went on, with Wasim finishing as the leading wicket-taker and receiving great support from Aqib Javed and Mushtaq Ahmed.

Waqar did not reappear until the first Test, at Edgbaston, by which time we were 2–0 up in the one-dayers and the tone of the series had already been set by headlines like 'It's war' after a very minor incident involving Javed Miandad and Ian Botham at The Oval. But soon the charge was 'Cheats', when Waqar and Wasim began to make the ball swing so extravagantly that they finished up with 43 wickets between them and effectively won the series.

All I will say is that, having played with Waqar at Surrey and against him for England, he is a world-class fast bowler who can take wickets at any stage of the game and turn it on its head. It is the sheer pace at which he bowls that enables him to swing the ball later than anyone else around. And Waqar can do that just as easily in the normal way with a shiny, new ball as he can by employing reverse swing with a battered old one.

I will not be sorry to see him back in my side next season, although it was a great challenge to bat against him. We had talked many times about what a good contest it would be if we got the chance to play against each other and that is exactly how it turned out. We did exchange the odd word here and there, but it was all in jest really and, once the game was over, I would go into their dressing room or he would come into ours to see me. It was good, competitive stuff played in the right spirit, and while I have no doubt that he will be reminding me next season of how many times he got me out I will be able to remind him of the runs I scored as well.

That was the most gratifying thing for me in a year which saw me get back in to the England side as a wicket-keeper who could bat and finish up opening the innings as well. Having always batted at number three, I was not too keen to open when I was first asked to do it in New Zealand, but I was happy enough to go in first if it meant being in the team. A century in the first Test gave me the confidence to do the job and made me feel part of the set-up rather than feeling that I was always playing for my place. And, ironically, when I was asked to keep wicket again, I would sooner have carried on just as an opener because it had gone so well.

I could appreciate that the selectors felt it would be best for the side if they played six batsmen and five bowlers, but I did feel sorry for Jack Russell who was being left out through no fault of his own. Some people said that he had a bad series but I think he probably made one mistake in his three Tests and was only dropped because there was no other all-rounder available.

As a general rule, I think you should play your best wicket-keeper, although I accepted the situation if it was felt to be for the good of the side. Unfortunately, my being the wicket-keeper coincided with me getting a couple of low scores, but I do not think it really affects my batting. It is just that I feel different when I have to keep wicket. Because I do not do it day in and day out, I am always working at it, always trying to do that little bit more. I do have confidence in my ability but I know that I have always got to perform at my very best to keep the standard at the required level and that does make it that much harder. And having established myself reasonably well as a batsman, I want to give myself the best opportunity to stay in the side.

My ambition is to play for my country for as long as possible – and that makes me no different from any other England player, including David Gower who has played in more Tests and scored more runs than anyone else. It was questionable, I suppose, whether he should have been recalled against Pakistan but once he did come back he did very well. We were all very happy for him when he broke Geoff Boycott's record at Old Trafford and we were even happier when he saw us through to victory at Headingley. It was a real pressure situation and he showed that he is not just a flamboyant player but one who can really concentrate on the job in hand. That was experience for you and, from the outside anyway, it was a big surprise when the selectors did not want him on the tour of India. I cannot comment on the reasons they gave, but I could understand why he and his supporters felt that he had been badly treated. They had picked a bloke to do a job for three Tests and he had done it well. And it seemed a shame that a player with so much natural talent could not fit into the England set-up.

Having played under Graham Gooch for three years now, I have to say that his methods are very good. He leads by example which I think is the best way to do it. His own performances have been quite outstanding and if he tells you to do something then you do it because you know very well that he would do it himself. He is not one of those people who says 'Go and do that' and then sits down and lets you get on with it.

Gooch's last great ambition, of course, is to win back the Ashes from Australia and I am sure that if he thinks David Gower has a part to play in that he will want him in the side. Every international game is very important, but to play against Australia is still the pinnacle as far as every England cricketer is concerned. And if we needed any extra motivation it is the memory of the last two series – in 1989 when we lost 4–0 and 1990–91 when we went down 3–0. Graham was injured at the start of that tour and hardly played, while no one else came out of it with flying colours . . . if you will pardon the expression!

Next season will also see the Benson and Hedges Cup become a straight knock-out competition, coloured clothing in the Sunday League and, most important of all, a full programme of four-day matches in the County Championship, which I am sure will be to the benefit of the England team. Four-day cricket is the nearest thing there is to Test cricket and it should produce better players. Middle-order batsmen, who will get more opportunity to play long innings, and spinners, who should have more chance to bowl, will benefit the most. It also means that each game should run its own course and, generally, the best team will win.

Finally, if I can finish on a personal note, 1992 saw Keith Fletcher taking over as England team manager from a certain Micky Stewart, who I've enjoyed working under, first at Surrey and more recently in the England team. There has been criticism of his methods, but all the training and practice is part of the game now. You have to be fitter and stronger to cope with the demands these days and, though people may suggest that it is too regimented, I do not think that is a bad thing as long as people are still encouraged to show their natural flair.

As for me, I grew up in a cricket atmosphere and Micky Stewart gave me all the advice and encouragement I could wish for. He never pushed me into first-class cricket but he said that if I did want to go into the game he would recommend it as a career. I will always be grateful for that.

SECTION

A

WORLD CUP 1992

The Triumph of Pakistan
Complete Score Cards,
Reports and Averages

Imran Khan delivers his victory speech after receiving the trophy from Sir Colin Cowdrey. (Patrick Eagar)

The fifth World Cup was played in Australia in February and March, 1992. The late inclusion of South Africa, who were welcomed in from the cold after 21 years in exile, brought about a rescheduling of the programme, and extended the number of matches that were to be played to 39. This was 12 more than in any previous World Cup, and, one would suggest, it took the tournament past saturation point.

Each side was to play each other once, with the top four sides in the league competing in the semi-finals. The matches were to be of 50 overs' duration, and no bowler was allowed to bowl more than ten overs. An interesting innovation was that the bowling side should use two white balls, one used exclusively at one end, and the other from the opposite end. This was an intelligent move and helped to counter delays as the ball was thrown to the umpire at the end of each over.

No reserve day was set aside for matches, except the semi-finals and final. The usual limitation on the number of overs applied if the bowling side failed to reach 50 overs in three-and-a-half hours. In the case of matches interrupted by rain, a minimum of 15 overs had to be bowled before a result could be declared.

The most controversial rule, and the one which was to blight the competition, was that if rain should curtail the number of overs that the side batting second should receive, then their target would be the number of runs scored by the side batting first from their equivalent number of *highest scoring overs*. In effect, the side who bowled first would be penalised for the 'good' overs that they bowled. Few saw the dangers of this at the outset. After all, Australia were the holders and the firm favourites, and the opening match was between the two hosts, in Auckland.

MATCH ONE
NEW ZEALAND v. AUSTRALIA, at Auckland

There was an eventful start to the World Cup. Craig McDermott bowled the opening over and began with two wides. His third delivery, the first legitimate one, bowled John Wright behind his legs. Jones hit the first boundary of the World Cup in the same over. The next, Reid's first, saw the first chance go begging as Moody put down Latham at slip. Within a couple of overs came the first controversial decision, Jones being adjudged leg before to a ball that looked as if it would go over the top of the stumps. The dramas completed, cricket in earnest began.

Crowe and Latham played attractively and positively. The 50 arrived in the 13th over, but the thick-set Latham, who had played some delightful shots, was taken at the wicket by the diving Healy three runs later. Crowe and Rutherford now began to run with purpose as the limitations of the Australian attack were exposed. Rutherford sped to 50 off 64 balls as he and Crowe added 118.

Crowe was now at his magisterial best, nor was he let down by his later partners. The New Zealand captain reached his hundred off 134 balls, and the man who had been openly criticised for his lack of leadership and form was once more a national hero.

The opening match of the tournament brings a surprise as New Zealand beat Australia. Martin Crowe hit a brilliant century and led his side with imagination. Crowe was to become the Player of the World Cup.
(Joe Mann/Allsport)

MATCH ONE – NEW ZEALAND v. AUSTRALIA
22 February, 1992 at Eden Park, Auckland

NEW ZEALAND

Batsman	How out	Runs
J.G. Wright	b McDermott	0
R.T. Latham	c Healy, b Moody	26
A.H. Jones	lbw, b Reid	4
M.D. Crowe (capt)	not out	100
K.R. Rutherford	run out	57
C.Z. Harris	run out	14
*I.D.S. Smith	c Healy, b McDermott	14
C.L. Cairns	not out	16
D.N. Patel		
G.R. Larsen		
W. Watson		
Extras	lb 6, w 7, nb 4	17
	(for 6 wickets)	248

AUSTRALIA

Batsman	How out	Runs
D.C. Boon	run out	100
G.R. Marsh	c Latham, b Larsen	19
D.M. Jones	run out	21
A.R. Border (capt)	c Cairns, b Patel	3
T.M. Moody	c and b Latham	7
M.E. Waugh	lbw, b Larsen	2
S.R. Waugh	c and b Larsen	38
*I.A. Healy	not out	7
C.J. McDermott	run out	1
P.L. Taylor	c Rutherford, b Watson	1
B.A. Reid	c Jones, b Harris	3
Extras	lb 6, w 2, nb 1	9
		211

(50 overs)

	O	M	R	W
McDermott	10	1	43	2
Reid	10	–	39	1
Moody	9	1	37	1
S.R. Waugh	10	–	60	–
P.L. Taylor	7	–	36	–
M.E. Waugh	4	–	27	–

(48.1 overs)

	O	M	R	W
Cairns	4	–	30	–
Patel	10	1	36	1
Watson	9	1	39	1
Larsen	10	1	30	3
Harris	7.1	–	35	1
Latham	8	–	35	1

FALL OF WICKETS
1–2, **2**–13, **3**–53, **4**–171, **5**–191, **6**–215

FALL OF WICKETS
1–62, **2**–92, **3**–104, **4**–120, **5**–125, **6**–199, **7**–200, **8**–205, **9**–206

Umpires: D.R. Shepherd & Khizer Hayat   Man of the Match – M.D. Crowe   *New Zealand won by 37 runs*

Nor did his popularity diminish. He had the inspired tactic of opening the bowling with off-spinner Patel. Cairns was dreadfully erratic, but Crowe changed his bowling frequently, suggesting variety where none occurred. Marsh was taken at cover, and Cairns ran out Jones. Border swung high to mid-wicket; Moody checked his shot and was caught and bowled; and Mark Waugh walked in front of a straight ball. Australia were in disarray.

Crowe manipulated his bowlers with shrewdness. Larsen was ungainly but niggardly, and Boon and Steve Waugh were faced with the task of scoring 96 from the last ten overs. Just as it seemed New Zealand might crack, Steve Waugh checked his shot, as Moody had done, and was caught and bowled. Boon reached his hundred and was immediately run out. Australia were doomed. The favourites had stumbled at the first fence.

MATCH TWO
ENGLAND v. INDIA, at Perth

A few hours after the drama in Auckland, England began their campaign with a victory over India. Gooch won the toss, and he and Botham began quietly against a tight opening spell from Kapil Dev and Prabhakar. Botham was out when he cut at Kapil Dev, but Smith was in regal form, hitting two sixes and eight fours in his 108-ball innings. He and Gooch added 100 in 21 overs before Gooch, who had been attacked by cramp, drove into the hands of extra cover. Hick came and went, and England were 137 for 3 in 32 overs.

Fairbrother batted busily, but when he and Smith went in rapid succession the last six overs produced a disappointing 38.

Srikkanth walloped the ball in his customary manner. DeFreitas was bowling short and being punished, but

England off to a winning start as Robin Smith cracks 91 in the victory over India at Perth.(Ben Radford/Allsport)

then Srikkanth played a wild shot and skied the ball to extra cover. Nevertheless, India had reached 63 in 16 overs, but in the next over, Azharuddin was out first ball as he jabbed at Reeve. Shastri and the immaculate Tendulkar restored sanity. They doubled the score in 14 overs, and it needed a superb delivery from Botham to account for Tendulkar.

Botham's spell was crucial. He had Kambli taken at mid-on by Hick who juggled with the ball and halted the Indian advance. Shastri hit high in the air. DeFreitas, the bowler, dropped the catch, but in the resultant chaos he ran Shastri out. Reeve returned with his strange mixture of good and bad deliveries and took two wickets. India had been strolling to victory. Now they were in disarray. There was a blend of wild running and crazy shots from the talented but inexperienced young tail-enders.

England edged home by nine runs.

A spectacular innings of 83 off 45 balls by Andy Waller of Zimbabwe failed to bring his side victory over Sri Lanka at New Plymouth.(Joe Mann/Allsport)

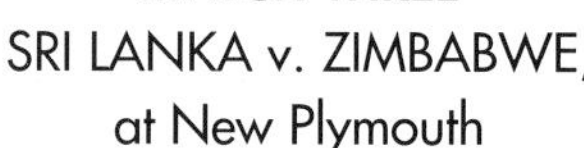

MATCH THREE
SRI LANKA v. ZIMBABWE, at New Plymouth

The two teams regarded as the minnows of the competition produced one of the most exhilarating and exciting games the World Cup has seen. Sri Lanka had suffered a great blow on the eve of the tournament when they lost their leading strike bowler Rumesh Ratnayake through injury. The limitations of their attack were shown as Zimbabwe scored at more than six runs an over.

Wicket-keeper Andy Flower carried his bat for 115, and, after three wickets had fallen for 82, Kevin Arnott hit a rapid 52. The spectacular batting came from Andy Waller who hit 83 off 45 balls and shared an unbroken fifth-wicket partnership of 145 in 13 overs with Flower. This was a World Cup record.

Sri Lanka made the ideal positive response, Mahanama and Samarasekera hitting 128 in under 21 overs for the first wicket. Veteran off-spinner John Traicos applied the brakes, and four wickets fell for 39 runs. Arjuna Ranatunga and Sanath Jayasuriya halted the slide, and Ranatunga began to dominate. He hit the winning four off the second ball of the last over to take his side to a memorable victory.

It was the first time that a team had scored over 300 runs when batting second to win a match in the World Cup, and the aggregate of 625 runs was only one short of the record for the competition.

MATCH FOUR
WEST INDIES v. PAKISTAN, at Melbourne

The loss of the outstanding bowler in world cricket, Waqar Younis, on the eve of the tournament came as a grievous blow to Pakistan, and his absence with a serious back injury was an obvious handicap in their opening game against West Indies in Melbourne.

West Indies surprised all by bowling spinners, Hooper and Harper, in tandem, but the pair were economical. Pakistan, who were missing skipper Imran Khan for this first game, began uneasily, and they had to rely on the improvisations of Javed to lift their run rate. He and Ramiz Raja shared an unbroken partnership of 123. Javed's 57 came off 61 balls while Ramiz, who had adopted the sheet anchor role, occupied 158 deliveries for his 102.

Pakistan's attack looked decidedly weak, and Haynes and Lara were soon in full flow. Wasim Haider, a mature medium-pacer, and Iqbal Sikander, a leg-spinner, were new to the international arena, and neither was able to penetrate. By the end of the 20th over, West Indies had scored 89; and by the end of the 30th, 139. Haynes was twice dropped, but Lara was quite magnificent and hit 88 off 101 balls with 11 fours. He was forced to retire when hit on the toe by a ball from Wasim Akram, but Haynes and Richardson stroked West Indies to victory with 3.1 overs to spare.

MATCH TWO – ENGLAND v. INDIA
22 February, 1992 at WACA Ground, Perth

ENGLAND

Batsman	Dismissal	Runs
G.A. Gooch (capt)	c Tendulkar, b Shastri	51
I.T. Botham	c More, b Kapil Dev	9
R.A. Smith	c Azharuddin, b Prabhakar	91
G.A. Hick	c More, b Banerjee	5
N.H. Fairbrother	c Srikkanth, b Srinath	24
*A.J. Stewart	b Prabhakar	13
C.C. Lewis	c Banerjee, b Kapil Dev	10
D.R. Pringle	c Srikkanth, b Srinath	1
D.A. Reeve	not out	8
P.A.J. DeFreitas	run out	1
P.C.R. Tufnell	not out	3
Extras	b 1, lb 6, w 13	20
	(for 9 wickets)	236

INDIA

Batsman	Dismissal	Runs
R.J. Shastri	run out	57
K. Srikkanth	c Botham, b DeFreitas	39
M. Azharuddin (capt)	c Stewart, b Reeve	0
S.R. Tendulkar	c Stewart, b Botham	35
V.G. Kambli	c Hick, b Botham	3
P.K. Amre	run out	22
Kapil Dev	c DeFreitas, b Reeve	17
S.T. Banerjee	not out	25
*K.S. More	run out	1
M. Prabhakar	b Reeve	0
J. Srinath	run out	11
Extras	lb 9, w 7, nb 1	17
		227

(50 overs)

	O	M	R	W
Kapil Dev	10	–	38	2
Prabhakar	10	3	34	2
Srinath	9	1	47	2
Banerjee	7	–	45	1
Tendulkar	10	–	37	–
Shastri	4	–	28	1

(49.2 overs)

	O	M	R	W
Pringle	10	–	53	–
Lewis	9.2	–	36	–
DeFreitas	10	–	39	1
Reeve	6	–	38	3
Botham	10	–	27	2
Tufnell	4	–	25	–

FALL OF WICKETS (England)
1–21, 2–121, 3–137, 4–197, 5–198, 6–214, 7–222, 8–223, 9–224

FALL OF WICKETS (India)
1–63, 2–63, 3–126, 4–140, 5–149, 6–187, 7–194, 8–200, 9–201

Umpires: P.J. McConnell & D.P. Buultjens — Man of the Match – I.T. Botham — *England won by 9 runs*

MATCH THREE – SRI LANKA v. ZIMBABWE
23 February, 1992, at Pukekura Park, New Plymouth

ZIMBABWE

Batsman	Dismissal	Runs
*A. Flower	not out	115
W.R. James	c Tillekeratne, b Wickremasinghe	17
A.J. Pycroft	c Ramanayake, b Gurusinha	5
D.L. Houghton (capt)	c Tillekeratne, b Gurusinha	10
K.J. Arnott	c Tillekeratne, b Wickremasinghe	52
A.C. Waller	not out	83
K.G. Duers		
I.P. Butchart		
E.A. Brandes		
M.P. Jarvis		
A.J. Traicos		
Extras	b 2, lb 6, w 13, nb 9	30
	(for 4 wickets)	312

SRI LANKA

Batsman	Dismissal	Runs
R.S. Mahanama	c Arnott, b Brandes	59
M.A.R. Samarasekera	c Duers, b Traicos	75
P.A. de Silva (capt)	c Houghton, b Brandes	14
A.P. Gurusinha	run out	5
A. Ranatunga	not out	88
S.T. Jayasuriya	c Flower, b Houghton	32
*H.P. Tillekeratne	b Jarvis	18
R.S. Kalpage	c Duers, b Brandes	11
C.P.H. Ramanayake	not out	1
K.I.W. Wijegunawardene		
A.G.D. Wickremasinghe		
Extras	lb 5, w 5	10
	(for 7 wickets)	313

(50 overs)

	O	M	R	W
Ramanayake	10	–	59	–
Wijegunawardene	7	–	54	–
Wickremasinghe	10	1	50	2
Gurusinha	10	–	72	2
Kalpage	10	–	51	–
Jayasuriya	3	–	18	–

(49.2 overs)

	O	M	R	W
Jarvis	9.2	–	61	1
Brandes	10	–	70	3
Duers	10	–	72	–
Butchart	8	–	53	–
Traicos	10	1	33	1
Houghton	2	–	19	1

FALL OF WICKETS (Zimbabwe)
1–30, 2–57, 3–82, 4–167

FALL OF WICKETS (Sri Lanka)
1–128, 2–144, 3–155, 4–167, 5–212, 6–273, 7–309

Umpires: P.D. Reporter & S.J. Woodward — Man of the Match – A. Flower — *Sri Lanka won by 3 wickets*

MATCH FOUR – WEST INDIES v. PAKISTAN
23 February, 1992 at MCG, Melbourne

PAKISTAN

Ramiz Raja	not out	102
Aamir Sohail	**c** Logie, **b** Benjamin	23
Inzamam-ul-Haq	**c** Hooper, **b** Harper	27
Javed Miandad (capt)	not out	57
Salim Malik		
Ijaz Ahmed		
Wasim Akram		
*Moin Khan		
Iqbal Sikander		
Wasim Haider		
Aqib Javed		
Extras	b 1, lb 3, w 5, nb 2	11
	(for 2 wickets)	**220**

WEST INDIES

D.L. Haynes	not out	93
B.C. Lara	retired hurt	88
R.B. Richardson (capt)	not out	20
C.L. Hooper		
K.L.T. Arthurton		
A.L. Logie		
R.A. Harper		
M.D. Marshall		
*D. Williams		
C.E.L. Ambrose		
W.K.M. Benjamin		
Extras	b 2, lb 8, w 7, nb 3	20
	(for no wicket)	**221**

(50 overs)

	O	M	R	W
Marshall	10	1	53	–
Ambrose	10	–	40	–
Benjamin	10	–	49	1
Hooper	10	–	41	–
Harper	10	–	33	1

(46.5 overs)

	O	M	R	W
Wasim Akram	10	–	37	–
Aqib Javed	8.5	–	42	–
Wasim Haider	8	–	42	–
Ijaz Ahmed	6	1	29	–
Iqbal Sikander	8	1	26	–
Aamir Sohail	6	–	35	–

FALL OF WICKETS

1–45, **2**–97

Umpires: S.G. Randell & I.D. Robinson — Man of the Match – B.C. Lara — *West Indies won by 10 wickets*

MATCH FIVE – NEW ZEALAND v. SRI LANKA
25 February, 1992 at Trust Bank Park, Hamilton

SRI LANKA

R.S. Mahanama	**c** and **b** Harris	80
M.A.R. Samarasekera	**c** Wright, **b** Watson	9
A.P. Gurusinha	**c** Smith, **b** Harris	9
P.A. Silva (capt)	run out	31
A. Ranatunga	**c** Rutherford, **b** Harris	20
S.T. Jayasuriya	run out	5
*H.P. Tillekeratne	**c** Crowe, **b** Watson	8
R.S. Kalpage	**c** Larsen, **b** Harris	11
C.P.H. Ramanayake	run out	2
S.D. Anurasiri	not out	3
G.P. Wickremasinghe	not out	3
Extras	b 1, lb 15, w 4, nb 5	25
	(for 9 wickets)	**206**

NEW ZEALAND

J.G. Wright	**c** and **b** Kalpage	57
R.T. Latham	**b** Kalpage	20
A.H. Jones	**c** Jayasuriya, **b** Gurusinha	49
M.D. Crowe (capt)	**c** Ramanayake, **b** Wickremasinghe	5
K.R. Rutherford	not out	65
C.Z. Harris	not out	5
D.N. Patel		
*I.D.S. Smith		
G.R. Larsen		
D.K. Morrison		
W. Watson		
Extras	lb 3, w 3, nb 3	9
	(for 4 wickets)	**210**

(50 overs)

	O	M	R	W
Morrison	8	–	36	–
Watson	10	–	37	3
Latham	3	–	13	–
Larsen	10	1	29	–
Harris	10	–	43	3
Patel	9	–	32	–

(48.2 overs)

	O	M	R	W
Ramanayake	9.2	–	46	–
Wickremasinghe	8	1	40	1
Anurasiri	10	1	27	–
Kalpage	10	–	33	2
Gurusinha	4	–	19	1
Ranatunga	4	–	22	–
Jayasuriya	2	–	14	–
de Silva	1	–	6	–

FALL OF WICKETS

1–18, **2**–50, **3**–120, **4**–172, **5**–172, **6**–181, **7**–195, **8**–199, **9**–202

FALL OF WICKETS

1–77, **2**–91, **3**–105, **4**–186

Umpires: P.D. Reporter & D.R. Shepherd — Man of the Match – K.R. Rutherford — *New Zealand won by 6 wickets*

MATCH FIVE
NEW ZEALAND v. SRI LANKA, at Hamilton

Having beaten Australia, New Zealand were unlikely to be too worried about their encounter with Sri Lanka who were put in to bat in cloudy, humid conditions. They suffered a setback when Samarasekera pulled a hamstring at the beginning of his innings, and it was soon apparent that fitness would be a significant factor in the World Cup. John Wright, too, suffered an injury although it did not prevent him from scoring a dominant 57.

Mahanama scored 80 off 132 balls, and in the 42nd over, Sri Lanka were 172 for 3 and seemingly set for a big score, but Harris had Ranatunga caught on the mid-wicket boundary and caught and bowled Mahanama next ball. Sri Lanka panicked, and six wickets went down for 30 runs to leave them with a disappointing 206.

New Zealand got off to a good start, but the middle order were troubled by spinners Kalpage and Anurasiri. Rutherford threw off the shackles to hit 65 as he and Jones scored 81 off 101 balls.

Tillekeratne unsuccessfully attempts to stump Rutherford, New Zealand v. Sri Lanka, at Hamilton. Rutherford hit 65 not out and took the individual award. (Joe Man/Allsport)

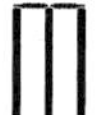

MATCH SIX
AUSTRALIA v. SOUTH AFRICA, at Sydney

It was inevitable that South Africa's entry into the World Cup would be an emotional one. What was not foreseen was that it would be a total disaster for Australia.

Winning the toss, Allan Border elected to bat first, and Marsh and Boon gave Australia a solid enough start with 42 from ten overs. Then Boon was run out, and South Africa began to bowl tightly and to field like tigers. McMillan and Snell probed; Donald demanded with his pace. Rhodes was brilliant in the field, and ran out McDermott in spectacular fashion. The Australian middle order disintegrated.

To add to Australia's woes, Healy injured a hamstring, and Boon took over behind the stumps. He dropped Wessels when the South African captain was on 23, but it mattered little. Australia's bowling was untidy, and their fielding sloppy.

Hudson was out at 74, but the two old warriors, Wessels and Kirsten, saw South Africa to victory with the greatest of ease.

South Africa's win evoked much passion. Australia had lost two matches, were bottom of the table and, unthinkably, faced elimination.

Richard Snell runs out David Boon as South Africa make a sensational entry into the competion by routing Australia in Sydney. (David Munden)

MATCH SIX – AUSTRALIA v. SOUTH AFRICA
26 February, 1992 at SCG, Sydney

AUSTRALIA

Batsman	Dismissal	Runs
G.R. Marsh	c Richardson, **b** Kuiper	25
D.C. Boon	run out	27
D.M. Jones	c Richardson, **b** McMillan	24
A.R. Border (capt)	**b** Kuiper	0
T.M. Moody	lbw, **b** Donald	10
S.R. Waugh	c Cronje, **b** McMillan	27
*I.A. Healy	c McMillan, **b** Donald	16
P.L. Taylor	**b** Donald	4
C.J. McDermott	run out	6
M.R. Whitney	not out	9
B.A. Reid	not out	5
Extras	lb 2, w 11, nb 4	17
	(for 9 wickets)	**170**

SOUTH AFRICA

Batsman	Dismissal	Runs
K.C. Wessels (capt)	not out	81
A.C. Hudson	**b** P.L. Taylor	28
P.N. Kirsten	not out	49
A.P. Kuiper		
W.J. Cronje		
J.N. Rhodes		
B.M. McMillan		
* D.J. Richardson		
R.P. Snell		
M.W. Pringle		
A.A. Donald		
Extras	b 5, w 6, nb 2	13
	(for 1 wicket)	**171**

(49 overs)

	O	M	R	W
Donald	10	–	34	3
Pringle	10	–	52	–
Snell	9	1	15	–
McMillan	10	–	35	2
Kuiper	5	–	15	2
Cronje	5	1	17	–

(46.5 overs)

	O	M	R	W
McDermott	10	1	23	–
Reid	8.5	–	41	–
Whitney	6	–	26	–
S.R. Waugh	4	1	16	–
P.L. Taylor	10	1	32	1
Border	4	–	13	–
Moody	4	–	15	–

FALL OF WICKETS

1–42, **2**–76, **3**–76, **4**–97, **5**–108, **6**–143, **7**–146, **8**–156, **9**–161

FALL OF WICKET

1–74

Umpires: B.L. Aldridge & S.U. Bucknor — Man of the Match – K.C. Wessels — *South Africa won by 9 wickets*

MATCH SEVEN – PAKISTAN v. ZIMBABWE
27 February, 1992 at Bellerive Oval, Hobart

PAKISTAN

Batsman	Dismissal	Runs
Ramiz Raja	c Flower, **b** Jarvis	9
Aamir Sohail	c Pycroft, **b** Butchart	114
Inzamam-ul-Haq	c Brandes, **b** Butchart	14
Javed Miandad	lbw, **b** Butchart	89
Salim Malik	not out	14
Wasim Akram	not out	1
Imran Khan (capt)		
*Moin Khan		
Iqbal Sikander		
Aqib Javed		
Mushtaq Ahmed		
Extras	lb 9, nb 4	13
	(for 4 wickets)	**254**

ZIMBABWE

Batsman	Dismissal	Runs
K.J. Arnott	c Wasim Akram, **b** Iqbal Sikander	7
* A. Flower	c Inzamam-ul-Haq, **b** Wasim Akram	6
A.J. Pycroft	**b** Wasim Akram	0
D.L. Houghton (capt)	c Ramiz Raja, **b** Aamir Sohail	44
A.H. Omarshah	**b** Aamir Sohail	33
A.C. Waller	**b** Wasim Akram	44
I.P. Butchart	c Javed Miandad, **b** Aqib Javed	33
E.A. Brandes	not out	2
A.J. Traicos	not out	8
W.R. James		
M.P. Jarvis		
Extras	b 3, lb 15, w 6	24
	(for 7 wickets)	**201**

(50 overs)

	O	M	R	W
Brandes	10	1	49	–
Jarvis	10	1	52	1
Omarshah	10	1	24	–
Butchart	10	–	57	3
Traicos	10	–	63	–

(50 overs)

	O	M	R	W
Wasim Akram	10	2	21	3
Aqib Javed	10	1	49	1
Iqbal Sikander	10	1	35	1
Mushtaq Ahmed	10	1	34	–
Aamir Sohail	6	1	26	2
Salim Malik	4	–	18	–

FALL OF WICKETS

1–29, **2**–63, **3**–208, **4**–253

FALL OF WICKETS

1–14, **2**–14, **3**–33, **4**–103, **5**–108, **6**–187, **7**–190

Umpires: S.G. Randell & D.P. Buultjens — Man of the Match – Aamir Sohail — *Pakistan won by 53 runs*

MATCH SEVEN
PAKISTAN v. ZIMBABWE, at Hobart

Imran Khan returned to the Pakistan side, but, nursing his injured shoulder, he did not bat nor did he bowl. Pakistan batted first, and they were restricted to 96 for 2 in their first 30 overs. Aamir Sohail and Javed Miandad then began to hit freely. Catches were missed, and the score climbed out of Zimbabwe's reach. Aamir went to three figures off 81 while Javed's 89 came from 94 balls.

Zimbabwe could never sustain the necessary momentum after losing their first three wickets for 33 runs. They floundered against the Pakistan spinners in mid innings, and only some late hitting from Waller and Butchart took them past 200.

MATCH EIGHT
ENGLAND v. WEST INDIES, at Melbourne

England emulated New Zealand in winning their second match in succession. They disposed of West Indies with a bewilderingly contemptuous ease that suddenly made them favourites to win the competition.

Inside 20 overs, England dismissed West Indies' four front-line batsmen for 55 runs, and this was a shock from which West Indies never recovered. Gooch had asked them to bat first, and while Lewis made the ball rear disconcertingly Pringle nagged the batsmen into inertia. Lara was caught behind second ball, and Richardson was taken at slip.

West Indies could never relax. They were confronted by five top-line bowlers and a sixth, Reeve, who, if not of the first flight, could still bowl ten overs for 23 runs. They did not survive their full quota of overs, and England faced a simple target.

Gooch and Botham scored 50 in 14 overs. Botham was strangely subdued and introspective, and Smith was out of touch, but Hick relished the more relaxed and undemanding situation. England strolled to victory with 10.1 overs to spare, an astonishing result.

MATCH NINE
INDIA v. SRI LANKA, at Mackay

This match was abandoned after only two balls.

MATCH EIGHT – ENGLAND v. WEST INDIES
27 February, 1992 at MCG, Melbourne

WEST INDIES

Batsman	Dismissal	Runs
D.L. Haynes	c Fairbrother, **b** DeFreitas	38
B.C. Lara	c Stewart, **b** Lewis	0
R.B. Richardson (capt)	c Botham, **b** Lewis	5
C.L. Hooper	c Reeve, **b** Botham	5
K.L.T. Arthurton	c Fairbrother, **b** DeFreitas	54
A.L. Logie	run out	20
R.A. Harper	c Hick, **b** Reeve	3
M.D. Marshall	run out	3
*D. Williams	c Pringle, **b** DeFreitas	6
C.E.L. Ambrose	c DeFreitas, **b** Lewis	4
W.K.M. Benjamin	not out	11
Extras	lb 4, w 3, nb 1	8
		157

(49.2 overs)

	O	M	R	W
Pringle	7	3	16	–
Lewis	8.2	1	30	3
DeFreitas	9	2	34	3
Botham	10	–	30	1
Reeve	10	1	23	1
Tufnell	5	–	20	–

FALL OF WICKETS
1–0, **2**–22, **3**–36, **4**–55, **5**–91, **6**–102, **7**–114, **8**–131, **9**–145

ENGLAND

Batsman	Dismissal	Runs
G.A. Gooch (capt)	st Williams, **b** Hooper	65
I.T. Botham	c Williams, **b** Benjamin	8
R.A. Smith	c Logie, **b** Benjamin	8
G.A. Hick	c and **b** Harper	54
N.H. Fairbrother	not out	13
*A.J. Stewart	not out	0
D.A. Reeve		
C.C. Lewis		
D.R. Pringle		
P.A.J. DeFreitas		
P.C.R. Tufnell		
Extras	lb 7, w 4, nb 1	12
	(for 4 wickets)	**160**

(39.5 overs)

	O	M	R	W
Ambrose	8	1	26	–
Marshall	8	–	37	–
Benjamin	9.5	2	22	2
Hooper	10	1	38	1
Harper	4	–	30	1

FALL OF WICKETS
1–50, **2**–71, **3**–126, **4**–156

Umpires: S.J. Woodward & K.E. Liebenberg   Man of the Match – C.C. Lewis   *England won by 6 wickets*

MATCH NINE – INDIA v. SRI LANKA
28 February, 1992 at Mackay, North Queensland

INDIA			SRI LANKA
K. Srikkanth	not out	1	R.S. Mahanama
Kapil Dev	not out	0	U.C. Hathurusinghe
M. Azharuddin (capt)			A.P. Gurusinha
A.D. Jadeja			P.A. de Silva (capt)
V.G. Kambli			A. Ranatunga
S.R. Tendulkar			S.T. Jayasuriya
P.K. Amre			*H.P. Tillekeratne
M. Prabhakar			R.S. Kalpage
*K.S. More			C.P.H. Ramanayake
S.T. Banerjee			K.I.W. Wijegunawardene
J. Srinath			A.G.D. Wickremasinghe
Extras		0	
	(for no wicket)	1	

(0.2 overs)

	O	M	R	W
Ramanayake	0.2	–	1	–

Umpires: D.R. Shepherd & I.D. Robinson

Match abandoned

MATCH TEN – NEW ZEALAND v. SOUTH AFRICA
29 February, 1992 at Eden Park, Auckland

SOUTH AFRICA			NEW ZEALAND		
K.C. Wessels (capt)	c Smith, b Watson	3	M.J. Greatbatch	b Kirsten	68
A.C. Hudson	b Patel	1	R.T. Latham	c Wessels, b Snell	60
P.N. Kirsten	c Cairns, b Watson	90	A.H. Jones	not out	34
W.J. Cronje	c Smith, b Harris	7	*I.D.S. Smith	c Kirsten, b Donald	19
*D.J. Richardson	c Larsen, b Cairns	28	M.D. Crowe (capt)	not out	3
A.P. Kuiper	run out	2	K.R. Rutherford		
J. N. Rhodes	c Crowe, b Cairns	6	C.Z. Harris		
B.M. McMillan	not out	33	D.N. Patel		
R.P. Snell	not out	11	G.R. Larsen		
T. Bosch			C.L. Cairns		
A.A. Donald			W. Watson		
Extras	lb 8, nb 1	9	Extras	b 1, w 5, nb 1	7
	(for 7 wickets)	190		(for 3 wickets)	191

(50 overs)

	O	M	R	W
Watson	10	2	30	2
Patel	10	1	28	1
Larsen	10	1	29	–
Harris	10	2	33	1
Latham	2	–	19	–
Cairns	8	–	43	2

(34.3 overs)

	O	M	R	W
Donald	10	–	38	1
McMillan	5	1	23	–
Snell	7	–	56	1
Bosch	2.3	–	19	–
Cronje	2	–	14	–
Kuiper	1	–	18	–
Kirsten	7	1	22	1

FALL OF WICKETS (South Africa)
1–8, 2–10, 3–29, 4–108, 5–111, 6–121, 7–162

FALL OF WICKETS (New Zealand)
1–114, 2–155, 3–179

Umpires: Khizer Hayat & P.D. Reporter

Man of the Match – M.J. Greatbatch

New Zealand won by 7 wickets

MATCH TEN
NEW ZEALAND v. SOUTH AFRICA, at Auckland

New Zealand marched on towards the semi-finals and South Africa were brought down from their heights of ecstasy following the triumph over Australia. Officially, this was the last day of summer in New Zealand, and the home side could not have ended the season with a more exhilarating performance nor a more emphatic victory.

South Africa chose to bat first, and they were soon in trouble on the slow pitch against the off-breaks of Patel and the fast medium pace of Watson. Hudson was static as a ball from Patel turned sharply, and Wessels fell to a flying catch by Smith. In the 15th over, Cronje dabbed at Harris' first ball, and South Africa were 29 for 3, and in deep trouble.

Richardson helped Kirsten to add 79 before Cairns, having been held back by Crowe, had the South African keeper taken at mid-on. In the same over, Kuiper was run out off a no-ball when both batsmen were at the bowler's end. Kirsten played valiantly until he was caught on the long-on boundary off the 129th ball he had received.

New Zealand were never likely to be daunted by the target that South Africa had set them. The pitch blunted Donald's pace, and Greatbatch and Latham, who reached a maiden 50 for New Zealand, virtually won the match with an opening stand of 114 in 17.5 overs. Greatbatch, playing instead of the injured Wright, was the first to leave, having hit 68 off 60 balls. Latham's 60 came off 69 balls, and New Zealand won with an astonishing 15.3 overs in hand.

MATCH ELEVEN
WEST INDIES v. ZIMBABWE, at Brisbane

West Indies recovered from the thrashing they had received from England by beating Zimbabwe with a confident and authoritative display. Simmons and Lara began purposefully, and Lara scored at a run a ball. When they had departed Richardson and Hooper batted with zest and technical precision to score 117 off 127 balls. The end of the innings was somewhat naive and careless, but a score of 264 had surely put the match beyond Zimbabwe's reach.

So it proved. Flower was yorked by Patterson, and Arnott forced to retire hurt after breaking a finger. Pycroft groped forward, and in spite of Houghton's courage and bustle, Zimbabwe were doomed. Even some late hitting from Omarshah could not disguise that.

MATCH TWELVE
AUSTRALIA v. INDIA, at Brisbane

For the first time the rain-rule came into operation and, arguably, it denied India victory. Australia batted first, began slowly and were lifted by Dean Jones who started his innings with a six and a four. India bowled well and fielded smartly, and, in spite of Jones' efforts, the Australian score was kept within bounds.

India's start was more laboured than Australia's had been. Srikkanth went for nothing, but Shastri and Azharuddin had just begun to accelerate when the rain arrived. The score was 45 for 1 in 16.2 overs. When the rain had stopped India found that they were chasing a target of 236, only two less than their original target, in three overs fewer than had been their initial quota. India, not Australia, were penalised for Kapil Dev bowling two maiden overs and an over in which only two runs were conceded.

The challenge sparked Azharuddin who played some glorious cricket as he raced to 93 off 103 balls before being run out. Manjrekar, too, batted well and hit two sixes. Nineteen runs were needed from the last two overs, and 13 were wanted from the last which, incomprehensibly, was bowled by Moody.

More glided the first two balls to the fine-leg boundary, and five were needed from four balls. Looking to glide again, More walked across his stumps and was bowled. Prabhakar pushed a single so that four runs were wanted from two balls. Srinath swung. He did not run, but his partner did and was run out. Srinath swung again at the final ball and hit high to long-on where Steve Waugh could not hold the catch. Waugh's throw was fast and straight, however, and Venkatapathy Raju was short of his line and the third run which would have given India a tie. It was the least that they deserved, but once again they had not helped themselves, and a side of great potential was on its way out of the competition.

ABOVE: Srinath swings at the last ball of the match, but the ball does not go quite far enough and India lose to Australia by one run. Venkatapathy Raju is the other batsman .(David Munden)

LEFT: Ali Omarshah played some good all-round cricket for Zimbabwe. Here he bats against West Indies at Hobart. David Williams is the wicket-keeper. (David Munden)

Australia v. India at Brisbane. (David Munden)

MATCH ELEVEN – WEST INDIES v. ZIMBABWE

29 February, 1992 at Woolloongabba, Brisbane

WEST INDIES

P.V. Simmons	**b** Brandes	21
B.C. Lara	c Houghton, **b** Omarshah	72
R.B. Richardson (capt)	c Brandes, **b** Jarvis	56
C.L. Hooper	c Pycroft, **b** Traicos	63
K.L.T. Arthurton	**b** Duers	26
A.L. Logie	run out	5
M.D. Marshall	c Houghton, **b** Brandes	2
*D. Williams	not out	8
W.K.M. Benjamin	**b** Brandes	1
A.C. Cummins		
B.P. Patterson		
Extras	b 1, lb 6, w 2, nb 1	10
	(for 8 wickets)	**264**

(50 overs)

	O	M	R	W
Brandes	10	1	45	3
Jarvis	10	1	71	1
Duers	10	–	52	1
Omarshah	10	2	39	1
Traicos	10	–	50	1

FALL OF WICKETS
1–78, **2**–103, **3**–220, **4**–221, **5**–239, **6**–254, **7**–255, **8**–264

ZIMBABWE

K.J. Arnott	retired hurt	16
*A. Flower	**b** Patterson	6
A.J. Pycroft	c Williams, **b** Benjamin	10
D.L. Houghton (capt)	c Patterson, **b** Hooper	55
A.C. Waller	c Simmons, **b** Benjamin	0
A.D. Campbell	c Richardson, **b** Hooper	1
A.H. Omarshah	not out	60
E.A. Brandes	c and **b** Benjamin	6
A.J. Traicos	run out	8
M.P. Jarvis	not out	5
K.G. Duers		
Extras	lb 9, w 5, nb 8	22
	(for 7 wickets)	**189**

(50 overs)

	O	M	R	W
Patterson	10	–	25	1
Marshall	6	–	23	–
Benjamin	10	2	27	3
Cummins	10	–	33	–
Hooper	10	–	47	2
Arthurton	4	–	25	–

FALL OF WICKETS
1–24, **2**–43, **3**–48, **4**–63, **5**–132, **6**–161, **7**–181

Umpires: S.J. Woodward & K.E. Liebenberg — Man of the Match – C.L. Hooper — *West Indies won by 75 runs*

MATCH TWELVE – AUSTRALIA v. INDIA

1 March, 1992 at Woolloongabba, Brisbane

AUSTRALIA

Batsman	Dismissal	Runs
M.A. Taylor	c More, **b** Kapil Dev	13
G.R. Marsh	**b** Kapil Dev	8
*D.C. Boon	c Shastri, **b** Venkatapathy Raju	43
D.M. Jones	c and **b** Prabhakar	90
S.R. Waugh	**b** Srinath	29
T.M. Moody	**b** Prabhakar	25
A.R. Border (capt)	c Jadeja, **b** Kapil Dev	10
C.L. McDermott	c Jadeja, **b** Prabhakar	2
P.L. Taylor	run out	1
M.G. Hughes	not out	0
M.R. Whitney		
Extras	lb 7, w 5, nb 4	16
	(for 9 wickets)	**237**

INDIA

Batsman	Dismissal	Runs
R.J. Shastri	c S.R. Waugh, **b** Moody	25
K. Srikkanth	**b** McDermott	0
M. Azharuddin (capt)	run out	93
S.R. Tendulkar	c S.R. Waugh, **b** Moody	11
Kapil Dev	lbw, **b** S.R. Waugh	21
S.V. Manjrekar	run out	47
A.D. Jadeja	**b** Hughes	1
*K.S. More	**b** Moody	14
J. Srinath	not out	8
M. Prabhakar	run out	1
Venkatapathy Raju	run out	0
Extras	lb 8, w 5	13
		234

(50 overs)

Bowler	O	M	R	W
Kapil Dev	10	2	41	**3**
Prabhakar	10	–	41	**3**
Srinath	8	–	48	**1**
Tendulkar	5	–	29	–
Venkatapathy Raju	10	–	37	**1**
Jadeja	7	–	34	–

(47 overs)

Bowler	O	M	R	W
McDermott	9	1	35	**1**
Whitney	10	2	36	–
Hughes	9	1	49	**1**
Moody	9	–	56	**3**
S.R. Waugh	10	–	50	**1**

FALL OF WICKETS

1–18, **2**–31, **3**–102, **4**–156, **5**–198, **6**–230, **7**–235, **8**–236, **9**–237

FALL OF WICKETS

1–6, **2**–53, **3**–86, **4**–128, **5**–194, **6**–199, **7**–216, **8**–231, **9**–232

Umpires: B.L. Aldridge & I.D. Robinson

Man of the Match – D.M. Jones

Australia won by 1 run (revised rate)

MATCH THIRTEEN – ENGLAND v. PAKISTAN

1 March, 1992 at Adelaide Oval

PAKISTAN

Batsman	Dismissal	Runs
Ramiz Raja	c Reeve, **b** DeFreitas	1
Aamir Sohail	c and **b** Pringle	9
Inzamam-ul-Haq	c Stewart, **b** DeFreitas	0
Javed Miandad (capt)	**b** Pringle	3
Salim Malik	c Reeve, **b** Botham	17
Ijaz Ahmed	c Stewart, **b** Small	0
Wasim Akram	**b** Botham	1
*Moin Khan	c Hick, **b** Small	2
Wasim Haider	c Stewart, **b** Reeve	13
Mushtaq Ahmed	c Reeve, **b** Pringle	17
Aqib Javed	not out	1
Extras	lb 1, w 8, nb 1	10
		74

ENGLAND

Batsman	Dismissal	Runs
G.A. Gooch (capt)	c Moin Khan, **b** Wasim Akram	3
I.T. Botham	not out	6
R.A. Smith	not out	5
G.A. Hick		
N.H. Fairbrother		
* A.J. Stewart		
D.A. Reeve		
C.C. Lewis		
D.R. Pringle		
P.A.J. DeFreitas		
G.C. Small		
Extras	b 1, lb 3, w 5, nb 1	10
	(for 1 wicket)	**24**

(40.2 overs)

Bowler	O	M	R	W
Pringle	8.2	5	8	**3**
DeFreitas	7	1	22	**2**
Small	10	1	29	**2**
Botham	10	4	12	**2**
Reeve	5	3	2	**1**

(8 overs)

Bowler	O	M	R	W
Wasim Akram	3	–	7	**1**
Aqib Javed	3	1	7	–
Wasim Haider	1	–	1	–
Ijaz Ahmed	1	–	5	–

FALL OF WICKETS

1–5, **2**–5, **3**–14, **4**–20, **5**–32, **6**–35, **7**–42, **8**–47, **9**–62

FALL OF WICKET

1–17

Umpires: P.J. McConnell & S.U. Bucknor

Match abandoned

MATCH THIRTEEN
ENGLAND v. PAKISTAN, at Adelaide

If India had suffered something of an injustice because of the rain, the match between England and Pakistan revealed the total farcicality of the rules in operation in the competition.

Pakistan, with Imran again unavailable, had to bat first on a wicket that was damp and treacherous. England bowled well, exploited the favourable conditions to the utmost, and Pakistan batted badly. DeFreitas took the first wicket, that of Ramiz Raja, with a long-hop which the batsman steered to cover, and only Salim Malik showed any indication that he could cope with the conditions.

Pringle and Botham were particularly demanding, and that Pakistan 'recovered' from the abyss of 47 for 8 was due only to some lusty hitting at the death.

Having bowled out their opponents for 74 in 40.2 overs, England appeared to have the easiest of tasks. After six overs, they were 17 for the loss of Gooch, and then it rained. When the rain stopped it was calculated that England now needed to reach 61 from 21 overs, but it rained again before the match could be restarted. It finally did get under way again, and by now England's target was 64 in 16. In effect, Pakistan were profiting from the overs in which they had managed to score, and England's 14 maiden overs and other overs of economy were being considered as never having happened. Luckily, only two overs were bowled before more rain ended the farce. Pakistan took a fortunate and, as it proved, highly valuable point.

MATCH FOURTEEN
SOUTH AFRICA v. SRI LANKA, at Wellington

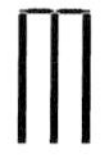

South Africa suffered an unexpected second defeat in New Zealand, and Sri Lanka, by dint of their victory, moved on to five points, level with England.

South Africa were put in to bat, and they could never generate a reasonable rate of scoring against an accurate seam attack. Wessels needed 94 balls for his 40, and Kirsten 85 for his 47, and as these two were the only significant contributors to the South African innings, a winning total did not look likely.

Sri Lanka did not start well, and the first glimpse of victory came when Ranatunga joined Mahanama in a stand of 67. Mahanama had provided the backbone to the innings with his 68 off 96 balls, and when he left Ranatunga took over. A former captain of Sri Lanka, he has spent some time in the wilderness, but he proved himself worthy of reinstatement with his performances in the World Cup. He hit six fours in his unbeaten 64, and although Sri Lanka trembled a little when Jayasuriya and Kalpage were out cheaply, Ramanayake hit the penultimate ball of the final over for four to win the match.

Jayasuriya clings on to a catch offered by Rhodes as Sri Lanka gain a surprise win over South Africa. (Joe Mann/Allsport)

MATCH FOURTEEN – SOUTH AFRICA v. SRI LANKA
2 March, 1992 at Basin Reserve, Wellington

SOUTH AFRICA

Batsman	How out	Runs
K.C. Wessels (capt)	c and **b** Ranatunga	40
A.P. Kuiper	**b** Anurasiri	18
P.N. Kirsten	**c** Hathurusinghe, **b** Kalpage	47
M.W. Rushmere	**c** Jayasuriya, **b** Ranatunga	4
J.N. Rhodes	**c** Jayasuriya, **b** Wickremasinghe	28
W.J. Cronje	**st** Tillekeratne, **b** Anurasiri	3
R.P. Snell	**b** Anurasiri	9
B.M. McMillan	not out	18
* D.J. Richardson	run out	0
O. Henry	**c** Kalpage, **b** Wickremasinghe	11
A.A. Donald	run out	3
Extras	lb 9, w 4, nb 1	14
		195

(50 overs)

	O	M	R	W
Ramanayake	9	2	19	–
Wickremasinghe	7	–	32	2
Anurasiri	10	1	41	3
Kalpage	10	–	38	1
Gurusinha	8	–	30	–
Ranatunga	6	–	26	2

FALL OF WICKETS

1–27, **2**–114, **3**–114, **4**–128, **5**–149, **6**–153, **7**–165, **8**–165, **9**–186

SRI LANKA

Batsman	How out	Runs
U.C. Hathurusinghe	**c** Wessels, **b** Donald	5
R.S. Mahanama	**c** Richardson, **b** McMillan	68
A.P. Gurusinha	lbw, **b** Donald	0
P.A. de Silva (capt)	**b** Donald	7
* H.P. Tillekeratne	**c** Rushmere, **b** Henry	17
A. Ranatunga	not out	64
S.T. Jayasuriya	**st** Richardson, **b** Kirsten	3
R.S. Kalpage	run out	5
C.P.H. Ramanayake	not out	4
G.P. Wickremasinghe		
S.D. Anurasiri		
Extras	b 1, lb 7, w 13, nb 4	25
	(for 7 wickets)	**198**

(49.5 overs)

	O	M	R	W
Donald	9.5	–	42	3
McMillan	10	2	34	1
Henry	10	–	31	1
Snell	10	1	33	–
Kuiper	5	–	25	–
Kirsten	5	–	25	1

FALL OF WICKETS

1–11, **2**–12, **3**–35, **4**–87, **5**–154, **6**–168, **7**–189

Umpires: S.J. Woodward & Khizer Hayat — Man of the Match – A. Ranatunga — *Sri Lanka won by 3 wickets*

MATCH FIFTEEN – NEW ZEALAND v. ZIMBABWE
3 March, 1992 at McLean Park, Napier

NEW ZEALAND

Batsman	How out	Runs
M.J. Greatbatch	**b** Duers	15
R.T. Latham	**b** Brandes	2
A.H. Jones	**c** Waller, **b** Butchart	57
M.D. Crowe (capt)	not out	74
C.L. Cairns	not out	1
K.R. Rutherford		
C.Z. Harris		
D.N. Patel		
* I.D.S. Smith		
G.R. Larsen		
D.K. Morrison		
Extras	b 7, lb 6	13
	(for 3 wickets)	**162**

(20.5 overs)

	O	M	R	W
Brandes	5	1	28	1
Duers	6	–	17	1
Omarshah	4	–	34	–
Butchart	4	–	53	1
Burmester	1.5	–	17	–

FALL OF WICKETS

1–9, **2**–25, **3**–154

ZIMBABWE

Batsman	How out	Runs
* A. Flower	**b** Larsen	30
A.C. Waller	**b** Morrison	11
D.L. Houghton (capt)	**b** Larsen	10
I.P. Butchart	**c** Cairns, **b** Larsen	3
E.A. Brandes	**b** Harris	6
A.J. Pycroft	not out	13
A.D. Campbell	**c** Crowe, **b** Harris	8
A.H. Omarshah	**b** Harris	7
M.G. Burmester	not out	4
A.J. Traicos		
K.G. Duers		
Extras	lb 9, w 3, nb 1	13
	(for 7 wickets)	**105**

(18 overs)

	O	M	R	W
Morrison	4	–	14	1
Cairns	2	–	27	–
Larsen	4	–	16	3
Harris	4	–	15	3
Latham	3	–	18	–
Crowe	1	–	6	–

FALL OF WICKETS

1–22, **2**–41, **3**–63, **4**–63, **5**–75, **6**–86, **7**–97

Umpires: K.E. Liebenberg & D.P. Buultjens — Man of the Match – M.D. Crowe — *New Zealand won by 48 runs (revised rate)*

MATCH FIFTEEN
NEW ZEALAND v. ZIMBABWE, at Napier

New Zealand maintained their 100 per cent record by beating Zimbabwe in a game which rain reduced to an 18-over slog. The home side struggled to 52 for 2 in 12 overs, and, with rain threatening, this was clearly not good enough. New Zealand had been put in, and, following a third break for rain, Martin Crowe and Andrew Jones extended their partnership to 129 in 14 overs. Crowe reached 50 off 31 balls, and Jones' 50 came off 56 balls.

Zimbabwe's bowlers were much handicapped by the dampness, and Butchart, who was hit for 53 in four overs, twice slipped and fell in his delivery stride. Their batsmen could not reach the required rate of scoring, and New Zealand claimed victory in a bizarre match.

MATCH SIXTEEN
INDIA v. PAKISTAN, at Sydney

India omitted Shastri because of slow scoring, and Jadeja moved up to open the innings. It was he who provided the aggression when Azharuddin chose to bat first. Srikkanth was more circumspect and faced 39 balls before edging the reliable and controlled Aqib to the keeper.

Wasim Akram was less controlled and offered a liberal sprinkling of wides. The Pakistan attack was steady rather than lethal, and Azharuddin played some exquisite shots as he and Jadeja added 61 in 15 overs. Azharuddin was out when he tried to cut a leg-break that turned more than expected, and Jadeja, who batted impressively, was held at mid-wicket three overs later. Sachin Tendulkar and Vinod Kambli, playing his first World Cup match, showed charm and elegance for 12 overs, and after the highly promising left-handed Kambli had departed, Tendulkar continued to flourish in company with the hard-hitting Kapil Dev. On a slow pitch and outfield, India's 216 was a reasonable score.

It was to prove far beyond Pakistan's reach. Inzamam-ul-Haq and Zahid Fazal failed, and only Aamir Sohail, who hit six fours, played with any freedom or style. Javed Miandad occupied 34 overs and faced 113 balls for his 40. In doing so, he virtually eclipsed any chance his side had of winning. He also managed to get embroiled in a verbal conflict with More who had an appeal rejected. It was an unsavoury incident in an emotional match.

India were worthy winners and looked a capable side. Pakistan remained the great under-achievers.

MATCH SEVENTEEN
WEST INDIES v. SOUTH AFRICA, at Christchurch

South Africa enhanced their chances of reaching the semi-finals with an excellent win over West Indies, a side struggling for consistency. One of the problems encountered by the South Africans had been the sluggish pitches. They had generally failed to adapt to them and had started slowly. At Lancaster Park, they were favoured by a pitch which had pace and bounce, but they still began slowly.

Wessels skied an intended pull to bring early worries, and the substance of the innings came from Kirsten who faced 91 balls for his 56, hit a five and two fours and finished with a runner because of a calf injury. If no batsman could generate an exciting rate of scoring, South Africa were helped by some poor West Indian ground fielding. This is, indeed, a side in transition.

Having reached 200 for the first time in the competition, South Africa then proceeded to demolish the top of the West Indian batting order. In the space of 11 balls, without conceding a run, Meyrick Pringle sent back Lara, Richardson, Hooper and Arthurton to reduce West Indies to 19 for 4. On top of this, Haynes was forced to retire hurt when hit three times on a hand that was already damaged. At 70 for 6, he returned.

With Kirsten unable to bowl because of his injury, Kuiper was pressed into service. Logie swung him for six and four and went on to make 61 off 69, but when he was caught in the deep West Indies were beaten.

Wasim Akram is stumped by More as India beat Pakistan in Sydney. (David Munden)

One of the great memories of the tournament – the fielding of South Africa's Jonty Rhodes. (Patrick Eagar)

MATCH SIXTEEN – INDIA v. PAKISTAN

4 March, 1992 at SCG, Sydney

INDIA

A.D. Jadeja	c Zahid Fazal, b Wasim Haider	46
K. Srikkanth	c Moin Khan, b Aqib Javed	5
M. Azharuddin (capt)	c Moin Khan, b Mushtaq Ahmed	32
V.G. Kambli	c Inzamam-ul-Haq, b Mushtaq Ahmed	24
S.R. Tendulkar	not out	54
S.V. Manjrekar	b Mushtaq Ahmed	0
Kapil Dev	c Imran Khan, b Aqib Javed	35
* K.S. More	run out	4
M. Prabhakar	not out	2
Venkatapathy Raju		
J. Srinath		
Extras	lb 3, w 9, nb 2	14
	(for 7 wickets)	**216**

(49 overs)

	O	M	R	W
Wasim Akram	10	–	45	–
Aqib Javed	8	2	28	2
Imran Khan	8	–	25	–
Wasim Haider	10	1	36	1
Mushtaq Ahmed	10	–	59	3
Aamir Sohail	3	–	20	–

FALL OF WICKETS
1–25, 2–86, 3–101, 4–147, 5–148, 6–208, 7–213

PAKISTAN

Aamir Sohail	c Srikkanth, b Tendulkar	62
Inzamam-ul-Haq	lbw, b Kapil Dev	2
Zahid Fazal	c More, b Prabhakar	2
Javed Miandad	b Srinath	40
Salim Malik	c More, b Prabhakar	12
Imran Khan (capt)	run out	0
Wasim Akram	st More, b Venkatapathy Raju	4
Wasim Haider	b Srinath	13
*Moin Khan	c Manjrekar, b Kapil Dev	12
Mushtaq Ahmed	run out	3
Aqib Javed	not out	1
Extras	lb 6, w 15, nb 1	22
		173

(48.1 overs)

	O	M	R	W
Kapil Dev	10	–	30	2
Prabhakar	10	1	22	2
Srinath	8.1	–	37	2
Tendulkar	10	–	37	1
Venkatapathy Raju	10	1	41	1

FALL OF WICKETS
1–8, 2–17, 3–105, 4–127, 5–130, 6–141, 7–141, 8–161, 9–166

Umpires: P.J. McConnell & D.R. Shepherd — Man of the Match – S.R. Tendulkar — *India won by 43 runs*

MATCH SEVENTEEN – WEST INDIES v. SOUTH AFRICA
5 March, 1992 at Lancaster Park, Christchurch

SOUTH AFRICA

Batsman	How out	Runs
K.C. Wessels (capt)	c Haynes, b Marshall	1
A.C. Hudson	c Lara, b Cummins	22
M.W. Rushmere	st Williams, b Hooper	10
A.P. Kuiper	b Ambrose	23
P.N. Kirsten	c Williams, b Marshall	56
J.N. Rhodes	c Williams, b Cummins	22
B.M. McMillan	c Lara, b Benjamin	20
R.P. Snell	c Haynes, b Ambrose	3
*D.J. Richardson	not out	20
M.W. Pringle	not out	5
A.A. Donald		
Extras	lb 8, w 3, nb 7	18
	(for 8 wickets)	200

WEST INDIES

Batsman	How out	Runs
D.L. Haynes	c Richardson, b Kuiper	30
B.C. Lara	c Rhodes, b Pringle	9
R.B. Richardson (capt)	lbw, b Pringle	1
C.L. Hooper	c Wessels, b Pringle	0
K.L.T. Arthurton	c Wessels, b Pringle	0
A.L. Logie	c Pringle, b Kuiper	61
M.D. Marshall	c Rhodes, b Snell	6
*D. Williams	c Richardson, b Snell	0
C.E.L. Ambrose	run out	12
A.C. Cummins	c McMillan, b Donald	6
W.K.M. Benjamin	not out	1
Extras	lb 9, w 1	10
		136

(50 overs)

	O	M	R	W
Ambrose	10	1	34	2
Marshall	10	1	26	2
Benjamin	10	–	47	1
Cummins	10	–	40	2
Hooper	10	–	45	1

(38.4 overs)

	O	M	R	W
Donald	6.4	2	13	1
Pringle	8	4	11	4
McMillan	8	2	36	–
Snell	7	2	16	2
Kuiper	9	–	51	2

FALL OF WICKETS
1–8, 2–52, 3–73, 4–119, 5–127, 6–159, 7–181, 8–187

FALL OF WICKETS
1–10, 2–19, 3–19, 4–19, 5–70, 6–70, 7–116, 8–117, 9–132

Umpires: B.L. Aldridge & S.G. Randell — Man of the Match – M.W. Pringle — *South Africa won by 64 runs*

MATCH EIGHTEEN
AUSTRALIA v. ENGLAND, at Sydney

Australia entered the World Cup as holders and clear favourites to retain the trophy. By the time they came to meet England, they had won only one of three encounters, and that was a somewhat fortuitous victory over India. For both morale and for keeping alive realistic hopes of reaching the semi-finals, Australia needed to beat England.

Border won the toss, and Australia batted. The atmosphere was humid, and there was the possibility of a storm. It never materialised, and the match went to its full quota of overs. In the third over, Pringle's inswinger beat Mark Taylor and trapped him leg before. Boon quickly found his touch, and Moody appeared to relish his promotion to open the innings in place of Marsh.

Boon is always regarded as a danger man by his opponents. His record has earned him respect. When he was run out by Fairbrother's direct hit as he and Moody hesitated over a run it was a boost for England and a severe blow to Australia. Moody and Jones now threatened to assert Australian control, particularly against Botham and Tufnell, who was later diagnosed as being unwell.

David Boon is run out, and another Australian collapse is on the way. Lewis is the fielder. (David Munden)

England gained composure with the bowling of DeFreitas, but it was a brilliant diving catch by Lewis at backward point off a hard cut by Jones that brought the breakthrough. Moody was bowled off his glove as he swept, and it was Border and Steve Waugh who attempted to keep the Australian score moving. They were doing well enough until, in the 38th over, Botham beat Border with an in-swinger.

Healy swept Tufnell for six, and then tried to hit Botham in the same direction and perished at mid-wicket. A quicker ball from Botham darted in at Peter Taylor and caught him directly in front, and before the over was completed, McDermott had tried to hit the ball over mid-on, only to be splendidly caught by DeFreitas. In seven deliveries, Botham had taken four wickets without conceding a run.

Eventually, England faced a target of 172, which, on a good wicket, was never likely to be demanding. Gooch and Botham soon eased any nerves there might have been with a partnership of 107 in 24 overs. Botham hit 53 off 77 balls, and there was no doubt that 'Beefy' was back and in business.

RIGHT: Botham roars an appeal as he traps Peter Taylor leg before for 0. (Patrick Eagar)

BELOW: Tom Moody unluckily plays on to Phil Tufnell. (David Munden)

MATCH EIGHTEEN – AUSTRALIA v. ENGLAND
5 March, 1992 at SCG, Sydney

AUSTRALIA

Batsman	How out	Runs
T.M. Moody	b Tufnell	51
M.A. Taylor	lbw, b Pringle	0
D.C. Boon	run out	18
D.M. Jones	c Lewis, b DeFreitas	22
S.R. Waugh	run out	27
A.R. Border (capt)	b Botham	16
* I.A. Healy	c Fairbrother, b Botham	9
P.L. Taylor	lbw, b Botham	0
C.J. McDermott	c DeFreitas, b Botham	0
M.R. Whitney	not out	8
B.A. Reid	b Reeve	1
Extras	b 2, lb 8, w 5, nb 4	19
		171

ENGLAND

Batsman	How out	Runs
G.A. Gooch (capt)	b S.R. Waugh	58
I.T. Botham	c Healy, b Whitney	53
R.A. Smith	not out	30
G.A. Hick	not out	7
N.H. Fairbrother		
* A.J. Stewart		
D.A. Reeve		
C.C. Lewis		
D.R. Pringle		
P.A.J. DeFreitas		
P.C.R. Tufnell		
Extras	lb 13, w 8, nb 4	25
	(for 2 wickets)	**173**

(49 overs)

	O	M	R	W
Pringle	9	1	24	1
Lewis	10	2	28	–
DeFreitas	10	3	23	1
Botham	10	1	31	4
Tufnell	9	–	52	1
Reeve	1	–	3	1

(40.5 overs)

	O	M	R	W
McDermott	10	1	29	–
Reid	7.5	–	49	–
Whitney	10	2	28	1
S.R. Waugh	6	–	29	1
P.L. Taylor	3	–	7	–
Moody	4	–	18	–

FALL OF WICKETS
1–5, **2**–35, **3**–106, **4**–114, **5**–145, **6**–155, **7**–155, **8**–155, **9**–164

FALL OF WICKETS
1–107, **2**–153

Umpires: S.U. Bucknor & Khizer Hayat — Man of the Match – I.T. Botham — *England won by 8 wickets*

MATCH NINETEEN – INDIA v. ZIMBABWE
7 March, 1992 at Trust Bank Park, Hamilton

INDIA

Batsman	How out	Runs
K. Srikkanth	b Burmester	32
Kapil Dev	lbw, b Brandes	10
M. Azharuddin (capt)	c Flower, b Burmester	12
S.R. Tendulkar	c Campbell, b Burmester	81
S.V. Manjrekar	c Duers, b Traicos	34
V.G. Kambli	b Traicos	1
A.D. Jadeja	c Omarshah, b Traicos	6
* K.S. More	not out	15
J. Srinath	not out	6
M. Prabhakar		
Venkatapathy Raju		
Extras	lb 3, w 3	6
	(for 7 wickets)	**203**

ZIMBABWE

Batsman	How out	Runs
* A. Fowler	not out	43
A.H. Omarshah	b Tendulkar	31
A.C. Waller	not out	13
A.J. Pycroft		
D.L. Houghton (capt)		
A.D. Campbell		
E.A. Brandes		
I.P. Butchart		
M.G. Burmester		
A.J. Traicos		
K.G. Duers		
Extras	b 1, lb 11, w 5	17
	(for 1 wicket)	**104**

(32 overs)

	O	M	R	W
Brandes	7	–	43	1
Duers	7	–	48	–
Burmester	6	–	36	3
Omarshah	6	1	38	–
Traicos	6	–	35	3

(19.1 overs)

	O	M	R	W
Prabhakar	3	–	14	–
Kapil Dev	4	–	6	–
Srinath	4	–	20	–
Tendulkar	6	–	35	1
Venkatapathy Raju	2.1	–	17	–

FALL OF WICKETS
1–23, **2**–43, **3**–69, **4**–168, **5**–170, **6**–182, **7**–184

FALL OF WICKET
1–79

Umpires: D.P. Buultjens & S.G. Randell — Man of the Match – S.R. Tendulkar — *India won by 55 runs (revised rate)*

MATCH NINETEEN
INDIA v. ZIMBABWE, at Hamilton

Rain was unkind to both India and Zimbabwe during the course of the World Cup, and it took its toll when the two sides met at Trust Bank Park. The match was initially reduced to 32 overs per innings, and India reached 203 thanks to another glorious knock by Sachin Tendulkar who hit a six and eight fours in his 78 off 76 balls. He and Manjrekar added 99 off 90 deliveries.

Zimbabwe maintained a good rate of scoring, with Andy Flower again impressive, but when rain arrived at the start of the 20th over the odds against them became impossible.

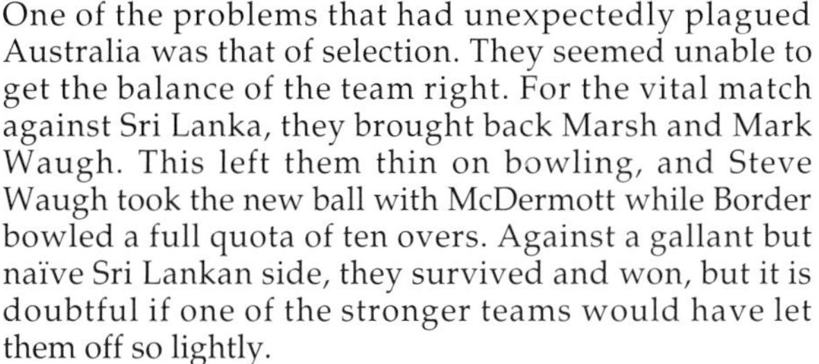

MATCH TWENTY
AUSTRALIA v. SRI LANKA, at Adelaide

One of the problems that had unexpectedly plagued Australia was that of selection. They seemed unable to get the balance of the team right. For the vital match against Sri Lanka, they brought back Marsh and Mark Waugh. This left them thin on bowling, and Steve Waugh took the new ball with McDermott while Border bowled a full quota of ten overs. Against a gallant but naïve Sri Lankan side, they survived and won, but it is doubtful if one of the stronger teams would have let them off so lightly.

Sri Lanka, put in first, in steaming heat, batted erratically and contributed to their own downfall. Mahanama did not respond to a call, but Samarasekera ran all the same, and Mahanama sacrificed himself, rather unwisely as he was in form. Aravinda de Silva, a batsman of immense talent upon whom the weight of captaincy seems very heavy, played his one good innings of the competition, but Sri Lanka's 189 was never enough to trouble Australia.

Moody and Marsh began with 120, and Australia had six overs to spare when the game was won.

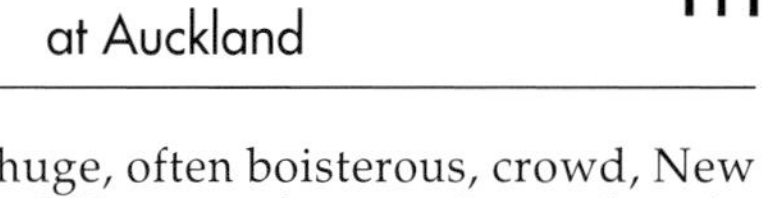

MATCH TWENTY-ONE
NEW ZEALAND v. WEST INDIES, at Auckland

To the delight of a huge, often boisterous, crowd, New Zealand gained their fifth win in five matches and, in the process, made West Indies' chances of qualifying for the semi-finals look slim.

Put in to bat and confronted by New Zealand's intelligent new-ball pairing of spin and medium pace, West Indies moved to 65 in the 19th over before they lost a wicket. Crowe's field-placing was always thoughtful, and, with Patel bowling particularly accurately, West Indies could never really break free. On paper, their batting line-up looks strong, but the middle order was one of promise rather than fulfilment. New Zealand bowled steadily, and they fielded with consistent enthusiasm and skill.

Ambrose and Marshall bowled beautifully at the start, but Greatbatch again showed astonishing belligerence. He hit Marshall for a huge six and unsettled Ambrose. In ten overs, New Zealand were 53, and when Greatbatch was third out, caught on the cover boundary, the score was 100 in the 25th over.

There was still much to do, but plenty of time in which to do it, and Martin Crowe played with measured calm and authority which gave both confidence and pride to his team. He, more than any man, had brought New Zealand to a position of eminence which few had envisaged, and they now seemed sure of a place in the last four.

Mark Greatbatch produced some of the most devastating hitting in the competition. Here he lashes out during his innings of 63 against West Indies at Auckland. (Joe Mann/Allsport)

MATCH TWENTY – SRI LANKA v. AUSTRALIA
7 March, 1992 at Adelaide Oval

SRI LANKA

R.S. Mahanama	run out	7
M.A.R. Samarasekera	c Healy, b P.L. Taylor	34
A.P. Gurusinha	lbw, b Whitney	5
P.A. de Silva (capt)	c Moody, b McDermott	62
A. Ranatunga	c Jones, b P.L. Taylor	23
S.T. Jayasuriya	lbw, b Border	15
* H.P. Tillekeratne	run out	5
R.S. Kalpage	run out	14
C.P.H. Ramanayake	run out	5
S.D. Anurasiri	not out	4
G.P. Wickremasinghe		
Extras	b 3, lb 6, w 1, nb 5	15
	(for 9 wickets)	**189**

(50 overs)

	O	M	R	W
McDermott	10	–	28	1
S.R. Waugh	7	–	34	–
Whitney	10	3	26	1
Moody	3	–	18	–
P.L. Taylor	10	–	34	2
Border	10	–	40	1

FALL OF WICKETS
1–8, 2–28, 3–72, 4–123, 5–151, 6–163, 7–166, 8–182, 9–189

AUSTRALIA

T.M. Moody	c Mahanama, b Wickremasinghe	57
G.R. Marsh	c Anurasiri, b Kalpage	60
M.E. Waugh	c Mahanama, b Wickremasinghe	26
D.C. Boon	not out	27
D.M. Jones	not out	12
A.R. Border (capt)		
S.R. Waugh		
* I.A. Healy		
P.L. Taylor		
C.J. McDermott		
M.R. Whitney		
Extras	lb 2, w 3, nb 3	8
	(for 3 wickets)	**190**

(44 overs)

	O	M	R	W
Wickremasinghe	10	3	29	2
Ramanayake	9	1	44	–
Anurasiri	10	–	43	–
Gurusinha	6	–	20	–
Ranatunga	1	–	11	–
Kalpage	8	–	41	1

FALL OF WICKETS
1–120, 2–130, 3–165

Umpires: P.D. Reporter & I.D. Robinson — Man of the Match – T.M. Moody — *Australia won by 7 wickets*

MATCH TWENTY-ONE – NEW ZEALAND v. WEST INDIES
8 March, 1992 at Eden Park, Auckland

WEST INDIES

D.L. Haynes	c and b Harris	22
B.C. Lara	c Rutherford, b Larsen	52
R.B. Richardson (capt)	c Smith, b Watson	29
C.L. Hooper	c Greatbatch, b Patel	2
K.L.T. Arthurton	b Morrison	40
A.L. Logie	b Harris	3
M.D. Marshall	b Larsen	5
* D. Williams	not out	32
W.K.M. Benjamin	not out	2
C.E.L. Ambrose		
A.C. Cummins		
Extras	lb 8, w 7, nb 1	16
	(for 7 wickets)	**203**

(50 overs)

	O	M	R	W
Patel	10	2	19	1
Harris	10	2	32	2
Morrison	9	1	33	1
Watson	10	2	56	1
Larsen	10	–	41	2
Latham	1	–	14	–

FALL OF WICKETS
1–65, 2–95, 3–100, 4–136, 5–142, 6–156, 7–201

NEW ZEALAND

M.J. Greatbatch	c Haynes, b Benjamin	63
R.T. Latham	c Williams, b Cummins	14
A.H. Jones	c Williams, b Benjamin	10
M.D. Crowe (capt)	not out	81
K.R. Rutherford	c Williams, b Ambrose	8
C.Z. Harris	c Williams, b Cummins	7
D.N. Patel	not out	10
* I.D.S. Smith		
G.R. Larsen		
D.K. Morrison		
W. Watson		
Extras	lb 7, w 5, nb 1	13
	(for 5 wickets)	**206**

(48.3 overs)

	O	M	R	W
Ambrose	10	1	41	1
Marshall	9	1	35	–
Cummins	10	–	53	2
Benjamin	9.3	3	34	2
Hooper	10	–	36	–

FALL OF WICKETS
1–67, 2–97, 3–100, 4–135, 5–174

Umpires: K.E. Liebenberg & P.J. McConnell — Man of the Match – M.D. Crowe — *New Zealand won by 5 wickets*

MATCH TWENTY-TWO
PAKISTAN v. SOUTH AFRICA, at Brisbane

The rain-rule farce struck again at Brisbane, and it could well have cost Pakistan a place in the semi-finals. On a good batting pitch, they had bowled well enough to restrict South Africa to 211 in their 50 overs. It must be said, however, that Wasim Akram again bowled with little control, and the Pakistan fielding was, for the most part, shoddy.

Having chosen to enter the World Cup without Rice and Cook, South Africa were finding batting something of a problem, and their innings relied on two stands, one of 67 between Hudson and Rushmere, and the other of 71 in 12 overs by Cronje and McMillan after four wickets had fallen for 29 runs.

All was going well for Pakistan as Inzamam-ul-Haq and Imran Khan began to hit the ball sweetly. After 22 overs they were 74 for 2, and 138 from 28 overs at this stage did not appear to be a difficult task. Then there was a thunderstorm. Play was suspended for an hour, and Pakistan's quota was reduced by 14 overs. Their target was reduced by only 18 runs.

The pressure was now very great indeed. Jonty Rhodes ran out Inzamam-ul-Haq in spectacular fashion. An over from Kuiper saw nine runs scored, a catch dropped and three wickets fall, including those of Salim Malik and Wasim Akram. With them went Pakistan's last hope.

MATCH TWENTY-THREE
ENGLAND v. SRI LANKA, at Ballarat

Not surprisingly, England beat Sri Lanka with some ease. They did not start well. Gooch was ponderous before he was beaten on the back foot. Smith hesitated and was run out, and Botham, having hit two sixes and five fours, missed as he aimed to cut. Hick hit 41 off 62 balls without ever suggesting conviction, and it was left to Stewart and Fairbrother to give the innings the impetus that it needed.

Stewart had been a surprise appointment as vice-captain in New Zealand, and his inclusion as wicket-keeper in the World Cup squad did not please many, yet he had prospered in New Zealand, and he had begun to shine in the World Cup. In nine overs, he and Fairbrother added 80. The Lancastrian hit two sixes and two fours in his 70 off 63 balls; Stewart settled for a six and seven fours in his 59 off 46 deliveries. Then came Chris Lewis with 20 off eight balls, including two sixes and a four, and Sri Lanka were staring at a massive target of 281.

Lewis fielded brilliantly off his bowling, had Mahanama caught at slip and Samarasekera taken at mid-on. He quickly added Gurusinha and de Silva, and the match was effectively at an end.

Graeme Hick is bowled by Ramanayake for 41, England v. Sri Lanka, Ballarat. (Patrick Eagar)

England v. Sri Lanka at Ballarat. (David Munden)

MATCH TWENTY-TWO – PAKISTAN v. SOUTH AFRICA
8 March, 1992 at Woolloongabba, Brisbane

SOUTH AFRICA

A.C. Hudson	c Ijaz Ahmed, b Imran Khan	54
K.C. Wessels (capt)	c Moin Khan, b Aqib Javed	7
M.W. Rushmere	c Aamir Sohail, b Mushtaq Ahmed	35
A.P. Kuiper	c Moin Khan, b Imran Khan	5
J.N. Rhodes	lbw, b Iqbal Sikander	5
W.J. Cronje	not out	47
B.M. McMillan	b Wasim Akram	33
*D.J. Richardson	b Wasim Akram	5
R.P. Snell	not out	1
M.W. Pringle		
A.A. Donald		
Extras	lb 8, w 2, nb 9	19
	(for 7 wickets)	211

(50 overs)	O	M	R	W
Wasim Akram	10	–	42	2
Aqib Javed	7	1	36	1
Imran Khan	10	–	34	2
Iqbal Sikander	8	–	30	1
Ijaz Ahmed	7	–	26	–
Mushtaq Ahmed	8	1	35	1

FALL OF WICKETS
1–31, 2–98, 3–110, 4–111, 5–127, 6–198, 7–207

PAKISTAN

Aamir Sohail	b Snell	23
Zahid Fazal	c Richardson, b McMillan	11
Inzamam-ul-Haq	run out	48
Imran Khan (capt)	c Richardson, b McMillan	34
Salim Malik	c Donald, b Kuiper	12
Wasim Akram	c Snell, b Kuiper	9
Ijaz Ahmed	c Rhodes, b Kuiper	6
*Moin Khan	not out	5
Mushtaq Ahmed	run out	4
Iqbal Sikander	not out	1
Aqib Javed		
Extras	lb 2, w 17, nb 1	20
	(for 8 wickets)	173

(36 overs)	O	M	R	W
Donald	7	1	31	–
Pringle	7	–	31	–
Snell	8	2	26	1
McMillan	7	–	34	2
Kuiper	6	–	40	3
Cronje	1	–	9	–

FALL OF WICKETS
1–50, 2–50, 3–135, 4–136, 5–156, 6–157, 7–163, 8–170

Umpires: B.L. Aldridge & S.U. Bucknor — Man of the Match – A.C. Hudson — *South Africa won by 20 runs (revised rate)*

MATCH TWENTY-THREE – ENGLAND v. SRI LANKA
9 March, 1992 at Eastern Oval, Ballarat

ENGLAND

G.A. Gooch (capt)	b Labrooy	8
I.T. Botham	b Anurasiri	47
R.A. Smith	run out	19
G.A. Hick	b Ramanayake	41
N.H. Fairbrother	c Ramanayake, b Gurusinha	63
*A.J. Stewart	c Jayasuriya, b Gurusinha	59
C.C. Lewis	not out	20
D.R. Pringle	not out	0
D.A. Reeve		
P.A.J. DeFreitas		
R.K. Illingworth		
Extras	b 1, lb 9, w 9, nb 4	23
	(for 6 wickets)	280

(50 overs)	O	M	R	W
Wickremasinghe	9	–	54	–
Ramanayake	10	–	42	1
Labrooy	10	1	68	1
Anurasiri	10	1	27	1
Gurusinha	10	–	67	2
Jayasuriya	1	–	12	–

FALL OF WICKETS
1–44, 2–80, 3–105, 4–164, 5–244, 6–268

SRI LANKA

R.S. Mahanama	c Botham, b Lewis	9
M.A.R. Samarasekera	c Illingworth, b Lewis	23
A.P. Gurusinha	c and b Lewis	7
P.A. de Silva (capt)	c Fairbrother, b Lewis	7
A. Ranatunga	c Stewart, b Botham	36
*H.P. Tillekeratne	run out	4
S.T. Jayasuriya	c DeFreitas, b Illingworth	19
G.F. Labrooy	c Smith, b Illingworth	19
C.P.H. Ramanayake	c and b Reeve	12
S.D. Anurasiri	lbw, b Reeve	11
G.P. Wickremasinghe	not out	6
Extras	lb 7, w 8, nb 6	21
		174

(44 overs)	O	M	R	W
Pringle	7	1	27	–
Lewis	8	–	30	4
DeFreitas	5	1	31	–
Botham	10	–	33	1
Illingworth	10	–	32	2
Reeve	4	–	14	2

FALL OF WICKETS
1–33, 2–46, 3–56, 4–60, 5–91, 6–119, 7–123, 8–156, 9–158

Umpires: Khizer Hayat & P.D. Reporter — Man of the Match – C.C. Lewis — *England won by 106 runs*

MATCH TWENTY-FOUR
WEST INDIES v. INDIA, at Wellington

Rain once more interfered with a match in which India were participants, but on this occasion they could have no cause for complaint. They chose to bat first when they won the toss and were given a sound start by Jadeja and Srikkanth. Azharuddin played with much of his elegant power and hit 61 off 83 balls, but Ambrose, returning for his second spell, cut short Tendulkar's innings with a superb delivery, and India lost their last seven wickets for 31 runs in 16 overs. Their total of 197 was a meagre effort in the circumstances.

With the weather uncertain, Lara went for quick runs and hit 41 off 37 deliveries so that when rain arrived at the end of the 11th over West Indies were 81 for the loss of Haynes. There were no more interruptions, and West Indies had to reach 195 in 46 overs. Lara's early blast and some enterprise from Arthurton and Hooper made this a relatively easy task.

MATCH TWENTY-FIVE
SOUTH AFRICA v. ZIMBABWE, at Canberra

Whatever lingering hopes of reaching the semi-finals Zimbabwe may have cherished disappeared when they became South Africa's fourth victims of the tournament. They were overpowered by the South African seam attack, and only some lively blows from the tail-enders took them to a totally inadequate 163.

There was never a need for South Africa to hurry, but Wessels was a little too slow for comfort, and his side were 71 for 1 after 25 overs. Realising that run rate could be important, Kirsten accelerated, and he and his captain added 112. Wessels fell when the match was all but decided.

MATCH TWENTY-FOUR – WEST INDIES v. INDIA
10 March, 1992 at Basin Reserve, Wellington

INDIA

A.D. Jadeja	c Benjamin, **b** Simmons	27
K. Srikkanth	c Logie, **b** Hooper	40
M. Azharuddin (capt)	c Ambrose, **b** Cummins	61
S.R. Tendulkar	c Williams, **b** Ambrose	4
S.V. Manjrekar	run out	27
Kapil Dev	c Haynes, **b** Cummins	3
P.K. Amre	c Hooper, **b** Ambrose	4
*K.S. More	c Hooper, **b** Cummins	5
M. Prabhakar	c Richardson, **b** Cummins	8
J. Srinath	not out	5
Venkatapathy Raju	run out	1
Extras	lb 6, w 5, nb 1	12
		197

(49.4 overs)

	O	M	R	W
Ambrose	10	1	24	2
Benjamin	9.4	–	35	–
Cummins	10	–	33	4
Simmons	9	–	48	1
Hooper	10	–	46	1
Arthurton	1	–	5	–

FALL OF WICKETS
1–56, **2**–102, **3**–115, **4**–166, **5**–171, **6**–173, **7**–180, **8**–186, **9**–193

WEST INDIES

D.L. Haynes	c Manjrekar, **b** Kapil Dev	16
B.C. Lara	c Manjrekar, **b** Srinath	41
P.V. Simmons	c Tendulkar, **b** Prabhakar	22
R.B. Richardson (capt)	c Srikkanth, **b** Srinath	3
K.L.T. Arthurton	not out	58
A.L. Logie	c More, **b** Venkatapathy Raju	7
C.L. Hooper	not out	34
* D. Williams		
C.E.L. Ambrose		
A.C. Cummins		
W.K.M. Benjamin		
Extras	lb 8, w 2, nb 4	14
	(for 5 wickets)	**195**

(40.3 overs)

	O	M	R	W
Kapil Dev	8	–	45	1
Prabhakar	9	–	55	1
Venkatapathy Raju	10	2	32	1
Srinath	9	2	23	2
Tendulkar	3	–	20	–
Srikkanth	1	–	7	–
Jadeja	0.3	–	5	–

FALL OF WICKETS
1–57, **2**–81, **3**–88, **4**–98, **5**–112

Umpires: S.G. Randell & S.J. Woodward — Man of the Match – A.C. Cummins — *West Indies won by 5 wickets (revised rate)*

MATCH TWENTY-FIVE – ZIMBABWE v. SOUTH AFRICA
10 March, 1992 at Manuka Oval, Canberra

ZIMBABWE

W.R. James	lbw, **b** Pringle	5
*A. Flower	c Richardson, **b** Cronje	19
A.J. Pycroft	c Wessels, **b** McMillan	19
D.L. Houghton (capt)	c Cronje, **b** Kirsten	15
A.C. Waller	c Cronje, **b** Kirsten	15
A.H. Omarshah	c Wessels, **b** Kirsten	3
E.A. Brandes	c Richardson, **b** McMillan	20
M.G. Burmester	c Kuiper, **b** Cronje	1
A.J. Traicos	not out	16
M.P. Jarvis	c and **b** McMillan	17
K.G. Duers	**b** Donald	5
Extras	lb 11, w 13, nb 4	28
		163

(48.3 overs)

	O	M	R	W
Donald	9.3	1	25	1
Pringle	9	–	25	1
Snell	10	3	24	–
McMillan	10	1	30	3
Cronje	5	–	17	2
Kirsten	5	–	31	3

FALL OF WICKETS

1–7, **2**–51, **3**–72, **4**–80, **5**–80, **6**–115, **7**–117, **8**–123, **9**–151

SOUTH AFRICA

K.C. Wessels (capt)	**b** Omarshah	70
A.C. Hudson	**b** Jarvis	13
P.N. Kirsten	not out	62
A.P. Kuiper	c Burmester, **b** Brandes	7
J.N. Rhodes	not out	3
W.J. Cronje		
B.M. McMillan		
M.W. Pringle		
R.P. Snell		
*D.J. Richardson		
A.A. Donald		
Extras	lb 4, w 2, nb 3	9
	(for 3 wickets)	**164**

(45.1 overs)

	O	M	R	W
Brandes	9.1	–	39	1
Jarvis	9	2	23	1
Burmester	5	–	20	–
Omarshah	8	2	33	1
Duers	8	1	19	–
Traicos	6	–	26	–

FALL OF WICKETS

1–27, **2**–139, **3**–151

Umpires: S.U. Bucknor & D.R. Shepherd — Man of the Match – P.N. Kirsten — *South Africa won by 7 wickets*

MATCH TWENTY-SIX – AUSTRALIA v. PAKISTAN
11 March, 1992 at WACA Ground, Perth

PAKISTAN

Aamir Sohail	c Healy, **b** Moody	76
Ramiz Raja	c Border, **b** Whitney	34
Salim Malik	**b** Moody	0
Javed Miandad	c Healy, **b** S.R. Waugh	46
Imran Khan (capt)	c Moody, **b** S.R. Waugh	13
Inzamam-ul-Haq	run out	16
Ijaz Ahmed	run out	0
Wasim Akram	c M.E. Waugh, **b** S.R. Waugh	0
*Moin Khan	c Healy, **b** McDermott	5
Mushtaq Ahmed	not out	3
Aqib Javed		
Extras	lb 9, w 16, nb 2	27
	(for 9 wickets)	**220**

(50 overs)

	O	M	R	W
McDermott	10	–	33	1
Reid	9	–	37	–
S.R. Waugh	10	–	36	3
Whitney	10	1	50	1
Moody	10	–	42	2
M.E. Waugh	1	–	13	–

FALL OF WICKETS

1–78, **2**–80, **3**–157, **4**–193, **5**–194, **6**–205, **7**–205, **8**–214, **9**–220

AUSTRALIA

T.M. Moody	c Salim Malik, **b** Aqib Javed	4
G.R. Marsh	c Moin Khan, **b** Imran Khan	39
D.C. Boon	c Mushtaq Ahmed, **b** Aqib Javed	5
D.M. Jones	c Aqib Javed, **b** Mushtaq Ahmed	47
M.E. Waugh	c Ijaz Ahmed, **b** Mushtaq Ahmed	30
A.R. Border (capt)	c Ijaz Ahmed, **b** Mushtaq Ahmed	1
S.R. Waugh	c Moin Khan, **b** Imran Khan	5
*I.A. Healy	c Ijaz Ahmed, **b** Aqib Javed	8
C.J. McDermott	lbw, **b** Wasim Akram	0
M.R. Whitney	**b** Wasim Akram	5
B.A. Reid	not out	0
Extras	lb 7, w 14, nb 7	28
		172

(45.2 overs)

	O	M	R	W
Wasim Akram	7.2	–	28	2
Aqib Javed	8	1	21	3
Imran Khan	10	1	32	2
Ijaz Ahmed	10	–	43	–
Mushtaq Ahmed	10	–	41	3

FALL OF WICKETS

1–13, **2**–31, **3**–116, **4**–122, **5**–123, **6**–130, **7**–156, **8**–162, **9**–167

Umpires: K.E. Liebenberg & P.D. Reporter — Man of the Match – Aamir Sohail — *Pakistan won by 48 runs*

MATCH TWENTY-SIX
AUSTRALIA v. PAKISTAN, at Perth

In retrospect, this was the most important match to be played in the qualifying rounds. By losing, Australia virtually forfeited their last chance of reaching the semi-finals while Pakistan, the most talented and most temperamental side in the World Cup, reasserted their challenge after a period of under-achievement.

Imran won the toss and chose to bat. Aamir Sohail and Ramiz Raja gave Pakistan a good start with 78 in 20 overs, but Salim Malik again failed. Javed Miandad, still suffering from the stomach disorder which had kept him out of the previous game, joined Aamir in a stand of 77, but the rest of the side made only small contributions. Once more, Pakistan's rich batting line-up had not produced the runs it should have done. Steve Waugh had bowled well at the close, but, McDermott apart, the Australian bowling looked far from menacing.

In contrast, Pakistan bowled a better length, and their attack, if not lethal, was more demanding than Australia's. Moody and Boon became victims of Aqib Javed's outswingers. Jones looked in total command until he lost patience against Mushtaq's leg-spin. Marsh batted 34 overs for 39 before waving his bat at Imran. Border flopped again, and Steve Waugh was taken down the leg side. The impetus had gone from the Australian innings, and Australia had all but gone from the World Cup.

MATCH TWENTY-SEVEN
NEW ZEALAND v. INDIA, at Dunedin

It is fair to say that little went right for India in the World Cup. They were badly hit by rain, and lost when they should have won. They omitted Shastri for slow scoring and then lost him altogether through injury. Azharuddin often seemed to lack the authority necessary to lead this talented side, and, too frequently, he played irresponsibly. Against New Zealand, he sent in Srikkanth to attack the opening off-spin of Patel, but Patel bowled Srikkanth with his third ball. More trouble followed when Jadeja pulled a hamstring in the eighth over and was forced to retire hurt. The chilly, damp weather was certainly no friend to India.

Azharuddin and Tendulkar added 127 in 30 overs, and it was batting of quality. Harris, one of the most successful bowlers in the competition, was made to look a very ordinary medium-pacer, and when Patel returned Azharuddin hit him straight for six. Unfortunately, in the same over, he pulled the off-spinner to the mid-wicket boundary where Greatbatch dived forward to take the catch.

Tendulkar, than whom there was no finer batsman in the competition, reached 84 off 105 balls before edging Harris to the wicket-keeper. Kapil Dev lashed the ball in familiar fashion, and 34 runs came from the last five overs, but against a highly confident New Zealand side 230 looked too frail a total.

Mark Greatbatch soon made this apparent. He lost Latham at 36, but by then he was well into his stride. His 73 came off 77 balls, and he hit four sixes and five fours. The man's power was astonishing. He was caught at deep mid-wicket in Venkatapathy Raju's second over by which time New Zealand had 25 overs in which to score 114 runs and confirm their place in the semi-finals.

More cleverly ran out Crowe, and Smith perished on the boundary. Rutherford and Harris were also dismissed, but there was never any doubt that New Zealand would claim their sixth win in a row.

MATCH TWENTY-EIGHT
ENGLAND v. SOUTH AFRICA, at Melbourne

Graham Gooch had limped off the field with a hamstring injury in the match against Sri Lanka, and he was unfit to play against South Africa. Alec Stewart led the side in his stead, and led by example. With Lewis again unable to bowl, England were a team of walking wounded.

Stewart chose to field when he won the toss. A far from fit DeFreitas took the new ball, and, as Small was unable to find length or direction, England laboured. Hudson and Wessels began with a partnership of 151 in 36 overs. The stand was broken when Hick, who was forced into action when Reeve slipped and bruised himself to such an extent that he was unable to continue bowling, caught and bowled Hudson off a leading edge.

Kirsten hit Illingworth for six, but then hit DeFreitas into the hands of deep square-leg. The loss of Kirsten rather denied South Africa the flourish they might have expected from the last ten overs, for Wessels batted until the 46th over without generating the power of acceleration that was called for.

Stewart and Botham seemed determined to end the game quickly, for they reached 62 after 12 overs. At this point, rain arrived, and, having needed 175 from 38 overs, England now found that they needed 164 from 29. This suddenly looked an impossible task as Botham rather lazily played over a ball, and Smith and Hick dabbled at wide-ish deliveries. At 64 for 3 in 15 overs, England looked beaten.

Hopes were restored in sensational fashion, as Stewart, in the sweetest of form, and Fairbrother, initially frenetic, added 66 in 13 overs. Stewart's wonderful innings came to an end when he was superbly run out by Rhodes, the fielder of the tournament.

Reeve came and carved ten as Fairbrother now assumed authority, but it was the dynamic Lewis who set the pulses beating faster with 33 off 22 balls. He and Fairbrother hit 50 off 37 balls, and England had almost snatched a famous victory. Lewis was run out by Rhodes, Pringle skied the ball with the scores level, and DeFreitas hit the run that was needed. Fairbrother remained unbeaten with 75 off 83 balls, and England were in the semi-finals.

MATCH TWENTY-SEVEN – NEW ZEALAND v. INDIA
12 March, 1992 at Carisbrook, Dunedin

INDIA

A.D. Jadeja	retired hurt	13
K. Srikkanth	c Latham, **b** Patel	0
M. Azharuddin (capt)	c Greatbatch, **b** Patel	55
S.R. Tendulkar	c Smith, **b** Harris	84
S.V. Manjrekar	c and **b** Harris	18
Kapil Dev	c Larsen, **b** Harris	33
S.T. Banerjee	c Greatbatch, **b** Watson	11
*K.S. More	not out	2
J. Srinath	not out	4
Venkatapathy Raju		
M. Prabhakar		
Extras	b 1, lb 4, w 4, nb 1	10
	(for 6 wickets)	**230**

(50 overs)

	O	M	R	W
Cairns	8	1	40	–
Patel	10	–	29	2
Watson	10	1	34	1
Larsen	9	–	43	–
Harris	9	–	55	3
Latham	4	–	24	–

FALL OF WICKETS

1–4, **2**–149, **3**–166, **4**–201, **5**–222, **6**–223

NEW ZEALAND

M.J. Greatbatch	c Banerjee, **b** Venkatapathy Raju	73
R.T. Latham	**b** Prabhakar	8
A.H. Jones	not out	67
M.D. Crowe (capt)	run out	26
* I.D.S. Smith	c sub, **b** Prabhakar	9
K.R. Rutherford	lbw, **b** Venkatapathy Raju	21
C.Z. Harris	**b** Prabhakar	4
C.L. Cairns	not out	4
D.N. Patel		
G.R. Larsen		
W. Watson		
Extras	b 4, lb 3, w 4, nb 8	19
	(for 6 wickets)	**231**

(47.1 overs)

	O	M	R	W
Kapil Dev	10	–	55	–
Prabhakar	10	–	46	3
Banerjee	6	1	40	–
Srinath	9	–	35	–
Venkatapathy Raju	10	–	38	2
Tendulkar	1	–	2	–
Srikkanth	1.1	–	8	–

FALL OF WICKETS

1–36, **2**–118, **3**–162, **4**–172, **5**–206, **6**–225

Umpires: P.J. McConnell & I.D. Robinson Man of the Match – M.J. Greatbatch *New Zealand won by 4 wickets*

MATCH TWENTY-EIGHT – ENGLAND v. SOUTH AFRICA
12 March, 1992 at MCG, Melbourne

SOUTH AFRICA

K.C. Wessels (capt)	c Smith, **b** Hick	85
A.C. Hudson	c and **b** Hick	79
P.N. Kirsten	c Smith, **b** DeFreitas	11
J.N. Rhodes	run out	18
A.P. Kuiper	not out	15
W.J. Cronje	not out	13
B.M. McMillan		
*D.J. Richardson		
R.P. Snell		
M.W. Pringle		
A.A. Donald		
Extras	b 4, lb 4, w 4, nb 3	15
	(for 4 wickets)	**236**

(50 overs)

	O	M	R	W
Pringle	9	2	34	–
DeFreitas	10	1	41	1
Botham	8	–	37	–
Small	2	–	14	–
Illingworth	10	–	43	–
Reeve	2.4	–	15	–
Hick	8.2	–	44	2

FALL OF WICKETS

1–151, **2**–170, **3**–201, **4**–205

ENGLAND

* A.J. Stewart (capt)	run out	77
I.T. Botham	**b** McMillan	22
R.A. Smith	c Richardson, **b** McMillan	0
G.A. Hick	c Richardson, **b** Snell	1
N.H. Fairbrother	not out	75
D.A. Reeve	c McMillan, **b** Snell	10
C.C. Lewis	run out	33
D.R. Pringle	c Kuiper, **b** Snell	1
P.A.J. DeFreitas	not out	1
G.C. Small		
R.K. Illingworth		
Extras	lb 3, w 1, nb 2	6
	(for 7 wickets)	**226**

(40.5 overs)

	O	M	R	W
Donald	9	1	43	–
Pringle	8	–	44	–
Snell	7.5	–	42	3
McMillan	8	1	39	2
Kuiper	4	–	32	–
Cronje	3	–	14	–
Kirsten	1	–	9	–

FALL OF WICKETS

1–63, **2**–63, **3**–64, **4**–132, **5**–166, **6**–216, **7**–225

Umpires: D.P. Buultjens & B.L. Aldridge Man of the Match – A.J. Stewart *England won by 3 wickets (revised rate)*

MATCH TWENTY-NINE
WEST INDIES v. SRI LANKA, at Berri

Sri Lanka's last hopes of finding a place among the élite in the World Cup were extinguished by Phil Simmons who hit 110 off 125 balls with two sixes and nine fours. Sri Lanka added to their own demise by dropping five catches so that the target which they chased was far in excess of what it should have been.

West Indies lost five wickets for 31 runs in 35 balls, and it was left to the big hitting of Ambrose and Benjamin to lift them to their winning score.

Sri Lanka never suggested that they would reach either the run rate or the target required to win the match, and only Samarasekera and Ranatunga hinted at substance. Ranatunga had been a sufferer as a bowler, having Simmons dropped off successive deliveries.

One must have sympathy for Sri Lanka. They have been shabbily treated since being granted Test status, and the itinerary they were given for the World Cup was horrendous, involving a vast amount of travel. They remain among the world's most pleasant and likeable cricketers.

Roshan Mahanama of Sri Lanka. (Allsport)

MATCH TWENTY-NINE – WEST INDIES v. SRI LANKA
13 March, 1992 at Berri, South Australia

WEST INDIES

D.L. Haynes	c Tillekeratne, b Ranatunga	38
B.C. Lara	c and b Ramanayake	1
P.V. Simmons	c Wickremasinghe, b Hathurusinghe	110
R.B. Richardson (capt)	run out	8
K.L.T. Arthurton	c Tillekeratne, b Hathurusinghe	40
A.L. Logie	b Anurasiri	0
C.L. Hooper	c Gurusinha, b Hathurusinghe	12
*D. Williams	c Tillekeratne, b Hathurusinghe	2
C.E.L. Ambrose	not out	15
W.K.M. Benjamin	not out	24
A.C. Cummins		
Extras	lb 9, w 3, nb 6	18
	(for 8 wickets)	268

SRI LANKA

R.S. Mahanama	c Arthurton, b Cummins	11
M.A.R. Samarasekera	lbw, b Hooper	40
U.C. Hathurusinghe	run out	16
P.A. de Silva (capt)	c and b Hooper	11
A. Ranatunga	c Benjamin, b Arthurton	24
A.P. Gurusinha	c Richardson, b Ambrose	10
*H.P. Tillekeratne	b Ambrose	3
R.S. Kalpage	not out	13
C.P.H. Ramanayake	b Arthurton	1
S.D. Anurasiri	b Benjamin	3
G.P. Wickremasinghe	not out	21
Extras	lb 8, w 14, nb 2	24
	(for 9 wickets)	177

(50 overs)

	O	M	R	W
Wickremasinghe	7	–	30	–
Ramanayake	7	1	17	1
Anurasiri	10	–	46	1
Gurusinha	1	–	10	–
Ranatunga	7	–	35	1
Kalpage	10	–	64	–
Hathurusinghe	8	–	57	4

(50 overs)

	O	M	R	W
Ambrose	10	2	24	2
Benjamin	10	–	34	1
Cummins	9	–	49	1
Hooper	10	1	19	2
Arthurton	10	–	40	2
Simmons	1	–	3	–

FALL OF WICKETS
1–6, 2–72, 3–103, 4–197, 5–199, 6–219, 7–223, 8–228

FALL OF WICKETS
1–56, 2–80, 3–86, 4–99, 5–130, 6–135, 7–137, 8–139, 9–149

Umpires: D.R. Shepherd & S.J. Woodward — Man of the Match – P.V. Simmons — *West Indies won by 91 runs*

MATCH THIRTY
AUSTRALIA v. ZIMBABWE, at Hobart

Finding a middle-order consistency which had hitherto eluded them, Australia trounced the pointless Zimbabwe side and kept alive their slim hopes of reaching the semi-finals. Zimbabwe contained Australia well in the early stages, and, in the 34th over, with the Waugh twins together, the home side were 144 for 4. Steve Waugh edged Burmester and Andy Flower, diving to his right, missed the catch. It was a costly slip, for the last ten overs of the Australian innings realised 106 runs, and Steve Waugh, scoreless when he was dropped, hit 55 of them.

Zimbabwe started with a confident partnership of 47, but Omarshah ran himself out, and then it was downhill all the way. Border crowded the bat in an effort to bowl out Zimbabwe as quickly as possible and improve his side's net run rate. He was successful.

MATCH THIRTY-ONE
NEW ZEALAND v. ENGLAND, at Wellington

England suffered their first defeat in the competition, and their first defeat in 13 one-day internationals. New Zealand established a World Cup record with their seventh win in as many matches. England were hampered by the absence of Gooch and Fairbrother with injury and illness, and by the necessity to field DeFreitas, Lewis and Reeve who were not fully fit. Lamb appeared for the first time after his injury, and it was difficult to understand why Tufnell, who was fit, did not play instead of one of the halt and lame.

Crowe asked England to bat first and his well-tried ploy of opening the bowling with Patel was again successful when the off-spinner bowled Botham through the gate. Stewart and Hick put on 70 in 55 balls, and England did not lose their second wicket until the 20th over by which time they had scored 95 and were looking set for a big score. The initiative was squandered as only 105 were made in the next 30 overs, 52 of them in singles.

If England wanted to blame the pitch for their ineptitude, New Zealand soon removed their alibi. Wright was out in the second over, but Greatbatch made 35 in 37 balls to give the innings great momentum from the start. When he was out in the 13th over the score was 64, and his colleagues' task was a comparatively simple one.

Jones and Crowe batted fluently and engagingly to add 108 in 138 balls, and the New Zealand skipper caressed his side to victory with 9.1 overs to spare.

MATCH THIRTY-TWO
INDIA v. SOUTH AFRICA, at Adelaide

Rain and misfortune haunted India to the last. Their match against South Africa was reduced to 30 overs, and they lost the toss. They also quickly lost Srikkanth when Kirsten leaped high at cover to take a catch one-handed.

Manjrekar was a little slow, but Azharuddin played a gem of an innings, hitting 79 off 77 balls. The real excitement came when he and Kapil Dev were together and lashed 71 in eight overs. Kapil Dev batted with the extravagance which few can emulate to score 42 off 29 deliveries.

Faced with the task of scoring at six runs an over, Wessels made a wise decision in dropping himself down the order. Kirsten moved up to open with Hudson, and the pair gave South Africa the best of starts. They scored 128 before Hudson was yorked.

South Africa needed 51 from six overs when Prabhakar, who bowled well throughout the competition, was brought back. Kirsten and Kuiper took 11 from his first over, but Kirsten ran out his partner, and then Kapil Dev yorked Kirsten who had batted 85 balls for his 84. Eighteen runs were needed from 17 balls, but there was no halting South Africa, and Cronje hit the first ball of the last over through mid-wicket for the winning boundary. South Africa were in the World Cup semi-finals at the first attempt.

If India could wed discipline to their talent, what a side they would be.

Alan Donald in action for South Africa against India at Adelaide. (Patrick Eagar)

ABOVE: Wessels and Cronje in triumphant mood as South Africa beat India and win a place in the semi-finals. (Patrick Eagar)

RIGHT: Amre and Pringle in a mix-up at the end of the Indian innings against South Africa.. (David Munden)

MATCH THIRTY – AUSTRALIA v. ZIMBABWE

14 March, 1992 at Bellerive Oval, Hobart

AUSTRALIA

T.M. Moody	run out	6
D.C. Boon	**b** Omarshah	48
D.M. Jones	**b** Burmester	54
A.R. Border (capt)	**st** Flower, **b** Traicos	22
M.E. Waugh	not out	66
S.R. Waugh	**b** Brandes	55
*I.A. Healy	lbw, **b** Duers	0
P.L. Taylor	not out	1
C.J. McDermott		
M.R. Whitney		
B.A. Reid		
Extras	b 2, lb 8, w 2, nb 1	13
	(for 6 wickets)	**265**

(46 overs)

	O	M	R	W
Brandes	9	–	59	1
Duers	9	1	48	1
Burmester	9	–	65	1
Omarshah	9	–	53	1
Traicos	10	–	30	1

FALL OF WICKETS

1–8, **2**–102, **3**–134, **4**–144, **5**–257, **6**–258

ZIMBABWE

A.H. Omarshah	run out	24
* A. Flower	**c** Border, **b** S.R. Waugh	20
A.D. Campbell	**c** M.E. Waugh, **b** Whitney	4
A.J. Pycroft	**c** M.E. Waugh, **b** S.R. Waugh	0
D.L. Houghton (capt)	**b** McDermott	2
A.C. Waller	**c** P.L. Taylor, **b** Moody	18
K.J. Arnott	**b** Whitney	8
E.A. Brandes	**c** McDermott, **b** P.L. Taylor	23
M.G. Burmester	**c** Border, **b** Reid	12
A.J. Traicos	**c** Border, **b** P.L. Taylor	3
K.G. Duers	not out	2
Extras	lb 11, w 8, nb 2	21
		137

(41.4 overs)

	O	M	R	W
McDermott	8	–	26	1
Reid	9	1	18	1
S.R. Waugh	7	–	28	2
Whitney	10	3	15	2
Moody	4	–	25	1
P.L. Taylor	3.4	–	14	2

FALL OF WICKETS

1–47, **2**–51, **3**–51, **4**–57, **5**–69, **6**–88, **7**–97, **8**–117, **9**–132

Umpires: B.L. Aldridge & P.D. Reporter — Man of the Match – S.R. Waugh — *Australia won by 128 runs*

MATCH THIRTY-ONE – NEW ZEALAND v. ENGLAND
15 March, 1992 at Basin Reserve, Wellington

ENGLAND

*A.J. Stewart (capt)	c Harris, b Patel	41
I.T. Botham	b Patel	8
G.A. Hick	c Greatbatch, b Harris	56
R.A. Smith	c Patel, b Jones	38
A.J. Lamb	c Cairns, b Watson	12
C.C. Lewis	c and b Watson	0
D.A. Reeve	not out	21
D.R. Pringle	c sub (Latham), b Jones	10
P.A.J. DeFreitas	c Cairns, b Harris	0
R.K. Illingworth	not out	2
G.C. Small		
Extras	b 1, lb 7, w 4	12
	(for 8 wickets)	**200**

NEW ZEALAND

M.J. Greatbatch	c DeFreitas, b Botham	35
J.G. Wright	b DeFreitas	1
A.H. Jones	run out	78
M.D. Crowe (capt)	not out	73
K.R. Rutherford	not out	3
C.Z. Harris		
*I.D.S. Smith		
C.L. Cairns		
D.N. Patel		
G.R. Larsen		
W. Watson		
Extras	b 1, lb 8, w 1, nb 1	11
	(for 3 wickets)	**201**

(50 overs)

	O	M	R	W
Patel	10	1	26	2
Harris	8	–	39	2
Watson	10	–	40	2
Cairns	3	–	21	–
Larsen	10	3	24	–
Jones	9	–	42	2

(40.5 overs)

	O	M	R	W
Pringle	6.2	1	34	–
DeFreitas	8.3	1	45	1
Botham	4	–	19	1
Illingworth	9	1	46	–
Hick	6	–	26	–
Reeve	3	–	9	–
Small	4	–	13	–

FALL OF WICKETS
1–25, **2**–95, **3**–135, **4**–162, **5**–162, **6**–169, **7**–189, **8**–195

FALL OF WICKETS
1–5, **2**–64, **3**–172

Umpires: S.G. Randell & I.D. Robinson — Man of the Match – A.H. Jones — *New Zealand won by 7 wickets*

MATCH THIRTY-TWO – INDIA v. SOUTH AFRICA
15 March, 1992 at Adelaide Oval

INDIA

K. Srikkanth	c Kirsten, b Donald	0
S.V. Manjrekar	b Kuiper	28
M. Azharuddin (capt)	c Kuiper, b Pringle	79
S.R. Tendulkar	c Wessels, b Kuiper	14
Kapil Dev	b Donald	42
V.G. Kambli	run out	1
P.K. Amre	not out	1
J. Srinath	not out	0
M. Prabhakar		
*K.S. More		
Venkatapathy Raju		
Extras	lb 7, w 6, nb 2	15
	(for 6 wickets)	**180**

SOUTH AFRICA

A.C. Hudson	b Srinath	53
P.N. Kirsten	b Kapil Dev	84
A.P. Kuiper	run out	7
J.N. Rhodes	c Venkatapathy Raju, b Prabhakar	7
K.C. Wessels (capt)	not out	9
W.J. Cronje	not out	8
B.M. McMillan		
*D.J. Richardson		
R.P. Snell		
A.A. Donald		
M.W. Pringle		
Extras	lb 10, nb 3	13
	(for 4 wickets)	**181**

(30 overs)

	O	M	R	W
Donald	6	–	34	2
Pringle	6	–	37	1
Snell	6	1	46	–
McMillan	6	–	28	–
Kuiper	6	–	28	2

(29.1 overs)

	O	M	R	W
Kapil Dev	6	–	36	1
Prabhakar	5.1	1	33	1
Tendulkar	6	–	20	–
Srinath	6	–	39	1
Venkatapathy Raju	6	–	43	–

FALL OF WICKETS
1–1, **2**–79, **3**–103, **4**–174, **5**–177, **6**–179

FALL OF WICKETS
1–128, **2**–149, **3**–157, **4**–163

Umpires: D.P. Buultjens & Khizer Hayat — Man of the Match – P.N. Kirsten — *South Africa won by 6 wickets*

MATCH THIRTY-THREE
PAKISTAN v. SRI LANKA, at Perth

Pakistan beat Sri Lanka, as expected, and entered the last round of matches still nursing hopes of reaching the semi-finals, but their performance again lacked conviction. They were profligate in bolstering Sri Lanka's score with 11 wides and six no-balls. They dropped catches, and fielded indifferently. They made hard work of reaching a moderate target, but they won.

The most promising stand of Sri Lanka's innings came when Samarasekera and de Silva added 51 in ten overs. The partnership was broken by Mushtaq Ahmed who drew Samarasekera forward and had him stumped. Gurusinha hit lustily, but 212 did not look a daunting score on a fast pitch.

Aamir Sohail was caught in the gully in the second over of the Pakistan innings, and Imran Khan found it difficult to get going. He and Ramiz Raja departed in quick succession, and Pakistan were 84 for 3 in the 24th over. Javed Miandad and Salim Malik, neither of whom had been at their best, nudged and pushed 101 runs in 21 overs, and they set up Pakistan's victory.

MATCH THIRTY-FOUR
NEW ZEALAND v. PAKISTAN, at Christchurch

Pakistan won their third match in succession, inflicted the first defeat upon New Zealand and then had to sit and wait for the result from Melbourne to see if they had qualified for the semi-finals.

Put in to bat on a fast wicket, New Zealand began as if this were to be a continuation of all that had gone before. Greatbatch hit Aqib Javed for 14 off three balls in the second over, but Aqib gained his revenge by accounting for Latham. Wasim Akram was erratic, but he was quick and he was dangerous. He dismissed both Jones and Crowe and took much of the heart out of the New Zealand batting.

The best piece of bowling, however, came from leg-spinner Mushtaq Ahmed who unsettled and dismissed Greatbatch, had Harris stumped off a wide and bowled ten immaculate overs for 18 runs. The New Zealand innings was in shreds, and although Larsen, playing his first innings of the tournament, and Morrison added 44 for the ninth wicket, the final score of 166 was scarcely a challenge to Pakistan.

Aamir Sohail hooked the first ball of Pakistan's innings into the hands of long-leg although some umpires would have called Morrison's delivery a no-ball as it appeared to be above shoulder height. In the third over, Morrison bowled Inzamam-ul-Haq with an in-cutter, and Pakistan were 9 for 2. Patel could have caught and bowled Javed when the batsman was on three, but the chance was missed, and Javed and Ramiz put on 115. Ramiz Raja batted exceptionally well, hit the highest score of the competition and won the match with his 16th boundary.

MATCH THIRTY-FIVE
ENGLAND v. ZIMBABWE, at Albury

The fifth World Cup had not really had an upset until the final round of matches, and for most of the time, it did not look as if there would be one then. Gooch returned to lead England, and all seemed right with his world when Zimbabwe were bowled out for 134 in 46.1 overs. Even without Lewis and Pringle, the England attack was too much for Zimbabwe and wickets were shared by all five bowlers.

The first indication of a surprise came when Gooch fell to the first ball of the England innings. Lamb looked distinctly out of touch, and Smith's form seemed to have deserted him. Hick's footwork was all awry, and he had the indignity of being yorked for nought, a salutary lesson from the country of his birth where he learned his cricket.

Stewart and Fairbrother added 52, and it appeared that the nightmare was over. Stewart was striking the ball well until he mis-hit the accurate Omarshah to cover, and DeFreitas and Fairbrother, still suffering from the effects of illness, soon followed. Progress had been tedious, and it even seemed probable that England would not reach the meagre target, and then Small clipped to mid-wicket on the first ball of the final over to give Zimbabwe a famous victory.

Brandes rightly won the individual award for breaking the back of the England innings and the hearts of the England supporters.

Asanka Gurusinha of Sri Lanka. (Allsport)

MATCH THIRTY-THREE – PAKISTAN v. SRI LANKA
15 March, 1992 at WACA Ground, Perth

SRI LANKA

Batsman	Dismissal	Runs
R.S. Mahanama	b Wasim Akram	12
M.A.R. Samarasekera	st Moin Khan, b Mushtaq Ahmed	38
U.C. Hathurusinghe	b Mushtaq Ahmed	5
P.A. de Silva (capt)	c Aamir Sohail, b Ijaz Ahmed	43
A.P. Gurusinha	c Salim Malik, b Imran Khan	37
A. Ranatunga	c sub, b Aamir Sohail	7
*H.P. Tillekeratne	not out	25
R.S. Kalpage	not out	13
H.C.P. Ramanayake		
G.P. Wickremasinghe		
K.I.J. Wijegunawardene		
Extras	lb 15, w 11, nb 6	32
	(for 6 wickets)	**212**

PAKISTAN

Batsman	Dismissal	Runs
Aamir Sohail	c Mahanama, b Ramanayake	1
Ramiz Raja	c Gurusinha, b Wickremasinghe	32
Imran Khan (capt)	c de Silva, b Hathurusinghe	22
Javed Miandad	c Wickremasinghe, b Gurusinha	57
Salim Malik	c Kalpage, b Ramanayake	51
Ijaz Ahmed	not out	8
Inzamam-ul-Haq	run out	11
Wasim Akram	not out	5
* Moin Khan		
Mushtaq Ahmed		
Aqib Javed		
Extras	lb 12, w 9, nb 8	29
	(for 6 wickets)	**216**

(50 overs)

	O	M	R	W
Wasim Akram	10	–	37	1
Aqib Javed	10	–	39	–
Imran Khan	8	1	36	1
Mushtaq Ahmed	10	–	43	2
Ijaz Ahmed	8	–	28	1
Aamir Sohail	4	–	14	1

(49.1 overs)

	O	M	R	W
Wijegunawardene	10	1	34	–
Ramanayake	10	1	37	2
Wickremasinghe	9.1	–	41	1
Gurusinha	9	–	38	1
Hathurusinghe	9	–	40	1
Kalpage	2	–	14	–

FALL OF WICKETS

1–29, **2**–48, **3**–99, **4**–132, **5**–158, **6**–187

FALL OF WICKETS

1–7, **2**–68, **3**–84, **4**–185, **5**–201, **6**–205

Umpires: K.E. Liebenberg & P.J. McConnell Man of the Match – Javed Miandad *Pakistan won by 4 wickets*

MATCH THIRTY-FOUR – NEW ZEALAND v. PAKISTAN
18 March, 1992 at Lancaster Park, Christchurch

NEW ZEALAND

Batsman	Dismissal	Runs
M.J. Greatbatch	c Salim Malik, b Mushtaq Ahmed	42
R.T. Latham	c Inzamam-ul-Haq, b Aqib Javed	6
A.H. Jones	b Wasim Akram	2
M.D. Crowe (capt)	c Aamir Sohail, b Wasim Akram	3
K.R. Rutherford	run out	8
C.Z. Harris	st Moin Khan, b Mushtaq Ahmed	1
D.N. Patel	c Mushtaq Ahmed, b Aamir Sohail	7
*I.D.S. Smith	b Imran Khan	1
G.R. Larsen	b Wasim Akram	37
D.K. Morrison	c Inzamam-ul-Haq, b Wasim Akram	12
W. Watson	not out	5
Extras	b 3, lb 23, w 12, nb 4	42
		166

PAKISTAN

Batsman	Dismissal	Runs
Aamir Sohail	c Patel, b Morrison	0
Ramiz Raja	not out	119
Inzamam-ul-Haq	b Morrison	5
Javed Miandad	lbw, b Morrison	30
Salim Malik	not out	9
Ijaz Ahmed		
Imran Khan (capt)		
Wasim Akram		
* Moin Khan		
Mushtaq Ahmed		
Aqib Javed		
Extras	lb 1, w 1, nb 2	4
	(for 3 wickets)	**167**

(48.2 overs)

	O	M	R	W
Wasim Akram	9.2	–	32	4
Aqib Javed	10	1	34	1
Mushtaq Ahmed	10	–	18	2
Imran Khan	8	–	22	1
Aamir Sohail	10	1	29	1
Ijaz Ahmed	1	–	5	–

(44.4 overs)

	O	M	R	W
Morrison	10	–	42	3
Patel	10	2	25	–
Watson	10	3	26	–
Harris	4	–	18	–
Larsen	3	–	16	–
Jones	3	–	10	–
Latham	2	–	13	–
Rutherford	1.4	–	11	–
Greatbatch	1	–	5	–

FALL OF WICKETS

1–23, **2**–26, **3**–39, **4**–85, **5**–88, **6**–93, **7**–96, **8**–106, **9**–150

FALL OF WICKETS

1–0, **2**–9, **3**–124

Umpires: S.U. Bucknor & S.G. Randell Man of the Match – Mushtaq Ahmed *Pakistan won by 7 wickets*

MATCH THIRTY-FIVE – ENGLAND v. ZIMBABWE

18 March, 1992 at Albury

ZIMBABWE

Batsman	How out	Runs
W.R. James	c and **b** Illingworth	13
*A. Flower	**b** DeFreitas	7
A.J. Pycroft	c Gooch, **b** Botham	3
K.J. Arnott	lbw, **b** Botham	11
D.L. Houghton (capt)	c Fairbrother, **b** Small	29
A.C. Waller	**b** Tufnell	8
A.H. Omarshah	c Lamb, **b** Tufnell	3
I.P. Butchart	c Fairbrother, **b** Botham	24
E.A. Brandes	st Stewart, **b** Illingworth	14
A.J. Traicos	not out	0
M.P. Jarvis	lbw, **b** Illingworth	6
Extras	lb 8, w 8	16
		134

(46.1 overs)

	O	M	R	W
DeFreitas	8	1	14	1
Small	9	1	20	1
Botham	10	2	23	3
Illingworth	9.1	–	33	3
Tufnell	10	2	36	2

FALL OF WICKETS

1–12, **2**–19, **3**–30, **4**–52, **5**–65, **6**–77, **7**–96, **8**–127, **9**–127

ENGLAND

Batsman	How out	Runs
G.A. Gooch (capt)	lbw, **b** Brandes	0
I.T. Botham	c Flower, **b** Omarshah	18
A.J. Lamb	c James, **b** Brandes	17
R.A. Smith	**b** Brandes	2
G.A. Hick	**b** Brandes	0
N.H. Fairbrother	c Flower, **b** Butchart	20
* A.J. Stewart	c Waller, **b** Omarshah	29
P.A.J. DeFreitas	c Flower, **b** Butchart	4
R.K. Illingworth	run out	11
G.C. Small	c Pycroft, **b** Jarvis	5
P.C.R. Tufnell	not out	0
Extras	b 4, lb 3, w 11, nb 1	19
		125

(49.1 overs)

	O	M	R	W
Brandes	10	4	21	4
Jarvis	9.1	–	32	1
Omarshah	10	3	17	2
Traicos	10	4	16	–
Butchart	10	2	32	2

FALL OF WICKETS

1–0, **2**–32, **3**–42, **4**–42, **5**–43, **6**–95, **7**–101, **8**–108, **9**–124

Umpires: B.L. Aldridge & Khizer Hayat — Man of the Match – E.A. Brandes — *Zimbabwe won by 9 runs*

MATCH THIRTY-SIX

AUSTRALIA v. WEST INDIES, at Melbourne

This match was scheduled to be the deciding encounter of the qualifying rounds. As it transpired, the only beneficiaries were Pakistan who were watching the game on television in Christchurch across the Tasman Sea.

Australia got a fine start as Boon and Moody took them to 107 in 25 overs. Moody hit into the hands of backward square-leg, and Boon became rather becalmed until reaching 100 off 146 balls before swiping wildly at the 147th that was bowled to him. The middle order again failed to capitalise. Jones was caught behind as he essayed a cut, Border missed a straight ball and Mark Waugh tried belligerence and was stumped. The final score was no more than respectable.

Desmond Haynes completed a disappointing World Cup when he hit a full toss to square-leg, and Simmons was leg before without scoring. The West Indian nerve seemed to have snapped, and only Lara, a batsman of dash and power, gave a glimpse of quality. Richardson struggled hard to survive. Arthurton shone briefly, and Logie and Hooper fell quickly to Whitney. When Lara was out in the 38th over West Indies were 137 for 7, and hope was gone.

Australia's victory gave them some restoration of pride, but they knew before the beginning of the match that Pakistan's win in Christchurch had eliminated them. Incredibly, neither Australia nor West Indies had won a place in the last four.

WORLD CUP FINAL TABLE

	P	W	L	Ab	Pts	Run Rate
New Zealand	8	7	1	–	14	+0.59
England	8	5	2	1	11	+0.47
South Africa	8	5	3	–	10	+0.14
Pakistan	8	4	3	1	9	+0.16
Australia	8	4	4	–	8	+0.20
West Indies	8	4	4	–	8	+0.07
India	8	2	5	1	5	+0.14
Sri Lanka	8	2	5	1	5	–0.68
Zimbabwe	8	1	7	–	2	–1.14

Thankfully, a place in the semi-finals was not decided by run rate, for the ruling here was as messy as that which governed rain interruptions. The run rate was calculated on the difference between bowling and batting rates with runs scored in abandoned matches disregarded.

David Boon skies the ball and is about to be caught by wicket-keeper Williams. Boon had scored 100 for Australia against West Indies at Melbourne, but Australia were out of the World Cup. (David Munden)

MATCH THIRTY-SIX – AUSTRALIA v. WEST INDIES
18 March, 1992 at MCG, Melbourne

AUSTRALIA

T.M. Moody	c Benjamin, b Simmons	42
D.C. Boon	c Williams, b Cummins	100
D.M. Jones	c Williams, b Cummins	6
A.R. Border (capt)	lbw, b Simmons	8
M.E. Waugh	st Williams, b Hooper	21
S.R. Waugh	b Cummins	6
*I.A. Healy	not out	11
P.L. Taylor	not out	10
C.J. McDermott		
M.R. Whitney		
B.A. Reid		
Extras	lb 3, w 3, nb 6	12
	(for 6 wickets)	216

(50 overs)

	O	M	R	W
Ambrose	10	–	46	–
Benjamin	10	1	49	–
Cummins	10	1	38	3
Hooper	10	–	40	1
Simmons	10	1	40	2

FALL OF WICKETS
1–107, 2–128, 3–141, 4–185, 5–189, 6–200

WEST INDIES

D.L. Haynes	c Jones, b McDermott	14
B.C. Lara	run out	70
P.V. Simmons	lbw, b McDermott	0
R.B. Richardson (capt)	c Healy, b Whitney	10
K.L.T. Arthurton	c McDermott, b Whitney	15
A.L. Logie	c Healy, b Whitney	5
C.L. Hooper	c M.E. Waugh, b Whitney	4
*D. Williams	c Border, b Reid	4
W.K.M. Benjamin	lbw, b S.R. Waugh	15
C.E.L. Ambrose	run out	2
A.C. Cummins	not out	5
Extras	b 3, lb 5, w 3, nb 4	15
		159

(42.4 overs)

	O	M	R	W
McDermott	6	1	29	2
Reid	10	1	26	1
Whitney	10	1	34	4
S.R. Waugh	6.4	–	24	1
P.L. Taylor	4	–	24	–
Moody	6	1	14	–

FALL OF WICKETS
1–27, 2–27, 3–59, 4–83, 5–99, 6–117, 7–128, 8–137, 9–150

Umpires: P.D. Reporter & D.R. Shepherd

Man of the Match – D.C. Boon

Australia won by 57 runs

SEMI-FINAL
NEW ZEALAND v. PAKISTAN, at Auckland

Martin Crowe won the toss, New Zealand batted, and for the first three-and-a-half hours, all went as the home side had dreamed. The weather had looked uncertain so that there was logic in Crowe's decision to desert his usual policy of chasing a target.

Greatbatch began with his customary panache and brought his total of World Cup sixes to 14 with two mighty clouts. In the tenth over, he was deceived by a slower ball from Aqib Javed, and three overs later Wright hit Mushtaq Ahmed to mid-wicket to cause New Zealand their one real moment of anxiety.

Crowe and Jones relieved tension with 48 in 68 balls before Jones became the second victim of leg-spinner Mushtaq. The New Zealand skipper continued to gather runs easily and elegantly without ever resorting to extravagance or giving way to any sense of impatience. He withstood the combined attack of Mushtaq and Wasim Akram, and by the time that Iqbal Sikander was introduced in the 28th over of the innings, Rutherford had overcome his initial uncertainty and was striking the ball cleanly. In 19 overs, Crowe and Rutherford put on 107 runs. Crowe hit three sixes and Rutherford one, and the crowd was in ecstasy.

At 194, in the 43rd over, Rutherford attempted to hook Wasim Akram and skied the ball to the keeper. As Crowe ran to the striker's end, he felt a sharp pain in his hamstring. After the next single he was hobbling, and Greatbatch came on as runner.

Symbolically, this was the point where all began to go wrong for Crowe and for New Zealand. The New Zealand captain had to endure the torture of seeing his runner being run out in a mix-up to deprive him of a century. His side still managed to pillage 56 from the last five overs, and Pakistan faced a formidable target of 263.

Aamir Sohail was caught backward of square-leg in the seventh over, and Ramiz Raja skied Watson to long-leg in the 22nd over. Imran was solid, but he lacked the form to punish the New Zealand medium-pace bowling even though he did hit two sixes. His 44 occupied 93 balls, and he was out when he pulled a ball into the hands of deep square-leg in the 34th over. In the next over, Salim Malik sliced the second ball he received into the hands of cover. Pakistan were now 140 for 4, and Inzamam-ul-Haq arrived at the crease with 123 needed from 15 overs.

He attacked from the start, and in ten overs, he and Javed, who hurried, scuttled and cajoled, put on 87 runs. Inzamam played a breath-taking innings, hitting a six and seven fours as he made 60 off 37 deliveries in 48 minutes. When he was run out by Harris' direct hit from cover Pakistan needed 36 from the last five overs. Wasim Akram slammed and went to leave 25 from just under four. This became 12 from two overs, and Moin Khan blasted Harris over long-off for six and pulled him to mid-wicket for four to end the match.

Pakistan were jubilant, and poor Martin Crowe, who had been forced to sit and watch his side lose, led his side on a tearful lap of honour. They deserved all the praise that was heaped upon them, for they had enriched the tournament with their attitude, their zest and performance. None had done more than their captain, who re-established himself as a truly great batsman and who revealed qualities of leadership which one had not seen before. He was unquestionably the Man of the World Cup.

Purposeful cricket from Andrew Jones, but defeat for New Zealand in the semi-finals. (Joe Mann/Allsport)

The precocious talent of Inzamam-ul-Haq as he ravages 60 off 37 balls to take Pakistan into the final with victory over New Zealand. Ian Smith is the wicket-keeper. (Joe Mann/Allsport)

SEMI-FINAL – NEW ZEALAND v. PAKISTAN

21 March, 1992 at Eden Park, Auckland

NEW ZEALAND

Batsman	Dismissal	Runs
M.J. Greatbatch	**b** Aqib Javed	17
J.G. Wright	**c** Ramiz Raja, **b** Mushtaq Ahmed	13
A.H. Jones	lbw, **b** Mushtaq Ahmed	21
M.D. Crowe (capt)	run out	91
K.R. Rutherford	**c** Moin Khan, **b** Wasim Akram	50
C.Z. Harris	**st** Moin Khan, **b** Iqbal Sikander	13
* I.D.S. Smith	not out	18
D.N. Patel	lbw, **b** Wasim Akram	8
G.R. Larsen	not out	8
D.K. Morrison		
W. Watson		
Extras	b 4, lb 7, w 8, nb 4	23
	(for 7 wickets)	**262**

PAKISTAN

Batsman	Dismissal	Runs
Aamir Sohail	**c** Jones, **b** Patel	14
Ramiz Raja	**c** Morrison, **b** Watson	44
Imran Khan (capt)	**c** Larsen, **b** Harris	44
Javed Miandad	not out	57
Salim Malik	**c** sub (Latham), **b** Larsen	1
Inzamam-ul-Haq	run out	60
Wasim Akram	**b** Watson	9
* Moin Khan	not out	20
Iqbal Sikander		
Mushtaq Ahmed		
Aqib Javed		
Extras	b 4, lb 10, w 1	15
	(for 6 wickets)	**264**

(50 overs)

	O	M	R	W
Wasim Akram	10	–	40	**2**
Aqib Javed	10	2	45	**1**
Mushtaq Ahmed	10	–	40	**2**
Imran Khan	10	–	59	–
Iqbal Sikander	9	–	56	**1**
Aamir Sohail	1	–	11	–

(49 overs)

	O	M	R	W
Patel	10	1	50	**1**
Morrison	9	–	55	–
Watson	10	2	39	**2**
Larsen	10	1	34	**1**
Harris	10	–	72	**1**

FALL OF WICKETS

1–35, **2**–39, **3**–87, **4**–194, **5**–214, **6**–221, **7**–244

FALL OF WICKETS

1–30, **2**–84, **3**–134, **4**–140, **5**–227, **6**–238

Umpires: D.R. Shepherd & S.U. Bucknor — Man of the Match – Inzamam-ul-Haq — *Pakistan won by 4 wickets*

SEMI-FINAL

ENGLAND v. SOUTH AFRICA, at Sydney

Hick survives an appeal for leg before first ball. Pringle is the bowler, Stewart the other batsman. England v. South Africa semi-final. (Patrick Eagar)

England were weakened by the absence of Pringle and Smith, both of whom were key players and both of whom were deemed unfit. South Africa were at full strength, and, judging the bowling conditions favourable, Wessels opted to field when he won the toss. What advantage there might have been was somewhat dissipated by Donald and Pringle who offered a liberal assortment of wides in the first two overs. In the third over, Donald produced a ball which came back sharply at Gooch, hit him on the thigh pad and went through to the wicket-keeper. Donald appealed, and Gooch was given out caught behind. It was a sad error by umpire Aldridge who otherwise coped well.

The England innings still had no foundation when Botham tried to cut a ball from Pringle and chopped it into his stumps. Stewart had begun tentatively, and Hick began with the greatest good fortune. He was hit on the front pad by Pringle's first ball, but umpire Aldridge rejected a most worthy appeal. Three balls later, Hick was caught at slip off a no-ball. It was apparent that the gods of the game were smiling on him.

Stewart was just getting into his stride when he tried to run McMillan down to third man and was acrobatically caught by Richardson who had not been seen as one of South Africa's strengths in the earlier matches. Hick was now batting splendidly and runs came smoothly at five an over. He hit 41 of the 73-run partnership with Fairbrother who was bowled by a leg-cutter. Four runs later, Hick fell to a tumbling catch by the exciting Jonty Rhodes at point. Hick hit nine fours and faced 90 balls for his 83.

Lamb, Lewis and Reeve continued the plunder. Reeve hit 25 off 14 balls, and 18 runs came from Donald's last over. South Africa had been tardy in bowling their overs, and they were to be heavily fined.

The opening attack of Botham and Lewis was poor in length and direction, but, as has been his wont over the years, Botham captured a wicket with a poor delivery, Wessels slicing a wide long-hop to backward point. Wessels reappeared to act as runner for Kirsten who had been injured in the field. Kirsten was bowled by a good delivery from DeFreitas, and Illingworth cut short a handsome-looking innings by Hudson who had enjoyed a good tournament.

Kuiper began to hit hard and often and made 36 off 44 balls. He sold his wicket cheaply, slogging wildly and unnecessarily at Illingworth. Rhodes was ebullient, hitting 43 off 38 balls, before driving Small high to point. Cronje had already fallen, caught on the square-leg boundary, but McMillan and Richardson scored at more than a run a ball.

A spectacular climax was in prospect when rain began to fall. South Africa were 231 for 6 with 13 balls remaining. The umpires asked the batsmen if they wished to leave the field. They did not. Gooch, on the other hand, agreed with the umpires that the conditions were unfit for play, and the sides left the field. Twelve minutes were lost, and it was announced that 22 runs were now needed from seven balls. As the players took the field, the target was readjusted to 21 runs needed from one ball. What should have been high drama had degenerated into low farce.

The England side was loudly booed, and South Africa were cheered. Those who should have been the recipients of the crowd's justified anger were the administrators whose rules had created this chaos. There was ample time and weather under the lights to play the game to its natural end. There was also a reserve day, but this, it was stated, was only for a completely new match. In any case, the television people had sold no advertising for this reserve day. As is now the custom in cricket, the last people to be considered were those who had paid to see the match.

One wonders what the crowd reaction would have been had Australia been in South Africa's position – or indeed what the reaction of the administrators would have been. More disturbingly, what would have happened had this semi-final been between India and Pakistan?

DeFreitas bowls Kirsten. (David Munden)

Kuiper pays the penalty for a wild swing and is bowled by Illingworth as Stewart leaps joyfully. (David Munden)

Low farce instead of high drama. The scoreboard as the players return to the field after the brief stoppage for rain. (Allsport)

SEMI-FINAL – ENGLAND v. SOUTH AFRICA
22 March, 1992 at SCG, Sydney

ENGLAND

G.A. Gooch (capt)	c Richardson, **b** Donald	2
I.T. Botham	**b** Pringle	21
* A.J. Stewart	c Richardson, **b** McMillan	33
G.A. Hick	c Rhodes, **b** Snell	83
N.H. Fairbrother	**b** Pringle	28
A.J. Lamb	c Richardson, **b** Donald	19
C.C. Lewis	not out	18
D.A. Reeve	not out	25
P.A.J. DeFreitas		
R.K. Illingworth		
G.C. Small		
Extras	b 1, lb 7, w 9, nb 6	23
	(for 6 wickets)	**252**

SOUTH AFRICA

K.C. Wessels (capt)	c Lewis, **b** Botham	17
A.C. Hudson	lbw, **b** Illingworth	46
P.N. Kirsten	**b** DeFreitas	11
A.P. Kuiper	**b** Illingworth	36
W.J. Cronje	c Hick, **b** Small	24
J.N. Rhodes	c Lewis, **b** Small	43
B.M. McMillan	not out	21
* D.J. Richardson	not out	13
R.P. Snell		
M.W. Pringle		
A.A. Donald		
Extras	lb 17, w 4	21
	(for 6 wickets)	**232**

(45 overs)

	O	M	R	W
Donald	10	–	69	2
Pringle	9	2	36	2
Snell	8	–	52	1
McMillan	9	–	47	1
Kuiper	5	–	26	–
Cronje	4	–	14	–

(43 overs)

	O	M	R	W
Botham	10	–	52	1
Lewis	5	–	38	–
DeFreitas	8	1	28	1
Illingworth	10	1	46	2
Small	10	1	51	2

FALL OF WICKETS
1–20, **2**–39, **3**–110, **4**–183, **5**–187, **6**–221

FALL OF WICKETS
1–26, **2**–61, **3**–90, **4**–131, **5**–176, **6**–206

Umpires: B.L. Aldridge & S.G. Randell — Man of the Match – G.A. Hick — *England won by 19 runs (revised rate)*

WORLD CUP FINAL – ENGLAND v. PAKISTAN
25 March, 1992 at MCG, Melbourne

PAKISTAN

Aamir Sohail	c Stewart, **b** Pringle	4
Ramiz Raja	lbw, **b** Pringle	8
Imran Khan (capt)	c Illingworth, **b** Botham	72
Javed Miandad	c Botham, **b** Illingworth	58
Inzamam-ul-Haq	**b** Pringle	42
Wasim Akram	run out	33
Salim Malik	not out	0
Ijaz Ahmed		
* Moin Khan		
Mushtaq Ahmed		
Aqib Javed		
Extras	lb 19, w 6, nb 7	32
	(for 6 wickets)	**249**

ENGLAND

G.A. Gooch (capt)	c Aqib Javed, **b** Mushtaq Ahmed	29
I.T. Botham	c Moin Khan, **b** Wasim Akram	0
* A.J. Stewart	c Moin Khan, **b** Aqib Javed	7
G.A. Hick	lbw, **b** Mushtaq Ahmed	17
N.H. Fairbrother	c Moin Khan, **b** Aqib Javed	62
A.J. Lamb	**b** Wasim Akram	31
C.C. Lewis	**b** Wasim Akram	0
D.A. Reeve	c Ramiz Raja, **b** Mushtaq Ahmed	15
D.R. Pringle	not out	18
P.A.J. DeFreitas	run out	10
R.K. Illingworth	c Ramiz Raja, **b** Imran Khan	14
Extras	lb 5, w 13, nb 6	24
		227

(50 overs)

	O	M	R	W
Pringle	10	2	22	3
Lewis	10	2	52	–
Botham	7	–	42	1
DeFreitas	10	1	42	–
Illingworth	10	–	50	1
Reeve	3	–	22	–

(49.2 overs)

	O	M	R	W
Wasim Akram	10	–	49	3
Aqib Javed	10	2	27	2
Mushtaq Ahmed	10	1	41	3
Ijaz Ahmed	3	–	13	–
Imran Khan	6.2	–	43	1
Aamir Sohail	10	–	49	–

FALL OF WICKETS
1–20, **2**–24, **3**–163, **4**–197, **5**–249, **6**–249

FALL OF WICKETS
1–6, **2**–21, **3**–59, **4**–69, **5**–141, **6**–141, **7**–180, **8**–183, **9**–208

Umpires: S.U. Bucknor & B.L. Aldridge — Man of the Match – Wasim Akram — *Pakistan won by 22 runs*

WORLD CUP FINAL
ENGLAND v. PAKISTAN, at Melbourne

The 1992 World Cup final at Melbourne. (Patrick Eagar)

Derek Pringle was able to take his place in the England side; Robin Smith was not. Pakistan brought back Ijaz Ahmed for Iqbal Sikander. Imran Khan won the toss, and Pakistan batted. The World Cup final has always been won by the side batting first.

This did not look as if it would be the case in 1992 when Pringle produced an opening spell of eight overs in which he conceded only 13 runs and captured the wickets of Aamir Sohail who edged to the keeper, and Ramiz Raja who shuffled in front of a straight ball. Imran Khan and Javed Miandad were at pains to give the innings foundation, and after 20 overs the score was a meagre 49 for 2.

In the next over Imran skied the ball on the leg side. Gooch called that he would take the catch, but he just failed to cling on to the ball as he fell. By the 30th over, the score had risen to 96, and Imran's calculated tactics were showing their worth. It had taken him nine overs to score 16; now he began to hit with relish. Javed Miandad pushed, dabbed and drove, and some frailties were apparent in both the England bowling and fielding. Imran and Javed had blunted the new-ball attack and scored 139 in 31 overs. Javed sustained a back injury and finished his innings with a runner. He was out when he made a violent reverse sweep off Illingworth and was caught at deep square-leg.

Imran followed four overs later, having hit 72 off 110 balls, but the platform had been provided for the hitters. Inzamam-ul-Haq and Wasim Akram did not allow the grip that Pakistan had taken on the game to weaken. The precocious Inzamam hit 42 off 35 balls, and Wasim Akram lashed 33 off 18 balls before being run out when he tried an impossible single on the last ball of the innings. The final 20 overs of the Pakistan innings had realised 153 runs, and this in spite of Pringle's continued accuracy and excellence which allowed only two runs from the final over in which Inzamam-ul-Haq and Wasim were dismissed.

Inzamam-ul-Haq just makes his ground as Stewart whips off the bails. (Patrick Eagar)

It was as if Wasim had been preparing himself for this day. He had enjoyed only a moderate tournament, but the great all-rounder was now fully charged, operating at maximum power. Botham was unfortunate to be judged caught behind; Stewart was fortunate to escape the same judgment. Stewart, who had proved himself in every department during the competition, fell to the demanding Aqib Javed who drew him forward and caught the edge with an away-swinger.

The introduction of leg-spinner Mushtaq Ahmed was

Botham is caught behind for nought off Wasim Akram. (Patrick Eagar)

Allan Lamb is bowled by Wasim Akram, and Pakistan have one hand on the World Cup. (David Munden)

all too much for Hick. He could not read the googly and was confused by the top-spinner. His footwork bordered on the grotesque and he was leg before to the googly which he tried to cut. That was in the 19th over, and in the 21st, Gooch swept against a leg-break and edged to square-leg where Aqib, diving forward, took a good catch. At 69 for 4, England were practically buried.

Fairbrother, who deserves the same sort of extended run in the Test side that Hick has enjoyed, played with wonderful spirit, and Lamb, whose tour had been spent much in the shadows, gave fine support. They added 72, but Imran had cleverly used Aamir Sohail's slow left-arm spin, and his support bowlers were escaping without severe punishment.

The game was decided after the second drinks break. Wasim Akram returned and knocked back Lamb's off stump with a ball which had first darted into him before moving back sharply. Next ball, Wasim moved the ball in viciously to Lewis and wrecked his stumps off an inside edge. This was fast bowling of the very highest quality, and the match now definitely belonged to Pakistan as had seemed likely for most of the day.

Fairbrother had to call for a runner, but then skied a ball towards square-leg which the wicket-keeper chased. Reeve was splendidly caught by Ramiz Raja, DeFreitas was run out by Salim Malik and Illingworth perished in the final over. Pakistan were comprehensive and worthy winners.

If Pakistan had been somewhat fortunate to reach the final so, ultimately, had England. Pakistan had moved into their best form at the right time while England had begun to look tired and jaded. They had played well throughout the tournament, but it was hard to judge why Illingworth was chosen ahead of the wicket-taker, Tufnell. Pakistan had a better balanced attack, and Imran led the side ably, 'a cool head at the top above a number of hotheads'.

The administration left much to be desired, and the organisation in Australia was not good. Above all, the competition was far too long, and the number of matches could have been reduced by half with benefit to all.

Lap of honour. Imran Khan leads his team in triumph. (Patrick Eagar)

WORLD CUP AVERAGES – AUSTRALIA

BATTING

	M	Inns	NO	Runs	HS	Av	100s	50s
D.C. Boon	8	8	1	368	100	52.57	2	–
D.M. Jones	8	8	1	276	90	39.42	–	2
M.E. Waugh	5	5	1	145	66*	36.25	–	1
G.R. Marsh	5	5	–	151	60	30.20	–	1
S.R. Waugh	8	7	–	187	55	26.71	–	1
T.M. Moody	8	8	–	202	57	25.25	–	2
M.R. Whitney	7	3	2	22	9*	22.00	–	–
I.A. Healy	7	6	2	51	16	12.75	–	–
A.R. Border	8	7	–	60	22	8.57	–	–
M.A. Taylor	2	2	–	13	13	6.50	–	–
B.A. Reid	6	4	2	9	5*	4.50	–	–
P.L. Taylor	7	6	2	17	10*	4.25	–	–
C.J. McDermott	8	5	–	9	6	1.80	–	–

Played in one match – M.G. Hughes 0*

BOWLING

	Overs	Mds	Runs	Wkts	Av	Best	Runs / Over
M.R. Whitney	66	12	215	9	23.88	4-34	3.25
P.L. Taylor	37.4	1	147	5	29.40	2-14	3.90
C.J. McDermott	73	5	246	8	30.75	2-29	3.36
T.M. Moody	49	2	225	7	32.14	3-56	4.59
S.R. Waugh	60.4	1	277	8	34.62	3-36	4.56
A.R. Border	14	–	53	1	53.00	1-40	3.78
B.A. Reid	54.4	2	210	3	70.00	1-18	3.84
M.E. Waugh	5	–	40	–	–	–	8.00

Bowled in one match – M.G. Hughes 9-1- 49-1

FIELDING FIGURES

9 – I.A. Healy; 5 – A.R. Border; 4 – M.E. Waugh; 2 – D.M. Jones, T.M. Moody, S.R. Waugh and C.J. McDermott; 1 – P.L. Taylor

WORLD CUP AVERAGES – INDIA

BATTING

	M	Inns	NO	Runs	HS	Av	100s	50s
M. Azharuddin	8	7	–	332	93	47.42	–	4
S.R. Tendulkar	8	7	1	283	84	47.16	–	3
R.J. Shastri	2	2	–	82	57	41.00	–	1
S. T.Banerjee	3	2	1	36	25*	36.00	–	–
J. Srinath	8	6	5	34	11	34.00	–	–
S.V. Manjrekar	6	6	–	154	47	25.66	–	–
A.D. Jadeja	6	5	1	93	46	23.25	–	–
Kapil Dev	8	8	1	161	42	23.00	–	–
K. Srikkanth	8	8	1	117	40	16.71	–	–
P.K. Amre	4	3	1	27	22	13.50	–	–
K.S. More	8	6	2	41	15*	10.25	–	–
V.G. Kambli	5	4	–	29	24	7.25	–	–
M. Prabhakar	8	4	1	11	8	3.66	–	–
Venkatapathy Raju	6	2	–	1	1	0.50	–	–

BOWLING

	Overs	Mds	Runs	Wkts	Av	Best	Runs/ Over
M. Prabhakar	57.1	5	245	12	20.41	3-41	4.28
Kapil Dev	58	2	251	9	27.88	3-41	4.32
J. Srinath	53.1	3	249	8	31.12	2-23	4.68
Venkatapathy Raju	48.1	3	208	5	41.60	2-38	4.31
S.T. Banerjee	13	1	85	1	85.00	1-45	6.53
S.R. Tendulkar	41	–	180	2	90.00	1-35	4.39
K. Srikkanth	2.1	–	15	–	–	–	6.94
A.D. Jadeja	7.3	–	39	–	–	–	5.20

Bowled in one match – R.J. Shastri 4-0-28-1

FIELDING FIGURES

7 – K.S. More (ct 6/st 1); 4 – K. Srikkanth; 3 – S.V. Manjrekar; 2 – S.R. Tendulkar, S.T. Banerjee and A.D. Jadeja; 1 – R.J. Shastri, M. Azharuddin, M. Prabhakar, Venkatapathy Raju and sub

WORLD CUP AVERAGES – ENGLAND

BATTING

	M	Inns	NO	Runs	HS	Av	100s	50s
N.H. Fairbrother	9	7	2	285	75*	57.00	–	3
D.A. Reeve	9	5	3	79	25*	39.50	–	–
A.J. Stewart	10	8	1	259	77	37.00	–	2
G.A. Hick	10	9	1	264	83	33.00	–	3
R.A. Smith	8	8	2	193	91	32.16	–	1
G.A. Gooch	8	8	–	216	65	27.00	–	3
I.T. Botham	10	10	1	192	53	21.33	–	1
C.C. Lewis	9	6	2	81	33	20.25	–	–
A.J. Lamb	4	4	–	79	31	19.75	–	–
R.K. Illingworth	6	3	1	27	14	13.50	–	–
D.R. Pringle	8	5	2	30	18*	10.00	–	–
P.A.J. DeFreitas	10	5	1	16	10	4.00	–	–

Played in five matches – G.C. Small 5
Played in four matches – P.C.R. Tufnell 3* & 0*

BOWLING

	Overs	Mds	Runs	Wkts	Av	Best	Runs / Over
D.A. Reeve	34.4	4	126	8	15.75	3-38	3.63
I.T. Botham	89	7	306	16	19.12	4-31	3.43
G.C. Small	35	3	127	5	25.40	2-29	3.62
P.A.J. DeFreitas	85.3	12	319	11	29.00	3-34	3.73
C.C. Lewis	50.4	5	214	7	30.57	4-30	4.22
D.R. Pringle	66.4	15	218	7	31.14	3-8	3.27
R.K. Illingworth	58.1	2	250	8	31.25	3-33	4.29
G.A. Hick	14.2	–	70	2	35.00	2-44	4.88
P.C.R. Tufnell	28	2	133	3	44.33	2-36	4.75

FIELDING FIGURES

9 – A.J. Stewart (ct 8/st 1); 6 – N.H. Fairbrother; 5 – G.A. Hick, D.A. Reeve and P.A.J. DeFreitas; 4 – I.T. Botham and C.C. Lewis; 3 – R.A. Smith and R.K. Illingworth; 2 – D.R. Pringle; 1 – G.A. Gooch and A.J. Lamb

WORLD CUP AVERAGES – NEW ZEALAND

BATTING

	M	Inns	NO	Runs	HS	Av	100s	50s
M.D. Crowe	9	9	5	456	100*	114.00	1	4
A.H. Jones	9	9	2	322	78	46.00	–	3
G.R. Larsen	9	2	1	45	37	45.00	–	–
M.J. Greatbatch	7	7	–	313	73	44.71	–	3
K.R. Rutherford	9	7	2	212	65*	42.40	–	3
R.T. Latham	7	7	–	136	60	19.42	–	1
J.G. Wright	4	4	–	71	57	17.75	–	1
I.D.S. Smith	9	5	1	61	19	15.25	–	–
D.N. Patel	9	3	1	25	10*	12.50	–	–
C.Z. Harris	9	6	1	44	14	8.80	–	–

Played in eight matches – W. Watson 5*
Played in five matches – C.L. Cairns 16*, 1* & 4*; D.K. Morrison 12
M.L. Su'a was in the New Zealand party but did not appear in the competition.

BOWLING

	Overs	Mds	Runs	Wkts	Av	Best	Runs / Over
C.Z. Harris	72.1	4	342	16	21.37	3-15	4.73
W. Watson	79	11	301	12	25.08	3-37	3.81
A.H. Jones	12	–	52	2	26.00	2-42	4.33
G.R. Larsen	76	7	262	9	29.11	3-16	3.44
D.N. Patel	79	8	245	8	30.62	2-26	3.10
D.K. Morrison	40	1	180	5	36.00	3-42	4.50
C.L. Cairns	25	1	161	2	80.50	2-43	6.44
R.T. Latham	23	–	136	1	136.00	1-35	5.91

Bowled in one match – M.D. Crowe 1-0-6-0; M.J. Greatbatch 1-0-5-0; K.R. Rutherford 1.4-0-11-0

FIELDING FIGURES

5 – I.D.S. Smith, C.L. Cairns and G.R. Larsen; 4 – C.Z. Harris and M.J. Greatbatch; 3 – R.T. Latham, M.D. Crowe and K.R. Rutherford; 2 – A.H. Jones, D.N. Patel and subs; 1 – J.G. Wright, W. Watson and D.K. Morrison

WORLD CUP AVERAGES – PAKISTAN

BATTING

	M	Inns	NO	Runs	HS	Av	100s	50s
Javed Miandad	9	9	2	437	89	62.42	–	5
Ramiz Raja	8	8	2	349	119*	58.16	2	–
Aamir Sohail	10	10	–	326	114	32.60	1	2
Imran Khan	8	6	–	185	72	30.83	–	1
Inzamam-ul-Haq	10	10	–	225	60	22.50	–	1
Salim Malik	10	9	3	116	51	19.33	–	1
Moin Khan	10	5	2	44	20*	14.66	–	–
Wasim Haider	3	2	–	26	13	13.00	–	–
Wasim Akram	10	8	2	62	33	10.33	–	–
Mushtaq Ahmed	9	4	1	27	17	9.00	–	–
Zahid Fazal	2	2	–	13	11	6.50	–	–
Ijaz Ahmed	7	4	1	14	8*	4.66	–	–

Played in ten matches – Aqib Javed 1* & 1*
Played in four matches – Iqbal Sikander 1*

BOWLING

	Overs	Mds	Runs	Wkts	Av	Best	Runs / Over
Wasim Akram	89.4	2	338	18	18.77	4-32	3.76
Mushtaq Ahmed	78	3	311	16	19.43	3-41	3.98
Aqib Javed	84.5	11	328	11	29.81	3-21	3.86
Imran Khan	60.2	2	251	7	35.85	2-32	4.16
Aamir Sohail	40	2	184	4	46.00	2-26	4.60
Iqbal Sikander	35	2	147	3	49.00	1-30	4.20
Wasim Haider	19	1	79	1	79.00	1-36	4.15
Ijaz Ahmed	36	1	149	1	149.00	1-28	4.50

Bowled in one match – Salim Malik 4-0-18-0

FIELDING FIGURES

14 – Moin Khan (ct 11/st 3); 4 – Ramiz Raja, Inzamam-ul-Haq and Ijaz Ahmed; 3 – Aamir Sohail and Salim Malik; 2 – Aqib Javed and Mushtaq Ahmed; 1 – Javed Miandad, Wasim Akram, Zahid Fazal, Imran Khan and sub

WORLD CUP AVERAGES – SOUTH AFRICA

BATTING

	M	Inns	NO	Runs	HS	Av	100s	50s
P.N. Kirsten	8	8	2	410	90	68.33	–	4
B.M. McMillan	9	5	3	125	33*	62.50	–	–
K.C. Wessels	9	9	2	313	85	44.71	–	3
A.C. Hudson	8	8	–	296	79	37.00	–	3
W.J. Cronje	8	6	3	102	47*	34.00	–	–
D.J. Richardson	9	5	2	66	28	22.00	–	–
J.N. Rhodes	9	8	1	132	43	18.85	–	–
M.W. Rushmere	3	3	–	49	35	16.33	–	–
A.P. Kuiper	9	8	1	113	36	16.14	–	–
R.P. Snell	9	4	2	24	11*	12.00	–	–

Played in nine matches – A.A. Donald 3
Played in seven matches – M.W. Pringle 5*
Played in one match – T. Bosch 0; O. Henry 11

BOWLING

	Overs	Mds	Runs	Wkts	Av	Best	Runs / Over
P.N. Kirsten	18	1	87	5	17.40	3-31	4.83
A.A. Donald	78	5	329	13	25.30	3-34	4.21
A.P. Kuiper	41	–	235	9	26.11	3-40	5.73
B.M. McMillan	73	7	306	11	27.81	3-30	4.19
M.W. Pringle	57	6	236	8	29.50	4-11	4.14
R.P. Snell	72.5	10	310	8	38.75	3-42	4.25
W.J. Cronje	20	1	85	2	42.50	2-17	4.25

Bowled in one match – O. Henry 10-0-31-1; T. Bosch 2.3-0-19-0

FIELDING FIGURES

15 – D.J. Richardson (ct 14/st 1); 7 – K.C. Wessels; 4 – J. N. Rhodes and B.M. McMillan; 3 – A.P. Kuiper and W.J. Cronje; 2 – P.N. Kirsten; 1 – R.P. Snell, A.A. Donald, M.W. Pringle and M.W. Rushmere

WORLD CUP AVERAGES – SRI LANKA

BATTING

	M	Inns	NO	Runs	HS	Av	100s	50s
A. Ranatunga	8	7	2	262	88*	52.40	–	2
M.A.R. Samarasekera	6	6	–	219	75	36.50	–	1
R.S. Mahanama	8	7	–	246	80	35.14	–	3
P.A. de Silva	8	7	–	175	62	25.00	–	1
R.S. Kalpage	7	6	2	67	14	16.75	–	–
S.T. Jayasuriya	6	5	–	74	32	14.80	–	–
H.P. Tillekeratne	8	7	1	80	25*	13.33	–	–
S.D. Anurasiri	5	4	2	21	11	10.50	–	–
A.P. Gurusinha	8	7	–	73	37	10.42	–	–
U.C. Hathurusinghe	4	3	–	26	16	8.66	–	–
C.P.H. Ramanayake	8	6	2	25	12	6.25	–	–

Played in eight matches – G.P. Wickremasinghe 3*, 6* & 21*
Played in three matches – K.I.W. Wijegunawardene did not bat
Played in one match – G.F. Labrooy 19

BOWLING

	Overs	Mds	Runs	Wkts	Av	Best	Runs / Over
U.C. Hathurusinghe	17	–	97	5	19.40	4-57	5.70
A. Ranatunga	18	–	94	3	31.33	2-26	5.22
G.P. Wickremasinghe	60.1	5	276	8	34.50	2-29	4.58
S.D. Anurasiri	50	3	184	5	36.80	3-41	3.68
A.P. Gurusinha	48	–	256	6	42.66	2-67	5.33
R.S. Kalpage	50	–	241	4	60.25	2-33	4.82
C.P.H. Ramanayake	64.4	5	265	4	66.25	2-37	4.09
S.T. Jayasuriya	6	–	44	–	–	–	7.33
K.I.W. Wijegunawardene	17	1	88	–	–	–	5.17

Bowled in one match – P.A. de Silva 1-0-6-0; G.F. Labrooy 10-1-68-1

FIELDING FIGURES

7 – H.P. Tillekeratne (ct 6/st 1); 4 – S.T. Jayasuriya and C.P.H. Ramanayake; 3 – R.S. Mahanama and R.S. Kalpage; 2 – A.P. Gurusinha and G.P. Wickremasinghe; 1 – P.A. de Silva, A. Ranatunga, S.D. Anurasiri and U.C. Hathurusinghe

South African and Sri Lanka teams congregate. (Allsport)

WORLD CUP AVERAGES – WEST INDIES

BATTING

	M	Inns	NO	Runs	HS	Av	100s	50s
B.C. Lara	8	8	1	333	88*	47.57	–	4
D.L. Haynes	7	7	1	251	93*	41.83	–	1
K.L.T. Arthurton	8	7	1	233	58*	38.83	–	2
P.V. Simmons	4	4	–	153	110	38.25	1	–
W.K.M. Benjamin	8	6	4	54	24*	27.00	–	–
C.L. Hooper	8	7	1	120	63	20.00	–	1
R.B. Richardson	8	8	1	132	56	18.85	–	1
A.L. Logie	8	7	–	101	61	14.42	–	1
D. Williams	8	6	2	52	32*	13.00	–	–
C.E.L. Ambrose	7	4	1	33	15*	11.00	–	–
A.C. Cummins	6	2	1	11	6	11.00	–	–
M.D. Marshall	5	4		16	6	4.00	–	–

Played in two matches – R.A. Harper 3
Played in one match – B.P. Patterson did not bat

BOWLING

	Overs	Mds	Runs	Wkts	Av	Best	Runs / Over
A.C. Cummins	59	1	246	12	20.50	4-33	4.16
W.K.M. Benjamin	79	8	297	10	29.70	3-27	3.75
P.V. Simmons	20	1	91	3	30.33	2-40	4.55
R.A. Harper	14	–	63	2	31.50	1-30	4.50
C.E.L. Ambrose	68	6	235	7	33.57	2-24	3.30
K.L.T. Arthurton	15	–	70	2	35.00	2-40	4.66
C.L. Hooper	80	2	312	8	39.00	2-19	3.90
M.D. Marshall	43	3	174	2	87.00	2-26	4.04

Bowled in one match – B.P. Patterson 10-0-25-1

FIELDING FIGURES

14 – D. Williams (ct 11/st 3); 4 – C.L. Hooper, D.L. Haynes and W.K.M. Benjamin; 3 – R.B. Richardson and A.L. Logie; 2 – B.C. Lara; 1 – K.L.T. Arthurton, R.A. Harper, C.E.L. Ambrose, P.V. Simmons and B.P. Patterson

WORLD CUP AVERAGES – ZIMBABWE

BATTING

	M	Inns	NOs	Runs	HS	Av	100s	50s
A. Flower	8	8	2	246	115*	41.00	1	–
A.C. Waller	8	8	2	192	83*	32.00	–	1
A.H. Omarshah	7	7	1	161	60*	26.83	–	1
D.L. Houghton	8	7	–	165	55	23.57	–	1
K.J. Arnott	5	5	1	94	52	23.50	–	1
I.P. Butchart	5	3	–	60	33	20.00	–	–
A.J. Traicos	8	5	3	35	16*	17.50	–	–
E.A. Brandes	8	6	1	71	23	14.20	–	–
M.P. Jarvis	5	3	1	28	17	14.00	–	–
W.R. James	4	3	–	35	17	11.66	–	–
M.G. Burmester	4	3	1	17	12	8.50	–	–
A.J. Pycroft	8	7	1	50	19	8.33	–	–
K.G. Duers	5	2	1	7	5	3.50	–	–
A.D. Campbell	4	3	–	13	8	4.33	–	–

BOWLING

	Overs	Mds	Runs	Wkts	Av	Best	Runs / Over
E.A. Brandes	70.1	7	354	14	25.28	4-21	5.04
I.P. Butchart	32	2	195	6	32.50	3-57	6.09
M.G. Burmester	21.5	–	138	4	34.50	3-36	6.32
A.J. Traicos	62	5	253	6	42.16	3-35	4.08
A.H. Omarshah	57	9	238	5	47.60	2-17	4.17
M.P. Jarvis	47.3	4	239	5	47.80	1-23	5.03
K.G. Duers	50	2	256	3	85.33	1-17	5.12

Bowled in one match – D.L. Houghton 2-0-19-1

FIELDING FIGURES

7 – A. Flower (ct 6/st 1); 3 – A.J. Pycroft, D.L. Houghton and K.G. Duers; 2 – A.C. Waller and E.A. Brandes; 1 – K.J. Arnott, A.H. Omarshah, A.D. Campbell, M.G. Burmester and W.R. James

SECTION B
AUSTRALIA

FAI Cup
Sheffield Shield
Australia v. India series
Benson and Hedges World Series –
Australia, India and West Indies
First-Class Averages
Form Charts
Comments by Ashley Mallett,
'Spin Australia'

Bellerive Oval, Hobart. (Pascal Rondeau/Allsport)

FAI CUP

11 October, 1991 *at WACA Ground, Perth*

Tasmania 121 (M.J. McCague 4 for 34)
Western Australia 125 for 0 (T.M. Moody 69 not out)

Western Australia won by 10 wickets

(*Man of the Match* – T. M. Moody)

12 October, 1991 *at Woolloongabba, Brisbane*

Victoria 135
Queensland 137 for 2 (T.J. Barsby 65 not out)

Queensland won by 8 wickets

(*Man of the Match* – S. Monty)

13 October, 1991 *at Woolloongabba, Brisbane*

Queensland 190 for 9
New South Wales 191 for 4 (S.R. Waugh 74)

New South Wales won by 6 wickets

(*Man of the Match* – S.R. Waugh)

at Adelaide Oval

South Australia 167 (P.C. Nobes 77)
Western Australia 169 for 4 (G.R. Marsh 67)

Western Australia won by 6 wickets

(*Man of the Match* – P.C. Nobes)

14 October, 1991 *at Adelaide Oval*

Tasmania 161 for 8 (D.C. Boon 57)
South Australia 159

Tasmania won by 2 runs

(*Man of the Match* – D.R. Gilbert)

15 October, 1991 *at North Sydney Oval*

New South Wales 310 for 5 (S.R. Waugh 126, M.E. Waugh 112)
Victoria 210 for 8 (S.P. O'Donnell 56)

New South Wales won by 100 runs

(*Man of the Match* – S.R. Waugh)

FAI CUP TABLES

Group A	P	W	L	Pts	Run Rate
Western Australia	2	2	–	4	4.14
Tasmania	2	1	1	2	2.82
South Australia	2	–	2	0	3.26
Group B					
New South Wales	2	2	–	4	5.37
Queensland	2	1	1	2	3.98
Victoria	2	–	2	0	3.45

SEMI-FINALS

19 October, 1991 *at WACA Ground, Perth*

Western Australia 166 for 9 (M.P. Lavender 61, C.J. McDermott 4 for 14)
v. Queensland

Match abandoned

20 October, 1991 *at North Sydney Oval*

New South Wales 250 for 6 (M.G. Bevan 93, M.A. Taylor 79)
Tasmania 233 for 8 (J. Cox 55)

New South Wales won by 17 runs

(*Man of the Match* – M.G. Bevan)

FINAL

26 October, 1991 *at North Sydney Oval*

New South Wales 199 for 9 (M.A. Taylor 50)

Western Australia 130 (D.R. Martyn 54)

New South Wales won by 69 runs

(*Man of the Match* – M.A. Taylor)

The Australian 50-over competition was condensed into a fortnight in October as a prelude to the busiest season in Australian cricket history. A superb bowling and fielding performance in the final brought the trophy to New South Wales for the third time after they had batted indifferently on a good pitch. Steve Waugh was the outstanding player of the tournament, being the leading run-scorer with 239 runs and the leading wicket-taker with seven. He and his twin brother Mark savaged the Victorian bowling in a third-wicket stand of 240 in two-and-a-half hours.

It was in this match that Victorian all-rounder Tony Dodemaide broke a rib, an injury that was to keep him out of cricket for a month.

South Australia began the season disastrously. They had already completed a two-week tour of Malaysia, an idea promulgated by coach Philpott and greatly encouraged by him, presumably to reward his charges for finishing second to last in the Shield table the previous year. There were rumblings that one particular South Australian player was disenchanted with his lot, especially as the coach had allegedly made promises to Paul Nobes which said coach had apparently neither the power nor the authority to honour. Nobes played in the FAI matches for South Australia, and then shifted himself and his family to Melbourne where he felt his efforts might be better appreciated. He had locked horns with the South Australia coach and selectors and had then been axed for 'cricket reasons only', although no other batsman in the side had averaged anywhere near his 57. The Australian Board ruled that, as he had played for South Australia, he could not play for Victoria in the same season. So Nobes took on the Board. The judge presided with wisdom, and common sense prevailed, but everyone knew that Nobes had been virtually forced out of South Australia.

SHEFFIELD SHIELD

1, 2, 3 and 4 November, 1991 *at Woolloongabba, Brisbane*

Queensland 588 for 5 dec. (A.R. Border 196, M. Hayden 149, D.M. Wellham 80, S.G. Law 64, G.M. Ritchie 53 not out) and 239 for 6 (D.M. Wellham 63 not out)

South Australia 554 (J.D. Siddons 149, T.J. Nielsen 88, G.A. Bishop 64, M.P. Faull 51, C.J. McDermott 6 for 150)

Match drawn

Queensland 2 pts., South Australia 0 pts.

at MCG, Melbourne

Victoria 434 for 8 dec. (D.M. Jones 243 not out) and 109 for 0 (D.J. Ramshaw 58 not out)

Tasmania 372 (J. Cox 82, D.J. Buckingham 73, S.K. Warne 4 for 75)

Match drawn

Victoria 2 pts., Tasmania 0 pts.

at WACA Ground, Perth

Western Australia 294 (M.P. Lavender 71, T.J. Zoehrer 58, D.R. Martyn 57, G.R. Marsh 53) and 259 for 5 (G.R. Marsh 98)

New South Wales 332 (M.E. Waugh 136, S.R. Waugh 115, T.M. Alderman 4 for 101)

Match drawn

New South Wales 2 pts., Western Australia 0 pts.

Dean Jones – phenomenal run-scoring for Victoria in the Sheffield Shield. (ASP)

Chris Matthews transferred from Western Australia to Tasmania and carried the islanders' attack almost single-handed. (David Cannon/Allsport)

Allan Border ended a two-year drought at the 'Gabba when he hit 196, but he was overshadowed by Matt Hayden who hit a century on his first-class debut. In spite of the performances of the imported Dirk Wellham and the rotund, returning Greg Ritchie, Hayden was to be Queensland's real star of the summer. Tall and robust, he showed a maturity beyond his years. He is solid and revealed the sort of temperament required to make the right selection of shots. New South Australian skipper Jamie Siddons hit a century in an innings which contained a record 78 extras.

Chris Matthews played his first game for Tasmania after transferring from Western Australia, but it was the super-talented Dean Jones who dominated the match in Melbourne. He hit 243 not out in 529 minutes.

Greg Matthews became the first player to be fined under the new misconduct laws when he reacted against a not out decision given in favour of Mark Lavender. The Waugh twins took New South to first innings points, battering the Western Australian bowling much as they had done the previous season.

8, 9, 10 and 11 November, 1991 *at Adelaide Oval*

South Australia 414 (J.D. Siddons 141, G.R. Blewett 63, D.R. Gilbert 4 for 88) and 93 for 1

Tasmania 426 (D.C. Boon 130, B.A. Cruse 100, J.C. Scuderi 4 for 50)

Match drawn

Tasmania 2 pts., South Australia 0 pts.

at SCG, Sydney

New South Wales 459 (G.R. Matthews 139, S.R. Waugh 88, S.M. Small 79)

Victoria 260 (D.M. Jones 68, D.J. Ramshaw 53) and 394 for 6 (D.M. Jones 144, D.S. Lehmann 66, D.J. Ramshaw 60)

Match drawn

New South Wales 2 pts., Victoria 0 pts.

After Siddons had hit his second century for South Australia, Boon and Cruse added 156 for Tasmania's second wicket. South Australian coach Philpott stated that off-spinner Tim May was the best of his type in the world. May bowled lots of overs – in this match he bowled 72 overs and took 2 for 108 – but he appeared about as predictable as Peter Taylor and about as effective. New captain Jamie Siddons also thinks the world of May. Trouble is, so do most of Australia's batsmen. They love facing May's flat, predictable off-spin. Soon May's figures were to reflect this with his first six wickets costing him more than 600 runs.

There were contrasting innings in Sydney. Greg Matthews whacked 139 off 172 deliveries while Ramshaw took 316 minutes to reach 50. Dean Jones hit his 15th century for Victoria when his side were asked to follow-on.

15, 16, 17 and 18 November, 1991 *at Woolloongabba, Brisbane*

New South Wales 119 (C.J. McDermott 5 for 54, C.G. Rackemann 4 for 35) and 230 (M.E. Waugh 60, M.A. Taylor 57, G.R.J. Matthews 50)
Queensland 268 (M.L. Hayden 64, M.R. Whitney 4 for 91) and 84 for 0

Queensland won by 10 wickets

Queensland 6 pts., New South Wales 0 pts.

at MCG, Melbourne

Victoria 514 for 8 dec. (D.M. Jones 214, W.N. Phillips 121)
South Australia 244 (A.M.J. Hilditch 103, P.R. Reiffel 4 for 44) and 246 (J.A. Brayshaw 90, A.M.J. Hilditch 50, M.G. Hughes 4 for 32, P.R. Reiffel 4 for 54)

Victoria won by an innings and 24 runs

Victoria 6 pts., South Australia 0 pts.

Queensland gained the season's first win, beating New South Wales inside three days. As in previous seasons, Queensland began well with McDermott bowling like the wind and Greg Rowell, whose action is not dissimilar to that of a young and taller Dennis Lillee, and skipper Carl Rackemann, again bowling with economy and guide, providing support.

A second double century by Dean Jones took Victoria to a position from which they could beat South Australia. He and Wayne Phillips shared a second-wicket stand of 302. Reiffel compensated for the disappointing form of Fleming, and Darren Berry kept wicket efficiently.

22, 23, 24 and 25 November, 1991 *at Bellerive Oval, Hobart*

Tasmania 138 (G. Rowell 7 for 46) and 180 (C.J. McDermott 4 for 65)
Queensland 447 (M.L. Hayden 108, D.M. Wellham 100, I.A. Healy 55 not out, C.D. Matthews 4 for 118)

Queensland won by an innings and 129 runs

Queensland 6 pts., Tasmania 0 pts.

at Adelaide Oval

South Australia 460 (J.C. Scuderi 125 not out, T.J. Nielsen 81, G.R. Blewett 78, D.W. Hookes 75, T.J. Zoehrer 5 for 58) and 180 for 6 dec.
Western Australia 338 for 5 dec. (T.M. Moody 168, D.R. Martyn 90) and 306 for 3 (G.R. Marsh 104, M.P. Lavender 58, T.M. Moody 54)

Western Australia won by 7 wickets

Western Australia 6 pts., South Australia 2 pts.

Pace bowler Greg Rowell returned the best bowling figures of his career as Queensland swept aside Tasmania. Star batsmen Hayden and Wellham shared a second-wicket stand of 167.

In the absence of the injured Siddons, South Australia were led by Hilditch. Joe Scuderi hit a maiden century, but the amazing accomplishment came from Tim Zoehrer who batted well, kept well and then added good-quality leg-spin which brought him seven wickets in the match. Zoehrer has just completed a second stint in Holland, and he is full of praise for the Dutch cricketers. Moody batted with his usual panache, and when Western Australia were set a not too difficult target Marsh saw his side home.

23, 24, 25 and 26 November, 1991 *at Lismore*

Indians 209 (S.R. Tendulkar 82, W.J. Holdsworth 4 for 38) and 147 (S.R. Tendulkar 59, M.R. Whitney 6 for 37)
New South Wales 364 (M.G. Bevan 115, M.E. Waugh 79, S.M. Small 58)

New South Wales won by an innings and 8 runs

Carl Rackemann, new captain of Queensland, a state still in search of the Shield. (Simon Brutes/Allsport)

This was the Indian tourists' only first-class game before the first Test. They had played three one-day matches and lost two of them. Tendulkar apart, their batting was lamentable. Michael Bevan hit a good century, but he failed to produce the consistency throughout the season that a batsman of his skill should.

29, 30 November, 1 and 2 December, 1991 *at Bellerive Oval, Hobart*

Tasmania 172 (S. Young 55, B. Julian 5 for 26) and 193 (D.J. Buckingham 110, B.A. Reid 6 for 55)

Western Australia 331 (D.R. Martyn 110, M.R.J. Veletta 84, C.D. Matthews 5 for 102) and 35 for 0

Western Australia won by 10 wickets

Western Australia 6 pts., Tasmania 0 pts.

Western Australia won their second match in succession. Brendon Julian returned the best bowling figures of his career, and Bruce Reid wrecked Tasmania in the second innings. He was to remain troubled by his back for much of the season, but there were times when he looked capable of almost anything. Following his tour of Zimbabwe, it was hoped that Jamie Cox would be a heavy scorer for Tasmania, but he had a disastrous summer. In this match, he scored 0 and 4. In the absence of Boon, Buckingham was the pick of the batsmen as he proved here. For the victors, Damien Martyn hit a maiden first-class hundred and revealed his undoubted class. He was later to be rewarded with a place in the party to tour Sri Lanka. Veletta led Western Australia in the absence of Marsh and although he was not to enjoy a bumper season with the bat, his captaincy proved fine.

Mike Veletta of Western Australia, a capable deputy wicket-keeper and deputy captain, and a reliable opening bat for the Shield winners. (Adrian Murrell/Allsport)

FIRST TEST MATCH
AUSTRALIA v. INDIA, at Brisbane

Playing in his record 126th Test match, Allan Border won the toss and asked India to bat. Australia chose Reiffel and Whitney ahead of Reid and Alderman, and Reiffel, not unexpectedly, was named as twelfth man. Peter Taylor was chosen as the spinner, a selection which emphasised Australia's weakness in this area.

Happily, five years ago, Ashley Mallett began *Spin Australia*, now sponsored by business man and cricket lover Sir Ronald Brierley and endorsed by the Australian Cricket Board. It embraces spinners from Test level to promising youngsters, and Ashley Mallett visits all Australian states, coaching senior and junior squads.

Mallett believes that the West Indian reliance on pace brought an imbalance to cricket, and that this imbalance was fostered by other nations who believed that the only way to fight fire was with fire. A spinner simply became a man who would bowl while the quick men rested.

'I know. My ambition was to take 100 Test wickets. I achieved that in 23 Tests. Dennis Lillee took the first 100 of his Test wickets in 22 Tests. In my final 15 Tests I took 32 wickets, Lillee took another 100. Times had changed. Strategy was different. If you tried to "buy" a wicket and were hit, you would be taken off. I could never

Craig McDermott wrecked India in the first Test match and was the leading wicket-taker in Australia. (Adrian Murrell/Allsport)

advocate spin to the exclusion of pace, for it was the combination of genuine pace and top-flight spin which made cricket in Australia great.'

As it transpired, Peter Taylor, a purely defensive spinner, was to take only one wicket in two Test matches.

India were initially wrecked by the pace of Craig McDermott. He dismissed both openers in a burst of seven overs, and Hughes accounted for Manjrekar and Vengsarkar. Azharuddin top-edged an ill-advised hook shot off Whitney who then bowled Tendulkar. India's much vaunted batting had wilted to 83 for 6.

Recovery was effected by Kapil Dev and Manoj Prabhakar, who was dropped by Border when on 22. The tail helped to sustain Prabhakar after Kapil Dev had been bowled for his 44 off 41 balls, and India were all out for 239 by the end of the day.

The second day was cut short by bad light which heralded rain, but before that point had been reached Australia had moved to within five runs of the Indian score for the loss of Marsh and Taylor. India did not capture a wicket until the afternoon session when Srinath, making his debut and bowling impressively, hit Marsh's middle and off stumps. The left-arm spinner Venkatapathy Raju also bowled well and claimed Taylor when the batsman swept once too often, but by then Australia had taken a firm grip on the game.

The Australians had batted drearily so that the tumble of wickets on the third day was rather unexpected. The middle order fell apart, but the last three wickets added 60 to give Australia a substantial lead. Kapil Dev finished with 4 for 80 to draw level with Ian Botham on 380 Test wickets. He bowled one inspired spell in which he clipped Border's off bail and knocked back Jones' off stump in the space of three outstanding deliveries. Mark Waugh was handicapped by a torn muscle in his left rib cage, an injury that was to keep him out of the beginning of the one-day series.

When India batted again Srikkanth was taken at short-leg off Hughes who then had Manjrekar taken in the same position and Vengsarkar leg before. Within an hour and a half the innings was in shreds as Azharuddin and Tendulkar both failed. Kapil Dev hit 25 off 24 balls, but he fell to McDermott, and India ended the day at 104 for 6.

Shastri had batted manfully throughout the disasters, but he added only four to his score next morning before being bowled by McDermott. Prabhakar again fought well to delay the inevitable which came with one-and-a-half days of the match remaining.

India's preparation for the game had been abysmal, and in spite of some spirited bowling which revived hopes on the third day, their display had reflected their preparation.

FIRST TEST MATCH – AUSTRALIA v. INDIA

29, 30 November, 1, 2 December, 1991 at Woolloongabba, Brisbane

INDIA

	FIRST INNINGS		SECOND INNINGS	
R.J. Shastri	c Waugh, b McDermott	8	c Healy, b McDermott	41
K. Srikkanth	c Boon, b McDermott	13	c Boon, b Hughes	0
S.V. Manjrekar	c and b Hughes	17	c Boon, b Hughes	5
D.B. Vengsarkar	c Waugh, b Hughes	5	lbw, b Hughes	0
M. Azharuddin (capt)	c Hughes, b Whitney	10	c Boon, b Hughes	12
S.R. Tendulkar	b Whitney	16	c Healy, b McDermott	7
Kapil Dev	b McDermott	44	c Waugh, b McDermott	25
M. Prabhakar	not out	54	c Healy, b Whitney	39
*K.S. More	c Whitney, b Hughes	19	lbw, b McDermott	1
Venkatapathy Raju	c Healy, b McDermott	12	c Healy, b Whitney	2
J. Srinath	c Healy, b McDermott	21	not out	12
Extras	b 1, lb 6, nb 13	20	lb 4, nb 8	12
		239		156

AUSTRALIA

	FIRST INNINGS		SECOND INNINGS	
G.R. Marsh	b Srinath	47	(2) not out	17
M.A. Taylor	c Vengsarkar, b Raju	94	(1) not out	35
D.C. Boon	c More, b Prabhakar	66		
A.R. Border (capt)	b Kapil Dev	28		
D.M. Jones	b Kapil Dev	0		
M.E. Waugh	c More, b Srinath	11		
*I.A. Healy	lbw, b Prabhakar	12		
P.L. Taylor	c Raju, b Srinath	31		
M.G. Hughes	b Kapil Dev	11		
C.J. McDermott	c Azharuddin, b Kapil Dev	8		
M.R. Whitney	not out	7		
Extras	lb 15, w 1, nb 9	25	lb 4, nb 2	6
		340	(for no wicket)	58

	O	M	R	W	O	M	R	W
McDermott	28.1	11	54	5	25	7	47	4
Whitney	21	2	82	2	17.2	3	55	2
Hughes	20	5	34	3	16	4	50	4
M.E. Waugh	1	–	6	–				
P.L. Taylor	18	3	56	–				

	O	M	R	W	O	M	R	W
Kapil Dev	34	9	80	4	9	–	23	–
Prabhakar	37	10	88	2	2	1	3	–
Srinath	24.4	4	59	3	9	5	6	–
Venkatapathy Raju	31	5	90	1	3	1	13	–
Tendulkar	1	–	8	–	1	–	5	–
Manjrekar	–	–	–	–	0.5	–	4	–

FALL OF WICKETS (India)

1–21, 2–24, 3–50, 4–53, 5–67, 6–83, 7–141, 8–186, 9–206
1–0, 2–14, 3–14, 4–32, 5–47, 6–87, 7–136, 8–140, 9–142

FALL OF WICKETS (Australia)

1–95, 2–178, 3–244, 4–244, 5–265, 6–278, 7–280, 8–301, 9–316

Umpires: P.J. McConnell & S.G. Randell

Australia won by 10 wickets

BENSON AND HEDGES WORLD SERIES
Phase One – Matches One to Seven

Mohammad Azharuddin deploys his troops in the Benson and Hedges World Series. Azharuddin failed to find form at the beginning of India's tour and came in for heavy criticism. (Joe Mann/Allsport)

To the astonishment of many, the Australian Board decided to play a full complement of World Series matches in 1991–92. This meant that a minimum of 39 one-day internationals would be played in Australia during the season plus a host of warm-up matches between countries competing in the World Cup. The Benson and Hedges World Series was played in two phases, the first seven matches in the first part of December, and the remaining five and the finals in the New Year.

The competition began on a spectacular note as West Indies, who played three one-day games and one first-class game outside the series, tied with India. India gave another miserable batting display, and only a patient innings of 33 off 113 balls by Shastri helped them to three figures. Haynes immediately fell to Kapil Dev, but it was the bowling of Srinath and debutant Subroto Banerjee which undermined the middle order. Srinath dismissed Hooper and Arthurton with successive balls, and Banerjee sent back Lara, Williams and Marshall in the space of 25 balls. Ambrose and Cummins added 37 for the ninth wicket before Ambrose was brilliantly run out by Shastri. With his front-line bowlers having exhausted their quotas, Azharuddin turned to Tendulkar. Patterson and Cummins took five off his first five deliveries, but the sixth had Cummins well caught at slip.

If the second match in the series lacked the excitement of the first, it did produce a great surprise. India were still short of their batting potential, but a vigorous, if crude, 60 off as many balls from Srikkanth, and some solidity from Amre, Tendulkar and Kapil Dev took them to 208. Srinath, Prabhakar and Kapil Dev wrecked the Australian innings beyond repair, and the left-arm spin of Shastri was all too much for the later batsmen.

Order was restored in Hobart where the Indian batting was once more a bitter disappointment. Electing to bat for

Sachin Tendulkar, India's batsman of the highest quality in all forms of cricket. (Joe Mann/Allsport)

the second match in succession, India owed all to Manjrekar and Tendulkar who shared a third-wicket stand of 102 and scored all but 61 of their side's runs. Boon and Marsh gave Australia a sound foundation in their search for a moderate target of 176, and Jones joined Boon in a stand worth 129, the pair being separated when only two runs were needed for victory. To the delight of his home state supporters, David Boon reached what proved to be the only century of the tournament.

Australia's batting was less assured against West Indies at Melbourne in front of a crowd of close to 60,000. Boon and Jones, the heroes of Hobart, went cheaply, and only Border, Marsh and Moody showed sufficient resilience. Marshall bowled at his best for West Indies. McDermott made significant inroads into the West Indian batting when he accounted for Best and Richardson, but the greatest contribution came from Steve Waugh. He held a return catch to account for Lara, trapped Hooper leg before and hit the stumps to run out both Arthurton and Marshall. West Indies were never quite in touch with the run rate in spite of Haynes' attempts to hold the innings together.

Azharuddin again chose to bat first in the fifth match, and on this occasion his batsmen relished the faster wicket of Adelaide. Srikkanth hit a blistering 82 off 88 balls, and only Shastri failed to contribute as India moved to an impressive 262 in their 50 overs. An opening partnership of 124 in 28 overs between Desmond Haynes and Philo Wallace appeared to make a West Indian victory something of a formality. Although Richardson went cheaply, Haynes and Lara added 57 in ten overs, and West Indies were moving relentlessly towards their target. At 205, Hooper hoisted Kapil Dev to mid-wicket where Manjrekar took a fine running catch. In the next over, Haynes top-edged Srinath to Shastri and Arthurton was caught at long-on. The cream of the West Indian batting had gone, and India now took control of the match, their pace bowlers sweeping them to victory.

Ever inconsistent, India batted poorly the following day and slumped to 69 for 6. Kapil Dev batted with uncharacteristic care to hit 39 in 17 overs, but 157 was a paltry score. Kapil Dev and Prabhakar made early strikes, but Jones and Border added 137, and Australia won a victory easier than the scores suggest.

An opening stand of 128 between Marsh and Boon set Australia on the path to success in the final match of the first phase. Steve Waugh and Ian Healy hit lustily, and West Indies were soon reduced to 70 for 4 by the Australian pace men. Hooper offered style and courage, but he could not prevent the inevitable.

The win meant that Australia had eight points from five games; India had five from five; and West Indies had only one point from their four matches. To add to West Indian woes, Ian Bishop was forced to return to the Caribbean with a back injury. The injury was to keep him out of the World Cup.

BENSON AND HEDGES WORLD SERIES – MATCH ONE – INDIA v. WEST INDIES

6 December, 1991 at WACA Ground, Perth

INDIA

Batsman	Dismissal	Runs
R.J. Shastri	c Lara, b Marshall	33
K. Srikkanth	c Hooper, b Patterson	3
S.V. Manjrekar	c Williams, b Cummins	15
S.R. Tendulkar	c Richardson, b Cummins	1
M. Azharuddin (capt)	c Lara, b Ambrose	6
P.K. Amre	run out	20
Kapil Dev	c Richardson, b Marshall	5
M. Prabhakar	run out	13
*K.S. More	c Richardson, b Ambrose	4
S.T. Banerjee	not out	2
J. Srinath	run out	0
Extras	lb 13, w 10, nb 1	24
		126

(47.4 overs)

	O	M	R	W
Patterson	10	1	28	1
Ambrose	8.4	3	9	2
Marshall	10	2	23	2
Cummins	9	1	21	2
Hooper	10	1	32	–

FALL OF WICKETS
1–8, 2–35, 3–41, 4–58, 5–74, 6–88, 7–111, 8–122, 9–125

WEST INDIES

Batsman	Dismissal	Runs
D.L. Haynes	c More, b Kapil Dev	0
P.A. Wallace	b Prabhakar	11
R.B. Richardson (capt)	c More, b Kapil Dev	12
B.C. Lara	c More, b Banerjee	14
C.L. Hooper	b Srinath	12
K.L.T. Arthurton	b Srinath	0
M.D. Marshall	c More, b Banerjee	7
*D. Williams	c Srikkanth, b Banerjee	5
C.E.L. Ambrose	run out	17
A.C. Cummins	c Azharuddin, b Tendulkar	24
B.P. Patterson	not out	8
Extras	lb 4, w 9, nb 3	16
		126

(41 overs)

	O	M	R	W
Kapil Dev	10	3	30	2
Prabhakar	10	1	30	1
Srinath	10	2	27	2
Banerjee	10	2	30	3
Tendulkar	1	–	5	1

FALL OF WICKETS
1–0, 2–23, 3–25, 4–55, 5–55, 6–61, 7–69, 8–76, 9–113

Umpires: R.J. Evans & P.J. McConnell — Man of the Match – C.E.L. Ambrose — *Match tied*

BENSON AND HEDGES WORLD SERIES – MATCH TWO – AUSTRALIA v. INDIA
8 December, 1991 at WACA Ground, Perth

INDIA

R.J. Shastri	c Jones, b S.R. Waugh	10
K. Srikkanth	c Moody, b S.R. Waugh	60
S.V. Manjrekar	run out	2
S.R. Tendulkar	c P.L. Taylor, b Moody	36
M. Azharuddin (capt)	c Healy, b Moody	6
P.K. Amre	c Jones, b McDermott	33
Kapil Dev	not out	25
M. Prabhakar	lbw, b S.R. Waugh	2
S.T. Banerjee	not out	6
*K.S. More		
J. Srinath		
Extras	b 1, lb 10, w 16, nb 1	28
	(for 7 wickets)	208

(50 overs)

	O	M	R	W
McDermott	10	1	40	1
Reid	10	2	16	–
O'Donnell	7	–	39	–
S.R. Waugh	10	1	46	3
P.L. Taylor	4	–	18	–
Moody	9	–	38	2

FALL OF WICKETS
1–49, 2–64, 3–95, 4–112, 5–158, 6–183, 7–193

AUSTRALIA

G.R. Marsh	c More, b Banerjee	15
D.C. Boon	c Kapil Dev, b Prabhakar	1
D.M. Jones	b Kapil Dev	1
A.R. Border (capt)	c More, b Srinath	32
T.M. Moody	c More, b Srinath	7
S.R. Waugh	c and b Shastri	5
S.P. O'Donnell	c Kapil Dev, b Shastri	10
*I.A. Healy	st More, b Shastri	3
P.L. Taylor	c Amre, b Shastri	6
C.J. McDermott	c Tendulkar, b Shastri	5
B.A. Reid	not out	1
Extras	lb 4, w 6, nb 5	15
		101

(37.5 overs)

	O	M	R	W
Kapil Dev	6	2	5	1
Prabhakar	6	2	19	1
Srinath	7	–	24	2
Banerjee	8	1	26	1
Shastri	6.5	1	15	5
Tendulkar	4	–	8	–

FALL OF WICKETS
1–3, 2–6, 3–52, 4–65, 5–68, 6–75, 7–84, 8–93, 9–99

Umpires: R.J. Evans & T.A. Prue — Man of the Match – K. Srikkanth — *India won by 107 runs*

BENSON AND HEDGES WORLD SERIES – MATCH THREE – INDIA v. AUSTRALIA
10 December, 1991 at Bellerive Oval, Hobart

INDIA

R.J. Shastri	lbw, b McDermott	0
K. Srikkanth	c Healy, b McDermott	7
S.V. Manjrekar	c Healy, b Reid	57
S.R. Tendulkar	c S.R. Waugh, b P.L. Taylor	57
Kapil Dev	c and b P.L. Taylor	3
P.K. Amre	b O'Donnell	8
M. Azharuddin (capt)	not out	21
S.T. Banerjee	c Jones, b McDermott	5
M. Prabhakar	run out	1
J. Srinath	not out	2
*K.S. More		
Extras	b 1, lb 7, w 4, nb 2	14
	(for 8 wickets)	175

(50 overs)

	O	M	R	W
Reid	10	1	24	1
McDermott	10	3	19	3
O'Donnell	10	1	35	1
S.R. Waugh	7	–	31	–
P.L. Taylor	10	–	43	2
Moody	3	–	15	–

FALL OF WICKETS
1–2, 2–18, 3–120, 4–134, 5–137, 6–151, 7–163, 8–168

AUSTRALIA

D.C. Boon	not out	102
G.R. Marsh	b Srinath	8
D.M. Jones	c Tendulkar, b Manjrekar	48
A.R. Border (capt)	not out	0
T.M. Moody		
S.R. Waugh		
S.P. O'Donnell		
*I.A. Healy		
P.L. Taylor		
C.J. McDermott		
B.A. Reid		
Extras	b 3, lb 4, w 7, nb 4	18
	(for 2 wickets)	176

(48.3 overs)

	O	M	R	W
Kapil Dev	10	3	21	–
Prabhakar	10	–	32	–
Srinath	10	1	37	1
Banerjee	6	–	41	–
Shastri	10	–	29	–
Srikkanth	2	–	7	–
Manjrekar	0.3	–	2	1

FALL OF WICKETS
1–45, 2–174

Umpires: S.G. Randell & C.D. Timmins — Man of the Match – D.C. Boon — *Australia won by 8 wickets*

BENSON AND HEDGES WORLD SERIES – MATCH FOUR – AUSTRALIA v. WEST INDIES

12 December, 1991 at MCG, Melbourne

AUSTRALIA

G.R. Marsh	c Richardson, **b** Marshall	43
D.C. Boon	**b** Marshall	8
D.M. Jones	c Williams, **b** Marshall	0
A.R. Border (capt)	**st** Williams, **b** Hooper	37
T.M. Moody	run out	51
S.R. Waugh	c Williams, **b** Cummins	8
*I.A. Healy	**b** Patterson	5
P.L.Taylor	c Lara, **b** Ambrose	3
C.J. McDermott	**lbw, b** Marshall	0
M.R. Whitney	not out	2
B.A. Reid	not out	2
Extras	lb 9, w 2, nb 3	14
	(for 9 wickets)	**173**

(50 overs)

	O	M	R	W
Ambrose	10	2	31	1
Patterson	10	–	49	1
Marshall	10	4	18	4
Cummins	10	1	35	1
Hooper	10	–	31	1

FALL OF WICKETS

1–21, **2**–29, **3**–97, **4**–103, **5**–141, **6**–154, **7**–159, **8**–167, **9**–170

WEST INDIES

D.L. Haynes	c and **b** P.L. Taylor	62
C.A. Best	c Border, **b** McDermott	5
R.B. Richardson (capt)	c S.R. Waugh, **b** McDermott	10
B.C. Lara	c and **b** S.R. Waugh	11
C.L. Hooper	lbw, **b** S.R. Waugh	0
K.L.T. Arthurton	run out	28
M.D. Marshall	run out	3
*D. Williams	run out	10
C.E.L. Ambrose	**b** P.L. Taylor	18
A.C. Cummins	**b** McDermott	6
B.P. Patterson	not out	1
Extras	b 1, lb 5, w 2, nb 2	10
		164

(49.1 overs)

	O	M	R	W
Reid	9	1	33	–
McDermott	9.1	2	23	3
Whitney	10	3	29	–
S.R. Waugh	6	–	16	2
Moody	5	–	21	–
P.L. Taylor	10	1	36	2

FALL OF WICKETS

1–9, **2**–34, **3**–64, **4**–64, **5**–119, **6**–124, **7**–129, **8**–145, **9**–162

Umpires: A.R. Crafter & P.J. McConnell — Man of the Match – S.R. Waugh — *Australia won by 9 runs*

BENSON AND HEDGES WORLD SERIES – MATCH FIVE – INDIA v. WEST INDIES

14 December, 1991, at Adelaide Oval

INDIA

R.J. Shastri	c Williams, **b** Ambrose	4
K. Srikkanth	**st** Williams, **b** Hooper	82
S.V. Manjrekar	c Wallace, **b** Arthurton	55
S.R. Tendulkar	c and **b** Arthurton	48
M. Azharuddin (capt)	not out	31
Kapil Dev	not out	21
P.K. Amre		
*K.S. More		
M. Prabhakar		
J. Srinath		
N.D. Hirwani		
Extras	b 5, w 11, nb 5	21
	(for 4 wickets)	**262**

(50 overs)

	O	M	R	W
Ambrose	10	1	35	1
Patterson	6	–	47	–
Marshall	10	–	59	–
Cummins	10	–	41	–
Hooper	10	–	52	1
Arthurton	4	–	23	2

FALL OF WICKETS

1–27, **2**–123, **3**–198, **4**–220

WEST INDIES

D.L. Haynes	c Shastri, **b** Srinath	89
P.A. Wallace	c Srinath, **b** Hirwani	52
R.B. Richardson (capt)	run out	2
B.C. Lara	lbw, **b** Shastri	29
C.L. Hooper	c Manjrekar, **b** Kapil Dev	12
K.L.T. Arthurton	c Amre, **b** Kapil Dev	5
M.D. Marshall	lbw, **b** Srinath	17
*D. Williams	c and **b** Prabhakar	3
C.E.L. Ambrose	**b** Kapil Dev	10
A.C. Cummins	**b** Kapil Dev	7
B.P. Patterson	not out	1
Extras	b 1, lb 11, w 9, nb 4	25
		252

(50 overs)

	O	M	R	W
Kapil Dev	10	1	54	4
Prabhakar	9	1	42	1
Srinath	10	–	35	2
Tendulkar	2	–	10	–
Hirwani	9	–	54	1
Shastri	10	–	45	1

FALL OF WICKETS

1–124, **2**–127, **3**–184, **4**–205, **5**–206, **6**–212, **7**–220, **8**–243, **9**–251

Umpires: D.B. Hair & L.J. King — Man of the Match – K. Srikkanth — *India won by 10 runs*

BENSON AND HEDGES WORLD SERIES – MATCH SIX – AUSTRALIA v. INDIA
15 December, 1991 at Adelaide Oval

INDIA

R.J. Shastri	lbw, **b** Reid	1
K. Srikkanth	c and **b** McDermott	3
S.V. Manjrekar	run out	12
S.R. Tendulkar	c Jones, **b** S.R. Waugh	21
P.K. Amre	c Healy, **b** Whitney	10
M. Azharuddin (capt)	c Healy, **b** Whitney	13
Kapil Dev	c Moody, **b** P.L. Taylor	39
M. Prabhakar	run out	17
*K.S. More	lbw, **b** McDermott	20
J. Srinath	run out	8
Venkatapathy Raju	not out	3
Extras	lb 6, w 4	10
		157

AUSTRALIA

D.C. Boon	**b** Kapil Dev	6
G.R. Marsh	**b** Prabhakar	3
D.M. Jones	not out	63
A.R. Border (capt)	c sub (Ganguly), **b** Venkatapathy Raju	76
T.M. Moody	c Tendulkar, **b** Venkatapathy Raju	0
S.R. Waugh	not out	0
*I.A. Healy		
P.L Taylor		
C.J. McDermott		
M.R. Whitney		
B.A. Reid		
Extras	lb 3, w 4, nb 3	10
	(for 4 wickets)	**158**

(48.4 overs)

	O	M	R	W
McDermott	8.4	–	29	2
Reid	10	1	32	1
Whitney	10	3	22	2
S.R. Waugh	10	1	27	1
P.L. Taylor	10	1	41	1

(40.5 overs)

	O	M	R	W
Kapil Dev	6	2	12	1
Prabhakar	6	–	20	1
Srinath	6	–	30	–
Shastri	10	–	34	–
Venkatapathy Raju	9	1	32	2
Srikkanth	2	–	24	–
Tendulkar	1.5	–	3	–

FALL OF WICKETS
1–2, **2**–4, **3**–37, **4**–41, **5**–64, **6**–69, **7**–119, **8**–133, **9**–149

FALL OF WICKETS
1–10, **2**–17, **3**–154, **4**–156

Umpires: A.R. Crafter & I.S. Thomas — Man of the Match – A.R. Border — *Australia won by 6 wickets*

BENSON AND HEDGES WORLD SERIES – MATCH SEVEN – AUSTRALIA v. WEST INDIES
18 December, 1991 at SCG, Sydney

AUSTRALIA

G.R. Marsh	c D.L. Haynes, **b** Cummins	82
D.C. Boon	**b** Arthurton	61
D.M. Jones	**b** Ambrose	2
S.R. Waugh	**b** Ambrose	34
T.M. Moody	run out	8
A.R. Border (capt)	**b** Hooper	1
*I.A. Healy	not out	17
P.L. Taylor	not out	2
C.J. McDermott		
M.R. Whitney		
B.A. Reid		
Extras	b 2, lb 15, w 4, nb 6	27
	(for 6 wickets)	**234**

WEST INDIES

D.L. Haynes	c Healy, **b** McDermott	9
P.A. Wallace	lbw, **b** Reid	2
R.B. Richardson (capt)	c Healy, **b** Reid	6
B.C. Lara	c S.R. Waugh, **b** Whitney	19
C.L. Hooper	c S.R. Waugh, **b** Moody	77
K.L.T. Arthurton	**b** S.R. Waugh	38
M.D. Marshall	**b** Whitney	7
*D. Williams	**b** Whitney	0
R.C. Haynes	c Moody, **b** McDermott	0
C.E.L. Ambrose	**b** S.R. Waugh	2
A.C. Cummins	not out	1
Extras	lb 13, w 4, nb 5	22
		183

(50 overs)

	O	M	R	W
Ambrose	10	3	26	2
Cummins	10	–	53	1
Marshall	9	2	39	–
R.C. Haynes	6	–	35	–
Hooper	10	–	42	1
Arthurton	5	1	22	1

(46.5 overs)

	O	M	R	W
Reid	10	2	29	2
McDermott	8	1	29	2
S.R. Waugh	6.5	–	33	2
Whitney	10	1	25	3
P.L. Taylor	5	–	32	–
Moody	7	–	22	1

FALL OF WICKETS
1–128, **2**–137, **3**–190, **4**–204, **5**–211, **6**–214

FALL OF WICKETS
1–13, **2**–17, **3**–36, **4**–70, **5**–146, **6**–177, **7**–177, **8**–178, **9**–181

Umpires: L.J. King & S.G. Randell — Man of the Match – G.R. Marsh — *Australia won by 51 runs*

12, 13, 14 and 15 December, 1991 *at SCG, Sydney*

Tasmania 144 for 7 dec. and 116 (P.J.S. Alley 4 for 25)
New South Wales 0 for 0 dec. and 212 (M.G. Bevan 52, S.M. Small 51, C.D. Matthews 5 for 50)

Tasmania won by 48 runs

Tasmania 6 pts., New South Wales 0 pts.

13, 14, 15 and 16 December, 1991 *at Woolloongabba, Brisbane*

Queensland 374 (T.J. Barsby 165, P.J.T. Goggin 91, P.W. Anderson 52) and 324 for 4 dec. (D.M. Wellham 167, M.L. Hayden 116)
Victoria 375 for 8 dec. (W.G. Ayres 115, D.S. Lehmann 65, D.J. Ramshaw 52) and 89 for 3

Match drawn

Victoria 2 pts., Queensland 0 pts.

Western Australia's Tim Zoehrer, the complete all-round cricketer, 579 runs, 15 wickets with his leg-breaks and 38 dismissals behind the stumps. (Adrian Murrell/Allsport)

New South Wales gave a debut to left-arm spinner David Freedman so that with Matthews and Freedman, Geoff Lawson was able to operate the best-balanced attack in Australia. Freedman fitted into the line-up well, took three wickets on his debut, and was to have much success. He doesn't make full use of his lead arm, but he is accurate and hard-working. Some believed he would be chosen for the tour of Sri Lanka, but he will need to prove his worth on all wickets before higher honours can be bestowed.

Lawson, the best Shield captain in the land for some years, again excelled in the rain-interrupted match with Tasmania. He forfeited New South Wales' first innings, the first time that this has been done in Australia, prepared to forgo two points for the big six. Holdsworth, Phil Alley, a giant left-armer who returned a career-best performance, McNamara and Freedman skittled Tasmania for 116, leaving New South Wales to make 260 to win. They fell to the burly Chris Matthews. Sheer boldness had demanded a New South Wales victory, but the gods were against Lawson and his men.

The match proved Lawson's innovative style. It was appreciated, and one hopes it will rub off on his successor Mark Taylor, who will also follow Border as Australia's captain . . . in time.

The demands of the World Series meant that Queensland gave a debut to Bruce Oxenford who looked capable but needs to work hard on his accuracy. He spins hard and is willing to learn. Deputising for the excellent Ian Healy was Peter Anderson, a top-flight replacement. He resembles an elongated Alan Knott, and any man resembling Knott as a keeper must be good, for Knott was easily the best keeper of my time. There was an aggressive innings from Trevor Barsby, a career-best from Peter Goggin, a century from Warren Ayres and a second-wicket stand of 248 between Hayden and Wellham, but the match was drawn.

20, 21, 22 and 23 December, 1991 *at Adelaide Oval*

New South Wales 225 (M.E. Waugh 94, J.C. Scuderi 7 for 79) and 342 (B.E. McNamara 80, M.A. Taylor 54)
South Australia 556 (D.W. Hookes 156, J.C. Scuderi 110, P.R. Sleep 70 not out, J.D. Siddons 68, G.R. Blewett 56) and 15 for 0

South Australia won by 10 wickets

South Australia 6 pts., New South Wales 0 pts.

at WACA Ground, Perth

Victoria 500 (D.M. Jones 204, W.G. Ayres 70, P.C. Nobes 51, D.S. Lehmann 51, T.J. Zoehrer 4 for 86) and 40 for 2
Western Australia 330 (D. Martyn 60, J. Langer 59) and 206 (W.S. Andrews 71)

Victoria won by 8 wickets

Victoria 6 pts., Western Australia 0 pts.

at Woolloongabba, Brisbane

Indians 454 for 9 dec. (C.S. Pandit 127, S.V. Manjrekar

110, Kapil Dev 80) and 177 for 2 dec. (M. Azharuddin 90 not out, D.B. Vengsarkar 82 not out)
Queensland 319 for 4 dec. (A.R. Border 85 not out, T.J. Barsby 83, G.M. Ritchie 68) and 273 (G.M. Ritchie 107, Venkatapathy Raju 6 for 81)
Indians won by 39 runs

at Bellerive Oval, Hobart

West Indians 235 (B.C. Lara 83) and 133 (S.K. Warne 4 for 42)
Australian XI 461 for 9 dec. (T.M. Moody 70, S.G. Law 68, C.D. Matthews 63, M.G. Bevan 58, W.N. Phillips 51, R.C. Haynes 4 for 106)
Australian XI won by an innings and 93 runs

Joe Scuderi, at last beginning to show consistency, excelled in the match at Adelaide. He hit 110 and had match figures of 10 for 165. This was only the third time in Shield history that a player had scored a century and taken ten wickets in the same match. The others were George Giffen, 1892–93, and Phil Carlson, 1978–79. Scuderi was named in the original 20-strong World Cup squad, but he could not make the final 14. The selectors had complimented him but were saying that if he achieves more consistent results, he will be rewarded with higher honours. He is a talented batsman and a more than useful medium-pace bowler, but how far he goes in the game depends upon how much he applies himself. He and David Hookes shared a fifth-wicket stand of 211 in South Australia's surprise victory. Hookes hit his 27th Shield hundred and became only the second batsman to reach 9,000 runs in Shield cricket.

In Perth, Dean Jones hit his third double century of the season. His batting had been in the Bradman mould – 243 not out, 68, 144, 214, 204 and 11 – 884 runs, average 176.80. Nobes, a hard-hitting batsman in the Ian Chappell fashion, played his first game for Victoria who surprised their opponents.

The Indian tourists gained a welcome win on the eve of the second Test, but their highest scorer was reserve keeper Pandit. Peter Taylor failed to take a wicket while the Indian spinners claimed ten of the 14 Queensland wickets to fall.

West Indies were soundly beaten in their one first-class match of the tour. A strong Australian XI scored consistently while the West Indians struggled against the leg-spin of Shane Warne who had match figures of 7 for 56. Warne had been engaged in a three-way battle for a place in the Victoria side. Peter McIntyre is another leg-spinner while Paul Jackson is an orthodox left-arm spinner. Warne and McIntyre both did well on the Australia 'B' tour of Zimbabwe. McIntyre thought Warne was transferring to New South Wales, but he stayed in Melbourne and was picked ahead of McIntyre and Jackson who languished in grade cricket. Jackson plugged away, but Warne won Test caps against India, bowling better than his 1 for 228 would suggest. Jackson was to replace Warne in the Victoria side, but Warne was chosen for the tour of Sri Lanka. Both McIntyre and Jackson may look elsewhere: McIntyre to Adelaide, a veritable haven for unwanted bowlers and the staging post for England; Jackson to Queensland where the northerners are in need of a class spinner.

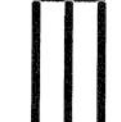
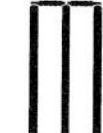

SECOND TEST MATCH
AUSTRALIA v. INDIA, at Melbourne

India fielded an unchanged side while Australia brought in Reid for Whitney. Electing to bat when they won the toss, India were soon in deep trouble. Reid's bounce and swing deceived both Srikkanth and Prabhakar, promoted to number three: the first was caught off a long hop while the second was out first ball, bowled behind his legs. Manjrekar was dropped at slip by Mark Taylor off Hughes, and he and Shastri went on to add 50. Shastri applied himself in exemplary fashion, but in the last over before lunch he was caught behind as Reid slanted the ball across him.

Shortly after the break Reid claimed his fourth victim when he had Manjrekar taken at slip off the shoulder of the bat. Azharuddin and Vengsarkar added 45 without conviction. Mark Waugh appealed that he had caught Azharuddin at slip, but the umpire gave the batsman the benefit because he was unsighted. Five minutes later, he was caught off another of his many reckless shots, lofting to cover. He had batted without responsibility or example.

Vengsarkar, clearly past his prime, lobbed a simple catch to leg. There was determination from Tendulkar

Bruce Reid celebrates one of his 12 wickets in the second Test. (Joe Mann/Allsport)

Kiran More in the middle of his defiant innings of 67 not out in the second Test at Melbourne. (Joe Mann/Allsport)

and Kapil Dev, and More and Venkatapathy Raju put on 77 for the ninth wicket, but India ended the day on a sad 243 for 9.

The second day saw India fight back, but it was a day soured by an umpiring controversy. More and Srinath added another 20 runs at a brisk rate before Srinath became Reid's sixth victim. Reid's performance in this Test moved Richie Benaud to class him alongside Alan Davidson. It is sad that he has been so troubled by injury.

Australia began slowly in reply and were rocked when Kapil Dev dismissed Boon and Border in the same over to close the gap between his number of Test wickets and that of record-holder Richard Hadlee. Kapil Dev had already made history during the year by becoming the first bowler to take 200 wickets in one-day internationals.

At 55 for 3, Australia were in some trouble, but the diligent Marsh and the more aggressive Jones added 108. Mark Waugh batted with enterprise, and Australia closed on 215 for 5. Shortly before he had fallen to Prabhakar's slower ball, Jones was involved in an incident which led to the Indian management complaining to the Australian Board and asking that King should not stand as umpire in the rest of the series.

Jones moved forward to play a ball from Venkatapathy Raju which lodged between wrist and thigh. As More advanced to catch it Jones knocked the ball away with his hand. The Indians appealed for 'handled ball', but umpire King ruled not out.

Tactically, Azharuddin had erred when, following Kapil Dev's fine burst, he had brought on Tendulkar rather than maintain the pressure with one of his front-line bowlers.

There was a delayed start to the third day, but then the Indian tactics were again at fault as, following Marsh's quick dismissal, Healy, Hughes and the tail realised 120 runs for the last four wickets. Healy, in particular, prospered through the absence of a third man for the quicker bowlers, and Hughes was fed much short-pitched bowling to his obvious delight.

By the end of the day, Australia were in total charge. Srikkanth went quickly, but Shastri and Manjrekar showed immense application before Shastri fell to a ball that he was forced to play and which moved late. Manjrekar batted in exemplary fashion before being caught at slip off an unplayable delivery, and Venkatapathy Raju, sent in too soon as night-watchman, and Azharuddin also fell before the close. Azharuddin played a desperately bad shot at Reid to cause further rumblings as to his suitability as captain and as to his ability to play the Australian pace bowlers.

India had ended the third day on 92 for 5, but they were encouraged by some exquisite shots from Tendulkar on the fourth morning. He became over-ambitious against Peter Taylor and lofted the off-spinner high to mid-on where Border took a good diving catch. This was Taylor's only Test wicket of the summer. More and Kapil Dev offered the resolute Vengsarkar some support, but when the veteran was last out India had totalled 213, and Australia were in sight of another four-day victory. The victory was achieved on the last ball of the day, and, to the surprise of no one, Bruce Reid, 12 for 126, was named Man of the Match.

Wicket-keeper Ian Healy plays one of his best innings in a Test match to help Australia into a commanding lead in the second Test. (Joe Mann/Allsport)

SECOND TEST MATCH – AUSTRALIA v. INDIA
26, 27, 28 and 29 December, 1991 at MCG, Melbourne

INDIA

	FIRST INNINGS		SECOND INNINGS	
R.J. Shastri	c Healy, **b** Reid	23	c Healy, **b** Reid	22
K. Srikkanth	c Boon, **b** Reid	5	lbw, **b** Reid	6
M. Prabhakar	**b** Reid	0	(9) c Healy, **b** Reid	17
S.V. Manjrekar	c Waugh, **b** Reid	25	(3) c M.A. Taylor, **b** McDermott	30
D.B. Vengsarkar	c Reid, **b** Hughes	23	(4) c sub (Whitney), **b** McDermott	54
M. Azharuddin (capt)	c Jones, **b** McDermott	22	(5) c M.A. Taylor, **b** Reid	2
S.R. Tendulkar	c Waugh, **b** Reid	15	c Border, **b** P.L. Taylor	40
Kapil Dev	c Hughes, **b** McDermott	19	c Healy, **b** Reid	12
*K.S. More	not out	67	(10) lbw, **b** Reid	12
Venkatapathy Raju	c Border, **b** Hughes	31	(6) c and **b** McDermott	1
J. Srinath	c Border, **b** Reid	14	not out	0
Extras	b 1, lb 8, w 6, nb 4	19	b 1, lb 6, nb 10	17
		263		**213**

AUSTRALIA

	FIRST INNINGS		SECOND INNINGS	
G.R. Marsh	c Vengsarkar, **b** Kapil Dev	86	(2) lbw, **b** Prabhakar	10
M.A. Taylor	c Tendulkar, **b** Prabhakar	13	(1) st More, **b** Raju	60
D.C. Boon	c Srikkanth, **b** Kapil Dev	11	not out	44
A.R. Border (capt)	**b** Kapil Dev	0	not out	5
D.M. Jones	c More, **b** Prabhakar	59		
M.E. Waugh	c More, **b** Shastri	34		
*I.A. Healy	lbw, **b** Kapil Dev	60		
P.L. Taylor	c More, **b** Prabhakar	11		
M.G. Hughes	c Tendulkar, **b** Kapil Dev	36		
C.J. McDermott	not out	16		
B.A. Reid	c Kapil Dev, **b** Prabhakar	3		
Extras	lb 9, nb 11	20	lb 3, nb 6	9
		349	(for 2 wickets)	**128**

	O	M	R	W	O	M	R	W
McDermott	30	6	100	2	29	8	63	3
Reid	26.2	7	66	6	29	9	60	6
Hughes	23	6	52	2	19	6	43	–
M.E. Waugh	8	1	16	–				
P.L. Taylor	6	–	20	–	11	3	40	1

	O	M	R	W	O	M	R	W
Kapil Dev	35	9	97	5	12	1	30	–
Prabhakar	34	7	84	4	11	–	38	1
Srinath	25	3	71	–	8	–	28	–
Venkatapathy Raju	17	3	52	–	6	–	17	1
Tendulkar	4	1	16	–				
Shastri	7	1	20	1	3	1	12	–

FALL OF WICKETS (India)
1–11, **2**–11, **3**–61, **4**–64, **5**–109, **6**–109, **7**–128, **8**–151, **9**–228
1–13, **2**–48, **3**–75, **4**–78, **5**–79, **6**–141, **7**–153, **8**–173, **9**–213

FALL OF WICKETS (Australia)
1–24, **2**–55, **3**–55, **4**–163, **5**–211, **6**–229, **7**–262, **8**–326, **9**–337
1–16, **2**–122

Umpires: L.J. King & T.A. Prue

Australia won by 8 wickets

THIRD TEST MATCH
AUSTRALIA v. INDIA, at Sydney

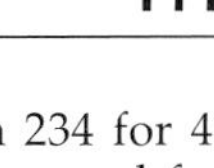

Australia made one change from the side which had been successful at Melbourne. They brought in leg-spinner Shane Warne for his Test debut in place of Peter Taylor. For India, Pandit replaced the injured More while Venkatapathy Raju and Srikkanth made way for Subroto Banerjee, who was playing his first Test, and Sidhu, who had arrived from India to strengthen the batting. Azharuddin won the toss and invited Australia to bat.

There was early reward for India when Banerjee, with his tenth ball in Test cricket, deceived Marsh and bowled him. Mark Taylor should have gone in the previous over, but he was badly dropped by Prabhakar off Srinath. Only 60 runs came before lunch, and in the afternoon, when 79 were scored, it began to look as if Australia were moving towards a big score. Banerjee stopped these ideas when he had Taylor caught behind and Mark Waugh taken in the gully. Jones was run out in the final session, and Australia closed on 234 for 4, Boon on 89. Boon had survived a confident appeal for leg before against Kapil Dev just before the end of play, another umpiring decision which did not please India.

The second day was India's best of the series. Border was twice close to being out before he was caught behind off Kapil Dev. Prabhakar had Healy taken at short-leg, Hughes caught low down by Pandit and yorked McDermott. Warne helped Boon to add 44 before Kapil Dev finished off the innings. Boon remained undefeated on 129, an innings occupying 444 minutes and containing 13 fours.

India were batting 40 minutes after lunch, and they immediately lost Sidhu, but their batsmen rarely looked troubled on a slowish pitch against an Australian attack which was soon deprived of Reid with a rib injury. Manjrekar looked most impressive until he was brilliantly caught at slip by Mark Waugh. India ended

Ravi Shastri hit a magnificent double century in the third Test and then missed the rest of the series through injury. (David Munden)

Kris Srikkanth was a successfully violent opening batsman in the Benson and Hedges World Series but failed in the Test matches. (Adrian Murrell/Allsport)

the second day at 103 for 2 with Shastri on 52, but their chances of winning the match were severely dented on the third day when only 35 overs were possible because of rain and bad light. The score advanced to 178; Shastri to 95.

On the fourth day, India's batsmen at last revealed their true abilities. Shastri scored 206 from 477 balls and hit two sixes and 17 fours. The precocious Tendulkar made 148 not out off 213 balls with 14 fours. In the hour after lunch, they hit 74, and their partnership of 196 for the fifth wicket was a record for India against Australia. Shastri became the first Indian batsman to hit a double century in a Test match against Australia.

India ended the fourth day on 445 for 7, but their hopes of leading Australia by 200 runs vanished on the last morning when they lost their last three wickets for the addition of 38 runs. Marsh was quickly out when he leg-glanced Kapil Dev to the keeper, and Boon slashed Srinath into the hands of gully. Although the pitch offered him only gentle turn, Shastri now threatened Australia with his left-arm spin. At tea, Australia were 109 for 5, and only Border, 18 not out, stood between India and success. Shastri soon accounted for Healy on the resumption, but Border remained resolute, and India were denied.

Man of the Series in the Benson and Hedges one-day matches and three Test centuries against India – David Boon. (David Munden)

THIRD TEST MATCH – AUSTRALIA v. INDIA
2, 3, 4, 5 and 6 January, 1992 at SCG, Sydney

AUSTRALIA

	FIRST INNINGS		SECOND INNINGS	
G.R. Marsh	b Banerjee	8	(2) c Pandit, b Kapil Dev	4
M.A. Taylor	c Pandit, b Banerjee	56	(1) c Kapil Dev, b Shastri	35
D.C. Boon	not out	129	c Azharuddin, b Srinath	7
M.E. Waugh	c Prabhakar, b Banerjee	5	lbw, b Prabhakar	18
D.M. Jones	run out	35	c Pandit, b Shastri	18
A.R. Border (capt)	c Pandit, b Kapil Dev	19	not out	53
*I.A. Healy	c sub (Srikkanth), b Prabhakar	1	c Prabhakar, b Shastri	7
M.G. Hughes	c Pandit, b Prabhakar	2	c Prabhakar, b Tendulkar	21
C.J. McDermott	b Prabhakar	1	c Vengsarkar, b Shastri	0
S.K. Warne	c Pandit, b Kapil Dev	20	not out	1
B.A. Reid	c Tendulkar, b Kapil Dev	0		
Extras	b 4, lb 14, w 1, nb 18	37	lb 4, w 1, nb 4	9
		313	(for 8 wickets)	173

INDIA

	FIRST INNINGS	
R.J. Shastri	c Jones, b Warne	206
N.S. Sidhu	c Waugh, b McDermott	0
S.V. Manjrekar	c Waugh, b Hughes	34
D.B. Vengsarkar	c Waugh, b McDermott	54
M. Azharuddin (capt)	c Boon, b McDermott	4
S.R. Tendulkar	not out	148
M. Prabhakar	c M. A. Taylor, b Hughes	14
Kapil Dev	c Marsh, b Hughes	0
*C.S. Pandit	run out	9
S.T. Banerjee	c Border, b McDermott	3
J. Srinath	run out	1
Extras	b 1, lb 4, nb 5	10
		483

	O	M	R	W	O	M	R	W
Kapil Dev	33	9	60	3	19	5	41	1
Prabhakar	39	12	82	3	25	10	53	1
Srinath	21	5	69	–	12	–	28	1
Banerjee	18	4	47	3				
Shastri	13	1	37	–	25	8	45	4
Tendulkar					1	–	2	1

	O	M	R	W
McDermott	51	12	147	4
Reid	4	–	10	–
Hughs	41.4	8	104	3
M.E. Waugh	14	5	28	–
Warne	45	7	150	1
Border	13	3	39	–

FALL OF WICKETS
1–22, **2**–117, **3**–127, **4**–210, **5**–248, **6**–251, **7**–259, **8**–269, **9**–313
1–9, **2**–31, **3**–55, **4**–85, **5**–106, **6**–114, **7**–164, **8**–171

FALL OF WICKETS
1–7, **2**–86, **3**–197, **4**–201, **5**–397, **6**–434, **7**–434, **8**–458, **9**–474

Umpires: P.J. McConnell & S.G. Randell

Match drawn

BENSON AND HEDGES WORLD SERIES
Phase Two – Matches Eight to Twelve

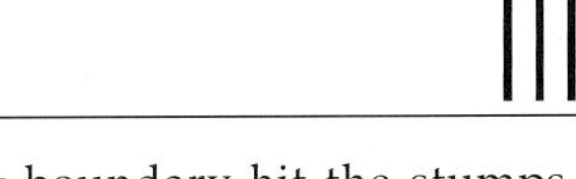

The second phase of matches in the World Series began with an abandonment because of rain in Melbourne. In Brisbane, two days later, West Indies kept alive their hopes of qualifying for the final with victory over India who had depended almost exclusively on Tendulkar for their run-getting. He spent too much of his time at the crease watching wickets fall at the other end, and he became a victim of the impressive Cummins. The fast bowler also claimed the debutant Ganguly who seemed rather over-awed by the occasion. West Indies were in some trouble at 24 for 2, but Richardson joined Haynes in a stand of 109 which brought his side to the brink of victory. It was the first time in the series that Richardson had shown his true ability.

With a narrow victory over Australia, West Indies moved into second place in the qualifying table. Richie Richardson confirmed that he had refound his form with an innings of 50 off 63 balls as he and Lara added 110 delightful runs for the third wicket. Thereafter only Carlisle Best who hit a brisk 30 offered serious resistance to the Australian attack. An opening stand of 70 in 17 overs seemed to have put Australia well on the way to victory, but Jones and Border fell in quick succession. Border was run out when a throw from substitute Anthony on the square-leg boundary hit the stumps. Boon and Mark Waugh steadied the innings with a partnership of 36, but Waugh played on, Moody was bowled by Ambrose and another collapse was in progress. Patterson returned to york Steve Waugh, and, in the space of 12 runs, Hooper ran out Boon and Healy with direct hits. Australia needed 41 from the last five overs with only two wickets left. Haynes took a tumbling catch to account for McDermott, and, with 13 needed from seven balls, Peter Taylor swept wildly at Hooper and was bowled.

Two days later, Australia did West Indies an immense favour by crushing India. Paul Reiffel made an impressive international debut to dismiss both Shastri and Srikkanth after the openers had given India a good start. From that point on, no Indian batsman remained long enough to play the substantial innings that was needed. Faced by a moderate target, Australia lost Marsh at 10, but Boon and Moody shared an unbroken partnership of 167 in which they devastated the Indian attack.

The 12th and final preliminary match had become a decider, for whoever won would qualify to meet Australia. Desmond Haynes and Philo Wallace

BENSON AND HEDGES WORLD SERIES – MATCH EIGHT – AUSTRALIA v. WEST INDIES

9 January, 1992 at MCG, Melbourne

WEST INDIES

D.L. Haynes	**c** S.R. Waugh, **b** P.L. Taylor	56
P.A. Wallace	**c** S.R. Waugh, **b** McDermott	22
B.C. Lara	run out	22
R.B. Richardson (capt)	run out	13
C.L. Hooper	**b** P.L. Taylor	7
K.L.T. Arthurton	not out	12
M.D. Marshall	**c** Healy, **b** Whitney	4
C.E.L. Ambrose	**b** McDermott	7
A.C. Cummins	not out	1
*D.Williams		
B.P. Patterson		
Extras	b 5, lb 9, w 1, nb 1	16
	(for 7 wickets)	**160**

(47 overs)

	O	M	R	W
McDermott	9	–	25	2
Whitney	10	–	28	1
Moody	5	–	28	–
S.R. Waugh	8	–	19	–
P.L. Taylor	10	1	28	2
M.E. Waugh	5	–	18	–

FALL OF WICKETS

1–33, **2**–97, **3**–113, **4**–128, **5**–137, **6**–144, **7**–159

AUSTRALIA

G.R. Marsh
D.C. Boon
D.M. Jones
A.R. Border (capt)
T.M. Moody
S.R. Waugh
M.E. Waugh
* I.A. Healy
P.L. Taylor
C.J. McDermott
M.R. Whitney

Umpires: A.R. Crafter & L.J. King — No award — *Match abandoned*

BENSON AND HEDGES WORLD SERIES – MATCH NINE – INDIA v. WEST INDIES

11 January, 1992 at Woolloongabba, Brisbane

INDIA

K. Srikkanth	**c** Marshall, **b** Cummins	4
N.S. Sidhu	**c** Hooper, **b** Marshall	1
S.V. Manjrekar	run out	1
S.R. Tendulkar	**c** sub (Anthony), **b** Cummins	77
M. Azharuddin (capt)	lbw, **b** Marshall	8
S.C. Ganguly	lbw, **b** Cummins	3
M. Prabhakar	**c** and **b** Patterson	14
Kapil Dev	**c** Marshall, **b** Patterson	28
*K.S. More	not out	11
Venkatapathy Raju	**c** Williams, **b** Cummins	8
J. Srinath	**c** Williams, **b** Cummins	0
Extras	b 4, lb 9, w 15, nb 8	36
		191

(48.3 overs)

	O	M	R	W
Ambrose	10	–	41	–
Marshall	10	–	30	2
Cummins	9.3	1	31	5
Patterson	9	–	52	2
Hooper	10	–	24	–

FALL OF WICKETS

1–14, **2**–20, **3**–21, **4**–35, **5**–62, **6**–85, **7**–161, **8**–178, **9**–191

WEST INDIES

D.L. Haynes	**c** sub (Amre), **b** Venkatapathy Raju	52
P.A. Wallace	**c** Srinath, **b** Prabhakar	4
B.C. Lara	**c** Manjrekar, **b** Srinath	4
R.B. Richardson (capt)	lbw, **b** Prabhakar	72
C.L. Hooper	not out	19
C.A. Best	not out	9
M.D. Marshall		
C.E.L. Ambrose		
A.C. Cummins		
* D. Williams		
B.P. Patterson		
Extras	b 2, lb 8, w 13, nb 9	32
	(for 4 wickets)	**192**

(48.3 overs)

	O	M	R	W
Kapil Dev	10	3	33	–
Prabhakar	9	1	39	2
Srinath	9	3	27	1
Tendulkar	7	–	27	–
Venkatapathy Raju	10	–	33	1
Srikkanth	3	–	21	–
Sidhu	0.3	–	2	–

FALL OF WICKETS

1–13, **2**–24, **3**–133, **4**–170

Umpires: D.B. Hair & S.G. Randell — Man of the Match – A.C. Cummins — *West Indies won by 6 wickets*

BENSON AND HEDGES WORLD SERIES – MATCH TEN – AUSTRALIA v. WEST INDIES
12 January, 1992 at Woolloongabba, Brisbane

WEST INDIES

D.L. Haynes	c Marsh, **b** Whitney	11
P.A. Wallace	c Whitney, **b** Moody	31
B.C. Lara	run out	69
R.B. Richardson (capt)	c Moody, **b** P.L. Taylor	50
C.L. Hooper	c and **b** S.R. Waugh	6
C.A. Best	**b** McDermott	30
M.D. Marshall	c Border, **b** S.R. Waugh	4
C.E.L. Ambrose	**b** McDermott	2
A.C. Cummins	c Boon, **b** S.R. Waugh	2
*D. Williams	not out	0
B.P. Patterson	lbw, **b** McDermott	0
Extras	lb 8, w 2	10
		215

AUSTRALIA

D.C. Boon	run out	77
G.R. Marsh	lbw, **b** Patterson	29
D.M. Jones	**b** Patterson	0
A.R. Border (capt)	run out	8
M.E. Waugh	**b** Cummins	17
T.M. Moody	**b** Ambrose	3
S.R. Waugh	**b** Patterson	3
*I.A. Healy	run out	11
P.L. Taylor	**b** Hooper	33
C.J. McDermott	c D.L. Haynes, **b** Hooper	10
M.R. Whitney	not out	1
Extras	b 1, lb 4, w 2, nb 4	11
		203

(49.3 overs)

	O	M	R	W
McDermott	9.3	2	36	**3**
Whitney	10	2	39	**1**
S.R. Waugh	10	2	31	**3**
Moody	6	–	29	**1**
P.L. Taylor	10	–	44	**1**
M.E. Waugh	4	–	28	–

(49 overs)

	O	M	R	W
Marshall	9	1	39	–
Ambrose	10	1	37	**1**
Cummins	10	–	49	**1**
Patterson	10	1	37	**3**
Hooper	10	–	36	**2**

FALL OF WICKETS

1–27, **2**–58, **3**–168, **4**–173, **5**–185, **6**–193, **7**–210, **8**–215, **9**–215

FALL OF WICKETS

1–70, **2**–73, **3**–84, **4**–120, **5**–135, **6**–141, **7**–152, **8**–164, **9**–200

Umpires: I.S. Thomas & C.D. Timmins — Man of the Match – B.C. Lara — *West Indies won by 12 runs*

BENSON AND HEDGES WORLD SERIES – MATCH ELEVEN – AUSTRALIA v. INDIA
14 January, 1992 at SCG, Sydney

INDIA

R.J. Shastri	**b** Reiffel	22
K. Srikkanth	**b** Reiffel	42
N.S. Sidhu	c Boon, **b** S.R. Waugh	1
S.V. Manjrekar	c Marsh, **b** Moody	16
S.R. Tendulkar	run out	31
M. Azharuddin (capt)	c Border, **b** McDermott	22
Kapil Dev	run out	7
M. Prabhakar	c and **b** Whitney	8
*C.S. Pandit	c Healy, **b** McDermott	2
Venkatapathy Raju	not out	6
J. Srinath	**b** S.R. Waugh	5
Extras	b 3, lb 5, w 4, nb 1	13
		175

AUSTRALIA

G.R. Marsh	**b** Prabhakar	3
D.C. Boon	not out	79
T.M. Moody	not out	87
A.R. Border (capt)		
M.E. Waugh		
S.R. Waugh		
* I.A. Healy		
P.L. Taylor		
C.J. McDermott		
P.R. Reiffel		
M.R. Whitney		
Extras	lb 5, w 2, nb 1	8
	(for 1 wicket)	**177**

(49.4 overs)

	O	M	R	W
McDermott	10	2	17	**2**
Whitney	10	1	36	**1**
Reiffel	10	1	27	**2**
S.R. Waugh	5.4	–	29	**2**
P.L. Taylor	9	–	40	–
Moody	5	–	18	**1**

(39.2 overs)

	O	M	R	W
Kapil Dev	6	–	11	–
Prabhakar	8	–	29	**1**
Tendulkar	2	–	14	–
Srinath	8	1	28	–
Shastri	8	–	40	–
Venkatapathy Raju	7	–	46	–
Manjrekar	0.2	–	4	–

FALL OF WICKETS

1–52, **2**–57, **3**–69, **4**–111, **5**–129, **6**–150, **7**–156, **8**–161, **9**–163

FALL OF WICKET

1–10

Umpires: D.B. Hair & T.A. Prue — Man of the Match – C.J. McDermott — *Australia won by 9 wickets*

BENSON AND HEDGES WORLD SERIES – MATCH TWELVE – WEST INDIES v. INDIA
16 January, 1992 at MCG, Melbourne

WEST INDIES		
D.L. Haynes	c Pandit, b Srinath	14
P.A. Wallace	run out	2
B.C. Lara	st Pandit, b Hirwani	11
R.B. Richardson (capt)	lbw, b Hirwani	20
C.L. Hooper	c Manjrekar, b Prabhakar	45
C.A. Best	b Srinath	29
M.D. Marshall	run out	0
*D. Williams	run out	3
C.E.L. Ambrose	not out	24
A.C. Cummins	not out	10
B.P. Patterson		
Extras	b 1, lb 8, w 6, nb 2	17
	(for 8 wickets)	175

INDIA		
R.J. Shastri	c Hooper, b Ambrose	11
K. Srikkanth	c Williams, b Ambrose	60
S.V. Manjrekar	c Williams, b Patterson	2
S.R. Tendulkar	not out	57
M. Azharuddin (capt)	c Lara, b Hooper	5
P.K. Amre	c sub (Anthony), b Hooper	18
Kapil Dev	not out	1
*C.S. Pandit		
M. Prabhakar		
J. Srinath		
N.D. Hirwani		
Extras	lb 11, w 2, nb 9	22
	(for 5 wickets)	176

(50 overs)	O	M	R	W
Prabhakar	9	1	20	1
Kapil Dev	10	2	27	–
Srinath	10	1	39	2
Hirwani	10	–	34	2
Tendulkar	10	1	38	–
Shastri	1	–	8	–

(46.4 overs)	O	M	R	W
Marshall	10	1	33	–
Ambrose	10	4	17	2
Cummins	10	–	47	–
Patterson	8	1	31	1
Hooper	8	–	35	2
Richardson	0.4	–	2	–

FALL OF WICKETS
1–21, 2–24, 3–45, 4–84, 5–127, 6–128, 7–138, 8–147

FALL OF WICKETS
1–20, 2–38, 3–100, 4–115, 5–169

Umpires: P.J. McConnell & C.D. Timmins   Man of the Match – S.R. Tendulkar   *India won by 5 wickets*

struggled to give West Indies a good start, and when Wallace was run out they had scored only 21 in 13 overs. No one was able to lift the tempo, and leg-spinner Hirwani captured the important wickets of Lara and Richardson in an economic spell. Not needing to score at a very fast rate, India owed much to Srikkanth and Tendulkar who took the pressure off their colleagues with a stand of 62. Srikkanth hit 60 off 84 balls, and Tendulkar ended with 57 off 88 balls as his side won with 3.2 overs remaining.

FINAL TABLE

	P	W	L	Ab	Tie	Pts
Australia	8	5	2	1	–	11
India	8	3	4	–	1	7
West Indies	8	2	4	1	1	6

BENSON AND HEDGES WORLD SERIES FINALS

Australia v. India

Australia entered the finals as strong favourites, and they did not disappoint. They overwhelmed India in the first match and narrowly won the second so that a third encounter was not needed. Electing to bat first at Melbourne, Australia batted with consistent relish and good sense to reach 233. Dean Jones, who had been dropped for the last of Australia's qualifying matches, and David Boon gave the innings substance with a partnership of 88 for the second wicket. Australia's attack looked rather weak on paper, but it proved far too good for the vaunted Indian batting. Srikkanth was responsible for Shastri being run out when he failed to respond to a call, but he made some amends with a belligerent 41. He was second out in the 19th over after which the Indian innings sank with little sign of a struggle.

Australia were below their best in the second final. Marsh hit 78 off 138 balls to provide the backbone to their innings, but it was a frantic 38 from Border which stemmed a late middle-order collapse brought about by the left-arm spinner Venkatapathy Raju. The Indian fieldsmen did not support their bowlers well, and chances were missed. A third-wicket partnership of 76 between Shastri and Tendulkar took India to within 88 of their target, but Azharuddin and Kapil Dev fell as another 33 were added. Amre, one of the least experienced men in the side, gave Tendulkar able support, and the Australians became ragged in the field and dropped catches. Whitney sprinted 20 yards to hold the third of his fine catches in the deep to remove Tendulkar, and it was Whitney who combined with McDermott to deny India the 17 runs they needed from the last two overs.

David Boon and Geoff Marsh were named as players of the finals, and Boon won the Player of the Series award. Australia took $100,000 in prize money from a competition which was watched by approximately 375,000 people. Ironically, the biggest attendance was for the Australia–West Indies game at Melbourne, 64,558, but the match was ruined by rain.

BENSON AND HEDGES WORLD SERIES – FIRST FINAL – AUSTRALIA v. INDIA
18 January, 1992 at MCG, Melbourne

AUSTRALIA

D.C. Boon	c Pandit, **b** Prabhakar	78
G.R. Marsh	c Azharuddin, **b** Tendulkar	21
D.M. Jones	c sub (Sidhu), **b** Kapil Dev	73
T.M. Moody	c Amre, **b** Shastri	13
M.E. Waugh	c Amre, **b** Shastri	3
A.R. Border (capt)	not out	28
S.R. Waugh	not out	5
*I.A. Healy		
P.L. Taylor		
C.J. McDermott		
M.R. Whitney		
Extras	lb 7, w 4, nb 1	12
	(for 5 wickets)	233

(50 overs)

	O	M	R	W
Kapil Dev	10	–	40	1
Prabhakar	10	2	53	1
Srinath	9	2	32	–
Tendulkar	6	–	29	1
Hirwani	5	–	34	–
Shastri	10	–	38	2

FALL OF WICKETS

1–54, **2**–142, **3**–169, **4**–176, **5**–216

INDIA

R.J. Shastri	run out	17
K. Srikkanth	c P.L. Taylor, **b** S.R. Waugh	41
S.V. Manjrekar	c Healy, **b** S.R. Waugh	18
S.R. Tendulkar	c Whitney, **b** Moody	4
M. Azharuddin (capt)	c Healy, **b** Moody	13
P.K. Amre	c Border, **b** P.L. Taylor	20
Kapil Dev	not out	20
M. Prabhakar	run out	0
* C.S. Pandit	c S.R. Waugh, **b** P.L. Taylor	0
J. Srinath	run out	0
N.D. Hirwani	c Marsh, **b** McDermott	4
Extras	lb 6, w 1, nb 1	8
		145

(42 overs)

	O	M	R	W
McDermott	8	–	27	1
Whitney	8	2	19	–
S.R. Waugh	7	–	32	2
Moody	10	–	34	2
P.L. Taylor	9	–	27	2

FALL OF WICKETS

1–37, **2**–72, **3**–79, **4**–84, **5**–114, **6**–130, **7**–135, **8**–136, **9**–136

Umpires: A.R. Crafter & T.A. Prue

Australia won by 88 runs

BENSON AND HEDGES WORLD SERIES – SECOND FINAL – AUSTRALIA v. INDIA
20 January, 1992 at SCG, Sydney

AUSTRALIA

G.R. Marsh	c Amre, **b** Srinath	78
D.C. Boon	**b** Prabhakar	20
D.M. Jones	**st** Pandit, **b** Venkatapathy Raju	9
T.M. Moody	c Tendulkar, **b**Venkatapathy Raju	15
M.E. Waugh	**st** Pandit, **b** Venkatapathy Raju	0
A.R. Border (capt)	run out	38
S.R. Waugh	**b** Prabhakar	5
*I.A. Healy	run out	11
P.L. Taylor	not out	8
C.J. McDermott	**b** Prabhakar	5
M.R. Whitney	not out	0
Extras	lb 9, w 3, nb 7	19
	(for 9 wickets)	208

(50 overs)

	O	M	R	W
Kapil Dev	10	1	42	–
Prabhakar	9	–	31	3
Srinath	7	1	30	1
Tendulkar	4	–	18	–
Shastri	10	1	46	–
Venkatapathy Raju	10	1	32	3

FALL OF WICKETS

1–47, **2**–74, **3**–114, **4**–117, **5**–168, **6**–175, **7**–192, **8**–200, **9**–208

INDIA

R.J. Shastri	c Whitney, **b** Moody	61
K. Srikkanth	c M.E. Waugh, **b** Whitney	11
S.V. Manjrekar	run out	10
S.R. Tendulkar	c Whitney, **b** S.R. Waugh	69
M. Azharuddin (capt)	c Whitney, **b** Border	11
Kapil Dev	**lbw**, **b** McDermott	2
P.K. Amre	c Jones, **b** McDermott	22
* C.S. Pandit	not out	5
M. Prabhakar	not out	4
Venkatapathy Raju		
J. Srinath		
Extras	lb 3, w 1, nb 3	7
	(for 7 wickets)	202

(50 overs)

	O	M	R	W
McDermott	9	1	37	2
Whitney	10	–	32	1
S.R. Waugh	10	1	40	1
Moody	10	1	31	1
P.L. Taylor	9	–	44	–
Border	2	–	15	1

FALL OF WICKETS

1–19, **2**–45, **3**–121, **4**–146, **5**–154, **6**–190, **7**–195

Umpires: P.J. McConnell & S.G. Randell   Men of the Finals – D.C. Boon & G.R. Marsh

Australia won by 6 runs

BENSON AND HEDGES WORLD SERIES AVERAGES

AUSTRALIA BATTING

	M	Inns	NO	Runs	HS	Av	100s	50s
D.C. Boon	10	9	2	432	102*	61.71	1	4
A.R. Border	10	8	2	220	76	36.66	–	1
G.R. Marsh	10	9	–	282	82	31.33	–	2
D.M. Jones	9	8	1	196	73	28.00	–	2
T.M. Moody	10	8	1	184	87*	26.28	–	2
P.L. Taylor	10	5	2	52	33	17.33	–	–
S.R. Waugh	10	7	2	60	34	12.00	–	–
I.A. Healy	10	5	1	47	17*	11.75	–	–
M.E. Waugh	5	3	–	20	17	6.66	–	–
C.J. McDermott	10	4	–	20	10	5.00	–	–

Played in eight matches – M.R. Whitney 2*, 1* & 0*
Played in five matches – B.A. Reid 1* & 2*
Played in two matches – S.P. O'Donnell 10
Played in one match – P.R. Reiffel did not bat

AUSTRALIA BOWLING

	Overs	Mds	Runs	Wkts	Av	Best	4/inn
C.J. McDermott	91.2	12	282	21	13.42	3-19	–
S.R. Waugh	80.3	5	304	16	19.00	3-31	–
M.R. Whitney	78	12	230	9	25.55	3-25	–
T.M. Moody	60	1	236	8	29.50	2-34	–
B.A. Reid	49	7	134	4	33.50	2-29	–
P.L. Taylor	86	3	353	10	35.30	2-27	–
S.P. O'Donnell	17	1	74	1	74.00	1-35	–
M.E. Waugh	9	–	46	–	–	–	–

Bowled in one match – P.R. Reiffel 10-1-27-2; A.R. Border 2-0-15-1

AUSTRALIA FIELDING FIGURES

11 – I.A. Healy; 9 – S.R. Waugh; 6 – M.R. Whitney; 5 – D.M. Jones; 4 – A.R. Border, T.M. Moody and P.L. Taylor; 3 – G.R. Marsh; 2 – D.C. Boon; 1 – C.J. McDermott and M.E. Waugh

BENSON AND HEDGES WORLD SERIES AVERAGES

INDIA BATTING

	M	Inns	NO	Runs	HS	Av	100s	50s
S.R. Tendulkar	10	10	1	401	77	44.55	–	4
K. Srikkanth	10	10	–	313	82	31.30	–	3
Kapil Dev	10	10	4	151	39	25.16	–	–
S.V. Manjrekar	10	10	–	189	57	18.80	–	2
P.K. Amre	8	7	–	131	33	18.71	–	–
R.J. Shastri	9	9	–	159	61	17.66	–	1
K.S. More	6	3	1	35	20	17.50	–	–
M. Azharuddin	10	10	2	136	31*	17.00	–	–
Venkatapathy Raju	4	3	2	17	8	17.00	–	–
S.T. Banerjee	3	3	2	13	6*	13.00	–	–
M. Prabhakar	10	8	1	59	17	8.42	–	–
C.S. Pandit	4	3	1	7	5*	3.50	–	–
J. Srinath	10	6	1	15	8	3.00	–	–

Played in three matches – N.D. Hirwani 4
Played in two matches – N.S. Sidhu 1 & 1
Played in one match – S.C. Ganguly 3

INDIA BOWLING

	Overs	Mds	Runs	Wkts	Av	Best	4/inn
S.V. Manjrekar	0.5	–	6	1	6.00	1-2	–
Venkatapathy Raju	36	2	143	6	23.83	3-32	–
S.T. Banerjee	24	3	97	4	24.25	3-30	–
M. Prabhakar	86	8	315	12	26.25	3-31	–
J. Srinath	88	11	309	11	28.09	2-24	–
Kapil Dev	88	17	275	9	30.55	4-54	1
R.J. Shastri	65.5	2	255	8	31.87	5-15	1
N.D. Hirwani	24	–	122	3	40.66	2-34	–
S.R. Tendulkar	37.5	1	152	2	76.00	1-5	–
K. Srikkanth	7	–	52	–	–	–	–

Bowled in one match – N.S. Sidhu 0.3 – 0 – 2 – 0

INDIA FIELDING FIGURES

8 – K.S. More (ct 7/st 1); 5 – C.S. Pandit (ct 2/st 3) and P.K. Amre (plus one as sub); 4 – S.R. Tendulkar; 3 – S.V. Manjrekar; 2 – R.J. Shastri, M. Azharuddin, Kapil Dev and J. Srinath; 1 – K. Srikkanth, M. Prabhakar, sub (S.C. Ganguly) and sub (N.S. Sidhu)

BENSON AND HEDGES WORLD SERIES AVERAGES

WEST INDIES BATTING

	M	Inns	NO	Runs	HS	Av	100s	50s
D.L. Haynes	8	8	–	293	89	36.62	–	4
C.L. Hooper	8	8	1	178	77	25.42	–	1
C.A. Best	4	4	1	73	30	24.33	–	–
R.B. Richardson	8	8	–	185	72	23.12	–	2
B.C. Lara	8	8	–	179	69	22.37	–	1
K.L.T. Arthurton	5	5	1	83	38	20.75	–	–
P.A. Wallace	7	7	–	124	52	17.71	–	1
C.E.L. Ambrose	8	7	1	80	24*	13.33	–	–
A.C. Cummins	8	7	3	51	24	12.75	–	–
B.P. Patterson	7	4	3	10	8*	10.00	–	–
M.D. Marshall	8	7	–	42	17	6.00	–	–
D. Williams	8	6	1	21	10	4.20	–	–

Played in one match – R.C. Haynes 0

WEST INDIES BOWLING

	Overs	Mds	Runs	Wkts	Av	Best	4/inn
K.L.T. Arthurton	9	1	45	3	15.00	2-23	–
C.E.L. Ambrose	68.4	14	196	9	21.77	2-9	–
A.C. Cummins	68.3	3	277	10	27.70	5-31	1
M.D. Marshall	68	10	241	8	30.12	4-18	1
B.P. Patterson	53	3	244	8	30.50	3-37	–
C.L. Hooper	68	1	252	7	36.00	2-35	–

Bowled in one match – R.C. Haynes 6-0-35-0; R.B. Richardson 0.4-0-2-0

WEST INDIES FIELDING FIGURES

10 – D. Williams (ct 8/st 2); 4 – R.B. Richardson and B.C. Lara; 3 – C.L. Hooper; 2 – D.L. Haynes, M.D. Marshall and sub (H.A.G. Anthony); 1 – P.A. Wallace, K.L.T. Arthurton and B.P. Patterson

10, 11, 12 and 13 January, 1992 *at SCG, Sydney*

New South Wales 331 (G.R.J. Matthews 85 not out, T.H. Bayliss 80, M.A. Taylor 50, G.J. Rowell 5 for 92, C.G. Rackemann 4 for 75) and 244 (T.H. Bayliss 75, G.R.J. Matthews 67, B. Oxenford 5 for 91)
Queensland 230 (P.J.T. Goggin 55, D.M. Wellham 53, G.R.J. Matthews 6 for 63) and 212 (G.R.J. Matthews 5 for 70)

New South Wales won by 133 runs

New South Wales 6 pts., Queensland 0 pts.

at WACA Ground, Perth

Western Australia 200 and 422 for 6 dec. (M.P. Lavender 172, M.R.J. Veletta 64, M.W. McPhee 54, C.D. Matthews 5 for 128)
Tasmania 358 (R.J. Tucker 72, S. Young 69) and 99 for 2 (B.A. Cruse 51 not out)

Match drawn

Tasmania 2 pts., Western Australia 0 pts.

New South Wales' victory over Queensland was a triumph for Greg Matthews. While Peter Taylor and Shane Warne were gaining international recognition Matthews just kept plugging away. His irresistible enthusiasm delighted his audiences, and he bowled beautifully throughout the year. Against Queensland, he became the first man since George Giffen to grab a double of 100 runs and ten wickets in a Shield match. His efforts were later to make him the first man this century to take 50 wickets and score 500 runs in Shield matches in a season.

A few years back Ashley Mallett said to Greg Matthews, 'You are still a batsman who can bowl a bit.' Greg was far from impressed, yet his bowling stride was so far apart that he found it impossible to drive over his front leg, like Jim Laker or Ray Illingworth, a much underrated bowler. Ashley suggested a shorter step at delivery. Greg tried it, and immediately it worked for him. There was little change in action, just a shorter step, and it helped enormously.

He has not, in recent times, appeared comfortable in the Test side. Some say he has raised the ire of skipper Allan Border and coach Bob Simpson. Sometimes the Matthews style of enthusiasm might rub the wrong way. Perhaps Greg may need to modify a little and the Aussie management bend a little. I hope things can be worked out, for Matthews is far and away Australia's best spinner. If he knows he is truly wanted in the Test side, he will do the job.

In Perth, Tasmania took first innings points, but Mark Lavender's career best 172 thwarted them in the second innings. Against his former state, Chris Matthews, as ever, toiled manfully, but he is the only strike bowler in the Tasmanian side liable to penetrate.

Wonderful all-round cricket from Greg Matthews for New South Wales against Queensland at Sydney, 10–13 January, 1992, and throughout the season. (Adrian Murrell/Allsport)

17, 18, 19 and 20 January, 1992 *at Bellerive Oval, Hobart*

Victoria 200 (W.N. Phillips 67, C.D. Matthews 5 for 48) and 246 for 5 dec. (W.G. Ayres 100 not out, A.I.C. Dodemaide 53 not out)
Tasmania 157 (A.I.C. Dodemaide 5 for 34) and 211 for 8 (J. Cox 55, M.G. Hughes 4 for 71)

Match drawn

Victoria 2 pts., Tasmania 0 pts.

at Woolloongabba, Brisbane

Queensland 275 (G.M. Ritchie 137, T.M. Alderman 5 for 51) and 355 for 8 (T.J. Barsby 99, M.L. Hayden 93, D.M. Wellham 64 not out)
Western Australia 444 (J.L. Langer 131, W.S. Andrews 87, D. Martyn 75, B. Oxenford 4 for 126)

Match drawn

Western Australia 2 pts., Queensland 0 pts.

Dodemaide showed his growing all-round strength for Victoria in Hobart, but O'Donnell again displayed poor form. In addition, he is a captain without flair and seems to have little idea of how to use his spinners.

Western Australia took first innings points against Queensland with newcomer Justin Langer, a left-hander of real class, giving a fine display. Hayden, Wellham, Ritchie and Barsby continued their feat of run-getting, inspired, no doubt, by Queensland's run bonus system. Barsby and Hayden began the second innings with a partnership of 199.

24, 25, 26 and 27 January, 1992 *at MCG, Melbourne*

Western Australia 397 (M.R.J. Veletta 99, W.S. Andrews 98, T.M. Moody 56) and 222 for 9 dec. (D. Martyn 105 not out)
Victoria 308 (D.S. Lehmann 148, M.J. McCague 4 for 44) and 95 for 2

Match drawn

Western Australia 2 pts., Victoria 0 pts.

Both sides were deprived of leading players because of Test calls. Mike Veletta was run out on 99, and Wayne Andrews, the tough, gritty left-hander, hit his highest score of the season. Darren Lehmann hit his first Shield century of the summer, his highest for Victoria, and he appears to have overtaken Bevan as the next batsman to be considered for Test recognition.

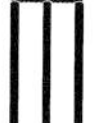

FOURTH TEST MATCH
AUSTRALIA v. INDIA, at Adelaide

Whitney replaced Reid in the Australian side, and India were forced to make a change, bringing in Srikkanth for the injured Shastri. India also brought back spinner Venkatapathy Raju for Banerjee, which was hard on one who had done well in his first Test match.

Azharuddin won the toss and asked Australia to bat first. It was a decision that amazed the pundits, but, on a pitch that was initially slow, India had instant success. The back of the Australian batting was broken before lunch. Marsh, uncertain against the outswinger, was bowled by a ball that moved in to him. As Srinath was having trouble with his run-up, Tendulkar was brought into the attack. He bowled Mark Taylor and had Border caught behind in the space of four deliveries. Kapil Dev bowled the solid Boon, and the out-of-form Mark Waugh and keeper Healy both fell cheaply. Australia were 81 for 6, and there was to be no effective recovery in spite of Dean Jones' 126-minute vigil. Venkatapathy Raju mopped up the tail, and Australia were all out for 145, dazed and bewildered.

Srikkanth was unfortunate to be given out caught off his arm, and three runs later, Manjrekar was adjudged leg before. India closed on 45 for 2.

On the second day, it looked as if India would go the same way as Australia had done. Within just over an hour, they had slumped to 70 for 6. Vengsarkar received a good ball and was taken at slip. Azharuddin and Tendulkar were leg before, and Sidhu, after a patient two-and-a-quarter hours, was caught off a steeply rising delivery. Kapil Dev and Prabhakar added 65, and the last four Indian wickets realised 155 runs in all. Craig McDermott claimed his eighth five-wicket haul in a Test match, but India led by 80 runs.

Marsh survived a run out appeal when Australia batted a second time, but he was bowled between bat and pad, and it may well be that his Test career is at an end. Australia ended the day with 36 on the board.

The best batting conditions of the match enabled Australia to prosper on the third day. They lost only the wicket of Mark Taylor during the day after he and Boon had added 221 in just over six hours. Taylor faced 303 balls and hit nine fours.

FOURTH TEST MATCH – AUSTRALIA v. INDIA
25, 26, 27, 28 and 29 January, 1992 at Adelaide Oval

AUSTRALIA

	FIRST INNINGS		SECOND INNINGS	
G.R. Marsh	b Prabhakar	8	(2) b Kapil Dev	5
M.A. Taylor	b Tendulkar	11	(1) c Venkatapathy Raju, b Kapil Dev	100
D.C. Boon	b Kapil Dev	19	run out	135
A.R. Border (capt)	c Pandit, b Tendulkar	0	not out	91
D.M. Jones	c Azharuddin, b Venkatapathy Raju	41	c Pandit, b Kapil Dev	0
M.E. Waugh	lbw, b Prabhakar	15	c Tendulkar, b Kapil Dev	0
*I.A. Healy	c Pandit, b Kapil Dev	1	c Srikkanth, b Kapil Dev	41
M.G. Hughes	c Manjrekar, b Kapil Dev	26	lbw, b Srinath	23
S.K. Warne	st Pandit, b Venkatapathy Raju	7	c Pandit, b Srinath	0
C.J. McDermott	b Venkatapathy Raju	0	b Venkatapathy Raju	21
M.R. Whitney	not out	0	c Srinath, b Venkatapathy Raju	12
Extras	lb 10, nb 7	17	lb 15, nb 8	23
		145		451

	O	M	R	W	O	M	R	W
Kapil Dev	23	11	33	3	51	12	130	5
Prabhakar	18	3	55	2	21	5	60	–
Srinath	10	2	26	–	37	13	76	2
Tendulkar	4	2	10	2	20	5	44	–
Venkatapathy Raju	11.4	7	11	3	56	15	121	2
Srikkanth					1	–	5	–

FALL OF WICKETS

1–13, 2–36, 3–39, 4–50, 5–77, 6–81, 7–117, 8–141, 9–145
1–10, 2–231, 3–277, 4–277, 5–277, 6–348, 7–383, 8–383, 9–409

INDIA

	FIRST INNINGS		SECOND INNINGS	
K. Srikkanth	c Healy, b McDermott	17	b McDermott	22
N.S. Sidhu	c Healy, b Hughes	27	lbw, b Hughes	35
S.V. Manjrekar	lbw, b Hughes	2	run out	45
D.B. Vengsarkar	c Waugh, b McDermott	13	(5) lbw, b Hughes	4
M. Azharuddin (capt)	lbw, b McDermott	1	(6) c M.A. Taylor, b McDermott	106
S.R. Tendulkar	lbw, b McDermott	6	(4) lbw, b Waugh	17
Kapil Dev	c Border, b Hughes	56	c Marsh, b Hughes	5
M. Prabhakar	lbw, b Whitney	33	lbw, b McDermott	64
*C.S. Pandit	c Boon, b McDermott	15	c Waugh, b McDermott	7
Venkatapathy Raju	not out	19	not out	8
J. Srinath	c Healy, b Whitney	21	c Warne, b McDermott	3
Extras	lb 5, nb 10	15	b 3, lb 9, nb 5	17
		225		333

	O	M	R	W	O	M	R	W
McDermott	31	9	76	5	29.1	8	92	5
Whitney	26.2	6	68	2	17	3	59	–
Hughes	18	5	55	3	23	5	66	3
Warne	7	1	18	–	16	1	60	–
M.E. Waugh	2	1	3	–	12	2	36	1
Border					3	–	8	–

FALL OF WICKETS

1–30, 2–33, 3–55, 4–64, 5–70, 6–70, 7–135, 8–174, 9–192
1–52, 2–72, 3–97, 4–102, 5–172, 6–182, 7–283, 8–291, 9–327

Umpires: D.B. Hair & P.J. McConnell

Australia won by 38 runs

Australia had now seized the initiative, and they began the fourth day on 245 for 2. Having batted for 352 minutes and hit 16 fours, Boon was run out in extraordinary fashion when he touched the ball to leg and was unaware that Pandit had run round to gather the ball. This was the start of a collapse as Jones was caught behind second ball and Mark Waugh was adjudged caught at third slip off bat and pad first ball. Healy played a characteristically jaunty knock, and McDermott and Whitney gave Border belligerent support before Venkatapathy Raju wrapped up the innings. Border had batted with quiet calm before accelerating in the final stages.

Needing 372 to win, India ended the penultimate day on 31 for 0, but they suffered a severe setback on the final morning when they lost four wickets within the first 90 minutes. Vengsarkar and Tendulkar could both feel aggrieved at being given out leg before, but, to their credit, the Indians never gave up the pursuit of victory. After his miserable tour Azharuddin suddenly displayed his brilliance. Between lunch and tea, he hit 80 off 103 balls out of the 121 runs scored in the session. At tea, India were 252 for 6, and an historic victory was a distinct possibility.

The match changed dramatically after the break when McDermott had Azharuddin caught at slip in his first over with the second new ball. McDermott also ended Prabhakar's brave knock, and completed another five-wicket haul when he accounted for Pandit and Srinath to give Australia victory with 41 balls and 38 runs to spare.

FIFTH TEST MATCH
AUSTRALIA v. INDIA, at Perth

Controversially, Australia omitted Marsh and Mark Waugh and brought in Wayne Phillips for his Test debut and Tom Moody. They also gave a first Test cap to Paul Reiffel as Warne was relegated to twelfth man. For India, More returned in place of Pandit. Border, who openly criticised the dropping of Marsh, his right-hand man, won the toss and chose to bat.

Both openers were out with only 21 scored, but Boon and Border repaired the damage with a stand of 117. Like Taylor, Border was taken at short-leg, and Jones was bemused by Venkatapathy Raju and taken at silly point. Boon remained resolute to end the day on 91 while Moody hit 42 in the total of 222 for 4.

Both the overnight batsmen fell to Prabhakar within the first hour of the second day. Boon had played another rock-like innings, batting 377 minutes and hitting 13 fours. Healy, Hughes and McDermott gave the Australian tail its customary buoyancy, but Prabhakar finished with five wickets and Srikkanth with a record five catches, four of them at short-leg.

McDermott and Hughes extracted considerable life and bounce from the wicket, and none of the Indian batsmen looked happy. Sidhu flashed wildly and paid the price while Srikkanth lived a charmed life until he mishooked McDermott. Manjrekar was brilliantly caught by Jones, diving to his left at gully. Vengsarkar was taken in the same area, and Azharuddin was caught behind fending off a short-pitched delivery. Throughout these disasters Tendulkar remained calm for 98 minutes, and India were 135 for 5.

The splendour of Tendulkar was never more apparent than in the first session of the third day when he hit 81 out of 98 runs scored and reached his hundred off 135 balls. His splendidly crafted innings ended when he was taken at slip off Whitney who destroyed the late order in which only More offered defiance. Tendulkar hit 16 fours in his innings and faced 161 balls. This was batsmanship of regal majesty.

Wayne Phillips of Victoria who won his first Test cap in the fifth match, at Perth. (Patrick Eagar)

Australia lost both openers for 31 when they batted a second time, and when Mark Taylor was leg before to Kapil Dev it gave the Indian all-rounder his 400th wicket in Test cricket, a mark which only Sir Richard Hadlee has reached. Kapil Dev was mobbed by his team-mates and the crowd rose to him. Thereafter, Boon and Jones took Australia safely to the close on 104 for 2.

The game moved out of India's reach on the fourth day. Boon was soon out, but Moody joined Jones in a partnership of 173 which quickly became exhilarating. Jones, outstanding in the Sheffield Shield but out of form in the Test series, reached his tenth Test century and, in his 150, hit a six and 14 fours. Moody's 101 came off only 149 balls and included nine fours. India's fielding wilted, and Border declared to give his bowlers 18 overs at the Indian batsmen before the close. Sidhu and Srikkanth survived and scored 55.

Sidhu was dropped by Reiffel on the last morning before becoming the Victorian's first Test victim, spectacularly caught in the gully. Whitney was brought into the attack 40 minutes before lunch and claimed Srikkanth with his third delivery. Reiffel had Tendulkar taken at slip, and Whitney had Vengsarkar caught in the same position, a dismissal which marked the end of Vengsarkar's long Test career. Manjrekar edged to the wicket-keeper, and Kapil Dev fell to the first ball he received. At lunch, India were 118 for 6, and with Azharuddin falling soon after the interval, India's humiliation was soon completed.

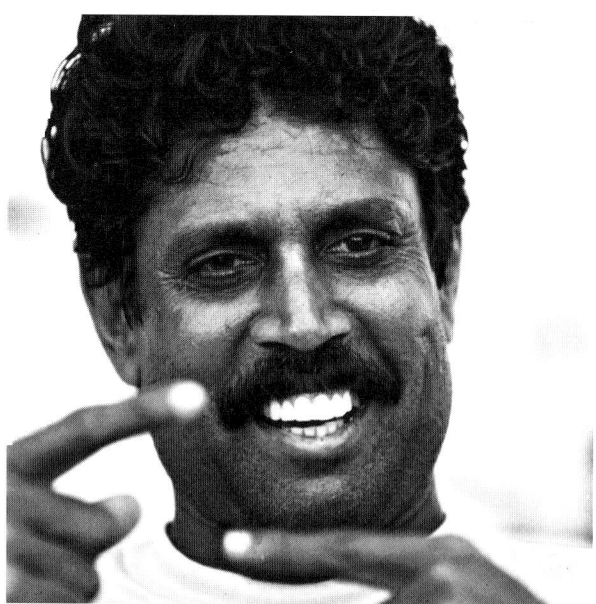

Only the second bowler to reach 400 wickets in Test cricket – Kapil Dev. (Ben Radford/Allsport)

FIFTH TEST MATCH – AUSTRALIA v. INDIA
1, 2, 3, 4 and 5 February, 1992 at WACA Ground, Perth

AUSTRALIA

	FIRST INNINGS		SECOND INNINGS	
M.A. Taylor	c Srikkanth, b Kapil Dev	2	(2) lbw, b Kapil Dev	16
W.N. Phillips	c More, b Prabhakar	8	(1) c Kapil Dev, b Srinath	14
D.C. Boon	c Sidhu, b Prabhakar	107	c Kapil Dev, b Prabhakar	38
A.R. Border (capt)	c Srikkanth, b Kapil Dev	59	(8) not out	20
D.M. Jones	c Srikkanth, b Venkatapathy Raju	7	(4) not out	150
T.M. Moody	c Vengsarkar, b Prabhakar	50	(5) c More, b Kapil Dev	101
*I.A. Healy	c More, b Srinath	28	(6) c More, b Venkatapathy Raju	7
M.G. Hughes	c Srikkanth, b Srinath	24	(7) c Tendulkar, b Srinath	11
P.R. Reiffel	c More, b Prabhakar	9		
C. J. McDermott	c Srikkanth, b Prabhakar	31		
M.R. Whitney	not out	1		
Extras	b 1, lb 7, nb 12	20	lb 4, nb 6	10
		346	(for 6 wkts., dec.)	367

	O	M	R	W	O	M	R	W
Kapil Dev	40	12	103	2	28	8	48	2
Prabhakar	32.5	9	101	5	32	4	116	1
Srinath	25	5	69	2	29.3	4	121	2
Tendulkar	5	2	9	–				
Venkatapathy Raju	23	6	56	1	24	5	78	1

FALL OF WICKETS

1–10, 2–21, 3–138, 4–145, 5–232, 6–259, 7–290, 8–303, 9–338
1–27, 2–31, 3–113, 4–286, 5–298, 6–315

INDIA

	FIRST INNINGS		SECOND INNINGS	
K. Srikkanth	c Boon, b McDermott	34	(2) c Jones, b Whitney	38
N.S. Sidhu	c Healy, b Hughes	5	(1) c Jones, b Reiffel	35
S.V. Manjrekar	c Jones, b Hughes	31	c Healy, b Whitney	8
S.R. Tendulkar	c Moody, b Whitney	114	c Moody, b Reiffel	5
D.B. Vengsarkar	c Taylor, b Hughes	1	c Moody, b Whitney	4
M. Azharuddin (capt)	c Healy, b McDermott	11	lbw, b Whitney	24
Venkatapathy Raju	c Taylor, b Whitney	1	(10) c Healy, b Whitney	8
Kapil Dev	c Hughes, b Whitney	4	(7) lbw, b Whitney	0
M. Prabhakar	c Reiffel, b Whitney	0	(8) c Healy, b McDermott	3
*K.S. More	c Healy, b Hughes	43	(9) c Taylor, b Whitney	1
J. Srinath	not out	5	not out	1
Extras	lb 14, nb 9	23	lb 11, nb 3	14
		272		141

	O	M	R	W	O	M	R	W
McDermott	21	6	47	2	20	8	44	1
Hughes	26.5	5	82	4	12	2	25	–
Reiffel	17	5	46	–	11	2	34	2
Whitney	23	4	68	4	12.1	3	27	7
Moody	2	–	15	–				

FALL OF WICKETS

1–25, 2–69, 3–100, 4–109, 5–130, 6–135, 7–159, 8–159, 9–240
1–82, 2–90, 3–97, 4–103, 5–111, 6–111, 7–126, 8–130, 9–134

Umpires: A.R. Crafter & T.A. Prue

Australia won by 300 runs

The end of a distinguished and lengthy Test career for Dilip Vengsarkar. (David Munden)

Man of the Match Michael Whitney returned the best figures of his career and his first ten-wicket match haul. McDermott was voted the International Cricketer of the Year, narrowly beating David Boon. India retreated quietly, beaten four matches to nil.

Mike Whitney who took 11 for 95 in the fifth Test in Perth. (Allsport)

TEST MATCH AVERAGES – AUSTRALIA v. INDIA

AUSTRALIA BATTING

	M	Inns	NO	Runs	HS	Av	100s	50s
D.C. Boon	5	9	2	556	135	79.42	3	1
A.R. Border	5	9	4	275	91*	55.00	–	3
M.A. Taylor	5	10	1	422	100	46.88	1	3
D.M. Jones	5	8	1	310	150*	44.28	1	1
G.R. Marsh	4	8	1	185	86	26.42	–	1
P.L. Taylor	2	2	–	42	31	21.00	–	–
M.R. Whitney	3	4	3	20	12	20.00	–	–
I.A. Healy	5	8	–	157	60	19.62	–	1
M.G. Hughes	5	8	–	154	36	19.25	–	–
M.E. Waugh	4	6	–	83	34	13.83	–	–
C.J. McDermott	5	7	1	77	31	12.83	–	–
S.K. Warne	2	4	1	28	20	9.33	–	–
B.A. Reid	2	2	–	3	3	1.50	–	–

Played in one Test – W.N. Phillips 8 & 14; T.M. Moody 50 & 101; P.R. Reiffel 9

AUSTRALIA BOWLING

	Overs	Mds	Runs	Wkts	Av	Best	10/m	5/inn
B.A. Reid	59.2	16	136	12	11.33	6-60	1	2
M.R. Whitney	116.5	21	359	17	21.11	7-27	1	1
C.J. McDermott	264.2	75	670	31	21.61	5-54	1	3
M.G. Hughes	199.3	46	511	22	23.22	4-50	–	–
P.R. Reiffel	28	7	80	2	40.00	2-34	–	–
M.E. Waugh	37	9	89	1	89.00	1-36	–	–
P.L. Taylor	35	6	116	1	116.00	1-40	–	–
S.K. Warne	68	9	228	1	228.00	1-150	–	–
A.R. Border	16	3	47	–	–	–	–	–

Bowled in one innings – T.M. Moody 2-0-15-0

AUSTRALIA FIELDING FIGURES

19 – I.A. Healy; 10 – M.E. Waugh; 8 – D.C. Boon; 7 – M.A. Taylor; 5 – A.R. Border and D.M. Jones; 4 – M.G. Hughes; 3 – T.M. Moody; 2 – G.R. Marsh; 1 – C.J. McDermott, M.R. Whitney (plus one as sub), S.K. Warne, B.A. Reid and P. Reiffel

INDIA BATTING

	M	Inns	NO	Runs	HS	Av	100s	50s
R.J. Shastri	3	5	–	300	206	60.00	1	–
S.R. Tendulkar	5	9	1	368	148*	46.00	2	–
K.S. More	3	6	1	143	67*	28.60	–	1
M. Prabhakar	5	9	1	224	64	28.00	–	2
S.V. Manjrekar	5	9	–	197	45	21.88	–	–
M. Azharuddin	5	9	–	192	106	21.33	1	–
N.S. Sidhu	3	5	–	102	35	20.40	–	–
Kapil Dev	5	9	–	165	56	18.33	–	1
D.B. Vengsarkar	5	9	–	158	54	17.55	–	1
K. Srikkanth	4	8	–	135	38	16.87	–	–
J. Srinath	5	9	4	78	21	15.60	–	–
Venkatapathy Raju	4	8	2	82	31	13.66	–	–
C.S. Pandit	2	3	–	31	15	10.33	–	–

Played in one Test – S.T. Banerjee 3

INDIA BOWLING

	Overs	Mds	Runs	Wkts	Av	Best	10/m	5/inn
R.J. Shastri	48	11	114	5	22.80	4-45	–	–
Kapil Dev	284	76	645	25	25.80	5-97	–	2
S.R. Tendulkar	36	10	94	3	31.33	2-10	–	–
M. Prabhakar	251.5	61	680	19	35.78	5-101	–	1
Venkatapathy Raju	171.4	42	438	9	48.66	3-11	–	–
J. Srinath	201.1	41	553	10	55.30	3-59	–	–

Bowled in one innings – S.T. Banerjee 18-4-47-3; S.V. Manjrekar 0.5-0-4-0; K. Srikkanth 1-0-5-0

INDIA FIELDING FIGURES

11 – K.S. More (ct 10/st 1) and C.S. Pandit (ct 10/st 1); 7 – K. Srikkanth (plus one as sub); 5 – S.R. Tendulkar; 4 – D.B. Vengsarkar and Kapil Dev; 3 – M. Azharuddin and M. Prabhakar; 2 – Venkatapathy Raju; 1 – S.V. Manjrekar, J. Srinath and N.S. Sidhu

NEW SOUTH WALES
First-Class Matches 1991–92

BATTING

	v. Western Australia (Perth) 1–4 November, 1991		v. Victoria (Sydney) 8–11 November, 1991		v. Queensland (Brisbane) 15–18 November, 1991		v. Indian XI (Lismore) 23–26 November, 1991		v. Tasmania (Sydney) 12–15 December, 1991		v. South Australia (Adelaide) 20–23 December, 1991		v. Queensland (Sydney) 10–13 January, 1992		v. South Australia (Sydney) 31 January – 3 February, 1992		v. Victoria (Melbourne) 13–16 February, 1992		v. Tasmania (Hobart) 29 February–3 March, 1992	
S.M. Small	0	–	79	–	0	1	58	–	–	51	42	15	0	11	19	–	17	37	10	–
M.A. Taylor	39	–	2	–	4	57	15	–	–	4	16	54	52	24			158	53		
S.R. Waugh	115	–	88	–	10	2	13	–							41	–	5	6		
M.E. Waugh	136	–	19	–	0	60	79	–			94	24			158	–	13	76		
M.G. Bevan	11	–	14	–	17	10	115	–	–	52			9	10	29	–	16	70	95	–
T.H. Bayliss	3	–	34	–	8	13			–	7	1	37	80	75	133	–	0	7	0	–
P.A. Emery	6	–	27	–	37*	0	3	–	–	10	36	8	20	21*	12	–	8	4*	7	–
G.R.J. Matthews	6	–	139	–	17	50	23	–	–	22	11	40	85*	67	19	–	33	4*	27	–
G.F. Lawson	4	–	27	–	6	24	2	–	–	4	7	28			0	–	12	–	1*	–
M.R. Whitney	0	–	0	–	0	1*	2*	–			0	0					0*	–		
W.J. Holdsworth	0*	–	0*	–	4	0	4	–	–	1	0*	33*	12	0	14	–	2	–	0	–
B.E. McNamara							18	–	–	13	6	80	14	3					43	–
D. Freedman									–	8	2	1	15	0	26*	–			0	–
P.J.S. Alley									–	21*			1	2						
G.S. Milliken													7	7	16	–				
M. Slater																			10	–
M. Haywood																			5	–
Byes			3			1				6		1		1	5					
Leg-byes	5		9			3	20			10	6	3	12	3	8		4	8	9	
Wides	1									1										
No-balls	6		18		16	8	12			2	4	18	24	20	8		12	8	10	
Total	332		459		119	230	364		0	212	225	342	331	244	488		280	273	217	
Wickets	10		10		10	10	10		0	10	10	10	10	10	10		10	6	10	
Result	D		D		L		W		L		L		W		W		D		W	
Points	2		2		0		–		0		0		6		6		0		6	

Fielding Figures

34 – P.A. Emery (ct 32/st 2)
19 – S.M. Small
17 – M.A. Taylor
16 – G.R.J. Matthews
9 – M.E. Waugh
8 – S.R. Waugh
7 – W.J. Holdsworth
6 – B.E. McNamara (plus one as sub)
4 – T.H. Bayliss and M.G. Bevan
2 – D. Freedman and M. Slater
1 – G.F. Lawson, G.S. Milliken, M. Haywood and P.J.S. Alley (as sub

BOWLING

	M.R. Whitney	W.J. Holdsworth	G.F. Lawson	G.R.J. Matthews	S.R. Waugh	M.E. Waugh	M.G. Bevan	T.H. Bayliss
v. Western Australia	20.2–4–54–3	19–1–80–2	24–4–66–2	29–16–26–1	12–5–33–0	6–3–11–2	8–1–20–0	
(Perth) 1–4 November, 1991	19–4–62–1	17–5–65–1	12–3–25–0	19–6–53–1	13–4–26–2	2–0–9–0		
v. Victoria	24–6–52–2	18–3–49–2	24–9–47–0	34–17–52–3	7–2–15–1	4.5–1–15–2	6–0–19–0	
(Sydney) 8–11 November, 1991	22–1–67–2	18–4–64–0	17–1–49–0	40–13–90–3	1–0–6–0	15–6–18–1	18–2–85–0	4–1–6–0
v. Queensland	28–6–91–4	14.5–1–52–3	23–10–60–2		17–4–51–1	3–0–11–0		
(Brisbane) 15–18 November, 1991	5–1–25–0	4–0–25–0		3–0–19–0			1.1–0–9–0	
v. Indian XI	19.3–4–45–3	17–3–38–4	14–3–23–0	18–4–56–1	13–6–24–2	7–2–19–0		
(Lismore) 23–26 November, 1991	19.4–7–37–6	6–2–23–1	7–0–23–1	14–4–37–2	6–1–20–0	3–1–7–0		
v. Tasmania		16–5–35–3	2.3–0–4–0	12.1–4–34–2				
(Sydney) 12–15 December, 1991		16.5–5–50–2		18–15–7–2				
v. South Australia	41–11–105–3	30–8–135–1	4.5–2–15–0	43–6–145–2				
(Adelaide) 20–23 December, 1991	2.5–0–14–0							
v. Queensland		12–2–49–1		26–8–63–6				
(Sydney) 10–13 January, 1992		17–1–62–0		34–13–70–5				0.4–0–1–2
v. South Australia (Sydney)		23.2–2–104–3	25–9–60–3	21–6–43–1	9–1–29–1	1–0–4–0		
31 January – 3 February, 1992		9–2–37–1	8–1–18–1	25.5–8–61–5	4–1–16–0			
v. Victoria	20–6–62–2	20–2–67–2	22–7–55–1	23–2–76–1	11–2–23–3	12–5–29–1		1–0–14–0
(Melbourne) 13–16 February, 1992	4–2–3–0	4–2–8–0						
v. Tasmania (Hobart)		12.2–5–33–6	15–4–20–0	5–2–8–2				
29 February – 3 March, 1992		16–4–55–3	21.5–8–33–3	21–7–31–2				
v. Western Australia		6–3–9–1	10–6–8–1	16–5–30–4				
(Sydney) 7–10 March, 1992		3–1–12–0	17–7–34–0	42–9–99–6			6–0–10–0	5–2–3–0
v. Western Australia	26–5–71–2	25–4–96–1	30–10–84–2	18.4–5–49–3	16–6–36–1	3–0–24–0		
(Perth) 28 March – 1 April, 1992	23.4–6–75–7	17–3–53–1	16–3–66–2	20–3–67–0	4–0–26–0	4–1–22–0		
Bowlers average	275–63–763–35 21.80	341.2–68–1201–38 31.60	293.1–87–690–18 38.33	482.4–153–116–52 21.46	113–32–305–11 27.72	60.5–19–169–6 28.16	39.1–3–143–0 –	10.4–3–24–2 12.00

v. Western Australia (Sydney) 7–10 March, 1992		v. Western Australia (Perth) 28 March – 1 April, 1992		M	Inns	NO	Runs	HS	Av
1	62*	10	98	12	18	1	511	98	30.05
			16	9	14	–	503	158	35.92
		113	68	7	10	–	461	115	46.10
		163	19	8	12	–	841	163	70.08
0	62*	0	20	11	16	1	530	115	35.33
20	11			10	15	–	429	133	28.60
7	–	30	0	12	17	3	236	37*	16.85
5	–	42	13	12	17	2	603	139	40.20
9*	–	1	4	11	14	2	129	28	10.75
		2	8	7	10	3	13	8	1.85
7	–	0	31*	12	16	5	108	33*	9.81
		15	–	6	8	–	192	80	24.00
20	–	6*	1	7	10	2	79	26*	9.87
				2	3	1	24	21*	12.00
				2	3	–	30	16	10.00
		62	26	2	3	–	98	62	32.66
		79	–	2	2	–	84	79	42.00
		2	4						
12	8	4	4						
	1								
8	4	24	6						
245	176	415	281						
10	2	10	10						
W		L							
6		–							

31 January, 1, 2 and 3 February 1992 *at SCG, Sydney*

South Australia 282 (D.W. Hookes 87, A.M.J. Hilditch 68) and 176 (G.R.J. Matthews 5 for 61)

New South Wales 488 (M.E. Waugh 158, T.H. Bayliss 133)

New South Wales won by an innings and 30 runs

New South Wales 6 pts., South Australia 0 pts.

Excluded from the Test side, Mark Waugh returned to New South Wales and shared a fourth-wicket stand of 178 with Trevor Bayliss who hit his one century of the summer. He had struggled when he should have had a bumper harvest of runs. New South Wales won with ease to make their qualification for the Shield final look assured.

4, 5 and 6 February, 1992 *at Bendigo*

Victoria 217 for 9 dec. (P.C. Nobes 53) and 180 for 9 dec. (Wasim Akram 5 for 47)

Pakistanis 194 for 9 dec. (Ijaz Ahmed 67, N. Maxwell 4 for 50) and 149 for 9

Match drawn

M.A. Taylor	B.E. McNamara	P.J.S. Alley	D. Freedman	S.M. Small	Byes	Leg-byes	Wides	No-balls	Total	Wkts
						4	1	12	234	10
					6	13		4	259	5
					1	10		10	260	10
2–1–1–0					5	3	1	26	394	6
						3		10	268	10
					4	2		8	84	0
					1	3			209	10
	1–1–0–0							2	147	10
	8–2–22–0	9–5–14–0	10–4–31–2		1	3	2		144	7
	7–1–18–1	13–2–25–4	6–1–14–1			2	1	8	116	10
	12.1–1–54–0		20–2–84–3		9	9		14	556	10
				2–1–1–0			1		15	0
	8–0–21–1	7–1–48–0	18–2–45–2		2	2	1	8	230	10
		7–1–33–0	19–6–40–3		2	4		16	212	10
			13–1–37–2			5		2	282	10
			21–9–37–3		2	5	1	2	176	10
						12	1	15	338	10
					5	1	1		17	0
	8–4–8–2				1	6		6	76	10
	12–5–16–2		1–1–0–0			2			137	10
			9.2–5–17–4			7			71	10
	10–2–16–2		18–4–60–2		3	15	1	8	252	10
			5–0–19–0		4	13	2	22	396	10
			7–0–25–0		4	6		24	344	10
2–1–1–0	66.1–16–155–8	36–9–120–4	147.2–35–409–22	2–1–1–0						
–	19.37	30.00	18.59	–						

QUEENSLAND

First-Class Matches 1991–92

BATTING

	v. South Australia (Brisbane) 1–4 November, 1991		v. New South Wales (Brisbane) 15–18 November, 1991		v. Tasmania (Hobart) 22–25 November, 1991		v. Victoria (Brisbane) 13–16 December, 1991		v. Indian XI (Brisbane) 20–23 December, 1991		v. New South Wales (Sydney) 10–13 January, 1992		v. Western Australia (Brisbane) 17–20 January, 1992		v. South Australia (Adelaide) 7–10 February, 1992		v. Western Australia (Perth) 13–16 February, 1992		v. Victoria (Melbourne) 29 February–3 March, 1992		v. Tasmania (Brisbane) 13–16 March, 1992	
T.J. Barsby	4	12	45	27*	46	–	165	5	83	22	6	49	14	99	6	67	5	43	32	19	14	85
M.L.. Hayden	149	5	64	43*	108	–	8	116	8	38	13	34	10	93	79	80	5	31	24	44	19	57
D.M. Wellham	80	63*	37	–	100	–	14	167			54	4	33	64*	34	28	83	6	25	22	60	0
A.R. Border	196	39*	2	–	20	–			85*	33					0	46	8	43				
S.G. Law	64	22	3	–	5	–	0	0			2	22	23	47	12	35*	15	4	42	82*	0	–
G.M. Ritchie	53*	6	25	–	18	–	8	26*	68	107	31	47	137	2	58	23*	30	22	40	41	6	–
I.A. Healy	–	48	49	–	55*	–									31	–	14	87*				
P.L. Taylor	–	12	8	–	7	–			–	12					29	–	22	2				
C.J. McDermott	–	–	17	–	18	–									5	–	19*	0				
C.G. Rackemann	–	–	0	–			0*	–	–	0	0	0	0	–	9	–	0	10	4*	–	5*	–
G.J. Rowell	–	–	5*	–	7	–	2	–			0*	5	2*	1	45*	–	2	2	0	–	30	–
B. Oxenford							10	–	–	9*	0	6*	20	0					3	–	1	–
S. Williams					29	–	16	–	–	14			4	16*								
P.J.T. Goggin							91	–	8	5	55	14	2	16					49	2	5	–
P.W. Anderson							52	–	–	1	39	3	7	0					34	13*	11	–
S. Prestwidge									48*	24	18	6										
M.A. Polzin																			0	–		
M.S. Kasprowicz																					10	–
Byes				4	4			1	1		2	2	5	11		5						1
Leg-byes	16	4	3	2	9		6	7	7	4	2	4	8	5	7	3	2	8	9	1	3	2
Wides		6			3					1	1		2	1	3			1	1			
No-balls	26	22	10	8	18		2	2	11	3	8	16	8		16	14	2	28	32	4	18	
Total	588	239	268	84	447		374	324	319	273	230	212	275	355	334	301	207	287	295	228	182	145
Wickets	5	6	10	0	10		10	4	4	10	10	10	10	8	10	4	10	10	10	5	10	1
Result	D		W		W		D		L		L		D		L		L		D		D	
Points	2		6		6		0		–		0		0		2		0		0		0	

BOWLING

	C.J. McDermott	G.J. Rowell	C.G. Rackemann	P.L. Taylor	A.R. Border	B. Oxenford	S. Williams	S.G. Law
v. South Australia (Brisbane) 1–4 November, 1991	45–7–150–6	31–8–89–1	34–5–124–1	42.1–14–122–0	19–6–52–0			
v. New South Wales (Brisbane) 15–18 November, 1991	14–3–54–5	8–0–30–1	8–1–35–4					
	24–8–57–3	11.5–2–58–2	21–9–59–3	19–3–52–2				
v. Tasmania (Hobart) 22–25 November, 1991	16–3–48–1	20–6–46–7					11.4–3–37–2	
	17–1–65–4	17–4–50–3		18.5–8–19–1			12–1–41–1	
v. Victoria (Brisbane) 13–16 December, 1991		43–8–132–3	35–9–59–3			22–2–89–0	29.2–10–77–2	3–2–5–0
		6–0–19–0	12–5–12–1			11–3–27–1	3–1–10–1	
v. Indian XI (Brisbane) 20–23 December, 1991			29–6–95–1	21–1–97–0		12–2–32–1	29.3–4–114–2	
				11–0–46–0		8–0–29–0	11–2–39–1	
v. New South Wales (Sydney) 10–13 January, 1992		37–9–92–5	34.5–12–75–4			12–1–55–0		1–0–3–0
		22–3–58–2	21–3–58–1			22.4–6–91–5		7–4–7–0
v. Western Australia (Brisbane) 17–20 January, 1992		40–9–97–1	38–14–69–3			41.1–7–126–4	34–6–133–1	2–1–8–0
v. South Australia (Adelaide) 7–10 February, 1992	18–2–58–6	7–0–44–1	10.4–3–22–3					
	37–6–124–4	18–1–64–1	32.4–6–117–1	42–6–126–0	23–4–63–0			1–0–1–0
v. Western Australia (Perth) 13–16 February, 1992	5–0–22–0	45–12–121–3	52–16–124–2	46–9–136–2	7–2–19–0			21–2–73–0
v. Victoria (Melbourne) 29 February – 3 March, 1992		27–6–86–2	27–4–89–5			23–3–81–0		16–5–27–0
		10–1–39–2	10–2–31–0			12–1–51–1		1–0–9–0
v. Tasmania (Brisbane) 13–16 March, 1992		30–8–74–1	30–5–74–2			25–4–116–2		22–9–54–0
Bowlers average	177–30–578–29–19.93	372.5–77–1099–35 31.40	395.1–100–1043–34 30.67	200–41–598–5 119.60	49–12–134–0 –	188.5–29–697–14 49.78	130.3–27–451–10 45.10	74–23–187–0 –

M	Inns	NO	Runs	HS	Av
11	21	1	848	165	42.40
11	21	2	1028	149	54.10
10	18	3	873	167	58.20
6	10	2	472	196	59.00
10	17	2	378	82*	25.20
11	19	3	748	137	46.75
5	6	2	284	87*	71.00
6	7	–	92	29	13.14
5	5	1	59	19*	14.75
10	11	3	28	10	3.50
10	12	4	101	45*	12.62
6	8	2	49	20	8.16
4	5	1	79	29	19.75
6	10	–	247	91	24.70
6	9	1	160	52	20.00
2	4	1	96	48*	32.00
1	1	–	0	0	0.00
1	1	–	10	10	10.00

7, 8, 9 and 10 February, 1992 *at Adelaide Oval*

Queensland 334 (M.L. Hayden 79, G.M. Ritchie 58, D.J. Hickey 4 for 96) and 301 for 4 dec. (M.L. Hayden 80, T.J. Barsby 67)

South Australia 130 (C.J. McDermott 6 for 58) and 506 for 6 (A.M.J. Hilditch 137, G.R. Blewett 98, P.R. Sleep 97 not out, J.D. Siddons 87, C.J. McDermott 4 for 124)

South Australia won by 4 wickets

South Australia 6 pts., Queensland 2 pts.

9, 10, 11 and 12 February, 1992 *at Devonport Oval*

Pakistanis 198 for 8 dec. (Ramiz Raja 50, S. Young 5 for 36) and 93 for 1 (Ramiz Raja 50 not out)

Tasmania 183 for 5 dec. (M. Atkinson 55 not out)

Match drawn

FIELDING FIGURES

18 – P.W. Anderson (ct 16/st 2)
17 – I.A. Healy
8 – A.R. Border
7 – C.G. Rackemann and B. Oxenford
6 – S.G. Law, M.L. Hayden and G.J. Rowell
5 – T.J. Barsby
4 – D.M. Wellham and P.L. Taylor
3 – G.M. Ritchie andP.J.T. Goggin (plus three as sub)
1 – S.Williams and S. Prestwidge (plus one as sub)

T.J. Barsby	G.M. Ritchie	D.M. Wellham	S. Prestwidge	P.J.T. Goggin	M.A. Polzin	M.L. Hayden	M.S. Kasprowicz	Byes	Leg-byes	Wides	No-balls	Total	Wkts
								1	16	1	60	554	10
											16	119	10
								1	3		8	230	10
									7		8	138	10
								2	3	1	10	180	9
								1	12		14	375	8
5–1–13–0	1–0–2–0	1–1–0–0						4	2		2	89	3
			25–3–113–2					2	1	5	9	454	9
	3–0–21–0		9–1–31–1	4–0–10–0					1		2	177	2
			22–2–94–0						12		24	331	10
			12–2–26–1					1	3		20	244	10
								5	6	11	14	444	10
									6		20	130	10
									11		20	506	6
								5	9	1	38	509	8
					17–3–52–1			5	10		16	350	8
	1–0–5–0			8–0–43–0	5–1–40–1			8	4	1		230	5
				8–1–35–0	9–3–35–0			1	11		8	400	6
5–1–13–0	5–0–28–0	1–1–0–0	68–8–264–4	12–0–53–0	22–4–92–2	8–1–35–0	9–3–35–0						
–	–	–	66.00	–	46.00	–	–						

Pakistan played two first-class matches as part of their preparation for the World Cup. They did not show to good advantage in either, and rain marred the game in Tasmania. Tasmania included Mark Atkinson, a diminutive wicket-keeper from New South Wales. He was to prove a magnificent keeper, and he also batted well. Tasmania has had some good keepers of late – Richard Coyle, a superb gloveman who struggled with his weight; Tim Coyle who decided to commit himself to coaching – and Atkinson, a busy keeper, has the ability and enthusiasm to press hard for a Test cap.

In Adelaide, Queensland made a solid 334 and rolled over South Australia for 130. They looked in good shape to reach the Shield final, but they did not enforce the follow-on, preferring to allow McDermott to rest. They hit a quick-fire 301 and set South Australia a target of 506. A first-wicket stand of 209 between Greg Blewett and veteran Andrew Hilditch set the pattern for the South Australian challenge. Queensland attacked, with men in catching positions and no one at third man. They also showed a lack of urgency. McDermott bowled manfully, but South Australia won the day, victory

FIELDING FIGURES

30 – T.J. Nielsen (ct 28/st 2)
10 – J.D. Siddons
8 – A.M.J. Hilditch
7 – G.R. Blewett
5 – P.R. Sleep
4 – D.W. Hookes
3 – D.J. Hickey, J.A. Brayshaw, C.J. Owen and G.A. Bishop
2 – J.C. Scuderi and T.B.A. May
1 – M.P. Faull, C.R. Miller, M.J. Minagall and C. Williamson

SOUTH AUSTRALIA
First-Class Matches 1991–92

BATTING

	v. Queensland (Brisbane) 1–4 November, 1991		v. Tasmania (Adelaide) 8–11 November, 1991		v. Victoria (Melbourne) 15–18 November, 1991		v. Western Australia (Adelaide) 22–25 November, 1991	
A.M.J. Hilditch	4	–	23	–	103	50	43	24
G.R. Blewett	18	–	63	31*	32	11	78	0
M.P. Faull	51	–					4	20*
J.D. Siddons	149	–	141	–	2	0		
G.A. Bishop	64	–	34	31	12	41		
D.W. Hookes	26	–	16	–	26	9	75	13
T.J. Nielsen	88	–	10	31*	3	1	81	35*
J.C. Scuderi	37	–	30	–			125*	36
T.B.A. May	33	–	43	–	0	8	6	–
D.J. Hickey	6	–	6*	–	13	10	1	–
S.P. George	0*	–						
C.R. Miller			23	–	0	4		
M.J. Minagall			9	–	11*	3*		
J.A. Brayshaw					23	90	16	40
G.H. Armstrong							2	5
C.J. Owen							0	–
P.R. Sleep								
C. Williamson								
P. Hutchinson								
Byes	1					3	6	
Leg-byes	16		10		11	6	5	5
Wides	1							
No-balls	60		6		8	10	18	2
Total	554		414	93	244	246	460	180
Wickets	10		10	1	10	10	10	6
Result		D		D		L		L
Points		0		0		0		2

BOWLING	D.J. Hickey	J.C. Scuderi	S.P. George	T.B.A. May	M.P. Faull	D.W. Hookes	G.R. Blewett	A.M.J. Hilditch
v. Queensland	28.3–1–129–1	33–6–143–2	20–3–72–0	43–5–151–0	4–1–22–1	9–2–33–0	2–0–22–0	
(Brisbane) 1–4 November, 1991	15–1–73–2	17–7–40–1	10–0–57–2	5–1–30–0			7–2–23–0	1–0–12–0
v. Tasmania (Adelaide)	44–11–121–2	4–-7–50–4		72–27–180–2				
8–11 November, 1991								
v. Victoria (Melbourne)	32–2–136–3			31–3–131–1		2–0–10–0	2–0–6–0	
15–18 November, 1991								
v. Western Australia (Adelaide)	22–3–34–1	22–4–54–0		28–5–110–1		6–0–23–0		
22–25 November, 1991	12.1–1–62–0	20–6–50–0		34–7–106–2	14–5–24–0	3–1–11–0		
v. New South Wales (Adelaide)	22–7–68–1	32.1–11–79–7		4–0–24–0				
20–23 December, 1991	8–1–31–1	32–10–86–3		45.3–9–135–3				
v. New South Wales (Sydney)	21–2–117–2	40–13–86–1		35–4–120–3				
31 January – 3 February, 1992								
v. Queensland (Adelaide)	23–2–96–4	30.1–5–96–2		24–8–52–0			5–1–10–0	
7–10 February, 1992	14–1–81–1	17–5–62–2		14–3–45–1			7–0–31–0	
v. Tasmania (Hobart)		36–12–81–1		21–6–50–1			6–1–17–0	
13–16 February, 1992		23–9–57–2		36–21–48–3				
v. Victoria (Adelaide)	25–3–95–2	26–7–66–1		32–5–112–0				
21–24 February, 1992		4–1–14–0					10–0–50–1	1–0–15–1
v. Western Australia (Perth)	39–6–131–2	31–11–89–2					7–1–30–0	
28 February–2 March, 1992							1.3–0–6–0	
Bowlers average	305.4–41–1234–22 56.09	403.2–114–1053–28 37.60	30–3–129–2 64.50	424.3–104–1222–17 71.88	18–6–46–1 46.00	20–3–77–0 –	47.3–5–195–1 195.00	2–0–27–1 27.00

v. New South Wales (Adelaide) 20–23 December, 1991		v. New South Wales (Sydney) 31 January – 3 February, 1992		v. Queensland (Adelaide) 7–10 February, 1992		v. Tasmania (Hobart) 13–16 February, 1992		v. Victoria (Adelaide) 21–24 February, 1992		v. Western Australia (Perth) 28 February–2 March, 1992		M	Inns	NO	Runs	HS	Av
6	1*	68	9	5	137	76	–	63	38	16	55	10	17	1	721	137	45.06
56	13*	11	11	34	98	86	–	6	7	16	0	10	18	2	571	98	35.68
												2	3	1	75	51	37.50
68	–	38	34	0	87	24	–	21	65	51	6	9	14	–	650	149	46.42
		10	22							19	37	5	9	–	270	64	30.33
156	–	87	26	5	3	14	5	4	49	51	1	10	17	–	530	156	31.17
32	–	1	0	1	14*	17	14*	23	9	20*	40	10	18	5	420	88	32.30
110	–	40	19	10	0	2	–	28	57	5	3	9	14	1	502	125*	38.61
6	–	7	6	20*	–	0	–	13*	13			9	12	2	155	43	15.50
1	–	11*	11	12	–			–	0*	1	9*	9	12	4	81	13	10.12
												1	1	1	0	0*	–
												2	3	–	27	23	9.00
												2	3	2	23	11*	23.00
19	–			1	39	75	–	101	0	52	60	7	12	–	516	101	43.00
												1	2	–	7	5	3.50
0	–	1	0	0	–							4	5	–	1	1	0.20
70*	–	1	28*	16	97*	0	–	33*	38	13	4	6	10	4	300	97*	50.00
						8*	13*					1	2	2	21	13*	–
						0	–	–	7*	11	14	3	4	1	32	14	10.66
9			2			2		8	2		2						
9		5	5	6	11	9		10	8	4	3						
	1		1			2											
14		2	2	20	20	10		6	6	34	16						
556	15	282	176	130	506	325	32	316	299	201	270						
10	0	10	10	10	6	10	0	7	9	10	10						
W		L		W		D		D		L							
6		0		6		0		0		0							

C.R. Miller	M.J. Minagall	J.D. Siddons	J.A. Brayshaw	C.J. Owen	P.R. Sleep	P. Hutchinson	C. Williamson	Byes	Leg-byes	Wides	No-balls	Total	Wkts
									16		26	588	5
									4	6	22	239	6
26–10–50–1	29.3–9–76–1							1	20		8	426	10
38–7–125–3	13–2–66–0	1–0–3–0	8–0–27–0						10	1	22	514	8
				19–3–53–2					4		26	338	5
				9–1–41–0				4	8			306	3
				15–2–48–1					6		4	225	10
				26–9–68–2	8–0–18–1			1	3		18	342	10
				22–5–67–3	19–2–85–1			5	8		8	488	10
				14–3–49–0	6–0–24–1				7	3	16	334	10
				11–5–40–0	12–6–34–0			5	3		14	301	4
			4–1–9–0	39.4–10–87–5	23–4–71–2				13	2	6	328	9
			9.5–3–17–2	22–4–68–2	16–6–42–1				8	1	8	240	10
				28–7–83–4	19–0–88–2				17		6	461	9
		6–0–4–0	11–2–47–2		1–0–6–0			2	1	1		175	4
				36.4–10–101–3	24–4–97–3			7	13	1	16	468	10
					2–2–0–0					1		6	0
64–17–175–4 43.75	42.3–11–142–1 142.00	7–0–43–0 –	19–2–74–2 37.00	116–28–366–8 45.75	123.3–29–371–12 30.91	107.4–20–346–12 28.83	39–10–113–3 37.66						

TASMANIA

First-Class Matches 1991–92

BATTING

	v. Victoria (Melbourne) 1–4 November, 1991		v. South Australia (Adelaide) 8–11 November, 1991		v. Queensland (Hobart) 22–25 November, 1991		v. Western Australia (Brisbane) 29 November–2 December, 1991		v. New South Wales (Sydney) 12–15 December, 1991		v. Western Australia (Perth) 10–13 January, 1992		v. Victoria (Hobart) 17–20 January, 1992		v. Pakistanis (Devonport) 9–11 February, 1992		v. South Australia (Hobart) 13–16 February, 1992		v. New South Wales (Hobart) 29 February–3 March, 1992		v. Queensland (Brisbane) 13–16 March, 1992	
R.J. Bennett	31	–	26	–	0	19					3	7										
B.A. Cruse	25	–	100	–	3	1	9	28	17	12	39	51*	10	3	31	–						
D.C. Boon	35*	–	130	–	22	8											34	24				
C.D. Matthews	40	–	18	–	10	29	24	1	5*	14	32	–	15	4	–	–	8	9	0	2	–	–
R.J. Tucker	7	–	0	–	0	26	1	24	14	0	72	9*	3	37	3*	–	75	8	0	6	35	–
J. Cox	82	–	6	–	41	3-	0	4	32	35	33	–	0	55	11	–	27	5	4	29	19	–
D.J. Buckingham	73	–	60	–	16	11	37	110	29	1	20	–	6	24	41	–	71*	82	11	10	69	–
G.A. Hughes	38	–	7	–									45	18	29	–	19	1	16	38	45	–
J.M. Holyman	2	–	38	–	0	14	6	9	–	11	20	–	19*	1								
D.R. Gilbert	2	–	12	–	20*	15	5	0*	–	3	10	–	0	–	–	–	–	3*	2	4		
G.D. Campbell	2*	–	0*	–	2	–											15	8				
P.T. McPhee					9	1*									–	–					–	–
D. Hills							12	2	6	21	23	27	41	17	0	–	44	33	17	5	106	–
M.G. Farrell							12	0	16	4									1	7		
S. Young							55	0	19	4	69	–	0	38*	–	–	7	38	12*	16	63	–
T.D. Bower							0*	0	–	0*	5*	–	5	2*					0	3		
M. Atkinson															55*	–	7	12	0	15*	–	–
D. Courtney																					19	–
M. Divenuto																					33*	–
Byes	5		1			2	1		1		6		6						1		1	
Leg-byes	7		20		7	3	8	3	3	2	12	3	5	10	3		13	8	6	2	11	
Wides						1	2		2	1	6		2	2	3		2	1				
No-balls	23		8		8	20		12		8	8	2			7		6	8	6		8	
Total	372		426		138	180	172	193	144	116	358	99	157	211	183		328	240	76	137	400	
Wickets	10		10		10	9†	10	10	7	10	10	2	10	8	5		9	10	10	10	6	
Result	D		D		L		L		W		D		D		D		D		L		D	
Points	0		2		0		0		6		2		0		–		2		0		2	

BOWLING

	D.R. Gilbert	G.D. Campbell	C.D. Matthews	R.J. Tucker	D.J. Buckingham	G.A. Hughes	B.A. Cruse	R.J. Bennett
v. Victoria (Melbourne)	33–8–81–3	30–6–96–1	34–8–81–1	26–6–73–1	23–2–88–2	2–0–4–0		
1–4 November, 1991	6–1–19–0	8–3–11–0	5–3–11–0	6–4–4–0	10–3–20–0	13–3–28–0	7–0–12–0	
v. South Australia (Adelaide)	29.5–8–88–4	35–11–108–0	30–7–89–2	23–7–34–2	23–3–81–2	2–1–4–0		
8–11 November, 1991		7–1–19–0		5–0–20–0	13–3–34–0	11–4–14–1	4–2–2–0	3–2–4–0
v. Queensland (Hobart)	30.4–5–81–2	18–3–62–1	39–7–118–4	13–1–39–3	13–1–49–0			
22–25 November, 1991								
v. Western Australia (Hobart)	26–8–60–1		36–8–102–5	14–5–45–1				
29 November–2 December, 1991			3–0–10–0		2.3–2–2–0			
v. New South Wales (Sydney)								
12–15 December, 1991	15–2–44–1		20–5–50–5	6–0–29–0				
v. Western Australia (Perth)	9–2–28–0		17–1–72–3	11–2–28–1	1–0–6–0			
10–13 January, 1992	23–8–53–0		37–5–128–5	11–2–30–0	6–0–39–0			
v. Victoria (Hobart)	13–5–24–1		27–8–48–5	15–5–43–3				
17–20 January, 1992	3–0–12–0		27–10–72–3	10–3–39–0		4–0–12–0		
v. Pakistanis (Devonport)	12–2–39–0		16–4–49–2	7–1–27–1				
9–11 February, 1992	7–0–32–1		4–0–8–0			1–0–4–0		
v. South Australia (Hobart)	32–7–84–0	6–0–18–0	37.2–9–89–4	11–4–33–1	5–4–13–0	1–1–0–0		
13–16 February, 1992	7–2–13–1	4–2–6–0	1–0–1–0					
v. New South Wales (Hobart)	18–5–46–1		28.3–4–89–6	11–3–21–3		1–0–5–0		
29 February–3 March, 1992								
v. Queensland (Brisbane)			18–3–53–5	9.2–2–42–3				
13–16 March, 1992			18–3–53–0	8–4–8–0				
	264.3–63–704–15 46.93	108–26–320–2 160.00	397.5–85–1123–50 22.46	186.2–49–515–19 27.10	96.3–18–332–4 83.00	35–9–71–1 71.00	11–2–14–0 –	3–2–4–0 –

M	Inns	NO	Runs	HS	Av
4	6	–	86	31	14.33
8	13	1	329	100	27.41
4	6	1	253	130	42.16
11	15	1	211	40	15.07
11	18	3	320	75	21.33
11	17	–	413	82	24.29
11	17	1	662	110	41.37
7	10	–	256	45	25.60
7	10	1	120	38	13.33
10	12	3	76	20*	8.44
4	5	2	27	15	9.00
3	2	1	10	9	10.00
8	14	–	354	106	25.28
3	6	–	40	16	6.66
8	12	2	321	69	32.10
5	8	4	15	5*	3.75
4	5	2	89	55*	29.66
1	1	–	19	19	19.00
1	1	1	33	33*	–

coming off the fourth ball of the last over. Their 506 was one run short of the record highest fourth-innings score to win a game.

A good spinner in operation and Queensland could not have lost this match. The imbalance in attack told dearly. Peter Taylor's spin was almost a non-event. People spoke of him as a liability as a Shield bowler, but an asset to the Australian limited-over squad. Paul Jackson is the spinner who might give the Queensland attack balance.

13, 14, 15 and 16 February, 1992 *at WACA Ground, Perth*

Queensland 207 (D.M. Wellham 83, J. Angel 4 for 46) and 287 (I.A. Healy 87 not out, T.M. Moody 4 for 61)
Western Australia 509 for 8 dec. (G.R. Marsh 88, M.P. Lavender 83, W.S. Andrews 67, D. Martyn 64, T.J. Zoehrer 57)

Western Australia won by an innings and 15 runs

Western Australia 6 pts., Queensland 0 pts.

FIELDING FIGURES

14 – J.M. Holyman (ct 13/st 1)
11 – M. Atkinson (ct 10/st 1)
7 – S. Young
6 – B.A. Cruse, R.J. Tucker and D.R. Gilbert
5 – D.J. Buckingham
4 – C.D. Matthews and M.G. Farrell
3 – D.C. Boon
2 – D. Hills and R.J. Bennett (plus two as sub)
1 – J. Cox, M. Divenuto, P.T. McPhee, D. Courtney, sub (Banks) and sub (Dykes)
†G.D. Campbell, absent hurt

P.T. McPhee	T.D. Bower	S. Young	M.G. Farrell	D. Hills	Byes	Leg-byes	Wides	No-balls	Total	Wkts
					2	9		22	434	8
					1	3		4	109	0
						10		6	414	10
									93	0
19–0–85–0					4	9	3	18	447	10
	30–6–78–1	16–5–31–0	4–2–9–1		1	5	1	8	331	0
	5–1–8–0	2–0–8–0	3–1–7–0						35	0
									0	0
	13–3–42–2	11.2–3–31–2			6	10	1	2	212	10
	21–10–37–3	19–8–27–2				2		10	200	10
	24–5–81–0	27–8–76–0			4	11	1	22	422	6
	13–3–31–0	23–8–49–1				5		6	200	10
	23–6–63–0	13–3–42–2			1	5	2	12	246	5
22–8–43–0		15–5–36–5				4	1	9	198	8
11–1–36–0		7–3–11–0			2			1	93	1
		22–4–77–2			2	9	2	10	325	10
		3–2–4–0		1–0–8–0					32	1
	6–2–14–0	7–2–18–0	3–1–15–0			9		10	217	10
16–2–71–2		5–1–13–0				3		18	182	10
13–4–52–0		12.1–4–29–1			1	2			145	1
81–15–287–2 143.50	135–36–354–6 59.00	182.3–56–452–15 30.13	10–4–31–1 31.00	1–0–8–0 –						

Shocked by their defeat in Adelaide, Queensland were routed by Western Australia in Perth, and the Westerners moved to the top of the Shield table. Queensland's main destroyer in the first innings was Joe Angel, a big man of pace with the devil in him.

Rain washed out the first day in Melbourne where Mark Taylor hit his first century against Victoria, so completing a hundred against each of New South Wales' five opposing states.

South Australia introduced a useful-looking pace bowler, Paul Hutchinson, in Hobart, and Blewett and Hilditch put on 168 for the first wicket, but South Australia's last six wickets went down for 35 runs.

VICTORIA

First-Class Matches 1991–92

BATTING

	v. Tasmania (Melbourne) 1–4 November, 1991		v. New South Wales (Sydney) 8–11 November, 1991		v. South Australia (Melbourne) 15–18 November, 1991		v. Queensland (Brisbane) 13–16 December, 1991	
G. Dowling	41	43*	5	10				
D.J. Ramshaw	14	58*	53	60	18	–	52	14
D.M. Jones	243*	–	68	144	214	–		
D.S. Lehmann	30	–	3	66	1	–	65	27*
S.P. O'Donnell	0	–	34	5	23	–		
G.J. Allardice	12	–	0	38*	37*	–	17	–
P.R. Reiffel	5	–	42*	29*	34	–	1	–
M.G. Hughes	12	–	8	–	0	–	27*	–
D.S. Berry	33	–	3	7	3	–	9*	–
S.K. Warne	11*	–	16	–	30*	–		
D.W. Fleming	–	–	7	–	–	–	–	–
W.N. Phillips					121	–	38	2
W.G. Ayres							115	28
G.R. Parker							1	10*
A.I.C. Dodemaide							23	–
P.C. Nobes								
J.A. Sutherland								
P.W. Jackson								
N.D. Maxwell								
D. Harris								
Byes	2	1	1	5			1	4
Leg-byes	9	3	10	3	10		12	2
Wides				1	1			
No-balls	22	4	10	26	22		14	2
Total	434	109	260	394	514		375	89
Wickets	8	0	10	6	8		8	3
Result	D		D		W		D	
Points	2		0		6		2	

FIELDING FIGURES

49 – D.S. Berry (ct 43/st 6)
12 – S.P. O'Donnell
11 – D.J. Ramshaw
9 – D.S. Lehmann
7 – P.C. Nobes
6 – D.M. Jones, W.N. Phillips and A.I.C. Dodemaide
4 – D.W. Fleming
2 – P.W. Jackson and N.D. Maxwell
1 – M.G. Hughes, P.R. Reiffel, G.R. Parker, S.K. Warne, J.A. Sutherland and W.G. Ayres

BOWLING	M.G. Hughes	D.W. Fleming	S.K. Warne	P.R. Reiffel	S.P. O'Donnell	D.M. Jones	D.S. Lehmann	A.I.C. Dodemaide
v. Tasmania (Melbourne) 1–4 November, 1991	32–5–80–1	32–7–82–0	47–14–75–4	28.1–8–61–2	20–5–50–2	8–5–11–0	3–2–1–0	
v. New South Wales (Sydney) 8–11 November, 1991	28–6–111–3	19–4–82–0	22–4–76–0	25–3–112–3	19.1–5–66–2			
v. South Australia (Melbourne) 15–18 November, 1991	33–8–73–3	17–6–35–0	25.3–3–67–3	28–9–44–4	5–0–14–0			
	21.1–6–32–4	14–3–35–1	17–6–43–0	22–5–54–4	18–4–73–1			
v. Queensland (Brisbane) 13–16 December, 1991	31–4–139–3	20.4–3–71–3		27–8–51–2			5–1–6–0	19–5–60–2
	9.3–0–34–2	10–2–43–0		12–3–38–0			18–4–62–0	12–2–40–0
v. Western Australia (Perth) 20–23 December, 1991	33.3–14–67–3	34–12–77–3				7–1–29–1	5–1–9–0	27–6–74–2
	20–4–76–3	19.3–5–55–3						12–3–28–2
v. Tasmania (Hobart) 17–20 January, 1992	30–11–38–3	20–6–48–0	14–7–26–2					35–18–34–5
	26–9–71–4	15–6–27–1	22–6–66–1		1–1–0–0			15–6–37–1
v. Western Australia (Melbourne) 24–27 January, 1992		33–7–100–1			25–7–68–1			37.1–12–81–2
		20–4–53–3			13–3–38–2			24–6–63–3
v. Pakistanis (Bendigo) 4–6 February, 1992		11–3–28–0			13–2–38–0			15–4–25–3
		6–1–12–0			12–4–26–1			16–7–30–3
v. New South Wales (Melbourne) 13–16 February, 1992	22.3–7–52–2		10–2–35–0	19–5–59–4	16–1–72–2			23–3–58–2
	9–0–55–0		20–8–78–1	10–0–37–0	2–0–19–0	2–0–7–1		21.5–1–69–4
v. South Australia (Adelaide) 21–24 February, 1992			35–15–67–1	28–5–92–1	13–7–23–0			30–15–55–2
			11–1–36–0	17–4–63–0	15–2–39–3			23–6–66–3
v. Queensland (Melbourne) 29 February–3 March, 1992				29–6–105–2	7–1–27–0			37–14–80–6
				4–0–24–0	12–4–40–1			13–2–58–3
Bowlers average	295.4–74–828–31–26.70	271.1–69–748–15 49.86	223.3–66–569–12 47.41	249.1–56–740–22 33.63	191.1–46–593–15 39.53	17–6–47–2 23.50	31–8–78–0 –	360–110–858–43 19.95

v. Western Australia (Perth) 20–23 December, 1991		v. Tasmania (Hobart) 17–20 January, 1992		v. Western Australia (Melbourne) 24–27 January, 1992		v. Pakistanis (Bendigo) 4–6 February, 1992		v. New South Wales (Melbourne) 13–16 February, 1992		v. South Australia (Adelaide) 21–24 February, 1992		v. Queensland (Melbourne) 29 February–3 March, 1992		M	Inns	NO	Runs	HS	Av
														2	4	1	99	43*	33.00
8	19*	28	19	9	19	39	35							8	15	2	445	60	34.23
204	11							54	–					5	7	1	938	243*	156.33
51	7*	18	34	148	23*	12	30	32	–	112	48	2	137*	11	19	4	846	148	56.40
31	–	0	1	8	–	9	13	45	–	87	23	27*	22	10	15	1	328	87	23.42
														4	5	2	104	38*	34.66
								6	–	27	–	1	1*	7	9	3	146	42*	24.33
7	–	0	–					23	–					7	7	1	77	27*	12.83
32	–	12	–	14	–	–	49	1	–	15	–	12	–	11	12	1	190	49	17.27
		10	–					10	–	14	–			6	6	2	91	30*	22.75
14	–	4*	–	0	–	–	14*							8	5	2	39	14*	13.00
		67	18	0	37			34	7*	30	23	123	4	7	13	1	504	123	42.00
70	–	38	100*	22	–	21	–	12	–	5	1	28	15	8	12	1	455	115	41.36
						28	2							2	4	1	41	28	13.66
16	–	3	58*	46	–	24*	4	32*	–	117*	–	0	–	8	10	4	318	117*	53.00
51	0	9	1	17	9*	53	0	61	3*	0	76*	103	21	7	14	3	404	103	36.72
6*	–			6	–									2	2	1	12	6*	12.00
				4*	–	–	2			20*	–	–	–	4	3	2	26	20*	26.00
						16*	12					20*	–	2	3	2	48	20*	48.00
										11	–	3	17	2	3	–	31	17	10.33
1			1	4		6	6		5		2	5	8						
3	1	5	5	6	1	4	5	12	1	17	1	10	4						
2	2		2					1	1	1		1							
4		6	12	24	6	5	8	15		6		16							
500	40	200	246	308	95	217	180	338	17	461	175	350	230						
10	2	10	5	10	2	6	9	10	0	9	4	8	5						
W		D		D		D		D		D		D							
6		2		0		–		2		2		2							

G.R. Parker	P.C. Nobes	W.N. Phillips	W.G. Ayres	G.J. Allardice	J.A. Sutherland	P.W. Jackson	N.D. Maxwell	Byes	Leg-byes	Wides	No-balls	Total	Wkts
								5	7		23	372	10
								3	9		18	459	10
									11		8	244	10
								3	6		10	246	10
7–1–41–0									6		2	374	10
		11–1–59–1	5–0–23–0	3–0–17–0				1	7		2	324	4
					22–8–64–1			1	9		4	330	10
					12–2–39–2				8	5		206	10
								6	5	2		157	10
									10	2		211	8
			26–5–71–2	21–6–69–3				2	6		6	397	10
			10–3–35–0	11–5–25–1				3	5		2	222	9
				15–4–51–2	18–4–50–4			1	1		4	194	9
				11–1–39–3	9–2–35–2			5	2	1	2	149	9
									4		12	280	10
									8		8	273	6
				32–12–61–2				8	10		6	316	7
				30–9–85–3				2	8		6	299	9
				20–9–32–1	22.1–6–42–1				9	1	32	295	10
	2–0–18–0			16–2–62–1	5–0–22–0				1		4	228	5
7–1–41–0 –	2–0–18–0 –	11–1–59–1 –	5–0–23–0 –	3–0–17–0 –	70–18–209–5 41.80	156–48–424–16 26.50	54.1–12–149–7 21.28						

WESTERN AUSTRALIA
First-Class Matches 1991–92

BATTING

	v. New South Wales (Perth) 1–4 November, 1991		v. South Australia (Adelaide) 22–25 November, 1991		v. Tasmania (Hobart) 29 November– 2 December, 1991		v. Victoria (Perth) 20–23 December, 1991		v. Tasmania (Perth) 10–13 January, 1992		v. Queensland (Brisbane) 17–20 January, 1992		v. Victoria (Melbourne) 24–27 January, 1992		v. Queensland (Perth) 13–16 February, 1992		v. South Australia (Perth) 28 February – 2 March, 1992		v. New South Wales (Sydney) 7–10 March, 1992		v. New South Wales (Perth) 28 March –	
M.J.R. Veletta	0	14	36	39	84	26*	8	7	11	64	27	–	99	0	46	–	121	–	1	101*	0	0
G.R. Marsh	53	98	1	104											88	–					30	0
M.P. Lavender	71	34	2	58	25	5*	33	13	41	172	11	–	10	6	83	–	10	–	6	0		
T.M. Moody	5	20	168	54*	5	–							56	23	21	–					78	1
D.R. Martyn	57	22	90	39*	110	–	60	21	13	24	75	–	20	105*	64	–	0	1*	2	21	41	57
W.S. Andrews	0	25*	6*	–	35	–	44	71	23	9	87	–	98	7	67	–	50	–	5	59	73	4
T.J. Zoehrer	58	23*	5*	–	36	–	5	13	19	36*	45	–	29	19	57	–	88	–	7	0	58	81
B. Julian	3	–	–	–	2	–	38*	4	0	5*	7	–	1	29	3	–	23	4*	10	3	54	13
M.J. McCague	18	–	–	–	3	–	34	3	10*	–			7	11			10	–				
J. Angel	7*	–									0	–	25*	0	13*	–	23	–	15*	12	11*	4
T.M. Alderman	5	–	–	–	14	–	1	5*	1	–	9	–	5	–	–	–	3*	–	0	0	6	0
B.A. Reid			–	–	1*	–									14*	–					0	1
G.M. Wood					1	–	15	32														
J. Langer							59	18	25	20	131	–	33	12			70	–	6	0	4	149
K.H. MacLeay							19	6														
M.W. McPhee									37	54	1	–					33	–	8	26		
P.A. Capes									8	–	15*	–										
S. Herzberg																			4	3		
Byes		6		4	1		1			4	5		2	3	5		7			3	4	4
Leg-byes	4	13	4	8	5		9	8	2	11	6		6	5	9		13		7	15	13	6
Wides	1				1			5		1	11				1		1	1		1	2	
No-balls	12	4	26		8	4	4		10	22	14		6	2	38		16			8	22	24
Total	294	259	338	306	331	35	330	206	200	422	444		397	222	509		468	6	71	252	396	344
Wickets	10	5	5	3	10	0	10	10	10	6	10		10	9	8		10	0	10	10	10	10
Result	D		W		W		L		D		D		D		W		W		L		W	
Points	0		6		6		0		0		2		2		6		6		0		–	

BOWLING

	T.M. Alderman	J. Angel	M.J. McCague	B. Julian	T.M. Moody	B.A. Reid	W.S. Andrews	T.J. Zoehrer
v. New South Wales	38.2–9–101–4	11–1–54–3	21–5–81–1	13–3–52–1	13–1–39–1			
(Perth) 1–4 November, 1991								
v. South Australia	28–6–69–0		19–2–74–0	14–0–56–1	14–3–48–1	34–8–112–2	12–1–32–1	22–3–58–5
(Adelaide) 22–25 November, 1991	6–3–12–1					6–1–16–0	13–2–55–3	18–3–79–2
v. Tasmania (Hobart)	16–3–34–0		17.3–6–47–2	16–6–26–5	12–6–12–1	15–6–22–1	1–1–0–0	7–1–22–0
29 November – 2 December, 1991			17–5–38–1	9–5–18–0	17–9–21–1	24–13–55–6	17–3–37–2	4–0–14–0
v. Victoria	26–9–62–1		32.5–5–106–2	36–10–119–3			12–3–49–0	32–10–86–4
(Perth) 20–23 December, 1991	7–0–24–0		5–2–10–1	2.3–1–5–1				
v. Tasmania	25–12–52–2		27–5–94–1	28–8–73–3			1–0–1–0	15–4–37–1
(Perth) 10–13 January, 1992	10–5–12–1		12–3–35–1					9–0–34–0
v. Queensland	23–9–51–5	24.4–6–60–3		20–6–41–0			11–2–27–2	
(Brisbane) 17–20 January, 1992	19–6–50–1	24–2–65–2		25–4–76–2			3–1–9–1	15–1–56–0
v. Victoria	33–10–79–3	15–3–57–0	22–9–44–4	1–1–0–0	24.4–11–42–3			22–6–69–0
(Melbourne) 24–27 January, 1992	6–2–18–0	8–2–18–1	3–0–16–0		3–0–10–0			9–3–26–1
v. Queensland	13–1–25–1	17–5–46–4		11.5–2–45–1	17–4–41–2	14–4–38–1		
(Perth) 13–16 February, 1992	7–2–26–0	23–4–78–2		21–9–40–2	30.4–13–61–4	24–9–40–2	3–0–22–0	2–0–7–0
v. South Australia	14–4–38–2	15.2–2–78–4	13–7–24–2	11–4–33–2			1–1–0–0	10–3–12–0
(Perth) 28 February – 2 March, 1992	15–7–37–1	24–5–97–4	23–5–65–2	15–3–50–2			2–0–4–1	9–6–12–0
v. New South Wales	21–7–45–2	16–5–41–2		16–3–54–2			5–2–15–0	12–2–30–0
(Sydney) 7–10 March, 1992	10–4–18–0	8–1–38–0		7–1–25–0				16–3–50–1
v. New South Wales	20–4–87–2	24.4–4–82–4		12–1–83–0	9–3–33–0	29–6–106–2	2–1–5–0	5–1–11–1
(Perth) 28 March – 1 April, 1992	19–1–73–3	13–0–73–2		4–2–13–0	5.2–1–19–1	24–6–61–3		10–1–38–0
	351.2–104–923–29 31.82	223.4–40–787–31 25.38	212.2–54–634–17 37.29	262.2–69–809–25 32.36	145.4–51–326–14 23.28	170–53–450–17 26.47	83–17–256–10 25.60	217–47–641–15 42.73

M	Inns	NO	Runs	HS	Av
11	19	2	684	121	40.23
4	7	–	374	104	53.42
10	17	1	580	172	36.25
6	10	1	431	168	47.88
11	19	3	822	110	51.37
11	17	2	663	98	44.20
11	17	3	579	88	41.35
11	16	3	199	54	15.30
7	8	1	96	34	13.71
7	10	5	110	25*	22.00
11	12	2	49	14	4.90
4	4	3	16	14*	16.00
2	3	–	48	32	16.00
7	12	–	527	149	43.91
1	2	–	25	19	12.50
4	6	–	159	54	26.50
2	2	1	23	15*	23.00
1	2	–	7	4	3.50

13, 14, 15 and 16 February, 1992 *at MCG, Melbourne*

New South Wales 280 (M.A. Taylor 158, P.R. Reiffel 4 for 59) and 273 for 6 dec. (M.E. Waugh 76, M.G. Bevan 70, M.A. Taylor 53, A.I.C. Dodemaide 4 for 69)
Victoria 338 (P.C. Nobes 61, D.M. Jones 54) and 17 for 0

Match drawn

Victoria 2 pts., New South Wales 0 pts.

at Bellerive Oval, Hobart

Tasmania 328 for 9 dec. (R.J. Tucker 75, D.J. Buckingham 71, P. Hutchinson 5 for 87) and 240 (D.J. Buckingham 82)
South Australia 325 (G.R. Blewett 86, A.M.J. Hilditch 76, J.A. Brayshaw 75, C.D. Matthews 4 for 89) and 32 for 1

Match drawn

Tasmania 2 pts., South Australia 0 pts.

FIELDING FIGURES

38 – T.J. Zoehrer
25 – M.J.R. Veletta
9 – W.S. Andrews and D.R. Martyn (ct 8/st 1)
8 – T.M. Alderman
6 – T.M. Moody and M.P. Lavender
5 – J. Langer
4 – M.J. McCague
3 – M.W. McPhee and B. Julian
2 – G.M. Wood and J. Angel
1 – G.R. Marsh, P.A. Capes, S. Herzberg and B.A. Reid

D.R. Martyn	K.H. MacLeay	P.A. Capes	M.W. McPhee	J. Langer	M.P. Lavender	S. Herzberg	Byes	Leg-byes	Wides	No-balls	Total	Wkts
								5	2	6	332	10
							6	5		18	460	10
5–0–13–0								5		2	180	6
							1	8	2		172	10
3–1–7–0								3		12	193	10
3–0–13–0	21–5–61–0						1	3	2	4	500	10
								1	2		40	2
5–2–11–0		27.3–5–72–3					6	12	6	8	358	10
7–2–15–0								3		2	99	2
4–2–10–0		20–4–73–0					5	8	2	8	275	10
3–0–10–1		22–4–61–0	1–0–12–0				11	5	1		355	8
2–1–7–0							4	6		24	308	10
				1–0–4–0	1–0–2–0		1			6	95	2
1–1–0–0								2		2	207	10
2–1–5–0								8	1	28	287	10
3–0–12–0								4		34	201	10
							2	3		16	270	10
3–0–15–1					13.1–2–33–3			12		8	245	10
					14–3–35–1		2	8	1	4	176	2
							4	4		24	415	10
								4		6	281	10
41–10–118–2 59.00	21–5–61–0 –	69.3–13–206–3 68.66	1–0–12–0 –	1–0–4–0 –	1–0–2–0 –	27.1–5–68–4 17.00						

21, 22, 23 and 24 February, 1992 *at Adelaide Oval*

Victoria 461 for 9 dec. (A.I.C. Dodemaide 117 not out, D.S. Lehmann 112, S.P. O'Donnell 87, P.R. Sleep 4 for 83) and 175 for 4 dec. (P.C. Nobes 76 not out)
South Australia 316 for 7 dec. (J.A. Brayshaw 101, A.M.J. Hilditch 63) and 299 for 9 (J.D. Siddons 65, J.C. Scuderi 57)

Match drawn

Victoria 2 pts., South Australia 0 pts.

Tony Dodemaide hit his first first-class hundred for Victoria and took five wickets in the match in Adelaide where South Australia narrowly escaped defeat.

28, 29 February, 1 and 2 March, 1992 *at WACA Ground, Perth*

South Australia 201 (J.A. Brayshaw 52, J. Angel 4 for 78) and 270 (J.A. Brayshaw 60, A.M.J. Hilditch 55, J. Angel 4 for 97)
Western Australia 468 (M.R.J. Veletta 121, T.J. Zoehrer 88, J.L. Langer 70, W.S. Andrews 50) and 6 for 0

Western Australia won by 10 wickets

Western Australia 6 pts., South Australia 0 pts.

29 February, 1, 2 and 3 March, 1992 *at Bellerive Oval, Hobart*

Tasmania 76 (W.J. Holdsworth 6 for 33) and 137
New South Wales 217 (M.G. Bevan 95, C.D. Matthews 6 for 89)

New South Wales won by an innings and 4 runs

New South Wales 6 pts., Tasmania 0 pts.

at MCG, Melbourne

Victoria 350 for 8 dec. (W.N. Phillips 123, P.C. Nobes 103, C.G. Rackemann 5 for 89) and 230 for 5 dec. (D.S. Lehmann 137 not out)
Queensland 295 (A.I.C. Dodemaide 6 for 80) and 228 for 5 (S.G. Law 82 not out)

Match drawn

Victoria 2 pts., Queensland 0 pts.

Western Australia confirmed their place in the final when they trounced South Australia. The match marked the end of David Hookes' career. He finished with a record 9,363 Shield runs from 120 games. His record cannot truly compare with that of Don Bradman or Peter Burge, but he has been a fabulous striker of the ball and deserves the accolades. He has delighted fans for years, hitting boldly, especially in Adelaide where the short, square boundaries suited his style. In Tests, he played only 23 times and failed to blossom, scoring just one century, against Sri Lanka.

New South Wales also kept alive their final hopes with victory in Tasmania. Wayne Holdsworth, a tearaway quick bowler with the Jeff Thomson attitude, 'move in and bowl flat out', wrecked Tasmania, taking 9 for 88 in the match. He bowls with genuine heart and

Farewell to David Hookes of South Australia, the leading run-scorer in Sheffield Shield history. (Allsport)

Daryl Foster, the master-mind of Western Australia cricket. (Tom Morris)

for 88 in the match. He bowls with genuine heart and with a desire to thrill team-mates and strike fear into the opposition. He tends to sling, but he slings mighty fast. When the rhythm is there and the mood is right Holdsworth is a threat to any batting line-up. Chris Matthews, too, bowled splendidly, but his batsmen let him down. Tasmania need a more balanced attack, and they could well turn to off-spinners Garry Goodman, the veteran, and the young and talented David Castle.

Phillips and Nobes began Victoria's innings with a partnership of 194, but the match against Queensland was drawn, and Victoria had slim hopes of reaching the final. For Queensland, the hopes now turn to their 100th anniversary summer, 1992–93. Consolation for the tough and talented Victoria side was that Tony Dodemaide became Sheffield Shield Player of the Year. Injury and loss of form have hampered him, but he is a very fine all-rounder and could now be on the threshold of great things.

7, 8, 9 and 10 March, 1992 *at SCG, Sydney*

New South Wales 245 (M. Haywood 79, M. Slater 62) and 176 for 2 dec. (S.M. Small 62 not out, M.G. Bevan 62 not out)
Western Australia 71 (D. Freedman 4 for 17, G.R.J. Matthews 4 for 30) and 252 (M.R.J. Veletta 101 not out, W.S. Andrews 59, G.R.J. Matthews 6 for 99)

New South Wales won by 98 runs

New South Wales 6 pts., Western Australia 0 pts.

New South Wales clinched their place in the final and owed much to the spin pairing of Matthews and Freedman. They needed to dismiss Western Australia for less than 130 in the second innings to host the final, but Mike Veletta thwarted them by carrying his bat through the 336-minute innings for his second century of the summer.

13, 14, 15 and 16 March, 1992 *at Woolloongabba, Brisbane*

Tasmania 400 for 6 dec. (D. Hills 106, S. Young 63, D.J. Buckingham 60)
Queensland 182 (D.M. Wellham 60, C.D. Matthews 5 for 53) and 145 for 1 (T.J. Barsby 85, M.L. Hayden 57 not out)

Match drawn

Tasmania 2 pts., Queensland 0 pts.

No play was possible on the last day of the last Shield match of the season, thwarting Tasmania of victory and a chance to climb off the bottom of the table. In Queensland's second innings, Hayden completed a thousand runs for the season.

SHEFFIELD SHIELD – FINAL TABLE

	P	W	L	D	Pts
Western Australia	10	4	2	4	28
New South Wales	10	4	3	3	28
Victoria	10	2	–	8	24
Queensland	10	2	3	5	16
South Australia	10	2	4	4	14
Tasmania	10	1	3	6	12

SHEFFIELD SHIELD FINAL
WESTERN AUSTRALIA v. NEW SOUTH WALES, at Perth

The hectic international programme told against the top sides, but Western Australia and New South Wales were the states with the necessary strength in depth. For much of the final, New South Wales seemed in control, but it was Justin Langer, with the highest score of his young career, and Tim Zoehrer who resurrected Western Australia's second innings when all looked lost. They added 191 after six wickets had fallen for 129. Then the Western Australian pace battery bowled their side to victory, capturing the last eight New South Wales wickets for 79 runs.

The victory was a triumph for coach Daryl Foster who knows the game thoroughly and knows how best to get his men to the right pitch, at the right time. He has worked with some great talent over the years, and he seems to have the balance right. A coach in cricket needs to understand that the game is tough enough to play when those who advise and guide keep it simple. Complicate the game of cricket, and it is damned near impossible to play.

Western Australia have worked tirelessly to such a point that these days the pendulum has swung right across the land, from Sydney to Perth. The benchmark for cricketing excellence is now in Western Australia; although New South Wales have only just been edged out by a small margin.

Sheffield Shield Player of the Year – Tony Dodemaide of Victoria. (David Munden)

One must feel sympathy for Geoff Lawson who would have loved to have ended his career by winning the Sheffield Shield. It was not to be. His captaincy will be missed. He has been a credit to the game and easily the most innovative of captains in first-class cricket in Australia for the past few years.

SHEFFIELD SHIELD FINAL – WESTERN AUSTRALIA v. NEW SOUTH WALES
28, 29, 30, 31 March, 1 April, 1992 at WACA Ground, Perth

WESTERN AUSTRALIA

	FIRST INNINGS		SECOND INNINGS	
G.R. Marsh (capt)	c Small, **b** Lawson	30	(2) c Emery, **b** Lawson	0
M.R.J. Veletta	c Matthews, **b** Whitney	0	(1) c Emery, **b** Whitney	0
J. Langer	c Matthews, **b** Lawson	4	(7) c M.E. Waugh, **b** Whitney	149
T.M. Moody	run out	78	(3) c Small, **b** Lawson	1
D.R. Martyn	c Emery, **b** S.R. Waugh	41	(4) c Bevan, **b** Holdsworth	57
W.S. Andrews	**b** Holdsworth	73	(6) lbw, **b** Whitney	4
*T.J. Zoehrer	c Emery, **b** Whitney	58	(8) c Matthews, **b** Whitney	81
B. Julian	**b** Matthews	54	(9) **b** Whitney	13
J. Angel	not out	11	(5) c Matthews, **b** Whitney	4
T.M. Alderman	**b** Matthews	6	c Emery, **b** Whitney	0
B.A. Reid	**b** Matthews	0	not out	1
Extras	b 4, lb 13, w 2, nb 22	41	b 4, lb 6, nb 24	34
		396		**344**

NEW SOUTH WALES

	FIRST INNINGS		SECOND INNINGS	
S.M. Small	c Veletta, **b** Angel	10	c Zoehrer, **b** Angel	98
M.A. Taylor	c Zoehrer, **b** Reid	16	lbw, **b** Alderman	9
S.R. Waugh	c Andrews, **b** Reid	113	c Veletta, **b** Reid	68
M.E. Waugh	c Reid, **b** Zoehrer	163	c Andrews, **b** Angel	19
M.G. Bevan	c Zoehrer, **b** Angel	0	run out	20
G.R.J. Matthews	c Zoehrer, **b** Alderman	42	c Veletta, **b** Alderman	13
*P.A. Emery	run out	30	c Veletta, **b** Alderman	0
D. Freedman	not out	6	c Moody, **b** Reid	1
G.F. Lawson (capt)	c Langer, **b** Alderman	1	c Moody, **b** Reid	4
W.J. Holdsworth	**b** Angel	0	not out	31
M.R. Whitney	c Veletta, **b** Angel	2	c Veletta, **b** Moody	8
Extras	b 4, lb 4, nb 24	32	lb 4, nb 6	10
		415		**281**

	O	M	R	W	O	M	R	W
Whitney	26	5	71	2	23.4	6	75	7
Holdsworth	25	4	96	1	17	3	53	1
Lawson	30	10	84	2	16	3	66	2
S.R. Waugh	16	6	36	1	4	–	26	–
Matthews	18.4	5	49	3	20	3	67	–
Freedman	5	–	19	–	7	–	25	–
M.E. Waugh	3	–	24	–	4	1	22	–

	O	M	R	W	O	M	R	W
Angel	24.4	4	82	4	13	–	73	2
Alderman	20	4	87	2	19	1	73	3
Reid	29	6	106	2	24	6	61	3
Moody	9	3	33	–	5.2	1	19	1
Andrews	2	1	5	–				
Julian	12	1	83	–	4	2	13	–
Zoehrer	5	1	11	1	10	1	38	–

FALL OF WICKETS
1–1, **2**–36, **3**–58, **4**–160, **5**–180, **6**–295, **7**–360, **8**–382, **9**–388
1–0, **2**–3, **3**–3, **4**–94, **5**–105, **6**–129, **7**–320, **8**–331, **9**–331

FALL OF WICKETS
1–16, **2**–56, **3**–260, **4**–271, **5**–350, **6**–400, **7**–404, **8**–410, **9**–413
1–39, **2**–157, **3**–202, **4**–210, **5**–225, **6**–225, **7**–226, **8**–236, **9**–255

Umpires: A.R. Crafter & T.A. Prue

Western Australia won by 44 runs

A credit to the game which he now leaves – Geoff Lawson. (Allsport)

FIRST-CLASS AVERAGES

BATTING

	M	Inns	NO	Runs	HS	Av	100s	50s
D.M. Jones	10	15	2	1248	243*	96.00	5	3
D.C. Boon	10	16	2	819	135	58.50	4	1
D.M. Wellham	10	18	3	873	167	58.20	2	6
A.R. Border	11	19	6	747	196	57.46	1	4
D.S. Lehmann	11	19	4	846	148	56.40	3	3
T.M. Moody	8	13	1	652	168	54.33	2	5
M.L. Hayden	11	21	2	1028	149	54.10	3	5
A.I.C. Dodemaide	8	10	4	318	117*	53.00	1	1
D.R. Martyn	11	19	3	822	110	51.37	2	6
M.E. Waugh	12	18	–	924	163	51.33	3	4
P.R. Sleep	6	10	4	300	97*	50.00	–	2
G.M. Ritchie	11	19	3	748	137	46.75	2	3
J.D. Siddons	9	14	–	650	149	46.42	2	3
A.M.J. Hilditch	10	17	1	721	137	45.06	2	5
W.S. Andrews	11	17	2	663	98	44.20	–	7
J. Langer	7	12	–	527	149	43.91	2	2
J.A. Brayshaw	7	12	–	516	101	43.00	1	4
S.R. Waugh	8	11	–	472	115	42.90	2	2
T.J. Barsby	11	21	1	848	165	42.40	1	4
D.J. Buckingham	11	17	1	662	110	41.37	1	5
W.G. Ayres	8	12	1	455	115	41.36	2	1
T.J. Zoehrer	11	17	3	579	88	41.35	–	5
M.R.J. Veletta	11	19	2	684	121	40.23	2	3
M.A. Taylor	14	24	1	925	158	40.21	2	7
G.R.J. Matthews	12	17	2	603	139	40.20	1	3
G.R. Marsh	8	15	1	559	104	39.92	1	4
J.C. Scuderi	9	14	1	502	125*	38.61	2	1
W.N. Phillips	9	16	1	577	123	38.46	2	2
I.A. Healy	11	15	2	485	87*	37.30	–	3
M.G. Bevan	12	17	1	588	115	36.75	1	5
P.C. Nobes	7	14	3	404	103	36.72	1	4
M.P. Lavender	10	17	1	580	172	36.25	1	3
G.R. Blewett	10	18	2	571	98	35.68	–	5
G.J. Allardice	4	5	2	104	38*	34.66	–	–
D.J. Ramshaw	8	15	2	445	60	34.23	–	4
T.J. Nielsen	10	18	5	420	88	32.30	–	2
S. Young	8	12	2	321	69	32.10	–	3
D.W. Hookes	10	17	–	530	156	31.17	1	2
S.M. Small	12	18	1	511	98	30.05	–	5
G.A. Bishop	5	9	–	270	64	30.00	–	1
T.H. Bayliss	10	15	–	429	133	28.60	1	2
S.G. Law	11	18	2	446	82*	27.87	–	3
B.A. Cruse	8	13	1	329	100	27.41	1	1
M.W. McPhee	4	6	–	159	54	26.50	–	1
G.A. Hughes	7	10	–	256	45	25.60	–	–
D. Hills	8	14	–	354	106	25.28	1	–
P.R. Reiffel	9	11	3	199	44	24.87	–	–
P.J.T. Goggin	6	10	–	247	91	24.70	–	1
J. Cox	11	17	–	413	82	24.29	–	2
B.E. McNamara	6	8	–	192	80	24.00	–	1
S.P. O'Donnell	10	15	1	328	87	23.42	–	1
J. Angel	7	10	5	110	25*	22.00	–	–
R.J. Tucker	11	18	3	320	75	21.33	–	2
P.W. Anderson	6	9	1	160	52	20.00	–	1
C.D. Matthews	12	16	1	274	63	18.26	–	1
D.S. Berry	11	12	1	190	49	17.27	–	–
S.K. Warne	9	11	4	120	30*	17.14	–	–
P.A Emery	12	17	3	236	37*	16.85	–	–
M.G. Hughes	12	15	1	231	36	16.50	–	–
T.B.A. May	9	12	2	155	43	15.50	–	–
B. Julian	11	16	3	199	54	15.30	–	1
P.L. Taylor	8	9	–	134	31	14.88	–	–
C.J. McDermott	10	12	2	136	31	13.60	–	–
J.M. Holyman	7	10	1	120	38	13.33	–	–
G.J. Rowell	10	12	4	101	45*	12.62	–	–
G.F. Lawson	11	14	2	129	28	10.75	–	–

(Qualification – 100 runs, average 10.00)

BOWLING

	Overs	Mds	Runs	Wkts	Av	Best	10/m	5/inn
D. Freedman	147.2	35	409	22	18.59	4-17	–	–
A.I.C. Dodemaide	360	110	858	43	19.95	6-80	–	2
C.J. McDermott	441.2	105	1248	60	20.80	6-58	2	6
B.A. Reid	261.2	76	697	33	21.12	6-55	1	2
G.R.J. Matthews	482.4	153	1116	52	21.46	6-63	2	4
M.R. Whitney	391.5	84	1122	52	21.57	7-27	1	3
C.D. Matthews	498.5	87	1182	53	22.30	6-89	–	6
T.M. Moody	148.4	52	341	14	24.35	4-61	–	–
M.G. Hughes	495.1	120	1839	53	25.26	4-32	–	–
J. Angel	223.4	40	787	31	25.38	4-46	–	–
W.S. Andrews	83	17	256	10	25.60	3-55	–	–
P.W. Jackson	156	48	424	16	26.50	3-39	–	–
R.J. Tucker	186.2	49	515	19	27.10	3-21	–	–
S.R. Waugh	125	35	342	12	28.50	3-23	–	–
P. Hutchinson	107.4	20	346	12	28.83	5-87	–	1
S. Young	182.3	56	452	15	30.13	5-36	–	1
C.G. Rackemann	395.1	100	1043	34	30.67	5-89	–	1
P.R. Sleep	123.3	29	371	12	30.91	4-83	–	–
G.J. Rowell	372.5	77	1099	35	31.40	7-46	1	2
P.R. Reiffel	304.1	67	915	29	31.55	4-44	–	–
W.J. Holdsworth	341.2	68	1201	38	31.60	6-33	–	1
T.M. Alderman	351.2	104	923	29	31.82	5-51	–	1
B. Julian	262.2	69	809	25	32.36	5-26	–	1
M.J. McCague	212.2	54	634	17	37.29	4-44	–	–
J.C. Scuderi	403.2	114	1053	28	37.60	7-79	1	1
G.F. Lawson	293.1	87	690	18	38.33	3-33	–	–
S.P. O'Donnell	191.1	46	593	15	39.53	3-39	–	–
S.K. Warne	312	82	853	20	42.65	4-42	–	–
T.J. Zoehrer	217	47	641	15	42.73	5-58	–	1
S. Williams	130.3	27	451	10	45.10	2-37	–	–
D.R. Gilbert	264.3	63	704	15	46.93	4-88	–	–
B. Oxenford	185.5	29	697	14	49.78	5-91	–	1
D.W. Fleming	271.1	69	748	15	49.86	3-53	–	–
D.J. Hickey	305.4	41	1234	22	56.09	4-96	–	–
T.B.A. May	424.3	104	1222	17	71.88	3-48	–	–

(Qualification – 10 wickets)

LEADING FIELDERS

49 – D.S. Berry (ct 43/st 6); 44 – I.A. Healy (ct 43/st 1); 38 – T.J. Zoehrer; 34 – P.A. Emery (ct 32/st 2); 30 – T.J. Nielsen (ct 28/st 2); 25 – M.R.J. Veletta; 24 – M.A. Taylor; 19 – M.E. Waugh and S.M. Small; 18 – P.W. Anderson (ct 16/st 2); 16 – G.R.J. Matthews; 14 – J.M. Holyman (ct 13/st 1); 13 – A.R. Border; 12 – S.P. O'Donnell; 11 – D.M. Jones, D.C. Boon, D.J. Ramshaw and M. Atkinson (ct 10/st 1); 10 – T.M. Moody and J.D. Siddons

SECTION

C

NEW ZEALAND

Shell Cup
Shell Shield
England tour, Test match series
and One-Day International series
Form Charts
First-Class Averages

Jeff Crowe – 1063 runs, average 62.52 – only the sixth batsman in history to score a thousand runs in a New Zealand season. (Sporting Pictures (UK) Ltd)

SHELL CUP

15 December, 1991 *at Basin Reserve, Wellington*

Wellington 204 for 9 (M.D. Crowe 86, P.S. Briasco 4 for 31)
Central Districts 208 for 5 (M.J. Greatbatch 78 not out, T.E. Blain 52 not out)

Central Districts (2 pts.) won by 5 wickets

at Carisbrook, Dunedin

Canterbury 239 for 5 (C.L. Cairns 62, P.G. Kennedy 57)
Otago 176 (M.H. Austen 65)

Canterbury (2 pts.) won by 63 runs

at Eden Park, Auckland

Auckland 265 for 3 (J.J. Crowe 130 not out, S.W. Brown 63)
Northern Districts 162 (M.N. Hart 52 not out, S.W. Brown 5 for 23)

Auckland (2 pts.) won by 103 runs

New Zealand's 50-over competition was compacted into the period of one month over Christmas and the New Year. Test cricketers took the individual honours in the first round of matches. Greatbatch and Blain shared an unbroken stand of 81 to take Central to victory. Blain's 52 came off 40 balls. Jeff Crowe heralded a superb season with 130 off 142 balls, and shared a second-wicket stand of 154 with Stephen Brown who had an outstanding match with bat and ball.

22 December, 1991 *at Eden Park, Auckland*

Auckland 164 (J.T.C. Vaughan 63)
Wellington 122

Auckland (2 pts.) won by 42 runs

27 December, 1991 *at Basin Reserve, Wellington*

Canterbury 219 for 9
Wellington 222 for 6 (J.D. Wells 58 not out)

Wellington (2 pts.) won by 4 wickets

at Molyneux Park, Alexandra

Auckland 233 for 4 (J.J. Crowe 86 not out, J.T.C. Vaughan 72)
Otago 110 (J.T.C. Vaughan 4 for 28)

Auckland (2 pts.) won by 123 runs

at Blake Park, Mt Maunganui

Central Districts 193 for 9 (R.G. Twose 72)
Northern Districts 120 (R.G. Twose 4 for 34)

Central Districts (2 pts.) won by 73 runs

The inspiring form of skipper Jeff Crowe and all-rounder Justin Vaughan brought Auckland three wins in as many matches and assured them of a place in the semi-finals. Warwickshire all-rounder Roger Twose won the individual award in the match at Blake Park.

29 December, 1991 *at Blake Park, Mt Maunganui*

Northern Districts 202 for 6
Wellington 203 for 7 (A.H. Jones 74, G.P. Burnett 67)

Wellington (2 pts.) won by 3 wickets

at Levin Domain, Levin

Central Districts 156
Otago 157 for 7 (M.J. Pawson 4 for 21)

Otago (2 pts.) won by 3 wickets

at Lancaster Park, Christchurch

Auckland v. Canterbury

Match abandoned

Auckland 1 pt., Canterbury 1 pt.

Andrew Jones and Graham Burnett put on 138 for Wellington's second wicket after Reid had fallen for 0. The win enhanced Wellington's chances of reaching the semi-finals.

1 January, 1992 *at Lancaster Park, Christchurch*

Northern Districts 178
Canterbury 181 for 3 (B.R. Hartland 103 not out)

Canterbury (2 pts.) won by 7 wickets

at Eden Park, Auckland

Auckland v. Central Districts

Match abandoned

Auckland 1 pt., Central Districts 1 pt.

at Basin Reserve, Wellington

Wellington v. Otago

Match abandoned

Wellington 1 pt., Otago 1 pt.

2 January, 1992 *at Pukekura Park, New Plymouth*

Central Districts 130 for 8
Canterbury 134 for 2 (B.R. Hartland 65 not out)

Canterbury (2 pts.) won by 8 wickets

4 January, 1992 *at Molyneux Park, Alexandra*

Northern Districts 212 (K.A. Wealleans 77, M.D. Bailey 75, A.J. Gale 5 for 43)
Otago 216 for 3 (K.R. Rutherford 115 not out)

Otago (2 pts.) won by 7 wickets

Two fine innings from Blair Hartland took Canterbury into the semi-finals. He hit his first century in the competition, against Northern Districts, his 103 not out coming off 111 balls, and he followed this with 65 not out off 118 balls against Central Districts. Rutherford's century against Northern failed to take his side into the semi-finals.

SHELL CUP FINAL TABLE

	P	W	L	Ab	Pts
Auckland	5	3	–	2	8
Canterbury	5	3	1	1	7
Central Districts	5	2	2	1	5
Wellington	5	2	2	1	5
Otago	5	2	2	1	5
Northern Districts	5	–	5	–	0

(Wellington and Central Districts qualified above Otago because of a higher average of runs)

SEMI-FINALS

8 January, 1992 *at Eden Park, Auckland*

Auckland 170 for 8
Wellington 171 for 5 (G.P. Burnett 78, A.H. Jones 51)
Wellington won by 5 wickets

at Lancaster Park, Christchurch

Canterbury 242 for 7 (R.T. Latham 80, P.G. Kennedy 56 not out)
Central Districts 111
Canterbury won by 131 runs

Wellington gained a surprise win over the hitherto unbeaten Auckland side who found run-getting difficult on a sluggish pitch. Only a late 38 not out off 35 balls from Chris Pringle took Auckland to a total that offered any challenge. Jones and Burnett added 117 after Martin Crowe and Reid had gone for ten, and Wellington won with nine balls to spare.

Emerging star Rod Latham played a significant part in Canterbury's victory in the Shell Cup final. (Joe Mann/Allsport)

SHELL CUP FINAL
CANTERBURY v. WELLINGTON, at Christchurch

Hartland and Latham began Canterbury's innings with a partnership of 110. Three wickets fell at that total, but Kennedy hit three sixes in his 56 off 48 balls, and Canterbury reached a formidable 242. Central Districts were never in contention.

Given full coverage by New Zealand television, the Shell Cup final produced what all commentators agreed was the most exciting match of the season. Lee Germon, Canterbury's 23-year-old skipper, won the toss and elected to bat first. His openers responded magnificently, putting on 93 in 13 overs before a very lively crowd numbering in excess of 10,000. To add to Wellington's woes, captain Gavin Larsen was injured in the fifth over and had to have eight stitches in a deep cut in the webbing of his left hand.

Wellington's bowling tightened, but Howell, Cairns, Kennedy and Petrie all hit hard to take Canterbury to a demanding 252. There seemed little hope for Wellington until Andrew Jones played a doughty innings of 67 off 99 balls. Stirling gave him excellent support in a stand of 52 but, at 195 for 7, Wellington looked beaten. Williams, 26 off 24 balls, thought otherwise, and he and Lincoln Doull added 49. Doull hit Petrie for six, and only nine runs were needed from ten balls. Doull got over-ambitious and was bowled as he attempted another six. Sears was soon out, and this brought Larsen to the wicket.

The Wellington captain was only to bat in an emergency, and now he found himself at the wicket with six runs needed from five deliveries. Unable to use his heavily bandaged left hand, he held the bat in his right hand and attempted to bat one-handed in a

One of New Zealand's main hopes for the future, all-rounder Chris Cairns, a cricketer of great enterprise. (Allsport)

SHELL CUP FINAL – CANTERBURY v. WELLINGTON
14 January, 1992 at Lancaster Park, Christchurch

CANTERBURY		
B.R. Hartland	run out	46
R.T. Latham	c McSweeney, b Stirling	38
L.G. Howell	c Stirling, b Jones	62
C.Z. Harris	c and b Jones	11
C.L. Cairns	c Wells, b Doull	24
P.G. Kennedy	b Sears	33
*L.K. Germon (capt)	b Sears	3
M.W. Priest	b Doull	3
R.G. Petrie	run out	16
N.J. Astle	c McSweeney, b Sears	1
M.B. Owens	not out	0
Extras	b 1, lb 8, w 5, nb 1	15
	(49.4 overs)	252

	O	M	R	W
Stirling	6	–	49	1
Sears	8.4	–	38	3
Doull	10	–	61	2
Jones	10	–	32	2
Williams	10	–	33	–
Crowe	5	–	30	–

FALL OF WICKETS
1–93, 2–99, 3–122, 4–186, 5–210, 6–216, 7–227, 8–251, 9–252

WELLINGTON		
M.D. Crowe	b Petrie	29
R.B. Reid	c Kennedy, b Owens	9
G.P. Burnett	b Priest	26
A.H. Jones	st Germon, b Astle	67
J.D. Wells	st Germon, b Priest	20
* E.B. McSweeney	b Owens	7
D.A. Stirling	c Hartland, b Astle	29
B.R. Williams	not out	26
L.J. Doull	b Petrie	17
M.J. Sears	b Cairns	2
G.R. Larsen (capt)	b Cairns	1
Extras	b 4, lb 5, w 7	16
	(49.4 overs)	249

	O	M	R	W
Petrie	10	1	72	2
Owens	10	1	51	2
Cairns	9.4	–	37	2
Priest	10	–	35	2
Astle	10	–	45	2

FALL OF WICKETS
1–27, 2–43, 3–79, 4–127, 5–142, 6–194, 7–195, 8–244, 9–247

Umpires: B.L. Aldridge & S.J. Woodward — Man of the Match – A.H. Jones — *Canterbury won by 3 runs*

left-handed stance. He squeezed a single from the first ball, but Williams could only manage a single from the next, and the fourth ball of the final over shattered Larsen's stumps. A courageous effort had failed, and Canterbury took the Cup for the first time in six years.

SHELL TROPHY

29, 30 November and 1 December, 1991 *at Queen Elizabeth Park, Masterton*

Northern Districts 172 (S.A. Thomson 51, S.W. Duff 4 for 13) and 238 for 6 dec. (B.A. Young 86 not out, K.A. Wealleans 58)
Central Districts 173 for 6 dec. and 238 for 6 (M.J. Greatbatch 81, R.G. Twose 79)

Central Districts won by 4 wickets

Central Districts 16 pts., Northern Districts 0 pts.

at Eden Park, Auckland

Otago 254 (K.R. Rutherford 79, M.H. Austen 73, S.W. Brown 5 for 57) and 289 (R.N. Hoskin 61, J.T.C. Vaughan 5 for 72)

Ervin McSweeney, veteran Wellington wicket-keeper, hit a century in the first first-class match of the season against Canterbury for whom Blair Hartland also hit a hundred. (David Munden).

Auckland 264 for 5 dec. (D.N. Patel 56 not out, S.W. Brown 56) and 283 for 5 (J.J. Crowe 102, S.W. Brown 62, D.N. Patel 51)

Auckland won by 5 wickets

Auckland 16 pts., Otago 0 pts.

at Lancaster Park, Christchurch

Wellington 286 (G.P. Burnett 63, E.B. McSweeney 63, D.A. Stirling 56 not out) and 266 (E.B. McSweeney 119, D.A. Stirling 70, R.M. Ford 6 for 35)
Canterbury 304 for 7 dec. (B.R. Hartland 127, R.T. Latham 50, G.R. Larsen 6 for 64) and 58 for 1

Match drawn

Canterbury 4 pts., Wellington 0 pts.

One of the earliest starts to a season in New Zealand cricket history saw Central Districts overcome the loss of the first day's play to beat Northern, although they were aided by White's generous declaration. The first century of the season was scored by Ervin McSweeney, now nearing the veteran stage, while Jeff Crowe's 137-ball century helped Auckland to victory over Otago.

6, 7 and 8 December, 1991 *at Basin Reserve, Wellington*

Auckland 173 (J.P. Millmow 5 for 49) and 291 for 7 dec. (J.G. Wright 100)
Wellington 125 and 340 for 5 (A.H. Jones 103, J.D. Wells 102, R.B. Reid 56)

Wellington won by 5 wickets

Wellington 12 pts., Auckland 4 pts.

at Burnside Park, Christchurch

Central Districts 134 (C.L. Cairns 4 for 28) and 178 (T.E. Blain 63, C.L. Cairns 4 for 38)
Canterbury 124 (D.J. Leonard 6 for 67) and 189 for 7 (R.T. Latham 62, B.R. Hartland 59, S.W. Duff 4 for 34)

Canterbury won by 3 wickets

Canterbury 12 pts., Central Districts 4 pts.

at Trust Bank, Hamilton

Otago 212 (R.L. Hayes 4 for 60) and 177 (M.H. Austen 56, R.P. de Groen 4 for 40)
Northern Districts 284 for 4 dec. (M.P. Maynard 142, S.A. Thomson 79 not out) and 106 for 2 (G.E. Bradburn 63 not out)

Northern Districts won by 8 wickets

Northern Districts 16 pts., Otago 0 pts.

Trailing by 48 on the first innings and punished by the 57th century of John Wright's career, Wellington seemed doomed to defeat against Auckland, but a remarkable second-wicket partnership of 168 between Jones and Wells changed the course of the match and brought the home side victory. The 21-year-old Jason Wells hit the first century of his career. Canterbury, too, recovered to win a low-scoring game in Christchurch while Matthew Maynard hit 142 off as many deliveries in Northern's win over Otago.

12, 13 and 14 December, 1991 *at Basin Reserve, Wellington*

Wellington 88 and 256 (J.D. Wells 86, A.H. Jones 53)
Central Districts 136 (M.J. Sears 6 for 48) and 212 for 3 (R.G. Twose 107 not out)

Central Districts won by 7 wickets

Central Districts 16 pts., Wellington 0 pts.

at Eden Park, Auckland

Auckland 244 (A.J. Hunt 68) and 424 for 4 dec. (D.N. Patel 204, J.J. Crowe 142 not out)
Nothern Districts 284 (M.P. Maynard 195, D.N. Patel 6 for 117) and 335 for 8 (M.P. Maynard 110, B.A. Young 82, D.N. Patel 4 for 116)

Match drawn

Northern Districts 4 pts., Auckland 0 pts.

at Centennial Park, Oamaru

Otago 350 for 7 dec. (K.R. Rutherford 133, R.N. Hoskin 53) and 198 for 7 dec. (M.J. Lamont 60)
Canterbury 295 for 9 dec. (C.Z. Harris 94 not out,

Matthew Maynard of Glamorgan enjoyed a spectacular season for Northern Districts. (Adrian Murrell/Allsport)

D.J. Boyle 84, R.T. Latham 68, J.K. Lindsay 5 for 72) and 257 for 5 (R.T. Latham 87, C.Z. Harris 65, N.A. Mallender 4 for 28)

Canterbury won by 5 wickets

Canterbury 12 pts., Otago 4 pts.

The inconsistent Wellington were well beaten at Basin Reserve where 15 wickets fell on the first day. Central's hero was the left-handed Roger Twose who hit the first century of his career. Canterbury came from behind to beat Otago who thus suffered their third defeat in as many matches. The main focus was on the game at Eden Park where Matthew Maynard hit 195 off 188 balls, with seven sixes and 24 fours. This was somewhat overshadowed by an astonishing innings from Dipak Patel who hit 204 off 155 deliveries in 163 minutes. He hit 12 sixes and 17 fours in an astonishing display and added 280 for the fourth wicket with Jeff Crowe. Patel had taken six wickets in the first innings and he now proceeded to take four more while Maynard hit his second century of the match, scoring 110 off 113 balls. Patel, who had never before reached 200, became the first player to hit a double century and take ten wickets in the same match in New Zealand. Maynard's feats were no less amazing, for Northern were 88 for 8 in their first innings before he and Simon Doull added 195 in 132 minutes. Doull made 44.

2, 3 and 5 January, 1992 *at Molyneux Park, Alexandra*

Northern Districts 266 (M.D. Bailey 60, K.A. Wealleans 56, N.A. Mallender 6 for 52) and 153 (J.W. Wilson 5 for 48)
Otago 203 (R.N. Hoskin 52, D.F. Potter 5 for 69) and 192 (K.R. Rutherford 55)

Northern Districts won by 24 runs

Northern Districts 16 pts., Otago 0 pts.

3, 4 and 5 January, 1992 *at Eden Park, Auckland*

Wellington 201 (E.J. Gray 51) and 199 (R.B. Reid 64, D.N. Patel 7 for 72)
Auckland 258 (J.J. Crowe 118, D.N. Patel 60, H.T. Davis 5 for 63) and 145 for 5

Auckland won by 5 wickets

Auckland 16 pts., Wellington 0 pts.

at Pukekura Park, New Plymouth

Central Districts 269 (M.W. Douglas 144, C.L. Cairns 4 for 66, R.G. Petrie 4 for 91) and 171 (C.D. Ingham 50, C.L. Cairns 7 for 34)
Canterbury 374 (R.G. Petrie 100, R.T. Latham 84, D.N. Askew 4 for 70) and 68 for 4

Canterbury won by 6 wickets

Canterbury 16 pts., Central Districts 0 pts.

Otago suffered their fourth defeat in a row while the success of Patel continued. He had match figures of 9 for 124 in Auckland's victory over Wellington and hit 60 off 73 balls. Significantly, there was also another century for skipper Jeff Crowe. There was a maiden first-class century for left-hander Mark Douglas of Central districts, but he was upstaged by Richard Petrie of Canterbury who went in as night-watchman and hit a century, having never before reached 50. Chris Cairns then produced the best bowling figures of his career to set up Canterbury's victory.

10, 11 and 12 January, 1992 *at Basin Reserve, Wellington*

Northern Districts 258 (K.A. Wealleans 108, B.A. Young 59, M.J. Sears 4 for 56) and 265 for 5 dec. (M.D. Bailey 77 not out, M.N. Hart 65 not out, M.P. Maynard 53)
Wellington 204 (D.A. Stirling 50, M.N. Hart 5 for 45) and 300 for 8 (R.B. Reid 84, R.A. Verry 76)

Match drawn

Northern Districts 4 pts., Wellington 0 pts.

at Carisbrook, Dunedin

Otago 305 for 8 dec. (R.N. Hoskin 80, K.R. Rutherford 64, D.N. Askew 4 for 88) and 168 for 7 dec.
Central Districts 159 (N.A. Mallender 7 for 39) and 211 for 9 (P.S. Briasco 56, N.A. Mallender 4 for 50)

Match drawn

Otago 4 pts., Central Districts 0 pts.

at Lancaster Park, Christchurch

Auckland 428 for 7 dec. (J.J. Crowe 128, A.P. O'Dowd 113, A.C. Parore 54 not out)
Canterbury 431 for 7 dec. (L.G. Howell 112, M.W. Priest 89, B.R. Hartland 89, P.G. Kennedy 74)

Match drawn

Canterbury 4 pts., Auckland 0 pts.

Wellington came very close to scoring the 320 in 342 minutes that they needed to beat Northern Districts, but they failed nobly. Central Districts' last pair, Askew and Auckram, denied Otago at Dunedin. Somerset's Neil Mallender continued to carry the Otago attack on his shoulders and bowled superbly. There was a run feast in Auckland where Jeff Crowe hit his fourth century in five matches and O'Dowd the first of his career. There was also a maiden first-class century for Lorne Howell.

16, 17 and 18 January, 1992 *at Trust Bank Park, Hamilton*

Central Districts 288 for 6 (S.W.J. Wilson 81, R.K. Brown 60 not out, T.E. Blain 59)
v. Northern Districts

Match abandoned

Central Districts 2 pts., Northern Districts 2 pts.

OPPOSITE: *Tony Blain – elegant behind the stumps and with the bat for Central Districts. (Adrian Murrell/Allsport)*

at Carisbrook, Dunedin

Auckland 127 (A.C. Parore 57 not out, J.W. Wilson 5 for 50) and 402 for 5 dec. (A.C. Parore 155 not out, A.P. O'Dowd 75 not out, B.A. Pocock 71)
Otago 301 and 135 for 7 (M.H. Austen 56, S.A. Robinson 53, R.J. Drown 4 for 6)

Match drawn

Otago 4 pts., Auckland 0 pts.

Adam Parore hit the first century of his career, 155 off 183 balls with 25 fours, in Auckland's drawn match with Otago.

20, 21 and 22 January, 1992 *at Trust Bank Park, Hamilton*

Northern Districts 311 (B.A. Young 129)
Canterbury 235 (L.K. Germon 85 not out, L.G. Howell 59, G.E. Bradburn 4 for 47)

Match drawn

Northern Districts 4 pts., Canterbury 0 pts.

at Eden Park, Auckland

Central Districts 354 for 5 dec. (P.S. Briasco 104, S.W.J. Wilson 94, M.W. Douglas 76 not out) and 222 for 1 dec. (R.G. Twose 107 not out, M.W. Douglas 103 not out)
Auckland 264 for 3 dec. (B.A. Pocock 101, S.J. Peterson 77, J.J. Crowe 50) and 233 for 7 (J.J. Crowe 77, S.J. Peterson 55)

Match drawn

Central Districts 4 pts., Auckland 0 pts.

21, 22 and 23 January, 1992 *at Petone Recreation Ground, Lower Hutt*

Wellington 142 (N.A. Mallender 5 for 39) and 205 (E.B. McSweeney 107, N.A. Mallender 5 for 37)
Otago 300 for 8 dec. (K.R. Rutherford 87, B.R. Williams 4 for 60) and 51 for 2

Otago won by 8 wickets

Otago 16 pts., Wellington 0 pts.

In a tedious encounter at Hamilton, Canterbury failed to take a point for the first time in the season. Young batted 367 minutes for his 129, and Hart batted nearly two-and-a-half hours for 22. Canterbury were a little quicker, but failed to take the points. Briasco and Wilson shared a third-wicket stand of 181 for Central Districts while Peterson and Pocock responded with an opening stand of 161 for Auckland. Twose and Douglas both hit their second centuries of the season and shared an unbroken stand of 207. The match always looked destined to be drawn.

Neil Mallender again bowled splendidly as Otago won their first match of the season, beating lowly Wellington.

25, 26 and 27 January,1992 *at Smallbone Park, Rotorua*

Northern Districts 231 (M.P. Maynard 92)
Auckland 72 (R.P. de Groen 5 for 18) and 92 for 1

Match drawn

Northern Districts 4 pts., Auckland 0 pts.

at Basin Reserve, Wellington

Wellington 134 (M.B. Owens 4 for 18, C.L. Cairns 4 for 61)
Canterbury 136 for 4 dec. (L.G. Howell 62 not out)

Match drawn

Canterbury 4 pts., Wellington 0 pts.

There was no play on the third day at Rotorua, and only a few overs were possible each day in Wellington.

1, 2 and 3 February, 1992 *at Carisbrook, Dunedin*

Wellington 214 (N.A. Mallender 5 for 44) and 227 for 5 dec. (S.J. Blackmore 107 not out)
Otago 200 (P.W. Dobbs 86, M.J. Sears 4 for 65) and 245 for 9 (M.H. Austen 68, M.J. Lamont 67)

Otago won by 1 wicket

Otago 12 pts., Wellington 4 pts.

at Lancaster Park, Christchurch

Northern Districts 385 (S.B. Doull 108, G.E. Bradburn 72, K.A. Wealleans 62, M.P. Maynard 50, M.B. Owens 4 for 74) and 51 for 2
Canterbury 397 (M.W. Priest 103, L.K. Germon 91, L.G. Howell 62, R.L. Hayes 4 for 55)

Match drawn

Canterbury 4 pts., Northern Districts 0 pts.

at Victoria Park, Wanganu

Central Districts 312 (S.W. Duff 164 not out, M.W. Douglas 63) and 248 for 8 dec. (M.W. Douglas 99, T.E. Blain 66, S.W. Brown 4 for 45)
Auckland 261 for 9 dec. (J.J. Crowe 68, A.J. Hunt 59, D.J. Leonard 4 for 84) and 225 (J.J. Crowe 88, S.W. Duff 4 for 57)

Central Districts won by 74 runs

Central Districts 16 pts., Auckland 0 pts.

In spite of Blackmore's century, Wellington lost to Otago whose final pair scored the ten runs needed for victory. A maiden first-class century by number nine Simon Doull, 108 off 109 balls, revived Northern Districts at Christchurch, but Germon and Priest added 205 for Canterbury's seventh wicket to claim the points.

The most sensational cricket was at Wanganu where Central Districts were 81 for 6, but Stu Duff hit 164 not out off 213 balls, the first century of his career. Douglas hit 99 off 101 balls in the second innings and Central took maximum points to move two points ahead of Canterbury in the table.

5, 6 and 7 February, 1992 *at McLean Park, Napier*

Wellington 220 (G.R. Larsen 70, D.N. Askew 4 for 42) and 295 for 4 dec. (G.P. Burnett 83 retired hurt, G.R. Larsen 56, E.B. McSweeney 50).
Central Districts 222 for 7 dec. (M.W. Douglas 86 not out, S.W. Duff 55) and 232 for 9 (R.G. Twose 83, M.J. Greatbatch 67)

Match drawn

Central Districts 4 pts., Wellington 0 pts.

at Lancaster Park, Christchurch

Canterbury 247 for 9 dec. (L.G. Howell 85, P.G. Kennedy 61) and 245 for 1 dec. (B.Z. Harris 133, D.J. Boyle 74 not out)
Otago 236 (D.S. McHardy 100, M.B. Owens 4 for 52) and 181 for 9 (D.S. McHardy 67, M.W. Priest 6 for 59)

Match drawn

Canterbury 4 pts., Otago 0 pts.

Asked to score 294 at more than four runs an over, Central were thankful to escape with a draw after a brave attempt to score the runs. They were 83 for 6 in their first innings, but were saved by Douglas and Duff again, the pair adding 134. Ben Harris' century gave Canterbury the chance of the victory that would have taken them to the top of the table. Otago slipped from 171 for 3 to 175 for 9, but Mallender and O'Dowda defied Priest, who had had a fine match, and Kember.

9, 10 and 11 February, 1992 *at Eden Park, Auckland*

Auckland 304 (J.T.C. Vaughan 81, J.J. Crowe 55, R.G. Petrie 5 for 70) and 86 for 2
Canterbury 131 (S.W. Brown 5 for 39, C. Pringle 4 for 52) and 257 (B.Z. Harris 122)

Auckland won by 8 wickets

Auckland 16 pts., Canterbury 0 pts.

at Fitzherbert Park, Palmerston North

Otago 362 for 9 dec. (N.A. Mallender 100 not out, J.W. Wilson 67, D.S. McHardy 53) and 194 for 4 dec. (D.S. McHardy 85 not out, S.A. Robinson 72 not out)
Central Districts 269 for 9 dec. (T.E. Blain 96, S.W. Duff 69, P.J. Marshall 6 for 59) and 198 for 9 (D.J. Leonard 67, J.W. Wilson 4 for 49)

Match drawn

Otago 4 pts., Central Districts 0 pts.

at Trust Bank Park, Hamilton

Wellington 370 for 3 dec. (G.P. Burnett 203 not out, R.A. Verry 132) and 146 for 5 dec.
Northern Districts 146 for 2 dec. (D.J. White 68 not out, S.A. Thomson 57 not out) and 371 for 4 (S.A. Thomson 126 not out, M.P. Maynard 102, G.E. Bradburn 52 not out)

Northern Districts won by 6 wickets

Northern Districts 12 pts., Wellington 4 pts.

Canterbury suffered their first defeat of the season in the Shell Trophy in their final match. In spite of Ben Harris' second century in successive matches, they were overwhelmed by Auckland and so lost the chance of winning the Trophy. The highlight of the match was that when he reached 30 in his first innings Jeff Crowe became only the sixth batsman to score 1,000 runs in a New Zealand season.

Unable to bowl through injury in the match against Central Districts, Neil Mallender compensated by hitting the first first-class century of his career. It capped what had been a magnificent season for him. The elegant Blain, a talent too long neglected by New Zealand selectors, and Duff, a newly developed batsman, saved Central Districts in the first innings, but, in the end, Central were denied the points that would have given them the Trophy.

They had to share the title with Northern Districts who won a remarkable game in Hamilton. Rain restricted play on the opening day after which Graham Burnett and Ross Verry put on 346 for Wellington's third wicket, the highest partnership for any Wellington wicket. Finally, Northern Districts were asked to make 371 in 85 overs, a formidable task. They reached their target in 76.4 overs thanks to a dynamic partnership of 208 in 149 minutes for the fourth wicket between Matthew Maynard and Shane Thomson. It was the highest fourth-innings total ever achieved by Northern Districts to win a match and it gave them a share of the title. This was the first time that two sides had shared the premier title in 85 years of cricket in New Zealand. It was a fitting end to Maynard's magnificent season.

The most exciting of New Zealand's Emerging Players, all-rounder Chris Harris. (Joe Mann/Allsport)

SHELL TROPHY FINAL TABLE

	P	W	L	D	1st inns lead	Pts
Central Districts (5)	10	3	2	5	6	62
Northern Districts (4)	10	3	1	6	6	62
Canterbury (2)	10	3	1	6	6	60
Auckland (1)	10	3	2	5	4	52
Otago (3)	10	2	4	4	5	33
Wellington (6)	10	1	5	4	2	14

(Northern Districts and Central Districts include two points for an abandoned match. Otago deducted 11 points and Wellington six for slow over rates.)
(1991 positions in brackets)

ENGLAND TOUR

2 January, 1992 *at Eden Park, Auckland*

Auckland 156 for 9 (P.C.R. Tufnell 4 for 25)
England XI 158 for 5

England XI won by 5 wickets

England began what was to be an arduous three months with a 50-over game against Auckland which they won with five wickets and a ball to spare. The most gratifying performance in the England side came from Phil Tufnell whose left-arm spin accounted for four front-line batsmen in ten overs.

3, 4 and 5 January, 1992 *at Trust Bank Park, Hamilton*

New Zealand Emerging Players 176 for 8 dec. (C.Z. Harris 60) and 153 (P.C.R. Tufnell 5 for 66)
England XI 434 for 4 dec. (G.A. Hick 129 retired hurt, G.A. Gooch 101 retired hurt, A.J. Lamb 88, R.C. Russell 50)

England XI won by an innings and 105 runs

Alec Stewart, already entrusted with the task of second wicket-keeper, was surprisingly named as vice-captain to Gooch at the start of the tour, and he led England against the Emerging Players even though Gooch was in the side. Stewart was dismissed for 0, but centuries came from Gooch and Hick, both of whom retired hurt with minor or imaginary injuries. Hick's century was a significant one, for he was still greatly struggling to earn his place in the England side.

In the young New Zealand players' first innings, left-hander Justin Vaughan had added 69 with Chris Harris when he edged a ball from Hick towards his stumps. Instinctively, he brushed the ball away with his hand and, on appeal, was given out 'handled ball'.

Apart from Hick's hundred, the most pleasing aspect of England's win was again the bowling of Tufnell. He received some criticism in the New Zealand press for his doubtful action, but the criticism was strongly refuted by the England management.

7, 8 and 9 January, 1992 *at McLean Park, Napier*

New Zealand Minor Associations XI 245 (K.R. Rutherford 64, D.V. Lawrence 5 for 52) and 260 (B.A. Young 80, P.C.R. Tufnell 4 for 65)
England XI 353 (G.A. Hick 113, R.C. Russell 57, S.N.J. Wilson 4 for 103) and 38 for 3

Match drawn

Trevor Franklin is one of the unluckiest of cricketers. The second ball of the match struck him on the forearm, and he was given out caught at short-leg, umpire McHarg having heard a crack. It transpired that the crack was Lawrence's delivery breaking Franklin's left arm. Pawson had suffered a fracture in the previous match, but Franklin was seen as Wright's opening partner in the Test series, and his loss was a great blow to New Zealand. Lawrence bowled with hostility and accuracy, and there was another fine performance from Tufnell when the aspiring players batted a second time.

The loss of Atherton with injury before the tour had deprived Gooch of a regular opening partner, and Hick was promoted in this match and responded with his second century in succession. He batted well after an uncertain start.

FIRST ONE-DAY INTERNATIONAL
NEW ZEALAND v. ENGLAND, at Auckland

An exacting World Cup schedule and a three-Test series in the immediate future did not detract the authorities from including three one-day internationals in the English itinerary. The first of these matches went in England's favour from beginning to end.

At the conclusion of the 15th over, New Zealand, having elected to bat first, were 45 for 1, and they lost Latham at the start of the 16th. When, in the 31st over, Crowe was beaten by Dermot Reeve's break-back, New Zealand were 81 for 5 and effectively doomed.

Two of New Zealand's 'young guns', both sons of former Test cricketers, added 84. Cairns was the more positive of the two, hitting a six and two fours in his 42, while Harris was more restrained. They could never really break free of the shackles that the England bowling and fielding imposed, and a target of 179 was never likely to tax the visitors.

This was the case as Gooch and Hick reached 60 without being separated after only ten overs. Hick was yorked in the 11th over, and Gooch clipped the ball to mid-wicket in the 19th, but by then England had reached 109. Robin Smith took total command. He hit a six and 11 fours and faced only 71 balls for his 61 to take England to victory with more than 16 overs to spare.

Reeve, relishing the international scene, took the individual award for his fine bowling which brought him three major scalps.

13, 14 and 15 January, 1992 *at Trafalgar Park, Nelson*

New Zealand XI 207 for 7 dec. (S.A. Thomson 76) and 266 for 3 dec. (B.A. Pocock 100 not out, S.A. Thomson 89 not out, M.W. Douglas 59)

England XI 159 for 3 dec. (A.J. Lamb 76 not out, A.J. Stewart 71 not out) and 316 for 8 (G.A. Hick 71, G.A. Gooch 64, A.J. Lamb 61 not out)

England XI won by 2 wickets

FIRST ONE-DAY INTERNATIONAL – NEW ZEALAND v. ENGLAND
11 January, 1992 at Eden Park, Auckland

NEW ZEALAND

J.G. Wright	c Stewart, b Lewis	6
R.T. Latham	lbw, b D.R. Pringle	25
M.D. Crowe (capt)	b Reeve	31
A.H. Jones	c Stewart, b Reeve	1
M.J. Greatbatch	c Hick, b Reeve	4
C.Z. Harris	not out	38
C.L. Cairns	c Hick, b D.R. Pringle	42
*I.D.S. Smith	c Gooch, b Lewis	2
C. Pringle	not out	9
G.R. Larsen		
D.K. Morrison		
Extras	lb 13, w 4, nb 3	20
	(for 7 wickets)	178

ENGLAND

G.A. Gooch (capt)	c Greatbatch, b Harris	47
G.A. Hick	b Cairns	23
R.A. Smith	not out	61
A.J. Lamb	c Crowe, b Harris	12
N.H. Fairbrother	not out	23
*A.J. Stewart		
D.A. Reeve		
C.C. Lewis		
D.R. Pringle		
P.A.J. DeFreitas		
P.C.R. Tufnell		
Extras	lb 6, w 3, nb 4	13
		179

(50 overs)

	O	M	R	W
DeFreitas	10	1	34	–
Lewis	8	–	33	2
D.R. Pringle	6	1	32	2
Reeve	10	3	20	3
Tufnell	10	3	17	–
Hick	6	–	29	–

(33.5 overs)

	O	M	R	W
C. Pringle	5	–	26	–
Morrison	5.5	–	35	–
Cairns	5	–	32	1
Larsen	9	3	36	–
Harris	8	–	40	2
Latham	1	–	4	–

FALL OF WICKETS
1–21, 2–45, 3–51, 4–61, 5–81, 6–165, 7–167

FALL OF WICKETS
1–64, 2–109, 3–123

Umpires: D.B. Cowie & S.J. Woodward | Man of the Match – D.A. Reeve | *England won by 7 wickets*

The major concern for the England tourists was the rib injury to David Lawrence which kept him out of the match against a New Zealand side once again filled with players who were pressing for Test places. Indeed, the injury was to prove serious enough to keep Lawrence out of the first two Tests.

Rain held up the start of England's last game before the first Test. There were two good, if somewhat fortunate, innings from Shane Thomson. Like Pocock, he benefited from some occasional bowling in the second innings. Set to make 315 to win in 270 minutes, England reached their target with eight minutes to spare.

FIRST TEST MATCH
NEW ZEALAND v. ENGLAND, at Christchurch

England had Neil Mallender on stand-by as cover for the injured David Lawrence, but he was not called upon as Dermot Reeve was given his first Test cap. Watson withdrew from the New Zealand squad with injury, and opening batsman Blair Hartland of Canterbury played in a Test match for the first time. Martin Crowe won the toss and asked England to bat first on a wicket which was tinged with green, but which was later to become placid.

Crowe's decision seemed valid when Gooch was caught behind in the third over, but there was insufficient sustained and accurate hostility to press home this advantage. Hick was never sure of himself, always vulnerable to the ball on the line of his body, and was leg before shortly before lunch, but by then he and Stewart had repaired the early damage.

Stewart had been slow to get under way, showing caution and care on and outside his off stump, but he gathered momentum and began to drive sweetly and clip the ball to leg effortlessly. Smith hit with thunder and displayed great power, but he was badly dropped by Crowe at slip off Thomson when on 44. It was a costly miss for, by tea, England were 214 for 2. Both Smith and Stewart were out in the final session. Smith was caught at slip when he drove at a wide delivery. He had hit a six and 16 fours in his three-hour innings and, with Stewart, had put England in a position of dominance.

Alex Stewart stroked a masterful 148, his second Test century, and his runs came off 265 balls and included 17 fours. It was also his second century in successive Tests, and it displayed admirable maturity, a blend of watchful defence and calculated aggression. He was out when he edged to slip, and no more runs were scored before the close.

Alec Stewart during his innings of 148 in the first Test match, New Zealand v. England, at Christchurch. Ian Smith is the wicket-keeper. (Ben Radford/Allsport)

If England were in a commanding position at the end of the first day, they were in an invincible position at the close of the second. In the first hour of the day, Lamb and Russell hit 67 in 15 overs. They were aided by a generous supply of long-hops, and Lamb reached 50 with the help of nine fours. His innings was marred by the running out of Russell, who was sent back and beaten by Wright's throw from mid-off. More sadly, Lamb became over-cautious as a century approached. He could well have knocked Patel out of the attack, but he lost his sense of adventure and his momentum and was bowled by one of the few deliveries that Patel was able to turn.

In contrast, Reeve played with pleasing zest in his first Test match and reached a competent 59 off 120 balls before chopping the ball into the hands of gully. By the time he was dismissed, he was being overshadowed by the uninhibited Chris Lewis. It is doubtful that Lewis will ever achieve consistency with bat or ball, but when the stars are right he is a joy to behold with either. In 86 minutes, off 73 balls, he hit 70 runs, 52 of them in boundaries. It was not slogging, but batting of high pedigree. Gooch declared when Lewis heaved across the line and missed, and New Zealand were three without loss at the close.

Rain delayed the start of the third day, but with the advantage of the extra hour, only 80 minutes' play were lost. There were no early panics for New Zealand although Gooch did miss a sharp, difficult chance at slip offered by Wright, and the opening pair hit 51. It was the introduction of Tufnell that brought about a change. In his fourth over, he frustrated Wright with two flat deliveries before tempting him with a highly flighted, wider ball. The batsman lunged and was taken at slip. One run later, Hartland, having made a confident debut, was caught at silly point off bat and pad.

A period of uncertainty followed. Jones shuffled across his stumps and was leg before to Lewis. Greatbatch hit Tufnell for two firm drives before being taken at short-leg, again off bat and pad. Thomson played a wretched shot and was bowled, and New Zealand were 91 for 5.

Martin Crowe had dropped down the order in an attempt to protect his damaged left index finger, but he was forced to the crease in this crisis. He batted for just under an hour before, vitally, Pringle had him taken at short-leg. Meanwhile, Patel, still to prove himself worthy of a Test place, had thrown caution to the wind and attacked Tufnell who lost his control in the closing stages. Patel reached his 50 with successive fours off the left-arm spinner, and New Zealand ended on 169 for 6, still 212 runs short of saving the follow-on.

The follow-on was not avoided on a fourth day which was a contrast in styles and fortunes. In 94 overs, only 224 runs were scored and only five wickets were taken. The morning session brought 107 of the day's runs. Patel and Cairns extended their seventh-wicket stand to 117 at little less than a run a minute. Patel looked set for his maiden Test century – this was only the second time he had passed 50 – when he called for a third run after playing the ball to deep mid-wicket, but Pringle's bowled return was fast and accurate, and Patel's dive was too late to save him. It was a cruel end to an innings which, in its belligerent attack on Tufnell, had heartened his colleagues. Patel faced 134 balls, hit two sixes and 11 fours.

Cairns became Reeve's first Test victim after another pugnacious innings, and DeFreitas took the last two wickets so that New Zealand followed-on 268 runs in arrears. In a confident opening partnership, Wright and Hartland scored 81 before Tufnell changed ends to have Hartland caught at silly mid-off at the end of the day.

Night-watchman Morrison fell without addition on the last morning, but Wright and Jones added 101 in 213 minutes, and the match seemed to be heading for a draw. Jones attempted to hook Pringle and gloved the ball to the wicket-keeper, and New Zealand went to tea on 201 for 3, with Wright on 99.

Gooch reintroduced Tufnell immediately after tea, and the left-armer teased Wright with two maidens. In his third over, Tufnell tossed the ball up, and, startlingly, Wright charged down the pitch, missed and was stumped by yards. He had batted for 400 minutes and faced 323 balls, making his end seem somewhat irrational.

Tufnell now had a grip on the New Zealand middle order. Greatbatch was brilliantly caught at silly point by the diving Smith, and Thomson, again in disarray, was leg before, offering no shot. Patel tried to adopt the tactics he had used in the first innings, but he succeeded only in lofting to extra cover. New Zealand entered the final hour of the match at 236 for 7, but within three overs, it was 241 for 8 as Cairns was taken at silly point. Lewis produced a ball that was too fast and lifted too sharply for Smith, and 32 minutes remained with the last pair together.

One of that last pair was Martin Crowe who appreciated the importance of runs as well as of time. England fielded tigerishly, and Crowe batted solidly and purposefully. Ten minutes remained, and New Zealand needed just four runs to save the match. Tufnell flighted a ball invitingly for Crowe who chanced his arm to hit the lofted straight drive that would have brought salvation, but he did not quite get to the pitch of the ball and sliced high to mid-off where Pringle calmly took the catch that brought England a remarkable victory.

With six wickets in the final session, Tufnell had achieved an outstanding best performance in Test cricket and was named Man of the Match. It was only New Zealand's third home Test defeat in 13 years, and it was one of the most astonishing Test matches in recent times.

FIRST TEST MATCH – NEW ZEALAND v. ENGLAND
18, 19, 20, 21 and 22 January, 1992 at Lancaster Park, Christchurch

ENGLAND

	FIRST INNINGS	
G.A. Gooch (capt)	c Smith, b Morrison	2
A.J. Stewart	c Crowe, b Morrison	148
G.A. Hick	lbw, b Cairns	35
R.A. Smith	c Greatbatch, b C. Pringle	96
A.J. Lamb	b Patel	93
* R.C. Russell	run out	36
D.A. Reeve	c Jones, b C. Pringle	59
C.C. Lewis	b C. Pringle	70
D.R. Pringle	c Greatbatch, b Patel	10
P.A.J. DeFreitas	not out	7
P.C.R. Tufnell		
Extras	b 5, lb 10, w 1, nb 8	24
	(for 9 wickets)	**580**

	O	M	R	W
Morrison	33	5	133	2
Cairns	30	3	118	1
C. Pringle	36	4	127	3
Thomson	15	3	47	–
Patel	46	5	132	2
Jones	3	–	8	–

FALL OF WICKETS
1–6, 2–95, 3–274, 4–310, 5–390, 6–466, 7–544, 8–571, 9–580

NEW ZEALAND

	FIRST INNINGS		SECOND INNINGS	
B.R. Hartland	c Smith, b Tufnell	22	c Smith, b Tufnell	45
J.G. Wright	c Lamb, b Tufnell	28	st Russell, b Tufnell	99
A.H. Jones	lbw, b Lewis	16	(4) c Russell, b D.R. Pringle	39
M.J. Greatbatch	c Stewart, b Tufnell	11	(6) c Smith, b Tufnell	0
S.A. Thomson	b Tufnell	5	(7) lbw, b Tufenll	0
D.N. Patel	run out	99	(8) c D.R. Pringle, b Tufnell	6
M.D. Crowe (capt)	c Stewart, b D.R. Pringle	20	(5) c D.R. Pringle, b Tufnell	48
C.L. Cairns	c Hick, b Reeve	61	(9) c Smith, b Tufnell	0
* I.D.S. Smith	lbw, b DeFreitas	20	(10) c Russell, b Lewis	1
D.K. Morrison	not out	8	(3) c Russell, b Lewis	0
C. Pringle	c Hick, b DeFreitas	6	not out	5
Extras	b 1, lb 7, nb 8	16	lb 4, nb 2	6
		312		**264**

	O	M	R	W	O	M	R	W
DeFreitas	32.4	16	54	2	23	6	54	–
Lewis	30	9	69	1	22	3	66	2
D.R. Pringle	15	2	54	1	21	5	64	1
Tufnell	39	10	100	4	46.1	25	47	7
Hick	3	–	11	–	14	8	11	–
Reeve	8	4	16	1	2	–	8	–
Smith					4	2	6	–

FALL OF WICKETS
1–51, 2–52, 3–73, 4–87, 5–91, 6–139, 7–256, 8–879, 9–306
1–81, 2–81, 3–182, 4–211, 5–222, 6–222, 7–236, 8–241, 9–250

Umpires: B.L. Aldridge & R.S. Dunne — Man of the Match – P.C.R. Tufnell — *England won by an innings and 4 runs*

24, 25 and 26 January, 1992 *at Pukekura Park, New Plymouth*

Central Districts 189 for 7 dec.
England XI 246 for 2 (G.A. Hick 115, A.J. Stewart 101 not out)
Match drawn

England's only game in between the first and second Tests was ruined by rain, no play being possible on the last day. Ian Botham, having arrived from the end of his pantomime run, took the first two wickets to fall. Hick hit a century off 75 balls. He and Stewart, who played another accomplished innings, added 178 for the second wicket.

The Young Gun combination of Cairns and Parore claims another victim in the second Test. (Ben Radford/Allsport)

Murphy Su'a bowls Allan Lamb to capture his first wicket in Test cricket. (Ben Radford/Allsport)

Graham Gooch drives the ball through the off side during his innings of 114 in the second Test. (Ben Radford/Allsport)

SECOND TEST MATCH
NEW ZEALAND v. ENGLAND, at Auckland

Although both Lawrence and Botham were available, England decided to rely upon the side that had won so dramatically in the first Test. New Zealand, on the other hand, left out Greatbatch, Thomson, Pringle and the injured Smith, bringing in Rutherford, Watson, Parore and Su'a, New Zealand's first Test cricketer of Polynesian descent.

Once more Crowe won the toss; once more he asked England to bat first. On a damp, green pitch, this was a justified decision and, had his side held all their catches, it could have been decisive. After four overs, England were 9 for 3, Gooch, Stewart and Smith all falling to catches behind the wicket within the space of eight balls. The third of these catches, which accounted for Smith, was a magnificent effort, one-handed at full stretch.

England were in further trouble when Murphy Su'a in his fourth over in Test cricket, forced Lamb onto the back foot and saw him drag the ball into his stumps. Hick meanwhile enjoyed the greatest of fortune. He was dropped at slip by Patel off Watson, and the usually safe Cairns put him down in the gully when he was on 20. Ten runs later, Cairns made amends when he trapped Hick leg before. Lewis and Reeve repaired some of the damage, and, on the second morning, resuming at 146 for 7, England owed much to Pringle who coaxed another 57 runs of which he scored 33. Cairns finished with his best figures in Test cricket, but New Zealand put down four vital catches, none of them difficult, and England scored 60 or 70 runs more than they should have done.

The match began to slip further and further away from New Zealand as it progressed. Lewis quickly sent back Hartland, and, at 13, Wright was hit on the hand and forced to retire. Jones hit a long-hop to cover point, and Rutherford gloved an attempted hook to the keeper. Wright returned and soon lost Crowe, taken at slip. The opener himself was next to go when he played on as he pushed forward to Pringle. Cairns drove at Tufnell in an attempt to remove the threatening silly point, but the ball hit Smith's boot and diverted into the hands of cover. Parore was the first of three wickets to fall at 139, offering no shot to a ball from Pringle. Patel was left static, and Morrison went first ball, pushing half forward.

New Zealand finished the day on 141 for 9, and they added just one run the next morning before Lewis claimed his fifth wicket. After that, the day belonged to Gooch. He had been suffering rather a lean period of late, but, with the help of two sixes and 15 fours, he hit 114 off 220 balls in 294 minutes on a pitch that was still assisting the bowlers. His principal partnership was one of 89 with Lamb who hit a belligerent 60 off 47 balls. England scored 138 in the Saturday afternoon session and took the match by the scruff of the neck.

Gooch reached his 16th Test hundred and was in gleeful mood when Reeve called him for an ambitious single and Watson ran him out. England ended the day on 272 for 6, and added another 49 on the fourth day, by the close of which they had virtually taken the match and the series. Needing 383 to win, New Zealand lost both openers without a run scored, and Jones was leg before to a ball that kept low with only seven scored. Crowe and Rutherford were defiant for 20 overs, and both played well against a pace attack that was rampant, high on success. Rutherford was dropped by Gooch at slip, but it proved an inexpensive miss, for the batsman pushed the ball into the hands of short-leg a few runs later. Crowe edged to slip, and New Zealand's cause was all but lost.

Before Crowe's departure Patel was caught in two minds about driving Tufnell and gave the bowler a return catch. Cairns, Parore and Su'a all showed defiance, remaining at the wicket for over an hour each. Su'a took the game into a fifth day, but New Zealand scored only another 11 runs as England took the last two wickets they needed.

The win gave England the series, their first in New Zealand since 1975. It was also New Zealand's first defeat in a home series since 1978–79 when they were beaten by Pakistan. John Wright, Javed Miandad and Imran Khan are the only ones from that series still playing Test cricket.

SECOND TEST MATCH – NEW ZEALAND v. ENGLAND

30, 31 January, 1, 2 and 3 February, 1992 at Eden Park, Auckland

ENGLAND

	FIRST INNINGS		SECOND INNINGS	
G.A. Gooch (capt)	c Parore, **b** Morrison	4	run out	114
A.J. Stewart	c Parore, **b** Cairns	4	c Parore, **b** Su'a	8
G.A. Hick	lbw, **b** Cairns	30	lbw, **b** Su'a	4
R.A. Smith	c Parore, **b** Cairns	0	**b** Morrison	35
A.J. Lamb	**b** Su'a	13	c Watson, **b** Patel	60
D.A. Reeve	c Parore, **b** Watson	22	lbw, **b** Watson	25
C.C. Lewis	c Cairns, **b** Watson	33	run out	23
*R.C. Russell	c Parore, **b** Cairns	33	c Hartland, **b** Cairns	24
D.R. Pringle	lbw, **b** Cairns	41	lbw, **b** Cairns	2
P.A.J. DeFreitas	c Crowe, **b** Cairns	1	c Wright, **b** Morrison	0
P.C.R. Tufnell	not out	6	not out	0
Extras	lb 11, nb 5	16	b 8, lb 16, nb 2	26
		203		**321**

NEW ZEALAND

	FIRST INNINGS		SECOND INNINGS	
B.R. Hartland	lbw, **b** Lewis	0	c Russell, **b** DeFreitas	0
J.G. Wright	**b** Pringle	15	lbw, **b** Lewis	0
A.H. Jones	c Smith, **b** DeFreitas	14	lbw, **b** DeFreitas	5
M.D. Crowe (capt)	c Hick, **b** Lewis	45	c Lamb, **b** DeFreitas	56
K.R. Rutherford	c Russell, **b** DeFreitas	26	c Stewart, **b** Pringle	32
D.N. Patel	lbw, **b** Lewis	24	c and **b** Tufnell	17
C.L. Cairns	c Hick, **b** Tufnell	1	c Russell, **b** Tufnell	24
*A.C. Parore	lbw, **b** Pringle	0	lbw, **b** Lewis	15
M.L. Su'a	not out	0	lbw, **b** DeFreitas	36
D.K. Morrison	lbw, **b** Lewis	0	run out	12
W. Watson	**b** Lewis	2	not out	5
Extras	nb 15	15	lb 1, nb 11	12
		142		**214**

	O	M	R	W	O	M	R	W
Morrison	17	2	55	1	21.4	6	66	2
Cairns	21	4	52	6	19	6	86	2
Watson	24	13	41	2	26	10	59	1
Su'a	21	8	44	1	10	3	43	2
Patel					22	7	43	1

	O	M	R	W	O	M	R	W
DeFreitas	16	2	53	2	27	11	62	4
Lewis	21	7	31	5	27	4	83	2
Pringle	15	7	21	2	7	2	23	1
Reeve	7	1	21	–				
Tufnell	4	2	16	1	17	5	45	2
Hick					1	1	0	–

FALL OF WICKETS

1–9, **2**–9, **3**–9, **4**–34, **5**–72, **6**–91, **7**–128, **8**–165, **9**–171
1–29, **2**–33, **3**–93, **4**–182, **5**–263, **6**–269, **7**–319, **8**–321, **9**–321

FALL OF WICKETS

1–2, **2**–35, **3**–91, **4**–102, **5**–123, **6**–124, **7**–139, **8**–139, **9**–139
1–0, **2**–0, **3**–7, **4**–77, **5**–109, **6**–118, **7**–153, **8**–173, **9**–203

Umpires: B.L. Aldridge & R.S. Dunne

Man of the Match – G.A. Gooch

England won by 168 runs

THIRD TEST MATCH
NEW ZEALAND v.ENGLAND, at Wellington

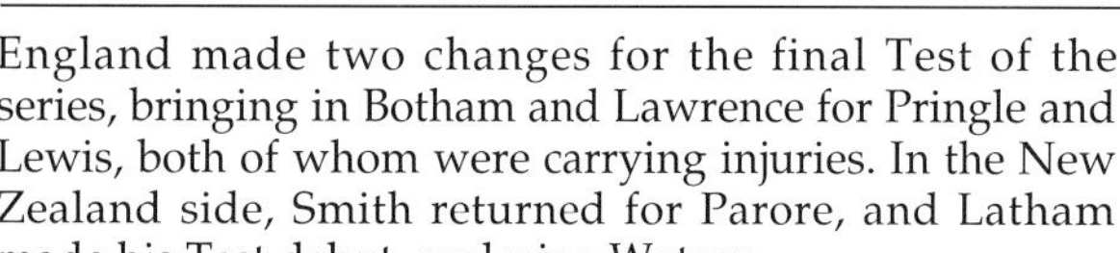

England made two changes for the final Test of the series, bringing in Botham and Lawrence for Pringle and Lewis, both of whom were carrying injuries. In the New Zealand side, Smith returned for Parore, and Latham made his Test debut, replacing Watson.

Gooch won the toss, and England batted on a good wicket of which they failed to take full advantage. Alec Stewart confirmed his growth in stature with his second century of the series, but England finished the opening day with 239 for 5. They churned another 66 runs on the second morning at under two an over, and by the close, New Zealand were 104 for 1. New Zealand were certainly in the stronger position, but once again they had been their own worst enemies, dropping several straightforward chances. The impressive Su'a was the main sufferer.

Jones and Wright extended their partnership to 241 on the third day, a record second-wicket stand for New Zealand in Test cricket. Wright batted 406 minutes and hit 15 fours in his 334-ball innings while Jones batted 56 minutes longer and also hit 15 fours. He faced 398 balls. It was Jones' first century against England and, if he has the reputation of being somewhat eccentric, he is a very fine player. For Wright, a century was fitting in what is likely to be his last Test match. He has served cricket and New Zealand well, and throughout his noble and plentiful career, he has remained a man of the utmost charm.

Accurate slow bowling from Tufnell and Hick prevented New Zealand from taking a complete grip on the game, but Crowe was able to declare on the fourth day with a lead of 127. England lost three wickets in clearing the arrears, the last of them being Stewart who again played admirably and took the individual award. Lamb hit a fiery century with two sixes and 19 fours, but he was fortunate that his opponents were chivalrous. He was given out caught at slip early in his innings, but Ian Smith pointed out that the ball had bounced before Crowe had taken it. Smith, one of the best of wicket-keepers, took three catches in what was his last Test match, for he announced his retirement after the World Cup.

Andrew Jones during his record-breaking partnership of 241 with John Wright. (Ben Radford/Allsport)

Allan Lamb in cavalier mood in the third Test match during his innings of 142. (Ben Radford/Allsport)

The game was moving amicably to a draw when David Lawrence, delivering the first ball of his third over, twisted his left knee in a worn foothold and fell to the ground, breaking his knee-cap as he landed. It was a chilling and terrible moment, and the brush with a television cameraman was born out of the deep concern, horror and anxiety of the England players. Lawrence, in great pain, was carried from the field on a stretcher and operated upon as soon as possible. It was an injury of such magnitude as to cast doubts on his future career. It was a sad end to a fine series in which England performed splendidly.

Small replaced Lawrence in England's World Cup squad from which, of those in New Zealand, Russell and Ramprakash were omitted.

Phil Tufnell beseeches the heavens in the third Test. Tufnell had an outstanding series and topped the England bowling averages. (Ben Radford/Allsport)

THIRD TEST MATCH – NEW ZEALAND v. ENGLAND

6, 7, 8, 9 and 10 February, 1992 at Basin Reserve, Wellington

ENGLAND

	FIRST INNINGS		SECOND INNINGS	
G.A. Gooch (capt)	b Patel	30	c Rutherford, b Cairns	11
A.J. Stewart	b Morrison	107	c Smith, b Patel	63
G.A. Hick	b Patel	43	c Smith, b Su'a	22
R.A. Smith	c Rutherford, b Patel	6	c and b Su'a	76
A.J. Lamb	c Smith, b Patel	30	c Latham, b Patel	142
D.A. Reeve	c Latham, b Su'a	18	b Su'a	0
D.V. Lawrence	c Rutherford, b Cairns	6		
I.T. Botham	c Cairns, b Su'a	15	(7) lbw, b Patel	1
*R.C. Russell	lbw, b Morrison	18	(8) not out	24
P.A.J. DeFreitas	lbw, b Morrison	3		
P.C.R. Tufnell	not out	2		
Extras	b 4, lb 12, nb 11	27	lb 13, nb 7	20
		305	(for 7 wickets, dec.)	359

	O	M	R	W	O	M	R	W
Morrison	22.1	6	44	3	23	5	63	–
Cairns	25	3	89	1	22	4	84	1
Su'a	36	10	62	2	33	10	87	3
Patel	34	10	87	4	41.3	12	112	3
Jones	1	–	7	–				

FALL OF WICKETS
1–83, 2–159, 3–169, 4–215, 5–235, 6–248, 7–277, 8–286, 9–298
1–17, 2–52, 3–127, 4–249, 5–249, 6–254, 7–359

NEW ZEALAND

	FIRST INNINGS		SECOND INNINGS	
B.R. Hartland	c Botham, b Lawrence	2	lbw, b Botham	19
J.G. Wright	c Reeve, b Tufnell	116	c Russell, b Botham	0
A.H. Jones	b Hick	143	(4) lbw, b Reeve	9
M.D. Crowe (capt)	b Tufnell	30	(3) not out	13
K.R. Rutherford	run out	8	not out	2
R.T. Latham	b Hick	25		
D.N. Patel	lbw, b Hick	9		
C.L. Cairns	c Russell, b Botham	33		
*I.D.S. Smith	b Hick	21		
M.L. Su'a	not out	20		
D.K. Morrison	not out	0		
Extras	b 1, lb 15, w 1, nb 8	25		0
		432	(for 3 wickets)	43

	O	M	R	W	O	M	R	W
DeFreitas	8	4	12	–				
Lawrence	27	7	67	1	2.1	1	4	–
Tufnell	71	22	147	2	9	5	12	–
Hick	69	27	126	4				
Botham	14	4	53	1	8	1	23	2
Reeve	3	1	11	–	4.5	2	4	1

FALL OF WICKETS
1–3, 2–244, 3–309, 4–312, 5–327, 6–340, 7–369, 8–404, 9–430
1–4, 2–24, 3–41

Umpires: B.L. Aldridge & R.S. Dunne — Man of the Match – A.J. Stewart — *Match drawn*

TEST MATCH AVERAGES – New Zealand v. England

NEW ZEALAND BATTING

	M	Inns	NO	Runs	HS	Av	100s	50s
M.L. Su'a	2	3	2	56	36	56.00	–	–
J.G. Wright	3	6	–	258	116	43.00	1	1
M.D. Crowe	3	6	1	212	56	42.40	–	–
A.H. Jones	3	6	–	226	143	37.66	1	–
D.N. Patel	3	5	–	155	99	31.00	–	1
C.L. Cairns	3	5	–	119	61	23.80	–	1
K.R. Rutherford	2	4	1	68	32	22.66	–	–
B.R. Hartland	3	6	–	88	45	14.66	–	–
I.D.S. Smith	2	3	–	42	21	14.00	–	–
D.K. Morrison	3	5	2	20	12	6.66	–	–

Played in one Test: M.J. Greatbatch 11 & 0; S.A. Thomson 5 & 0; C. Pringle 6 & 5*; A.C. Parore 0 & 15; W. Watson 2 & 5*; R.T. Latham 25

NEW ZEALAND BOWLING

	Overs	Mds	Runs	Wkts	Av	Best	10/m	5/inn
M.L. Su'a	100	31	236	8	29.50	3-87	–	–
W. Watson	50	23	100	3	33.33	2-41	–	–
D.N. Patel	143.3	34	374	10	37.40	4-87	–	–
C.L. Cairns	117	20	429	11	39.00	6-52	–	1
D.K. Morrison	116.5	24	361	8	45.12	3-44	–	–

Bowled in one innings: C. Pringle 36–4–127–3; S.A. Thomson 15–3–47–0

NEW ZEALAND FIELDING FIGURES

6 – A.C. Parore; 4 – I.D.S. Smith; 3 – K.R. Rutherford; 2 – M.D. Crowe, M.J. Greatbatch, C.L. Cairns and R.T. Latham; 1 – B.R. Hartland, J.G. Wright, A.H. Jones, M.L. Su'a and W. Watson

ENGLAND BATTING

	M	Inns	NO	Runs	HS	Av	100s	50s
A.J. Lamb	3	5	–	338	142	67.60	1	1
A.J. Stewart	3	5	–	330	148	66.00	2	1
R.A. Smith	3	5	–	213	96	42.60	–	2
C.C. Lewis	2	3	–	126	70	42.00	–	1
R.C. Russell	3	5	1	135	36	33.75	–	–
G.A. Gooch	3	5	–	161	114	32.30	1	–
G.A. Hick	3	5	–	134	43	26.80	–	–
D.A. Reeve	3	5	–	124	59	24.80	–	1
D.R. Pringle	2	3	–	53	41	17.66	–	–
P.A.H. DeFreitas	3	4	1	11	7*	3.66	–	–

Played in three Tests: P.C.R. Tufnell 6*, 0* & 2*
Played in one Test: I.T. Botham 15 & 1; D.V. Lawrence 6

ENGLAND BOWLING

	Overs	Mds	Runs	Wkts	Av	Best	10/m	5/inn
P.C.R. Tufnell	186.1	69	367	16	22.93	7-47	1	1
C.C. Lewis	100	23	249	10	24.90	5-31	–	1
I.T. Botham	22	5	76	3	25.33	2-23	–	–
P.A.J. DeFreitas	106.4	39	235	8	29.37	4-62	–	–
D.A. Reeve	24.5	8	60	2	30.00	1-4	–	–
D.R. Pringle	58	16	162	5	32.40	2-21	–	–
G.A. Hick	87	36	148	4	37.00	4-126	–	–
D.V. Lawrence	29.1	8	71	1	71.00	1-67	–	–

Bowled in one innings: R.A. Smith 4–2–6–0

ENGLAND FIELDING FIGURES

9 – R.C. Russell (ct 8/st 1); 5 – R.A. Smith; 4 – G.A. Hick; 3 – A.J. Stewart; 2 – A.J. Lamb and D.R. Pringle; 1 – D.A. Reeve, I.T. Botham and P.C.R. Tufnell

SECOND ONE-DAY INTERNATIONAL
NEW ZEALAND v. ENGLAND, at Carisbrook, Dunedin

Both sides were pared to their World Cup squads, and Su'a played in his first one-day international. Crowe won the toss, and New Zealand batted. The pitch was slow and run-scoring was never easy. Ken Rutherford took the individual award for hitting 52 off 86 balls, which was a fine achievement. He was out when he was sent back as he looked for a second run. This was the second such mishap in the New Zealand innings, for, in the seventh over, with the score on 14, Latham suffered the same fate.

England were faced with a moderate target, but they did not find the task easy. Morrison accounted for Hick with a good delivery, but it was Larsen who caused problems as he dismissed Gooch and Smith. Latham also bowled well, and when he had Botham taken at cover and bowled Stewart second ball, there were hints of a New Zealand victory. Indeed, the game went to the last over, and it was the strength of Pringle and Reeve that took the day.

Man of the Match Ken Rutherford. (Adrian Murrell/Allsport)

SECOND ONE-DAY INTERNATIONAL – NEW ZEALAND v. ENGLAND
12 February, 1992 at Carisbrook, Dunedin

NEW ZEALAND

R.T. Latham	run out	12
A.H. Jones	b Botham	20
M.J. Greatbatch	c Stewart, b Reeve	10
M.D. Crowe (capt)	c sub (Ramprakash), b Illingworth	29
K.R. Rutherford	run out	52
C.Z. Harris	b Pringle	32
C.L. Cairns	b Lewis	3
* I.D.S. Smith	not out	5
M.L. Su'a	not out	4
G.A. Larsen		
D.K. Morrison		
Extras	b 1, lb 12, w 3, nb 3	19
	(for 7 wickets)	**186**

(50 overs)

	O	M	R	W
Pringle	10	2	31	1
Lewis	9	–	32	1
Reeve	8	1	19	1
Botham	6	1	27	1
Illingworth	9	1	33	1
Tufnell	8	–	31	–

FALL OF WICKETS
1–14, 2–35, 3–54, 4–89, 5–163, 6–170, 7–180

ENGLAND

G.A. Gooch (capt)	c Smith, b Larsen	24
G.A. Hick	lbw, b Morrison	7
R.A. Smith	b Larsen	17
A.J. Lamb	lbw, b Latham	40
I.T. Botham	c Rutherford, b Latham	28
* A.J. Stewart	b Latham	0
D.A. Reeve	not out	31
C.C. Lewis	c Greatbatch, b Morrison	18
D.R. Pringle	not out	14
R.K. Illingworth		
P.C.R. Tufnell		
Extras	lb 2, w 9	9
	(for 7 wickets)	**188**

(49.1 overs)

	O	M	R	W
Morrison	7	–	27	2
Su'a	8	1	35	–
Larsen	10	1	24	2
Cairns	6.1	–	36	–
Harris	10	1	39	–
Latham	8	1	25	3

FALL OF WICKETS
1–21, 2–54, 3–63, 4–108, 5–108, 6–131, 7–165

Umpires: B.L. Aldridge & R.S. Dunne — Man of the Match – K.R. Rutherford — *England won by 3 wickets*

THIRD ONE-DAY INTERNATIONAL
NEW ZEALAND v. ENGLAND, at Christchurch

England completed a triumphant tour of New Zealand with a crushing victory in the third one-day international. Their elation was tempered by the fact that Allan Lamb tore a hamstring, and the injury raised doubts as to whether or not he should be retained in the World Cup party.

Crowe again won the toss, but he elected to field. The England innings was marked by two spectacular innings. Ian Botham hit two sixes and 11 fours in his 79 off 73 balls, while Robin Smith hit 13 fours in his 85 which came from 71 balls.

New Zealand's bowling was severely mauled, and when Lewis and Pringle reduced the home side to 23 for 3 in the tenth over there was never any doubt as to the result. Pringle was particularly impressive, and his form allowed Small a comfortable entry into the attack only 48 hours after arriving as replacement for the injured Lawrence.

Lewis bowled at a brisk pace and hit Wright on the head in his fifth over, forcing the batsman to retire. Wright returned at the fall of the fifth wicket.

'Goodbye to all that' – Retirement for one of the world's finest wicket-keepers, Ian Smith. (Sporting Pictures (UK) Ltd)

THIRD ONE-DAY INTERNATIONAL – NEW ZEALAND v. ENGLAND
15 February, 1992 at Lancaster Park, Christchurch

ENGLAND

I.T. Botham	c Greatbatch, b Latham	79
G.A. Hick	c Greatbatch, b Larsen	18
R.A. Smith	c Smith, b Cairns	85
* A.J. Stewart (capt)	c Crowe, b Su'a	13
A.J. Lamb	c Harris, b Watson	25
G.A. Gooch	not out	22
C.C. Lewis	c Latha, b Watson	0
D.R. Pringle	c Watson, b Cairns	5
D.A. Reeve	not out	2
R.K. Illingworth		
G.C. Small		
Extras	lb 2, w 4	6
	(for 7 wickets)	255

NEW ZEALAND

R.T. Latham	c Reeve, b Lewis	0
J.G. Wright	c Hick, b Reeve	36
M.J. Greatbatch	b Pringle	5
M.D. Crowe (capt)	c Stewart, b Pringle	6
K.R. Rutherford	c sub (Ramprakash), b Botham	37
C.Z. Harris	run out	37
C.L. Cairns	c Smith, b Illingworth	6
* I.D.S. Smith	c sub (DeFreitas), b Small	27
M.L. Su'a	not out	12
G.R. Larsen	not out	3
W. Watson		
Extras	lb 6, w 6, nb 3	0
	(for 8 wickets)	184

(40 overs)

	O	M	R	W
Cairns	6	–	37	2
Watson	8	1	64	2
Larsen	6	2	34	1
Su'a	5	–	35	1
Harris	8	–	35	–
Latham	7	–	48	1

(40 overs)

	O	M	R	W
Lewis	6	1	21	1
Pringle	6	2	11	2
Small	8	–	46	1
Reeve	5	–	26	1
Botham	7	1	36	1
Illingworth	8	–	38	1

FALL OF WICKETS
1–60, **2**–125, **3**–166, **4**–220, **5**–228, **6**–231, **7**–248

FALL OF WICKETS
1–4, **2**–20, **3**–23, **4**–92, **5**–100, **6**–112, **7**–148, **8**–171

Umpires: R.L. McHarg & S.J. Woodward | Man of the Match – I.T. Botham | *England won by 71 runs*

England wicket-keeper Jack Russell in a reflective mood at Auckland (Ben Radford/Allsport)

AUCKLAND

First-Class Matches 1991–92

BATTING

	v. Otago (Auckland) 29 November – 1 December, 1991		v. Wellington (Wellington) 6–8 December, 1991		v. Northern Districts (Auckland) 12–14 December, 1991		v. Wellington (Auckland) 3–5 January, 1992		v. Canterbury (Christchurch) 10–12 January, 1992		v. Otago (Dunedin) 16–18 January, 1992		v. Central Districts (Auckland) 20–22 January, 1992		v. Northern Districts (Rotorua) 25–27 January, 1992		v. Central Districts (Wanganui) 1–3 February, 1992		v. Canterbury (Auckland) 9–11 February, 1992	
T.J. Franklin	0	4	14	34	12	12	14	44												
J.G. Wright	26	6	48	100	19	38	5	18												
J.J. Crowe	36	102	7	28	24	142*	118	16	128	–	18	18	50	77	13	37*	68	88	55	38
D.N. Patel	56*	51	27	15	6	204	60	0							0	–				
S.W. Brown	56	62	9	5	4	2	1	18*	28	–	0	10					0	27	12	–
J.T.C. Vaughan	20	25*	17	37	27	11*					0	28	6*	36	4	–	40	4	81	11*
A.J. Hunt	50*	15*	0	26	68	–	2	29*	19	–	5	–	–	8	5	–	59	1	21	–
I.D.S. Smith	–	–	33*	14*																
C. Pringle	–	–	0	–	23	–									1	–	20	11	9	–
D.K. Morrison	–	–	5	–			–	–												
W. Watson	–	–			2*	–	5	–	–	–					0	–				
M.H. Richardson			4	7*	23	–														
A.C. Parore					27	–	2	–	54*	–	57*	155*	–	24*	3	–			41	–
A.P. O'Dowd							29	–	113	–	5	75*	11*	5	16*	–	26	20	0	6*
I.D. Fisher							12*	–												
S.J. Peterson									10	–	0	27	77	55	12	15	0	41	26	26
B.A. Pocock									1	–	14	71	101	5	14	32*	8	4	26	2*
M.L. Su'a									15*	–	1	–			0	–				
M.R. Pringle									35	–										
M.J. Haslam									–	–	3	–	–	–			7*	0	1*	–
R.J. Drown											1	–	–	–			16*	4	0	–
M. O'Rourke													–	5						
P.J. Wiseman													–	4*						
J. Mills																	1	17*		
Byes	9	6		7	1	4		9	6			4	7			1			8	2
Leg-byes	9	9	9	13	7	10	4	10	16		17	8	4	13	2	5	7	2	6	
Wides	1	3		1		1					2	2			1				5	
No-balls	1			4	1		6	1	3		4	4	8	1	1	2	9	6	13	1
Total	264	283	173	291	244	424	258	145	428		127	402	264	233	72	92	261	225	304	86
Wickets	5	5	10	7	10	4	9†	5	7		10	5	3	7	10	1	9	10	10	2
Result	W		L		D		W		D		D		D		D		L		W	
Points	16		4		0		16		0		0		0		0		0		16	

BOWLING

	D.K. Morrison	C. Pringle	W. Watson	S.W. Brown	D.N. Patel	J.T.C. Vaughan	M.H. Richardson	A.J. Hunt
v. Otago (Auckland)	17–4–59–3	22.1–4–67–2	13.1–8–25–0	24–7–57–5	8–2–40–0			
29 November – 1 December, 1991	25–4–66–1	30.5–7–89–3		15–7–29–1	8–4–22–0	26–6–72–5		
v. Wellington (Wellington)	19–5–38–3	13.3–3–34–3		9–2–23–2		10–3–25–2		
6–8 December, 1991	21.5–3–49–3	25–2–101–0		20.3–4–65–1	11–0–32–0	19.1–6–50–1	7–0–28–0	3–2–5–0
v. Northern Districts (Auckland)		29–11–83–3	16–4–62–0		25.2–3–117–6		3–0–11–0	2–1–4–0
12–14 December, 1991		13–4–29–2	11–2–38–0		37–11–116–4		16–3–78–2	16–3–73–0
v. Wellington (Auckland)	10–1–23–2		30–14–51–3	12–1–31–1	23–6–52–2			1–0–1–0
3–5 January, 1992			39–19–67–3	5–0–28–0	31.5–12–72–7			3–2–1–0
v. Canterbury (Christchurch)			30–6–91–0	30–9–79–3				9–3–23–0
10–12 January, 1992								
v. Otago (Dunedin)				21–7–72–3		15–4–52–2		11–3–37–0
16–18 January, 1992				3–0–11–0		1–0–4–0		8–3–29–1
v. Central Districts (Auckland)								14–5–32–1
20–22 January, 1992								12.1–1–39–0
v. Northern Districts (Rotorua)		18–5–50–0	30–12–53–3		11–1–32–3	7–4–7–1		
25–27 January, 1992								
v. Central Districts (Wanganui)		32–6–80–3		23–4–111–3		16–5–52–2		
1–3 February, 1992		24–8–73–1		7–0–41–0				3–0–14–1
v. Canterbury (Auckland)		23.1–5–52–4		19–8–39–5		3–1–3–0		
9–11 February, 1992		21.3–6–61–3		17–2–45–1		25–10–58–2		
Bowlers average	92.5–17–235–12 19.58	252.1–61–719–24 29.95	169.1–65–387–9 43.00	205.3–51–631–25 25.24	155.1–39–483–22 21.95	122.1–39–323–15 21.53	26–3–117–2 58.50	82.1–23–258–3 86.00

M	Inns	NO	Runs	HS	Av
4	8	–	134	44	16.75
4	8	–	260	100	32.50
10	19	2	1063	142*	62.52
5	9	1	419	204	52.37
8	14	1	234	62	18.00
8	15	4	347	81	31.54
10	14	3	308	68	28.00
2	2	2	47	33*	–
6	6	–	64	23	10.66
3	1	–	5	5	5.00
5	3	1	7	5	3.50
2	3	1	34	23	17.00
7	8	4	363	155*	90.75
7	12	4	306	113	38.25
1	1	1	12	12*	–
6	11	–	289	77	26.27
6	11	1	278	101	27.80
3	3	1	16	15*	8.00
1	1	–	35	35	35.00
5	4	2	11	7*	5.50
4	3	1	21	16*	10.50
1	1	–	5	5	5.00
1	1	1	4	4*	–
1	2	1	17	17*	17.00

FIELDING FIGURES

17 – A.C. Parore (ct 16/st 1)
14 – A.J. Hunt
13 – J.J. Crowe
10 – J.T.C. Vaughan
9 – I.D.S. Smith
6 – Subs
5 – J. Mills
4 – T.J. Franklin, D.N. Patel, S.W. Brown and B.A. Pocock
3 – R.J. Drown and S.J. Peterson
2 – A.P. O'Dowd and M.J. Haslam
1 – J.G. Wright, W. Watson ,M.L. Su'a and C. Pringle
† D. K. Morrison absent ill

Trevor Franklin of Auckland (Simon Bruty/Allsport)

I.D. Fisher	M.L. Su'a	S.J. Peterson	M.J. Haslam	R.J. Drown	M. O'Rourke	P.J. Wiseman	Byes	Leg-byes	Wides	No-balls	Total	Wkts
								6		6	254	10
							1	10		6	289	10
								5		7	125	10
							2	8	1	3	340	5
							2	5		2	284	10
								1		1	335	8
17–6–37–1								6	1	2	201	10
9–2–29–0								2		1	199	10
	28.4–4–111–1	8–0–41–0	27–9–72–3				3	11		11	431	7
	25–6–57–3		17–5–25–0	27–11–50–2				8		3	301	10
	13–8–24–0		15–5–60–2	10–7–6–4				1			135	7
	3–0–20–0	32–10–87–1	22–9–41–1	29–5–79–2	29–8–82–0		1	12	1	6	354	5
		15–1–71–0	6–2–12–0	15–2–49–1	11–2–49–0			2			222	1
	21.1–2–88–3							1	1	11	231	10
			5–1–17–0	24–11–41–2			1	10			312	10
			11.5–0–66–2	17–4–45–4				9		2	248	8
				13–3–30–1				7	1	1	131	10
			10–2–29–3	19–6–59–1				5		3	257	10
26–8–66–1 66.00	87.5–20–280–7 40.00	11–0–61–0 –	132.5–33–427–11 38.81	138–53–284–15 18.93	44–7–128–3 42.66	40–10–131–0 –						

CANTERBURY
First-Class Matches 1991–92

BATTING	v. Wellington (Christchurch) 29 November – 1 December, 1991		v. Central Districts (Christchurch) 6–8 December, 1991		v. Otago (Oamaru) 12–14 December, 1991		v. Central Districts (New Plymouth) 3–5 January, 1992		v. Auckland (Christchurch) 10–12 January, 1992		v. Northern Districts (Hamilton) 20–22 January, 1992		v. Wellington (Wellington) 25–27 January, 1992		v. Northern Districts (Christchurch) 1–3 February, 1992		v. Otago (Christchurch) 5–7 February, 1992		v. Auckland (Auckland) 9–11 February, 1992	
B.R. Hartland	127	–	0	59	13	0			89	–			9	–						
D.J. Boyle	4	–	7	14	84	5	12	0	19	–	9	–	7	–	0	–	3	74*	5	6
L.G. Howell	44	37*	0	0	0	34			112	–	59	–	62*	–	62	–	85	–	4	28
R.T. Latham	50	7	27	62	68	87	84	32			28	–	0	–						
C.Z. Harris†	17	–	18	23*	94*	65							27	–	37	–	4	24*	20	–
P.G. Kennedy	6	–	23	5	15	30*	11	20	74	–	34	–	17*	–	6	–	61	–	24	23
M.W. Priest	26*	–	2	0	0	–	25	–	89	–	1	–	–	–	103	–	7	–	26	0
C.L. Cairns	0	–	5	10*	3	26*	9	–					–	–						
L.K. Germon	20*	–	36*	–	12	–	20	–	18*	–	85*	–	–	–	91	–	14	–	4	35
R.G. Petrie	–	11*	3	1	1	–	100	–	0	–					12	–	2	–	2	0
R.M. Ford	–	–	0	–	–	–			–	–	0	–	–	–	0	–				
A. Nathu							25	0												
B.Z. Harris							33	5*	0	–	1	–			45	–	8	133	0	122
N.J. Astle							18	4*	5*	–									37	12
M.B. Owens							5*	–					–	–	1*	–	5*	–	0*	4*
M.F. Sharpe†									–	–	6	–							0	8
S.P. Fleming											0	–			10	–	25	–	–	11
H.J. Kember											1	–					2*	–		
Byes				7		4			3		5		1		1		6		1	
Leg-byes	8	2	1	6	3	6	14	6	11		5		3		24		10	8	7	5
Wides													2				1		1	
No-balls	2	1	2	2	2		18	1	11		1		8		5		14	5	1	3
Total	304	58	124	189	295	257	374	68	431		235		136		397		247	245	131	257
Wickets	7	1	10	7	9	5	10	4	7		10		4		10		9	1	10	10
Result	D		W		W		W		D		D		D		D		D		L	
Points	4		12		12		16		4		0		4		4		4		0	

BOWLING	C.L. Cairns	R.M. Ford	R.G. Petrie	M.W. Priest	C.Z. Harris	R.T. Latham	P.G. Kennedy	D.J. Boyle
v. Wellington (Christchurch)	27.3–8–79–3	24–12–37–2	25–4–67–3	31–13–56–1	12–4–24–0	6–2–18–1		
29 November – 1 December, 1991	14–2–45–2	23.3–10–35–6	17–3–45–0	26–7–103–0		6–1–18–0	3–1–14–0	
v. Central Districts (Christchurch)	17.4–8–28–4	15–3–38–0	14–3–28–2		13–5–24–1		3–1–6–2	
6–8 December 1991	23–10–38–4	18–7–35–2	10–1–30–0	28–9–46–3			17–6–20–1	
v. Otago (Oamaru)	24–7–71–2	31–11–65–2	19–3–69–1	20–3–68–1	22.5–6–54–1	3–2–8–0		
12–14 December, 1991	9–3–21–1	8–1–26–1	14–5–38–3	25–4–61–2	9.2–2–31–0			3–0–12–0
v. Central Districts (New Plymouth)	23–4–66–4		21.3–5–91–4	14–2–38–1				
3–5 January, 1992	18.5–3–34–7		8–1–28–0	39–21–49–3				8–3–16–0
v. Auckland (Christchurch)		36–10–65–0	26–8–61–1	33–9–96–3			15–3–54–0	
10–12 January, 1992								
v. Northern Districts (Hamilton)		33–6–85–3		44–17–87–1		15–7–20–3	8–3–10–0	
20–22 January, 1992								
v. Wellington (Wellington)	20–2–61–4	23–8–33–1			8–5–12–1			
25–27 January, 1992								
v. Northern Districts (Christchurch)		18–3–46–0	29–5–100–3	26–8–70–2	25–5–69–0		4–1–22–1	
1–3 February, 1992			5–1–13–2		1–1–0–0			
v. Otago (Christchurch)			19–2–50–2	22–7–52–3	13–2–43–0		4–1–8–0	
5–7 February, 1992 ·			9–1–33–0	31–14–59–6				
v. Auckland (Auckland)			22.2–3–70–5	8–3–30–0	16–6–24–1		12–4–20–0	
9–11 February, 1992			2–0–11–0	12–3–40–2				2.5–2–9–0
Bowlers average	177–47–443–31 14.29	229.3–71–465–17 27.35	240.5–45–734–26 28.23	359–120–855–28 30.53	120.1–36–281–4 70.25	30–12–64–4 16.00	66–20–154–4 38.50	13.5–5–37–0 –

M	Inns	NO	Runs	HS	Av
5	7	–	297	127	42.42
10	15	1	249	84	17.78
9	13	1	527	112	43.91
6	10	–	445	87	44.50
7	10	3	329	94*	47.00
10	14	2	349	74	29.08
10	11	1	279	103	27.90
4	6	2	53	26*	13.25
10	10	4	335	91	55.83
8	10	1	132	100	14.66
7	3	–	0	0	0.00
1	2	–	25	25	12.50
6	9	1	347	133	43.37
3	5	2	76	37	25.33
5	5	5	15	5*	–
3	3	–	14	8	4.66
4	4	–	46	25	11.50
2	2	1	3	2*	3.00

FIELDING FIGURES

34 – L.K. Germon (ct 31/st 3)
9 – L.G. Howell
8 – R.T. Latham and D.J. Boyle
6 – P.G. Kennedy and S.P. Fleming
5 – M.W Priest
4 – C.Z. Harris and B.R. Hartland
3 – A. Nathu and M.B. Owens
2 – R.G. Petrie
1 – C.L. Cairns, B.Z. Harris, R.M. Ford, N.T. Astle and sub (D.J. Murray)

†In the final match of the season C.Z. Harris was called up for international duty, and S.P. Fleming replaced him in the second innings

Mark Priest of Canterbury. (David Munden)

M.B. Owens	N.J. Astle	M.F. Sharpe	H.J. Kember	B.Z. Harris	Byes	Leg-byes	Wides	No-balls	Total	Wkts
						5		2	286	10
						6	1	3	266	9
					4	6	1	3	134	10
					6	3		1	178	10
					5	10	4	3	350	7
					5	4		1	198	7
16–2–49–1	11–4–17–0					8	2	8	269	10
13–3–37–0					5	2		6	171	10
	19–8–32–0	32–10–98–3			6	16		3	428	7
		28.4–8–64–2	29–15–29–1		3	13		3	311	10
13.1–3–18–4					4	6		16	134	10
29.1–6–74–4						4	1	17	385	10
3–0–27–0				2–1–11–0			2	3	51	2
18.5–3–52–4			11–4–24–1			7	1	7	236	10
14–6–31–1			20–7–48–2		5	5		1	181	9
20–3–53–1	29–15–42–1	24–7–51–2			8	6	5	13	304	10
4–1–13–0		5–2–11–0			2			1	86	2
131.1–27–354–15 23.60	59–27–91–1 91.00	89.4–27–224–7 32.00	60–26–101–4 25.25	2–1–11–0 –						

CENTRAL DISTRICTS

First-Class Matches 1991–92

BATTING

	v. Northern Districts (Masterton) 29 November – 1 December, 1991		v. Canterbury (Christchurch) 6–8 December, 1991		v. Wellington (Wellington) 12–14 December, 1991		v. Canterbury (New Plymouth) 3–5 January, 1992		v. Otago (Dunedin) 10–12 January, 1992		v. Northern Districts (Hamilton) 16–18 January, 1992		v. Auckland (Auckland) 20–22 January, 1992		v. England XI (New Plymouth) 24–26 January, 1992		v. Auckland (Wanganui) 1–3 February, 1992		v. Wellington (Napier) 5–7 February, 1992		v. Otago (Palmerston North) 9–11 February, 1992	
R.G. Twose	25	79	23	16	5	107*	16	24	5	43	8	–	11	107*	13	–	0	6	33	83	12	37
C.D. Ingham	11	20	20	31	2	19	0	50	2	20	6	–	7	10	13	–	4	18				
M.J. Greatbatch	30	81	15	0	6	47	9	5							4	–	30	5	4	67	27	–
M.W. Douglas	31	4	4	5	13	26*	144	1	28	7	9	–	76*	103*	5	–	63	99	86*	2	3	5
S.W.J. Wilson	19*	4	2	23	5	8	9	31	2	32	81	–	94	–	12	–	5	6	15	10	26	3
T.E. Blain	3	24*	34	63	47	–	4	1	0	0	59	–	42	–	45	–	5	66	5	41	96	12
P.S. Briasco	47	8	2	0	4	–	7	1	5	56	11	–	104	–	41	–	7	4	9	10	13	6
S.W. Duff	1*	4*	2	20	0	–	22	38	32	22	39*	–	–	–	36*	–	164*	22	55	4	69	29
D.J. Leonard	–	–	17	3	46	–	22	6	3	4	–	–	–	–	10*	–	15	4*	0	0*	1	67
C.L. Auckram	–	–	0	7*	1*	–	14*	0*	0*	0*	–	–	–	–	–	–						
D.W. Lamason	–	–																				
D.N. Askew			1*	0	3	–	4	1	31	15*	–	–	–	–	–	–	8	–	–	5		
R.K. Brown									38	–	60*	–	0*	–					0	2	–	2
M.J. Pawson															0	7*	–	3*	0	0	0	0
J.B.M. Furlong																					4*	27
R.P. Wixon																					1*	5
Byes		8	4	6				5	6		5		1				1		1			
Leg-byes	4	5	6	3	4	5	8	2	6	6	9		12	2			10	9	8	2	15	1
Wides		1	1				2			1			1							1	2	4
No-balls	2		3	1			8	6	1	5	1		6					2	6	2		
Total	173	238	134	178	136	212	269	171	159	211	288		354	222	189		312	248	222	232	269	198
Wickets	6	6	10	10	10	3	10	10	10	9	6		5	1	7		10	8	7	9	9	9
Result	W		L		W		L		D		Ab.		D		D		W		D		D	
Points	16		4		16		0		0		2		4		–		16		4		0	

BOWLING

	D.J. Leonard	C.L. Auckram	R.G. Twose	D.W. Lamason	S.W. Duff	C.D. Ingham	S.W.J. Wilson	D.N. Askew
v. Northern Districts (Masterton)	15–7–40–2	14–6–36–2	15–4–42–2	8–2–36–0	11.4–6–13–4			
29 November – 1 December, 1991	13–7–26–1	8–3–30–0	9–2–22–1	14–5–44–1	23–8–59–3	4–0–35–0	1–0–2–0	
v. Canterbury (Christchurch)	18.3–2–67–6	7–2–14–0	12–7–11–2					6–1–27–2
6–8 December, 1991	16–4–39–0	8–2–26–0	16–9–24–1		28–14–34–4			17.5–2–53–2
v. Wellington (Wellington)	12.2–5–26–3	8–3–15–2	12–4–22–3					9–5–22–2
12–14 December, 1991	14–1–45–2	17–6–39–3	16–5–32–1		23–6–61–1			15–3–56–3
v. Canterbury (New Plymouth)	26–4–88–3	19.4–2–73–3	16–2–52–0		31–13–77–0			27–6–70–4
3–5 January, 1992	8–2–21–1				5–1–10–1			5.3–0–31–2
v. Otago (Dunedin)	22–9–52–2	24–4–76–0	15–3–44–2		11–4–19–0			24–4–88–4
10–12 January, 1992	16–2–49–1	9–2–25–2	9–1–26–1		11–2–34–3			8–2–28–0
v. Northern Districts (Hamilton)								
16–18 January, 1992								
v. Auckland (Auckland)	16–10–16–0	16–3–51–1	7–0–28–0		27–3–74–0			7–2–29–0
20–22 January, 1992	13–3–54–3	5–0–31–0	7–0–34–0		19–4–60–2	2–0–11–1		2–1–12–0
v. England XI (New Plymouth)	13–2–39–2	10–1–45–0	5–1–21–0		10–0–77–0			4–0–37–0
24–26 January, 1992								
v. Auckland (Wanganui)	23–9–84–4		11–3–23–2		27–9–46–1			7–2–13–0
1–3 February, 1992	11–2–59–1		7–3–18–1		17.3–3–57–4	3–0–16–1		6–2–23–0
v. Wellington (Napier)	19–4–43–3		17–5–33–1		24–13–35–1			19–6–42–4
5–7 February, 1992	7–0–37–0				3–2–4–0		8–1–53–0	
v. Otago (Palmerston North)	22–4–67–0		14–8–23–3		38–8–95–1			
9–11 February, 1992	4–1–13–0				15–7–19–3		3–0–29–0	
Bowlers average	288.5–78–865–34 25.44	145.4–34–1 461–13 35.46	188–57–455–20 22.75	22–7–80–1 80.00	324.1–103–774–28 27.64	9–0–62–2 31.00	11–1–82–0 –	157.2–36–531–23 23.08

	M	Inns	NO	Runs	HS	Av
	11	20	2	653	107*	36.27
	9	16	–	233	50	14.56
	8	14	–	330	81	23.57
	11	20	4	714	144	44.62
	11	19	1	387	94	21.50
	11	18	1	547	96	32.17
	11	18	–	335	104	18.61
	11	17	5	559	164*	46.58
	11	14	3	198	67	18.00
	8	7	6	22	14*	22.00
	1	–	–	–	–	–
	9	9	2	68	31	9.71
	5	7	3	102	60*	25.50
	3	5	2	10	7*	3.33
	1	2	2	31	27*	–
	1	2	2	6	5*	–

FIELDING FIGURES

29 – T.E. Blain (ct 26/st 3)
10 – M.J. Greatbatch and S.W. Duff
9 – P.S. Briasco
8 – M.W. Douglas
7 – R.G. Twose
5 – C.D. Ingham and S.W.J. Wilson
3 – D.N. Askew
2 – D.J. Leonard
1 – C.L. Auckram, R.K. Brown, M.J. Pawson and sub (D.W. Lamason)

Roger Twose of Central Districts (David Munden)

P.S. Briasco	R.K. Brown	M.J. Pawson	M.W. Douglas	M.J. Greatbatch	T.E. Blain	J.B.M. Furlong	R.P. Wixon	Byes	Leg-byes	Wides	No-balls	Total	Wkts
								2	3			172	10
5–0–19–0									1			238	6
5–2–4–0									1		2	124	10
1–1–0–0								7	6		2	189	7
1–0–2–0									1	1	1	88	0
7–1–13–0									10	1	2	256	10
									14		18	374	10
									6		1	68	4
6–3–13–0									13	1		305	8
								3	3		4	168	7
													Ab.
13–4–29–2	6–0–26–0							7	4		8	264	3
5–1–18–0									13		1	233	7
2–0–24–0									3			246	2
9–4–12–1		21–5–76–1							7		9	261	9
		12–5–45–2	1–0–5–1						2		6	225	10
6–2–14–0		11–0–33–0						8	12		7	220	10
10–5–13–1	8–2–30–0		5–0–29–2	8–0–57–0	9–0–56–1			7	9			295	4
3–1–8–0		19.4–2–55–3		10–1–33–0	43–20–67–2			1	13		17	362	9
2–0–2–0	3–0–28–0	4–0–13–0	3–0–62–0	4–2–12–0	13–3–14–1			1	1	2	2	194	4
75–24–171–4 42.75	17–2–84–0 –	67.4–12–222–6 37.00	9–0–96–3 32.00	8–0–57–0 –	9–0–56–1 56.00	14–3–45–0 –	56–23–81–3 27.00						

NORTHERN DISTRICTS
First-Class Matches 1991–92

BATTING

BATTING	v. Central Districts (Masterton) 29 November – 1 December, 1991		v. Otago (Hamilton) 6–8 December, 1991		v. Auckland (Auckland) 12–14 December, 1991		v. Otago (Alexandra) 3–5 January, 1992		v. Wellington (Wellington) 10–12 January, 1992		v. Central Districts (Hamilton) 16–18 January, 1992		v. Canterbury (Hamilton) 20–22 January, 1992		v. Auckland (Rotorua) 25–27 January, 1992		v. Canterbury (Christchurch) 1–3 February, 1992		v. Wellington (Hamilton) 9–11 February, 1992	
K.A. Wealleans	29	58	24	28	3	2	56	6	108	28	–	–	21	–	4	–	62	–	0	16
D.J. White	1	0	5	2	20	39	30	28	0	5	–	–	7	–	30	–	14	19	68*	23
G.E. Bradburn	0	19	18	83*	7	37	14	33	1	0	–	–	0	–	27	–	72	–	–	52*
S.A. Thomson	51	22	79*	9*	2	16	5	15	6	13					32	–	6	0*	57*	126*
M.P. Maynard	26	27	142	–	195	110	22	23	20	53	–	–	31	–	92	–	50	–	–	102
B.A. Young	49*	86*	7*	–	3	82	42	13	59	–	–	–	129	–	20	–	1	2*	4	24
M.N. Hart	7	2	–	–	1	46	20	6*	20	65*	–	–	22	–	2	–	38	25	–	–
D.J. Nash	0	23*			0	0*														
S.B. Doull	4	–	–	–	44	0*	1	8			–	–	23	–	8	–	108	–	–	–
R.P. de Groen	0	–	–	–	0*	–			0*	–	–	–	15*	–	1	–	5	–	–	–
R.L. Hayes	0	–	–	–			0*	0	10	–	–	–	2	–	0*	–	0*	–	–	–
M.D. Bailey			–	–	0	1	60	8	1	77*	–	–	18	–	2	–	7	–	–	–
D.F. Potter							2	4	4	–	–	–								
B.S. Oxenham													24	–						
Byes	2				2		1	3	2	3			3						2	6
Leg-byes	3	1	6	4	5	1	8	4	10	4			13		1		4		1	12
Wides							4	2	1	2					1		1	2		5
No-balls			3		2	1	1		16	15			3		11		17	3	14	5
Total	172	238	284	106	284	335	266	153	258	265			311		231		385	51	146	371
Wickets	10	6	4	2	10	8	10	10	10	5			10		10		10	2	2	4
Result	L		W		D		W		D		Ab.		D		D		D		W	
Points	0		16		4		16		4		2		4		4		0		12	

BOWLING

BOWLING	R.P. de Groen	R.L. Hayes	S.B. Doull	G.E. Bradburn	S.A. Thomson	D.J. Nash	M.N. Hart	D.F. Potter
v. Central Districts (Masterton)	14–3–32–1	9–2–31–0	18–4–44–3	8–1–27–0	10–4–21–1	4.3–2–14–1		
29 November – 1 December, 1991	15–5–37–1	11–0–41–2	6–2–29–0	14–0–56–2	11.1–0–62–0			
v. Otago (Hamilton)	24–5–72–3	19–6–60–4	18–4–42–1	4–0–14–0	13–7–9–2			
6–8 December, 1991	22–10–40–4	10–2–20–1	13–3–34–1	23–14–29–1	5–2–12–0		7.5–2–31–3	
v. Auckland (Auckland)	22–6–56–3		20–3–49–3	21–4–58–2	13–4–35–1	13–5–35–1	3–2–3–0	
12–14 December, 1991	18–3–81–0		4–1–11–1	35–12–123–1	6.5–1–25–0	8–2–30–0	30–8–140–2	
v. Otago (Alexandra)		15–6–21–0	17–5–36–1	9–4–25–1	17–6–31–3		1–0–9–0	27.4–9–69–5
3–5 January, 1992		11–2–23–0	8.3–0–36–3	6–0–33–0	8–0–16–2		6–1–15–1	16–4–62–3
v. Wellington (Wellington)	16–5–27–1	14–3–41–0		9.4–4–33–3	7–3–11–0		21–6–45–5	20–6–40–1
10–12 January, 1992	13–2–51–0	15–6–28–2		22–6–60–1	7–0–27–1		30.5–7–87–3	7–1–25–0
v. Central Districts (Hamilton)	24–8–43–2	18–3–61–1	20–4–59–2	18–4–24–0			17–7–38–1	15–4–46–0
16–18 January, 1992								
v. Canterbury (Hamilton)	29–7–76–3	17–7–62–1	11–6–22–1	34.2–14–47–4			13–8–18–1	
20–22 January, 1992								
v. Auckland (Rotorua)	21–12–18–5	6–2–14–0	20.4–8–35–5	1–0–3–0				
25–27 January, 1992	4–2–6–0	8–3–13–0	3–2–3–0	5–1–17–0	7–1–35–1		5–2–12–0	
v. Canterbury (Christchurch)	27–6–52–1	21.5–5–55–4	17–3–56–0	42–12–90–2	9–0–34–0		43–12–85–2	
1–3 February, 1992								
v. Wellington (Hamilton)	27–9–62–1	24–5–79–0	16.1–4–48–1	24–6–60–1	13–0–49–0		29–14–38–0	
9–11 February, 1992	5–2–11–0	12–1–55–1	8–1–26–2	4–2–10–0			14–6–40–2	
Bowlers average	281–85–664–25 26.56	210.5–53–605–16 37.81	204.2–50–530–24 22.08	279.4–84–709–19 37.31	127–28–367–11 33.36	25.3–9–79–2 39.50	220.4–75–561–20 28.05	85.4–24–242–9 26.88

M	Inns	NO	Runs	HS	Av
10	15	–	445	108	29.66
10	16	1	291	68*	19.40
10	14	2	343	72	28.58
8	15	5	439	126*	43.90
10	13	–	893	195	68.69
10	14	4	521	129	52.10
10	12	2	254	65*	25.40
2	4	2	23	23*	11.50
9	8	1	196	108	28.00
9	6	2	21	15*	5.25
9	7	3	12	10	3.00
9	9	1	174	77*	21.75
3	3	–	10	4	3.33
1	1	–	24	24	24.00

FIELDING FIGURES

31 – B.A. Young (ct 30/st 1)
14 – M.P. Maynard (ct 12/st 2)
11 – G.E. Bradburn and M.N. Hart
7 – M.D. Bailey
6 – K.A. Wealleans
5 – D.J. White
4 – S.A. Thomson
2 – D.J. Nash and D.F. Potter (plus one as sub)
1 – R.P. de Groen, S.B. Doull and B.S. Oxenham (plus one as sub)

Thomson of Nothern Districts (UPA)

M.D. Bailey	M.P. Maynard	Byes	Leg-byes	Wides	No-balls	Total	Wkts
			4		2	173	6
		8	5	1		238	6
			15			212	10
			11			177	10
		1	7		1	244	10
		4	10	1		424	4
			12	1	1	203	10
			7	1		192	10
		1	6	3	1	204	10
		1	21		1	300	8
	1–0–3–0	5	9		1	288	6
		5	5		1	235	10
			2	1	1	72	10
		1	5		2	92	1
		1	24		5	397	10
4–0–16–0		3	15		4	370	3
			4			146	5
4–0–16–0 –	1–0–3–0 –						

OTAGO

First-Class Matches 1991–92

BATTING

	v. Auckland (Auckland) 29 November – 1 December, 1991		v. Northern Districts (Hamilton) 6–8 December, 1991		v. Canterbury (Oamaru) 12–14 December, 1991		v. Northern Districts (Alexandra) 3–5 January, 1992		v. Central Districts (Dunedin) 10–12 January, 1992		v. Auckland (Dunedin) 16–18 January, 1992		v. Wellington (Wellington) 21–23 January, 1992		v. Wellington (Dunedin) 1–3 February, 1992		v. Canterbury (Christchurch) 5–7 February, 1992		v. Central Districts (Palmerston North) 9–11 February, 1992	
M.H. Austen	73	3	2	56	36	0	11	21	40*	9	10	56	24	–	14	68	3	0	31	0
P.W. Dobbs	20	4	27	0	5	19			3	1*					86	21	3	32	13	23
K.R. Rutherford	79	32	18	3	133	44	42	55	64	49	41	0	87	8*						
M.J. Lamont	20	26	20	11	0	60	5	25	35	34	24	8	49	23	1	67	3	14	12	8
I.S. Billcliff	0	34	44	0	48	13	30	16	19	5	45	5	20	–	45	1	26	35	12	0
R.N. Hoskin	14	61	0	29	53	0	52	20	80	36	47	4	48	5						
N.A. Mallender	0	20	7	19*	–	13*	6	7	0	10			20*	–	12	1	49	6*	100*	–
K.J. McKnight	15	8	24	26																
J.K. Lindsay	6	18	2	2	–	–					8	0*	16*	–						
E.J. Marshall	13*	47	19*	8	4	23*														
K.R. O'Dowda	2	19*					4	3*	–	–							0*	0*	0*	–
D.J. Hunter			34	12	–	–														
S.A. Robinson					49*	16	0	25	35	2	41	53	5	6*	9	21	4	13	35	72*
K.J. Burns							18	0												
J.W. Wilson							1	9			47*	8*	14	–	4	16	20	2	67	–
A.J. Gale							20*	3	5*	6*	14	–	0	–	10	2*	1	0	0	–
R.T. King											1	0			7	16	12	1		
D.S. McHardy															0	11	100	67	53	85*
P.J. Marshall									10	6*	12	–	–	–	3*	9*			8	–
Byes		1			5	5				3			3	1		1		5	1	1
Leg-byes	6	10	15	11	10	4	12	7	13	3	8	1	6	2	6	11	7	5	13	1
Wides					4		1	1	1				1		1		1			2
No-balls	6	6			3	1	1			4	3		7	6	2		7	1	17	2
Total	254	289	212	177	350	198	203	192	305	168	301	135	300	51	200	245	236	181	362	194
Wickets	10	10	10	10	7	7	10	10	8	7	10	7	8	2	10	9	10	9	9	4
Result	L		L		L		L		D		D		W		W		D		D	
Points	0		0		4		0		4		4		16		12		0		4	

BOWLING

	N.A. Mallender	K.R. O'Dowda	E.J. Marshall	M.H. Austen	J.K. Lindsay	D.J. Hunter	I.S. Billcliff	J.W. Wilson
v. Auckland (Auckland)	17–2–53–3	16–4–60–1	18–5–60–1	10.3–1–42–0	12–3–31–0			
29 November – 1 December, 1991	15–1–44–0	10–0–55–2	14.3–2–66–1	15–1–22–1	15–0–81–0			
v. Northern Districts (Hamilton)	15–8–20–1		19–4–62–1	19–4–70–0	16–3–68–1	18–4–58–1		
6–8 December, 1991	6–2–10–1		8–2–25–1		8–1–48–0	6–0–15–0	0.4–0–0.4–0	
v. Canterbury (Oamaru)	22–4–59–3		19–8–47–0	17–6–49–1	23–7–72–5	17–0–65–0		
12–14 December, 1991	13–4–28–4		7.2–0–61–0	11–3–38–0	21–1–100–1	7–3–20–0		
v. Northern Districts (Alexandra)	25–5–52–6	21–5–58–2		12–4–22–0				17–1–66–0
3–5 January, 1992	22–6–43–2	13–2–33–1		4–1–8–1				23.5–7–48–5
v. Central Districts (Dunedin)	23.1–10–39–7	14–2–51–0						
10–12 January, 1992	25–10–50–4	7–2–13–0		7–2–21–0				
v. Auckland (Dunedin)					2–1–1–0			18.5–5–50–5
16–18 January, 1992				3–0–19–0	34–11–96–2			33–8–108–3
v. Wellington (Wellington)	21–2–39–5			4.1–0–13–1	4–1–3–0			9–3–19–0
21–23 January, 1992	22–6–37–5			3.5–0–13–2	22–7–41–0			13–3–25–1
v. Wellington (Dunedin)	23–7–44–5							19–4–52–3
1–3 February, 1992	11–3–20–0						6–3–7–1	8–3–17–1
v. Canterbury (Christchurch)	17–4–42–3	19–1–80–2		6–1–20–0				16–3–47–3
5–7 February, 1992	7.3–0–23–0	9.3–2–34–0					9–0–38–0	15–3–41–0
v. Central Districts (Palmerston		17–5–48–0		11–2–36–0				23–6–40–1
North) 9–11 February, 1992		11–1–54–2		7–1–26–0				16–3–49–4
	284.4–74–603–49	137.3–24–486–10	85.5–21–321–4	130.3–26–399–6	157–35–541–9	48–7–158–1	15.4–3–49–1	211.4–49–562–26
Bowlers average	12.30	48.60	80.25	66.50	60.11	158.00	49.00	21.61

M	Inns	NO	Runs	HS	Av
10	19	1	457	73	25.38
7	14	1	257	86	19.76
7	14	1	655	133	50.38
10	20	–	445	67	22.25
10	19	–	398	48	20.94
7	14	–	449	80	32.07
9	15	5	270	100*	27.00
2	4	–	73	26	18.25
5	7	2	52	18	10.40
3	6	3	114	47	38.00
5	7	5	28	19*	14.00
2	2	–	46	34	23.00
8	16	3	386	72*	29.69
1	2	–	18	18	9.00
6	10	2	188	67	23.50
7	11	4	61	20*	8.71
3	6	–	37	16	6.16
3	6	1	316	100	63.20
5	6	3	48	12	16.00

FIELDING FIGURES

28 – S.A. Robinson
12 – R.N. Hoskin
8 – K.R. Rutherford and M.J. Lamont
5 – I.S. Billcliff and J.W. Wilson
4 – A.J. Gale
2 – M.H. Austen, K.R. O'Dowda, K.J. McKnight and R.T. King (plus two as sub)
1 – E.J. Marshall and K.J. Burns

Neil Mallender of Otago (David Munden)

A.J. Gale	K.R. Rutherford	D.S. McHardy	M.J. Lamont	P.W. Dobbs	R.T. King	P.J. Marshall	Byes	Leg-byes	Wides	No-balls	Total	Wkts
							9	9	1	1	264	5
							6	9	3		283	5
								6		3	284	4
								4			106	2
								3		2	295	9
							4	6			257	5
28.2–10–59–2							1	8	4	1	266	10
16–8–14–1							3	4	2		153	10
17–4–33–2					8–3–24–1		6	8		1	159	10
23–4–40–0	10–4–26–3				18–3–55–1			6	1	5	212	9
13–3–31–1	1–1–0–0				11–3–28–3			17	2	4	127	10
22.5–5–65–0	10–2–33–0				17–3–69–0		4	8	2	4	402	5
10–1–24–1					17–3–40–3			4	2	13	142	10
14–2–44–1					9–1–37–0		2	6	4	6	205	10
20–7–50–1		1–0–10–1			15–4–50–0			8	3	3	214	10
2-2-0-0	9-0-78-2	9-0-49-1	8-1-35-0	1-1-0-0	4–0–7–0		5	9	2	1	227	5
18–2–41–0		1–0–1–0					6	10	1	14	247	9
10–1–33–0			15–2–67–1				1	8		5	245	1
28–7–65–2			1–0–6–0		23–6–59–6			15	2		269	9
6–3–22–1		2–1–13–1			8–2–33–1			1	4		198	9
228.1–59–521–12 43.41	21–7–59–3 19.66	13–1–102–4 25.50	25–2–122–2 61.00	8–1–35–0 –	1–1–0–0 –	130–28–402–15 26.80						

WELLINGTON

First-Class Matches 1991–92

BATTING

	v. Canterbury (Christchurch) 29 November – 1 December, 1991		v. Auckland (Wellington) 6–8 December, 1991		v. Central Districts (Wellington) 12–14 December, 1991		v. Auckland (Auckland) 3–5 January, 1992		v. Northern Districts (Wellington) 10–12 January, 1992		v. Otago (Wellington) 21–23 January, 1992		v. Canterbury (Wellington) 25–27 January, 1992		v. Otago (Dunedin) 1–3 February, 1992		v. Central Districts (Napier) 5–7 February, 1992		v. Northern istricts (Hamilton) 9–11 February, 1992	
G.P. Burnett	63	2	10	21	7	5			11	1*	33	6	12	–	45	4	8	83*	203	47
R.B. Reid	1	10	16	56	13	23	9	61	38	84										
M.E.L. Lane	0	23*			8	11														
J.D. Wells	29	2	1	102	1	86			23	25	8	22	7	–	40	39	28	–	2	–
G.R. Larsen	9	18	8	24*	8	7	4	24*					22	–	1	2	70	56	0*	–
J.R. Murtagh	0	0	8	1			41	44	7	22	0	3								
E.B. McSweeney	63	119	21	19*	17	30	3	14	31	9	15	107	6	–	24	25	15	50	–	5
E.J. Gray	25	11	18	–	0	2	51	0												
D.A. Stirling	56*	70	12	–	0	11			50	23										
L.J. Doull	27	1																		
J.P. Millmow	6	0*	3*	–	16	0														
A.H. Jones			8	103	0	53	48	14					5	–						
M.J. Sears			8	–	15*	15*	22	0	6	14	17	12	9	–	6	–	9*	–	–	23*
S.A. Kellett							8	22												
M.D. Crowe							3	5					23	–						
P.W. O'Rourke							0	12							26	–	1	–		
H.T. Davis							3*	0	1*	–	5	5	11*	–			0	–	–	–
R.A. Verry									26	76	9	6	12	–	13	21	31	15	132	0
B.R. Williams									0	20	1	21	1	–	33	–	1	11*	–	22*
G.J. MacKenzie									0	3*	8	3	0	–	0*	–			–	–
S.P. Blackmore											26	0			6	107*	27	31	11	27
M.C. Goodson											1*	2*								
G.R. Baker															6	12*	3	33*	–	18
C.D. Lee																			–	–
Byes				2					1	1		2	4			5	8	7	3	
Leg-byes	5	6	5	8	1	10	6	2	6	21	4	6	6		8	9	12	9	15	4
Wides		1		1	1	1	1		3		2	4			3	2				
No Balls	2	3	7	3	1	2	2	1	1	1	13	6	16		3	1	7	4		
Total	286	266	125	340	88	256	201	199	204	300	142	205	134		214	227	220	295	370	146
Wickets	10	9	10	5	10	10	10	10	10	8	10	10	10		10	5	10	4	3	5
Result	D		W		L		L		D		L		D		L		D		L	
Points	0		12		0		0		0		0		0		4		0		4	

BOWLING

	J.P. Millmow	D.A. Stirling	L.J. Doull	G.R. Larsen	E.J. Gray	A.H. Jones	M.J. Sears	P.W. O'Rourke
v. Canterbury (Christchurch)	22–7–48–1	17–3–61–0	10–0–58–0	38–14–64–6	21–6–65–0			
29 November – 1 December, 1991	6–0–28–1	6–0–28–0						
v. Auckland (Wellington)	21–7–49–5	10–2–43–0		172–8–39–3			15–3–33–2	
6–8 December, 1991	18–3–44–3	23–4–63–1		20–7–46–0	18–4–40–2	8–0–30–0	9–1–48–0	
v. Central Districts (Wellington)	7–1–22–1	15–4–45–1		19–11–15–1	3–2–2–0		19.1–6–48–6	
12–14 December, 1991		12–4–34–0		14–9–19–0	20.2–5–67–1	16–2–47–1	12–1–40–1	
v. Auckland (Auckland)				13.2–6–36–0	16–5–60–2	7–1–21–2	15–5–43–0	11.4–4–19–0
3–5 January, 1992				9–2–14–3	23–9–39–1	1–0–9–0	10–5–22–1	
v. Northern Districts (Wellington)		17.5–1–47–2					14–0–56–4	
10–12 January, 1992		6–0–26–0					16–2–51–3	
v. Otago (Wellington)							19–1–56–0	
21–23 January, 1992							4–0–16–1	
v. Canterbury (Wellington)				11–6–12–0			18–4–51–0	
25–27 January, 1992								
v. Otago (Dunedin)				24–11–29–2			25–8–65–4	22.5–7–42–3
1–3 February, 1992				8–3–11–1			9–4–26–2	14.5–6–36–2
v. Central Districts (Napier)				17–7–36–3			14–5–44–0	20–6–61–1
5–7 February, 1992				9–0–58–1			4–0–35–0	4.4–0–32–1
v. Northern Districts (Hamilton)				11–5–17–0			5–1–20–0	
9–11 February, 1992							20–1–64–1	
	74–18–191–11	106.5–18–327–4	10–0–58–0	210.4–89–396–20	101.2–31–273–6	32–3–107–3	228.1–47–718–25	74–23–190–7
Bowlers average	17.36	81.75	–	19.80	45.50	35.66	28.72	27.14

	M	Inns	NO	Runs	HS	Av
	9	17	3	561	203*	40.07
	5	10	–	311	84	31.10
	2	4	1	42	23*	14.00
	9	15	–	415	102	27.66
	8	14	3	253	70	23.00
	5	10	–	126	44	12.60
	10	18	1	573	119	33.70
	4	7	–	107	51	15.28
	4	7	1	222	70	37.00
	1	2	–	28	27	14.00
	3	5	2	25	16	8.33
	4	7	–	231	103	33.00
	9	13	4	156	23*	17.33
	1	2	–	30	22	15.00
	2	3	–	31	23	10.33
	3	4	–	39	26	9.75
	6	7	3	25	11*	6.25
	6	11	–	341	132	31.00
	6	9	2	110	33	15.71
	5	6	2	14	8	3.50
	4	8	1	235	107*	33.57
	1	2	2	3	2*	–
	3	5	2	72	33*	24.00
	1	–	–	–	–	–

FIELDING FIGURES

26 – E.B. McSweeney (ct 23/st 3)
8 – G.P. Burnett
4 – B.R. Williams, S.P. Blackmore and J.R. Murtagh (plus two as sub)
3 – H.T. Davis, S.A. Kellett, E.J. Gray, J.D. Wells and D.A. Stirling
2 – G.R. Larsen, A.H. Jones, R.B. Reid, R.A. Verry, M.J. Sears and G.R. Baker
1 – J.P. Millmow, G.J. MacKenzie and P.W. O'Rourke

Evan Gray of Wellington. (Sporting Pictures UK Ltd)

H.T. Davis	S.A. Kellett	G.J. MacKenzie	B.R. Williams	M.C. Goodson	J.D. Wells	M.D. Crowe	C. Lee	Byes	Leg-byes	Wides	No-balls	Total	Wkts
									8		2	304	7
									2		1	58	1
									9			173	0
								7	13	1	4	291	7
									4			136	10
									5			212	3
21.2–3–63–5	1–0–12–0								4			136	10
13.3–4–42–0								9	10		1	145	5
14–3–47–2		20–4–58–2	23–10–38–0					2	10	1	16	258	10
10–1–58–1		17–1–62–1	18–4–61–0					3	4	2	15	265	5
19–5–62–1		19–5–70–1	40–18–60–4	18–4–42–2	1–0–1–0			3	6	1	7	300	8
6–0–24–0		1.5–0–8–1						1	2		6	51	2
9–2–29–1		6–3–12–2	7–2–12–1		2.2–0–10–0			1	3	2	8	136	4
		15–3–44–1	10–3–14–0						6	1	2	200	10
		14–1–55–1	15–1–105–3					1	11			245	9
8–1–44–1			4.4–0–28–0					1	8		6	222	7
9.2–0–55–3			8.5–0–50–3						2	1	2	232	9
3–0–22–2		9–0–46–0	17.2–9–38–0					2	1		14	146	2
8–2–53–0		19–2–82–2	20–0–92–0		9.4–0–62–1			6	12	5	5	371	4
121.1–21–499–16 31.18	1–0–12–0 –	120.5–19–437–11 39.72	163.5–47–498–11 45.27	18–4–42–2 21.00	1–0–1–0 –	2.2–0–10–0 –	9.4–0–62–1 62.00						

ENGLAND IN NEW ZEALAND

First-Class Matches 1992

BATTING

	v. Emerging Players (Hamilton) 3–5 January		v. Minor Associations XI (Napier) 7–9 January		v. New Zealand XI (Napier) 13–15 January		First Test Match (Christchurch) 18–22 January		v. Central Districts (New Plymouth) 24–26 January		Second Test Match (Auckland) 30 January – 3 February		Third Test Match (Wellington) 6–10 February	
G.A. Gooch	101*	–	42	–	3	64	2	–	8	–	4	114	30	11
A.J. Stewart	0	–	46	–	71*	2	148	–	101*	–	4	8	107	63
R.C. Russell	50	–	57	–	–	0	36	–	–	–	33	24	18	24*
G.A. Hick	129*	–	113	–	0	71	35	–	115	–	30	4	43	22
R.A. Smith	17	–	15	4	0	35	96	–	–	–	0	35	6	76
A.J. Lamb	88	–			76*	61*	93	–			13	60	30	142
M.R. Ramprakash	10*	–	13	5	–	0			19*	–				
C.C. Lewis	22*	–			–	36	70	–			33	23		
P.A.J. DeFreitas	–	–			–	–	7*	–			1	0	3	–
D.V. Lawrence	–	–	4	–									6	–
P.C.R. Tufnell	–	–	2	–			–	–			6*	0*	2*	–
N.H. Fairbrother			9	14*					–	–				
D.A. Reeve			42*	6*	–	42	59	–	–	–	22	25	18	0
D.R. Pringle			0	9	–	1*	10	–	–	–	41	2		
I.T. Botham									–	–			15	1
R.K. Illingworth									–	–				
Byes	4						5							
Leg-byes	4		6		3	3	10		3		11	16	12	13
Wides			2		2		1							
No-balls	9		2		4	1	8				5	2	11	7
Total	434		353	38	159	316	580		246		203	321	305	359
Wickets	4		10	3	3	8	9		2		10	10	10	7
Result	W		D		W		W		D		W		D	

BOWLING

	P.A.J. DeFreitas	C.C. Lewis	D.R. Pringle	D.A. Reeve	P.C.R. Tufnell	G.A. Hick	D.V. Lawrence	G.A. Gooch
v. Emerging Players	18–7–38–2	16–5–35–0			21–7–34–1	10–5–18–0	18–7–28–2	11–6–14–2
(Hamilton) 3–5 January	10–3–24–0	11.5–3–37–2			23–4–66–5	4–2–4–0	12–5–15–2	
v. Minor Associations XI			24–5–65–1	23–6–61–2	22.2–6–58–2		22–5–52–5	
(Napier) 7–9 January			23–6–57–2	10–2–45–1	38–14–65–4	30–14–39–1	12–3–34–0	
v. New Zealand XI	20–7–60–1	20–7–48–2	17–7–20–1	13.1–7–19–2		15–0–50–0		
(Nelson) 13–15 January	6–1–15–0	8–3–12–0	7–2–20–1	7–0–20–0		11–3–53–0		8–2–64–0
First Test Match	32.4–16–54–2	30–9–69–1	15–2–54–1	8–4–16–1	39–10–100–4	3–0–11–0		
(Christchurch) 18–22 January	23–6–54–0	22–3–66–2	21–5–64–1	2–0–8–0	46.1–25–47–7	14–8–11–0		
v. Central Districts			20–6–37–2	19–6–49–1				8–4–7–1
(New Plymouth) 24–26 January								
Second Test Match	16–2–53–2	21–7–31–15	15–7–21–2	7–1–21–0	4–2–16–1			
(Auckland) 30 January – 3 February	27–11–62–4	27–4–83–2	7–2–23–1		17–5–45–2	1–1–0–0		
Third Test Match	8–4–12–0			3–1–11–0	71–22–147–2	69–27–126–4	27–7–67–1	
(Wellington) 6–10 February				4.5–2–4–1	9–5–12–0		2.1–1–4–0	
	160.4–57–372–11	155.5–41–381–14	149–42–361–12	97–29–254–8	290.3–100–590–28	156–60–312–5	93.1–28–200–10	27–12–85–3
Bowlers average	33.81	27.21	30.08	31.75	21.07	62.40	20.00	28.33

M	Inns	NO	Runs	HS	Av
7	10	1	379	114	42.11
7	10	2	550	148	68.75
7	8	1	242	57	34.57
7	10	1	562	129*	62.44
7	10	–	284	96	28.40
5	8	2	563	142	93.83
4	5	2	47	19*	15.66
4	5	1	184	70	46.00
5	4	1	11	7*	3.66
3	2	–	10	6	5.00
5	4	3	10	6*	10.00
2	2	1	23	14*	23.00
6	8	2	214	59	35.66
5	6	1	63	41	12.60
2	2	–	16	15	8.00
1	–	–	–	–	–

FIELDING FIGURES

23 – R.C. Russell (ct 22/st 1)
10 – G.A. Hick
8 – A.J. Stewart
7 – R.A. Smith
3 – A.J. Lamb, D.A. Reeve, P.C.R. Tufnell, G.A. Gooch and M.R. Ramprakash
2 – D.R. Pringle
1 – C.C. Lewis and I.T. Botham

M.R. Ramprakash	R.A. Smith	A.J. Stewart	A.J. Lamb	R.C. Russell	I.T. Botham	R.K. Illingworth	Byes	Leg-byes	Wides	No-balls	Total	Wkts
								9	5		176	8
							5	2		7	153	9
							3	6		11	245	10
4–1–11–0							2	7		11	260	9
								10		1	207	7
8–1–29–1	7–2–27–0	2–0–9–0	1–0–6–0	1–0–5–0			1	5	1		266	2
							1	7		8	312	10
	4–2–6–0						1	7		13	264	10
				16–4–40–2	21–7–53–1			3		7	189	7
										15	142	10
								1		11	214	10
					14–4–53–1							
					8–1–23–2							
12–2–40–1 40.00	11–4–33–0 –	2–0–9–0 –	1–0–6–0 –	1–0–5–0 –	38–9–116–5 23.20	21–7–53–1 53.00						

FIRST-CLASS AVERAGES

BATTING

	M	Inns	NO	Runs	HS	Av	100s	50s
M.P. Maynard	10	13	–	893	195	68.69	4	3
D.S. McHardy	3	6	1	316	100	63.20	1	3
J.J. Crowe	10	19	2	1063	142*	62.52	4	5
L.K. Germon	10	10	4	335	91	55.83	–	2
A.C. Parore	9	12	4	420	155*	52.80	1	2
B.A. Young	11	16	4	606	129	50.50	1	4
S.A. Thomson	10	19	6	607	126*	46.69	1	5
S.W. Duff	11	17	5	559	164*	46.58	1	2
L.G. Howell	10	15	2	583	112	44.84	1	4
C.Z. Harris	8	12	3	403	94*	44.77	–	3
D.N. Patel	8	14	1	574	204	44.15	1	4
K.R. Rutherford	10	20	2	787	133	43.72	1	5
B.Z. Harris	6	9	1	347	133	43.37	2	–
M.W. Douglas	12	22	4	773	144	42.94	2	5
R.T. Latham	7	11	–	470	87	42.72	–	5
G.P. Burnett	9	17	3	561	203*	40.07	1	2
A.P. O'Dowd	7	12	4	306	113	38.25	1	1
E.J. Marshall	3	6	3	114	47	38.00	–	–
J.G. Wright	7	14	–	518	116	37.00	2	1
D.A. Stirling	4	7	1	222	70	37.00		3
R.G. Twose	11	20	2	653	107*	36.27	2	2
A.H. Jones	7	13	–	457	143	35.15	2	1
B.A. Pocock	8	15	3	409	110*	34.08	2	1
T.E. Blain	12	19	2	574	96	33.76	–	4
E.B. McSweeney	10	18	1	573	119	33.70	2	2
S.P. Blackmore	4	8	1	235	107*	33.57	1	–
R.N. Hoskin	7	14	–	449	80	32.07	–	4
S.B. Doull	10	10	2	252	108	31.50	1	–
R.B. Reid	5	10	–	311	84	31.10	–	3
M.D. Crowe	5	9	1	243	56	30.37	–	1
J.T.C. Vaughan	10	18	4	425	81	30.35	–	1
J.D. Wells	10	17	–	508	102	29.88	1	2
S.A. Robinson	8	16	3	386	72*	29.69	–	2
P.G. Kennedy	10	14	2	349	74	29.08	–	2
G.E. Bradburn	11	16	2	397	72	28.35	–	3
A.J. Junt	10	14	3	308	68	28.00	–	3
M.W. Priest	10	11	1	279	103	27.90	1	1
K.A. Wealleans	11	17	–	460	108	27.05	1	3
N.A. Mallender	9	15	5	270	100*	27.00	1	–
R.A. Verry	6	11	–	290	132	26.36	1	–
S.J. Peterson	6	11	–	289	77	26.27	–	2
B.R. Hartland	9	15	–	386	127	25.73	1	2
R.K. Brown	5	7	3	102	60*	25.50	–	1
M.H. Austen	10	19	1	457	73	25.38	–	4
J.W. Wilson	6	10	2	188	67	23.50	–	1
G.R. Larsen	8	14	3	253	70	23.00	–	2
M.J. Lamont	11	22	–	504	67	22.90	–	2
M.D. Bailey	9	9	1	174	77*	21.75	–	2
M.J. Greatbatch	10	17	–	366	81	21.52	–	2
I.D.S. Smith	5	7	2	105	33*	21.00	–	–
I.S. Bilcliff	10	19	–	398	48	20.94	–	–
S.W.J. Wilson	12	21	1	414	94	20.70	–	2
M.N. Hart	12	15	2	263	65*	20.23	–	1
P.W. Dobbs	7	14	1	257	86	19.76	–	1
D.J. White	10	16	1	291	68*	19.40	–	1
C.L. Cairns	8	11	2	172	61	19.11	–	1
P.S. Briasco	11	18	–	335	104	18.61	1	1
D.J. Leonard	11	14	3	198	67	18.00	–	1
D.J. Boyle	10	15	1	249	84	17.78	–	2
S.W. Brown	9	16	1	266	62	17.73	–	2
M.J. Sears	9	13	4	156	23*	17.33	–	–
B.R. Williams	6	9	2	110	33	15.71	–	–
E.J. Gray	4	7	–	107	51	15.28	–	1
T.J. Franklin	5	9	–	134	44	14.88	–	–
R.G. Petrie	8	10	1	132	100	14.66	1	–
C.D. Ingham	8	10	1	132	100	14.66	1	–
J.R. Murtagh	5	10	–	126	44	12.60	–	–

(Qualification – 100 runs, average 10.00)

BOWLING

	Overs	Mds	Runs	Wkts	Av	Best	10/m	5/inn
N.A. Mallender	284.4	74	603	49	12.30	7-39	2	5
J.P. Millmow	74	18	191	11	17.36	5-49	–	1
R.J. Drown	138	53	284	15	18.93	4-6	–	–
G.R. Larsen	210.4	89	396	20	19.80	6-64	–	1
C.L. Cairns	294	67	872	42	20.76	7-34	1	2
J.W. Wilson	211.4	49	562	26	21.61	5-48	–	2
R.G. Twose	188	57	455	20	22.75	3-22	–	–
S.B. Doull	204.2	50	551	24	22.95	5-35	–	1
D.N. Askew	157.2	35	531	23	23.08	4-42	–	–
M.B. Ownes	131.1	27	354	15	23.60	4-18	–	–
J.T.C. Vaughan	159.5	52	434	18	24.11	5-72	–	1
D.J. Leonard	288.5	78	865	34	25.44	6-67	–	1
R.P. de Groen	281	85	664	25	26.56	5-18	–	1
D.N. Patel	298.4	73	857	32	26.78	7-72	1	2
P.J. Marshall	130	28	402	15	26.80	6-59	–	1
S.W. Brown	216.3	53	677	25	27.08	5-39	–	2
S.W. Duff	324.1	103	774	28	27.64	4-13	–	–
R.G. Petrie	240.5	45	734	26	28.23	5-70	–	1
R.M. Ford	243.3	74	516	18	28.66	6-35	–	1
M.J. Sears	228.1	47	718	25	28.72	6-48	–	1
D.K. Morrison	209.4	41	596	20	29.80	3-38	–	–
M.N. Hart	254.4	77	695	23	30.21	5-45	–	1
M.W. Priest	359	120	855	28	30.53	6-69	–	1
H.T. Davis	122.1	21	499	16	31.18	5-63	–	1
C. Pringle	315.1	70	941	29	32.44	4-52	–	–
M.L. Su'a	238.5	56	738	21	35.14	3-54	–	–
C.L. Auckram	145.4	34	461	13	35.46	3-39	–	–
R.L. Hayes	236.5	53	711	20	35.55	4-55	–	–
G.E. Bradburn	309.4	86	808	21	38.47	4-47	–	–
M.J. Haslam	132.5	33	427	11	38.31	3-29	–	–
G.J. Mackenzie	120.5	19	437	11	39.72	2-12	–	–
S.A. Thomson	148	31	441	11	40.09	3-31	–	–
W. Watson	219.1	88	487	12	40.58	3-51	–	–
A.J. Gale	228.1	59	521	12	43.41	2-33	–	–
B.R. Williams	163.5	47	498	11	45.27	4-60	–	–
K.R. O'Dowda	137.3	24	486	10	48.60	2-54	–	–

LEADING FIELDERS

34 – L.K. Germon (ct 31/st 3); 31 – T.E. Blain (ct 28/st 3) and B.A. Young (ct 30/.st 1); 28 – S.A. Robinson; 26 – E.B. McSweeney (ct 23/st 3); 23 – A.C. Parore (ct 22/st 1); 15 – I.D.S. Smith; 14 – M.N. Hart, A.J. Hunt and M.P. Maynard (ct 12/st 2); 13 – G.E. Bradburn and J.J. Crowe; 12 – M.J. Greatbatch and R.N. Hoskin; 11 – S.W. Duff and K.R. Rutherford; 10 – R.T. Latham and J.T.C. Vaughan

SECTION

D

SOUTH AFRICA

Nissan Shield
Castle Cup
President's Cup
UCBSA Bowl
Benson and Hedges Night Series
All first-class matches
First-class averages

South Africa return to Test cricket. The party that went to West Indies to play South Africa's first Test match for 22 years.
Back row (l to r) – C. Smith, J.N. Rhodes, M.W. Rushmere, R.P. Snell, T. Bosch, M.W. Pringle, W.J. Cronje, O. Henry, M.J. Procter
Front row (l to r) – A.C. Hudson, D.J. Richardson, A.P. Kuiper, A. Jordaan, K.C. Wessels, P.N. Kirsten, A.A. Donald, C.J.P.G. van Zyl. (Patrick Eagar)

In anticipation of their return to the fold of international cricket, South Africa restructured their season for 1991–92. The Currie Cup, the premier competition now known as the Castle Cup, was extended to include Border, while the 'A' teams of the Castle Cup sides no longer competed in the Bowl, but played for the President's Cup. The third first-class competition, the Bowl, had Eastern and Western Transvaal joining Griqualand West. The Nissan Shield, the 55-over knock-out tournament, was open to 16 teams, and from the second round to the semi-finals was played on a two-leg basis. The Benson and Hedges day/night competition remained unchanged.

There was an alteration to the points scoring system in the first-class matches with six points awarded for a win and two for a first-innings lead.

Friendly Matches

12, 13 and 14 September, 1991 *at Centurion Park, Verwoerdburg*

Northern Transvaal 269 for 2 dec. (V.F. du Preez 111 not out, M. Yachad 102) and 271 for 6 dec. (L.P. Vorster 83, A.M. Ferreira 63, M.J.R. Rindel 59)
Western Province 261 for 6 dec. (T.N. Lazard 150 not out, L. Seeff 54) and 283 for 4 (J.B. Commins 85, A.P. Kuiper 66)

Western Province won by 6 wickets

21, 22 and 23 September, 1991 *at Harmony Ground, Virginia*

Orange Free State 222 (J.M. Arthur 76) and 200 for 7 dec.
Transvaal 123 (N.W. Pretorius 4 for 24) and 198 (D.J. Cullinan 57, N.W. Pretorius 4 for 51)

Orange Free State won by 101 runs

27, 28 and 29 September, 1991 *at Boland Park, Worcester*

Eastern Province 392 (T.G. Shaw 105, R.E. Bryson 100, K.C. Wessels 79, H. Barnard 4 for 110) and 328 for 3 dec. (K.C. Wessels 168, P.G. Amm 124)
Boland 233 (L.J. Koen 90, T.G. Shaw 5 for 64) and 187 (B.N. Schultz 4 for 59)

Eastern Province won by 300 runs

25, 26 and 27 October, 1991 *at Victoria Club, Cradock*

Eastern Province 333 for 5 dec. (K.C. Wessels 212, D.J. Richardson 55 not out) and 221 for 3 dec. (M.W. Rushmere 100 not out, E.A.E. Baptiste 61)
Griqualand West 252 (W.E. Schonegevel 96 not out, M.N. Angel 67) and 147 (T.G. Shaw 4 for 31)

Eastern Province won by 155 runs

The early-season friendly matches saw maiden first-class centuries for Eastern Province bowlers Shaw and Bryson, and a career-best innings from Wayne Schonegevel who carried his bat for Griqualand West against Eastern Province. Kepler Wessels scored heavily.

17, 18 and 19 March, 1992 *at Newlands, Cape Town*

Western Province 188 (P.Carrick 6 for 70) and 243 for 9 dec. (T.N. Lazard 100)
Yorkshire 123 (C.R. Matthews 6 for 22) and 182 (R.J. Blakey 64, A.A. Metcalfe 50, D.B. Rundle 5 for 56)

Western Province won by 126 runs

29, 30 and 31 March, 1992 *at Kingsmead, Durban*

Natal 344 for 8 dec. (I.B. Hobson 92, M.B. Logan 64, J. Payn 63, A.R. Roberts 4 for 63) and 187 for 8 dec.
Northamptonshire 248 (R.J. Bailey 76, T.J. Packer 4 for 57) and 265 for 8 (A. Fordham 84, N.A. Felton 80, N.A. Stanley 54 not out)

Match drawn

2, 3 and 4 April, 1992 *at Brackenfell*

Boland 277 (N.M. Snyman 103, M. Erasmus 51 not out) and 347 for 8 dec. (M. Erasmus 103 not out, P.A. Booth 4 for 82)
Warwickshire 347 for 7 dec. (J.D. Ratcliffe 104, M. Asif Din 76, N.M.K. Smith 56 not out) and 161 for 6 (A.J. Moles 88 not out)

Match drawn

South Africa's return to international cricket allowed English counties to make pre-season tours. They found the opposition strong. Yorkshire lost their last seven wickets for 28 runs when they lost to Western Province. Against Natal, Fordham and Felton began Northamptonshire's attempt to score 284 to win with a partnership of 148, but the county fell short of their target.

First Round

NISSAN SHIELD

23 November, 1991 *at Brackenfell*

Border 247 for 7 (D.O. Nosworthy 69, I.L. Howell 50)
Boland 200

Border won by 47 runs

at PAM Brink Stadium, Springs

Griqualand West 202 for 7 (M.J. Cann 106 not out)
Eastern Transvaal 203 for 5 (P.A. Cottey 66)

Eastern Transvaal won by 5 wickets

at Pietersburg CC, Pietersburg

Orange Free State 282 for 3 (P.J.R. Steyn 127 not out, W.J. Cronje 83)
Northern Transvaal Country Districts 96 (A.A. Donald 5 for 25)

Orange Free State won by 186 runs

at Addison Park, Empangeni

Transvaal 254 for 7 (M.J. Mitchley 84, S.J. Cook 63, C.E.B. Rice 55)
Natal Country Districts 106 (S. Jacobs 4 for 6)

Transvaal won by 148 runs

at Witrand Cricket Field, Potchefstroom

Western Transvaal 162
Western Province 164 for 2 (T.N. Lazard 65, K.C. Jackson 51 not out)

Western Province won by 8 wickets

at King William's Town

Eastern Province 266 for 7 (M.W. Rushmere 139)
Border Country Districts 189 for 9 (D.H. Howell 60, M. Dilley 50, B.N. Schultz 4 for 26)

Eastern Province won by 77 runs

at Landau Recreation Club, Witbank

Natal 364 for 2 (M.B. Logan 115 retired hurt, A.C. Hudson 107, J.N. Rhodes 61)
Eastern Transvaal Country Districts 184 for 6 (B.W. Marais 56, C. Gilbert 53 not out)

Natal won by 180 runs

at Graaff Reinet

Eastern Province Country Districts 126 for 9 (E.A. Moseley 4 for 12)
Northern Transvaal 127 for 1 (P.H. Barnard 61 not out)

Northern Transvaal won by 9 wickets

The minor associations failed to cause any surprises. There was a distinct Glamorgan flavour at Springs where Cann, the Griqualand West captain, and Cottey shared the Man of the Match award. Logan and Hudson put on 241 for Natal's first wicket against Eastern Transvaal Country Districts. Logan was forced to retire at 245.

Second Round
First Leg

14 December, 1991 *at Buffalo Park, East London*

Border 227 for 8 (A.G. Lawson 81, B.M. Osborne 62)
Eastern Transvaal 192 for 9 (R.A. Moxham 64)

Border won by 35 runs

at Springbok Park, Bloemfontein

Orange Free State 225 for 8 (W.J. Cronje 79, P.J.R. Steyn 52)
Transvaal 176 (D.J. Cullinan 61)

Orange Free State won by 49 runs

15 December, 1991 *at St George's Park, Port Elizabeth*

Western Province 261 for 8 (T.N. Lazard 105, K.C. Jackson 58)
Eastern Province 263 for 4 (M.W. Rushmere 108 not out, K.C. Wessels 57)

Eastern Province won by 6 wickets

at Kingsmead, Durban

Northern Transvaal 200 (L.J. Barnard 70, M.J.R. Rindel 66, D. Norman 4 for 23)
Natal 200 for 9 (A.C. Hudson 79)

Natal won on losing fewer wickets with scores level

Second Leg

21 December, 1991 *at PAM Brink Stadium, Springs*

Border 156 for 3 (B.M. Osborne 62 not out)
Eastern Transvaal 136 (B.C. Fourie 5 for 16)

Border won by 20 runs

at Wanderers, Johannesburg

Orange Free State 233 for 5 (W.J. Cronje 82 not out, P.J.R. Steyn 53)
Transvaal 177

Orange Free State won by 56 runs

at Newlands, Cape Town

Eastern Province 215 for 5 (M. Michau 94, D.J. Richardson 51 not out)
Western Province 203 (K.C. Jackson 59)

Eastern Province won by 12 runs

at Centurion Park, Verwoerdburg

Northern Transvaal 171 for 4 (L.P. Vorster 93 not out)
Natal 106 for 6

Northern Transvaal won on faster scoring rate

Third Leg

22 December, 1991 *at Centurion Park, Verwoerdburg*

Natal 193 for 7
Northern Transvaal 197 for 5 (M.D. Haysman 74)

Northern Transvaal won by 5 wickets

Orange Free State began to emerge as the strongest of the one-day sides with the formidable pace trio of Donald, Franklyn Stephenson and van Zyl posing problems for the opposition. Only one of the ties went to a third leg when Northern Transvaal won on a faster scoring rate once rain had brought an abrupt end to the second-leg match at Centurion Park.

Semi-Finals
First Leg

11 January, 1992 *at Springbok Park, Bloemfontein*

Orange Free State 212 for 9 (L.J. Wilkinson 91)
Border 190 for 5

Orange Free State won by 22 runs

12 January, 1992 *at Centurion Park, Verwoerdburg*

Eastern Province 199 (L.J. Koen 63)
Northern Transvaal 168 (P.H. Barnard 50)

Eastern Province won by 31 runs

Second Leg

18 January, 1992 *at Buffalo Park, East London*

Orange Free State 232 for 5 (L.J. Wilkinson 102)
Border 196 for 7 (A.G. Lawson 99 not out)

Orange Free State won by 36 runs

at St George's Park, Port Elizabeth

Eastern Province 240 for 8 (L.J. Koen 86, T. Bosch 5 for 56)
Northern Transvaal 167 for 7 (M. Yachad 56)

Eastern Province won on faster scoring rate

Orange Free State and Eastern Province qualified for the Nissan Shield final without too many tremors. Wilkinson's 91 off 107 balls set up the Free State's first-leg win although Omar Henry took the individual award for his 3 for 26 in 11 overs. Wilkinson and Cronje added 77 off 78 balls in the second match. In the second leg of the tie between Eastern Province and Northern Transvaal, rain ended play with 12 overs unbowled, but Eastern won on a faster scoring rate.

FINAL
Eastern Province v. Orange Free State

The powerful Free State attack proved too much for Eastern Province who decided to bat first when they won the toss. The home side never recovered from the loss of their first four wickets for 28 runs, and the only effective stand of the innings was one of 37 between Richardson and Bryson.

Corrie van Zyl took the individual award while Hansie Cronje took the Man of the Series award. In the competition, Cronje had scores of 83, 79, 82 not out, 46, 40 and 32 not out, and he handled his side admirably.

NISSAN SHIELD FINAL – EASTERN PROVINCE v. ORANGE FREE STATE
1 February, 1992 at St George's Park, Port Elizabeth

EASTERN PROVINCE

K.C. Wessels (capt)	b Player	13
M.W. Rushmere	b Stephenson	3
M.C. Venter	c Henry, b Stephenson	8
L.J. Koen	c Radley, b van Zyl	0
M. Michau	c Radley, b van Zyl	13
*D.J. Richardson	not out	36
E.A.E. Baptiste	c Radley, b Donald	2
T.G. Shaw	c Cronje, b Player	0
R.E. Bryson	c Arthur, b van Zyl	22
P.A. Rayment	lbw, b van Zyl	10
B.N. Schultz	run out	0
Extras	lb 4, w 8, nb 1	13
		120

ORANGE FREE STATE

P.J.R. Steyn	c Michau, b Schultz	9
J.M. Arthur	c Rushmere, b Shaw	45
W.J. Cronje (capt)	not out	32
L.J. Wilkinson	lbw, b Baptiste	0
F.D. Stephenson	c Schultz, b Shaw	22
C.J.P.G. van Zyl	not out	7
G.F.J. Liebenberg		
O. Henry		
B.T. Player		
* P.J.L. Radley		
A.A. Donald		
Extras	w 7, nb 2	9
	(for 4 wickets)	124

(50 overs)

	O	M	R	W
Donald	8	3	14	1
Stephenson	9	1	22	2
van Zyl	11	2	24	4
Player	11	3	21	2
Henry	11	1	35	–

(33 overs)

	O	M	R	W
Bryson	8	1	31	–
Schultz	7	1	39	1
Baptiste	7	1	14	1
Rayment	2	–	11	–
Shaw	9	2	29	2

FALL OF WICKETS
1–16, 2–27, 3–28, 4–28, 5–52, 6–60, 7–62, 8–99, 9–112

FALL OF WICKETS
1–10, 2–70, 3–70, 4–105

Umpires: S.B. Lambson & K.E. Liebenberg Man of the Match – C.J.P.G. van Zyl *Orange Free State won by 6 wickets*

CASTLE CUP

15, 16, 17 and 18 November, 1991 *at Kingsmead, Durban*

Natal 238 for 9 dec. (M.B. Logan 68) and 193 (A.L. Hobson 5 for 84)
Eastern Province 398 (M. Michau 130, M.C. Venter 119) and 34 for 1

Eastern Province won by 9 wickets

Eastern Province 6 pts., Natal 0 pts.

at Springbok Park, Bloemfontein

Orange Free State 464 for 7 dec. (C.J.P.G. van Zyl 119, P.J.R. Steyn 109, O. Henry 64 not out) and 17 for 0
Border 250 (A.G. Lawson 117 not out, B.M. Osborne 83, F.D. Stephenson 5 for 40) and 227 (E.A.N. Emslie 62 not out, O. Henry 5 for 56)

Orange Free State won by 10 wickets

Orange Free State 6 pts., Border 0 pts.

at Wanderers, Johannesburg

Transvaal 143 (S. Elworthy 5 for 61, E.A. Moseley 4 for 24) and 193 (N.E. Wright 86, S. Elworthy 4 for 50)
Northern Transvaal 200 (S. Jacobs 4 for 40) and 138 for 3 (P.H. Barnard 57)

Northern Transvaal won by 7 wickets

Northern Transvaal 6 pts., Transvaal 0 pts.

The first round of matches in South Africa's premier competition produced outright results in all three contests. Indeed, the game at Springbok Park was decided with a day to spare, the newcomers offering little opposition to the strength of Orange Free State. Steyn hit 109 off 186 balls and, with van Heerden, added 127 for the second wicket to give the platform for the home side's big score. Acting captain Corrie van Zyl then hit the first century of his career. Border's consolation was that Andrew Lawson hit a century and carried his bat on the occasion of his first-class debut. He is only the third player to carry his bat on the occasion of his first-class debut in South Africa.

A stand of 258 for the fourth wicket between Venter and Michau after three wickets had fallen for 16 put Eastern Province in a commanding position over Natal, a position which they never relinquished, while a weakened Transvaal side were no match for their northern neighbours in a low-scoring game over in three days.

28, 29, 30 November and 1 December, 1991 *at St George's Park, Port Elizabeth*

Eastern Province 307 (L.J. Koen 121 not out, W.K. Watson 4 for 36) and 189 for 1 (M.W. Rushmere 83 not out, K.C. Wessels 54 not out)

Former Nottinghamshire pace bowler Kenny Watson was the spearhead of the Border attack. He underwent a serious brain operation at the end of the season and was forced to retire from first-class cricket. (Adrian Murrell/Allsport)

Border 103 (R.E. Bryson 6 for 48) and 389 (I.L. Howell 115 not out, D.O. Nosworthy 53, L.M. Fuhri 50, R.E. Bryson 5 for 111)

Eastern Province won by 9 wickets

Eastern Province 6 pts., Border 0 pts.

at Centurion Park, Verwoerdburg

Northern Transvaal 220 (M.D. Haysman 93) and 210 (L.P. Vorster 75, M. Yachad 66, M.W. Pringle 6 for 37)
Western Province 220 (T.N. Lazard 108 not out, T. Bosch 6 for 54) and 189 (T.N. Lazard 56, T. Bosch 5 for 50, E.A. Moseley 4 for 43)

Northern Transvaal won by 21 runs

Northern Transvaal 6 pts., Western Province 1 pt.

at Springbok Park, Bloemfontein

Natal 244 (A.R. Wormington 63 not out, F.D. Stephenson 4 for 34, A.A. Donald 4 for 77) and 168 (J.N. Rhodes 56, O. Henry 4 for 60)
Orange Free State 446 (J.M. Arthur 82, W.J. Cronje 76, F.D. Stephenson 76, L.J. Wilkinson 64)

Orange Free State won by an innings and 34 runs

Orange Free State 6 pts., Natal 0 pts.

Border fought back bravely against Eastern Province after being forced to follow-on. Ian Howell hit a career best 115 not out, but the home side still won comfortably. Bryson had 11 wickets in the match. Tertius Bosch had 11 wickets in a match for the first time as Northern Transvaal won a closely contested match against Western Province. Lazard carried his bat throughout Western's first innings, but his side floundered against the pace of Bosch and Ezra Moseley when chasing a target of 211. They lost their last seven wickets for 58 runs. Consistent batting and a very strong attack were too much for Natal who were overwhelmed by Orange Free State.

26, 27, 28 and **29** December, 1991 *at Buffalo Park, East London*

Border 245 (P.N. Kirsten 107, E.A. Moseley 5 for 50, T. Bosch 4 for 71) and 266 (B.M. Osborne 69, P.N. Kirsten 54, K.S. McEwan 54, E.A. Moseley 6 for 66)
Northern Transvaal 460 for 6 dec. (M. Yachad 169, P.H. Barnard 117) and 52 for 1

Northern Transvaal won by 9 wickets

Northern Transvaal 6 pts., Border 0 pts.

at Kingsmead, Durban

Natal 272 (J.N. Rhodes 64, E.L.R. Stewart 57, B.M. McMillan 5 for 60, M.W. Pringle 4 for 60) and 206 (A.C. Hudson 52)
Western Province 320 (T.N. Lazard 130) and 162 for 7 (G. Kirsten 56)

Western Province won by 3 wickets

Western Province 6 pts., Natal 0 pts.

at Wanderers, Johannesburg

Transvaal 227 (N.E. Wright 60, R.E. Bryson 4 for 63) and 260 for 6 (S.J. Cook 88)
Eastern Province 451 (M.W. Rushmere 177, E.A.E. Baptiste 63, R.E. Bryson 61 not out, R.P. Snell 4 for 70)

Match drawn

Eastern Province 2 pts., Transvaal 0 pts.

Peter Kirsten returned to lead Border who were also assisted by Ken McEwan who had been lured out of retirement at the age of 39, but the efforts of these two great players could not prevent Border from being defeated by Northern Transvaal. The pace bowling of Moseley and Bosch, and an opening stand of 264 between Yachad and Barnard, proved too much for Border. Terry Lazard hit another century for Western Province, and this time saw his efforts rewarded with a narrow victory over Natal. Mark Rushmere's highest first-class score could not bring victory for Eastern Province over Transvaal.

1, 2, 3 and **4** January, 1992 *at Buffalo Park, East London*

Natal 159 (J.N. Rhodes 52, I.L. Howell 6 for 38) and 214 (A.C. Hudson 65, E.L.R. Stewart 55, S.J. Base 5 for 38)

Ken McEwan came out of retirement to assist Border in their first season in the Castle Cup. (Sporting Pictures (UK) Ltd)

Border 257 (B.M. Osborne 92, R.K. McGlashan 4 for 72) and 118 for 1 (P.N. Kirsten 60 not out, B.M. Osborne 54 not out)

Border won by 9 wickets

Border 6 pts., Natal 0 pts.

at St George's Park, Port Elizabeth

Orange Free State 401 (W.J. Cronje 112, F.D. Stephenson 71, J.M. Arthur 59) and 213 for 3 dec. (P.J.R. Steyn 95, J.M. Arthur 51)
Eastern Province 326 (K.C. Wessels 115, D.J. Richardson 72) and 291 for 5 (K.C. Wessels 147 not out, M.C. Venter 86)

Eastern Province won by 5 wickets

Eastern Province 6 pts., Orange Free State 2 pts.

at Newlands, Cape Town

Transvaal 223 (D.J. Cullinan 73, M.W. Pringle 5 for 57) and 266 for 8 dec. (C.E.B. Rice 80 not out, A.J. McClement 5 for 86)
Western Province 221 and 272 for 6 (A.P. Kuiper 89, K.C. Jackson 61, C.E. Eksteen 4 for 87)

Western Province won by 4 wickets

Western Province 6 pts., Transvaal 2 pts.

A season of supreme achievement for Kepler Wessels – captain of Castle Cup winners Eastern Province, captain of South Africa, and top of the first-class batting averages. (David Munden)

Ezra Moseley took 36 wickets for Northern Transvaal and was one of the most feared bowlers in the Castle Cup and one-day competitions. (Adrian Murrell/Allsport)

Both Natal and Border had lost the first three matches, but it was Border who came out better in the meeting of the two bottom sides. Splendid batting from Bradley Osborne and some inspirational play from skipper Peter Kirsten gave Border their first Castle Cup win. In the battle of the giants, Eastern Province beat Orange Free State after trailing on the first innings. Free State's renowned attack was blunted by Kepler Wessels who hit a century in each innings and steered his side to victory after Hansie Cronje's somewhat generous declaration. A fine all-round performance from Clive Rice won the Transvaal skipper the individual award in the New Year match in Cape Town, but it was Kuiper's explosive innings which won the game for Western Province.

Western Province's leading pace bowler Meyrick Pringle, 31 first-class wickets at 13.61 runs apiece. (Patrick Eagar)

24, 25, 26 and 27 January, 1992 *at Centurion Park, Verwoerdburg*

Natal 143 (P.S. de Villiers 4 for 21, E.A. Moseley 4 for 41) and 272 (J.N. Rhodes 131, S. Elworthy 6 for 85)
Northern Transvaal 207 (M. Yachad 95, T.J. Packer 5 for 67) and 138

Natal won by 70 runs

Natal 6 pts., Northern Transvaal 2 pts.

at Wanderers, Johannesburg

Orange Free State 329 (J.M. Arthur 120, L.J. Wilkinson 63, W.J. Cronje 57, C.E. Eksteen 5 for 83) and 136 (S. Jacobs 5 for 26, C.E. Eksteen 4 for 44)
Transvaal 258 (C.E.B. Rice 53, L. Seeff 53, A.A. Donald 4 for 64) and 210 for 8 (B.T. Player 6 for 43)

Transvaal won by 2 wickets

Transvaal 6 pts., Orange Free State 2 pts.

at Newlands, Cape Town

Western Province 335 (A.P. Kuiper 122, B.M. McMillan 88, S.J. Base 4 for 80, W.K. Watson 4 for 83) and 32 for 3
Border 155 (M.W. Pringle 6 for 42) and 209 (K.S. McEwan 54)

Western Province won by 7 wickets

Western Province 6 pts., Border 0 pts.

Transvaal's left-arm spinner Clive Eksteen, a highly successful season. (David Munden)

The fifth round of matches in the Castle Cup produced the surprises. Northern Transvaal, with a maximum point record, took their expected first-innings lead over pointless Natal. Batting again, Natal were well served by Jonty Rhodes who hit the second, and higher, century of his career. Northern Transvaal still needed a mere 209 to win, but the loss of seven wickets for 51 runs to a varied attack was a position from which they could never hope to recover.

Century stands for the first two wickets put Orange Free State in a dominant position against Transvaal, and they eventually took a first-innings lead of 71, but Jacobs and Eksteen dismissed the visitors cheaply when they batted a second time, and Rice's men ground out a brave victory. Western Province's win over Border was less surprising.

7, 8, 9 and 10 February, 1992 *at Buffalo Park, East London*

Transvaal 405 for 5 dec. (R.F. Pienaar 98, D.J. Cullinan 79, D.R. Laing 71 not out, S. Jacobs 54 not out)
Border 199 and 399 for 5 (K.S. McEwan 134 not out, D.H. Howell 100 not out, A.G. Lawson 68)

Match drawn

Transvaal 2 pts., Border 0 pts.

at St George's Park, Port Elizabeth

Western Province 263 (G. Kirsten 91, E.O. Simons 50, E.A.E. Baptiste 5 for 30, B.N. Schultz 4 for 66) and 235 (G. Kirsten 52, E.O. Simons 51, P.A. Rayment 5 for 41)
Eastern Province 328 (G.C. Victor 83, L.J. Koen 72, E.O. Simons 5 for 93) and 151 for 8

Match drawn

Eastern Province 2 pts., Western Province 0 pts.

at Springbok Park, Bloemfontein

Orange Free State 375 (G.F.J. Liebenberg 115, F.D. Stephenson 100, J.M. Arthur 59) and 243 for 8 dec. (F.D. Stephenson 59, C.J.P.G. van Zyl 58 not out)
Northern Transvaal 292 (V.F. du Preez 132, B.T. Player 4 for 67) and 182 (L.P. Vorster 54, J.F. Venter 4 for 41)

Orange Free State won by 144 runs

Orange Free State 6 pts., Northern Transvaal 0 pts.

With the World Cup team having departed, sides were short of their leading players. In East London, Border were forced to follow-on by Transvaal, but David Howell and Ken McEwan shared an unbroken sixth-wicket partnership of 242 to save the game. This was McEwan's first century since his return to first-class cricket. In search of 171 in 38 overs to beat Western Province, Eastern Province lost their bearings. Orange Free State kept alive their cup hopes by crushing Northern Transvaal. Gerhardus Liebenberg hit a career best 115 off 197 balls with 19 fours, and Franklyn Stephenson had 12 fours in his two-hour century which came off 125 balls.

21, 22, 23 and 24 February, 1992 *at Kingsmead, Durban*

Transvaal 355 (D.R. Laing 97, B. McBride 84, T.J. Packer 5 for 69) and 215 for 3 (N.E. Wright 90, R.F. Pienaar 57)
Natal 134 (M.B. Logan 53, G.C. Yates 5 for 46) and 433 (M.B. Logan 150, E.L.R. Stewart 121, D.N. Crookes 61, C.E. Eksteen 5 for 90)

Transvaal won by 7 wickets

Transvaal 6 pts., Natal 0 pts.

at Centurion Park, Verwoerdburg

Northern Transvaal 129 (P.A. Rayment 6 for 25) and 145 (R.E. Bryson 5 for 48)
Eastern Province 189 (E.A. Moseley 4 for 51, P.S. de Villiers 4 for 58) and 88 for 3

Eastern Province won by 7 wickets

Eastern Province 6 pts., Northern Transvaal 0 pts.

at Newlands, Cape Town

Orange Free State 372 for 7 dec. (G.F.J. Liebenberg 104, L.J. Wilkinson 67, J.F. Venter 63 not out) and 167 (J.F. Venter 82, C.R. Matthews 4 for 41, E.O. Simons 4 for 45)
Western Province 197 (F.D. Stephenson 5 for 39) and 155 for 4 (M.F. Voss 56)
Match drawn

Orange Free State 2 pts., Western Province 0 pts.

In spite of a tremendous fight-back by Natal, Transvaal finished their season on a winning note. Eastern Province demolished Northern Transvaal and so won the Castle Cup. It was the third time in four years that they had won or shared the title. Orange Free State were unlucky not to share the 1991–92 title with Eastern Province. Liebenberg's second century in successive matches and Franklyn Stephenson's bowling had put them in a strong position at Newlands, but there was rain on the last day.

The season ended on a sad note with Kenny Watson, the Border and former Nottinghamshire pace bowler, being forced to retire following a serious brain operation.

CASTLE CUP FINAL TABLE

	P	W	L	D	Pts
Eastern Province	6	4	–	2	28
Orange Free State	6	3	2	1	24
Northern Transvaal	6	3	3	–	20
Western Province	6	3	1	2	19
Transvaal	6	2	2	2	16
Border	6	1	4	1	6
Natal	6	1	5	–	6

Dave Richardson of Eastern Province, number one choice as South Africa's wicket-keeper. (David Munden)

PRESIDENT'S CUP

18, 19 and 20 October, 1991 *at UPE, Port Elizabeth*

Natal 'B' 290 (G.M. Walsh 117, A.L. Hobson 4 for 81) and 117 for 5
Eastern Province 'B' 292 for 7 dec. (A. Peters 62, M.P. Stonier 54)
Match drawn

Eastern Province 'B' 2 pts., Natal 'B' 0 pts.

at Centurion Park, Verwoerdburg

Northern Transvaal 'B' 217 (A.M. Ferreira 93) and 275 for 9 dec. (B.J. Somerville 63, N.T. Day 59, G.D. Stevenson 5 for 76)
Transvaal 'B' 228 (D.R. Laing 61) and 248 for 7 (J.J. Strydom 73 not out, P.J. Botha 55, D.W. McCosh 4 for 60)
Match drawn

Transvaal 'B' 2 pts., Northern Transvaal 'B' 0 pts.

at RJE Burt Oval, Constantia

Western Province 'B' 82 for 5 dec. and 235 for 7 dec. (F. Davids 51, C.A. van Ee 4 for 66)
Orange Free State 'B' 82 for 1 dec. (D. Jordaan 54 not out) and 193 (J.M. Truter 56, A.J. McClement 4 for 72)
Western Province 'B' won by 42 runs

Western Province 'B' 6 pts., Orange Free State 'B' 1 pt.

Greg Walsh hit the sixth first-class century of his career, but three days proved inadequate time for two of the first-round matches in the President's Cup to produce a result. In Constantia, captains defied the rain by limiting their first innings to ten overs and sharing the points. Western Province 'B' eventually came out on top.

29, 30 November and 1 December, 1991 *at Kingsmead, Durban*

Natal 'B' 300 for 7 dec. (B.A. Nash 129 not out, J. Nel 52, H.C. Bakkes 4 for 44) and 185 for 5 dec. (J. Payn 53 not out)
Orange Free State 'B' 245 (D. Jordaan 118, R.K. McGlashan 4 for 84) and 167 (G.F.J. Liebenberg 84, R.K. McGlashan 5 for 63)
Natal 'B' won by 73 runs

Natal 'B' 6 pts., Orange Free State 'B' 0 pts.

at Wanderers, Johannesburg

Eastern Province 'B' 365 (P.C. Strydom 67, A. Peters 51, T.C. Webster 6 for 65) and 167 for 4 dec. (C.B. Rhodes 79 not out)
Transvaal 'B' 256 for 7 dec. (H.A. Manack 66, P.A. Rayment 4 for 72) and 34 for 2
Match drawn

Eastern Province 'B' 2 pts., Transvaal 'B' 0 pts.

at Newlands, Cape Town

Northern Transvaal 'B' 180 and 159 (I.A. Hoffman 58)
Western Province 'B' 413 for 8 dec. (M.F. Voss 115, F.B. Touzel 69, F. Davids 63, T.J. Mitchell 59 not out)

Western Province 'B' won by an innings and 74 runs

Western Province 'B' 6 pts., Northern Transvaal 'B' 0 pts.

A maiden first-class century for Michael Voss put Western Province 'B' in charge of the game at Newlands. Western's second win in as many matches gave them a valuable early lead in the President's Cup.

13, 14 and 15 December, 1991 *at Centurion Park, Verwoerdburg*

Northern Transvaal 'B' 318 (M.B. Mare 88, V.F. du Preez 57) and 131 (R.L. Malamba 4 for 21, S.J.S. Kimber 4 for 38)
Natal 'B' 194 (A.J. Forde 64, C. van Noordwyk 4 for 65) and 121 for 7 (C. van Noordwyk 4 for 43)

Match drawn

Northern Transvaal 'B' 2 pts., Natal 'B' 0 pts.

at Wanderers, Johannesburg

Transvaal 'B' 209 (J.J. Strydom 59, A.J. McClement 5 for 65) and 310 for 6 dec. (P.J. Botha 95, W.V. Rippon 65, J.J. Strydom 58)
Western Province 'B' 279 for 6 dec. (H.F. Gibbs 81, L.F. Bleekers 68) and 242 for 7 (M.F. Voss 65)

Western Province 'B' won by 3 wickets

Western Province 'B' 6 pts., Transvaal 'B' 0 pts.

at Springbok Park, Bloemfontein

Eastern Province 'B' 240 (K.G. Bauermeister 64, H.C. Bakkes 6 for 28) and 287 for 8 dec. (G.C. Victor 127)
Orange Free State 'B' 232 (C.J. van Heerden 61, A.L. Hobson 5 for 86, B.S. Forbes 4 for 36) and 261 (B.S. Forbes 5 for 65)

Eastern Province 'B' won by 34 runs

Eastern Province 'B' 6 pts., Orange Free State 'B' 0 pts.

Western Province 'B' strengthened their hold on the Cup when they scored at nearly six runs an over to win in Johannesburg.

9, 10 and 11 January, 1992 *at University of OFS Oval, Bloemfontein*

Northern Transvaal 'B' 220 (M.B. Mare 87) and 199 (V.F. du Preez 58, P.S. de Villiers 50, H.C. Bakkes 4 for 58)
Orange Free State 'B' 325 for 7 dec. (D. Jordaan 100, R.A. Brown 57) and 96 for 4

Orange Free State 'B' won by 6 wickets

Orange Free State 'B' 6 pts., Northern Transvaal 'B' 0 pts.

10, 11 and 12 January, 1992 *at Wanderers, Johannesburg*

Transvaal 'B' 282 for 9 dec. (V.B.N. Vermeulen 78, S.J.S. Kimber 5 for 63) and 219 for 7 dec. (P.J. Botha 55)
Natal 'B' 241 for 8 dec. and 166 for 5 (J. Payn 67)

Match drawn

Transvaal 'B' 2 pts., Natal 'B' 0 pts.

at Plumstead, Cape Town

Western Province 'B' 338 for 8 dec. (F. Davids 146, H.H. Gibbs 90) and 281 for 9 dec. (F.B. Touzel 132, F. Davids 66, B.S. Forbes 4 for 41, N.C. Johnson 4 for 86)
Eastern Province 'B' 193 for 9 dec. and 194 for 2 (G.C. Victor 79 not out, M.P. Stonier 73 not out)

Match drawn

Western Province 'B' 2 pts., Eastern Province 'B' 0 pts.

Mark Davis of Northern Transvaal 'B' was given out 'handled ball' for 0 when he opened his side's second innings in the match at Bloemfontein. He is only the sixth South African to be adjudged out in this manner. His side was well beaten. Western Province 'B' won the President's Cup when they took first-innings points in the drawn match in Cape Town. Davids and Touzel both hit maiden first-class centuries in this match.

24, 25 and 26 January, 1992 *at St George's Park, Port Elizabeth*

Northern Transvaal 'B' 413 (G.R. Grobler 122, Q. Jacobs 89) and 234 for 9 dec. (V.F. du Preez 97, A.L. Hobson 5 for 59)
Eastern Province 'B' 297 (G.C. Victor 112) and 189 for 8 (D.J. Callaghan 69)

Match drawn

Northern Transvaal 'B' 2 pts., Eastern Province 'B' 0 pts.

at Jan Smuts Stadium, Pietermaritzburg

Natal 'B' 256 (G.W. Bashford 79 not out) and 210 for 7 dec.
Western Province 'B' 204 (T.J. Mitchell 61, W.F. Stelling 53, R.J. Varner 4 for 42) and 167 for 5 (M.F. Voss 64 not out)

Match drawn

Natal 'B' 2 pts., Western Province 'B' 0 pts.

at Springbok Park, Bloemfontein

Orange Free State 'B' 421 for 6 dec. (F.C.J. Cronje 152 not out, N.R. Davis 83, A. Wessels 50 not out)
Transvaal 'B' 183 (F.J.C. Cronje 5 for 29) and 414 for 6 (M.J. Mitchley 156, G.A. Pollock 115, P.J. Botha 75)

Match drawn

Orange Free State 'B' 2 pts., Transvaal 'B' 0 pts.

In the match at Port Elizabeth, Grobler and Jacobs shared a seventh-wicket stand of 142. Both batsmen made their highest scores in first-class cricket. In Bloemfontein, Frans Cronje became the ninth player in first-class cricket in South Africa to score 150 and take five wickets in an innings. His 152 not out was the first century of his career. Forced to follow-on, Transvaal 'B' were saved by skipper Mark Mitchley who hit the highest score of his career and shared an opening stand of 229 with Botha. Anthony Pollock then reached a maiden first-class century.

PRESIDENT'S CUP FINAL TABLE

	P	W	L	D	Pts
Western Province 'B'	5	3	–	2	20
Eastern Province 'B'	5	1	–	4	10
Orange Free State 'B'	5	1	3	1	9
Natal 'B'	5	1	–	4	8
Northern Transvaal 'B'	5	–	2	3	4
Transvaal 'B'	5	–	1	4	4

UNION CRICKET BOARD OF SOUTH AFRICA BOWL

18, 19 and 20 October, 1991 *at Brackenfell*

Western Transvaal 205 (C.W. Henderson 7 for 102) and 52 for 1
Boland 326 for 6 dec. (N.M. Snyman 137, W.S. Truter 57)

Match drawn

Boland 2 pts., Western Transvaal 0 pts.

at De Beers Country Club, Kimberley

Griqualand West 296 (G.C. Abbott 127, H.F. Wilson 81, T.A. Marsh 4 for 22) and 159 for 7 (G.C. Abbott 62, M.J. Cann 60, P.D. de Vaal 4 for 52)
Eastern Transvaal 265 (P.J. Grobler 69, M.J. Cann 4 for 74, M.N. Angel 4 for 75)

Match drawn

Griqualand West 2 pts., Eastern Transvaal 0 pts.

Left-arm slow bowler Claude Henderson opened the Bowl season with a career-best bowling performance for Boland. Glen Abbott hit the highest score of his career.

29, 30 November and 1 December, 1991 *at Brackenfell*

Boland 402 for 7 dec. (N.M. Snyman 134, M. Erasmus 98, C.P. Dettmer 66, J.G. de Villiers 59, S.E. Mitchley 4 for 51) and 176 for 7 dec. (W.S. Truter 56, P.D. de Vaal 4 for 60)
Eastern Transvaal 271 for 8 dec. (C.R. Norris 68, K.A. Moxham 67) and 86 for 4

Match drawn

Boland 2 pts., Eastern Transvaal 0 pts.

at Witrand Cricket Field, Potchefstroom

Western Transvaal 168 (M.N. Angel 5 for 30) and 248 (A.J. van Deventer 67, I.M. Kidson 4 for 49)
Griqualand West 428 for 3 dec. (W.E. Schonegevel 153 not out, G.C. Abbott 115, C.S.N. Marais 106)

Griqualand West won by an innings and 12 runs

Griqualand West 6 pts., Western Transvaal 0 pts.

Having lost his opening partner Cann at eight, Wayne Schonegevel shared stands of 169 with Marais, and 192 with Abbott as Griqualand West trounced Western Transvaal. Both Schonegevel and Marais scored maiden first-class centuries.

3, 4 and 5 January, 1992 *at Witrand Cricket Field, Potchefstroom*

Eastern Transvaal 440 for 8 dec. (P.D. de Vaal 100 not out, P.J. Grobler 60, T.A. Marsh 51 not out)
Western Transvaal 146 and 257 (H.M. de Vos 74, P.D. de Vaal 7 for 94)

Eastern Transvaal won by an innings and 37 runs

Eastern Transvaal 6 pts., Western Transvaal 0 pts.

at De Beers Country Club, Kimberley

Boland 349 (P.A. Koen 101, M. Erasmus 72) and 182 for 6 dec. (M. Erasmus 67 not out, N.M. Snyman 51)
Griqualand West 264 (C.W. Henderson 4 for 43) and 268 for 3 (G.C. Abbott 112 not out, C.S.N. Marais 64)

Griqualand West won by 7 wickets

Griqualand West 6 pts., Boland 2 pts.

Batting at number seven, Eastern Transvaal's skipper Peter de Vaal hit 100 not out. It was his first century in a first-class career which had begun for South African Universities in 1965–66. The left-hander was 46 years 32 days old, the oldest maiden centurion in South African cricket history. With his left-arm spin, he then returned match figures of 10 for 126, thereby becoming the second oldest cricketer in the world to perform the double of a century and ten wickets in a match. Emmott Robinson of Yorkshire was the oldest when he accomplished the feat against Hampshire in 1930.

24, 25 and 26 January, 1992 *at Witrand Cricket Field, Potchefstroom*

Western Transvaal 96 and 354 (A.J. van Deventer 80, H.G. Prinsloo 64, J.J. Scholtz 56, D.B. Blignaut 50)
Boland 362 for 8 dec. (K.J. Bridgens 130 not out, J.S. Roos 81) and 92 for 1

Boland won by 9 wickets

Boland 6 pts., Western Transvaal 0 pts.

at PAM Brink Stadium, Springs

Griqualand West 182 and 139 (C.S.N. Marais 58, G. Radford 4 for 43)
Eastern Transvaal 226 (K.A. Moxham 101, P. McLaren 6 for 50) and 96 for 3

Eastern Transvaal won by 7 wickets

Eastern Transvaal 6 pts., Griqualand West 0 pts.

A fourth pointless match left Western Transvaal as the only one of the four sides without hope of winning the Bowl.

7, 8 and 9 February, 1992 *at PAM Brink Stadium, Springs*

Boland 404 for 9 dec. (W. van As 155, K.J. Bridgens 64) and 189 for 5 (N.M. Snyman 58, W.S. Truter 50)
Eastern Transvaal 329 (K.A. Moxham 122, P.A. Cottey 76, B. Chedburn 5 for 64)

Match drawn

Boland 2 pts., Eastern Transvaal 0 pts.

at De Beers Country Club, Kimberley

Griqualand West 279 (G.C. Abbott 70, C.S.N. Marais 60, J.P.B. Mulder 4 for 41) and 228 for 7 dec. (G.C. Abbott 60, H.F. Wilson 55)
Western Transvaal 335 (J.P.B. Mulder 119, D.P. le Roux 65, J.J. Scholtz 54, M.N. Angel 5 for 108) and 146 for 6 (M.J. Cann 4 for 54)

Match drawn

Western Transvaal 2 pts., Griqualand West 0 pts.

Western Transvaal took their first points thanks to Mulder's century on the occasion of his first-class debut. Only two points separated three teams as they went into the final round.

21, 22 and 23 February, 1992 *at Brackenfell*

Boland 289 (C.P. Dettmer 97, J.S. Roos 52, I.M. Kidson 5 for 70) and 193 (W.S. Truter 52, M.N. Angel 4 for 41, P. McLaren 4 for 82)
Griqualand West 166 (M.J. Cann 60) and 247 for 7 (G.C. Abbott 76, C.S.N. Marais 73)

Match drawn

Boland 2 pts., Griqualand West 0 pts.

at PAM Brink Stadium, Springs

Eastern Transvaal 268 (P.J. Grobler 81, B. Randall 57, P.A. Cottey 55, J.P.B. Mulder 4 for 78) and 228 for 2 dec. (C.R. Norris 69 not out, J.E. Burger 52 not out, P.A. Cottey 52)
Western Transvaal 174 (J.P.B. Mulder 59, G. Radford 4 for 24) and 241 (H.M. de Vos 54 not out, L.C.R. Jordaan 4 for 50)

Eastern Transvaal won by 81 runs

Eastern Transvaal 6 pts., Western Transvaal 0 pts.

Stubborn resistance from Abbott and Marais denied Boland victory over Griqualand West and cost them the Bowl. Eastern Transvaal took a commanding lead over Western Transvaal and then scored briskly. Western resisted strongly in their second innings, and de Vaal used nine bowlers in an effort to force victory. Eventually Lucas Jordaan effected the necessary breakthrough with his left-arm spin, and Eastern Transvaal won the match and the Bowl.

UCBSA BOWL FINAL TABLE

	P	W	L	D	Pts
Eastern Transvaal	6	3	–	3	18
Boland	6	1	1	4	16
Griqualand West	6	2	1	3	14
Western Transvaal	6	–	4	2	2

BENSON AND HEDGES NIGHT SERIES

16 October, 1991 *at Kingsmead, Durban*

Natal 208 for 7 (J.N. Rhodes 60, R.M. Bentley 60)
Border 198 for 9 (B.M. Osborne 65, P.N. Kirsten 51)

Natal (4 pts.) won by 10 runs

18 October, 1991 *at Buffalo Park, East London*

Border 131 for 1 (P.N. Kirsten 71 not out, A.G. Lawson 50 not out)
Northern Transvaal 133 for 5

Northern Transvaal (4 pts.) won by 5 wickets

at Springbok Park, Bloemfontein

Eastern Province 162 for 6
Orange Free State 165 for 5

Orange Free State (4 pts.) won by 5 wickets

23 October, 1991 *at Newlands, Cape Town*

Western Province 203 for 6
Impalas 204 for 2 (M.J. Cann 60, N.M. Snyman 54)

Impalas (4 pts.) won by 8 wickets

25 October, 1991 *at Centurion Park, Verwoerdburg*

Northern Transvaal 129
Orange Free State 40 for 2

Match abandoned

Northern Transvaal 2 pts., Orange Free State 2 pts.

30 October, 1991 *at Springbok Park, Bloemfontein*

Border 174 for 4
Orange Free State 170 for 9 (F.D. Stephenson 53, B.C. Fourie 4 for 28)

Border (4 pts.) won by 4 runs

The outstanding performance of the first month of the floodlit series was Impalas' win over Western Province. Cann and Snyman gave them a fine start with a partnership of 91, but it was Koen's violent hitting that made victory possible.

1 November, 1991 *at Buffalo Park, East London*

Border 47 (E.O. Simons 4 for 3)
Western Province 51 for 2

Western Province (4 pts.) won by 8 wickets

at Kingsmead, Durban

Transvaal 158 for 8 (D.J. Cullinan 51)
Natal 132

Transvaal (4 pts.) won by 26 runs

6 November, 1991 *at St George's Park, Port Elizabeth*

Impalas 150 (P.A. Rayment 4 for 29)
Eastern Province 151 for 4

Eastern Province (4 pts.) won by 6 wickets

at Centurion Park, Verwoerdburg

Northern Transvaal 187 for 5 (M.D. Haysman 96)
Western Province 190 for 4 (T.N. Lazard 77 not out, J.B. Commins 50)

Western Province (4 pts.) won by 6 wickets

8 November, 1991 *at Wanderers, Johannesburg*

Border 202 for 8 (B.M. Osborne 69, H.A. Page 4 for 36)
Transvaal 205 for 4 (R.F. Pienaar 87)

Transvaal (4 pts.) won by 6 wickets

E.O. Simons performed the fourth hat-trick in the history of the competition when he sent back Palframan and Fourie with the last two balls of his first over and van Vuuren with the first ball of his second. With the first ball of his third he had Howell caught so that Border were all out for 47, the lowest score ever made in the series.

9 December, 1991 *at Springbok Park, Bloemfontein*

Western Province 209 for 9 (B.M. McMillan 57, A.A. Donald 4 for 32)
Orange Free State 182 for 8 (J.M. Arthur 126 not out)

Western Province (4 pts.) won by 27 runs

10 December, 1991 *at Centurion Park, Verwoerdburg*

Northern Transvaal 157 for 8 (M. Yachad 90)
Natal 158 for 0 (A.C. Hudson 87 not out, M.B. Logan 58 not out)

Natal (4 pts.) won by 10 wickets

11 December, 1991 *at Buffalo Park, East London*

Border 154 for 9 (D.O. Nosworthy 57)
Eastern Province 115 for 3

Border (4 pts.) won on faster scoring rate

12 December, 1991 *at Wanderers, Johannesburg*

Orange Free State 217 for 8 (W.J. Cronje 108)
Transvaal 145 (S. Jacobs 61)

Orange Free State (4 pts.) won by 72 runs

17 December, 1991 *at St George's Park, Port Elizabeth*

Eastern Province 221 for 8 (K.C. Wessels 76, M.W. Rushmere 57)
Northern Transvaal 188 for 9 (M.D. Haysman 59, B.N. Schultz 4 for 32)

Eastern Province (4 pts.) won by 33 runs

18 December, 1991 *at Newlands, Cape Town*

Transvaal 178 (R.F. Pienaar 62, C.E.B. Rice 58, M.W. Pringle 5 for 36)
Western Province 181 for 3 (T.N. Lazard 78)

Western Province (4 pts.) won by 7 wickets

19 December, 1991 *at Kingsmead, Durban*

Orange Free State 214 for 7 (W.J. Cronje 97)
Natal 151 (A.C. Hudson 61, B.T. Player 4 for 24)

Orange Free State (4 pts.) won by 63 runs

At the Christmas break, Western Province held a two-point lead over Orange Free State who had played one game more. John Arthur hit the fifth highest score ever recorded in the series and finished on the losing side. His skipper Hansie Cronje scored heavily for Orange Free State.

5 February, 1992 *at Kingsmead, Durban*

Natal 200 for 6 (B.A. Nash 60 not out, E.L.R. Stewart 53)
Impalas 201 for 4 (M.J. Cann 87 not out, W.S. Truter 50)

Impalas (4 pts.) won by 6 wickets

12 February, 1992 *at Newlands, Cape Town*

Western Province 181 for 7 (D.B. Rundle 75)
Natal 176 for 8 (I.B. Hobson 55)

Western Province (4 pts.) won by 5 runs

13 February, 1992 *at Springbok Park, Bloemfontein*

Orange Free State 200 for 7 (P.J.R. Steyn 66, J.M. Arthur 65)
Impalas 201 for 5 (C.S.N. Marais 61)

Impalas (4 pts.) won by 5 wickets

14 February, 1992 *at St George's Park, Port Elizabeth*

Eastern Province 215 for 5 (D.J. Callaghan 61)
Transvaal 124

Eastern Province (4 pts.) won by 91 runs

26 February, 1992 *at St George's Park, Port Elizabeth*

Natal 202 for 5 (E.L.R. Stewart 86 not out)
Eastern Province 204 for 7 (D.J. Callaghan 78)

Eastern Province (4 pts.) won by 3 wickets

27 February, 1992 *at Buffalo Park, East London*

Impalas 116 for 3
v. Border

Match abandoned

Impalas 2 pts., Border 2 pts.

28 February, 1992 *at Wanderers, Johannesburg*

Northern Transvaal 199 for 6 (M.J.R. Rindel 55 not out)
Transvaal 200 for 9 (G.A. Pollock 94 not out)

Transvaal (4 pts.) won by 1 wicket

4 March, 1992 *at Centurion Park, Verwoerdburg*

Northern Transvaal 209 for 6 (M.J.R. Rindel 50 not out)
Impalas 211 for 5 (G.C. Abbott 68 not out, W.S. Truter 64)

Impalas (4 pts.) won by 5 wickets

5 March, 1992 *at Newlands, Cape Town*

Western Province 213 for 8 (G. Kirsten 56)
Eastern Province 148 (G.C. Victor 56)

Western Province (4 pts.) won by 65 runs

6 March, 1992 *at Wanderers, Johannesburg*

Impalas 209 for 4 (N.M. Snyman 51)
Transvaal 213 for 2 (R.F. Pienaar 72 not out, H.A. Page 57)

Transvaal (4 pts.) won by 8 wickets

The surprise side of the series was Impalas. They won three of their last five games to move into second place and condemn the much-favoured Orange Free State to fifth place, thereby not qualifying for the semi-finals.

BENSON AND HEDGES NIGHT SERIES FINAL TABLE

	P	W	L	Ab	Pts	Run Rate
Western Province	7	6	1	–	24	4.30
Impalas	7	4	2	1	18	4.52
Eastern Province	7	4	3	–	16	4.02
Transvaal	7	4	3	–	16	3.94
Orange Free State	7	3	3	1	14	4.37
Border	7	2	4	1	10	3.48
Natal	7	2	5	–	8	4.02
Northern Transvaal	7	1	5	1	6	3.97

Semi-Finals
First Leg

10 March, 1992 *at St George's Park, Port Elizabeth*

Eastern Province 257 (P.G. Amm 108, L.J. Koen 56)
Impalas 86

Eastern Province won by 171 runs

11 March, 1992 *at Wanderers, Johannesburg*

Transvaal 198 for 9 (D.J. Cullinan 104 not out)
Western Province 201 for 7 (T.N. Lazard 88)

Western Province won by 3 wickets

Second Leg

13 March, 1992 *at St George's Park, Port Elizabeth*

Eastern Province 275 for 3 (L.J. Koen 74 not out, P.G. Amm 69, D.J. Callaghan 59)
Impalas 159

Eastern Province won by 116 runs

at Newlands, Cape Town

Transvaal 140
Western Province 141 for 6 (H.A. Page 4 for 25)

Western Province won by 4 wickets

Final

Both Eastern Province and Western Province reached the final without the need of playing a third leg. Eastern Province were well served by Philip Amm who had returned after injury to lead the side in the absence of Wessels who was on international duty. The World Cup squad returned to South Africa in time for the final. Amm was to end the season as the leading run scorer for Eastern Province with 364 runs in the series. Lazard hit 445 for Western Province. Schultz's 18 wickets put him at the top of the list.

A record three centuries were scored in the final, in which Kepler Wessels took the individual award. Eastern Province won in the last over.

The South African season, which had begun with the friendly match between Northern Transvaal and Western Province on 12 September, ended three days after the Benson and Hedges final with the last day of the friendly between Boland and Warwickshire. This was the longest season in South African cricket history.

BENSON AND HEDGES NIGHT SERIES FINAL – WESTERN PROVINCE v. EASTERN PROVINCE

1 April, 1992 at Wanderers, Johannesburg

WESTERN PROVINCE

T.N. Lazard	not out	108
K.C. Jackson	**b** Bryson	12
G. Kirsten	**c** and **b** Shaw	7
A.P. Kuiper	not out	107
H.H. Gibbs		
E.O. Simons		
D.B. Rundle		
M.W. Pringle		
C.R. Matthews (capt)		
* R.J. Ryall		
V.A. Barnes		
Extras	lb 7, w 1, nb 2	10
	(for 2 wickets)	**244**

(45 overs)

	O	M	R	W
Bryson	9	–	59	1
Schultz	9	1	47	–
Shaw	9	–	30	1
Baptiste	9	1	47	–
Rayment	9	–	54	–

FALL OF WICKETS

1–27, **2**–51

EASTERN PROVINCE

K.C. Wessels (capt)	**c** and **b** Barnes	103
P.G. Amm	**c** and **b** Rundle	33
M.W. Rushmere	run out	64
D.J. Callaghan	**c** Kirsten, **b** Pringle	24
L.J. Koen	not out	5
* D.J. Richardson	not out	4
E.A.E. Baptiste		
P.A. Rayment		
R.E. Bryson		
T.G. Shaw		
B.N. Schultz		
Extras	lb 6, w 7	13
	(for 4 wickets)	**246**

(44.1 overs)

	O	M	R	W
Pringle	8	–	45	1
Matthews	8	1	38	–
Rundle	9	–	44	1
Simons	8.1	–	49	–
Barnes	8	–	47	1
Kuiper	3	–	17	–

FALL OF WICKETS

1–72, **2**–212, **3**–232, **4**–242

Umpires: S.B. Lambson & R.E. Koertzen

Man of the Match – K.C. Wessels

Eastern Province won by 6 wickets

FIRST-CLASS AVERAGES

BATTING

	M	Inns	NO	Runs	HS	Av	100s	50s
K.C. Wessels	5	8	2	795	212	132.50	4	2
F.J.C. Cronje	4	6	3	278	152*	92.66	1	–
M. Erasmus	8	14	6	547	103*	68.37	1	4
G.G. Abbott	7	13	1	754	127	62.83	3	4
W.J. Cronje	4	7	1	332	112	55.33	1	2
M. Yachad	6	11	1	553	169	55.30	2	2
M.W. Rushmere	6	11	2	490	177	54.44	2	1
P.N. Kirsten	3	6	1	267	107	53.40	1	2
K.S. McEwan	4	7	1	313	134*	53.16	1	2
G.C. Victor	8	15	3	635	127	52.91	2	2
T.N. Lazard	8	15	2	674	150*	51.84	4	1
P.J. Grobler	6	8	2	310	81	51.65	–	3
N.M. Snyman	7	13	–	656	137	50.46	3	2
G.A. Pollock	3	6	1	250	115	50.00	1	–
L.J. Koen	7	11	2	448	121*	49.77	1	2
F.D. Stephenson	6	9	–	430	100	47.77	1	3
D. Jordaan	5	9	1	379	118	47.37	2	1
J.N. Rhodes	4	8	–	378	131	47.25	1	3
J.M. Arthur	7	13	1	566	120	47.16	1	5
D.H. Howell	3	6	1	231	100*	46.20	1	–
P.C. Strydom	4	5	–	230	69	46.00	–	2
K.A. Moxham	5	7	–	318	122	45.42	2	1
V.F. du Preez	7	14	1	588	132	45.23	2	3
J.P.B. Mulder	2	4	–	179	119	44.75	1	1
P.D. de Vaal	6	6	2	178	100*	44.50	1	–
G.F.J. Liebenberg	7	12	1	476	115	43.27	2	1
V.D. Westhuizen	3	6	2	173	46*	43.25		
A.P. Kuiper	5	10	1	384	122	42.66	1	2
W.N. van As	4	8	1	296	155	42.28	1	–
O. Henry	4	6	1	207	64*	41.40	–	1
C.E.B. Rice	4	7	1	248	80*	41.33	–	2
M.C. Venter	7	11	1	406	119	40.60	1	1
D.J. Cullinan	7	13	1	472	79	39.33	–	3
T.J. Mitchell	6	11	5	231	61	38.50	–	2
A.J. van Deventer	6	11	1	379	80	37.90	–	2
B.M. Osborne	6	12	1	414	92	37.63	–	4
G. Kirsten	8	16	2	525	91	37.50	–	3
R.E. Bryson	7	7	1	224	100	37.33	1	1
C.S.N. Marais	7	13	–	483	106	37.15	1	4
E.L.R. Stewart	5	10	–	371	121	37.10	1	2
H.F. Wilson	7	13	4	326	81	36.22	–	2
D.J. Richardson	5	6	1	181	72	36.20	–	2
P.A. Cottey	5	7	–	253	76	36.14	–	3
R.F. Pienaar	6	11	–	397	98	36.09	–	2
W.E. Schonegevel	7	12	2	359	153*	35.90	1	1
S.J. Cook	4	7	–	250	88	35.71	–	1
F. Davids	7	13	–	463	146	35.61	1	3
L. Seeff	3	6	1	176	54	35.20	–	2
H.H. Gibbs	6	11	–	385	90	35.00	–	2
F.B. Touzel	5	9	–	315	132	35.00	1	1
C.R. Norris	6	8	1	245	69*	35.00	–	2
C.J. van Heerden	6	9	1	277	61	34.62	–	1
M.B. Logan	7	14	–	482	150	34.42	–	2
E.A.E. Baptiste	7	9	1	273	63	34.12	–	2
K.J. Bridgens	7	12	1	372	130*	33.81	1	1
H.M. de Vos	6	11	2	302	74	33.55	–	2
G.W. Bashford	4	7	2	166	79*	33.20	–	1
A.G. Lawson	6	12	1	364	117*	33.09	1	1
M.J. Mitchley	5	10	–	330	156	33.00	1	–
P.A. Koen	6	10	3	231	101	33.00	1	–
C.B. Rhodes	5	8	1	230	79*	32.85	–	1
C.P. Dettmer	8	15	1	458	97	32.71	–	2
D.R. Laing	8	12	1	356	97	32.36	–	3
L.P. Vorster	7	13	1	386	83	32.16	–	4
N.E. Wright	6	11	–	352	90	32.00	–	3
B.A. Nash	6	12	1	351	129*	31.90	1	–
W.S. Truter	7	13	1	375	57	31.25	–	–
C.J.P.G. van Zyl	6	9	1	249	119	31.12	1	1
P.J.R. Steyn	7	13	1	372	109	31.00	1	1
M.P. Stonier	5	9	1	248	73*	31.00	–	2
W.V. Rippon	2	4	–	123	65	30.75	–	1
A.M. Ferreira	4	9	1	244	93	30.50	–	2

BATTING continued

	M	Inns	NO	Runs	HS	Av	100s	50s
J.J. Strydom	7	14	3	333	73*	30.27	–	3
S.E. Mitchely	6	8	2	181	45	30.16	–	–
K.G. Bauermeister	4	6	1	149	64	29.80	–	1
J.S. Roos	7	12	1	326	81	29.63	–	2
D.P. le Roux	3	6	–	174	65	29.00	–	1
M.F. Voss	9	17	1	463	115	28.93	1	3
P.J. Botha	7	14	–	405	95	28.92	–	4
M.B. Mare	6	12	–	347	88	28.91	–	2
M.N. Angel	7	10	4	171	67	28.50	–	1
I.L. Howell	6	10	1	254	115*	28.22	1	–
A.C. Hudson	3	6	–	169	65	28.16	–	2
L.F. Bleekers	6	11	2	251	68	27.88	–	2
T.G. Shaw	7	7	1	167	105	27.83	1	–
J. Payn	7	14	1	359	67	27.61	–	3
A. Peters	3	5	–	138	62	27.60	–	2
B.M. McMillan	4	7	–	192	88	27.42	–	1
J.M. Truter	5	9	1	217	56	27.12	–	1
V.B.N. Vermeulen	2	4	–	106	78	26.50	–	1
L.J. Wilkinson	6	9	–	238	67	26.44	–	3
M. Michau	6	9	1	211	130	26.37	1	–
B.J. Somerville	5	10	–	260	63	26.00	–	1
P.H. Barnard	6	12	2	259	117	25.90	1	1
H.C. Bakkes	7	10	4	155	44	25.83	–	–
H.A. Manack	7	12	–	309	66	25.75	–	1
M.J. Cann	7	13	–	334	60	25.69	–	2
E.O. Simons	6	10	2	205	51	25.62	–	2
G.M. Walsh	6	12	1	281	117*	25.54	1	–
J.F. Venter	8	14	2	306	82	25.50	–	2
P.G. Amm	6	12	1	279	124	25.36	1	–
M.J.R. Rindel	7	13	2	275	59	25.00	–	1
I.B. Hobson	3	6	–	149	92	24.83	–	1
A.R. Wormington	5	9	2	173	63*	24.71	–	1
M.D. Haysman	6	10	–	245	93	24.50	–	1
G. Grobler	6	11	–	269	122	24.45	1	–
S.J. Palframan	6	10	1	220	49*	24.44	–	–
B. McBride	6	7	1	146	84	24.33	–	1
R.A. Brown	5	8	–	191	57	23.87	–	1
P.S. de Villiers	3	6	–	141	50	23.50	–	1
B. Randall	6	9	–	211	57	23.44	–	1
R.E. Veenstra	5	6	1	117	43	23.40	–	–
J.J. Scholtz	6	12	1	256	56	23.27	–	2
J.B. Commins	3	6	–	138	85	23.00	–	1
J. Nel	4	8	–	175	52	21.87	–	1
L.J. Wenzler	4	7	1	131	32	21.83	–	2
N.T. Day	4	8	–	173	59	21.62	–	1
A.J. Forde	6	12	1	237	64	21.54	–	1
P.E. Smith	5	9	4	105	27*	21.00	–	–
J.G. de Villiers	4	7	–	146	59	20.85	–	1
D.N. Crookes	4	8	2	125	61	20.83	–	1
M.A. Fletcher	4	7	–	144	39	20.57	–	–
R.J. Varner	5	10	2	158	41	19.75	–	–
P.A. Tullis	8	11	3	157	37	19.62	–	–
N.C. Johnson	4	8	2	117	39	19.50	–	–
H. Pangarkar	3	6	–	166	36	19.33	–	–
H.G. Prinsloo	5	10	1	158	64	17.55	–	1
P.W.E. Rawson	7	14	2	209	32	17.41	–	–
R.J. Ryall	8	10	2	137	23*	17.12	–	–
D.B. Rundel	8	15	2	220	42	16.92	–	–
B.E. van der Vyver	4	7	–	113	30	16.14	–	–
K.C. Jackson	8	15	–	242	61	16.13	–	1
J.D. du Toit	4	8	–	128	37	16.00	–	–
C.M. Casalis	5	9	–	143	32	15.88	–	–
R.K. McGlashan	7	12	1	174	32	15.81	–	–
B.M. White	4	8	–	125	34	15.62	–	–
S. Jacobs	5	9	2	104	54*	14.85	–	1
R.V. Jennings	7	12	3	130	29	14.44	–	–
D.J. van Schalkwyk	6	10	1	130	35	14.44	–	–
D.O. Nosworthy	5	9	–	129	53	14.33	–	1
I.A. Hoffmann	4	8	–	109	58	13.62	–	1
T.J. Packer	6	12	2	131	32	13.10	–	–
S. Elworthy	6	9	–	104	30	11.55	–	–

(Qualification – 100 runs, average 10.00)
(one match – Q. Jacobs 89 & 41)

BOWLING

	Overs	Mds	Runs	Wkts	Av	Best	10/m	5/inn
R.L. Malamba	68.1	17	175	13	13.46	4-21	–	–
M.W. Pringle	179.1	42	422	31	13.61	6-37	–	3
P. McLaren	84.5	15	249	15	16.60	6-50	–	1
P.S. de Villiers	99.2	32	202	12	16.83	4-21	–	–
E.A. Moseley	244.2	56	608	36	16.88	6-68	1	2
C.R. Matthews	217.5	52	482	28	17.21	6-22	–	1
B.S. Forbes	141.5	33	381	22	17.31	5-65	–	1
B.M. McMillan	136.5	43	290	16	18.12	5-60	–	1
T.J. Packer	165.3	43	458	25	18.32	5-67	–	1
R.E. Bryson	249.2	52	760	41	18.53	6-48	1	3
F.D. Stephenson	219.3	60	488	25	19.52	5-39	–	2
P.D. de Vaal	226.5	65	590	29	20.34	7-94	1	1
G. Radford	105	28	317	15	21.13	4-24	–	–
F.J.C. Cronje	79.2	14	275	13	21.15	5-29	–	1
T.A. Marsh	118.4	39	276	13	21.23	4-22	–	–
E.A.E. Baptiste	309.5	100	596	28	21.28	5-30	–	1
T. Bosch	184.4	22	535	24	22.29	6-54	1	2
H.C. Bakkes	193	57	448	20	22.40	6-28	–	1
B.A.S. Chedburn	110.5	19	360	16	22.50	5-64	–	1
P.A. Rayment	200	54	503	22	22.86	6-25	–	2
C.J. van Heerden	130.1	33	276	12	23.00	3-19	–	–
C.E. Eksteen	388	159	736	32	23.00	5-83	–	2
D.W. McCosh	99.3	11	338	14	24.14	4-60	–	–
I.M. Kidson	202.4	49	510	21	24.28	5-70	–	1
L.C.R. Jordaan	224.4	95	469	19	24.68	4-50	–	–
A.A. Donald	137.5	27	402	16	25.12	4-64	–	–
B.T. Player	190	56	454	18	25.22	6-43	–	1
A.J. McClement	198.5	46	530	21	25.23	5-65	–	2
O. Henry	193	75	437	17	25.70	5-56	–	1
K.G. Bauremeister	123.1	24	363	14	25.92	3-33	–	–
I.A. Hoffmann	81.3	22	260	10	26.00	3-47	–	–
S. Jacobs	165.5	43	451	17	26.52	5-26	–	1
V.A. Barnes	164.3	39	398	15	26.53	3-44	–	–
E.O. Simons	176.5	41	460	17	27.05	5-93	–	1
S.J. Base	170.5	32	515	19	27.10	5-38	–	1
B.N. Schultz	238	64	597	22	27.13	4-59	–	–
C.W. Henderson	293	87	792	29	27.31	7-102	1	–
S. Elworthy	223.4	38	741	27	27.44	6-85	–	2
T.G. Shaw	251.2	87	559	20	27.95	5-64	–	1
A. Pollock	105	21	365	13	28.07	3-38	–	–
C. van Noordwyk	127	22	423	15	28.20	4-43	–	–
M.N. Angel	289	66	790	28	28.21	5-30	–	2
M.J. Cann	218.4	58	554	19	29.15	4-54	–	–
C.A. van Ee	78.4	13	293	10	29.30	4-66	–	–
R.P. Snell	123.2	33	295	10	29.50	4-70	–	–
H. Barnard	197	38	624	21	29.71	4-110	–	–
S.J.S. Kimber	139.4	31	360	12	30.00	5-63	–	1
R.K. McGlashan	236.4	50	761	25	30.44	5-63	–	1
L.D. Botha	112	25	338	11	30.72	3-17	–	–
G.D. Stevenson	72.4	8	311	10	31.10	5-76	–	1
C.J.P.G. van Zyl	184	59	438	14	31.28	3-67	–	–
W.K. Watson	163	54	345	11	31.36	4-36	–	–
A.L. Hobson	315.5	69	982	31	31.67	5-59	–	1
G. Grobler	140.4	30	412	13	31.69	3-19	–	–
D.G. Payne	243	48	762	24	31.75	3-33	–	–
J.R. Meyer	109	14	392	12	32.66	3-49	–	–
D.R. Laing	206.4	61	536	16	33.50	3-34	–	–
M. Erasmus	169.1	36	439	13	33.76	3-46	–	–
J.F. Venter	172.2	34	536	15	35.73	4-41	–	–
A. Manack	125	19	395	11	35.90	3-59	–	–
R.A. Lyle	177.2	28	575	16	35.93	3-42	–	–
D.N. Crookes	137	18	508	14	36.28	3-69	–	–
N.W. Pretorius	185.5	37	620	16	38.75	4-24	–	–
I.L. Howell	227.2	72	558	14	39.85	6-38	–	1
P.W.E. Rawson	206.5	69	488	12	40.66	3-52	–	–
D.B. Rundle	329.4	87	746	17	43.88	5-56	–	1
B.C. Fourie	170	31	537	11	48.81	3-47	–	–

(Qualification – 10 wickets)

LEADING FIELDERS

42 – R.J. Ryall (ct 39/st 3); 33 – R.V. Jennings (ct 32/st 1); 30 – B. McBride (ct 27/st 3); 26 – C.S.N. Marais (ct 22/st 4); 25 – P.A. Tullis (ct 24/st 1); 24 – D.J. Richardson (ct 21/st 3); 23 – B. Randall (ct 18/st 5); 20 – P.J.L. Radley; 16 – C.F. Spilhaus (ct 14/st 2); G.W. Bashford; (ct 13/st 3); S.J. Palframan (ct 13/st 3) and K.J. Bridgens; 15 – T.A. Marsh; 14 – R.A. Brown (ct 13/st 1); 13 – H.M. de Vos (ct 12/st 1); 12 – L.J. Koen and J.A. Teeger; 11 – G.C. Victor 10 – Y. Begg (ct 9/st 1); N.T. Day and M.D. Haysman

INDIA

Irani Cup
One-Day International Series, India v. South Africa
Duleep Trophy
Ranji Trophy
First-Class Averages

A capacity crowd watches India play South Africa in the one-day international at Gwalior. (David Munden)

IRANI CUP

HARYANA v. REST OF INDIA, at Faridabad

India's domestic season began with the Irani Cup, the match in which the Ranji Trophy holders take on the rest of India. Led by former Test wicket-keeper Syed Kirmani, the Rest of India included several players anxious to win a place in the national side. Raman, who has played Test cricket but has failed to establish himself, shared a second-wicket stand of 202 with Kambli, pressing hard for Test recognition. Another aspirant to Test cricket, Amre, also hit a century. Forgotten man Chetan Sharma bowled well on a docile wicket which Haryana's batsmen enjoyed as much as their opponents.

Haryana suffered a mid-innings collapse as three wickets fell for six runs, but then Kapil Dev and Jadeja added 239. Kapil Dev then led the rout of the Rest of India when they batted a second time and made another significant contribution with the bat when his side chased a target of 204 for victory.

Maninder Singh showed a welcome return to form, bowling with economy and guile.

Ajay Jadeja – a century for Haryana in the Irani Cup and a place in the Indian World Cup squad. (David Munden)

IRANI CUP – HARYANA v. REST OF INDIA

2, 3, 4, 5 and 6 October, 1991 at Nahar Singh Stadium, Faridabad

REST OF INDIA

	FIRST INNINGS		SECOND INNINGS	
W.V. Raman	c Yadav, b Kapil Dev	149	c Yadav, b C.M. Sharma	23
J. Arun Lal	c Yadav, b Jadeja	4	b C.M. Sharma	0
V.G. Kambli	c Jain, b C.M. Sharma	116	lbw, b Jadeja	16
P.K. Amre	c Yadav, b C.M. Sharma	120	lbw, b Kapil Dev	40
Sneha Ganguly	c Yadav, b Kapil Dev	6	c Yadav, b Kapil Dev	4
Saurath Ganguly	lbw, b Jain	20	lbw, b Kapil Dev	0
*S.M.H. Kirmani (capt)	lbw, b C.M. Sharma	30	c Yadav, b Kapil Dev	2
S.T. Banerjee	b C.M. Sharma	13	st Yadav, b Jain	13
J. Srinath	c Kapil Dev, b Jain	18	(10) b Jain	17
P.S. Vaidya	not out	1	(9) b Jain	16
Maninder Singh	not out	44	not out	3
Extras	b 17, lb 11, w 4, nb 5	37	b 5, lb 1, w 1, nb 3	10
	(for 9 wickets dec.)	**518**		**144**

HARYANA

	FIRST INNINGS		SECOND INNINGS	
N. Goel	c Kirmani, b Srinath	54	b Maninder Singh	51
D. Sharma	c Vaidya, b S.T. Banerjee	50	b Maninder Singh	31
A. Jadeja	lbw, b Srinath	131	lbw, b Maninder Singh	13
Amarjeet Kaypee	lbw, b Srinath	0	lbw, b Vaidya	1
A. Banerjee	c Kirmani, b Srinath	1	lbw, b Maninder Singh	0
Kapil Dev (capt)	c and b S.T. Banerjee	135	c Raman, b Maninder Singh	53
Rajesh Puri	lbw, b Srinath	18	not out	36
*V.S. Yadav.	b Maninder Singh	1		
C.M. Sharma	not out	19	(8) not out	4
P. Jain	c Maninder Singh, b S.T. Banerjee	1		
Y. Bhandari	c Kirmani, b S.T. Banerjee	0		
Extras	b 10, lb 27, nb 12	49	b 9, lb 6, w 3	18
		459	(for 6 wickets)	**207**

	O	M	R	W	O	M	R	W
C.M. Sharma	39	7	90	4	15	1	45	2
Jadeja	21	5	72	1	7	–	20	1
Kapil Dev	33	9	80	2	7	3	26	4
Bhandari	27	3	104	–	14.1	3	47	3
Jain	45	8	115	2				
D. Sharma	12	–	29	–				

	O	M	R	W	O	M	R	W
Srinath	41	9	120	5	3	1	5	–
Vaidya	31	3	107	–	12	–	45	1
S.T. Banerjee	31	7	70	4	9	1	46	–
Maninder Singh	52	17	121	1	24.4	2	79	5
Saurath Ganguly	2	–	4	–	3	–	17	–

FALL OF WICKETS

1–24, **2**–226, **3**–317, **4**–346, **5**–383, **6**–474, **7**–481, **8**–498, **9**–512
1–1, **2**–20, **3**–53, **4**–77, **5**–83, **6**–95, **7**–96 , **8**–120, **9**–129

FALL OF WICKETS

1–113, **2**–150, **3**–150, **4**–156, **5**–395, **6**–438, **7**–439, **8**–439, **9**–457
1–57, **2**–87, **3**–90, **4**–92, **5**–140, **6**–203

Umpires: S.D. Shah & S.K. Sharma

Haryana won by 4 wickets

ONE-DAY INTERNATIONAL SERIES
INDIA v. SOUTH AFRICA

A record crowd of 100,000 people gathered for the historic first one-day international between India and South Africa at Eden Gardens, Calcutta. (David Munden)

Pakistan were scheduled to play five one-day international matches in India in October and November, 1991, but on the eve of the tour, General Zahid Ali Akbar, President of the Cricket Board of Pakistan, informed his counterpart in India that the trip had been cancelled because of worsening relations between the two countries.

The cancellation left a gap in the Indian cricket programme. India had supported South Africa's re-entry into international cricket, and they were quick to invite South Africa to play a one-day series in India as a prelude to the World Cup. So history was made, and at Calcutta on 10 November, 1991, before a crowd estimated at 100,000, South Africa returned to international cricket to the most ecstatic of welcomes.

Put in to bat, South Africa lost Hudson to the sixth ball of the innings when he was caught behind as he pushed forward to Kapil Dev. Cook fell at 28, and with Wessels concentrating on building an innings, South Africa took 24 overs to reach 50. Cook had taken 49 balls for his 17, and Kirsten went quickly when he tried to cut a ball that kept low. Wessels chopped a delivery into his stumps to end his 96-ball innings, and the main impetus of the innings came from Kuiper who hit 43 off 69 balls before clouting a full toss into the hands of Amre on the leg-side boundary. Amre – like the entire South African team, with the exception of Wessels – was making his debut in a one-day international.

India faced a modest target, but by the end of the third over they were 6 for 2, rocked by Donald's pace and fire. With the score on eight, Tendulkar, having scored three, was stranded in mid-pitch. Hudson returned the ball to bowler Snell who failed to gather it, and Tendulkar was reprieved. He went on to hit a six and eight fours before being taken at mid-off. By then, Amre had established himself, and he, too, hit a six and eight fours in a most promising innings, 55 off 78 balls. He was out with the scores level, but the winning leg-bye came three balls later.

This was a highly emotional occasion, and the result was of secondary importance. Clive Rice was quoted as saying, 'Having been on the sidelines for 21 years, I now know how Neil Armstrong felt when he stood on the moon.' It was an apt comparison, for many of the South Africans were obviously deeply affected by the occasion. Rice is 42 years old, and he has been one of the great captains of the post-war era. It was good that he was at last able to enjoy an honour that his ability, character and demeanour had earned him.

Tendulkar and Donald were jointly named as Man of the Match, which was appropriate at this historic moment.

The second match in the series was less edifying than the first. Eksteen, Matthews and Yachad made their debuts for South Africa; Srikkanth replaced Shastri in the Indian side. The capacity crowd was unruly, and two Indian outfielders, Srikkanth and Sidhu, were struck by articles thrown from the crowd. There were also complaints that the Indian bowlers had been tampering with the ball. A diplomatic incident was avoided by apologies after the game.

An opening stand of 130 in 28 overs between Sidhu

Adrian Kuiper pulls a ball from Venkatapathy Raju during his innings of 43 in the one-day international at Calcutta. More is the wicket-keeper. (David Munden)

and Srikkanth gave India a strong early advantage. Manjrekar hit 52 off as many deliveries, and South Africa faced a target of 224 in 45 overs. They lost Cook in the first over, but Yachad, who broke a finger during his 77-ball innings, and Wessels added 94. The rate was never really quick enough. Wessels' knock occupied 96 balls. The Indians took some fine catches, and the later South African batsmen were content to play out time.

In the last match of the series, South Africa came out of the shadows to pull off a sensational win. Leading India in the absence of Azharuddin, Shastri hit 11 fours in his 109 before being run out on the last ball of the innings. He shared a stand of 175 for the second wicket with Manjrekar who batted in spectacular fashion, hitting two sixes and eight fours and facing only 81 balls for his century.

South Africa faced a daunting task, but Cook and Wessels provided a sound start. Kirsten joined Wessels in a stand of 111 and was then partnered by Kuiper, dropped when on 18, in a stand which realised 105 in 12 pulsating overs, and which brought victory to South Africa.

Wessels and Manjrekar were named as Men of the Series. More importantly, South Africa were truly back in the fold.

Richardson unsuccessfully attempts to stump Manjrekar in the second match at Lahore. Skipper Rice is at slip. (David Munden)

FIRST ONE-DAY INTERNATIONAL – INDIA v. SOUTH AFRICA
10 November, 1991 at Eden Gardens, Calcutta

SOUTH AFRICA

S.J. Cook	lbw, b Srinath	17
A.C. Hudson	c More, b Kapil Dev	0
K.C. Wessels	b Tendulkar	50
P.N. Kirsten	b Venkatapathy Raju	7
A.P. Kuiper	c Amre, b Prabhakar	43
C.E.B. Rice (capt)	b Prabhakar	14
R.P. Snell	c Amre, b Kapil Dev	16
B.M. McMillan	run out	2
*D.J. Richardson	not out	4
T.G. Shaw	not out	0
A.A. Donald		
Extras	lb 13, w 11	24
	(for 8 wickets)	177

INDIA

R.J. Shastri	c Richardson, b Donald	0
N.S. Sidhu	c McMillan, b Donald	6
S.V. Manjrekar	b Donald	1
S.R. Tendulkar	c Snell, b Donald	62
M. Azharuddin (capt)	st Richardon, b Shaw	16
P.K. Amre	lbw, b Donald	55
Kapil Dev	b Kuiper	11
M. Prabhakar	not out	12
* K.S. More	not out	0
Venkatapathy Raju		
J. Srinath		
Extras	lb 2, w 11, nb 2	15
	(for 7 wickets)	178

(47 overs)

	O	M	R	W
Kapil Dev	9	2	23	2
Prabhakar	10	1	26	2
Srinath	10	–	39	1
Venkatapathy Raju	10	–	32	1
Shastri	3	–	17	–
Tendulkar	5	–	27	1

(40.4 overs)

	O	M	R	W
Donald	8.4	–	29	5
Snell	6	–	35	–
McMillan	6	–	30	–
Shaw	10	–	46	1
Rice	5	–	14	–
Kuiper	5	–	22	1

FALL OF WICKETS
1–3, **2**–28, **3**–49, **4**–109, **5**–151, **6**–156, **7**–167, **8**–176

FALL OF WICKETS
1–1, **2**–3, **3**–20, **4**–60, **5**–116, **6**–148, **7**–177

Man of the Match – S.R. Tendulkar & A.A. Donald *India won by 3 wickets*

SECOND ONE-DAY INTERNATIONAL – INDIA v. SOUTH AFRICA
12 November, 1991 at Roop Singh Stadium, Gwalior

INDIA

K. Srikkanth	c Yachad, b Snell	68
N.S. Sidhu	c Eksteen, b Rice	61
S.V. Manjrekar	not out	52
S.R. Tendulkar	c Richardson, b Matthews	4
M. Azharuddin (capt)	c Kirsten, b Donald	19
Kapil Dev	b Donald	3
P.K. Amre	b Donald	4
M. Prabhakar		
*K.S. More		
Venkatapathy Raju		
J. Srinath		
Extras	b 1, w 10, nb 1	12
	(for 6 wickets)	223

SOUTH AFRICA

S.J. Cook	c More, b Kapil Dev	0
M. Yachad	lbw, b Venkatapathy Raju	31
K.C. Wessels	c More, b Srinath	71
P.N. Kirsten	lbw, b Prabhakar	2
A.P. Kuiper	c Azharuddin, b Kapil Dev	21
C.E.B. Rice (capt)	c sub (Pandit), b Venkatapathy Raju	12
*D.J. Richardson	c Kapil Dev, b Venkatapathy Raju	5
R.P. Snell	c Manjrekar, b Srinath	2
C.R. Matthews	not out	10
C.E. Eksteen	not out	6
A.A. Donald		
Extras	b 3, lb 14, w 5, nb 3	25
	(for 8 wickets)	185

(45 overs)

	O	M	R	W
Donald	9	1	36	3
Snell	9	–	43	1
Matthews	9	–	41	1
Eksteen	2	–	18	–
Rice	9	–	46	1
Kuiper	7	–	38	–

(45 overs)

	O	M	R	W
Kapil Dev	9	3	27	2
Prabhakar	9	1	19	1
Srinath	9	–	34	2
Tendulkar	7	–	31	–
Venkatapathy Raju	9	–	43	3
Srikkanth	2	–	14	–

FALL OF WICKETS
1–130, **2**–144, **3**–159, **4**–202, **5**–218, **6**–223

FALL OF WICKETS
1–0, **2**–94, **3**–97, **4**–144, **5**–145, **6**–162, **7**–164, **8**–167

Umpires: S.K. Bansal & R.V. Ramani Man of the Match – S.V. Manjrekar & K.C. Wessels *India won by 38 runs*

THIRD ONE-DAY INTERNATIONAL – INDIA v. SOUTH AFRICA

12 November, 1991 at Jawaharlal Nehru Stadium, New Delhi

INDIA

R.J. Shastri (capt)	run out	109
K. Srikkanth	**st** Richardson, **b** Kirsten	53
S.V. Manjrekar	**c** McMillan, **b** Rice	105
S.R. Tendulkar	**c** Cook, **b** Donald	1
Kapil Dev	not out	3
D.B. Vengsarkar		
P.K. Amre		
*C.S. Pandit		
M. Prabhakar		
Venkatapathy Raju		
J. Srinath		
Extras	b 4, lb 5, w 6, nb 1	16
	(for 4 wickets)	**287**

(50 overs)

	O	M	R	W
Donald	10	–	55	1
Snell	10	1	56	–
Matthews	10	1	50	–
McMillan	8	–	40	–
Rice	9	–	54	1
Kirsten	3	–	23	1

FALL OF WICKETS

1–86, **2**–261, **3**–264, **4**–287

SOUTH AFRICA

S.J. Cook	**c** Prabhakar, **b** Srinath	35
K.C. Wessels	lbw, **b** Venkatapathy Raju	90
P.N. Kirsten	not out	86
A.P. Kuiper	not out	63
A.C. Hudson		
C.E.B. Rice (capt)		
B.M. McMillan		
*D.J. Richardson		
R.P. Snell		
C.R. Matthews		
A.A. Donald		
Extras	b 2, lb 5, w 4, nb 3	14
	(for 2 wickets)	**288**

(46.4 overs)

	O	M	R	W
Kapil Dev	8	–	37	–
Prabhakar	8.4	–	64	–
Srinath	10	–	69	1
Tendulkar	6	–	38	–
Venkatapathy Raju	10	–	48	1
Srikkanth	4	–	25	–

FALL OF WICKETS

1–72, **2**–183

Umpires: S. Banerjee & P.D. Reporter

Man of the Match – P.N. Kirsten

South Africa won by 8 wickets

DULEEP TROPHY FINAL – NORTH ZONE v. WEST ZONE

21, 22, 23, 24 and 25 January, 1992 at Sardar Patel Stadium, Valsad

NORTH ZONE

	FIRST INNINGS		SECOND INNINGS	
A. Jadeja	**c** Patil, **b** Kuruvilla	3	**c** Kambli, **b** Narula	66
M. Nayyar	**c** Jedhe, **b** Narula	23	**b** Amin	0
R. Puri	**b** Narula	58	**b** Kuruvilla	1
A.K. Sharma	**c** Mongia, **b** Narula	11	lbw, **b** Kuruvilla	4
K.P. Bhaskar	lbw, **b** Kuruvilla	21	lbw, **b** Kuruvilla	104
A. Kaypee	run out	23	**b** Kuruvilla	72
*V. Yadav	**c** Amin, **b** Kuruvilla	28	**c** Jedhe, **b** Kuruvilla	4
C.M. Sharma (capt)	**c** sub, **b** Amin	10	(9) **c** Mongia, **b** Narula	24
V. Razdan	**c** Mongia, **b** Narula	33	(8) **c** Narula, **b** Jedhe	50
Maninder Singh	**b** Narula	28	not out	44
A.S. Wassan	not out	11	**b** Kuruvilla	14
Extras	b 12, lb 11, nb 7	30	lb 10	10
		279		**393**

	O	M	R	W	O	M	R	W
Kuruvilla	31	12	60	3	30.3	7	98	6
Amin	17	3	55	1	14	5	22	1
Narula	23.4	4	48	5	30	6	96	2
Patil	23	5	69	–	29	2	90	–
Radia	5	–	24	–	7	–	34	–
Sugwekar					3	–	11	–
Jedhe					10	4	32	1

FALL OF WICKETS

1–10, **2**–44, **3**–56, **4**–94, **5**–140, **6**–174, **7**–192, **8**–192, **9**–262
1–18, **2**–19, **3**–25, **4**–128, **5**–237, **6**–255, **7**–264 , **8**–307, **9**–348

WEST ZONE

	FIRST INNINGS		SECOND INNINGS	
M.H. Parmar	**c** Yadav, **b** C.M. Sharma	31	**c** Bhaskar, **b** Wassan	3
K.S. Chavan	run out	0	**c** Puri, **b** Maninder Singh	37
S.V. Jedhe	lbw, **b** C.M. Sharma	13	**c** Yadav, **b** Razdan	44
V.G. Kambli	**c** Yadav, **b** C.M. Sharma	27	**c** Yadav, **b** C.M. Sharma	58
S.S. Sugwekar (capt)	**b** C.M. Sharma	5	**c** Bhaskar, **b** Razdan	29
*N.R. Mongia	lbw, **b** C.M. Sharma	52	**st** Yadav, **b** Maninder Singh	22
M.S. Narula	**b** Razdan	0	**b** Razdan	1
B.M. Radia	lbw, **b** C.M. Sharma	39	**st** Yadav, **b** Maninder Singh	1
S.S. Patil	**b** Jadeja, **b** Wassan	8	run out	0
K.D. Amin	lbw, **b** Wassan	11	lbw, **b** Maninder Singh	0
A. Kuruvilla	not out	1	not out	6
Extras	lb 4, w 1, nb 19	24	b 8, lb 3, nb 8	19
	penalty runs	5		
		216		**220**

	O	M	R	W	O	M	R	W
Wassan	16	1	47	2	11	–	52	1
Razdan	14	2	40	1	22	6	46	3
C.M. Sharma	21.3	3	65	6	18	3	56	1
Jadeja	5	–	23	–				
Maninder Singh	16	5	32	–	29.3	7	55	4

FALL OF WICKETS

1–9, **2**–37, **3**–69, **4**–83, **5**–92, **6**–97, **7**–178, **8**–195, **9**–209
1–5, **2**–73, **3**–128, **4**–162, **5**–196, **6**–206, **7**–206, **8**–207, **9**–207

Umpires: S.B. Kulkarni & D.V. Pathak

North Zone won by 236 runs

DULEEP TROPHY

QUARTER-FINAL

8, 9, 10 and 11 January, 1992 *at Wankhede Stadium, Bombay*

Central Zone 173 (V. Prasad 6 for 40) and 268 (Abhay Sharma 59, S.S. Lahore 53, Sanjeeva Sharma 53)
South Zone 491 (Robin Singh 108, A.R. Kumble 88 not out, N.V. Sridhar 56, Zakir Hussain 51, P.S. Vaidya 5 for 113)

South Zone won by an innings and 50 runs

Central Zone derived no advantage from winning the toss as they were routed by the medium pace of Prasad and the off-spin of Arshad Ayub. Former international all-rounder Robin Singh hit a sparkling century, and Test leg-spinner Kumble hit strongly to the close of South Zone's innings to put his side in a commanding position.

SEMI-FINALS

15, 16, 17, 18 and 19 January, 1992 *at Wankhede Stadium, Bombay*

East Zone 185 (R.R. Kulkarni 4 for 27) and 142 (S.S. Patil 5 for 36, A. Kuruvilla 4 for 59)
West Zone 682 for 9 dec. (V.G. Kambli 208, S.S. Sugwekar 158, K.S. Chavan 123, S.V. Jedhe 57, N.R. Mongia 55, Abinash Kumar 5 for 153)

West Zone won by an innings and 355 runs

at BRC Complex, Udhna

South Zone 220 (A.S. Wassan 6 for 72) and 230 (C.M. Sharma 5 for 80)
North Zone 533 (V. Yadav 201, A.K. Sharma 89, C.M. Sharma 57)

North Zone won by an innings and 83 runs

The semi-finals provided overwhelming victories for West Zone, who won an hour after lunch on the fourth day, and for North Zone, who also had more than a day to spare. There were double centuries for Kambli, the outstanding batsman of the season, and for Vijay Yadav. Yadav, the 24-year-old Haryana wicket-keeper, was making his debut in the competition, and he batted nearly nine hours for his 201.

FINAL
NORTH ZONE v. WEST ZONE, at Valsad

Chetan Sharma decided to bat when he won the toss, but North Zone found run-getting far from easy and struggled to score at two and a half an over as medium-pacer Mukesh Narula produced a particularly fine spell. It was only the consistent application of the later batsmen which took North Zone to a reasonable score.

West Zone found themselves in even greater difficulties as Chetan Sharma bowled in the manner which had once seen him as Kapil Dev's new-ball partner.

Leading by 63 on the first innings, North Zone suffered a set-back when they batted a second time, losing three leading batsmen for 25 runs. Jadeja and Bhaskar stopped the rot with a stand of 103, and centurion Bhaskar, so often so close to inclusion in the national side, was joined by Kaypee in a fifth-wicket stand of 109. Both men fell to the impressive Kuruvilla, but North Zone were able to set the West a target of 457 to win.

They never looked likely to succeed and North Zone retained the trophy with ease.

The outstanding batsman of the Indian season – the 20-year-old left-hander Vinod Kambli. (David Munden)

Skipper of Tamil Nadu Woorkeri Raman scored prolifically. (Ben Radford/Allsport)

RANJI TROPHY

WEST ZONE

6, 7, 8 and 9 December, 1991 *at Baroda Rayon Ground, Surat*

Bombay 554 for 4 dec. (V.G. Kambli 179 not out, J.B. Jadhav 139, J.V. Paranjpe 106) and 272 for 6 dec. (J.B. Jadhav 63, S.S. Talpade 50 not out)
Gujarat 242 and 121 for 6

Match drawn

Bombay 20 pts., Gujarat 7 pts.

at Municipal Corporation Ground, Rajkot

Baroda 290 (K.S. Chavan 84, M.S. Narula 77, B.M. Radia 5 for 104) and 252 for 8 (K.S. Chavan 111)
Saurashtra 499 (S.S. Tanna 253 not out, C.C. Mankad 54, B. Dutta 53, S. Patel 6 for 106) and 9 for 0

Match drawn

Saurashtra 15 pts., Baroda 9 pts.

Kambli confirmed his challenge for a place in the national side and shared a stand of 206 with Paranjpe who scored a century on his debut. Patel, a medium-pace bowler, took six wickets on his debut, but the outstanding performance came from Tanna who carried his bat for 253 in 168.5 overs.

13, 14, 15 and 16 December, 1991 *at Wankhede Stadium, Bombay*

Bombay 511 for 9 dec. (V.G. Kambli 262, Iqbal Khan 105, B.M. Radia 5 for 136) and 227 for 8 (V.G. Kambli 55)
Saurashtra 380 (B.M. Jadeja 129, B. Dutta 110, S.S. Patil 4 for 86) and 62 for 6

Match drawn

Bombay 19 pts., Saurashtra 12 pts.

at Sardar Patel Stadium, Valsad

Gujarat 361 for 9 dec. (M.H. Parmar 147, B.H. Mistry 50) and 157 (B.H. Mistry 50, S.V. Ranjane 4 for 67)
Maharashtra 502 for 8 dec. (Abhijit Deshpande 217, S.V. Jedhe 118, S.S. Sugwekar 63) and 17 for 1

Maharashtra won by 9 wickets

Maharashtra 21 pts., Gujarat 5 pts.

The success of the left-handed Vinod Kambli continued with the highest score of his career in the drawn game at Bombay. Maharashtra's win owed much to Abhijit Deshpande who hit a double century and shared a second-wicket stand of 287 with Jedhe.

20, 21, 22 and 23 December, 1991 *at Poona Club, Pune*

Saurashtra 345 (B. Dutta 76, B.S. Pujara 71, A.N. Pandya 71) and 264 for 9 dec. (B.M. Radia 71, B.S. Pujara 55, S.V. Ranjane 4 for 54)
Maharashtra 498 (S.S. Sugwekar 180, S.V. Jedhe 123, Abhijit Deshpande 57) and 23 for 0

Match drawn

Maharashtra 16 pts., Saurashtra 9 pts.

at Motibaug Palace Ground, Baroda

Bombay 268 (S.S. Talpade 79, V.G. Kambli 57, M.S. Narula 4 for 57) and 339 (S.S. Dighe 71 not out, S.S. Hattangadi 53, M.S. Narula 5 for 90)
Baroda 404 (K.S. Chavan 129, A.C. Bedade 102, R.B. Parikh 76, A. Kuruvilla 4 for 96) and 187 for 4 (T.B. Arothe 70)

Match drawn

Baroda 16 pts., Bombay 11 pts.

Jedhe and Sugwekar shared a third-wicket partnership of 193 as Maharashtra had the better of the drawn game at Pune. Baroda needed 204 in 28 overs to beat Bombay and made a spirited bid to get the runs.

27, 28, 29 and 30 December, 1991 *at Chatrapati Shivaji Stadium, Kolhapur*

Baroda 224 (R.B. Parikh 62, S.J. Jadhav 4 for 38) and 312 (T.B. Arothe 109, K.S. Chavan 88)
Maharashtra 328 (S.S. Sugwekar 90, S.C. Gudge 61) and 209 for 4 (S.S. Sugwekar 65 not out, S.V. Jedhe 60)

Maharashtra won by 6 wickets

Maharashtra 17 pts., Baroda 7 pts.

at Rajkot Municipal Ground, Rajkot

Saurashtra 422 for 7 dec. (B. Dutta 139, C.C. Mankad 65 not out, B.M. Jadeja 62) and 237 (B.S. Pujara 73, M. Parmar 53)
Gujarat 358 (M.H. Parmar 152, N.Y. Laliwala 60) and 81 for 3

Match drawn

Saurashtra 17 pts., Gujarat 13 pts.

Maharashtra gained their second victory of the season with a good all-round team performance. At Rajkot, Mukund Parmar hit a magnificent 152 but he could not prevent Saurashtra from taking a first-innings lead in a match which was eventually drawn.

2, 3, 4 and 5 January, 1992 *at Wankhede Stadium, Bombay*

Maharashtra 237 for 9 dec. (M.D. Gunjal 61) and 319 (S.S. Bhave 117, S.J. Jadhav 64, A. Kuruvilla 5 for 60)
Bombay 641 for 9 dec. (V.G. Kambli 182, S.V. Bahutule 111 not out, Iqbal Khan 76, R.R. Kulkarni 69, S.S.

Talpade 66, S.S. Bighe 54, S.J. Jadhav 4 for 138)

Bombay won by an innings and 85 runs

Bombay 22 pts., Maharashtra 5 pts.

at Motibaug Palace Ground, Baroda

Baroda 383 (A.D. Gaekwad 143, M.S. Narula 57, B. Mistry 5 for 77) and 251 for 5 dec. (A.C. Bedade 72)
Gujarat 367 (B. Mistry 138 not out, N. Bakriwala 68, Maqbul Malam 51, J.J. Martin 5 for 51) and 116 for 4 (M.H. Parmar 67 not out)

Match drawn

Baroda 14 pts., Gujarat 11 pts.

Against all expectation, Bombay beat Maharashtra by an innings to snatch the West Zone title. A century by the 18-year-old all-rounder Sairaj Bahutule, his first in first-class cricket, built upon the earlier magnificence of Kambli and took Bombay to a first-innings lead of 404 runs. Even this did not seem sufficient to win the game, but a remarkable spell of straight, hostile fast bowling from Abey Kuruvilla brought about a collapse in the last session of the match as Maharashtra lost their last six wickets for 83 runs.

WEST ZONE FINAL TABLE

	P	W	L	D	Pts
Bombay	4	1	–	3	72
Maharashtra	4	2	1	1	59
Saurashtra	4	–	–	4	53
Baroda	4	–	1	3	46
Gujarat	4	–	1	3	36

SOUTH ZONE

3, 4, 5 and 6 November, 1991 *at Panji Gymkhana, Panji*

Hyderabad 535 for 8 dec. (Abdul Azeem 158, M.V. Sridhar 140, Arshad Ayub 70, Ehthesham Ali 67, A. Shetty 4 for 184)
Goa 103 (Arshad Ayub 6 for 16) and 165 (R.M.H. Binny 102)

Hyderabad won by an innings and 267 runs

Hyderabad 25 pts., Goa 2 pts.

Roger Binny had moved to Goa to lead the side, but his valiant century could not save Goa from a crushing defeat. Arshad Ayub had a fine all-round match for Hyderabad for whom Abdul Azeem and Sridhar shared a second-wicket stand of 215.

12, 13, 14 and 15 November, 1991 *at Arlem Breweries Ground, Arlem, Margao*

Goa 154 and 261 (A. Gaekwad 80, R.M.H. Binny 62 not out, N.P. Parikhar 53, K.N.A. Padmanabhan 4 for 96)
Kerala 183 (A. Shetty 6 for 55) and 233 for 4 (B. Ramprakash 81 not out, V. Narayan Kutty 51)

Kerala won by 6 wickets

Kerala 14 pts., Goa 6 pts.

Goa gave an improved performance in their second match, but an unbroken partnership of 127 between Sunder and Ramprakash took Kerala to victory.

22, 23, 24 and 25 November, 1991 *at M.A. Chidambaram Stadium, Madras*

Tamil Nadu 600 for 6 dec. (W.V. Raman 206, Robin Singh 100 not out, M. Senthilnathan 71, A. Kripal Singh 67)
Kerala 162 (S.Subramaniam 4 for 47) and 301 (B. Ramprakash 152, D. Vasu for 20, Ashish Kapoor 4 for 86)

Tamil Nadu won by an innings and 137 runs

Tamil Nadu 22 pts., Kerala 3 pts.

at BGML Sports Complex, Kolar Gold Fields

Goa 169 and 161 (R.M.H. Binny 63, A.R. Kumble 4 for 61)
Karnataka 324 (R.S. Dravid 126, A. Shetty 5 for 78) and 7 for 0

Karnataka won by 10 wickets

Karnataka 15 pts., Goa 3 pts.

Inspired by a double century from skipper Woorkeri Raman, Tamil Nadu built up a huge score and overwhelmed Kerala. Karnataka entered the competition with a sound win over Goa for whom Shetty again bowled well.

29, 30 November, 1 and 2 December, 1991 *at District Stadium, Bijapur*

Karnataka 603 (A.R. Kumble 154 not out, S.M.H. Kirmani 150, R.S. Dravid 128, C. Saldanha 88)
Kerala 189 (A. Raghuram Bhat 5 for 67) and 172 (P.T. Subramaniam 56 not out)

Karnataka won by an innings and 242 runs

Karnataka 25 pts., Kerala 2 pts.

at Gymkhana, Secunderabad

Andhra 322 (V. Vijayasarathy 98, O. Vinod Kumar 75, Arshad Ayub 6 for 82) and 164 (Arshad Ayub 6 for 59)
Hyderabad 575 for 8 dec. (Abdul Azeem 208, Zakir Hussain 108, M.V. Sridhar 105)

Hyderabad won by an innings and 89 runs

Hyderabad 24 pts., Andhra 3 pts.

at M.A. Chidambaram Stadium, Madras

Tamil Nadu 604 for 7 dec. (V.B. Chandrasekhar 144, N. Gautam 129, Robin Singh 121 not out, A. Kripal Singh 52)

Goa 201 (Ishan Bakhle 80, S. Subramaniam 5 for 69, Ashish Kapoor 4 for 60) and 123 (D. Vasu 4 for 39)

Tamil Nadu won by an innings and 280 runs

Tamil Nadu 25 pts., Goa 2 pts.

A career-best innings by Anil Kumble and centuries from the veteran Kirmani and from Dravid, his second in successive matches, set Karnataka on the way to trouncing Kerala. Hyderabad also trounced Andhra thanks to a double century from Abdul Azeem, who shared a second-wicket stand of 284 with Sridhar, and 12 wickets from Test off-spinner Arshad Ayub. Tamil Nadu followed the pattern of the dominant sides with three centurions, Robin Singh hitting his second hundred in succession.

6, 7, 8 and 9 December, 1991 *at Municipal Ground, Tellicherry*

Hyderabad 380 (Zakir Hussain 86, M.V. Sridhar 75, K.N.A. Padmanabhan 5 for 112) and 339 (Ehtesham Ali 106, Zakir Hussain 52, Suresh Kumar 6 for 93)
Kerala 461 (P.T. Subramaniam 89, P.G. Sunder 81, B. Ramprakash 81, P.V. Ranganathan 60, F.V. Rashid 59, M.V. Ramanamurthy 5 for 60) and 182 for 4 (P.G. Sunder 58 not out, B. Ramprakash 57)

Match drawn

Kerala 16 pts., Hyderabad 16 pts.

Kerala gave Hyderabad a surprisingly hard game in a dour struggle in which neither side could seize the initiative.

13, 14, 15 and 16 December, 1991 *at M.A. Chidambaram Stadium, Madras*

Hyderabad 529 (Zakir Hussain 161, R.A. Swarup 131, Arshad Ayub 81, N. Rajesh Yadav 71, D. Vasu 4 for 141) and 83 for 1 dec.
Tamil Nadu 420 (N. Gautam 68, Mujibur Rehman 61, D. Vasu 53, S. Subramaniam 53, Arshad Ayub 5 for 172) and 47 for 2

Match drawn

Hyderabad 12 pts., Tamil Nadu 8 pts.

at Vishakhapatnam Steel Plant Ground, Ukkunagram

Karnataka 461 (K.A. Jeshwanth 151, C. Saldanha 71, A.R. Kumble 64, V. Vijayasaradhi 4 for 98)
Andhra 140 (O. Vinod Kumar 56, A.R. Kumble 6 for 41) and 247 (A. Pathak 101)

Karnataka won by an innings and 74 runs

Karnataka 22 pts., Andhra 3 pts.

After losing three wickets cheaply, Hyderabad recovered as Swarup and Zakir Hussain added 191, and the tail wagged strongly. Tamil Nadu batted more consistently in a match that always looked to be heading for a draw.

Karnataka, too, recovered from early shocks, and they owed much to a fine all-round performance from Anil Kumble. The leg-spinner performed the hat-trick in the first innings when he dismissed Vijayasaradhi, Vincent Kumar and Vivekanand with the third, fourth and fifth balls of his 23rd over.

19, 20, 21 and 22 December, 1991 *at Municipal Stadium, Cuddapash*

Goa 327 (C.R. Radhakrishnan 182, G.V.V. Gopalaraju 6 for 122) and 243 (D. Avinash 71)
Andhra 279 (A. Shetty 6 for 89) and 295 for 2 (Mohammad F. Rehman 136 not out, A. Pathak 126)

Andhra won by 8 wickets

Andhra 20 pts., Goa 7 pts.

Having led on the first innings and looked in control for most of the match, Goa were beaten by a second-wicket stand of 230 between Mohammad F. Rehman and A. Pathak.

26, 27, 28 and 29 December, 1991 *at Medical College Ground, Calicut*

Andhra 251 (Sudhakar Reddy 91 not out, B. Ramprakash 5 for 63) and 94 (B. Ramprakash 6 for 30, K.N.A. Padmanabhan 4 for 38)
Kerala 226 (P.G. Sunder 66, K.N.A. Padmanabhan 59, V. Vijayasaradhi 5 for 68, G.V.V. Gopalaraju 4 for 91) and 125 for 4

Kerala won by 6 wickets

Kerala 17 pts., Andhra 7 pts.

27, 28, 29 and 30 December, 1991 *at Gymkhana, Secunderabad*

Hyderabad 563 (Zakir Hussain 139, V. Jaisimha 115, M.V. Sridhar 83, N. Rajesh Yadav 75 not out)
Karnataka 301 for 8 dec. (C. Saldanha 84, Arjun Raja 56) and 202 for 8 (S.M.H. Kirmani 62, Arshad Ayub 5 for 76)

Match drawn

Hyderabad 15 pts., Karnataka 9 pts.

Sudhakar Reddy had the rare distinction of carrying his bat through both innings, but he still finished on the losing side.

Zakir Hussain hit his third hundred of the season, and Kirmani declared Karnataka's innings and was forced to follow-on, confident that he could deny Hyderabad victory and gain sufficient points to reach the knock-out stage of the competition.

2, 3, 4 and 5 January, 1992 *at S.V. University Ground, Tirupathi*

Tamil Nadu 503 for 9 dec. (W.V. Raman 122, A. Kripal Singh 122, V. Vijayasaradhi 5 for 142)
Andhra 204 (M. Venkataramana 4 for 69) and 133 (S. Subramaniam 7 for 45)

Tamil Nadu won by an innings and 166 runs

Tamil Nadu 25 pts., Andhra 2 pts.

Tamil Nadu moved above Karnataka in the table with the expected domination of Andhra.

6, 7, 8 and 9 February, 1992 *at Bhadravathi*

Tamil Nadu 172 and 139 (A. Raghuram Bhat 4 for 39, A.R. Kumble 4 for 50)
Karnataka 209 for 8 dec. (R.S. Dravid 61 not out, Arjun Raja 56, D. Vasu 5 for 45) and 106 for 9 (D. Vasu 5 for 42)

Karnataka won by 1 wicket

Karnataka 17 pts., Tamil Nadu 9 pts.

Karnataka beat Tamil Nadu in a tense game on a poor wicket, but they were edged out of a place in the quarter-finals. They owed the ultimate victory to the last pair, Venkatesh Prasad and Raghuram Bhat who came together at 97 for 9, but Tamil Nadu's bowlers collected enough points in a match in which batting points were not won.

SOUTH ZONE FINAL TABLE

	P	W	L	D	Pts
Hyderabad	5	2	–	3	92
Tamil Nadu	5	3	1	1	89
Karnataka	5	4	–	1	88
Kerala	5	2	2	1	52
Andhra	5	1	4	–	35
Goa	5	–	5	–	20

CENTRAL ZONE

21, 22, 23 and 24 November, 1991 *at Green Park, Kanpur*

Vidarbha 210 (P.B. Hingnikar 62, R.P. Singh 5 for 51) and 240 (A.W. Zaidi 4 for 47)
Uttar Pradesh 496 for 5 dec. (A. Gautam 144 not out, S. Chaturvedi 97, S.S. Khandkar 92, V.S. Yadav 62)

Uttar Pradesh won by an innings and 46 runs

Uttar Pradesh 22 pts., Vidarbha 1 pt.

Uttar Pradesh opened their Central Zone programme in convincing fashion, outplaying Vidarbha.

28, 29, 30 November and 1 December, 1991 *at Vidarbha CA Ground, Nagpur*

Vidarbha 190 (P.B. Hingnikar 74, D.K. Nilose 5 for 68, S.S. Lahore 4 for 60) and 503 (S. Gujar 221, U.I. Ghani 140, D.K. Nilose 5 for 152)
Madhya Pradesh 476 (P.K. Dwivedi 114, A.R. Khurasia 99, A. Prabhakar 57 not out, P.S. Vaidya 4 for 130) and 218 for 3 (A.R. Khurasia 99 not out)

Madhya Pradesh won by 7 wickets

Madhya Pradesh 20 pts., Vidarbha 6 pts.

Vidarbha staged a remarkable recovery against Madhya Pradesh, but they were still well beaten. They trailed by 286 runs on the first innings and were 92 for 4 in their second when Ghani joined Gujar in a stand of 253. Madhya Pradesh scored the 218 that they needed to win in 22.3 overs, an astonishing performance, and Khurasia finished on 99 for the second time in the match.

5, 6, 7 and 8 December, 1991 *at K.D. Singh Babu Stadium, Lucknow*

Uttar Pradesh 532 for 9 dec. (G. Pandey 178, G. Sharma 100 not out, R.P. Singh 98, A. Gautam 58, R. Rathore 4 for 103) and 250 for 6 dec. (R. Sapru 81, V. Vats 55)
Rajasthan 411 (G. Rhoda 116, V. Joshi 89, A. Beg 70, G. Sharma 5 for 86) and 14 for 1

Match drawn

Uttar Pradesh 15 pts., Rajasthan 12 pts.

at Roop Singh Stadium, Gwalior

Madhya Pradesh 427 (K.K. Patel 202, S.M. Patil 55) and 47 for 0
Railways 417 (Yusuf Ali Khan 125, Abhay Sharma 85, R.K. Chauhan 6 for 210) and 11 for 0

Match drawn

Madhya Pradesh 7 pts., Railways 5 pts.

The outstanding feature of the match at Lucknow was the all-round performance of Gopal Sharma who hit a century at number ten and shared a ninth-wicket stand of 196 with R.P. Singh. Gopal Sharma then took five wickets with his off-breaks. At Gwalior, K.K. Patel hit a double century, and Chauhan (92) and Lahoroe (80.5) sent down all but 23 of the 195.5 overs bowled in Railways' innings.

12, 13, 14 and 15 December, 1991 *at Northern Railway Ground, Bikaner*

Vidarbha 312 (P. Rawat 79, U.I. Ghani 58, Y.T. Ghare 52) and 297 for 4 dec. (S. Gujar 98, Y.T. Ghare 71, A.V. Sarwate 63)
Rajasthan 238 and 210 for 8 (V. Joshi 77 not out, A. Sinha 61, P.V. Gandhe 5 for 53)

Match drawn

Vidarbha 14 pts., Rajasthan 9 pts.

at Karnali Stadium, Delhi

Railways 304 (Sanjeev Sharma 111 not out, Yashpal Sharma 52, G. Sharma 4 for 89) and 279 for 5 dec. (Yusuf Ali Khan 116 not out, Sanjeev Sharma 57 not out)
Uttar Pradesh 370 (R. Sapru 94, S. Chaturvedi 57, G. Pandey 54 not out, A. Gautam 50, Sanjeev Sharma 5 for 70) and 80 for 2

Match drawn

Uttar Pradesh 13 pts., Railways 9 pts.

At Delhi, Sanjeev Sharma, former Test bowler, hit 168 without being dismissed and took five wickets in 23.3 overs.

19, 20, 21 and 22 December, 1991 *at Nehru Stadium, Indore*

Madhya Pradesh 546 (S.M. Patil 157, M. Sahni 90, K.K. Patel 74, C.P. Singh 59) and 251 for 7 dec. (S.M. Patil 119, D.K. Nilose 50)
Uttar Pradesh 554 for 7 dec. (R. Sapru 139, V.S. Yadav 97, V. Vats 92, S.S. Khandkar 66, A. Gautam 55 not out, R.K. Chauhan 4 for 187)

Match drawn

Uttar Pradesh 15 pts., Madhya Pradesh 12 pts.

at Vidarbha CA Ground, Nagpur

Vidarbha 104 (D. Mishra 6 for 34, Sanjeev Sharma 4 for 63) and 382 (P.B. Hingnikar 115, S. Gujar 92, P. Rawat 67, Sanjeev Sharma 4 for 140)
Railways 426 (Yashpal Sharma 144, Abhay Sharma 143, P.S. Vaidya 5 for 93) and 61 for 0

Railways won by 10 wickets

Railways 18 pts., Vidarbha 5 pts.

In the clash of the giants, veteran batsman Sandeep Patil hit a century in each innings for Madhya Pradesh, but he could not prevent Uttar Pradesh from winning the points battle. Yashpal and Abhay Sharma shared a fifth-wicket partnership of 263 as Railways overwhelmed Vidarbha who again effected a brave recovery through skipper Hingnikar.

26, 27, 28 and 29 December, 1991 *at Mansarovar, Jaipur*

Madhya Pradesh 397 (P.K. Dwivedi 114, A.V. Vijayvirgiya 68, S.M. Patil 51, Perminder Singh 4 for 92) and 290 for 3 dec. (S.M. Patil 77 not out, P.K. Dwivedi 67 not out, A.R. Khurasia 59)
Rajasthan 213 (M. Amer 56, A. Sinha 55, R.K. Chauhan 4 for 58) and 148 for 5 (S.S. Lahore 4 for 56)

Match drawn

Madhya Pradesh 19 pts., Rajasthan 9 pts.

1, 2, 3 and 4 January, 1992 *at Palam Ground, Delhi*

Rajasthan 274 (Parminder Singh 65, A. Sinha 57, K. Bharatan 4 for 28) and 192 (Yashpal Sharma 4 for 4)
Railways 515 (Yashpal Sharma 100, K. Bharatan 99, Sanjeev Sharma 70, S. Sawant 58)

Railways won by an innings and 49 runs

Railways 22 pts., Rajasthan 4 pts.

In spite of the mighty efforts of skipper Yashpal Sharma, the former Test player, and in spite of the of the fact that they had won two of their four matches, Railways failed to qualify for the knock-out stage of the Ranji Trophy, another condemnation of a points system which gives too little credit for a victory.

CENTRAL ZONE FINAL TABLE

	P	W	L	D	Pts
Uttar Pradesh	4	1	–	3	65
Madhya Pradesh	4	1	–	3	58
Railways	4	2	–	2	54
Rajasthan	4	–	1	3	34
Vidarbha	4	–	3	1	26

EAST ZONE

21, 22, 23 and 24 November, 1991 *at VSS Stadium, Sambalpur*

Bihar 384 (S. Chatterjee 142, K.V.P. Rao 72, R. Biswal 5 for 91, S. Kumar 4 for 117)
Orissa 64 (Avinash Kumar 5 for 19, V. Venkatram 5 for 32) and 178 (P. Mohapatra 60, K.V.P. Rao 5 for 40)

Bihar won by an innings and 142 runs

Bihar 17 pts., Orissa 3 pts.

at Eden Gardens, Calcutta

Assam 177 (S. Sen Sharma 5 for 63) and 225 (L.S. Rajput 70, S. Mukherjee 6 for 85)
Bengal 339 (C. Raja Venkat 69, M. Das 61, A.O. Malhotra 61, Sneha Ganguly 50, S. Chakraborty 5 for 91) and 65 for 1

Bengal won by 9 wickets

Bengal 17 pts., Assam 6 pts.

Predictably, the two strongest East Zone sides had easy victories in their opening matches.

28, 29, 30 November and 1 December, 1991 *at Polytechnic Ground, Agartala*

Tripura 104 (K.V.P. Rao 5 for 25, Avinash Kumar 4 for 35) and 74 (K.V.P. Rao 4 for 17)
Bihar 412 for 5 dec. (H. Gidwani 160, Adil Hussain 125, S.S. Karim 62)

Bihar won by an innings and 234 runs

Bihar 24 pts., Tripura 2 pts.

at BOS Engineering College Ground, Cuttack

Assam 203 (Rajesh Singh 4 for 44, Sushil Kumar 4 for 69) and 246 (Zahir Alam 69, L.S. Rajput 60, Sushil Kumar 6 for 84)
Orissa 411 (A. Ray 125, Rajesh Singh 59, R. Bora 4 for 110) and 39 for 0

Orissa won by 10 wickets

Orissa 17 pts., Assam 3 pts.

Bihar achieved victory inside three days and virtually

assured themselves of a place in the later stages of the competition. Gidwani shared a third-wicket partnership of 233 with Adil Hussain, and then added 117 with Karim.

5, 6, 7 and 8 December, 1991 *at MECON, Ranchi*

Assam 649 for 9 dec. (R. Bora 235, S.K. Kulkarni 200 not out, G. Dutta 55, Avinash Kumar 6 for 198) and 222 for 7 (Zaheer Alam 94, L.S. Rajput 50, K.V.P. Rao 4 for 64)
Bihar 454 (Adil Hussain 128, P. Khanna 107, H. Gidwani 91, G. Dutta 6 for 92)

Match drawn

Bihar 13 pts., Assam 12 pts.

at Eden Gardens, Calcutta

Tripura 124 (A. Debburman 50, Sen Sharma 4 for 17) and 89 (S. Mukherjee 4 for 12)
Bengal 435 for 9 dec. (Sneha Ganguly 136, S.J. Kalyani 63, C. Raja Venkat 59, M. Das 51, J. Arun Lal 51)

Bengal won by an innings and 222 runs

Bengal 25 pts., Tripura 4 pts.

While Bengal took maximum points against Tripura, Bihar encountered unexpectedly strong opposition from Assam who made the highest score in the association's history. Bora and Kulkarni both hit double centuries and shared a fourth-wicket partnership of 259, another Assam record. Bihar still managed to gather more points by virtue of their second-innings bowling.

12, 13, 14 and 15 December, 1991 *at Keenan Stadium, Jamshedpur*

Bihar 310 (P. Khanna 83, S.S. Karim 63, Adil Hussain 54, S. Das 52, S. Mukherjee 4 for 65, U. Chatterjee 4 for 83) and 246 for 6 dec. (S.S. Karim 102 not out)
Bengal 234 (S.J. Kalyani 82, S. Mukherjee 51 not out) and 53 for 2

Match drawn

Bihar 12 pts., Bengal 8 pts.

at BOS Engineering College Ground, Cuttack

Tripura 117 (Sushil Kumar 4 for 19) and 208 (R. Biswal 4 for 40)
Orissa 414 (R. Biswal 107, S. Chowdhary 73, D. Lenka 55, M. Bhatt 51)

Orissa won by an innings and 89 runs

Orissa 23 pts., Tripura 4 pts.

The battle between the two leading East Zone teams went marginally in favour of Bihar while Orissa gained their second victory of the season, beating lowly Tripura inside three days.

19, 20, 21 and 22 December, 1991 *at Baripada Stadium, Baripada*

Bengal 514 for 4 dec. (A.O. Malhotra 151, C. Raja Venkat 140 not out, J. Arun Lal 130, S.J. Kalyani 52) and 259 for 3 dec. (A.O. Malhotra 101 not out, J. Arun Lal 99)
Orissa 225 (M. Bhatt 69, Sen Sharma 5 for 65, U. Chatterjee 4 for 69) and 187 for 4 (M. Bhatt 86)

Match drawn

Bengal 19 pts., Orissa 7 pts.

at Nehru Stadium, Guwahati

Assam 684 for 7 dec. (Zaheer Alam 257, L.S. Rajput 239)
Tripura 129 (G. Dutta 9 for 52) and 83 (H. Barua 5 for 38, G. Dutta 5 for 44)

Assam won by an innings and 472 runs

Assam 25 pts., Tripura 2 pts.

Bengal skipper Ashok Malhotra hit a century in each innings as his side finished their campaign and qualified for the knock-out section of the Ranji Trophy. Team-mate Arun Lal was close to emulating him, being caught on 99. The honours of the last round, however, went to Assam. They beat the record score they had established in the previous match, and Zaheer Alam and Rajput put on 475 for the second wicket, a record for any Assam wicket and the highest partnership of the season. Alam's 257 was the highest score ever made for Assam, and Dutta's 9 for 52 was the best bowling performance for the province and the best return of the season. Assam's margin of victory was also a record and the largest of the season.

EAST ZONE FINAL TABLE

	P	W	L	D	Pts
Bengal	4	2	–	2	69
Bihar	4	2	–	2	69
Orissa	4	2	1	1	50
Assam	4	1	2	1	46
Tripura	4	–	4	–	12

NORTH ZONE

28, 29, 30 and 31 October, 1991 *at Nahar Singh Stadium, Faridabad*

Haryana 567 for 9 dec. (A. Jadeja 256, A. Kaypee 200)
Services 161 (Chinmoy Sharma 63, D. Sharma 4 for 25, Y. Bhandari 4 for 55) and 194 (Chinmoy Sharma 67 not out, K.S. Roshan 61)

Haryana won by an innings and 212 runs

Haryana 24 pts., Services 1 pt.

Ajaysingh Jadeja and Amarjeet Kaypee put on 405 for Haryana's third wicket. Jadeja hit the highest score of his career.

2, 3, 4 and 5 November, 1991 *at Air Force Sports Complex, Palam, Delhi*

Delhi 543 for 6 dec. (M. Prabhakar 134, V. Razdan 100 not out, Bantoo Singh 72, Kirti Azad 67, Sanjay Sharma 65 not out, K.P. Bhaskar 52)
Services 180 (Harpreet Singh 4 for 55) and 216 (K.M. Roshan 50)

Delhi won by an innings and 147 runs

Delhi 21 pts., Services 2 pts.

Delhi made their start to the Ranji Trophy much as expected, with three century partnerships in their innings.

9, 10, 11 and 12 November, 1991 *at Gandhi Grounds, Amritsar*

Services 164 (M.I. Singh 5 for 60) and 117 (Bhupinder Singh snr 7 for 38)
Punjab 566 for 9 dec. (D. Pandove 170, Bhupinder Singh jnr 103, N.S. Sidhu 77, Chinmoy Sharma 4 for 95)

Punjab won by an innings and 285 runs

Punjab 25 pts., Services 2 pts.

Services suffered their third innings defeat in succession as Punjab took maximum points. The match was completed inside three days.

15, 16, 17 and 18 November, 1991 *at Police Ground, Dharamshala*

Services 258 (Chinmoy Sharma 64, S.K. Bhatnagar 62) and 339 (Chinmoy Sharma 133, Anil Sen 4 for 98)
Himachal Pradesh 222 (R. Bittu 131 not out, S. Subramaniam 4 for 48) and 240 (R. Nayyar 55, Shambu Sharma 51, M.V. Rao 4 for 46)

Services won by 135 runs

Services 16 pts., Himachal Pradesh 8 pts.

at Government College for Boys Ground, Ludhiana

Jammu & Kashmir 203 (M.I. Singh 4 for 38) and 84 (M.I. Singh 7 for 33)
Punjab 393 (Gursharan Singh 191, K. Mohan 70, V. Rathore 54, A. Gupta 4 for 93)

Punjab won by an innings and 106 runs

Punjab 24 pts., Jammu & Kashmir 4 pts.

The entry of Himachal Pradesh into the tournament allowed Services to redeem some pride while the other weak side in the North Zone, Jammu & Kashmir, were trounced by Punjab inside three days. The outstanding performance came from Ramesh Bittu who carried his bat through Himachal's first innings.

20, 21, 22 and 23 November, 1991 *at Maulana Azad Stadium, Jammu*

Jammu & Kashmir 473 (V. Bhaskar 130, A. Gupta 124, R. Nayyar 5 for 117)
Himachal Pradesh 142 (R. Nayyar 59, Abdul Qayyum 5 for 45) and 267 (R. Nayyar 109, Abdul Qayyum 6 for 122)

Jammu & Kashmir won by an innings and 64 runs

Jammu & Kashmir 24 pts., Himachal Pradesh 6 pts.

21, 22, 23 and 24 November, 1991

Delhi 315 (R. Vinayak 76, Sanjay Sharma 57, A.K. Sharma 51)
Punjab 100 (Kirti Azad 4 for 20) and 175 (Maninder Singh 7 for 43)

Delhi won by an innings and 40 runs

Delhi 23 pts., Punjab 5 pts.

Jammu & Kashmir hit the highest score in their history as they achieved an innings victory over Himachal Pradesh who are flattered by first-class status. Ashwini Gupta and Vidya Bhaskar shared a record fourth-wicket stand of 224. Delhi brushed aside Punjab's challenge with Maninder Singh returning match figures of 10 for 64.

26, 27, 28 and 29 November, 1991 *at TIT Senior Secondary School Ground, Bhiwani*

Jammu & Kashmir 189 (Kawaljit Singh 53) and 69 (Deepak Sharma 4 for 12, C.M. Sharma 4 for 45)
Haryana 377 (V.S. Yadav 82, A. Jadeja 65, A. Gupta 5 for 134)

Haryana won by an innings and 119 runs

Haryana 24 pts., Jammu & Kashmir 4 pts.

at Gandhi Grounds, Amritsar

Punjab 396 (Gursharan Singh 75, K. Mohan 75, M. Arora 72 not out, A. Sen 4 for 117)
Himachal Pradesh 128 and 150 (Balsinder Singh 73, Jaideep Singh 5 for 62)

Punjab won by an innings and 118 runs

Punjab 24 pts., Himachal Pradesh 4 pts.

Haryana and Punjab accounted for weak opposition inside three days.

1, 2, 3 and 4 December, 1991 *at Nehru Stadium, Gurgaon*

Punjab 240 (S. Chopra 108, D. Pandove 51, P. Jain 5 for 75) and 304 for 6 dec. (Gursharan Singh 72, S. Chopra 64, Bhupinder Singh jnr 63 not out, V. Rathore 54)
Haryana 506 (A. Jadeja 228, A. Kaypee 72, R. Puri 70, C.M. Sharma 52, Jaideep Singh 4 for 120) and 15 for 1

Match drawn

Haryana 14 pts., Punjab 6 pts.

at Indira Stadium, Una

Delhi 475 for 7 dec. (K.P. Bhaskar 178, A.K. Sharma 159, Sanjay Sharma 58 not out)
Himachal Pradesh 86 (Maninder Singh 5 for 14, V. Razdan 4 for 55) and 226 (R. Bittu 76, Maninder Singh 5 for 73)

Delhi won by an innings and 163 runs

Delhi 23 pts., Himachal Pradesh 3 pts.

Punjab completed their programme with the first drawn match in the North Zone. Ajay Jadeja hit his second double century of the season for Haryana whose 14 points from the match seemed likely to ensure them a place in the quarter-finals ahead of Punjab. As expected, Delhi overwhelmed Himachal Pradesh inside three days.

2, 3, 4 and 5 December, 1991 *at Air Force Sports Complex, Palam, Delhi*

Services 283 (K.M. Roshan 104 not out, Chinmoy Sharma 50, M. Qaiser 4 for 56) and 363 (D. Ahuja 86, K.D. Pandey 76, G.S. Thapa 50, Abdul Qayyum 5 for 103)
Jammu & Kashmir 369 (A. Gupta 183 not out, S.C. Sadangi 4 for 62) and 229 (A. Gupta 55, S. Subramaniam 4 for 74)

Services won by 48 runs

Services 16 pts., Jammu & Kashmir 9 pts.

7, 8, 9 and 10 December, 1991 *at Ferozeshah Kotla Ground, Delhi*

Jammu & Kashmir 161 (R. Bali 56, V. Razdan 5 for 67) and 211 (Maninder Singh 6 for 93)
Delhi 569 for 6 dec. (M. Nayyar 172, A.K. Sharma 169, Sanjay Sharma 80)

Delhi won by an innings and 197 runs

Delhi 25 pts., Jammu & Kashmir 3 pts.

at Nahar Singh Stadium, Faridabad

Himachal Pradesh 86 (C.M. Sharma 4 for 25) and 256 (R. Nayyar 91, C.M. Sharma 4 for 101)
Haryana 444 (A. Jadeja 199, V.S. Yadav 82)

Haryana won by an innings and 102 runs

Haryana 24 pts., Himachal Pradesh 4 pts.

Ashwini Gupta hit the highest individual score ever recorded for Jammu & Kashmir but still finished on the losing side. Himachal Pradesh suffered their fifth successive defeat, with Ajay Jadeja continuing his magnificent form for Haryana.

12, 13, 14 and 15 December, 1991 *at Ferozeshah Kotla Ground, Delhi*

Haryana 336 (R. Puri 136, A. Kaypee 90, A. Wassan 6 for 92) and 303 for 4 (A. Kaypee 118 not out, R. Puri 77 not out)
Delhi 322 (K.P. Bhaskar 85, C.M. Sharma 5 for 118)

Match drawn

Haryana 11 pts., Delhi 10 pts.

With both Delhi and Haryana having already qualified for the quarter-finals, the final match in North Zone was a dour struggle for the top spot. Haryana were 65 for 4, but Kaypee and Puri added 191. The same pair added 181 in the second innings, but the scoring rate barely reached three runs an over, and the match was drawn.

NORTH ZONE FINAL TABLE

	P	W	L	D	Pts
Delhi	5	4	–	1	102
Haryana	5	3	–	2	97
Punjab	5	3	1	1	84
Jammu & Kashmir	5	1	4	–	44
Services	5	2	3	–	37
Himachal Pradesh	5	–	5	–	25

PRE-QUARTER-FINALS

13, 14, 15, 16 and 17 February, 1992 *at Nehru Stadium, Pune*

Maharashtra 757 for 7 dec. (S.S. Shave 229, M.D. Gunjal 162, S.V. Jedhe 156, S.J. Jadhav 77 not out, S.V. Ranjane 64 not out)
Bihar 270 (H. Gidwani 99, P. Khanna 71) and 424 for 7 (S.S. Karim 176, S. Kumar 90, S. Chatterjee 79)

Match drawn

Maharashtra qualified for quarter-finals on first-innings lead

15, 16, 17, 18 and 19 February, 1992 *at Gymkhana, Secunderabad*

Hyderabad 409 (Abdul Azeem 130, M.V. Ramanamurthy 72, C. Jai Kumar 66, S.S. Lahore 5 for 116) and 249 (C. Jai Kumar 59, S.M. Patil 5 for 86)
Madhya Pradesh 535 (A.R. Khurasia 132, A.V. Vijayvirgiya 85, P.K. Dwivedi 67, K.K. Patel 54, Arshad Ayub 5 for 203) and 127 for 3 (S.M. Patil 65)

Madhya Pradesh won by 7 wickets

A stand of 228 for the second wicket between Shave and Jedhe, and of 282 for the fourth between Jedhe and Gunjal put Maharashtra in an impregnable position against Bihar who, forced to follow on, died courageously.

Madhya Pradesh skipper Sandeep Patil gave an inspiring lead to his side in the victory over Hyderabad. He took on the role of main strike bowler in Hyderabad's second innings, and promoted himself to opener to lash a whirlwind 65 as his side chased 124 to win. The target was reached in 23.4 overs.

QUARTER-FINALS

28, 29 February, **1, 2** and **3** March, 1992 *at Wankhede Stadium, Bombay*

Madhya Pradesh 230 (R.K. Chauhan 55 not out) and 373 (A.R. Khurasia 104, A.V. Vijayvirgiya 52, R.K. Chauhan 51, A. Kuruvilla 4 for 73, Iqbal Khan 4 for 107)
Bombay 721 for 8 dec. (D.B. Vengsarkar 284, J.V. Paranjpe 118, J.B. Jadhav 110, Iqbal Khan 52, S.S. Lahore 4 for 169)

Bombay won by an innings and 118 runs

at Ferozeshah Kotla Ground, Delhi

Bengal 237 (Saurav Ganguly 74 not out, V. Razdan 4 for 53) and 228 (Saurav Ganguly 51, Maninder Singh 7 for 57)
Delhi 633 (Bantoo Singh 164, A.S. Wassan 110, V. Razdan 101, R. Vinayak 67, A.K. Sharma 64, U. Chatterjee 5 for 169)

Delhi won by an innings and 168 runs

at Nehru Stadium, Pune

Haryana 673 for 9 dec. (A. Kaypee 131, V. Yadav 129, A. Bannerjee 83, R. Puri 63, S.J. Jadhav 6 for 179) and 95 for 0
Maharashtra 557 (S.S. Bhave 231 not out, A.P. Deshpande 86, S.S. Sugwekar 59, M.D. Gunjal 59, Y. Bhandari 4 for 194)

Match drawn

Haryana qualified for semi-finals on first-innings lead

at Green Park, Kanpur

Tamil Nadu 349 (M. Senthilnathan 109, D. Vasu 84) and 628 (M. Gautam 190, V.B. Chandrasekhar 131, W.V. Raman 110, M. Senthilnathan 59, G. Pandey 7 for 167)
Uttar Pradesh 203 (G. Pandey 55 not out, A. Kapoor 4 for 41) and 77 for 0

Match drawn

Tamil Nadu qualified for semi-finals on first-innings lead

The quarter-finals of the Ranji Trophy were decided much as had been predicted. In Bombay, Vengsarkar won the toss and asked Madhya Pradesh to bat first on a wicket which helped his seam bowlers. By the end of the first day, Bombay were batting, and on the second, they took total control. Vengsarkar went on to reach the fourth – and highest – double century of his career.

Delhi, too, overwhelmed their opponents. Razdan hit his second century of the season, and Wassan the first of his career in the run deluge which was led by Bantoo Singh, who, in 1991, helped Ealing to win the Middlesex League. Maninder Singh again showed a complete return of confidence and form with his left-arm spin.

The holders, Haryana, had a much closer contest, but just edged out Maharashtra on the first innings.

Vivek Razdan – two centuries and 30 wickets for Delhi. (Ben Radford/Allsport)

Surendra Bhave battled throughout Maharashtra's innings to carry his bat, but the last four wickets fell for 30 runs.

Having gained a first-innings lead against Uttar Pradesh, Tamil Nadu then played a holding game.

SEMI-FINALS

13, 14, 15 and **16** March, 1992 *at Wankhede Stadium, Bombay*

Delhi 516 (K.P. Bhaskar 221, Kirti Azad 66, Maninder Singh 56, A. Kuruvilla 4 for 124) and 574 (A.K. Sharma 259 not out, Maninder Singh 78, Kirti Azad 60)
Bombay 254 (S.S. Dighe 61, Maninder Singh 5 for 63) and 182 for 3 (S.S. Dighe 100 not out)

Match drawn

Delhi entered final on first-innings lead

at Nahar Singh Stadium, Faridabad

Tamil Nadu 507 (W.V. Raman 226, D. Vasu 58) and 340 (W.V. Raman 120, M. Senthilnathan 68, Y. Bhandari 4 for 111)
Haryana 375 (A. Kaypee 82, V.S. Yadav 59 not out, C.M. Sharma 52, S. Subramaniam 4 for 71) and 233 for 7 (A. Kaypee 71)

Match drawn

Tamil Nadu entered final on first-innings lead

Pillai Bhaskar, so close to the national side for some seasons, was one run short of his career best for Delhi, but, with the all-round cricket of Maninder Singh, and with Ajay Sharma's career-best innings in Delhi's second knock, the North Zone champions ousted the West Zone champions from the Ranji Trophy.

A double century and a second-innings century from Woorkeri Raman, Tamil Nadu's captain, were sufficient to deny Haryana a place in the final.

RANJI TROPHY FINAL
DELHI v. TAMIL NADU, at Delhi

Winning the toss and batting first on a placid pitch, Delhi batted dourly on the opening day to reach 234 for 3 at under three runs an over. In contrast, they sparkled on the second day as Ajay Sharma, 30 not out overnight, reached 175 with 25 fours and two sixes off 320 balls. The real impetus to the innings was given by pace bowler Vivek Razdan whose batting had been one of the revelations of the season. He hit two sixes and 14 fours in his 93 which came off 148 balls.

Delhi's innings closed early on the third morning, and by the end of the day, Tamil Nadu had lost four wickets, including that of Raman, for 225. What was needed was a big innings from someone, but it never transpired. Wasu and Kapoor promised more than they achieved, and Maninder Singh ended a glorious season by gnawing away at the tail.

With a first-innings lead of 83, Delhi were unlikely to loosen their grip on the trophy. So it proved, as Bantoo Singh hit his second century in the Trophy's knock-out stage.

Bowler of the year, Maninder Singh took 72 wickets in first-class cricket and brought himself back into contention for regaining his Test place. (Alan Cozzi)

RANJI TROPHY FINAL – DELHI v. TAMIL NADU
27, 28, 29, 30 and 31 March, 1992 at Ferozeshah Kotla Ground, Delhi

DELHI

	FIRST INNINGS		SECOND INNINGS	
M. Nayyar	lbw, **b** Gautam	26	**b** Venkataramana	85
R. Lamba	c Raman, **b** Subramaniam	80	c Raman, **b** Wasu	6
M. Prabhakar	c Gautam, **b** Kapoor	56		
A.K. Sharma	c Sanjay, **b** Wasu	175	**b** Venkataramana	6
K.P. Bhaskar	c Sanjay, **b** Wasu	14	not out	31
*R. Vinayak	c Robin Singh, **b** Wasu	6	not out	5
Kirti Azad (capt)	c Raman, **b** Wasu	5		
Bantoo Singh	c Sanjay, **b** Gautam	10	(3) lbw, **b** Subramaniam	123
V. Razdan	c and **b** Robin Singh	93		
Maninder Singh	not out	8		
A.S. Wassan	**b** Robin Singh	4		
Extras	b 6, lb 15, w 2, nb 32	55	b 6, lb 1, w 2, nb 8	17
		532	(for 4 wickets)	273

	O	M	R	W	O	M	R	W
Wasu	42	10	106	4	15	2	36	1
Robin Singh	30.2	5	97	2	13	–	42	–
Subramaniam	44	10	124	1	24	8	58	1
Gautam	13	9	38	2				
Kapoor	25	5	85	1	8	1	29	–
Venkataramana	18	3	61	–	19	1	74	2
Srikkanth					5	–	27	–

FALL OF WICKETS
1–67, **2**–184, **3**–188, **4**–238, **5**–281, **6**–290, **7**–305, **8**–453, **9**–455
1–30, **2**–190, **3**–204, **4**–262

TAMIL NADU

	FIRST INNINGS	
V.B. Chandrasekhar	c Bantoo Singh, **b** Wassan	59
K. Srikkanth	**b** Maninder Singh	13
W.V. Raman (capt)	lbw, **b** Prabhakar	82
N. Gautam	c A.K. Sharma, **b** Prabhakar	22
M. Senthilnathan	c Bhaskar, **b** Maninder Singh	54
Robin Singh	c A.K. Sharma, **b** Razdan	28
D. Wasu	**b** Maninder Singh	63
A. Kapoor	not out	61
M. Venkataramana	lbw, **b** Maninder Singh	12
S. Subramaniam	c Vinayak, **b** Prabhakar	13
*M. Sanjay	c sub, **b** Maninder Singh	9
Extras	b 9, lb 3, nb 16	28
	penalty runs	5
		449

	O	M	R	W
Prabhakar	42	14	108	3
Wassan	26	4	91	1
Razdan	14	6	54	1
Maninder Singh	51.1	12	130	5
Kirti Azad	12	4	31	–
A.K. Sharma	1	–	2	–
Nayyar	8	2	16	–

FALL OF WICKETS
1–57, **2**–156, **3**–189, **4**–201, **5**–265, **6**–318, **7**–379, **8**–397, **9**–422

Umpires: D. Krishna & W.K. Ramaswamy

Match drawn – Delhi won Ranji Trophy by virtue of their first-innings lead

FIRST-CLASS AVERAGES

BATTING

	M	Inns	NO	Runs	HS	Av	100s	50s
V.G. Kambli	7	12	1	1218	262	110.72	5	3
A.K. Sharma	9	12	1	1037	259*	94.27	4	3
A. Jadeja	8	12	1	1036	256	94.18	4	2
S.S. Bhave	6	10	3	651	231*	93.00	3	–
A. Gautam	5	6	2	365	144*	91.25	1	3
W.V. Raman	9	13	–	1137	226	87.46	6	1
Zaheer Alam	3	5	–	432	257	86.40	1	2
Yusuf Ali Khan	4	7	3	324	125	81.00	2	–
V. Yadav	10	12	3	714	201	79.33	2	3
G.K. Pandey	6	8	3	389	178	77.80	1	2
S.S. Sugwekar	8	11	1	753	180	75.30	2	4
S.M. Patil	6	11	2	675	157	75.00	2	4
Abdul Azeem	6	9	–	650	208	72.22	3	–
A. Kaypee	10	15	2	938	200	72.15	3	5
Sanjeev Sharma	5	7	2	360	111*	72.00	1	3
C.R. Venkatraman	5	7	2	354	140*	70.80	1	2
Adil Hussain	4	5	–	339	128	67.80	2	1
B. Dutta	4	7	–	474	139	67.71	2	2
S.S. Karim	6	9	1	529	176	66.12	2	2
Zakir Hussain	8	11	–	716	161	65.09	3	3
A.R. Khurasia	6	11	2	584	132	64.08	2	3
P.S. Rawat	2	4	1	189	79	63.00	–	2
K.P. Bhaskar	10	13	1	749	221	62.41	3	2
Yashpal Sharma	4	5	–	309	144	61.80	2	1
B.H. Mistry	4	7	2	307	138*	61.40	1	2
Gurusharan Singh	5	7	–	427	191	61.00	1	2
H. Gidwani	5	7	–	426	160	60.85	1	2
A.O. Malhotra	5	7	1	364	151	60.66	2	1
A. Gupta	5	9	1	483	183*	60.37	2	1
S.J. Jadhav	6	8	2	362	77*	60.33	–	2
A. Pathak	3	6	–	357	126	59.50	2	–
Sanjay Sharma	7	8	2	351	80	58.50	–	4
M.V. Sridhar	7	10	1	523	140	58.11	2	3
P.K. Dwivedi	6	9	1	457	114	57.12	2	2
S.V. Jedhe	8	13	2	622	156	56.54	3	2
S.K. Talpade	5	6	1	282	79	56.40	–	3
K.S. Chavan	6	11	–	619	129	56.27	3	2
U.R. Radhakrishnan	2	4	–	223	182	55.75	1	–
L.S. Rajput	5	9	–	498	239	55.33	1	3
S.S. Dighe	6	10	3	384	100*	54.85	1	3
P.T. Subramaniam	5	10	4	327	89	54.50	–	2
S.R. Kulkarni	4	77	1	326	200*	54.33	1	–
A.R. Kumble	7	10	2	431	154*	53.87	1	2
S. Chatterjee	5	7	1	320	142	53.33	1	1
B. Ramprakash	5	10	1	476	152	52.88	1	3
Bantoo Singh	7	9	1	423	164	52.87	2	1
P.G. Sunder	5	10	3	368	81	52.57	–	3
V.B. Chandrasekhar	8	12	1	572	144	52.00	2	1
A.D. Gaekwad	4	7	2	259	143	51.80	1	–
A. Deshpande	6	10	1	465	217	51.66	1	2
R. Bora	4	7	–	354	235	50.57	1	–
S.S. Tanna	4	8	2	303	253*	50.50	1	–
R. Chanda	2	3	1	101	48	50.50	–	–
R.A. Swarup	5	6	1	250	131	50.00	1	–
Abhay Sharma	5	7	–	348	143	49.71	1	2
M.H. Parmar	6	11	1	496	152	49.60	2	1
M. Senthilnathan	8	11	–	545	109	49.54	1	4
Chinmoy Sharma	5	10	1	443	133	49.22	1	4
S. Chopra	3	5	–	244	108	48.80	1	1
Iqbal Khan	6	10	1	439	105	48.77	1	3
S. Chaturvedi	5	8	2	292	97	48.66	–	2
J.B. Jadhav	6	10	–	486	139	48.60	2	1
Saurav Ganguly	2	4	1	145	74*	48.33	–	2
S.G. Gujar	5	10	–	483	221	48.30	1	2
R.S. Dravid	7	10	1	434	128	48.22	2	1
C. Saldanha	5	8	1	335	88	47.85	–	3
Robin Singh	10	14	2	573	121*	47.75	3	–
M. Nayyar	9	12	–	573	172	47.75	1	2
N.R. Yadav	6	8	3	235	75*	47.00	–	2
Rajesh Puri	10	15	2	611	136	47.00	1	4
R.R. Kulkarni	7	9	4	232	69	46.40	–	1
P. Khanna	5	7	–	324	107	46.28	1	2
Maninder Singh	11	11	5	274	78	45.66	–	2
N. Gautam	8	12	–	543	190	45.25	2	1
V.S. Yadav	5	7	2	224	97	44.80	–	2
P.B. Hingnikar	4	8	–	354	115	44.25	1	2
N. Bakriwala	2	4	1	132	68	44.00	–	1
V. Razdan	10	11	1	438	101	43.80	2	2
A. Roy	3	4	–	175	125	43.75	1	–
K.K. Patel	6	12	1	474	202	43.09	1	2
M.D. Gunjal	6	8	–	344	162	43.00	1	2
Arshad Ayub	8	11	2	386	81	42.88	–	2
M.S. Sahni	5	7	2	211	90	42.20	–	1
M. Bhatt	3	5	–	211	86	42.20	–	3
Gopal Sharma	5	5	2	126	100*	42.00	1	–
R.V. Sapru	6	8	–	336	139	42.00	1	2
C.C. Mankad	4	7	3	167	65*	41.75	–	2
A. Prabhakar	4	4	1	124	57*	41.33	–	1
V. Joshi	4	7	1	241	89	40.16	–	2
N.Y. Laliwala	4	6	1	200	60	40.00	–	1
R.K. Chauhan	6	8	2	239	55*	39.83	–	2
T.B. Arothe	4	8	–	318	109	39.75	1	1
J. Arun Lal	7	13	1	474	130	39.50	1	2
Ehtesham Ali Khan	6	8	–	313	106	39.12	1	1
V.I. Ghani	4	7	–	272	140	38.85	1	1
R.M.H. Binny	5	10	1	346	102	38.44	1	2
Bhupinder Singh jnr	4	6	1	191	103	38.20	1	1
A.C. Bedade	4	8	–	303	102	37.87	1	1
A.D. Sinha	4	7	–	263	61	37.57	–	3
Sneha Ganguly	7	11	2	337	136	37.44	1	1
Sudhakar Reddy	4	7	3	149	91*	37.25	–	1
S.G. Gudge	5	6	2	149	61	37.25	–	1
Pratap Singh	5	6	2	148	98	37.00	–	1
M.S. Narula	5	10	3	255	77*	36.42	–	2
V.S. Vats	5	7	–	254	92	36.28	–	2
J.V. Paranjpe	5	9	–	325	118	36.11	2	–
M.F. Rehman	5	10	1	323	136*	35.88	1	–
B.M. Jadeja	4	7	–	251	129	35.85	1	1
R. Nayyar	5	10	–	358	109	35.80	1	3
S.V. Bahutule	6	8	2	213	111*	35.50	1	–
S.S. Khandkar	6	9	–	319	92	35.44	–	2
D.M. Pandove	5	7	–	247	170	35.28	1	1
B.S. Pujara	4	8	1	246	73	35.14	–	3
A.V. Vijayvirgiya	6	12	1	383	85	34.81	–	3
R. Bittoo	5	10	1	312	131*	34.66	1	1
N.R. Goel	8	12	2	346	54	34.60	–	2
V.M. Jaisimha	8	11	–	377	115	34.27	1	1
Krishna Mohan	5	7	–	236	75	33.71	–	2
D. Vasu	10	15	1	469	84	33.50	–	4
S. Subramaniam	8	8	3	167	53	33.40	–	1
R.B. Parikh	4	8	–	264	76	33.00	–	2
D. Lenka	4	6	1	165	55	33.00	–	1
Y.T. Ghare	2	4	–	132	71	33.00	–	2
D. Gautam	4	7	2	162	55	32.40	–	1
S.M.H. Kirmani	8	12	–	386	150	32.16	1	1
K.M. Roshan	5	10	1	282	104*	31.33	1	2
A.S. Wassan	10	10	3	219	110	31.28	1	–
A. Kripal Singh	7	11	1	312	117	31.20	1	2
K.D. Pandey	2	4	–	124	76	31.00	–	1
C.M. Sharma	10	13	2	340	57	30.90	–	3
S. Chowdhary	3	5	1	123	73	30.75	–	1
M. Das	5	7	1	184	61	30.66	–	2
V. Rathore	5	7	–	212	54	30.28	–	2
M.V. Ramanamurthy	6	8	2	181	72	30.16	–	1
K.A. Jeshwant	5	7	–	211	151	30.14	1	–
A.V. Sarwate	2	4	–	120	63	30.00	–	1
D.K. Nilose	6	10	2	240	50	30.00	–	1
V. Bhaskar	5	8	–	237	130	29.62	1	1
S.V. Ranjane	6	7	2	147	64*	29.40	–	1
O.V. Kumar	5	10	–	294	75	29.40	–	2
S.P. Mukherjee	5	5	1	117	51*	29.25	–	1
S.S. Lahore	7	9	2	204	53	29.14	–	1
R.B. Biswal	5	8	–	233	107	29.12	1	–
Kirti Azad	8	9	–	259	67	28.77	–	3

FIRST-CLASS AVERAGES

BATTING (continued)

	M	Inns	NO	Runs	HS	Av	100s	50s
S.J. Kalyani	6	11	1	287	82	28.70	–	3
P.R. Mohapatra	3	6	1	139	60	27.80	–	1
A. Beg	4	6	1	138	70	27.60	–	1
I. Bakhie	2	4	–	109	80	27.25	–	1
D. Ahuja	2	4	–	109	86	27.25	–	1
P.V. Shashikant	4	6	2	108	43	27.00	–	–
A.N. Pandya	4	7	–	189	71	27.00	–	1
A.S. Shetty	5	10	3	188	42	26.85	–	–
B.M. Radia	6	9	1	214	71	26.75	–	1
A.R. Kapoor	8	10	1	235	61*	26.11	–	1
M.S. Arora	4	6	1	129	72*	25.80	–	1
M.T. Kaore	2	4	–	103	40	25.75	–	–
K.V.P. Rao	5	6	2	102	72	25.50	–	1
P.V. Ranganathan	5	10	1	229	60	25.44	–	1
P. Kumar	4	8	3	125	32*	25.00	–	–
Parminder Singh	4	7	–	172	65	24.57	–	1
R. Vinayak	7	9	1	188	76	23.50	–	2
V. Vijayasarathy	5	9	–	211	98	23.44	–	1
Dhanraj Singh	4	7	1	138	37*	23.00	–	–
D. Das	4	7	–	159	49	22.71	–	–
H. Joshi	4	7	1	133	42	22.16	–	–
A.S. Banerjee	6	8	–	175	83	21.87	–	1
S. Das	4	5	–	108	52	21.60	–	1
Kamaljit SIngh	5	9	–	194	53	21.55	–	1
A.R. Bali	5	9	–	194	56	21.55	–	1
M. Subramaniya	5	10	2	171	49*	21.37	–	–
V. Arjun Raja	5	7	–	149	56	21.28	–	2
C.P. Singh	4	5	–	106	59	21.20	–	1
K.B. Kala	4	5	–	106	48	21.20	–	–
Brijender Sharma	4	8	1	148	73	21.14	–	1
Sanjay Sharma	5	9	1	169	41*	21.12	–	–
G. Khoda	4	8	–	168	116	21.00	1	–
N.R. Mongia	6	10	1	188	55	20.88	–	2
S. Bhatnagar	5	9	–	187	62	20.77	–	1
K.V.S.D. Kamaraju	5	10	1	181	37	20.11	–	–
K.G. Sekhar	4	5	–	100	39	20.00	–	–
M. Sanjay	6	9	2	130	43	18.57	–	–
J.K. Deb Burman	4	8	–	145	48	18.12	–	–
K.N.A. Panmanabhan	5	7	–	126	59	18.00	–	1
P.S. Vaidya	6	11	2	158	35	17.55	–	–
Rajinder Singh	4	7	–	119	42	17.00	–	–
S.S. Hattangadi	4	7	–	119	53	17.00	–	1
S.V. Mehra	5	6	–	101	45	16.83	–	–
Deepak Sharma	6	9	–	151	50	16.77	–	1
R. Vats	4	8	1	116	33	16.57	–	–
G.S. Thapa	4	8	–	131	50	16.37	–	1
A. Gaekwad	4	8	–	130	80	16.25	–	1
M.V. Rao	5	10	–	158	31	15.80	–	–
R. Vivekananda	5	9	–	141	40	15.66	–	–
H.B.P. Angle	5	10	–	154	41	15.40	–	–
T.P. Ajit Kumar	5	10	–	150	30	15.00	–	–
R. Jaswant	5	10	1	135	29	15.00	–	–
Feroze Rashid	5	8	–	119	59	14.87	–	1
S.S. Patil	7	10	1	130	32*	14.44	–	–
K. Narayanan	5	10	–	129	51	12.90	–	–
Arup Deb Burman	4	8	–	101	50	12.62	–	1
A. Qayyum	5	9	–	103	45	11.44	–	–

(Qualification – 100 runs, average 10.00)

Also batted: D.B. Vengsarkar 284 & 6; M. Prabhakar 134 & 56; Kapil Dev 135; P.K. Amre 120 & 40; C.L. Jaikumar 66 & 59; S. Kumar 90 & 17

BOWLING

	Overs	Mds	Runs	Wkts	Av	Best	10/m	5/inn
M. Inder Singh	94.1	17	248	23	10.78	7-33	1	2
G. Dutta	92.4	17	278	20	13.90	9-52	1	3
R. Anath	111	30	260	18	14.44	3-33	–	–
Maninder Singh	588.4	204	1231	72	17.09	8-43	2	8
Bhupinder Singh snr	118	16	346	20	17.30	7-39	–	1
K.V.P. Rao	164	34	449	24	18.70	5-25	–	2
Jaideep Singh	117.5	35	302	16	18.87	5-62	–	1
A.R. Kumble	294.4	84	662	33	20.06	6-41	–	1
D. Vasu	347.3	91	861	41	21.00	5-39	1	3
M.V. Ramanamurthy	131	26	360	17	21.17	5-60	–	1
S. Mukherjee	197.3	63	467	22	21.22	6-85	–	1
C.M. Sharma	356.4	67	1088	50	21.76	6-65	–	4
Deepak Sharma	201.5	43	503	23	21.86	4-12	–	–
S. Subramaniam	350.2	109	848	38	22.31	7-45	–	2
A. Kuruvilla	350.4	66	1158	51	22.70	6-98	–	2
A.R. Bhat	189.1	48	445	19	23.42	5-67	–	1
Harpreet Singh	66.2	11	237	10	23.70	4-20	–	–
V. Razdan	239.5	55	731	30	24.36	5-67	–	1
S.J. Jadhav	289.3	81	641	26	24.65	6-179	–	1
S. Sen Sharma	209.3	45	577	23	25.08	5-63	–	2
M.S. Narula	126.1	24	433	17	25.47	5-48	–	2
Arshad Ayub	471.1	112	1317	49	26.87	6-16	1	6
Abinash Kumar	312.3	71	834	31	26.90	6-198	–	3
R.R. Kulkarni	176.3	30	597	22	27.13	4-27	–	–
A.S. Wassan	298.5	55	969	35	27.68	6-72	–	2
A. Qayyum	180.1	24	612	22	27.81	6-122	1	3
Pratap Singh	182.5	35	529	19	27.84	5-51	–	1
S. Kumar	255.4	84	566	20	28.30	6-84	1	1
S.V. Mehra	103.4	14	372	13	28.61	3-62	–	–
Sanjeev Sharma	211.1	34	667	23	29.00	5-70	–	1
U. Chatterjee	188.5	55	466	16	29.12	5-169	–	1
B. Ramprakash	233	43	614	21	29.23	6-30	1	2
A. Kapoor	286	69	833	28	29.75	4-41	–	–
Brijender Sharma	83.2	7	298	10	29.80	3-28	–	–
V. Prasad	150	22	511	17	30.05	6-40	–	1
S.V. Ranjane	171	35	575	19	30.26	4-54	–	–
Sanjay Sharma	178.1	40	428	14	30.57	3-30	–	–
S. Patel	85.5	12	339	11	30.81	6-106	–	1
V. Venkatram	130.1	32	309	10	30.90	5-32	–	1
S.C. Sadangi	114.5	16	371	12	30.91	4-62	–	–
G.K. Pandey	135.5	23	374	12	31.16	7-167	–	1
A.W. Zaidi	220	41	692	22	31.45	4-47	–	–
V. Vijayasarathy	189.2	21	637	20	31.85	5-68	–	2
P. Jain	347.3	99	836	26	32.15	5-75	–	1
K.N.A. Padmanabhan	258.5	49	839	26	32.26	5-112	–	1
R.B. Biswal	218.3	45	558	17	32.82	5-91	–	1
A.S. Shetty	279.2	58	729	22	33.13	6-55	–	3
A. Gupta	175.1	21	603	18	33.50	5-134	–	1
N.R. Yadav	96.1	10	376	11	34.18	3-18	–	–
R.T. Yeravedekar	213.1	46	685	20	34.25	3-55	–	–
Chinmoy Sharma	110.3	15	352	10	35.20	4-95	–	–
B.M. Radia	210.5	26	706	20	35.30	5-104	–	2
G.V.V. Gopalaraju	151	11	575	16	35.93	6-122	–	1
P.V. Gandhe	144.4	24	468	13	36.00	5-53	–	1
S.S. Lahore	348.4	98	869	24	36.20	5-116	–	1
M. Venkataramana	146	24	474	13	36.45	4-69	–	–
S.S. Patil	303.1	81	895	24	37.29	5-36	–	1
Gopal Sharma	283.2	72	715	19	37.63	5-86	–	1
K.D. Amin	136	22	456	12	38.00	3-88	–	–
R.K. Chouhan	282.2	54	823	21	39.19	6-210	–	1
P.S. Vaidya	208	20	802	20	40.10	5-93	–	2
Y.S. Bhandari	314.3	48	935	23	40.65	4-55	–	–
B.H. Mistry	122.3	25	413	10-	41.30	5-77	–	1
A. Sen	180	15	629	15	41.93	4-98	–	–
M. Subramaniya	193	23	645	15	43.00	4-48	–	–
H.B.P. Angle	175.5	28	588	13	45.23	3-61	–	–
D.K. Nilose	128.5	8	557	12	46.41	5-68	1	2
R. Jaswant	161	18	523	11	47.54	3-43	–	–
S.V. Bahutule	200.4	48	678	14	48.42	3-5	–	–
Robin Singh	154.5	16	503	10	50.30	2-82	–	–
D.T. Patel	152.4	27	515	10	51.50	3-87	–	–

(Qualification – 10 wickets)

LEADING FIELDERS

43 – V. Yadav (ct 37/st 6); 25 – N.R. Mongia (ct 24/st 1); 21 – S.S. Karim (ct 16/st 5); 18 – K.K. Patel (ct 14/st 4); 17 – M. Das (ct 12/st 5); 15 – K.P. Bhaskar, S.S. Dighe (ct 13/st 2) and S.M.H. Kirmani (ct 11/st 4); 14 – R. Vinayak (ct 11/st 3); 13 – N.H. Phadnis and R.S. Dravid; 12 – R.A. Aslam (ct 8/st 4) and W.V. Raman; 11 – Abhay Sharma (ct 10/st 1), Arun Sharma, D. Vasu, A. Kripal Singh, S.V. Jedhe and R. Vivekananda (ct 9/st 2); 10 – Maninder Singh, U.S. Kumar, R.V. Saprula and V. Rathore

SECTION

F

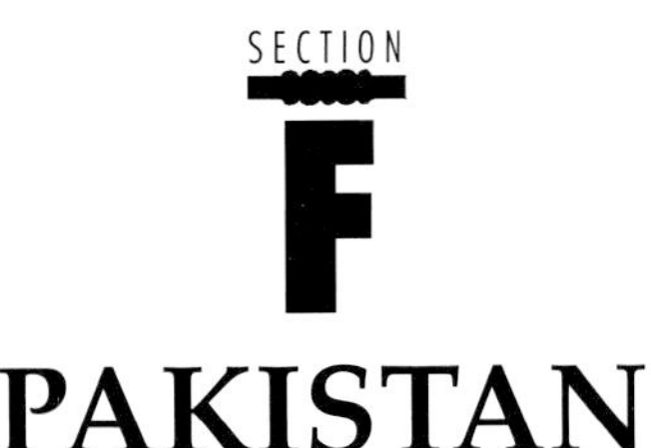

PAKISTAN

One-Day Series v. West Indies
Test and One-Day Series
v. Sri Lanka
Quaid-e-Azam Trophy
BCCP Patron's Trophy
First-Class Averages

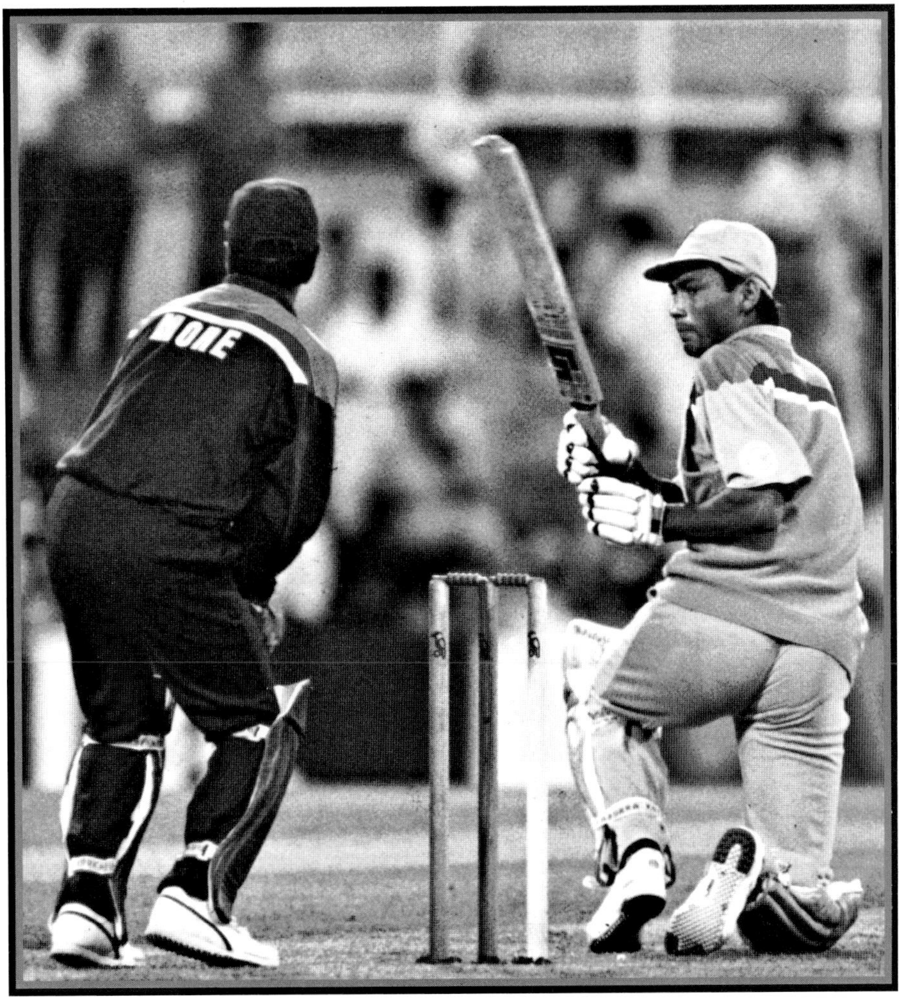

Wasim Haider – good all-round cricket for Pakistan International Airlines earned him international recognition. (David Munden)

ONE-DAY INTERNATIONAL SERIES
PAKISTAN v. WEST INDIES

The international season in Pakistan began with a brief visit from West Indies. West Indies introduced two new players to international cricket in opener Philo Wallace and pace bowler Anderson Cummins. Following the failures in Sharjah, Phil Simmons, Clayton Lambert, Jeff Dujon, Courtney Walsh and Winston Benjamin were axed. Desmond Haynes returned to the side, but Richie Richardson retained the captaincy. Malcolm Marshall was also back in the side.

Imran Khan, ever a rule to himself in Pakistan cricket, arranged a training session on the eve of the series even though the Quaid-e-Azam Trophy, Pakistan's premier domestic competition, was in progress. He took this move without consulting the Pakistan Board, and he received considerable criticism, particularly as he himself has not seen fit to play domestic cricket in his own country for more than a decade.

Games were scheduled to be 40 overs per innings, but Pakistan's failure to bowl the stipulated number of overs before lunch reduced the first encounter to 34 overs. Batting first on winning the toss, West Indies were given a good start by Haynes and Wallace who put on 55. Lara made 54 off 59 balls, and the visitors reached 170. Pakistan made an abject reply. Aamir Sohail was run out

Moin Khan established himself as Pakistan's first-choice wicket-keeper. (Ben Radford/Allsport)

FIRST ONE-DAY INTERNATIONAL – PAKISTAN v. WEST INDIES
20 November, 1991 at National Stadium, Karachi

WEST INDIES

D.L. Haynes	lbw, b Mushtaq Ahmed	45
P.A. Wallace	b Mushtaq Ahmed	22
R.B. Richardson (capt)	b Aqib Javed	2
B.C. Lara	c Javed Miandad, b Wasim Akram	54
C.L. Hooper	c Mushtaq Ahmed, b Wasim Akram	17
K.L.T. Arthurton	b Wasim Akram	4
*D. Williams	not out	5
I.R. Bishop	not out	3
C.E.L. Ambrose		
B.P. Patterson		
A.C. Cummins		
Extras	lb 10, w 5, nb 3	18
	(for 6 wickets)	170

(34 overs)

	O	M	R	W
Imran Khan	8	1	30	–
Wasim Akram	6	–	27	3
Aqib Javed	7	–	38	1
Mushtaq Ahmed	8	–	43	2
Waqar Younis	5	–	22	–

FALL OF WICKETS
1–55, 2–58, 3–126, 4–152, 5–156, 6–167

PAKISTAN

Aamir Sohail	run out	1
Ramiz Raja	c Williams, b Patterson	11
Zahid Fazal	c Lara, b Patterson	17
Salim Malik	run out	16
Javed Miandad	c Richardson, b Ambrose	31
Imran Khan (capt)	c Arthurton, b Hooper	15
Wasim Akram	st Williams, b Hooper	0
* Moin Khan	c Richardson, b Ambrose	18
Mushtaq Ahmed	c Bishop, b Hooper	6
Waqar Younis	not out	11
Aqib Javed	b Hooper	2
Extras	lb 5, w 8, nb 5	18
		146

(33.5 overs)

	O	M	R	W
Bishop	6	2	23	–
Ambrose	7	–	28	2
Patterson	8	–	29	2
Cummins	5	–	27	–
Hooper	7.5	–	34	4

FALL OF WICKETS
1–8, 2–25, 3–45, 4–57, 5–82, 6–82, 7–119, 8–129, 9–134

Umpires: Khizer Hayat & Riazuddin — Man of the Match – B.C. Lara — *West Indies won by 24 runs*

Sixteen wickets in four innings in the Test series against Sri Lanka for Waqar Younis. Then he was ruled out of the World Cup through back injury. (David Munden)

in the second over, and Salim Malik was also run out when he responded to a suicidal call by Javed. Half the side were out for 82 and only seven overs remained. Javed and Moin Khan added 37, but Javed was caught at mid-on, and the run rate became well out of Pakistan's reach.

Asked to bat first in the second match, West Indies were again given a good start by Haynes and Wallace. Pakistan failed to meet the required run rate, Salim Malik was run out once more, falling the ball after debutant Inzamam-ul-Haq had been bowled by Marshall. Imran was solid, but when Wasim Akram was out in the 34th over Pakistan needed 51 runs in 4.4 overs to win the match. Imran was out in the penultimate over, and Waqar Younis and Mushtaq Ahmed faced the last over needing ten for victory. They managed eight from the first five balls. Mushtaq hit the final ball into the covers and was run out by Richardson when he attempted the second run that would have won the game. Under the rules of the series the match was tied.

The deciding game of the series was marred by crowd disturbances. A fourth-wicket stand of 93 between Hooper and Lara gave substance to West Indies' innings, but Ramiz Raja and Inzamam-ul-Haq, Pakistan's positive find of the series, responded with an opening partnership of 65. Zahid Fazal also batted with confidence, but Ambrose, Cummins and Marshall exposed the weaknesses of Pakistan's middle order, and West Indies won with ease.

SECOND ONE-DAY INTERNATIONAL – PAKISTAN v. WEST INDIES
22 November, 1991 at Qaddafi Stadium, Lahore

WEST INDIES

Batsman	Dismissal	Runs
D.L. Haynes	b Aqib Javed	69
P.A. Wallace	lbw, b Imran Khan	32
R.B. Richardson (capt)	c Aamir Sohail, b Aqib Javed	14
B.C. Lara	b Wasim Akram	18
C.L. Hooper	c Inzamam-ul-Haq, b Wasim Akram	22
K.L.T. Arthurton	not out	5
M.D. Marshall	not out	2
*D. Williams		
I.R. Bishop		
C.E.L. Ambrose		
B.P. Patterson		
Extras	b 2, lb 11, w 9, nb 2	24
	(for 5 wickets)	**186**

PAKISTAN

Batsman	Dismissal	Runs
Aamir Sohail	c and b Patterson	13
Ramiz Raja	c Williams, b Marshall	26
Inzamam-ul-Haq	b Marshall	20
Salim Malik	run out	0
Imran Khan (capt)	c Richardson, b Patterson	51
Ijaz Ahmed	c Williams, b Ambrose	27
Wasim Akram	b Marshall	12
* Moin Khan	c and b Ambrose	7
Waqar Younis	not out	12
Mushtaq Ahmed	run out	1
Aqib Javed		
Extras	lb 6, w 9, nb 2	17
	(for 9 wickets)	**186**

(39 overs)

	O	M	R	W
Imran Khan	8	–	19	1
Wasim Akram	7	–	36	2
Waqar Younis	8	–	47	–
Mushtaq Ahmed	8	–	22	–
Aqib Javed	8	–	49	2

(39 overs)

	O	M	R	W
Bishop	7	–	41	–
Ambrose	8	1	28	2
Patterson	8	–	44	2
Marshall	8	–	39	3
Hooper	8	1	28	–

FALL OF WICKETS
1–53, **2**–85, **3**–134, **4**–178, **5**–183

FALL OF WICKETS
1–27, **2**–69, **3**–69, **4**–70, **5**–117, **6**–136, **7**–171, **8**–180, **9**–186

Umpires: Khizer Hayat & Riazuddin — Man of the Match – D.L. Haynes — *Match tied*

Consistently exciting form in the one-day international series from Ramiz Raja. (Alan Cozzi)

Prominent in the revival of Lahore and for PIA – Aamir Malik, the leading run-scorer in Pakistan, 1991–92. (Adrian Murrell/Allsport)

THIRD ONE-DAY INTERNATIONAL – PAKISTAN v. WEST INDIES

24 November, 1991 at Iqbal Stadium, Faisalabad

WEST INDIES

D.L. Haynes	c Moin Khan, b Aqib Javed	8
P.A. Wallace	b Aqib Javed	36
R.B. Richardson (capt)	c Wasim Akram, b Aqib Javed	5
B.C. Lara	c Moin Khan, b Inzamam-ul-Haq	45
C.L. Hooper	c Zahid Fazal, b Aqib Javed	57
K.L.T. Arthurton	not out	29
M.D. Marshall	not out	7
R.C. Haynes		
*D. Williams		
C.E.L. Ambrose		
A.C. Cummins		
Extras	lb 7, w 10	17
	(for 5 wickets)	**204**

(40 overs)

	O	M	R	W
Imran Khan	8	–	36	–
Wasim Akram	8	1	43	–
Mushtaq Ahmed	8	–	33	–
Aqib Javed	8	1	31	4
Waqar Younis	5	–	30	–
Inzamam-ul-Haq	3	–	24	1

FALL OF WICKETS
1–42, 2–52, 3–52, 4–145, 5–186

PAKISTAN

Ramiz Raja	c and b R.C. Haynes	29
Inzamam-ul-Haq	c Lara, b Cummins	60
Zahid Fazal	c Cummins, b Ambrose	53
Salim Malik	b Hooper	10
Imran Khan (capt)	c Lara, b Cummins	14
Ijaz Ahmed	c Richardson, b Ambrose	4
Wasim Akram	b Marshall	0
* Moin Khan	not out	7
Waqar Younis	c and b Marshall	0
Mushtaq Ahmed	not out	5
Aqib Javed		
Extras	lb 3, w 2	5
	(for 8 wickets)	**187**

(40 overs)

	O	M	R	W
Ambrose	8	–	35	2
Cummins	8	1	27	2
Marshall	8	–	44	2
R.C. Haynes	8	–	34	1
Hooper	8	–	44	1

FALL OF WICKETS
1–65, 2–106, 3–126, 4–161, 5–175, 6–175, 7–175, 8–175

Umpires: Khizer Hayat & Athar Zaidi

Man of the Match – C.L. Hooper

West Indies won by 17 runs

SRI LANKA TOUR

Led by Aravinda de Silva, Sri Lanka toured Pakistan in December and January, playing three Test matches and five one-day internationals. Of the 16-strong party, only wicket-keeper Ashley de Silva and medium-pace bowler Gallage Wickremasinghe had not appeared in Test cricket although both had played in one-day internationals. Former captain Arjuna Ranatunga was recalled to the side.

7, 8, and 9 December, 1991 *at National Stadium, Karachi*

Sri Lankans 222 for 7 dec. (P.A. de Silva 69 not out) and 195 for 4 (H.P. Tillekeratne 56 not out)
BCCP President's XI 221 for 8 dec. (Shahid Saeed 67 not out)
Match drawn

FIRST TEST MATCH
PAKISTAN v. SRI LANKA, at Sialkot

The decision to play the first Test match in the north of Pakistan at a time when rain and bad light were likely to disrupt play was strongly criticised, and the critics were proved right. Bad light curtailed each day, and rain ended the match when Pakistan were in sight of victory. Sri Lanka gave a first Test cap to Wickremasinghe and, rather surprisingly, batted when they won the toss.

Fifty-five for the loss of Samarasekera at lunch, Sri Lanka lost four wickets as 73 runs were scored in the post-lunch period. It was Aqib Javed who brought about the collapse, having Hathurusinghe taken at square leg after an innings which lasted two hours 21 minutes, knocking back Gurusinha's leg stump and trapping Ranatunga leg before. Aravinda de Silva fell to a sizzling ball from Waqar Younis, but Jayasuriya and Tillekeratne took Sri Lanka to 191 before play ended early.

Jayasuriya, 60 not out overnight, was bowled by Akram Raza the following morning, and it was the off-spinner and pace man Waqar Younis who brought the Sri Lankan innings to a close. Ramiz and Shoaib lifted the tempo of the match, scoring at three an over and reaching 72 before another enforced early finish. The Sri

FIRST TEST MATCH – PAKISTAN v. SRI LANKA
12, 13, 14, 16 and 17 December, 1991 at Jinnah Park Stadium, Sialkot

SRI LANKA

	FIRST INNINGS		SECOND INNINGS	
M.A.R. Samarasekera	c Moin Khan, b Waqar	19	b Waqar	6
U.C. Hathurusinghe	c Akram Raza, b Aqib	17	c Ramiz, b Wasim	7
A.P. Gurusinha	b Aqib	33	lbw, b Aqib	23
P.A. de Silva (capt)	b Waqar	31	c sub (Ijaz Ahmed), b Akram Raza	19
A. Ranatunga	lbw, b Aqib	0	c Moin Khan, b Waqar	0
S.T. Jayasuriya	b Akram Raza	77	not out	35
*H.P. Tillekeratne	c Akram Raza, b Waqar	49	not out	42
R.J. Ratnayake	b Waqar	13		
C.P.H. Ramanayake	b Akram Raza	0		
S.D. Anurasiri	not out	3		
G.P. Wickremasinghe	b Waqar	0		
Extras	b 5, lb 11, nb 12	28	nb 5	5
		270	(for 5 wickets)	**137**

PAKISTAN

	FIRST INNINGS	
Ramiz Raja	c Tillekeratne, b Anurasiri	98
Shoaib Mohammad	c and b Wickremasinghe	43
Zahid Fazal	c and b Ratnayake	36
Salim Malik	c Gurusinha, b Anurasiri	101
Javed Miandad	c Jayasuriya, b Anurasiri	1
Imran Khan (capt)	not out	93
Wasim Akram	not out	20
*Moin Khan		
Akram Raza		
Waqar Younis		
Aqib Javed		
Extras	lb 6, nb 25	31
	(for 5 wickets, dec.)	**423**

	O	M	R	W	O	M	R	W
Wasim Akram	32	7	47	–	13	4	31	1
Waqar Younis	30.5	5	84	5	14.4	1	43	2
Aqib Javed	23	4	70	3	7	3	22	1
Akram Raza	24	10	37	2	11	3	34	1
Imran Khan	9	1	16	–				
Salim Malik					1	–	7	–

	O	M	R	W
Ratnayake	31	4	100	1
Ramanayake	33	9	75	–
Wickremasinghe	27	3	120	1
Hathurusinghe	1	–	3	–
Anurasiri	61	21	106	3
de Silva	4	–	13	–

FALL OF WICKETS
1–21, **2**–70, **3**–89, **4**–89, **5**–128, **6**–229, **7**–244, **8**–245, **9**–270
1–6, **2**–33, **3**–58, **4**–58, **5**–58

FALL OF WICKETS
1–128, **2**–169, **3**–232, **4**–233, **5**–365

Umpires: Khizer Hayat & Ikram Rabbani

Match drawn

Lankan innings had lasted until the second afternoon and had occupied nearly 120 overs.

Pakistan, too, struggled on the third day, adding 171 runs in 78.2 overs for the loss of four wickets. Ramiz and Shoaib completed a record first-wicket stand for Pakistan against Sri Lanka, and Ramiz gave a polished display for 262 minutes before becoming becalmed in the 90s. Imran and Salim Malik lifted Pakistan's hopes on the fourth day with a record partnership of 132. Salim, the only man to be out on the fourth day, reached his ninth Test hundred off 201 balls and hit ten fours. He batted for 287 minutes. Imran hit nine fours and three sixes in his 235-minute innings and denied himself a century by his declaration. He was rewarded with the wicket of Samarasekera before the close.

Sri Lanka were in deep trouble against Waqar Younis on the last morning and were reduced to 58 for 5, but resolution from Jayasuriya and Tillekeratne and the rain saved them from defeat.

SECOND TEST MATCH
PAKISTAN v. SRI LANKA, at Gujranwala

Gujranwala had an unhappy debut as a Test ground. Put in to bat, Pakistan made 109 for 2 from 36 overs on the first day after which there was no more play.

27, 28 and 29 December, 1991 *at Qaddafi Stadium, Lahore*

Punjab Governor's XI 251 for 9 dec. (Aamir Sohail 71, Tahir Shah 61, Wasim Haider 50 not out) and 222 for 2 (Aamir Sohail 102)

Sri Lankans 219 for 9 dec. (A. Ranatunga 50, Salim Jaffer 4 for 71)

Match drawn

SECOND TEST MATCH – PAKISTAN v. SRI LANKA
20, 21, 22, 24 and 25 December, 1991 at Municipal Stadium, Gujranwala

PAKISTAN

	FIRST INNINGS	
Ramiz Raja	not out	51
Shoaib Mohammad	c Tillekeratne, b Ratnayake	1
Zahid Fazal	c Tillekeratne, b Wickremasinghe	21
Javed Miandad	not out	20
Salim Malik		
Imran Khan (capt)		
*Moin Khan		
Wasim Akram		
Waqar Younis		
Salim Jaffer		
Aqib Javed		
Extras	lb 10, nb 6	16
	(for 2 wickets)	109

SRI LANKA

R.S. Mahanama
U.C. Hathurusinghe
A.P. Gurusinha
A. Ranatunga
P.A. de Silva (capt)
S.T. Jayasuriya
*H.P. Tillekeratne
R.J. Ratnayake
C.P.H. Ramanayake
S.D. Anurasiri
G.P. Wickremasinghe

	O	M	R	W
Ratnayake	13	3	39	1
Ramanayake	10	2	16	–
Wickremasinghe	7	2	27	1
Hathurusinghe	2	1	6	–
Anurasiri	1	–	2	–
Gurusinha	2	–	9	–
Ranatunga	1	1	0	–

FALL OF WICKETS
1–3, **2**–59

Umpires: Khizer Hayat & Athar Zaidi

Match abandoned as a draw

THIRD TEST MATCH
PAKISTAN v. SRI LANKA, at Faisalabad

Put in to bat, Sri Lanka seemed to have survived disaster when Mahanama and Hathurusinghe put on 81 for the first wicket, but some furious and impressive fast bowling in the final session sent them sliding to 205 for 9. Jayasuriya, who had been hit on the neck, finished the day with 50 not out. On the second morning, he hit 31 of the 35 runs scored for the last wicket, and he was head and shoulders above any other Sri Lankan batsman in the series.

On a very restricted second day, Pakistan made 117 for 2, and on the third, they collapsed ignominiously against a spirited attack. Sri Lanka's hero was the fast medium-pace bowler Wickremasinghe who, in his third Test match, took 5 for 73. Twenty years old, he remains his country's hope for the future. Leading by 19 runs on the first innings, Sri Lanka closed on 68 for 3.

Inevitably, it was the pace bowling of the incomparable Waqar Younis that brought Pakistan back into the match. He, Wasim and Aqib demolished Sri Lanka who lost their last five wickets for 29 runs to leave Pakistan with the task of scoring 185 to win the Test. Medium-pacer Kapila Wijegunawardene took three wickets in eight balls. His victims were Javed, Salim Malik and Imran, and Pakistan closed at 95 for 4. Sri Lanka dreamed of their first away victory in a Test match.

They were thwarted by Zahid Fazal and Wasim Akram who halted the decline on the fourth evening and extended their partnership to 89 on the last morning. Zahid, having made his highest score in Test cricket, was caught off Gurusinha, and Wasim followed seven runs later. Moin and Shoaib, batting low in the order because of an injured finger, carried Pakistan to 171 for 6 at lunch and calmed nerves. Shoaib edged a ball from Ratnayake into his stumps shortly after the break, but Moin and Waqar completed the victory, which was not a convincing one for Pakistan, and, in truth, Sri Lanka derived much honour and praise for their fight.

THIRD TEST MATCH – PAKISTAN v. SRI LANKA
2, 3, 4, 6 and 7 January, 1992 at Iqbal Stadium, Faisalabad

SRI LANKA

	FIRST INNINGS		SECOND INNINGS	
R.S. Mahanama	c Moin, **b** Salim Jaffer	58	lbw, **b** Waqar	8
U.C. Hathurusinghe	**b** Waqar	49	c Zahid, **b** Waqar	20
A.P. Gurusinha	c Zahid, **b** Wasim	3	lbw, **b** Aqib Javed	14
P.A. de Silva (capt)	c Moin, **b** Salim Jaffer	12	lbw, **b** Waqar	38
A. Ranatunga	lbw, **b** Salim Jaffer	0	(8) c Miandad, **b** Wasim	6
S.T. Jayasuriya	run out	81	c Salim Malik, **b** Waqar	45
*H.P. Tillekeratne	c Shoaib, **b** Waqar	11	c Moin Khan, **b** Aqib	14
R.J. Ratnayake	lbw, **b** Waqar	4	(9) not out	5
S.D. Anurasiri	c Shoaib, **b** Waqar	0	(10) **b** Wasim	0
K.I.W. Wijegunawardene	lbw, **b** Wasim	2	(5) **b** Waqar	2
G.P. Wickremasinghe	not out	1	**b** Wasim	0
Extras	b 3, lb 6, w 2, nb 8	19	lb 3, nb 10	13
		240		**165**

PAKISTAN

	FIRST INNINGS		SECOND INNINGS	
Ramiz Raja	lbw, **b** Wickremasinghe	63	lbw, **b** Wickremasinghe	8
Shoaib Mohammad	lbw, **b** Wickremasinghe	30	(7) **b** Ratnayake	7
Zahid Fazal	lbw, **b** Wijegunawardene	13	(2) c Anurasiri, **b** Gurusinha	78
Javed Miandad	c Gurusinha, **b** Wickremasinghe	14	(3) c Gurusinha, **b** Wijegunawardene	2
Salim Malik	c Tillekeratne, **b** Gurusinha	4	(4) c Gurusinha, **b** Wijegunawardene	4
Imran Khan (capt)	**b** Wijegunawardene	22	(5) lbw, **b** Wijegunawardene	0
Wasim Akram	lbw, **b** Gurusinha	13	(6) c de Silva, **b** Wijegunawardene	54
*Moin Khan	lbw, **b** Wickremasinghe	3	not out	22
Waqar Younis	lbw, **b** Wickremasinghe	6	not out	1
Salim Jaffer	not out	8		
Aqib Javed	c sub (M.S. Atapattu), **b** Wijegunawardene	10		
Extras	lb 8, w 1, nb 26	35	b 2, lb 3, nb 7	12
		221	(for 7 wickets)	**188**

	O	M	R	W	O	M	R	W
Wasim Akram	22	8	62	**2**	18	2	71	**3**
Waqar Younis	21	1	87	**4**	17	3	65	**5**
Aqib Javed	12.1	3	46	–	8	4	7	**2**
Salim Jaffer	17	4	36	**3**	8	2	19	–

	O	M	R	W	O	M	R	W
Ratnayake	13	2	40	–	9.3	–	43	**1**
Wijegunawardene	31.2	13	47	**3**	17.2	1	52	**4**
Wickremasinghe	32	9	73	**5**	26	5	52	**1**
Anurasiri	10	2	28	–	6	1	18	–
Gurusinha	15	9	19	**2**	12	5	18	**1**
Ranatunga	3	2	2	–				
Hathurusinghe	2	–	4	–				

FALL OF WICKETS (Sri Lanka)

1–81, **2**–89, **3**–130, **4**–130, **5**–150, **6**–179, **7**–185, **8**–193, **9**–205
1–28, **2**–43, **3**–67, **4**–72, **5**–105, **6**–136, **7**–146, **8**–160, **9**–165

FALL OF WICKETS (Pakistan)

1–102, **2**–110, **3**–141, **4**–146, **5**–162, **6**–186, **7**–196, **8**–197, **9**–205
1–31, **2**–52, **3**–60, **4**–60, **5**–149, **6**–156, **7**–179

Umpires: Khalid Aziz & Shakoor Rana

Pakistan won by 3 wickets

TEST MATCH AVERAGES – PAKISTAN v. SRI LANKA

PAKISTAN BATTING

	M	Inns	NO	Runs	HS	Av	100s	50s
Ramiz Raja	3	4	1	220	98	73.33	–	3
Imran Khan	3	3	1	115	93*	57.50	–	2
Wasim Akram	3	3	1	87	54	43.50	–	1
Zahid Fazal	3	4	–	148	78	37.00	–	1
Salim Malik	3	3	–	109	101	36.33	1	–
Moin Khan	3	1	1	25	22*	25.00	–	–
Shoaib Mohammad	3	4	–	81	43	20.25	–	–
Javed Miandad	3	4	1	37	20*	12.33	–	–
Waqar Younis	3	2	1	7	6	7.00	–	–

Played in three Tests – Aqib Javed 10
Played in two Tests – Salim Jaffer 8*
Played in one Test – Akram Raza did not bat

PAKISTAN BOWLING

	Overs	Mds	Runs	Wkts	Av	Best	10/m	5/inn
Waqar Younis	83.3	10	279	16	17.43	5-65	–	2
Salim Jaffer	25	6	55	3	18.33	3-36	–	–
Akram Raza	35	13	71	3	23.66	2-37	–	–
Aqib Javed	50.1	14	145	6	24.16	3-70	–	–
Wasim Akram	86	21	211	6	35.16	3-71	–	–

Bowled in one innings – Imran Khan 9-1-16-0; Salim Malik 1-0-7-0

PAKISTAN FIELDING FIGURES

5 – Moin Khan; 2 – Shoaib Mohammad, Zahid Fazal and Akram Raza; 1 – Ramiz Raja, Javed Miandad, Salim Malik and sub (Ijaz Ahmed)

SRI LANKA BATTING

	M	Inns	NO	Runs	HS	Av	100s	50s
S.T. Jayasuriya	3	4	1	238	81	79.33	–	2
H.P. Tillekeratne	3	4	1	116	49	38.66	–	–
R.S. Mahanama	2	2	–	66	58	33.00	–	1
P.A. de Silva	3	4	–	100	38	25.00	–	–
U.C. Hathurusinghe	3	4	–	93	49	23.35	–	–
A.P. Gurusinha	3	4	–	73	33	18.25	–	–
R.J. Ratnayake	3	3	1	22	13	11.00	–	–
A. Ranatunga	3	4	–	6	6	1.50	–	–
S.D. Anurasiri	3	3	1	3	3*	1.50	–	–
G.P. Wickremasinghe	3	3	1	1	1*	0.50	–	–

Played in two Tests – C.P.H. Ramanayake 0
Played in one Test – K.I.W. Wijegunawardene 2 & 2; M.A.R. Samarasekera 19 & 6

SRI LANKA BOWLING

	Overs	Mds	Runs	Wkts	Av	Best	5/inn
K.I.W. Wijegunawardene	38.4	14	99	7	14.14	4-52	–
A.P. Gurusinha	29	14	46	3	15.33	2-19	–
G.P. Wickremasinghe	92	19	272	8	34.00	5-73	1
S.D. Anurasiri	78	24	154	3	51.33	3-106	–
R.J. Ratnayake	66.3	9	222	3	74.00	1-39	–
A. Ranatunga	4	3	2	–	–	–	–
U.C. Hathurusinghe	5	1	13	–	–	–	–
C.P.H. Ramanayake	43	11	91	–	–	–	–

Bowled in one innings – P.A. de Silva 4-0-13-0

SRI LANKA FIELDING FIGURES

4 – H.P. Tillekeratne and A.P. Gurusinha; 1 – P.A. de Silva, R.J. Ratnayake, S.D. Anurasiri, G.P. Wickremasinghe and sub (M.S. Atapattu)

FIRST ONE-DAY INTERNATIONAL – PAKISTAN v. SRI LANKA

10 January, 1992 at Sargodha Stadium, Sargodha

SRI LANKA

R.S. Mahanama	lbw, **b** Waqar Younis	5
U.C. Hathurusinghe	**c** Moin Khan, **b** Imran Khan	6
A.P. Gurusinha	**c** Imran Khan, **b** Akram Raza	37
P.A. de Silva (capt)	**c** Wasim Akram, **b** Waqar Younis	19
S.T. Jayasuriya	run out	26
*H.P. Tillekeratne	not out	37
M.S. Atapattu	**b** Aqib Javed	4
R.S. Kalpage	not out	5
C.P.H. Ramanayake		
G.P. Wickremasinghe		
K.I.W. Wijegunawardene		
Extras	b 1, lb 5, w 7, nb 3	16
	(for 6 wickets)	155

(40 overs)

	O	M	R	W
Wasim Akram	8	–	33	–
Waqar Younis	8	2	13	2
Aqib Javed	8	1	26	1
Imran Khan	8	–	35	1
Akram Raza	8	–	42	1

FALL OF WICKETS
1–11, **2**–27, **3**–69, **4**–79, **5**–118, **6**–138

PAKISTAN

Ramiz Raja	**c** Mahanama, **b** Wijegunawardene	74
Zahid Fazal	**b** Ramanayake	9
Javed Miandad	not out	60
Salim Malik	not out	9
Inzamam-ul-Haq		
Imran Khan (capt)		
* Moin Khan		
Wasim Akram		
Akram Raza		
Waqar Younis		
Aqib Javed		
Extras	lb 1, w 2, nb 2	5
	(for 2 wickets)	157

(36.5 overs)

	O	M	R	W
Ramanayake	6	1	19	1
Wijegunawardene	8	–	41	1
Wickremasinghe	5	–	14	–
Gurusinha	4	–	21	–
Jayasuriya	6.5	–	29	–
Kalpage	7	1	32	–

FALL OF WICKETS
1–19, **2**–131

Umpires: Khizer Hayat & Amanullah Khan — Man of the Match – Ramiz Raja — *Pakistan won by 8 wickets*

ONE-DAY INTERNATIONAL SERIES
PAKISTAN v. SRI LANKA

If Pakistan came out of the Test series with little credit in the eyes of their supporters, they reasserted themselves in the one-day series which they won with ease. Put in to bat in the first match, Sri Lanka found themselves under constant pressure from the Pakistan attack, and their meagre score of 155 never troubled the home side. Javed returned to form, and he and Ramiz flayed the Sri Lankan bowling.

The visitors did well to restrict Pakistan to 210 in the second encounter, and they looked as if they might win the game when Mahanama and Gurusinha were in full flow, but Gurusinha hooked nonchalantly into the hands of the only man on the leg side, de Silva drove rashly at leg-spinner Mushtaq Ahmed and Mahanama was forced to retire hurt at 128 for 4 with cramp and dehydration. With him went Sri Lanka's hopes.

Pakistan took the series when they won the third match. Javed was again in masterly form, and he and Salim Malik and Wasim Akram hit 61 in the last five overs of the Pakistan innings. Sri Lanka began boldly in reply, but the customary collapse followed.

A brilliant opening stand of 149 between Ramiz Raja and Inzamam-ul-Haq seemed to put Pakistan on the road to a big score at Multan, but Imran changed his batting order in an attempt to give practice before the World Cup. The opportunities were not taken, and Pakistan finished with a disappointing 205. An exciting second-wicket stand of 157 between Samarasekera and Gurusinha set up Sri Lanka's victory, but they still took until the last over to clinch it, and even then they had a fright when de Silva was out to a dreadful shot.

Sri Lanka were totally outplayed in the final match. Inzamam-ul-Haq hit his second century in succession, and Salim Malik also reached three figures. The pair shared a second-wicket stand of 204.

Kalpage and Hathurusinghe made their one-day international debuts in the series. Kalpage and Labrooy were called in as replacements for the injured Rumesh Ratnayake. They were not in the original party.

SECOND ONE-DAY INTERNATIONAL – PAKISTAN v. SRI LANKA
13 January, 1992 at National Stadium, Karachi

PAKISTAN

Batsman	How out	Runs
Ramiz Raja	c Labrooy, b Jayasuriya	35
Inzamam-ul-Haq	run out	48
Javed Miandad	b Wijegunawardene	29
Salim Malik	b Labrooy	36
Imran Khan (capt)	not out	44
Wasim Akram	c Kalpage, b Wijegunawardene	7
Ijaz Ahmed	not out	1
*Moin Khan		
Mushtaq Ahmed		
Waqar Younis		
Aqib Javed		
Extras	lb 4, w 1, nb 5	10
	(for 5 wickets)	210

(40 overs)

	O	M	R	W
Ramanayake	6	2	17	–
Labrooy	8	1	56	1
Wickremasinghe	5	1	26	–
Wijegunawardene	8	–	43	2
Kalpage	8	–	37	–
Jayasuriya	5	–	27	1

FALL OF WICKETS
1–89, 2–89, 3–150, 4–160, 5–194

SRI LANKA

Batsman	How out	Runs
R.S. Mahanama	retired hurt	60
U.C. Hathurusinghe	b Wasim Akram	14
A.P. Gurusinha	c Wasim Akram, b Waqar Younis	13
P.A. de Silva (capt)	c sub (Akram Raza), b Mushtaq Ahmed	24
S.T. Jayasuriya	lbw, b Waqar Younis	0
*H.P. Tillekeratne	not out	29
R.S. Kalpage	b Mushtaq Ahmed	3
G.F. Labrooy	b Imran Khan	13
C.P.H. Ramanayake	b Wasim Akram	4
K.I.W. Wijegunawardene	run out	7
G.P. Wickremasinghe	b Wasim Akram	0
Extras	lb 10, w 3, nb 1	14
		181

(36.1 overs)

	O	M	R	W
Wasim Akram	6.1	–	31	3
Waqar Younis	8	1	38	2
Aqib Javed	6	–	19	–
Imran Khan	8	–	44	1
Mushtaq Ahmed	8	–	39	2

FALL OF WICKETS
1–46, 2–66, 3–109, 4–111, 5–134, 6–155, 7–167, 8–178, 9–181

Umpires: Mahboob Shah & Riazuddin

Man of the Match – Imran Khan

Pakistan won by 29 runs

THIRD ONE-DAY INTERNATIONAL – PAKISTAN v. SRI LANKA
15 January, 1992 at Niaz Stadium, Hyderabad

PAKISTAN

Ramiz Raja	c Labrooy, **b** Ramanayake	12
Inzamam-ul-Haq	c Atapattu, **b** Labrooy	60
Javed Miandad	not out	115
Salim Malik	c de Silva, **b** Wijegunawardene	40
Wasim Akram	not out	7
Ijaz Ahmed		
Imran Khan (capt)		
*Moin Khan		
Mushtaq Ahmed		
Waqar Younis		
Aqib Javed		
Extras	lb 2, w 2, nb 3	7
	(for 3 wickets)	**241**

(40 overs)

	O	M	R	W
Ramanayake	8	2	26	1
Wijegunawardene	8	–	49	1
Labrooy	6	–	51	1
Madurasinghe	8	2	34	–
Gurusinha	2	–	13	–
Jayasuriya	8	–	66	–

FALL OF WICKETS
1–27, **2**–134, **3**–220

SRI LANKA

U.C. Hathurusinghe	c Ijaz Ahmed, **b** Imran Khan	19
M.A.R. Samarasekera	c Moin Khan, **b** Aqib Javed	43
P.A. de Silva (capt)	c Moin Khan, **b** Aqib Javed	2
* H.P. Tillekeratne	**b** Wasim Akram	44
S.T. Jayasuriya	lbw, **b** Imran Khan	0
A.P. Gurusinha	c Salim Malik, **b** Mushtaq Ahmed	15
G.F. Labrooy	lbw, **b** Imran Khan	7
M.S. Atapattu	not out	19
C.P.H. Ramanayake	**b** Wasim Akram	1
K.I.W. Wijegunawardene	c Imran Khan, **b** Aqib Javed	1
M.A.W.R. Madurasinghe	not out	3
Extras	lb 14, w 8, nb 6	28
	(for 9 wickets)	**182**

(40 overs)

	O	M	R	W
Wasim Akram	8	–	34	2
Waqar Younis	8	–	42	–
Aqib Javed	8	1	30	3
Imran Khan	8	3	15	3
Mushtaq Ahmed	8	–	47	1

FALL OF WICKETS
1–70, **2**–72, **3**–80, **4**–80, **5**–119, **6**–127, **7**–167, **8**–174, **9**–177

Umpires: Shakeel Khan & Taufiq Khan — Man of the Match – Javed Miandad — *Pakistan won by 59 runs*

An all-round cricketer of outstanding quality, Asif Mujtaba excelled with bat, with ball and in the field. He also led Karachi Whites against Bahawalpur. (Alan Cozzi)

Iqbal Sikander, 14 for 94 for Karachi Whites against Bahawalpur. (David Munden).

FOURTH ONE-DAY INTERNATIONAL – PAKISTAN v. SRI LANKA

17 January, 1992 at Qasim Bagh Stadium, Multan

PAKISTAN

Ramiz Raja	st Tillekeratne, b Jayasuriya	52
Inzamam-ul-Haq	c sub (Kalpage), b Jayasuriya	101
Ijaz Ahmed	c de Silva, b Ramanayake	31
Wasim Akram	c Hathurusinghe, b Wijegunawardene	6
*Moin Khan	not out	2
Mushtaq Ahmed	b Ramanayake	1
Javed Miandad		
Imran Khan (capt)		
Salim Malik		
Waqar Younis		
Aqib Javed		
Extras	lb 5, w 5, nb 2	12
	(for 5 wickets)	205

(40 overs)

	O	M	R	W
Ramanayake	8	1	30	2
Wijegunawardene	6	1	37	1
Gurusinha	2	–	14	–
Madurasinghe	8	1	36	–
Anurasiri	8	–	42	–
Jayasuriya	8	–	41	2

FALL OF WICKETS
1–149, 2–180, 3–196, 4–201, 5–205

SRI LANKA

M.A.R. Samarasekera	c Inzamam-ul-Haq, b Mushtaq Ahmed	76
U.C. Hathurusinghe	c Moin Khan, b Waqar Younis	2
A.P. Gurusinha	st Moin Khan, b Mushtaq Ahmed	74
P.A. de Silva (capt)	c Inzamam-ul-Haq, b Aqib Javed	18
*H.P. Tillekeratne	run out	10
S.T. Jayasuriya	lbw, b Aqib Javed	5
M.S. Atapattu	not out	5
C.P.H. Ramanayake	not out	0
S.D. Anurasiri		
K.I.W. Wijegunawardene		
M.A.W.R. Madurasinghe		
Extras	b 1, lb 7, w 5, nb 3	16
	(for 6 wickets)	206

(39.4 overs)

	O	M	R	W
Wasim Akram	8	–	31	–
Waqar Younis	8	1	36	1
Aqib Javed	7.4	1	40	2
Imran Khan	6	–	40	–
Mushtaq Ahmed	8	–	37	2
Inzamam-ul-Haq	2	–	14	–

FALL OF WICKETS
1–4, 2–161, 3–161, 4–183, 5–192, 6–203

Umpires: Shakoor Rana & Mian Aslam — Man of the Match – Inzamam-ul-Haq — *Sri Lanka won by 4 wickets*

Mohsin Kamal took 6 for 20 for PNSC in the second innings against United Bank in Karachi and completed the only hat-trick of the season. (Chris Cole/Allsport)

A thrilling young batsman – Inzamam-ul-Haq. (Alan Cozzi)

FIFTH ONE-DAY INTERNATIONAL – PAKISTAN v. SRI LANKA
19 January, 1992 at Rawalpindi Stadium, Rawalpindi

PAKISTAN

Ramiz Raja	b Wijegunawardene	5
Inzamam-ul-Haq	c Wickremasinghe, b Ramanayake	117
Salim Malik	c Jayasuriya, b Ramanayake	102
Javed Miandad	run out	19
Ijaz Ahmed	not out	4
Wasim Akram	not out	16
Imran Khan (capt)		
*Moin Khan		
Mushtaq Ahmed		
Waqar Younis		
Aqib Javed		
Extras	b 1, lb 2, w 5	8
	(for 4 wickets)	271

(40 overs)

	O	M	R	W
Ramanayake	8	1	48	2
Wijegunawardene	8	–	68	1
Wickremasinghe	6	–	32	–
Madurasinghe	8	–	54	–
Gurusinha	3	–	23	–
Jayasuriya	7	–	43	–

FALL OF WICKETS
1–5, 2–209, 3–251, 4–251

SRI LANKA

R.S. Mahanama	lbw, b Aqib Javed	18
M.A.R. Samarasekera	b Waqar Younis	13
A.P. Gurusinha	c Ramiz Raja, b Aqib Javed	16
P.A. de Silva (capt)	run out	17
* H.P. Tillekeratne	c Ramiz Raja, b Mushtaq Ahmed	36
S.T. Jayasuriya	run out	3
M.S. Atapattu	run out	3
C.P.H. Ramanayake	b Waqar Younis	26
K.I.W. Wijegunawardene	c Imran Khan, b Wasim Akram	0
M.A.W.R. Madurasinghe	not out	6
G.P. Wickremasinghe	st Moin Khan, b Inzamam-ul-Haq	5
Extras	lb 4, w 5, nb 2	11
		154

(38.3 overs)

	O	M	R	W
Wasim Akram	8	2	20	1
Waqar Younis	8	–	42	2
Aqib Javed	6	–	25	2
Imran Khan	8	–	30	–
Mushtaq Ahmed	8	–	29	1
Inzamam-ul-Haq	0.3	–	4	1

FALL OF WICKETS
1–31, 2–39, 3–63, 4–75, 5–84, 6–91, 7–117, 8–130, 9–149

Umpires: Javed Akhtar & Siddiq Khan — Man of the Match – Inzamam-ul-Haq — *Pakistan won by 117 runs*

QUAID-E-AZAM TROPHY

19, 20, 21 and 22 October, 1991 *at National Stadium, Karachi*

Karachi Whites 339 for 6 (Asif Mujtaba 105 not out, Azam Khan 53) and 267 for 2 dec. (Azam Khan 135 not out, Basit Ali 64)
Karachi Blues 288 for 8 (Ameer-ud-din 120, Munir-ul-Haq 77, Mohsin Mirza 5 for 48) and 284 (Ameer-ud-din 66, Tahir Mahmood 51, Mohsin Mirza 8 for 92)

Karachi Whites won by 34 runs

Karachi Whites 10 pts., Karachi Blues 0 pts.

at Montgomery Biscuit Factory Ground, Sahiwal

Bahawalpur 302 for 8 (Umer Rashid 87, Murtaza Hussain 67 not out, Shakeel Ahmed 57, Nadeem Nazar 5 for 102) and 415 for 8 (Shahid Anwar 161, Bilal Rana 59 not out, Shakeel Ahmed 55, Nadeem Nazar 4 for 178)
Multan 305 for 9 (Manzoor Elahi 85, Zahoor Elahi 76, Aamir Bashir 68, Mohammad Altaf 5 for 77) and 94 for 3

Match drawn

Multan 5 pts., Bahawalpur 0 pts.

at Pindi Club Ground, Rawalpindi

Lahore 199 (Aamir Malik 63, Tanqir Hussain 4 for 31, Zahir Shah 4 for 59) and 139 (Mohammad Riaz 6 for 63)
Rawalpindi 197 (Mohammad Asif 5 for 66) and 144 for 3 (Naseer Ahmed 70)

Rawalpindi won by 7 wickets

Rawalpindi 10 pts., Lahore 0 pts.

at Iqbal Stadium, Faisalabad

Faisalabad 297 for 4 (Mohammad Ramzan 144, Nadeem Arshad 71, Shahid Nawaz 54 not out) and 182 (Zakir Khan 6 for 67)
Peshawar 336 for 8 (Sagheer Abbas 156 not out) and 146 for 6

Peshawar won by 4 wickets

Peshawar 10 pts., Faisalabad 0 pts.

Pakistan's premier domestic competition was played in two-and-a-half months at the end of 1991. With the national side engaged in Test and one-day series against Sri Lanka and in preparation for the World Cup, the tournament was once again bereft of its leading players. Asif Mujtaba, the most accomplished all-round cricketer outside the national side, led the defending champions, Karachi Whites, to victory in their opening match. Mohammad Ramzan of Faisalabad hit a maiden first-class century.

26, 27, 28 and 29 October, 1991 *at National Stadium, Karachi*

Sargodha 284 (Rizwan Umer 151) and 216 (Iqbal Sikander 6 for 36)
Karachi Whites 363 for 6 (Aamir Hanif 163 not out, Azam Khan 63, Salim Yousuf 52) and 138 for 6 (Naeem Khan 4 for 74)

Karachi Whites won by 4 wickets

Karachi Whites 10 pts., Sargodha 0 pts.

at Montgomery Biscuit Factory Ground, Sahiwal

Multan 337 (Zahoor Elahi 126, Manzoor Elahi 50, Nadeem Khan 4 for 130) and 234 (Haaris Khan 5 for 83)
Karachi Blues 322 (Rizwan-uz-Zaman 74, Ameer-ud-din 72, Rashid Latif 51, Zahoor Elahi 4 for 64) and 252 for 3 (Ameer-ud-din 122, Rizwan-uz-Zaman 60, Iqbal Salim 59 not out)

Karachi Blues won by 7 wickets

Karachi Blues 10 pts., Multan 0 pts.

at Bahawal Stadium, Bahawalpur

Bahawalpur 199 (Shakeel Ahmed 55, Shahid Anwar 54, Raja Sarfraz 7 for 64) and 133
Rawalpindi 74 (Shehzad Arshad 6 for 14) and 142 (Mohammad Zahid 4 for 20)

Bahawalpur won by 116 runs

Bahawalpur 10 pts., Rawalpindi 0 pts.

at Arbab Niaz Stadium, Peshawar

Peshawar 204 (Jehangir Khan 51, Farrukh Zaman 51) and 320 (Sher Ali 93, Nasir Khan 59, Jehangir Khan 51, Mohammad Asif 5 for 65)
Lahore 287 (Shahid Saeed 67, Ali Zia 61, Farrukh Zaman 5 for 90) and 46 for 0

Match drawn

Lahore 5 pts., Peshawar 0 pts.

After two rounds of matches Karachi Whites remained the only side with two victories to their credit. A maiden century from Aamir Hanif and some excellent leg-spin from Iqbal Sikander were the main ingredients in the Whites' victory.

3, 4, 5 and 6 November, 1991 *at National Stadium, Karachi*

Karachi Whites 202 (Iqbal Sikander 52, Nadeem Afzal 5 for 77) and 159 (Naseer Shaukat 7 for 62)
Faisalabad 156 (Shahid Mahboob 5 for 53) and 208 for 5 (Mohammad Ramzan 68, Shahid Mahboob 4 for 78)

Faisalabad won by 5 wickets

Faisalabad 10 pts., Karachi Whites 0 pts.

at Bahawal Stadium, Bahawalpur

Bahawalpur 151 (Shahzad Arshad 50 not out, Nadeem Khan 5 for 56) and 286 (Murtaza Hussain 51, Nadeem Khan 5 for 92)
Karachi Blues 166 (Mohammad Zahid 4 for 27) and 114 (Sajid Ali 63, Bilal Rana 3 for 55)

Bahawalpur won by 157 runs

Bahawalpur 10 pts., Karachi Blues 0 pts.

at Pindi Club Ground, Rawalpindi

Multan 259 (Mohammad Riaz 5 for 52) and 147 (Raja Afaq 4 for 48)
Rawalpindi 274 (Nadeem Abbasi 72 not out, Ghaffar Kazmi 67, Masood Anwar 65, Masood Anwar 4 for 74) and 135 for 4 (Ghaffar Kazmi 50 not out)

Rawalpindi won by 6 wickets

Rawalpindi 10 pts., Multan 0 pts.

at LCCA Ground, Lahore

Sargodha 343 (Salim Malik 86, Rizwan Umer 68, Maqsood Ahmed 61, Sajjad Akbar 50, Nadeem Ghauri 4 for 114) and 320 for 9 dec. (Arshad Pervez 65, Rizwan Umer 64, Mohammad Hussain 58, Sohail Khan 6 for 109)
Lahore 347 for 8 (Shahid Saeed 109, Mansoor Rana 79, Aamir Malik 61, Mohammad Nawaz 4 for 65) and 266 for 7 (Shahid Saeed 72, Ali Zia 58, Aamir Malik 50)

Match drawn

Lahore 5 pts., Sargodha 0 pts.

Karachi Whites were surprisingly beaten by Faisalabad whereas Bahawalpur and Rawalpindi gained their second victories to draw level with the reigning champions.

9, 10, 11 and 12 November, 1991 *at National Stadium, Karachi*

Karachi Whites 272 for 8 (Mohsin Mirza 58 not out, Sohail Mehdi 50 not out) and 260 for 8 dec. (Aamir Kurshid 73, Asif Mujtaba 69 not out)
Peshawar 195 (Javed Khan 68, Athar Laeeq 5 for 60) and 268 (Sagheer Abbas 103 not out, Mohammad Salim 63, Athar Laeeq 4 for 56, Shahid Mahboob 4 for 84)

Karachi Whites won by 69 runs

Karachi Whites 10 pts., Peshawar 0 pts.

at Pindi Club Ground, Rawalpindi

Rawalpindi 301 for 7 (Shahid Javed 105 not out, Haaris Khan 5 for 114) and 221 (Shahid Javed 60, Naseer Ahmed 50, Nadeem Khan 5 for 72, Haaris Khan 4 for 69)
Karachi Blues 200 (Munir-ul-Haq 53, Tahir Mahmood 52, Mohammad Riaz 5 for 66) and 175 (Sajid Ali 68, Shakeel Ahmed 5 for 60, Raja Afaq 4 for 42)

Rawalpindi won by 147 runs

Rawalpindi 10 pts., Karachi Blues 0 pts.

at Montgomery Biscuit Factory Ground, Sahiwal

Faisalabad 245 (Naseer Shaukat 75, Masood Anwar 7 for 69) and 395 for 6 (Ijaz Ahmed 100, Mohammad Ramzan 72, Nadeem Arshad 52 not out)
Multan 251 (Masroor Hussain 80, Raja Arhad 55, Tanvir Afzal 5 for 90)

Match drawn

Multan 5 pts., Faisalabad 0 pts.

at Sargodha Stadium, Sargodha

Bahawalpur 256 (Bilal Rana 77, Aziz-ur-Rehman 5 for 62) and 354 (Umar Rasheed 147 not out, Sajjad Akbar 5 for 142)
Sargodha 265 and 28 for 1

Match drawn

Sargodha 5 pts., Bahawalpur 0 pts.

Karachi Whites and Rawalpindi drew clear at the top of the table. Whites were saved in their first innings by an unbroken ninth-wicket stand of 102 between Mohsin Mirza and Sohail Mehdi. The veteran Sagheer Abbas came close to snatching the game for Peshawar.

16, 17, 18 and 19 November, 1991 *at Montgomery Biscuit Factory Ground, Sahiwal*

Sargodha 279 for 9 (Mohammad Nawaz 77, Mohammad Hussain 53, Masood Anwar 5 for 78) and 345 (Azhar Sultan 75, Rizwan Umer 60, Pervez Shah 58, Nadeem Nazar 4 for 151)
Multan 353 for 7 (Mohammad Shafiq 68, Zahoor Elahi 63, Raja Arshad 56, Sajjad Akbar 4 for 128) and 70 for 2

Match drawn

Multan 5 pts., Sargodha 0 pts.

at Arbab Niaz Stadium, Peshawar

Peshawar 142 (Mohammad Hasnain 5 for 36, Nadeem Khan 4 for 50) and 316 (Javed Khan 70, Mohammad Salim 59)
Karachi Blues 154 (Kabir Khan 7 for 69) and 245 (Iqbal Salim 80, Munir-ul-Haq 54, Kabir Khan 5 for 63, Shahid Hussain 5 for 66)

Peshawar won by 59 runs

Peshawar 10 pts., Karachi Blues 0 pts.

at Bagh-e-Jinnah Ground, Faisalabad

Faisalabad 306 for 5 (Mohammad Ramzan 133, Shahid Nawaz 61) and 360 (Bilal Ahmed 126, Sami-ul-Haq 99, Zahir Shah 5 for 73)
Rawalpindi 322 for 6 (Naseer Ahmed 101 not out, Masood Anwar 80, Tanvir Afzal 4 for 138) and 63 for 1

Match drawn

Rawalpindi 5 pts., Faisalabad 0 pts.

at LCCA Ground, Lahore

Bahawalpur 292 (Bilal Rana 92, Tanvir Mehdi 5 for 88) and 241 (Shahid Anwar 77, Umer Rashid 60, Tanvir Mehdi 7 for 74)
Lahore 398 for 4 (Aamir Malik 162, Shahid Saeed 141) and 136 for 4 (Shahid Saeed 75)

Lahore won by 6 wickets

Lahore 10 pts., Bahawalpur 0 pts.

Twelve wickets from Tanvir Mehdi and a second-wicket partnership of 291 between Shahid Saeed and Aamir Malik set up Lahore's first victory of the season.

23, 24, 25 and 26 November, 1991 *at National Stadium, Karachi*

Karachi Whites 194 (Moin-ul-Atiq 50) and 182 (Moin-ul-Atiq 79)
Lahore 251 for 9 (Ashraf Ali 107 not out) and 126 for 4 (Shahid Saeed 65)

Lahore won by 6 wickets

Lahore 10 pts., Karachi Whites 0 pts.

at Sargodha Stadium, Sargodha

Sargodha 190 (Pervez Shah 84, Baqar Rizvi 6 for 75, Mohammad Hasnain 4 for 55) and 132 (Mohammad Hasnain 8 for 61)
Karachi Blues 54 (Naeem Khan 6 for 19) and 137 (Naeem Khan 5 for 86)

Sargodha won by 131 runs

Sargodha 10 pts., Karachi Blues 0 pts.

at Montgomery Biscuit Factory Ground, Sahiwal

Peshawar 182 (Zahid Ahmed 67, Nadeem Nazar 4 for 39) and 237 (Sher Ali 76, Masood Anwar 4 for 53, Nadeem Nazar 4 for 69)

Multan 362 for 8 (Zahoor Elahi 138, Masroor Hussain 80, Manzoor Elahi 73, Zahid Ahmed 4 for 48) and 59 for 2

Multan won by 8 wickets

Multan 10 pts., Peshawar 0 pts.

at Bahawal Stadium, Bahawalpur

Faisalabad 225 (Mohammad Ramzan 74, Ijaz Ahmed 67, Murtaza Hussain 6 for 37) and 114 (Bilal Rana 7 for 57)
Bahawalpur 264 for 7 (Shehzad Arshad 65 not out, Shakeel Ahmed 51) and 76 for 2

Bahawalpur won by 8 wickets

Bahawalpur 10 pts., Faisalabad 0 pts.

Karachi Whites suffered a second defeat, and they were not helped by the policy of fielding a constantly changing side. Multan beat Peshawar to claim their first win of the season. Zahoor Elahi and Masroor Hussain shared a first-wicket stand of 150.

30 **November, 1, 2** **and 3 December, 1991** *at Iqbal Stadium, Faisalabad*

Faisalabad 299 (Naseer Shaukat 68, Mohammad Ashraf 67, Nadeem Arshad 58, Mohammad Ramzan 50) and 95 (Baqar Rizvi 5 for 50, Mohammad Hussain 4 for 20)
Karachi Blues 153 (Amir-ud-din 72, Fazal Hussain 7 for 41) and 148 (Rashid Latif 53, Saadat Gul 4 for 40)

Faisalabad won by 93 runs

Faisalabad 10 pts., Karachi Blues 0 pts.

at LCCA Ground, Lahore

Lahore 131 (Masood Anwar 5 for 12) and 374 for 3 dec. (Shahid Saeed 161, Aamir Malik 87, Ashraf Ali 56 not out, Ali Zia 55 not out)
Multan 318 for 8 (Tariq Mahboob 80, Manzoor Elahi 77, Tanvir Mehdi 4 for 76)

Match drawn

Multan 5 pts., Lahore 0 pts.

at Arbab Niaz Stadium, Peshawar

Sargodha 122 (Shahid Hussain 6 for 40, Farukh Zaman 4 for 59) and 149 for 7
Peshawar 176 (Wasim Yousif 64 not out, Naeem Khan 5 for 52)

Match drawn

Peshawar 5 pts., Sargodha 0 pts.

at National Stadium, Karachi

Rawalpindi 320 for 9 (Naseer Ahmed 55, Sabih Azhar 54, Ghaffar Kazmi 54, Asif Mujtaba 5 for 76) and 287 (Arif Butt 91, Naseer Ahmed 74, Asif Mujtaba 5 for 47, Sohail Mehdi 4 for 95)
Karachi Whites 310 (Asif Mujtaba 105, Aamir Hanif 65, Shakil Ahmed 4 for 94) and 59 for 3

Match drawn

Rawalpindi 5 pts., Karachi Whites 0 pts.

Lahore recovered too late to cause any damage to Multan while a brilliant all-round performance from Asif Mujtaba failed to bring a point for Karachi Whites. Asif had match figures of 10 for 123 and hit 127 for once out.

7, 8, 9 **and 10 December, 1991** *at Bahawal Stadium, Bahawalpur*

Bahawalpur 102 (Iqbal Sikander 7 for 34) and 155 (Iqbal Sikander 7 for 60)
Karachi Whites 227 (Asif Mujtaba 72) and 31 for 2

Karachi Whites won by 8 wickets

Karachi Whites 10 pts., Bahawalpur 0 pts.

at LCCA Ground, Lahore

Lahore 334 for 4 (Aamir Malik 132 not out, Mansoor Rana 85) and 319 (Ashraf Ali 87, Nadeem Khan 5 for 128, Haaris Khan 4 for 86)
Karachi Blues 338 for 3 (Iqbal Salim 172 not out, Munir-ul-Haq 111) and 188 for 5 (Iqbal Salim 75, Amir-ud-din 54, Nadeem Ghauri 4 for 57)

Match drawn

Karachi Blues 5 pts., Lahore 0 pts.

at Iqbal Stadium, Faisalabad

Sargodha 180 (Asad Malik 68, Saadat Gul 5 for 52) and 273 (Azhar Sultan 60, Sajjad Akbar 58 not out, Rashid Wali 5 for 64)
Faisalabad 233 (Shahid Nawaz 112) and 53 for 2

Match drawn

Faisalabad 5 pts., Sargodha 0 pts.

at Pindi Club Ground, Rawalpindi

Peshawar 165 (Raja Afaq 5 for 59, Shakeel Ahmed 4 for 34) and 91 (Shakeel Ahmed 6 for 35)
Rawalpindi 229 (Naseer Ahmed 77, Arshad Khan 4 for 63, Shahid Hussain 4 for 66) and 30 for 0

Rawalpindi won by 10 wickets

Rawalpindi 10 pts., Peshawar 0 pts.

Karachi Whites made sure of a place in the semi-finals with an emphatic win over Bahawalpur. They were inspired by skipper Asif Mujtaba and by the leg-spin bowling of Iqbal Sikander who took ten or more wickets in a match for the eighth time. Rawalpindi owed much to left-arm spinner Shakeel Ahmed as they, too, confirmed their place in the semi-finals.

14, 15, 16 and **17** December, 1991 *at National Stadium, Karachi*

Karachi Whites 244 (Iqbal Sikander 51) and 362 (Manzoor Akhtar 182, Ghulam Ali 71)
Multan 360 for 9 (Zahoor Elahi 148, Aamir Hanif 6 for 125) and 26 for 0

Match drawn

Multan 5 pts., Karachi Whites 0 pts.

at Arbab Niaz Stadium, Peshawar

Peshawar 186 (Mohammad Altaf 4 for 45)
Bahawalpur 257 (Shakeel Ahmed, 84, Farrukh Zaman 5 for 94, Arshad Khan 5 for 98)

Match drawn

Bahawalpur 5 pts., Peshawar 0 pts.

at LCCA Ground, Lahore

Lahore 246 (Kashif Khan 92 not out, Naved Nazir 4 for 68) and 257 for 7 dec. (Tariq Javed 75, Ali Zia 55)
Faisalabad 210 (Sami-ul-Haq 62 not out) and 87 for 6

Match drawn

Lahore 5 pts., Faisalabad 0 pts.

at Sargodha Stadium, Sargodha

Sargodha 194 (Sabih Azhar 5 for 69, Naeem Akhtar 4 for 64) and 84 (Sabih Azhar 6 for 40)
Rawalpindi 103 (Naeem Khan 7 for 42) and 121 (Mohammad Hasnain 5 for 28)

Sargodha won by 54 runs

Sargodha 10 pts., Rawalpindi 0 pts.

Lahore's first-innings lead over Faisalabad took them into the semi-finals. Kashif Khan hit the highest score of his career, being deprived of his century when Nadeem Ghauri was run out in the 80th over after helping to add 58 for the last wicket.

FINAL TABLE

	P	W	L	D	Pts
Rawalpindi	8	4	2	2	50
Karachi Whites	8	4	2	2	40
Bahawalpur	8	3	2	3	35
Lahore	8	2	1	5	35
Multan	8	1	2	5	35
Sargodha	8	2	1	5	25
Faisalabad	8	2	2	4	25
Peshawar	8	2	3	3	25
Karachi Blues	8	1	6	1	15

SEMI-FINALS

21, 22, 23 and **24** December, 1991 *at Qaddafi Stadium, Lahore*

Lahore 371 (Aamir Malik 84, Tariq Javed 80, Shahid Saeed 64, Ali Zia 61 not out) and 254 for 5 (Tariq Javed 72, Mansoor Rana 70 not out, Aamir Malik 64)
Rawalpindi 201 (Naeem Akhtar 57)

Match drawn

at National Stadium, Karachi

Bahawalpur 161 (Athar Laeeq 5 for 69, Hamayun Fida Hussain 4 for 51) and 291 (Imran Zia 55)
Karachi Whites 297 for 7 (Azam Khan 109, Asif Mujtaba 76) and 157 for 1 (Ghulam Ali 94)

Karachi Whites won by 9 wickets

Lahore entered the final by virtue of their first-innings lead over Rawalpindi who had won the toss and put their opponents in to bat. Shahid Saeed and Tariq Javed established a commanding position with an opening stand of 121, and there were fine innings by Aamir Malik and Ali Zia. Rawalpindi were all out shortly after lunch on the third day, but Ashraf Ali, who led Lahore well, did not enforce the follow-on. Play was brought to an early close on the last day through bad light.

Karachi Whites won a crucial toss at Karachi, and quickly accounted for Bahawalpur on a damp wicket. An enterprising innings from Asif Mujtaba gave Karachi a substantial first-innings lead. He shared a fourth-wicket stand of 159 with centurion Azam Khan who hit nine fours. Bahawalpur recovered well in their second innings, and Karachi Whites were left to make 156 on the final day. Ghulam Ali was in blistering form and hit 94 in a first-wicket partnership of 144 with Azam Khan. Ghulam hit 16 fours.

FINAL

27, 28, 29, 30 and **31** December, 1991 *at National Stadium, Karachi*

Karachi Whites 364 (Ghulam Ali 164, Aamir Hanif 121) and 306 (Moin-ul-Atiq 88, Manzoor Akhtar 71, Shahid Ali Khan 4 for 54)
Lahore 288 (Fayyaz Shah 79, Ashraf Ali 61, Ali Zia 56, Athar Laeeq 5 for 119) and 43 for 0

Match drawn

Karachi Whites retained the Quaid-e-Azam Trophy by virtue of their first-innings lead in the drawn final. Lahore needed to score 383 in 40 overs on the last afternoon. Dropped catches on the fourth day cost Lahore what chances they had. Annoyed by controversial umpiring decisions, Lahore refused to attend the presentation ceremony.

In the absence of Asif Mujtaba, who was unwell, Iqbal Sikander led Karachi Whites, but the outstanding contributions came from Ghulam Ali and Aamir Hanif who shared a third-wicket stand of 247 after the Whites had been put in to bat.

BCCP PATRON'S TROPHY

4, 5, 6 and 7 January, 1992 *at National Stadium, Karachi*

United Bank 271 (Mansoor Akhtar 74, Rashid Latif 51) and 147 (Fakhruddin Baloch 4 for 45)
PACO 303 for 3 (Ghulam Ali 136, Aamir Hanif 104 not out) and 116 for 2 (Shahid Saeed 55 not out)

PACO won by 8 wickets

PACO 10 pts., United Bank 0 pts.

at KDA Ground

PNSC v. PIA

Match abandoned

No points

at Qaddafi Stadium, Lahore

Pakistan Universities 102 (Habib Baloch 6 for 48, Barkatullah 4 for 52) and 336 (Rizwan Umer 149)
National Bank 300 (Shahid Anwar 81, Ameer Akbar 56) and 142 for 2 (Sajid Ali 68, Shahid Anwar 62 not out)

National Bank won by 8 wickets

National Bank 10 pts., Pakistan Universities 0 pts.

at Jinnah Park Stadium, Sialkot

ADBP 250 (Mansoor Rana 76, Nadeem Ghauri 5 for 69) and 59 for 2
Habib Bank 267 (Shakeel Ahmed 64, Qasim Shera 5 for 52)

Match drawn

Habib Bank 5 pts., ADBP 0 pts.

The Patron's Trophy, competed for by departmental teams, was condensed into the first two months of 1992. For PACO, Ghulam Ali and Aamir Hanif displayed the form that they had shown for Karachi Whites.

12, 13, 14 and 15 January, 1992 *at Agha Khan Gymkhana Ground, Karachi*

United Bank 343 for 5 (Basit Ali 74, Mansoor Akhtar 74, Aamir Basheer 71, Raees Ahmed 56) and 296 (Aamir Basheer 93, Saifullah 80, Pervez Shah 72, Mohsin Kamal 6 for 60)
PNSC 259 (Sohail Miandad 126, Aamir Ishaq 67, Raees Ahmed 4 for 26) and 303 for 5 (Sohail Miandad 99, Mohammad Javed 60)

Match drawn

United Bank 5 pts., PNSC 0 pts.

at Iqbal Stadium, Faisalabad

PACO 246 (Shahid Saeed 89, Shahid Nawaz 62, Asif Mujtaba 5 for 38) and 121 (Ghulam Ali 55, Iqbal Sikander 5 for 29)
PIA 288 (Aamir Malik 104, Rizwan-uz-Zaman 52, Shahid Mahboob 7 for 109) and 82 for 1

PIA won by 9 wickets

PIA 10 pts., PACO 0 pts.

at Bagh-e-Jinnah Ground, Lahore

Habib Bank 349 for 7 (Shaukat Mirza 88, Moin-ul-Atiq 59, Naved Anjum 52)
Pakistan Universities 149 (Nadeem Ghauri 5 for 24, Naved Anjum 4 for 62) and 218 for 5 (Mushid Jamshid 85, Ahmed Munir 50)

Match drawn

Habib Bank 5 pts., Pakistan Universities 0 pts.

at LCCA Ground, Lahore

ADBP 282 (Zahoor Elahi 67, Saeed Anwar 50, Iqbal Qasim 6 for 78)
National Bank 285 for 5 (Saeed Azad 97, Sajid Ali 64)

Match drawn

National Bank 5 pts., ADBP 0 pts.

Bad weather hit the second round of matches. There was no play possible on the first day in Lahore, nor on the second at the LCCA Ground. Aamir Ishaq and Sohail Miandad began PNSC's innings with a stand of 163.

18, 19, 20 and 21 January, 1992 *at Montgomery Biscuit Factory Ground, Sahiwal*

PNSC 333 for 8 (Aamir Ishaq 123, Nasir Wasti 71, Mehmood Hamid 63, Shahid Mahboob 4 for 111) and 409 for 5 (Mehmood Hamid 115 not out, Nasir Wasti 67, Aamir Ishaq 56)
PACO 296 (Ghulam Ali 83, Ayaz Jilani 53, Amin Lakhani 7 for 119)

Match drawn

PNSC 5 pts., PACO 0 pts.

at Iqbal Stadium, Faisalabad

PIA 303 for 9 (Aamir Malik 142, Zahid Ahmed 58, Sajid Khan 53) and 183 (Tanvir Mehdi 5 for 58)
United Bank 306 for 5 (Basit Ali 107) and 183 for 7 (Basit Ali 96)

United Bank won by 3 wickets

United Bank 10 pts., PIA 0 pts.

at Qaddafi Stadium, Lahore

Pakistan Universities 89 (Zakir Khan 6 for 36) and 169 (Zakir Khan 5 for 64)

ADBP 222 for 9 dec. (Ghaffar Kazmi 79 not out, Asad-ullah-Butt 6 for 91) and 38 for 0

ADBP won by 10 wickets

ADBP 10 pts., Pakistan Universities 0 pts.

at LCCA Ground, Lahore

National Bank 151 (Naved Anjum 9 for 45) and 298 (Sajid Ali 143, Tahir Shah 54, Sarmad Khan 6 for 121)
Habib Bank 375 (Aamir Sohail 124, Naved Anjum 115, Shahid Javed 71 not out, Barkatullah 4 for 71, Iqbal Qasim 4 for 89) and 75 for 1

Habib Bank won by 9 wickets

Habib Bank 10 pts., National Bank 0 pts.

Aamir Malik continued his outstanding form, but two splendid innings from Basit Ali won the match for United Bank. A spectacular all-round performance from discarded Test man Naved Anjum was the feature of Habib Bank's win over National Bank.

25, 26, 27 and 28 January, 1992 *at LCCA Ground, Lahore*

PACO 161 (Ghulam Ali 57, Iqbal Qasim 4 for 44)
National Bank 177 for 4 (Shahid Anwar 59)

Match drawn

National Bank 5 pts., PACO 0 pts.

at Iqbal Stadium, Faisalabad

PNSC 93 (Naeed Khan 5 for 25, Naved Anjum 5 for 58)
Habib Bank 165 for 8 (Nadeem Afzal 4 for 81)

Match drawn

Habib Bank 5 pts., PNSC 0 pts.

at Model Town Ground, Lahore

PIA v. Pakistan Universities

Match abandoned

No points

at KRL Ground, Rawalpindi

United Bank v. ADBP

Match abandoned

No points

1, 2, 3 and 4 February, 1992 *at Bagh-i-Jinnah Ground, Lahore*

PACO 216 (Umar Rasheed 71, Naved Anjum 4 for 59)
Habib Bank 183 (Mohammad Zahid 4 for 47)

Match drawn

PACO 5 pts., Habib Bank 0 pts.

at Iqbal Stadium, Faisalabad

PNSC 231 and 271 for 2 (Sohail Jaffer 84 not out, Aamir Ishaq 66)
National Bank 298 (Ameer Akbar 79, Shahid Anwar 68, Tahir Shah 62, Sajjad Akbar 6 for 118)

Match drawn

National Bank 5 pts., PNSC 0 pts.

at LCCA Ground, Lahore

United Bank 279 for 6 (Basit Ali 134, Raees Ahmed 59)
Pakistan Universities 93 (Masood Anwar 6 for 23) and 54 (Masood Anwar 6 for 24, Tauseef Ahmed 4 for 24)

United Bank won by an innings and 132 runs

United Bank 10 pts., Pakistan Universities 0 pts.

at KRL Ground, Rawalpindi

PIA 298 (Rizwan-uz-Zaman 95, Sajid Khan 65, Javed Hayat 7 for 81) and 51 for 2
ADBP 248 for 9 (Mansoor Rana 93, Iqbal Sikander 5 for 85)

Match drawn

ADBP 3 pts., PIA 3 pts.

In the fourth and fifth rounds of matches, no game was able to escape the rain, but United Bank managed to achieve a remarkable victory over the weak Universities side even though play was possible only on the last two days.

8, 9, 10 and 11 February, 1992 *at LCCA Ground, Lahore*

ADBP 287 for 7 (Zahoor Elahi 90, Yahya Toor 4 for 83)
PACO 270 (Kamran Khan 109, Aamir Hanif 52, Javed Hayat 6 for 104)

Match drawn

ADBP 5 pts., PACO 0 pts.

at Qaddafi Stadium, Lahore

PNSC 375 (Nasir Wasti 134, Mehmood Hamid 84, Asad-ullah-Butt 4 for 122) and 189 for 5 (Sohail Jaffer 51)
Pakistan Universities 259 for 6 (Mushid Jamshid 79, Aziz-ur-Rehman 50 not out, Ahmed Munir 50) and 185 for 7 (Mohsin Kamal 4 for 72)

Match drawn

PNSC 5 pts., Pakistan Universities 0 pts.

at KRL Ground, Rawalpindi

National Bank 337 for 8 (Tahir Shah 89, Ameer Akbar 68, Sajid Ali 53)
PIA 240 (Aamir Malik 83, Iqbal Qasim 5 for 81)

Match drawn

National Bank 5 pts., PIA 0 pts.

at Iqbal Stadium, Faisalabad

Habib Bank 357 for 7 (Shaukat Mirza 139, Shahid Javed 89, Moin-ul-Atiq 65) and 178 (Tauseef Ahmed 7 for 46)
United Bank 186 (Saifullah 59, Nadeem Ghauri 5 for 71) and 187 (Masood Anwar 56, Nadeem Ghauri 4 for 51, Naved Anjum 4 for 68)

Habib Bank won by 162 runs

Habib Bank 10 pts., United Bank 0 pts.

Habib Bank's win over United Bank assured them of a place in the final while National Bank looked likely to join them after taking first-innings points in the rain-affected match in Rawalpindi. They owed much to the wiles of veteran left-arm spinner Iqbal Qasim.

15, 16, 17 and 18 February, 1992 *at Qaddafi Stadium, Lahore*

Pakistan Universities 295 for 6 (Aziz-ur-Rehman 84 not out, Idrees Baig 78, Shahid Mahboob 4 for 94) and 289 (Mushid Jamshid 117, Idrees Baig 71, Ata-ur-Rehman 8 for 87)
PACO 347 for 7 (Abadullah Khan 90, Umar Rasheed 56, Yahya Toor 51 not out, Asaf-ukkah-Butt 4 for 142) and 239 for 1 (Ghulam Ali 102 not out, Kamran Khan 56 not out)

PACO won by 9 wickets

PACO 10 pts., Pakistan Universities 0 pts.

at LCCA Ground, Lahore

PNSC 282 for 9 (Sohail Miandad 67, Raja Afaq 6 for 85)
ADBP 285 for 3 (Mansoor Rana 124 not out, Zahoor Elahi 121)

Match drawn

ADBP 5 pts., PNSC 0 pts.

at National Stadium, Karachi

PIA 255 for 9 (Naved Anjum 6 for 84) and 294 for 5 (Rizwan-uz-Zaman 142, Aamir Malik 52)
Habib Bank 191 (Wasim Haider 5 for 50) and 197 for 8 (Moin-ul-Atiq 50, Ashfaq Ahmed 6 for 69)

Match drawn

PIA 5 pts., Habib Bank 0 pts.

at KRL Ground, Rawalpindi

United Bank 284 (Basit Ali 72, Raees Ahmed 53, Hafeez-ur-Rehman 4 for 104)
National Bank 218 (Saeed Azad 61, Shahid Anwar 60, Tauseef Ahmed 6 for 112)

Match drawn

United Bank 5 pts., National Bank 0 pts.

At a late hour, the BCCP decided that there were to be no semi-finals and that the two leading teams, Habib Bank and National Bank, would contest the final. The decision did not please PACO and United Bank. The reason for the alteration to the schedule was the number of protests that had not been judged. BCCP also suggested that the approach of Ramadan did not allow time for the semi-finals, but as Ramadan did not begin until 5 March, this was hardly a valid reason.

FINAL TABLE

	P	W	L	D	Ab	Pts
Habib Bank	7	2	–	5	–	35
National Bank	7	1	1	5	–	30
United Bank	7	2	2	2	1	30
PACO	7	2	1	4	–	25
ADBP	7	1	–	5	1	23
PIA	7	1	1	3	2	18
PNSC	7	–	–	6	1	10
Pakistan Universities	7	–	4	2	1	0

FINAL

23, 24, 25, 26 and 27 February, 1992 *at Qaddafi Stadium, Lahore*

Habib Bank 379 (Agha Zahid 72, Anwar Miandad 67, Shakeel Ahmed 50, Iqbal Qasim 4 for 48) and 390 (Shaukat Mirza 141)
National Bank 246 (Shahid Tanvir 84, Saeed Azad 51, Shakeel Khan 4 for 47) and 20 for 1

Match drawn

Habib Bank took the Patron's Trophy by virtue of their first-innings lead. The game began late because of the non-arrival of umpire Riazuddin. Ninety minutes later Shakoor Rana deputised when it was discovered that Riazuddin had not been informed that he was to stand in the final. Chaos plagued domestic cricket in Pakistan until the end.

A solid foundation from Shakeel Ahmed and Moin-ul-Atiq made it possible for Habib Bank to reach 175 for 3 on the first day. Three wickets fell for two runs, but skipper Agha Zahid and Anwar Miandad prevented a collapse, and with a late flourish from Naved Anjum, six fours in his 43, Habib Bank reached 379. Naved then dismissed Wasim Arif, and National Bank were 17 for 1 at the close of the second day.

Naved Anjum and Shakeel Khan blighted any hope National Bank had on the third day, and Nadeem Ghauri stifled the run-scoring, sending down 28 overs to take 1 for 39. Habib Bank used the fourth day, and much of the fifth, for batting practice, deciding to hold on to their advantage and the trophy.

FIRST-CLASS AVERAGES

BATTING

	M	Inns	NO	Runs	HS	Av	100s	50s
Aamir Sohail (HB)	3	5	–	386	124	77.20	2	1
Mansoor Rana (L/ADBP)	10	13	4	618	124*	68.66	1	5
Zahoor Elahi (M/ADBP)	14	21	4	1103	148	64.88	4	4
Aamir Malik (L/PIA)	13	22	2	1269	162	63.45	4	8
Sahid Saeed (L/PACO)	14	24	3	1222	161	58.19	3	8
Shaukat Mirza (HB)	7	9	1	442	141	55.25	2	1
Ghulam Ali (KW/PACO)	12	20	1	988	164	52.00	3	5
Ashraf Ali (L)	9	14	5	461	107*	51.22	1	3
Mahmood Hamid (PNSC)	6	9	2	347	115*	49.57	1	2
Basit Ali (KW/UB)	7	12	–	594	134	49.50	2	4
Mujahid Jamshed (U)	6	12	–	586	149	48.83	2	2
Masroor Hussain (M)	7	12	3	420	80	46.66	–	2
Ali Zia (L)	7	11	2	412	61*	45.77	–	6
Mohammad Ramzan (F)	8	16	–	721	144	45.06	2	4
Sohail Miandad (PNSC)	6	10	–	440	126	44.00	1	2
Iqbal Salim (KB)	8	16	2	603	172*	43.07	1	3
Tariq Javed (L)	5	10	1	385	80	42.77	–	3
Aamir Ishaq (PNSC)	6	10	–	426	123	42.60	1	3
Azam Khan (KW)	9	18	3	627	135*	41.80	2	2
Nasir Wasti (PNSC)	6	9	–	374	134	41.55	1	2
Asif Mujtaba (KW/PIA)	14	25	7	735	105*	40.83	2	3
Sajid Ali (KB/NB)	12	18	–	729	143	40.50	1	5
Shahid Anwar	17	27	2	1002	161	40.08	1	7
Ameer-ud-din (KB)	8	16	–	640	122	40.00	2	4
Ghaffar Kazmi (R/ADBP)	11	15	4	415	79*	37.72	–	4
Umar Rasheed (B/PACO)	15	22	3	706	147*	37.15	1	4
Sagheer Abbas (P/PIA)	10	15	3	438	156*	36.50	2	–
Rizwan-uz-Zaman (KB/PIA)	9	17	1	582	142	36.37	1	4
Aamir Hanif (KW/PACO)	15	24	3	757	163*	36.04	3	2
Raees Ahmed (UB)	6	10	–	359	59	35.90	–	3
Shahid Javed (R/HB)	16	26	6	718	105*	35.90	1	3
Tahir Shah (NB)	9	11	1	359	89	35.90	1	3
Moin-ul-Atiq (KW/HB)	12	19	–	673	88	35.42	–	6
Manzoor Elahi (M/ADBP)	14	16	–	562	85	35.12	–	4
Naseer Ahmed (R)	9	15	1	486	101*	34.71	1	5
Sohail Jaffer (PNSC)	6	10	1	307	84*	34.11	–	2
Tariq Mahboob (M)	8	13	3	334	80	33.40	–	2
Shakeel Ahmed (B/HB)	15	26	1	827	84	33.08	–	7
Shahid Nawaz (F/PACO)	11	19	3	523	112	32.68	1	3
Naved Anjum (HB)	9	12	1	354	115	32.18	1	1
Mohammad Salim (P)	8	14	2	386	63	32.16	–	2
Saeed Azad (KW/NB)	9	13	1	368	97	30.66	–	3
Pervez Shah (S/UB)	11	19	3	481	84	30.06	–	3
Mohammad Ashraf (F)	7	14	3	314	67	28.54	–	1
Rizwan Umar (S/U)	9	17	–	481	151	28.29	1	3
Bilal Rana (B)	8	15	1	393	92	28.07	–	3
Azhar Sultan (S)	8	15	–	407	75	27.13	–	3
Sajjad Akbar (S/PNSC)	14	23	7	430	67*	26.87	–	3
Sher Ali (P)	8	14	–	376	93	26.85	–	2
Munir-ul-Haq (KB)	8	16	–	414	111	25.87	1	3
Aamir Bashir (M/UB)	14	20	–	504	93	25.20	–	3
Ijaz Ahmed (F)	7	13	–	324	100	24.92	1	1
Salim Taj (R)	9	17	2	373	42	24.86	–	–
Arshad Pervez (S/HB)	9	16	2	337	65	24.07	–	1
Mohammad Hasnain (S)	8	16	–	384	58	24.00	–	2
Mohammad Nawaz (S)	8	16	1	354	77	23.60	–	1
Raja Arshad (M/UB)	11	17	1	376	56	23.50	–	2
Rashid Latif (KB/UB)	11	18	4	303	53	21.64	–	3
Aziz-ur-Rehman (S/U)	11	21	2	401	84*	21.10	–	2
Bilal Ahmed (F/ADBP)	13	21	2	389	126	20.47	1	–

(Qualification – 300 runs)

BOWLING

	Overs	Mds	Runs	Wkts	Av	Best	10/m	5/inn
Shakeel Ahmed (R)	116.5	18	342	24	14.25	6-35	1	2
Fazal Hussain (F)	96.1	20	250	16	15.62	7-41	–	1
Naved Anjum (HB)	241.4	48	748	47	15.91	9-45	1	3
Mohammad Altaf (B)	142.1	33	362	21	17.23	5-77	–	1
Mohammad Hasnain (KB)	132.2	16	486	28	17.35	8-61	1	2
Waqar Younis (Pakistan)	83.3	10	279	16	17.43	5-65	–	2
Iqbal Qasim (NB)	229.4	55	515	28	18.39	6-78	–	2
Mohsin Mirza (KW)	209.3	51	483	26	18.57	8-92	1	2
Bilal Rana (B)	185.3	38	558	30	18.60	7-57	1	2
Javed Hayat (ADBP)	95.4	18	299	16	18.68	7-81	–	2
Mohsin Kamal (PNSC)	81	8	301	16	18.81	6-60	–	1
Naeem A. Khan (S/NB)	280	37	964	48	20.08	7-42	2	5
Saadat Gul (F)	135.5	27	452	22	20.54	5-52	–	1
Iqbal Sikander (KW/PIA)	307.1	56	887	42	21.11	7-34	1	5
Zahir Shah (R)	99.3	5	338	16	21.12	5-73	–	1
Mohammad Riaz (R)	204.1	45	587	26	22.57	6-63	–	3
Masood Anwar (M/UB)	684.4	176	1672	72	23.22	6-23	1	4
Zakir Khan (P/ADBP)	203.2	47	583	25	23.32	6-36	1	3
Sabih Azhar (R)	140.2	29	421	18	23.38	6-40	1	2
Shahid Hussain (P)	194.3	32	516	22	23.45	6-40	–	2
Shahid Mahboob (KW/PACO)	264	42	857	36	23.80	7-109	–	2
Mohammad Zahid (B/PACO)	279.3	55	837	35	23.91	4-20	–	–
Asif Mujtaba (KW/PIA)	269	70	694	29	23.93	5-38	1	2
Nadeem Afzal (F/PNSC)	139.3	22	506	21	24.09	5-77	–	1
Raja Afaq (R/ADBP)	229.3	36	702	29	24.20	6-85	–	2
Shahid A. Khan (L/U)	198	38	540	22	24.54	4-54	–	–
Farrukh Zaman (P)	184.3	24	595	24	24.79	5-90	–	2
Tanvir Mehdi (L/UB)	314.3	42	1134	45	25.20	7-74	1	3
Nadeem Ghauri (L/HB)	516	143	1363	54	25.24	5-24	–	4
Athar Laeeq (KW)	248.5	44	760	30	25.33	5-60	–	3
Kabir Khan (P)	165.1	25	558	22	25.36	7-69	1	2
Naseer Shaukat (F)	94	7	387	15	25.80	7-62	–	1
Barkatullah (KB/NB)	180.2	27	612	23	26.60	4-52	–	–
Baqar Rizvi (KB)	85.3	2	428	16	26.75	6-75	–	2
Habib Baloch (NB)	105	10	435	16	27.18	6-48	–	1
Tanvir Afzal (F)	173.1	20	521	19	27.42	5-90	–	1
Tauseef Ahmed (UB)	251	53	715	26	27.50	7-46	–	2
Haaris A.Khan (KB)	379	70	1056	38	27.78	5-83	–	2
Ata-ur-Rehman (L/PACO)	149.3	24	480	17	28.23	8-87	–	1
Pervez Shah (S/UB)	137	30	433	15	28.86	3-23	–	–
Nadeem Khan (KB/NB)	451.1	70	1493	49	30.46	5-56	1	4
Naeem Akhtar (R)	192	37	552	18	30.66	4-64	–	–
Hafeez-ur-Rehman (NB)	153	15	510	16	31.87	4-104	–	–
Aamir Hanif (KW/PACO)	175	32	539	16	33.68	6-125	–	1
Naved Nazir (F)	201.4	52	543	16	33.93	5-64	–	1
Mohammad Asif (L/ADBP)	320	61	837	24	34.87	5-65	–	2
Aziz-ur-Rehman (S/U)	194	26	569	16	35.56	5-62	–	1
Asadullah Butt (U)	187.5	34	676	19	35.57	6-91	–	1
Zahid Ahmed (P/PIA)	166	29	538	15	35.86	4-48	–	–
Sajjad Akbar (S/PNSC)	444.3	56	1301	36	36.13	6-118	–	2
Manzoor Elahi (M/ADBP)	201.1	36	560	15	37.33	2-21	–	–
Nadeem Naazir (M)	423.3	46	1494	39	38.30	5-102	–	1
Amin Lakhani (PNSC)	192	33	641	15	42.73	7-119	–	1

(Qualification – 15 wickets)

LEADING FIELDERS

29 – Ashraf Ali (L) (ct 26/st 3); 26 – Bilal Ahmed (F/ADBP) (ct 22/st 4); 25 – Wasim Arif (NB) (ct 16/st 9); 23 – Rashid Latif (KB/UB) (ct 14/st 9); 22 – Tahir Rasheed (HB) (ct 18/st 4); 19 – Asif Mujtaba (KW/PIA); 18 – Nadeem Abbasi (R) (ct 15/st 3); Sanaullah (PACO); and Iqbal Salim (KB) (ct 14/st 4); 16 – Sajid Ali (KB/NB) and Mohammad Zahid (B/PACO); 15 – Aamir Iqbal (KW) (ct 14/st 1); Mohammad Shafiq (M) (ct 9/st 6); Shakeel Ahmed (B/HB) (ct 13/st 2); Kashif Khan (L); and Zahoor Elahi (M/ADBP); 14 – Manzoor Elahi (M/ADBP); 13 – Haider Nisar (PIA) (ct 9/st 4); Azam Khan (KW); and Iqbal Imam (KB/UB); 12 – Dildar Malik (M) (ct 11/st 1); Salim Yousuf (KW); Naseer Ahmed (R); and Aamir Hanif (KW/PACO)

Abbreviations for team names used

ADBP – Agricultural Development Bank of Pakistan; B – Bahawalpur; F – Faisalabad; HB – Habib Bank; KB – Karachi Blues; KW – Karachi Whites; L – Lahore; M – Multan; NB – National Bank; P – Peshawar; PACO – Pakistan Automobile Corporation; PIA – Pakistan International Airlines; PNSC – Pakistan National Shipping Corporation; R – Rawalpindi; S – Sargodha; U – Pakistan Universities; UB – United Bank

ZIMBABWE

Australia 'B' team tour
Zimbabwe v. South Africa
Durham CCC tour
Facts and figures by John R. Ward

Kevin Arnott – a consistently good season for Zimbabwe. (David Munden)

AUSTRALIA 'B' TOUR

FIRST ONE-DAY INTERNATIONAL
ZIMBABWE v. AUSTRALIA 'B'

Australia sent a very strong 'B' side to Zimbabwe in an effort to prepare both countries for the World Cup and to help Zimbabwe in their advance towards Test status. The Australians were led by Mark Taylor who had two other players rich in Test experience, Moody and Steve Waugh, in his side. The party began their brief tour with the first of three one-day internationals and, obviously not yet acclimatised, they struggled against some good off-spin bowling and brilliant fielding after they had elected to bat first.

Arnott and Flower gave Zimbabwe a solid start, scoring 95 before Flower was run out by Moody, and there was never any doubt that the home side would win.

The tourists won a non-first-class game against Zimbabwe 'B'.

SECOND ONE-DAY INTERNATIONAL
ZIMBABWE v. AUSTRALIA 'B'

Zimbabwe, eager to give players experience for the World Cup, made three changes for the second of the one-day internationals. Put in to bat, Australia lost two wickets cheaply, but Law and Steve Waugh batted excitingly in a stand of 97. Waugh's 116 came off 126 balls.

Arnott and Andy Flower again gave Zimbabwe a fine start against some erratic bowling, but the medium pace of Tucker and the leg-spin of McIntyre tore apart the middle order, and the home side sank to a miserable defeat.

FIRST ONE-DAY INTERNATIONAL – ZIMBABWE v. AUSTRALIA 'B'
8 September, 1991 at Harare Sports Club

AUSTRALIA 'B'

M.A. Taylor (capt)	c Traicos, b Omarshah	10
T.M. Moody	c Omarshah, b Peall	42
S.G. Law	c and b Peall	31
S.R. Waugh	b Traicos	4
M.G. Bevan	c Flower, b Traicos	2
R.J. Tucker	b Traicos	25
*T.J. Nielsen	c Jarvis, b Campbell	17
S.K. Warne	c Pycroft, b Traicos	3
P.R. Reiffel	b Burmester	11
W.J. Holdsworth	c Omarshah, b Burmester	16
D.J. Hickey	not out	6
Extras	lb 2, w 3, nb 1	6
		173

(49.1 overs)

	O	M	R	W
Jarvis	10	1	39	–
Burmester	8.1	1	29	2
Omarshah	7	–	37	1
Peall	10	–	28	2
Traicos	10	1	20	4
Campbell	4	–	18	1

FALL OF WICKETS
1–24, 2–66, 3–82, 4–94, 5–98, 6–135, 7–139, 8–142, 9–166

ZIMBABWE

K.J. Arnott	c Warne, b Holdsworth	85
* A. Flower	run out	30
A.D.R. Campbell	c Moody, b Waugh	4
A.J. Pycroft	c Waugh, b Holdsworth	9
D.L. Houghton (capt)	not out	12
G.A. Paterson	not out	10
A.H. Omarshah		
M.G. Burmester		
S.G. Peall		
A.J. Traicos		
M.P. Jarvis		
Extras	b 1, lb 3, w 16, nb 6	26
	(for 4 wickets)	176

(44.3 overs)

	O	M	R	W
Holdsworth	10	–	39	2
Hickey	5.3	–	26	–
Reiffel	7	–	28	–
Warne	10	2	33	–
Bevan	3	–	19	–
Waugh	5	–	18	1
Tucker	4	–	9	–

FALL OF WICKETS
1–95, 2–105, 3–142, 4–154

Umpires: K. Kanjee & E. Gilmour

Zimbabwe won by 6 wickets

THIRD ONE-DAY INTERNATIONAL
ZIMBABWE v. AUSTRALIA 'B'

Houghton again asked Australia to bat first and was rewarded by three quick wickets. Typically, the visitors continued to attack, and Waugh and Bevan added 110, with Waugh reaching his century off 115 balls. He was then dropped twice and fell eventually to the last ball of the innings.

Pycroft played one of his very best innings for Zimbabwe and hit 100 off 108 balls. He and Butchart added 73 and gave Zimbabwe hope of victory, but a brilliant catch at fine-leg by Holdsworth accounted for Butchart and effectively turned the course of the match.

Andy Pycroft played one of his finest innings for Zimbabwe in the third one-day international match against Australia 'B'. (David Munden)

SECOND ONE-DAY INTERNATIONAL – ZIMBABWE v. AUSTRALIA 'B'
15 September, 1991 at Bulawayo Athletic Club

AUSTRALIA 'B'

M.A. Taylor (capt)	c Omarshah, **b** Jarvis	12
T.M. Moody	run out	6
S.G. Law	c Waller, **b** Omarshah	53
S.R. Waugh	not out	116
M.G. Bevan	c and **b** Jarvis	28
R.J. Tucker	lbw, **b** Jarvis	14
*T.J. Nielsen	c Houghton, **b** Butchart	2
P.R. Reiffel	**b** Jarvis	2
S.K. Warne	not out	3
P.E. McIntyre		
W.J. Holdsworth		
Extras	lb 2, w 5, nb 1	8
	(for 7 wickets)	**244**

ZIMBABWE

K.J. Arnott	c Nielsen, **b** Warne	61
* A. Flower	**b** McIntyre	49
N.P. Hough	**b** Tucker	18
D.L. Houghton (capt)	c Moody, **b** Tucker	14
A.J. Pycroft	not out	30
A.C. Waller	c Moody, **b** Tucker	3
I.P. Butchart	st Nielsen, **b** McIntyre	0
A.H. Omarshah	st Nielsen, **b** McIntyre	7
S.G. Peall	**b** Tucker	6
M.P. Jarvis	**b** Waugh	1
A.J. Traicos	run out	3
Extras	b 2, lb 2, w 11, nb 2	17
		209

(50 overs)

	O	M	R	W
Jarvis	10	–	46	**4**
Butchart	10	–	51	**1**
Omarshah	10	–	60	**1**
Peall	10	–	53	–
Traicos	10	–	32	–

(48.4 overs)

	O	M	R	W
Holdsworth	5	2	16	–
Reiffel	7.4	–	34	–
Warne	10	1	37	**1**
Waugh	6	1	25	**1**
McIntyre	10	–	52	**3**
Tucker	10	–	41	**4**

FALL OF WICKETS
1–11, **2**–28, **3**–125, **4**–175, **5**–220, **6**–223, **7**–226

FALL OF WICKETS
1–106, **2**–141, **3**–143, **4**–166, **5**–182, **6**–182, **7**–193, **8**–200, **9**–203

Umpires: K. Kanjee & E. Gilmour

Australia 'B' won by 35 runs

THIRD ONE-DAY INTERNATIONAL – ZIMBABWE v. AUSTRALIA 'B'

22 September, 1991 at Harare Sports Club

AUSTRALIA 'B'

M.A. Taylor (capt)	b Jarvis	5
T.M. Moody	c Houghton, b Omarshah	17
S.G. Law	b Brandes	3
S.R. Waugh	c Omarshah, b Butchart	116
M.G. Bevan	run out	55
R.J. Tucker	c Traicos, b Butchart	19
* T.J. Nielsen	c Houghton, b Butchart	9
P.R. Reiffel	run out	9
S.K. Warne	not out	11
W.J. Holdsworth		
P.E. McIntyre		
Extras	lb 2, w 1, nb 1	4
	(for 8 wickets)	248

ZIMBABWE

K.J. Arnott	c Nielsen, b Waugh	25
A. Flower	c Waugh, b Tucker	21
D.L. Houghton (capt)	b Warne	24
A.J. Pycroft	run out	104
*W.R. James	run out	1
A.H. Omarshah	run out	19
I.P. Butchart	c Holdsworth, b Tucker	17
E.A. Brandes	b Tucker	4
A.J. Traicos	c Waugh, b Tucker	0
M.P. Jarvis	c and b Waugh	12
A.G. Huckle	not out	1
Extras	lb 7, w 1, nb 4	12
		240

(50 overs)

	O	M	R	W
Brandes	10	1	30	1
Jarvis	10	–	55	1
Omarshah	9	–	53	1
Huckle	5	–	33	–
Traicos	10	–	43	–
Butchart	6	–	32	3

(49.5 overs)

	O	M	R	W
Holdsworth	6	–	21	–
Reiffel	8.5	1	37	–
Tucker	10	–	41	4
Waugh	10	1	52	2
Warne	6	–	32	1
McIntyre	9	–	50	–

FALL OF WICKETS

1–19, 2–26, 3–39, 4–149, 5–185, 6–203, 7–219, 8–248

FALL OF WICKETS

1–50, 2–50, 3–92, 4–97, 5–170, 6–208, 7–214, 8–214, 9–230

Umpires: R. Suchet & I.D. Robinson

Australia 'B' won by 8 runs

FIRST INTERNATIONAL MATCH

ZIMBABWE v. AUSTRALIA 'B', at Bulawayo

Weakened by the absence of Brandes and Duers, Zimbabwe also chose to leave out Traicos to give experience to the young off-spinner Peall. In spite of the thinness of his attack, Houghton asked Australia to bat first on a moist wicket. The pitch quickly dried, and the visitors were soon scoring freely. Moody and Steve Waugh joined together in a third-wicket partnership of 240, the highest stand for this wicket in first-class cricket in Zimbabwe.

Moody reached his century off 173 balls, and Waugh, having hit his first 50 off 41 deliveries, moved to three figures off 136 balls. Australia ended the first day at 409 for 7, and on the second morning, Reiffel and Hickey plundered 60 off six overs for the last wicket.

Grant Flower began brightly, but he became more and more introspective, and his innings of 74 occupied 234 balls. His slowness increased the pressure on his partners, and, having finished the second day at 171 for 7, Zimbabwe were soon following-on on the third morning.

Arnott batted with great fluency in an opening stand of 94, but Grant Flower was even more cautious than he had been in the first innings, and he batted 363 balls for his 84. On the last morning, wickets fell quickly, and only a pugnacious last-wicket stand by Peall and Jarvis helped Zimbabwe to avoid an innings defeat.

FIRST INTERNATIONAL MATCH – ZIMBABWE v. AUSTRALIA 'B'

16, 17, 18 and 19 September, 1991 at Bulawayo Athletic Club

AUSTRALIA 'B'

	FIRST INNINGS		SECOND INNINGS	
J. Cox	c A. Flower, b Jarvis	8	not out	6
M.A. Taylor (capt)	c Houghton, b Omarshah	31	not out	14
T.M. Moody	c Waller, b Davies	141		
S.R. Waugh	b Omarshah	119		
M.G. Bevan	c Davies, b Omarshah	54		
*T.J. Nielsen	c Pycroft, b Peall	13		
P.R. Reiffel	not out	54		
S.K. Warne	c A. Flower, b Omarshah	0		
P.E. McIntyre	b Davies	2		
W.J. Holdsworth	b Jarvis	7		
D.J. Hickey	c Houghton, b Jarvis	32		
Extras	b 1, lb 6, w 3, nb 12	22		0
		483	(for no wicket)	**20**

ZIMBABWE

	FIRST INNINGS		SECOND INNINGS	
G.W. Flower	c Taylor, b Hickey	74	(2) lbw, b Reiffel	84
K.J. Arnott	c Taylor, b Reiffel	4	(1) c Taylor, b McIntyre	60
A.D.R. Campbell	c Waugh, b Holdsworth	35	run out	9
* A. Flower	c Moody, b Waugh	20	c Moody, b Reiffel	17
A.J. Pycroft	lbw, b Waugh	0	lbw, b Warne	30
D.L. Houghton (capt)	c Nielsen, b Hickey	21	b Warne	5
A.C. Waller	b Hickey	8	c Taylor, b Reiffel	12
S.G. Davies	c Nielsen, b Reiffel	5	(10) lbw, b Reiffel	1
A.H. Omarshah	lbw, b Reiffel	5	(8) lbw, b Reiffel	4
S.G. Peall	not out	6	(9) not out	41
M.P. Jarvis	c Nielsen, b Reiffel	2	c Reiffel, b Warne	17
Extras	lb 5, nb 8	13	b9, lb 8, w 1, nb 11	29
		193		**309**

	O	M	R	W	O	M	R	W
Jarvis	28.2	6	112	3	3	–	10	–
Davies	17	–	84	2	1	1	0	–
Omarshah	24	3	113	4	4	2	9	–
Peall	20	2	100	1				
G. Flower	13	1	67	–				
Waller					0.3	–	1	–

	O	M	R	W	O	M	R	W
Holdsworth	9	4	17	1	23	4	53	–
Reiffel	17.4	4	34	4	25	8	43	5
Hickey	18	2	46	3	18	6	37	–
Warne	20	5	42	–	24.4	8	76	3
McIntyre	13	5	19	–	21	9	40	1
Bevan	10	2	28	–	7	3	27	–
Waugh	8	6	2	2	6	4	2	–
Moody					4	1	14	–

FALL OF WICKETS

1–29, **2**–55, **3**–295, **4**–331, **5**–371, **6**–387, **7**–387, **8**–410, **9**–423

FALL OF WICKETS

1–24, **2**–75, **3**–127, **4**–127, **5**–161, **6**–164, **7**–171, **8**–182, **9**–189

1–94, **2**–107, **3**–145, **4**–200, **5**–206, **6**–229, **7**–237, **8**–258, **9**–260

Umpires: K. Kanjee & I.D. Robinson

Australia 'B' won by 10 wickets

SECOND INTERNATIONAL MATCH

ZIMBABWE v. AUSTRALIA 'B', at Harare

Zimbabwe made five changes from the side that had been heavily beaten in the first match, but this did not save them from another crushing defeat. Their batsmen floundered against a varied attack, and by mid-afternoon on the first day, they were 88 for 7. Traicos then offered Houghton solid support, and the pair added 67. Houghton moved to the eighth century of his career before the close when he was engaged in a very useful partnership with Jarvis. Houghton had reached his hundred when he took 13 off an over from Hickey, and Jarvis hit the highest score of his career.

Moody and Taylor gave Australia a brisk and bright start, and Moody looked to be heading for a most attractive century until he was well caught and bowled low down by Burmester. It was the bowler's first wicket in first-class cricket. Australia ended the second day leading by 46 runs with five wickets in hand.

Tucker had played with good sense, and Warne and McIntyre bolstered the score with a vigorous last-wicket

One of Zimbabwe's hopes for the future – A.D. Campbell. (David Munden)

SECOND INTERNATIONAL MATCH
ZIMBABWE v. AUSTRALIA 'B', at Harore

stand of 45. Zimbabwe began their second innings resolutely enough, but the advent of leg-spinner Warne brought about a collapse which only Houghton looked like halting. The 22-year-old Warne returned the best figures of his very short career, and within a few months he was to win his first Test cap.

Warne's glory did not end there. He opened the Australian second innings, and 23 runs came in one over from Brandes: four byes, seven to Law, and then three successive fours for Warne.

SECOND INTERNATIONAL MATCH – ZIMBABWE v. AUSTRALIA 'B'
21, 23, 24 and 25 September, 1991 at Harare Sports Club

ZIMBABWE

	FIRST INNINGS		SECOND INNINGS	
K.J. Arnott	lbw, **b** McIntyre	31	**b** Warne	47
G.W. Flower	c Nielsen, **b** Hickey	4	lbw, **b** Warne	27
A.D.R. Campbell	c Law, **b** McIntyre	15	c Moody, **b** Warne	7
*A. Flower	c Nielsen, **b** Hickey	3	**b** Warne	6
D.L. Houghton (capt)	not out	105	not out	57
N.P. Hough	c Warne, **b** Hickey	4	c Moody, **b** Waugh	5
E.A. Brandes	c Taylor, **b** McIntyre	7	c Moody, **b** Bevan	4
M.G. Burmester	c Waugh, **b** McIntyre	2	c Taylor, **b** Warne	5
A.J. Traicos	**b** Hickey	13	run out	6
A.G. Huckle	lbw, **b** Warne	1	lbw, **b** Warne	0
M.P. Jarvis	c Waugh, **b** Hickey	33	c Nielsen, **b** Reiffel	0
Extras	w 2, nb 19	21	lb 3, nb 12	15
		239		**179**

	O	M	R	W	O	M	R	W
Hickey	24.4	4	72	5				
Reiffel	20	4	66	–	15.5	3	36	1
Waugh	6	2	7	–	7	2	10	–
McIntyre	24	10	42	4	22	6	54	–
Tucker	2	–	8	–				
Warne	17	5	40	1	36	10	49	7
Bevan	2	–	4	–	9	1	27	1

FALL OF WICKETS
1–7, 2–52, 3–61, 4–62, 5–75, 6–86, 7–88, 8–155, 9–164
1–69, 2–83, 3–98, 4–99, 5–105, 6–117, 7–144, 8–163, 9–174

AUSTRALIA 'B'

	FIRST INNINGS		SECOND INNINGS	
M.A. Taylor (capt)	c Hough, **b** Brandes	41		
T.M. Moody	c and **b** Burmester	85		
S.G. Law	c Campbell, **b** Brandes	94	(1) lbw, **b** Brandes	13
S.R. Waugh	**b** Brandes	11		
M.G. Bevan	lbw, **b** Jarvis	20		
R.J. Tucker	c Traicos, **b** Burmester	62	(3) not out	1
* T.J. Nielsen	lbw, **b** Brandes	9		
P.R. Reiffel	c Traicos, **b** Brandes	4		
S.K. Warne	not out	35	(2) not out	18
D.J. Hickey	c and **b** Brandes	3		
P.E. McIntyre	run out	15		
Extras	lb 1, w 1, nb 2	4	b 4	4
		383	(for 1 wicket)	**36**

	O	M	R	W	O	M	R	W
Brandes	31.3	3	95	6	2	–	22	1
Jarvis	25	4	90	1	1.3	–	10	–
Burmester	14.3	5	24	2				
Huckle	13	1	74	–				
Traicos	21	4	72	–				
G. Flower	5	–	16	–				
Hough	2	–	11	–				

FALL OF WICKETS
1–124, 2–129, 3–157, 4–200, 5–285, 6–304, 7–328, 8–332, 9–338
1–30

Umpires: I.D. Robinson & R. Suchet

Australia 'B' won by 9 wickets

ONE-DAY INTERNATIONAL
ZIMBABWE v. SOUTH AFRICA

This match was played the day before both sides flew to Australia for the World Cup. It was the first ever meeting between the two countries, and the first contact between teams from either country since Rhodesia became independent as Zimbabwe. Although later termed 'unofficial' by Dr Ali Bacher, the game attracted an audience of nearly ten thousand, the largest crowd ever to attend a cricket match in Zimbabwe.

Put in to bat, Zimbabwe began nervously, and they encountered disaster when Donald yorked Flower and Campbell with successive deliveries. Some erratic running and fielding marked the next stages of the game, and it came as little surprise when James was run out by Rhodes. The later batsmen promised more than they achieved, and although Waller hit 27 off 36 balls, a total of 170 looked inadequate as a test for South Africa.

So it proved. Jarvis and Brandes bowled well, and Wessels was dropped before he had scored. Jarvis was particularly unlucky not to dismiss Kirsten, but eventually the South African batsmen gained the upper hand. Kirsten and Cronje added 98 in 119 minutes, and Kuiper hit strongly to bring victory in the last over.

The match was played under World Cup rules and regulations.

DURHAM TOUR

As preparation for their entry into first-class cricket, Durham CCC toured Zimbabwe in February. With Zimbabwe engaged in the World Cup, the opposition that Durham encountered was hardly the strongest. The results of the matches are listed below.

3 February, 1992 *at Harare South Sports Club*

Zimbabwe 274 for 4 (A. Flower 90, A.J. Pycroft 83 not out)
Durham 151 for 8 (M.P. Jarvis 4 for 17)

Zimbabwe won by 123 runs

4 February, 1992 *at Alexandra Sports Club*

Durham 206 for 4 (P. Bainbridge 64)
Zimbabwe 207 for 8

Zimbabwe won by 2 wickets

6 February, 1992 *at Old Hararians Sports Club*

Zimbabwe Under-19s 152
Durham 155 for 4 (M.P. Briers 63 not out)

Durham won by 6 wickets

ONE-DAY INTERNATIONAL – ZIMBABWE v. SOUTH AFRICA
5 February, 1992 at Harare Sports Club

ZIMBABWE

W.R. James	run out	27
* A. Flower	b Donald	5
A.D.R. Campbell	b Donald	0
A.J. Pycroft	c Richardson, b Bosch	21
D.L. Houghton (capt)	c Cronje, b Henry	14
A.C. Waller	c Richardson, b Bosch	27
A.H. Omarshah	c Richardson, b Donald	11
I.P. Butchart	lbw, b Cronje	10
E.A. Brandes	not out	14
A.J. Traicos	c Richardson, b Pringle	4
M.P. Jarvis	run out	7
Extras	lb 5, w 19, nb 6	30
		170

(49.3 overs)

	O	M	R	W
Donald	10	2	29	3
Pringle	10	–	35	1
Bosch	9.3	–	44	2
Kuiper	6	1	12	–
Henry	10	1	27	1
Cronje	4	–	18	1

FALL OF WICKETS
1–20, 2–20, 3–54, 4–81, 5–83, 6–107, 7–134, 8–134, 9–158

SOUTH AFRICA

K.C. Wessels (capt)	lbw, b Brandes	19
A.C. Hudson	c Flower, b Brandes	8
P.N. Kirsten	c Omarshah, b Traicos	64
W.J. Cronje	c Waller, b Omarshah	47
A.P. Kuiper	not out	23
J.N. Rhodes	not out	1
* D.J. Richardson		
O. Henry		
M.W. Pringle		
A.A. Donald		
T. Bosch		
Extras	lb 4, w 4, nb 1	9
	(for 4 wickets)	**171**

(49.2 overs)

	O	M	R	W
Brandes	10	3	26	2
Jarvis	10	1	29	–
Omarshah	10	1	32	1
Butchart	10	–	32	–
Traicos	9	–	43	1
Houghton	0.2	–	5	–

FALL OF WICKETS
1–21, 2–31, 3–129, 4–166

Umpires: I.D. Robinson & K. Kanjee

Man of the Match – P.N. Kirsten

South Africa won by 6 wickets

8 February, 1992 *at Harare South Country Club*

Durham 200 for 7
Zimbabwe Country Districts 199 for 7 (M.H. Dekker 67)

Durham won by 1 run

9 February, 1992 *at Harare Sports Club*

Zimbabwe XI 200 for 6
Durham 187 (G.K. Brown 51)

Zimbabwe XI won by 13 runs

11, 12 and 13 February, 1992 *at Mutare Sports Club*

Manicaland Select XI 220 (J.P. Brent 52, G. Wigham 4 for 36, D.A. Graveney 4 for 39) and 286 for 2 dec. (N.P. Hough 200 not out)
Durham 300 for 7 dec. (M.P. Briers 74, I. Smith 69, P. Bainbridge 52) and 209 for 3 (W. Larkins 119, I. Smith 55 not out)

Durham won by 7 wickets

16 February, 1992 *at Harare Sports Club*

Durham 120
ZCU President's XI 121 for 1 (S. Dudhia 65 not out)

ZCU President's XI won by 9 wickets

18, 19, 20 and 21 February, 1992, *at Harare Sports Club*

Zimbabwe 'B' 230 (J.A. Rennie 84, P.W. Henderson 5 for 51, S.J.E. Brown 4 for 45) and 127 (P.J. Berry 4 for 47)
Durham 447 for 6 dec. (S. Hutton 143, P.W.G. Parker 100 not out, G.K. Brown 65, J.D. Glendenen 51, P.J. Berry 51 not out)

Durham won by an innings and 90 runs

23 February, 1992 *at Bulawayo Athletic Club*

Zimbabwe XI 144
Durham 147 for 6 (W. Larkins 69, H. Streak 5 for 19)

Durham won by 4 wickets

24, 25 and 26 February, 1992 *at Bulawayo Athletic Club*

Durham 316 for 6 dec. (M.P. Briers 132 not out, W. Larkins 71) and 202 for 4 dec. (P. Bainbridge 79 not out, S. Hutton 54)
Zimbabwe XI 262 for 6 dec. (G.J. Crocker 63 not out, G.C. Martin 61) and 205 for 9 (M.H. Dekker 66)

Match drawn

SHARJAH

The Sharjah Cup –
One-Day International
tournament between India,
Pakistan and West Indies

Aqib Javed of Pakistan who produced the best bowling performance ever recorded in a one-day international in the Sharjah Cup final. His seven wickets included a hat-trick. (David Munden)

THE SHARJAH CUP

Richie Richardson led West Indies for the first time and played two magnificent captain's innings. He pulls a ball to the boundary during his century against Pakistan. Moin Khan is the keeper. (David Munden)

Three nations contested the Sharjah Cup in 1991, and the favourites, Pakistan, received a shock in the opening match. They batted indifferently on a good pitch against a West Indies side which was captained for the first time by Richie Richardson. Aided by a plethora of extras, Pakistan made 215, but were bowled out in the 49th over. In contrast to their poor batting, Pakistan bowled splendidly with, inevitably, Waqar Younis to the fore. Only Richardson offered resistance, and eight wickets fell for 158. Ian Bishop then gave his skipper confident support, and 45 were added before Bishop fell to Waqar. The limping Richardson still managed to steer his side to victory and completed a memorable and courageous hundred in the process.

Worse was to follow for Pakistan who, the following day, were well beaten by India. This was the first time that India had beaten Pakistan in Sharjah for six years. India included two players new to international cricket, Kambli and Srinath, but the heroes were Prabhakar,

Aqib Javed attempts to run out Manjrekar but misses the stumps. (David Munden)

Manjrekar and Tendulkar who lashed 52 off 40 deliveries.

Prabhakar was again a major contributor to an Indian victory in the third match of the tournament. Navjot Singh Sidhu and Manjrekar laid the foundations of India's impressive score with a second-wicket partnership of 128. Lara, 45 off 44 balls, and Lambert raised West Indies' hopes, but the combined wiles of leg-spinner Kumble and medium-pacer Prabhakar saw the last six wickets fall for 50 runs.

Pakistan needed to beat West Indies in the fourth match to have any chance of qualifying for the final. They batted unevenly, and Ambrose bowled at his menacing best, but Ramiz Raja and Imran Khan added 137 from 169 balls for the third wicket. Wasim Akram then hit Ambrose for a six and two fours in the 48th over

Salim Malik is bowled by Hooper for 1. Pakistan v. West Indies. Dujon is the keeper. (David Munden)

to boost the scoring rate. Richie Richardson played another innings of outstanding quality for West Indies, but he had little support, and the last over arrived with West Indies 12 short of victory and their last pair together. Ian Bishop hit Waqar Younis for six over long-on, and only two were needed from three balls. Bishop refused a bye which would have levelled the scores, and Waqar was lucky to escape being called for a wide. Bishop missed the last ball and was bowled.

India reached the final and eliminated West Indies in the process when they won their third match in a row. Sachin Tendulkar displayed his all-round worth with four wickets for 34 runs in ten overs, his best performance in a one-day international.

The sixth match produced one of the epic encounters between India and Pakistan which Sharjah expects. Pakistan included Aamir Sohail, Zahid Fazal and Saeed Anwar who had arrived from Pakistan only the previous day, and it was left-hander Aamir Sohail who took the individual award for his 91 which included a six and four fours. He and Salim Malik added 91 in 17 overs. Kambli and Shastri gave India a wonderful start with 124 in 27.4 overs, but three wickets fell quickly. Tendulkar and Manjrekar belligerently reasserted the Indian cause, but Tendulkar was brilliantly caught by substitute Mushtaq Ahmed, and Kapil Dev went first ball. Twelve runs were needed from the last over, and Waqar Younis' pace and accuracy denied Prabhakar and More.

Aamir Sohail hit 91 for Pakistan against India within hours of arriving as replacement for injured Javed Miandad. (David Munden)

LEAGUE TABLE

	P	W	L	Pts	Run Rate
India	4	3	1	6	4.7
Pakistan	4	2	2	4	4.6
West Indies	4	1	3	2	4.2

The Sharjah Cup final proved to be a less exciting encounter than the previous match between India and Pakistan, but it was among the most historic of one-day matches. Zahid Fazal and Salim Malik added 171 for Pakistan's third wicket, and the stand only came to an end when Zahid, two short of his century, was carried off on a stretcher suffering from cramp. India faced a daunting task, and in Aqib Javed's first over, they lost Navjot Singh Sidhu. With the third, fourth and fifth balls of his third over, Aqib dismissed Shastri, Azharuddin and Tendulkar, a formidable trio, to perform the hat-trick. Aqib finished with figures of 7 for 37, the best performance ever recorded in a one-day international, beating Winston Davis' 7 for 51 in the World Cup of 1983.

SHARJAH CUP – MATCH ONE – PAKISTAN v. WEST INDIES
17 October, 1991 at Sharjah CA Stadium

PAKISTAN

Ramiz Raja	c Logie, b Patterson	49
Sajid Ali	c Dujon, b Ambrose	11
Ijaz Ahmed	lbw, b Hooper	9
Salim Malik	b Hooper	1
Javed Miandad	b Simmons	47
Imran Khan (capt)	c Logie, b Patterson	11
Wasim Akram	run out	16
* Moin Khan	c Hooper, b Bishop	18
Mushtaq Ahmed	lbw, b Ambrose	4
Waqar Younis	b Bishop	9
Aqib Javed	not out	1
Extras	lb 15, w 17, nb 7	39
		215

(48.3 overs)

	O	M	R	W
Ambrose	9	1	33	2
Bishop	9.3	–	40	2
Patterson	10	–	48	2
Hooper	10	–	33	2
Benjamin	9	–	38	–
Simmons	1	–	8	1

FALL OF WICKETS
1–25, 2–54, 3–59, 4–132, 5–150, 6–171, 7–185, 8–199, 9–212

WEST INDIES

P.V. Simmons	run out	14
C.B. Lambert	c Moin Khan, b Wasim Akram	0
R.B. Richardson (capt)	not out	106
B.C. Lara	c Moin Khan, b Waqar Younis	5
A.L. Logie	c Moin Khan, b Waqar Younis	11
C.L. Hooper	run out	23
* P.J.L. Dujon	c Moin Khan, b Imran Khan	15
W.K.M. Benjamin	lbw, b Waqar Younis	1
C.E.L. Ambrose	lbw, b Imran Khan	1
I.R. Bishop	lbw, b Waqar Younis	19
B.P. Patterson	not out	1
Extras	b 4, lb 4, w 8, nb 5	21
	(for 9 wickets)	217

(47.3 overs)

	O	M	R	W
Wasim Akram	8.3	1	37	1
Aqib Javed	10	2	32	–
Waqar Younis	9	–	48	4
Mushtaq Ahmed	10	–	54	–
Imran Khan	10	–	38	2

FALL OF WICKETS
1–6, 2–38, 3–49, 4–70, 5–121, 6–152, 7–157, 8–158, 9–203

Umpires: W.A.U. Wickremasinghe & B.C. Cooray — Man of the Match – R.B. Richardson — *West Indies won by 1 wicket*

SHARJAH CUP – MATCH TWO – PAKISTAN v. INDIA
18 October, 1991 at Sharjah CA Stadium

INDIA

R.J. Shastri	run out	22
N.S. Sidhu	**b** Wasim Akram	38
S.V. Manjrekar	lbw, **b** Waqar Younis	72
M. Azharuddin (capt)	**b** Waqar Younis	32
S.R. Tendulkar	not out	52
Kapil Dev	not out	10
V.G. Kambli		
* K.S. More		
M. Prabhakar		
Venkatapathy Raju		
J. Srinath		
Extras	lb 4, w 3, nb 5	12
	(for 4 wickets)	**238**

PAKISTAN

Sajid Ali	c More, **b** Prabhakar	5
Ramiz Raja	run out	35
Javed Miandad	lbw, **b** Venkatapathy Raju	61
Salim Malik	lbw, **b** Shastri	19
Imran Khan (capt)	**b** Prabhakar	1
Ijaz Ahmed	c and **b** Venkatapathy Raju	4
Wasim Akram	**b** Srinath	14
* Moin Khan	not out	17
Akram Raza	c Azharuddin, **b** Kapil Dev	0
Waqar Younis	**b** Prabhakar	6
Aqib Javed	**b** Prabhakar	4
Extras	w 2, nb 10	12
		178

(50 overs)

	O	M	R	W
Imran Khan	10	–	44	–
Aqib Javed	10	3	38	–
Waqar Younis	10	–	65	2
Wasim Akram	10	–	42	1
Akram Raza	10	–	45	–

(44 overs)

	O	M	R	W
Prabhakar	7.4	1	25	4
Kapil Dev	8	–	30	1
Srinath	9	1	31	1
Shastri	10	1	53	1
Venkatapathy Raju	10	–	39	2

FALL OF WICKETS

1–44, **2**–93, **3**–149, **4**–193

FALL OF WICKETS

1–8, **2**–84, **3**–124, **4**–129, **5**–129, **6**–139, **7**–155, **8**–156, **9**–166

Umpires: W.A.U. Wickremasinghe & P.W. Vidanagamage — Man of the Match – S.V. Manjrekar — *India won by 60 runs*

SHARJAH CUP – MATCH THREE – INDIA v. WEST INDIES
19 October, 1991 at Sharjah CA Stadium

INDIA

N.S. Sidhu	**st** Dujon, **b** Hooper	98
R.J. Shastri	**st** Dujon, **b** Hooper	6
S.V. Manjrekar	**c** Hooper, **b** Bishop	56
M. Azharuddin (capt)	**c** and **b** Simmons	12
S.R. Tendulkar	run out	22
V.G. Kambli	not out	23
Kapil Dev	**c** Simmons, **b** Bishop	7
M. Prabhakar	not out	2
* K.S. More		
Venkatapathy Raju		
A.R. Kumble		
Extras	lb 2, w 7, nb 5	14
	(for 6 wickets)	**240**

WEST INDIES

P.V. Simmons	lbw, **b** Shastri	20
C.B. Lambert	**c** and **b** Kumble	66
R.B. Richardson (capt)	**c** Azharuddin, **b** Shastri	28
B.C. Lara	**b** Prabhakar	45
A.L. Logie	lbw, **b** Kumble	4
C.L. Hooper	lbw, **b** Kumble	17
K.L.T. Arthurton	**st** More, **b** Kumble	2
*P.J.L. Dujon	lbw, **b** Prabhakar	0
C.E.L. Ambrose	lbw, **b** Prabhakar	0
I.R. Bishop	**c** Shastri, **b** Prabhakar	23
B.P. Patterson	not out	3
Extras	b 2, lb 7, nb 4	13
		221

(50 overs)

	O	M	R	W
Ambrose	10	2	32	–
Bishop	10	–	49	2
Patterson	10	–	47	–
Hooper	10	–	46	2
Simmons	8	–	49	1
Arthurton	2	–	15	–

(48.5 overs)

	O	M	R	W
Kapil Dev	9	–	50	–
Prabhakar	9.5	–	30	4
Shastri	10	–	38	2
Kumble	10	–	50	4
Venkatapathy Raju	10	–	44	–

FALL OF WICKETS

1–33, **2**–161, **3**–181, **4**–184, **5**–216, **6**–232

FALL OF WICKETS

1–54, **2**–116, **3**–123, **4**–132, **5**–171, **6**–175, **7**–185, **8**–186, **9**–194

Umpires: B.C. Cooray & P.W. Vidanagamage — Man of the Match – M. Prabhakar — *India won by 19 runs*

SHARJAH CUP – MATCH FOUR – PAKISTAN v. WEST INDIES
21 October, 1991 at Sharjah CA Stadium

PAKISTAN

Ramiz Raja	c Logie, b Ambrose	90
Sajid Ali	c Dujon, b Ambrose	7
Javed Miandad	b Ambrose	2
Salim Malik	c Logie, b Hooper	10
Imran Khan (capt)	c Hooper, b Ambrose	77
Ijaz Ahmed	not out	14
Wasim Akram	c Patterson, b Bishop	19
*Moin Khan	b Ambrose	0
Akram Raza	not out	1
Waqar Younis		
Aqib Javed		
Extras	lb 8, w 7, nb 1	16
	(for 7 wickets)	236

(50 overs)

	O	M	R	W
Ambrose	10	–	53	5
Bishop	10	1	44	1
Walsh	10	–	48	–
Hooper	10	–	30	1
Patterson	10	1	53	–

FALL OF WICKETS
1–17, 2–62, 3–200, 4–202, 5–229, 6–229, 7–229

WEST INDIES

P.V. Simmons	b Aqib Javed	8
C.B. Lambert	b Aqib Javed	7
R.B. Richardson (capt)	c Ijaz Ahmed, b Waqar Younis	122
B.C. Lara	lbw, b Aqib Javed	0
C.L. Hooper	lbw, b Waqar Younis	13
A.L. Logie	run out	0
* P.J.L. Dujon	run out	53
I.R. Bishop	b Waqar Younis	16
C.E.L. Ambrose	lbw, b Waqar Younis	0
C.A. Walsh	b Wasim Akram	0
B.P. Patterson	not out	1
Extras	lb 6, w 9	15
		235

(50 overs)

	O	M	R	W
Wasim Akram	10	–	59	1
Aqib Javed	10	2	54	3
Akram Raza	10	–	40	–
Waqar Younis	10	1	39	4
Ijaz Ahmed	7	–	24	–
Imran Khan	3	–	13	–

FALL OF WICKETS
1–16, 2–32, 3–32, 4–56, 5–57, 6–211, 7–217, 8–220, 9–227

Umpires: B.C. Cooray & P.W. Vidanagamage Man of the Match – R.B. Richardson *Pakistan won by 1 run*

SHARJAH CUP – MATCH FIVE – INDIA v. WEST INDIES
22 October, 1991 at Sharjah CA Stadium

WEST INDIES

P.V. Simmons	c Prabhakar, b Kapil Dev	14
C.B. Lambert	lbw, b Tendulkar	11
R.B. Richardson (capt)	c Azharuddin, b Tendulkar	16
C.L. Hooper	run out	8
A.L. Logie	c More, b Tendulkar	0
K.L.T. Arthurton	c and b Prabhakar	59
* P.J.L. Dujon	c More, b Tendulkar	0
I.R. Bishop	c and b Prabhakar	14
W.K.M. Benjamin	lbw, b Kapil Dev	9
C.E.L. Ambrose	not out	4
B.P. Patterson	run out	1
Extras	lb 3, w 4, nb 2	9
		145

(46.2 overs)

	O	M	R	W
Kapil Dev	8	1	23	2
Prabhakar	8.2	–	32	2
Tendulkar	10	1	34	4
Kumble	10	2	24	–
Venkatapathy Raju	10	1	29	–

FALL OF WICKETS
1–24, 2–39, 3–47, 4–47, 5–78, 6–78, 7–129, 8–130, 9–143

INDIA

W.V. Raman	lbw, b Bishop	0
N.S. Sidhu	c Logie, b Benjamin	44
S.V. Manjrekar	lbw, b Bishop	43
M. Azharuddin (capt)	not out	19
S.R. Tendulkar	not out	11
V.G. Kambli		
Kapil Dev		
* K.S. More		
M. Prabhakar		
A.R. Kumble		
Venkatapathy Raju		
Extras	b 8, lb 4, w 18	30
	(for 3 wickets)	147

(37.3 overs)

	O	M	R	W
Ambrose	8	1	22	–
Bishop	7	2	28	2
Benjamin	9	–	34	1
Patterson	6.3	–	16	–
Hooper	6	–	24	–
Arthurton	1	–	11	–

FALL OF WICKETS
1–0, 2–108, 3–108

Umpires: W.A.U. Wickremasinghe & P.W. Vidanagamage Man of the Match – S.R. Tendulkar *India won by 7 wickets*

SHARJAH CUP – MATCH SIX – PAKISTAN v. INDIA
23 October, 1991 at Sharjah CA Stadium

PAKISTAN

Aamir Sohail	c Tendulkar, b Kapil Dev	91
Saeed Anwar	run out	1
Zahid Fazal	b Venkatapathy Raju	39
Salim Malik	c Azharuddin, b Srinath	42
Imran Khan (capt)	b Prabhakar	43
Wasim Akram	b Srinath	2
Ijaz Ahmed	run out	9
* Moin Khan	not out	1
Akram Raza	not out	0
Waqar Younis		
Aqib Javed		
Extras	b 1, lb 5, w 16, nb 7	29
	(for 7 wickets)	257

INDIA

R.J. Shastri	b Waqar Younis	77
V.G. Kambli	c Moin Khan, b Aqib Javed	40
S.V. Manjrekar	c Ijaz Ahmed, b Wasim Akram	49
M. Azharuddin (capt)	b Akram Raza	0
S.R. Tendulkar	c sub (Mushtaq Ahmed), b Salim Malik	49
Kapil Dev	lbw, b Wasim Akram	0
M. Prabhakar	not out	19
* K.S. More	run out	1
A.R. Kumble		
Venkatapathy Raju		
J. Srinath		
Extras	b 1, lb 3, w 12, nb 2	18
	(for 7 wickets)	253

(50 overs)

	O	M	R	W
Kapil Dev	9	2	31	1
Prabhakar	10	–	62	1
Srinath	8	–	55	2
Tendulkar	6	–	20	–
Kumble	7	–	35	–
Venkatapathy Raju	10	–	48	1

(50 overs)

	O	M	R	W
Wasim Akram	9	–	44	2
Aqib Javed	10	1	36	1
Imran Khan	2	–	17	–
Akram Raza	10	–	43	1
Waqar Younis	10	–	59	1
Aamir Sohail	6	–	34	–
Salim Malik	3	–	16	1

FALL OF WICKETS
1–4, **2**–90, **3**–181, **4**–202, **5**–214, **6**–255, **7**–257

FALL OF WICKETS
1–124, **2**–133, **3**–134, **4**–219, **5**–219, **6**–240, **7**–253

Umpires: B.C. Cooray & W.A.U. Wickremasinghe — Man of the Match – Aamir Sohail — *Pakistan won by 4 runs*

SHARJAH CUP FINAL – PAKISTAN v. INDIA
25 October, 1991 at Sharjah CA Stadium

PAKISTAN

Aamir Sohail	c Kapil Dev, b Prabhakar	1
Sajid Ali	c More, b Kapil Dev	10
Zahid Fazal	retired hurt	98
Salim Malik	c Azharuddin, b Prabhakar	87
Imran Khan (capt)	c Manjrekar, b Kapil Dev	13
Ijaz Ahmed	not out	16
Wasim Akram	b Kapil Dev	3
* Moin Khan	c More, b Prabhakar	5
Akram Raza		
Waqar Younis		
Aqib Javed		
Extras	lb 15, w 10, nb 4	29
	(for 6 wickets)	262

INDIA

R.J. Shastri	lbw, b Aqib Javed	15
N.S. Sidhu	c Moin Khan, b Aqib Javed	21
S.V. Manjrekar	c Waqar Younis, b Aqib Javed	52
M. Azharuddin (capt)	lbw, b Aqib Javed	0
S.R. Tendulkar	lbw, b Aqib Javed	0
V.G. Kambli	run out	30
Kapil Dev	b Aqib Javed	8
M. Prabhakar	c Aamir Sohail, b Aqib Javed	7
* K.S. More	not out	26
J. Srinath	c Wasim Akram, b Akram Raza	14
Venkatapathy Raju	run out	2
Extras	lb 5, w 8, nb 2	15
		190

(50 overs)

	O	M	R	W
Prabhakar	10	2	54	3
Kapil Dev	10	–	36	3
Tendulkar	5	–	24	–
Srinath	10	–	49	–
Shastri	8	–	39	–
Venkatapathy Raju	7	–	45	–

(46 overs)

	O	M	R	W
Wasim Akram	10	3	21	–
Imran Khan	4	–	24	–
Aqib Javed	10	1	37	7
Waqar Younis	9	2	28	–
Akram Raza	9	–	56	1
Ijaz Ahmed	2	–	11	–
Salim Malik	2	–	8	–

FALL OF WICKETS
1–6, **2**–23, **3**–223, **4**–230, **5**–247, **6**–262

FALL OF WICKETS
1–32, **2**–47, **3**–47, **4**–47, **5**–100, **6**–129, **7**–132, **8**–143, **9**–177

Umpires: W.A.U. Wickremasinghe & P.W. Vidanagamage — Man of the Match – Aqib Javed — *Pakistan won by 72 runs*

SECTION I

WEST INDIES

Red Stripe Cup
England 'A' tour
West Indies v. South Africa,
one-day internationals and
Test match
First-Class Averages

Courtney Walsh leaves the field at the end of the Test match against South Africa. Walsh took a record 36 wickets in the Red Stripe Cup. (Shaun Botterill)

RED STRIPE CUP

Jeff Dujon, dropped from the West Indian side, helped Jamaica to win the Red Stripe Cup but announced that this would be his last season. (David Munden)

24, 25, 26 and 27 January, 1992 *at Queen's Park Oval, Port of Spain, Trinidad*

Trinidad & Tobago 250 (B.C. Lara 135, P.V. Simmons 50, O.D. Gibson 7 for 78) and 208 for 4 dec. (P.V. Simmons 77, C.G. Yorke 65)
Barbados 109 (A.H. Gray 4 for 23, R. Dhanraj 4 for 35) and 309 for 7 (R.I.C. Holder 123, C.O. Browne 62 not out)

Match drawn

Trinidad & Tobago 8 pts., Barbados 4 pts.

at Recreation Ground, Antigua

Windward Islands 193 (N.F. Williams 50, W.K.M. Benjamin 4 for 65) and 248 (J.R. Murray 102, C.E.L. Ambrose 4 for 70, H.A.G. Anthony 4 for 67)
Leeward Islands 242 (R.B. Richardson 62) and 200 for 2 (K.L.T. Arthurton 97 not out, R.D. Jacobs 52 not out)

Leeward Islands won by 8 wickets

Leeward Islands 16 pts., Windward Islands 0 pts.

at Sabina Park, Kingston, Jamaica

Guyana 173 (S. Dhaniram 81, R.C. Haynes 4 for 21) and 232 (C.B. Lambert 57, R.A. Harper 57, C.A. Walsh 5 for 51)
Jamaica 171 (J.C. Adams 57, L.A. Joseph 6 for 51) and 235 for 4 (J.C. Adams 102 not out, P.J.L. Dujon 66 not out)

Jamaica won by 6 wickets

Jamaica 16 pts., Guyana 5 pts.

The West Indian authorities attempted to squeeze the Red Stripe Cup into the period between the Benson and Hedges World Series and the World Cup in Australia, but the competition was still bereft of some of the Caribbean's leading cricketers. Viv Richards and Gordon Greenidge, hurt by the attitude of the World Cup selectors, decided to retire from domestic cricket. Dujon, too, announced that this would be his last season while Eldine Baptiste and Ezra Moseley played professional cricket in South Africa. Malcolm Marshall remained in Australia to play grade cricket for Waverley, and of the World Cup squad, only Simmons and Roger Harper played in as many as three Red Stripe Cup matches.

In spite of a career best bowling performance from young pace man Ottis Gibson, Barbados, the reigning champions, struggled against Trinidad in the opening match. Brian Lara hit his highest Cup score, and Barbados, needing 360 for victory, were saved by acting skipper Roland Holder and by Courtney Browne who hit the highest score of his career.

Leeward Islands crushed Windward Islands for whom wicket-keeper Junior Murray, seen as a future Test player, hit a maiden first-class century.

Jamaica began their campaign in fine style with victory over Guyana. Jimmy Adams, the 24-year-old left-hander, heralded his outstanding season with an innings of 102 not out which made victory possible.

Phil Simmons hit the first double century of his career, Trinidad v Guyana, and earned a recall to the Test side. (David Munden)

31 January, 1, 2 and 3 February, 1992 *at Kensington Oval, Bridgetown, Barbados*

Windward Islands 379 (D.A. Joseph 61, J.D. Charles 54, W.N. Reid 4 for 112) and 201 (J.R. Murray 65, A.C. Cummins 4 for 56)
Barbados 499 (D.L. Haynes 246, W.N. Reid 78, P.A. Wallace 66, C.A. Davis 6 for 101) and 82 for 3

Barbados won by 7 wickets

Barbados 16 pts., Windward Islands 0 pts.

at Guaracara Park, Pointe-a-Pierre, Trinidad

Trinidad & Tobago 358 (P.V. Simmons 202, A.H. Gray 55, R.A. Harper 6 for 92)
Guyana 193 (C.B. Lambert 53, A.H. Gray 5 for 49) and 387 for 6 (C.B. Lambert 144, R.A. Harper 62 not out, R. Seeram 58)

Match drawn

Trinidad & Tobago 8 pts., Guyana 4 pts.

at Sabina Park, Kingston, Jamaica

Leeward Islands 389 (K.L.T. Arthurton 117, L.L. Harris 85, C.A. Walsh 4 for 51, R.C. Haynes 4 for 75) and 171 (A.C.H. Walsh 77, B.P. Patterson 5 for 44)
Jamaica 324 (R.G. Samuels 104, N.O. Perry 57, H.A.G. Anthony 4 for 71) and 79 for 3

Match drawn

Leeward Islands 8 pts., Jamaica 4 pts.

Desmond Haynes hit his first double century in the West Indies in his first innings of the season for Barbados. He and Wallace shared an opening stand of 136 and provided the platform for Barbados' resounding victory.

Phil Simmons hit the first double century of his career, but once again Trinidad failed to sustain their advantage and were denied victory by Lambert and Roger Harper.

Jamaica's young left-handed opening batsman Robert Samuels hit a maiden first-class hundred in Jamaica's drawn match with Leewards.

7, 8, 9 and 10 February, 1992 *at Kensington Oval, Bridgetown, Barbados*

Leeward Islands 246 (R.D. Jacobs 78, S.C. Williams 66, V.D. Walcott 4 for 49) and 175
Barbados 315 (D.L. Haynes 135, R.I.C. Holder 72, P.A. Wallace 55) and 110 for 7

Barbados won by 3 wickets

Barbados 16 pts., Leeward Islands 0 pts.

at Mindoo Phillip Park, St Lucia

Windward Islands 106 (C.G. Butts 7 for 29) and 207 (L.D. John 63, L.A. Joseph 4 for 52)
Guyana 354 (C.B. Lambert 125, R.A. Harper 74)

Guyana won by an innings and 41 runs

Guyana 16 pts., Windward Islands 0 pts.

8, 9, 10 and 11 February, 1992

at Queen's Park Oval, Port of Spain, Trinidad

Jamaica 324 (J.C. Adams 99, R.G. Samuels 94, R.C. Haynes 51, R. Dhanraj 4 for 92) and 175 (E.C. Antoine 6 for 49)
Trinidad & Tobago 186 (P.V. Simmons 57, C.A. Walsh 6 for 62)

Match drawn

Jamaica 8 pts., Trinidad & Tobago 4 pts.

Another century from Desmond Haynes set Barbados on the way to victory over Leeward Islands although they struggled nervously to reach a meagre target in their second innings. The win took them to the top of the table, eight points ahead of Jamaica who were thwarted by the weather in Trinidad. Once again Jamaica owed much to their two young left-handers, Adams and Samuels, and to the pace bowling of skipper Courtney Walsh.

Guyana kept their hopes of winning the Cup alive with a resounding victory over Windward Islands who suffered their third defeat in as many matches. There was a second century in succession for Clayton Lambert, another to be neglected by the West Indian selectors.

14, 15, 16 and **17 February, 1992** *at Kensington Oval, Bridgetown, Barbados*

Jamaica 296 (J.C. Adams 118, R.W. Staple 79) and 183 (V.D. Walcott 5 for 41)
Barbados 187 (S.L. Campbell 62, C.A. Walsh 4 for 48) and 148 (C.A. Walsh 4 for 37)

Jamaica won by 144 runs

Jamaica 16 pts., Barbados 0 pts.

at Queen's Park, Grenada

Trinidad & Tobago 131 (S. Ragoonath 67, N.F. Williams 5 for 33)
Windward Islands 135 for 2 (L.D. John 64)

Match drawn

Windward Islands 8 pts., Trinidad & Tobago 4 pts.

at Bourda, Georgetown, Guyana

Leeward Islands 350 (L.L. Harris 98, H.A.G. Anthony 71, L.A. Joseph 5 for 80) and 55 for 2
Guyana 161 (K.C.G. Benjamin 4 for 33) and 243 (S. Chanderpaul 90, V.A. Walsh 6 for 77)

Leeward Islands won by 8 wickets

Leeward Islands 16 pts., Guyana 0 pts.

Put in to bat, Jamaica lost Samuels and Palmer for five, but Adams and Staple added 182, a stand which was to have a significant influence on the outcome of the match. It enabled Jamaica to come close to 300 on a difficult wicket, and the bowling of Walsh and Perry gave them a stranglehold on the game. Walsh was the ultimate hero although Adams was named Man of the Match, for it was the Jamaican captain who bowled his side to their first ever victory at Kensington Oval and generally inspired his side. The win took Jamaica to the top of the league, four points ahead of Leeward Islands who crushed Guyana. The diminutive Vaughn Walsh, a pace bowler who had troubled Barbados in the previous round, took a career best 6 for 77, and wicket-keeper Livingstone Harris hit the highest score of his career.

The game in Grenada was ruined by rain. No play at all was possible on the first day.

21, 22, 23 and **24 February, 1992** *at Albion Sports Complex, Berbice, Guyana*

Guyana 256 (N.E.F. Barry 71, S. Chanderpaul 66) and 183 for 3 (C.B. Lambert 68, N.A. McKenzie 67)
Barbado 404 for 9 dec. (F.L. Reiffer 126, C.A. Best 79, R.I.C. Holder 71, A. Nandu 4 for 119)

Match drawn

Barbados 8 pts., Guyana 4 pts.

at Sabina Park, Kingston, Jamaica

Windward Islands 130 (J.R. Murray 60, C.A. Walsh 4 for 57) and 113 (C.A. Walsh 5 for 17)
Jamaica 411 for 8 dec. (J.C. Adams 128 not out, D.S. Morgan 77, R.G. Samuels 74, R.W. Staple 58)

Jamaica won by an innings and 168 runs

Jamaica 16 pts., Windward Islands 0 pts.

22, 23, 24 and **25 February, 1992**

at Warner Park, St Kitts

Trinidad & Tobago 322 (C.G. Yorke 91, K.A. Williams 69, J. Maynard 4 for 52) and 115 (H.A.G. Anthony 4 for 23)
Leeward Islands 478 (W. Davis 99, L.L. Harris 82, N.C. Guishard 79, K.C.G. Benjamin 52 not out, E.C. Antoine 6 for 117)

Leeward Islands won by an innings and 41 runs

Leeward Islands 16 pts., Trinidad & Tobago 0 pts.

David Williams of Trinidad took over from Dujon as the West Indies wicket-keeper. (Allsport)

When Courtney Walsh trapped Cuffy leg before on the third day of what was scheduled as a four-day match he had cause for double celebration. The wicket gave Jamaica victory over Windward Islands and the Red Stripe Cup, and it brought his personal total for the competition for the season to 36 wickets so establishing a new record for domestic cricket in the Caribbean. The previous record was 35 wickets by Curtly Ambrose in 1988 in the Red Stripe Cup.

Jamaica's triumph was well deserved and the team received an emotional reception from a crowd of 8,000 at Sabina Park. Walsh's personal achievement was an embarrassment to the West Indian selectors who had omitted him from the World Series and World Cup squads. Once more the individual award in the final match went to Jimmy Adams who hit his third century in five matches.

Barbados were held at Berbice while Leeward Islands won easily in St Kitts to confirm second place.

RED STRIPE CUP – FINAL TABLE

	P	W	L	D	Pts
Jamaica (5)	5	3	–	2	60
Leeward Islands (3)	5	3	1	1	56
Barbados (1)	5	2	1	2	44
Guyana (4)	5	1	2	2	29
Trinidad & Tobago (2)	5	–	1	4	24
Windward Islands (6)	5	–	4	1	8

(1991 positions in brackets)

(Points system: 16 points for a win; 8 points for first innings lead in match drawn; 4 points for loss on first innings in match drawn; 5 points for lead in first innings in match lost.)

ENGLAND 'A' TOUR

The England 'A' side were deprived of their captain, Martyn Moxon, through injury. John Stephenson came into the side, and Hugh Morris took over the captaincy. Another to be forced to withdraw through injury was wicket-keeper Warren Hegg. The side played five matches in Bermuda before moving to the West Indies. All matches in Bermuda were played at Somerset Cricket Club. The results were as follows –

22 February, 1992

Bermuda CBC President's XI 86 (J.P. Stephenson 4 for 31)
England 'A' 88 for 4

England 'A' won by 6 wickets

22 February, 1992 (20 overs)

England 'A' 138 for 7 (M.D. Moxon 56 not out)
Bermuda CBC President's XI 79 for 3

England 'A' won on faster scoring rate

23 February, 1992

Bermuda 145 for 8
England 'A' 147 for 1 (J.P. Stephenson 74 not out, G.P. Thorpe 59 not out)

England 'A' won by 9 wickets

25 February, 1992

Bermuda Select XI 183 for 7 (N. Gibbons 84)
England 'A' 185 for 3 (D.J. Bicknell 89, H. Morris 51)

England 'A' won by 7 wickets

27 February, 1992

England 'A' 192 for 5 (N. Hussain 61, M.R. Ramprakash 59)
Devonshire 76

England 'A' won by 116 runs

4 March, 1992 *at Kensington Oval, Bridgetown, Barbados*

Barbados 171 for 9 (P.A. Wallace 50)
England 'A' 172 for 4 (P. Johnson 56)

England 'A' won by 6 wickets

6, 7 and 8 March, 1992 *at Queen's Park, Grenada*

England 'A' 263 (H. Morris 54, M.R. Ramprakash 53, I.B.A. Allen 4 for 60) and 178 for 5 dec. (M.R. Ramprakash 74 not out, I.B.A. Allen 4 for 56)
Windward Islands 233 for 8 dec. (J. Eugene 68) and 89 for 4

Match drawn

England 'A' beat Barbados in a 50-over match and then engaged in the first of two first-class matches before the first representative game. By chance, their first-class fixtures were against the two sides who had finished fifth and sixth in the Red Stripe Cup. Handicapped by injuries, England 'A' had the better of the drawn match with Windwards, but it was a dour encounter, and a result never looked likely.

10, 11 and 12 March, 1992 *at Guaracara Park, Pointe-a-Pierre, Trinidad*

Trinidad & Tobago 257 (K.A. Williams 98, M.P. Carew 61, S. Ragoonath 51, J.P. Stephenson 4 for 26) and 188 (I.D.K. Salisbury 4 for 21, D.E. Malcolm 4 for 68)
England 'A' 406 for 7 dec. (H. Morris 135, P. Johnson 71, G.P. Thorpe 57, E.C. Antoine 4 for 112)

Match drawn

The England side gave a good account of themselves in Trinidad with Hugh Morris grafting his way to his first century in England colours in what was a sluggish pitch. England 'A' batted into the last morning, but they came close to forcing victory until held up by Jumadeen and Elvin who added 42 for the eighth wicket.

FIRST INTERNATIONAL MATCH
WEST INDIES 'A' v. ENGLAND 'A'

England's injury woe continued with Malcolm pulling out of the side shortly before the start of the first representative match. At first he was scarcely missed. Morris won the toss, put West Indies in to bat, and saw two wickets fall in the first six overs. Stephenson, who had taken a career best bowling performance against Trinidad, soon had Best leg before, and the dangerous Adams was out to the last ball before lunch. Eugene went shortly after the break, but Holder batted with authority until beaten in the flight by Salisbury. Morris ran out Murray, and at tea, West Indies were 163 for 7.

That was really the high point of England's success, for, inspired by Gray, West Indies conjured 103 runs from their last three wickets. On a wicket of doubtful quality, Darren Bicknell batted well, but the home side's quick bowlers made the ball lift menacingly, and England trailed by 37 runs on the first innings.

When West Indies batted again Carlisle Best who has never been able to establish himself in the senior side played a chanceless innings while everyone else struggled on a pitch of uneven bounce. John Stephenson again bowled well, moving the ball sufficiently at his medium pace. Walsh declared at the overnight score, and England had the last day in which to score 279 to win.

They never looked like saving the game on a pitch on which the ball now tended to scuttle through low as is evidenced by the number of batsmen either bowled or leg before. The game was over shortly after tea, and the only significant resistance to the West Indian pace men came from Thorpe and Johnson who scored 77 in 19 overs.

Best was named Man of the Match, and the pitch was widely condemned.

FIRST INTERNATIONAL MATCH – WEST INDIES 'A' v. ENGLAND 'A'
14, 15, 16 and 17 March, 1992 at Queen's Park Oval, Port of Spain, Trinidad

WEST INDIES 'A'

	FIRST INNINGS		SECOND INNINGS	
C.B. Lambert	c Rhodes, b Pick	4	c Morris, b Pick	0
R.G. Samuels	c Rhodes, b Munton	0	lbw, b Cork	14
C.A. Best	lbw, b Stephenson	11	st Rhodes, b Salisbury	71
J.C. Adams	c Rhodes, b Pick	27	c Morris, b Salisbury	37
R.I.C. Holder	c and b Salisbury	54	b Salisbury	8
J. Eugene	c Thorpe, b Cork	12	b Stephenson	1
*J.R. Murray	run out	16	c Ramprakash, b Stephenson	10
A.H. Gray	b Cork	50	lbw, b Stephenson	6
L.A. Joseph	lbw, b Pick	27	c Morris, b Stephenson	4
K.C.G. Benjamin	c Johnson, b Cork	5	not out	24
C.A. Walsh (capt)	not out	20	not out	16
Extras	b 2, lb 1, w 4, nb 16	23	b 26, lb 12, w 2, nb 10	50
		249	(for 9 wickets dec.)	241

	O	M	R	W	O	M	R	W
Pick	13.5	1	62	3	10	3	25	1
Cork	16	4	61	3	12	3	19	1
Stephenson	18	7	39	1	22	6	57	4
Salisbury	10	2	38	1	28	9	79	3
Munton	17	3	46	1	9	4	23	–

FALL OF WICKETS
1–4, 2–13, 3–34, 4–66, 5–101, 6–140, 7–146, 8–212, 9–223
1–12, 2–30, 3–119, 4–143, 5–153, 6–175, 7–189, 8–193, 9–211

ENGLAND 'A'

	FIRST INNINGS		SECOND INNINGS	
D.J. Bicknell	c Lambert, b Gray	54	b Joseph	10
H. Morris (capt)	c Adams, b Gray	19	lbw, b Walsh	6
M.R. Ramprakash	run out	22	b Benjamin	7
P. Johnson	c Gray, b Benjamin	4	lbw, b Walsh	35
G.P. Thorpe	c Murray, b Walsh	27	lbw, b Joseph	37
J.P. Stephenson	c Holder, b Benjamin	37	c Murray, b Joseph	0
*S.J. Rhodes	c Lambert, b Joseph	3	b Best	9
D.G. Cork	c Gray, b Benjamin	2	b Joseph	0
I.D.K. Salisbury	lbw, b Joseph	0	b Benjamin	13
T.A. Munton	b Joseph	15	not out	9
R.A. Pick	not out	0	b Benjamin	0
Extras	b 7, lb 6, nb 16	29	b 12, lb 7, nb 3	22
		212		148

	O	M	R	W	O	M	R	W
Walsh	21	6	35	1	13	3	35	2
Joseph	22.2	4	61	3	16	6	30	4
Gray	18	2	36	2	12	2	32	–
Benjamin	24	8	49	3	13.5	6	26	3
Best	9	2	18	–	5	2	6	1
Adams					1	1	0	–

FALL OF WICKETS
1–48, 2–87, 3–96, 4–123, 5–148, 6–158, 7–166, 8–166, 9–212
1–14, 2–29, 3–29, 4–106, 5–106, 6–106, 7–110, 8–130, 9–148

Umpires: C.E. Cumberbatch & F. Ali

West Indies 'A' won by 130 runs

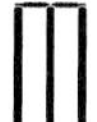

SECOND INTERNATIONAL MATCH
WEST INDIES 'A' v. ENGLAND 'A'

In spite of losing Bicknell in the opening over, England 'A' had the basis of a good score when they reached the end of a rain-shortened first day on 190 for 5, but off-spinner Nehemiah Perry had a spell of 5.1 overs during which he took three wickets without conceding a run on the second morning to bring the England innings to an abrupt end. England off-spinner Robin Croft was also to the fore. He bowled Lambert with his first ball in international cricket and produced an admirable spell which restricted West Indies to 142 for 4 on the second day.

Holder and Murray extended their partnership to 77 on the third morning, but once again it was the resolute batting of the West Indian tail which thwarted England, and the home side took a valuable 61-run lead. England began their second innings positively and were 46 for the loss of Morris when rain arrived.

After half an hour on the last morning Ramprakash was taken at short-leg where Lambert held five fine catches, and this signalled an England collapse. Joseph and Benjamin were accurate and aggressive, and Perry again bowled his off-spinners with control and cunning.

England were outplayed, and this time there was no alibi to be offered by the pitch. West Indies won the game, and the series, shortly after lunch. Perry, 9 for 73 in the match, took the individual award.

SECOND INTERNATIONAL MATCH – WEST INDIES 'A' v. ENGLAND 'A'
21, 22, 23 and 24 March, 1992 at Arnos Vale, St Vincent

ENGLAND 'A'

	FIRST INNINGS		SECOND INNINGS	
D.J. Bicknell	c Murray, **b** Joseph	4	(2) **b** Benjamin	20
H. Morris (capt)	c Best, **b** Gray	48	(1) c Murray, **b** Perry	23
M.R. Ramprakash	c Gray, **b** Perry	41	c Lambert, **b** Benjamin	5
P. Johnson	lbw, **b** Gray	56	c Murray, **b** Joseph	3
G.P. Thorpe	c Murray, **b** Benjamin	19	c Murray, **b** Gray	14
J.P. Stephenson	c Lambert, **b** Perry	6	c Lambert, **b** Perry	25
*S.J. Rhodes	c Lambert, **b** Perry	18	c Best, **b** Perry	2
R.D.B. Croft	c Murray, **b** Joseph	17	c Gray, **b** Walsh	0
D.G. Cork	**b** Perry	7	not out	3
T.A. Munton	c Best, **b** Perry	4	**b** Walsh	0
S.L. Watkin	not out	0	c Lambert, **b** Perry	0
Extras	b 1, lb 6, nb 14	21	b 2, lb 5, w 1, nb 5	13
		241		**108**

WEST INDIES 'A'

	FIRST INNINGS		SECOND INNINGS	
C.B. Lambert	**b** Croft	17	c Ramprakash, **b** Croft	21
R.G. Samuels	c Ramprakash, **b** Croft	54	not out	15
C.A. Best	c Morris, **b** Croft	1	not out	12
J.C. Adams	c Rhodes, **b** Watkin	23		
R.I.C. Holder	st Rhodes, **b** Croft	77		
*J.R. Murray	lbw, **b** Stephenson	44		
N.O. Perry	c and **b** Stephenson	1		
A.H. Gray	**b** Munton	16		
L.A. Joseph	c and **b** Stephenson	22		
K.C.G. Benjamin	not out	17		
C.A. Walsh (capt)	c and **b** Stephenson	4		
Extras	b 5, lb 8, nb 13	26		
		302	(for 1 wicket)	**48**

	O	M	R	W	O	M	R	W
Joseph	22	5	58	2	10	3	25	1
Benjamin	20	4	28	1	7	3	9	2
Walsh	21	8	37	–	10	5	14	2
Gray	15	2	52	2	11	2	27	1
Perry	24.1	9	47	5	12	7	26	4
Best	1	–	12	–				

	O	M	R	W	O	M	R	W
Munton	21	3	69	1	4	–	27	–
Cork	13	2	45	–	2	–	12	–
Watkin	16	3	54	1				
Croft	33	9	90	4	3	1	9	1
Ramprakash	5	1	9	–				
Stephenson	11.1	4	22	4				

FALL OF WICKETS

1–4, **2**–92, **3**–114, **4**–154, **5**–183, **6**–191, **7**–230, **8**–230, **9**–238
1–44, **2**–52, **3**–55, **4**–63, **5**–96, **6**–99, **7**–105, **8**–105, **9**–105

FALL OF WICKETS

1–36, **2**–38, **3**–102, **4**–108, **5**–185, **6**–187, **7**–250, **8**–254, **9**–296
1–32

Umpires: G.T. Johnson & D.M. Archer

West Indies 'A' won by 9 wickets

THIRD INTERNATIONAL MATCH
WEST INDIES 'A' v. ENGLAND 'A'

With considerable patience England 'A' reached 260 for 4 on the opening day of the final match of the series. They owed much to Ramprakash who curbed his natural attacking instincts and batted for more than five hours. Without Joseph, the West Indian attack did not look so formidable, but Kenneth Benjamin bowled impressively on the second morning to bring the England innings to an abrupt close in spite of a good knock from Morris.

Lambert batted with great panache, and West Indies closed on 146 for 1. He added only three to his overnight score before becoming the first of John Stephenson's five victims on the third day. One of the features of the tour was Stephenson's remarkable success with the ball, and his bowling in Bridgetown brought him his first five-wicket haul of his career.

Hugh Morris set a challenging declaration on the last afternoon, asking West Indies to make 208 in 39 overs, but the game meandered to a draw.

Carlisle Best played an outstanding innings for West Indies 'A' against England 'A' in the first match at Port of Spain. (Allsport)

THIRD INTERNATIONAL MATCH – WEST INDIES 'A' v. ENGLAND 'A'
28, 29, 30 and 31 March, 1992 at Kensington Oval, Bridgetown, Barbados

ENGLAND 'A'

	FIRST INNINGS		SECOND INNINGS	
D.J. Bicknell	b Benjamin	21	c Murray, b Walsh	14
J.P. Stephenson	c Gray, b Benjamin	26	(6) c sub, b Benjamin	3
M.R. Ramprakash	b Walsh	86	lbw, b Walsh	0
P. Johnson	b Benjamin	43	lbw, b Benjamin	9
N. Hussain	lbw, b Benjamin	5	c Holder, b Perry	27
H. Morris (capt)	c Murray, b Gray	73	(2) b Walsh	47
*S. J. Rhodes	c Murray, b Gray	12	b Gray	17
I.D.K. Salisbury	not out	21	not out	18
T.A. Munton	lbw, b Walsh	2	(10) not out	3
R.A. Pick	c Best, b Benjamin	7	(9) run out	6
D.E. Malcolm	b Benjamin	0		
Extras	lb 14, w 2, nb 30	46	b 3, lb 7, nb 17	27
		342	(for 8 wickets, dec.)	171

WEST INDIES 'A'

	FIRST INNINGS		SECOND INNINGS	
C.B. Lambert	lbw, b Stephenson	83	c Rhodes, b Stephenson	17
R.G. Samuels	c Hussain, b Pick	19	c Stephenson, b Salisbury	32
C.A. Best	c Munton, b Salisbury	34	not out	21
J.C. Adams	c Johnson, b Stephenson	1	not out	6
R.I.C. Holder	c Hussain, b Stephenson	40		
*J.R. Murray	not out	47		
A.H. Gray	c Morris, b Stephenson	11		
N.O. Perry	c Rhodes, b Pick	7		
K.C.G. Benjamin	run out	25		
C.A. Walsh (capt)	b Stephenson	6		
O.D. Gibson	c and b Salisbury	0		
Extras	b 4, lb 4, nb 25	33	b 3, lb 1, nb 2	6
		306	(for 2 wickets)	97

	O	M	R	W	O	M	R	W
Gray	26	4	74	2	11	–	39	1
Gibson	18	1	75	–				
Walsh	28	8	45	2	21	4	41	3
Benjamin	26.5	10	72	6	18	–	55	2
Perry	19	7	38	–	6	1	26	1
Best	9	3	22	–	1	1	0	–
Adams	2	1	2	–				

	O	M	R	W	O	M	R	W
Malcolm	22	4	78	–	6	–	17	–
Munton	14	4	40	–				
Pick	10	1	46	2	4	–	14	–
Salisbury	28.3	5	81	2	10	–	36	1
Stephenson	27	9	53	5	11	1	26	1

FALL OF WICKETS (England 'A')
1–51, 2–62, 3–135, 4–145, 5–290, 6–305, 7–306, 8–314, 9–342
1–54, 2–54, 3–70, 4–89, 5–98, 6–125, 7–142, 8–160

FALL OF WICKETS (West Indies 'A')
1–66, 2–151, 3–154, 4–179, 5–203, 6–218, 7–256, 8–294, 9–304
1–58, 2–81

Umpires: D.M. Archer & L.H. Barker

Match drawn

John Stephenson in training. He surprised all with his medium pace bowling and took 15 wickets in the 'A' series. (Alan Cozzi)

INTERNATIONAL SERIES AVERAGES – WEST INDIES 'A' v ENGLAND 'A'

WEST INDIES 'A' BATTING

	M	Inns	NO	Runs	HS	Av	100s	50s
R.I.C. Holder	3	4	–	179	77	44.75	–	2
J.R. Murray	3	4	1	117	47*	39.00	–	–
C.A. Best	3	6	2	150	71	37.50	–	1
K.C.G Benjamin	3	4	2	71	25	35.50	–	–
R.G. Samuels	3	6	1	134	54	26.80	–	1
C.B. Lambert	3	6	–	157	83	26.16	–	1
J.C. Adams	3	5	1	94	37	23.50	–	–
C.A. Walsh	3	4	2	46	20*	23.00	–	–
A.H. Gray	3	4	–	83	50	20.75	–	1
L.A. Joseph	2	3	–	53	27	17.66	–	–
N.O. Perry	2	2	–	8	7	4.00	–	–

Played in one match – J. Eugene 12 & 1; O.D. Gibson 0

WEST INDIES 'A' BOWLING

	Overs	Mds	Runs	Wkts	Av	Best	10/m	5/inn
N.O. Perry	61.1	24	137	10	13.70	5-47	–	1
K.C.G. Benjamin	109.4	31	239	17	14.05	6-72	–	1
L.A. Joseph	70.2	18	174	10	17.40	4-30	–	–
C.A. Walsh	114	34	207	10	20.70	3-41	–	–
A.H. Gray	93	12	260	8	32.50	2-36	–	–
C.A. Best	25	8	58	1	58.00	1-6	–	–
J.C. Adams	3	2	2	–	–	–	–	–

Bowled in one innings – O.D. Gibson 18-1-75-0

WEST INDIES 'A' FIELDING FIGURES

11 – J.R. Murray; 7 – C.B. Lambert; 5 – A.H. Gray; 4 – C.A. Best; 2 – R.I.C. Holder; 1 – J.C. Adams and sub

ENGLAND 'A' BATTING

	M	Inns	NO	Runs	HS	Av	100s	50s
H. Morris	3	6	–	216	73	36.00	–	1
M.R. Ramprakash	3	6	–	161	86	26.83	–	1
I.D.K. Salisbury	2	4	2	52	21*	26.00	–	–
P. Johnson	3	6	–	150	56	25.00	–	1
G.P. Thorpe	2	4	–	97	37	24.25	–	–
D.J. Bicknell	3	6	–	123	54	20.50	–	1
J.P. Stephenson	3	6	–	97	37	16.16	–	–
S.J. Rhodes	3	6	–	61	18	10.16	–	–
T.A. Munton	3	6	2	33	15	8.25	–	–
R.A. Pick	2	4	1	13	7	4.33	–	–
D.G. Cork	2	4	1	12	7	4.00	–	–

Played in one match – R.D.B. Croft 17 & 0; S.L. Watkin 0* & 0; D.E. Malcolm 0; N. Hussain 5 & 27

ENGLAND 'A' BOWLING

	Overs	Mds	Runs	Wkts	Av	Best	10/m	5/inn
J.P. Stephenson	89.1	27	197	15	13.13	5-53	–	1
R.D.B. Croft	36	10	99	5	19.80	4-90	–	–
R.A. Pick	37.5	5	147	6	24.50	3-62	–	–
I.D.K. Salisbury	76.3	16	234	7	33.42	3-79	–	–
D.G. Cork	43	9	137	4	34.25	3-61	–	–
T.A. Munton	65	14	205	2	102.50	1-46	–	–
D.E. Malcolm	28	4	95	–	–	–	–	–

Bowled in one innings – S.L. Watkin 16-3-54-1; M.R. Ramprakash 5-1-9-0

ENGLAND 'A' FIELDING FIGURES

8 – S.J. Rhodes (ct 6/st 2); 5 – H. Morris; 4 – J.P. Stephenson; 3 – M.R. Ramprakash; 2 – N. Hussain, P. Johnson and I.D.K. Salisbury; 1 – T.A. Munton and G.P. Thorpe

SOUTH AFRICA TOUR
ONE-DAY INTERNATIONAL SERIES

The West Indian season was scheduled to end with the tour by the England 'A' side, but the return of South Africa to the international fold brought about a hastily arranged extension in order to accommodate an historic brief tour by a party from South Africa. Three one-day internationals and a Test match were arranged. This was the first time that a South African side had visited the Caribbean, and the first occasion that the two nations had met in an official Test match.

Carried along by the euphoria surrounding the achievement of South Africa in reaching the semi-final of the World Cup, the selectors rather unwisely announced an unchanged party to make the trip to West Indies. To re-enter the Test arena without the services of Jim Cook and the leadership of Clive Rice, arguably the best captain cricket has seen in the past 20 years, was, one felt, a grave error. Unhappily, Brian McMillan, South Africa's best all-rounder, was forced to withdraw from the side through injury, and his place was taken by Cornelius van Zyl.

The West Indies were not without their problems. Richardson, blamed for the failure in the World Cup and, allegedly, for a rift with Dujon which caused the Jamaican wicket-keeper to be omitted from the World Cup squad, was booed by the Sabina Park crowd. In contrast, the South Africans were given a rapturous reception. They were, however, soundly beaten in all three one-day international matches.

Against some alert fielding, but bowling which failed in control and consistency, Phil Simmons batted spectacularly at Kingston. He hit five sixes and 12 fours and reached his hundred off 113 balls. Lara had began positively with 50 off 68 balls, and South Africa were left with a mighty task. They began well enough and were 79 for 1 in the 20th over, but the loss of Hudson and Kirsten in the space of three overs sparked a collapse, and the last seven wickets fell in 12 overs.

At Port of Spain, West Indies gained a crushing victory to take the series. Put in to bat, South Africa were never at ease against some lively bowling, and they did not help themselves with some poor shots. Wessels lost concentration and slashed at a widish delivery while Kirsten cut a long-hop to third man. Rhodes played well to hit 45 off 71 balls, but South Africa's total was

FIRST ONE-DAY INTERNATIONAL – WEST INDIES v. SOUTH AFRICA
at Sabina Park, Kingston, Jamaica, 7 April, 1992

WEST INDIES

D.L. Haynes	c Henry, **b** Donald	9
B.C. Lara	c Wessels, **b** Henry	50
P.V. Simmons	c Wessels, **b** Kuiper	122
R.B. Richardson (capt)	lbw, **b** Kuiper	30
K.L.T. Arthurton	c Wessels, **b** Donald	27
C.L. Hooper	not out	19
W.K.M. Benjamin	c Wessels, **b** Kuiper	8
C.E.L. Ambrose	not out	0
*D. Williams		
A.C. Cummins		
B.P. Patterson		
Extras	b 1, lb 5, w 12, nb 4	22
	(for 6 wickets)	**287**

SOUTH AFRICA

K.C. Wessels (capt)	run out	8
A.C. Hudson	c and **b** Patterson	50
P.N. Kirsten	c Lara, **b** Patterson	15
A.P. Kuiper	st Williams, **b** Hooper	15
W.J. Cronje	**b** Cummins	42
J.N. Rhodes	**b** Cummins	17
R.P Snell	run out	1
*D.J. Richardson	c Arthurton, **b** Benjamin	5
C.J.P.G. van Zyl	c Ambrose, **b** Benjamin	0
O. Henry	**b** Benjamin	1
A.A. Donald	not out	5
Extras	lb 8, w 10, nb 3	21
		180

(50 overs)

	O	M	R	W
Donald	10	1	47	2
Snell	10	1	55	–
van Zyl	8	–	53	–
Henry	10	–	53	1
Cronje	3	–	18	–
Kirsten	4	–	22	–
Kuiper	5	–	33	3

(42.2 overs)

	O	M	R	W
Ambrose	7	1	20	–
Patterson	7	2	17	2
Benjamin	9.2	–	45	3
Cummins	9	–	34	2
Hooper	8	–	44	1
Simmons	2	–	12	–

FALL OF WICKETS
1–32, **2**–104, **3**–210, **4**–239, **5**–278, **6**–286

FALL OF WICKETS
1–10, **2**–79, **3**–82, **4**–121, **5**–153 **6**–155, **7**–161, **8**–169, **9**–174

Umpires: L.H. Barker & C.E. Cumberbatch   Man of the Match – P.V. Simmons   *West Indies won by 107 runs*

Ken Benjamin appeals. His performances for West Indies 'A' earned him a Test cap against South Africa. (Shaun Botterill)

SECOND ONE-DAY INTERNATIONAL – WEST INDIES v. SOUTH AFRICA
at Queen's Park Oval, Port of Spain, Trinidad, 11 April, 1992

SOUTH AFRICA

K.C. Wessels (capt)	c Williams, **b** Ambrose	1
A.C. Hudson	run out	6
P.N. Kirsten	c Benjamin, **b** Cummins	9
A.P. Kuiper	c Lara, **b** Harper	19
W.J. Cronje	run out	22
J.N. Rhodes	run out	45
*D.J. Richardson	c Arthurton, **b** Cummins	6
R.P. Snell	c Arthurton, **b** Cummins	8
O. Henry	not out	8
M.W. Pringle	**b** Ambrose	1
A.A. Donald	**b** Ambrose	0
Extras	lb 10, w 15, nb 2	27
		152

(43.4 overs)

	O	M	R	W
Ambrose	7.4	–	24	3
Patterson	9	2	30	–
Cummins	9	–	40	3
Benjamin	8	–	21	–
Harper	10	–	27	1

WEST INDIES

D.L. Haynes	not out	59
B.C. Lara	not out	86
P.V. Simmons		
R.B. Richardson (capt)		
K.L.T. Arthurton		
R.A. Harper		
*D. Williams		
C.E.L. Ambrose		
W.K.M. Benjamin		
A.C. Cummins		
B.P. Patterson		
Extras	b 1, lb 1, w 2, nb 5	9
		154

(25.5 overs)

	O	M	R	W
Donald	8	1	49	–
Pringle	7	–	32	–
Henry	4.5	–	41	–
Snell	6	–	30	–

FALL OF WICKETS

1–17, **2**–24, **3**–36, **4**–67, **5**–96, **6**–118, **7**–138, **8**–146, **9**–152

Umpires: L.H. Barker & C.E. Cumberbatch Man of the Match – B.C. Lara *West Indies won by 10 wickets*

completely inadequate. Haynes and Lara confirmed this when they romped to victory.

The following day, South Africa again found it difficult to master the West Indian attack although Rushmere and Hudson began promisingly. Wessels and Kirsten added 68 in 18 overs but lacked authority. With ten overs remaining, South Africa were 129 for 2, but three wickets fell quickly, and once more the final total was inadequate. Haynes was bowled by the first ball of the innings, but Simmons hit his third century in his last four one-day international innings. He hit two sixes and 10 fours and reached 103 out of 172 in the 40th over, his last 50 coming off 32 balls.

History is made. Kepler Wessels and Richie Richardson toss up before the first-ever Test match between West Indies and South Africa. (Patrick Eagar)

THIRD ONE-DAY INTERNATIONAL – WEST INDIES v. SOUTH AFRICA
at Queen's Park Oval, Port of Spain, Trinidad, 12 April, 1992

SOUTH AFRICA

A.C. Hudson	c Williams, b Harper	30
M.W. Rushmere	c and b Harper	29
K.C. Wessels (capt)	b Benjamin	45
P.N. Kirsten	c Harper, b Benjamin	28
A.P. Kuiper	c Richardson, b Patterson	2
W.J. Cronje	run out	23
* D.J. Richardson	not out	17
C.J.P.G. van Zyl	not out	3
R.P. Snell		
T. Bosch		
M.W. Pringle		
Extras	lb 8, w 3, nb 1	12
	(for 6 wickets)	189

(50 overs)

	O	M	R	W
Ambrose	10	1	39	–
Patterson	10	2	35	1
Benjamin	10	1	37	2
Cummins	10	–	39	–
Harper	10	–	31	2

FALL OF WICKETS
1–54, 2–67, 3–135, 4–139, 5–142, 6–185

WEST INDIES

D.L. Haynes	b Pringle	0
B.C. Lara	c Pringle, b Kuiper	35
P.V. Simmons	c Bosch, b Snell	104
R.B. Richardson (capt)	not out	37
K.L.T. Arthurton	not out	1
R.A. Harper		
*D. Williams		
C.E.L. Ambrose		
W.K.M. Benjamin		
A.C. Cummins		
B.P. Patterson		
Extras	lb 7, w 4, nb 2	13
	(for 3 wickets)	190

(43 overs)

	O	M	R	W
Pringle	5	3	6	1
Bosch	6	–	47	–
Snell	10	2	45	1
van Zyl	10	–	40	–
Kuiper	7	–	28	1
Kirsten	5	–	17	–

FALL OF WICKETS
1–0, 2–78, 3–182

Umpires: L.H. Barker & C.E. Cumberbatch — Man of the Match – P.V. Simmons — *West Indies won by 7 wickets*

TEST MATCH
WEST INDIES v. SOUTH AFRICA

Kepler Wessels leads South Africa onto the field at Kensington Oval. (Patrick Eagar)

SOUTH AFRICA
BATTING RUNS H.O. B
RUSHMERE 3 C 7
HUDSON 163 B 9
WESSELS 59 C 7
KIRSTEN 11 C 9
CRONJE 5 C 6
KUIPER 34 C 11
RICHARDSON 8 C 16
SNELL
PRINGLE
DONALD
BOSCH
SCORE
RUNS 315 WKTS 7
BATTING
8 NO 9
6 RUNS 0
EXTRAS 26
RUNS REQUIRED
OVERS 38
REMAINING OVERS 65
INNINGS TOTALS
WEST INDIES 1ST 262
1ST
2ND
WEST INDIES
FIELDING
1 HAYNES
2 SIMMONS
3 LARA
4 RICHARDSON
5 ARTHURTON
6 ADAMS
7 AMBROSE
8 WILLIAMS
9 BENJAMIN
10 WALSH
11 PATTERSON

The scoreboard showing the two teams at Bridgetown. (Shaun Botterill)

The first Test match to be played between West Indies and South Africa aroused much interest around the world of cricket, but the attendance at Kensington Oval was bitterly disappointing. Angered by the omission of fast bowler Cummins from the West Indian side, the Bajans announced that they would boycott the match in protest, and they kept their word. There were two Test debutants in the West Indian side, Adams and Kenneth Benjamin, while Wessels, once of Australia, was the only South African with Test match experience. Wessels won the toss and asked West Indies to bat first.

This seemed an unwise decision as the home side raced to 99 at little under five runs an over. Both openers then fell in quick succession. Simmons hit impetuously to mid-off, and Haynes also drove rashly at Snell. Lara was dropped first ball, but he survived to suggest his class with some elegant shots before being splendidly caught down the leg side by wicket-keeper Richardson at 137.

Richardson and Arthurton regained the initiative for West Indies with a partnership of 82 runs in brisk time. Richardson was out shortly before tea. Arthurton reached his first half century in Test cricket, but in the final session West Indies collapsed, losing their last six wickets for 22 runs in ten overs. Hudson and Rushmere took South Africa safely to the close.

Andrew Hudson on the way to his century. (Shaun Botterill)

Rushmere fell to the eighth ball of the second day, but in the next 33 overs Hudson and Wessels added 135. Wessels played a necessarily positive innings while Hudson settled to become the rock of the South African reply. Kenneth Benjamin could find no rhythm on his Test debut, and Arthurton had to be brought into the attack. Hudson was badly dropped by Walsh at long leg off Ambrose, but the bowler gained some compensation when Wessels sliced to Adams at backward point.

Hudson had first been dropped when he was on 22, and in the over following the dismissal of Wessels, he was put down by wicket-keeper Williams another who, though rich in one-day internationals, was playing his first Test. Hudson had scored 66 when missed off Patterson, and although Kirsten and Cronje fell shortly before tea, South Africa ended the day in a strong position at 254 for 4. Andrew Hudson had reached an historic landmark by becoming not only the first batsman to score a century for South Africa on the country's return to Test cricket, but the first South African to score a century on the occasion of his Test debut.

Hudson was seventh out. He batted with remarkable and highly commendable application, facing 384 balls and hitting 20 fours. Like Hudson, Adams made a fine Test debut, returning figures of 4 for 43 with his slow left-arm bowling, the best bowling performance of his career, and capturing a wicket, that of Cronje, in his first over.

The South African lead was not as big as they might have hoped for, but West Indies lost three wickets in clearing the arrears, and they might have lost four had Lara been given not out when he dislodged a bail with his foot as he leg-glanced a ball from Bosch. This proved

Jimmy Adams ends a magnificent season with an invaluable innings of 79 not out on his Test debut. He drives Donald past cover. (Patrick Eagar)

Donald wrecks Arthurton's stumps.(Shaun Botterill/Allsport)

to be only a minor discouragement to the South Africans, however, for Donald and Snell, now following the inspiring example of Hudson's eight-and-a-half-hour innings, bowled with control and zest. Richardson was palpably leg before to the first ball after tea, and although Lara and Arthurton added 52 in under an hour, both were dismissed, and with Williams and Ambrose falling in the last overs of the day, the West Indian innings was in tatters by the close at 184 for 7.

South Africa enjoyed the rest day with the majority of correspondents believing them to be on the brink of victory. The last three West Indian wickets proved harder to capture than the visitors must have anticipated. Donald soon trapped Benjamin, but Walsh offered some good support to Adams before being caught behind off Snell's second delivery of the day. In the last 50 minutes before lunch, Adams and Patterson brought West Indies back into the match. Patterson denied anything straight, and Adams punished anything loose. Both were missed off Pringle, Patterson in the gully by Hudson, and Adams by the bowler himself off a very difficult chance. Patterson was eventually bowled by Bosch, but by then he had helped Adams to add 62 runs in 17 overs. Adams played only because Hooper had an injured hand, but his 221-minute innings was the longest by a West Indian in the match. This was an exemplary Test debut.

Hudson was out to the second ball of the innings when South Africa went in search of 201 to win the match. Rushmere also fell to Ambrose, but Wessels, whose field placings in the closing stages of the West Indian innings had been somewhat naive, and Kirsten negotiated all further problems. South Africa ended the day on 122 for 2, victory in sight.

In the first hour of the last day, Courtney Walsh crowned his memorable season by taking the wickets of Wessels, Kirsten and Kuiper in the space of 27 balls at a personal cost of six runs. Only a leg-bye had been added to the overnight score when Wessels drove at Walsh and was wonderfully caught by Lara low to his left. Cronje was all nerves, and both he and Kuiper were spectacularly caught behind by Williams. The departure of Kirsten after his three-and-three-quarter-hour, 168-ball innings marked the end for South Africa. Snell was taken by short-leg. Pringle was yorked by Ambrose who had Richardson caught behind in his next over. He bowled Donald first ball, and South Africa had lost eight wickets for 26 runs in 95 minutes. Ambrose and Walsh had bowled magnificently, and the fielding was electric. Richardson and his team joined hands in a lap of honour which symbolised their unity and helped to silence the critics. Hudson and Ambrose were named as joint Man of the Match, but there were no losers in this epic Test match which was the most memorable of returns from the wilderness for South Africa.

Williams dives to take a spectacular catch to dismiss Kuiper off Walsh. (Patrick Eagar)

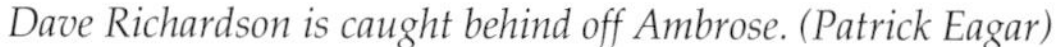

Dave Richardson is caught behind off Ambrose. (Patrick Eagar)

Ambrose bowls Donald and West Indies have beaten South Africa by 52 runs. (Patrick Eagar)

TEST MATCH – WEST INDIES v. SOUTH AFRICA

18, 19, 20, 22 and 23 April, 1992 at Kensington Oval, Bridgetown, Barbados

WEST INDIES

	FIRST INNINGS		SECOND INNINGS	
D.L. Haynes	c Wessels, **b** Snell	58	c Richardson, **b** Snell	23
P.V. Simmons	c Kirsten, **b** Snell	35	c Kirsten, **b** Bosch	3
B.C. Lara	c Richardson, **b** Bosch	17	c Richardson, **b** Donald	64
R.B. Richardson (capt)	c Richardson, **b** Snell	44	lbw, **b** Snell	2
K.L.T. Arthurton	c Kuiper, **b** Pringle	59	**b** Donald	22
J.C. Adams	**b** Donald	11	not out	79
*D. Williams	c Hudson, **b** Donald	1	lbw, **b** Snell	5
C.E.L. Ambrose	not out	6	c Richardson, **b** Donald	6
K.C.G. Benjamin	**b** Snell	1	lbw, **b** Donald	7
C.A. Walsh	**b** Pringle	6	c Richardson, **b** Snell	13
B.P. Patterson	run out	0	**b** Bosch	11
Extras	lb 7, nb 17	24	b 17, lb 11, nb 20	48
		262		**283**

SOUTH AFRICA

	FIRST INNINGS		SECOND INNINGS	
M.W. Rushmere	c Lara, **b** Ambrose	3	(2) **b** Ambrose	3
A.C. Hudson	**b** Benjamin	163	(1) c Lara, **b** Ambrose	0
K.C. Wessels (capt)	c Adams, **b** Ambrose	59	c Lara, **b** Walsh	74
P.N. Kirsten	c Lara, **b** Benjamin	11	**b** Walsh	52
W.J. Cronje	c Lara, **b** Adams	5	c Williams, **b** Ambrose	2
A.P. Kuiper	c Williams, **b** Patterson	34	c Williams, **b** Walsh	0
*D.J. Richardson	c Ambrose, **b** Adams	8	c Williams, **b** Ambrose	2
R.P. Snell	run out	6	c Adams, **b** Walsh	0
M.W. Pringle	c Walsh, **b** Adams	15	**b** Ambrose	4
A.A. Donald	st Williams, **b** Adams	0	(11) **b** Ambrose	0
T. Bosch	not out	5	(10) not out	0
Extras	b 4, lb 6, w 1, nb 25	36	b 4, lb 3, nb 4	11
		345		**148**

	O	M	R	W	O	M	R	W
Donald	20	1	67	**2**	25	3	77	**4**
Bosch	15	2	43	**1**	24.3	7	61	**2**
Pringle	18.4	2	61	**2**	16	–	43	–
Snell	18	3	84	**4**	16	1	74	**4**

	O	M	R	W	O	M	R	W
Ambrose	39	19	47	**2**	24.4	7	34	**6**
Patterson	23	4	79	**1**	7	1	26	–
Walsh	27	7	71	–	22	10	31	**4**
Benjamin	25	3	87	**2**	9	2	21	–
Arthurton	3	–	8	–				
Adams	21.4	5	43	**4**	5	–	16	–
Simmons					5	1	13	–

FALL OF WICKETS

1–99, **2**–106, **3**–137, **4**–219, **5**–240, **6**–241, **7**–250, **8**–258, **9**–262
1–10, **2**–66, **3**–68, **4**–120, **5**–139, **6**–164, **7**–174, **8**–196, **9**–221

FALL OF WICKETS

1–14, **2**–139, **3**–168, **4**–187, **5**–279, **6**–293, **7**–312, **8**–316, **9**–336
1–0, **2**–27, **3**–123, **4**–130, **5**–131, **6**–142, **7**–142, **8**–147, **9**–148

Umpires: D.M. Archer & S.U. Bucknor

West Indies won by 52 runs

FIRST-CLASS AVERAGES

BATTING

	M	Inns	NO	Runs	HS	Av	100s	50s
D.L. Haynes	3	5	–	490	246	98.00	2	1
P.V. Simmons	4	6	–	424	202	70.66	1	3
J.C. Adams	9	16	5	770	128*	70.00	3	3
K.L.T. Arthurton	3	6	1	335	117	67.00	1	2
S. Chanderpaul	2	4	1	168	90	56.00	–	2
R.A. Harper	3	5	1	203	74	50.75	–	3
J.R. Murray	9	15	3	575	102	47.91	1	2
B.C. Lara	4	6	–	282	135	47.00	1	1
C.B. Lambert	8	15	–	646	144	43.06	2	4
R.I.C. Holder	8	13	–	555	123	42.69	1	4
L.L. Harris	5	7	–	291	98	41.57	–	3
R.G. Samuels	8	15	1	560	104	40.00	1	3
F.L. Reiffer	3	5	–	181	126	36.20	1	
R.B. Richardson	2	3	–	108	62	36.00	–	1
S.C. Williams	3	6	1	180	66	36.00	–	1
W. Davis	3	5	–	175	99	35.00	–	1
R.D. Jacobs	5	9	2	227	78	32.42	–	2
K.A. Williams	5	8	1	220	98	31.42	–	2
C.A. Best	7	13	3	314	79	31.40	–	2
R.W. Staple	4	7	–	219	79	31.28	–	2
H.A.G. Anthony	5	7	1	183	71	30.50	–	1
M.P. Carew	3	5	–	149	61	29.80	–	1
N.C. Guishard	5	7	2	145	79	29.00	–	1
L.D. John	5	9	–	257	64	28.55	–	2
F.R. Redwood	3	5	1	111	38*	27.75	–	–
N.E.F. Barry	5	8	–	215	71	26.87	–	1
C.A. Davis	6	9	5	107	28	26.75	–	–
C.G. Yorke	5	8	–	212	91	26.50	–	2
A.C.H. Walsh	5	9	1	211	77	26.37	–	1
P.J.L. Dujon	4	7	2	129	66*	25.80	–	1
K.C.G. Benjamin	8	12	5	177	52*	25.28	–	1
C.G. Butts	5	7	1	151	47	25.16	–	–
D.A. Joseph	6	11	–	255	61	23.18	–	1
P.A. Wallace	5	9	–	206	66	22.88	–	2
S. Dhaniram	4	7	–	155	81	22.14	–	1
J.D. Charles	6	11	3	174	54	21.75	–	1
S. Ragoonath	6	9	–	190	67	21.11	–	2
A.H. Gray	8	10	–	210	55	21.00	–	2
R. Seeram	4	7	–	143	58	20.42	–	1
R.C. Haynes	5	7	–	140	51	20.00	–	1
J. Eugene	3	6	–	119	68	19.83	–	1
N.O. Perry	7	9	2	137	57	19.57	–	1
N.A. McKenzie	3	6	–	115	67	19.16	–	1
C.O. Browne	5	9	2	126	62*	18.00	–	1
W.N. Reid	4	6	–	106	78	17.66	–	1
L.A. Joseph	7	11	1	170	37*	17.00	–	–
T.Z. Kentish	6	8	1	118	37	16.85	–	–
N.F. Williams	5	8	–	123	50	15.37	–	1
R.A.M. Smith	6	8	–	115	33	14.37	–	–
C.A. Walsh	9	12	2	129	22	12.90	–	–

(Qualification – 100 runs, average 10.00)

BOWLING

	Overs	Mds	Runs	Wkts	Av	Best	10/m	5/inn
C.A. Walsh	349.1	101	716	50	14.32	6-62	–	3
C.E.L. Ambrose	144.1	47	241	16	15.06	6-34	–	1
L.A. Joseph	201.2	45	579	33	17.54	6-51	–	2
V.D. Walcott	161.1	38	425	21	20.23	5-41	–	1
K.C.G. Benjamin	276	68	677	33	20.51	6-72	–	1
N.O. Perry	168.1	53	364	17	21.41	5-47	–	1
V.A. Walsh	97	15	354	16	22.12	6-77	–	1
R.C. Haynes	171.5	48	378	17	22.23	4-21	–	–
H.A.G. Anthony	126.1	12	464	20	23.20	4-23	–	–
V.C. Drakes	82	13	281	12	23.41	3-17	–	–
C.G. Butts	163.3	35	405	17	23.82	7-29	–	1
E.C. Antoine	197.4	40	566	23	24.60	6-49	–	2
C.A. Davis	148.4	26	499	19	26.26	6-101	–	1
O.D. Gibson	144	15	496	18	27.55	7-78	–	1
A.H. Gray	257.4	43	703	25	28.12	5-49	–	1
N.F. Williams	102.5	12	306	10	30.60	5-33	–	1
I.B.A. Allen	146.1	27	454	14	32.42	4-56	–	–
R. Dhanraj	173.5	36	516	15	34.40	4-35	–	–
W.N. Reid	150	40	372	10	37.20	4-214		
112	–	–						

(Qualification – 10 wickets)

LEADING FIELDERS

26 – J.R. Murray; 19 – C.O. Browne; 16 – D. Williams (ct 12/st 4); 15 – R.D. Jacobs; 14 – P.J.L. Dujon (ct 12/st 2) and R.C. Haynes; 13 – C.B. Lambert; 9 – A.H. Gray; 8 – C. A. Best and R.A. Harper

SECTION J ENGLAND

Britannic Assurance County Championship
Benson and Hedges Cup
Sunday League NatWest Trophy Pakistan tour,
Cornhill Test and Texaco Trophy series,
Tetley Bitter Challenge Tilcon Trophy
Joshua Tetley Festival Trophy Seeboard Trophy
First-class averages First-class and one-day form charts

The birth of a first-class county. Paul Parker faces the first ball in first-class cricket by a Durham player. Oxford University v. Durham, Oxford, 14 April. (David Munden)

The season begins. Gooch leads Essex onto the field for the start of the match between the Champion County and England 'A'. Behind Gooch are Garnham, Foster, Shahid and Prichard, with others reluctant to leave the warmth of the pavilion. (Patrick Eagar)

13, 14, 15 and 16 April *at Lord's*

England 'A' 456 for 7 dec. (D.J. Bicknell 115, M.D. Moxon 71, P. Johnson 53, H. Morris 51)
Essex 317 for 8 dec. (D.R. Pringle 102 not out, G.A. Gooch 75, M.E. Waugh 61)
Match drawn

14, 15 and 16 April *at Cambridge*

Leicestershire 279 for 2 dec. (N.E. Briers 120, J.J. Whitaker 73 not out, T.J. Boon 51) and 0 for 0 dec.
Cambridge University 0 for 0 dec. and 146 (S.W. Johnson 50)
Leicestershire won by 133 runs

at Oxford

Durham 286 for 2 dec. (J.D. Glendenen 117, P.W.G. Parker 103)
Oxford University 105 for 2 (J.E.R. Gallian 53)
Match drawn

At Lord's, Neil Foster bowled from the Pavilion End, Darren Bicknell went onto the back foot and played the ball into the covers. The England season had begun. The talented Surrey left-hander went on to reach an admirable century, the season's first, and there was a good innings from skipper Martyn Moxon who may well reassert his challenge for a recall to the England side. Essex looked with embarrassment at the prospect of following-on when they collapsed after a blank third day, but Derek Pringle gave a reminder that he is an all-rounder with the ninth century of his career.

In weather that was cold and unwelcoming, Leicestershire and Cambridge University contrived a result with the forfeiture of innings after the loss of the

The season begins. Spectators in The Parks to watch Oxford University and the newcomers Durham. (Simon Bruty/Allsport)

John Glendenen (Durham) – a century on his first-class debut against Oxford University. (USPA)

second day's play. Skipper Briers shared in two century partnerships. Durham began their first-class career with a first-wicket stand of 222 in The Parks. Paul Parker and John Glendenen both hit centuries. Glendenen was making his first-class debut and hit a six and 17 fours.

17, 18 and 20 April *at Cambridge*

Middlesex 238 for 3 dec. (M.A. Roseberry 101) and 123 for 2 dec. (K.R. Brown 53 not out)
Cambridge University 109 for 1 dec. and 113 for 3

Match drawn

at Oxford

Worcestershire 413 for 4 dec. (A.C.H. Seymour 133, T.M. Moody 100 not out, T.S. Curtis 76, D.A. Leatherdale 67) and 162 for 7 dec. (N.V. Radford 66)
Oxford University 227 (J.E.R. Gallian 112, R.K. Illingworth 4 for 79)

Match drawn

There was a blank first day at Fenner's, and on the Saturday Mark Roseberry hit three sixes and ten fours in a good launch to the season. At Oxford, Seymour hit a century in his first match for Worcestershire, sharing an opening partnership of 181 with Tim Curtis, while Jason Gallian, who had captained Young Australia, made a maiden first-class century for the University.

SUNDAY LEAGUE

19 April *at Derby*

Derbyshire 121 (M.C.J. Ilott 4 for 15)
Essex 122 for 2

Essex (4 pts.) won by 8 wickets

at Durham University

Durham 246 for 4 (D.M. Jones 114, W. Larkins 59)
Lancashire 237 (N.J. Speak 58)

Durham (4 pts.) won by 9 runs

at Southampton

Gloucestershire 150 for 6
Hampshire 151 for 4 (R.A. Smith 61)

Hampshire (4 pts.) won by 6 wickets

Mike Roseberry began the season in top form for Middlesex. His consistency was to bring him more than 2000 first-class runs and a place in the England 'A' side. (USPA)

at Canterbury

Kent 163 (N.R. Taylor 51)
Somerset 164 for 6 (M.N. Lathwell 55)

Somerset (4 pts.) won by 4 wickets

at Leicester

Middlesex 207 for 7 (M.A. Roseberry 59)
Leicestershire 197 (L. Potter 52)

Middlesex (4 pts.) won by 10 runs

at Trent Bridge

Nottinghamshire 187 for 9
Sussex 191 for 3 (K. Greenfield 77, J.W. Hall 77)

Sussex (4 pts.) won by 7 wickets

at The Oval

Surrey 166 for 9 (K.M. Curran 4 for 21)
Northamptonshire 168 for 5

Northamptonshire (4 pts.) won by 5 wickets

at Edgbaston

Glamorgan 180 for 6 (I.V.A. Richards 68, A. Dale 51, T.A. Munton 4 for 16)
Warwickshire 181 for 4 (A.J. Moles 96 not out)

Warwickshire (4 pts.) won by 6 wickets

at Worcester

Yorkshire 160 for 9
Worcestershire 153 for 7 (T.S. Curtis 50)

Yorkshire (4 pts.) won by 7 runs

The competitive season began with a full round of Sunday League matches. Most attention was on Durham, and the newcomers did not disappoint. Dean Jones hit 114 in 103 minutes, with eight fours and four sixes, and Botham ran out Hegg in the last over to give the home side a dramatic win. Gus Fraser made a welcome and economic return for Middlesex who won at Leicester. Fraser's return was doubly welcome as Ricardo Ellcock had announced his retirement because of injury. Sussex surprisingly beat the reigning champions Nottinghamshire. Hall and Greenfield hit 144 in 28 overs for the first wicket to set up Sussex's victory.

BENSON AND HEDGES CUP

21 April *at Durham University*

Durham 196 for 9 (I.T. Botham 86, M. Frost 4 for 26)
Glamorgan 197 for 6 (C.S. Cowdrey 78)

Glamorgan (2 pts.) won by 4 wickets

(Gold Award – I.T. Botham)

at Chelmsford

Essex 61 (P.A.J. DeFreitas 5 for 16)
Lancashire 65 for 2

Lancashire (2 pts.) won by 8 wickets

(Gold Award – P.A.J. DeFreitas)

at Cheltenham

Gloucestershire 110
Leicestershire 111 for 0 (T.J. Boon 54 not out, N.E. Briers 51 not out)

Leicestershire (2 pts.) won by 10 wickets

(Gold Award – V.J. Wells)

at Canterbury

Kent 231 for 7 (M.V. Fleming 69, J.I. Longley 57)
Somerset 194 (R.J. Harden 76, M.J. McCague 5 for 43, M.A. Ealham 4 for 29)

Kent (2 pts.) won by 37 runs

(Gold Award – M.V. Fleming)

at Lord's

Minor Counties 165 for 9
Middlesex 167 for 3 (M.A. Roseberry 84)

Middlesex (2 pts.) won by 7 wickets

(Gold Award – M.A. Roseberry)

at Forfar

Northamptonshire 235 for 6 (A. Fordham 103, J.W. Govan 4 for 55)
Scotland 190 for 9 (B.M.W. Patterson 96)

Northamptonshire (2 pts.) won by 45 runs

(Gold Award – A. Fordham)

at Hove

Sussex 246 for 7 (J.W. Hall 81, A.P. Wells 61)
Surrey 238 for 8 (D.J. Bicknell 71)

Sussex (2 pts.) won by 8 runs

(Gold Award – J.W. Hall)

at Edgbaston

Yorkshire 188 for 6
Warwickshire 185 (R.G. Twose 62, P.W. Jarvis 4 for 34)

Yorkshire (2 pts.) won by 3 runs

(Gold Award – R.J. Blakey)

at Worcester

Worcestershire 232 for 5 (T.M. Moody 70 not out, T.S. Curtis 62)
Derbyshire 164 (P.J. Newport 5 for 31)

Worcestershire (2 pts.) won by 68 runs

(Gold Award – T.M. Moody)

The Benson and Hedges Cup opened in fine weather, produced some excellent cricket and witnessed at least one surprising result.

Glamorgan beat Durham in the last over, but the sensation was at Chelmsford where Essex, favourites to win the cup, were put in to bat and were bowled out in 25.3 overs for 61 runs, their lowest score in a one-day competition. DeFreitas bowled the first over of the match and trapped Gooch leg before with his fourth ball. Two deliveries later, Waugh was taken at slip. Essex never recovered. DeFreitas bowled splendidly to take five wickets in the Benson and Hedges Cup for the first time and to produce the best bowling against Essex in the history of the competition. Essex batted poorly on a pitch which encouraged the seam bowlers, and the game was over by mid-afternoon.

Leicestershire brushed aside Gloucestershire, winning with more than 20 overs to spare, and Vincent Wells, newly signed from Kent, took the Gold Award for his 3 for 13 in 11 overs. His old county were roused from the depths of 87 for 4 by Matthew Fleming, and Mark Ealham and Martin McCague then bowled out Somerset for 194, the last eight wickets falling for 21 runs.

Minor Counties promised more than they achieved at Lord's, and Roseberry steered Middlesex to an easy win. Alan Fordham hit his first century in the competition and took the Gold Award in Forfar, but he was run close by Patterson who hit Scotland's highest score in the Benson and Hedges Cup

Hall and Greenfield gave Sussex a good start against Surrey, and skipper Alan Wells brought an increase in tempo in the middle order. Darren Bicknell continued his fine form of early season, and, in the 38th over, Surrey were 146 for 1. Nine overs later, they were 189 for 7. Sussex bowled well and fielded excitingly. When Stephenson began the last over Surrey still needed 15 to win, a task that was beyond them.

There was a stirring finish at Edgbaston where left-hander Roger Twose, who had had such a good season in New Zealand, and Tim Munton took 13 runs off the penultimate over to bring Warwickshire in sight of victory over Yorkshire, but Twose was caught at mid-wicket off the first ball of the final over, and Yorkshire won by three runs. Jarvis had cut away the foundations of the Warwickshire innings, and Blakey's five catches behind the stumps earned him the Gold Award.

Tom Moody took his fourth Gold Award as Worcestershire swept aside Derbyshire.

23 April *at Derby*

Glamorgan 155 for 9 (D.E. Malcolm 4 for 43)
Derbyshire 159 for 6 (P.D. Bowler 66 not out)

Derbyshire (2 pts.) won by 4 wickets

(Gold Award – P.D. Bowler)

at Cheltenham

Minor Counties 212 for 7 (N.A. Folland 63, J.D. Love 57, C.W.J. Athey 4 for 57)
Gloucestershire 213 for 3 (G.D. Hodgson 103 not out)

Gloucestershire (2 pts.) won by 7 wickets

(Gold Award – G.D. Hodgson)

at Southampton

Hampshire 177
Essex 136 (N. Hussain 55, M.D. Marshall 4 for 20)

Hampshire (2 pts.) won by 41 runs

(Gold Award – M.D. Marshall)

at Old Trafford

Scotland 219 for 5 (I.L. Philip 80, B.M.W. Patterson 63)
Lancashire 221 for 4 (N.J. Speak 64, G.D. Mendis 51)

Lancashire (2 pts.) won by 6 wickets

(Gold Award – I.L. Philip)

at Leicester

Sussex 237 for 7 (K. Greenfield 62, A.P. Wells 55 not out)
Leicestershire 240 for 5 (N.E. Briers 98, T.J. Boon 59)

Leicestershire (2 pts.) won by 5 wickets

(Gold Award – N.E. Briers)

at Trent Bridge

Kent 228 for 9 (M.R. Benson 66, C.C. Lewis 5 for 46)
Nottinghamshire 167 (B.C. Broad 64)

Kent (2 pts.) won by 61 runs

(Gold Award – M.R. Benson)

at Taunton

Somerset 143
Yorkshire 120

Somerset (2 pts.) won by 23 runs

(Gold Award – G.D. Rose)

at The Oval

Surrey 307 for 4 (G.P. Thorpe 78, D.J. Bicknell 70, M.A. Lynch 65)
Middlesex 238 (R.E. Bryson 4 for 56)

Surrey (2 pts.) won by 69 runs

(Gold Award – D.J. Bicknell)

at Oxford

Combined Universities 173 for 6 (R.R. Montgomerie 75, A. Storie 53 not out)
Worcestershire 174 for 6

Worcestershire (2 pts) won by 4 wickets

(Gold Award – J. Snape)

Good bowling and a solid innings from Peter Bowler took Derbyshire to victory over Glamorgan while Dean Hodgson hit his first century in the Benson and Hedges Cup and took his first Gold Award as Gloucestershire beat Minor Counties. For Essex disaster followed upon disaster. Their bowlers did an admirable job in dismissing Hampshire for 177, the last seven wickets going down for 53 runs, but again Essex began disastrously, losing Gooch, Waugh and Stephenson for five. In spite of Hussain's half-century, there was no

Benson and Hedges Cup. Combined Universities v. Worcestershire, at Oxford. John Crawley, the Universities skipper, takes evasive action as Steve Rhodes drives. (David Munden)

effective recovery, and the favourites faced elimination from the competition. Surprisingly, Malcolm Marshall's Gold Award was his first.

Scotland scored well at Old Trafford, with Philip and Patterson putting on 144 for the first wicket, but Lancashire never looked like being beaten.

Leicestershire's good form continued as they beat Sussex comfortably to head Group A. Boon and Briers laid the foundation of their victory with an opening partnership of 135. Sussex made their task harder by sending down 19 wides and three no-balls.

Like Leicestershire, Kent won their second match to take the lead in Group C. Their victory over Nottinghamshire was based on a good team performance, and they excelled in the field. Chris Lewis took five wickets in a Benson and Hedges Cup match for the first time, but the Gold Award went to Mark Benson for his 66 and intelligent captaincy.

Somerset occupied 55 overs at Taunton for their 143, which certainly did not appear to be a winning score, but the Yorkshire batsmen found the sluggish pitch even harder to cope with and were bowled out for 120 in the 52nd over.

Middlesex began their game against Surrey at The Oval under a cloud. England batsman Mark Ramprakash had been fined the maximum amount permitted by the TCCB for his behaviour at Cambridge in Middlesex's first match of the season. Ramprakash had used abusive language at one of the undergraduates and rightly paid the price. Middlesex's troubles deepened when the game began, for Darren Bicknell and Monte Lynch opened the Surrey innings with a partnership of 140 in 24 overs. Stewart, Thorpe and Brown all plundered runs, and, faced with a formidable 307, Middlesex were never in contention.

Worcestershire led Group D after easily disposing of the Combined Universities in The Parks.

25, 27 and 28 April *at Cambridge*

Essex 315 for 8 dec. (M.A. Garnham 82 not out, P.J. Prichard 71, N.V. Knight 62, J.J.B. Lewis 58) and 195 for 3 dec. (N.V. Knight 104 not out, J.J.B. Lewis 70)
Cambridge University 75 (T.D. Topley 5 for 15) and 41 for 3

Match drawn

25, 26, 27 and 28 April *at Old Trafford*

Lancashire 397 (G.D. Lloyd 132, P.A.J. DeFreitas 55 not out, M.A. Ealham 4 for 81, A.P. Igglesden 4 for 85) and 213 for 5 dec. (G. Fowler 66)
Kent 300 for 7 dec. (S.A. March 78, R.P. Davis 54 not out, M.R. Benson 53, M. Watkinson 4 for 60) and 192 for 8

Match drawn

Lancashire 7 pts., Kent 7 pts.

at Trent Bridge

Warwickshire 249 (R.G. Twose 55, A.J. Moles 51) and 263 (D.P. Ostler 102)

Nottinghamshire 311 (E.E. Hemmings 52 not out, R.A. Pick 52, P.A. Smith 5 for 79) and 202 for 2 (B.C. Broad 104, M.A. Crawley 64 not out)

Nottinghamshire won by 8 wickets

Nottinghamshire 23 pts., Warwickshire 6 pts.

at Taunton

Gloucestershire 344 (T.H.C. Hancock 102, C.W.J. Athey 65, M.C.J. Ball 54, A.R. Caddick 4 for 96)
Somerset 348 for 9 dec. (G.D. Rose 85, A.N. Hayhurst 54, A. Payne 51 not out, M.C.J. Ball 4 for 103)

Match drawn

Somerset 5 pts., Gloucestershire 4 pts.

25, 27, 28 and 29 April *at Durham University*

Durham 164 (P.W.G. Parker 77) and 318 (P.W.G. Parker 117, I.T. Botham 105, D.J. Millns 5 for 69)
Leicestershire 342 (T.J. Boon 110, B.F. Smith 100 not out) and 142 for 3

Leicestershire won by 7 wickets

Leicestershire 23 pts., Durham 3 pts.

at Southampton

Hampshire 468 for 2 dec. (T.C. Middleton 153, V.P. Terry 141, R.A. Smith 107 not out, D.I. Gower 55 not out) and 0 for 0 dec.
Sussex 169 for 2 dec. (B.T.P. Donelan 68 not out, D.M. Smith 61) and 149 (S.D. Udal 8 for 50)

Hampshire won by 150 runs

Hampshire 20 pts., Sussex 1 pt.

at Lord's

Middlesex 341 (M.W. Gatting 170, J.E. Emburey 57, S. Bastien 5 for 95) and 179 for 2 dec. (M.A. Roseberry 86)
Glamorgan 255 for 3 dec. (H. Morris 146, R.D.B. Croft 51) and 237 for 6 (S.P. James 94, J.E. Emburey 4 for 77)

Match drawn

Glamorgan 6 pts., Middlesex 5 pts.

at The Oval

Yorkshire 495 for 9 dec. (M.D. Moxon 141, A.A. Metcalfe 73, P.W. Jarvis 62, A.P. Grayson 57, N.M. Kendrick 4 for 89)
Surrey 164 (D. Gough 4 for 43, P. Carrick 4 for 60) and 64 for 2

Match drawn

Yorkshire 8 pts., Surrey 2 pts.

at Worcester

Worcestershire 345 (G.A. Hick 92, D.J. Capel 5 for 61) and 282 for 9 dec. (D.A. Leatherdale 60, A.R. Roberts 4 for 101)
Northamptonshire 354 (A.J. Lamb 101, D. Ripley 60 not out, P.J. Newport 5 for 102) and 180 for 7 (A.J. Lamb 66, R.K. Illingworth 4 for 43)

Match drawn

Worcestershire 6 pts., Northamptonshire 5 pts.

The weather was not kind to the opening round of matches in the Britannic Assurance County Championship. Lancashire did not start well against Kent, but Graham Lloyd hit the highest score of his career to revive them and to claim the four batting points. On a bleak second day, nearly 44 overs were lost, and on the third, Kent were indebted to Marsh and Davis who added 115 after six wickets had fallen for 167. Eventually, Kent were asked to make 311 in 75 overs, but they were quickly in trouble, and it was a defiant seventh-wicket stand between Ealham and Davis that saved them.

Front-runners in the Championship race for most of 1991, Warwickshire suffered defeat in their opening match of the new campaign. They batted with tedium on the Saturday to reach 230 for 9, yet by the end of the second day they appeared to have seized the initiative by reducing Nottinghamshire to a point where they were still 13 runs in arrears with their last pair together. That last pair proved most obdurate, however, and on the third day, they extended their partnership to 109. Hemmings hit seven fours, and Pick struck Booth for two sixes in the 100th over to claim the fourth batting point. Warwickshire's agonies were compounded when Munton broke a finger in trying to take a catch. Dominic Ostler hit the second century of his career in little over four hours, but Warwickshire lost their last seven second-innings wickets for 73 runs, and Nottinghamshire were left to score 202 in 73 overs. Small bowled eight balls before retiring with hamstring trouble, and Broad hit 17 boundaries in his 104 which made the home side's victory a formality.

There was rain on a dour first day at Taunton. Put in to bat, Gloucestershire crawled. They were 74 for 4, but the second day saw a remarkable transformation as Tim Hancock hit a maiden first-class century in 155 minutes. His 102 came out of 147 runs scored while he was at the wicket, and with Ball making the highest score of his career, Gloucestershire's revival was complete. The weather reduced play on each day, nor did it relent on the final day which was notable for the 18-year-old Payne hitting a fifty on the occasion of his debut. Fast bowler Caddick was most impressive on his Championship debut.

There was no romantic beginning for Durham who were well beaten by Leicestershire. Durham elected to bat, but they quickly succumbed to the Mullally, Wells and Millns seam attack. Boon and Smith both hit centuries as Leicestershire built up a big lead. Boon hit 15 fours and faced 236 balls while Smith reached a maiden first-class hundred in 321 minutes. Ben Smith, a young player of exciting promise, had a mixed match, for, following this century, he injured tendons in an ankle while fielding and was out of the game for some weeks. Parker, with his second century of the season, and Botham, who reached his hundred off 98 balls, gave Durham hope with a fifth-wicket stand of 178, but the newcomers lost their last six wickets for 28 runs, and Leicestershire won with ease.

At the end of the first day at Southampton, Hampshire were 334 for 1. Terry and Middleton began the innings with a partnership of 246 after Sussex had won the toss and asked the home county to bat first. Robin Smith completed the third century of the innings, and Gower hit a fifty before Nicholas declared. There was no play on the third day, and casual bowling aided Sussex to a declaration which was followed by Hampshire's forfeiture of their second innings. Set to make 300 to win, Sussex collapsed against the off-spin of Shaun Udal, considered by Ray Illingworth as the most promising of his type in the country. Udal took 8 for 50, by far the best performance of his short career.

There were remarkable events at Lord's where Middlesex were bowled out in 95.4 overs on the first day. They were 129 for 6 before Gatting and Emburey added 148. Gatting was at his belligerent best and hit 27 fours in his 170 which was made in 339 minutes. Stephen James hit his highest score in the Championship, but the loss of the third day through rain hindered any chance of a result.

The same could be said of the game at The Oval where Moxon and Metcalfe put on 221 for Yorkshire's first wicket. Unfortunately, Moxon broke a finger shortly before the end of his innings and was out of the game for the next few weeks, a severe blow to Yorkshire. Murphy and Kendrick added 60 for Surrey's tenth wicket to save them from complete humiliation just as the rain saved them from defeat.

Graeme Hick gave encouragement to the England selectors with an innings of 92 which included 15 fours, but he was outshone by Allan Lamb, another who was trying to hold on to his England place. Lamb hit 100 off 176 balls, and Northamptonshire took a narrow first-innings lead. They were fortunate to survive in the end, however, as they lost their way in search of a target of 274 in 53 overs and were saved by Ripley and Bailey.

There was no play on the final day at Fenner's where Essex were thankful that their batsmen scored some runs. Nick Knight hit the second and higher century of his career, and Jonathan Lewis gave further evidence of his immense talent.

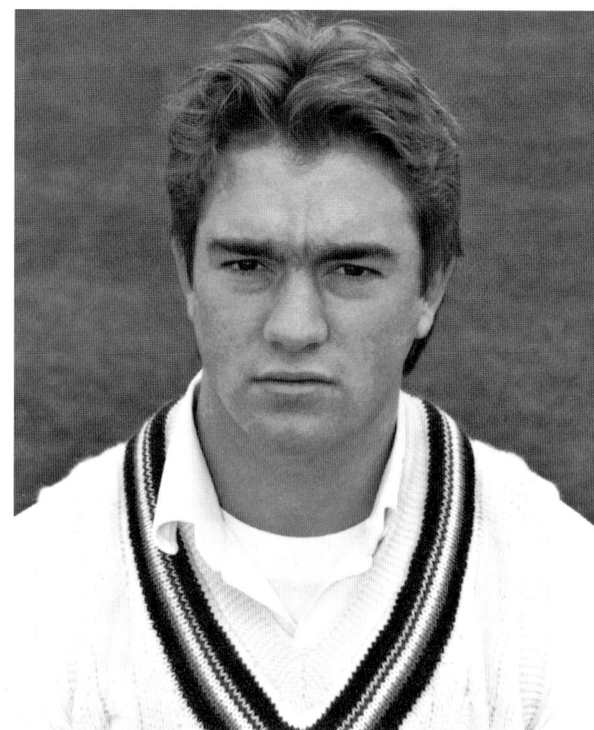

Gloucestershire's Tim Hancock – a maiden first-class century against Somerset. (David Munden)

Shaun Udal took 8 for 50 as Hampshire beat Sussex at Southampton, 25–29 April. (Patrick Eagar)

Tony Middleton of Hampshire, the first batsman to reach a thousand runs for the season. (Patrick Eagar)

SUNDAY LEAGUE

26 April *at Gateshead Fell*

Durham 232 for 7 (I.T. Botham 67)
Leicestershire 224 for 9

Durham (4 pts.) won by 8 runs

at Chelmsford

Surrey 84 for 9
Essex 88 for 0

Essex (4 pts.) won by 10 wickets

at Lord's

Glamorgan 181 for 5 (H. Morris 67)
Middlesex 184 for 2 (M.R. Ramprakash 88 not out, M.A. Roseberry 71 not out)

Middlesex (4 pts.) won by 8 wickets

at Hove

Sussex v. Yorkshire

Match abandoned

Sussex 2 pts., Yorkshire 2 pts.

at Worcester

Northamptonshire 207 for 7 (R.J. Bailey 69, A. Fordham 50)
Worcestershire 208 for 3 (G.A. Hick 83 not out)

Worcestershire (4 pts.) won by 7 wickets

Only Worcester and Gateshead escaped the rain. The match at Chelmsford was reduced to a ten-over slog, and Essex, like Durham, who hit 96 from their last 11 overs, and Middlesex, won their second match in succession.

BENSON AND HEDGES CUP

30 April *at Derby*

Combined Universities 164 for 7 (J.E.R. Gallian 50)
Derbyshire 167 for 1 (K.J. Barnett 84 not out, P.D. Bowler 55)

Derbyshire (2 pts.) won by 9 wickets

(Gold Award – K.J. Barnett)

at Lord's

Middlesex 249 for 7 (M.A. Roseberry 74)
Gloucestershire 162

Middlesex (2 pts.) won by 87 runs

(Gold Award – P.N. Weekes)

at Worcester

Worcestershire 173 (T.S. Curtis 60, P. Bainbridge 4 for 38)
Durham 177 for 7

Durham (2 pts.) won by 3 wickets

(Gold Award – P.Bainbridge)

30 April and 1 May *at Chelmsford*

Essex 388 for 7 (G.A. Gooch 127, J.P. Stephenson 66, N.A. Foster 62, J.W. Govan 4 for 71)
Scotland 116 (M.C.J. Ilott 4 for 31)

Essex (2 pts.) won by 272 runs

(Gold Award – G.A. Gooch)

at Leicester

Leicestershire 96 (M.A. Feltham 5 for 30, R.E. Bryson 4 for 31)
Surrey 100 for 4

Surrey (2 pts.) won by 6 wickets

(Gold Award – M.A. Feltham)

at Marlow

Minor Counties 220 for 8
Sussex 201 (D.M. Smith 61)

Minor Counties (2 pts.) won by 19 runs

(Gold Award – K.A. Arnold)

at Edgbaston

Warwickshire 209 for 7 (M. Asif Din 71 not out)
Nottinghamshire 210 for 3 (P.R. Pollard 76 not out, P. Johnson 76)

Nottinghamshire (2 pts.) won by 7 wickets

(Gold Award – P. Johnson)

at Leeds

Kent 203 for 9 (M.V. Fleming 66)
Yorkshire 133

Kent (2 pts.) won by 70 runs

(Gold Award – M.V. Fleming)

1 May *at Southampton*

Hampshire 197 for 6 (D.I. Gower 118 not out)
Northamptonshire 191 for 5 (R.J. Bailey 109 not out)

Hampshire (2 pts.) won by 6 runs

(Gold Award – D.I. Gower)

The third round of matches in the Benson and Hedges Cup produced the first major surprise of the season as Minor Counties gained their fifth victory in the history of the competition with a win over Sussex at Marlow. The success was based on fine teamwork, with five batsmen reaching 30 and none making 40. Arnold, Greensword and Conn all bowled splendidly, and on the second day, Sussex were never in touch.

Several matches carried over to a second day because of rain, and there were comfortable wins for Derbyshire, Middlesex and Surrey who routed Leicestershire in 27.5 overs.

Durham won nobly against Worcestershire. They declined the offer of bad light and won by three wickets with 19 balls to spare as gloom enveloped the ground. The ultimate hero was Ian Smith who made 29 not out, but there were also fine efforts by McEwan, Fothergill and Glendenen.

There was spectacular cricket at Chelmsford where Essex kept their hopes of qualifying for the quarter-finals alive by scoring at a furious rate against Scotland. The game started 25 minutes late, but Gooch hit a hundred before lunch off 108 balls. He and Stephenson put on 193 for the first wicket. Foster hit 62 off 27 balls and was then injured and out of the game for some weeks. Scotland stuck to their task bravely, but Essex's 388 for 7 was a record for the competition as was their margin of victory. Gooch's century was his tenth in the Benson and Hedges Cup, and he collected the Gold Award for the 20th time.

Nottinghamshire beat Warwickshire with two balls to spare and owed much to Johnson who was dropped twice and survived to hit 76 off 86 balls. He and Pollard shared a third-wicket stand of 143 in 31 overs. Piper, the Warwickshire wicket-keeper, dislocated a finger.

Hampshire narrowly beat Northamptonshire in a match reduced to 33 overs by bad weather. Gower and Smith added 114 in 19 overs for Hampshire's second wicket, and Gower reached his highest score in the competition off 95 balls. Bailey responded with a 94-ball century, but his side could not manage 13 off the last over.

At Headingley, attention focused on the debut for Yorkshire of Indian Test star Sachin Tendulkar. Craig McDermott had been Yorkshire's first overseas signing, but injury had prevented him from fulfilling his contract, and Tendulkar had replaced him. Tendulkar bowled well and took 2 for 21 in his 11 overs, but he was disappointingly run out for 7, and Kent won comfortably.

Benson and Hedges Cup at Marlow. Minor Counties v. Sussex on the last day of April. (David Munden)

SUNDAY LEAGUE

2 May *at Cambridge*

Durham 271 for 6 (W. Larkins 73, I.T. Botham 72, J.D. Glendenen 60)
Combined Universities 220 for 5 (J.E.R. Gallian 50)
Durham (2 pts.) won by 51 runs
(Gold Award – W. Larkins)

at Cardiff

Worcestershire 244 for 7 (T.M. Moody 80)
Glamorgan 147
Worcestershire (2 pts.) won by 97 runs
(Gold Award – S.R. Lampitt)

at Old Trafford

Hampshire 241 for 4 (R.A. Smith 109)
Lancashire 203 (N.J. Speak 82)
Hampshire (2 pts.) won by 38 runs
(Gold Award – R.A. Smith)

at Leicester

Middlesex 325 for 5 (M.R. Ramprakash 108 not out, J.D. Carr 70, D.L. Haynes 67)
Leicestershire 226 for 8
Middlesex (2 pts.) won by 99 runs
(Gold Award – M.R. Ramprakash)

at Northampton

Essex 264 (G.A. Gooch 119, M.E. Waugh 100, C.E.L. Ambrose 4 for 31)
Northamptonshire 198 (A. Fordham 69, A.J. Lamb 53, P.M. Such 4 for 43)
Essex (2 pts.) won by 66 runs
(Gold Award – M.E. Waugh)

at Taunton

Warwickshire 236 for 6 (D.P. Ostler 65 not out, T.A. Lloyd 51)
Somerset 236 for 8 (A.N. Hayhurst 78, G.D. Rose 58)
Warwickshire (2 pts.) won by losing fewer wickets in a match in which scores finished level
(Gold Award – N.M.K. Smith)

at The Oval

Surrey 299 for 3 (M.A. Lynch 105, A.J. Stewart 71 not out, D.J. Bicknell 55)
Minor Counties 131 for 6
Surrey (2 pts.) won by 168 runs
(Gold Award – M.A. Lynch)

at Hove

Gloucestershire 224 for 7 (C.W.J. Athey 56 not out, G.D. Hodgson 54)
Sussex 225 for 6 (J.W. Hall 70, K. Greenfield 53)
Sussex (2 pts.) won by 4 wickets
(Gold Award – F.D. Stephenson)

at Leeds

Yorkshire 193 for 9
Nottinghamshire 194 for 3 (P. Johnson 79 not out)
Nottinghamshire (2 pts.) won by 7 wickets
(Gold Award – P. Johnson)

Durham kept alive their hopes of qualifying for the final stages of the Benson and Hedges Cup with a victory in which their batting rather than their bowling again proved to be their strength. In the same group (D) Worcestershire assured themselves of a place in the quarter-finals with a comfortable win over Glamorgan.

Hampshire, too, became qualifiers by beating Lancashire at Old Trafford. Hampshire lost Terry for 0, but Robin Smith and Tony Middleton added 134 for the second wicket. Robin Smith reached his third century in the competition and took his third Gold Award.

In the closely fought Group A, there were wins for Middlesex, Surrey and Sussex. Middlesex hit 153 from their last 15 overs and Ramprakash hit his first hundred in the competition. He and Carr added 147 for the fifth wicket, and Leicestershire could never match Middlesex's scoring rate. Surrey again scored heavily to account for Minor Counties and virtually make certain of a place in the quarter-finals, while Sussex recovered from the trauma at Marlow to beat Gloucestershire in the final over after Greenfield and Hall had given them a fine start with 113 for the first wicket.

Essex kept alive their hopes of an improbable placing by scoring at a brisk rate against Northamptonshire. Gooch and Mark Waugh added 206 in 33 overs for the second wicket, but Essex lost their last nine wickets for 27 runs in seven overs as batsmen perished in search of quick runs. Waugh's first Benson and Hedges hundred came off 98 balls while Gooch faced 119 balls. Incredibly, Gooch's Benson and Hedges record for 1992 was 0, 0, 127 and 119. Like Ambrose, Such recorded his best figures in the competition and Northamptonshire were well beaten in a match which finished at 8.25 p.m.

The main excitement was at Taunton where Somerset reached the last over needing four to win. The over was bowled by off-spinner Neil Smith, and he maintained an impeccable length and direction. Three runs were scampered, and Snell was run out off the fifth ball. Mallender drove and missed the last delivery, and was bowled, to give Warwickshire victory having lost fewer wickets.

This result kept open the question as to who would qualify from Group C along with Kent. Nottinghamshire's acting captain Paul Johnson again led his side by example in a comfortable win over Yorkshire. Johnson won his second Gold Award in two days for his 79 off 59 balls.

SUNDAY LEAGUE

3 May *at Cardiff*

Glamorgan 169 for 8 (I.V.A. Richards 75)
Worcestershire 170 for 2 (T.M. Moody 80 not out, G.A. Hick 80)

Worcestershire (4 pts.) won by 8 wickets

at Old Trafford

Hampshire 209 for 7 (V.P. Terry 66)
Lancashire 210 for 6 (N.J. Speak 65)

Lancashire (4 pts) won by 4 wickets

at Leicester

Leicestershire 189 for 8 (J.J. Whitaker 68)
Essex 193 for 7 (M.E. Waugh 86)

Essex (4 pts.) won by 3 wickets

at Lord's

Gloucestershire 108
Middlesex 111 for 1 (D.L. Haynes 59 not out)

Middlesex (4 pts.) won by 9 wickets

at Northampton

Kent 221 for 9 (J.I. Longley 71, M.R. Benson 68)
Northamptonshire 137

Kent (4 pts.) won by 84 runs

at Taunton

Somerset 199 for 8 (R.P. Snell 62)
Warwickshire 177 (A.J. Moles 60)

Somerset (4 pts.) won by 22 runs

at Leeds

Yorkshire 167 for 7 (R.J. Blakey 72)
Nottinghamshire 171 for 1 (D.W. Randall 91 not out, B.C. Broad 62)

Nottinghamshire (4 pts.) won by 9 wickets

Essex and Middlesex moved clear at the top of the Sunday League with three wins in as many matches. Only two Gloucestershire batsmen reached double figures at Lord's and Middlesex won with 14.3 overs to spare. Essex were harder pressed after a middle-order collapse, and they were indebted to an unbroken partnership between Garnham and Alastair Fraser to take them to victory in the final over.

Moody and Hick added 166 for Worcestershire's second wicket at Cardiff, and Benson and Longley put on 124 in 17 overs for Kent's second wicket in the victory over Northamptonshire who batted without Allan Lamb, injured. Longley's 71 was his highest score in any competition.

Broad and Randall scored 120 for Nottinghamshire's first wicket to set up victory over Yorkshire, while both Speak and DeFreitas hit their Sunday League best scores in Lancashire's win over Hampshire. Lancashire needed 34 from five overs before DeFreitas hit 49 not out off 38 balls to bring them to victory with seven balls to spare.

At Taunton, Warwickshire wicket-keeper Piran Holloway took four catches but saw his side lose to Somerset for whom South African Richard Snell hit 62 off 54 balls.

3 May *at Arundel*

Pakistanis 253 for 3 (Aamir Sohail 104 retired, Salim Malik 84)
Lavinia, Duchess of Norfolk's XI 240 for 4 (P.D. Bowler 82, T.J.G. O'Gorman 69)

Pakistanis won by 13 runs

4 May *at Canterbury*

Pakistanis 281 for 6 (Salim Malik 95, Asif Mujtaba 69 not out)
Kent 241 (M.V. Fleming 74)

Pakistanis won by 40 runs

Pakistan's tour of England began with two 50-over matches, at Arundel and at Canterbury on Bank Holiday Monday when no other first-class counties were playing. Their batting showed to good effect in both matches.

BENSON AND HEDGES CUP

5 May *at Jesmond*

Derbyshire 281 for 9 (J.E. Morris 121)
Durham 201 (W. Larkins 58, D.G. Cork 4 for 26)

Derbyshire (2 pts.) won by 80 runs

(Gold Award – J.E. Morris)

at Cardiff

Glamorgan 277 for 5 (S.P. James 135, A. Dale 53)
Combined Universities 156 for 9

Glamorgan (2 pts.) won by 121 runs

(Gold Award – S.P. James)

at Glasgow (Hamilton Crescent)

Scotland 151 for 5 (G.N. Reifer 63 not out)
Hampshire 16 for 2

Match abandoned

Scotland 1 pt., Hampshire 1 pt.

at Stone

Leicestershire 289 for 8 (N.E. Briers 102, J.J. Whitaker 73)
Minor Counties 253 (N.A. Folland 52, D.J. Millns 4 for 51)

Leicestershire (2 pts.) won by 36 runs

(Gold Award – N.E. Briers)

at Trent Bridge

Nottinghamshire 224 (B.C. Broad 83, M.A. Crawley 57, N.A. Mallender 4 for 49)
Somerset 227 for 6 (A.N. Hayhurst 95)

Somerset (2 pts.) won by 4 wickets

(Gold Award – A.N. Hayhurst)

at Hove

Sussex 141 (D.W. Headley 4 for 19)
Middlesex 145 for 0 (M.A. Roseberry 70 not out, D.L. Haynes 66 not out)

Middlesex (2 pts.) won by 10 wickets

5 and 6 May *at Canterbury*

Kent 209 for 7 (M.R. Benson 62)
Warwickshire 182 (T.A. Lloyd 61)

Kent (2 pts.) won by 27 runs

(Gold Award – C.L. Hooper)

at Northampton

Lancashire 257 for 8 (N.H. Fairbrother 79, M. Watkinson 76)
Northamptonshire 249 for 7 (A.J. Lamb 108 not out, N.A. Felton 82)

Lancashire (2 pts.) won by 8 runs

(Gold Award – A.J. Lamb)

at The Oval

Gloucestershire 252 for 5 (G.D. Hodgson 80, A.J. Wright 62)
Surrey 253 for 8 (D.J. Bicknell 78)

Surrey (2 pts.) won by 2 wickets

(Gold Award – G.D. Hodgson)

The final round of matches in the zonal section of the Benson and Hedges Cup saw Derbyshire and Durham engaged in what was, in effect, a straightforward knock-out contest for the second spot in Group D. Durham had been expected to win, but, put in to bat, Derbyshire prospered after Morris had been dropped behind the stumps by Fothergill when on six. Morris went on to make 121 off 118 balls, and his innings included four sixes and 11 fours. Bishop hit a lusty 42, and Durham could never score briskly enough against the accuracy of Mortensen and Cork. Krikken held four catches behind the wicket – one a brilliant one-hander to account for Botham – and was awarded his county cap.

Stephen James hit his first century in the Benson and Hedges Cup as Glamorgan trounced Combined Universities, and Nigel Briers was another to hit his first century in the competition. He and Whitaker added 186 for Leicestershire's second wicket, but Minor Counties again performed most creditably.

Somerset scored quickly enough in beating Nottinghamshire to claim a place in the quarter-finals. They had to win inside 51 overs, and, in fact, they won in 49.4 overs. Nottinghamshire had been well served by Broad and Crawley who put on 132 for the second wicket, but Neil Mallender took three wickets in six balls to blunt the middle order. Hayhurst and MacLeay then began Somerset's innings with a partnership of 91, and Tavaré and Rose kept up the necessary momentum.

Middlesex routed Sussex to reach the last eight, and Kent ended with the only 100 per cent record when they beat Warwickshire.

Lancashire had to beat Northamptonshire to qualify for the knock-out stage, and Fairbrother and Watkinson put on 99 for the fifth wicket to give the basis of a respectable score. The cost was high, however, for Watkinson tore a hamstring and was unable to bowl. This gave Lancashire acute problems, and skipper Fairbrother took on the responsibility himself, sharing the fifth-bowler duties with Atherton and sending down six overs of medium pace. Lamb was in particularly aggressive mood as he and Felton added 144 for Northamptonshire's third wicket, but darkness descended, and play had to be resumed on the next morning with Northamptonshire needing 35 off 25 balls. Williams was run out by Speak's throw, and Ripley fretted painfully before being leg before to Austin who, with DeFreitas, had given Fairbrother some leeway. The Lancashire captain bowled the last over with 22 needed. Lamb hit 4, 2, 2, 4, but the fifth ball only brought a single, and Walker could make no contact with the final delivery.

Surrey finished top of Group A by beating Gloucestershire, but they stumbled on the second morning when they lost four wickets quickly.

BENSON AND HEDGES CUP – ZONAL ROUND

GROUP A	P	W	L	Ab	Pts	Run Rate
Surrey	5	4	1	–	8	82.55
Middlesex	5	4	1	–	8	74.48
Leicestershire	5	3	2	–	6	63.45
Sussex	5	2	3	–	4	63.83
Minor Counties	5	1	4	–	2	59.45
Gloucestershire	5	1	4	–	2	58.74
GROUP B	**P**	**W**	**L**	**Ab**	**Pts**	**Run Rate**
Hampshire	4	3	–	1	7	70.58
Lancashire	4	3	1	–	6	64.87
Essex	4	2	2	–	4	64.31
Northamptonshire	4	1	3	–	2	73.48
Scotland	4	–	3	1	1	51.21
GROUP C	**P**	**W**	**L**	**Ab**	**Pts**	**Run Rate**
Kent	4	4	–	–	8	65.98
Somerset	4	2	2	–	4	62.11
Nottinghamshire	4	2	2	–	4	61.39
Warwickshire	4	1	3	–	2	61.51
Yorkshire	4	1	3	–	2	48.03

BENSON AND HEDGES CUP – ZONAL ROUND

GROUP D	P	W	L	Ab	Pts	Run Rate
Worcestershire	4	3	1	–	6	63.45
Derbyshire	4	3	1	–	6	62.02
Durham	4	2	2	–	4	64.95
Glamorgan	4	2	2	–	4	58.96
Combined Universities	4	–	4	–	0	54.01

6, 7 and 8 May *at Worcester*

Pakistanis 374 for 4 dec. (Ramiz Raja 172, Salim Malik 91) and 93 (P.J. Newport 5 for 22)
Worcestershire 303 for 5 dec. (T.S. Curtis 85, W.P.C. Weston 64 not out) and 166 for 5

Worcestershire won by 5 wickets

7, 8 and 9 May *at Oxford*

Nottinghamshire 324 for 4 dec. (M.A. Crawley 110 not out, M. Saxelby 73, P.R. Pollard 72) and 100 for 0 (G.F. Archer 50 not out)
Oxford University 161 (C.L. Keey 60, K.E. Cooper 4 for 41)

Match drawn

The Pakistan touring side's first first-class match of the season ended in a surprising defeat. They gave an exciting display of batting on the opening day when Ramiz Raja hit 172 off 206 balls with 28 fours. He and Salim Malik shared a third-wicket stand of 165 in 135 minutes. Their bowling was less impressive, and Worcestershire gained much credit through the batting of Philip Weston who hit a maiden first-class fifty. Inexplicably, the tourists collapsed when they batted a second time. Asif Mujtaba had been injured in the field and was unable to bat, and Shoaib Mohammad was last man out, having batted through the Pakistani innings for 46. Needing 165 to win, Worcestershire batted for more than 56 overs to score the runs.

Nottinghamshire introduced Graeme Archer to first-class cricket, and Stephen Bramhall, a former Lancashire wicket-keeper, played his first game for them at Oxford. There was no play on the third day because of rain.

7, 8, 9 and 10 May *at Lord's*

Lancashire 343 (N.J. Speak 93, P.A.J. DeFreitas 69, W.K. Hegg 63) and 113 for 3 dec. (M.A. Atherton 51 not out)
Middlesex 493 for 8 dec. (M.R. Ramprakash 108, M.W. Gatting 103, J.E. Emburey 78, D.L. Haynes 62)

Match drawn

Middlesex 7 pts., Lancashire 5 pts.

at Leeds

Yorkshire 250 (S.R. Tendulkar 86, R.J. Blakey 72) and 74 for 1
Hampshire 397 for 8 dec. (K.D. James 116, D.I. Gower 68, T.C. Middleton 55, C.A. Connor 51)

Match drawn

Hampshire 7 pts., Yorkshire 5 pts.

7, 8, 9 and 11 May *at Chelmsford*

Leicestershire 223 (L.Potter 70, N.E. Briers 51) and 312 for 7 (N.E. Briers 99, T.J. Boon 82)
Essex 424 for 4 dec. (G.A. Gooch 160, P.J. Prichard 102, J.P. Stephenson 91)

Match drawn

Essex 7 pts., Leicestershire 3 pts.

at Canterbury

Kent 244 (M.R. Benson 75, N.R. Taylor 57, S.J.E. Brown 7 for 105) and 263 for 3 dec. (C.L. Hooper 115 not out, N.R. Taylor 78 not out)
Durham 239 (R.M. Ellison 5 for 77) and 145 for 3 (P. Bainbridge 61 not out, J.D. Glendenen 57 not out)

Match drawn

Durham 6 pts., Kent 5 pts.

at Northampton

Northamptonshire 375 (A. Fordham 192) and 147 for 3 dec.
Surrey 279 for 6 dec. (D.J. Bicknell 99, G.P. Thorpe 64) and 142 for 5

Match drawn

Northamptonshire 6 pts., Surrey 6 pts.

at Hove

Somerset 264 (G.D. Rose 65, A.G. Robson 4 for 37) and 253 for 5 (R.J. Bartlett 72, A.N. Hayhurst 55)
Sussex 346 (F.D. Stephenson 133, A.P. Wells 61, N.A. Mallender 5 for 86)

Match drawn

Sussex 6 pts., Somerset 6 pts.

at Edgbaston

Warwickshire 235 (A.J. Moles 50, J.D. Ratcliffe 50, D.E. Malcolm 4 for 83) and 178 for 1 (A.J. Moles 86 not out)
Derbyshire 85 (T.A. Munton 5 for 44, A.A. Donald 4 for 22) and 327 (D.G. Cork 72 not out, J.E. Morris 69, K.J. Barnett 57, P.A. Smith 6 for 91)

Warwickshire won by 9 wickets

Warwickshire 22 pts., Derbyshire 4 pts.

9, 10 and 11 May *at Cardiff*

Pakistanis 354 for 5 dec. (Aamir Sohail 124, Shoaib

Mohammad 58) and 0 for 0 dec.
Glamorgan 0 for 0 dec. and 148 (Mushtaq Ahmed 4 for 26, Wasim Akram 4 for 46)

Pakistanis won by 206 runs

On Saturday 9 May, 21 overs were bowled at Chelmsford, but not a ball was bowled anywhere else in first-class cricket in the country. On the first day at Lord's, Speak and DeFreitas had scored 137 for Lancashire's fifth wicket, and on the second day, Gatting again batted with dominance to hit 103 off 143 balls. Ramprakash completed his century on the last morning.

Sachin Tendulkar hit 12 fours and rescued Yorkshire from the depths of 27 for 3. Kevan James hit the eighth century of his career, and Cardigan Connor his first fifty.

A dour Leicestershire side lost Whitaker with a cracked cheek-bone and could barely score at two an over on the opening day at Chelmsford. In contrast, Essex reached 400 in the 100th over. Gooch hit a century before lunch, and he and Stephenson put on 238 for the first wicket. Prichard then hit 102 off 122 balls, but the weather and an opening partnership of 147 between Boon and Briers denied Essex victory.

The two outstanding features of the match at Canterbury were the bowling of left-arm medium-pacer Simon Brown, and the batting of West Indian Test player Carl Hooper. The former Northamptonshire bowler Brown took 7 for 105, a career-best performance, while Hooper reached his first century for Kent off 82 balls, so setting the pace for the season's fastest hundred. The rain made any prospect of a result unlikely.

Left-arm pace bowler Simon Brown took 7 for 105 as Durham drew with Kent at Canterbury, 7–11 May. (Tom Morris)

Carl Hooper hits Phil Bainbridge for six during his innings of 115 not out in his first championship match for Kent, v. Durham, at Canterbury. Graveney and wicket-keeper Fothergill look on. Hooper reached his hundred off 82 balls. (Tom Morris)

Fordham hit two sixes and 28 fours in his 192 against Surrey for whom Darren Bicknell once more showed excellent form. He played on to leg-spinner Roberts when on 99. As elsewhere, rain was the winner.

Somerset gave a first-class debut to slow left-arm bowler Andrew Cottam, son of Bob Cottam, the former England seam bowler. Robson, formerly of Surrey, had a career-best bowling performance for Sussex who were rescued by their new overseas cricketer Franklyn Stephenson, formerly of Nottinghamshire. Sussex were 128 for 7 before Stephenson hit 133, an innings which included 17 fours. Cottam had skipper Alan Wells stumped by Burns to claim his first first-class wicket.

Warwickshire achieved the only victory of the round thanks mainly to the pace bowling of Munton and Donald who bowled out Derbyshire in under 32 overs. Derbyshire fared better in their second innings, but Moles and Ratcliffe provided the basis of a nine-wicket victory on the last day.

Pakistan won their first match in the Tetley Bitter Challenge with the help of innings forfeitures at Cardiff. Butcher, the Glamorgan captain, played his first game of the season and aggravated a knee injury which meant that he had to undergo a cartilage operation. Aamir Sohail hit a six and 14 fours in his 124, and Glamorgan collapsed against the pace of Wasim Akram and the leg-spin of Mushtaq Ahmed and were bowled out in 61 overs.

SUNDAY LEAGUE

10 May *at Derby*

Derbyshire 153 for 7
Gloucestershire 103

Derbyshire (4 pts.) won by 50 runs

at Chelmsford

Northamptonshire 180 for 5
Essex 183 for 6

Essex (4 pts.) won by 4 wickets

at Canterbury

Kent 94 for 2
v. Durham

Match abandoned

Kent 2 pts., Durham 2 pts.

at Trent Bridge

Nottinghamshire 174 for 4 (D.W. Randall 55)
Surrey 177 for 4

Surrey (4 pts.) won by 6 wickets

at Hove

Somerset 141 for 7
Sussex 144 for 2 (M.P. Speight 87 not out)

Sussex (4 pts.) won by 8 wickets

at Worcester

Warwickshire 171 for 9 (T.A. Lloyd 62, S.R. Lampitt 4 for 40)
Worcestershire 171 for 4 (T.M. Moody 78, G.A. Hick 60)

Match tied

Worcestershire 2 pts., Warwickshire 2 pts.

The vagaries of the weather meant that only at Worcester could a complete 40-over match be played, and this match provided the drama of the day. The Warwickshire hero was once more Neil Smith who had bowled so well in a tense finish at Taunton in the Benson and Hedges Cup eight days earlier. Warwickshire made a patchy 171, but Neil Smith bowled Curtis for 1. Moody and Hick added 125 to place Worcestershire in a winning position before Hick was caught off Paul Smith. Worcestershire needed five to win from the last two overs, but Munton exerted pressure by bowling a maiden to Leatherdale who was then bowled by the second ball of the last over, from Neil Smith. The scores were level when the off-spinner bowled the last ball, and Moody was run out in attempting what would have been the winning run.

The innings of the day came from Martin Speight who hit an unbeaten 87 which included eight fours and a six. His knock helped Sussex to beat Somerset and maintain their challenge on the leaders Essex who won their fourth match in succession.

12, 13 and 14 May *at Cambridge*

Warwickshire 319 for 8 dec. (T.L. Penney 102 not out, M. Burns 78, R.M. Pearson 5 for 108) and 105 for 2 dec. (A.J. Moles 50)
Cambridge University 206 for 8 dec. (J.P. Arscott 65 not out) and 154 for 8

Match drawn

at Oxford

Middlesex 290 for 5 dec. (M.A. Roseberry 108 retired hurt, P.N. Weekes 95, P. Farbrace 51 not out) and 143 for 1 dec. (J.D. Carr 75 not out)
Oxford University 222 for 8 dec. (C.L. Keey 57 not out, R.R. Montgomerie 51) and 212 for 5 (R.R. Montgomerie 103 not out, C.L. Keey 64)

Oxford University won by 5 wickets

13, 14 and 15 May *at Taunton*

Somerset 163 and 169 (Mushtaq Ahmed 5 for 46)
Pakistanis 240 (Salim Malik 89, A.R. Caddick 6 for 73) and 93 for 5

Pakistanis won by 5 wickets

Richard Pearson, the England Under-19 off-spinner, took five wickets an innings for the first time as Cambridge University drew with Warwickshire. He might have fared better had not Mike Burns, third choice wicket-keeper, and Trevor Penney, the Zimbabwe batsman newly qualified for Warwickshire, not added 124 for the seventh wicket. Penney reached a maiden first-class century in England.

Aided by a generous declaration, Oxford University gained their first victory over a county since 1974. Roseberry and Weekes revived Middlesex after early failures, but the hero of the match was Richard Montgomerie whose century took Oxford to victory. This was Phil Tufnell's last appearance for Middlesex for a month, for he was operated upon for appendicitis.

A career best bowling performance by Andrew Caddick could not prevent the Pakistan tourists from racing to victory at Taunton.

14, 15, 16 and 17 May *at Cardiff*

Glamorgan 224 (M.P. Maynard 88) and 193 (P.A. Cottey 112 not out, S.J.E. Brown 5 for 66)
Durham 521 for 9 dec. (W. Larkins 143, P.W.G. Parker 124, D.M. Jones 94, R.D.B. Croft 5 for 105)

Durham won by an innings and 104 runs

Durham 24 pts., Glamorgan 3 pts.

at Leeds

Gloucestershire 411 (G.D. Hodgson 124, M.W. Alleyne 88 not out, A.J. Wright 51, C.A. Walsh 51) and 142 (P.J. Hartley 5 for 48)

Durham claimed their first victory in the county championship when they beat Glamorgan by an innings and 104 runs at Cardiff, 14–18 May. Wayne Larkins was one of their heroes with an innings of 143. (USPA)

Yorkshire 272 (S.R. Tendulkar 92, R.J. Blakey 66, C.A. Walsh 4 for 77) and 134 (C.A. Walsh 7 for 27)

Gloucestershire won by 147 runs

Gloucestershire 23 pts., Yorkshire 5 pts.

14, 15, 16 and 18 May *at Chelmsford*

Kent 166 (M.C.J. Ilott 4 for 56) and 274 (G.R. Cowdrey 82 not out, C.L. Hooper 74, M.R. Benson 53, J.H. Childs 5 for 69)
Essex 526 (N. Shahid 132, M.E. Waugh 120, D.R. Pringle 80, N. Hussain 77, R.M. Ellison 6 for 95)

Essex won by an innings and 86 runs

Essex 24 pts., Kent 3 pts.

at Derby

Derbyshire 251 (P.D. Bowler 91, J.E. Morris 55, N.V. Radford 5 for 67) and 433 for 7 dec. (C.J. Adams 121, P.D. Bowler 112, S.C. Goldsmith 100 not out, N.V. Radford 6 for 88)
Worcestershire 470 for 9 dec. (T.S. Curtis 228 not out)

Match drawn

Worcestershire 6 pts., Derbyshire 4 pts.

at Leicester

Lancashire 485 (N.J. Speak 232, N.H. Fairbrother 65, G.D. Lloyd 56, D.J. Millns 4 for 123)
Leicestershire 258 (T.J. Boon 139, A.A. Barnett 5 for 78) and 182 (W.K.M. Benjamin 72)

Lancashire won by an innings and 45 runs

Lancashire 24 pts., Leicestershire 4 pts.

at Northampton

Northamptonshire 282 (A. Fordham 88, N.A. Felton 64, K.P. Evans 5 for 27) and 296 (J.P. Taylor 74 not out, D.J. Capel 52, C.C. Lewis 5 for 74)
Nottinghamshire 342 (C.C. Lewis 134) and 237 for 7 (P. Johnson 95, J.P. Taylor 4 for 76)

Nottinghamshire won by 3 wickets

Nottinghamshire 24 pts., Northamptonshire 6 pts.

14, 16 and 18 May *at Oxford*

Hampshire 331 for 4 dec. (T.C. Middleton 121, J.R. Ayling 121) and 111 for 5 dec.
Oxford University 133 and 148 (S.D. Udal 5 for 47)

Hampshire won by 161 runs

at Cambridge

Surrey 381 for 5 dec. (G.P. Thorpe 114, A.J. Stewart 71, M.A. Lynch 61, R.I, Alikhan 54) and 179 for 2 dec. (D.M. Ward 112 not out)
Cambridge University 161 (J.P. Crawley 62, R.E. Bryson 5 for 48) and 259 (J.P. Arscott 79)

Surrey won by 141 runs

16 May *at Hove*

Pakistanis 230 for 9 (Aamir Sohail 54, Ramiz Raja 53 retired hurt)
Sussex 233 for 7 (F.D. Stephenson 71, M.P. Speight 57)
Sussex won by 3 wickets

17 May *at Hove*

Pakistanis 321 for 2 (Inzamam-ul-Haq 157 not out, Zahid Fazal 83 not out, Shoaib Mohammad 68)
Sussex 236 (N.J. Lenham 50, Mushtaq Ahmed 4 for 35)
Pakistanis won by 85 runs

Durham claimed their first victory in the County Championship, winning in fine style at Cardiff. Electing to bat first, Glamorgan faltered against the medium pace of debutant Paul Henderson. Durham gained a massive advantage through a second-wicket stand of 206 between Wayne Larkins and Dean Jones. A century from Paul Parker then took them to an impregnable position. The game was decided when Brown and Botham reduced Glamorgan to 40 for 6 in their second innings. Tony Cottey hit a brave 112 to restore some pride to the home side, but Durham won inside three days.

Essex, too, needed only three days in which to overwhelm Kent who fell to Ilott and Pringle on the opening day. Mark Waugh and Nasser Hussain added 142 runs for Essex's third wicket, and this was followed by Shahid's career best 132, an innings which included a six and 17 fours and some chances which were missed before the batsman had reached double figures. There was some mighty hitting by Pringle towards the close of the innings. Kent lost Taylor retired hurt as they strove to avoid an innings defeat. Hooper batted at his most graceful and was given able support by Cowdrey, but Childs saw that Essex were not denied.

An opening stand of 104 between Hinks and Hodgson gave Gloucestershire's innings a sound start at Headingley, and there were later flamboyant gestures from Alleyne and Walsh. It seemed as though Sachin Tendulkar would reach his first century for Yorkshire, but he was deceived by off-spinner Ball when 92. On a wicket which was not giving the umpires much cause for concern, Gloucestershire were languishing at 90 for 8 before Jack Russell hit sensibly. The pitch was now such that Yorkshire never looked to have a remote chance of reaching a target of 282, and they were destroyed by the pace of Walsh who took 7 for 27 in 20 overs.

There were fewer fireworks at Derby where the home side were bowled out on the first day after some rather stodgy batting. Tim Curtis hit 23 fours and faced 477 balls in a knock which occupied the whole of the Worcestershire innings. It was again a heavy performance with only 235 runs coming from the first 100 overs. On the last day, there were three Derbyshire centurions, and Adams and Goldsmith hit career best scores.

In spite of Tim Boon's century, Leicestershire were forced to follow-on and were beaten inside three days by Lancashire for whom left-arm spinner Barnett took eight wickets. The outstanding performance of the match came from Nick Speak who hit the first double century of his career. His 231 came off 251 balls in 270 minutes, and he hit two sixes and 38 fours.

Fordham and Felton shared an opening stand of 133 for Northamptonshire against Nottinghamshire, but Kevin Evans took four wickets in 13 balls and finished with a career best 5 for 27 to tilt the game in favour of the visitors. Chris Lewis hit the second century of his career to put Nottinghamshire in a good position, and the position would have been even stronger but for Paul Taylor. Batting at number ten, he hit a career best 74 not out as 144 runs were added for the last two wickets. Nottinghamshire moved to victory with some alarms on the last day.

Jonathan Ayling hit a maiden first-class century for Hampshire in The Parks where Middleton continued his astonishing start to the season with another hundred.

SUNDAY LEAGUE

17 May *at Derby*

Derbyshire 152 for 5
Worcestershire 153 for 3 (G.A. Hick 51 not out)
Derbyshire (4 pts.) won by 7 wickets

at Northampton

Northamptonshire 194 for 3 (D.J. Capel 97 not out, K.M. Curran 80 not out)
Lancashire 198 for 6 (M.A. Atherton 76)
Lancashire (4 pts.) won by 4 wickets

at Trent Bridge

Middlesex 257 for 5 (K.R. Brown 73 not out, J.D. Carr 68, D.L. Haynes 63)
Nottinghamshire 256 for 8 (P. Johnson 90, D.W. Randall 68)
Middlesex (4 pts.) won by 1 run

at Taunton

Somerset 184 for 7 (R.J. Harden 53)
Hampshire 87 (A.R. Caddick 4 for 20)
Somerset (4 pts.) won by 97 runs

at The Oval

Surrey 241 for 5 (D.J. Bicknell 102, A.J. Stewart 54)
Kent 246 for 7 (C.L. Hooper 90, T.R. Ward 56, G.R. Cowdrey 56)
Kent (4 pts.) won by 3 wickets

at Edgbaston

Warwickshire 217 for 5 (R.G. Twose 100)
Leicestershire 117 for 8

Warwickshire (4 pts.) won by 100 runs

Capel and Curran added 164 in 28 overs for Northamptonshire's fourth wicket, but their side were beaten by Lancashire. At Trent Bridge, Kevin Cooper faced his first ball of the season which was the last of the match between Nottinghamshire and Middlesex. The home side needed three to win, but Cooper could only manage a single. Caddick again bowled with impressive speed and accuracy as Somerset routed Hampshire, and Kent beat Surrey with some ease in spite of Darren Bicknell's century.

19, 20, 21 and 22 May *at Gloucester*

Worcestershire 270 (T.M. Moody 118, D.A. Leatherdale 56, M. Davies 4 for 75) and 145 (M.C.J. Ball 4 for 47)
Gloucestershire 206 (R.D. Stemp 6 for 67) and 210 for 7 (R.C. Russell 72 not out, R.D. Stemp 5 for 79)

Gloucestershire won by 3 wickets

Gloucestershire 22 pts., Worcestershire 7 pts.

at Southampton

Hampshire 522 for 9 dec. (T.C. Middleton 221, V.P. Terry 131, N.M. Kendrick 6 for 164) and 2 for 0
Surrey 184 (M.D. Marshall 6 for 58) and 369 (M.P. Bicknell 88, D.J. Bicknell 71, G.P. Thorpe 50)

Hampshire won by 10 wickets

Hampshire 24 pts., Surrey 1 pt.

at Leicester

Middlesex 467 (J.E. Emburey 102, D.W. Headley 91, M.W. Gatting 86, M.A. Roseberry 51) and 6 for 0
Leicestershire 248 (J.D.R. Benson 122, J.E. Emburey 4 for 44) and 224 (J.D.R. Benson 58, N.E. Briers 53, V.J. Wells 50 not out, J.E. Emburey 4 for 45)

Middlesex won by 10 wickets

Middlesex 23 pts., Leicestershire 5 pts.

20, 21 and 22 May *at Swansea*

Glamorgan 346 for 5 dec. (I.V.A. Richards 127, M.P. Maynard 62) and 167 for 6 dec. (A. Dale 67 not out)
Warwickshire 248 (N.M.K. Smith 67, A.J. Moles 66, R.D.B. Croft 6 for 103) and 172 (D.A. Reeve 79, R.D.B. Croft 8 for 66)

Glamorgan won by 93 runs

Glamorgan 24 pts., Warwickshire 4 pts.

at Canterbury

Kent 480 for 7 dec. (G.R. Cowdrey 127, S.A. Marsh 125, M.R. Benson 78, T.R. Ward 53) and 153 for 2 dec. (N.R. Taylor 83 not out, T.R. Ward 53)
Yorkshire 340 for 7 dec. (S.A. Kellett 90, C. White 63 not out, P.J. Hartley 61 not out, D. Byas 51) and 292 for 8 (R.J. Blakey 95 not out, D. Byas 82)

Match drawn

Kent 7 pts., Yorkshire 6 pts.

at Blackpool

Lancashire 327 for 7 dec. (I.D. Austin 115 not out, N.J. Speak 61, W.K. Hegg 59, M. Jean-Jacques 4 for 46) and 273 for 2 dec. (M.A. Atherton 140 not out, N.J. Speak 64, S.P. Titchard 54)
Derbyshire 300 for 9 dec. (C.J. Adams 72, S.C. Goldsmith 60 not out, P.D. Bowler 53) and 301 for 5 (P.D. Bowler 104 not out, J.E. Morris 98)

Derbyshire won by 5 wickets

Derbyshire 23 pts., Lancashire 8 pts.

at Trent Bridge

Sussex 365 (M.P. Speight 166, N.J. Lenham 60, J.A. Afford 4 for 117) and 208 for 8 dec. (J.A. Afford 6 for 68)
Nottinghamshire 249 (K.P. Evans 50, I.D.K. Salisbury 5 for 69) and 294 for 8 (M.A. Crawley 76, M. Saxelby 54, I.D.K. Salisbury 4 for 122)

Match drawn

Nottinghamshire 8 pts., Sussex 5 pts.

at Taunton

Essex 259 (J.P. Stephenson 113 not out, A.P. van Troost 6 for 48) and 314 for 2 dec. (J.P. Stephenson 159 not out, P.J. Prichard 55)
Somerset 275 (M.N. Lathwell 76, R.J. Harden 72, M.C. Ilott 4 for 76) and 302 for 6 (M.N. Lathwell 79, R.J. Harden 68, J.H. Childs 4 for 91)

Somerset won by 4 wickets

Somerset 23 pts., Essex 7 pts.

Electing to bat first at Gloucester, Worcestershire were soon in trouble, losing openers Curtis and Seymour for 8. Moody and Leatherdale revived the visitors' fortunes with a partnership of 181 before left-arm spinner Mark Davies took four wickets to wipe out the middle order. Worcestershire seemed totally in command at the end of the first day, however, when Gloucestershire were 27 for 3. There was some dogged batting on the second day, but Stemp's career best gave Worcestershire a first innings lead of 64. They then fell to the home side's balanced attack, and, needing 210 to win, Gloucestershire were taken to victory by the calm of Russell and the lusty hitting of Walsh. The game was over in three days.

Middleton and Terry began Hampshire's innings against Surrey with a partnership of 269. Tony Middleton reached the first double hundred of his career, and it was his third century in four first-class innings. He faced 447 balls and hit a six and 19 fours.

Terry's innings occupied 262 balls, but he later had the misfortune to dislocate a thumb while fielding. Neil Kendrick took a patient career best of 6 for 164. Only David Ward offered serious resistance to the pace of Malcolm Marshall, but Surrey did avoid the indignity of an innings defeat and of defeat in three days. Martin Bicknell saved them with the highest score of his career.

Middlesex found the Grace Road pitch slow and difficult and were 249 for 7 when Dean Headley joined John Emburey. The pair added 160 and put their side in a position of dominance. They then played a major role with the ball as Middlesex triumphed early on the last day.

At Swansea, there was a fine match. Glamorgan scored at a brisk rate on the opening day and declared at the end of the hundredth over. Their innings revolved around Viv Richards' chanceless 127 which came off only 129 balls and included four sixes and 15 fours. It was the great man's 112th century, and he shared three-figure stands with Maynard and Cottey. Unfortunately, Richards pulled a hamstring while fielding, an injury which was to keep him out of the side for the next few matches. Warwickshire were bemused by the off-spin of Robert Croft, and they would have fared worse but for Neil Smith's hard hitting. Croft's figures were, in fact, the best of his career, but he improved upon them in the second innings with a splendid performance which brought him 8 for 66. Needing 266 from 72 overs, Warwickshire lost six wickets for 92 runs before Reeve and Paul Smith added 69 in 30 overs of defiance. With seven overs remaining, Croft had Reeve caught at mid-wicket, but the last over arrived with Glamorgan still needing two wickets for their first championship win of the season. With his fourth ball, Croft had Paul Smith taken at short-leg off a ball which turned appreciably, and with the penultimate ball of the match, he trapped Munton leg before.

Without Moxon and Jarvis, both injured, and Metcalfe, dropped, Yorkshire gave a first-class debut to Bradley Parker. Kent were 192 for 5 before Cowdrey and Marsh added 235. Marsh's 125 was a career best while Graham Cowdrey, having taken 117 balls to reach 50, went from 85 to 109 in five successive balls – two sixes followed by three fours. Yorkshire batted soundly in reply and were eventually asked to make 294 runs in 72 overs to win the match. They seemed to be in command, but they lost their way somewhat and needed three off the last ball with Hartley on strike. He was run out in going for the second run which would have levelled the scores.

Ian Austin enjoyed some good fortune in reaching the second century of his career which revived Lancashire after a poor start against Derbyshire who took maximum batting points thanks to robust work from their middle order. Michael Atherton hit a faultless 140, aided by some generous bowling in the later stages, and declared to set Derbyshire a target of 301 in 69 overs. John Morris hit 98 off 94 balls while Peter Bowler hit his second championship century of the week, a coolly controlled innings, and Derbyshire won with 11 balls to spare.

Having won their first two championship matches, Nottinghamshire ran into trouble against Sussex for whom Martin Speight hit 166 in 257 minutes to lift them from 186 for 6 to 365 all out. Nottinghamshire stumbled against the leg-spin of Ian Salisbury and were set a target of 325 in 80 overs. Left-arm spinner Afford had returned a career best 6 for 68, an indication that the wicket was aiding the slow bowlers, and the home side were brave in their chase. In the end, it was the Nottinghamshire tail-enders, French and Field-Buss, who thwarted Sussex.

Essex opening batsman John Stephenson hit a century in each innings but finished on the losing side at Taunton. He was on the field for the entire match. Van Troost took five wickets in 17 balls and claimed a career best 6 for 48, but Mark Ilott bowled Essex back into contention just as Somerset appeared to be dominating the game. Prichard was generous in his declaration, offering Somerset a target of 299 at four runs an over. Disaster struck Essex, already without Gooch, Pringle and Foster, when Ilott broke down with a groin strain in his third over. Childs dismissed Harden and Rose in the same over, but Lathwell had given his side an exuberant start. Snell straight drove Childs for the winning six with four overs to spare.

TEXACO TROPHY

Robin Smith won the individual award in the first Texaco Trophy match at Lord's for his innings of 85. Moin Khan is the wicket-keeper. (Patrick Eagar)

Allan Lamb shared a partnership of 98 with Smith, Texaco Trophy, Lord's 20 May. (David Munden)

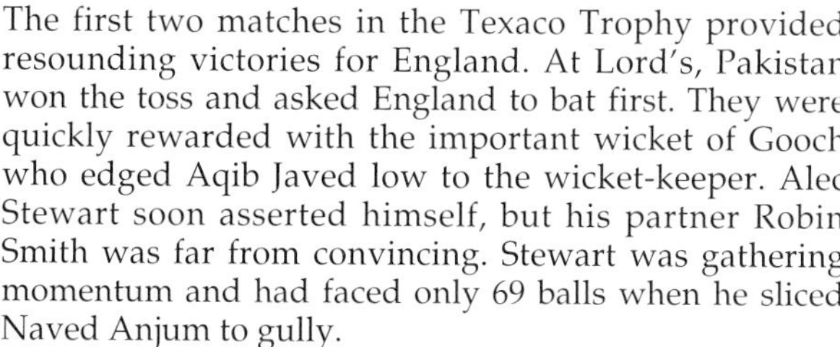

The first two matches in the Texaco Trophy provided resounding victories for England. At Lord's, Pakistan won the toss and asked England to bat first. They were quickly rewarded with the important wicket of Gooch who edged Aqib Javed low to the wicket-keeper. Alec Stewart soon asserted himself, but his partner Robin Smith was far from convincing. Stewart was gathering momentum and had faced only 69 balls when he sliced Naved Anjum to gully.

Lamb and Smith then added 98 before Smith, who had battled well against a lack of timing for 117 balls, edged to the keeper. Lamb was out four overs later, having batted with confident aggression. There was an enjoyable flourish from the enthusiastic Fairbrother, but, in truth, the Pakistan bowling was never more than pedestrian and the fielding was that of a side who had to endure this penance before being allowed to bat.

Pringle caught and bowled Ramiz Raja in his opening over, and Salim Malik, having suggested that he might win the match off his own bat, was caught behind when he dabbled at Botham's away swinger. The match was virtually decided when Javed Miandad was well caught at square-leg. Aamir Sohail was run out by DeFreitas' sharp throw when he attempted a second run to mid-wicket, and Inzamam-ul-Haq gave a thin edge onto his pad from whence it rebounded into the hands of Botham. The left-handers Asif Mujtaba and Wasim Akram added 83 pleasant runs, but it was a stand of only academic interest.

Pakistan were well beaten, but there were hints that the batting of Aamir Sohail and Salim Malik was of a class above anything that was seen on the England side.

At The Oval, England won the second one-day international even more decisively than they had won the first. Pakistan were greatly weakened by the absence of Wasim Akram, and, with Wasim's stress fracture of the shin threatening his place on the tour, they faced the prospect of entering the first Test without both of their

Alec Stewart drives through the covers during his exciting century in the second Texaco Trophy match, The Oval, 22 May. (David Munden)

leading bowlers, Wasim and Waqar. Ata-ur-Rehman was flown from Pakistan as a replacement.

The England innings was given all its impetus by Alec Stewart who batted with eagerness and supreme confidence for 171 minutes, hit ten fours and faced 145 balls. It was the ideal limited-over innings. There was a superb frolic by Fairbrother who hit 63 off 65 balls although it seemed unnecessary that he should continue to bat after badly pulling a hamstring. The injury was to mar much of his season. The injury came when he was on 35, and he finished his innings with a runner.

Hick made a spectacular 71 off 51 balls, but, in the light of later decisions, it was hard to see how he survived an appeal for leg before first ball. He and Fairbrother added 94 in 11 overs.

Asif Mujtaba fails to run out Neil Fairbrother in the second Texaco Trophy match. Fairbrother was later injured. (David Munden)

TEXACO TROPHY – FIRST ONE-DAY INTERNATIONAL– ENGLAND v. PAKISTAN
20 May, 1992 at Lord's

ENGLAND

G.A. Gooch (capt)	c Moin Khan, b Aqib Javed	9
*A.J. Stewart	c Asif Mujtaba, b Naved Anjum	50
R.A. Smith	c Moin Khan, b Aqib Javed	85
A.J. Lamb	c Javed Miandad, b Naved Anjum	60
N.H. Fairbrother	c Asif Mujtaba, b Aqib Javed	25
G.A. Hick	b Wasim Akram	3
I.T. Botham	not out	10
C.C. Lewis	not out	6
D.R. Pringle		
P.A.J. DeFreitas		
R.K. Illingworth		
Extras	lb 14, w 9, nb 7	30
	(for 6 wickets)	278

PAKISTAN

Aamir Sohail	run out	36
Ramiz Raja	c and b Pringle	0
Salim Malik	c Stewart, b Botham	24
Javed Miandad (capt)	c Hick, b Pringle	7
Inzamam-ul-Haq	c and b Botham	2
Asif Mujtaba	c Smith, b Hick	52
Wasim Akram	st Stewart, b Illingworth	34
Naved Anjum	c Hick, b Pringle	3
*Moin Khan	c Stewart, b Pringle	11
Mushtaq Ahmed	not out	7
Aqib Javed	b Hick	8
Extras	lb 8, w 5, nb 2	15
		199

(55 overs)

	O	M	R	W
Wasim Akram	11	–	39	1
Aqib Javed	11	–	54	3
Naved Anjum	11	–	48	2
Mushtaq Ahmed	11	–	56	–
Asif Mujtaba	11	–	67	–

(54.2 overs)

	O	M	R	W
DeFreitas	9	2	17	–
Pringle	11	1	42	4
Lewis	8	1	35	–
Botham	11	–	45	2
Illingworth	11	–	36	1
Hick	3.2	–	7	2
Fairbrother	1	–	9	–

FALL OF WICKETS
1–20, **2**–115, **3**–213, **4**–238, **5**–250, **6**–265

FALL OF WICKETS
1–0, **2**–49, **3**–74, **4**–78, **5**–78, **6**–161, **7**–164, **8**–181, **9**–184

Umpires: B.J. Meyer & D.R. Shepherd

Man of the Match – R.A. Smith

England won by 79 runs

TEXACO TROPHY – SECOND ONE-DAY INTERNATIONAL– ENGLAND v. PAKISTAN

22 May, 1992 at The Oval

ENGLAND

G.A. Gooch (capt)	run out	25
*A.J. Stewart	b Aqib Javed	103
R.A. Smith	b Mushtaq Ahmed	7
A.J. Lamb	st Moin Khan, b Aamir Sohail	11
N.H. Fairbrother	b Tanvir Mehdi	63
G.A. Hick	not out	71
I.T. Botham	not out	2
C.C. Lewis		
D.R. Pringle		
P.A.J. DeFreitas		
R.K. Illingworth		
Extras	lb 8, w 9, nb 3	20
	(for 5 wickets)	302

PAKISTAN

Aamir Sohail	b Illingworth	32
Ramiz Raja	c sub (Ramprakash), b DeFreitas	86
Salim Malik	b Pringle	26
Inzamam-ul-Haq	lbw, b Pringle	15
Javed Miandad (capt)	lbw, b Botham	38
Asif Mujtaba	lbw, b Illingworth	29
Naved Anjum	run out	6
*Moin Khan	c and b Lewis	15
Mushtaq Ahmed	c Illingworth, b Lewis	8
Tanvir Mehdi	b DeFreitas	0
Aqib Javed	not out	0
Extras	lb 4, w 3, nb1	8
		263

(55 overs)

	O	M	R	W
Aqib Javed	10	–	70	1
Naved Anjum	9	–	37	–
Tanvir Mehdi	11	–	72	1
Mushtaq Ahmed	11	–	47	1
Aamir Sohail	11	–	52	1
Asif Mujtaba	3	–	16	–

(50.5 overs)

	O	M	R	W
DeFreitas	10.5	–	59	2
Lewis	8	–	47	2
Botham	11	–	52	1
Illingworth	11	–	58	2
Pringle	9	1	35	2
Hick	1	–	8	–

FALL OF WICKETS

1–71, 2–81, 3–108, 4–202, 5–295

FALL OF WICKETS

1–81, 2–144, 3–148, 4–174, 5–220, 6–232, 7–249, 8–263, 9–263

Umpires: M.J. Kitchen & R. Palmer — Man of the Match – A.J. Stewart — *England won by 39 runs*

Pakistan began as if they could win the match, scoring 132 for the loss of Aamir Sohail in the first 25 overs, but the loss of three wickets in eight overs after tea tilted the game emphatically and irretrievably in England's favour. There were some histrionics from Botham, and he and Javed appeared to engage in some verbal exchanges of a less than friendly nature, but, happily, there were no repercussions.

23, 24 and 25 May *at Leicester*

Leicestershire 256 (Mushtaq Ahmed 5 for 49) and 269 (N.E. Briers 123)

Pakistanis 393 for 8 dec. (Asif Mujtaba 95, Ramiz Raja 65, Inzamam-ul-Haq 57, Naved Anjum 56) and 133 for 2 (Inzamam-ul-Haq 61 not out)

Pakistanis won by 8 wickets

23, 25 and 26 May *at Derby*

Derbyshire 500 for 9 dec. (P.D. Bowler 155, J.E. Morris 120, K.J. Barnett 71, C.C. Lewis 4 for 88)

Nottinghamshire 347 (R.T. Robinson 97, P. Johnson 75, I.R. Bishop 4 for 70, D.E. Malcolm 4 for 71) and 342 for 1 (M.A. Crawley 160 not out, B.C. Broad 117)

Match drawn

Derbyshire 7 pts., Nottinghamshire 5 pts.

at Stockton

Northamptonshire 420 for 9 dec. (D. Ripley 104, K.M. Curran 82, A.J. Lamb 58, S.J.E. Brown 5 for 124) and 95 for 2

Durham 258 (P. Bainbridge 92 not out) and 253 (D.M. Jones 157)

Northamptonshire won by 8 wickets

Northamptonshire 24 pts., Durham 5 pts.

at Gloucester

Somerset 257 (A.N. Hayhurst 97, C.J. Tavaré 74, C.A. Walsh 5 for 55) and 140 (R.J. Harden 56, C.A. Walsh 5 for 30)

Gloucestershire 177 (R.C. Russell 58 not out, H.R.J. Trump 7 for 52) and 203 (S.G. Hinks 60, H.R.J. Trump 7 for 52)

Somerset won by 17 runs

Somerset 23 pts., Gloucestershire 5 pts.

at Old Trafford

Hampshire 349 for 5 dec. (K.D. James 98, D.I. Gower 74, T.C. Middleton 73) and 316 for 4 dec. (T.C. Middleton 138 not out, D.I. Gower 71)

Lancashire 322 for 6 dec. (G.D. Lloyd 102 not out, W.K. Hegg 80, N.J. Speak 58, K.J. Shine 5 for 58) and 171 (S.P. Titchard 73, M.A. Atherton 52, K.J. Shine 8 for 47)

Hampshire won by 172 runs

Hampshire 22 pts., Lancashire 6 pts.

at Lord's

Middlesex 486 for 7 dec. (M.R. Ramprakash 233, P.N. Weekes 89 not out, M.A. Roseberry 63, J.D. Carr 52)
Surrey 188 (M.A. Lynch 51, N.F. Williams 4 for 31) and 227 for 9 (N.M. Kendrick 55, C.W. Taylor 4 for 50)

Match drawn

Middlesex 8 pts., Surrey 3 pts.

at Hove

Sussex 335 (A.P. Wells 144, M.A. Ealham 4 for 67) and 368 for 1 dec. (N.J. Lenham 222 not out, J.W. Hall 99)
Kent 368 for 7 dec. (C.L. Hooper 121, G.R. Cowdrey 62) and 338 for 6 (M.R. Benson 117, N.R. Taylor 61)

Kent won by 4 wickets

Kent 22 pts., Sussex 7 pts.

at Edgbaston

Warwickshire 313 for 8 dec. (P.C.L. Holloway 102 not out, T.M. Moody 4 for 50) and 189 (P.J. Newport 5 for 45)
Worcestershire 208 (T.M. Moody 54) and 242 (G.A. Hick 70, T.S. Curtis 54, A.A. Donald 5 for 69)

Warwickshire won by 52 runs

Warwickshire 24 pts., Worcestershire 5 pts.

The Pakistan touring side shook off their defeats in the Texaco Trophy and beat Leicestershire in the Tetley Bitter Challenge match so claiming another £2000 in prize money. They needed 133 in 35 overs on the last afternoon and won with 20 balls to spare.

Derbyshire batted into the second day to score 500 against Nottinghamshire, who gave Chris Lewis a severe reprimand for arriving 50 minutes late for the match. Peter Bowler hit his third championship century in six days, and John Morris scored 103 between lunch and tea. Nottinghamshire just failed to avert the follow-on, but Chris Broad and Mark Crawley began their second innings with a stand of 230, and Crawley reached the highest score of his career.

Dean Jones hit his first century for Durham, but he could not prevent his side being beaten by Northamptonshire. Ripley and Curran had put the visitors into a strong position with a seventh-wicket stand of 161, but Jones frustrated Northamptonshire as he rescued Durham from the depths of 112 for 7 after they had been forced to follow-on. The visitors had only nine overs in which to score 92 runs to win, and victory came when Bailey hit Botham's last ball of the match for four.

At Gloucester, Harvey Trump, the Somerset off-spinner, had figures of 7 for 52 in either innings. These were career best performances, and it was the first time that he had taken ten or more wickets in a match. In spite of Walsh's fine bowling, Gloucestershire were beaten. They lost their last five second innings wickets for 16 runs, all to Trump, who performed the first hat-trick of his career when he dismissed Russell, Ball and Walsh with successive deliveries.

Hampshire went to the top of the Britannic Assurance County Championship when they overwhelmed Lancashire at Old Trafford. The first innings had seen honours even as Middleton and James began Hampshire's task with a partnership of 164, and Lloyd and Hegg replied with a sixth-wicket stand of 169 for Lancashire. The prolific Middleton scored his fifth century of the summer, and Lancashire were left two sessions in which to score 344 to win. They made 123 without loss in the first, and nine runs were added after tea before the first wicket fell. They lost all ten wickets for 39 runs in 90 minutes, and Hampshire won with 8.5

Mark Ramprakash hit 233 for Middlesex against Surrey at Lord's, 23–25 May, and he earned a recall to the England side. Disciplinary problems were to mar his season. (USPA)

overs to spare. Kevin Shine, the young medium pace bowler, produced the best figures of the season and the best of his career, 8 for 47, and took four wickets in five balls, including the hat-trick. His victims were Lloyd, Hegg and Austin. Martin was out second ball.

Mark Ramprakash hit the first double century of his career, a splendid innings, as Middlesex savaged Surrey at Lord's. Forced to follow-on, Surrey promoted Kendrick to opener, and he batted 68 overs for his 55. It was somewhat surprising that Gatting did not recall Taylor, the left-arm seamer, during the last 20 overs. He had caused much damage early on, and Surrey's final pair were able to survive the last 13 balls to draw the match.

Warwickshire wicket-keeper Piran Holloway hit a maiden first-class century against Worcestershire, at Edgbaston, 23–25 May. He also had six dismissals in the Sunday League match against Hampshire, 15 June, but most of his cricket was limited to Sundays. (David Munden)

There was an exciting finish at Hove where Hooper hit Salisbury for six to give Kent victory over Sussex with four balls to spare. Hooper had earlier hit an elegant hundred for the visitors while skipper Alan Wells held the Sussex innings together with 144 off 294 balls. On the last morning, Kent bowled 63 overs before lunch, most of them from occasional bowlers. Lenham helped himself to the first double century of his career, and Hall showed his exasperation when he fell to Cowdrey for 99. Needing 336 in what turned out to be 54 overs, Kent were given the ideal start by skipper Benson who equalled the fastest hundred of the season, reaching three figures off 82 balls.

Warwickshire were 215 for 8 on the opening day against Worcestershire, but Donald joined Piran Holloway, the young reserve wicket-keeper, in an unbroken partnership of 98. The left-handed Holloway reached the first century of his career when he reverse swept Hick for four. Worcestershire ultimately needed 295 from 80 overs, and they were never quite in touch against the pace of Donald.

SUNDAY LEAGUE

24 May *at Derby*

Derbyshire 202 for 7 (P.D. Bowler 63)
Nottinghamshire 186

Derbyshire (4 pts.) won by 16 runs

at Stockton

Durham 124 (D.J. Capel 4 for 41)
Northamptonshire 127 for 4

Northamptonshire (4 pts.) won by 6 wickets

at Chelmsford

Glamorgan 194 for 5 (M.P. Maynard 75)
Essex 195 for 2 (G.A. Gooch 75, J.P. Stephenson 59)

Essex (4 pts.) won by 8 wickets

at Gloucester

Somerset 165 for 8 (R.J. Harden 50)
Gloucestershire 145 for 4 (M.W. Alleyne 58 not out, R.C. Russell 56 not out)

Gloucestershire (4 pts.) won on faster scoring rate

at Canterbury

Kent 219 for 8 (T.R. Ward 55)
Middlesex 221 for 3 (D.L. Haynes 95 not out, M.R. Ramprakash 57)

Middlesex (4 pts.) won by 7 wickets

at The Oval

Surrey 196 (D.M. Ward 63, G.P. Thorpe 51)
Sussex 200 for 5 (J.W. Hall 61, K. Greenfield 50)

Sussex (4 pts.) won by 5 wickets

at Edgbaston

Warwickshire 251 for 4 (T.A. Lloyd 68, A.J. Moles 56, R.G. Twose 54)
Lancashire 61 for 3

Match abandoned

Warwickshire 2 pts., Lancashire 2 pts.

at Leeds

Hampshire 211 for 5 (R.A. Smith 77, T.C. Middleton 66)
Yorkshire 152

Hampshire (4 pts.) won by 59 runs

Middlesex and Essex maintained their 100 per cent records in the Sunday League. Gooch and Stephenson put on 128 for Essex's first wicket against Glamorgan, and Haynes batted throughout the 38.4 overs of the Middlesex innings.

27 and 28 May *at Luton*

Pakistanis 332 for 3 dec. (Shoaib Mohammad 107 not out, Javed Miandad 105 retired, Inzamam-ul-Haq 102)
England Amateur XI 174 (S.J. Dean 80, Asif Mujtaba 5 for 22) and 142 (N.A. Folland 76, Asif Mujtaba 5 for 25)

Pakistanis won by an innings and 16 runs

Waqar Younis played his first match of the tour as did Ata-ur-Rehman, newly arrived for Pakistan.

BENSON AND HEDGES CUP

QUARTER-FINALS

27 May *at Southampton*

Middlesex 206 (D.L. Haynes 89, S.D. Udal 4 for 40)
Hampshire 207 for 4 (T.C. Middleton 65)

Hampshire won by 6 wickets

(Gold Award –S.D. Udal)

at Canterbury

Kent 193 (I.R. Bishop 4 for 30)
Derbyshire 160 for 9 (K.J. Barnett 73)

Kent won by 33 runs

(Gold Award –R.P. Davis)

at The Oval

Surrey 305 for 7 (D.J. Bicknell 86, A.J. Stewart 64, M.A. Lynch 54)
Lancashire 230 (S.P. Titchard 82)

Surrey won by 75 runs

(Gold Award –M.P. Bicknell)

at Worcester

Somerset 256 for 9 (M.N. Lathwell 93, T.M. Moody 4 for 59)
Worcestershire 246 (T.M. Moody 80, T.S. Curtis 78)

Somerset won by 10 runs

(Gold Award –T.M. Moody)

Hampshire brushed aside Middlesex with surprising ease to reach the semi-final of the Benson and Hedges

Benson and Hedges Cup quarter-final at Southampton, Hampshire v. Middlesex. David Gower is run out, but Hampshire win with ease. (Patrick Eagar)

Cup. With their score on 176 for 4 after 40 overs, Middlesex looked set for a huge total, but substitute Wood ran round the boundary to fling himself and hold on to Haynes' hook off Connor. Next ball, Carr drove into the hands of extra cover. Two runs later, Weekes fell to Udal whose off-spin proved all too much for the Middlesex late order. Hampshire excelled in the field, and their batting had a consistency that made the result inevitable. There was flourish from James, who had captured the wickets of Roseberry and Gatting with his left-arm seam, solidity from Middleton and Smith, and elegance from Gower until he was run out one short of his fifty. Nicholas finished the job with four overs to spare.

A sluggish pitch at Canterbury did not make run-getting easy, but there was some strange cricket. Choosing to bat first, Kent were disconcerted by the early loss of Ward, but Taylor had just begun to break free from the shackles of Bishop, Mortensen and the pitch when he lobbed a gentle delivery from Goldsmith to mid-on where Morris held the easiest of catches at the third attempt. Benson was totally out of touch, but Hooper looked to be thriving before he attempted to dab Bishop to third-man and was splendidly caught by Krikken. Worse followed, and in the 47th over, Kent were 149 for 8. Davis stood firm, and McCague, a rather controversial selection, belted the ball happily for 30 off 27 deliveries. He missed a ball from Goldsmith in the last over of the innings, but he had, it transpired, played a match-winning innings. Bowler, Morris and O'Gorman all failed to score, and Derbyshire were 10 for 3. Chris Adams attempted to infuse some positivity into the Derbyshire, but he was caught on the square-leg boundary off Hooper. Strangely, Barnett never seemed capable of breaking the shackles imposed by the spin duet of Hooper and Davis, and brave as his 73 may seem, he never once seized the initiative nor looked like saving his side. Davis, a staunch innings, three catches and 1 for 17 in his 11 overs deservedly took the Gold Award although McCague and Hooper were also in contention.

Darren Bicknell, 86 off 117 balls, and Monte Lynch, 54 off 66 balls, gave Surrey a riotous start on a flat fast pitch at The Oval. Stewart, Brown and Ward maintained the momentum, and Surrey passed 300 and looked impregnable. Their authority was compounded when Martin Bicknell quickly removed Atherton and Speak, and Lancashire, without the injured Fairbrother, could never get to terms with the required run rate.

Mark Lathwell enjoyed some good fortune in reaching his highest score in any competition, but Somerset suffered a mid-innings collapse and were indebted to the aggression of Rose and Snell for their 256 for 9. Curtis and Moody began with a stand of 140, and Worcestershire appeared to be cruising to victory. At 198 for 1, eight overs remaining, victory seemed even more certain. Then Curtis was run out, and Hick, Leatherdale and D'Oliveira fell to Mallender. Two of the wickets came in Mallender's 11th and final over, and he also ran out Curtis. Moreover, he took the heart out of Worcestershire, and Somerset won by 10 runs.

Matthew Fleming bowls Ian Bishop, and Kent scent victory over Derbyshire in the Benson and Hedges Cup quarter-final at Canterbury. (Tom Morris)

Somerset's exciting young batsman Mark Lathwell played a prominent part in the victory over Worcestershire at New Road. (David Munden)

29, 30 May and 1 June *at Swansea*

Leicestershire 246 for 6 (T.J. Boon 69, L. Potter 65)
v. Glamorgan

Match drawn

Leicestershire 2 pts., Glamorgan 2 pts.

at Southampton

Durham 306 (J.D. Glendennen 64, I.T. Botham 51, C.A. Connor 5 for 58) and 87 for 2
Hampshire 210 (K.D. James 62, J.R. Wood 57, J. Wood 5 for 68)

Match drawn

Durham 8 pts., Hampshire 6 pts.

at Old Trafford

Somerset 376 for 9 dec. (M.N. Lathwell 74, N.D. Burns 73 not out, R.P. Snell 55)
Lancashire 313 for 7 (N.J. Speak 102, M. Watkinson 96, G. Fowler 56)

Match drawn

Lancashire 8 pts., Somerset 7 pts.

at Northampton

Derbyshire 180 for 0 dec. (P. Bowler 90 not out, K.J. Barnett 82 not out) and 0 for 0 dec.
Northamptonshire 0 for 0 dec. and 181 for 2 (R.J. Bailey 72, N.A. Felton 58 not out)

Northamptonshire 16 pts., Derbyshire 1 pts.

at The Oval

Sussex 300 for 6 dec. (A.P. Wells 165 not out, J.A. North 53 not out, M.P. Bicknell 4 for 47)
Surrey 396 for 8 dec. (A.J. Stewart 140, M.A. Lynch 71, G.P. Thorpe 53)

Match drawn

Sussex 7 pts., Surrey 6 pts.

at Worcester

Worcestershire v. Gloucestershire

Match abandoned

No points

at Oxford

Oxford University v. Yorkshire

Match abandoned

30, 31 May and 1 June *at Lord's*

Pakistanis 327 for 4 dec. (Asif Mujtaba 123, Salim Malik 68) and 5 for 0
Middlesex 222 for 8 dec. (M.A. Roseberry 111 not out, Mushtaq Ahmed 4 for 73)

Match drawn

A prolific scorer for Lancashire in a troubled season, Nick Speak. (Alan Cozzi)

Rain savaged the Britannic Assurance County Championship programme with no play possible on the final day at Swansea or Southampton. The most interesting feature of the game at Southampton was the performance of the Durham seamer John Wood, who has played for Griqualand West in one-day matches. In his championship debut, he had Middleton caught behind with his first delivery and Gower taken at slip with the last ball of the same over.

Lathwell again sparkled for Somerset, and Lancashire were revived by Watkinson and Speak who added 163 for the sixth wicket in 34 overs after five wickets had fallen for 115. DeFreitas was no-balled for bowling two consecutive bouncers at Neil Burns.

Martin Bicknell began spiritedly for Surrey, but was banned after persistently running on the pitch. Alan Wells and North shared an unbroken stand of 134 for Sussex's seventh wicket, and Alec Stewart hit a welcome century on the eve of the first Test. Ligertwood, an opening batsman/wicket-keeper, made his first-class debut for Surrey.

Only 11 overs were possible before the third day at Northampton, but Kim Barnett was strongly criticised for setting the home side a meagre target of 181 in 50 overs after Derbyshire were fed friendly bowling on the last morning. Northamptonshire achieved a ludicrous 16 points with 13.3 overs to spare.

Asif Mujtaba assured himself of a place in the Pakistani side for the first Test with a century in the rain-ruined match at Lord's.

SUNDAY LEAGUE

31 May *at Swansea*

Glamorgan 264 for 3 (M.P. Maynard 122 not out, S.P. James 74)
Leicestershire 205 for 7 (A. Dale 4 for 27)
Glamorgan (4 pts.) won by 59 runs

at Southampton

Durham 200 for 7 (I.T. Botham 64, D.J. Jones 55, S.D. Udal 4 for 64)
Hampshire 212 for 8 (R.A. Smith 78, D.I. Gower 56)
Hampshire (4 pts.) won by 2 wickets

at Canterbury

Yorkshire 161 for 8
Kent 157
Yorkshire (4 pts.) won by 4 runs

at Old Trafford

Lancashire 77 (A.R. Caddick 4 for 18)
Somerset 79 for 1
Somerset (4 pts.) won by 9 wickets

at Northampton

Derbyshire 189 for 7 (T.J.G. O'Gorman 69, K.J. Barnett 50)
Northamptonshire 190 for 2 (A. Fordham 81, N.A. Felton 62)
Northamptonshire (4 pts.) won by 8 wickets

at Trent Bridge

Nottinghamshire 177 for 7 (C.L. Cairns 55 not out)
Gloucestershire 181 for 1 (G.D. Hodgson 84 not out)
Gloucestershire (4 pts.) won by 9 wickets

at Hove

Warwickshire 175 for 7 (R.G. Twose 71)
Sussex 176 for 2 (A.P. Wells 55 not out)
Sussex (4 pts.) won by 8 wickets

at Worcester

Essex 172 for 9
Worcestershire 173 for 8 (T.S. Curtis 67, T.M. Moody 65)
Worcestershire (4 pts.) won by 2 wickets

With Middlesex engaged against the Pakistan touring side, Essex lost the opportunity to go clear at the top of the Sunday League table when they were beaten by Worcestershire, who hit seven from Waugh's last over. It was Essex's first Sunday defeat of the season. James and Maynard hit 148 in 20 overs for Glamorgan's third wicket against Leicestershire, and Smith and Gower put on 135 in 22 overs for Hampshire's second wicket in the win over Durham. There were sensations at Old Trafford where Lancashire, 55 for 2, were bowled out for 77. Impressive pace bowler Caddick had his best figures in the Sunday League for Somerset while wicket-keeper Burns took five catches behind the stumps. Sussex maintained their unbeaten run with a comfortable win over Warwickshire.

Andy Moles of Warwickshire is run out as Sussex maintain their early season challenge in the Sunday League, Hove, 31 May. (Philip Wilcox)

2, 3 and 4 June *at Darlington*

Somerset 270 (A.N. Hayhurst 76, M.N. Lathwell 53, S.J.E. Brown 4 for 71) and 192 for 6 dec. (M.N. Lathwell 50)
Durham 250 for 8 dec. (C.W. Scott 57 not out) and 213 for 2 (W. Larkins 92, D.M. Jones 78)

Durham won by 8 wickets

Durham 23 pts., Somerset 6 pts.

at Chelmsford

Essex 310 for 7 dec. (N. Shahid 96, N.V. Knight 70, M.E. Waugh 52, S.L. Watkin 4 for 80) and 102 for 4 (J.P. Stephenson 60)
Glamorgan 289 (M.P. Maynard 82, I.V.A. Richards 51, J.H. Childs 6 for 82)

Match drawn

Essex 8 pts., Glamorgan 6 pts.

at Basingstoke

Yorkshire 210 (P-J. Bakker 4 for 38) and 222 for 7
Hampshire 351 for 9 dec. (D.I. Gower 155, K.D. James 59, J.D. Batty 4 for 75)

Match drawn

Hampshire 7 pts., Yorkshire 3 pts.

at Tunbridge Wells

Worcestershire 327 for 6 dec. (T.S. Curtis 140 not out, D.A. Leatherdale 91, M.A. Ealham 4 for 78) and 210 for 6 dec. (T.M. Moody 100, A.C.H. Seymour 62)
Kent 250 for 1 dec. (T.R. Ward 140 not out, N.R. Taylor 67 not out) and 190 for 3 (M.R. Benson 84 not out, T.R. Ward 59)

Match drawn

Kent 4 pts., Worcestershire 3 pts.

at Northampton

Northamptonshire 117 (V.J. Wells 4 for 26) and 238 (V.J. Wells 4 for 68)
Leicestershire 77 and 112 (K.M. Curran 4 for 20)

Northamptonshire won by 166 runs

Northamptonshire 20 pts., Leicestershire 4 pts.

at Trent Bridge

Middlesex 401 for 2 dec. (M.A. Roseberry 148, D.L. Haynes 114, M.W. Gatting 65 not out)
Nottinghamshire 211 (D.W. Randall 63, P.H. Edmonds 4 for 48, J.E. Emburey 4 for 55) and 53 for 0

Match drawn

Middlesex 8 pts., Nottinghamshire 2 pts.

at The Oval

Derbyshire 249 (M.P. Bicknell 4 for 56) and 244 for 1 dec. (K.J. Barnett 140 not out, T.J.G. O'Gorman 63 not out)
Surrey 253 for 9 dec. (G.P. Thorpe 70) and 69 for 3

Match drawn

Surrey 6 pts., Derbyshire 6 pts.

at Hove

Warwickshire 340 for 5 dec. (A.J. Moles 122, D.P. Ostler 108, D.A. Reeve 57) and 224 for 6 dec.
Sussex 315 (A.P. Wells 115, D.M. Smith 82, J.W. Hall 54, N.M.K. Smith 4 for 101) and 250 for 8 (D.M. Smith 82, J.W. Hall 54, N.M.K. Smith 4 for 101)

Sussex won by 2 wickets

Sussex 22 pts., Warwickshire 8 pts.

at Oxford

Lancashire 314 for 3 dec. (G. Fowler 106, M.A. Atherton 65, G.D. Lloyd 56 not out) and 119 for 8 dec. (J.E.R. Gallian 4 for 29)
Oxford University 104 (M. Watkinson 5 for 16) and 116 for 8

Match drawn

Rain again interfered with the Britannic Assurance County Championship programme. There was no play on the last day at Chelmsford where there were some minor innings of charm and some excellent bowling from the left-arm spin of John Childs. Another 41-year-old left-arm spinner made his mark at Trent Bridge. Phil Edmonds came out of retirement to assist Middlesex in the absence of Tufnell. He combined with his former England spin partner John Emburey to bowl out Nottinghamshire and force them to follow-on, but there was no play possible on the final day. On the first day, Haynes and Roseberry had shared an opening stand of 266.

Durham claimed their second championship win of their first season in first-class cricket. Somerset reached 150 for 1 on the opening day, but Brown and Henderson gnawed at their middle order to keep their total within bounds. Durham's innings never got into its stride and owed its impetus to keeper Scott's fifty which included seven fours. Needing 213 in 42 overs on the last afternoon, Durham were indebted to Larkins and Jones who scored 175 in 113 minutes for their first wicket. Victory came with three overs to spare.

Championship leaders Hampshire were denied victory at Basingstoke by some stubborn Yorkshire batting, and the weather. In the first innings, Bakker had a spell of 4 for 5, including the wicket of Tendulkar for only the second duck of his career. David Gower made his highest score for Hampshire.

There was some rather grim batting by Worcestershire at Tunbridge Wells. Curtis batted into the second day for his 140. He and Leatherdale added 164 for the fourth wicket. Kent showed far greater enterprise as Taylor and Ward added 171 in 48 overs for the second wicket, but Kent's valiant attempt to score 288 at just under five runs an over in their second innings was thwarted by rain.

A green pitch at Northampton, 22 wickets fell on the first day, and the game was completed on the second. Felton was the only batsman on either side to reach 20 on the Tuesday while Bailey batted two and a half hours for 42 in the second Northamptonshire innings. Needing

279 to win, Leicestershire were bowled out in 24 overs.

Derbyshire barely reached two runs an over on the first day at The Oval, and Surrey were only marginally better on the second. Some friendly offerings to Barnett and O'Gorman set up a declaration, but rain ended all speculation.

Moles and Ostler put on 193 for Warwickshire's second wicket against Sussex, but Alan Wells hit his third consecutive century to keep his side in touch. Again there were friendly offerings to force a declaration, and Sussex were asked to score 250 in 49 overs. They reached their target with a leg-bye off the fifth ball of the last over.

Oxford University, 103 for 5, lost their last five wickets for one run against Lancashire.

FIRST TEST MATCH
ENGLAND v. PAKISTAN, at Edgbaston

The first Test match between England and Pakistan was a delight only for the statisticians. There was no play possible on the first day, and on the second day, play began at 2.45. Aamir Sohail hit DeFreitas' first ball for three, Ramiz Raja faced the second and then the players left the field because of bad light which soon turned to rain.

England omitted leg-spinner Salisbury, a surprise choice, and Munton from their thirteen, and Pakistan gave first Test caps to Aamir Sohail, Ata-ur-Rehman, who deputised for the injured Wasim Akram, and Inzamam-ul-Haq. Gooch won the toss and asked Pakistan to bat first, but by Saturday morning, this decision had lost any relevance.

By lunch on the Saturday, Pakistan were 95 for 1, the adventurous Aamir Sohail having mishooked a bouncer from DeFreitas. Asif Mujtaba gave some indication of why he was the leading run-scorer on the tour until he played loosely at the same bowler, and DeFreitas claimed his third wicket when he had Ramiz Raja leg before. That was the end of England's success for the day. At the close, Pakistan were 290 for 3, Javed Miandad, 99, and Salim Malik, 80, having added 180 rich runs in 220 minutes.

The feast did not end there. Javed and Salim were eventually parted when they had 322, a record for either side for any wicket in Test matches between Pakistan and England. The runs came in 370 minutes. This was batting of top quality in approach and manner.

Salim Malik made his highest score in Test cricket off 297 balls. He hit a six and 19 fours. Javed was left unbeaten on 153, his 23rd Test century in his 113th Test. He faced 337 balls and hit 19 fours, and he declared just after he had given Inzamam-ul-Haq his first taste of batting in a Test match.

England soon lost a wicket when Gooch lobbed a bat and pad catch to short-leg. Graeme Hick hit his first half-century in Test cricket. It was not an innings of great conviction, but it pleased those who had lobbied strongly for his retention in the side. Hick was caught in the gully off Waqar Younis who bowled well within himself and without his old fluency of movement on his return to the international scene after his back injury.

The most pleasing aspect of the England innings was another masterly display by Alec Stewart who batted with style, purpose and supreme confidence. He reached 94 in under three hours before the close when, with Smith 10, England were 170 for 2.

The last day saw Smith and Stewart extend their third-wicket partnership to a record 227. In his first Test against Pakistan, Robin Smith hit his seventh Test century. Once again, he was not at his most fluent, but he has the capacity for battling through uneasy periods. He is a gutsy cricketer. He fell to the leg-spinner Mushtaq Ahmed who, rather surprisingly, sent down 50 overs in a match which was doomed to be drawn from

Ramiz Raja is leg before to DeFreitas. (Patrick Eagar)

A rare chance goes begging. Javed Miandad is dropped by Robin Smith. (Adrian Murrell/Allsport)

the second day. One learned that this was at the request of manager Intikhab Alam, a Test leg-spinner of great worth, who believed that the inexperienced Mushtaq would benefit from the practice. He was to be proved right.

Smith was, in fact, the last man out. Having batted for 351 minutes and faced 261 balls, Alec Stewart skied a pull to mid-on to give young Ata-ur-Rehman his first wicket in Test cricket. He claimed his second two balls later when he had Ramprakash caught behind. Stewart's 190 was the highest of his four Test centuries, and it included 31 fours and won him the Man-of-the-Match award. He was both composed and entertaining. If the style is the man, he is a man of warmth, honesty and charm.

Lamb drove to extra cover to give Ata-ur-Rehman a third wicket, and Lewis was bowled by Mushtaq. Botham had a groin strain and did not appear after the third day. England passed the Pakistan score, but doubts as to quality persisted.

The record breakers – Salim Malik and Javed Miandad. (David Munden)

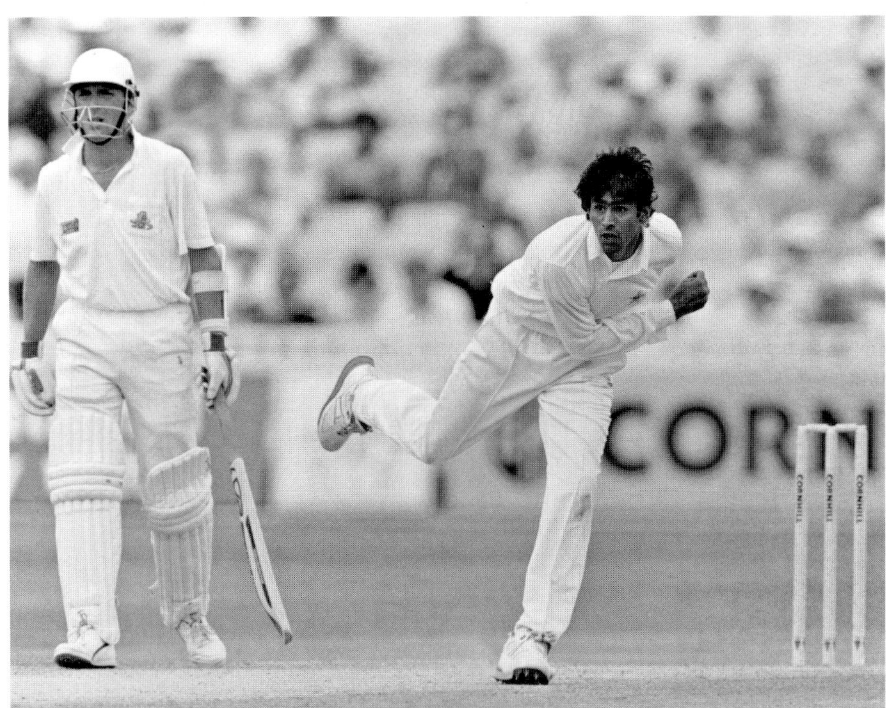

Alec Stewart, who made his highest Test score, is pictured with Ata-ur-Rehman, who bowled well on his Test debut. (Patrick Eagar)

Success at last for Mushtaq Ahmed – Robin Smith is leg before for 127. (Patrick Eagar)

FIRST CORNHILL TEST MATCH – ENGLAND v. PAKISTAN
4, 5, 6, 7 and 8 June, 1992 at Edgbaston, Birmingham

PAKISTAN

Aamir Sohail	c Stewart, b DeFreitas	18
Ramiz Raja	lbw, b DeFreitas	47
Asif Mujtaba	c Russell, b DeFreitas	29
Javed Miandad (capt)	not out	153
Salim Malik	lbw, b DeFreitas	165
Inzamam-ul-Haq	not out	8
*Moin Khan		
Mushtaq Ahmed		
Waqar Younis		
Aqib Javed		
Ata-ur-Rehman		
Extras	b 2, lb 5, nb 19	26
	(for 4 wickets, dec.)	**446**

	O	M	R	W
DeFreitas	33	6	121	4
Lewis	33	3	116	–
Pringle	28	2	92	–
Botham	19	6	52	–
Hick	13	1	46	–
Gooch	10	5	9	–
Ramprakash	1	–	3	–

FALL OF WICKETS
1–33, **2**–96, **3**–110, **4**–432

ENGLAND

G.A. Gooch (capt)	c Asif Mujtaba, b Aqib Javed	8
A.J. Stewart	c Salim Malik, b Ata-ur-Rehman	190
G.A. Hick	c Javed Miandad, b Waqar Younis	51
R.A. Smith	lbw, b Mushtaq Ahmed	127
M.R. Ramprakash	c Moin Khan, b Ata-ur-Rehman	0
A.J. Lamb	c Javed Miandad, b Ata-ur-Rehman	12
C.C. Lewis	b Mushtaq Ahmed	24
*R.C. Russell	not out	29
D.R. Pringle	not out	0
I.T. Botham		
P.A.J. DeFreitas		
Extras	b 5, lb 5, w 1, nb 7	18
	(for 7 wickets, dec.)	**459**

	O	M	R	W
Waqar Younis	24	2	96	1
Aqib Javed	16	3	86	1
Mushtaq Ahmed	50	8	156	2
Ata-ur-Rehman	18	5	69	3
Asif Mujtaba	8	1	29	–
Aamir Sohail	2	–	8	–
Salim Malik	1	–	5	–

FALL OF WICKETS
1–28, **2**–121, **3**–348, **4**–348, **5**–378, **6**–415, **7**–446

Umpires: M.J. Kitchen & B.J. Meyer

Match drawn

5, 6 and 8 June *at Chesterfield*

Durham 241 for 3 dec. (D.M. Jones 93 not out, P.W.G. Parker 75)
Derbyshire 31 for 0

Match drawn

No points

at Tunbridge Wells

Essex 342 for 4 dec. (P.J. Prichard 133, N. Hussain 75 not out) and 0 for 0 dec.
Kent 0 for 0 dec. and 343 for 6 (N.R. Taylor 90, C.L. Hooper 86, M.R. Benson 67, G.R. Cowdrey 57 not out)

Kent won by 4 wickets

Kent 17 pts., Essex 4 pts.

at Old Trafford

Lancashire 298 (N.J. Speak 144, C.A. Walsh 6 for 42) and 70 for 0 dec.
Gloucestershire 29 for 1 dec. and 148 for 1 (S.G. Hinks 88 not out, G.D. Hodgson 50)

Match drawn

Gloucestershire 4 pts., Lancashire 3 pts.

at Lord's

Middlesex 102 (V.J. Wells 4 for 27) and 265 for 2 dec. (M.A. Roseberry 102, D.L. Haynes 94)
Leicestershire 128 for 5 (N.F. Williams 4 for 45) and 141 for 5 (B.F. Smith 67 not out)

Match drawn

Leicestershire 4 pts., Middlesex 2 pts.

at Middlesbrough

Yorkshire 312 for 7 dec. (M.D. Moxon 117, S.A. Kellett 87)
Somerset 167 (R.J. Bartlett 56, P. Carrick 6 for 58) and 57 for 0

Match drawn

Yorkshire 7 pts., Somerset 3 pts.

On 5 June, the only ground on which play was possible was at Tunbridge Wells, and there, only 4.2 overs were bowled. The game finally got underway again at 12.30 on the Saturday, and then Essex played with considerable panache considering the damp conditions and sluggish pitch. Although not at his most fluent, Prichard hit a six and 12 fours in his four-hour century, and Hussain and Foster provided the dash which enabled Foster to offer Kent a generous target on the Monday morning, 343 in 92 overs. Childs was soon introduced into the attack and quickly accounted for Ward, but Taylor hit 16 fours in his 90 off 102 balls. Then came the silky qualities of Carl Hooper who combined with Cowdrey to score 125 in 20 overs. Kent won with 20 balls to spare, and for Essex there was a sad coda when Hussain was suspended for a serious breach of discipline by the County Club. It appeared that this was a culmination in a series of events concerning Hussain.

There was no play on the first two days at Chesterfield, and the attempts at a one-innings game on the final day were dashed by the weather.

Speak's third century of the season helped Lancashire to respectability on the Saturday, but the declarations in search of a result came to nought when rain ended Gloucestershire's attempt to score 340 runs in 94 overs. Lancashire, for whom problems seemed to be growing, lost skipper Fairbrother who was carried off with the recurrence of his hamstring trouble.

Middlesex lost four middle-order wickets while not a run was scored on the Saturday, and were bowled out for 102. Briers surprised many people by declaring with a lead of only 26. He was hoping for a breakthrough on the Saturday evening, but Haynes and Roseberry began Middlesex's second innings with a partnership of 195, and Leicestershire made a very poor attempt to score 240 in 43 overs, which was the target offered by Mike Gatting.

Moxon and Kellett began Yorkshire's innings with a partnership of 203. Moxon did not declare until the last morning, but Carrick's spin routed Somerset who were forced to follow-on. Byas took four catches at slip, and Tendulkar three at silly mid-off in the Somerset innings. The match marked Moxon's return to the Yorkshire side after injury, and the White Rose county looked a better team for his presence and leadership.

SUNDAY LEAGUE

7 June at Chesterfield

Durham 197 for 6 (D.M. Jones 67)
Derbyshire 201 for 3 (P.D. Bowler 77 not out, K.J. Barnett 53)

Derbyshire (4 pts.) won by 7 wickets

at Chelmsford

Essex 229 for 7 (M.E. Waugh 105 not out)
Kent 223 for 9 (M.R. Benson 64)

Essex (4 pts.) won by 6 runs

at Basingstoke

Hampshire 153 (J. Boiling 5 for 24)
Surrey 157 for 1 (D.J. Bicknell 74 not out, G.P. Thorpe 53 not out)

Surrey (4 pts.) won by 9 wickets

at Old Trafford

Lancashire 199 for 7 (G. Fowler 57, M.W. Alleyne 4 for 35)
Gloucestershire 202 for 5 (A.J. Wright 59 not out)

Gloucestershire (4 pts.) won by 5 wickets

at Lord's

Middlesex 235 for 3 (J.D. Carr 104 not out, D.L. Haynes 84)
Warwickshire 179 for 8 (T.A. Lloyd 71)

Middlesex (4 pts.) won by 56 runs

at Hove

Glamorgan 188 (F.D. Stephenson 4 for 22)
Sussex 192 for 6 (K. Greenfield 79)

Sussex (4 pts.) won by 4 wickets

at Middlesbrough

Somerset 252 for 3 (G.D. Rose 88, R.J. Harden 76 not out)
Yorkshire 256 for 5 (D. Byas 80, M.D. Moxon 57, C. White 52 not out)

Yorkshire (4 pts.) won by 5 wickets

J.D. Carr came out of retirement and played a vital part in Middlesex's record run in the Sunday League. (USPA)

Middlesex and Essex continued to head the Sunday League table. Essex had a narrow victory over Kent and were indebted to Mark Waugh's century off 84 balls. He hit three sixes and eight fours. Middlesex overwhelmed Warwickshire as Carr hit his first Sunday League hundred and shared a stand of 135 in 21 overs with Haynes for the third wicket. For Warwickshire everything went wrong as Paul Smith dislocated his shoulder, and Gladstone Small injured his index finger. Hampshire collapsed against the off-spin of Boiling, and Surrey, led by Ian Greig, won with ease. Speak was deservedly awarded his county cap by Lancashire who fell to Mark Alleyne's best Sunday League bowling performance. Sussex kept in touch with the leaders by beating Glamorgan, and Byas and White hit 119 in 15 overs to give Yorkshire victory over Somerset.

TILCON TROPHY, at Harrogate

9 June

Sussex 214 for 8 (M.P. Speight 71)
Durham 177 (N.J. Lenham 4 for 32)

Sussex won by 37 runs

10 June

Glamorgan 175 (H. Morris 82, M.A. Robinson 5 for 27)
Yorkshire 167 (S. Bastien 4 for 29)

Glamorgan won by 8 runs

FINAL

Glamorgan 291 for 5 (P.A. Cottey 91, S. Dhaniran 65 not out)
Sussex 169 (S. Bastien 4 for 31)

Glamorgan won by 122 runs

10, 11 and 12 June *at Trent Bridge*

Nottinghamshire 116 (Wasim Akram 4 for 9) and 212 (P. Johnson 60, Aqib Javed 4 for 51)
Pakistanis 163 (Inzamam-ul-Haq 53, K.P. Evans 4 for 54) and 167 for 2 (Aamir Sohail 58, Shoaib Mohammad 50)

Pakistanis won by 8 wickets

The important factor in Pakistan's comfortable win over Nottinghamshire before lunch on the third day was the form of Wasim Akram who had match figures of 6 for 33 to convince that he had recovered from the injury which, at one time, looked as if it might cut short his tour. Reserve wicket-keeper Rashid Latif took eight catches in the match.

BENSON AND HEDGES CUP

SEMI-FINALS

10 June *at Southampton*

Somerset 218 for 8 (G.D. Rose 65, C.A. Connor 4 for 32)
Hampshire 219 for 4 (V.P. Terry 89 not out)

Hampshire won by 6 wickets

(Gold Award - V.P. Terry)

at Canterbury

Surrey 198 (G.P. Thorpe 82)
Kent 199 for 8 (C.L. Hooper 50)

Kent won by 2 wickets

(Gold Award - M.V. Fleming)

There was no fairy tale ending for Somerset at Southampton. They troubled Hampshire only briefly, and the favourites entered the final with more ease than 11 balls and six wickets would suggest. Somerset suffered a severe setback when the excitingly promising Lathwell perished in Marshall's second over. Hayhurst had to retire for a time when hit on the finger by a ball from Marshall, and Somerset could achieve no sort of rhythm in their batting. The spark of hope came when Rose hit 65 off 61 deliveries including three sixes, one out of the ground. Connor returned to dismiss both Rose and Snell, and although Burns batted admirably, Somerset's total always looked 20 or 30 short of causing Hampshire any real problems. There was instant encouragement for Somerset when the prolific Middleton was caught at slip off Mallender in the opening over of Hampshire's innings, but Terry and Smith were soon scoring freely. Smith was run out when Terry sent him back. Gower quickly established authority, and although both he and Nicholas were dismissed, the result was never in doubt.

Alec Stewart chose to bat first when he won the toss at Canterbury, but his side struggled painfully at the outset. Both Darren Bicknell and Lynch fell when they tried to cut Igglesden, and Stewart, having survived confident appeals for a catch in the gully and leg before, clipped Ealham's slower ball to mid-on. In the 11th over, Surrey were 27 for 3, and the loss of the likeable Ward at 41 gave them serious problems. Igglesden and Ealham bowled their full quota of overs, and the spinners Hooper and Davis did the same, surely a tactic unique in the competition. Thorpe, so often frustrating, batted with great good sense, pushing the singles rather than attempting lavish hits. He and Brown added 50, and Feltham showed aggression. McCague and Fleming had the uncomfortable responsibility of bowling the last 11 overs, and Surrey's 198 was way beyond what had looked possible earlier. Ward quickly fell to the fast and lively Martin Bicknell, and Benson became more and more becalmed. Taylor was smartly caught by Stewart, and there were doubts as to Kent's survival. Then

Neil Kendrick is bowled by Martin McCague for 24 in the Benson and Hedges Cup semi-final at Canterbury. (Tom Morris)

Fleming joined Hooper, and when the West Indian was at the crease it looked a completely different game. Fleming drove Boiling straight for six, and the next ball produced three wides. This is the over which wins the match for Kent, one thought, and next ball Hooper top edged his sweep to fine leg, and this, one thought, is the over which wins the game for Surrey. Marsh went for three, and Kent were 139 for 6. Fleming hit thrillingly, and when he was out 16 were needed from 16 balls with two wickets remaining. Kent's hero arrived in the shape of McCague. Martin Bicknell produced a dreadful short ball in the final over when seven were needed, and McCague drove the ball through the covers with ferocity. It was the shot of the match, and he and Davis scrambled the remaining three comfortably. Kent fielded magnificently, and Ealham, in particular, caught the eye. It was this, as much as anything, which tilted the game in their favour.

12, 13 and 15 June *at Hartlepool*

Essex 360 (G.A. Gooch 113, M.E. Waugh 75, N.A. Foster 54) and 309 for 6 dec. (G.A. Gooch 86, J.P. Stephenson 81, P.J. Prichard 66)
Durham 300 for 7 dec. (P. Bainbridge 60, D.M. Jones 57, I.T. Botham 55 not out, P.W.G. Parker 55, J.H. Childs 4 for 85) and 179 (N.A. Foster 4 for 49)

Essex won by 190 runs

Essex 23 pts., Durham 8 pts.

at Colwyn Bay

Glamorgan 296 (I.V.A. Richards 68, D.K. Morrison 4 for 55) and 298 for 2 dec. (S.P. James 152 not out, H. Morris 104)
Lancashire 295 (P.A.J. DeFreitas 72, N.J. Speak 71) and 242 for 7 (M.A. Atherton 69, G.D. Lloyd 52)

Match drawn

Glamorgan 7 pts., Lancashire 7 pts.

at Leicester

Sussex 171 (D.J. Millns 4 for 35) and 103
Leicestershire 251 (J.J. Whitaker 74, B.F. Smith 56) and 24 for 0

Leicestershire won by 10 wickets

Leicestershire 23 pts., Sussex 5 pts.

at The Oval

Surrey 301 for 9 dec. (M.A. Lynch 107, N.M. Kendrick 51) and 169 for 5 dec. (G.P. Thorpe 69 not out)
Worcestershire 195 for 7 dec. (S.R. Lampitt 71 not out) and 219 for 7 (G.A. Hick 73, N.M. Kendrick 4 for 60)

Match drawn

Surrey 7 pts., Worcestershire 5 pts.

at Edgbaston

Hampshire 290 (T.C. Middleton 124, P.A. Smith 5 for 63) and 182 for 3 dec. (T.C. Middleton 77)
Warwickshire 216 for 9 dec. (A.J. Moles 95) and 198 for 8 (D.P. Ostler 65, R.G. Twose 51)

Match drawn

Hampshire 7 pts., Warwickshire 5 pts.

at Harrogate

Derbyshire 227 (P.D. Bowler 60, P. Carrick 4 for 58, J.D. Batty 4 for 84) and 74 (J.D. Batty 4 for 34)
Yorkshire 305 (S.R. Tendulkar 89, M.D. Moxon 64, C. White 53, I.R. Bishop 5 for 37)

Yorkshire won by an innings and 4 runs

13, 14 and 15 June *at Northampton*

Northamptonshire 193 (R.J. Bailey 51, Wasim Akram 5 for 43) and 213 (D. Ripley 64, Wasim Akram 5 for 74)
Pakistanis 287 for 8 dec. (Shoaib Mohammad 59, Ramiz Raja 55) and 129 for 3

Pakistanis won by 7 wickets

Essex gained a very welcome victory over Durham and moved to within 20 points of leaders Hampshire with a game in hand. Gooch and Waugh added 157 for Essex's third wicket, and Foster hit 54 off 36 balls as the visitors raced to 360 in 93 overs. The left-handed Stewart Hutton, making his first-class debut, opened the Durham innings and made 43. Consistent batting took the home side to maximum batting points in brisk time, but Essex began their second innings at a phenomenal rate, Gooch and Stephenson hitting 152 in 24 overs.

Gooch was able to declare early on the Monday morning and set Durham a target of 370 in 87 overs on a good pitch. They lost Bainbridge with a broken arm, hit by a ball from Ilott, and were bowled out in 50.2 overs.

Warren Hegg claimed five dismissals for Lancashire against Glamorgan, and he was then forced to retire with a hamstring injury. Daniel Morrison returned his best figures since joining Lancashire and took three wickets in four balls at one stage. Lancashire trailed by one run on the first innings, and James, who hit his first championship century, and Morris began Glamorgan's second innings with a partnership of 250. Needing 300 in 58 overs, Lancashire fell well short of their target.

Sussex were 65 for 6 at lunch on the first day at Leicester, and the match was all over on the second day. Millns and the seam bowlers thrived on a green wicket, but there was some good batting from Whitaker and Smith.

Lynch and Kendrick added 131 for Surrey's seventh wicket against Worcestershire and took their side to maximum batting points. Lynch's century included 15 fours. In contrast, Worcestershire offered nothing but tedium. They were 91 for 7 and only 157 for 7 after 100 overs. That they should be offered a target at all was an insult to the paying customer, but they needed 276 in 68 overs and finished 57 short with three wickets standing.

Tony Middleton hit his fifth century of the season, and Hampshire wicket-keeper Aymes was injured in the game at Edgbaston in which Warwickshire hung on for a draw to deny the championship leaders.

The Yorkshire spinners destroyed Derbyshire at Harrogate to bring their county their first championship win of the season. Yorkshire, who lost their last four wickets for two runs, were well served by another pleasing innings from Sachin Tendulkar. For Derbyshire, left-arm spinner Sladdin laboured for 45 overs in succession to finish with 2 for 119.

Wasim Akram proved himself totally fit as the tourists brushed aside Northamptonshire. Wasim took ten wickets in the match, and victory came early on the Monday.

SUNDAY LEAGUE

14 June *at Hartlepool*

Essex 220 for 8 (P.J. Prichard 83)
Durham 205 for 8 (D.M. Jones 100)

Essex (4 pts.) won by 15 runs

at Colwyn Bay

Glamorgan 196 for 4 (H. Morris 96 not out, P.A. Cottey 51 not out)
Lancashire 197 for 4 (G. Fowler 51)

Lancashire (4 pts.) won by 6 wickets

at Swindon

Kent 171
Gloucestershire 156 for 9

Kent (4 pts.) won by 15 runs

at Leicester

Sussex 235 for 6 (A.P. Wells 62, F.D. Stephenson 55 not out)
Leicestershire 166 for 9 (I.D.K. Salisbury 5 for 30)

Sussex (4 pts.) won by 69 runs

at Bath

Nottinghamshire 162 for 6
Somerset 163 for 3 (A.N. Hayhurst 56)

Somerset (4 pts.) won by 7 wickets

at The Oval

Worcestershire 200 (T.M. Moody 51)
Surrey 201 for 6 (A.D. Brown 84, D.M. Ward 51)

Surrey (4 pts.) won by 4 wickets

at Edgbaston

Warwickshire 226 for 6 (R.G. Twose 66, D.A. Reeve 50 not out)
Hampshire 186 (M.C.J. Nicholas 53)

Warwickshire (4 pts) won by 40 runs

at Leeds

Yorkshire 236 for 2 (S.A. Kellett 118 not out)
Derbyshire 165 (C.J. Adams 58)

Yorkshire (4 pts.) won by 71 runs

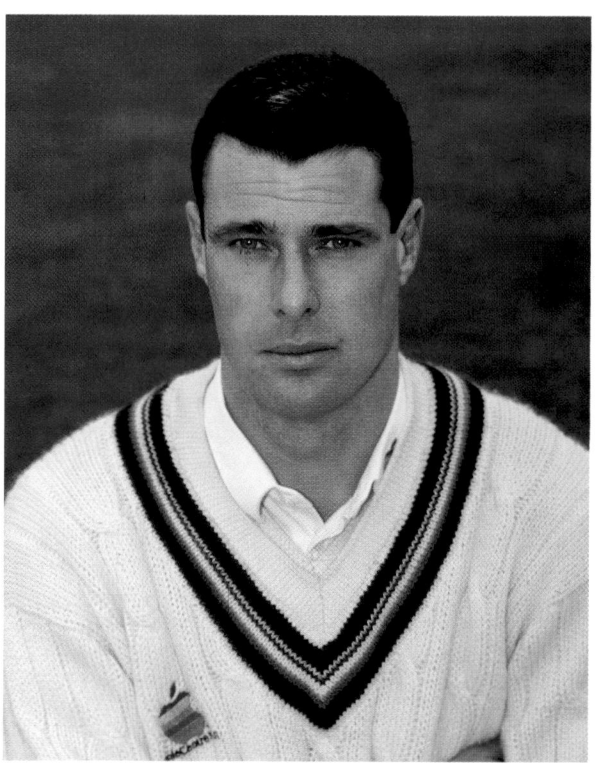

A career best 8 for 107 for Gloucestershire's Andy Babington versus Kent, 16–18 June. (David Munden)

With Middlesex idle, both Essex and Sussex moved above them in the Sunday League. Essex recovered from the loss of Gooch to the third ball of the match, and from the loss of Stephenson and Waugh at 46, to make a challenging 220 at Hartlepool. Jones hit 100 off 115 balls, but economic bowling in the closing overs from Pringle and Ilott gave Essex the match. Morris and Cottey shared an unbroken stand of 100, but Glamorgan lost to Lancashire with eight balls to spare.

At Swindon, there was controversy as Babington allegedly threw the ball at Fleming after he had caught and bowled the Kent player. Babington was spoken to by the umpires. On the eve of the second Test, Ian Salisbury produced his best bowling performance in the Sunday League to give Sussex victory over Leicestershire. Earlier Franklyn Stephenson had hit 50 off 36 balls. Nottinghamshire, the reigning champions, continued with their Sunday misery while Surrey beat Worcestershire with a five in the last over. The splendid Piran Holloway had four catches and two stumpings for Warwickshire who beat Hampshire for whom Bobby Parks made a welcome return. Kellett hit a maiden Sunday League century at Headingley.

16, 17 and 18 June *at Bristol*

Kent 507 (G.R. Cowdrey 147, S.A. Marsh 86, M.V. Fleming 65, M.A. Ealham 58, C.L. Hooper 52, A.M. Babington 8 for 107) and 96 for 0 dec. (M.A. Ealham 67 not out)
Gloucestershire 263 for 6 dec. (A.J. Wright 128, S.G. Hinks 50) and 272 for 9 (G.D. Hodgson 76, M.W. Alleyne 69, R.P. Davis 7 for 99)

Match drawn

Kent 6 pts., Gloucestershire 5 pts.

at Leicester

Leicestershire 450 for 7 dec. (P.A. Nixon 107 not out, W.K.M. Benjamin 71, N.E. Briers 63) and 140 for 5 dec.
Hampshire 282 for 3 dec. (V.P. Terry 99, K.D. James 67) and 294 for 9 (D.I. Gower 80, V.P. Terry 69, G.J. Parsons 5 for 79)

Match drawn

Leicestershire 5 pts., Hampshire 5 pts.

at Trent Bridge

Nottinghamshire 199 and 392 for 5 dec. (D.W. Randall 133 not out, C.L. Cairns 102 not out, P. Johnson 62)
Lancashire 292 (P.J. Martin 80, C.L. Cairns 6 for 70) and 103 for 3

Match drawn

Lancashire 7 pts., Nottinghamshire 4 pts.

at Bath

Northamptonshire 307 for 8 dec. (D. Ripley 107 not out, K.M. Curran 61) and 266 (N.A. Felton 86, A. Fordham 71, A.R. Caddick 4 for 56)
Somerset 250 for 3 dec. (M.N. Lathwell 86, G.D. Rose 55 not out, A.N. Hayhurst 53) and 147 for 3

Match drawn

Somerset 6 pts., Northamptonshire 5 pts.

at Coventry

Middlesex 304 (M.W. Gatting 117, D.L. Haynes 67, R.G. Twose 6 for 63) and 299 for 2 dec. (M.W. Gatting 163 not out, D.L. Haynes 72)
Warwickshire 251 for 3 dec. (T.A. Lloyd 84 not out, A.J. Moles 55) and 126 (J.E. Emburey 5 for 23, C.W. Taylor 4 for 50)

Middlesex won by 226 runs

Middlesex 21 pts., Warwickshire 7 pts.

at Worcester

Worcestershire 407 for 5 dec. (T.S. Curtis 124, G.R. Haynes 66, D.A. Leatherdale 66, S.R. Lampitt 66) and 83 for 2
Glamorgan 150 (P.J. Newport 4 for 34) and 339 (H. Morris 123, P.J. Newport 5 for 101)

Worcestershire won by 8 wickets

Worcestershire 24 pts., Glamorgan 2 pts.

at Leeds

Essex 223 (M.A. Robinson 5 for 48) and 83 (M.A. Robinson 4 for 20)
Yorkshire 361 (S.R. Tendulkar 93, C. White 69, D. Byas 55)

Yorkshire won by an innings and 55 runs

Yorkshire 23 pts., Essex 5 pts.

at Cambridge

Derbyshire 348 for 4 dec. (C.J. Adams 80, P.D. Bowler 75, J.E. Morris 73, K.M. Krikken 55, T.J.G. O'Gorman 51 not out) and 158 for 5 dec. (A.E. Warner 55)
Cambridge University 200 (J.P. Crawley 65, R.W. Sladdin 6 for 58) and 183 for 4 (J.P. Crawley 92)

Match drawn

There seemed every reason to suppose that Tony Wright was correct in his decision to ask Kent to bat first on a grassy wicket at Bristol when the visitors lost their first three wickets for 23 runs. By the end of the day, the position had changed dramatically. Graham Cowdrey hit the highest score of his career, and he and Marsh added 137 in rapid time for the sixth wicket, and Kent, 456 for 8 at the end of the first day, were not dismissed until the second morning. Remarkably, Andy Babington ended with by far the best bowling figures of his career, missing only numbers one and eleven in his 8 for 107.

Wright's century held Gloucestershire together and to keep the game alive he declared 244 runs in arrears. Benson asked Gloucestershire to make 341 to win in 102 overs on the last day, and Richard Davis' slow left-arm spin nearly brought victory. He returned a career best of 7 for 99, but Smith and reserve wicket-keeper Williams held out for the last six overs to deny the visitors.

Leicestershire, too, batted into the second day against Hampshire. Wicket-keeper Paul Nixon, edging out the excellent Whitticase on batting ability, hit a maiden first-class century off 157 balls. Tony Middleton became the first batsman to reach a thousand runs in the season, and, ultimately, the game came alive when Hampshire were asked to score 309 in 68 overs. Led by Gower, they made a brave attempt, but they fell 15 runs short with their last pair together.

Nottinghamshire were bundled out by Lancashire at Trent Bridge and trailed by 93 runs on the first innings in spite of Chris Cairns returning his best bowling figures for them. Randall hit a match-saving century and, with Chris Cairns, shared an unbroken partnership of 203 in 37 overs for the sixth wicket. Cairns' innings lasted 114 balls and included five sixes, but, like the paying customers, he clearly disapproved of Robinson's delayed declaration which effectively killed the game.

At Bath, Northamptonshire made a splendid recovery after being put in by Somerset and being reduced to 51 for 4. Their heroes were Curran and, particularly, Ripley whose 107 not out was made in three hours. Unfortunately, Northamptonshire's decision to bat on too long on the last morning ended any hope of a result, and the game died.

For the first time in his career, Mike Gatting hit a century in each innings of a match. He and Haynes added 161 for the second wicket, but Middlesex then lost seven wickets for 48 runs. Roger Twose returned the best bowling figures of his career, having one spell of 6 for 11. Andy Lloyd batted well to keep Warwickshire's hopes alive, but a second Gatting hundred, a bristling affair of 163 off 169 balls with six sixes, reasserted Middlesex's dominance. The home side were asked to make 333 in 74 overs, but for no apparent reason they collapsed against Emburey and Taylor and were all out in 36.3 overs for 126, their last six wickets falling for eight runs in 19 balls.

Worcestershire batted into the second day against Glamorgan, and Tim Curtis became the second player to reach a thousand runs in the season. Hugh Morris made a spirited effort to save the visitors, but to no avail.

The sensation took place at Headingley. Choosing to bat first, Essex, for whom Hussain returned after suspension, performed indifferently against Hartley and Robinson and were all out for 223 in the 86th over. By the close, though, three Yorkshire wickets had been captured for 44 runs, and Essex seemed in command.

The second day brought a total reversal of fortune. Sachin Tendulkar made his highest score for Yorkshire, and White and Batty added 92 for the ninth wicket. Essex lost Prichard, Stephenson and Hussain for 11 runs before the close, and these three leading batsmen scored only a single between them. There was no recovery on the last morning as Essex dissolved to 40 for 8, salvaging only a hint of pride in a ninth-wicket stand of 41 between Ilott and Andrew.

Left-arm spinner Sladdin took a career best 6 for 58 at Fenner's, and Cambridge University captain John Crawley made his highest score for the light blues.

Mike Gatting, a century in each innings against Warwickshire at Coventry, and a splendidly pugnacious season for Middlesex. (Alan Cozzi)

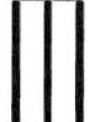

SECOND TEST MATCH
ENGLAND v. PAKISTAN, at Lord's

England made two changes from the side which played at Edgbaston, leg-spinner Salisbury coming in for his first Test at the expense of Ramprakash, and Malcolm replacing Pringle. Wasim Akram was deemed fit for Pakistan and took the place of Ata-ur-Rehman.

Gooch won the toss, England batted, and all seemed serene. Wasim Akram bowled from the Pavilion End, and Gooch steered him through the slips for two. In the fourth over, Gooch square-drove Aqib Javed for the first four of the match. Javed seemed too reluctant to change the bowling, and Aqib, one felt, bowled two overs more than he should have done in his first spell. But Waqar Younis looked to have none of the pace nor the control of line to which one has become accustomed. The outfield was smooth and fast, the gaps plentiful, and placement seemed easy as the ball was pushed through the covers. Fifty came up in the 16th over, and Gooch reached his fifty in the 24th over. It came from 70 balls and included 10 fours, two of them in one over from Mushtaq Ahmed. At lunch, England were 108 for 0, Gooch 57, Stewart 38, and they were in total command.

Gooch hit three fours after lunch, two of them in one over from Waqar, but suddenly the complexion of the game changed. Gooch went back to a ball from Wasim which came through very quickly, and he edged the ball onto his leg stump. Waqar found pace and rhythm, and an air of menace was apparent as Javed, alive to the situation, made intelligent field placing adjustments. Stewart was fortunate to survive a leg before appeal against Waqar, and Hick adopted an aggressive policy without ever looking sure of himself. Having faced 21 balls, he tried to pull Waqar and sliced the ball gently to mid-on. Robin Smith played one thunderous square-cut off Waqar Younis, but then, deceived by the angle of delivery, he pushed at a ball from Wasim Akram and was taken at third slip by Rashid Latif, substituting for Ramiz Raja. It was an astonishing catch, taken as the fielder flung himself to his left.

Shortly before tea, Javed introduced the left-arm spin of Asif Mujtaba, and Stewart, having played with discipline and confidence, drove early at a half-volley and gave extra-cover a simple catch.

England resumed after tea on 197 for 4, and, with Pakistan now rampant, they soon declined into deep trouble. In successive overs, Waqar Younis accounted for Botham and Lewis with inswinging yorkers of high pace, and higher quality. Lamb was comprehensively bowled when he misread an off-cutter, and the fiercely

Allan Lamb has his stumps shattered by Waqar Younis. (Patrick Eagar)

Botham dives at slip to catch Javed Miandad and give Ian Salisbury his first Test wicket. (Patrick Eagar)

enthusiastic and competitive Waqar claimed his fifth wicket when he had DeFreitas taken at slip. Mushtaq justly claimed the last two wickets, and England were all out in 322 minutes for 255, having been 123 for 0 and 172 for 2. Shocked and shattered, they took the field, and from the last seven overs of the day, Pakistan plundered 31 runs.

Play was possible only before lunch on the second day. During that time, Pakistan advanced to 123 for the loss of Ramiz Raja, bowled by a break-back from the inconsistent Lewis.

Saturday was bright and clear. Aamir Sohail flashed wildly at a widish delivery from DeFreitas and was caught behind without addition to the overnight score. He had played so brilliantly on the Friday that this was a dreadful waste. Aamir has so much class. He needs only maturity and self-discipline to make him one of the greatest batsmen in the world. Ian Salisbury earned a mighty first scalp in Test cricket when Javed Miandad edged a leg-break and Botham took a good catch at slip. At lunch, Pakistan were 209 for 3.

This seemed to be a dominant position, but between lunch and tea, five wickets fell for the addition of 65 runs. The first three went to Devon Malcolm who bowled his first spell of the day from the Nursery End. He generated a lively pace, and his speed and unpredictable ability unsettled batsmen. Both Asif Mujtaba, who hit his first fifty in Test cricket, and Inzaman-ul-Haq were caught when they mistimed pull shots, and when Salim Malik lofted a drive to mid-off, Malcolm had taken three wickets for four runs in 13 balls.

DeFreitas is caught at slip off Waqar, and the England first innings nears its close. (Adrian Murrell/Allsport)

Devon Malcolm is bowled by Wasim Akram for 0, and Pakistan require 138 to win. (Patrick Eagar)

Wasim took Pakistan into the lead before he got tangled up against Salisbury and was bowled between his legs. Mushtaq edged DeFreitas to the keeper, and, after tea, Moin edged to third slip, and Waqar was yorked. Pakistan led by 38, and England were back in the game. They had just cleared the arrears when Gooch pushed half forward, was beaten as the ball moved back and was leg before. Salisbury came in as night-watchman, and England closed at 52 for 1.

Salisbury played his part well and batted for an hour on the Sunday morning before he was adjudged leg before to Wasim. It was the advent of the leg-spinner Mushtaq Ahmed which brought doom to England. Hick pushed forward defensively and was caught behind off a ball which turned sharply enough to take the edge. Smith was bowled round his legs as he tried to glance, and Lamb was leg before to a ball that kept low. The frailty of England's middle-order batting against leg-spin of top quality was transparently obvious.

After lunch, it was Waqar Younis and Wasim Akram who blasted away the last vestiges of English resistance. Botham, whose role in the match was difficult to ascertain, was leg before, beaten for pace as he played across the line. Lewis was comprehensively yorked after being missed by the keeper, and the last three wickets went down in four balls to Wasim Akram, the first and last to yorkers, the second to a diving catch by second slip. We had seen great bowling, and Pakistan needed 138 to win, a simple task.

Throughout the collapse of the England batting, Alec

Stewart had shown sense, resolution and, when the opportunity allowed, aggression. He carried his bat through the 249 minutes of the England innings, the sixth English batsman to carry his bat through a Test innings. It was an heroic and mighty performance, eminently in context with this match.

Almost immediately, the Pakistan quest for 138 runs began to look a formidable task. Three times Chris Lewis found the bat's edge, and Hick at second slip and Russell behind the stumps, accepted the chances offered by Ramiz, Asif Mujtaba and Javed Miandad before they had scored. At the other end, Aamir Sohail showed little inclination to dampen his natural appetite for runs and scored 16 of the 18 runs on the board by the time the third wicket fell.

Salim, we felt, would restore sanity, and a boundary suggested this, but Salisbury, bowling from the Nursery End, spun a ball right across Salim, who played loosely and was caught at short gully. Aamir Sohail and Inzamam-ul-Haq added 21, and they were batting with increasing authority, particularly after Botham had missed Aamir in the gully off Lewis and then survived a chance to Russell off Salisbury. Russell's keeping to Salisbury was below the expected standard.

Problems seemed to have been negotiated, but England were then presented with two gifts. Aamir played the ball to third man and went for a comfortable second run, but Inzamam hesitated, and Malcolm's throw to Russell was hard and fast. Russell threw to Lewis, the bowler, and the dreaming Inzamam was run out. In the next over, Salisbury turned a ball a long way, but slowly and high. It hit Aamir on the waist and spun back towards the stumps. The batsman aimed to kick it away and missed. Pakistan were 68 for 6, and England scented an historic victory.

For Pakistan, things did not improve. Gooch had had to operate with three bowlers, neither DeFreitas nor, it appeared, Botham being fit to bowl, but Salisbury had Moin caught bat and pad at silly mid-on, it was judged, and Mushtaq was taken at slip off Malcolm, 95 for 8.

Ramiz Raja is caught at slip off Chris Lewis, and a Pakistan collapse begins. (Patrick Eagar)

When Mushtaq departed Wasim Akram was on 22. He had shown from the start of his innings a positivity and unrelenting concentration, and he was now joined by his fellow pace-man Waqar Younis who came to the wicket breathing determination and belligerence. He pushed the tiring Lewis for two, and, with the field in, drove him over the top to the Pavilion rails. Wasim Akram drove Lewis mightily for four, and with eight overs of the day remaining, Pakistan were 113 for 8.

It was important to Pakistan, and indeed to England, that the game should be finished that day. Salisbury came on at the Pavilion End, and Wasim swept him for four. Waqar pushed him to mid-wicket for three, and there were two byes. The scores drew level, and Wasim Akram, Man of the Match, drove Salisbury violently through the covers. Pakistan's two great fast bowlers had won their side the match with bat and ball.

Nobody scored a century in a match which lasted three days and one session. Neither side had reached 300, and 17 wickets fell on the last day. And this was the greatest match of the season, and for many a season. Those who advocate four-day cricket and mammoth scores on benign pitches might note this.

Robin Smith dives to catch Moin Khan, and Pakistan are 81 for 7. (Adrian Murrell/Allsport)

Wasim Akram celebrates a famous victory. (Patrick Eagar)

SECOND CORNHILL TEST MATCH – ENGLAND v. PAKISTAN
18, 19, 20 and 21 June, 1992 at Lord's

ENGLAND

	FIRST INNINGS		SECOND INNINGS	
G.A. Gooch (capt)	b Wasim	69	lbw, b Aqib	13
A.J. Stewart	c Javed, b Asif	74	not out	69
G.A. Hick	c Javed, b Waqar	13	(4) c Moin, b Mushtaq	11
R.A. Smith	c sub (Rashid Latif), b Wasim	9	(5) b Mushtaq	8
A.J. Lamb	b Waqar	30	(6) lbw, b Mushtaq	12
I.T. Botham	b Waqar	2	(7) lbw, b Waqar	6
C.C. Lewis	lbw, b Waqar	2	(8) b Waqar	15
*R.C. Russell	not out	22	(9) b Wasim	1
P.A.J. DeFreitas	c Inzamam, b Waqar	3	(10) c Inzamam, b Wasim	0
I.D.K. Salisbury	hit wkt, b Mushtaq	4	(3) lbw, b Wasim	12
D.E. Malcolm	lbw, b Mushtaq	0	b Wasim	0
Extras	b 6, lb 12, nb 9	27	b 5, lb 8, nb 15	28
		255		175

PAKISTAN

	FIRST INNINGS		SECOND INNINGS	
Aamir Sohail	c Russell, b DeFreitas	73	b Salisbury	39
Ramiz Raja	b Lewis	24	c Hick, b Lewis	0
Asif Mujtaba	c Smith, b Malcolm	59	c Russell, b Lewis	0
Javed Miandad (capt)	c Botham, b Salisbury	9	c Russell, b Lewis	0
Salim Malik	c Smith, b Malcolm	55	c Lewis, b Salisbury	12
Inzamam-ul-Haq	c and b Malcolm	0	run out	8
Wasim Akram	b Salisbury	24	not out	45
*Moin Khan	c Botham, b DeFreitas	12	c Smith, b Salisbury	3
Mushtaq Ahmed	c Russell, b DeFreitas	4	c Hick, b Malcolm	5
Waqar Younis	b Malcolm	14	not out	20
Aqib Javed	not out	5		
Extras	b 4, lb 3, nb 7	14	b 2, lb 5, w 1, nb 7	9
		293	(for 8 wickets)	141

	O	M	R	W	O	M	R	W
Wasim Akram	19	5	49	2	17.4	2	66	4
Aqib Javed	14	3	40	–	12	3	23	1
Waqar Younis	24	1	91	5	13	3	40	2
Mushtaq Ahmed	19.1	5	57	2	9	1	32	2
Asif Mujtaba	3	3	0	1	1	–	1	–

	O	M	R	W	O	M	R	W
DeFreitas	26	8	58	3				
Malcolm	15.5	1	70	4	15	2	42	1
Lewis	29	7	76	1	16	3	43	3
Salisbury	23	3	73	2	14.1	–	49	3
Botham	5	2	9	–				

FALL OF WICKETS (England)

1–123, 2–153, 3–172, 4–197, 5–213, 6–221, 7–232, 8–242, 9–247
1–40, 2–73, 3–108, 4–120, 5–137, 6–148, 7–174, 8–175, 9–175

FALL OF WICKETS (Pakistan)

1–43, 2–123, 3–143, 4–228, 5–228, 6–235, 7–263, 8–271, 9–276
1–6, 2–10, 3–18, 4–41, 5–62, 6–68, 7–81, 8–95

Umpires: B. Dudleston & J.H. Hampshire

Pakistan won by 2 wickets

19, 20 and 22 June *at Bristol*

Warwickshire 253 (D.P. Ostler 83, T.L. Penney 55) and 205 for 9 dec. (D.A. Reeve 72, C.A. Walsh 4 for 60)
Gloucestershire 199 (M.W. Alleyne 55, R.J. Scott 50, A.A. Donald 5 for 44) and 184 (T.A. Munton 4 for 60)

Warwickshire won by 75 runs

Warwickshire 23 pts., Gloucestershire 5 pts.

at Bournemouth

Hampshire 300 for 8 dec. (M.C.J. Nicholas 81) and 80 (M.C. Ilott 4 for 19)
Essex 149 (N. Hussain 63) and 310 (M.A. Garnham 60 not out, D.R. Pringle 51)

Essex won by 79 runs

Essex 19 pts., Hampshire 8 pts.

at Old Trafford

Lancashire 456 for 3 dec. (M.A. Atherton 135, N.J. Speak 111, G.D. Lloyd 103 not out, S.P. Titchard 68 not out) and 190 for 2 dec. (N.J. Speak 74 not out)
Middlesex 306 for 3 dec. (M.W. Gatting 126 retired hurt, M.R. Ramprakash 69) and 309 for 9 (J.D. Carr 80, M.R. Ramprakash 63, K.R. Brown 56, P.J. Martin 4 for 45)

Match drawn

Lancashire 5 pts., Middlesex 5 pts.

at Trent Bridge

Northamptonshire 326 for 9 dec. (N.A. Felton 64, A.R. Roberts 62, R.J. Bailey 54, D. Ripley 54) and 272 for 5 dec. (A. Fordham 119)
Nottinghamshire 302 for 3 dec. (B.C. Broad 159 not out, R.T. Robinson 52) and 297 for 8 (R.T. Robinson 100, P.R. Pollard 69)

Nottinghamshire won by 2 wickets

Nottinghamshire 23 pts., Northamptonshire 4 pts.

at Bath

Somerset 376 for 9 dec. (M.N. Lathwell 114, R.J. Harden 73) and 20 for 1
Surrey 116 (N.A. Mallender 5 for 29) and 276 (J.D. Robinson 53)

Somerset won by 9 wickets

Somerset 24 pts., Surrey 3 pts.

at Horsham

Durham 300 for 8 dec. (S. Hutton 78, W. Larkins 53, F.D. Stephenson 4 for 65) and 190 for 3 dec. (D.M. Jones 89 not out, M.P. Briers 62 not out)
Sussex 151 for 4 dec. (J.W. Hall 82 not out) and 340 for 6 (N.J. Lenham 118, D.M. Smith 67, A.P. Wells 65)

Sussex won by 4 wickets

Sussex 20 pts., Durham 5 pts.

at Worcester

Worcestershire 386 for 9 dec. (T.S. Curtis 197, P.J. Newport 61) and 144 for 4 dec.
Yorkshire 234 for 9 dec. (R.J. Blakey 57, N.V. Radford 4 for 41) and 207 (C. White 79 not out, P.J. Newport 4 for 69)

Worcestershire won by 89 runs

Worcestershire 23 pts., Yorkshire 5 pts.

at Oxford

Glamorgan 317 for 5 dec. (S.P. James 111, R.D.B. Croft 51 not out, C.S. Cowdrey 50, P.A. Cottey 50) and 136 for 1 dec. (A. Dale 76 not out, J. Bishop 51 not out)
Oxford University 183 (G.B.T. Lovell 64, D.J. Foster 4 for 73) and 153 for 6 (G.B.T. Lovell 110 not out)

Match drawn

19, 20 and 21 June *at Cambridge*

Kent 300 for 5 dec. (J.I. Longley 110, R.M. Ellison 64) and 160 for 6 dec.
Cambridge University 200 (J.P. Crawley 65, R.W. Sladdin 6 for 58) and 183 for 4 (J.P. Crawley 92)

Match drawn

20, 21 and 22 June *at Dundee (Broughty Ferry)*

Scotland 390 for 6 dec. (G. Salmond 118, I.L. Philip 79, B.M.W. Patterson 55) and 213 for 4 dec. (G. Salmond 95)
Ireland 280 (M.P. Rea 89, C. McCrum 70, J.W. Govan 6 for 70) and 276 for 8 (D.A. Lewis 122 not out)

Match drawn

Playing in his first championship match, Zimbabwe batsman Trevor Penney joined with Dominic Ostler to rescue Warwickshire on the opening day at Bristol. There was some tidy bowling from Gloucestershire's promising left-arm spinner Mark Davies, once with Glamorgan, but it was the pace men who dominated, and Munton, Donald and Small proved too much for Gloucestershire on the last afternoon.

Essex appeared to be heading for their second innings defeat in succession at Bournemouth. Rain shortened the first day, but Hampshire, who had been put in to bat reached 300 on the Saturday morning.

Essex lost Prichard and Waugh for 0, and, in spite of Hussain's 63, they never fully recovered and were bowled out for 149. At the close of play on Saturday, they were 105 for 4 in their second innings and an innings defeat loomed. Early on the Monday, Essex's position worsened, and when the seventh wicket fell they had a lead of only 13 runs. Garnham and Pringle then came together in a stand of 107. Pringle had spent 11 overs before getting off the mark, but Garnham later scored freely. There was further spirited resistance from Foster and Childs, and Hampshire were left 31 overs in which to score 160 to win the match. The last three Essex wickets had realised 145 runs. Middleton was caught behind before a run was scored, but Terry and Gower seemed in control before Gower fell to a breathtaking catch by Prichard at deep cover. The fielder flung himself to his left to hold the ball, and from that point, Hampshire faltered. Their last nine wickets fell for 49 runs, with Ilott and Childs their chief tormentors. Essex claimed a famous victory with 19 balls to spare, and they moved to fourth in the championship table, nine points behind the leaders Hampshire with a game in hand.

Mark Ilott, 4 for 19 in Essex's dramatic victory over Hampshire at Bournemouth, 22 June. A victory that changed the course of the season. (Alan Cozzi)

There were plenty of runs at Old Trafford, but not quite the same excitement on a placid pitch. Speak and Atherton added 233 for Lancashire's second wicket, and Speak reached his thousand runs for the season, the third player to pass the mark. Middlesex found run-getting equally simple, but Gatting was forced to retire hurt when, having hit his third consecutive century, he was struck in the face by a ball from Fletcher. With Middlesex needing 341 from 66 overs on the last afternoon, Gatting bravely batted at number seven and scored 27. Middlesex fell short of their target, and their last pair survived Watkinson's last over to save the match.

Excitingly, Nottinghamshire did reach their target of 297 in 68 overs against Northamptonshire. There had been centuries from Broad and Fordham, but the decisive hundred came from Tim Robinson who reached three figures off 97 balls as his side chased their target. Twenty-six were wanted from the final three overs, but Mark Crawley hit leg-spinner Roberts for a six and a four in an over which cost 17 runs. Five were needed from the last over, bowled by Ambrose, and they came in five singles so that victory arrived with a ball to spare.

The maiden first-class century which Mark Lathwell had been promising from the first ball of the season arrived against Surrey at Bath. The Somerset opener's innings lasted three-and-a-quarter hours, and he faced 163 balls and hit 12 fours. He is an exciting young man, and he is well supported and encouraged by his more senior opening partner, Andy Hayhurst, with whom he put on 139. A rather spineless Surrey side wilted before Neil Mallender, and although they offered sterner resistance in their second innings, they never looked like avoiding defeat.

Sussex and Durham defied the rain with declarations which left Sussex a target of 340 in 65 overs. Lenham had a twisted ankle and batted throughout his innings with a runner. He hit 19 fours and batted most bravely for 165 balls. Skipper Alan Wells gave the innings its impetus with a ferocious 65 off 37 balls, but the last over arrived with Sussex still 12 runs short of victory. Moores took a single off Hughes' first ball, and two leg-byes followed. Franklyn Stephenson then swept Hughes over square-leg for six, and the next ball saw a scampered single. Moores was caught at long-off, and two were needed off the last ball. Stephenson obliged with another pull which brought a most exciting victory.

Tim Curtis hit his fourth first-class century of the season, and eventually asked Yorkshire to make 296 in 71 overs. Tendulkar and White put on 70 for the fifth wicket, but once Tendulkar was dismissed, the batting collapsed, the last six wickets falling for 49 runs.

There were maiden first-class centuries in the matches involving the universities, for Lovell of Oxford and for Longley of Kent.

SUNDAY LEAGUE

21 June *at Derby*

Middlesex 212 for 5 (J.D. Carr 53 not out)
Derbyshire 190 (C.J. Adams 61)

Middlesex (4 pts.) won by 22 runs

at Ebbw Vale

Glamorgan 167 for 7
Yorkshire 171 for 6 (M.D. Moxon 53)

Yorkshire (4 pts.) won by 4 wickets

at Bournemouth

Essex 175 for 6 (J.P. Stephenson 54)
Hampshire 178 for 2 (T.C. Middleton 72, V.P. Terry 62)

Hampshire (4 pts.) won by 8 wickets

at Bristol

Gloucestershire 171 (A.J. Wright 51)
Warwickshire 172 for 8

Warwickshire (4 pts.) won by 2 wickets

at Old Trafford

Leicestershire 248 for 9 (P.E. Robinson 104, J.J. Whitaker 59, J.D.R. Benson 51)
Lancashire 153

Leicestershire (4 pts.) won by 95 runs

at Trent Bridge

Nottinghamshire 204 for 5 (R.T. Robinson 71)
Northamptonshire 207 for 2 (A. Fordham 89, N.A. Felton 77 not out)

Northamptonshire (4 pts.) won by 8 wickets

at Bath

Somerset 217 (R.J. Harden 90 not out)
Surrey 218 for 6 (D.J. Bicknell 107 not out)

Surrey (4 pts.) won by 4 wickets

at Horsham

Durham 275 for 4 (W. Larkins 84, D.M. Jones 74 not out, J.D. Glendenen 64)
Sussex 270 for 9 (J.A. North 56)

Durham (4 pts.) won by 5 runs

With their seventh victory in as many matches, Middlesex moved into a very strong position at the top of the Sunday League alongside Essex who were well beaten by Hampshire. This was Essex's second defeat of the season. Moxon hit Chris Cowdrey for four fours in one over as he led Yorkshire to victory over Glamorgan, and Warwickshire won off the last ball at Bristol. Former Yorkshire batsman Phil Robinson hit a century on his debut for Leicestershire. His runs came off 93 balls and included three sixes and nine fours. He reached his hundred with a six off Martin. It was his first one-day century. Fordham and Felton set up Northants' win over Nottinghamshire with an opening stand of 149. Darren Bicknell hit 107 off 116 balls to take Surrey to victory over Somerset, and Sussex, needing 111 off the last ten overs to beat Durham, fell six runs short of their target before a huge crowd at Horsham.

NATWEST TROPHY – ROUND ONE

24 June *at Beaconsfield*

Sussex 327 for 6 (A.P. Wells 119, D.M. Smith 62)
Buckinghamshire 126

Sussex won by 201 runs

(Man of the Match – A.P. Wells)

at Derby

Derbyshire 280 for 6 (P.D. Bowler 111, C.J. Adams 106 not out, J.H. Jones 4 for 54)
Berkshire 139 (D.G. Cork 5 for 18)

Derbyshire won by 114 runs

(Man of the Match – D.G. Cork)

at Chelmsford

Essex 361 for 8 (N. Hussain 108, N.V. Knight 81 not out, G.A. Gooch 77)
Cumberland 200 for 8 (S. Sharp 75, S.M. Dutton 61)

Essex won by 161 runs

(Man of the Match – N. Hussain)

at Swansea

Surrey 239 for 6 (D.M. Ward 101 not out, A.J. Stewart 60, S.R. Barwick 5 for 26)
Glamorgan 243 for 6 (M.P. Maynard 87, H. Morris 55)

Glamorgan won by 4 wickets

(Man of the Match – M.P. Maynard)

at Bristol

Gloucestershire 272 for 4 (A.J. Wright 107 not out, C.W.J. Athey 57)
Cheshire 68 (C.A. Walsh 6 for 21)

Gloucestershire won by 204 runs

(Man of the Match – C.A. Walsh)

at Southampton

Dorset 218 for 3 (G.S. Calway 105, R. Richings 74 not out)
Hampshire 219 for 1 (V.P. Terry 108 not out, R.A. Smith 59 not out)

Hampshire won by 9 wickets

(Man of the Match – G.S. Calway)

at Dublin

Durham 305 for 6 (W. Larkins 113, M.P. Briers 54 not out)
Ireland 116 (S.M. McEwan 4 for 41)

Durham won by 189 runs

(Man of the Match – S.M. McEwan)

at Canterbury

Kent 266 for 7 (M.R. Benson 58, M.V. Fleming 53)
Devon 166 for 8

Kent won by 100 runs

(Man of the Match – M.V. Fleming)

at Leicester

Leicestershire 293 for 7 (P.E. Robinson 73)
Norfolk 161 (C.J. Rogers 51)

Leicestershire won by 132 runs

(Man of the Match – P.E. Robinson)

at Northampton

Northamptonshire 234 for 4 (K.M. Curran 78 not out, D.J. Capel 72 not out)
Cambridgeshire 166 for 6 (N.J. Adams 104 not out)

Northamptonshire won by 68 runs

(Man of the Match – N.J. Adams)

at Trent Bridge

Nottinghamshire 307 for 7 (P. Johnson 78, B.C. Broad 72, D.W. Randall 55)
Worcestershire 250 (S.J. Rhodes 54, K.P. Evans 4 for 43, M.G. Field-Buss 4 for 62)

Nottinghamshire won by 57 runs

(Man of the Match – C.C. Lewis)

at Christchurch, Oxford

Lancashire 283 for 5 (M.A. Atherton 109 not out, M. Watkinson 82)
Oxfordshire 88

Lancashire won by 195 runs

(Man of the Match - M. Watkinson)

at St George's, Telford

Middlesex 294 for 7 (M.A. Roseberry 112, D.L. Haynes 101, G.J. Toogood 6 for 47)
Shropshire 149 (D.W. Headley 5 for 20)

Middlesex won by 145 runs

(Man of the Match – G.J. Toogood)

at Taunton

Scotland 245 for 2 (I.L. Philip 102 not out, B.M.W. Patterson 61, G.N. Reifer 55)
Somerset 246 for 2 (R.J. Harden 108 not out, C.J. Tavaré 60 not out)

Somerset won by 8 wickets

(Man of the Match – R.J. Harden)

at Edgbaston

Staffordshire 172 for 9 (S.D. Myles 60, A.A. Donald 5 for 28)
Warwickshire 173 for 2 (R.G. Twose 107 not out)

Warwickshire won by 8 wickets

(Man of the Match – A.A. Donald)

at Leeds

Northumberland 137
Yorkshire 138 for 2

Yorkshire won by 8 wickets

(Man of the Match – G.R. Morris)

The first round matches in the NatWest Trophy were all completed on the scheduled day. The round produced a record 16 centuries, 13 of them by batsmen who had not previously scored a hundred in this competition. The three who had previously reached three figures in the tournament were Paul Terry, Wayne Larkins and Desmond Haynes.

There were brave performances from the Minor Counties, but no surprises. Nor was it really a surprise that Glamorgan beat the 1991 runners-up Surrey who, without the intelligent influence of Ian Greig and the pace of Waqar Younis, looked a limp side. The most likeable and enthusiastic David Ward hit his first century in the competition and took three sixes off one over from Dale, but Glamorgan won in the last over.

Another side for whom life was not going well, Worcestershire, were savaged by Nottinghamshire who scored 58 from the last four overs. Haynes and Radford both conceded eight runs an over from their ten-over stints. Lewis, 32 from 15 balls, was one of those who pulsated at the close, and he also held four catches to equal the competition record.

24, 25 and 26 June *at Cambridge*

Pakistanis 446 for 5 dec. (Inzamam-ul-Haq 200 not out, Shoaib Mohamad 56, Zahid Fazal 51) and 46 for 1
Oxford & Cambridge Universities 164 (J.P. Crawley 70, Mushtaq Ahmed 5 for 56) and 327 (G.B.T. Lovell 96, J.E.R. Gallian 89, Asif Mujtaba 4 for 73, Mushtaq Ahmed 4 for 91)

Pakistanis won by 9 wickets

26, 27 and 28 June *at Derby*

Warwickshire 121 (I.R. Bishop 4 for 32, D.G. Cork 4 for 41) and 174 (D.A. Reeve 60, S.J. Base 5 for 35)
Derbyshire 343 (T.J.G. O'Gorman 75, J.E. Morris 74, P.A. Smith 4 for 67)

Derbyshire won by an innings and 48 runs

Derbyshire 24 pts., Warwickshire 3 pts.

at Ilford

Essex 510 for 2 dec. (M.E. Waugh 219 not out, N. Hussain 172 not out, P.J. Prichard 50)
Lancashire 212 (G.D. Lloyd 61, J.H. Childs 5 for 50) and 261 (G.D. Lloyd 76, S.P. Titchard 74)

Essex won by an innings and 37 runs

Essex 24 pts., Lancashire 2 pts.

at Bristol

Gloucestershire 352 for 9 dec. (G.D. Hodgson 68, C.W.J. Athey 57, M.C.J. Ball 53 not out, J. Boiling 4 for 119) and 178 (J. Boiling 6 for 84)
Surrey 300 for 5 dec. (D.J. Bicknell 81, G.P. Thorpe 75, J.D. Robinson 65 not out) and 232 for 6 (D.M. Ward 82)

Surrey won by 4 wickets

Surrey 22 pts., Gloucestershire 5 pts.

at Lord's

Middlesex 355 for 5 dec. (M.W. Gatting 90, M.A. Roseberry 85, M.R. Ramprakash 68, D.L. Haynes 54) and 234 for 6 dec. (D.L. Haynes 84, M.A. Roseberry 67)
Somerset 290 for 7 dec. (A.N. Hayhurst 97, C.J. Tavaré 53) and 144 for 5 (R.J. Harden 58, K.H. MacLeay 50)

Match drawn

Middlesex 7 pts., Somerset 4 pts.

at Luton

Northamptonshire 499 for 5 dec. (R.J. Bailey 165, A. Fordham 137, A.J. Lamb 109 retired ill)
Glamorgan 176 (C.E.L. Ambrose 4 for 53) and 139 (A.R. Butcher 59 not out, D.J. Capel 4 for 41)

Northamptonshire won by an innings and 184 runs

Northamptonshire 24 pts., Glamorgan 1 pt.

at Worcester

Sussex 289 (F.D. Stephenson 87 not out, J.W. Hall 59, N.V. Radford 4 for 77) and 194 for 7 dec. (P. Moores 61 not out)
Worcestershire 208 (W.P.C. Weston 56, S.J. Rhodes 51, F.D. Stephenson 4 for 78) and 195 (G.A. Hick 131, F.D. Stephenson 7 for 29)

Sussex won by 80 runs

Sussex 23 pts., Worcestershire 6 pts.

27, 28 and 29 June *at Gateshead Fell*

Kent 392 (G.R. Cowdrey 115, C.L. Hooper 97, J. Wood 4 for 92) and 235 for 6 dec. (N.J. Llong 92, N.R. Taylor 50 not out)
Durham 329 for 8 dec. (W. Larkins 90, S. Hutton 76,

P.W.G. Parker 72 not out, R.P. Davis 7 for 64) and 216 for 5 (M.P. Briers 56 not out)

Match drawn

Durham 8 pts., Kent 6 pts.

at Southampton

Pakistanis 406 for 1 dec. (Asif Mujtaba 154 not out, Javed Miandad 142 retired hurt, Salim Malik 50 not out)
Hampshire 162 (D.I. Gower 55, Mushtaq Ahmed 5 for 64) and 230 (K.D. James 69, Wasim Akram 4 for 38)

Pakistanis won by an innings and 14 runs

at Trent Bridge

Nottinghamshire 300 for 4 dec. (W.A. Dessaur 148, J.R. Wileman 109) and 179 for 3 dec. (C.C. Lewis 62, P. Johnson 60 not out, M.A. Crawley 51 not out)
Cambridge University 153 (J.E. Hindson 5 for 42) and 164 (J.A. Afford 5 for 75)

Nottinghamshire won by 162 runs

Phil Tufnell returned to the Middlesex side at the end of June and fought his way back into the Test XI. (Alan Cozzi)

Derbyshire beat Warwickshire inside two days. Derbyshire's seam attack twice proved too much for the visitors who were 34 for 5 in their first innings and 28 for 5 in their second, positions from which they never recovered. In contrast, Derbyshire offered consistent middle-order batting.

Essex, too, won in two days, claiming the extra half hour on the Saturday. Gooch and Prichard began at a furious rate, and, at lunch, Essex were 187 for 2 from 39 overs. In the afternoon, Waugh and Hussain added 215 in 38 overs. When Gooch finally declared Waugh and Hussain had put on 347 in 64 overs, a record for the Essex third wicket. Batting looked more difficult when Lancashire were at the crease, and Atherton fell to Ilott before the close. On the Saturday, Lancashire lost 19 wickets to the varied and aggressive Essex attack well supported by a tigerish group of close catchers. Essex's most impressive victory took them to the top of the table.

Surrey notched their first championship win of the season, and they owed much to James Boiling, the off-spinner, who returned his best bowling figures for both an innings and a match. Gloucestershire set them a task of scoring 231 in 46 overs, and, with Ward hitting three sixes and eight fours, Surrey won with five balls to spare.

Phil Tufnell returned to the Middlesex side and took three wickets in Somerset's first innings. The most exciting part of this drawn match was provided by Haynes and Roseberry on the Saturday evening. They scored 120 in the last 65 minutes of the day.

The same day that his son Mark made his first-class debut for Surrey, Alan Butcher returned, briefly, to lead Glamorgan. It was not a happy return as his side were beaten by an innings. Fordham hit his second century in succession, and he and Bailey added 206 for Northamptonshire's second wicket. Lamb could not continue his innings on the second day because of a severe attack of hay fever. The home side added 83 in 35 minutes, and by the end of the day, Glamorgan were 98 for 7. The match was all over within 40 minutes on the third day.

At Worcester, Sussex, whose last three wickets added 109, set the home side a target of 273 in 72 overs. Worcestershire were soon in trouble as Stephenson reduced them to 5 for 3. Wickets continued to tumble, but in the midst of the debris, Graeme Hick hit his first century of the season. He was particularly severe on Salisbury before falling to a loose shot off North. In the end, Franklyn Stephenson was not to be denied.

The first first-class match at Gateshead ended in a draw. Durham lost Dean Jones after he was hit in the mouth by a ball from McCague. The main features of the match were a career best bowling performance from Richard Davis and an opening partnership of 169 by Larkins and Hutton.

The two matches involving the Pakistani tourists saw Inzamam-ul-Haq hit three sixes and 24 fours in his double century, and a feast of runs in the victory over Hampshire. Javed Miandad reached 100 off 120 balls, and Hampshire lost their last eight first innings wickets for 34 runs. Their second innings was soured by controversy. Nicholas was given out by umpire Tolchard, caught bat and pad at forward short-leg. He began to leave the wicket, and then disputed the decision with umpire Palmer. The umpires debated, and Tolchard rescinded his decision to the great consternation of the Pakistanis. After the match, manager Khalid Mahmood stated that his players were very unhappy and that the ball had been caught cleanly. 'Is this kind of behaviour going to be tolerated from players?' he queried. In the light of what was to happen in the Old Trafford Test, it is well to remember the incident involving Nicholas.

Slow left-arm bowler Hindson, medium-pacer Pennett and opening batsman Wileman made their first-class debuts for Nottinghamshire against Cambridge University. Dessaur and Wileman shared an opening stand of 234, Wileman hitting a century on his debut.

An impressive newcomer to the Nottinghamshire side – David Pennett. (Tom Morris)

SUNDAY LEAGUE

28 June *at Derby*

Leicestershire 232 for 8 (P.E. Robinson 59, J.J. Whitaker 55)
Derbyshire 233 for 5 (P.D. Bowler 87 not out, C.J. Adams 75)

Derbyshire (4 pts.) won by 5 wickets

at Ilford

Lancashire 238 for 7 (N.J. Speak 68, M.A. Atherton 57)
Essex 242 for 3 (G.A. Gooch 79, M.E. Waugh 61 not out, P.J. Prichard 60)

Essex (4 pts.) won by 7 wickets

at Bristol

Surrey 206 for 6 (M.A. Lynch 58)
Gloucestershire 189

Surrey (4 pts.) won by 17 runs

at Lord's

Middlesex 245 for 4 (M.W. Gatting 68, D.L. Haynes 54)
Somerset 203 (P.N. Weekes 4 for 37)

Middlesex (4 pts.) won by 42 runs

at Luton

Northamptonshire 262 for 5 (A. Fordham 88, R.J. Bailey 52 not out)
Glamorgan 263 for 3 (I.V.A. Richards 87 not out, M.P. Maynard 61, A. Dale 55 not out)

Glamorgan (4 pts.) won by 7 wickets

at Worcester

Worcestershire 186 for 6 (T.S. Curtis 77 not out, G.A. Hick 55)
Sussex 178 (A.P. Wells 64)

Worcestershire (4 pts.) won by 8 runs

at Scarborough

Yorkshire 224 for 5 (R.J. Blakey 105 not out, S.A. Kellett 77)
Warwickshire 203 for 8 (D.P. Ostler 54, T.L. Penney 53 not out)

Yorkshire (4 pts.) won by 21 runs

Middlesex and Essex continued their winning ways and, with Worcestershire beating Sussex, they drew clear of the rest of the field. Gooch became only the second player to reach 7000 runs in the Sunday League. Sussex lost their last five wickets for six runs in 17 balls, and Warwickshire keeper Holloway had three stumpings at Scarborough.

30 June, 1 and 2 July *at Derby*

Gloucestershire 281 (M.W. Alleyne 78 not out, G.D. Hodgson 50, D.G. Cork 5 for 103, A.E. Warner 4 for 52) and 29 for 0 dec.
Derbyshire 0 for 0 dec. and 303 for 9 (P.D. Bowler 77, T.J.G. O'Gorman 70 not out, J.E. Morris 50)

Match drawn

Derbyshire 4 pts., Gloucestershire 3 pts.

at Ilford

Middlesex 273 (J.D. Carr 102, T.D. Topley 4 for 67) and 185 for 3 dec. (M.A. Roseberry 70 not out, M.W. Gatting 69)
Essex 204 for 8 (P.J. Prichard 53) and 255 for 2 (N.V. Knight 109, M.E. Waugh 94 not out)

Essex won by 8 wickets

Essex 22 pts., Middlesex 6 pts.

at Maidstone

Kent 359 (M.R. Benson 131, M.V. Fleming 63, C.L. Cairns 5 for 76) and 55 for 1 dec.
Nottinghamshire 113 for 3 dec. and 266 (M.A. Crawley 102 not out, D.W. Randall 66, A.P. Igglesden 4 for 32)

Kent won by 35 runs

Kent 20 pts., Nottinghamshire 2 pts.

at Leicester

Worcestershire 232 for 9 dec. (P.J. Newport 75 not out, D.J. Millns 6 for 87) and 0 for 0 dec.
Leicestershire 0 for 0 dec. and 234 for 1 (N.E. Briers 122 not out, T.J. Boon 97)

Leicestershire won by 9 wickets

Leicestershire 20 pts., Worcestershire 2 pts.

at Arundel

Hampshire 271 for 9 dec. (K.D. James 59) and 0 for 0 dec.
Sussex 0 for 0 dec. and 141 (R.J. Maru 4 for 8)

Hampshire won by 130 runs

Hampshire 18 pts., Sussex 4 pts.

at The Oval

Northamptonshire 312 for 8 dec. (D.J. Capel 103, A.J. Lamb 56, M.P. Bicknell 6 for 107) and 102 for 6 dec.
Surrey 164 for 2 dec. (M.A. Lynch 69 not out) and 252 for 5 (D.M. Ward 103 not out)

Surrey won by 5 wickets

Surrey 20 pts., Northamptonshire 4 pts.

at Lord's

Oxford University 182 for 7 dec. and 115 for 1 dec. (J.E.R. Gallian 66)
Cambridge University 60 for 7 dec. and 238 for 3 (J.P. Crawley 106 not out, R.M. Wight 62 not out)

Cambridge University won by 7 wickets

Rain interrupted all matches, and it took the ingenuity of captains to produce results. Even forfeitures could not bring a result at Derby where there was no play on the second day and where Gloucestershire set the home side a target of 311 in 72 overs. With 13 overs left, Derbyshire were 229 for 7, but there was no conviction or positivity in Gloucestershire's approach, retaining defensive field-placings.

In contrast, Essex completed a wonderful Ilford week with a stunning victory over Middlesex. The Middlesex first innings stretched into the second day with Carr facing 175 balls for his 102. Essex declared on the last morning as soon as they reached 200, and Gatting finally asked Essex to make 255 in 43 overs. Essex were without Gooch, Pringle and the injured Stephenson, but the make-shift opening pair of Prichard and Knight began with 71 in 14 overs. Prichard was taken at slip off Taylor, but Waugh now joined Knight in a blistering stand of 152 which brought Essex to the brink of victory. Knight made the highest score of his career, an innings of real

Nick Knight – a fine century as Essex beat Middlesex at Ilford. (Alan Cozzi)

quality. His hundred came off 115 balls. Waugh hit nine fours and two sixes and finished the job.

At Maidstone, Kent set Nottinghamshire a target of 302 from 70 overs, a task which looked hopeless when they were reduced to 46 for 4. Randall and Crawley added 94, and French joined Crawley in a stand of 63. When Crawley, on 91, was joined by last man Pennett 4.5 overs were left. Crawley reached his second hundred of the season, but with eight balls remaining, Pennett was leg before to Hooper, and Kent were victorious by 35 runs.

Ever-improving pace bowler David Millns put Leicestershire on top against a rather slow-scoring Worcestershire. Curtis offered a generous target of 233 in 77 overs, but his spinners, Illingworth and Stemp, bowled poorly. Briers, dropped three times, and Boon put on 213 for the first wicket, and Leicestershire romped home with seven overs to spare.

Sussex lost their last seven wickets for 57 runs in drizzle and fading light at Arundel, but Surrey sparkled as they raced to their second victory in succession, beating Northamptonshire by five wickets at The Oval. Surrey needed 251 in 48 overs and won with seven balls to spare. Their hero was David Ward who reached 50 off 29 balls, and a hundred off 70 balls, the fastest of the season. He hit two sixes and 14 fours.

All credit should go to the two captains in the Varsity match, Lovell and Crawley, for achieving the first result since 1986. Having won the toss, Oxford University scored 153 for 6 from the 60 overs possible on the first day. They batted on for half an hour on the second day, and then reduced Cambridge to 26 for 4 before rain ended play. Only 23 overs had been possible. On a full last day, spirited batting from Lovell and Montgomerie gave Oxford 115 for the first wicket and a declaration which left Cambridge to make 238 in 52 overs. The crucial turn of the match was when Crawley was twice dropped on 20, and Wight was also put down. These were expensive misses. The pair added 166 in 24 overs to win the match for Cambridge with an over to spare. It was exciting stuff. Crawley made his first century for Cambridge and hit a six and 13 fours off the 124 balls he faced.

John Crawley – a match-winning century for Cambridge in the Varsity match and some fine performances for Lancashire. (USPA)

THIRD TEST MATCH
ENGLAND v. PAKISTAN, at Old Trafford

Atherton, Gower and Munton replaced Lamb, Botham and the injured DeFreitas in the England side while Pakistan were unchanged. Javed Miandad won the toss, and Pakistan batted. Against an attack that was as weak in practice as it looked on paper, they made 131 for 1 in 27 overs before lunch. The one wicket that fell was of very doubtful quality. Having hit seven fours and faced only 58 balls, Ramiz Raja was adjudged caught behind by umpire Roy Palmer, standing in his first Test. Malcolm appealed for leg before. Gooch remained impassive at first slip. Russell threw the ball up in appeal, and Palmer raised his finger, judging that Ramiz had got an inside edge onto his pad.

Aamir Sohail was 60 not out at lunch, and he added another 70 to his score in the afternoon session. His maiden Test hundred had come from 127 balls, and, at tea, Pakistan were 252 for 2, Asif Mujtaba having been well taken, head high at point, by Atherton. Having batted for 343 minutes and faced 284 balls, Aamir Sohail was bowled between bat and pad by Lewis for a quite enchanting 205, an innings studded with 32 scintillating fours. Pakistan ended the day on 388 for 3, and the game was already out of England's reach.

On the Friday, it rained, and no play was possible. Pakistan continued to flourish on the Saturday. By lunch time, they were 480 for 5. Javed Miandad had increased his overnight 59 to 88 before edging to slip to give Munton his first Test wicket, and, three overs later,

Aamir Sohail hooks a ball to the boundary during his double century. (Ben Radford/Allsport)

Moin, having batted capably, mishooked Malcolm to square-leg.

In the afternoon session, Gooch looked by far the best of the England bowlers, and he was rewarded with three wickets, one being the precious one of Salim Malik, beaten by the inswinger. Javed's declaration came with his side's score at 505, scored at almost a run a minute, off 126 overs.

Gooch and Stewart faced a difficult time, with Wasim Akram and Waqar Younis bowling with great pace and equally great menace. It was at this point, however, that Pakistan's troubles began. Gooch was dropped in the gully when 8, and the same fielder, Inzamam, put down Stewart, a more difficult chance, when the Surrey man was 14. The Stewart miss was not costly, for almost immediately Inzamam made amends by taking him at second slip. Atherton's return to Test cricket lasted only three balls, for the third moved across and he was caught behind. Now came the miss of the series. Gooch cut Aqib straight into the hands of Salim Malik at slip, the easiest of chances, and the catch was dropped. England entered the rest day on a trembling 72 for 2.

Monday was a bad day for Pakistan, and for cricket.

Wasim Akram is stumped by Russell off Gooch. (David Munden)

Tim Munton's first Test wicket. Javed Miandad is caught at slip by Hick. (David Munden)

The visitors had early success when Aqib trapped Smith leg before. Gower made his return to Test cricket, and thick-edged his second ball past third slip for four. His third he drove majestically to the boundary. On 15, he edged Aqib Javed to Salim Malik at slip, and the fielder put down a chance as simple as the one from which he had reprieved Gooch on the Saturday evening.

With a cover drive, Gower went past Boycott's record 8114 runs for England. It was a moment of history and beauty in a grim day in the sun. The Pakistan frustration grew as they celebrated Inzamam's 'catch' at slip off Gower, but the umpires ruled, rightly, that the ball had not carried. There were times in the series when Pakistan had cause for grievance; this was not one of them.

Gooch was adjudged caught down the leg side. The umpires inspected the ball for tampering, and match referee Conrad Hunte also inspected it during the interval, England 195 for 4, but no action was taken, nor it seems did the referee find anything about which to complain.

Gower went to his third ball after lunch, and Hick, tormented by Waqar, was bowled middle stump by Aqib who produced an inspired spell which also accounted for Russell, taken at second slip. England were 256 for 7, still 249 runs in arrears.

They were saved by Lewis, Salisbury, a certain amount of good fortune and the indiscipline of the

Gower edges a ball short of Inzamam-ul-Haq, and debate follows. (Patrick Eagar)

Geoff Boycott and David Gower, the man who passed Boycott's Test batting record at Old Trafford. (Ben Radford/Allsport)

David Gower plays the shot that makes him England's leading run-scorer in Test cricket. (Adrian Murrell/Allsport)

Pakistan side who conceded 35 extras. The indiscipline reached its peak when Aqib Javed bowled consistently short at number eleven Malcolm and was warned by umpire Palmer. Both Aqib and Javed remonstrated with the umpire, and the feud continued at the end of the over when Aqib threw his sweater on the ground and aimed a kick at it. He and Javed also intimated that the sweater had been returned to Aqib in an insulting manner by the umpire. Malcolm was bowled in the next Aqib over, and the day's play, thankfully, was at an end.

Referee Hunte later fined Aqib half his match fee for his behaviour, and reprimanded both Javed and manager Intikhab who, nevertheless, continued to make comments on the events which were not complimentary to the umpire. Hunte also gave a gentle rebuke to the England management although few could tell why.

The soul of the game was now as dead as was the contest itself. On the final day, Ramiz Raja looked as if he might score a century, but he semeed weak in stamina. He hit 11 fours, faced 138 balls and batted for 199 minutes. One would like to remember two glorious left-handers at opposite ends of their careers, Aamir Sohail and David Gower, and forget the rest.

THIRD CORNHILL TEST MATCH – ENGLAND v. PAKISTAN
2, 3, 4, 6 and 7 July, 1992 at Old Trafford, Manchester

PAKISTAN

	FIRST INNINGS		SECOND INNINGS	
Aamir Sohail	b Lewis	205	c Smith, b Lewis	1
Ramiz Raja	c Russell, b Malcolm	54	c Hick, b Lewis	88
Asif Mujtaba	c Atherton, b Lewis	57	c Atherton, b Lewis	40
Javed Miandad (capt)	c Hick, b Munton	88	not out	45
*Moin Khan	c Gower, b Malcolm	15	(7) not out	11
Salim Malik	b Gooch	34	(5) b Gooch	16
Inzamam-ul-Haq	c Gooch, b Malcolm	26		
Wasim Akram	st Russell, b Gooch	0	(6) c Atherton, b Gooch	13
Waqar Younis	not out	2		
Mushtaq Ahmed	c Lewis, b Gooch	6		
Aqib Javed				
Extras	b 9, lb 4, w 2, nb 3	18	b 8, lb 5,wb 5, nb 7	25
	(for 9 wickets, dec.)	505	(for 5 wickets, dec.)	239

ENGLAND

	FIRST INNINGS	
G.A. Gooch (capt)	c Moin, b Waqar Younis	78
A.J. Stewart	c Inzamam, b Wasim Akram	15
M.A. Atherton	c Moin, b Wasim Akram	0
R.A. Smith	lbw, b Aqib Javed	11
D.I. Gower	c Moin, b Wasim Akram	73
G.A. Hick	b Aqib Javed	22
C.C. Lewis	c Moin, b Wasim Akram	55
*R.C. Russell	c Aamir, b Aqib Javed	4
I.D.K. Salisbury	c Aamir, b Wasim Akram	50
T.A. Munton	not out	25
D.E. Malcolm	b Aqib Javed	4
Extras	b 8, lb 8, w 2, nb 35	53
		390

	O	M	R	W	O	M	R	W
Malcolm	31	3	117	3	12	2	57	–
Lewis	24	5	90	2	17	5	46	3
Munton	30	6	112	1	17	6	26	–
Salisbury	20	–	117	–	13	–	67	–
Gooch	18	2	39	3	16	5	30	2
Hick	3	–	17	–	2	2	0	–

	O	M	R	W
Wasim Akram	36	4	128	5
Waqar Younis	32	6	96	1
Aqib Javed	21.4	1	100	4
Asif Mujtaba	1	1	0	–
Mushtaq Ahmed	10	1	50	–

FALL OF WICKETS
1–115, **2**–241, **3**–378, **4**–428, **5**–432, **6**–492, **7**–497, **8**–497, **9**–505
1–1, **2**–143, **3**–148, **4**–195, **5**–217

FALL OF WICKETS
1–41, **2**–42, **3**–93, **4**–186, **5**–200, **6**–252, **7**–256, **8**–315, **9**–379

Umpires: D.R. Shepherd & R. Palmer

Match drawn

3, 4 and 6 July *at Stockton*

Gloucestershire 259 for 4 dec. (A.J. Wright 83 not out, C.W.J. Athey 56, R.J. Scott 51 not out)
Durham 227 for 7 (W. Larkins 74, M. Davies 4 for 73)

Match drawn

No points

at Neath

Surrey 316 for 6 dec. (D.M. Ward 138, G.P. Thorpe 93) and 232 for 5 dec. (G.P. Thorpe 69 not out)
Glamorgan 250 for 6 dec. (S.P. James 105, H. Morris 58) and 248 (M.P. Maynard 66, H. Morris 58, M.P. Bicknell 5 for 43)

Surrey won by 50 runs

Surrey 22 pts., Glamorgan 5 pts.

at Southampton

Hampshire 261 for 6 dec. (T.C. Middleton 71, V.P. Terry 52) and 0 for 0 dec.
Nottinghamshire 0 for 0 dec. and 262 for 5 (R.T. Robinson 95, D.W. Randall 93)

Nottinghamshire won by 5 wickets

Nottinghamshire 18 pts., Hampshire 3 pts.

at Maidstone

Kent 193 (G.R. Cowdrey 77, D.K. Morrison 6 for 48, P.J. Martin 4 for 67) and 113 for 1 dec. (T.R. Ward 56 not out, M.A. Ealham 54)
Lancashire 11 for 0 dec. and 242 for 6 (S.P. Titchard 71, G. Fowler 52)

Match drawn

Lancashire 4 pts., Kent 1 pt.

at Northampton

Sussex 251 for 8 dec.
Northamptonshire 0 for 0 dec.

Match drawn

Northamptonshire 3 pts., Sussex 3 pts.

at Taunton

Somerset 299 for 8 dec. (R.J. Harden 166 not out, C.J. Tavare 59) and 0 for 0 dec.
Derbyshire 0 for 0 dec. and 301 for 4 (P.D. Bowler 147 not out, J.E. Morris 109)

Derbyshire won by 6 wickets

Derbyshire 18 pts., Somerset 3 pts.

at Edgbaston

Essex 275 for 7 dec. (P.J. Prichard 74, J.J.B. Lewis 60 not out, N.A. Foster 54) and 0 for 0 dec.
Warwickshire 0 for 0 dec. and 204 for 7 (D.A. Reeve 54 not out)

Match drawn

Warwickshire 3 pts., Essex 3 pts.

at Sheffield

Yorkshire 207 for 5 dec. (C. White 74 not out)
Leicestershire 132 for 6 (P.W. Jarvis 4 for 32)

Match drawn

No points

On Friday, 3 July, there was play possible only at Neath and Maidstone; 75 overs were bowled at the first, and 32 at the second. At Stockton, no play was possible until the final day, and then Durham could not manage a target of 260 in 46 overs. Gloucestershire's reserve wicket-keeper, Richard Williams, had two catches and three stumpings, and once again proved himself most capable.

David Ward hit 96 in an afternoon session shortened by rain on the opening day at Neath. He and Thorpe added 211 in 46.4 overs, and Ward's innings included 25 fours. Sparkling batting by James, who went to his century with a six off Boiling, kept Glamorgan in contention, but there was a minor collapse, and Maynard declared when the third batting point arrived. Eventually, the home side were asked to make 299 in 68 overs. They reached 247 for 6 at which point Martin Bicknell took four wickets in 11 balls for no runs to win the match for Surrey.

Forfeitures brought a result at Southampton where Nottinghamshire chased a target of 262 in 57 overs and won with 14 balls to spare. Their victory was founded on a fourth-wicket partnership of 153 between Randall and Robinson.

Kent went from 5 for 0 to 5 for 3 on the shortened first day at Maidstone, and Morrison, the New Zealand pace bowler, returned his best figures for Lancashire. There were manipulations in order to try to get a result, in spite of the rain, and Kent scored 113 from nine overs in their second innings. Lancashire were left 90 overs in which to score 296, and they were given a good start by Fowler and Titchard, but thereafter they lost their way.

No play on the first day and only 7.3 overs on the second condemned Sussex and Northamptonshire to playing for crumbs at Northampton. At Taunton, Richard Harden hit the highest score of his career and finished on the losing side. Derbyshire were asked to make 300 in 85 overs, and some spirited batting from Bowler and Morris, who added 259 in 43 overs, and some very wayward bowling saw them reach their target with an astonishing 32.5 overs to spare.

In contrast, Warwickshire showed little appetite for attempting to score 276 in 66 overs against Essex and Leicestershire, needing 208 in 47 overs to beat Yorkshire, declined to 68 for 6 and were saved by Wells and Nixon.

SUNDAY LEAGUE

5 July *at Stockton*

Gloucestershire 226 for 5 (A.J. Wright 93)
Durham 228 for 4 (D.M. Jones 81 not out, J.D. Glendenen 52)

Durham (4 pts.) won by 6 wickets

at Llanelli

Glamorgan 234 for 5 (H. Morris 98, M.P. Maynard 72)
Surrey 235 for 3 (A.D. Brown 113, G.P. Thorpe 56 not out)

Surrey (4 pts.) won by 7 wickets

at Southampton

Hampshire 172 for 7 (V.P. Terry 69)
Nottinghamshire 148 for 9

Hampshire (4 pts.) won by 24 runs

at Maidstone

Kent v. Lancashire
Match abandoned

Kent 2 pts., Lancashire 2 pts.

at Lord's

Worcestershire 181 for 4 (T.S. Curtis 69, D.B. D'Oliveira 58)
Middlesex 183 for 1 (M.W. Gatting 88 not out, M.A. Roseberry 76 not out)

Middlesex (4 pts.) won by 9 wickets

at Tring

Northamptonshire 226 for 5 (A.J. Lamb 120, N.A. Felton 61)
Sussex 152 for 9

Northamptonshire (4 pts.) won by 74 runs

at Taunton

Derbyshire 160 for 9
Somerset 162 for 5 (A.N. Hayhurst 54)

Somerset (4 pts.) won by 5 wickets

at Edgbaston

Warwickshire 214 for 5 (A.J. Moles 63)
Essex 190 (D.R. Pringle 52, N.M.K. Smith 4 for 25)

Warwickshire (4 pts.) won by 24 runs

at Sheffield

Yorkshire 148 for 7
Leicestershire 152 for 4 (J.J. Whitaker 82 not out)

Leicestershire (4 pts.) won by 6 wickets

While Essex were being beaten at Edgbaston, Middlesex won their ninth Sunday League game of the season so establishing a record for the best start to a season in the league. Curtis batted throughout the 40 overs for his 69. Roseberry and Gatting added 151 for Middlesex's second wicket in 22 overs to take their side to victory with 11 overs to spare. Maynard and Morris put on 139 in 23 overs for Glamorgan's second wicket at Llanelli, but Alistair Brown hit a century off 82 balls to give Surrey victory. The match at Tring was reduced to 25 overs, but Lamb, dropped by England, hit 120 off 62 balls, reaching his century off 48 balls, the second fastest in Sunday League history.

NATWEST TROPHY – ROUND TWO

9 July *at Chelmsford*

Lancashire 318 for 8 (G. Fowler 66, N.J. Speak 60)
Essex 319 for 9 (J.P. Stephenson 75, M.A. Garnham 53 not out)

Essex won by 1 wicket

(Man of the Match – M.A. Garnham)

at Southampton

Hampshire 243 for 9 (V.P. Terry 109)
Kent 244 for 8 (T.R. Ward 92)

Kent won by 2 wickets

(Man of the Match – M.A. Ealham)

at Uxbridge

Middlesex 259 for 8 (M.W. Gatting 57, S.P. Hughes 4 for 41)
Durham 260 for 4 (P.W.G. Parker 69, I.T. Botham 63 not out, J.D. Glendenen 57)

Durham won by 6 wickets

(Man of the Match – P.W.G. Parker)

at Northampton

Northamptonshire 325 for 7 (A. Fordham 78, A.J. Lamb 69)
Yorkshire 192 (R.J. Blakey 64, C.E.L. Ambrose 4 for 7)

Northamptonshire won by 133 runs

(Man of the Match – C.E.L. Ambrose)

at Taunton

Gloucestershire 235 (A.J. Wright 71, S.G. Hinks 67, A.R. Caddick 6 for 30)
Somerset 213 (M.N. Lathwell 85, C.A. Walsh 4 for 34)

Gloucestershire won by 22 runs

(Man of the Match – A.R. Caddick)

9 and 10 July *at Derby*

Leicestershire 201 for 9
Derbyshire 103 (W.K.M. Benjamin 5 for 32)

Leicestershire (4 pts.) won by 98 runs

(Man of the Match – D.J. Millns)

at Trent Bridge

Nottinghamshire 194 (C.L. Cairns 77)
Glamorgan 197 for 8 (M.P. Maynard 60)

Glamorgan won by 2 wickets

(Man of the Match – S.L. Watkin)

at Edgbaston

Sussex 150
Warwickshire 151 for 7
Warwickshire won by 3 wickets
(Man of the Match -- R.G. Twose)

The second round of the NatWest Trophy produced some pulsating finishes, but there have been none more exciting in the short history of one-day cricket than that at Chelmsford. Gooch won the toss and asked Lancashire to bat. Atherton was caught at cover, but the second-wicket stand between Fowler and Speak realised 91 in 21 overs. Fowler was dropped by Gooch who also put down Fairbrother and seemed unable to take anything cleanly. He had a most uneasy day in the field, for his bowling, too, lacked its usual miserliness. Stephenson was the leading Essex wicket-taker, but he was expensive as Watkinson and Lloyd hit 57 off eight overs, and Austin and Fitton took 40 from the last 20 deliveries. To win, Essex had to record the highest second innings total a side has made to win a tie in this competition. Lancashire had included DeFreitas after a fitness test shortly before the game, but he bowled only three balls before indicating that he was unfit to continue. One sympathised with Lancashire, but the wound was mostly self-inflicted. Gooch and Stephenson began with an effortless 123 in 26 overs, which made the daunting target seem as nothing, but they fell in successive overs. A bottom edge from Gooch stuck in between Hegg's pads, and, Stephenson, 75 for 94 balls, mishit to DeFreitas at cover. Waugh and Prichard continued serenely in worsening light. At 179 for 2 in the 38th over, the umpires conferred but allowed play to continue. Waugh was immediately bowled, and three balls later the players left the field. Many in the crowd left, believing play to be over for the day, but, after 30 minutes, the Essex innings continued in difficult conditions. Five wickets fell for 45 runs, and when Topley joined Garnham 91 were needed from ten overs. With furious running and some hitting that was both sensible and audacious they added 54 before Topley was run out. This had been a stand of heroic proportions, but Essex still needed 23 off the last two overs, and only Childs, not noted for his batting skills, to support Garnham. The last over arrived with Essex still 14 short of victory, and when Garnham accepted a single off the first ball it seemed that Lancashire must be victors. Atherton was the bowler, and Childs, a left-hander perhaps better suited to cope with leg-breaks, clouted him to long-on for four. The next ball he clouted straight for four. They were hits of immense courage. The next ball he pushed for a single, and Garnham drove the fifth past long-off's fingers for the winning four. Man of the Match Garnham had hit 53 off 37 balls, and Essex had won a famous victory.

Trevor Penney – a most useful addition to the Warwickshire side. (David Munden)

Kent, too, had a fine win at Southampton, beating Hampshire with five balls to spare, the county they were to meet in the Benson and Hedges final two days later. Hampshire, in spite of Terry's century, were somewhat disappointed by their 243 for 9 in 60 overs, and when Ward hit 92 off 146 balls Kent needed 70 from the last 12 overs with six wickets in hand. They quickly lost two wickets, and it needed the coolness of Ealham to keep Kent afloat. Marsh was bowled in the 55th over with 33 still needed, and Davis also fell, but eight off the 59th over sealed the match.

Durham overcame adversity to beat Middlesex, the real surprise of the round. Wood fell as he ran up to deliver the first ball and was unable to take any part in the match. This strained Durham's bowling resources, but no one played a big innings for Middlesex, and Hughes cut down the tail of his old county to keep their score within bounds. Larkins went for 0, but Glendenen kept the score moving, and Parker and Botham added 123 in 26 overs to bring their side to the point of victory. Skipper Parker had an inspired match, taking three catches as well as scoring 69.

Yorkshire fell apart against Northamptonshire. Their bowling was wayward, and their fielding disintegrated as the home side plundered 102 runs from the last ten overs. A dispirited Yorkshire side then lost both openers for 3, and Curtly Ambrose returned figures of 8.3–4–7–4.

Caddick, Somerset's fast bowler from New Zeland, also had splendid figures against Gloucestershire, but he ended on the losing side. Facing a moderate 235, Somerset were 147 for 1. Then Lathwell, who had again been in fine form, mistimed a drive off Scott and was caught. Walsh was recalled, and wickets fell in each of the next three overs. Burns offered resistance, but Walsh and Smith bowled Gloucestershire to victory.

The match at Derby went into the second day. Leicestershire made a meagre 209, but Derbyshire, without the injured Barnett, lost Bowler and Morris for 7 just before the premature close, and there was no recovery on the second morning.

Watkin bowled Glamorgan to a position of strength at Trent Bridge, helping to reduce Nottinghamshire to 43 for 5. Chris Cairns played an innings of immense character to take them to 194. Glamorgan's innings was almost the reverse of their hosts. They seemed to be cruising to victory at 138 for 3, but they faltered against Cairns and Pick, and it was left to Metson to rouse them. They still required nine from Lewis' last over, with Watkin and Bastien together. Seven came off the first five deliveries, and Bastien crashed the last for four.

It was a more dour struggle at Edgbaston where Warwickshire won with 6.3 overs to spare. Roger Twose took the individual award for his 3 for 39, which blunted Sussex's charge in the closing overs, and his 38.

BENSON AND HEDGES CUP FINAL

Hampshire v. Kent, at Lord's

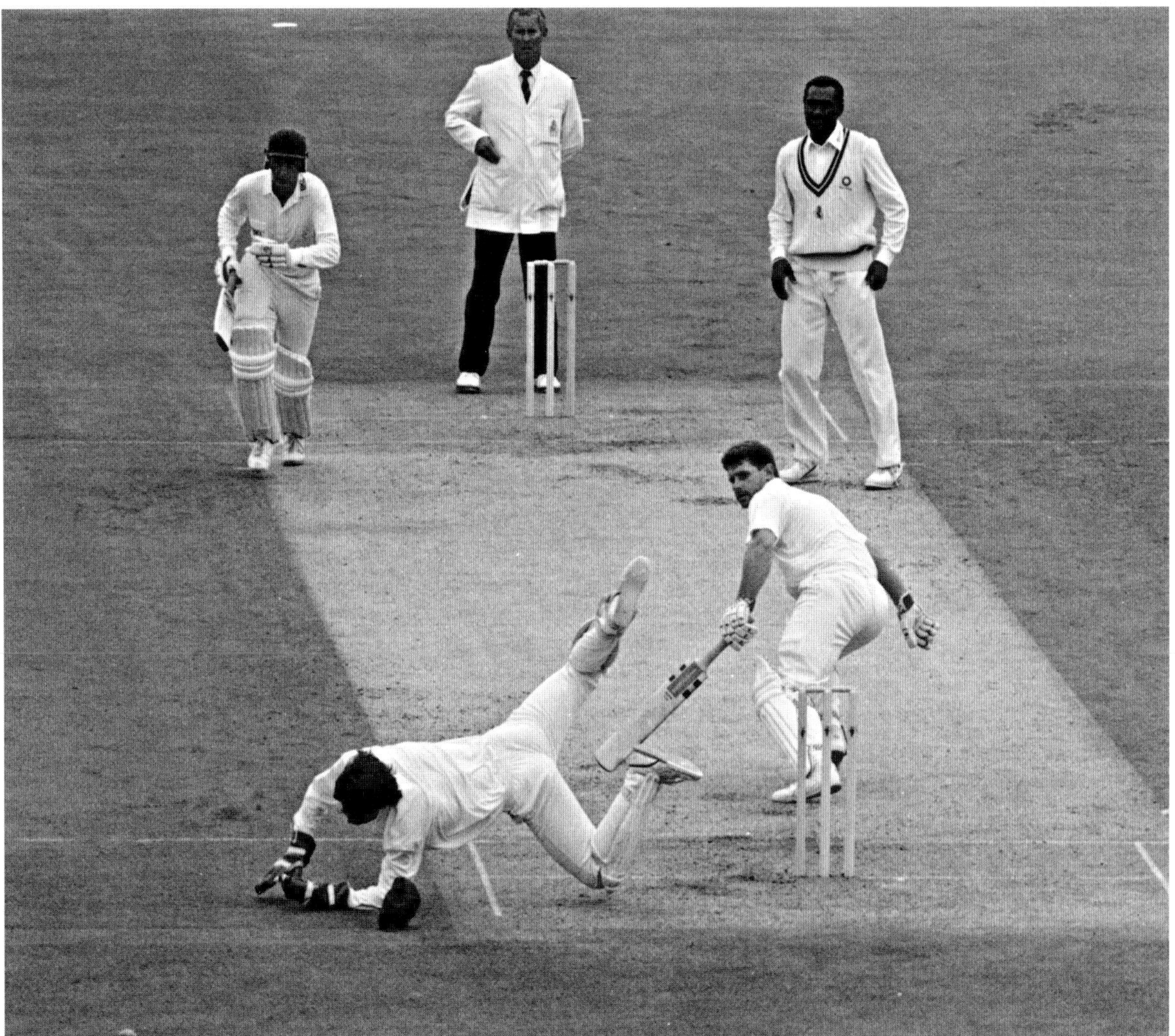

Smith turns Hooper past Marsh, and he and Gower set off for a run. Smith was to take the Gold Award for his 90. (Patrick Eagar)

1992 BENSON and HEDGES CUP

PRIZE STRUCTURE

£115,150 of the £596,148 Benson and Hedges sponsorship of this event will go in prize money for teams or individuals.

The breakdown is as follows:

- The Champions will win £27,500 (and hold, for one year only, the Benson and Hedges Cup)
- For the Runners-up £13,500
- For the losing Semi-finalists £6,750
- For the losing Quarter-finalists £3,375

ADDITIONAL TEAM AWARDS

The winners of all matches in the group stages of the Cup will receive £850.

INDIVIDUAL GOLD AWARDS

There will be a Benson and Hedges Gold Award for the outstanding individual performance at all matches throughout the Cup.

These will be:

- In the group matches £150
- In the Quarter-finals £250
- In the Semi-finals £300
- In the Final £550

The playing conditions and Cup records are on the reverse.

HOLDERS:
WORCESTERSHIRE COUNTY CRICKET CLUB

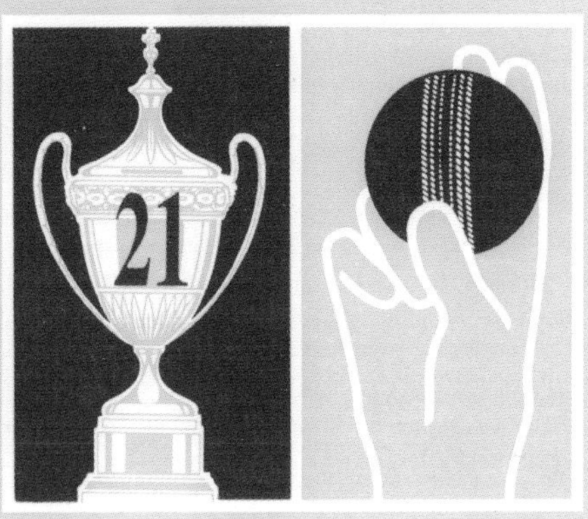

MARYLEBONE CRICKET CLUB

50p | 50p

FINAL

HAMPSHIRE v. KENT

at Lord's Ground, Saturday & Sunday, July 11th & 12th, 1992

Any alterations to teams will be announced over the public address system

HAMPSHIRE

	Batsman	How out	Runs
1	V. P. Terry	b Igglesden	41
2	T. C. Middleton	l b w b Hooper	27
3	R. A. Smith	run out	90
4	D. I. Gower	l b w b Fleming	29
†5	M. C. J. Nicholas	c Ealham b Fleming	25
6	M. D. Marshall	not out	29
7	K. D. James	not out	2
*8	R. J. Parks		
9	S. D. Udal		
10	J. R. Ayling		
11	C. A. Connor		
	B , l-b 3, w 3, n-b 4,		10
		Total...	253

FALL OF THE WICKETS

1...68 2...86 3...171 4...205 5...234 6... 7... 8... 9... 10...

Bowling Analysis	O.	M.	R.	W.	Wd	N b
Igglesden	11	1	39	1	...	2
Ealham	9	0	46	0	...	2
McCague	11	0	43	0	1	...
Hooper	11	1	41	1	...	...
Davis	5	0	18	0	...	...
Fleming	8	0	63	2	2	...
...	...	...	...	...	...	...

KENT

	Batsman	How out	Runs
1	T. R. Ward	c Parks b Marshall	5
†2	M. R. Benson	b James	59
3	N. R. Taylor	c Parks b Ayling	8
4	C. L. Hooper	b Udal	28
5	G. R. Cowdrey	c Gower b Marshall	27
6	M. V. Fleming	c Nicholas b Ayling	32
*7	S. A. Marsh	b Udal	7
8	M. A. Ealham	b Connor	23
9	M. J. McCague	b Udal	0
10	R. P. Davis	c Gower b Marshall	1
11	A. P. Igglesden	not out	1
	B 1, l-b 11, w 5, n-b 4,		21
		Total...	212

FALL OF THE WICKETS

1...17 2...38 3...116 4...116 5...171 6...182 7...186 8...194 9...204 10...212

Bowling Analysis	O.	M	R	W	Wd	N-b
Connor	9.3	2	27	1	2	...
Marshall	10	1	33	3	1	2
Ayling	11	0	38	2	1	2
James	11	1	35	1	...	...
Udal	11	0	67	3	1	...
...	...	...	...	...	...	...
...	...	...	...	...	...	...

† Captain * Wicket-keeper

Umpires—J. H. Hampshire & M. J. Kitchen

Scorers—V. H. Isaacs, J. Foley & E. Solomon

Toss won by—Kent who elected to field

RESULT—Hampshire won by 41 runs

The playing conditions for the Benson & Hedges Cup Competition are printed on the back of this score card.

Reproduced by kind permission of MCC.

For the second year in succession, the Benson and Hedges Cup final, the great mid-season event, was spoiled by bad weather, and play went over into the Sunday.

Kent were encouraged by their victory over Hampshire in the NatWest Trophy two days earlier, and kept to the side that had taken them through the early rounds of the competition, which meant omitting Ellison. Hampshire brought in Ayling for Maru, and, happily, retained Parks instead of bringing back Aymes who was fit again. One rejoiced for Parks in his benefit year. He is a very good keeper who lost his place to an inferior keeper who is a marginally better batsman, and it was just that his worthy career should be crowned in this way.

Benson won the toss and asked Hampshire to bat. There was no immediate gain. Igglesden was quick and moved the ball appreciably, but Ealham was neither as accurate nor as taxing as he had been in the previous rounds. Fifty came up in the 15th over, and Benson had already turned to Hooper's off-breaks in an effort to stem the flow of runs. It was the West Indian who achieved the break-through.

Middleton had been tucking the ball away off his legs efficiently, but he tried to sweep Hooper and was leg before. Benson recalled Igglesden and five overs later he bowled Terry who attempted to cut a ball that was too close to him. Gower now joined Smith in a fruitful partnership.

It should have been broken when Smith, on 40, clipped Davis to square-leg, but Benson failed to hold a difficult chance. This was unfortunate for Davis who never quite found the rhythm that had marked his bowling for most of the season, and he was only to bowl five overs of his quota although one feels that Benson erred in his lack of confidence here.

Gower was content to play a secondary role, but the score kept moving, and 85 were added in 20 overs before Gower drove at Fleming and missed. It should not be imagined that this stand was uninterruped. Drizzle began in the lunch hour, and, after one abortive attempt to restart, play did not begin in earnest until 4.35. Conditions were not pleasant for anybody.

Hampshire increased the pace. Nicholas and Marshall pounded away, and Smith hit a six and six fours in his 108-ball innings. He was run out in the 54th over, but one already had the suspicion that he had done enough to win Hampshire the cup. Kent had six balls and scored four runs before everyone called it a day.

The batting conditions were much improved on the Sunday, but Kent found it hard to settle against Connor and Marshall to whom this Lord's final meant so much. With the score on 17, Ward pushed forward at Marshall and got a faint edge to the wicket-keeper. Marshall rested after seven overs, but Ayling and James offered no respite. The grunting Ayling gave Parks his second catch when he found the edge of Taylor's bat as the Kent man attempted to cut. After 20 overs, Kent were 43 for 2.

Smith is run out by Fleming. (David Munden)

Benson had negotiated the early difficult period, but he was unable to lift the tempo. Hooper, however, was as elegantly masterful as ever, and, in 16 overs, 78 runs were added. In effect, for the only time in the match, Hampshire were not in control. Then, just before lunch, Benson, judging the time to hit badly, swung at James, and his 91-ball innings was at an end. Worse followed, for in the next over, the last before lunch, when extra care should have been taken, Hooper played a careless shot at Udal and was bowled.

Cowdrey has qualities, but he is not a big hitter, and much depended on Fleming. He hit 32 off 34 balls in a stand of 55 before Nicholas jubilantly took him head high at mid-on. Marsh was bowled by Udal, and Cowdrey, forsaking what comes naturally, skied the ball back over the bowler's head. Ealham offered an exciting coda with a six and two fours, but the end had long since been nigh when he was bowled as he jumped out to drive.

Hampshire were worthy winners. For Nicholas, it was compensation for having missed the NatWest final in 1991; for Malcolm Marshall, it was a dream realised. Not surprisingly, Robin Smith took the Gold Award.

ABOVE: Marsh is bowled by Udal for 7. (Patrick Eagar)

BELOW: Ealham is bowled by Connor, and Hampshire are winners of the Benson and Hedges Cup. (Patrick Eagar)

ABOVE: Cardigan Connor fails in his attempt to run out Mark Ealham. (David Munden)

BELOW: Mark Nicholas holds aloft the Benson and Hedges Cup. Jim Elkins, in blazer, and M.J. Stewart are among those who applaud. (Tom Morris)

12 July *at Edgbaston*

Warwickshire 197 for 8 (J.D. Ratcliffe 72)
Transvaal 198 for 2 (S.J. Cook 101 not out)

Transvaal won by 8 wickets

at Glasgow (Titwood)

Pakistanis 235 (Aamir Sohail 70)
Scotland 108 (Mushtaq Ahmed 6 for 43)

Pakistanis won on faster scoring rate

SUNDAY LEAGUE

12 July *at Moreton-in-Marsh*

Gloucestershire 176 for 7 (M.W. Alleyne 58)
Northamptonshire 98 (A.M. Babington 4 for 21)

Gloucestershire (4 pts.) won by 78 runs

at Old Trafford

Middlesex 201 for 5 (D.L. Haynes 84, J.D. Fitton 4 for 26)
Lancashire 199 for 9

Middlesex (4 pts.) won by 2 runs

at Leicester

Worcestershire 171 (T.M. Moody 66, L. Potter 4 for 33)
Leicestershire 165

Worcestershire (4 pts.) won by 6 runs

at Taunton

Durham 263 for 4 (D.M. Jones 83, P.W.G. Parker 82, W. Larkins 52)
Somerset 252 for 8 (A.N. Hayhurst 73)

Durham (4 pts.) won by 11 runs

at The Oval

Derbyshire 208 for 8 (J.E. Morris 78, M.P. Bicknell 4 for 48)
Surrey 212 for 7 (A.J. Stewart 86)

Surrey (4 pts.) won by 3 wickets

at Scarborough

Yorkshire 162 for 5
Essex 163 for 7

Essex (4 pts.) won by 3 wickets

Middlesex made it ten Sunday League wins in a row, a record, with Desmond Haynes hitting 84 off 91 balls. Lancashire were always just out of touch. Essex kept Middlesex in sight, and Gooch became the leading run scorer in Sunday League history. Jones and Parker put on 141 in 18.3 overs for Durham's third wicket against Somerset, who fought back well. There was real excitement at The Oval where Morris hit 78 off 77 balls for Derbyshire and was then the first of a Martin Bicknell hat-trick.

13 July *at Taunton*

Somerset 260 for 7 (M.N. Lathwell 60, R.J. Harden 64 not out, G.T.J. Townsend 59)
Transvaal 60 for 0

Match abandoned

14, 15 and 16 July *at Southend*

Gloucestershire 356 for 8 dec. (G.D. Hodgson 147, A.J. Wright 69, M.C. Ilott 5 for 79) and 230 for 4 dec. (C.W.J. Athey 94)
Essex 252 (M.E. Waugh 74, C.A. Walsh 4 for 46) and 335 for 6 (M.E. Waugh 125 not out, G.A. Gooch 55)

Essex won by 4 wickets

Essex 20 pts., Gloucestershire 8 pts.

at Portsmouth

Hampshire 158 (D.I. Gower 54) and 182 (I.R. Bishop 7 for 34)
Derbyshire 474 for 4 dec. (P.D. Bowler 241 not out, T.J.G. O'Gorman 95, D.G. Cork 65 not out)

Derbyshire won by an innings and 135 runs

Derbyshire 24 pts., Hampshire 2 pts.

at Southport

Leicestershire 257 (T.J. Boon 76, V.J. Wells 51, M. Watkinson 6 for 82, D.K. Morrison 4 for 70) and 181
Lancashire 280 (G. Fowler 62, N.H. Fairbrother 51, G.J. Parsons 4 for 34, D.J. Millns 4 for 65) and 150 (C.J. Hawkes 4 for 18, G.J. Parsons 4 for 25)

Leicestershire won by 8 runs

Leicestershire 23 pts., Lancashire 7 pts.

at Uxbridge

Northamptonshire 369 (K.M. Curran 82, A.J. Lamb 65, N.A. Felton 52) and 163 for 5 dec. (N.A. Felton 57)
Middlesex 220 for 5 dec. (D.L. Haynes 127 not out, M.R. Ramprakash 54) and 253 for 7 (J.D. Carr 72, D.L. Haynes 61, J.E. Emburey 50 not out)

Match drawn

Middlesex 6 pts., Northamptonshire 6 pts.

at Trent Bridge

Nottinghamshire 400 for 8 dec. (M.A. Crawley 115, C.L. Cairns 62, P. Johnson 58, K.P. Evans 55 not out, D.W. Randall 51) and 176 for 2 dec. (R.T. Robinson 64 not out, P. Johnson 51 not out)
Worcestershire 318 for 6 dec. (G.A. Hick 213 not out) and 262 for 5 (D.A. Leatherdale 112, N.V. Radford 73 not out)

Worcestershire won by 5 wickets

Worcestershire 22 pts., Nottinghamshire 6 pts.

at Guildford

Surrey 301 for 8 dec. (G.P. Thorpe 52) and 76
Kent 117 (J.E. Benjamin 5 for 29, M.P. Bicknell 4 for 47) and 332 (C.L. Hooper 131, T.R. Ward 103, M.P. Bicknell 4 for 62)

Kent won by 72 runs

Kent 19 pts., Surrey 8 pts.

at Sheffield

Yorkshire 301 for 6 dec. (S.A. Kellett 59, C. White 54 not out, D. Byas 52) and 62 for 0 dec.
Warwickshire 88 for 0 dec. and 276 for 7 (D.A. Reeve 74, R.G. Twose 66)

Warwickshire won by 3 wickets

Warwickshire 18 pts., Yorkshire 2 pts.

at Chester-le-Street

Pakistanis 308 for 7 dec. (Asif Mujtaba 79, Aamir Sohail 53, Moin Khan 53) and 338 for 6 dec. (Aamir Sohail 90, Javed Miandad 67, Ramiz Raja 59)
Durham 341 for 4 dec. (D.M. Jones 134 not out, W. Larkins 118) and 198 (D.M. Jones 105, Waqar Younis 5 for 22)

Pakistanis won by 107 runs

A career best 241 not out for Peter Bowler for Derbyshire in their victory over Hampshire at Portsmouth. (Sporting Pictures (UK) Ltd)

Essex tightened their grip at the top of the table with a spectacular win over Gloucestershire at Southchurch Park. Gooch asked Gloucestershire to bat first, but it brought Essex no success. Hinks was forced to retire hurt, and Athey went for 10, but Dean Hodgson played an admirable innings, the highest of his career with 19 fours, and Gloucestershire batted into the second day, leaving Essex with just one bowling point. Gooch and Waugh apart, the Essex batting looked anything but secure against Walsh, and Gloucestershire took a first-innings lead of 104. Wright eventually asked Essex to make 335 in 61 overs, a very difficult task. The first ten overs produced 52 runs, but both Gooch and Stephenson were out at 81. Waugh and Prichard added 77, but the loss of Prichard, Garnham and Shahid in quick succession, two of them run out, tilted the game in Gloucestershire's favour. Foster then played a magnificent innings in support of the rampant Waugh. When Walsh was brought back to stem the flow of runs he was hit for 15 in his first over, Foster putting him over mid-wicket for four and six. The partnership added 116 in 16 overs before Foster fell to Smith for 40, but Waugh, whose outstanding knock brought him 128 off 110 balls, and Lewis saw Essex home with 13 balls to spare.

Second-place Hampshire suffered wretchedly in comparison. They were 110 for 2 and were bowled out for 158, and then saw Peter Bowler hit the highest score of his career, and of the season. He showed the utmost application, sharing stands of 259, 93 and 110 with O'Gorman, Adams and Cork. He batted for 471 minutes, faced 387 balls and hit 26 fours. Hampshire's misery was completed when Ian Bishop crushed them with the best bowling performance of his career.

Leicestershire achieved victory over Lancashire in a manner which rivalled Essex with its sensational quality. Watkinson mixed his medium pace and his off-breaks to good effect, and Lancashire, generally on top, arrived on the last day with 159 to get to win, and ample time in which to get them. Victory looked certain when, with Speak and Lloyd together, Lancashire were 100 for 2. Briers then introduced veteran medium-pacer Parsons and slow left-arm bowler Hawkes, who was playing in his second county match. Lancashire collapsed before them, and Leicestershire won a thrilling victory by eight runs.

There were no such thrills at Uxbridge where the bat dominated, and John Emburey eventually kept Northamptonshire at bay. There was also a glut of runs at Trent Bridge. Nottinghamshire seemed in total command as Mark Crawley hit his fourth century of the summer, and the home side batted into the second day to reach 400. Graeme Hick responded with his highest score for two seasons. He seemed back to his best, hitting 213 off 275 balls, an innings that included four sixes and 24 fours. He fared differently in the second innings, being out first ball to Cairns when Worcestershire, in search of 259 in 58 overs, lost their first three wickets for one run. Leatherdale and Philip Weston added 116, and 130 were needed in the final 20 overs. Leatherdale reached his first century of the season and was out with 32 wanted. Radford, promoted in the order, struck 73 off 60 balls and blasted his side to victory.

Kent gained an incredible win at Guildford. They were forced to follow-on 184 in arrears, Benjamin producing a career best bowling performance. Astonishingly, on the Wednesday evening, Ward hit 102 in 95 balls out of an opening partnership of 117. He hit four sixes and ten fours. His opening partner, Benson, made 14. On the last morning, Carl Hooper played an innings which was both exquisite and purposeful. He guided Kent to a position where they had not only avoided an innings defeat, but had set Surrey a token target of 149 in 43 overs. Surrey were handicapped in that David Ward had sustained a broken thumb, but this could not explain what happened after Stewart and Darren Bicknell scored 28 from the first five overs. Kent relied on their seam bowlers and dynamic fielding, and the Surrey batsmen did the rest.

After very slow going on the first two days at Sheffield, Yorkshire set Warwickshire a target of 276 in 91 overs, which was reached with three balls to spare. The match saw Phil Carrick reach a thousand wickets in first-class cricket.

Dean Jones hit a century in each innings for Durham against the Pakistan tourists. He and Larkins shared a second-wicket stand of 162 on the second day but Waqar Younis led Pakistan to their seventh win in nine games against the counties. Dean Jones reached a thousand runs for the season, but he batted with a suspected broken finger in the second innings.

17, 18 and 20 July *at Southend*

Sussex 429 for 9 dec. (D.M. Smith 213, P. Moores 109, J.H. Childs 4 for 101) and 104 (P.M. Such 6 for 17)
Essex 303 for 1 dec. (J.P. Stephenson 123 not out, G.A. Gooch 102, P.J. Prichard 68 not out) and 231 for 2 (G.A. Gooch 108 not out, M.E. Waugh 85 not out)

Essex won by 8 wickets

Essex 22 pts., Sussex 4 pts.

at Cheltenham

Yorkshire 364 (M.D. Moxon 183, S.A. Kellett 50) and 30 for 2
Gloucestershire 257 (J.T.C. Vaughan 80, P.J. Hartley 5 for 66)

Match drawn

Yorkshire 8 pts., Gloucestershire 6 pts.

at Portsmouth

Hampshire 338 for 9 dec. (R.A. Smith 79, M.D. Marshall 70, S.L. Watkin 6 for 97) and 167 for 9 dec. (R.A. Smith 56)
Glamorgan 208 (M.P. Maynard 73, K.J. Shine 4 for 36) and 284 for 6 (D.L. Hemp 84 not out, S.P. James 73, S.D. Udal 4 for 89)

Match drawn

Hampshire 8 pts., Glamorgan 5 pts.

at Leicester

Somerset 327 (R.P. Snell 81, C.J. Tavaré 69, G.D. Rose 59, D.J. Millns 5 for 64) and 108 for 6
Leicestershire 270 (P.A. Nixon 68, W.K.M. Benjamin 53)

Match drawn

Somerset 7 pts., Leicestershire 6 pts.

at Uxbridge

Middlesex 202 (J.D. Carr 64, P.J. Newport 4 for 59) and 321 (M.A. Roseberry 118, M.W. Gatting 66, K.R. Brown 50, N.V. Radford 5 for 48)
Worcestershire 346 (G.A. Hick 168) and 118 for 8 (T.S. Curtis 60, P.C.R. Tufnell 4 for 24)

Match drawn

Worcestershire 7 pts., Middlesex 6 pts.

at Northampton

Northamptonshire 345 for 8 dec. (A. Fordham 122, N.A. Felton 66, D.J. Capel 59, A.A. Barnett 5 for 82) and 223 for 2 dec. (A. Fordham 81, R.J. Bailey 76 not out)
Lancashire 298 (W.K. Hegg 76 not out) and 23 for 2

Match drawn

Northamptonshire 8 pts., Lancashire 6 pts.

at Trent Bridge

Nottinghamshire 431 for 6 dec. (R.T. Robinson 164 not out, C.C. Lewis 107)
Durham 147 (M.P. Briers 53, C.L. Cairns 4 for 41) and 265 for 3 (D.M. Jones 154 not out, W. Larkins 57)

Match drawn

Nottinghamshire 8 pts., Durham 2 pts.

at Guildford

Warwickshire 372 for 6 dec. (D.P. Ostler 192, T.L. Penney 70 not out, R.G. Twose 55) and 198 for 9 dec. (J.E. Benjamin 4 for 81)
Surrey 341 for 6 dec. (G.P. Thorpe 86, A.J. Stewart 67, M.A. Lynch 63, A.D. Brown 56) and 131 for 7 (M.A. Feltham 50, A.A. Donald 6 for 49)

Match drawn

Surrey 6 pts., Warwickshire 6 pts.

18, 19 and 20 July *at Derby*

Derbyshire 216 (C.J. Adams 51, Wasim Akram 5 for 59) and 212 for 5 dec. (P.D. Bowler 79)
Pakistanis 197

Match drawn

Peter Such took a career best 6 for 17 as Essex beat Sussex at Southend and went 51 points clear at the top of the Britannic Assurance County Championship. (Sporting Pictures (UK) Ltd)

Mark Crawley Nottinghamshire. (Tom Morris)

Essex went 51 points clear at the top of the Britannic Assurance County Championship with another remarkable win to conclude Southend week. Winning the toss and batting first, Sussex batted into the second day as David Smith hit the first double century of his career which has spanned three counties. Peter Moores hit 109 off 187 balls and shared in a fifth-wicket partnership of 251 which seemed to put Sussex in an impregnable position. Essex's positive approach was never better exemplified than in the batting of Gooch and Stephenson who scored 179 in 35 overs for the first wicket. Indeed, Essex reached 300 in 66 overs, and Gooch declared, 126 in arrears, so that Sussex were batting again before the end of the second day. Resuming on the Monday at 63 for 2, but without Moores who had an injured toe, Sussex gave a most inept display. Rooted to the crease against Such and Childs, they allowed the spinners to control the game and were bowled out for 104. Such returned the best bowling figures of his career. Gooch then hit his second century of the match, and Waugh hit 85 off 84 balls as Essex hit 231 off 39.3 overs to win the game by mid-afternoon.

Martin Moxon hit two sixes and 23 fours in his fine 183 for Yorkshire against Gloucestershire, but rain on the last day ruined the match. Rain also blighted Glamorgan's heroic bid for victory at Portsmouth. Hampshire had dominated for most of the first two days, and Nicholas set Glamorgan a target of 298 in 72 overs on the final afternoon. James and Morris began with a stand of 110, but Maynard and Richards went cheaply as five wickets fell for 53 runs. At 237 for 6, Metson joined Hemp who had stood firm through the disasters, and the pair took Glamorgan to within 14 runs of victory with 29 balls left when a violent storm ended the match.

Rain also settled the argument at Leicester where Snell, who had batted better than he had bowled for Somerset, hit 81 off 72 balls. Hick played another innings which helped the selectors in their decision to retain him in the England side. His 168 occupied six hours and helped resurrect Worcestershire from an uncertain position to a first-innings lead of 144. Middlesex responded with a second-wicket stand of 184 between Gatting and Roseberry, and Tufnell and Emburey came close to bowling them to victory, but there was a lethargy in the Middlesex cricket which suggested a lack of belief or interest.

Fordham and Felton began the match at Northampton with a stand of 155, but rain on the last day thwarted either the home side or Lancashire claiming a result.

Tim Robinson shared century stands with Lewis and Cairns as Nottinghamshire piled up the runs against Durham. Lewis' 107 was his second century of the summer and the third of his career. Durham were forced to follow-on, but Dean Jones' third century in four innings saved them from defeat.

It was rain that saved Surrey at Guildford. Dominic Ostler hit the highest score of his career, 192 off 243 balls, and although Surrey got to near parity on the first innings, they were crumbling before Donald in their second when rain ended the match. Rain caused problems, too, at Derby where only five overs were possible on the last day.

ABOVE: *Jimmy Cook leads out Transvaal for their match against MCC at Lord's, 19 July. MCC's International XI won by 7 wickets – Transvaal were bowled out for 115, and MCC International XI were 116 for 3. (Patrick Eagar)*

SUNDAY LEAGUE

19 July *at Southend*

Sussex 239 for 6 (A.P. Wells 110 not out, J.W. Hall 52)
Essex 240 for 2 (M.E. Waugh 69 not out, J.P. Stephenson 64, P.J. Prichard 52 not out, G.A. Gooch 50)

Essex (4 pts.) won by 8 wickets

at Cheltenham

Yorkshire 200 (S.R. Tendulkar 63)
Gloucestershire 203 for 7 (C.W.J. Athey 51)

Gloucestershire (4 pts.) won by 3 wickets

at Portsmouth

Hampshire 129
Glamorgan 133 for 3 (H. Morris 51 not out)

Glamorgan (4 pts.) won by 7 wickets

at Canterbury

Kent 235 for 9 (T.R. Ward 51)
Worcestershire 199 for 9 (N.V. Radford 55)

Kent (4 pts.) won by 36 runs

at Leicester

Leicestershire 200 for 8
Somerset 202 for 1 (M.N. Lathwell 96, A.N. Hayhurst 67 not out)

Somerset (4 pts.) won by 9 wickets

at Northampton

Northamptonshire 221 for 5 (A. Fordham 54)
Middlesex 222 for 2 (M.W. Gatting 96, D.L. Haynes 84 not out)

Middlesex (4 pts.) won by 8 wickets

at Trent Bridge

Durham 211 for 7
Nottinghamshire 190 for 9 (R.T. Robinson 51)

Durham (4 pts.) won by 21 runs

at The Oval

Surrey 132 (A.A. Donald 4 for 23)
Warwickshire 135 for 4

Warwickshire (4 pts.) won by 6 wickets

With six matches still to play, Middlesex looked almost certain to win the Sunday League for the first time. They romped to victory over Northamptonshire with 20 balls to spare and maintained a four-point lead over Essex who had played two games more. Essex had a good win over Sussex, who had been early contenders. Alan Wells hit a hundred off 92 balls, but the four Essex batsmen who went to the wicket each passed fifty, and Essex won with 19 balls to spare. The woe of holders Nottinghamshire continued, and Lathwell and Hayhurst shared an opening stand of 169 in 30 overs in Somerset's victory over Leicestershire.

OPPOSITE: *One of the outstanding discoveries of the season, the Somerset fast bowler Andrew Caddick. (David Munden)*

21, 22 and 23 July *at Derby*

Derbyshire 334 for 3 dec. (C.J. Adams 112 not out, J.E. Morris 82, T.J.G. O'Gorman 68 not out) and 66 for 2
Middlesex 216 for 2 dec. (M.A. Roseberry 100 not out, D.L. Haynes 70)

Match drawn

Derbyshire 4 pts., Middlesex 3 pts.

at Cardiff

Yorkshire 348 for 8 dec. (R.J. Blakey 125 not out, M.D. Moxon 103) and 102 for 2 dec. (D. Byas 68 not out)
Glamorgan 200 for 6 dec. (S.P. James 80) and 219 for 9 (A. Dale 59 not out)

Match drawn

Glamorgan 4 pts., Yorkshire 4 pts.

at Cheltenham

Hampshire 167 (T.C. Middleton 64, C.A. Walsh 6 for 33) and 274 for 8 dec. (R.S.M. Morris 64)
Gloucestershire 339 for 8 dec. (M.W. Alleyne 86, R.C. Russell 75, G.D. Hodgson 56) and 95 for 7 (S.D. Udal 4 for 36)

Match drawn

Gloucestershire 7 pts., Hampshire 2 pts.

at Canterbury

Kent 275 (M.A. Ealham 40, A.R. Caddick 4 for 105) and 160 for 8 dec. (A.R. Caddick 6 for 52)
Somerset 133 (M.J. McCague 5 for 23) and 220 (M.N. Lathwell 72, R.P. Davis 6 for 75)

Kent won by 82 runs

Kent 23 pts., Somerset 4 pts.

at Leicester

Durham 145 (D.J. Millns 5 for 41, A.D. Mullally 4 for 39) and 116 (D.J. Millns 5 for 46, W.K.M. Benjamin 4 for 34)
Leicestershire 256 (N.E. Briers 93) and 6 for 0

Leicestershire won by 10 wickets

Leicestershire 23 pts., Durham 4 pts.

at Northampton

Northamptonshire 334 (A.J. Lamb 209) and 218 for 4 dec. (A.J. Lamb 107, A. Fordham 75)
Warwickshire 316 for 7 dec. (T.L. Penney 100 not out) and 206 for 5 (R.G. Twose 78, A.J. Moles 66)

Match drawn

Warwickshire 8 pts., Northamptonshire 7 pts.

at The Oval

Surrey 333 for 4 dec. (P.D. Atkins 99, M.A. Lynch 97 not out, D.J. Bicknell 60) and 219 for 7 dec. (A.D. Brown 111, M.G. Field-Buss 4 for 71)

Nottinghamshire 201 for 2 dec. (P. Johnson 107 not out, R.T. Robinson 73 not out) and 352 for 7 (M.A. Crawley 95, P. Johnson 78, P.R. Pollard 74, M.A. Feltham 4 for 118)

Nottinghamshire won by 3 wickets

Nottinghamshire 19 pts., Surrey 4 pts.

at Hove

Sussex 342 for 5 dec. (J.W. Hall 140 not out, D.M. Smith 105, J.D. Fitton 4 for 81) and 302 for 3 dec. (M.P. Speight 119 not out, J.W. Hall 71)

Lancashire 349 for 8 dec. (G.D. Lloyd 96, N.J. Speak 59, S.P. Titchard 54) and 238 for 9 (J.P. Crawley 65, N.J. Speak 62, P.J. Martin 52 not out, E.S.H. Giddins 5 for 54)

Match drawn

Sussex 7 pts., Lancashire 6 pts.

at Kidderminster

Worcestershire 448 for 6 dec. (T.M. Moody 178, D.B. D'Oliveira 100) and 186 for 5 dec. (S.R. Lampitt 63, S.J. Rhodes 62 not out)

Essex 300 for 5 dec. (M.E. Waugh 138 not out, N. Hussain 78) and 0 for 0.

Match drawn

Worcestershire 6 pts., Essex 5 pts.

Chris Adams – exciting cricket for Derbyshire and a well-deserved county cap. (Sporting Pictures (UK) Ltd)

A first day restricted by rain dampened any real chance of a result at Derby, but Adams and O'Gorman shared an unbroken stand of 192 for the home side's fourth wicket off 57 overs. Both young players received their county caps. Haynes and Roseberry put on 147 for Middlesex's first wicket, but rain returned on the last day to end the match.

At Cardiff, there were centuries for Yorkshire's Blakey and Moxon who shared a fourth-wicket stand of 117. On the last afternoon, Moxon asked Glamorgan to score 251 in 65 overs, but 12 overs were lost to rain. Glamorgan were well served by Maynard's 38 off 34 balls, but when he was out they were 134 for 5. Dale and Croft added 62. Croft was caught off Batty, and three wickets then fell at 217 when Metson was run out, and Jarvis dismissed Watkin and Barwick with successive deliveries. Frost stayed with Dale for the last four overs to save the game.

Courtney Walsh returned match figures of 9 for 90 as Gloucestershire mostly held the upper hand against Hampshire, but they were nearly beaten on the last day when Nicholas' challenge of 103 off nine overs provoked some bizarre dismissals.

The pitch at Canterbury, short of water, gave the TCCB inspectors cause for concern as 19 wickets fell on the second day. A shortened first day saw Kent move to 195 for 7, and some violent hitting by the tail took them to 275 on the second morning. A mixture of pace and spin then proved far too much for Somerset who were asked to make 303 in 90 overs on the last day. They reached 81 in 18 overs without loss, but both openers were out just before lunch, Lathwell again having sparkled with 72 off 69 balls. Thereafter Davis, bowling from the Pavilion End, dominated, and Kent moved to a comfortable victory. This was rather hard on Caddick who took 10 for 157 in the match, including a career best 6 for 52 in Kent's second innings.

The Leicestershire seam attack totally destroyed Durham and ended Dean Jones' season in England. He sustained a broken finger and returned to Australia for treatment prior to the tour of Sri Lanka. On a green wicket, Millns thrived, and Leicestershire maintained their slender challenge to Essex at the top of the table.

Allan Lamb hit 209 in 314 minutes and 107 against some rather friendly bowling in the second innings for Northamptonshire against Warwickshire. Trevor Penney hit his first championship century for the visitors, but Warwickshire fell short of their target of 237 off 47 overs, and the match was drawn.

Nottinghamshire kept alive their championship hopes with a fine win at The Oval. Only 52 overs were possible on the first day, but Surrey made up for lost time on the second, Lynch declaring when three short of his century with the score at 333 of 89 overs. Lynch hit 97 off 78 balls, but while he was hitting cleanly Atkins was becalmed in the 90s for nearly an hour as he searched for his maiden century. He played an uppish shot off Pennett on 99 and was caught by Randall. Robinson and Johnson, who hit 107 off 151 balls, shared an unbroken stand of 185 before Robinson declared 132 runs in arrears. Lynch eventually set Nottinghamshire the formidable target of 352 in 68 overs. They were given a splendid start by Pollard and Crawley who put on 159. Johnson hit 78 off 63 balls, but with 11 balls to go, 25 runs were needed. Greg Mike arrived and hit Feltham for three sixes. He was dismissed, and six were needed from the last over. French was bowled by Bryson's first ball, but Evans hit a four and a single, and Cairns scrambled a single off the last ball to win the game.

At Hove, Smith and Hall hit 172 off 59 overs, and Hall reached the highest score of his career. Lancashire's batsmen kept pace with Sussex, and Martin Speight hit a second-innings century off Lancashire bowling which was in search of a declaration. When it came it offered Lancashire the chance to score 296 in 71 overs. Crawley and Speak added 118 for the second wicket, but pace bowler Giddins had career best bowling figures as Lancashire slumped, and they were only saved from defeat by Martin.

Batsmen prospered on a placid wicket at Kidderminster. Moody and D'Oliveira, neither of whom had enjoyed the best of seasons, hit centuries, and Waugh responded for Essex. Worcestershire's declaration left Essex 53 overs in which to score 335, but rain prevented the chase from beginning.

Martin Speight – the fastest century of the season, Sussex v. Lancashire, Hove, 21 July. (David Munden)

BELOW: *Aamir Sohail is caught by Atherton off Mallender for 23. This was Mallender's first Test wicket. He had a remarkable debut, having match figures of 8 for 122. (David Munden)*

FOURTH TEST MATCH

ENGLAND v. PAKISTAN, at Leeds

England chose a side for the ground and the conditions. John Childs had been called into the party, but no spinner was played, so Mallender, a surprise choice for his first Test cap, Munton, Lewis and Pringle formed an all-seam attack. Russell was omitted, and Stewart kept wicket. This was a move that was aimed at strengthening the batting, but, in truth, Russell's keeping had been below standard in the series.

Javed won the toss and chose to bat first. The Headingley pitch offered its usual difficulties for the batsmen, real or imaginary, and it was not long before wickets began to tumble. The first day was to be fractured by rain, and the extra hour was taken. At the end of it, Pakistan were 165 for 8. Their predicament could have been much worse, for the eighth wicket had fallen at 128 before Mushtaq Ahmed joined the admirable Salim Malik in a rearguard action.

Lewis bowled without zest or accuracy at the outset and wasted the new ball, but Mallender showed good control and adapted to the conditions intelligently, fully justifying his selection. He claimed his first Test wicket when Aamir Sohail, who had played with his natural aggression, dabbed lamely, low to first slip.

Ramiz had seemed totally lacking in confidence, and he retreated into introspection. Asif Mujtaba, whose technical proficiency gave hope that he could cope with abnormal conditions, played securely enough and until he pushed forward, bat a little away from his body, and was bowled off an inside edge. Pringle struck the vital blows in a fine spell, bowling Ramiz, nearly two hours at the crease, with an in-swinger and, vitally, having Javed taken at short-leg off bat and pad.

This was no pitch for Inzamam, and he edged Munton to second slip. This was also no pitch for Wasim who was run out when Salim, rightly, declined a third run to Gooch at mid-wicket. Lewis, summoning more energy in his later spell, had Moin taken at slip, and Waqar fell in the same position to give Mallender his third wicket of the day. At last, Salim found a reliable partner in Mushtaq.

They extended their partnership to 64 on the second morning before Mushtaq was yorked by Lewis. Five runs later, Aqib provided Hick with his fourth catch at slip. Salim Malik was left unbeaten on 82 which had occupied 227 minutes and included 12 fours. He had had his problems early in his innings, but he survived with determination. Never afraid to attack when the chance arrived, he shamed the majority of his colleagues with his application. This was an innings of great character.

Mallender strikes again. Asif Mujtaba is bowled. (Patrick Eagar)

Pakistan's hero Salim Malik who made scores of 82 and 84 without being dismissed. (David Munden)

England had fielded well and bowled intelligently; now, in 50 minutes before lunch, they batted with confidence. Gooch and Atherton raised the fifty in ten overs. Aqib and Waqar did not bowl the right line or length, and no wicket fell in the afternoon session in which England scored 76 runs. At tea, Gooch was 59 and Atherton was 54, and England were 130 for 0.

Having batted for 228 minutes and hit a six and nine fours, Atherton was beaten off the pitch and bowled as he played back to Wasim Akram. Smith was soon busy, and England ended the day in total command, 216 for 1, with Gooch seven short of his century.

England were most fortunate with the weather on the second day. The sun shone, and batting seemed easier, but Gooch had played very, very well. He was intent at all times on pushing well forward, and he showed great discipline in countering the vagaries of the pitch. His century was very much deserved, as inspiring as it was invaluable.

Smith was out in the 91st over, driving a widish delivery to extra-cover, but, at 270 for 2, England were riding high. Eight overs later, with the score on 292, Stewart was beaten by a swinging delivery of full length and was leg before. This was the beginning of a remarkable spell from the incomparable Waqar Younis who, in seven overs of sustained pace, took five wickets for 13 runs.

England's last seven wickets went down for 28 runs. Gooch was bowled between bat and pad as he misread Mushtaq's googly. Ramprakash swept and missed the same kind of delivery. Hick, painfully ill-at-ease, had his

Gooch and Atherton discuss a point during their opening partnership of 168. (Patrick Eagar)

ABOVE: *Inzamam-ul-Haq brings the England innings to a close as he catches Munton off Mushtaq Ahmed. (Adrian Murrell/Allsport)*

BELOW: *Asif Mujtaba is given out caught at slip by Hick off Mallender for 11. (Patrick Eagar)*

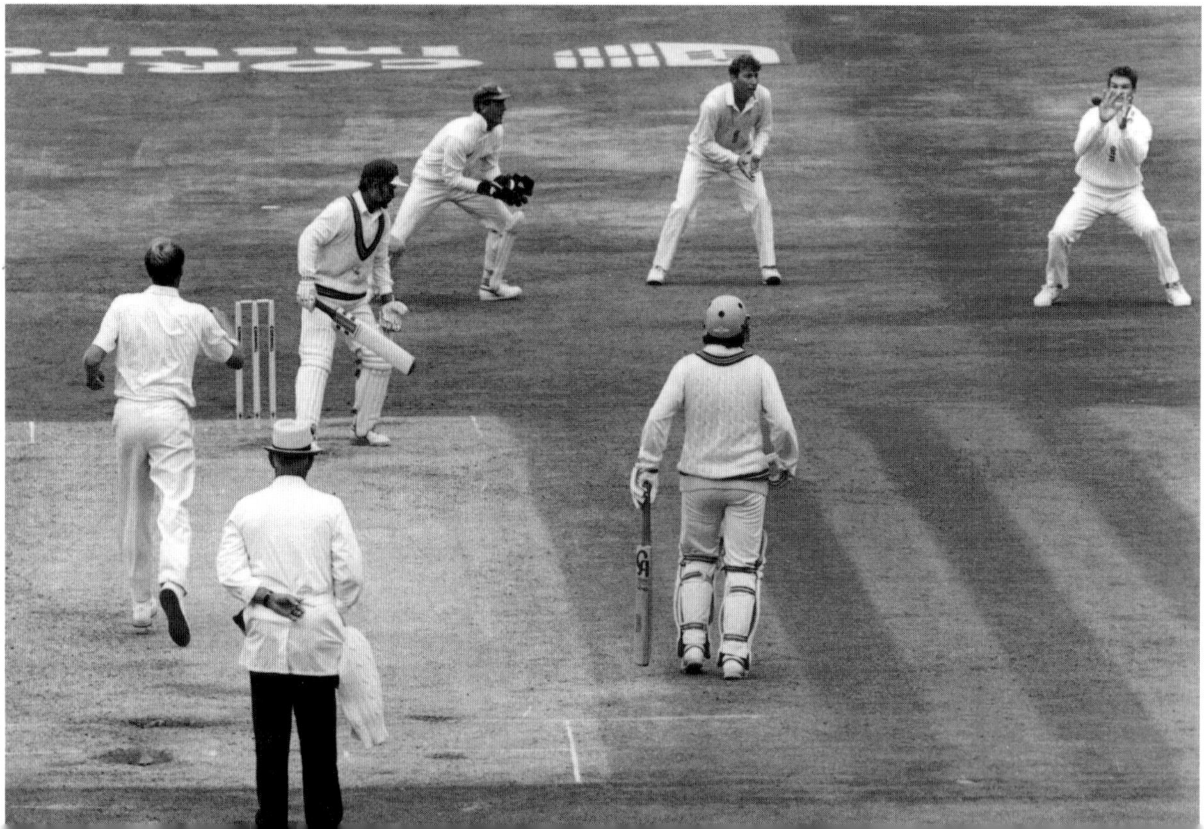

stumps shattered by Waqar's yorker, which also accounted for Lewis. Pringle offered no shot and was bowled, and Mallender fell to one that kept low. Munton spooned Mushtaq to silly point, and Gower was marooned on 18. Having looked forward to a lead of somewhere close to 250, England led by 123, and Pakistan were just back in the game.

It must be said that the Pakistanis felt somewhat aggrieved by decisions which had not gone in their favour, and one must give them some sympathy. Before the series began, they were convinced, rightly or wrongly, that they would not win the rubber because of the umpiring. This view festered as the series got underway. As Mike Brearley pointed out in a most intelligent and perceptive article in the *Observer*, there was a hint of 'subliminal prejudice' in the umpiring. This was, and is, not aimed solely at the Pakistanis, but at later order batsmen in contrast to those at the top of the order. Gooch, Atherton and Smith were given reprieves which were not given to Ramprakash or Lewis.

There was more cause for concern when Pakistan batted a second time. Aamir Sohail played wildly at a wide delivery, but Asif Mujtaba was adjudged caught at slip when the ball lobbed gently off his boot. The suggestion was that he got a faint inside edge onto his boot in going through with this shot. There was no doubt about Javed who played back and away from his body to give Stewart a straightforward catch. It was a very poor shot at any time. In the circumstances, it was unforgivable. Ramiz had batted purposefully and made 63 out 96 before flicking a catch to square-leg where Atherton dived to hold on to the ball. Two more runs were scored before the close, and the advantage was still very much with England.

Salim and Inzamam made certain that England would have to bat again when, on the fourth morning, they took the score to 147 before Inzamam was taken at short-leg off Pringle, who exploited the conditions admirably and bowled intelligently. He also accounted for Wasim Akram, who batted belligerently until he pulled a drive to mid-on. Moin stayed with Salim while 28 were added, but the rest of the tail disappointed. Once again, Salim Malik was left unbeaten. His 84 was another masterly innings, and no praise can be too high for his batting in this match.

The prized wicket of Javed Miandad, caught behind off Mallender for 4. (Patrick Eagar)

Pakistan were all out at ten past two, and England had a day and a half in which to score 99 to win. There were shivers of fear when two wickets fell at 27. Atherton was leg before, and Smith was splendidly taken low at mid-wicket. Had Gooch been given run out by umpire Ken Palmer, England's plight would have bordered on the desperate. The umpire ruled 'no' although television later cruelly informed that Gooch was more than a yard short of the line.

Gooch was finally taken at silly point, and Stewart pushed forward and edged to the keeper to cause a flutter of uncertainty, but Gower kept his head and Ramprakash thrashed to bring a welcome victory.

Gooch is caught by Asif Mujtaba off Mushtaq for 37, but England win by six wickets. (David Munden)

FOURTH CORNHILL TEST MATCH – ENGLAND v. PAKISTAN

23, 24, 25 and 26 July at Headingley, Leeds

PAKISTAN

	FIRST INNINGS		SECOND INNINGS	
Aamir Sohail	c Atherton, b Mallender	23	c Stewart, b Mallender	1
Ramiz Raja	b Pringle	17	c Atherton, b Munton	63
Asif Mujtaba	b Mallender	7	c Hick, b Mallender	11
Javed Miandad (capt)	c Smith, b Pringle	6	c Stewart, b Mallender	4
Salim Malik	not out	82	not out	84
Inzamam-ul-Haq	c Hick, b Munton	5	c Smith, b Pringle	19
Wasim Akram	run out	12	c Ramprakash, b Pringle	17
*Moin Khan	c Hick, b Lewis	2	c Hick, b Mallender	3
Waqar Younis	c Hick, b Mallender	6	(10) b Mallender	3
Mushtaq Ahmed	b Lewis	11	(9) lbw, b Pringle	0
Aqib Javed	c Hick, b Munton	0	run out	0
Extras	b 1, lb 2, w 7, nb 16	26	b 4, lb 1, w 2, nb 9	16
		197		221

	O	M	R	W	O	M	R	W
Lewis	23	6	48	2	16	3	55	–
Mallender	23	7	72	3	23	7	50	5
Pringle	17	6	41	2	19	2	66	3
Munton	10.3	3	22	2	10	–	40	1
Gooch	6	3	11	–	1	–	5	–

FALL OF WICKETS

1–34, 2–54, 3–60, 4–68, 5–80, 6–111, 7–117, 8–128, 9–192
1–11, 2–53, 3–64, 4–96, 5–147, 6–177, 7–205, 8–206, 9–213

ENGLAND

	FIRST INNINGS		SECOND INNINGS	
G.A. Gooch (capt)	b Mushtaq	135	c Asif, b Mushtaq	37
M.A. Atherton	b Wasim Akram	76	lbw, b Waqar Younis	5
R.A. Smith	c Javed, b Aqib	42	c sub (Zahid Fazal), b Waqar Younis	0
*A.J. Stewart	lbw, b Waqar Younis	8	(5) c Moin, b Mushtaq	2
D.I. Gower	not out	18	(4) not out	31
M.R. Ramprakash	lbw, b Mushtaq	0	not out	12
G.A. Hick	b Waqar Younis	1		
C.C. Lewis	lbw, b Waqar Younis	0		
D.R. Pringle	b Waqar Younis	0		
N.A. Mallender	b Waqar Younis	1		
T.A Munton	c Inzamam, b Mushtaq	0		
Extras	b 1, lb 15, w 1, nb 23	39	b 5, lb 3, nb 4	12
		320	(for 4 wickets)	99

	O	M	R	W	O	M	R	W
Wasim Akram	36	12	80	1	17	4	36	–
Aqib Javed	16	3	48	1				
Waqar Younis	30	3	117	5	12	2	28	2
Mushtaq Ahmed	29.5	6	60	3	13.4	3	27	2
Aamir Sohail	2	2	0	–				

FALL OF WICKETS

1–168, 2–170, 3–292, 4–298, 5–298, 6–303, 7–305, 8–305, 9–313
1–27, 2–27, 3–61, 4–65

Umpires: M.J. Kitchen & K.E. Palmer

England won by 6 wickets

24, 25 and 27 July *at Abergavenny*

Glamorgan 276 (H. Morris 71, A. Dale 67, G.D. Rose 4 for 59) and 308 for 5 dec. (H. Morris 117, M.P. Maynard 57)
Somerset 250 for 5 dec. (A.N. Hayhurst 70) and 293 for 8 (N.D. Burns 71 not out, G.D. Rose 50)

Match drawn

Somerset 7 pts., Glamorgan 5 pts.

at Cheltenham

Sussex 324 (N.J. Lenham 83, A.P. Wells 63, D.M. Smith 61, C.A. Walsh 4 for 39) and 242 for 9 dec. (N.J. Lenham 52, M.C.J. Ball 5 for 101)
Gloucestershire 221 (G.D. Hodgson 82, B.T.P. Donelan 6 for 77) and 346 for 6 (C.W.J. Athey 181, R.C. Russell 57)

Gloucestershire won by 4 wickets

Gloucestershire 22 pts., Sussex 8 pts.

at Leicester

Leicestershire 193 (T.J. Boon 58, N.A. Foster 4 for 47, M.C. Ilott 4 for 73) and 230 (N.E. Briers 61, T.J. Boon 52, S.J.W. Andrew 4 for 54)
Essex 75 and 280 (P.J. Prichard 106, D.J. Millns 5 for 67)

Leicestershire won by 68 runs

Leicestershire 21 pts., Essex 4 pts.

at Lord's

Middlesex 366 (M.A. Roseberry 173, M.W. Gatting 90, P.J. Berry 7 for 113) and 159 for 3 dec. (M.A. Roseberry 81)
Durham 232 (P.J. Berry 76, P.C.R. Tufnell 5 for 83, J.E. Emburey 4 for 94) and 118 (J.E. Emburey 5 for 43)

Middlesex won by 175 runs

Middlesex 23 pts., Durham 3 pts.

at Edgbaston

Nottinghamshire 415 for 7 dec. (R.T. Robinson 189, M. Saxelby 66, G.W. Mike 61 not out) and 197 for 3 dec. (P. Johnson 107 not out, R.T. Robinson 84)
Warwickshire 266 for 8 dec. and 229 (K.J. Piper 62 not out, D.P. Pennett 4 for 58)

Nottinghamshire won by 117 runs

Nottinghamshire 23 pts., Warwickshire 5 pts.

at Worcester

Derbyshire 246 (J.E. Morris 67, P.D. Bowler 50, R.K. Illingworth 4 for 56, S.R. Lampitt 4 for 57) and 285 for 2 dec. (C.J. Adams 140 not out, P.D. Bowler 100 not out)
Worcestershire 266 for 9 dec. (T.S. Curtis 86) and 162 for 3 (T.S. Curtis 96, W.P.C. Weston 50 not out)

Match drawn

Worcestershire 7 pts., Derbyshire 5 pts.

Hugh Morris hit his fourth championship hundred of the season and enabled Maynard to declare and set Somerset the task of scoring 335 in 67 overs. At 134 for 4, they were behind the asking rate, but a brisk fifty from Rose, and the aggression of Burns and Lefebvre brought a stronger challenge. Lefebvre was run out, and Watkin had Caddick caught behind so that eventually Burns and Trump held on for a draw and kept Glamorgan bottom of the table.

At Cheltenham, Gloucestershire managed a thrilling win over Sussex. The visitors scored freely on the opening day. Gloucestershire began well enough in reply, but the off-breaks of Donelan and the leg-spin of Salisbury brought about a collapse, and Sussex led by 103 on the first innings. They built on this, and Alan Wells was able to ask Gloucestershire to make 346 in what became 92 overs. Athey and Alleyne added 87 in 21 overs for the second wicket after Hodgson had retired hurt in the first over, and Wright had been dismissed at 38. The crucial stand, however, was that between Athey and Russell who added 180 for the fourth wicket. The partnership was broken when Athey, who made his highest score for Gloucestershire and hit 25 fours, was caught at long-leg. His formidable innings had taken his county to within 32 runs of victory, but Walsh was immediately bowled, and Russell was out at 321. Vaughan thumped 19, and Ball hit the first ball of the last over for four and victory.

The top-of-the-table clash at Leicester went in favour of the home side who chose to bat and were bundled out by the Essex pace attack. They found themselves batting again before the end of the first day on which 20 wickets fell. The Leicestershire seamers routed Essex in 23.4 overs, and the game seemed to be getting out of the visitors' reach when Leicestershire reached 170 for 2 in their second innings. Ilott, Waugh and Andrew led a revival, and Essex finally had the daunting task of making 349 to win. By the end of Saturday, that looked a distinct possibility as Prichard and Stephenson had scored 103. They were separated at 121, but Waugh and Prichard took the score to 184 with lunch in sight. Waugh, in his last championship game before joining the Australian side, was splendidly caught behind by Nixon. This was the first of four wickets to fall in 12 overs which reduced Essex to 212 for 5 and only token defiance to come. Prichard batted with his customary stylish discipline, but the bowling of Millns and Wells, in particular, and some fine fielding took Leicestershire to within 31 points of Essex.

Middlesex brushed aside Durham. Mike Roseberry hit a six and 13 fours in the highest score of his career while off-break bowler Phil Berry, formerly of Yorkshire had career bests with bat and ball. He also took all three Middlesex wickets to fall in the second innings to finish with match figures of 10 for 191. The spin combination of Tufnell and Emburey twice proved too much for the newcomers to first-class cricket.

Nottinghamshire maintained their championship challenge with a roistering win over Warwickshire. Robinson and Saxelby took the score from 102 for 4 to 254, and Mike, who hit a career best, helped Robinson to add 134 for the seventh wicket. Warwickshire declared as soon as the follow-on was avoided, and Johnson hit 107 off 66 balls from mostly friendly bowlers. The home side

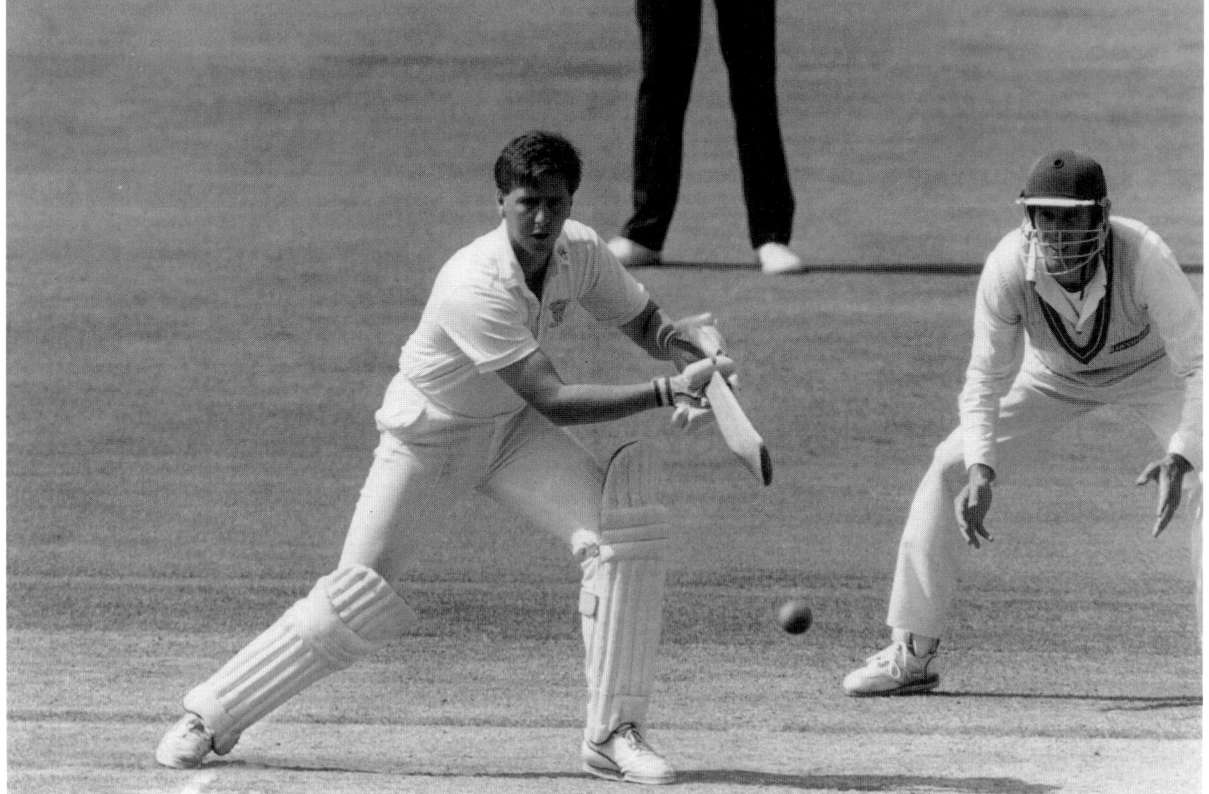

Phil Berry batting for Durham against Middlesex at Lord's, 24–27 July, the match in which Berry had career best performances with both bat and ball. (Jan Traylen/Patrick Eagar)

found the target of 347 beyond them as Pennett and Mike, two inexperienced seamers, did the initial damage. Pennett finished with the best figures of his short career.

At Worcester, the home side found a target of 266 in 51 overs beyond their ambition and settled for a draw after three batsmen had been stumped. Curtis and Philip Weston put on 156 for the first wicket. The excitement had come in the morning when, against some generous bowling, Bowler hit his sixth championship hundred of the summer and Chris Adams hit the fastest century in Derbyshire's history, 57 minutes. He hit six sixes and 20 fours.

SUNDAY LEAGUE

26 August *at Pontypridd*

Glamorgan 246 for 2 (I.V.A. Richards 109 not out, H. Morris 104 not out)
Derbyshire 30 for 0

Match abandoned

Glamorgan 2 pts., Derbyshire 2 pts.

at Cheltenham

Gloucestershire 232 for 6 (C.W.J. Athey 105)
Sussex 140

Gloucestershire (4 pts.) won by 92 runs

at Old Trafford

Surrey 168 for 9
Lancashire 100 for 2

Lancashire (4 pts.) won on faster scoring rate

at Leicester

Kent 245 for 7 (N.R. Taylor 71)
Leicestershire 183 for 8 (M.J. McCague 4 for 35)

Kent (4 pts.) won by 62 runs

at Lord's

Durham 198 for 7
Middlesex 202 for 3 (D.L. Haynes 70)

Middlesex (4 pts.) won by 7 wickets

at Taunton

Somerset 236 for 6 (R.J. Harden 53)
Northamptonshire 176

Somerset (4 pts.) won by 60 runs

at Edgbaston

Warwickshire 262 for 4 (D.P. Ostler 60 not out, A.J. Moles 55, R.G. Twose 54)
Nottinghamshire 183 for 4 (R.T. Robinson 54)

Warwickshire (4 pts.) won on faster scoring rate

at Worcester

Worcestershire 176 for 5 (T.M. Moody 53)
Hampshire 177 for 4

Hampshire (4 pts.) won by 6 wickets

There was something of a monotony about the Sunday League as, with Essex idle, Middlesex won their 12th match in succession and took an eight-point lead at the top of the table. This meant that Essex were the only side capable of overtaking them although most sides had four matches to play. The unluckiest side of the day was Glamorgan. Viv Richards hit 109 off 88 balls, and he and Morris added 194 in 25 overs against Derbyshire, and then came the rain.

29 and 30 July *at Marlow*

Pakistanis 226 (Zahid Fazal 93, Waqar Younis 57, G.S. Calway 4 for 30) and 198 for 3 dec. (Shoaib Mohammad 63 not out)
Minor Counties 175 for 2 dec. (N.A. Folland 84 not out) and 252 for 9 (I. Cockbain 87 not out, G.S. Calway 57, Mushtaq Ahmed 6 for 43)

Minor Counties won by 1 wicket

29 July *at Jesmond*

Rest of the World XI 319 for 6 (S.R. Tendulkar 100, D.N. Patel 58 not out)
England XI 320 for 6 (J.E. Morris 72, C.C. Lewis 66)

England XI won by 4 wickets

30 July *at Jesmond*

England XI 272 for 8 (N.H. Fairbrother 84)
Rest of World XI 232 (D.L. Haynes 52)

England XI won by 40 run

NATWEST TROPHY

QUARTER-FINALS

29 July *at Swansea*

Northamptonshire 224 for 8 (R.J. Bailey 98 not out)
Glamorgan 141

Northamptonshire won by 83 runs

(Man of the Match – R.J. Bailey)

at Cheltenham

Gloucestershire 236 for 7 (C.W.J. Athey 59, J.T.C. Vaughan 54 not out)
Essex 240 for 4 (G.A. Gooch 105 not out, P.J. Prichard 58)

Essex won by 6 wickets

(Man of the Match – G.A. Gooch

at Leicester

Leicestershire 249 (J.J. Whitaker 63)
Durham 204 (P.W.G. Parker 54)

Leicestershire won by 45 runs

(Man of the Match – J.D.R. Benson)

at Edgbaston

Warwickshire 224 (A.J. Moles 76)
Kent 161 (M.R. Benson 57)

Warwickshire won by 63 runs

(Man of the Match – G.C. Small)

Northamptonshire reached the semi-final of the NatWest Trophy for the third year in succession although their win over Glamorgan was not as easy as it may appear. A low, slow pitch made run-getting a difficult task, and Rob Bailey held the Northamptonshire innings together with a gritty, disciplined knock. Responsibility rested heavily upon him when Dale dismissed Lamb with his first delivery, the Northants captain dragging the ball onto his own wicket. Bailey faced 161 balls and hit a six and six fours. Glamorgan did not start well, and they lost Richards for 2. They needed 130 from the last 20 overs, but when Maynard was sixth out after making 41 off 58 balls their hopes disappeared. Capel and Ambrose bowled particularly well for the visitors.

At the beautiful College ground in Cheltenham, Essex gave a highly professional performance and won with 17 balls to spare. Gloucestershire chose to bat first and found the going hard against some very accurate bowling. Hodgson and Athey put on 51 for the first wicket, but it occupied 23 overs and included only two fours. Foster dismissed Hodgson in what was his 12th and last over. The following day, Foster was to have an exploratory operation on his knee and did not play again in the season. Wright was bowled by Topley for 10, and, at lunch, Gloucestershire were 112 for 2 from 39 overs, Athey having reached his fifty-two overs earlier. This seemed a reasonable platform for a good score, but, in the 42nd over, Alleyne was caught and bowled by Stephenson. In the next over, a dreaming Scott was run out by Waugh, and Athey's long innings came to an end in the 44th over to leave Gloucestershire at 128 for 5. Russell and Walsh hit briefly, but the real boost to the innings came from Vaughan and Ball who scored 53 from the last six overs as the Essex fielding became ragged and the bowling lacking in concentration. Vaughan batted with admirable enthusiasm and skill.

The Essex innings had a surprise beginning. Gooch was most unhappy against Walsh while Stephenson was supremely confident. In the sixth over, with the score on 22, a ball from Babington was half-hit by Stephenson and went through to Russell. Gooch called for an impossible run, and Stephenson was forced to offer himself for self-sacrifice. Gooch became introspective, but Prichard was not. At tea, Essex were 110 for 1 from

25 overs, and in the ten overs after the break, Gooch scored just seven. His fifty came in the 35th over by which time both Prichard, who played with flair and correctness, and Waugh, in his last innings for Essex, were out. Hussain hit hard, but once too often, as 66 were added in 16 overs. Gooch was now firing on all cylinders. He reached his hundred with a six off Walsh in the 57th over, and Essex were in the semi-finals. Gooch became the first man to win nine awards in the 60-over competition, but an award should also go to Cheltenham and the Gloucestershire club for the excellent facilities provided for the paying customers. Would that all grounds showed such concern for those who watch.

There was a great blow for Leicestershire when they lost the services of David Millns with an injured foot shortly before the start of the match against Durham. Millns had been in fine form and was being widely tipped for a place in the England side at The Oval. Benson took his place against Durham and proceeded to play such a significant part in his county's victory that he took the individual award. Put in to bat, Leicestershire soon lost Briers, but they were lifted when Whitaker and Robinson added 74 for the third wicket. Equally important was the stand of 62 in 12 overs between Potter and Benson who hit 42. At 99 for 1, Durham were in a good position, but Larkins then drove Benson to long-on, and the same bowler had the veteran Geoff Cook, in the side because of injuries to others, stumped. When Botham was insanely run out in a mix-up with Parker, Durham were on a slide, and they were never able to apply the breaks.

At Edgbaston, there was rather a dire struggle which was won most comfortably, with 7.1 overs to spare, by Warwickshire. Theirs was more of a solid team performance with adequate and consistent batting which was never inspired. As Small and Donald removed Ward, Taylor, Hooper and Cowdrey with only 35 scored, Kent were never able to make a fight of the game not to provide it with any batting of distinction. They limped to 102 for 7 and succumbed with only the briefest of flourishes.

31 July, 1 and 2 August *at Taunton*

Somerset 356 (C.J. Tavaré 99, A.N. Hayhurst 86, M.N. Lathwell 55, R.J. Harden 52, I.D.K. Salisbury 5 for 61) and 232 for 7 dec. (C.J. Tavaré 55)

Sussex 310 for 7 dec. (M.P. Speight 122, A.P. Wells 103) and 159 for 4 (J.W. Hall 73 not out)

Match drawn

Sussex 8 pts., Somerset 7 pts.

31 July, 1 and 3 August *at Durham University*

Durham 189 (J.E. Benjamin 6 for 30) and 357 (I. Smith 74, M.P. Bicknell 5 for 120)

Surrey 431 (A.D. Brown 175, P.D. Atkins 60) and 116 for 3 (G.P. Thorpe 60 not out)

Surrey won by 7 wickets

Surrey 24 pts., Durham 4 pts.

Tim Boon is stumped by Fothergill, but Leicestershire went on to beat Durham in the NatWest Trophy quarter-final. (David Munden)

at Swansea

Glamorgan 354 for 7 dec. (S.P. James 91, R.D.B. Croft 60 not out) and 255 for 4 dec. (M.P. Maynard 113 not out, P.A. Cottey 65 not out)
Kent 300 for 6 dec. (C.L. Hooper 100, T.R. Ward 85) and 273 (T.R. Ward 118, R.D.B. Croft 6 for 112)

Glamorgan won by 36 runs

Glamorgan 21 pts., Kent 6 pts.

at Edgbaston

Warwickshire 433 for 7 dec. (R.G. Twose 233, A.J. Moles 91, T.L. Penney 50 not out, A.D. Mullally 5 for 119)
Leicestershire 169 (L. Potter 56, T.A. Munton 5 for 46) and 140 (T.A. Munton 7 for 64)

Warwickshire won by an innings and 124 runs

Warwickshire 24 pts., Leicestershire 1 pt.

at Headingley

Lancashire 399 for 8 dec. (N.H. Fairbrother 166 not out, N.J. Speak 59, G.D. Lloyd 56, P. Carrick 4 for 129) and 182 for 3 dec. (M.A. Atherton 53 not out)
Yorkshire 300 for 3 dec. (S.A. Kellett 91, M.D. Moxon 90, S.R. Tendulkar 56 not out) and 283 for 6 (S.A. Kellett 89, R.J. Blakey 63)

Yorkshire won by 4 wickets

Yorkshire 23 pts., Lancashire 5 pts.

1, 2 and 3 August *at Chelmsford*

Essex 357 for 9 dec. (G.A. Gooch 141, N. Shahid 86 not out, Wasim Akram 4 for 102) and 188 (J.J.B. Lewis 55, Wasim Akram 4 for 48)
Pakistanis 353 for 6 dec. (Salim Malik 153 not out, Javed Miandad 91, Shoaib Mohammad 50) and 196 for 3 (Asif Mujtaba 62 not out, Salim Malik 50)

Pakistanis won by 7 wickets

One must ponder as to why, over what was for many a holiday weekend, there were only five county matches scheduled whereas, the following mid-week with the fifth Test match depriving counties of leading players, there was a full programme of nine games.

At Taunton, Somerset began well against Sussex. For the most part, they scored briskly, and Tavaré, in search of his first century of the season, hit ten fours before being caught at slip off Salisbury for 99. Salisbury bowled his leg-breaks well, and there was unflagging endeavour from Stephenson and Giddins. On the Saturday, Alan Wells and Martin Speight added 161 in 37 overs for the fourth wicket. Both men found the boundary regularly and batted with great purpose. The final day was a disappointment. Somerset faltered and Sussex found the task of scoring 279 in 52 overs beyond their capabilities and ambitions.

Joey Benjamin had the best bowling figures of his career, and Durham were bowled out for 189 on the opening day against Surrey. To compound the home side's misery, Alistair Brown hit the second successive hundred of his very short first-class career, making a sizzling 120 off 88 balls before the end of the day. There was no respite for Durham on the second morning as Brown continued to flog the bowling, his 175 came off 164 balls. It was a brilliant innings, giving immense pleasure to all who saw it. A first-innings lead of 242 put Surrey in an impregnable position, and they continued to prosper as Durham slipped to 58 for 3. A fifth-wicket stand of 89 between Botham and Smith ended early on the last morning, but there was a last-wicket stand of 80 between Graveney and Simon Brown, a career best 47 not out, to delay Surrey's fourth championship win of the season.

Alistair Brown gained a regular place in the Surrey side in late July and played several outstanding attacking innings. He launched a violent assault on the Durham bowlers and scored 175, 31 July–2 August. (Sporting Pictures (UK) Ltd)

Glamorgan found run-scoring hard on the first day against Kent. James provided the backbone of their innings, batting five-and-a-quarter hours for his 91. Maynard declared ten minutes before lunch on the second day after rain had delayed the start. The Kent innings was a great contrast. Ward and Taylor hit 118 in 26 overs for the second wicket, and then came Hooper's glorious 100 off 75 balls with two sixes and 13 fours. With some fireworks from Fleming, Kent reached 300 in 56.1 overs. Joke bowling on the Monday morning allowed Glamorgan to add 112 runs in five overs to their score, and enabled Maynard to set Kent the task of scoring 310 from 64 overs. Maynard himself had hit 34 in one over. Ward started Kent's challenge at a furious rate and had hit four sixes and 14 fours before charging fatally at Barwick and being stumped. No one could give him adequate support, and the most impressive off-spin of Croft accounted for five of the first six wickets. In spite of bravery from Ellison and Davis, Glamorgan claimed their second win of the season.

Leicestershire's championship dreams suffered a dreadful awakening at Edgbaston. Moles and Twose began the Warwickshire innings with a partnership of 285. Twose, whose rise to eminence had begun in New Zealand, ended the day on 233, and Leicestershire had only two wickets. Twose hit 29 fours and two sixes in what was his first century in the championship. He did not add to his score on the Saturday by the end of which Leicestershire were 60 for 4 in their second innings. There was no reprieve. Munton finished with match figures of 12 for 110, a career best, and Leicestershire finished with one point as Warwickshire moved into third place.

Neil Fairbrother hit his first century for more than a year, a buoyant affair, as Lancashire scored 399 on the first day against Yorkshire. Moxon and Kellett responded with an opening partnership of 169, and Moxon declared as soon as his side had taken four batting points. Eventually asked to make 282 in 59 overs, Yorkshire owed much to Kellett and Blakey who added 121 for the fourth wicket. There was a slight panic towards the close, but they won with eight balls to spare.

Gooch hit his fifth century in six innings in all types of cricket for Essex as they took on the Pakistanis at Chelmsford. He and Stephenson shared an opening partnership of 99 before Stephenson was bemused by Mushtaq Ahmed's googly. Shahid apart, the rest of the Essex side was uneasy against the mixture of pace and spin, and Wasim's later burst caused mayhem. A dynamic innings from Salim Malik, who shared a stand of 133 for the fourth wicket with Javed, brought the tourists to near parity. Wasim bowled Gooch on the Sunday evening, and the same combination of pace and spin duly helped the Pakistanis to their eighth win of the tour and the £50,000 jackpot provided by Tetley Bitter.

At Edgbaston, Warwickshire beat Leicestershire by an innings and 124 runs, 31 July–2 August, to keep alive their championship hopes. One of their heroes was Tim Munton who had career best match figures of 12 for 110. Here he has Nixon caught at slip by Moles. (Philip Wilcox)

SUNDAY LEAGUE

2 August *at Leek*

Warwickshire 204 (T.A. Lloyd 50)
Derbyshire 208 for 2 (C.J. Adams 75 not out, J.E. Morris 68 not out)

Derbyshire (4 pts.) won by 8 wickets

at Durham University

Surrey 330 for 6 (D.J. Bicknell 125, A.D. Brown 75)
Durham 230 for 7 (M.P. Briers 69, I.T. Botham 52)

Surrey (4 pts.) won by 100 runs

at Swansea

Kent 263 for 8 (M.R. Benson 64)
Glamorgan 216 for 9 (S.P. James 69, H. Morris 67, M.J. McCague 4 for 41)

Kent (4 pts.) won by 47 runs

at Southampton

Middlesex 181 for 7 (D.L. Haynes 77)
Hampshire 182 for 5 (T.C. Middleton 64 not out)

Hampshire (4 pts.) won by 5 wickets

at Trent Bridge

Leicestershire 244 for 8 (P.A. Nixon 60, C.L. Cairns 4 for 30)
Nottinghamshire 248 for 3 (M.A. Crawley 94 not out, D.W. Randall 91)

Nottinghamshire (4 pts.) won by 7 wickets

at Worcester

Gloucestershire 174 for 8 (M.W. Alleyne 55)
Worcestershire 175 for 4 (T.S. Curtis 70)

Worcestershire (4 pts.) won by 6 wickets

at Leeds

Lancashire 264 for 3 (N.J. Speak 102 not out, N.H. Fairbrother 64 not out)
Yorkshire 260 for 6 (S.R. Tendulkar 107, R.J. Blakey 86)

Lancashire (4 pts.) won by 4 runs

3 August *at Hove*

Sussex 206 for 7 (J.W. Hall 58, P. Moores 57)
Hampshire 210 for 2 (T.C. Middleton 78 not out, R.A. Smith 55)

Hampshire (4 pts.) won by 8 wickets

By beating Middlesex at Southampton, Hampshire breathed some life into the Sunday League. Roseberry, Gatting and Carr all failed to reach double figures and left Middlesex below par for the pitch. Hampshire batted with reasonable consistency and won with an over to spare. Hampshire had the unique distinction of winning two 'Sunday' League games in two days when they trounced Sussex on the Monday. McCague performed the hat-trick as Kent beat Glamorgan. Darren Bicknell and Alistair Brown started Surrey's overwhelming of Durham with a partnership of 117, and Chris Adams was again in violent mood for Derbyshire as he and John Morris added 128 in 12 overs against Warwickshire without being separated. Sachin Tendulkar hit his first century for Yorkshire, and he and Blakey hit 176 in 24 overs. Yorkshire then lost their way, and 17 were needed from DeFreitas' last over. Ten came off the first five balls, but Jarvis' attempt to hit the last ball for six ended short of the line and produced only two.

4, 5 and 6 August *at Ilkeston*

Derbyshire 268 (D.G. Cork 56, J.E. Morris 50, W.K.M. Benjamin 4 for 55, R.P. Gofton 4 for 81) and 264 for 3 dec. (K.J. Barnett 117 not out, J.E. Morris 107)
Leicestershire 160 (N.E. Briers 73 not out, F.A. Griffith 4 for 33) and 223

Derbyshire won by 139 runs

Derbyshire 23 pts., Leicestershire 5 pts.

at Durham University

Durham 214 (W. Larkins 67, M.A. Robinson 6 for 57) and 155 (C.W. Scott 64, P.W. Jarvis 4 for 43, M.A. Robinson 4 for 44)
Yorkshire 108 (S.P. Hughes 5 for 25, I.T. Botham 4 for 72) and 263 for 5 (S.R. Tendulkar 100)

Yorkshire won by 5 wickets

Yorkshire 20 pts., Durham 6 pts.

at Chelmsford

Northamptonshire 444 for 9 dec. (A.J. Lamb 83, A. Fordham 65, D.J. Capel 61, N.A. Felton 51, P.M. Such 5 for 114)
Essex 273 (N.V. Knight 69, J.P. Stephenson 64, N. Hussain 52) and 158 (N.G.B. Cook 7 for 34)

Northamptonshire won by an innings and 13 runs

Northamptonshire 23 pts., Essex 5 pts.

at Canterbury

Kent 369 (T.R. Ward 150, G.R. Cowdrey 76 not out, C.L. Hooper 65) and 242 for 7 dec. (G.R. Cowdrey 60, S.A. Marsh 52 not out)
Middlesex 331 for 9 dec. (J.C. Pooley 69) and 229 for 6 (M.W. Gatting 102 not out, D.L. Haynes 68)

Match drawn

Middlesex 8 pts., Kent 7 pts.

at Lytham

Lancashire 376 for 3 dec. (J.P. Crawley 172, N.J. Speak 95, N.H. Fairbrother 66 not out) and 167 for 5 dec. (G.D. Lloyd 59, N.M. Kendrick 4 for 46)
Surrey 253 for 2 dec. (D.J. Bicknell 120 not out, G.P. Thorpe 66) and 204 (A.D. Brown 62, M.P. Bicknell 58 not out, M. Watkinson 4 for 60)

Lancashire won by 86 runs

Lancashire 20 pts., Surrey 3 pts.

at Worksop

Gloucestershire 335 (C.W.J. Athey 133, R.J. Scott 65, J.T.C. Vaughan 50, E.E. Hemmings 4 for 78) and 112 (E.E. Hemmings 4 for 30)
Nottinghamshire 302 for 8 dec. (C.L. Cairns 107 not out, P. Johnson 98) and 135 (C.A. Walsh 5 for 33)

Gloucestershire won by 10 runs

Gloucestershire 21 pts., Nottinghamshire 6 pts.

at Taunton

Somerset 278 (K.H. MacLeay 74) and 264 for 9 M.N. Lathwell 71, N.D. Burns 68, P.A. Booth 4 for 29)
Warwickshire 276 (T.L. Penney 89, T.A. Lloyd 50) and 260 for 9

Match drawn

Somerset 7 pts., Warwickshire 6 pts.

at Eastbourne

Sussex 360 (M.P. Speight 179, F.D. Stephenson 80, S.L. Watkin 4 for 92) and 192 for 8 dec. (A.P. Wells 74 not out)
Glamorgan 281 for 8 dec. (I.D.K. Salisbury 4 for 75) and 199 for 5 (H. Morris 104 not out)

Match drawn

Sussex 7 pts., Glamorgan 7 pts.

at Worcester

Worcestershire 335 for 9 dec. (P.J. Newport 60, I.J. Turner 4 for 103) and 178 for 3 dec. (G.A. Hick 63, W.P.C. Weston 53 not out)
Hampshire 261 for 8 dec. (M.D. Marshall 58) and 251 for 6 (V.P. Terry 113, M.C.J. Nicholas 71)

Match drawn

Worcestershire 6 pts., Hampshire 6 pts.

Having reached the semi-finals of the NatWest Trophy and moved into a position to challenge Essex in the championship, Leicestershire appeared suddenly to have gone into reverse. They bowled efficiently enough on the opening day at Ilkeston to dismiss Derbyshire for 268, but on the second day they wilted and lost their last eight wickets for 60 runs. Skipper Nigel Briers carried his bat through the 59.1 overs of the innings for 73. Barnett and Morris then showed that the pitch held no terrors as they added 180 for the second wicket. Asked to make 363 in 91 overs, Leicestershire offered no resistance and sank to a second massive defeat in succession.

The decline of Durham continued. Electing to bat when they won the toss, they slid from 114 for 1 to 214 all out as Mark Robinson returned the best bowling figures of his career and Paul Jarvis gave able support. Yorkshire's joy was short-lived as they were bowled out for 108 by Hughes and Botham, but Durham failed to benefit from the reprieve their bowlers had given them. They were 68 for 8 before Scott and Graveney put on 86. Robinson finished with match figures of 10 for 101, and Yorkshire sighted victory as they moved to 85 for 2 by the close. On the last day, Tendulkar hit a century off 96 balls. His runs came out of 155 scored while he was at the crease, and he hit 16 exquisitely executed fours to assure his side of victory.

Mark Robinson, ten wickets for Yorkshire against Durham, 4–6 August, and a highly successful season. (David Munden)

The beautiful Durham University ground with the cathedral in the background. Sachin Tendulkar plays a ball from Botham on his way to his first century in first-class cricket for Yorkshire, 4–6 August. (Ken Kelly)

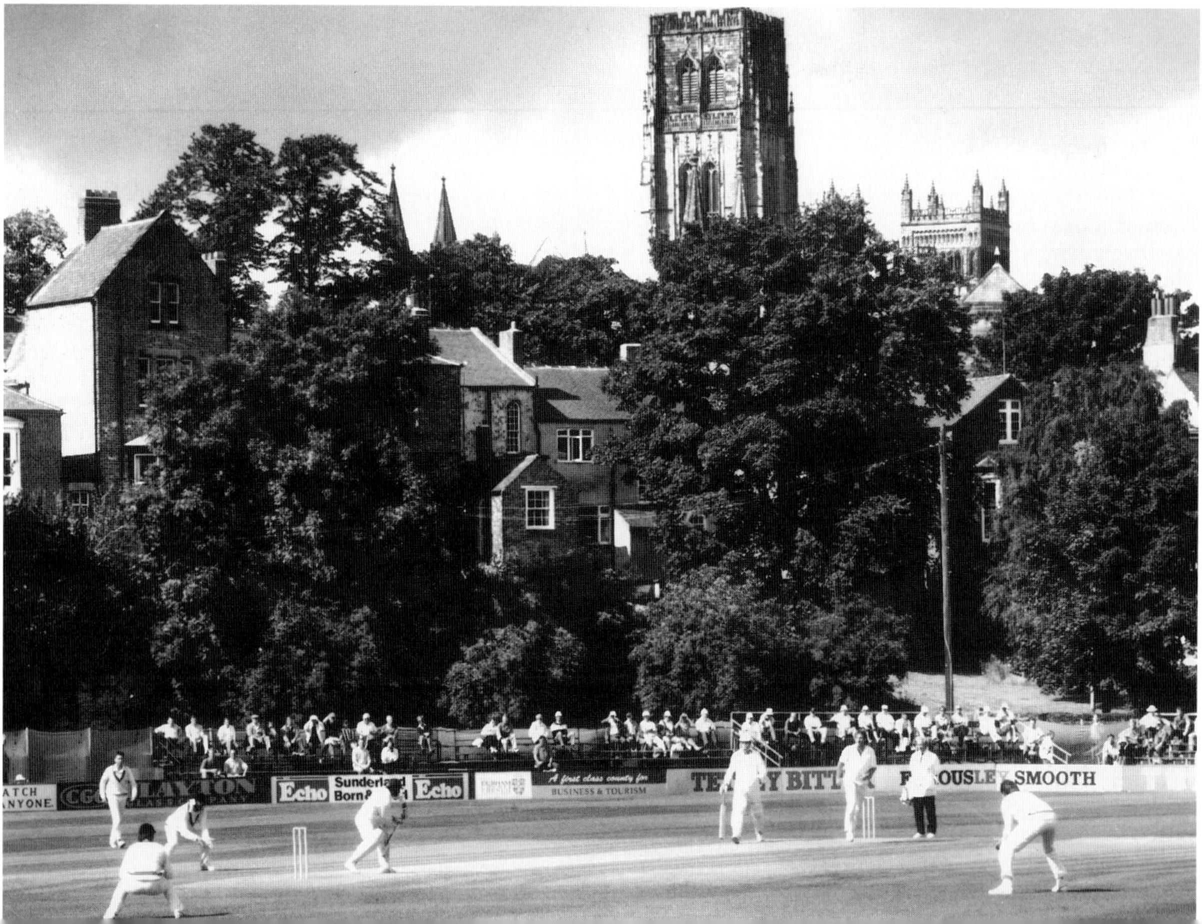

Cricket at Canterbury. (Sporting Pictures (UK) Ltd)

Allan Lamb's statement that Northamptonshire still had a chance of winning the championship gained some credibility when his side beat Essex by an innings. He refused to accept the pitch originally selected for the match at Chelmsford, won the toss and saw his side bat with consistency and vigour to reach 366 for 7 on the opening day. There was more lusty hitting by Ambrose on the second morning before Lamb declared. Essex started positively with Prichard and Stephenson scoring 113 for the first wicket. Three men were out quickly before Hussain and Knight added 88. Hussain drove rashly at Penberthy and was superbly caught at slip by Lamb. Knight stayed until the end of the day, but he was out early on the second morning, and Essex narrowly failed to save the follow-on. On a pitch now offering generous help to spin, they collapsed before Nick Cook who had his best return in 14 seasons of cricket. Northamptonshire moved to fifth place in the table, but Essex still led Leicestershire and Warwickshire by 30 points.

At Canterbury, there was another fine innings from Trevor Ward whose 150 came off 196 balls. He and Hooper added 160 for the third wicket at five runs an over. At one time on the second day, Middlesex, 158 for 5, were in some danger of having to follow-on, but Jason Pooley, given all too few first team opportunities, played soundly and sensibly for 69, and his side reached a healthy total. It soon became apparent that the game would end in a last-day run-chase, and Middlesex were set 281 in 49 overs. With 13 overs remaining, they had eight wickets standing and needed 89 to win. The scene changed as four wickets fell in five overs, and Gatting, unbeaten on 102 off 92 balls, saw his side thwarted.

John Crawley batted almost all of the first day at Lytham, faced 345 balls, hit 18 fours and made the highest score of his career, 172. It was a studious rather than brilliant innings, but it was a remarkable achievement for this talented young man who shared stands of 161 with Speak, and 152 with Fairbrother. Surrey found equal enjoyment in the pitch on the second day which rain reduced to two sessions. Darren Bicknell hit a six and ten fours in his second first-class hundred of the season, and, on the last day, Surrey were asked to make 291 in 66 overs. By the 32nd over, they were 83 for 5, hope of victory gone. Brown and Martin Bicknell added 89 in 16 overs before four wickets fell in six overs. Boiling stayed with Martin Bicknell for nearly 11 overs, but Watkinson had Boiling caught behind with 13 balls of the match remaining.

With two games in hand of Essex, Nottinghamshire, just 32 points adrift of the leaders, seemed the side most likely to stop the reigning champions from retaining the title. On a dour first day at Worksop, Athey and Scott put on 167 for the fourth wicket, and Gloucestershire reached 295 for 6. They were pepped up somewhat by an eighth-wicket stand of 92 between Vaughan and Ricardo Williams, who hit a career best 44. The home county were 107 for 5 before Johnson found an ally in Cairns. The pair added 147 in 27 overs, and the New Zealander all-rounder reached his second century of the season off 111 balls. He hit three sixes and 16 fours. Hemmings and Evans then bowled Nottinghamshire into a winning position, for a target of

146 in 45 overs did not seem too demanding even on a pitch which was giving help to the bowlers. The loss of three leading batsmen for eight runs undermined the Nottinghamshire innings. Robinson, Randall and Crawley made 108 between them, but no one else reached double figures, and Walsh bowled Gloucestershire to victory by ten runs.

Both Hayhurst and Harden were forced to retire hurt at Taunton after being hit by Donald who bowled at a great pace. Warwickshire let slip the advantage that they seemed to have at one time, and their frustration became greater when they failed by seven runs to reach a target of 267 in 60 overs. Indeed, at the end, they were happy to draw.

The constantly impressive Martin Speight hit the highest score of his career for Sussex against Glamorgan at Eastbourne. He hit 25 fours and shared a stand of 137 with Moores, and one of 137 with Stephenson. Glamorgan kept in touch on the second day and claimed three Sussex wickets cheaply before the close. Needing 272 in 54 overs on the last afternoon, Glamorgan fell well short in spite of Morris' excellent century, and Sussex could not take wickets.

Worcestershire batted with a certain lack of adventure against Hampshire and declared on the second morning. Hampshire batted more positively, and Nicholas forfeited a fourth batting point in an attempt to keep the game alive. Curtis set a target of 254 in 61 overs. Nicholas hit 71 off 73 balls as he and Terry added 126 in 19 overs, but Terry, after a splendidly attacking 113, was bowled off the last ball of the match as he attempted to hit Newport for the winning four.

FIFTH TEST MATCH
ENGLAND v. PAKISTAN, at The Oval

Rashid Latif, who fielded as substitute at Headingley, was fined for showing dissent by throwing down his cap when an appeal was rejected in the fourth Test. Moin Khan was not charged, although there were suggestions from some quarters that he had scuffed up the pitch at Headingley. Rashid replaced Moin for the fifth Test at The Oval so winning his first Test cap. Pakistan made one other change, bringing in the dependable Shoaib Mohammad for the exciting Inzamam-ul-Haq who had not fulfilled his great promise.

England dropped Hick and Munton, and retained Ramprakash. Malcolm returned, as did Phil Tufnell, who had missed much of the season through illness but was showing good form in county matches. Neil Mallender, the hero of Headingley with match figures of 8 for 123 on his debut, and the equally impressive Pringle were retained although some felt that Salisbury should have been recalled to bowl at The Oval.

Gooch won the toss, and England batted. Five runs came from Wasim's first over, and Waqar bowled one over for three runs. By the end of the third over in which Gooch swatted Wasim for the first four of the match, England had scored 15, and it was left to Aqib Javed to halt the scoring with the day's first maiden. It was also Aqib who separated the openers, Gooch lobbing the ball to short-leg in the 12th over. Three overs later, Stewart was the unwise victim of over-indulgence. He had carved a short-pitched ball from Wasim to the cover boundary, but, intoxicated, he rashly tried to hook with two men back and was caught at deep backward square-leg. Lunch arrived with England 89 for 2 off 27 overs, Smith 12, Atherton 17.

Derek Pringle had his stumps wrecked by Wasim Akram twice in the match. (Patrick Eagar)

Malcolm shatters Ramiz's stumps. (Patrick Eagar)

In the post-lunch period, Smith became becalmed, enduring hardships against the pace of Wasim and the delightful wrist spin of Mushtaq. He survived until the tea interval was approaching and then lost patience to Mushtaq, charged down the wicket and was bowled between bat and pad. Had he not been bowled, he would surely have been stumped by the impressive Rashid. Gower could make no contact with the first six balls he received, but he hung on, and at tea, England were 149 for 3.

Suddenly, it seemed that Gower would bring elegance and panache to the England innings. Atherton completed a grim, but worthy, fifty in the third over after tea. It was an innings of great determination, but one begged for some light at the other end. Just as there were suggestions that Gower would provide this light, he chopped on to Aqib Javed. England were now 182 for 4, and the rot had set in. The last six wickets were to go down in eight overs for 17 runs.

The arch-destroyer was Wasim Akram who, in the space of 22 balls, took five wickets for eight runs. Ramprakash was leg before to a full pitch. Lewis played back and around a break-back, and, in the same over, Pringle was bowled by a yorker which swung late and could be deemed unplayable.

Atherton's 190-ball innings came to an end when he pushed at a rather wide delivery from Waqar Younis. One should pause for a moment to give praise to Atherton. He had missed the tours of both New Zealand and of West Indies with the 'A' side because of a back injury, but he had fought back with great resolution and technical competence. He provides England with a much-needed stability.

Two runs and one over after the fall of Atherton, Wasim Akram bowled Mallender with a ball of full length, and in his next over, he wrecked Malcolm's stumps. On a blameless wicket, in ideal batting conditions, England had been bowled out for 207, and we had witnessed fast bowling of the highest quality and some batting that was palpably short of international standards. In five overs before the close, with Smith behind the stumps in place of Stewart who had bruised his foot in taking a ball from Wasim on the in-step, Pakistan scored 16.

There were great efforts on the part of England to remain in the game on the second day, but Pakistan ended it with a lead of 68 and six wickets in hand. Mallender could find neither the length nor the direction that he had found at Headingley, but The Oval was less conducive to his type of bowling than Leeds had been. Tufnell bowled well, but it would have been easier for him had he had spin support at the other end – the Cricket Writers' Club Young Cricketer of the Year, Ian Salisbury, for example, or Robert Croft – and the selection of Pringle, who was neither fully fit nor suitable for The Oval, was hard to justify.

Pakistan went along quite merrily, Aamir Sohail hitting ten fours, until Malcolm was summoned at mid-day. He had bowled two wayward overs on the Thursday evening, and he now delivered the widest of wides, but in his second over, he fired a very fast, straight ball of full length at Ramiz and scattered his stumps. He also accounted for Aamir Sohail who edged very low to Stewart and was given out after the umpires had consulted.

At lunch, Pakistan were 100 for 2, and between lunch and tea, Shoaib and Javed added 89 in 29 overs. Javed should have fallen to Tufnell. He went down the wicket to the Middlesex spinner and was beaten by the flight and the turn. Stewart swept the ball across the stumps and failed to take off the bails with Javed well out of his ground. He removed them at the second attempt, but by then Shepherd was wagging his finger, not raising it. Stewart was being asked to do two things for England that he does not do for his county, open and keep wicket, and the price you can pay for a non-specialist keeper is high.

In this case, it was not excessive, for, after tea, with the score on 197, Javed drove straight and ankle high to the bowler Lewis whose claim for a catch was upheld. Javed had every right to wait for the umpires' decision, for, even with the aid of a television replay, it was hard to discern whether or not the ball had carried. Nevertheless, Javed was booed as he left the field. The British public had been well brainwashed, and Javed's reputation as a dissenter was well secured.

Having held the innings together for 200 minutes, Shoaib gave Tufnell a return catch, and a deserved wicket. Salim and Asif Mujtaba were sometimes beaten, but they scored 61 in the last-hour-and-a-half of the day.

Salim Malik was soon out on the Saturday morning, Malcolm just trimming off his bail, and, six overs later, Wasim edged to the keeper. There were even hopes that Pakistan's lead might be kept in bounds, but Rashid Latif's batting was a revelation. He was confident, stylish, technically sound and very keen to play his shots. He lost Asif Mujtaba, who had again played sensibly, in the 118th over, run out by Smith's direct hit

Another victim for Malcolm as Salim Malik has his off-bail clipped. (David Munden)

A decisive blow for Pakistan. David Gower is bowled by a magnificent ball from Waqar Younis for 1. (Adrian Murrell/Allsport)

from mid-wicket, but he was last out when he miscued to cover and 48 runs had come from the last ten overs of the innings.

Gooch and Stewart began England's second innings with the knowledge that 173 runs were needed to make Pakistan bat again. There were no immediate alarms, but after Wasim had bowled five overs with the new ball, he was replaced by Waqar. The fifth ball of his first over thudded into Stewart's pads as he tried to turn it to leg, and umpire Bird's finger was up almost before the bowler appealed. The next ball thudded into Atherton's pads and Waqar's appeal was justifiably confident, but this time Mr Bird said 'no'. Atherton did clip a boundary to square-leg, but, perhaps ever mindful of the in-swinger, he edged Waqar's away-swinger to the keeper.

Mushtaq was now bowling in tandem with Waqar, and Gooch hit him high over mid-on. If this gave England some joy, it was not to last long. In the last over before tea, Waqar had Gooch very well taken at slip off an away-swinger that moved a little, but late. Pakistan were jubilant, and even the most avid of England supporters believed that once Gooch had gone an end was open.

Worse was to follow. In his first over after tea, Waqar bowled a ball which seemed to be slanted across the left-handed Gower. The batsman offered no shot, and the ball hit the off-stump. This was an astonishing delivery, and only a bowler of Waqar's ability, of which there have been very few, could have made the ball hold its line in such a manner. In an eight-over spell either side of tea, he had taken 4 for 31 and broken England.

Ramprakash and Smith added 33 in 11 overs before Ramprakash pushed forward at Mushtaq's googly and was taken, presumably pad and glove, at short-leg. The Pakistani close fielders appealed immediately, and umpire Shepherd had no hesitation in giving Ramprakash out, but it was difficult to see what the ball had made contact with that provoked the appeal and the verdict. Lewis and Smith saw out the rest of the day, and England closed on 137 for 5. Smith had reached a dogged 59. He was never comfortable, but he is a fighter.

Waqar Younis began his Sunday morning spell with three maidens, and then he rested. Eleven overs into the morning, and England had added 16 to their overnight score. Lewis had been playing sensibly, but he suddenly cracked under the pressure, leapt forward at Mushtaq and was stumped by yards. It was an unbelievable shot in the circumstances, and one must question Lewis' rating as a Test all-rounder both on grounds of consistent performance and temperament.

The end was in sight. Pringle played down the wrong line, most obviously, and was bowled. Mallender edged to second slip where Aamir knocked the ball up, and Mushtaq dived forward to catch the ball in front of first slip. Tufnell's stumps were wrecked first ball. Waqar had returned, and he claimed his fifth wicket when his famous yorker demolished Malcolm's leg stump. The last five wickets had fallen for 21 runs of which Smith had scored 16 and at least made Pakistan bat again. His 84 not out had come off 179 balls, and he batted for 239 minutes. He had not been at his best during the summer, and he rarely played with conviction or fluency, but, as in this innings, he battled, and he showed grit and determination which are admirable qualities.

Pakistan needed two to win. Ramprakash bowled a wide, and Aamir slashed his first legal delivery to the cover boundary. A ten-wicket victory was an apt indication of the gap in quality between the two sides. The most surprising thing about the series was that England had reached the final Test on level terms. Indeed, some might argue that they might even have reached it in the lead. That Pakistan did not win the rubber more conclusively than two to one was due in the main part to their own temperamental flaws in the matter of discipline. This is a truly great side, and one hopes that they can now gain just a little more maturity and self-knowledge.

Sadly, much nonsense was written and spoken about ball-tampering. There were legal proceedings, and writs flew. The saddest aspect of all this was that somehow it tended to make the British public believe that England had really won on points. It created a smoke screen which obscured the frailties of England selection, technique and general management. We were not in the same class as Pakistan, and that we came so close to them for much of the series was due in no small measure to the relentless dedication of Graham Gooch as batsman. He was rightly named England's Man of the Series. For Pakistan, the honour was shared between Wasim Akram and Waqar Younis. To have watched them bowl in this series was an experience which one should long cherish.

Men of the series – Waqar Younis and Wasim Akram. (Patrick Eagar)

FIFTH CORNHILL TEST MATCH – ENGLAND v. PAKISTAN
6, 7, 8 and 9 August, 1992 at The Oval, Kennington

ENGLAND

	FIRST INNINGS		SECOND INNINGS	
G.A. Gooch (capt)	c Asif, b Aqib Javed	20	c Aamir, b Waqar	24
*A.J. Stewart	c Ramiz, b Wasim	31	lbw, b Waqar	8
M.A. Atherton	c Rashid, b Waqar	60	c Rashid, b Waqar	4
R.A. Smith	b Mushtaq	33	not out	84
D.I. Gower	b Aqib Javed	27	b Waqar	1
M.R. Ramprakash	lbw, b Wasim	12	c Asif, b Mushtaq	17
C.C. Lewis	lbw, b Wasim	4	st Rashid, b Mushtaq	14
D.R. Pringle	b Wasim	1	b Wasim	1
N.A. Mallender	b Wasim	4	c Mushtaq, b Wasim	3
P.C.R. Tufnell	not out	0	b Wasim	0
D.E. Malcolm	b Wasim	2	b Waqar	0
Extras	b 4, lb 8, w 1, nb 10	23	b 1, lb 8, nb 9	18
		207		174

PAKISTAN

	FIRST INNINGS		SECOND INNINGS	
Aamir Sohail	c Stewart, b Malcolm	49	not out	4
Ramiz Raja	b Malcolm	19	not out	0
Shoaib Mohammad	c and b Tufnell	55		
Javed Miandad (capt)	c and b Lewis	59		
Salim Malik	b Malcolm	40		
Asif Mujtaba	run out	50		
Wasim Akram	c Stewart, b Malcolm	7		
*Rashid Latif	c Smith, b Mallender	50		
Waqar Younis	c Gooch, b Malcolm	6		
Mushtaq Ahmed	c Lewis, b Mallender	9		
Aqib Javed	not out	0		
Extras	b 2, lb 6, w 4, nb 24	36	w 1	1
		380	(for no wicket)	5

	O	M	R	W	O	M	R	W
Wasim Akram	22.1	3	67	6	21	6	36	3
Waqar Younis	16	4	37	1	18	5	52	5
Aqib Javed	16	6	44	2	9	2	25	–
Mushtaq Ahemd	24	7	47	1	23	6	46	2
Aamir Sohail					1	–	6	–

	O	M	R	W	O	M	R	W
Mallender	28.5	6	93	2				
Malcolm	29	6	94	5				
Lewis	30	8	70	1				
Tufnell	34	9	87	1				
Pringle	6	–	28	–				
Ramprakash					0.1	–	5	–

FALL OF WICKETS (England)
1–39, 2–57, 3–138, 4–182, 5–190, 6–196, 7–199, 8–203, 9–205
1–29, 2–46, 3–55, 4–55, 5–92, 6–153, 7–159, 8–173, 9–173

FALL OF WICKETS (Pakistan)
1–64, 2–86, 3–197, 4–214, 5–278, 6–292, 7–332, 8–342, 9–359

Umpires: H.D. Bird & D.R. Shepherd

Pakistan won by 8 wickets

TEST MATCH AVERAGES – ENGLAND v. PAKISTAN

ENGLAND BATTING

	M	Inns	NO	Runs	HS	Av	100s	50s
A.J. Stewart	5	8	1	397	190	56.71	1	2
D.I. Gower	3	5	2	150	73	50.00	–	1
G.A. Gooch	5	8	–	384	135	48.00	1	2
R.A. Smith	5	8	1	314	127	44.85	1	1
M.A. Atherton	3	5	–	145	76	29.00	–	2
R.C. Russell	3	4	2	56	29*	28.00	–	–
T.A. Munton	2	2	1	25	25*	25.00	–	–
I.D.K. Salisbury	2	3	–	66	50	22.00	–	1
G.A. Hick	4	5	–	98	51	19.60	–	1
A.J. Lamb	2	3	–	54	30	18.00	–	–
C.C. Lewis	5	7	–	114	55	16.28	–	1
M.R. Ramprakash	3	5	1	31	17	7.75	–	–
I.T. Botham	2	2	–	8	6	4.00	–	–
N.A. Mallender	2	3	–	8	4	2.66	–	–
P.A.J. DeFreitas	2	2	–	3	3	1.50	–	–
D.E. Malcolm	3	5	–	6	4	1.20	–	–
D.R. Pringle	3	4	1	2	1	0.66	–	–

Played in one Test – P.C.R. Tufnell 0* & 0

ENGLAND BOWLING

	Overs	Mds	Runs	Wkts	Av	Best	10/m	5/inn
G.A. Gooch	51	15	94	5	18.80	3-39	–	1
N.A. Mallender	74.5	20	215	10	21.50	5-50	–	1
P.A.J. DeFreitas	59	14	179	7	25.57	4-121	–	–
D.E. Malcolm	102.5	14	380	13	29.23	5-94	–	1
C.C. Lewis	188	40	544	12	45.33	3-43	–	–
D.R. Pringle	70	10	227	5	45.40	3-66	–	–
T.A. Munton	67.3	15	200	4	50.00	2-22	–	–
I.D.K. Salisbury	70.1	3	306	5	61.20	3-49	–	–
M.R. Ramprakash	1.1	–	8	–	–	–	–	–
I.T. Botham	24	8	61	–	–	–	–	–
G.A. Hick	18	3	63	–	–	–	–	–

Bowled in one innings – P.C.R. Tufnell 34–9–87–1

ENGLAND LEADING FIELDERS

10 – G.A. Hick; 7 – R.C. Russell (ct 6/st 1) and R.A. Smith; 5 – A.J. Stewart and M.A. Atherton; 4 – C.C. Lewis; 2 – G.A. Gooch and I.T. Botham; 1 – D.I. Gower, M.R. Ramprakash, D.E. Malcolm and P.C.R. Tufnell

PAKISTAN BATTING

	M	Inns	NO	Runs	HS	Av	100s	50s
Salim Malik	5	8	2	488	165	81.33	1	3
Javed Miandad	5	8	2	364	153*	60.66	1	2
Aamir Sohail	5	9	1	413	205	51.62	1	1
Ramiz Raja	5	9	1	312	88	39.00	–	3
Asif Mujtaba	5	8	–	253	59	31.62	–	3
Wasim Akram	4	7	1	118	45*	19.66	–	–
Inzamam-ul-Haq	4	6	1	66	26	13.20	–	–
Waqar Younis	5	6	2	51	20*	12.75	–	–
Moin Khan	4	6	1	46	15	9.20	–	–
Mushtaq Ahmed	5	6	–	35	11	5.83	–	–
Aqib Javed	5	4	2	5	5*	2.50	–	–

Played in one Test – Shoaib Mohammad 55; Rashid Latif 50; Ata-ur-Rehman did not bat

PAKISTAN BOWLING

	Overs	Mds	Runs	Wkts	Av	Best	10/m	5/inn
Wasim Akram	168.5	36	462	21	22.00	6-67	–	2
Waqar Younis	166	29	557	22	25.31	5-52	–	3
Asif Mujtaba	13	5	30	1	30.00	1-0	–	–
Mushtaq Ahmed	178.4	37	475	15	31.66	3-32	–	–
Aqib Javed	104.4	21	366	9	40.66	4-100	–	–
Aamir Sohail	5	2	14	–	–	–	–	–

Bowled in one innings – Salim Malik 1–0–5–0; Ata-ur-Rehman 18–5–69–3

PAKISTAN LEADING FIELDERS

7 – Moin Khan; 5 – Javed Miandad; 4 – Asif Mujtaba and Inzamam-ul-Haq; 3 – Rashid Latif (ct 2/st 1) and Aamir Sohail; 2 – Salim Malik, Mushtaq Ahmed and Ramiz Raja

ABOVE: Ramprakash is given out caught at forward short-leg off Mushtaq Ahmed. (David Munden)

7, 8 and 10 August *at Canterbury*

Hampshire 288 (M.C.J. Nicholas 59, T.C. Middleton 52) and 70 (M.J. McCague 8 for 26)
Kent 252 for 6 dec. (M.V. Fleming 100 not out) and 109 for 1 (T.R. Ward 63)

Kent won by 9 wickets

Kent 22 pts., Hampshire 5 pts.

at Old Trafford

Lancashire 349 for 5 dec. (G.D. Lloyd 101, N.J. Speak 71, N.H. Fairbrother 70 not out) and 0 for 0 dec.
Worcestershire 0 for 0 dec. and 197 for 8

Match drawn

Lancashire 4 pts., Worcestershire 2 pts.

at Lord's

Gloucestershire 322 for 9 dec. (G.D. Hodgson 64, N.F. Williams 4 for 64) and 141 (N.F. Williams 8 for 75)
Middlesex 251 for 8 dec. (M.W. Gatting 86) and 213 for 5 (J.D. Carr 66, J.C. Pooley 56 not out)

Middlesex won by 5 wickets

Middlesex 21 pts., Gloucestershire 6 pts.

at Northampton

Northamptonshire 224 (N.A. Felton 103, C.S. Pickles 4 for 40) and 174 for 7 dec.
Yorkshire 158 (D.J. Capel 4 for 61) and 174 for 5

Match drawn

Northamptonshire 6 pts., Yorkshire 5 pts.

at Trent Bridge

Glamorgan 334 for 8 dec. (A. Dale 150 not out, D.L. Hemp 51) and 12 for 0 dec.
Nottinghamshire 17 for 0 dec. and 322 (M.A. Crawley 88, P.R. Pollard 75, B.N. French 55, S.R. Barwick 4 for 67)

Glamorgan won by 7 runs

Glamorgan 20 pts., Nottinghamshire 3 pts.

at Eastbourne

Derbyshire 248 (J.E. Morris 68) and 142 (E.S.H. Giddins 5 for 32)
Sussex 230 and 161 for 6

Sussex won by 4 wickets

Sussex 22 pts., Derbyshire 6 pts.

at Edgbaston

Durham 136 (A.A. Donald 7 for 37) and 238 for 4 (W. Larkins 77, P. Bainbridge 71 not out)
Warwickshire 314 for 6 dec. (R.G. Twose 65, T.A. Lloyd 60, A.J. Moles 51)

Match drawn

Warwickshire 8 pts., Durham 1 pt.

Martin McCague, 8 for 26, Kent v. Hampshire, 7–10 August, and an inspired last month of the season. (David Munden)

A dull first day at Canterbury gave no indication of what was to come later in the match. The gloom and the rain robbed the game of 33 overs on the Saturday, but a highly attractive century from Fleming lit the darkness and took Kent to a third batting point in the 69th over. Hampshire closed at 7 for 0, but on the Monday, they were routed by Martin McCague who took a career best 8 for 26 with a devastating spell of fast bowling. McCague had begun the season in indifferent manner and was unsure of a regular place in the Kent side, but in the middle of July, he had seemed to find an extra yard of pace. He had also discovered more control and hostility. His outstanding performance, the season's best, made a Kent victory a formality.

A century by Lloyd for Lancashire on the first day was followed by a blank second day. The inevitable forfeitures followed. Needing 350 in 83 overs, Worcestershire fell far short of expectations and settled for a draw. This was not a good day for Lancashire who, following a season of turmoil, discontent and no success, announced that cricket manager Alan Ormrod was being dismissed. Later it was revealed that Fowler and Allott were not to be retained. The cavalier style usually associated with soccer clubs did no credit to the county or its committee.

Neil Williams emulated McCague with a career best eight-wicket performance which set Middlesex on the path to victory over Gloucestershire. Gatting conceded a first-innings lead of 71, but Williams reduced

Gloucestershire to 94 for 9 in their second innings. A last-wicket stand of 47 between Russell and Walsh meant that Middlesex required 213 for victory. This looked a little remote when Haynes, Roseberry and Gatting were dismissed for 56. Carr and Brown added 73, but it was eventually Pooley who brought Middlesex to their target, with Gloucestershire regretting dropped catches.

Nigel Felton's first championship century of the season saved Northamptonshire from embarrassment on the opening day against Yorkshire who, in their turn, struggled on a green wicket. Rain and some dogged resistance from White saved Yorkshire on the last afternoon in spite of losing Byas with a broken nose, the batsman being caught unawares by an Ambrose bouncer.

Adrian Dale – an excellent all-round season, and a career best 150 for Glamorgan against Nottinghamshire, 7–10 August. (David Munden)

Nottinghamshire's championship hopes suffered a further setback in a thrilling game at Trent Bridge. Glamorgan had seemed to be in early decline on the opening day when they slipped to 214 for 7. They were revived by a career best 150 from Adrian Dale who gained staunch support from the tail as, with them, he raised the score to 334 for 8. There was no play on the Saturday, and discussion between the captains led to Nottinghamshire being set a target of 330 in 100 overs. They began cautiously, with Pollard supplying the foundation to the innings with his 75. It was Crawley and Randall who gave the impetus with a stand of 86, but the home county found themselves needing 73 from the last eight overs in poor light. French and Hemmings hit 48 in six overs. Hemmings was bowled when he attempted a big hit, but French made 55 off 39 balls and was still there with 11 needed off the last over. He was stumped off the third ball so that Paul Johnson, his left arm in plaster after sustaining a broken bone in the Sunday League game, came to the wicket with eight needed from three balls. Johnson swung one-handed at Barwick and was leg before to give Glamorgan victory by seven runs with two balls to spare.

It took some bold hitting from Stephenson to take Sussex to a nervous victory over Derbyshire, but they had been well served by the consistently impressive Giddins and by Ian Salisbury.

Allan Donald was far too quick for Durham on the opening day at Edgbaston, and Warwickshire, second in the table, looked sure of victory before being thwarted by Larkins and Bainbridge on the last day.

SUNDAY LEAGUE

9 August *at Bristol*

Leicestershire 205 (P.E. Robinson 88, A.M. Smith 4 for 38)
Gloucestershire 209 for 1 (M.W. Alleyne 134 not out)

Gloucestershire (4 pts.) won by 9 wickets

at Canterbury

Hampshire 172 for 9 (T.C. Middleton 71)
Kent 176 for 4 (G.R. Cowdrey 51 not out)

Kent (4 pts.) won by 6 wickets

at Old Trafford

Lancashire v. Worcestershire

Match abandoned

Lancashire 2 pts., Worcestershire 2 pts.

at Lord's

Middlesex 236 for 6 (M.W. Gatting 89, M.A. Roseberry 57)
Essex 142 (D.W. Headley 4 for 23)

Middlesex (4 pts.) won by 94 runs

at Northampton

Northamptonshire 222 for 9 (K.M. Curran 62, P.W. Jarvis 5 for 29)
Yorkshire 157 (M.D. Moxon 53)

Northamptonshire (4 pts.) won by 65 runs

at Trent Bridge

Nottinghamshire 158 for 6 (P.R. Pollard 61)
Glamorgan 148 for 7 (C.L. Cairns 4 for 26)

Nottinghamshire (4 pts.) won by 10 runs

at Eastbourne

Derbyshire 183 for 7 (T.J.G. O'Gorman 55, J.E. Morris 51)
Sussex 124 (P. Moores 56)

Derbyshire (4 pts.) won by 59 runs

at Edgbaston

Durham 190 for 6 (J.D. Glendenen 78)
Warwickshire 173

Durham (4 pts.) won by 17 runs

12 August *at Canterbury*

Kent v. Nottinghamshire

Match abandoned

Kent 2 pts., Nottinghamshire 2 pts.

By trouncing Essex in a most emphatic manner, Middlesex virtually dispelled any lingering doubt that they would win the Sunday League. Put in to bat, they quickly lost Haynes, caught behind off Topley, but Gatting, practically running before the ball was hit, and Roseberry added 151 in 25 overs. The Essex bowling frayed, and their fielding became ragged. Apart from a stylish 40 from Prichard, the acting captain, they offered little resistance. Mark Alleyne hit his first Sunday League century as Gloucestershire beat Leicestershire, and Nottinghamshire won only their third Sunday game of the season to leave Leicestershire at the bottom of the table. They paid a hard price, for Paul Johnson had a knuckle fractured by a ball from Darren Foster before he had scored, and so a key batsman was lost for the rest of the season.

NATWEST TROPHY

SEMI-FINALS

12 and 13 August *at Leicester*

Essex 226 for 8 (P.J. Prichard 87)
Leicestershire 229 for 5 (N.E. Briers 88)

Leicestershire won by 5 wickets

(Man of the Match – N.E. Briers)

at Edgbaston

Warwickshire 149
Northamptonshire 152 for 7 (N.A. Felton 58)

Northamptonshire won by 3 wickets

(Man of the Match – N.A. Felton)

Short of the injured Millns, Leicestershire called the BBC's cricket correspondent Jonathan Agnew out of retirement to play in the semi-final against Essex at Grace Road, and he played a noble part, bowling his 12 overs for 31 runs and the wicket of Lewis. This was an excellent performance in a match which had too many unsatisfactory features for the comfort of the spectators and the commentators. There was heavy rain in the morning, and the match began six hours late. A delay was understandable; the length of the delay was not. When the umpires inspected at mid-day they announced that they would see how the drying-up operations would succeed. As there appeared to be no sign of any drying-up operations save one man with a fork, this was hard for an increasingly restless crowd to understand. The crowd's restlessness could well be appreciated, for the facilities offered to the paying public at Grace Road border on the barbaric. There is room in plenty; imaginative development and maintenance there is not. When play was finally about to begin, the umpires insisted on matting being laid on old wickets, a task which could have been deemed necessary hours earlier.

Briers won the toss and asked Essex to bat. This was a wise decision for the pitch certainly posed problems. Stephenson was out to the first ball he received. He attempted to sway from a delivery from Mullally, but the ball touched his glove and he was taken at slip by Benson. More significantly, Benson held on to an edge from Gooch who had made eight, and Essex were 17 for 2. Lewis had hung on with an air of desperation until caught behind off Agnew at 50, but Prichard and Hussain then batted with admirable sense and style to add 112 in 27 overs. This partnership appeared to be taking Essex to a commanding position, but, unaccountably, when Parsons returned for his second spell Hussain charged wildly and insanely and was bowled. Parsons claimed Pringle in his next over, and just as it seemed that Prichard would score a hundred and lead Essex into a final, vital assault on the bowling he was bowled by Potter when he tried to cut a ball too close to him. Bad light ended play with Essex 188 for 6 from 52 overs.

Action in the NatWest Trophy semi-final at Grace Road. Boon and Garnham collide, and Topley looks on. Leicestershire were the victors over favourites Essex. (David Munden)

Mostly through Topley and Ilott, Essex added 38 runs for the loss of two wickets in their last eight overs. Briers and Boon began solidly and scored 52 for the first wicket. Briers, who was the backbone of the Leicestershire innings, was twice dropped by Gooch, once on 26, and then, a more difficult chance, on 61. His survival probably won Leicestershire the match. He and Whitaker put on 86 in 27 overs, but the run rate was slowed by Such and Stephenson. The promotion of Benjamin in an attempt to lift the rate failed, for he skied Pringle to mid-on. By now, Essex were bowling in steady rain with what amounted to a bar of soap. Gooch twice enquired of umpires Oslear and Plews as to whether conditions were suitable for a continuation. They consulted and continued. This was something of a contradiction to their first-day statement that, in a limited-over match, conditions should be the same for both sides. With only two days set aside for this important game, this was patently impossible, and in sunshine on the first day, no cricket was played because the ground was damp.

Robinson added spice to the Leicestershire innings with a vigorous and important 15 before being caught by Gooch. Essex's woes came on apace when Garnham was hit in the face by an edge from Benson and was taken to hospital. Arguably, the unfortunate Garnham should have held the ball that hit him. Benson had another escape when Prichard, who had taken over behind the stumps, missed a chance off Ilott. Briers, who well deserved the individual award for his coolness and quiet leadership, hit high to deep mid-wicket where Hussain took a fine catch. Only three runs were needed off the last over, but Stephenson bowled four balls to Potter from which the batsman failed to score. The fifth was adjudged a wide, to the anger of Stephenson and close fielders, and the batsman crossed. Benson sliced wide of Prichard, and Leicestershire were in the NatWest final for the first time.

There was less excitement and no controversy at Edgbaston, although the paying customer was again poorly served. Play began at 1.25, and there might have been a possibility of a result in one day had not Northamptonshire bowled their overs so tardily and the umpires not decided to come off for debatable bad light at 7.30, only to return in pale sunshine 20 minutes later.

Northamptonshire bowled with professional accuracy, and Warwickshire batted with a melancholy dullness. No one could break the shackles. After 18 overs, they were 45 for 3. There were only ten fours in the entire innings, which lasted 59.2 overs, and strokes were at a minimum. At 99 for 7, Warwickshire looked totally demoralised, but Small, with Piper and Donald, conjured 44 from the eighth and ninth wickets.

Northamptonshire were 47 for 2 from 23 overs when play ended on the Wednesday, and the game continued on its somnolent way the next morning. At 87, Lamb was caught behind off Small, and Felton, after playing with the utmost care for his 58, slogged at Neil Smith and was caught. Curran enlivened proceedings with a six and two fours, but he was fifth out with 27 still needed. Northamptonshire made heavy weather of this, losing two wickets, including that of Penberthy to the luckless Donald's last delivery, before winning with 4.1 overs to spare.

14, 15 and 17 August *at Chesterfield*

Derbyshire 207 and 334 for 4 (K.J. Barnett 160, T.J.G. O'Gorman 62 not out, J.E. Morris 55)

Kent 295 (T.R. Ward 87, N.R. Taylor 71, I.R. Bishop 5 for 60)

Match drawn

Kent 7 pts., Derbyshire 6 pts.

at Hartlepool

Glamorgan 396 for 6 dec. (H. Morris 126, P.A. Cottey 91, A. Dale 68)

Durham 201 (I.T. Botham 54, D.J. Foster 5 for 87) and 313 (W. Larkins 140, P. Bainbridge 56, M.P. Briers 52)

Match drawn

Glamorgan 8 pts., Durham 4 pts.

at Colchester

Nottinghamshire 249 (C.L. Cairns 82 not out, P.R. Pollard 65, J.P. Stephenson 6 for 54, D.R. Pringle 4 for 55) and 130 (P.M. Such 6 for 39, J.H. Childs 4 for 59)

Essex 416 for 5 dec. (P.J. Prichard 136, J.P. Stephenson 74, J.J.B. Lewis 53 not out)

Essex won by an innings and 37 runs

Essex 24 pts., Nottinghamshire 3 pts.

at Bournemouth

Hampshire 260 (K.D. James 74, R.A. Smith 62, K.M. Curran 6 for 45) and 100 (J.P. Taylor 7 for 23)

Northamptonshire 338 for 8 dec. (A.J. Lamb 160, D. Ripley 57, M.D. Marshall 4 for 49) and 23 for 0

Northamptonshire won by 10 wickets

Northamptonshire 22 pts., Hampshire 5 pts.

at Uxbridge

Yorkshire 286 (S.R. Tendulkar 82, P.C.R. Tufnell 4 for 92) and 194 for 4 dec. (S.R. Tendulkar 77 not out)

Middlesex 250 for 6 dec. (D.L. Haynes 83, P.N. Weekes 64 not out) and 234 for 4 (M.R. Ramprakash 94)

Middlesex won by 6 wickets

Middlesex 23 pts., Yorkshire 5 pts.

at The Oval

Leicestershire 216 (V.J. Wells 56, N.M. Kendrick 6 for 61) and 267 for 5 dec. (R.P. Gofton 75)

Surrey 218 (M.A. Lynch 106, G.J. Parsons 6 for 70, A.D. Mullally 4 for 56) and 193 (M.A. Lynch 58, L. Potter 4 for 73)

Leicestershire won by 72 runs

Leicestershire 22 pts., Surrey 6 pts.

15, 16 and 17 August *at Bristol*

Pakistanis 357 for 8 dec. (Ramiz Raja 135, Shoaib Mohamad 66, Inzamam-ul-Haq 65) and 184 for 4 dec. (Inzamam-ul-Haq 54 not out)

Gloucestershire 123 (Aqib Javed 5 for 34, Wasim Akram 5 for 44) and 126 (Wasim Akram 6 for 32)

Pakistanis won by 292 runs

Rain on the last morning of the match at Chesterfield frustrated hopes of an exciting finish. There was no agreement between the captains, and Barnett batted on to reach 160.

Glamorgan had far the better of the drawn match between the two bottom of the table sides. They batted excitingly on the opening day, scoring at nearly four runs an over, with Hugh Morris hitting his sixth championship hundred of the season. On the Saturday, Durham succumbed to the Glamorgan seam attack and were forced to follow-on. A defiantly aggressive knock by Wayne Larkins on the Monday saved Durham from defeat.

The vital meeting between Essex and Nottinghamshire at Colchester provided some fine cricket for very large crowds. Nottinghamshire chose to bat first after a delayed start, and they were bowled out for 249 on a good wicket. They would have fared more badly but for an excellent knock from Chris Cairns who scored 82 of the 141 runs scored for the fall of the last five wickets. Most praise, however, must go to the Essex seam attack who performed outstandingly to dismiss their close rivals for such a low score. John Stephenson, laying further claim to be recognised as an all-rounder, took a career best 6 for 54. Essex batted in an urgent manner and had taken maximum bonus points by Saturday evening, having reached 302 for 4 in 70 overs. Stephenson and Prichard added 130 for the second wicket, and the pace quickened all the time with Prichard reaching a delightful 136. On the last morning, Pringle and Lewis hit strongly, and Gooch declared shortly before lunch. He soon had his spinners in action, and Such soon had Pollard caught behind by Alistair Brown, who deputised for the injured Garnham and had a quite magnificent match. In Such's next over, he hit Robinson on the pad, and the ball bounced head-high. As short-leg went to catch it, there was a shout of 'Leave it!' Robinson, too late, tried to brush the ball away, but it rolled back onto his stumps and dislodged a bail. Broad became the first victim of the ring of young close catchers, and soon Nottinghamshire were 55 for 5. Lewis and Cairns held up the spinners for over an hour, but Lewis was well caught in the gully, and Cairns was brilliantly taken by Prichard, low at leg slip. Evans and French offered resistance until Evans lost patience against Such and was bowled. Childs dismissed French and Afford with successive balls, and the roar from the crowd must have been heard as far away as Southend. Such and Childs had bowled with intelligence and skill, and they had been magnificently supported in the field. After three first-class defeats and a disappointing loss in the NatWest Trophy semi-final, Essex had reaffirmed their intention to retain the title.

At Bournemouth, Hampshire lost their last six wickets for 22 runs, and Northamptonshire took a grip on the match that they never relinquished. Lamb dominated the Northamptonshire innings, reaching his century off 125 balls and rallying his side after Marshall had struck two early blows. Taylor captured the wicket of James before the close on Saturday, and he continued his work on the Monday when Hampshire lost five wickets in seven balls after lunch. Taylor returned the best figures of his career, 7 for 23, and the left-arm pace bowler claimed four of his wickets in one over. The win took Northamptonshire into third place, 37 points behind the leaders.

Rain greatly affected the match at Uxbridge where Sachin Tendulkar, close to saying goodbye to Yorkshire, played two splendid innings. Moxon's declaration left Middlesex 46 overs in which to score 231. They lost Haynes and Roseberry cheaply, but Ramprakash played an innings of superbly controlled aggression. He was bowled when he tried to hit Carrick for the six which would have given him his century and Middlesex victory, a victory that was achieved with five balls to spare.

Leicestershire lost their last seven wickets for 31 runs against Surrey on the opening day at The Oval. Left-arm spinner Neil Kendrick returned the best bowling figures of his career. Surrey fared no better on the Saturday as Lynch alone offered serious resistance. He hit two sixes and 16 fours in a powerful display which shamed his colleagues. Surrey were to falter again on the last afternoon when, with the game looking as it it would be drawn, Briers turned to the irregular bowling of Boon who caught Benjamin's return lob, had Lynch caught behind and retired after three overs, all maidens, with two wickets. Potter's left-arm spin did the rest, and Leicestershire were again in second place, 32 points behind Essex who had a game in hand.

A bubbling century by Ramiz, and the pace bowling of Wasim Akram took the Pakistani tourists to a splendid ninth win in their last match against a county side.

A career best bowling performance by Northamptonshire's Paul Taylor against Hampshire at Bournemouth, 14–17 August, kept his county's championship challenge alive. Consistently good form from the left-arm pace bowler earned him a place in the side to tour India. (Alan Cozzi)

SUNDAY LEAGUE

16 August *at Chesterfield*

Derbyshire 257 for 5 (C.J. Adams 141 not out, P.D. Bowler 56)
Kent 209 (T.R. Ward 65, A.E. Warner 4 for 23)

Derbyshire (4 pts.) won by 48 runs

at Hartlepool

Glamorgan 216 for 7 (M.P. Maynard 65, S.P. James 63)
Durham 200 for 9 (S. Hutton 70)

Glamorgan (4 pts.) won by 16 runs

at Colchester

Essex 176 for 7 (G.A. Gooch 55)
Nottinghamshire 165 for 6 (B.C. Broad 63)

Essex (4 pts.) won by 11 runs

at Bournemouth

Hampshire 255 for 3 (T.C. Middleton 98, R.A. Smith 61)
Northamptonshire 174 (R.J. Bailey 64, S.D. Udal 4 for 51)

Hampshire (4 pts.) won by 81 runs

at Uxbridge

Yorkshire 194 for 6 (S.A. Kellett 68)
Middlesex 195 for 5 (J.D. Carr 60 not out, M.R. Ramprakash 58)

Middlesex (4 pts.) won by 5 wickets

at Taunton

Worcestershire 125 (K.H. MacLeay 5 for 20)
Somerset 126 for 8

Somerset (4 pts.) won by 2 wickets

at The Oval

Surrey 207 for 5 (A.J. Stewart 105 not out)
Leicestershire 210 for 5 (J.J. Whitaker 118 not out)

Leicestershire (4 pts.) won by 5 wickets

at Hove

Lancashire 173 (C.C. Remy 4 for 31)
Sussex 175 for 4 (N.J. Lenham 81 not out, A.P. Wells 56)

Sussex (4 pts.) won by 6 wickets

What had been apparent for several weeks was confirmed at Uxbridge on 16 August when Middlesex beat Yorkshire with 13 balls to spare and won the Sunday League. A partnership of 107 in 20 overs between Carr and Ramprakash, both of whom had contributed much to the triumph, was at the heart of the Middlesex win. Their record of 14 wins in 15 matches was an incredible achievement, form and energy had never flagged, and others were left trailing. Chris Adams continued his season of success with another blistering display for Derbyshire. He hit 141, the county's highest score in the 40-over competition, off 102 balls. He hit ten sixes and seven fours. From the last ten overs of the Derbyshire innings, 114 runs were scored. There were two century-makers at The Oval where Whitaker took Leicestershire to victory with two balls to spare.

Middlesex ran away with the Sunday League. Their success was finally confirmed when they beat Yorkshire at Uxbridge, 16 August. Gatting displays the financial reward and the champagne. (Mark Leech)

18, 19 and 20 August *at Chesterfield*

Glamorgan 170 (P.A. Cottey 62, D.E. Malcolm 5 for 45) and 366 (M.P. Maynard 176, A. Dale 82, H. Morris 52)
Derbyshire 334 for 8 dec. (I.R. Bishop 90, F.A. Griffith 81, P.D. Bowler 67, S.D. Thomas 5 for 80) and 22 for 2

Match drawn

Derbyshire 6 pts., Glamorgan 3 pts.

at Colchester

Surrey 292 (M.A. Lynch 102, D.J. Bicknell 53, P.M. Such 4 for 22, D.R. Pringle 4 for 63) and 10 for 0
Essex 229 (J.J.B. Lewis 66, M.A. Garnham 59, M.P. Bicknell 4 for 53)

Match drawn

Surrey 7 pts., Essex 6 pts.

at Bristol

Gloucestershire 346 (J.T.C. Vaughan 99, T.H.C. Hancock 82, D.J. Capel 4 for 65) and 176 for 8 dec.
Northamptonshire 251 for 6 dec. (R.J. Bailey 91) and 232 (R.J. Bailey 96)

Gloucestershire won by 39 runs

Gloucestershire 22 pts., Northamptonshire 7 pts.

at Bournemouth

Hampshire 386 for 9 dec. (M.C.J. Nicholas 95, J.R. Ayling 57, A.N. Aymes 53, J.E. Emburey 5 for 105)
Middlesex 115 (J.R. Ayling 5 for 12) and 346 for 9 (M.W. Gatting 93, J.D. Carr 77 not out, M.A. Roseberry 52, S.D. Udal 4 for 101)

Match drawn

Hampshire 8 pts., Middlesex 2 pts.

at Leicester

Kent 502 for 4 dec. (N.R. Taylor 144, M.R. Benson 139, C.L. Hooper 62 not out, M.V. Fleming 58)
Leicestershire 181 (.J. McCague 7 for 52) and 183 (T.J. Boon 72, A.P. Igglesden 5 for 41)

Kent won by an innings and 138 runs

Kent 24 pts., Leicestershire 1 pt.

at Weston-super-Mare

Somerset 328 (R.P. Snell 75, A.R. Caddick 54, G.D. Rose 51, R.D. Stemp 5 for 112) and 175 for 4 dec. (N.A. Folland 82 not out)
Worcestershire 250 for 5 dec. (D.B. D'Oliveira 65, G.R. Haynes 64) and 130 for 2 (W.P.C. Weston 66 not out)

Match drawn

Worcestershire 7 pts., Somerset 5 pts.

at Edgbaston

Warwickshire 203 (A.J. Moles 86, R.G. Twose 53, M. Watkinson 4 for 41) and 187 (D.P. Ostler 56, M. Watkinson 6 for 62)
Lancashire 415 for 8 dec. (M.A. Atherton 130, J.P. Crawley 74, N.J. Speak 52)

Lancashire won by an innings and 25 runs

Lancashire 24 pts., Warwickshire 3 pts.

at Scarborough

Nottinghamshire 152 (C.L. Cairns 69) and 353 for 8 (B.C. Broad 120, R.T. Robinson 63, C.L. Cairns 61)
Yorkshire 404 for 9 dec. (R.J. Blakey 112 not out, P.J. Hartley 69, P.W. Jarvis 55)

Match drawn

Yorkshire 8 pts., Nottinghamshire 4 pts.

The end of an innings. First-class cricket at Dean Park, Bournemouth, for the last time. Hampshire v. Middlesex, 18–20 August. (Allsport)

There was no play on the final day at Colchester, but Essex suffered little as Leicestershire were routed by Kent who moved into second place in the Britannic

Assurance County Championship, 25 points behind Essex. With Taylor and Benson sharing a second-wicket stand of 235, Kent reached 414 for 3 on the opening day after being put in by Briers. Taylor batted with great fluency; Benson's innings lasted over six hours and was a monument to grit rather than to form. McCague, who had undergone something of a metamorphosis in mid-season, routed Leicestershire on the second day as his golden vein of form continued, and the varied Kent attack finished the job early on the last day.

Derbyshire bowled out Glamorgan on the first day at Chesterfield and then limped to 167 for 5. They were revived by Griffith and Bishop who added 142. Griffith, in one of his infrequent appearances, hit the highest score of his career. The main honours went to Darren Thomas, Glamorgan's medium-pace bowler who is still a student. He took 5 for 80 on his championship debut. Maynard hit 176 off 195 balls to put the game beyond Derbyshire's reach on the final day.

Northamptonshire's hopes of catching Essex were severely set back at Bristol where Gloucestershire won a good contest. At 113 for 6, the home side were in deep trouble on the first day, but Hancock and Vaughan added 141. Hancock was the more aggressive of the two, but both played with commendable determination, and Vaughan, who hit 13 fours, was unfortunate to be caught off Cook when one short of what would have been a maiden century. Having led by example, Bailey declared Northamptonshire's innings closed when 95 runs behind. Bailey also led the way when his side was set a target of 272 in 55 overs on the last afternoon. Felton was run out in the second over, and thereafter nobody remained long enough with Bailey to make a significant stand. The left-arm spin of Davies and the medium-pace of Vaughan brought the innings to a close after Walsh had inflicted early wounds.

The last first-class match to be played at Dean Park, Bournemouth saw Gatting and Carr thwart Hampshire and force a draw for Middlesex. Middlesex left out Ramprakash for disciplinary reasons, the second time in the season that the player had been censured for his behaviour. Hampshire scored freely on the first day, and Nicholas was denied his first century of the season by Emburey, but they were boosted by Ayling and Aymes who added 111 for the seventh wicket. Inexplicably, Middlesex collapsed on the second day. They lost their last six wickets for 24 runs, with Ayling taking a career best 5 for 12. Following-on, Middlesex fared much better, but the match dragged to a gloomy conclusion amid the thoughts that first-class cricket would no longer be played on one of the loveliest grounds in England.

Weston-super-Mare is another ground about whose future there are rumours. The only notable feature of the game between Somerset and Worcestershire was an innings of 82 by the left-handed Devon captain Folland, who is considering the offer of a contract from Somerset. With neither captain seemingly willing to gamble, the game meandered to a draw.

Warwickshire were all but eclipsed from the championship race when they suffered an innings defeat at the hands of Lancashire. All had begun well, with Moles and Twose opening with a stand of 111, but then Mike Watkinson performed the hat-trick as he sent back Twose, Ostler and Penney. With Paul Smith unable to bat because of an infection, Warwickshire were bundled out for 203. Things got worse for them as they dropped catches and allowed Lancashire to pass 400, with acting captain Atherton hitting a somewhat dour 130 off 268 balls. When Warwickshire batted again Mike Watkinson completed the best match figures of his career, bowling seam initially and off-breaks towards the close. There was also some impressively aggressive bowling from the medium-pace youngster Glen Chapple.

There was no romantic farewell to Yorkshire from Sachin Tendulkar although his side came close to beating Nottinghamshire. He had Pollard caught behind on the first day when Yorkshire shot out the visitors for 152 and closed on 144 for 5. Blakey found an admirable partner in Hartley on the second day, and the pair added 135 for the eighth wicket. Leading by 252, Yorkshire looked as if they might force an innings victory. They were thwarted by Chris Broad, who batted five-and-three-quarter hours for his 120, and by stern resistance throughout the Nottinghamshire order.

TEXACO TROPHY

MATCHES THREE TO FIVE

There were two things which bewildered about the second phase of the Texaco Trophy. The first was how three one-day matches could be scheduled for *after* the Test series; and the second was the composition of the England squad for these matches. Having been beaten more comprehensively in the Test series than a two-one margin would suggest, one would have believed that the selectors would have shown some imagination and initiative in their choice for these three anti-climactic one-day matches, giving promising youngsters a sniff of international cricket. They chose instead to recall most of the World Cup squad. Out went Gower and Ramprakash, and back came Lamb, Botham, Hick, Illingworth and Small, at least four of whom have no international future. The reasoning advanced was that the World Cup squad had performed well and could win the Texaco Trophy in which England already led two matches to nil. With due respect to charming and generous sponsors, in three or four years' time, who will remember, or care, who won the Texaco Trophy? They are games of instant enjoyment, nothing more.

In the first match, Pakistan were without Javed. Salim won the toss and asked England to bat. Gooch and Stewart gave their side a blistering start, and the run rate increased throughout the innings. Smith hit 77 off 72 balls; Fairbrother 62 off 63; and Hick 63 off 42. England reached 363 for 7, the highest score ever made in a limited-over international.

ABOVE: Rashid Latif is stumped by Stewart off Illingworth, Texaco Trophy at Trent Bridge. (David Munden)

BELOW: Success at last for Pakistan in the Texaco Trophy match at Trent Bridge. Gooch is bowled by Waqar. (Patrick Eagar)

Pakistan, who had flown Ijaz Ahmed from Pakistan to bolster their side for some obscure reason, lost their first three wickets for 27 runs, and there was never a remote chance of there being a proper contest.

At Lord's, Javed returned, Gooch dropped out, and England brought in Reeve, and, astonishingly, Blakey as wicket-keeper. Richard Blakey was not in the original squad, but was called up after the victory at Trent Bridge. How he won recognition ahead of several other keepers will remain an enigma. The weather was grim, and, in very difficult conditions, Pakistan made 204 for 5. Play stopped and started, and England had two overs before the game was finally abandoned for the day during which time Botham hit Wasim's first three balls to the boundary, was dropped by substitute Shoiab, and Stewart was leg before to Waqar.

England batted in improved conditions on the Sunday and looked to be heading for victory, but, in a thrilling finish, Pakistan, in the inevitable form of Wasim and Waqar, took the last four England wickets for ten runs to win by three runs.

Waqar Younis bowls Illingworth to win the Texaco Trophy match at Lord's, 23 August. (Adrian Murrell/Allsport)

TEXACO TROPHY – THIRD ONE-DAY INTERNATIONAL – ENGLAND v. PAKISTAN

20 August, 1992 at Trent Bridge, Nottingham

ENGLAND

G.A. Gooch (capt)	b Waqar Younis	42
* A.J. Stewart	c Wasim Akram, b Waqar Younis	34
R.A. Smith	c Ramiz Raja, b Aqib Javed	77
N.H. Fairbrother	b Aqib Javed	62
A.J. Lamb	lbw, b Waqar Younis	16
G.A. Hick	b Wasim Akram	63
I.T. Botham	c Ramiz Raja, b Waqar Younis	24
C.C. Lewis	not out	1
P.A.J. DeFreitas	not out	5
R.K. Illingworth		
G.C. Small		
Extras	b 4, lb 12, w 18, nb 5	39
	(for 7 wickets)	**363**

PAKISTAN

Aamir Sohail	c Botham, b Lewis	17
Ramiz Raja	c Gooch, b DeFreitas	0
Salim Malik (capt)	c Small, b Illingworth	45
Asif Mujtaba	c Lewis, b DeFreitas	1
Inzamam-ul-Haq	run out	10
Ijaz Ahmed	c Gooch, b Botham	23
Wasim Akram	lbw, b Illingworth	1
* Rashid Latif	st Stewart, b Illingworth	29
Waqar Younis	c Hick, b DeFreitas	13
Mushtaq Ahmed	not out	14
Aqib Javed	c Stewart, b Small	2
Extras	lb 5, w 5	10
		165

(55 overs)

	O	M	R	W
Wasim Akram	11	–	55	1
Aqib Javed	11	–	55	2
Waqar Younis	11	–	73	4
Mushtaq Ahmed	11	1	58	–
Ijaz Ahmed	4	–	29	–
Aamir Sohail	3	–	34	–
Asif Mujtaba	4	–	43	–

(46.1 overs)

	O	M	R	W
DeFreitas	11	1	33	3
Lewis	8	2	24	1
Botham	11	1	41	1
Small	5.1	–	28	1
Illingworth	11	1	34	3

FALL OF WICKETS

1–84, **2**–95, **3**–224, **4**–250, **5**–269, **6**–353, **7**–357

FALL OF WICKETS

1–2, **2**–22, **3**–27, **4**–60, **5**–87, **6**–98, **7**–103, **8**–129, **9**–153

Umpires: B. Dudleston & D.R. Shepherd　　Man of the Match – R.A. Smith　　*England won by 198 runs*

During the lunch interval, the umpires changed the ball, but no explanation was offered as to why this was done. The mystery served only to compound rumours and allegations and sour the series more.

On the Monday, at Old Trafford, where far more people attended than had arrived for the Test match, England belatedly included Cork of Derbyshire, and he was by far the most impressive of the bowlers. With Javed and Salim both absent injured, Ramiz Raja captained Pakistan. He won the toss, and Pakistan batted.

There were excellent innings from Aamir Sohail, who was run out in a piece of dreadful cricket, and from Inzamam-ul-Haq. Pakistan's 254 looked a reasonable score, but Gooch and Stewart went off in a blaze of glory, hitting 98 from 15 overs. Smith followed with 85 off 91 balls, and England won with more than 11 overs to spare.

It was all great entertainment for a home crowd, but in the context of the season and in view of England's position in Test cricket, the three games were, in truth, full of sound and fury, signifying nothing.

Dominic Cork – an impressive debut for England in the Texaco Trophy match at Old Trafford. (David Munden)

TEXACO TROPHY – FOURTH ONE-DAY INTERNATIONAL – ENGLAND v. PAKISTAN

22 and 23 August, 1992 at Lord's

PAKISTAN

Aamir Sohail	c Stewart, b DeFreitas	20
Ramiz Raja	c Stewart, b Botham	23
Salim Malik	st Blakey, b Illingworth	48
Javed Miandad (capt)	not out	50
Inzamam-ul-Haq	c Blakey, b Reeve	16
Wasim Akram	b DeFreitas	23
Naved Anjum	not out	4
*Moin Khan		
Waqar Younis		
Mushtaq Ahmed		
Aqib Javed		
Extras	b 2, lb 17, w 11	20
	(for 5 wickets)	204

(50 overs)

	O	M	R	W
DeFreitas	10	2	39	2
Lewis	10	–	49	–
Botham	10	1	33	1
Reeve	10	1	31	1
Illingworth	10	–	43	1

FALL OF WICKETS

1–32, 2–91, 3–102, 4–137, 5–189

ENGLAND

I.T. Botham	st Moin Khan, b Aamir Sohail	40
A.J. Stewart (capt)	lbw, b Waqar Younis	0
R.A. Smith	c Moin Khan, b Aqib Javed	4
N.H. Fairbrother	b Aqib Javed	33
A.J. Lamb	c Moin Khan, b Mushtaq Ahmed	55
G.A. Hick	b Aamir Sohail	8
*R.J. Blakey	b Waqar Younis	25
D.A. Reeve	not out	6
C.C. Lewis	c sub (Asif Mujtaba), b Wasim Akram	1
P.A.J. DeFreitas	c Mushtaq Ahmed, b Wasim Akram	0
R.K. Illingworth	b Waqar Younis	4
Extras	lb 8, w 11, nb 6	25
		201

(49.2 overs)

	O	M	R	W
Wasim Akram	10	2	41	2
Waqar Younis	9.2	–	36	3
Mushtaq Ahmed	10	1	34	1
Aqib Javed	9	–	39	2
Aamir Sohail	5	–	22	2
Naved Anjum	6	–	21	–

FALL OF WICKETS

1–15, 2–30, 3–72, 4–111, 5–139, 6–172, 7–191, 8–193, 9–193

Umpires: J.H. Hampshire & K.E. Palmer — Man of the Match – Javed Miandad — *Pakistan won by 3 runs*

TEXACO TROPHY – FIFTH ONE-DAY INTERNATIONAL – ENGLAND v. PAKISTAN

24 August, 1992 at Old Trafford, Manchester

PAKISTAN

Aamir Sohail	run out	87
Ramiz Raja (capt)	run out	37
Shoaib Mohammad	**b** Reeve	9
Inzamam-ul-Haq	lbw, **b** Cork	75
Asif Mujtaba	**c** Smith, **b** DeFreitas	10
Wasim Akram	not out	15
Naved Anjum	not out	12
*Moin Khan		
Waqar Younis		
Mushtaq Ahmed		
Aqib Javed		
Extras	lb 6, w 2, nb 1	9
	(for 5 wickets)	254

(55 overs)

	O	M	R	W
DeFreitas	11	1	52	1
Cork	11	1	37	1
Botham	11	–	43	–
Reeve	11	1	57	1
Illingworth	11	–	59	–

FALL OF WICKETS
1–69, 2–90, 3–189, 4–210, 5–240

ENGLAND

G.A. Gooch (capt)	**b** Aamir Sohail	45
*A.J. Stewart	**st** Moin Khan, **b** Aamir Sohail	51
R.A. Smith	not out	85
N.H. Fairbrother	**b** Waqar Younis	15
A.J. Lamb	**c** Moin Khan, **b** Waqar Younis	2
G.A. Hick	not out	42
I.T. Botham		
D.A. Reeve		
P.A.J. DeFreitas		
R.K. Illingworth		
D.G. Cork		
Extras	lb 7, w 3, nb 5	15
	(for 4 wickets)	255

(43.4 overs)

	O	M	R	W
Wasim Akram	9.4	1	45	–
Waqar Younis	8	–	58	2
Aqib Javed	6	–	42	–
Mushtaq Ahmed	9	–	48	–
Aamir Sohail	7	–	29	2
Naved Anjum	4	–	26	–

FALL OF WICKETS
1–98, 2–101, 3–149, 4–159

Umpires: H.D. Bird & M.J. Kitchen — Man of the Match – R.A. Smith — *England won by 6 wickets*

21, 22 and 24 August *at Swansea*

Gloucestershire 272 for 8 dec. (R.C. Russell 66 not out) and 31 for 0 dec.
Glamorgan 3 for 0 dec. and 32 for 0

Match drawn

Glamorgan 2 pts., Gloucestershire 2 pts.

at Leicester

Nottinghamshire 168 (G.J. Parsons 4 for 50, W.K.M. Benjamin 4 for 66) and 261 for 4 dec. (B.C. Broad 122, G.F. Archer 52 not out)
Leicestershire 252 (N.E. Briers 70) and 134 for 6 (N.E. Briers 66 not out, J.A. Afford 4 for 35)

Match drawn

Leicestershire 7 pts., Nottinghamshire 5 pts.

at Northampton

Kent 196 (S.A. Marsh 65) and 141 for 1 dec. (T.R. Ward 95 not out)
Northamptonshire 85 for 2 dec. and 108 for 1 (N.A. Felton 50 not out)

Match drawn

Northamptonshire 4 pts., Kent 1 pt.

at Weston-super-Mare

Somerset 370 for 8 dec. (C.J. Tavaré 115, A.N. Hayhurst 82, M.N. Lathwell 73) and 0 for 0 dec.
Hampshire 47 for 1 dec. and 52 for 1

Match drawn

Somerset 4 pts., Hampshire 3 pts.

at Hove

Middlesex 445 for 7 dec. (D.L. Haynes 177, M.W. Gatting 73, J.D. Carr 51) and 63 for 0 dec.
Sussex 187 for 3 dec. (J.W. Hall 81) and 79 for 1

Match drawn

Middlesex 4 pts., Sussex 2 pts.

at Worcester

Durham 199 (N.V. Radford 5 for 60) and 199 for 2 (P.W.G. Parker 94, P. Bainbridge 65 not out)
Worcestershire 294 for 6 dec. (D.B. D'Oliveira 81, T.S. Curtis 50)

Match drawn

Worcestershire 7 pts., Durham 3 pts.

at Bradford (Park Avenue)

Yorkshire 341 (S.A. Kellett 78, D. Byas 70, N.M. Kendrick 5 for 60) and 0 for 0 dec.
Surrey 39 for 1 dec. and 306 for 9 (G.P. Thorpe 79)

Surrey won by 1 wicket

Surrey 19 pts., Yorkshire 3 pts.

After a generally uninterrupted first day, matches were ruined by rain, and the agreements and forfeitures of captains could not bring a result. Chris Tavaré hit his first century of the summer, making 106 out of 117 runs scored in the afternoon session at Weston-super-Mare. Haynes hit his third century of the season and shared a second-wicket stand of 178 with Gatting. Most significantly, Chris Broad scored his second hundred in successive matches for Nottinghamshire and was then told that his services, along with those of Hemmings and Cooper, would no longer be required. Mike Hendrick, who had succeeded John Birch as manager earlier in the year, stated that Nottinghamshire had many young players of talent they wished to develop, but there was more than a whiff of politics in the decision to sack Broad, a very strong candidate for a Test place now that his ban was close to being lifted.

The return to the restored Park Avenue ground in Bradford brought defeat for Yorkshire, but Moxon's declaration was an intelligent one, and it nearly brought success for his side. He asked Surrey to make 303 in 93 overs. At 199 for 6, the odds were very much with Yorkshire. Feltham and Martin Bicknell added 69, but Bicknell was run out by Moxon and Feltham was leg before to Jarvis at the same score. Kendrick and Bryson added 14, and Boiling stayed with Kendrick to win the match with two balls to spare.

Jamie Hall, the Sussex opener, who had enjoyed a consistent season, was awarded his county cap, and, most regrettably, the last round of three-day matches in the county championship came to an end. One can only hope that sense will once more prevail and that the paying customer will be considered, and that, in the not-too-distant future, the three-day format will be reinstated.

SUNDAY LEAGUE

23 August *at Bristol*

Gloucestershire 43 for 1
v. Glamorgan

Match abandoned

Gloucestershire 2 pts., Glamorgan 2 pts.

at Southampton

Derbyshire 143 for 2 (P.D. Bowler 70 not out, K.J. Barnett 55)
Hampshire 120 for 3

Hampshire (4 pts.) won on faster scoring rate

at Leicester

Leicestershire 171 for 7 (M.I. Gidley 55 not out)
v. Northamptonshire

Match abandoned

Leicestershire 2 pts., Northamptonshire 2 pts.

at Trent Bridge

Lancashire 151 for 3 (N.J. Speak 60)
v. Nottinghamshire

Match abandoned

Nottinghamshire 2 pts., Lancashire 2 pts.

at Weston-super-Mare

Somerset 51 for 0
v. Essex

Match abandoned

Somerset 2 pts., Essex 2 pts.

at Hove

Middlesex 220 for 9 (D.L. Haynes 65, C.C. Remy 4 for 49)
v. Sussex

Match abandoned

Sussex 2 pts., Middlesex 2 pts.

at Edgbaston

Warwickshire 36 for 2
v. Kent

Match abandoned

Warwickshire 2 pts., Kent 2 pts.

at Worcester

Durham 94 for 5
v. Worcestershire

Worcestershire 2 pts., Durham 2 pts.

at Scarborough

Yorkshire 204 (C. White 63)
Surrey 141 for 1 (A.D. Brown 105 not out)

Surrey (4 pts.) won on faster scoring rate

Rain ruined the penultimate round of Sunday League matches, and results could only be achieved at Scarborough where Alistair Brown hit a century off 65 balls with three sixes and 13 fours, and at Southampton. The abandoned match at Hove meant that Middlesex would not be able to beat Sussex's Sunday League record of 14 wins, one loss and one 'no result' of 1982. Middlesex would only be able to equal the record if they won their last match.

26, 27, 28 and 29 August *at Derby*

Derbyshire 320 for 9 dec. (K.J. Barnett 68, P.D. Bowler 66, K.M. Krikken 57 not out, A.R. Caddick 5 for 77) and 0 for 0 dec.

Somerset 0 for 0 dec. and 199 (K.H. MacLeay 73, R.J. Turner 56 retired hurt, D.G. Cork 4 for 61)

Derbyshire won by 121 runs

Derbyshire 20 pts., Somerset 4 pts.

at Darlington

Hampshire 303 for 6 dec. (T.C. Middleton 127 not out, J.R. Ayling 90) and 229 for 5 dec. (M.C.J. Nicholas 95 not out, K.D. James 57)
Durham 250 for 4 dec. (P. Bainbridge 84, I. Smith 68 not out, P.W.G. Parker 68) and 194 for 8 (P. Bainbridge 83, K.J. Shine 6 for 68)

Match drawn

Durham 5 pts., Hampshire 5 pts.

at Canterbury

Kent 189 (C.A. Walsh 5 for 50) and 383 (N.R. Taylor 96, S.A. Marsh 70, M.V. Fleming 67, C.L. Hooper 56, C.A. Walsh 4 for 69)
Gloucestershire 175 (M.J. McCague 5 for 42) and 164 (M.J. McCague 5 for 44, R.P. Davis 5 for 61)

Kent won by 233 runs

Kent 21 pts., Gloucestershire 5 pts.

at Old Trafford

Lancashire 384 for 6 dec. (M.A. Atherton 119, G.D. Lloyd 77 not out, N.H. Fairbrother 67) and 0 for 0 dec.
Yorkshire 0 for 0 dec. and 121 for 3

Match drawn

Lancashire 4 pts., Yorkshire 2 pts.

at Northampton

Middlesex 95 (J.P. Taylor 5 for 24) and 105 (J.P. Taylor 5 for 30)
Northamptonshire 203 (A. Fordham 91, N.F. Williams 5 for 49)

Northamptonshire won by an innings and 3 runs

Northamptonshire 22 pts., Middlesex 4 pts.

at Hove

Sussex 204 (P. Moores 73, M.C. Ilott 5 for 60) and 279 (M.P. Speight 126, D.R. Pringle 4 for 47)
Essex 405 for 8 dec. (J.J.B. Lewis 133, D.R. Pringle 112 not out, G.A. Gooch 77) and 80 for 1

Essex won by 9 wickets

Essex 24 pts., Sussex 3 pts.

at Edgbaston

Glamorgan 316 (A. Dale 127, P.A. Cottey 67 not out, S.P. James 64, P.A. Smith 5 for 73) and 0 for 0 dec.
Warwickshire 0 for 0 dec. and 256 for 4 (D.P. Ostler 60, T.A. Lloyd 53, R.G. Twose 51)

Match drawn

Warwickshire 4 pts., Glamorgan 4 pts.

at Worcestershire

Worcestershire 162 (C.L. Cairns 4 for 50, C.C. Lewis 4 for 64) and 32 for 1
Nottinghamshire 321 for 9 dec. (C.C. Lewis 70 not out, D.W. Randall 66, C.L. Cairns 58, R.K. Illingworth 4 for 111)

Match drawn

Nottinghamshire 8 pts., Worcestershire 5 pts.

26, 27 and 28 August *at Scarborough*

Pakistanis 253 for 6 dec. (Shoaib Mohammad 105 not out)
World XI 385 for 8 dec. (P.R. Sleep 182, D.N. Patel 72)

Match drawn

The rain did not relent, particularly in the north of England, where the Pakistanis ended their tour in dampness and comedy. There was no play on the first day at Derby or Old Trafford, nor, on the second day, at these two grounds and Northampton, Edgbaston and Worcester. Efforts to revive the game at Derby were successful. Innings were forfeited, and Derbyshire bowled out Somerset on the last afternoon. They were not successful at Old Trafford where Mike Atherton created a record by hitting his fourth Roses century in consecutive seasons at the Manchester ground. Rain returned on the last afternoon after a declaration had set Yorkshire a daunting task.

Only 35 overs were possible on the first day at Darlington, and 52 on the second. Tony Middleton completed his fifth championship hundred of the season, and Ayling reached his best championship score. The match was kept alive by declarations, and the odds were very much in favour of Hampshire when Shine claimed his sixth wicket, bowling McEwan to reduce Durham to 178 for 8. At this point, with 17.1 overs remaining, the umpires took the players off the field although only the lightest of rain was falling. Umpire White argued that he and Burgess were trying to protect the pitch, but Mark Nicholas, the Hampshire skipper, was rightly very upset. Eight overs were lost, and Hampshire could not regain their momentum when play resumed.

Walsh dealt a blow to Kent's championship chances when he helped bowl them out for 189 on the first day at Canterbury, but Gloucestershire fared no better, losing their last five wickets for 12 runs on the second day. Reprieved, Kent scored freely and the pace of McCague and the spin of Davis took them to victory on the last day.

Northamptonshire, too, kept their slim championship hopes alive. Their seam attack disposed of Middlesex for 95 on the first day, and, after a blank second day, the home side made 203 which proved enough to give them an innings victory on a green wicket. A match scheduled for four days was over in two, and no one said a word.

The efforts of Kent and Northamptonshire appeared to matter little, however, as Essex moved resolutely towards retaining their title. At Hove, Gooch won the toss, asked Sussex to bat first. They were quickly reduced to 130 for 8 by the Essex seam attack, but, as he had done at Southend a few weeks earlier, Moores showed his capabilities in dealing with the Essex bowlers and took his side past 200. By the end of a restricted second day, Essex were 195 for 2. Gooch and Lewis had added 131 for the second wicket. Prichard and Garnham went early on the third morning, but Pringle joined Lewis in a stand of 105 which secured the fourth batting point. Hussain was unable to bat, having broken a finger while fielding, but Lewis' patient second hundred of his very short career and Pringle's more aggressive second of the season took Essex to a very strong position. Childs gave a further glimpse of victory by dismissing Hall before the close. At 113 for 7, still 88 in arrears, Sussex looked a well beaten side. Speight and Stephenson thought otherwise and batted commendably in a stand of 136. Speight was last out, having given the England captain more indication of his worth. Gooch and Prichard took Essex to victory, and the champions were one victory away from retaining their title. There had been eight leg before decisions in the Sussex first innings.

At Edgbaston, Adrian Dale hit 18 fours and a six in his 127, his third championship century of the season. His six was a hook off Paul Smith which brought him his hundred. His innings was in two halves which were separated by 44½ hours. Rain on the last day thwarted Warwickshire when, with 9.2 overs and 61 runs needed, play was brought to a close.

Rain was even more destructive at Worcester, but Nottinghamshire could take comfort from the all-round form of Chris Lewis who had begun to hint at consistency.

at Canterbury

Kent 235 for 7 (T.R. Ward 73)
Sussex 159 (A.P. Wells 52, M.J. McCague 4 for 45)

Kent (4 pts.) won by 76 runs

at Old Trafford

Derbyshire 155 for 6 (P.D. Bowler 91 not out)
Lancashire 157 for 5

Lancashire (4 pts.) won by 5 wickets

at Leicester

Leicestershire v. Hampshire

Match abandoned

Leicestershire 2 pts., Hampshire 2 pts.

at Northampton

Northamptonshire 235 for 3 (R.J. Bailey 63 not out)
Warwickshire 195 for 8

Northamptonshire (4 pts.) won by 40 runs

at The Oval

Surrey 268 for 4 (A.J. Stewart 103 not out, G.P. Thorpe 84)
Middlesex 193 for 9 (J.D. Carr 56, J.E. Benjamin 4 for 44)

Surrey (4 pts.) won on faster scoring rate

at Worcester

Worcestershire v. Nottinghamshire

Match abandoned

Worcestershire 2 pts., Nottinghamshire 2 pts.

SUNDAY LEAGUE

30 August *at Darlington*

Durham v. Yorkshire

Match abandoned

Durham 2 pts., Yorkshire 2 pts.

at Chelmsford

Gloucestershire 239 for 8 (G.D. Hodgson 73, M.W. Alleyne 68, R.J. Scott 50 not out, J.P. Stephenson 5 for 58)
Essex 106 for 4

Gloucestershire (4 pts.) won on faster scoring rate

at Cardiff

Glamorgan v. Somerset

Match abandoned

Glamorgan 2 pts., Somerset 2 pts.

SUNDAY LEAGUE – FINAL TABLE, 1992

	P	W	L	Nr	Pts
Middlesex (11)	17	14	2	1	58
Essex (6)	17	11	5	1	46
Hampshire (17)	17	10	6	1	42
Surrey (8)	17	10	7	–	40
Somerset (9)	17	9	6	2	40
Kent (10)	17	8	5	4	40
Worcestershire (4)	17	7	6	4	36
Gloucestershire (13)	17	8	8	1	34
Durham (–)	17	7	7	3	34
Warwickshire (5)	17	7	7	3	34
Sussex (12)	17	7	8	2	32
Lancashire (2)	17	6	7	4	32
Northamptonshire (3)	17	7	9	1	30
Derbyshire (15)	17	7	9	1	30
Yorkshire (7)	17	6	9	2	28
Glamorgan (16)	17	4	10	3	22
Nottinghamshire (1)	17	3	11	3	18
Leicestershire (14)	17	3	12	2	16

Warwickshire and Worcestershire no result columns include one match that was tied. The 1991 positions are in brackets.

The Sunday League came to a suitable, soggy, anti-climactic conclusion. Middlesex, the champions, lost to Surrey who climbed into fourth place as a result and claimed some prize money. Essex, already confirmed as runners-up, lost to Gloucestershire in a damp Chelmsford, but Gooch, Pringle, Ilott and Such were rested prior to the vital championship match against Hampshire.

Haynes ended as leading scorer in the Sunday League, with, remarkably, Dean Jones 183 runs behind him in second place. Darren Bicknell, Matthew Maynard, Hugh Morris and James Whitaker all scored heavily. Martin Bicknell was among the leading wicket-takers who were headed by Sean Udal, 31 wickets, and Martin McCague, 27.

One could not mourn the passing of the 40-over slog, but one dreaded more the coming of its 50-over Technicolor replacement.

Jamie Hall, Sussex, a fine season as opening bat and a county cap. (Sporting Pictures (UK) Ltd)

31 August, 1, 2 and 3 September *at Chelmsford*

Hampshire 233 (P.M. Such 4 for 23) and 229 (A.N. Aymes 65)
Essex 298 (P.J. Prichard 82, I.J. Turner 5 for 81) and 165 for 2 (J.P. Stephenson 83 not out, P.J. Prichard 55 not out)

Essex won by 8 wickets

Essex 22 pts., Hampshire 6 pts.

at Cardiff

Glamorgan 268 (H. Morris 80, P.A. Cottey 58, I.D.K. Salisbury 4 for 79)
Sussex 146 for 7

Match drawn

Glamorgan 6 pts., Sussex 4 pts.

at Bristol

Gloucestershire 302 for 7 dec. (G.D. Hodgson 81, T.H.C. Hancock 74, J.T.C. Vaughan 51) and 0 for 0 dec.
Leicestershire 0 for 0 dec. and 24 for 0

Match drawn

Gloucestershire 4 pts., Leicestershire 3 pts.

at Trent Bridge

Nottinghamshire 166 (M. Saxelby 57, D.G. Cork 5 for 36) and 385 (G.F. Archer 117, C.C. Lewis 82)
Derbyshire 330 (K.J. Barnett 156 not out) and 222 for 8 (P.D. Bowler 61, J.A. Afford 4 for 91)

Derbyshire won by 2 wickets

Derbyshire 23 pts., Nottinghamshire 4 pts.

at The Oval

Surrey 557 (G.P. Thorpe 216, A.D. Brown 129, A.J. Stewart 76, A.P. van Troost 6 for 104)
Somerset 352 (G.D. Rose 132, M.A. Feltham 4 for 75) and 124 for 3

Match drawn

Surrey 6 pts., Somerset 2 pts.

at Worcester

Worcestershire 409 for 7 dec. (G.A. Hick 146, S.J. Rhodes 116 not out)
Warwickshire 210 for 6 (A.J. Moles 85 not out)

Match drawn

Worcestershire 5 pts., Warwickshire 4 pts.

at Scarborough

Yorkshire 508 (D. Byas 100, S.A. Kellett 96, P.W. Jarvis 80, M.D. Moxon 77) and 171 for 3 dec. (M.D. Moxon 101 not out)

Northamptonshire 359 for 8 dec. (D.J. Capel 89, R.J. Bailey 85, K.M. Curran 50, M.A. Robinson 6 for 62) and 298 for 8 (A. Fordham 93, D.J. Capel 66, R.J. Bailey 58, J.D. Batty 4 for 95)

Match drawn

Yorkshire 5 pts., Northamptonshire 3 pts.

At 3.35 pm, on Thursday, 3 September, John Stephenson dabbed a ball from Robin Smith to backward point, and he and Paul Prichard ran through for a single with arms raised in triumph. Essex had beaten Hampshire by eight wickets and retained the Britannic Assurance County Championship. The match was fought tenaciously from start to finish. Hampshire won the toss and took first innings on a pitch which was sluggish after rain on the Sunday. They found run-getting very difficult, and when James nudged on to Topley the score was 35, and 21 overs had passed. Middleton was painfully slow, and it was something of a merciful release when he was caught behind off Ilott. Gower, Nicholas and Marshall flickered briefly, but Childs and Such extracted some turn from the pitch, and the batsmen were surrounded by ravenous close fielders. Udal's 44 was the main reason why Hampshire's last three wickets realised 65 runs, but Essex could be well pleased with their first day's work – Hampshire all out for 233, and the home side had maximum bowling points.

The loss of openers Gooch and Stephenson for 50 did not seem to disturb Essex too much, for Lewis, in his crouching, tenacious manner, and Prichard, all style and fluency, added 92. They seemed to be moving serenely towards a dominant lead when Ayling had Lewis caught behind, and Turner bowled Knight who pushed forward half-heartedly. At 185 for 4, Prichard and Garnham together, all was bright and urgent, but they fell in successive overs by Turner, who was to claim the best return of his career. Pringle, Topley and Ilott all surrendered without playing a shot in anger, and Essex were 219 for 9, a first-innings lead remote, a third batting point beyond the horizon. Hampshire had been handicapped by the loss of Shine through injury, but Ayling had bowled steadily, and Udal and Turner had mesmerised the late middle order. Now came a remarkable change. In 17 overs, Such and Childs added 79 priceless runs in a manner often comic but ever defiant and brave. Both made the highest scores of their careers, Childs 43, Such 35 not out, and although they narrowly failed to win the third batting point, they gave Essex a very valuable lead. Childs played two wonderful shots, a straight drive for six and a cover drive of which Gower would have been proud. Such was less correct. He retreated rapidly towards square-leg when facing Marshall who, instead of bowling straight, followed the batsman. Such, almost lying on the ground, threw his bat at the ball and smeared it to the off-side boundary. The crowd loved it. Hampshire were less amused, noticeably wicket-keeper Aymes.

Bad light ended play early, but it seemed that Essex would win on the third day when Hampshire lost six wickets before clearing the arrears. Childs was finding some quick turn, and he bowled Nicholas and had Marshall caught close in, but Ayling helped Aymes in a stand of 56 before he, too, fell to Childs. Udal and Aymes added a spirited 53, and Aymes continued to delay Essex until the final morning. A target of 165 was more than Essex had expected or would have wished for. The loss of Gooch and Lewis, both to Turner, for 32 added to the tension, but Stephenson and Prichard, having seen off the menace of Marshall's pace, attacked the spinners Turner and Udal, and Essex claimed their sixth championship in 13 years.

The match at Chelmsford drew all the attention, particularly as the games at Cardiff and Bristol were ruined by rain. There was no play on the last day at Cardiff, and little at Bristol. There was also no play on the last day at Worcester where the home side had been 43 for 3 until rallied first by Hick and then by Rhodes who hit his first century of the season.

At Trent Bridge, in the wake of the bewildering culling, Nottinghamshire chose to bat first and lost their last eight wickets for 35 runs. Kim Barnett carried his bat through the 126.4 overs of the Derbyshire innings to give his side a formidable lead. Nottinghamshire fought back strongly. Graeme Archer reached a maiden first-class century, and he and Chris Lewis took the score from 144 for 6 to 312 before Lewis was bowled by Griffith. Archer hit three sixes and 11 fours, and he was first out on the last morning, but Nottinghamshire added another 73 runs to frustrate Derbyshire, who were left to make 222 in 62 overs. Peter Bowler became the first batsman to reach 2000 runs, and he

Alan Fordham – an outstanding season for Northamptonshire in all forms of cricket. (Alan Cozzi)

was third out with the score at 172. A dramatic collapse followed, prompted by some excellent spin bowling from Afford. Four wickets fell for six runs. Cork played sensibly, but he was out at 213, and Bishop followed five runs later. Griffith and Warner eventually saw Derbyshire home, and into fourth place, with 17 balls to spare.

Graham Thorpe hit his first championship century of the season and turned it into the first double hundred of his career. He and Brown hit 211 in 34 overs for the fifth wicket. In another whirlwind hundred, Brown hit three sixes and 14 fours while Thorpe hit 16 boundaries. Thorpe is a compact, technically sound left-hander with a wide range of shots. He has been hailed as an England batsman, but, at present, he is an August player. His runs inevitably come late in the season. Surrey fell apart at the close, but they still reached their highest score of the season. Somerset, thanks to Rose's dedicated grim century, almost saved the follow-on, but, in any case, rain thwarted Surrey on the last day.

Allan Lamb was suspended for two games by the Northamptonshire Committee for allowing his name to be associated with an article in a national newspaper alleging ball-tampering and 'cheating'. He missed the Sunday League game, and the game against Yorkshire at Scarborough where his side fought a game battle. Moxon and Kellett began with a partnership of 140, and Byas and Jarvis hit 133 for the seventh wicket on the second day to take Yorkshire to a massive 508, Byas hitting his first hundred of the season and Jarvis a career best 80. Northamptonshire were set-back by a brisk spell from their former bowler Mark Robinson. Robinson finished with six wickets, but sound middle-order batting saved Northamptonshire from having to follow-on. They were eventually asked to score 321 in 60 overs. With 11 overs remaining, they were 242 for 2, but Batty removed Bailey and Curran in successive balls, and the innings fell apart. Six wickets fell in the last 11 overs, and Northamptonshire were happy to draw.

JOSHUA TETLEY FESTIVAL TROPHY
at Scarborough

4 September

Nottinghamshire 238 for 5 (P.R. Pollard 68, M. Saxelby 54)
Hampshire 242 for 1 (T.C. Middleton 109 not out, R.M.F. Cox 68, J.R. Ayling 55 not out)
Hampshire won by 9 wickets

Essex retain the Britannic Assurance County Championship. Celebrations at Chelmsford after the victory over Hampshire, 3 September. (Mike Hewitt/Allsport)

5 September

Durham 244 for 6 (W. Larkins 103)
Yorkshire 248 for 1 (S.A. Kellett 109 not out, M.D. Moxon 108)

Yorkshire won by 9 wickets

The final could not be played because of rain, and the trophy was shared between Hampshire and Yorkshire. Moxon and Kellett hit 217 for Yorkshire's first wicket against Durham.

SEEBOARD TROPHY
at Hove

4 September

Kent 254 for 9 (G.R. Cowdrey 91, N.R. Taylor 51, R.E. Bryson 5 for 39)
Surrey 250 for 7 (A.D. Brown 78)

Kent won by 4 runs

Early disaster for Leicestershire. Tim Boon is run out for 3. (David Munden)

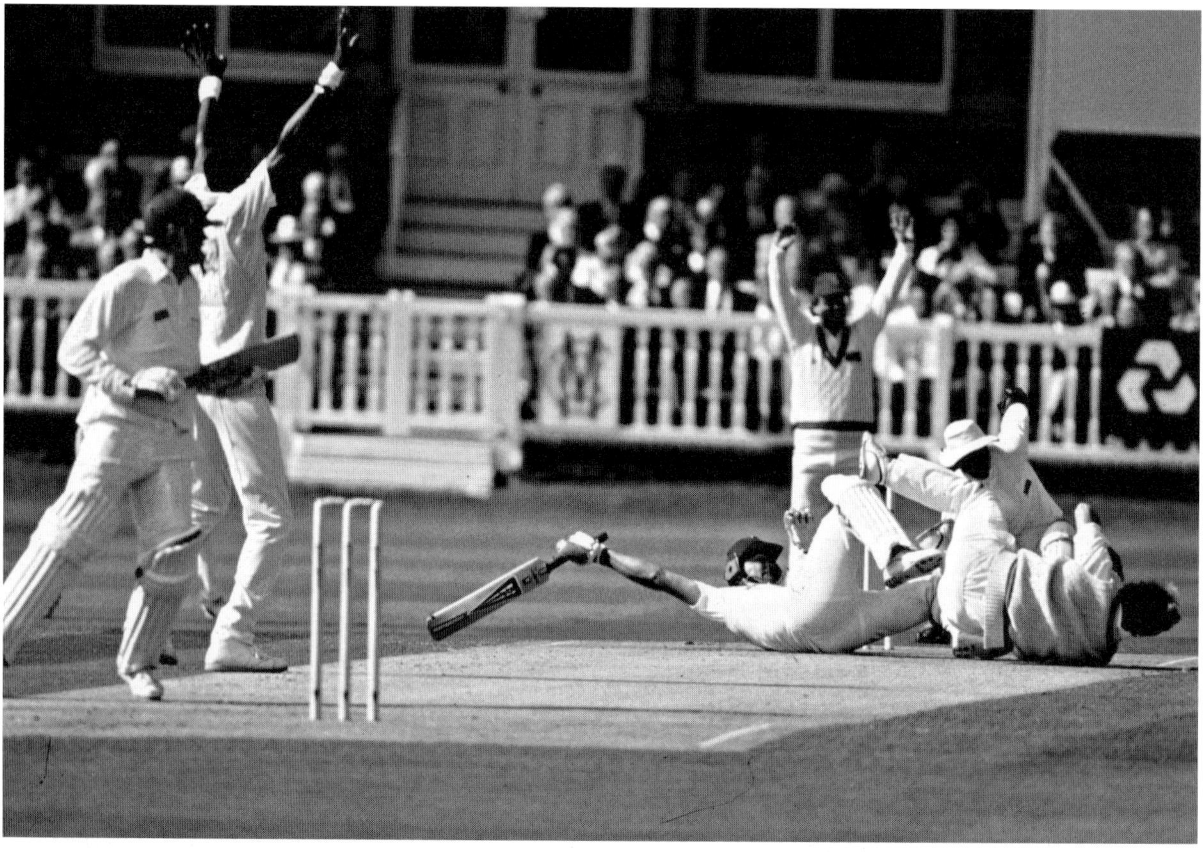

5 September

Sussex 237 (A.P. Wells 79, F.D. Stephenson 62)
Gloucestershire 222 (G.D. Hodgson 69, F.D. Stephenson 5 for 36)

Sussex won by 15 runs

The final could not be played because of rain. Kent beat Sussex when the sides had a bowl-out at unguarded stumps. Bill Athey did not appear for Gloucestershire. It had been announced that he had refused a new contract and would be leaving the county.

NATWEST TROPHY FINAL
NORTHAMPTONSHIRE v. LEICESTERSHIRE
at Lord's

NatWest announced their continued sponsorship of the 60-over knock-out competition towards the end of the 1992 final, and one hopes for these generous sponsors that they will be better served in the future than they were by the poor fare offered by Leicestershire and Northamptonshire in 1992. For the first time, rows of empty seats were to be seen at a major Lord's final. There were two main reasons for this. Firstly, Leicestershire, in particular, and Northamptonshire are

ABOVE: *James Whitaker gets a ball away during his fine innings of 84. (David Munden)*

BELOW: *Phil Robinson in aggressive mood, but he saw too little of the bowling in the closing stages. (David Munden)*

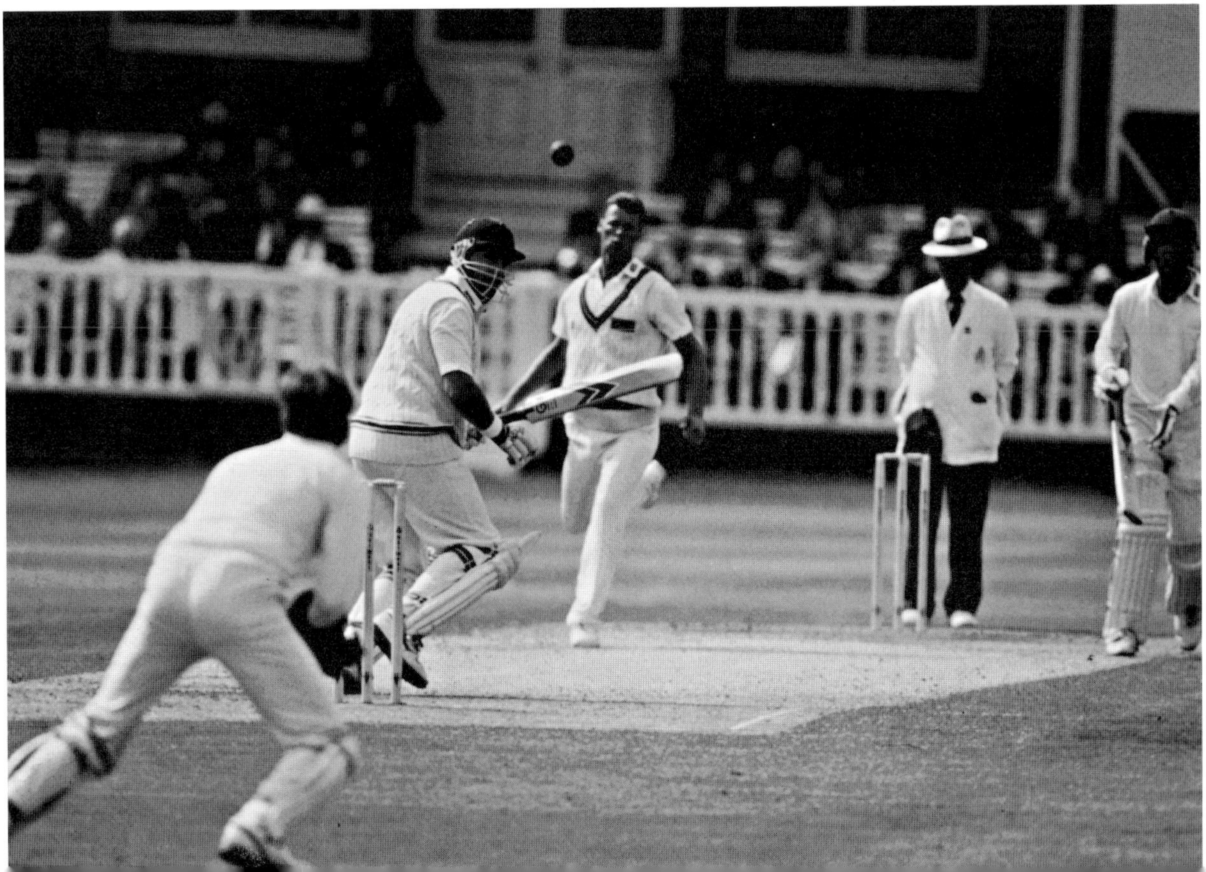

poorly supported sides; secondly, in a time of deepest recession, there are very many people who cannot afford £35 for a ticket. Administrators might care to note this. Once you lose the paying customer, it is very hard to get him back. Even in the garden behind the Warner Stand, the scene of picnics and friendly gatherings, there was not the usual bubble and excitement. This was, indeed, a low-key final. It certainly was on the field.

Northamptonshire won the toss. It was no surprise that Lamb asked Leicestershire to bat first, but he gained little advantage from his tactic. There was no extravagant movement similar to that which Northamptonshire had suffered against DeFreitas two years earlier. Indeed, neither Ambrose nor Taylor appeared to swing the ball, and batting was not an arduous task on a benign pitch. What wounds were to come Leicestershire's way were to be self-inflicted.

Ambrose opened the bowling from the Nursery End, and Boon pushed the ball for a single. He scored a single in the second over and another in the third, and when Briers pushed the ball to leg in the same over the batsmen went for an insane run, and Boon was run out by Curran's under-arm throw from short-leg. This dampened what spirit Leicestershire may have possessed, and after ten overs the score was 16.

The first boundary arrived in the eighth over when Whitaker mis-hit Taylor over square-leg. When Curran and Capel replaced the opening bowlers the run rate increased. Three fours came in two overs, and Briers twice drove Capel sweetly, but just as Leicestershire seemed to be gaining in confidence they threw away another wicket. Briers was run out by Bailey's direct hit on the stumps from square-leg. It was the 20th over, and the score was 45.

Whitaker and Robinson now gave Leicestershire their best hope of victory. They added 130 in 34 overs, but just as they tried to accelerate, the wickets fell. Whitaker skied the

Benson is bowled by Ambrose. (Patrick Eagar)

Nigel Felton chops on to Mullally. (David Munden)

ball to long-off after hitting 84 off 160 balls, a responsible innings which eventually promised more than it achieved. In the next over, Benson, who had a nightmare match, had his off-stump knocked back. Potter, Benjamin and Robinson fell in the space of 11 balls, and from their last ten overs, Leicestershire managed a meagre 46 runs. Northamptonshire had bowled tightly, and their fielding had hovered between the brilliant and the downright sloppy.

The Leicestershire bowling never suggested more than the pedestrian. Mullally was unable to control width in his first over, and Millns and Potter were to have similar problems. Fordham showed great purpose from the beginning of his innings, but he was dropped at slip by Benson who put down Bailey, on two, in a similar manner, diving sideways for a ball of waist height. Leicestershire's success came in the eighth over when Felton chopped on to Mullally, but they badly missed Wells who had been taken ill the previous evening. Millns, having just returned to the side after injury, looked far from fit and was not the force he had been for most of the season.

Fordham and Bailey added 144 in 35 overs, and the game had long been decided when Fordham mis-hit the ball high to mid-on. Lamb entered to hit 24 off 22 balls, including four vigorous fours, and Northamptonshire won with 10.2 overs to spare. Bailey had punctuated his forward lunge with some clean and powerful hitting, and, after offering the early chance, never looked in trouble.

Much of the cricket was of poor standard, and this was a disappointing final in every way.

ABOVE: *Fordham's positive innings comes to an end when he skies Mullally. (David Munden)*

BELOW: *Allan Lamb holds the trophy. A bearded Alan Curtis, announcer supreme, stands in the background. (Patrick Eagar)*

NATWEST TROPHY FINAL – NORTHAMPTONSHIRE v. LEICESTERSHIRE
5 September, 1992 at Lord's

LEICESTERSHIRE

T.J. Boon	run out	3
N.E. Briers (capt)	run out	25
J.J. Whitaker	c Taylor, b Curran	84
P.E. Robinson	c Felton, b Ambrose	62
J.D.R. Benson	b Ambrose	0
L. Potter	c Capel, b Curran	12
W.K.M. Benjamin	b Curran	0
*P.A. Nixon	not out	7
G.J. Parsons	not out	1
SD.J. Millns		
A.D. Mullally		
Extras	b 1, lb 8, w 3, nb 2	14
	(for 7 wickets)	208

(60 overs)	O	M	R	W
Ambrose	12	–	35	2
Taylor	7	1	19	–
Capel	11	3	39	–
Curran	12	1	41	3
Cook	12	–	43	–
Penberthy	6	–	22	–

FALL OF WICKETS
1–3, 2–45, 3–175, 4–178, 5–197, 6–198, 7–200

NORTHAMPTONSHIRE

A. Fordham	c Potter, b Mullally	91
N.A. Felton	b Mullally	6
R.J. Bailey	not out	72
A.J. Lamb (capt)	not out	24
D.J. Capel		
K.M. Curran		
A.L. Penberthy		
*D. Ripley		
C.E.L. Ambrose		
J.P. Taylor		
N.G.B. Cook		
Extras	lb 9, w 9	18
	(for 2 wickets)	211

(49.4 overs)	O	M	R	W
Benjamin	12	–	65	–
Mullally	10	2	22	2
Millns	10	–	43	–
Parsons	9	1	31	–
Potter	4	–	18	–
Benson	4.4	1	23	–

FALL OF WICKETS
1–29, 2–173

Umpires: D.J. Constant & D.R. Shepherd — Man of the Match – A. Fordham — *Northamptonshire won by 8 wickets*

7, 8, 9 and 10 September *at Derby*

Derbyshire 226 (T.J.G. O'Gorman 64, C.J. Adams 60, D.R. Pringle 5 for 63) and 309 (C.J. Adams 135, J.E. Morris 55, M.C. Ilott 6 for 87)
Essex 96 (G.A. Gooch 53, I.R. Bishop 6 for 18) and 442 for 6 (G.A. Gooch 123 not out, J.P. Stephenson 97, M.A. Garnham 66, N. Shahid 51)

Essex won by 4 wickets

Essex 20 pts., Derbyshire 6 pts.

at Canterbury

Glamorgan 158 (A.P. Igglesden 5 for 45) and 389 (P.A. Cottey 141, I.V.A. Richards 76, A. Dale 50, M.V. Fleming 4 for 63)
Kent 219 (N.R. Taylor 74, S.A. Marsh 60) and 242 (T.R. Ward 53, S.D. Thomas 5 for 79)

Glamorgan won by 86 runs

Glamorgan 21 pts., Kent 6 pts.

at Old Trafford

Sussex 563 (A.P. Wells 143, N.J. Lenham 136, P. Moores 74, B.T.P. Donelan 68, A.A. Barnett 4 for 148)
Lancashire 174 (G.D. Lloyd 56, I.D.K. Salisbury 6 for 29) and 207 (J.P. Crawley 93, I.D.K. Salisbury 5 for 54)

Sussex won by an innings and 182 runs

Sussex 24 pts., Lancashire 2 pts.

at Trent Bridge

Surrey 207 (C.C. Lewis 4 for 65) and 411 (G.P. Thorpe 100, A.J. Stewart 85, D.J. Bicknell 77, M.A. Lynch 70, A.D. Brown 50 not out, C.C. Lewis 6 for 90)
Nottinghamshire 357 (K.P. Evans 104, C.C. Lewis 52, M.P. Bicknell 5 for 89) and 262 for 5 (R.T. Robinson 129 not out, G.F. Archer 66)

Nottinghamshire won by 5 wickets

Nottinghamshire 23 pts., Surrey 5 pts.

at Taunton

Somerset 534 (R.J. Harden 126, C.J. Tavaré 124, A.N. Hayhurst 102, N.D. Burns 54, M.N. Lathwell 50, S.P. Hughes 4 for 112) and 25 for 2
Durham 219 (I. Smith 110, N.A. Mallender 5 for 65, A.R. Caddick 4 for 62) and 339 (W. Larkins 117, J.A. Daley 88, I.T. Botham 74, A.R. Caddick 4 for 53)

Somerset won by 8 wickets

Somerset 24 pts., Durham 3 pts.

8, 9, 10 and 11 September *at Lord's*

Warwickshire 476 (T.L. Penney 151, R.G. Twose 84, K.J. Piper 72) and 57 for 2

Middlesex 201 (N.M.K. Smith 5 for 61) and 328 (K.R. Brown 106, M.W. Gatting 71, A.A. Donald 5 for 36)

Warwickshire won by 8 wickets

Warwickshire 24 pts., Middlesex 5 pts.

Essex gave further evidence of their quality and total commitment when they gained a remarkable victory over Derbyshire in the penultimate round of county championship matches. Having won the toss, they asked Derbyshire to bat first and bowled them out for 226, the wickets falling to the seamers, Pringle, Ilott and Topley. Essex's contentment was short-lived as they were routed by Ian Bishop. They were all out for 96 of which Gooch, batting at number six, scored 53. Twenty wickets fell on the first day, and another ten fell on the second when Derbyshire were bowled out for 309. Mark Ilott took six wickets for 84, a career best, but the star of the day was the aggressively entertaining Chris Adams. He and Morris added 163 in 41 overs for the fourth wicket, and Adams reached his century off 116 balls. He is a very fine fielder as well as being a batsman full of strokes, and he is one to whom England should look in the near future. Essex were left with more than two days to bat to save the game, or to score an improbable 440 for victory. They closed at 46 for 0, and Knight and Lewis were both out quickly on the third morning. When Prichard was out at 85 it seemed that Derbyshire were in sight of a three-day win, but Shahid joined Stephenson in a stand worth 88. Both were dismissed before the end of play, but Gooch and Garnham were together with the score on 283 for 5, and there was a hint of the unexpected. Essex completed an exceptional victory on the last afternoon, having lost only one more wicket, that of Garnham who helped Gooch to add 129 for the sixth wicket. Pringle partnered Gooch while the remaining 84 runs were scored. Gooch faced 298 balls and was at the crease for 373 minutes. The Essex innings lasted for more than nine hours. There was batting of the highest quality, and a professionalism that has no equal in the county championship. Only two other counties have bettered Essex's score to win a match in the fourth innings. The remarkable thing was that, with the title already won, Essex were still able to summon the resources and concentration to achieve this memorable win. Gooch's 123 not out was the 98th first-class century of his career.

Fortunes changed, too, at Canterbury. Led by the pace of Igglesden, Kent bowled out Glamorgan for 158, but they lost five wickets for 55 runs before Taylor and Marsh took them into the second day with a stand of 113. They led by 61 on the first innings and seemed in control until Viv Richards and Tony Cottey added 142 in 46 overs for Glamorgan's fifth wicket. Cottey hit his highest score in the championship, and Kent, losing Ward and Taylor, ended the day on 119 for 2, needing another 210 runs for victory. On the last day, they fell apart against the Glamorgan seam attack. There were five wickets for Darren Thomas, who had quickly shown his qualities in the county game after a handful of matches.

Jimmy Daley – a young hope for Durham at the end of a disappointing first season. (Sporting Pictures (UK) Ltd)

Sussex overwhelmed the troubled Lancashire inside three days at Old Trafford. A third-wicket stand of 263 between Lenham and Alan Wells formed the basis of Sussex's victory. Ian Salisbury took a career best 6 for 29 and finished with match figures of 11 for 83, another career best. A stylish innings from John Crawley was Lancashire's only riposte.

Trent Bridge saw a match of revivals. Surrey slumped before Lewis and Evans on the first day. They were bowled out for 207, with Bryson and Boiling adding 84 for the last wicket. Nottinghamshire seemed to have lost the initiative when they descended to 233 for 8, but Steve Bramhall then joined Kevin Evans in a partnership of 124 in 48 overs. Evans hit nine fours in his second championship hundred. Trailing by 150, Surrey bounced back after the early loss of David Ward. Darren Bicknell and Thorpe added 174, and Stewart, Lynch and Brown appeared to take the game out of Nottinghamshire's reach before the last six Surrey wickets went down for 35 runs. Chris Lewis had a particularly good all-round match. It looked as if his efforts would come to nothing when Nottinghamshire, in search of 262 to win, lost three wickets for 39 runs, but Robinson and Archer added 132, and Robinson played a captain's innings to take his side to victory.

With five of their first six batsmen reaching fifty, and three of those going on to make centuries, Somerset took a strong grip on the game against lowly Durham. The visitors had some consolation in that Ian Smith hit a maiden first-class century, but he could not save his side from having to follow-on. Larkins, too, hit a hundred, and Jimmy Daley, a teenager making his first-class debut, scored 88. The pair added 201 for the fourth

Durham wicket, and Somerset were forced to bat again, but they still won inside three days.

At Lord's, Roger Twose was awarded his county cap for another stirring innings, the culmination of an excellent season, but the real honours for Warwickshire went to Trevor Penney, who hit a career best 151, and to Keith Piper, who shared an eighth-wicket stand of 192. The last 20 overs of the partnership realised 111 runs. Middlesex ended the second day on 161 for 7, and they followed-on early on the third day. Some belligerence from Gatting and a rearguard action from Keith Brown, who hit his first century of the summer, could not save Middlesex from defeat although Warwickshire did have to bat again.

12, 13, 14 and 15 September *at Gateshead Fell*

Durham 312 (J.D. Glendenen 76, P.W.G. Parker 70, W. Larkins 53, M. Watkinson 5 for 63) and 271 (J.A. Daley 80 not out, P.W.G. Parker 52, P.A.J. DeFreitas 6 for 94)
Lancashire 562 (M.A. Atherton 199, P.J. Martin 133, I.D. Austin 58, P. Bainbridge 5 for 100) and 24 for 0

Lancashire won by 10 wickets

Lancashire 24 pts., Durham 6 pts.

at Cardiff

Glamorgan 307 (I.V.A. Richards 85, M.P. Maynard 57, S.P. James 52, R.W. Sladdin 4 for 102) and 0 for 0 dec.
Derbyshire 0 for 0 dec. and 244 (R.D.B. Croft 6 for 49)

Glamorgan won by 63 runs

Glamorgan 20 pts., Derbyshire 4 pts.

at Bristol

Essex 128 (C.A. Walsh 7 for 38) and 382 (G.A. Gooch 101, J.P. Stephenson 93, J.J.B. Lewis 53)
Gloucestershire 326 (M.W. Alleyne 93, M.G.N. Windows 71, S.J.W. Andrew 4 for 58) and 187 for 3 (M.W. Alleyne 73 not out, R.J. Scott 73)

Gloucestershire won by 7 wickets

Gloucestershire 23 pts., Essex 2 pts.

at Southampton

Hampshire 231 (R.A. Smith 87) and 261 for 5 dec. (M.C.J. Nicholas 88 not out, R.S.M. Morris 74, T.C. Middleton 50)
Worcestershire 228 for 8 dec. and 254 for 7 (S.J. Rhodes 107, S.R. Lampitt 69)

Match drawn

Worcestershire 6 pts., Hampshire 5 pts.

at Leicester

Leicestershire 352 (B.F. Smith 86, T.J. Boon 81, W.K.M. Benjamin 71) and 240 for 5 dec. (T.J. Boon 97)
Northamptonshire 303 for 7 dec. (R.J. Bailey 167 not out) and 290 for 4 (A.J. Lamb 122 not out, K.M. Curran 52)

Northamptonshire won by 6 wickets

Northamptonshire 23 pts., Leicestershire 6 pts.

at Taunton

Nottinghamshire 265 (G.F. Archer 83 not out, R.T. Robinson 74) and 188 (M. Saxelby 64, H.R.J. Trump 4 for 53)
Somerset 616 for 7 dec. (R.J. Harden 187, C.J. Tavaré 125, R.J. Turner 101 not out, K.P. Evans 4 for 96)

Somerset won by an innings and 163 runs

Somerset 24 pts., Nottinghamshire 4 pts.

at The Oval

Middlesex 441 (M.A. Roseberry 120, M.R. Ramprakash 117, J.D. Carr 114, R.E. Bryson 5 for 117) and 32 for 0 dec.
Surrey 141 for 3 dec. (A.J. Stewart 51 not out) and 325 for 9 (D.J. Bicknell 87, A.J. Stewart 52, P.C.R. Tufnell 5 for 130)

Match drawn

Middlesex 4 pts., Surrey 0 pts.

at Hove

Yorkshire 232 (C. White 71 not out, S.A. Kellett 63, I.D.K. Salisbury 7 for 54) and 259 (M.D. Moxon 50, I.D.K. Salisbury 5 for 84, E.S.H. Giddins 4 for 65)
Sussex 432 (N.J. Lenham 135, J.W. Hall 90) and 61 for 4 (P.W. Jarvis 4 for 27)

Sussex won by 6 wickets

Sussex 23 pts., Yorkshire 2 pts.

at Edgbaston

Kent 603 for 8 dec. (T.R. Ward 153, M.R. Benson 122, C.L. Hooper 102, G.R. Cowdrey 88, N.R. Taylor 78, N.M.K. Smith 4 for 160)
Warwickshire 289 (T.A. Lloyd 76, D.A. Reeve 51, A.P. Igglesden 5 for 91) and 171 (R.G. Twose 52, R.P. Davis 5 for 41, C.L. Hooper 4 for 57)

Kent won by an innings and 143 runs

Kent 24 pts., Warwickshire 4 pts.

Any hopes that Durham may have had of climbing off the bottom of the championship table with a win in the last match of the season vanished when Lancashire scored 562 at Gateshead Fell. Durham, encouraged by an opening partnership of 104 between Larkins and Parker, made 312, and they reduced Lancashire to 220 for 6 just before the close of the second day. On the Monday, Martin and Atherton added 243 for the seventh wicket. Both batsmen reached career best scores, and Martin's 133 off 192 balls was his maiden first-class century. DeFreitas and Austin disposed of Durham on the last day, and Lancashire moved to an easy victory. It lifted them to

12th in the table, but it offered little comfort in a restless and unhappy season in which politics seemed to dominate. Durham's early brightness had long disappeared, and their first season in first-class cricket ended with them 36 points adrift at the bottom of the championship. There was a ray of hope – a young batsman named Jimmy Daley, born in Sunderland and not an ageing import.

Glamorgan finished two places below Lancashire as a result of their victory over Derbyshire. There was no play possible on the first two days at Cardiff, and there were forfeitures of innings. Glamorgan owed much to Croft who took 6 for 49 in 7.3 overs. One of the mysteries of the selectors' policy was the omission of Croft from both of the winter tours. One feels that he is now the best off-spinner in the country, and he needs reward and encouragement.

Put in to bat, Essex, the champions, were bowled out cheaply by Courtney Walsh, who exploited conditions favouring pace bowling. Mark Alleyne and Matthew Windows built on the work of Gloucestershire's acting captain with some competent batting. Windows, on his first-class debut, was particularly impressive. Gooch hit his 99th first-class hundred to give thoughts of another mighty Essex recovery, but Gloucestershire were not to be denied and claimed their sixth win of the season.

Hampshire were denied. Nicholas revitalised the match against Worcestershire by setting the visitors a target of 265 at approximately four runs an over. A stand of 166 in 34 overs for the fifth wicket between Rhodes, who found batting form late in the season, and Lampitt gave Worcestershire a glimpse of victory, but tight bowling by Marshall and Udal denied them. In a miserable season, Worcestershire suffered only four defeats as opposed to Essex's six, but Essex took the title, and only Durham finished below Worcestershire. A bolder, more positive, less cautious approach might well have brought better rewards.

Nigel Briers, who had gained much praise for what he had achieved with Leicestershire's limited resources, set Northamptonshire a target of 290 in 66 overs. A century by Allan Lamb, ending the season defiantly as ever, gave the visitors victory and third place in the championship. Lamb had been a consistent scorer in the batting, but Bailey, who led the side very well in Lamb's absence, enjoyed a splendid season and is an underrated batsman.

With three batsmen making their highest scores of the season, Somerset overwhelmed Nottinghamshire. Off-spinner Trump took the last four wickets in 14 balls to win the game for Somerset, whose season had promised more than it achieved.

Rain seriously disrupted the match at The Oval, and the third day saw some rather meaningless circket with the Middlesex innings not ending until after lunch, and the players showing a reluctance to take the field late in the day after a brief stoppag347e for bad light. There was a criticism of this attitude, which brought a change of heart on the last day and an exciting finish. Surrey were asked to make 333 in 92 overs, and the chase, against bowlers with the craft of Emburey and Tufnell, brought four stumpings to wicket-keeper Keith Brown. When the last over began both sides had a chance of victory, but Middlesex captured wickets with the first and fourth balls, and Boiling was happy to keep out Tufnell's last two deliveries and earn a draw.

One of the happiest aspects of the season had been the revival of Sussex. They were a side with character and dash, and they played entertainingly. Ian Salisbury ended the season on a triumphant note, taking 12 for 138, to better his career best performance of the previous match. Yorkshire were twice bewildered by him, and there was another impressive bowling performance from the young pace bowler Giddins, a real talent to be nurtured. There was some fine batting by Lenham and Hall, some good wicket-keeping from Moores, and, as all season, most capable leadership from Alan Wells. Yorkshire produced an unlikely hero in Peter Hartley who took a career best eight wickets on the third day and outshone Jarvis who did take the four wickets to fall in the second innings.

An opening partnership of 290 between Ward and Benson, and a beautifully struck century by Hooper took Kent to 468 for 3 by the 100th over against Warwickshire. Declaring on the second day at 603 for 8, Kent reduced the home side to 121 for 5 by the close and enforced the follow-on on the third day. Warwickshire held out until the last morning when, in the space of 55 minutes, Kent's admirable spinners captured the last five wickets to give their side the runners-up spot in the championship. Kent have a well-balanced attack, some solid and, at times, sparkling batting, and they were deserving of their second spot. In his last match as captain, another of the season's mysteries, Andy Lloyd was caught at slip by Davis off Hooper, and Benson caught Donald at silly point off Davis, who also had Ostler stumped and Munton taken at mid-on. Piper was aggressive, as was Small, but when Small was caught at long-off by Ellison off Hooper the season was over.

BRITANNIC ASSURANCE COUNTY CHAMPIONSHIP FINAL TABLE

					Bonus Pts		
	P	W	L	D	Bat.	Bowl.	Pts
Essex (1)	22	11	6	5	60	64	300
Kent (6)	22	9	3	10	60	55	259
Northamptonshire (10)	22	8	4	10	60	58	248
Nottinghamshire (4)	22	7	7	8	54	58	224
Derbyshire (3)	22	7	6	9	47	63	222
Warwickshire (2)	22	6	8	8	55	68	219
Sussex (11)	22	6	7	9	60	61	217
Leicestershire (16)	22	7	7	8	39	60	211
Somerset (17)	22	5	4	13	64	62	206
Gloucestershire (13)	22	6	6	10	48	58	202
Middlesex (15)	22	5	3	14	62	60	202
Lancashire (8)	22	4	6	12	73	51	188
Surrey (5)	22	5	7	10	56	50	186
Glamorgan (12)	22	5	4	13	53	49	182
Hampshire (9)	22	4	6	12	61	57	182
Yorkshire (14)	22	4	6	12	56	52	172
Worcestershire (7)	22	3	4	15	54	65	167
Durham (–)	22	2	10	10	46	53	131

The match between Gloucestershire and Worcestershire was abandoned. The 1991 positions are in brackets.

FIRST-CLASS AVERAGES

BATTING

	M	Inns	NO	Runs	HS	Av	100s	50s
M.E. Waugh	16	24	7	1314	219*	77.29	4	6
D.M. Jones	14	23	7	1179	157	73.68	4	5
G.A. Gooch	18	29	3	1850	160	71.15	8	7
M.W. Gatting	24	36	6	2000	170	66.66	6	10
P.C.L. Holloway	2	3	1	133	101*	66.50	1	–
P.D. Bowler	24	38	7	2044	241*	65.93	6	11
J.A Daley	2	4	1	190	88	63.33	–	2
N.H. Fairbrother	12	18	7	689	166*	62.63	1	5
A.J. Lamb	18	28	4	1460	209	60.83	6	5
N.J. Speak	22	36	3	1892	232	57.33	4	12
R.J. Turner	7	10	5	286	101*	57.20	1	1
M.A. Roseberry	25	41	5	2044	173	56.77	9	8
R.T. Robinson	19	33	5	1547	189	55.25	4	8
W.A. Dessaur	2	3	–	164	148	54.66	1	–
N.R. Taylor	21	35	7	1508	144	53.85	1	11
G.A. Hick	17	27	2	1337	213*	53.48	4	5
M.D. Moxon	19	28	2	1385	183	53.26	5	5
T.L. Penney	16	24	7	904	151	53.17	3	4
K.J. Barnett	19	29	5	1270	160	52.91	4	4
G.R. Cowdrey	21	31	6	1291	147	51.64	3	7
M.A. Atherton	21	37	6	1598	199	51.54	5	7
G.D. Lloyd	23	37	10	1399	132	51.44	4	10
G.P. Thorpe	24	41	4	1895	216	51.21	3	13
V.P. Terry	11	17	2	766	141	51.06	3	3
T.S. Curtis	23	41	5	1829	228*	50.80	4	7
R.J. Harden	20	33	5	1387	187	49.53	3	6
T.C. Middleton	24	40	4	1780	221	49.44	6	7
A.D. Brown	11	16	1	740	175	49.33	3	3
R.J. Bailey	23	39	7	1572	167*	49.12	2	8
A.P. Wells	22	35	5	1465	165*	48.83	5	4
T.R. Ward	21	37	3	1648	153	48.47	5	9
C. White	19	26	8	859	79*	47.72	–	7
G.F. Archer	7	13	3	475	117	47.50	1	4
C.L. Hooper	21	32	4	1329	131	47.46	5	7
D.I. Gower	20	33	7	1225	155	47.11	1	8
H. Morris	23	37	3	1597	146	46.97	6	6
P.A. Cottey	20	28	5	1076	141	46.78	2	6
J.J.B. Lewis	13	20	4	746	133	46.62	1	7
S.R. Tendulkar	16	25	2	1070	100	46.52	1	7
J.C. Pooley	3	6	2	186	69	46.50	–	2
R.J. Blakey	21	32	9	1065	125*	46.30	2	5
P. Johnson	19	29	4	1147	107*	45.88	2	10
D.L. Haynes	20	35	2	1513	177	45.84	3	10
J.P. Crawley	17	29	3	1175	172	45.19	2	7
M.R. Benson	21	35	2	1482	139	44.90	4	6
P. Bainbridge	17	30	9	923	92*	43.95	–	8
A. Fordham	23	41	2	1710	192	43.84	4	7
J.P. Stephenson	21	37	5	1401	159*	43.78	3	8
P.J. Prichard	23	38	4	1485	136	43.67	4	9
B.C. Broad	14	27	3	1040	159*	43.33	5	–
M.A. Lynch	23	40	6	1465	107	43.08	3	8
R.C. Russell	20	34	11	985	75	42.82	–	5
T.M. Moody	11	19	2	724	178	42.58	4	1
A.J. Stewart	19	33	4	1234	190	42.55	2	8
D. Ripley	22	31	10	891	107*	42.42	2	4
D.R. Pringle	16	17	5	509	112*	42.41	2	2
J.I. Longley	3	4	–	169	110	42.25	1	–
A. Dale	22	33	5	1159	150*	41.39	2	7
J.E. Morris	23	33	–	1358	120	41.15	3	12
C.J. Adams	23	33	6	1109	140*	41.07	4	4
C.L. Cairns	21	30	6	984	107*	41.00	2	6
R.G. Twose	23	38	3	1412	233	40.34	1	10
P.W.G. Parker	20	35	2	1331	124	40.33	3	8
M.R. Ramprakash	20	33	3	1199	233	39.96	3	5
R.R. Montgomerie	9	15	3	477	103*	39.75	1	1
S.P. James	24	39	4	1376	152*	39.31	3	6
J.W. Hall	20	34	5	1125	140*	38.79	1	8
C.J. Tavaré	21	32	2	1157	125	38.56	3	6
M. Saxelby	8	13	1	462	73	38.50	–	5
P.N. Weekes	17	21	7	539	95	38.50	–	3
J.D. Carr	25	39	7	1228	114	38.57	2	8
N.E. Briers	24	42	6	1372	123	38.11	3	9
T.J. Boon	24	41	3	1448	139	38.10	2	10
M.P. Maynard	23	36	4	1219	176	38.09	2	7
M.P. Speight	20	33	2	1180	179	38.06	5	–
C.C. Lewis	17	26	4	836	134*	38.00	2	5
R.A. Smith	17	28	3	950	127	38.00	2	5
S.A. Kellett	22	36	1	1326	96	37.88	–	9
N. Hussain	20	26	3	866	172*	37.65	1	5
W.P.C. Weston	14	23	5	675	66*	37.50	–	5
W. Larkins	22	41	–	1536	143	37.46	4	8
P.W. Jarvis	15	14	4	374	80	37.40	–	3
M.C.J. Nicholas	21	32	5	1003	95*	37.14	–	6
M.A. Crawley	25	44	9	1297	160*	37.05	4	5
N.D. Burns	22	33	12	772	73*	36.76	–	4
M.N. Lathwell	19	33	1	1176	114	36.75	1	11
N.J. Lenham	20	34	2	1173	222*	36.65	4	3
D.M. Ward	18	30	6	879	138	36.62	3	1
W.K. Hegg	18	24	7	618	80	36.35	–	4
D.J. Bicknell	24	42	5	1340	120*	36.21	2	7
A.J. Moles	23	41	3	1359	122	35.76	1	12
T.J.G. O'Gorman	24	37	8	1031	95	35.55	–	8
S.J. Rhodes	24	34	11	815	116*	35.43	2	2
F.A. Griffith	7	10	3	248	81	35.42	–	1
G.B.T. Lovell	9	13	1	422	110*	35.16	1	2
D.P. Ostler	22	37	2	1225	192	35.00	3	4
G.D. Hodgson	21	36	1	1224	147	34.97	2	8
D.A. Reeve	17	28	4	833	79	34.70	–	7
D.M. Smith	19	33	2	1076	213	34.70	2	5
G. Fowler	11	20	2	623	106	34.61	1	4
S.A. Marsh	22	30	4	896	125	34.46	1	6
M. Asif Din	2	3	–	103	40	34.33	–	–
S.C. Goldsmith	10	11	3	273	100*	34.12	1	1
P. Moores	21	30	5	851	109	34.04	1	3
D.W. Randall	19	29	3	882	133*	33.92	1	5
J.T.C. Vaughan	11	18	4	473	99	33.78	–	4
MA. Feltham	13	19	6	437	50	33.61	–	1
A.N. Hayhurst	23	38	2	1197	102	33.25	1	9
K.D. James	23	37	2	1149	116	32.82	1	8
G.W. Mike	5	6	2	130	61*	32.50	–	1
F.D. Stephenson	18	25	4	680	133	32.38	1	2
M.W. Alleyne	22	36	3	1065	93	32.27	–	7
N.V. Knight	20	30	6	774	109	32.25	2	3
C.W.J. Athey	20	32	–	1022	181	31.93	2	4
S.P. Titchard	14	24	3	668	74	31.80	–	6
N.A. Felton	22	37	3	1076	103	31.64	1	9
I.V.A. Richards	14	23	–	722	127	31.59	1	4
J.E.R. Gallian	9	15	–	468	112	31.20	1	3
G.D. Rose	22	34	4	930	132	31.00	1	6
I.T. Botham	17	25	2	713	105	31.00	1	4
J.P. Arscott	10	14	3	341	79	31.00	–	3
V.J. Wells	17	23	6	526	56	30.94	–	3
S.G. Hinks	10	16	3	402	88*	30.92	–	3
D.G. Cork	19	21	2	578	72*	30.42	–	3
D. Byas	20	30	4	784	100	30.15	1	–
P.R. Pollard	19	33	3	900	75	30.00	–	5
D.B. D'Oliveira	13	20	2	536	100	29.77	1	2
D.J. Capel	23	34	4	892	103	29.73	1	5
P.M. Crawley	4	6	2	118	45	29.50	–	–
P.A. Nixon	16	25	7	529	107*	29.38	1	1
I. Smith	12	16	1	435	110	29.00	1	2
I.D. Austin	8	10	2	230	115*	28.75	1	1
N. Shahid	15	21	1	561	132	28.05	1	3
R.M. Wight	10	17	3	388	62*	27.71	–	2
N.J. Long	4	5	–	137	92	27.40	–	1
P.J. Martin	22	24	5	492	133	27.33	1	2
P.D. Atkins	7	14	–	382	99	27.28	–	2
D.A. Leatherdale	23	39	3	982	112	27.27	1	5
R.P. Snell	16	20	4	436	81	27.25	–	3
T.H.C. Hancock	10	17	1	436	102	27.25	1	2

FIRST-CLASS AVERAGES

BATTING (continued)

	M	Inns	NO	Runs	HS	Av	100s	50s
R.D.B. Croft	24	34	10	650	60*	27.08	–	3
R.J. Bartlett	8	13	–	352	72	27.07	–	2
S. Hutton	8	15	–	406	78	27.06	–	2
R.J. Scott	19	31	3	751	73	26.82	–	4
J.J. Whitaker	22	34	3	830	74	26.77	–	2
K.H. MacLeay	12	19	3	427	74	26.68	–	3
M.V. Fleming	21	32	2	797	100*	26.56	1	4
A.C.H. Seymour	11	21	–	556	133	26.47	1	1
J.E. Emburey	23	27	6	554	102	26.38	1	3
A.A. Metcalfe	11	17	1	422	73	26.37	–	1
G.R. Haynes	9	13	2	288	66	26.18	–	2
R.S.M. Morris	5	9	1	209	74	26.12	–	2
L. Potter	23	36	4	834	96	26.06	–	4
B.F. Smith	15	20	3	441	100*	25.94	1	3
K.R. Brown	25	37	7	776	106	25.86	1	3
A.J. Wright	19	33	3	772	128	25.73	1	3
C. Keey	8	13	1	308	64	25.66	–	3
M.D. Marshall	19	25	5	513	70	25.65	–	2
K. Greenfield	6	10	2	205	48	25.62	–	–
J.D. Robinson	9	17	5	307	65*	25.58	–	2
N.M.K. Smith	12	20	2	454	67	25.22	–	1
K.M. Curran	21	30	1	730	82	25.17	–	5
P.A.J. DeFreitas	13	14	1	325	72	25.00	–	3
M.P. Bicknell	19	26	8	447	88	24.83	–	2
T.A. Lloyd	23	39	2	919	84*	24.83	–	5
P.J. Newport	22	25	6	467	75*	24.57	–	3
D.W. Headley	17	14	3	270	91	24.54	–	1
J.R. Wood	10	13	1	294	57	24.50	–	1
R.J. Parks	7	10	3	169	33	24.14	–	–
R.P. Davis	18	24	11	312	54*	24.00	–	1
J.R. Ayling	18	26	1	593	121	23.72	1	2
MA. Garnham	24	28	4	569	82*	23.70	–	5
N.G.B. Cook	17	11	6	118	37	23.60	–	–
S.R. Lampitt	19	29	5	565	71*	23.54	–	4
R.E. Bryson	11	13	2	257	76	23.36	–	1
N.A. Foster	11	14	–	326	54	23.28	–	2
R.M. Ellison	19	22	8	323	64	23.07	–	1
J.D.R. Benson	18	28	1	623	122	23.07	1	1
C.W. Scott	18	24	5	433	57*	22.78	–	2
G.T.J. Townsend	7	13	1	272	49	22.66	–	–
G.K. Brown	4	6	–	136	48	22.66	–	–
J.D. Glendenen	17	28	1	607	117	22.48	1	3
C.M. Wells	6	7	1	133	39	22.16	–	–
B.T.P. Donelan	16	25	6	421	68*	22.15	–	2
E.E. Hemmings	7	11	5	132	52*	22.00	–	1
K.P. Evans	19	24	4	438	104	21.90	1	2
N.V. Radford	22	19	7	261	73*	21.75	–	2
D.L. Hemp	12	17	2	326	84*	21.73	–	2
C.C. Remy	7	9	–	192	47	21.33	–	–
S.D. Udal	23	29	10	400	44	21.05	–	–
R.K. Illingworth	20	20	6	294	43	21.00	–	–
G.W. Jones	6	12	–	249	44	20.75	–	–
G.D. Mendis	5	8	1	145	45	20.71	–	–
W.K.M. Benjamin	20	25	3	453	72	20.59	–	4
M.A. Ealham	17	27	5	452	67*	20.54	–	4
I.R. Bishop	20	21	2	388	90	20.42	–	1
K.J. Piper	19	25	8	345	72	20.29	–	2
R.P. Gofton	5	8	1	142	75	20.28	–	1
M. Watkinson	20	25	1	482	96	20.08	–	1
A.R. Caddick	20	19	6	261	54*	20. 07	–	1
C.E.L. Ambrose	18	20	10	200	49*	20.00	–	–
A.N. Aymes	18	23	5	359	65	19.94	–	2
C.P. Metson	23	28	6	437	46*	19.86	–	–
A.A. Donald	21	22	10	234	41	19.50	–	–
J.P. Carroll	5	9	–	175	92	19.44	–	1
J.D. Fitton	8	9	2	136	48*	19.42	–	–
J.D. Ratcliffe	7	14	–	272	50	19.42	–	1
A.P. Grayson	6	6	–	116	57	19.33	–	1
M.P. Briers	16	28	4	460	62*	19.16	–	4
N.M. Kendrick	17	21	5	306	55	19.12	–	2

	M	Inns	NO	Runs	HS	Av	100s	50s
J. Boiling	19	21	11	190	29	19.00	–	–
A.R. Roberts	14	19	3	304	62	19.00	–	1
P.A. Smith	19	27	5	416	45	18.90	–	–
A.M. Smith	12	14	5	169	51*	18.77	–	1
S.J.E. Brown	20	24	13	202	47*	18.36	–	–
S.W. Johnson	9	13	2	201	50	18.27	–	1
R.A. Pick	10	12	4	145	52	18.12	–	1
A.M. Brown	7	8	–	144	43	18.00	–	–
M.I. Gidley	5	10	2	143	39	17.87	–	–
P.J. Hartley	20	23	3	353	69	17.65	–	2
J.P. Taylor	23	19	8	188	74*	17.09	–	1
P.J. Berry	9	15	3	205	76	17.08	–	1
P.W. Henderson	5	7	–	119	46	17.00	–	–
A.R.C. Fraser	18	20	7	218	33	16.76	–	–
D.A. Graveney	21	29	9	333	36	16.65	–	–
G.C. Small	17	17	6	181	31*	16.45	–	–
C.S. Pickles	6	9	1	131	49	16.37	–	–
S. Bramhall	8	10	3	114	37*	16.28	–	–
B.N. French	17	20	4	260	55	16.25	–	1
A.E. Warner	17	15	2	210	55	16.15	–	1
K.M. Krikken	23	27	3	383	57*	15.95	–	2
A.C.S. Pigott	17	19	7	191	27*	15.91	–	–
C.A. Connor	16	13	5	127	51	15.87	–	1
M.B. Loye	10	14	1	195	46	15.00	–	–
A.M. Hooper	10	19	1	268	48	14.88	–	–
R.J. Maru	8	11	3	119	27	14.87	–	–
I.D.K. Salisbury	20	22	3	279	50	14.68	–	1
S.N. Warley	7	10	2	117	35	14.62	–	–
D.J. Millns	17	19	9	144	33*	14.40	–	–
J.D. Batty	18	15	4	155	49	14.09	–	–
H.R.J. Trump	18	18	7	154	28	14.00	–	–
M.C.J. Ball	12	21	6	204	54	13.60	–	2
N.F. Williams	17	17	3	186	56*	13.28	–	–
P. Carrick	19	25	5	261	46	13.05	–	–
A.L. Penberthy	10	14	1	164	33	12.61	–	–
A. Storie	7	10	1	113	29	12.55	–	–
P.N. Hepworth	10	15	1	173	38	12.35	–	–
T.A. Munton	19	19	7	148	47	12.33	–	–
J.H. Childs	22	17	8	110	43	12.22	–	–
N.A. Mallender	17	21	5	190	29*	11.87	–	–
G.J. Parsons	14	14	2	142	35	11.83	–	–
N.F. Sargeant	14	19	4	176	30	11.73	–	–
R.C. Williams	7	11	1	117	44	11.70	–	–
C.A. Walsh	18	27	3	280	51	11.66	–	1
J.E. Benjamin	18	18	8	116	42	11.60	–	–
P.M. Such	15	13	3	113	35*	11.30	–	–
S.P. Hughes	20	25	5	224	42	11.20	–	–
M. Davies	19	23	10	145	32*	11.15	–	–
D.K. Morrison	14	12	1	113	30	10.27	–	–
R.W. Sladdin	13	16	3	131	39*	10.07	–	–
T.D. Topley	11	12	2	100	29	10.00	–	–
D.E. Malcolm	19	19	4	150	26	10.00	–	–

(Qualification – 100 runs, average 10.00)

(P.R. Sleep 182; D.A. Lewis 122* & 4; J.R. Wileman 109; G. Salmond 118 & 95; N.A. Folland 82* & 22; M.P. Rea 89 & 26; C. McCrumb 70 & 39; I.L. Philip 79 & 28)

BOWLING

	Overs	Mds	Runs	Wkts	Av	Best	10/m	5/inn
C.A. Walsh	587.2	138	1469	92	15.96	7-27	2	8
I.R. Bishop	482.5	116	1118	64	17.46	7-34	–	4
J.R. Ayling	356.2	78	989	48	20.60	5-12	–	1
D.J. Millns	468.5	107	1526	74	20.62	6-87	1	6
R.P. Davis	582	150	1609	74	21.74	7-64	–	5
A.A. Donald	575.2	139	1647	74	22.25	7-37	–	6
S.D. Thomas	113.2	18	404	18	22.44	5-79	–	2
M.A. Robinson	413.5	79	1134	50	22.68	6-57	1	3
V.J. Wells	301	93	751	33	22.75	4-26	–	–
N.A. Mallender	436.3	94	1282	55	23.30	5-29	–	4

FIRST-CLASS AVERAGES

BOWLING (continued)

	Overs	Mds	Runs	Wkts	Av	Best	10/m	5/inn
G.J. Parsons	343.2	92	955	39	24.48	6-70	–	2
N.G.B. Cook	308.1	90	939	38	24.71	7-34	1	1
F.A. Griffith	113	31	373	15	24.86	4-33	–	–
D.R. Pringle	425.5	98	1177	47	25.04	5-63	–	1
D.J. Capel	446	91	1214	48	25.29	5-61	–	1
P.M. Such	411.5	126	1015	40	25.37	6-17	–	3
J.E. Emburey	854.5	249	2069	81	25.54	5-23	–	3
M.P. Bicknell	628.5	116	1823	71	25.67	6-107	–	4
P.J. Newport	618.2	131	1770	68	26.02	5-22	–	4
R.J. Maru	204.2	75	444	17	26.11	4-8	–	–
C.E.L. Ambrose	543.4	151	1307	50	26.14	4-53	–	–
J.R. Robinson	93.4	14	341	13	26.23	3-22	–	–
N.R. Williams	437	86	1283	48	26.72	8-75	1	2
M.J. McCague	457.2	86	1430	53	26.98	8-26	1	5
A.R. Caddick	587.4	99	1918	71	27.01	6-52	1	3
J.H. Childs	684.2	206	1822	67	27.19	6-82	–	3
I.J. Turner	182.4	51	519	19	27.31	5-81	–	1
M.D. Marshall	528	134	1348	49	27.51	6-58	–	1
K.M. Curran	452.4	96	1376	50	27.52	6-45	–	1
C.S. Pickles	120.1	26	387	14	27.64	4-40	–	–
E.S.H. Giddins	247.5	52	857	31	27.64	5-32	–	2
N.V. Radford	532.2	99	1670	60	27.83	6-88	1	4
R.G. Twose	249.3	50	794	28	28.35	6-63	–	1
D.G. Cork	450.4	74	1366	48	28.45	5-36	–	2
I.D.K. Salisbury	772.4	176	2520	87	28.96	7-54	2	6
M.V. Fleming	251	46	696	24	29.00	4-63	–	–
P.W. Jarvis	393.4	89	1164	40	29.10	4-27	–	–
P. Carrick	630.1	202	1375	47	29.25	6-58	–	1
M. Davies	560.5	143	1661	56	29.66	4-73	–	–
J.A. North	96.3	14	331	11	30.09	3-51	–	–
N.A. Foster	256	63	724	24	30.16	4-47	–	–
P.J. Hartley	550.4	101	1690	56	30.17	8-111	–	3
J.P. Taylor	648.2	119	2072	68	30.47	7-23	1	3
M.E. Waugh	184.4	31	671	22	30.50	3-38	–	–
A.E. Warner	367.5	86	888	29	30.62	4-52	–	–
A.P. Igglesden	489.4	93	1413	46	30.71	5-41	–	3
N.M. Kendrick	596.1	170	1567	51	30.72	6-61	–	3
C.C. Lewis	594.3	119	1633	53	30.81	6-90	1	2
S.L. Watkin	689.3	148	2126	68	31.26	6-97	–	1
J.A. Afford	509.1	128	1599	51	31.35	6-68	1	2
G.W. Mike	90.2	17	314	10	31.40	3-48	–	–
J. Wood	134.2	17	334	17	31.41	5-68	–	1
R.D.B. Croft	657.2	124	2152	68	31.64	8-66	1	5
W.K.M. Benjamin	489	102	1498	47	31.87	4-34	–	–
P.A.J. DeFreitas	349.5	65	1091	34	32.08	6-94	–	1
A. Dale	234	62	644	20	32.20	3-30	–	–
K.J. Shine	333.5	49	1290	40	32.25	8-47	1	3
C.M. Wells	119	26	323	10	32.30	3-26	–	–
H.R.J. Trump	558	134	1584	49	32.32	7-52	1	2
P.A. Smith	373	57	1362	42	32.42	6-91	–	4
T.D. Topley	240.4	54	779	24	32.45	5-15	–	1
J.T.C. Vaughan	202.4	44	588	18	32.66	3-46	–	–
M. Watkinson	666	140	2178	66	33.00	6-62	1	4
G.C. Small	367.2	83	1003	30	33.43	3-43	–	–
E.E. Hemmings	259.5	95	602	18	33.44	4-30	–	–
D.K. Morrison	335.4	52	1209	36	33.58	6-48	–	1
M.A. Ealham	407.1	71	1243	37	33.59	4-67	–	–
T.A. Munton	640.4	176	1725	51	33.82	7-64	1	3
S.J.E. Brown	509.1	75	1973	58	34.01	7-105	–	3
M.A. Crawley	220.4	56	647	19	34.05	3-18	–	–
F.D. Stephenson	466.2	93	1375	40	34.37	7-29	1	1
O.H. Mortensen	338.4	87	795	23	34.56	2-22	–	–
S.D. Udal	692.2	177	2012	58	34.68	8-50	–	2
A.M. Smith	249.2	35	835	24	34.79	3-53	–	–
J.E.R. Gallian	208	41	628	18	34.88	4-29	–	–
J. Boiling	591.1	156	1579	45	35.08	6-84	1	1
C.L. Cairns	592.3	110	1974	56	35.25	6-70	–	2
A.D. Mullally	518.2	125	1485	42	35.35	5-119	–	1
M.C. Ilott	675.3	145	2264	64	35.37	6-87	–	3
S.J.W. Andrew	265	45	849	24	35.37	4-54	–	–

	Overs	Mds	Runs	Wkts	Av	Best	10/m	5/inn
J.D. Fitton	171.1	38	465	13	35.76	4-81	–	–
R.W. Sladdin	499.3	138	1396	39	35.79	6-58	–	1
M.W. Alleyne	138.1	32	502	14	35.85	3-25	–	–
K.P. Evans	596.4	132	1723	48	35.89	5-27	–	1
S.R. Lampitt	379.3	44	1257	35	35.91	4-57	–	–
P.C.R. Tufnell	595.2	146	1559	43	36.25	5-83	–	2
D. Gough	255.1	53	910	25	36.40	4-43	–	–
A.P. van Troost	175.4	20	766	21	36.47	6-48	–	2
D.E. Malcolm	451.1	64	1648	45	36.62	5-45	–	2
D.J. Foster	191.3	27	820	22	37.27	5-87	–	1
C.L. Hooper	499.5	114	1307	35	37.34	4-57	–	–
R.K. Illingworth	635.3	185	1580	42	37.61	4-43	–	–
R.D. Stemp	336.5	80	1054	28	37.64	6-67	1	3
D.B. Pennett	296.2	51	981	26	37.73	4-58	–	–
P.J. Berry	178.3	27	649	17	38.17	7-113	1	1
M.C.J. Ball	322	61	1072	28	38.28	5-101	–	1
J.P. Stephenson	251.5	51	854	22	38.81	6-54	–	1
R.M. Wight	231.3	39	748	19	39.94	3-65	–	–
A.C.S. Pigott	363	74	1063	27	39.37	3-34	–	–
J.E. Benjamin	582.2	94	1780	45	39.55	6-30	–	2
L. Potter	360.1	80	1075	27	39.81	4-73	–	–
P-J. Bakker	162	48	441	11	40.09	4-38	–	–
P.J. Martin	520.1	129	1490	37	40.27	4-45	–	–
C.M. Tolley	239	56	726	18	40.33	3-38	–	–
P.W. Henderson	96	14	405	10	40.50	3-59	–	–
D.W. Headley	385	74	1258	31	40.58	3-31	–	–
P. Bainbridge	188.1	39	569	14	40.64	5-100	–	1
C.W. Taylor	409.2	82	1425	35	40.71	4-50	–	–
R.M. Ellison	401.5	80	1204	29	41.51	6-95	–	2
J.D. Batty	426	87	1408	33	42.66	4-34	–	–
P.A. Booth	279.4	74	814	19	42.84	4-29	–	–
D.A. Graveney	380.4	87	1201	28	42.89	3-22	–	–
C.A. Connor	417.2	69	1386	32	43.31	5-58	–	1
I.D. Austin	164.5	41	522	12	43.50	3-44	–	–
I.T. Botham	346	70	1144	26	44.00	4-72	–	–
R.P. Snell	339.1	60	1194	27	44.22	3-29	–	–
A.M. Babington	188	21	753	17	44.29	8-107	–	1
G.D. Rose	392.1	83	1250	28	44.64	4-59	–	–
M.A. Feltham	326.1	61	1125	25	45.00	4-75	–	–
S.R. Barwick	602	155	1627	36	45.19	4-67	–	–
S.M. McEwan	226	44	800	17	47.05	3-52	–	–
A.A. Barnett	595	84	2165	46	47.06	5-78	–	2
B.T.P. Donelan	404	85	1323	28	47.25	6-77	–	1
R.A. Pick	254.1	50	865	18	47.88	3-33	–	–
R.J. Scott	267.4	39	959	20	47.95	2-9	–	–
A.R. Roberts	323.2	60	1056	22	48.00	4-101	–	–
A.J. Murphy	178.4	34	531	11	48.27	3-97	–	–
D.A. Reeve	267	80	632	13	48.61	2-4	–	–
N.M.K. Smith	332.3	63	1178	24	49.08	5-61	–	1
S.P. Hughes	548.3	98	1672	34	49.17	5-25	–	1
P.N. Weekes	222	51	595	12	49.58	3-61	–	–
M.P.W. Jeh	233.5	38	846	17	49.76	3-44	–	–
S. Bastien	305.3	73	954	19	50.21	5-95	–	1
M.P. Briers	144.3	22	621	12	51.75	3-109	–	–
M.B. Abington	146.4	23	530	10	53.00	3-33	–	–
D.B. D'Oliveira	153.4	29	536	10	53.60	2-44	–	–
M.G. Field-Buss	169	29	590	11	53.63	4-71	–	–
S.W. Johnson	164	27	541	10	54.10	3-62	–	–
R.E. Bryson	333.4	41	1256	23	54.60	5-48	–	2
A.R.C. Fraser	426.4	90	1273	23	55.34	3-16	–	–
K.D. James	264.3	65	781	14	44.78	2-23	–	–
R.M. Pearson	402.3	64	1279	20	63.95	5-108	–	1
M. Frost	198.1	29	833	13	64.07	3-100	–	–
A.N. Jones	161.5	17	745	11	67.72	3-76	–	–

(Qualification – 10 wickets)

FIRST-CLASS AVERAGES

LEADING FIELDERS

71 – D. Ripley (ct 66/st 5); 57 – K.M. Krikken (ct 52/st 5); 54 – C.P. Metson (ct 49/st 5); 52 – S.A. Marsh (ct 44/st 8); 51 – S.J. Rhodes (ct 46/st 5); 50 A.N. Aymes (ct 47/st 3) and K.R. Brown (ct 39/st 11); 49 – R.J. Blakey (ct 44/st 5); 45 – M.A. Garnham (ct 42/st 3), P.A. Nixon (ct 40/st 5) and B.N. French (ct 40/st 5); 44 – N.D. Burns (ct 41/st 3); 43 – R.C. Russell (ct 40/st 3) and K.J. Piper (ct 41/st 2); 41 – N.F. Sargeant (ct 35/st 6) and J.D. Carr; 39 – W.K. Hegg (ct 33/st 6) and P. Moores (ct 32/st 7); 32 – G.A. Hick; 30 – D. Byas and J.D.R. Benson; 29 – C.W. Scott (ct 27/st 2); 27 – M.E. Waugh; 25 – C.L. Hooper and T.R. Ward; 24 – N. Hussain, A.P. Wells, M.A. Atherton and M.A. Lynch; 23 – M.W. Alleyne, S.A. Kellett and R.J. Parks (ct 21/st 2); 22 – R.J. Bailey and A.J. Stewart; 21 – G.D. Lloyd, P.R. Pollard, D.P. Ostler and J.E. Emburey; 20 – S.P. James, C.J. Adams, P. Whitticase (ct 19/st 1) and M.A. Crawley

Young Cricketer of the Year Ian Salisbury finished the season with a flourish. (David Munden)

Britannic Assurance Cricketer of the Year – Paul Prichard, Essex. (Sporting Pictures (UK) Ltd)

English Counties Form Charts

The games covered are:

Sunday League (SL)
Tilcon Trophy (TT)
Benson and Hedges Cup (B & H)
National Westminster Bank Trophy (NW)
Joshua Tetley Festival (JT)
Seeboard Trophy (SB)

Once again averages are not produced as it is felt that they have little relevance in limited-over cricket where batsmen often sacrifice wickets for quick runs and bowlers are ordered to contain rather than capture wickets.
In the batting tables a blank indicates that a batsman did not *play* in a game, a dash (–) that he did not *bat*.

DERBYSHIRE CCC

BATTING	v. Essex (Derby) 19 April SL	v. Worcestershire (Worcester) 21 April B+H	v. Glamorgan (Derby) 23 April B+H	v. Combined Universities (Derby) 30 April B+H	v. Durham (Jesmond) 5 May B+H	v. Gloucestershire (Derby) 10 May SL	v. Worcestershire (Derby) 17 May SL	v. Nottinghamshire (Derby) 24 May SL	v. Kent (Canterbury) 27 May B+H	v. Northamptonshire (Northampton) 31 May SL	v. Durham (Chesterfield) 7 June SL	v. Yorkshire (Leeds) 14 June SL	Runs
K.J. Barnett	31	31	36	84*	28	40	33	6	73	50	53	35	641
P.D. Bowler	13	10	66*	55	8	44	0	63	0	11	77*	0	837
J.E. Morris	30	17	20	21*	121	0	42		0	9		0	602
T.J.G. O'Gorman	11	21	9	–	37	12	30	28	0	69	15	14	418
C.J. Adams	0	10	0	–	1	10	17	1	18	27	20*	58	684
K.M. Krikken	5	37*	4	–	5	1	–	27	6	0*	–	3	194
D.G. Cork	3	0	8*	–	5*	1*		0	0	–		8	84
I.R. Bishop	1*	0	6	–	42	12	–	36*	20	1	–	19	177
A.E. Warner	3	4	–	–	13	20*	18*	8*	22*	14	–	0	154
D.E. Malcolm	0	8	–	–	2						–		23
O.H. Mortensen	0	4	–	–	–	–	–	–	5*	–	–	3*	14
R.W. Sladdin						–							3
S.C. Goldsmith							7*	20	9	1*	20	16	143
S.J. Base							–						19
M. Jean-Jacques								–					–
A.M. Brown											–		–
F.A. Griffith													5
I.G. Steer													–
Byes		1			4					2		4	
Leg-byes	11	12	3	2	9	8	4	6	4	2	7	3	
Wides	8	9	7	2	5	3	1	7	2	2	8	1	
No-balls	5			3	1	2			1	1	1	1	
Total	121	164	159	167	281	153	152	202	160	189	201	165	
Wickets	10	10	6	1	9	7	5	7	9	7	3	10	
Result	L	L	W	W	W	W	-L	W	L	L	W	L	
Points	0	0	2	2	2	4	0	4	–	0	4	0	

BATTING	v. Middlesex (Derby) 21 June SL	v. Berkshire (Derby) 24 June NW	v. Leicestershire (Derby) 28 June SL	v. Somerset (Taunton) 5 July SL	v. Leicestershire (Derby) 9 & 10 July NW	v. Surrey (The Oval) 12 July SL	v. Glamorgan (Pontypridd) 26 July SL	v. Warwickshire (Leek) 2 August SL	v. Sussex (Eastbourne) 9 August SL	v. Kent (Chesterfield) 16 August SL	v. Hampshire (Southampton) 23 August SL	v. Lancashire (Old Trafford) 30 August SL	Runs
K.J. Barnett	6						6*	41	1	1	55	31	641
P.D. Bowler	15	111	87*	5	4	9	20*	15	7	56	70*	91*	837
J.A. Morris	6	31	35	33	0	78		68*	51	27	13	0	602
T.J.G. O'Gorman	41	1	8	4	0	44	–	–	55	11	–	8	418
C.J. Adams	61	106*	75	3	30	23	–	75*	0	141*		8	684
K.M. Krikken	19	–	–	24	18	1	–	–	28*	16	–	–	194
D.G. Cork	5	4	9	20	11		–	–	6	0*		4	84
I.R. Bishop		6		23	0	10	–	–	1*	–	–		177
A.E. Warner	2	0*	0*	6*	21	4	–		17	–	0*	2	154
D.E. Malcolm		–	–		10*	3*		–		–	–	–	23
O.H. Mortensen	2*	–			0	–	–	–	–	–		–	14
R.W. Sladdin				3*			–		–		–		3
S.C. Goldsmith	8	0	2	33	0	27							143
S.J. Base	13		–			6*							19
M. Jean-Jacques													–
A.M. Brown			–				–	–					–
F.A. Griffith				1							–	4*	5
I.G. Steer											–		–
Byes		3	1						4				
Leg-byes	3	8	13	1	1	3		6	5	1	3	3	
Wides	7	6	3		3		4	2	7	4	1	4	
No-balls	2	4		4	5			1	1		1		
Total	190	280	233	160	103	208	30	208	183	257	143	155	
Wickets	10	6	5	9	10	8	0	2	7	5	2	6	
Result	L	W	W	L	L	L	Ab.	W	W	W	L	L	
Points	0	–	4	0	–	0	2	4	4	4	0	0	

FIELDING FIGURES

29 – K.M. Krikken
15 – C.J. Adams
11 – K.J. Barnet
9 – P.D. Bowler
7 – J.E. Morris
4 – T.J.G. O'Gorman and D.G. Cork
3 – S.C. Goldsmith, A.E. Warner and S.J. Base
2 – R.W. Sladdin and sub
1 – O.H. Mortensen, A.M. Brown and F.A. Griffith

DERBYSHIRE CCC

BOWLING

		I.R. Bishop	O.H. Mortensen	A.E. Warner	D.E. Malcolm	D.G. Cork	K.J. Barnett	R.W. Sladdin	S.J. Base	S.C. Goldsmith	M. Jean-Jacques	P.D. Bowler	C.J. Adams	F.A. Griffith	Byes	Leg-byes	Wides	No-balls	Total	Wkts
v. Essex (Derby) 19 April	SL	6–1–14–1	8–1–26–1	5–1–32–0	8–0–21–0	7.5–0–29–0											4		122	2
v. Worcestershire (Worcester) 21 April	B+H	11–0–26–0	11–0–44–2	11–3–29–2	11–0–76–0	11–0–47–0										10	11		232	5
v. Glamorgan (Derby) 23 April	B+H	11–1–29–1	11–4–26–2	11–1–26–1	11–0–43–4	11–0–27–0										4	7		155	9
v. Combined Universities (Derby) 30 April	B+H	11–3–18–3	11–3–20–0	9–1–34–2	6–1–27–1	11–0–28–0	7–0–26–1									11	11	3	164	7
v. Durham (Jesmond) 5 May	B+H	9–1–44–0	10–1–39–3	9–0–34–1	9–0–46–0	9.2–0–26–4										12	14	7	201	10
v. Gloucestershire (Derby) 10 May	SL	7–0–18–3	8–1–22–0	5–0–16–2		6–0–26–3		4–1–15–1							1	5	4	3	103	10
v. Worcestershire (Derby) 17 May	SL	8–0–28–0	7–0–32–0	8–1–25–2					8–0–31–1	6.4–0–31–0						6	3	4	153	3
v. Nottinghamshire (Derby) 24 May	SL	7.5–0–31–3	8–0–22–0	8–0–44–3		8–0–40–2				4–0–23–1	4–0–20–0					6	4		186	10
v. Kent (Canterbury) 27 May	B+H	11–2–30–4	11–3–17–1	11–1–39–3		11–1–42–0	5–0–33–0			5.1–0–25–2						7	7	1	193	10
v. Northamptonshire (Northampton) 31 May	SL	8–1–18–0	8–0–33–0	7–0–40–1		8–0–48–1				7.4–0–48–0						3	6	4	190	2
v. Durham (Chesterfield) 7 June	SL	8–0–25–2	8–2–37–1	8–0–24–0	8–0–52–3					8–0–48–0						11	6		197	6
v. Yorkshire (Leeds) 14 June	SL	8–0–47–0	8–1–20–0	8–0–57–1		8–0–48–0				5–0–39–1		3–0–21–0				4	3		236	2
v. Middlesex (Derby) 21 June	SL		8–0–27–1	8–2–22–1		8–0–48–1			8–0–58–0	8–0–42–2						15	2	4	212	5
v. Berkshire (Derby) 24 June	NW	10–2–24–0	3–2–1–1	11–2–25–0	9–1–29–2	9.5–4–18–5				3–0–5–0		3–0–12–0	3–1–15–1		3	7	9	6	139	10
v. Leicestershire (Derby) 28 June	SL			8–0–31–2	8–0–47–2	8–0–45–1			8–0–56–1	8–0–41–2						12	8	5	232	8
v. Somerset (Taunton) 5 July	SL	8–0–38–2		7.2–1–23–0		8–0–34–1		8–0–28–0		3–0–14–1				5–0–21–1	1	3	9		162	5
v. Leicestershire (Derby) 9 & 10 July	NW	12–1–37–0	12–2–43–0	12–2–40–2	12–0–39–2	12–1–36–3										6	9	1	201	9
v. Surrey (The Oval) 12 July	SL	7.3–0–57–1	8–2–16–1	8–2–46–2	8–0–55–0				8–0–31–1						2	5	5	2	212	7
v. Glamorgan (Pontypridd) 26 July	SL	8–2–34–0	8–0–65–0	8–0–28–1		8–0–56–0		8–0–59–1								4	3	1	246	2
v. Warwickshire (Leek) 2 August	SL	6–1–20–2	8–0–30–1		8–0–47–2	6–0–39–3	4–0–23–2						4–0–40–0		1	4	12	2	204	10
v. Sussex (Eastbourne) 9 August	SL	6–0–22–3	8–1–9–1	6.2–0–26–1		7–0–27–1		8–1–35–2								5	3		124	10
v. Kent (Chesterfield) 16 August	SL	7–0–35–1	8–0–30–1	6.2–0–23–4	8–0–66–2	8–0–43–1										12	4	2	209	10
v. Hampshire (Southampton) 23 August	SL	7–0–42–1		5–0–25–0	3.4–0–32–0									3–0–20–2		1	10	1	120	3
v. Lancashire (Old Trafford) 30 August	SL		5–1–29–1	6.3–0–22–3	5–0–19–0	3–0–35–0							1–0–1–0	3–0–41–1		10	3		157	5
Wickets		27	17	34	18	26	3	4	3	9	0	0	1	4						

DURHAM CCC

BATTING

BATTING	v. Lancashire (Durham) 19 April SL	v. Glamorgan (Durham) 21 April B+H	v. Leicestershire (Gateshead) 26 April SL	v. Worcestershire (Worcester) 30 April B+H	v. Combined Universities (Cambridge) 2 May B+H	v. Derbyshire (Jesmond) 5 May B+H	v. Kent Canterbury) 10 May SL	v. Northamptonshire (Stockton) 24 May SL	v. Hampshire (Southampton) 31 May SL	v. Derby (Chesterfield) 7 June SL	v. Sussex (Harrogate) 10 June TT	v. Essex (Hartlepool) 14 June SL	v. Sussex (Horsham) 21 June SL	Runs
I.T. Botham	14	86	67	2	72	6	–	8	64			27		627
W. Larkins	59	0	17	19	73	58	–	4	8	3	20	3	86	784
D.M. Jones	114	6	21	13	6	0	–	26	55	67	8	100	74*	760
P. Bainbridge	35	22	3	5	16	27	–	2	5	57	2	41		242
P.W.G. Parker	11*	22	16	9	22	22	–	2	42*	17	31	10	19	521
J.D. Glendenen	–	7	38	45	60	20	–	35	2	14			64	670
A.R. Fothergill	–		42*	17	12*	3	–	4	8	11*		4	0*	203
S.M. McEwan	–	12*	7*	29*	1*	9	–	18				0	–	125
S.P. Hughes	–	3	–	–	–	0	–	0	1*	–	5	5*	–	26
D.A. Graveney	–	13	11			21	–	11*	–	–	2	2*	–	52
S.J.E. Brown	–	4*	–	–	–	2*	–	1	–	–				10
C.W. Scott		3									0			16
I. Smith				29*					19	8	35*	3		237
P.J. Berry					–									15
P.W. Henderson										3*			–	13
S. Hutton											41			148
M.P. Briers											17		16	218
J. Wood											3		–	11
G. Wigham												–		–
G. Cook														79
J.A. Daley														8
Byes		4									1			
Leg-byes	10	7	5	4	3	12		12	3	11	9	4	10	
Wides	1	7	5	2	5	14		1	2	6	3	5	6	
No-balls	2			3	1	7						1		
Total	246	196	232	177	271	201		124	209	197	177	205	275	
Wickets	4	9	7	7	6	10		10	7	6	10	8	4	
Result	W	L	W	W	W	L	Ab.	L	L	L	L	L	W	
Points	4	0	4	2	2	0	2	0	0	0	–	0	4	

BATTING	v. Ireland (Dublin) 24 June NW	v. Gloucestershire (Stockton) 5 July SL	v. Middlesex (Uxbridge) 9 July NW	v. Somerset (Taunton) 12 July SL	v. Nottinghamshire (Trent Bridge) 19 July SL	v. Middlesex (Lord's) 26 July SL	v. Leicestershire (Leicester) 29 July NW	v. Surrey (Durham) 2 August SL	v. Warwickshire (Edgbaston) 9 August SL	v. Glamorgan (Hartlepool) 16 August SL	v. Worcestershire (Worcester) 23 August SL	v. Yorkshire (Darlington) 30 August SL	v. Yorkshire (Scarborough) 5 September JT	Runs
I.T. Botham		23	63*	27	19	48	5	52	10	9			25*	627
W. Larkins	113	20	0	52	47	9	41	9	29	9	2		103	784
D.M. Jones	46	81*	25	83	35									760
P. Bainbridge							6				5		16	242
P.W.G. Parker	10	19	69	82	23	1	54						40	521
J.D. Glendenen	18	52	57	4*	33*	28	39	28	78	15	33			670
A.R. Fothergill	4	–	–	–	27	20*	7	39	5	0				203
S.M. McEwan	34*	–	–	–	0	1*		–	1*	13*	–			125
S.P. Hughes	–	–	–	–	–	–	2	–	–	10*	–			26
D.A. Graveney	–	–						–	–	2	–		–	52
S.J.E. Brown		–	–	–	–	–	3*		–				–	10
C.W. Scott											8*		5	16
I. Smith	3	23*	12*	0*		23	2	3	26	18	3		30	237
P.J. Berry						6	9						–	15
P.W. Henderson					10*								–	13
S. Hutton									8*	70	29*			148
M.P. Briers	54*			–	8			69	22	32	0			218
J. Wood	–		–					4*		4	–			11
G. Wigham														–
G. Cook						49	16	14						79
J.A. Daley													8	8
Byes		1		1			1		1					
Leg-byes	9	6	12	10	2	4	9	6	7	7	5		9	
Wides	14	1	17	3	5	8	10	5	3	6	9		8	
No-balls		2	5	1	2	1		1		5				
Total	305	228	260	263	211	198	204	230	190	200	94		244	
Wickets	6	4	4	4	7	7	10	7	6	9	5		6	

FIELDING FIGURES

27 – A.R. Fothergill (ct 21/st 6)
13 – P.W. G. Parker
10 – W. Larkins
8 – D.M. Jones, S.P. Hughes and I.T. Botham
6 – D.A. Graveney and I. Smith
5 – J.D. Glendenen
4 – S.M. McEwan
3 – P. Bainbridge
2 – S. Hutton and M.P. Briers
1 – C.W. Scott (st 1), G. Cook, P.W. Henderson and sub

DURHAM CCC

BOWLING

		S.M. McEwan	S.J.E. Brown	S.P. Hughes	I.T. Botham	P. Bainbridge	D.A. Graveney	P.J. Berry	D.M. Jones	I. Smith	P.W. Henderso	J. Wood	G. Wigham	M.P. Briers	P.W.G. Parker	Byes	Leg-byes	Wides	No-balls	Total	Wkts
v. Lancashire (Durham) 19 April	SL	8–0–35–3	8–0–32–3	7.1–0–31–2	8–0–57–1	6–0–60–0	2–0–13–0									1	8	4	1	237	10
v. Glamorgan (Durham) 21 April	B+H	7–0–32–0	10–0–36–2	10.2–2–32–2	11–2–21–2	5–0–30–0	11–1–41–0										5	3	3	197	6
v. Leicestershire (Gateshead) 26 April	SL	4–0–31–0	4–0–29–0	8–0–46–3	8–0–30–2	8–0–41–2	8–0–41–1									1	5	2	1	224	9
v. Worcestershire (Worcester) 30 April	B+H	11–2–45–3	11–1–27–1	9.4–1–30–1	10–2–27–1	11–0–38–4										2	4	5		173	10
v. Combined Universities (Cambridge) 2 May	B+H	7–0–23–0	5–2–14–0	8–0–31–2	7–2–20–0	10–0–41–0		11–0–49–0	7–0–34–2								8	8		220	5
v. Derbyshire (Jesmond) 5 May	B+H	11–1–54–2	11–1–52–1	11–0–52–2	11–1–46–1	10–1–51–1	1–0–13–0									4	9	5	1	281	9
v. Kent (Canterbury) 10 May	SL	5–1–27–0	3–0–21–1		6–0–12–1	1–0–10–0	5–0–19–0										5	1		94	2
v. Northamptonshire (Stockton) 24 May	SL		5–0–25–0	8–0–22–0	5–0–19–1	7–1–32–1	5.3–0–29–2											4		127	4
v. Hampshire (Southampton) 31 May	SL		7–0–36–1	8–0–37–1	8–0–30–2	7–0–53–1	8–0–33–1			2–0–17–0							6	5		212	8
v. Derbyshire (Chesterfield) 7 June	SL		7–0–23–0	7–0–35–0		8–0–41–1	8–0–44–1		0.1–0–4–0	2–0–17–1	5–0–30–0						7	8	1	201	3
v. Sussex (Harrogate) 10 June	TT			8–2–21–2		8–0–25–0	11–2–41–2		7–0–34–0	11–2–34–3		10–0–48–0				5	6	5	2	214	8
v. Essex (Hartlepool) 14 June	SL	7–0–44–2		8–1–34–2		8–1–39–0	4–0–19–1			5–0–37–0			8–1–43–1				4	2	1	220	8
v. Sussex (Horsham) 21 June	SL	8–0–50–0		8–0–51–2			8–1–40–3				8–0–60–0	8–0–58–2				4	7	2		270	9
v. Ireland (Dublin) 24 June	NW	12–1–41–4		6–0–9–1						12–1–40–2		7–1–22–2		0.2–0–0–1			4	11	1	116	10
v. Gloucestershire (Stockton) 5 July	SL	5–2–13–0	8–0–56–0	8–0–47–1	8–1–34–2				6–0–37–1	5–0–33–0							6	1	1	226	5
v. Middlesex (Uxbridge) 9 July	NW	12–1–45–1	12–2–43–1	12–3–41–4	12–0–53–1				2–0–16–0	10–0–50–0						5	6	13		259	8
v. Somerset (Taunton) 12 July	SL	8–0–47–1	8–0–61–2	8–0–49–1	8–0–37–3									8–0–48–0		1	9	6		252	8
v. Nottinghamshire (Trent Bridge) 19 July	SL	8–1–26–1	8–0–27–1	8–0–37–2	8–0–41–1						8–0–47–3					2	10	7		190	9
v. Middlesex (Lord's) 26 July	SL	8–0–40–1	7–0–40–0	8–0–31–1	7.5–0–49–0			8–0–35–1								3	4	3		202	3
v. Leicestershire (Leicester) 29 July	NW		11.3–1–53–1	12–2–34–3	12–2–54–1	8–0–29–1		11–0–48–0		5–0–24–0							7	6		249	10
v. Surrey (Durham) 2 August	SL	6–0–57–0		8–0–72–2	5–0–39–1		8–0–51–2			2–0–18–0		5–0–26–0		5–0–47–1		4	16	11	1	330	6
v. Warwickshire (Edgbaston) 9 August	SL	8–0–27–3	8–0–43–3	7.1–0–26–3	4–0–17–0		8–0–36–1			3–0–17–0							7	5		173	10
v. Glamorgan (Hartlepool) 16 August	SL	5–0–38–0		7–1–27–1	6–0–36–0		8–0–40–2			8–1–32–3		6–0–33–1				1	9	5	1	216	7
v. Worcestershire (Worcester) 23 August	SL																				Ab.
v. Yorkshire (Darlington) 30 August	SL																				Ab.
v. Yorkshire (Scarborough) 5 September	JT		10–0–62–1		10–2–29–0	3–0–21–0	10–0–42–0	4–0–27–0		3–0–18–0	8–0–39–0				0.1–0–4–0	3	3	6		248	1
Wickets		21	18	38	20	11	16	1	3	9	3	5	1	2	0						

ESSEX CCC

BATTING

BATTING	v. Derbyshire (Derby) 19 April SL	v. Lancashire (Chelmsford) 21 April B+H	v. Hampshire (Southampton) 23 April B+H	v. Surrey (Chelmsford) 26 April SL	v. Scotland (Chelmsford) 30 April & 1 May B+H	v. Northamptonshire (Northampton) 2 May B+H	v. Leicestershire (Leicester) 3 May SL	v.Northamptonshire (Chelmsford) 10 May SL	v. Glamorgan (Chelmsford) 24 May SL	v. Worcestershire (Worcester) 31 May SL	v. Kent (Chelmsford) 7 June SL	v. Durham (Hartlepool) 14 June SL	v. Hampshire (Bournemouth) 21 June SL	Runs
G.A. Gooch	19	0	0	48*	127	119	49	48	75	17		0		968
J.P. Stephenson	49	8	1	38*	66	10	1	6	59	15	30	23	54	567
M.E. Waugh	37*	0	2	–	34	100	86	45	29*	47	105*	22	28	766
N. Hussain	13*	15	55	–	20	2	11	8	27*	30	1		4	400
P.J. Prichard	–	6	18		25	5	5	25	–	17	22	83	22	697
N.V. Knight	–		2	–	18*	2	5	35	–	10	27	28	29*	339
D.R. Pringle	–	6	23	–	9	1	2	1*	–	0		37	11	209
M.A. Garnham	–	17*	8	–	12*	2	13*	8*	–	5	6	4	14*	204
T.D. Topley	–	4		–	–	5	–	–	–	4*	2*	6*	–	71
M.C. Ilott	–	0	5*	–	–			–			–	–	–	33
P.M. Such	–	0	3	–		1*	–	–	–	9*	–	–	–	13
N.A. Foster		2	0	–	62						11		0	104
A.G.J. Fraser						6	9*		–	3				31
N. Shahid											10	10		102
J.H. Childs														14
J.J.B. Lewis														31
A.D. Brown														–
K.A. Butler														5
S.J.W. Andrew														–
Byes			1						1	1	6			
Leg-byes		2	9		7	8	8	5	1	11	3	4	3	
Wides	4	1	7	1	8	3	4		1	2	6	2	9	
No-Balls			2	1				2	2	1		1	1	
Total	122	61	136	88	388	264	193	183	195	172	229	220	175	
Wickets	2	10	10	0	7	10	7	6	2	9	7	8	6	
Result	W	L	L	W	W	W	W	W	W	L	W	W	L	
Points	4	0	0	4	2	2	4	4	4	0	4	4	0	

BATTING	v. Cumberland (Chelmsford) 24 June NW	v. Lancashire (Ilford) 28 June SL	v. Warwickshire (Edgbaston) 5 July SL	v. Lancashire (Chelmsford) 9 July NW	v. Yorkshire (Scarborough) 12 July SL	v. Sussex (Southend) 19 July SL	v. Gloucestershire (Cheltenham) 29 July NW	v. Middlesex (Lord's) 9 August SL	v. Leicestershire (Leicester) 12 & 13 August NW	v. Nottinghamshire (Colchester) 16 August SL	v. Somerset (Weston-super-Mare) 23 August SL	v. Gloucestershire (Chelmsford) 30 August SL	Runs
G.A. Gooch	77	79		49	43	50	105*		8	55			968
J.P. Stephenson				75	3	64	11	5	0	24	–	25	567
M.E. Waugh	24	61*	43	25	0	69*	9						766
N. Hussain	108	2	16			–	30	12	40	6	–		400
P.J. Prichard	23	60	7	28	33	52*	58	40	87	47	–	34	697
N.V. Knight	81*	19*	6	1	11			29	8	13	–	15	339
D.R. Pringle	10	–	52	16	21	–	14*		3	3	–		209
M.A. Garnham	5	–	1	53*	33*	–	–	0	8		–	15*	204
T.D. Topley	1	–	0*	15	4*	–	–	8	19*	3*	–	–	71
M.C. Ilott	9*				–	–	–	7	10*	2*	–		33
P.M. Such		–				–	–	0*	–	–	–		13
N.A. Foster	–		18	11		–	–						104
A.G.J. Fraser			1					12				–	31
N. Shahid	18	–	30	12	6			11			–	5	102
J.H. Childs		–		13*	–			1				–	14
J.J.B. Lewis			7						21	3	–	–	31
A.D. Brown										–			–
K.A. Butler												5*	5
S.J.W. Andrew												–	–
Byes							3	3		4			
Leg-byes	3	15	5	13	8	3	5	7	9	4		3	
Wides	2	4	4	5	1	2	3	7	10	8			
No-Balls		2		3			2		3	4		4	
Total	361	242	190	319	163	240	240	142	226	176		106	
Wickets	8	3	10	9	7	2	4	10	8	7		4	
Result	W	W	L	W	W	W	W	L	L	W	Ab.	L	
Points	–	4	0	–	4	4	–	0	–	4	2	0	

FIELDING FIGURES

20 – M.A. Garnham (ct 17/st 3)
10 – N.V. Knight
9 – P.J. Prichard and T.D. Topley
8 – G.A. Gooch, J.P. Stephenson and N. Hussain
5 – M.E. Waugh and N. Shahid
4 – N.A. Foster and D.R. Pringle
3 – P.M. Such
2 – M.C. Ilott, J.H. Childs and J.J.B. Lewis
1 – A.D. Brown

ESSEX CCC

BOWLING

		M.C. Ilott	D.R. Pringle	T.D. Topley	J.P. Stephenson	G.A. Gooch	P.M. Such	N.A. Foster	M.E. Waugh	A.G.J. Fraser	N. Shahid	J.H. Childs	S.J.W. Andrew	Byes	Leg-byes	Wides	No-balls	Total	Wkts
v. Derbyshire (Derby) 19 April	SL	7.1–1–15–4	7–0–22–2	8–0–22–2	8–0–22–1	4–0–16–0	4–0–13–1								11	8	5	121	10
v. Lancashire (Chelmsford) 21 April	B+H	5.5–0–13–0	8–5–7–0	4–0–8–1				11–1–36–1							1	5	1	65	2
v. Hampshire (Southampton) 23 April	B+H	11–1–27–3	10.4–0–40–2		11–0–47–2		11–2–32–2	11–1–25–1							6	14	2	177	10
v. Surrey (Chelmsford) 26 April	SL	2–0–15–2	2–0–16–3	2–0–22–0	2–0–10–3			2–0–16–1						2	3	5		84	9
v. Scotland (Chelmsford) 30 April & 1 May	B+H	10–1–31–4	7.4–3–15–1	5–2–15–1	5–0–17–1			0.2–0–0–0	7.5–0–31–3						7	11	3	116	10
v. Northamptonshire (Northampton) 2 May	B+H		9–2–16–1	11–2–40–3	8–0–35–1	7–1–28–0	11–0–43–4			5.1–0–31–1					5	5		198	10
v. Leicestershire (Leicester) 3 May	SL		8–0–34–1	8–0–32–1	8–0–29–2		8–0–46–1			8–0–39–2					9	6		189	8
v. Northamptonshire (Chelmsford) 10 May	SL	8–1–38–2	8–0–41–1	8–1–34–0	8–0–44–2	1–0–8–0								4	11	5	2	180	5
v. Glamorgan (Chelmsford) 24 May	SL		8–0–35–2	8–1–25–0	7–0–40–0		5–0–28–1		6–0–36–0	6–0–24–1				1	5	10	3	194	5
v. Worcestershire (Worcester) 31 May	SL		8–1–25–1	8–0–32–2	8–0–38–0		8–1–48–1		7.4–1–26–3					1	3	1		173	8
v. Kent (Chelmsford) 7 June	SL	8–0–45–3		8–0–21–1	8–1–46–1		4–0–24–0	6–0–35–0	6–0–38–2					6	8	8		223	9
v. Durham (Hartlepool) 14 June	SL	8–0–40–3	8–0–37–2	6–1–31–1	6–0–23–1		6–0–30–0		6–0–40–1						4	5	1	205	8
v. Hampshire (Bournemouth) 21 June	SL	8–1–28–1	4–0–10–0	8–0–40–0	3–0–19–0		6–0–41–0	5–0–23–0	2–0–14–0						3	3		178	2
v. Cumberland (Chelmsford) 24 June	NW	11–2–23–2	6–1–18–0	11–1–47–3		5–0–17–0	12–3–37–1		12–1–51–1		3–3–0–1			1	6	2	4	200	8
v. Lancashire (Ilford) 28 June	SL		8–0–58–2	8–0–34–1			8–0–56–1		8–0–49–1			8–1–30–2			11	2	2	238	7
v. Warwickshire (Edgbaston) 5 July	SL		8–0–53–1	8–1–36–1				8–0–35–0	8–0–49–2	8–0–33–1					8	1	4	214	5
v. Lancashire (Chelmsford) 9 July	NW		12–3–50–2	8–0–51–2	12–0–78–3	4–0–22–0		12–1–47–0				12–1–51–0			19	6	10	318	8
v. Yorkshire (Scarborough) 12 July	SL	8–1–36–1		4–0–20–0	8–2–22–1	8–1–24–2			8–0–31–1			4–0–20–0			9	2	2	162	5
v. Sussex (Southend) 19 July	SL	7–0–55–1	8–1–39–1	7–0–53–0	2–0–14–0		8–0–29–2	8–0–44–1							5	13	2	239	6
v. Gloucestershire (Cheltenham) 29 July	NW	12–0–67–2	12–0–50–0	12–0–30–1	10–1–42–2			12–3–25–1	2–0–13–0						9	6	2	236	7
v. Middlesex (Lord's) 9 August	SL	8–0–33–1		7–1–35–2	7–0–44–1		8–0–45–0			6–0–37–1		3–0–32–0		3	7	8	4	236	6
v. Leicestershire (Leicester) 12 & 13 August	NW	12–2–36–2	12–2–35–1	12–1–58–2	11.5–1–56–0		12–0–37–0								7	5	4	229	5
v. Nottinghamshire (Colchester) 16 August	SL	7–1–44–1	8–2–28–0	8–0–36–1	8–1–18–2	1–0–7–0	8–0–28–1							1	3	4	2	165	6
v. Somerset (Weston-super-Mare) 23 August	SL	2–0–12–0	3–0–16–0		2–0–17–0		1.2–0–6–0									2		51	0
v. Gloucestershire (Chelmsford) 30 August	SL			8–0–40–0	8–0–58–5					8–0–44–1		8–0–50–0	8–0–41–1		6	10	3	239	8

GLAMORGAN CCC

BATTING	v. Warwickshire (Edgbaston) 19 April SL	v. Durham (Durham) 21 April B+H	v. Derbyshire (Derby) 23 April B+H	v. Middlesex (Lord's) 26 April SL	v. Worcestershire (Cardiff) 2 May B+H	v. Worcestershire (Cardiff) 3 May SL	v. Combined Universities (Cardiff) 5 May B+H	v. Essex (Chelmsford) 24 May SL	v. Leicestershire (Swansea) 31 May SL	v. Sussex (Hove) 7 June SL	v. Yorkshire (Harrogate) 10 June TT	v. Sussex (Harrogate) 11 June TT	v. Lancashire (Colwyn Bay) 14 June SL	Runs
M.P. Maynard	11	1	11	49	16	22	32	75	122*	47	28	35	25	961
H. Morris	20	0	32	67	40	1	14	19	5	1	82	31	96*	921
I.V.A. Richards	68	1	48		1	75				40			2	569
A. Dale	51	30				18	53	48	19	20			–	379
C.S. Cowdrey	9	78	6	3	44	0	11	17	27*	1			14	217
P.A. Cottey	7*	38	8		2	1	8*	2*	–	12	0	91	51*	301
R.D.B. Croft	0	30*	24*	1*	1	24	3*	1*	–		32	–	–	225
C.P. Metson	1*	6*	7	–	14	15*	–	–	–	15*	8	–	–	120
S.L. Watkin	–	–	0	–				–		2	0	–		22
S.R. Barwick	–	–	7		5	6	–	–	–	3	3	–	–	24
M. Frost	–	–	1*	–	4				–					11
S.P. James			0	48	1		135	13	74	35	0	49	1	637
S. Kirnon				1										1
D.L. Hemp				1*							3	5		23
D.J. Foster				–		–	–		–	0			–	23
S. Bastien					3*	0*	–	–			0*	–		10
S. Dhaniram											13	65*		78
A.D. Shaw														–
S.D. Thomas														–
Byes	2							1	1	4				
Leg-byes	8	5	4	8	6	3	9	5	11	3	4	10	4	
Wides	3	5	7	2	3	4	8	10	4	1	2	5	3	
No-balls		3		1	7		4	3	1	4	2			
Total	180	197	155	181	147	169	277	194	264	188	175	291	196	
Wickets	6	6	9	5	10	8	5	5	3	10	10	5	4	
Result	L	W	L	L	L	L	W	L	W	L	W	W	L	
Points	0	2	0	0	0	0	2	0	4	0	–	–	0	

BATTING	v. Yorkshire (Ebbw Vale) 21 June SL	v. Surrey (Swansea) 24 June NW	v. Northamptonshire (Luton) 28 June SL	v. Surrey (Llanelli) 5 July SL	v. Nottinghamshire (Trent Bridge) 9 & 10 July NW	v. Hampshire (Portsmouth) 19 July SL	v. Derbyshire (Pontypridd) 26 July SL	v. Northamptonshire (Swansea) 29 July NW	v. Kent (Swansea) 2 August SL	v. Nottinghamshire (Trent Bridge) 9 August SL	v. Durham (Hartlepool) 16 August SL	v. Gloucestershire (Bristol) 23 August SL	v. Somerset (Cardiff) 30 August SL	Runs
M.P. Maynard	45	87	61	72	60	15	5	41	18	18	65	–		961
H. Morris	38	55	5	98	26	51*	104*	29	67	14	26	–		921
I.V.A. Richards	15	16	87*	45*	25	23	109*	2	10		2			569
A. Dale		16	55*	0	20	8*	–	5	2	28	6	–		378
C.S. Cowdrey	1				6									217
P.A. Cottey	0	24	–	1	17	–	–	9	12	18		–		301
R.D.B. Croft	31*	17*	–	0*	2	–	–	16	1	16	26*	–		225
C.P. Metson	15	0*	–	–	21	–		1	5	6*	6	–		120
S.L. Watkin	7*	–	–	–	4*	–		9						22
S.R. Barwick	–	–	–	–	–	–	–	0*	0	–				24
M. Frost				–		–	–		6*	–		–		11
S.P. James	5	19	38	7		29	20	11	69	20	63	–		637
S. Kirnon														1
D.L. Hemp										10	4	–		23
D.J. Foster	–	–	–					2	10*	9*	2*			23
S. Bastien					7*						–	–		10
S. Dhaniram														78
A.D. Shaw							–							–
S.D. Thomas							–				–	–		–
Byes				2						1	1			
Leg-byes	6	4	11	4	1	1	4	7	5	3	9			
Wides	1	5	6	4	8	3	3	9	11	5	5			
No-balls	3			1		3	1				1			
Total	167	243	263	234	197	133	246	141	216	148	226			
Wickets	7	6	3	5	8	3	2	10	9	7	7			
Result	L	W	W	L	W	W	Ab.	L	L	L	W	Ab.	Ab.	
Points	0	–	4	0	–	4	2	–	0	0	4	2	2	

FIELDING FIGURES

32 – C.P. Metson (ct 23/st 9)
15 – M.P. Maynard
8 – R.D.B. Croft
5 – P.A. Cottey, C.S. Cowdrey and S.P. James
4 – I.V.A. Richards, H. Morris and S.R. Barwick
3 – S.L. Watkin
2 – M. Frost
1 – D.J. Foster, S.D. Thomas, D.L. Hemp and sub

GLAMORGAN CCC

BOWLING

		M. Frost	S.L. Watkin	C.S. Cowdrey	R.D.B. Croft	A. Dale	S.R. Barwick	I.V.A. Richards	D.J. Foster	S. Kirnon	S. Bastien	H. Morris	P.A. Cottey	M.P. Maynard	S. Dhaniram	S.D. Thomas	Byes	Leg-byes	Wides	No-balls	Total	Wkts
v. Warwickshire (Edgbaston) 19 April	SL	8–0–33–0	8–1–25–2	5–0–24–0	8–0–27–1	3–0–17–0	7.2–0–47–0										1	7	7		181	4
v. Durham (Durham) 21 April	B+H	11–4–26–4	11–6–20–2	7–0–39–0	9–0–28–1	6–0–40–2	11–0–32–0										4	7	7		196	9
v. Derbyshire (Derby) 23 April	B+H	9–0–41–1	10–4–49–3		11–4–15–0		11–1–33–1	11–5–18–1										3	7		159	6
v. Middlesex (Lord's) 26 April	SL	5–0–21–1	7–0–32–0	4–0–26–0	8–0–37–0				5.3–0–42–0	2–0–20–0								6	6		184	2
v. Worcestershire (Cardiff) 2 May	B+H	10–1–42–0		6–0–35–1	6–0–39–0		11–2–32–2	11–0–45–3			11–2–44–0						1	6	16		244	7
v. Worcestershire (Cardiff) 3 May	SL			3.2–0–18–0	2–0–17–0	6–0–29–0	8–0–32–1	1–0–6–0	6–0–40–0		8–0–25–1							3	4	1	170	2
v. Combined Universities (Cardiff) 5 May	B+H				11–3–28–3	9–2–24–1	11–2–29–2		11–0–42–2		11–2–29–1	1–0–1–0	1–0–1–0					2	7	3	156	9
v. Essex (Chelmsford) 24 May	SL		8–0–40–0	3–0–15–1	3–0–25–0	8–1–30–0	8–0–49–0				5–0–32–1			0.4–0–2–0			1	1	1	2	195	2
v. Leicestershire (Swansea) 31 May	SL	7–0–40–0		5–0–20–2	6–0–26–0	8–1–27–4	6–0–36–0		8–0–45–0									11	5	1	205	7
v. Sussex (Hove) 7 June	SL		8–1–32–0	6–0–23–1		4–0–26–0	7.2–0–40–0		6–0–32–3				8–0–30–2				6	3	6	1	192	6
v. Yorkshire (Harrogate) 10 June	TT		11–4–32–2		8–1–16–0		11–1–31–3				10.3–2–29–4		3–0–21–0		11–2–31–1			7	6		167	10
v. Sussex (Harrogate) 11 June	TT		8–1–23–1		11–1–52–1		8.5–0–29–2				9–0–31–4				7–0–28–1			6	8	1	169	10
v. Lancashire (Colwyn Bay) 14 June	SL			6–0–42–1	8–0–30–0	8–0–34–0	5.4–0–36–2	5–0–26–0	6–0–28–1									1	2	1	197	4
v. Yorkshire (Ebbw Vale) 21 June	SL		8–0–37–2	8–1–40–2	8–3–16–0		7.4–0–32–1		7–0–41–0								4	1	3	3	171	6
v. Surrey (Swansea) 24 June	NW		11–2–38–0		12–2–33–0	11–1–50–1	12–3–26–5	7–0–28–0			7–0–56–0							8	7		239	6
v. Northamptonshire (Luton) 28 June	SL		8–0–45–0		8–0–71–1	8–0–31–1	8–0–61–0		8–0–45–2									9	2	1	262	5
v. Surrey (Llanelli) 5 July	SL	6.4–0–48–1	8–0–48–0		5–0–35–0	8–0–41–1	8–0–40–1						2–0–13–0				1	9	1	2	235	3
v. Nottinghamshire (Trent Bridge) 9 & 10 July	NW		12–3–21–3			12–0–46–2	12–3–48–2	11.3–1–31–2			12–1–42–1						2	4	7		194	10
v. Hampshire (Portsmouth) 19 July	SL	5.5–1–25–1	8–0–31–1		2–0–6–0	6–0–27–2	8–3–16–3	7–1–12–3									1	11	7		129	10
v. Derbyshire (Pontypridd) 26 July	SL	4–0–16–0														3.4–0–14–0			4		30	0
v. Northamptonshire (Swansea) 29 July	NW		12–1–43–2		10–0–45–1	6–1–14–1	12–3–36–2	8–0–39–0	12–3–40–1									7	5	4	224	8
v. Kent (Swansea) 2 August	SL	8–1–52–3			8–1–50–1	8–0–34–2	8–0–53–1		8–0–66–0									8	11	4	263	8
v. Nottinghamshire (Trent Bridge) 9 August	SL	7–0–35–2			4–0–26–1	6–0–23–0	6–0–28–2		6–2–24–1				2–0–9–0				2	11	2		158	6
v. Durham (Hartlepool) 16 August	SL					8–0–55–1		8–0–43–3	8–1–37–2		8–0–24–1					8–1–34–1		7	6	5	200	9
v. Gloucestershire (Bristol) 23 August	SL	6–1–20–0				1–0–4–1					5–1–18–0							1	2		43	1
v. Somerset (Cardiff) 30 August	SL																					Ab.
Wickets		13	19	8	10	19	30	12	12	0	13	0	2	0	2	1						

GLOUCESTERSHIRE CCC

BATTING	v. Hampshire (Southampton) 19 April SL	v. Leicestershire (Cheltenham) 21 April B+H	v. Minor Counties (Cheltenham) 23 April B+H	v. Middlesex (Lord's) 30 April B+H	v. Sussex (Hove) 2 May B+H	v. Middlesex (Lord's) 3 May SL	v. Surrey (The Oval) 5 & 6 May B+H	v. Derbyshire (Derby) 10 May SL	v. Somerset (Gloucester) 24 May SL	v. Nottinghamshire (Trent Bridge) 31 May SL	v. Lancashire (Old Trafford) 7 June SL	v. Kent (Swindon) 14 June SL	v. Warwickshire (Bristol) 21 June SL	Runs
M.W. Alleyne	16	1	–	4	24	7	20	10	58*	–	18	25	19	722
S.G. Hinks	16	20	28	26	11	2	42	8	2	39	12	7		284
C.W.J. Athey	41	9	13	17	56*	3	27	11	4	46*	47	4	5	713
A.J. Wright	27	0	33	13	36	9	62	12	2	–	59*	20	51	697
J.T.C. Vaughan	20	12	–	8	4	2								158
R.C. Russell	13*	15	18*	7	30	42	8*	3	56*	–		15		355
T.H.C. Hancock	5	12	–	12	1		–				3		8	50
M.C.J. Ball	2*	1	–	13	–	0	–	5		–				67
A.M. Smith	–	7				3	–	0	–	–	–	1*	1*	36
A.M. Babington	–	27	–	8*	–	0*	–	2*	–		–	2*	6	54
M.J. Gerrard	–	1*	–											2
G.D. Hodgson			103*	26	54	25	80	38	13	84*	40	45	9	836
C.A. Walsh				13	0*	8	–	1	–	–		9	8	79
R.J. Scott								0	–	–	12*	6	18	271
M. Davies									–					2
R.I. Dawson										–	–	14	17	166
R.C.J. Williams											–		17	17
R.C. Williams														–
Byes							1	1				1	2	
Leg-byes	6	2	8	5	3	3	6	5	7	7	7	3	4	
Wides	2	3	8	8	5	2	2	4	2	4	3	4	6	
No-balls	2		2	2		2	4	3	1	1	1			
Total	150	110	213	162	224	108	252	103	145	181	202	156	171	
Wickets	6	10	3	10	7	10	5	10	4	1	5	9	10	
Result	L	L	W	L	L	L	L	L	W	W	W	L	L	
Points	0	0	2	0	0	0	0	0	4	4	4	0	0	

BATTING	v. Cheshire (Bristol) 24 June NW	v. Surrey (Bristol) 28 June SL	v. Durham (Stockton) 5 July SL	v. Somerset (Taunton) 9 July NW	v. Northamptonshire (Moreton-in-Marsh) 12 July SL	v. Yorkshire (Cheltenham) 19 July SL	v. Sussex (Cheltenham) 26 July SL	v. Essex (Cheltenham) 29 July NW	v. Worcestershire (Worcester) 2 August SL	v. Leicestershire (Bristol) 9 August SL	v. Glamorgan (Bristol) 23 August SL	v. Essex (Chelmsford) 30 August SL	v. Sussex (Hove) 5 September SB	Runs
M.W. Alleyne	25	31	32	17	58	41	0	26	55	134*	17*	68	16	722
S.G. Hinks			4	67										284
C.W.J. Athey	57	49	38	8	12	51	105	59	1	39*	0*	11		713
A.J. Wright	107*	24	93	71	17	26	16	10	9	–	–			697
J.T.C. Vaughan				11			1*	54*	6	–		5	35	158
R.C. Russell	13*	4		20	26*	41*	21	11	4	–	–	1	7	355
T.H.C. Hancock												5	4	50
M.C.J. Ball	–	19				0*	–	16*	4*	–	–	1	6	67
A.M. Smith	–	5	–	6	13*	–	–	–	–	–	–	–		36
A.M. Babington	–	0	–	1*		–	–	–		–	–	–	8	54
M.J. Gerrard		0*			–								1*	2
G.D. Hodgson	29	1	12	0	22	8	13	25	22	22	23	73	69	836
C.A. Walsh	–			10	10	2		17	1		–			79
R.J. Scott	25	16	39*	4	7	23	25*	1	34*	–	–	50*	11	271
M. Davies					–								2	2
R.I. Dawson	–	24	0*		4	5	35		19	–	–	6	42	166
R.C.J. Williams			–											17
R.C. Williams			–											–
Byes	1	2				1							5	
Leg-byes	6	5	6	6	5	3	7	9	10	10	1	6	8	
Wides	9	9	1	14	2	2	7	6	6	4	2	10	6	
No-balls			1				2	2	3			3	2	
Total	272	189	226	235	176	203	232	236	174	209	43	239	222	
Wickets	4	10	5	10	7	7	6	7	8	1	1	8	10	
Result	W	L	L	W	W	W	W	L	L	W	Ab.	W	L	
Points	–	0	0	–	4	4	4	–	0	4	2	4	–	

FIELDING FIGURES

25 – R.C. Russell (ct 23/st 2)
9 – M.W. Alleyne
8 – C.W.J. Athey
7 – A.J. Wright
6 – M.C.J. Ball
5 – T.H.C. Hancock, G.D. Hodgson and A.M. Babington
4 – A.M. Smith, C.A. Walsh and R.I. Dawson
2 – S.G. Hinks and R.C.J. Williams
1 – M.J. Gerrard, J.T.C. Vaughan, M. Davies, R.J. Scott and sub

GLOUCESTERSHIRE CCC

BOWLING

		A.M. Smith	A.M. Babington	M.J. Gerrard	J.T.C. Vaughan	M.C.J. Ball	M.W. Alleyne	C.W.J. Athey	C.A. Walsh	R.J. Scott	T.H.C. Hancock	R.C. Williams	M. Davies	Byes	Leg-byes	Wides	No-balls	Total	Wkts
v. Hampshire (Southampton) 19 April	SL	6.3–0–32–0	8–0–25–1	8–0–24–1	7–1–22–1	8–0–32–1	1–0–6–0								10		5	151	4
v. Leicestershire (Cheltenham) 21 April	B+H	3–0–10–0	5–0–21–0	5.5–1–21–0	7–0–16–0	9–2–24–0	5–0–18–0								1	4	1	111	0
v. Minor Counties (Cheltenham) 23 April	B+H		11–4–32–2	8–1–32–0	10–1–36–1	4–1–18–0	11–3–34–0	11–1–57–4							3	3		212	7
v. Middlesex (Lord's) 30 April	B+H		11–2–27–2		10–0–64–1	9–0–39–1	10–1–38–0	3–0–15–0	11–1–58–1					1	7	2	1	249	7
v. Sussex (Hove) 2 May	B+H		11–0–32–1		10–0–61–3	10–0–41–0	8.1–0–34–0	4–0–18–0	11–1–34–1						5	2	6	225	6
v. Middlesex (Lord's) 3 May	SL	7–0–28–0	4–0–24–0		2.3–0–11–0	6–0–31–0			6–0–15–1						2	2	4	111	1
v. Surrey (The Oval) 5 & 6 May	B+H	11–0–39–0	11–1–48–1			9–0–53–1	8–0–25–1	5–0–32–0	10.4–0–46–2						10	5	4	253	8
v. Derbyshire (Derby) 10 May	SL	7–0–34–0	6–0–18–0			2–0–11–1	5–0–19–2		8–0–33–1	8–0–30–0					8	3	2	153	7
v. Somerset (Gloucester) 24 May	SL	8–1–33–1	8–1–35–2				8–0–33–0		8–0–32–2	8–0–27–2				1	4	5	2	165	8
v. Nottinghamshire (Trent Bridge) 31 May	SL	8–0–42–0				7.1–0–21–1	8–0–35–0	0.5–0–8–0	8–2–28–3	8–0–36–2					7	6		177	7
v. Lancashire (Old Trafford) 7 June	SL	8–0–51–2	8–1–37–0				8–1–35–4			8–0–36–1	8–0–36–0				4	2	1	199	7
v. Kent (Swindon) 14 June	SL	8–1–18–2	8–1–33–2				8–0–31–2		8–0–35–2	8–0–48–0				1	5	1	2	171	10
v. Warwickshire (Bristol) 21 June	SL	7–0–33–1	8–1–31–1				8–0–39–1		8–0–23–3	7–0–31–0	2–0–9–0				6	1		172	8
v. Cheshire (Bristol) 24 June	NW	7–0–22–0	8–3–8–3			4–2–9–0			10.4–3–21–6	5–3–4–1					4	4	2	68	10
v. Surrey (Bristol) 28 June	SL	6–0–38–1	7–0–24–0	8–0–35–2		4–0–19–0	8–0–47–1			7–0–41–1					2	5		206	6
v. Durham (Stockton) 5 July	SL	8–0–42–1	6.1–0–40–0				8–0–40–1	4–0–23–0		7–0–44–1		6–0–32–0		1	6	1	2	228	4
v. Somerset (Taunton) 9 July	NW	12–1–45–3	11–1–46–1		7–0–16–0		5–0–22–0	2–0–11–0	11.4–2–34–4	7–0–32–2					7	3	1	213	10
v. Northamptonshire (Moreton-in-Marsh) 12 July	SL	5–0–18–0	8–1–21–4				5.1–0–16–1		6–2–16–1	8–2–23–3					4	9	2	98	10
v. Yorkshire (Cheltenham) 19 July	SL	6–1–20–2	7–0–39–3			8–0–39–1	6–0–35–0		7.5–3–38–1	5–0–23–1					6	9		200	10
v. Sussex (Cheltenham) 26 July	SL	3–0–11–0	6–1–18–1		8–0–31–3	7–1–24–0	4.4–1–23–2			8–1–23–2					10	7		140	10
v. Essex (Cheltenham) 29 July	NW	3.1–1–23–0	8–1–36–0		9–0–41–0	4–0–24–1	9–0–22–1		12–2–43–0	12–0–43–1				3	5	3	2	240	4
v. Worcestershire (Worcester) 2 August	SL	3.4–0–19–1			6–2–21–0	7–1–33–2	8–0–41–0		7–1–30–1	5–0–23–0					8	6		175	4
v. Leicestershire (Bristol) 9 August	SL	8–0–38–4	8–0–40–2		8–3–25–0	4–0–29–0	8–0–47–0			4–0–23–0					3	7	3	205	10
v. Glamorgan (Bristol) 23 August	SL																		Ab.
v. Essex (Chelmsford) 30 August	SL	4–0–21–0	6–1–25–0			8–0–37–1				6–0–20–1					3		4	106	4
v. Sussex (Hove) 5 September	SB		7–0–45–1	10–2–34–1	8.3–0–46–1	10–0–39–2	1–0–10–0			3–0–21–0			10–0–38–3		4	4		237	10
Wickets		18	27	4	10	12	16	4	29	18	0	0	3						

HAMPSHIRE CCC

BATTING	v. Gloucestershire (Southampton) 19 April SL	v. Essex (Southampton) 23 April B+H	v. Northamptonshire (Southampton) 1 May B+H	v. Lancashire (Old Trafford) 2 May B+H	v. Lancashire (Old Trafford) 3 May SL	v. Scotland (Glasgow) 5 May B+H	v. Somerset (Taunton) 17 May SL	v. Yorkshire (Leeds) 24 May SL	v. Middlesex (Southampton) 27 May B+H	v. Durham (Southampton) 31 May SL	v. Surrey (Basingstoke) 7 June SL	v. Somerset (Southampton) 10 June B+H	v. Warwickshire (Edgbaston) 14 June SL	v. Essex (Bournemouth) 21 June SL	Runs
V.P. Terry	37	14	0	0	66	11*	2					89*	29	62	637
R.A. Smith	61	42	40	109	40		17	77	23	78		44	11		893
D.I. Gower	13	6	118*	44*	37	0	27	8	49	56	25	42	1	15*	570
J.R. Ayling	20*	14	8	18*	39	1*	13	2*	0*		1		8	–	369
M.C.J. Nicholas	5	19	4	5	5	–		1*	37*	20	2	7	53	23*	328
M.D. Marshall	0*	1	4	–	7	–	2	19	–		5	–	9	–	156
K.D. James	–		13		0	–	4	24	30	6	24	13*	38	–	193
A.N. Aymes	–	11	–	–	5*	–	4	–	–	3*	18	–			84
S.D. Udal	–	3*	–	–	–	–	1*	–	–	9	17	–	0	–	43
I.J. Turner	–														–
C.A. Connor	–	0	–	–	–	–	0	–	–	2	7	–	6	–	16
T.C. Middleton		41		48		2		66	65	7	42	1		72	966
R.J. Maru		4	–	–	0*	–	4	–	–	8*		–	0	–	20
J.R. Wood							2			12	5				96
P-J. Bakker										–	0*				14
R.J. Parks													14*	–	29
R.M.F. Cox															73
R.S.M. Morris															4
J.N. Bovill															–
Byes															
Leg-byes	10	6	3	8	6	1	6	5	1	6	5	12	9	3	
Wides		14	7	5	3	1	2	7	2	5	2	2	6	3	
No-balls	5	2		4	1		3	2				9	2		
Total	151	177	197	241	209	16	87	211	207	212	153	219	186	178	
Wickets	4	10	6	4	7	2	10	5	4	8	10	4	10	2	
Result	W	W	W	W	L	Ab.	L	W	W	W	L	W	L	W	
Points	4	2	2	2	0	1	0	4	–	4	0	–	0	4	

BATTING	v. Dorset (Southampton) 24 June NW	v. Nottinghamshire (Southampton) 5 July SL	v. Kent (Southampton) 9 July NW	v. Kent (Lord's) 11 July B+H	v. Glamorgan (Portsmouth) 19 July SL	v. Worcestershire (Worcester) 26 July SL	v. Middlesex (Southampton) 2 August SL	v. Sussex (Hove) 3 August SL	v. Kent (Canterbury) 9 August SL	v. Northamptonshire (Bournemouth) 16 August SL	v. Derbyshire (Southampton) 23 August SL	v. Leicestershire (Leicester) 30 August SL	v. Nottinghamshire (Scarborough) 4 September JT	Runs
V.P. Terry	108*	69	109	41										637
R.A. Smith	59*		14	90	38		34	55		61				893
D.I. Gower	–		6	29	10		13	44		27	0			570
J.R. Ayling	–	5		–	16	45	23	15*	26	28*	32*		55*	369
M.C.J. Nicholas	–	1	25	25	5	38*	2	–	8	29*	14*		–	328
M.D. Marshall	–	13*	7	29*	0	23*	18	–	19	–	–			156
K.D. James		24	4	2*	1		9*	–	1	–	–		–	193
A.N. Aymes					20*	–	–	–	23	–	–		–	84
S.D. Udal	–	0*	2	–	1	–	–	–	10	–	–		–	43
I.J. Turner						–	–	–	–	–	–		–	–
C.A. Connor	–	–	–	–	0	–	–	–	1	–	–		–	16
T.C. Middleton	38	34	43	27	5	27	64*	78*	71	98	28		109*	966
R.J. Maru	–	–	4											20
J.R. Wood		4				35			4		34		–	96
P–J. Bakker					14	–								14
R.J. Parks	–	5	10*	–										29
R.M.F. Cox						5							68	73
R.S.M. Morris									4*					4
J.N. Bovill													–	–
Byes			1		1		4	8		1				
Leg-byes	8	11	7	3	11	2	13	6	3	5	1		5	
Wides	4	4	11	3	7	1	1	4		6	10		5	
No-balls	2	2		4		1	1		2		1			
Total	219	172	243	253	129	177	182	210	172	255	120		242	
Wickets	1	7	9	5	10	4	5	2	9	3	3		1	
Result	W	W	L	W	L	W	W	W	L	W	W	Ab.	W	
Points	–	4	–	–	0	4	4	4	0	4	4	2	–	

FIELDING FIGURES

15 – A.N. Aymes (ct 12/st 3)
11 – R.A. Smith and R.J. Maru
9 – S.D. Udal
8 – K.D. James, D.I. Gower and R.J. Parks
7 – M.D. Marshall, C.A. Connor and T.C. Middleton
6 – V.P. Terry
5 – J.R. Ayling
3 – I.J. Turner, J.R. Wood and M.C.J. Nicholas
1 – sub

HAMPSHIRE CCC

BOWLING

		M.D. Marshall	C.A. Connor	I.J. Turner	J.R. Ayling	S.D. Udal	K.D. James	R.J. Maru	R.A. Smith	P-J. Bakker	J.N. Bovill	Byes	Leg-byes	Wides	No-balls	Total	Wkts
v. Gloucestershire (Southampton) 19 April	SL	8–0–34–2	8–1–26–1	8–2–20–1	5–1–18–1	8–1–35–1	3–0–11–0						6	2	2	150	6
v. Essex (Southampton) 23 April	B+H	11–3–20–4	9–1–23–0		9–2–25–2	11–1–27–3		9.3–1–31–1				1	9	7	2	136	10
v. Northamptonshire (Southampton) 1 May	B+H	7–0–34–1	7–0–34–2		6–0–40–1	7–0–42–1	3–0–18–0	3–0–16–0				1	6	2		191	5
v. Lancashire (Old Trafford) 2 May	B+H	10–3–28–3	10.3–2–35–2		11–0–54–0	11–0–40–3		11–3–35–1					11	4	1	203	10
v. Lancashire (Old Trafford) 3 May	SL	8–0–31–0	6.5–0–47–1		6–0–37–1	8–0–32–2	2–0–12–0	8–0–44–1				1	6	11		210	6
v. Scotland (Glasgow) 5 May	B+H	7–3–17–0	11–4–26–1		11–2–42–1	11–1–23–2	4–0–20–0	11–4–19–1					4	2	2	151	5
v. Somerset (Taunton) 17 May	SL	8–0–29–1	8–1–30–1		8–0–47–0	8–0–43–3		8–0–30–2					5	5	2	184	7
v. Yorkshire (Leeds) 24 May	SL	4–0–15–1	7–0–29–1		4–0–23–0	7–0–30–3	8–1–11–1	8–0–41–1	0.2–0–0–1				3	3	1	152	10
v. Middlesex (Southampton) 27 May	B+H	5–2–11–0	9.4–1–38–2		10–0–37–0	11–1–40–4	7–1–25–2	10–0–54–1					1		3	206	10
v. Durham (Southampton) 31 May	SL		8–0–26–1			8–0–64–4	8–0–32–1	8–0–43–0		8–0–41–1			3	2		209	7
v. Surrey (Basingstoke) 7 June	SL	8–0–30–0	7–0–33–0		5.3–0–18–0	8–1–28–1	3–0–16–0			4–0–25–0			7	2	3	157	1
v. Somerset (Southampton) 10 June	B+H	11–3–37–1	11–3–32–4			11–0–58–1	11–0–58–0	11–1–26–1					7	12	3	218	8
v. Warwickshire (Edgbaston) 14 June	SL	8–0–36–2	7–0–44–1		6–0–44–0	6–0–33–3	5–1–15–0	8–0–43–0				1	10	10		226	6
v. Essex (Bournemouth) 21 June	SL	8–1–34–2	8–1–30–1		7–0–28–1	6–0–30–1	5–0–22–0	6–0–28–1					3	9	1	175	6
v. Dorset (Southampton) 24 June	NW	12–3–26–0	12–3–29–3		12–0–70–0	12–2–44–0		12–1–39–0				2	8	7	2	218	3
v. Nottinghamshire (Southampton) 5 July	SL	7–0–26–2	8–0–35–2		6–0–18–0	5–0–18–1	8–1–25–3	6–0–24–1					2	5	2	148	9
v. Kent (Southampton) 9 July	NW	12–0–43–2	11.1–2–37–3			12–0–39–3	12–3–56–0	12–0–61–0					8	3	10	244	8
v. Kent (Lord's) 11 July	B+H	10–1–33–3	9.3–2–27–1		11–0–38–2	11–0–67–3	11–1–35–1					1	11	5	4	212	10
v. Glamorgan (Portsmouth) 19 July	SL	8–1–29–0	7–2–21–0		8–0–26–1	4–1–15–1	4–0–13–1			6–0–28–0			1	3	3	133	3
v. Worcestershire (Worcester) 26 July	SL	8–1–19–2	7–1–34–0	5–0–24–0	6–0–24–2	8–0–41–1				6–0–28–0			6	3	1	176	5
v. Middlesex (Southampton) 2 August	SL	8–0–44–1	8–0–29–1	3–0–15–1	8–0–20–1	8–0–40–1	5–0–32–1						1	1	1	181	7
v. Sussex (Hove) 3 August	SL	8–0–33–2	8–0–39–1	6–0–28–0	4–0–35–1	8–0–42–2	6–0–26–0						3	2		206	7
v. Kent (Canterbury) 9 August	SL	8–0–41–1	7–0–27–0	4–0–19–0	8–0–44–0	4–0–23–1	8–0–17–2						5	1	3	176	4
v. Northamptonshire (Bournemouth) 16 August	SL	8–0–23–1	7.2–0–30–3	5–1–31–2	4–0–7–0	8–0–51–4	6–0–27–0					1	4	7		174	10
v. Derbyshire (Southampton) 23 August	SL	5–0–29–0	7–0–34–0	1–0–3–0		7–0–51–2	4–0–23–0						3	1	1	143	2
v. Leicestershire (Leicester) 30 August	SL																Ab.
v. Nottinghamshire (Scarborough) 4 September	JT		10–1–41–2	10–0–40–1	3–0–13–0	9–0–47–0	10–0–45–2				8–2–46–0		6	1		238	5
Wickets		31	32	5	14	51	14	11	1	1	0						

KENT CCC

BATTING

	v. Somerset (Canterbury) 19 April SL	v. Somerset (Canterbury) 21 April B+H	v. Nottinghamshire (Trent Bridge) 23 April B+H	v. Yorkshire (Leeds) 30 April & 1 May B+H	v. Northamptonshire (Northampton) 3 May SL	v. Warwickshire (Canterbury) 5 & 6 May B+H	v. Durham Canterbury) 10 May SL	v. Surrey (The Oval) 17 May SL	v. Middlesex (Canterbury) 24 May SL	v. Derbyshire (Canterbury) 27 May B+H	v. Yorkshire (Canterbury) 31 May SL	v. Essex (Chelmsford) 7 June SL	v. Surrey (Canterbury) 10 June B+H	v. Gloucestershire (Swindon) 14 June SL	Runs
T.R. Ward	45	6	29	21	8	12	45	56	55	6	13	27	4	0	693
M.R. Benson	17	7	66	7	68	62	0	4	29	36	6	64	17	12	774
N.R. Taylor	51	45	48	15			30*		11	29	34	18	41	10	618
G.R. Cowdrey	12	7	15	16	5	7	–	56	31	1	3	5	2	3	453
M.V. Fleming	0	69	0	66	18	29	–	0	37	22	3	19	40	40	594
S.A. Marsh	22	14*	26	0	4	9	–	11	11	3	6		3	34	315
J.I. Longley	1	57	10		71	9		1*							149
R.M. Ellison	2			3			–		17*						34
M.A. Ealham	4	13	6*	26	2	12*	–	6*	12	0	34	0	5	6*	340
R.P. Davis	1	–	1		2*	–	–	–	4*	12	26	2	12*	3	110
A.P. Igglesden	3*	–	–	4*	1*	–				0*	12*		–		30
M.J. McCague			10	11*	1	13*	–	–	–	30	2	16	7*	11	147
C.L. Hooper				17	36	39	13*	90	5	39	3	6	50	23	520
N.J. Llong								11				44*		20	121
G.R. Kersey												0*			0
C. Penn															
Byes			1	4		4			1		3	6	3	1	
Leg-byes	2	8	9	8	2	5	5	3	4	7	7	8	7	5	
Wides	2	1	3	5	3	7	1	2	1	7	3	8	8	1	
No-balls	1	4	4			1		6	1	1	2			2	
Total	163	231	228	203	221	209	94	246	219	193	157	223	199	171	
Wickets	10	7	9	9	9	7	2	7	8	10	10	9	8	10	
Result	L	W	W	W	W	W	Ab.	W	L	W	L	L	W	W	
Points	0	2	2	2	4	2	2	4	0	–	0	0	–	4	

BATTING

	v. Devon (Canterbury) 24 June NW	v. Lancashire (Maidstone) 5 July SL	v. Hampshire (Southampton) 9 July NW	v. Hampshire (Lord's) 11 & 12 July B+H	v. Worcestershire (Canterbury) 19 July SL	v. Leicestershire (Leicester) 26 July SL	v. Warwickshire (Edgbaston) 29 July NW	v. Glamorgan (Swansea) 2 August SL	v. Hampshire (Canterbury) 9 August SL	v. Nottinghamshire (Canterbury) 12 August SL	v. Derbyshire (Chesterfield) 16 August SL	v. Warwickshire (Edgbaston) 23 August SL	v. Sussex (Canterbury) 30 August SL	v. Surrey (Hove) 4 September SB	Runs
T.R. Ward			92	5	51	37	4	26	6		65	–	73	7	693
M.R. Benson	58		11	59	36	15	57	64	8		10	–	38	23	774
N.R. Taylor	43		15	8	28	71	3	1	35		11	–	20	51	618
G.R. Cowdrey	33		6	27	33	23	3	10	51*		11	–	2	91	453
M.V. Fleming	53		1	32	38	9	11	36	45*		10	–	9	7	594
S.A. Marsh	10		13	7	16	27	7	32	–		11	–	36*	13	315
J.I. Longley															149
R.M. Ellison	–											–		12*	34
M.A. Ealham	6		33*	23	9	22*	19	41	–		43*	–	0	18	340
R.P. Davis	–		9	1	4	–	22	1*			3	–	–	7	110
A.P. Igglesden			–	1*	2*		7*	–	–			–	–		30
M.J. McCague	4*		3*	0	1*	–	14	22*	–		1		1*		147
C.L. Hooper	22		40	28	9	5	5	7	22		11	–	46	4	520
N.J. Llong	13*					18*			–		15				121
G.R. Kersey															0
C. Penn														6*	
Byes				1		5									
Leg-byes	15		8	11	7	6	6	8	5		12		3	7	
Wides	9		3	5	1	7	3	11	1		4		6	7	
No-balls			10	4				4	3		2		1	1	
Total	266		244	212	235	245	161	263	176		209		235	254	
Wickets	7		8	10	9	7	10	8	4		10		7	9	
Result	W	Ab.	W	L	W	W	L	W	W	Ab.	L	Ab.	W	W	
Points	–	2	–	–	4	4	–	4	4	2	0	2	4	–	

FIELDING FIGURES

28 – S.A. Marsh (ct 23/st 5)
12 – R.P. Davis
10 – C.L. Hooper
9 – M.A. Ealham
8 – M.R. Benson
7 – G.R. Cowdrey
6 – T.R. Ward
4 – M.V. Fleming
3 – A.P. Igglesden
2 – M.J. McCague, R.M. Ellison and N.R. Taylor
1 – G.R. Kersey and sub

KENT CCC

BOWLING

		R.M. Ellison	M.A. Ealham	M.V. Fleming	A.P. Igglesden	R.P. Davis	G.R. Cowdrey	M.J. McCague	C.L. Hooper	N.J. Llong	T.R. Ward	C. Penn	Byes	Leg-byes	Wides	No-balls	Total	Wkts
v. Somerset (Canterbury) 19 April	SL	7.2–0–43–2	8–0–27–0	7–0–22–1	8–0–30–2	6–0–21–0	3–0–12–0						4	5	1		164	6
v. Somerset (Canterbury) 21 April	B+H		10–1–29–4	9–0–34–0	9–2–31–0	11–1–31–0	3–0–14–0	10.4–0–43–5					1	11	3	3	194	10
v. Nottinghamshire (Trent Bridge) 23 April	B+H		11–0–38–2	6–0–26–1	9–2–24–3	11–2–40–2		8–0–34–1						5	5	3	167	10
v. Yorkshire (Leeds) 30 April & 1 May	B+H	11–0–27–2	8–2–20–0	5–0–10–0	7–2–13–1			6.5–0–26–3	11–2–28–3					9	5	1	133	10
v. Northamptonshire (Northampton) 3 May	SL		5–0–20–1	2–0–11–1	8–0–32–2	8–0–23–2		4.4–0–21–1	8–0–23–2					7	3		137	9A
v. Warwickshire (Canterbury) 5 & 6 May	B+H		8–1–26–0	8–0–37–2	11–3–34–1	11–3–22–0		5–0–19–1	11–0–29–2				4	11	5		182	10
v. Durham (Canterbury) 10 May	SL																	Ab.
v. Surrey (The Oval) 17 May	SL		8–0–56–1	8–0–41–2		8–0–68–0		8–0–41–1	8–0–32–0					3	5		241	5
v. Middlesex (Canterbury) 24 May	SL	1–0–12–0	8–0–34–0	8–0–42–1		7–0–41–0		6.4–0–48–1	8–0–34–1				4	6	2		221	3
v. Derbyshire (Canterbury) 27 May	B+H		8–2–19–2	8–0–43–1	11–1–35–1	11–4–17–1		6–0–22–2	11–3–20–2					4	2	1	160	9
v. Yorkshire (Canterbury) 31 May	SL		5–0–17–0	7–0–40–2	8–0–23–0	8–0–22–0		4–0–17–2	8–0–37–1					5	8		161	8
v. Essex (Chelmsford) 7 June	SL		8–0–57–1	8–0–49–1		8–0–64–2		8–0–33–2	8–0–17–1				6	3	6		229	7
v. Surrey (Canterbury) 10 June	B+H		11–2–30–2	5–0–32–2	11–2–24–2	11–1–45–1		5.5–0–23–3	11–1–39–0					5		1	198	10
v. Gloucestershire (Swindon) 14 June	SL		8–0–27–0	8–0–37–2		8–0–21–1		8–0–39–2	8–0–28–1				1	3	4		156	9
v. Devon (Canterbury) 24 June	NW	7–1–21–0	7–0–28–0	7–3–14–0		12–0–40–2	3–1–4–2	8–0–16–2	12–6–19–1	4–0–11–1			1	12	5	4	166	8
v. Lancashire (Maidstone) 5 July	SL																	Ab.
v. Hampshire (Southampton) 9 July	NW		12–1–34–0	9–0–34–3	12–0–33–1	8–0–47–1		7–0–44–2	12–1–43–0				1	7	11		243	9
v. Hampshire (Lord's) 11 & 12 July	B+H		9–0–46–0	8–0–63–2	11–1–39–1	5–0–18–0		11–0–43–0	11–1–41–1					3	3	4	253	5
v. Worcestershire (Canterbury) 19 July	SL		8–0–32–2		8–1–46–0	8–0–35–3	1–0–5–0	5–0–26–2	8–0–30–1		1–0–11–1		2	12	6		199	9
v. Leicestershire (Leicester) 26 July	SL		8–0–30–1	8–0–40–1		8–0–28–0		8–0–35–4	8–0–39–1				1	10	6		183	8
v. Warwickshire (Edgbaston) 29 July	NW		12–0–33–2	2–0–10–2	12–3–30–0	12–0–42–1		11–0–44–2	11–0–48–1				2	15	8	1	224	10
v. Glamorgan (Swansea) 2 August	SL		6–0–25–0	8–0–45–2	8–0–48–2	2–0–16–0		8–0–41–4	8–0–36–0					5	11		216	9
v. Hampshire (Canterbury) 9 August	SL		8–2–24–3	8–0–25–2	8–0–34–1			8–0–36–2	8–0–50–0					3		2	172	9
v. Nottinghamshire (Canterbury) 12 August	SL																	Ab.
v. Derbyshire (Chesterfield) 16 August	SL		8–0–54–1	8–0–61–0		8–0–46–1		8–0–76–2	8–1–19–0					1	4		257	5
v. Warwickshire (Edgbaston) 23 August	SL	5–0–22–1			4–1–13–1									1	2		136	2
v. Sussex (Canterbury) 30 August	SL		3–0–16–0	6–0–22–1	7–0–30–0	4.4–0–22–2		7–0–45–4	3–0–20–0					4	1		159	10
v. Surrey (Hove) 4 September	SB	10–3–38–0	10–2–30–1	7–0–43–0		4–0–30–1			10–0–55–1			9–0–40–1	8	6	5	2	250	7
Wickets		5	23	29	18	20	2	48	19	1	1	1						

A. A.J. Lamb absent hurt

LANCASHIRE CCC

BATTING	v. Durham (Durham) 19 April SL	v. Essex (Chelmsford) 21 April B+H	v. Scotland (Old Trafford) 23 April B+H	v. Hampshire (Old Trafford) 2 May B+H	v. Hampshire (Old Trafford) 3 May SL	v. Northamptonshire (Northampton) 5 & 6 May B+H	v. Northamptonshire (Northampton) 17 May SL	v. Warwickshire (Edgbaston) 24 May SL	v. Surrey (The Oval) 27 May B+H	v. Somerset (Old Trafford) 31 May SL	v. Gloucestershire (Old Trafford) 7 June SL	v. Glamorgan (Colwyn Bay) 14 June SL	Runs
G. Fowler	27	22	36							5	57	51	390
M.A. Atherton	11			24	35	8	76	5	9	13	42	45	608
G.D. lloyd	4	–	23*	1	18	4	1	7	26	14	30	30	351
N.H. Fairbrother	2	6*	26	44	9	79	2				7		322
N.J. Speak	58	9*	64	82	65	1	9	36*	2	6	12	25	788
M. Watkinson	37	–	10*	2	7	76	30	1*	25	3	2	–	387
I.D. Austin	27	–	–	20	1	1	14*	–	33	3	15	–	228
P.A.J. DeFreitas	33	–	–	8*	49*	24	41	–	3	5		41*	228
W.K. Hegg	22	–	–	0	8*	10*	10*	–	19	0*	18*	–	145
P.J.W. Allott	2			3	–	1*	–	–	9	0		–	18
D.K. Morrison	0*	–	–	0	–	–	–		0*		–		0
G.D. Mendis		21	51	3		31							106
A.A. Barnett		–	–		–		–						–
S.P. Titchard								5	82	20		1*	146
P.J. Martin								–					34
R. Irani								–					3
J.D. Fitton									14	0	9*	–	108
S.D. Fletcher											–		6
J.P. Crawley													14
J. Stanworth													–
G. Yates													–
Byes	1				1	1	3	2	2				
Leg-byes	8	1	7	11	6	9	6	5	4	2	4	1	
Wides	4	5	4	4	11	10	5		2	6	2	2	
No-balls	1	1		1		2	1				1	1	
Total	237	65	221	203	210	257	198	61	230	77	199	197	
Wickets	10	2	4	10	6	8	6	3	10	10	7	4	
Result	L	W	W	L	W	W	W	Ab.	L	L	L	W	
Points	0	2	2	0	4	2	4	2	–	0	0	4	

BATTING	v. Leicestershire (Old Trafford) 21 June SL	v. Oxfordshire (Oxford) 24 June NW	v. Essex (Ilford) 28 June SL	v. Kent (Maidstone) 5 July SL	v. Essex (Chelmsford) 9 July NW	v. Middlesex (Old Trafford) 12 July SL	v. Surrey (Old Trafford) 26 July SL	v. Yorkshire (Leeds) 2 August SL	v. Worcestershire (Old Trafford) 9 August SL	v. Sussex (Hove) 16 August SL	v. Nottinghamshire (Trent Bridge) 23 August SL	v. Derbyshire (Old Trafford) 30 August SL	Runs
G. Fowler	10	3	16		66	11	49*	28		9			390
M.A. Atherton	3	109*	57		8	27		46		24	32	34	608
G.D. lloyd	21	7	7		24	28	2	6		15	42*	41	351
N.H. Fairbrother					28		4*	64*		24		27*	322
N.J. Speak	28	35	68		60	9	40	102*		4	60	13	788
M. Watkinson	18	82	21		40	7	–	–		3	–	23	387
I.D. Austin	12	3*	27*		33*	31	–	–		2	–	6*	228
P.A.J. DeFreitas			4		0			–		20		0	228
W.K. Hegg	2	–	15*		7	34	–	–				–	145
P.J.W. Allott	3						–	–					18
D.K. Morrison		–			–								0
G.D. Mendis													106
A.A. Barnett													–
S.P. Titchard	10	20	8										146
P.J. Martin	6	–	–			10*	–			18*	–	–	34
R. Irani						3	–				–	–	3
J.D. Fitton	19*	–	–		17*	13	–	–		36	–	–	108
S.D. Fletcher						6*							6
J.P. Crawley										6	8		14
J. Stanworth											–		–
G. Yates											–		–
Byes	5									1			
Leg-byes	8	3	11		19	11	2	11		2	4	10	
Wides	8	21	2		6	5		7		8	5	3	
No-balls			2		10	4	3			1			
Total	153	283	238		318	199	100	264		173	151	157	
Wickets	10	5	7		8	9	2	3		10	3	5	
Result	L	W	L	Ab.	L	L	W	W	Ab.	L	Ab.	W	
Points	[illegible]	[illegible]	[illegible]	[illegible]	[illegible]	[illegible]	[illegible]	[illegible]	[illegible]	[illegible]	[illegible]	[illegible]	

FIELDING FIGURES

25 – W.K. Hegg (ct 23/st 2)
7 – M. Watkinson
6 – N.H. Fairbrother
4 – N.J. Speak3 – I.D. Austin and P.J. Martin
2 – D.K. Morrison, M.A. Atherton, P.A.J. DeFreitas, S.P. Titchard and J.D. Fitton
1 – G.D. Mendis, G.D. Lloyd, G. Fowler, R. Irani, P.J.W. Allott and sub

LANCASHIRE CCC

BOWLING

		P.J.W. Allott	D.K. Morrisc	P.A.J. DeFrei	I.D. Austin	M. Watkinsc	M.A. Athert	A.A. Barnet	N.H. Fairbr	P.J. Martin	R. Irani	J.D. Fitton	S.D. Fletch	Byes	Leg-byes	Wides	No-balls	Total	Wkts
v. Durham (Durham) 19 April	SL	8–0–30–1	8–0–43–1	8–0–53–1	7–0–46–0	5–0–34–0	4–0–30–1								10	1	2	242	4
v. Essex (Chelmsford) 21 April	B+H		7–1–17–2	8–2–16–5	3.3–1–7–0	7–0–19–2									2	1		61	10
v. Scotland (Old Trafford) 23 April	B+H		11–0–41–1	11–1–35–2	11–0–45–0	11–0–33–1		11–1–53–0							12	7		219	5
v. Hampshire (Old Trafford) 2 May	B+H	11–3–39–1	11–0–48–1	11–2–39–1	9–0–34–0	9–0–51–1	4–0–22–0								8	5	4	241	4
v. Hampshire (Old Trafford) 3 May	SL	8–0–23–0	8–0–46–1	8–0–34–2	8–0–42–1	5–0–37–2		3–0–21–0							6	3	1	209	7
v. Northamptonshire (Northampton) 5 & 6 May	B+H	11–1–41–1	11–1–35–1	11–2–35–2	11–1–44–2		5–0–38–0		6–0–50–0					1	5	2		249	7
v. Northamptonshire (Northampton) 17 May	SL	6–0–13–1	6–0–41–1	8–0–39–1	8–0–39–0	8–0–42–0		4–0–19–0							1	1		194	3
v. Warwickshire (Edgbaston) 24 May	SL	8–0–33–0		8–0–52–1	8–0–45–2	8–0–67–1				6–0–28–0	2–0–15–0			1	10	1	2	251	4
v. Surrey (The Oval) 27 May	B+H	11–1–56–1	6–0–44–0	11–0–51–2	11–0–56–0	5–0–33–0						11–0–56–2		1	8	5		305	7
v. Somerset (Old Trafford) 31 May	SL	0.4–0–1–0		8–0–40–1	4.1–0–18–0	6.2–2–19–0									1		1	79	1
v. Gloucestershire (Old Trafford) 7 June	SL		8–0–46–0		8–1–28–2	8–0–42–0						8–0–34–1	7.1–0–45–2		7	3	1	202	5
v. Glamorgan (Colwyn Bay) 14 June	SL	8–1–36–0		8–0–44–1	8–0–41–0	8–0–31–1						8–1–40–2			4	3		196	4
v. Leicestershire (Old Trafford) 21 June	SL	5–0–16–0			8–0–38–3	8–0–52–1	3–0–28–1			8–0–65–1		8–0–46–1			3	3		248	9
v. Oxfordshire (Oxford) 24 June	NW		8.1–3–17–3		9–2–27–2	7–2–17–3				9–1–26–2		1–1–0–0			1	5	1	88	10
v. Essex (Ilford) 28 June	SL			8–0–56–1	8–0–32–1	8–0–55–0				8–0–42–0		6–0–42–1			15	4	2	242	3
v. Kent (Maidstone) 5 July	SL																		Ab.
v. Essex (Chelmsford) 9 July	NW		12–0–72–2	0.3–0–5–0	12–1–58–0	12–2–39–2	11.2–0–83–2					12–0–49–1			13	5	3	319	9
v. Middlesex (Old Trafford) 12 July	SL				7–0–47–0	7–0–40–0				8–0–30–0	3–0–21–1	7–0–26–4	4–0–32–0		5	3		201	5
v. Surrey (Old Trafford) 26 July	SL	8–1–24–0			8–0–37–2	8–0–42–3				8–0–33–2		8–1–22–2			10	1		168	9
v. Yorkshire (Leeds) 2 August	SL	8–1–32–0		8–0–53–3	8–0–41–0	8–0–53–1						8–0–68–1			13	1		260	6
v. Worcestershire (Old Trafford) 9 August	SL																		Ab.
v. Sussex (Hove) 16 August	SL			8–0–38–0	7.4–0–32–0	8–0–34–1				8–0–28–2		7–0–40–0			3	4		175	4
v. Nottinghamshire (Trent Bridge) 23 August	SL																		Ab.
v. Derbyshire (Old Trafford) 30 August	SL			7–1–31–1	6–0–31–1	6–0–32–0				6–0–17–2		6–0–41–1			3	4		155	6
Wickets		5	13	24	16	19	4	0	0	9	1	16	2						

LEICESTERSHIRE CCC

BATTING

	v. Middlesex (Leicester) 19 April SL	v. Gloucestershire (Cheltenham) 21 April B+H	v. Sussex (Leicester) 23 April B+H	v. Durham (Gateshead) 26 April SL	v. Surrey (Leicester) 30 April & 1 May B+H	v. Middlesex (Leicester) 2 May B+H	v. Essex (Leicester) 3 May SL	v. Minor Counties (Stone) 5 May B+H	v. Warwickshire (Edgbaston) 17 May SL	v. Glamorgan (Swansea) 31 May SL	v. Sussex (Leicester) 14 June SL	v. Lancashire (Old Trafford) 21 June SL	v. Norfolk (Leicester) 24 June NW	v. Derbyshire (Derby) 28 June SL	Runs
N.E. Briers	18	51*	98	36	19	30	38	102	29	43	20	7	21	20	799
J.D.R. Benson	22	–	23*	45	1	14	1	10	0	42	11	51	11	0	427
J.J. Whitaker	42	–	7	0	26	40	68	73		5	20	59	42	55	977
L. Potter	52	–	1	21	4	0	0	9	9	7		5	41	37	345
B.F. Smith	10	–	2	31							24	2	49	12	216
V.J. Wells	10	–	18*	4	0	19	29*	19	4	21		3*	6*	10*	206
P. Whitticase	3	–	–	7	17	12			15*						64
P.N. Hepworth	1						0	11*	4	8*					24
G.J. Parsons	19	–	–	11	1	2*	24*		14*		31*	2		5*	137
D.J. Millns	11*	–	–	2*	3*	0*		6*			3		–		56
A.D. Mullally	2*	–	–	9*	11	–	–	–	–	–	5*	1*	–	–	30
T.J. Boon		54*	59	49	0	48	3	3	9	17					399
P.A. Nixon					5		4	0	17	45*	21	5	17*	8	358
W.K.M. Benjamin						45	7	39	6	0	2	3	1	1	142
R.P. Gofton										–	2				4
M.I. Gidley											10				104
P.E. Robinson												104	73	59	595
J.P. Agnew															–
Byes	2		1	1	4	2		2			1		8		
Leg-byes	3	1	9	5		8	9	8	6	11	11	3	10	12	
Wides	1	4	19	2	5	4	6	5	3	5	5	3	14	8	
No-balls	1	1	3	1		2		2	1	1				5	
Total	197	111	240	224	96	226	189	289	117	205	166	248	293	232	
Wickets	9	0	5	9	10	8	8	8	8	7	9	9	7	8	
Result	L	W	W	L	L	L	L	W	L	L	L	W	W	L	
Points	0	2	2	0	0	0	0	2	0	0	0	4	–	0	

BATTING

	v. Yorkshire (Sheffield) 5 July SL	v. Derbyshire (Derby) 9 & 10 July NW	v. Worcestershire (Leicester) 12 July SL	v. Somerset (Leicester) 19 July SL	v. Kent (Leicester) 26 July SL	v. Durham (Leicester) 29 July NW	v. Nottinghamshire (Trent Bridge) 2 August SL	v. Gloucestershire (Bristol) 9 August SL	v. Essex (Leicester) 12 & 13 August NW	v. Surrey (The Oval) 16 August SL	v. Northamptonshire (Leicester) 23 August SL	v. Hampshire (Leicester) 30 August SL	v. Northamptonshire (Lord's) 5 September NW	Runs
N.E. Briers	0	28	34	18	29	7	21	3	88	0	14		25	799
J.D.R. Benson	2		6	39		42	48	19	25*	13	2		0	427
J.J. Whitaker	82*	0	49	46	15	63	22	3	46	118*	12		84	977
L. Potter	1*		8	10	47*	31	40	2	7*		1		12	345
B.F. Smith	37	10	18	17						4				216
V.J. Wells	–	21	10		7	0					25			206
P. Whitticase								10						64
P.N. Hepworth														24
G.J. Parsons	–	5	1	6	3	3	0*	0*	–	–	9*		1*	137
D.J. Millns		29*		2*									–	56
A.D. Mullally	–	1*	0*	–	–	0	–	1	–	–	–		–	30
T.J. Boon		17			1	25	25	46	31	9			3	399
P.A. Nixon	–	32	19	27*	14	10	60		–	42*	25		7*	358
W.K.M. Benjamin	–	2	8			24*		3	1				0	142
R.P. Gofton				0	2*		–			–	–			4
M.I. Gidley					8		14	17		–	55*			104
P.E. Robinson	19	40	3	24	40	31	5	88	15	14	18		62	595
J.P. Agnew									–					–
Byes					1		2				1		1	
Leg-byes	8	6	8	6	10	7	3	3	7	5	5		8	
Wides	2	9		2	6	6	3	7	5	2	4		3	
No-balls	1	1	1	3			1	3	4	3			2	
Total	152	201	165	200	183	249	244	205	229	210	171		208	
Wickets	4	9	10	8	8	10	8	10	5	5	7		7	
Result	W	W	L	L	L	W	L	L	W	W	Ab.	Ab.	L	
Points	4	–	0	0	0	–	0	0	–	4	2	2	–	

FIELDING FIGURES

15 – P.A. Nixon (ct 12/st 3)
12 – J.D.R. Benson
10 – N.E. Briers
7 – P. Whitticase (ct 5/st 2) and V.J. Wells
6 – J.J. Whitaker, A.D. Mullally and T.J. Boon
5 – L. Potter
4 – P.E. Robinson
3 – B.F. Smith, G.J. Parsons, D.J. Millns and W.K.M. Benjamin
2 – M.I. Gidley and R.P. Gofton
1 – P.N. Hepworth

LEICESTERSHIRE CCC

BOWLING

BOWLING		A.D. Mullally	G.J. Parsons	V.J. Wells	D.J. Millns	J.D.R. Benson	P.N. Hepworth	L. Potter	W.K.M. Benjamin	T.J. Boon	R.P. Gofton	M.I. Gidley	J.P. Agnew	Byes	Leg-byes	Wides	No-balls	Total	Wkts
v. Middlesex (Leicester) 19 April	SL	8–1–50–1	8–0–35–3	7–0–36–0	6–0–30–1	8–0–29–0	3–0–24–1								3	2		207	7
v. Gloucestershire (Cheltenham) 21 April	B+H	8–4–8–1	3.5–0–13–1	11–5–13–3	11–3–36–2	6–0–27–2		8–2–11–1							2	3		110	10
v. Sussex (Leicester) 23 April	B+H	8–0–37–0	11–3–31–1	7–0–42–1	7–1–34–1	11–0–39–2		11–1–44–1							10	8		237	7
v. Durham (Gateshead) 26 April	SL	8–0–42–2	8–1–32–1	8–0–44–1	8–0–45–1	8–0–64–2									5	5		232	7
v. Surrey (Leicester) 30 April & 1 May	B+H	6–2–18–0	6–2–16–2	4–0–27–0	6–0–31–2									4	4	4		100	4
v. Middlesex (Leicester) 2 May	B+H	11–0–64–1	10–0–62–0	7–0–44–0	10–0–55–3	2–0–17–0		4–0–37–0	11–5–37–1						9		3	325	5
v. Essex (Leicester) 3 May	SL	7.1–1–20–2	4–0–21–0	4–0–28–0		6–0–35–2	8–0–34–1	2–0–19–0	8–1–28–2						8	4		193	7
v. Minor Counties (Stone) 5 May	B+H	11–1–47–1		9–0–44–2	11–0–51–4	2–0–9–0	11–2–44–2		10.3–0–48–1						10	8	6	253	10
v. Warwickshire (Edgbaston) 17 May	SL	4–0–14–0	4–0–21–0	7–0–27–1		5–0–32–1	8–0–42–0		8–1–47–1	4–0–23–1					11	5		217	5
v. Glamorgan (Swansea) 31 May	SL	8–1–18–1		8–0–59–0		3–0–23–0	2–0–15–0	2–0–30–0	8–0–43–0	1–0–18–0	8–0–46–1			1	11	4	1	264	3
v. Sussex (Leicester) 14 June	SL	7–1–39–1	8–0–25–1		8–0–66–0				8–1–30–1		6–0–41–1	3–0–22–0		5	7	2		235	6
v. Lancashire (Old Trafford) 21 June	SL	8–0–31–2	5–0–29–3	8–0–34–2				8–0–33–1	5–1–13–1					5	8	8		153	10
v. Norfolk (Leicester) 24 June	NW	11–1–49–2		9–0–15–2	10–3–22–3	4.1–0–18–2		12–1–32–1	7–1–19–0					1	5	18	1	161	10
v. Derbyshire (Derby) 28 June	SL	7–0–42–0	8–0–61–0	7–0–29–0		1–0–10–0		8–0–45–1	7.5–0–32–2					1	13	3		233	5
v. Yorkshire (Sheffield) 5 July	SL	8–2–25–0	8–1–34–2	8–1–28–2				8–0–31–1	8–0–20–2					1	9	3		148	7
v. Derbyshire (Derby) 9 & 10 July	NW	7–1–22–2		5–0–19–0	8–0–29–3				10.3–0–32–5						1	3	5	103	10
v. Worcestershire (Leicester) 12 July	SL	8–1–33–0	8–0–46–1	7.3–0–35–3				8–0–33–4	7–2–19–1					2	3	7		171	10
v. Somerset (Leicester) 19 July	SL	6–0–23–0	6–0–45–0		7–0–37–0	2–0–14–0		8–1–32–0			6.4–0–33–1				18	9		202	1
v. Kent (Leicester) 26 July	SL	8–0–38–2	8–0–39–1	8–1–37–2				8–0–39–1			5–0–56–0	3–0–25–1		5	6	7		245	7
v. Durham (Leicester) 29 July	NW	10–2–33–2	3–0–24–0	8.5–2–38–3		12–1–44–2		12–0–37–0	10–3–18–1					1	9	10		204	10
v. Nottinghamshire (Trent Bridge) 2 August	SL	8–0–49–0	8–0–51–2			3.3–0–22–0		4–0–27–0			8–0–44–0	8–0–42–1		6	7	5		248	3
v. Gloucestershire (Bristol) 9 August	SL	8–0–39–0	7–0–34–1			3–0–27–0		8–0–37–0	7.3–0–37–0			5–0–25–0			10	4		209	1
v. Essex (Leicester) 12 & 13 August	NW	12–0–41–1	12–3–29–2			3–0–26–0		9–0–50–1	12–1–40–3				12–2–31–1		9	10	3	226	8
v. Surrey (The Oval) 16 August	SL	8–0–40–2	8–0–38–0			8–0–48–0					8–0–40–0	8–0–35–1			6	4	2	207	5
v. Northamptonshire (Leicester) 23 August	SL																		Ab.
v. Hampshire (Leicester) 30 August	SL																		Ab.
v. Northamptonshire (Lord's) 5 September	NW	10–2–22–2	9–1–31–0		10–0–43–0	4.4–1–23–0		4–0–18–0	12–0–65–0						9	9		211	2
Wickets		25	21	22	20	13	4	12	21	1	3	3	1						

MIDDLESEX CCC

BATTING

BATTING	v. Leicestershire (Leicester) 19 April SL	v. Minor Counties (Lord's) 21 April B+H	v. Surrey (The Oval) 23 April B+H	v. Glamorgan (Lord's) 26 April SL	v. Gloucestershire (Lord's) 30 April B+H	v. Leicestershire (Leicester) 2 May B+H	v. Gloucestershire (Lord's) 3 May SL	v. Sussex (Hove) 5 May B+H	v. Nottinghamshire (Trent Bridge) 17 May SL	v. Kent (Canterbury) 24 May SL	v. Hampshire (Southampton) 27 May B+H	v. Warwickshire (Lord's) 7 June SL	v. Derbyshire (Derby) 21 June SL	Runs
M.A. Roseberry	59	84	5	71*	74	29	10	70*	4	19	25	1	25	912
J.D. Carr	29	16	48	7	6	70	–	–	68	–	34	104*	53*	731
M.W. Gatting	9	38	16	6	4	37	34*	–	24	25	11	9		703
M.R. Ramprakash	11	19*	39	88	41	108*	–	–	1	57	4		18	649
K.R. Brown	40	9*	31	–	33	1	–	–	73*	13*	10	28*	7	438
P.N. Weekes	17	–	20	–	44*	1*	–	–	13*	–	0	–	23	216
R.J. Sims	25	–		–								–	27*	65
J.E. Emburey	7*	–	19	–	6	–	–	–	–	–	10	–	–	93
N.F. Williams	5*	–	22	–	2*	–	–	–	–	–	8	–	–	46
A.R.C. Fraser	–	–	2	–	–	–	–	–	–	–	0*	–	–	12
N.G. Cowans	–													–
S.A. Sylvester			0											0
P.C.R. Tufnell			15*											16
D.W. Headley				–	–	–	–	–	–	–	11	–	–	32
D.L. Haynes					28	67	59*	66*	63	95*	89	84	38	1210
C.W. Taylor														3
Byes					1					4				
Leg-byes	3		7	6	7	9	2	1	5	6	1	5	15	
Wides	2		14	6	2		2	3	2	2		4	2	
No-balls		1			1	3	4	5	4		3		4	
Total	207	167	238	184	249	325	111	145	257	221	206	235	212	
Wickets	7	3	10	2	7	5	1	0	5	3	10	3	5	
Result	W	W	L	W	W	W	W	W	W	W	L	W	W	
Points	4	2	0	4	2	2	4	2	4	4	–	4	4	

BATTING	v. Shropshire (Telford) 24 June NW	v. Somerset (Lord's) 28 June SL	v. Worcestershire (Lord's) 5 July SL	v. Durham (Uxbridge) 9 July NW	v. Lancashire (Old Trafford) 12 July NW	v. Northamptonshire (Northampton) 19 July SL	v. Durham (Lord's) 26 July SL	v. Hampshire (Southampton) 2 August SL	v. Essex (Lord's) 9 August SL	v. Yorkshire (Uxbridge) 16 August SL	v. Sussex (Hove) 23 August SL	v. Surrey (The Oval) 30 August SL	Runs
M.A. Roseberry	112	35	76*	14	27	11	44	3	57	21	29	7	912
J.D. Carr	15	42*	–	45	18	–	20*	6	19	60*	15	56	731
M.W. Gatting		68	88*	57	9	96	48	1	89	2	24	8	703
M.R. Ramprakash	29	23	–	46	3	19*		23		58	41	21	649
K.R. Brown	2	15*	–	44*	25*	–	10*	47	19	0*	11	20	438
P.N. Weekes	2	–	–	0	27*	–	–	0	29	20	6	14	216
R.J. Sims	13*						–		0*				65
J.E. Emburey	0	–	–	4	–	–	–	17*	0*	–		30*	93
N.F. Williams	–	–	–	4	–	–	–	4*	–	–	1	0	46
A.R.C. Fraser	–	–	–	1*	–	–	–	–	–	–	9	0	12
N.G. Cowans													–
S.A. Sylvester													0
P.C.R. Tufnell											1*		16
D.W. Headley	7*	–	–		–	–	–	–	–	–	4*		32
D.L. Haynes	101	54	16	20	84	84*	70	77	1	21	65	28	1210
C.W. Taylor				–								3*	3
Byes				5			3		3				
Leg-byes	6	4	1	6	5	6	4	1	7	9	10	5	
Wides	6	4	2	13	3	6	3	1	8	4	4	1	
No-balls	1							1	4				
Total	294	245	183	259	201	222	202	181	236	195	220	193	
Wickets	7	4	1	8	5	2	3	7	6	5	9	9	
Result	W	W	W	L	W	W	W	L	W	W	Ab.	L	
Points	–	4	4	–	4	4	4	0	4	4	2	0	

FIELDING FIGURES

29 – K.R. Brown (ct 18/st 11)
15 – J.D. Carr
11 – M.W. Gatting
10 – N.F. Williams
9 – M.R. Ramprakash
8 – J.E. Emburey
7 – P.N. Weekes
6 – M.A. Roseberry
5 – D.W. Headley and D.L. Haynes
1 – N.G. Cowans, R.J. Sims and sub

MIDDLESEX CCC

BOWLING

		N.G. Cowans	N.F. Williams	A.R.C. Fraser	J.E. Emburey	P.N. Weekes	J.D. Carr	S.A. Sylvester	P.C.R. Tufnell	D.W. Headley	M.W. Gatting	D.L. Haynes	M.A. Roseberry	M.R. Ramprakash	C.W. Taylor	Byes	Leg-byes	Wides	No-balls	Total	Wkts
v. Leicestershire (Leicester) 19 April	SL	7–1–44–2	8–1–32–2	8–1–25–0	8–0–34–2	7–0–44–1	2–0–13–1									2	3	1	1	197	9
v. Minor Counties (Lord's) 21 April	B+H		11–2–25–3	11–2–50–0	11–5–14–3	6–2–13–1	5–0–21–0	11–1–31–1								2	9	4	3	165	9
v. Surrey (The Oval) 23 April	B+H		11–2–40–0	11–1–52–2	10–1–45–1	2–0–10–0	5–0–29–0	6–0–52–0	10–0–65–0							1	13	6	1	307	4
v. Glamorgan (Lord's) 26 April	SL		8–1–34–3	8–1–25–0	7–0–48–0					7–0–34–1	3–0–32–0						8	2	1	181	5
v. Gloucestershire (Lord's) 30 April	B+H		5.2–2–11–2	11–3–30–3	8–1–25–3	11–0–64–2	4–1–10–0			4–0–17–0							5	8	2	162	10
v. Leicestershire (Leicester) 2 May	B+H		11–0–36–3	10–2–37–2	11–0–35–1	11–1–38–0				9–1–47–0		2–0–21–1	1–0–2–0			2	8	4	2	226	8
v. Gloucestershire (Lord's) 3 May	SL		8–1–19–2	6.2–1–16–2	6–1–15–2	8–0–26–1				8–0–29–1							3	2	2	108	10
v. Sussex (Hove) 5 May	B+H		11–1–39–1	8–2–23–1	8.5–1–23–1		11–1–25–3			10–4–19–4							12	5	4	141	10
v. Nottinghamshire (Trent Bridge) 17 May	SL		6–0–48–0	6–0–57–0	8–0–44–2	5–1–18–1	8–0–42–3			6–0–42–1							5	1	4	256	8
v. Kent (Canterbury) 24 May	SL		8–0–28–2	6–0–33–0	8–1–39–2	8–0–53–1	6–0–42–2			4–1–19–0						1	4	1	1	219	8
v. Hampshire (Southampton) 27 May	B+H		8–1–28–0	10–1–35–0	9–0–56–0	11–2–29–2	5–1–18–1			8–0–40–0							1	2		207	4
v. Warwickshire (Lord's) 7 June	SL		8–1–53–1	7–1–21–0	8–0–34–2	8–1–31–3				6–0–35–2							5	1	1	179	8
v. Derbyshire (Derby) 21 June	SL		6–2–16–1	8–0–33–2	7.4–0–34–1	2–0–25–0	8–1–29–2			8–0–50–3							3	7	2	190	10
v. Shropshire (Telford) 24 June	NW			7–3–10–1	11–3–26–1	12–6–23–0	2–1–2–0			8.1–4–20–5		2–0–7–0	4–0–22–1	12–2–38–2			1	9	6	149	10
v. Somerset (Lord's) 28 June	SL		7–0–38–0	8–1–39–2	6.4–0–39–3	8–1–37–4				8–0–46–1							4	7	1	203	10
v. Worcestershire (Lord's) 5 July	SL		8–0–25–0	8–2–22–1	6–0–33–1	5–0–36–1	6–0–23–1			7–1–28–0							14	1	3	181	4
v. Durham (Uxbridge) 9 July	NW		10–0–55–1	12–1–45–1	10.3–1–36–0	10–0–47–1	5–1–11–0								11–1–54–1		12	17	5	260	4
v. Lancashire (Old Trafford) 12 July	SL		6–0–33–1	8–0–40–3	7–0–47–1	5–1–14–1	3–0–19–0			7–0–35–2							11	5	4	199	9
v. Northamptonshire (Northampton) 19 July	SL		8–0–46–1	8–1–34–2	8–1–37–0	8–0–40–2	3–0–15–0			5–0–37–0						3	9	6		221	5
v. Durham (Lord's) 26 July	SL		4–0–27–1	7–0–35–1	8–0–44–0	8–0–37–1	7–0–30–0			6–0–21–3							4	8	1	198	7
v. Hampshire (Southampton) 2 August	SL		8–0–26–1	6–1–21–0	7–0–38–2	8–0–33–1	4–0–15–0			6–0–32–1						4	13	1	1	182	5
v. Essex (Lord's) 9 August	SL		8–1–29–0	6–0–17–1	5–0–22–1	8–0–41–3				6.1–0–23–4						3	7	7		142	10
v. Yorkshire (Uxbridge) 16 August	SL		5–0–18–1	6–0–29–0	7–0–39–1	8–0–40–2	8–0–34–2			6–0–26–0							8	6		194	6
v. Sussex (Hove) 23 August	SL																				Ab.
v. Surrey (The Oval) 30 August	SL		8–0–55–2	8–0–32–0	8–0–33–2	5–0–60–0	3–0–33–0								7–0–46–0	1	8	4		268	4
Wickets		2	28	24	32	28	15	1	0	28	0	1	1	2	1						

NORTHAMPTONSHIRE CCC

BATTING	v. Surrey (The Oval) 19 April SL	v. Scotland (Forfar) 21 April B+H	v. Worcestershire (Worcester) 26 April SL	v. Hampshire (Southampton) 1 May B+H	v. Essex (Northampton) 2 May B+H	v. Kent (Northampton) 3 May SL	v. Lancashire (Northampton) 5 & 6 May B+H	v. Essex (Chelmsford) 10 May SL	v. Lancashire (Northampton) 17 May SL	v. Durham (Stockton) 24 May SL	v. Derbyshire (Northampton) 31 May SL	v. Nottinghamshire (Trent Bridge) 21 June SL	v. Cambridgeshire (Northampton) 24 June NW	Runs
A. Fordham	11	103	50	7	69	36	3	26	1	5	81	89	15	925
N.A. Felton	30	31	33	3	5	6	82	28	–	27	62	77*	14	762
R.J. Bailey	46*	4	69	109*	4	18	21	19	0	33*	–	18	18	806
A.J. Lamb	24	44	28	9	53	–	108*		14	42	33*		26	714
D.J. Capel	8	7	11	25	44	6	14	38	97*	16	1*	13*	72*	598
K.M. Curran	29	12	8*	29	3		2		80*	0*	–	–	78*	481
R.G. Williams	9*	18*	0	0*	1	5	7							40
D. Ripley	–	–	2*	–	2	24*	4	11*	–	–	–	–	–	113
A.L. Penberthy	–	7*	1								–	–		149
J.P. Taylor	–	–	–	–	3	8	–	–	–	–	–	–	–	20
A. Walker	–	–	–	–	3*		0*	–	–	–	–	–	–	6
C.E.L. Ambrose				–	1	12		–	–	–	–	–	–	46
N.A. Stanley						1		9						10
N.G.B. Cook						11	–	–						16
M.B. Loye								27*						27
A.R. Roberts									–	–		–	–	4
W.M. Noon														13
R.M. Pearson														–
J.N. Snape														11
M.N. Bowen														9
T.C. Walton														–
Byes				1			1	4						
Leg-byes	8	2	4	6	5	7	5	11	1		3	3	3	
Wides	2	7	1	2	5	3	2	5	1	4	6	7	6	
No-balls	1							2			4		2	
Total	168	235	207	191	198	137	249	180	194	127	190	207	234	
Wickets	5	6	7	5	10	9†	7	5	3	4	2	2	4	
Result	W	W	L	L	L	L	L	L	L	W	W	W	W	
Points	4	2	0	0	0	0	0	0	0	4	4	4	–	

BATTING	v. Glamorgan (Luton) 28 June SL	v. Sussex (Tring) 5 July SL	v. Yorkshire (Northampton) 9 July NW	v. Gloucestershire (Moreton-in-Marsh) 12 July SL	v. Middlesex (Northampton) 19 July SL	v. Somerset (Taunton) 26 July SL	v. Glamorgan (Swansea) 9 July NW	v. Yorkshire (Northampton) 9 August SL	v. Warwickshire (Edgbaston) 12 & 13 August NW	v. Hampshire (Bournemouth) 16 August SL	v. Leicestershire (Leicester) 23 August SL	v. Warwickshire (Northampton) 30 August SL	v. Leicestershire (Lord's) 5 September NW	Runs
A. Fordham	88	14	78	1	54	27	33	6	6	31	–		91	925
N.A. Felton	14	61	48	39	26	17	2	45	58	0	–	48	6	762
R.J. Bailey	52*	1	24	10	22	27	98*	7	7	64	–	63*	72*	806
A.J. Lamb	10	120	69	0	41	9	8	26*	26	0			24*	714
D.J. Capel	26	6	18	1	22	26	21	46	24	17	–	39	–	598
K.M. Curran	41	4*	28	6	19*		19	62	14	20	–	27*	–	481
R.G. Williams														40
D. Ripley	19*	–	3*	11		28	6		3*				–	113
A.L. Penberthy		–	36	0	19*	14	13	10	2	4		43	–	149
J.P. Taylor	–	–	–	1	–	8	–		–				–	20
A. Walker	–							–		3	–			6
C.E.L. Ambrose	–	–	4*	14*	–	7	8		–				–	46
N.A. Stanley														10
N.G.B. Cook		–	–	0		4*	–	0		1*	–	–	–	16
M.B. Loye												–		27
A.R. Roberts	–					4								4
W.M. Noon					–			0		13	–	–		13
R.M. Pearson					–									–
J.N. Snape								6	5*		–	–		11
M.N. Bowen										9	–	–		9
T.C. Walton											–	–		
Byes					3			1		1				
Leg-byes	9	5	10	4	9	3	7	3	2	4		7	9	
Wides	2	14	4	9	6	1	5	10	3	7		7	9	
No-balls	1	1	3	2		1	4		2			1		
Total	262	226	325	98	221	176	224	222	152	174		235	211	
Wickets	5	5	7	10	5	10	8	9	7	10		3	2	
Result	W	W	W	L	L	L	W	W	W	L	Ab.	W	W	
Points	4	4	–	0	0	0	–	4	–	0	2	4	–	

FIELDING FIGURES

26 - D.J. Ripley
10 - D.J. Capel
9 - J.P. Taylor
7 - A.J. Lamb and R.J. Bailey
6 - N.A. Felton and A. Fordham
5 - A.L. Penberthy and N.G.B. Cook
4 - W.M. Noon (ct 3/st 1) and K.M. Curran
3 - A.R. Roberts
2 - C.E.L. Ambrose
1 - J.N. Snape and M.B. Loye
† - A.J. Lamb absent hurt

NORTHAMPTONSHIRE CCC

BOWLING

		J.P. Taylor	A. Walker	K.M. Curran	A.L. Penberthy	D.J. Capel	R.G. Williams	C.E.L. Ambrose	N.G.B. Cook	A. Fordham	A.R. Roberts	R.J. Bailey	N.A. Felton	R.M. Pearson	J.N. Snape	M.N. Bowen	T.C. Walton	Byes	Leg-byes	Wides	No-balls	Total	Wkts
v. Surrey (The Oval) 19 April	SL	8–0–45–2	8–0–37–1	8–2–21–4	8–1–28–0	8–0–28–1													7	5		166	9
v. Scotland (Forfar) 21 April	B+H	10–2–25–0	9–0–25–0	9–0–32–2	8–1–36–1	8–1–33–1	11–1–35–1											2	2	4		190	9
v. Worcestershire (Worcester) 26 April	SL	7.5–1–30–1	7–0–24–1	8–0–42–1	4–0–32–0	8–0–44–0	4–0–24–0												12	3		208	3
v. Hampshire (Southampton) 1 May	B+H	6–0–29–0	7–0–50–2	6–0–44–1		3–0–21–0	4–0–23–0	7–1–27–3											3	7		197	6
v. Essex (Northampton) 2 May	B+H	11–1–30–1	11–1–49–2	10–0–64–2		11–0–76–0	1–0–6–0	11–2–31–4											8	3		264	10
v. Kent (Northampton) 3 May	SL	8–0–39–1				8–0–44–0	7–0–54–1	8–2–29–3	8–0–43–2	1–0–10–0									2	3		221	9
v. Lancashire (Northampton) 5 & 6 May	B+H	11–0–38–3	11–1–56–2	11–0–52–2		11–1–52–1			11–0–49–0									1	9	10	2	257	8
v. Essex (Chelmsford) 10 May	SL	8–0–38–3	5.2–0–46–0			8–0–40–2		8–0–31–0	3–0–23–0										5		2	183	6
v. Lancashire (Northampton) 17 May	SL	8–1–31–1	8–1–26–3	8–0–47–0		1–0–7–0		7.3–0–37–0			7–1–41–1							3	6	5	1	198	6
v. Durham (Stockton) 24 May	SL	7.3–1–15–2	6–0–17–1	8–0–29–2		8–1–41–4		6–1–10–0											12	1		124	10
v. Derbyshire (Northampton) 31 May	SL	7–1–19–1	8–1–26–1	8–0–57–1	4–0–27–1	5–0–23–0		8–0–33–3										2	2	2	1	189	7
v. Nottinghamshire (Trent Bridge) 21 June	SL	8–0–39–1	8–0–41–1	7–0–31–1		5–0–27–0		8–0–44–0			4–0–21–1							1		1		204	5
v. Northamptonshire (Northampton) 24 June	NW	6–3–8–2	10–1–46–0	9–0–32–2				10–5–5–0			12–0–23–1	12–3–27–0	1–0–20–0						5	4	2	166	6
v. Glamorgan (Luton) 28 June	SL	8–1–46–0	7–0–57–1	6–0–41–0		4–0–36–1		7–0–44–0			6–0–28–0								11	6		263	3
v. Sussex (Tring) 5 July	SL	5–0–25–1		2–0–8–1	5–0–32–1	5–0–36–0		1–0–4–0	5–0–34–2			2–0–4–2							9	2		152	9
v. Yorkshire (Northampton) 9 July	NW	7–1–29–1		8–0–33–3		12–1–54–1		8.3–4–7–4	12–0–45–1			3–0–12–0							12	4		192	10
v. Gloucestershire (Moreton-in-Marsh) 12 July	SL	8–1–34–0		8–0–33–1	8–0–29–2	4–0–19–1		8–1–33–1	4–0–23–2										5	2		176	7
v. Middlesex (Northampton) 19 July	SL	7–0–34–0		7–0–48–0	5–0–35–0	8–1–30–2		7.4–0–51–0						2–0–18–0					6	6		222	2
v. Somerset (Taunton) 26 July	SL	8–1–48–2			8–0–50–2	8–1–36–0		8–0–45–0	8–0–49–1									1	7	3	1	236	6
v. Glamorgan (Swansea) 29 July	NW	12–1–41–3		7–1–19–2	7.1–0–29–2	12–1–21–3		9–3–14–0	4–0–10–0										7	9		141	10
v. Yorkshire (Northampton 9 August	SL		6–0–22–1		8–0–32–1	6.5–0–20–2			8–0–33–2						8–0–40–2			3	7	5	2	157	10
v. Warwickshire (Edgbaston) 12 & 13 August	NW	12–2–34–2		12–1–28–2	12–4–28–1	12–1–34–2		11.2–3–21–2										1	3	10	3	149	10
v. Hampshire (Bournemouth) 16 August	SL		6–0–56–1	8–0–52–1	6–0–30–1	6–0–29–0			8–0–37–0							6–0–45–0		1	5	6		255	3
v. Leicestershire (Leicester) 23 August	SL		7–2–30–0						8–2–20–2			2–0–12–1			8–0–43–0	7–0–33–1	8–0–27–2	1	5	4		171	7
v. Warwickshire (Northampton) 30 August	SL				8–0–41–1				8–0–22–2			4–0–28–1			8–1–33–3	5–0–20–0	7–0–36–1	2	13	8		195	8
v. Leicestershire (Lord's) 5 September	NW	7–1–19–0		12–1–41–3	6–0–22–0	11–3–39–0		12–0–35–2	12–0–43–0									1	8	3	2	208	7
Wickets		27	17	31	13	21	2	22	14	0	3	4	0	0	5	1	3						

NOTTINGHAMSHIRE CCC

BATTING

BATTING	v. Sussex (Trent Bridge) 19 April SL	v. Kent (Trent Bridge) 23 April B+H	v. Warwickshire (Edgbaston) 30 April & 1 May B+H	v. Yorkshire (Leeds) 2 May B+H	v. Yorkshire (Leeds) 3 May SL	v. Somerset (Trent Bridge) 5 May B+H	v. Surrey (Trent Bridge) 10 May SL	v. Middlesex (Trent Bridge) 17 May SL	v. Derbyshire (Derby) 24 May SL	v. Gloucestershire (Trent Bridge) 31 May SL	v. Somerset (Bath) 14 June SL	v. Northamptonshire (Trent Bridge) 21 June SL	Runs
B.C. Broad	31	64	26	19	62	83	1	21	18	6	32	29	535
D.W. Randall	0	0	7*	4*	91*	0	55	68	48		15		477
P. Johnson	0	39	76	79*	11*	20	48	90	1	0		8	551
P.R. Pollard	41	3	76*	39	–	5	47*					24	488
C.C. Lewis	38	5	–	–	–	26	17	14	21	39	27		239
C.L. Cairns	14	16	–	–	–	1	–	18	8	55*	4	30*	314
M. Saxelby	25				–		1*	9	12	10			153
K.P. Evans	0	6	–	–	–	2	–	7*	10*		–	–	95
B.N. French	22*	10	–	–	–	5	–	17	7	4*	1*	1*	87
E.E. Hemmings	3	4	–	–	–	5*	–						12
R.A. Pick	–	3*	–	–	–	5	–			–	–	–	56
M.A. Crawley		4	0	44		57		1		24	27	39	370
K.E. Cooper								1*	1				2
J.A. Afford								–					–
R.T. Robinson									48	15	25	71	324
M.G. Field-Buss									2	–	–	–	20
G.W. Mike										11			59
W.A. Dessaur											13*		29
D.B. Pennett												–	14
G.F. Archer													43
S. Bramhall													1
M.P. Dowman													2
L. Walker													12
Byes			7	1		1					1	1	
Leg-byes	6	5	10	3	1	7	2	5	6	7	14		
Wides	6	5	5	4	6	3	3	1	4	6	3	1	
No-balls	1	3	3	1		4		4					
Total	187	167	210	194	171	224	174	256	186	177	162	204	
Wickets	9	10	3	3	1	10	4	8	10	7	6	5	
Result	L	L	W	W	W	L	L	L	L	L	L	L	
Points	0	0	2	2	4	0	0	0	0	0	0	0	

BATTING	v. Worcestershire (Trent Bridge) 24 June NW	v. Hampshire (Southampton) 5 July SL	v. Glamorgan (Trent Bridge) 9 & 10 July NW	v. Durham (Trent Bridge) 19 July SL	v. Warwickshire (Edgbaston) 26 July SL	v. Leicestershire (Trent Bridge) 2 August SL	v. Glamorgan (Trent Bridge) 9 August SL	v. Kent (Canterbury) 12 August SL	v. Essex (Colchester) 16 August SL	v. Lancashire (Trent Bridge) 23 August SL	v. Worcestershire (Worcester) 30 August SL	v. Hampshire (Scarborough) 4 September JT	Runs
B.C. Broad	72		8						63	–			535
D.W. Randall	55	5	5			91	23		10	–			477
P. Johnson	78	27	6	11	23	34	0*						551
P.R. Pollard	28	22		9	36	9*	61		20*			68	488
C.C. Lewis	32		4			–			16				239
C.L. Cairns	14	0	77	26		–	23		28	–			314
M. Saxelby					42*					–		54	153
K.P. Evans	6*	30	10	18	–		6						95
B.N. French	8*		12										87
E.E. Hemmings						–							12
R.A. Pick	–	24	24*									–	56
M.A. Crawley		2	4	1	8*	94*	9*		8*	–		48*	370
K.E. Cooper													2
J.A. Afford					–							–	–
R.T. Robinson	5	14	30	51	54	2	0		9	–			324
M.G. Field-Buss	–	10*	1	7			–		–	–		–	20
G.W. Mike				26*	0	–	21		1	–			59
W.A. Dessaur		3										13	29
D.B. Pennett		2*		12*	–		–			–		–	14
G.F. Archer				9	–				–	–		34	43
S. Bramhall				1	–	–	–		–	–			1
M.P. Dowman												2	2
L. Walker												12*	12
Byes			2	2		6	2		1				
Leg-byes	3	2	4	10	8	7	11		3			6	
Wides	3	5	7	7	12	5	2		4			1	
No-balls	3	2							2				
Total	307	148	194	190	183	248	158		165			238	
Wickets	7	9	10	9	4	3	6		6			5	
Result	W	L	L	L	L	W	W	Ab.	L	Ab.	Ab.	L	
Points		0		0	0	4	4	2	0	2	2	–	

FIELDING FIGURES

8 – C.L. Cairns
7 – S. Bramhall (ct 4/st 3) and R.T. Robinson
6 – B.N. French and D.W. Randall
5 – M.A. Crawley and C.C. Lewis
3 – P. Johnson and B.C. Broad
2 – E.E. Hemmings, M. Saxelby, M.G. Field-Buss and P.R. Pollard
1 – K.E. Cooper, R.A. Pick, D.B. Pennett, K.P. Evans and sub

NOTTINGHAMSHIRE CCC

BOWLING

Match		R.A. Pick	C.C. Lewis	K.P. Evans	C.L. Cairns	E.E. Hemmings	M. Saxelby	M.A. Crawley	K.E. Cooper	J.A. Afford	M.G. Field-Buss	G.W. Mike	D.B. Pennett	M.P. Dowman	G.F. Archer	Byes	Leg-byes	Wides	No-balls	Total	Wkts
v.Sussex (Trent Bridge) 19 April	SL	7.2–0–27–1	6–0–30–0	8–0–28–2	5–0–40–0	8–0–32–0	4–0–25–0										9	3		191	3
v. Kent (Trent Bridge) 23 April	B+H	11–0–38–1	11–1–46–5	11–2–38–2	8–0–38–1	9–1–38–0		5–0–20–0								1	9	3	4	228	9
v. Warwickshire (Edgbaston) 30 April & 1 May	B+H	11–3–29–2	11–0–50–2	11–2–45–0	10–1–41–1	11–2–21–1		1–0–7–0									16	1	5	209	7
v. Yorkshire (Leeds) 2 May	B+H	10–2–35–3	11–2–27–0	10–0–32–1	6–0–42–0	11–1–32–3		7–0–15–0								2	8	7		193	9
v. Yorkshire (Leeds) 3 May	SL	7–0–39–2	8–0–36–0	8–0–31–3	6–2–21–1	8–0–27–1	3–0–12–0										1	5	1	167	7
v. Somerset (Trent Bridge) 5 May	B+H	8–0–25–0	8–1–46–2	9.4–0–61–0	11–1–34–1	11–1–46–2		2–0–10–0									5	3	6	227	6
v. Surrey (Trent Bridge) 10 May	SL	8–1–38–2	8–0–34–1	7.2–0–49–0	8–0–23–0	4–0–26–0											7	2	2	177	4
v. Middlesex (Trent Bridge) 17 May	SL		7–0–45–0	7–0–39–0	8–0–51–2		2–0–19–1	2–0–28–0	7–0–38–0	6–0–32–1							5	2	4	257	5
v. Derbyshire (Derby) 24 May	SL		8–1–34–3	6–0–43–0	8–0–29–1		4–0–14–0		7–0–36–0		7–0–40–1						6	7		202	7
v. Gloucestershire (Trent Bridge) 31 May	SL	6.3–0–29–0	8–0–33–0		8–0–36–0		3–0–16–0				8–0–33–1	6–0–27–0					7	4	1	181	1
v. Somerset (Bath) 14 June	SL	5–0–35–1	7.2–0–29–0	6–0–25–0	8–0–23–1			3–0–15–0			8–0–29–1					1	6	7		163	3
v. Northamptonshire (Trent Bridge) 21 June	SL	8–0–28–1		7–0–33–0	6–0–33–0			4.5–0–28–1			8–0–45–0		5–0–37–0				3	7		207	2
v. Worcestershire (Trent Bridge) 24 June	NW	12–1–53–0	10–0–53–1	10.4–1–43–4	12–0–28–1						12–1–62–4					5	6	16	1	250	10
v. Hampshire (Southampton) 5 July	SL	8–0–34–2		8–1–22–2	8–1–24–2			4–0–21–0			4–1–22–0		8–0–38–0				11	4	2	172	7
v. Glamorgan (Trent Bridge) 9 & 10 July	NW	12–0–66–2	12–0–44–1	12–3–25–0	12–2–38–2						12–4–23–3						1	8		197	8
v. Durham (Trent Bridge) 19 July	SL			8–0–53–2	8–0–53–2						8–0–38–0	8–0–37–1	8–0–28–2				2	5	2	211	7
v. Warwickshire (Edgbaston) 26 July	SL			8–0–58–1			5–0–22–0	8–0–42–1		3–0–27–0		8–0–46–1	8–1–55–0			1	11	6	1	262	4
v. Leicestershire (Trent Bridge) 2 August	SL		8–0–39–0		8–1–30–4	8–0–50–1		7–0–41–3				5–0–43–0	4–0–36–0			2	3	3	1	244	8
v. Glamorgan (Trent Bridge) 9 August	SL			5–0–28–0	7–0–26–4			5–0–19–1			5–0–28–1	6–1–25–1	3–0–18–0			1	3	5		148	7
v. Kent (Canterbury) 12 August	SL																				Ab.
v. Essex (Colchester) 16 August	SL		8–1–34–1		8–1–27–1			8–0–33–0			8–0–41–2	8–0–33–1				4	4	8	4	176	7
v. Lancashire (Trent Bridge) 23 August	SL				6–0–43–0			6–0–36–0			4–0–25–1	3.2–0–18–1	6–0–25–1				4	5		151	3
v. Worcestershire (Worcester) 30 August	SL.																				Ab.
v. Hampshire (Scarborough) 4 September	JT	10–0–40–0						7–0–31–0		8–0–53–0	7–0–41–0		9–1–32–0	7–0–36–1	0.2–0–4–0		5	5		242	1
Wickets		17	16	17	24	8	1	6	0	1	14	5	3	1	0						

SOMERSET CCC

BATTING

BATTING	v. Kent (Canterbury) 19 April SL	v. Kent (Canterbury) 21 April B+H	v. Yorkshire (Taunton) 23 April B+H	v. Warwickshire (Taunton) 2 May B+H	v. Warwickshire (Taunton) 3 May SL	v. Nottinghamshire (Trent Bridge) 5 May B+H	v. Sussex (Hove) 10 May SL	v. Hampshire (Taunton) 17 May SL	v. Gloucestershire (Gloucester) 24 May SL	v. Worcestershire (Worcester) 27 May B+H	v. Lancashire (Old Trafford) 31 May SL	v. Yorkshire (Middlesbrough) 7 June SL	v. Hampshire (Southampton) 10 June B+H	Runs
M.N. Lathwell	55	4						17	6	93	14	39	1	591
R.J. Bartlett	4	3	3	22	0	4	0	14	24			37		111
C.J. Tavare	0	30	17	9	28	31	5	11	18	31	36*		28	479
R.J. Harden	14	76	19	10	2	12	4	53	50	15	–	76*	13	746
A.N. Hayhurst	28	37	6	78	4	95	15	9	24	10	27*	–	11	747
G.D. Rose	34*	4	28	58	44	18	37	34	5	30	–	88	65	575
K.H. MacLeay	3	16	23	5	22	43	33	11	10	0	–	–	25	286
N.D. Burns	16*	2	16	26*	6	0*	21*	14*	15	15	–	–	39*	270
N.A. Mallender	–	2	14*	0	2*	–	17	–	0*	6*	–	–	11	91
A.R. Caddick	–	1*	6	–			–	–		6*	–	–	1*	18
H.R.J. Trump	–	1	1	–	–	–	–		–	1	–	–	–	18
G.T.J. Townsend			1											34
R.P. Snell				17	62	10*		9*		31	–	1*	2	237
A. Payne					6*									6
A.C. Cottam						–								–
R.P. Lefebvre							2*		1*					3
N.A. Folland														3
K.J. Parsons														–
Byes	4	1		1	1				1					
Leg-byes	5	11	6	4	16	5	4	5	4	8	1	7	7	
Wides	1	3	3	5	6	3	3	5	5	10		2	12	
No-balls		3		1		6		2	2		1	2	3	
Total	164	194	143	236	199	227	141	184	165	256	79	252	218	
Wickets	6	10	10	8	8	6	7	7	8	9	1	3	8	
Result	W	L	W	L	W	W	L	W	L	W	W	L	L	
Points	4	0	2	0	4	2	0	4	0	–	4	0	–	

BATTING	v. Nottinghamshire (Bath) 14 June SL	v. Surrey (Bath) 21 June SL	v. Scotland (Taunton) 24 June NW	v. Middlesex (Lord's) 28 June SL	v. Derbyshire (Taunton) 5 July SL	v. Gloucestershire (Taunton) 9 July NW	v. Durham (Taunton) 12 July SL	v. Leicestershire (Leicester) 19 July SL	v. Northamptonshire (Taunton) 26 July SL	v. Worcestershire (Taunton) 16 August SL	v. Essex (Weston-supe-Mare) 23 August SL	v. Glamorgan (Cardiff) 30 August SL	Runs
M.N. Lathwell	22	13	12	33	21	85	33	96		22	25*		591
R.J. Bartlett													111
C.J. Tavare	10	2	60*	21	33	2	41	12*	45	9	–		479
R.J. Harden	25*	90*	108*	32	27	39	28	–	53				746
A.N. Hayhurst	56	31	47	24	54	21	73	67*	0	6	24*		747
G.D. Rose	36*	1	–	14	8*	2	26	–	42	1	–		575
K.H. MacLeay	–	40*	–	9	6*	8	3	–	3*	26	–		286
N.D. Burns	–	30	–	13	0	24	14*	–	19*	0	–		270
N.A. Mallender	–	–	–	7		1	12*	–		19*	–		91
A.R. Caddick	–	–	–		–	0	–	–	–	4*	–		18
H.R.J. Trump			–	14*	–	1*		–	–	–	–		18
G.T.J. Townsend									33				34
R.P. Snell	–	–	–	24	–	19	6	–	29	27	–		237
A. Payne													6
A.C. Cottam													–
R.P. Lefebvre	–	–		0	–		0		–				3
N.A. Folland										3			3
K.J. Parsons											–		–
Byes	1		4		1		1		1				
Leg-byes	6	2	5	4	3	7	9	18	7	4			
Wides	7	6	10	7	9	3	6	9	3	5	2		
No-balls		2		1		1			1				
Total	163	217	246	203	162	213	252	202	236	126	51		
Wickets	3	5	2	10	5	10	8	1	6	8	0		
Result	W	L	W	L	W	L	L	W	W	W	Ab.	Ab.	
Points	4	0	–	0	4	–	0	4	4	4	2	2	

FIELDING FIGURES

26 – N.D. Burns (ct 24/st 2)
12 – K.H. MacLeay
8 – R.J. Harden and C.J. Tavare
7 – M.N. Lathwell
6 – H.R.J. Trump
4 – A.R. Caddick and G.D. Rose
3 – N.A. Mallender and R.P. Lefebvre
2 – R.P. Snell, A.N. Hayhurst and N.A. Folland
1 – R.J. Bartlett

SOMERSET CCC

BOWLING

		N.A. Mallender	G.D. Rose	A.R. Caddick	K.H. MacLeay	H.R.J. Trump	A.N. Hayhurst	R.P. Snell	A.C. Cottam	R.P. Lefebvre	Byes	Leg-byes	Wides	No-balls	Total	Wkts
v. Kent (Canterbury) 19 April	SL	6.4–0–22–2	4–0–21–0	7–0–30–1	7–0–40–1	8–0–24–1	6–0–24–3					2	2	1	163	10
v. Kent (Canterbury) 21 April	B+H	10–0–61–1	8–3–21–3	8–2–33–1	8–1–21–0	11–1–36–0	10–3–51–2					8	1	4	231	7
v. Yorkshire (Taunton) 23 April	B+H	11–4–18–1	10.5–2–31–3	11–4–20–2		11–0–23–2	8–0–24–2					4	5	2	120	10
v. Warwickshire (Taunton) 2 May	B+H	11–1–39–0	7–0–50–0	11–1–29–1		11–0–40–2	4–0–29–1	11–2–40–1				9	5		236	6
v. Warwickshire (Taunton) 3 May	SL	8–1–14–1	5–0–22–1		4–0–20–2	8–0–54–1	6.1–0–29–2	8–0–28–1			1	9	6		177	10
v. Nottinghamshire (Trent Bridge) 5 May	B+H	11–2–49–4	7–1–14–1		8–0–27–0	6–0–26–0	5–0–19–2	11–0–47–2	7–0–34–0		1	7	3	4	224	10
v. Sussex (Hove) 10 May	SL	7–1–31–0		7–0–29–1	7–0–20–0	3–0–16–0	2–0–17–0			6.3–0–27–1		4	1		144	2
v. Hampshire (Taunton) 17 May	SL	6.4–0–16–3	4–1–12–1	8–1–20–4	6–0–10–1			4–0–23–0				6	2	3	87	10
v. Gloucestershire (Gloucester) 24 May	SL	7–1–27–3	6–1–15–1		8–1–22–0		6–0–36–0			5.3–0–38–0		7	2	1	145	4
v. Worcestershire (Worcester) 27 May	B+H	11–1–48–3	3–0–17–0	11–0–37–1	10–0–41–0	3–0–17–0	6–0–31–2	10.4–0–47–3			2	6	1	2	246	10
v. Lancashire (Old Trafford) 31 May	SL	4–0–19–1		5.3–0–18–4	8–1–17–2	5–1–8–2		5–1–13–1				2	6		77	10
v. Yorkshire (Middlesbrough) 7 June	SL	8–0–43–0		8–0–53–0	8–0–32–2	4–0–30–1	5–0–43–0	6–0–53–1				2	4	1	256	5
v. Hampshire (Southampton) 10 June	B+H	9–2–44–1	11–1–23–2	11–0–45–0	8–0–27–0	5–0–26–0		10.1–0–42–0				12	2	9	219	4
v. Nottinghamshire (Bath) 14 June	SL	7–0–32–0	6–0–25–2	4–0–15–1	8–0–24–1			8–0–30–1		7–0–21–1	1	14	3		162	6
v. Surrey (Bath) 21 June	SL	7–0–40–0	3–0–29–0	8–0–45–0	5–0–27–1		2–0–14–1	8–0–27–2		6.4–0–31–2		5	4	1	218	6
v. Scotland (Taunton) 24 June	NW	12–2–47–1	3–0–13–0	12–2–58–1	10–2–30–0	9–0–26–0	2–0–15–0	12–0–48–0				8	5	1	245	2
v. Middlesex (Lord's) 28 June	SL	5–1–19–0			8–0–46–2	8–0–53–1	3–0–16–1	8–0–56–0		8–0–51–0		4	4		245	4
v. Derbyshire (Taunton) 5 July	SL		5–0–16–2	8–0–26–2	8–0–31–1	7–0–28–0		8–0–40–2		4–0–18–2		1		4	160	9
v. Gloucestershire (Taunton) 9 July	NW	12–2–32–0	8–2–24–1	12–2–30–6	9–0–49–1	4–0–21–0	4.4–0–22–2	10–0–51–0				6	14		235	10
v. Durham (Taunton) 12 July	SL	8–0–33–0	8–1–63–2	8–0–40–0	6–0–44–1		2–0–11–0	2–0–17–0		6–0–44–1	1	10	3	1	263	4
v. Leicestershire (Leicester) 19 July	SL	8–0–36–0	1–0–10–1	8–0–44–1	8–0–29–2	7–0–40–1		8–0–35–1				6	2	3	200	8
v. Northamptonshire (Taunton) 26 July	SL		8–0–34–2	8–0–39–1	6–0–29–2	3–0–15–0		7–0–24–2		7–0–32–1		3	1	1	176	10
v. Worcestershire (Taunton) 16 August	SL	8–0–20–1	4–0–13–0	7–1–25–1	7.3–0–20–5	8–0–26–1		4–0–13–1				8	2	1	125	10
v. Essex (Weston-super-Mare) 23 August	SL															Ab.
v. Glamorgan (Cardiff) 30 August	SL															Ab.
Wickets		22	22	28	24	12	18	18	0	8						

SURREY CCC

BATTING

	v. Northamptonshire (The Oval) 19 April SL	v. Sussex (Hove) 21 April B+H	v. Middlesex (The Oval) 23 April B+H	v. Essex (Chelmsford) 26 April SL	v. Leicestershire (Leicester) 30 April & 1 May B+H	v. Minor Counties (The Oval) 2 May B+H	v. Gloucestershire (The Oval) 5 & 6 May B+H	v. Nottinghamshire (Trent Bridge) 10 May SL	v. Kent (The Oval) 17 May SL	v. Sussex (The Oval) 24 May SL	v. Lancashire (The Oval) 27 May B+H	v. Hampshire (Basingstoke) 7 June SL	v. Kent (Canterbury) 10 June B+H	Runs
D.J. Bicknell	21	71	70	15	37*	55	78	36	102		86	74*	13	1122
A.D. Brown	0	26	29*	22	6*	30	22	13	37	14	41	18	16	833
A.J. Stewart	28	41	40	1	0	71*	46	4	54	32	64		5	757
G.P. Thorpe	5	3	78	6	28	14*	14	26	20	51	11	53*	82	686
D.M. Ward	22	9	4*	1	12	–	18	46*	4*	63	27*	–	7	566
M.A. Lynch	25	23	65	5	5	105	21	41*	15	3	54		9	600
M.A. Feltham	9	20*	–		–	–	4	–	1*	0	0		35	161
R.E. Bryson	20	0	–	3*	–	–	18*	–	–					60
M.P. Bicknell	14*	19	–		–	–	5	–	–	6	7	–	0	91
J. Boiling	4	7*	–	–	–		8*	–	–	0*	–	–	1	29
J.E. Benjamin	6*	–	–	7	–	–	–	–	–		–		0*	24
I.A. Greig				7								–		40
J.D. Robinson				7						12		–		118
M.A. Butcher										6				11
N.M. Kendrick										1	1*	–	24	26
D.G.C. Ligertwood												–		–
A.J. Murphy												–		9
N.F. Sargeant														2
A.J. Hollioake														22
A.W. Smith														40
Byes		2	1	2	4					1	1			
Leg-byes	7	9	13	3	4	16	10	7	3	2	8	7	5	
Wides	5	4	6	5	4	7	5	2	5	3	5	2		
No-balls		4	1			1	4	2		2		3	1	
Total	166	238	307	84	100	299	253	177	241	196	305	157	198	
Wickets	9	8	4	9	4	3	8	4	5	10	7	1	10	
Result	L	L	W	L	W	W	W	W	L	L	W	W	L	
Points	0	0	2	0	2	2	2	4	0	0	–	4	–	

BATTING

	v. Worcestershire (The Oval) 14 June SL	v. Somerset (Bath) 21 June SL	v. Glamorgan (Swansea) 24 June NW	v. Gloucestershire (Bristol) 28 June SL	v. Glamorgan (Llanelli) 5 July SL	v. Derbyshire (The Oval) 12 July SL	v. Warwickshire (The Oval) 19 July SL	v. Lancashire (Old Trafford) 26 July SL	v. Durham (Durham) 2 August SL	v. Leicestershire (The Oval) 16 August SL	v. Yorkshire (Scarborough) 23 August SL	v. Middlesex (The Oval) 30 August SL	v. Kent (Hove) 4 September SB	Runs
D.J. Bicknell	6	107*	21	44	30	1	14		125	33	13	30	40	1122
A.D. Brown	84	23		2	113	33	11	14	75	8	105*	13	78	833
A.J. Stewart			60	3		86	5		9	105*		103*		757
G.P. Thorpe	12	11	3	38	56*		26	34	3*	13	15*	84		686
D.M. Ward	51	26	101*	35	3*	15			45	7	–	23*	47	566
M.A. Lynch		28	27	58	20	11	14	12	16	29	–	2	12	600
M.A. Feltham	8*	4	4	14*	–	12	14	11	–	0*	–		11	161
R.E. Bryson	–							19			–		0*	60
M.P. Bicknell	5*			5*	–	9*	3	18*	–	–	–	–		91
J. Boiling	–	–	–	–	–	4*	5	0	–	–	–	–	–	29
J.E. Benjamin	–	–	–	–	–	–	11	–		–	–	–		24
I.A. Greig	6							27						40
J.D. Robinson	26	8	4		–	27	10	21	3*					118
M.A. Butcher		1*	4*											11
N.M. Kendrick			–		–									26
D.G.C. Ligertwood														–
A.J. Murphy		–		–		–	9*			–		–	–	9
N.F. Sargeant								1			–		1	2
A.J. Hollioake									22			–	0	22
A.W. Smith													40*	40
Byes	1				1	2			4		2	1	8	
Leg-byes	2	5	8	2	9	5	3	10	16	6	4	8	6	
Wides		4	7	5	1	5	7	1	11	4	2	4	5	
No-balls		1			2	2			1	2			2	
Total	201	218	239	206	235	212	132	168	330	207	141	268	250	
Wickets	6	6	6	6	3	7	10	9	6	5	1	4	7	
Result	W	W	L	W	W	W	L	L	W	L	W	W	L	
Points	4	4	–	4	4	4	0	0	4	0	4	4	–	

FIELDING FIGURES

28 – A.J. Stewart (ct 26/st 2)
12 – D.M. Ward
11 – G.P. Thorpe, M.A. Feltham and J.A. Boiling
8 – M.A. Lynch
7 – D.J. Bicknell and J.E. Benjamin
5 – A.D. Brown
4 – J.D. Robinson
3 – M.P. Bicknell and N.M. Kendrick
2 – N.F. Sargeant and A.J. Hollioake
1 – A.J. Murphy, I.A. Greig, D.G.C. Ligertwood and W.A. Smith

SURREY CCC

BOWLING

		R.E. Bryson	M.P. Bicknell	J.E. Benjamin	J. Boiling	M.A. Feltham	I.A. Greig	J.D. Robinson	M.A. Lynch	G.P. Thorpe	N.M. Kendrick	M.A. Butcher	A.J. Murphy	A.J. Hollioake	Byes	Leg-byes	Wides	No-balls	Total	Wkts
v. Northamptonshire (The Oval) 19 April	SL	8–0–30–2	8–0–28–0	7.4–0–47–0	8–0–30–1	8–1–25–1										8	2	1	168	5
v. Sussex (Hove) 21 April	B+H	11–0–62–0	11–0–55–1	11–0–59–1	11–0–38–1	11–1–28–3										4	1	2	246	7
v. Middlesex (The Oval) 23 April	B+H	11–0–56–4	11–0–50–1	11–1–46–2	11–0–35–0	11–0–44–3										7	14		238	10
v. Essex (Chelmsford) 26 April	SL	1–0–13–0		1.4–0–22–0	2–0–12–0		2–0–27–0	2–0–14–0									1	1	88	0
v. Leicestershire (Leicester) 30 April & 1 May	B+H	8–1–31–4	4–1–16–0	6–0–15–1		9.5–1–30–5									4		5		96	10
v. Minor Counties (The Oval) 2 May	B+H	11–2–25–1	11–1–30–0	11–2–19–1	11–1–20–2	7–2–14–2			4–1–13–0							10	5	9	131	6
v. Gloucestershire (The Oval) 5 & 6 May	B+H	11–0–58–1	11–2–45–1	11–1–57–2	11–1–49–0	11–3–36–1									1	6	2	4	252	5
v. Nottinghamshire (Trent Bridge) 10 May	SL	6–0–35–1	6–1–12–1	6–0–31–0	8–0–40–1	7–0–30–1				3–0–24–0						2	3		174	4
v. Kent (The Oval) 17 May	SL	7–0–55–1	8–0–68–2	8–0–34–2	8–0–47–1	8–0–39–0										3	2	6	246	7
v. Sussex (The Oval) 24 May	SL		8–0–39–0		7–0–36–0	7.5–0–40–1		2–0–14–1	2–0–16–0		8–0–29–0	5–0–23–3				3	2		200	5
v. Lancashire (The Oval) 27 May	B+H		10–0–43–3	7–0–47–0	11–2–48–2	9–0–35–3					11–0–51–1				2	4	2		230	10
v. Hampshire (Basingstoke) 7 June	SL		8–0–22–2		8–0–24–5			8–0–28–1			8–0–35–0		7.5–0–39–2			5	2		153	10
v. Kent (Canterbury) 10 June	B+H		10.5–2–24–2	11–2–25–1	11–0–46–2	11–0–47–1					11–0–47–2				3	7	8		199	8
v. Worcestershire (The Oval) 14 June	SL	7.5–0–44–2	8–0–47–3	8–0–27–1	8–0–41–1	8–0–34–2										7	6	3	200	10
v. Somerset (Bath) 21 June	SL			8–0–47–0	8–0–26–2	8–1–24–3		3–0–28–0				8–0–55–0	5–0–35–0			2	6	2	217	5
v. Glamorgan (Swansea) 24 June	NW			12–2–39–0	12–2–37–2	5.1–0–39–0		1–0–8–0	5–0–28–2		12–1–51–1	12–3–37–0				4	5		243	6
v. Gloucestershire (Bristol) 28 June	SL		8–0–36–1	8–0–34–2	8–0–40–1	7.3–0–37–1							8–1–35–2		2	5	9		189	10
v. Glamorgan (Llanelli) 5 July	SL		8–2–33–3	7–0–47–1	7–1–33–0	5–0–35–0		5–0–35–0			8–0–45–1				2	4	4	1	234	5
v. Derbyshire (The Oval) 12 July	SL		8–0–48–4	8–0–32–0	8–0–40–0	8–0–27–2							8–0–58–1			3			208	8
v. Warwickshire (The Oval) 19 July	SL		8–2–25–1	8–2–31–0		8–1–27–1		3–0–19–1					6.5–0–30–1			3	2	3	135	4
v. Lancashire (Old Trafford) 26 July	SL	8–1–32–1	8–0–29–1	2.3–0–15–0	3–0–9–0		1–0–13–0									2		3	100	2
v. Durham (Durham) 2 August	SL		8–0–48–1		8–0–48–3	8–0–45–0		7–0–46–1						8–0–37–1		6	5	1	230	7
v. Leicestershire (The Oval) 16 August	SL		8–1–35–2	8–1–37–0	8–0–37–2	7.4–0–55–1							8–0–41–0			5	2	3	210	5
v. Yorkshire (Scarborough) 23 August	SL	7.2–0–58–1	8–1–36–2	8–0–32–3	8–0–32–1	8–0–35–1									1	10	4		204	10
v. Middlesex (The Oval) 30 August	SL		8–1–38–3	8–0–44–4									7–0–49–2	7–0–57–0		5	1		193	9
v. Kent (Hove) 4 September	SB	10–1–39–5			10–0–53–2	10–1–40–2							10–0–75–0	10–1–40–0		7	7	1	254	9
Wickets		23	34	21	29	34	0	4	2	0	5	3	8	1						

SUSSEX CCC

BATTING

BATTING	v. Nottinghamshire (Trent Bridge) 19 April SL	v. Surrey (Hove) 21 April B+H	v. Leicestershire (Leicester) 23 April B+H	v. Yorkshire (Hove) 26 April SL	v. Minor Counties (Marlow) 30 April & 1 May B+H	v. Gloucestershire (Hove) 2 May B+H	v. Middlesex (Hove) 5 May B+H	v. Somerset (Hove) 10 May SL	v. Surrey (The Oval) 24 May SL	v. Warwickshire (Hove) 31 May SL	v. Glamorgan (Hove) 7 June SL	v. Durham (Harrogate) 9 June TT	v. Glamorgan (Harrogate) 11 June TT	v. Leicestershire (Leicester) 14 June SL	Runs
K. Greenfield	77	47	62		31	53	0	20	50	29	79		4	4	567
J.W. Hall	77	81	10		20	70	8	4	61	23	7	10	12	17	701
M.P. Speight	9	14	39				14	87*	41	47*	19	71	21	44	638
A.P. Wells	12*	61	55*		15	2	35	28*	14	55*	7	43	36	62	1023
C.M. Wells	4*				6	16	4	–							30
F.D. Stephenson	–	3	21		4	34	16	–	4	–	12	0	7	55*	331
R. Hanley	–														3
J.A. North	–	11*	9							–	7*			9*	111
A.R. Hansford	–	–	–		4*										9
A.C.S. Pigott	–	13	5		6	–	17	–	–	–	–			–	98
I.D.K. Salisbury	–					–	2*	–	–	–	–	22*		–	86
P. Moores		0	10		5	1*	15	–	9*	–	3*	3	37	7	348
B.T.P. Donelan		9*	8*						–			0	16*		34
A.N. Jones		–	–		24							10*	0		39
D.M. Smith					61	21						28	15		232
N.J. Lenham					2	15*	9	–	16*	–	42	9	6	23	298
A.G. Robson						–	0	–	–	–	–	–	0	–	5
C.C. Remy															41
E.S.H. Giddins															4
Byes					1					2	6	5		5	
Leg-byes	9	4	10		9	5	12	4	3	18	3	6	6	7	
Wides	3	1	8		13	2	5	1	2	2	6	5	8	2	
No-balls		2				6	4				1	2	1		
Total	191	256	237		201	225	141	144	200	176	192	214	169	235	
Wickets	3	7	7		10	6	10	2	5	2	6	8	10	6	
Result	W	W	L	Ab.	L	W	L	W	W	W	W	W	L	W	
Points	4	2	0	2	0	2	0	4	4	4	4	–	–	4	

BATTING	v. Durham (Horsham) 21 June SL	v. Buckinghamshire (Beaconsfield) 24 June NW	v. Worcestershire (Worcester) 28 June SL	v. Northamptonshire (Tring) 5 July SL	v. Warwickshire (Edgbaston) 9 & 10 July NW	v. Essex (Southend) 19 July SL	v. Gloucestershire (Cheltenham) 26 July SL	v. Hampshire (Hove) 3 August SL	v. Derbyshire (Eastbourne) 9 August SL	v. Lancashire (Hove) 16 August SL	v. Middlesex (Hove) 23 August SL	v. Kent (Canterbury) 30 August SL	v. Gloucestershire (Hove) 5 September SB	Runs
K. Greenfield	1	19	6	26	0	1	17	18	19				4	567
J.W. Hall	19	47	42	14	0	52	9	58		2	–	14	44	701
M.P. Speight	38	28	19	18	1	23	26	30	2	8	–	26	13	638
A.P. Wells	36	119	64	31	47*	110*	3	1	0	56	–	52	79	1023
C.M. Wells										–	–			30
F.D. Stephenson	10	12	4	34	40	0		6	1			6	62	331
R. Hanley									3					3
J.A. North	56		3	8									8	111
A.R. Hansford	5*													9
A.C.S. Pigott	6	3*	1	0	0	7*	2	17*	17*	–	–	4*	0*	98
I.D.K. Salisbury		–	0	1	4	–	27*	10*	7	–	–	6	7	86
P. Moores	42	14*	24	2	0	24	6	57	56	21*	–	7	5	348
B.T.P. Donelan						–			1				0	34
A.N. Jones					5									39
D.M. Smith		62			22					0	–	23		232
N.J. Lenham	43	–	8	6*	14	2	15			81*	–	0	7	298
A.G. Robson	1*	–	0*	1*		–	3	–						5
C.C. Remy							14	4	8	–	–	15		41
E.S.H. Giddins							1	–	2	–	–	1		4
Byes	4	5			4									
Leg-byes	7	8	6	9	4	5	10	3	5	3		4	4	
Wides	2	9	1	2	1	13	7	2	3	4		1	4	
No-Balls		1			8	2								
Total	270	327	178	152	150	239	140	206	124	175		159	237	
Wickets	9	6	10	9	10	6	10	7	10	4		10	10	
Result	L	W	L	L	L	L	L	L	L	W	Ab.	L	W	
Points	0	–	0	0	–	0	0	0	0	4	2	0	–	

FIELDING FIGURES

22 – P. Moores (ct 20/st 2)
12 – M.P. Speight (ct 11/st 1)
10 – I.D.K. Salisbury
9 – A.P. Wells
8 – K. Greenfield
6 – F.D. Stephenson
5 – A.C.S. Pigott
4 – J.W. Hall and D.M. Smith
3 – A.N. Jones, A.G. Robson and C.M. Wells
2 – N.J. Lenham and E.S.H. Giddins
1 – R. Hanley, B.T.P. Donelan, A.R. Hansford and J.A. North

SUSSEX CCC

BOWLING

		C.M. Wells	F.D. Stephenson	I.D.K. Salisbury	A.C.S. Pigott	J.A. North	A.R. Hansford	A.N. Jones	B.T.P. Donelan	K. Greenfield	A.G. Robson	N.J. Lenham	A.P. Wells	E.S.H. Giddins	C.C. Remy	Byes	Leg-byes	Wides	No-balls	Total	Wkts
v. Nottinghamshire (Trent Bridge) 19 April	SL	8–1–28–1	8–0–38–2	8–0–26–0	8–0–45–2	2–0–14–0	6–0–30–1										6	6	1	187	9
v. Surrey (Hove) 21 April	B+H		11–0–54–2		11–0–39–3	5–0–20–0	8–0–30–1	9–1–43–1	11–1–41–1							2	9	4	4	238	8
v. Leicestershire (Leicester) 23 April	B+H		11–1–32–1		9.5–0–49–1	4–0–24–3	11–0–48–0	1–0–8–0	7–0–32–0	9–0–37–0						1	9	19	3	240	5
v. Yorkshire (Hove) 26 April	SL																				Ab.
v. Minor Counties (Marlow) 30 April & 1 May	B+H	11–3–32–1	11–1–28–3		11–0–59–2		11–1–44–1	11–0–51–0									6	7	3	220	8
v. Gloucestershire (Hove) 2 May	B+H	8–1–41–1	11–0–41–3	11–2–43–2	11–1–49–0					3–0–15–0	11–1–32–1						3	5		224	7
v. Middlesex (Hove) 5 May	B+H	8–0–31–0	9–2–27–0	5.3–0–26–0	8–1–25–0						11–3–29–0	3–0–6–0					1	3	5	145	0
v. Somerset (Hove) 10 May	SL	7–1–16–3	7–2–31–1	7–0–32–0	7–0–35–0						7–1–23–2						4	3		141	7
v. Surrey (The Oval) 24 May	SL		8–2–37–2	8–0–40–1	8–0–39–1				8–0–39–2		8–0–38–2					1	2	3	2	196	10
v. Warwickshire (Hove) 31 May	SL		8–1–40–1	8–1–35–1	8–0–41–1	8–0–41–1					8–1–14–2						4	6	3	175	7
v. Glamorgan (Hove) 7 June	SL		7.4–1–22–4	8–0–33–1	8–0–46–2	2–0–16–0				6–0–36–2	8–0–28–0					4	3	1	4	188	10
v. Durham (Harrogate) 9 June	TT		9.3–3–20–3					6–0–34–1	10–1–24–1		3–0–19–0	11–0–32–4	9–0–38–1			1	9	3		177	10
v. Glamorgan (Harrogate) 11 June	TT		11–0–56–2					11–1–24–0	7–0–36–1	7–0–46–1	9–0–70–0	10–2–49–0					10	5		291	5
v. Leicestershire (Leicester) 14 June	SL		8–2–21–1	8–0–30–5	8–1–29–2	3–0–5–0				5–0–35–0	8–1–34–1					1	11	5		166	9
v. Durham (Horsham) 21 June	SL		8–0–43–0		8–0–65–1	1–0–13–0	6–0–50–0			7–0–39–1	6–0–34–0	4–0–21–1					10	6		275	4
v. Buckinghamshire (Beaconsfield) 24 June	NW		9–4–8–3	12–4–28–3	8–0–18–2					12–5–33–1	10–1–29–1					4	6	1	2	126	10
v. Worcestershire (Worcester) 28 June	SL		8–2–24–0	5–0–33–1	8–0–39–0	7–0–34–1				4–0–20–0	8–0–30–1						6	4	1	186	6
v. Northamptonshire (Tring) 5 July	SL		5–0–22–3		5–0–35–0	4–0–46–0	4–0–46–0			2–0–41–1	5–0–31–0						5	14	1	226	5
v. Warwickshire (Edgbaston) 9 & 10 July	NW		12–2–35–2	9–1–21–1	12–1–31–3			9–0–31–0				11.3–3–24–1				1	8	4	1	151	7
v. Essex (Southend) 19 July	SL		6–0–39–0	8–0–32–2	5.5–0–57–0				2–0–23–0	2–0–17–0	6–0–31–0	7–0–38–0					3	2		240	2
v. Gloucestershire (Cheltenham) 26 July	SL			6–0–47–0	8–0–45–2						8–2–23–0	6–0–55–0		8–0–37–3	4–0–18–1		7	7	2	232	6
v. Hampshire (Hove) 3 August	SL		6–0–30–0	8–0–31–1	7.4–0–46–1					2–0–13–0	5–0–14–0			5–0–37–0	4–0–25–0	8	6	4		210	2
v. Derbyshire (Eastbourne) 9 August	SL		8–1–41–2	8–1–25–0	8–1–34–2				5–0–33–0					6–0–23–1	5–0–18–1	4	5	7	1	183	7
v. Lancashire (Hove) 16 August	SL	8–0–27–1		8–3–10–1	5.3–0–34–2							2–0–16–1		8–0–52–0	8–0–31–4	1	2	8	1	173	10
v. Middlesex (Hove) 23 August	SL	8–0–31–0		8–0–38–1	8–0–49–3									8–0–43–1	8–0–49–4		10	4		220	9
v. Kent (Canterbury) 30 August	SL		7–0–54–2	7–0–40–2	3–0–21–0							7–0–41–2		7–0–54–0	2–0–22–0		3	6	1	235	7
v. Gloucestershire (Hove) 5 September	SB		10–0–36–5	9–0–32–1	9.1–0–37–2	4–0–21–1			10–0–36–0			7–0–47–1				5	8	6	2	222	10
Wickets		7	42	23	32	6	3	2	5	6	10	10	1	5	10						

WARWICKSHIRE CCC

BATTING

BATTING	v. Glamorgan (Edgbaston) 19 April SL	v. Yorkshire (Edgbaston) 21 April B+H	v. Nottinghamshire (Edgbaston) 30 April & 1 May B+H	v. Somerset (Taunton) 2 May B+H	v. Somerset (Taunton) 3 May SL	v. Kent (Canterbury) 5 & 6 May B+H	v. Worcestershire (Worcester) 10 May SL	v. Leicestershire (Edgbaston) 17 May SL	v. Lancashire (Edgbaston) 24 May SL	v. Sussex (Hove) 31 May SL	v. Middlesex (Lord's) 7 June SL	v. Hampshire (Edgbaston) 14 June SL	v. Gloucestershire (Bristol) 21 June SL	Runs
A.J. Moles	96*	1	8	15	60	13	19	21	56	1	18	26	38	698
M. Asif Din	6	42	71*	5	9	10	22		1*	4				174
T.A. Lloyd	21	21	11	51	5	61	62	16	68	9	71	2	0	630
D.P. Ostler	0	14	16	65*	31	10	1	28	47	0	0	49	17	506
R.G. Twose	10	62	28	45	0	5	6	100	54	71	32	66	48	895
T.L. Penney	33*	17	5		13			10*				8	0	267
P.A. Smith	–	13	37	9	15*	17	18	7*	–	3	–	3*	8	199
N.M.K. Smith	–	3	11	32	14	5	9	–	11*	30	8	1	14*	230
K.J. Piper	–	1	0*											31
G.C. Small	–	1	–	–	6	20*	10*	–	–	8*	–			85
T.A. Munton	–	3*		–	5	3	0	–	–	–	9*	–	–	21
A.A. Donald				–		10	0	–	–	–			1*	34
P.C.L. Holloway				0*	3	8	8	19	–	36*	0	–	0	183
D.A. Reeve											20	50*	39	324
D.R. Brown											14	–		14
G. Welch														29
M. Burns														1
W.G. Khan														7
Byes	1				1	4	1		1			1		
Leg-byes	7	4	16	9	9	11	8	11	10	4	5	10	6	
Wides	7	3	1	5	6	5	5	5	1	6	1	10	1	
No-Balls			5				2		2	3	1			
Total	181	185	209	236	177	182	171	217	251	175	179	226	172	
Wickets	4	10	7	6	10	10	10	5	4	7	8	6	8	
Result	W	L	L	W	L	L	Tie	W	Ab.	L	L	W	W	
Points	4	0	0	2	0	0	2	4	2	0	0	4	4	

BATTING	v. Staffordshire (Edgbaston) 24 June NW	v. Yorkshire (Scarborough) 28 June SL	v. Essex (Edgbaston) 5 July SL	v. Sussex (Edgbaston) 9 & 10 July NW	v. Surrey (The Oval) 19 July SL	v. Nottinghamshire (Edgbaston) 26 July SL	v. Kent (Edgbaston) 29 July NW	v. Derbyshire (Leek) 2 August SL	v. Durham (Edgbaston) 9 August SL	v. Northamptonshire (Edgbaston) 12 & 13 August NW	v. Kent (Edgbaston) 23 August SL	v. Northamptonshire (Northampton) 30 August SL	Runs
A.J. Moles	21	11	63	11	27	55	76	14	4	19	10	15	698
M. Asif Din								4					174
T.A. Lloyd	37	12	13	40	–	44	12	50		10	14*		630
D.P. Ostler	0*	54	14	0	17	60*	30	16	8	6	9*	14	506
R.G. Twose	107*	22	42	38	11	54	10	47	1	15	0	21	895
T.L. Penney		53*	40*	6	32*	13*	6	10	14	7	–	0	267
P.A. Smith	–	14	–		–	–		21	20		–	14*	199
N.M.K. Smith	–	2	4*	21*	–	–	12		44	8	–	1	230
K.J. Piper				7			11			12			31
G.C. Small	–	–	–	6*		–	10	1		23			85
T.A. Munton	–			–	–		0	0	1	0	–	–	21
A.A. Donald	–		–	–	–	–	9*			14*	–		34
P.C.L. Holloway	–	3	–		17	–		18	20*		–	51	183
D.A. Reeve	–	29	25	8	23*	17	22		25	18		48	324
D.R. Brown													14
G. Welch		1*						4*	23		–	1*	29
M. Burns									1				1
W.G. Khan												7	7
Byes				1		1	2	1		1		2	
Leg-byes	2	1	8	8	3	11	15	4	7	3	1	13	
Wides	1	1	1	4	2	6	8	12	5	10	2	8	
No-balls	1		4	1	3	1	1	2		3			
Total	173	203	214	151	135	262	224	204	173	149	36	195	
Wickets	2	8	5	7	4	4	10	10	10	10	2	8	
Result	W	L	W	W	W	W	W	L	L	L	Ab.	L	
Points	–	0	4	–	4	4	–	0	0	–	2	0	

FIELDING FIGURES

27 – P.C.L. Holloway (ct 21/st 6)
10 – T.L. Penney (ct 9/st 1)
9 – K.J. Piper
7 – D.P. Ostler
6 – A.J. Moles and N.M.K. Smith
5 – R.G. Twose, T.A. Lloyd and D.A. Reeve
3 – M. Asif Din
2 – G.C. Small and P.A. Smith
1 – T.A. Munton and A.A. Donald

WARWICKSHIRE CCC BOWLING

Match		R.G. Twose	T.A. Munton	P.A. Smith	A.J. Moles	G.C. Small	N.M.K. Smith	M. Asif Din	A.A. Donald	T.L. Penney	D.P. Ostler	D.R. Brown	D.A. Reeve	G. Welch	T.A. Lloyd	Byes	Leg-byes	Wides	No-balls	Total	Wkts
v. Glamorgan (Edgbaston) 19 April	SL	5–0–30–0	8–2–16–4	7–0–47–1	4–0–13–0	8–0–24–1	8–0–40–0									2	8	3		180	6
v. Yorkshire (Edgbaston) 21 April	B+H		11–2–34–1	9–1–43–2	4–0–18–0	11–4–31–2	11–4–21–1	9–0–32–0									9	4		188	6
v. Nottinghamshire (Edgbaston) 30 April & 1 May	B+H	4–0–22–0		11–2–42–1	6–1–19–0	11–2–42–0	10.4–2–34–1	1–0–8–0	11–1–26–0							7	10	5	3	210	3
v. Somerset (Taunton) 2 May	B+H		11–2–46–1	11–0–59–1		11–2–38–0	11–0–45–3		11–0–43–2							1	4	5	1	236	8
v. Somerset (Taunton) 3 May	SL	8–1–27–2	8–0–31–1	8–0–50–3		8–0–25–2	8–0–49–0									1	16	6		199	8
v. Kent (Canterbury) 5 & 6 May	B+H	9–1–27–0	11–1–33–1	8–0–41–2	5–0–17–1	8–1–27–0	3–0–22–1		11–3–33–2								5	7	1	209	7
v. Worcestershire (Worcester) 10 May	SL		8–2–13–0	8–0–50–1	2–0–12–0	8–0–26–0	6–0–39–2		8–0–25–0								6	4		171	4
v. Leicestershire (Edgbaston) 17 May	SL	3–0–10–0	6–3–7–1	8–0–24–1		8–0–25–2	7–1–18–1		6–0–21–2	1–0–2–0	1–0–4–0						6	3	1	117	8
v. Lancashire (Edgbaston) 24 May	SL		5–0–20–1			2–0–6–0	7–0–28–2										2	5		61	3
v. Sussex (Hove) 31 May	SL		7.5–0–47–0	6–0–31–0		8–0–49–0	6–0–13–0		7–1–16–1							2	18	2		176	2
v. Middlesex (Lord's) 7 June	SL	7.3–0–55–1	8–0–37–2	2.4–0–20–0	1.2–0–8–0	5.3–0–32–0	8–0–52–0					6–0–26–0					5	4		235	3
v. Hampshire (Edgbaston) 14 June	SL	3–0–18–1	6–0–22–0	6–0–50–2			7.1–0–30–3					8–2–21–3	8–0–36–0				9	6	2	186	10
v. Gloucestershire (Bristol) 21 June	SL	8–0–27–1	7–1–19–3	5–1–25–3			8–0–43–1		8–0–32–0				4–0–19–0			2	4	6		171	10
v. Staffordshire (Edgbaston) 24 June	NW	8–0–30–2	12–3–27–0	2–0–15–0		12–3–34–0	10–1–21–1		12–3–28–5				4–0–9–0			1	7	8	1	172	9
v. Yorkshire (Scarborough) 28 June	SL	3–0–22–0		6–0–45–0		6–0–31–0	8–0–33–1						6–0–28–0	6–1–24–1	5–0–37–2	1	3	1	1	224	5
v. Essex (Edgbaston) 5 July	SL	3–0–9–0		5–0–27–2		8–0–52–1	6.5–0–25–4		8–0–40–0				7–0–32–2				5	4		190	10
v. Sussex (Edgbaston) 9 & 10 July	NW	12–0–39–3	10–1–23–1			11–3–29–0	2–0–13–0		11–4–17–2				8–3–21–0			4	4	1	8	150	10
v. Surrey (The Oval) 19 July	SL	4–0–18–0	7–0–27–3	7–1–29–1					8–0–23–4				8–0–32–2				3	7		132	10
v. Nottinghamshire (Edgbaston) 26 July	SL	4–0–17–0		5.4–0–40–1		8–0–37–1	6–0–35–0		6–0–28–2				6–0–18–0				8	12		183	4
v. Kent (Edgbaston) 29 July	NW	9–2–41–3	10–0–26–1			12–1–28–3	1–0–5–0		10.5–4–22–2				10–1–33–0				6	3		161	10
v. Derbyshire (Leek) 2 August	SL	7–0–34–0	6–0–28–0	6–0–52–1		3–0–17–0		2–0–23–0						7.5–0–48–1			6	2	1	208	2
v. Durham (Edgbaston) 9 August	SL	5–0–34–1	8–0–26–1	7–0–39–1			3–0–21–0						8–0–40–2	8–0–22–0		1	7	3		190	6
v. Northamptonshire (Edgbaston) 12 & 13 August	NW	5–0–16–0	11–3–17–1			12–3–30–1	3.5–0–17–1		12–0–41–2				12–4–29–2				2	3	2	152	7
v. Kent (Edgbaston) 23 August	SL																				Ab.
v. Northamptonshire (Northampton) 30 August	SL	4–0–31–0	8–2–35–0	8–0–48–1			8–0–48–0						4–0–24–0	8–1–42–1			7	7	1	235	3
Wickets		14	22	24	1	13	22	0	24	0	0	3	8	3	2						

WORCESTERSHIRE CCC

BATTING

BATTING	v. Yorkshire (Worcester) 19 April SL	v. Derbyshire (Worcester) 21 April B+H	v. Combined Universities (Oxford) 23 April B+H	v. Northamptonshire (Worcester) 26 April SL	v. Durham (Worcester) 30 April B+H	v. Glamorgan (Cardiff) 2 May B+H	v. Glamorgan (Cardiff) 3 May SL	v. Warwickshire (Worcester) 10 May SL	v. Derbyshire (Derby) 17 May SL	v. Somerset (Worcester) 27 May B+H	v. Essex (Worcester) 31 May SL	v. Surrey (The Oval) 14 June SL	Runs
T.S. Curtis	50	62	48	16	60	26	2	1	19	78	67	30	774
T.M. Moody	7	70*	14	8	8	80	80*	78	31	80	65	51	721
G.A. Hick	44	44	6	83*	26	39	80	60	51*	29	5	2	607
D.A. Leatherdale	6	1	14	46	14	14	0*	21	5	4	2	37	279
D.B. D'Oliveira	11			40*		8	–	1*	34*	3	9	7	331
S.J. Rhodes	0	2	17	–	0	25	–	–	–	1	16*	2	153
N.V. Radford	12	–	12*	–	5	4*	–	–	–	13		0	206
S.R. Lampitt	12*	23*	–		4	22	–	–	–	5	1	19*	130
R.K. Illingworth	2*	–	14*	–	5*	–	–	–	–	1	–	5	51
P.J. Newport	–	–	–	–	9	–	–	–	–	2	1*	5	41
R.D. Stemp	–		–										–
A.C.H. Seymour		9	23		17								58
G.R. Dilley		–											–
M.J. Weston				–			–	–	–		1		19
G.R. Haynes				–	14	3*				19*	1	26	97
P.A. Neale													1
C.M. Tolley													0
Byes	2		4		2	1				2	1		
Leg-byes	3	10	2	12	4	6	3	6	6	6	3	7	
Wides	4	11	16	3	5	16	4	4	3	1	1	6	
No-balls			4				1		4	2		3	
Total	153	232	174	208	173	244	170	171	153	246	173	200	
Wickets	7	5	6	3	10	7	2	4	3	10	8	10	
Result	L	W	W	W	L	W	W	Tie	W	L	W	L	
Points	0	2	2	4	0	2	4	2	4	–	4	0	

BATTING	v. Nottinghamshire (Trent Bridge) 24 June NW	v. Sussex (Worcester) 28 June SL	v. Middlesex (Lord's) 5 July SL	v. Leicestershire (Leicester) 12 July SL	v. Kent (Canterbury) 19 July SL	v. Hampshire (Worcester) 26 July SL	v. Gloucestershire (Worcester) 2 August SL	v. Lancashire (Old Trafford) 9 August SL	v. Somerset (Taunton) 16 August SL	v. Durham (Worcester) 23 August SL	v. Nottinghamshire (Worcester) 30 August SL	Runs
T.S. Curtis	12	77*	69	14	42	18	70		13	–		774
T.M. Moody			15	66	15	53						721
G.A. Hick	14	55		17	37		14		1			607
D.A. Leatherdale	32	29	11	13	7	3	19		1	–		279
D.B. D'Oliveira	37	2	58	12	3	20	48		38	–		331
S.J. Rhodes	54	0	–	15	4	–	–		17	–		153
N.V. Radford	32				55	49*	10*		14	–		206
S.R. Lampitt	14	0	10*	6		14*	0*			–		130
R.K. Illingworth	12*	–	–	1*	8*	–	–		3			51
P.J. Newport	9	–	–	7	1				7*	–		41
R.D. Stemp			–							–		–
A.C.H. Seymour						9						58
G.R. Dilley												–
M.J. Weston		6*			7	–	–		5	–		19
G.R. Haynes	5	6	–	8			–		15	–		97
P.A. Neale	1											1
C.M. Tolley		–	–	0	0*	–	–		0	–		0
Byes	5			2	2							
Leg-byes	6	6	14	3	12	6	8		8			
Wides	16	4	1	7	6	3	6		2			
No-balls	1	1	3			1			1			
Total	250	186	181	171	199	176	175		125			
Wickets	10	6	4	10	9	5	4		10			
Result	L	W	L	W	L	L	W	Ab.	L	Ab.	Ab.	
Points	–	4	0	4	0	0	4	2	0	2	2	

FIELDING FIGURES

33 – S.J. Rhodes (ct 25/st 8)
10 – D.A. Leatherdale
9 – T.S. Curtis
8 – G.A. Hick
7 – D.B. D'Oliveira
5 – T.M. Moody and S.R. Lampitt
4 – N.V. Radford
3 – R.K. Illingworth, G.R. Haynes and C.M. Tolley
2 – M.J. Weston and P.J. Newport
1 – P.A. Neale

WORCESTERSHIRE CCC

BOWLING

		P.J. Newport	T.M. Moody	S.R. Lampitt	N.V. Radford	R.K. Illingworth	R.D. Stemp	G.R. Dilley	G.A. Hick	M.J. Weston	G.R. Haynes	D.B. D'Oliveira	C.M. Tolley	D.A. Leatherdale	Byes	Leg-byes	Wides	No-balls	Total	Wkts
v. Yorkshire (Worcester) 19 April	SL	8–1–19–2	8–0–33–2	7–0–21–2	5–0–29–0	8–1–28–1	4–0–22–1									8	2		160	9
v. Derbyshire (Worcester) 21 April	B+H	11–1–31–5	4–1–10–0	9–1–28–1	7.4–0–26–2	11–3–23–2		7–0–33–0							1	12	9		164	10
v. Combined Universities (Oxford) 23 April	B+H	11–0–37–1	10–3–24–1		8–1–31–1	11–3–29–1	11–2–29–0		4–0–17–0						1	5	6		173	6
v. Northamptonshire (Worcester) 26 April	SL	8–0–49–1			8–0–43–2	8–0–41–2				8–0–30–0	8–0–40–0					4	1		207	7
v. Durham (Worcester) 30 April	B+H	10.5–0–45–2		9–1–28–1	10–0–37–0	11–4–22–2			2–0–8–0		9–1–33–1					4	2	3	177	7
v. Glamorgan (Cardiff) 2 May	B+H	11–1–38–1		8–1–30–3	8.5–4–15–2	11–2–34–2					11–2–22–2	1–0–2–0				6	3	7	147	10
v. Glamorgan (Cardiff) 3 May	SL	8–1–25–1		8–0–44–2	8–0–47–0	8–0–23–1				8–0–27–0						3	4		169	8
v. Warwickshire (Worcester) 10 May	SL	8–0–37–0		8–1–40–4	8–0–22–2	8–0–31–1				8–1–32–0					1	8	5	2	171	9
v. Derbyshire (Derby) 17 May	SL	8–0–38–0	4–0–10–0	8–2–25–2	8–1–30–1	4–0–21–1				8–1–24–0						4	1		152	5
v. Somerset (Worcester) 27 May	B+H	11–2–38–2	11–0–59–4	9–0–57–2	3–0–18–0	11–0–38–1					10–1–38–0					8	10		256	9
v. Essex (Worcester) 31 May	SL	8–1–36–3	6–0–25–1	4–0–23–0		8–0–30–3				8–0–28–0	6–0–18–1				1	11	2	1	172	9
v. Surrey (The Oval) 14 June	SL	8–1–28–0	5–0–23–1	4.2–0–28–3	3–0–19–0	4–0–20–0			7–0–48–0		8–0–32–0				1	2			201	6
v. Nottinghamshire (Trent Bridge) 24 June	NW	12–1–32–1		12–0–64–2	10–1–81–2	12–2–25–1			4–0–22–0		10–0–80–0					3	3	3	307	7
v. Sussex (Worcester) 28 June	SL	6–1–27–3		7.3–0–40–2		8–0–38–0				4–0–18–1	6–2–18–0		8–0–31–3			6	1		178	10
v. Middlesex (Lord's) 5 July	SL	7–0–32–0		6–0–45–0		4–0–24–0	2–0–23–0				4–0–22–0		5–0–33–0	1–0–3–0		1	2		183	1
v. Leicestershire (Leicester) 12 July	SL	7.4–0–38–3		2–0–18–0		8–2–23–2			8–0–36–1		6–0–14–0		8–1–28–3			8		1	165	10
v. Kent (Canterbury) 19 July	SL	8–0–39–1			6–1–23–1	8–0–44–1			8–0–45–1	3–0–34–0			6–0–43–3			7	1		235	9
v. Hampshire (Worcester) 26 July	SL		6–0–36–0	5–0–36–0	6.2–1–26–1	8–0–27–1				8-0-23-0			6-0-27-1			2	1	1	177	4
v. Gloucestershire (Worcester) 2 August	SL			8-0-33-2	6-0-32-1	8-0-31-1				8-1-28-2	6-0-22-0		4-0-18-1		1	10	6	3	174	8
v. Lancashire (Old Trafford) 9 August	SL																			Ab.
v. Somerset (Taunton) 16 August	SL	6-1-15-2				8-1-16-2			3.3-0-13-1	8-0-20-2	8-0-28-0		6-0-30-1			4	5		126	8
v. Durham (Worcester) 23 August	SL	2–0–7–0			8–0–27–3		3–0–13–0			8–0–27–2	2–0–15–0					5	9		94	5
v. Nottinghamshire (Worcester) 30 August	SL																			Ab.
Wickets		28	9	26	18	25	1	0	3	7	4	0	12	0						

YORKSHIRE CCC

BATTING	v. Worcestershire (Worcester) 19 April SL	v. Warwickshire (Edgbaston) 21 April B+H	v. Somerset (Taunton) 23 April B+H	v. Sussex (Hove) 26 April SL	v. Kent (Leeds) 30 April & 1 May B+H	v. Nottinghamshire (Leeds) 2 May B+H	v. Nottinghamshire (Leeds) 3 May SL	v. Hampshire (Leeds) 24 May SL	v. Kent (Canterbury) 31 May SL	v. Somerset (Middlesbrough) 7 June SL	v. Glamorgan (Harrogate) 10 June TT	v. Derbyshire (Leeds) 14 June SL	v. Glamorgan (Ebbw Vale) 21 June SL	Runs
M.D. Moxon	13	0	3							57	14	30	53	494
A.A. Metcalfe	17	25	14		11	29	18	0	39					202
R.J. Blakey	9	12	5		39	29	72	2	28	31	3	49	29	638
D. Byas	43	26	19		16	31	1	45	28	80	37	–	1	493
S.A. Kellett	31	40	36		8	0		10	4	18	13	118*	2	684
C.S. Pickles	26*	37*	9		15	13	14*	15			9	–	11*	163
P. Carrick	3	13*	3*		0	18	–	11	4*	–			2*	60
P.J. Hartley	5	–	1		6*	5	1	1	1	1*		–	–	81
D. Gough	1	–	6		5	7*	0*	2	0	–	5	–	–	37
P.W. Jarvis	2	–	3						–					58
A.P. Grayson	–	22	10		11		8				16*			67
S.R. Tendulkar					7	16	40	16	33	10	40	32*	34	580
M.A. Robinson					0		–	3		–	0	–	–	5
C. White						26	6	40*	11	52*	15	–	28	375
J.D. Batty						2*			0*	–	2	–		5
C.A. Chapman														13
Byes						2			4				4	
Leg-byes	8	9	4		9	8	1	3	1	2	7	4	1	
Wides	2	4	5		5	7	5	3	8	4	6	3	3	
No-balls			2		1		1	1		1			3	
Total	160	188	120		133	193	167	152	161	256	167	236	171	
Wickets	9	6	10		10	9	7	10	8	5	10	2	6	
Result	W	W	L	Ab.	L	L	L	L	W	W	L	W	W	
Points	4	2	0	2	0	0	0	0	4	4	–	4	4	

BATTING	v. Northumberland (Leeds) 24 June NW	v. Warwickshire (Scarborough) 28 June SL	v. Leicestershire (Sheffield) 5 July SL	v. Northamptonshire (Northampton) 9 July NW	v. Essex (Scarborough) 12 July SL	v. Gloucestershire (Cheltenham) 19 July SL	v. Lancashire (Leeds) 2 August SL	v. Northamptonshire (Northampton) 9 August SL	v. Middlesex (Uxbridge) 16 August SL	v. Surrey (Scarborough) 23 August SL	v. Durham (Darlington) 30 August SL	v. Durham (Scarborough) 5 September JT	Runs
M.D. Moxon	34	10	13	2	41	26	24	53	9	4		108	494
A.A. Metcalfe									6	43		–	202
R.J. Blakey	–	105*	9	64	3	19	86	22	22			–	638
D. Byas	24*	3	7	32	28	29	9	1		14		19*	493
S.A. Kellett	38	77	38	0	27	13	1	9	68	24		109*	684
C.S. Pickles	–					0	6*	0	2	6		–	163
P. Carrick	–	–	4	0	–		–	2				–	60
P.J. Hartley	–	7*	4*	0	13*	17	–		–	19		–	81
D. Gough	–	–	5*	4	–	0	–			2			37
P.W. Jarvis				11	–	17	11*	7	6*	1		–	58
A.P. Grayson													67
S.R. Tendulkar	32*	15	41	21	13	63	107	13	47				580
M.A. Robinson	–	–	–	1*				1	–			–	5
C. White	–	1	14	41	24*	0	2	32*	20*	63		–	375
J.D. Batty		–	–		–	1*		0	–	0*			5
C.A. Chapman										13			13
Byes		1	1					3		1		3	
Leg-byes	2	3	9	12	9	6	13	7	8	10		3	
Wides	7	1	3	4	2	9	1	5	6	4		6	
No-balls	1	1			2			2					
Total	138	224	148	192	162	200	260	157	194	204		248	
Wickets	2	5	7	10	5	10	6	10	6	10		1	
Result	W	W	L	L	L	L	L	L	L	L	Ab.	W	
Points	–	4	0	–	0	0	0	0	0	0	2	–	

FIELDING FIGURES

24 – R.J. Blakey (ct 21/st 3)
9 – J.D. Batty
8 – M.D. Moxon
6 – P. Carrick and P.J. Hartley
5 – S.R. Tendulkar and D. Byas
4 – S.A. Kellett, C.S. Pickles and C. White
3 – M.A. Robinson and P.W. Jarvis
2 – A.A. Metcalfe and D. Gough

YORKSHIRE CCC

BOWLING

		P.W. Jarvis	D. Gough	P.J. Hartley	C.S. Pickles	P. Carrick	M.D. Moxon	M.A. Robinson	S.R. Tendulkar	J.D. Batty	A.P. Grayson	Byes	Leg-byes	Wides	No-balls	Total	Wkts
v. Worcestershire (Worcester) 19 April	SL	8–2–22–2	8–1–23–2	8–0–31–1	4–0–24–0	8–0–34–1	4–0–14–1					2	3	4		153	7
v. Warwickshire (Edgbaston) 21 April	B+H	11–1–34–4	11–3–31–2	10.1–3–32–3	11–0–55–0	11–0–29–1							4	3		185	10
v. Somerset (Taunton) 23 April	B+H	11–3–14–3	9–1–29–2	11–2–28–2	11–1–30–1	11–2–23–0	2–0–13–0						6	3		143	10
v. Sussex (Hove) 26 April	SL																Ab.
v. Kent (Leeds) 30 April & 1 May	B+H		8–1–29–2	10–3–39–1	7–2–28–0	11–1–28–1		8–1–46–1	11–2–21–2			4	8	5		203	9
v. Nottinghamshire (Leeds) 2 May	B+H		7–1–35–0	9–3–29–1	8.1–3–16–1	11–0–32–0			9–0–44–1	7–0–34–0		1	3	4	1	194	3
v. Nottinghamshire (Leeds) 3 May	SL		6–0–29–0	8–0–33–1	6.3–0–48–0	8–0–37–0		6–0–23–0					1	6		171	1
v. Hampshire (Leeds) 24 May	SL		8–1–38–1	6–0–36–1	4–0–19–0	8–0–42–2		8–0–39–0	6–0–32–0				5	7	2	211	5
v. Kent (Canterbury) 31 May	SL	8–1–37–1	8–0–33–1	8–0–39–2		8–0–17–2				8–0–21–3		3	7	3	2	157	10
v. Somerset (Middlesbrough) 7 June	SL		5–0–38–1	8–0–43–0		8–0–32–1		8–0–59–0	3–0–24–0	8–0–49–1			7	2	2	252	3
v. Glamorgan (Harrogate) 10 June	TT		10–2–29–2		8–2–28–3			8.3–2–27–5	6–2–22–0	11–3–32–0	11–2–33–0		4	2	2	175	10
v. Derbyshire (Leeds) 14 June	SL		8–1–30–3	7–0–19–3	7–0–34–0			5–0–8–0	5.3–0–28–2	5–1–39–1		4	3	1	1	165	10
v. Glamorgan (Ebbw Vale) 21 June	SL		8–0–32–0	8–1–22–3	8–1–34–1	8–1–30–1		8–0–43–2					6	1	3	167	7
v. Northumberland (Leeds) 24 June	NW		11–3–18–2	10–2–33–1	12–2–40–2	12–4–20–1		11.4–4–18–3					8	4	13	137	10
v. Warwickshire (Scarborough) 28 June	SL		8–0–26–2	8–1–39–1		8–0–55–2		8–0–32–0		8–0–50–3			1	1		203	8
v. Leicestershire (Sheffield) 5 July	SL		8–2–13–2	8–1–31–1		8–0–41–1	0.1–0–4–0	7–1–30–0		8–1–25–0			8	2	1	152	4
v. Northamptonshire (Northampton) 9 July	NW	12–0–53–2	12–1–73–2	12–0–71–0		12–1–45–0		12–1–73–0					10	4	3	325	7
v. Essex (Scarborough) 12 July	SL	7–0–33–2	6–1–20–1	7.4–0–27–2		5–0–22–0	6–0–20–0			7–0–33–1			8	1		163	7
v. Gloucestershire (Cheltenham) 19 July	SL	7.3–0–36–0	6–0–37–1	8–0–40–0	5–1–22–0		5–0–32–2			8–1–32–2		1	3	2		203	7
v. Lancashire (Leeds) 2 August	SL	8–0–59–0	8–0–53–1	8–0–43–0	8–0–44–1	8–0–54–1							11	7		264	3
v. Northamptonshire (Northampton) 9 August	SL	8–0–29–5			8–0–62–2	8–1–44–0	1–0–5–1	7–0–32–0		8–1–46–1		1	3	10		222	9
v. Middlesex (Uxbridge) 16 August	SL	7–0–37–1		8–1–40–2	5–0–24–1			5–0–20–0	6.5–0–18–1	7–0–47–0			9	4		195	5
v. Surrey (Scarborough) 23 August	SL	5–1–32–0	3–0–27–0	5.1–0–14–0	4–0–32–0					3–0–30–1		2	4	2		141	1
v. Durham (Darlington) 30 August	SL																Ab.
v. Durham (Scarborough) 5 September	JT	10–0–52–3		10–0–45–0	10–0–62–1	10–0–51–1		10–1–25–0					9	8		244	6
Wickets		23	27	25	13	15	4	11	6	13	0						

English Counties Form Charts

The games covered are:

Britannic Assurance County Championships
Matches against touring and representative sides

In the batting table a blank indicates that a batsman did not play in a game, a dash (–) that he did not *bat*. A dash (–) is placed in the batting averages if a player had 2 innings or less, and in the bowling figures if no wicket was taken.

PAKISTANIS IN ENGLAND, 1992

First-Class Matches

BATTING	v. Worcestershire (Worcester) 6–8 May		v. Glamorgan (Cardiff) 9–11 May		v. Somerset (Taunton) 13–15 May		v. Leicestershire (Leicester) 23–25 May		v. Middlesex (Lord's) 30 May – 1 June		First Test Match (Edgbaston) 4–8 June		v. Nottinghamshire (Trent Bridge) 10–12 June	
Ramiz Raja	172	5	41	–	10	12	65	29	37*	–	47	–		
Aamir Sohail	36	11	124	–	37	8	24	–			18	–	47	58
Shoaib Mohammad	17	46	58	–	1	14	25	13	43	1*			16	50*
Salim Malik	91	7	41*	–	89	18*			68	–	165	–		
Inzamam-ul-Haq	33*	7	16	–	6	0*	57	61*			8*	–	53	–
Asif Mujtaba	19*	–					95	27*	123	–	29	–	8	33
Wasim Akram	–	4	21*	–	30	–							8	–
Rashid Latif	–	2					16	–					8	–
Mushtaq Ahmed	–	4	–	–	4	–	8*	–	–	–	–	–		
Salim Jaffer	–	1*	–	–			–	–						
Aqib Javed	–	0			0	–			–	–	–	–	3	–
Javed Miandad			35	–	30	35			14	–	153*	–		
Moin Khan			–	–	0	–			2*	–	–	–		
Tanvir Mehdi			–	–	13*	0	–	–					8	–
Zahid Fazal							26	–	21*	3*			0	9*
Naved Anjum							56	–					4	–
Waqar Younis									–	–	–	–		
Ata-ur-Rehman									–	–	–	–	1*	–
Ijaz Ahmed														
Byes		1	1		8		6				2			4
Leg-byes	1	2	12		6	1	13	3	7	1	5			5
Wides		1					2						2	2
No-balls	5	2	5		6	5			12		19		5	6
Total	374	93	354	0	240	93	393	133	327	5	446		163	167
Wickets	4	9†	5	0	10	5	8	2	4	0	4		10	2
Result	L		W		W		W		D		D		W	

BATTING	v. Northamptonshire (Northampton) 13–15 June		Second Test Match (Lord's) 18–22 June		v. Oxbridge (Cambridge) 24–26 June		v. Hampshire (Southampton) 27–29 June		Third Test Match (Old Trafford) 2–7 July		v. Durham (Chester-le-Street) 14–16 July		v. Derbyshire (Derby) 18–20 July	
Ramiz Raja	55	26	24	0			31	–	54	88	14	59	7	–
Aamir Sohail	34	33	73	39	43	0	6*	–	205	1	53	90	2	–
Shoaib Mohammad	59	18			56	22*								
Salim Malik	45	–	55	12			50*	–	34	16	23	40	21	–
Inzamam-ul-Haq	33	4*	0	8	200*	–	–	–	26	–			43	–
Asif Mujtaba	20	39*	59	0	48	24*	154*	–	57	40	79	8	40	–
Wasim Akram	9	–	24	45*			–	–	0	13	21	27	26	–
Rashid Latif					2*	–								
Mushtaq Ahmed			4	5	–	–	–	–	6	–	10*	–	12	–
Salim Jaffer					–	–								
Aqib Javed	2*	–	5*	–			–	–	–	–	–	–		
Javed Miandad			9	0			142*	–	88	45*	25	67	6	–
Moin Khan	6	–	12	3	22	–	–	–	15	11*	53	29*	35*	–
Tanvir Mehdi					–	–								
Zahid Fazal					51	–								
Naved Anjum														
Waqar Younis	19*	–	14	20*			–	–	2*	–	23*	–	2	–
Ata-ur-Rehman	–	–			–	–					–	–	0	–
Ijaz Ahmed														
Byes	2	1	4	2	8		2		9	8				
Leg-byes	3	1	3	5	2		9		4	5	2	13	2	
Wides				1	6		6		2	5	1	2		
No-balls			7	1	8		6		3	7	4	3	1	
Total	287	122	293	141	446	46	406		506	239	308	338	197	
Wickets	8	3	10	8	5	1	1		9	5	7	6	10	
Result	W		W		W		W		D		W		D	

BATTING	Fourth Test Match (Leeds) 23–27 July		v. Essex (Chelmsford) 1–3 August		Fifth Test Match (The Oval) 6–10 August		v. Gloucestershire (Bristol) 15–17 August		v. World XI (Scarborough) 26–28 August		M	Inns	NO	Runs	HS	Av
Ramiz Raja	17	63	4	22	19	0*	135	–			16	26	2	1036	172	43.16
Aamir Sohail	23	1			49	4*	46	30	15	–	17	28	2	1110	205	42.69
Shoaib Mohammad			50	32	55	–	66	14	105*	–	12	21	4	761	105*	44.76
Salim Malik	82*	84*	153*	50	40	–	–	–			15	21	6	1184	165	78.93
Inzamam-ul-Haq	5	19					65	54*	38	–	15	21	7	736	200*	52.27
Asif Mujtaba	7	11	25	62*	50	–			17	–	16	25	6	1074	154*	56.52
Wasim Akram	12	17	10	25*	7	–	0	–			14	18	3	299	45*	19.93
Rashid Latif			–	–	50	–	2	42	14*	–	8	8	2	136	50	22.66
Mushtaq Ahmed	11	0	–	–	9	–	0*	–	–	–	17	12	3	73	12	8.11
Salim Jaffer											4	1	1	1	1*	–
Aqib Javed	0	0			0*	–	–	–	–	–	14	8	3	10	5*	2.00
Javed Miandad	6	4	91	–	59	–					12	17	3	809	153*	57.78
Moin Khan	2	3							44	–	13	14	4	237	53	23.70
Tanvir Mehdi											5	3	1	21	13*	10.50
Zahid Fazal			5	–					0	–	6	8	3	115	51	23.00
Naved Anjum			6*	–			0	6*	5	–	5	6	2	77	56	19.25
Waqar Younis	6	3			6	–					10	9	4	95	23*	19.00
Ata-ur-Rehman			–	–					–	–	9	2	1	1	1*	1.00
Ijaz Ahmed							36	31			1	2	–	67	36	33.50
Byes	1	4	5	4	2											
Leg-byes	2	1	2		6		3	5	4							
Wides	7	2	1		4	1										
No-balls	16	9	1	1	24		4	2	11							
Total	197	221	353	196	380	5	357	184	253							
Wickets	10	10	6	3	10	0	8	4	6							
Result	L		W		W		W		D							

FIELDING FIGURES

29 – Moin Khan (ct 28/st 1)
28 – Rashid Latif (ct 26/st 2)
22 – Inzamam-ul-Haq
13 – Aamir Sohail
10 – Subs
8 – Javed Miandad
7 – Zahid Fazal
5 – Asif Mujtaba, Wasim Akram and Mushtaq Ahmed
4 – Salim Malik
3 – Ata-ur-Rehman and Ramiz Raja
2 – Tanvir Mehdi and Shoaib Mohammad
1 – Aqib Javed, Waqar Younis, Naved Anjum and Ijaz Ahmed

† Asif Mujtaba absent hurt

PAKISTANIS IN ENGLAND

BOWLING

	Wasim Akram	Aqib Javed	Mushtaq Ahmed	Salim Jaffer	Shoaib Mohammad	Aamir Sohail	Salim Malik	Tanvir Mehdi	Naved Anjum	Zahid Fazal	Asif Mujtaba	Waqar Younis	Ata-ur-Rehman	Inzamam-ul-Haq	Rashid Latif	Moin Khan	Byes	Leg-byes	Wides	No-balls	Total	Wkts
v. Worcestershire (Worcester)	18–2–75–0	14–2–30–2	28–5–71–3	21–2–71–0	7–0–16–0	4–0–29–0											4	7	3	16	303	5
6–8 May	14–3–27–2	17–4–47–0	11–3–24–1	14–2–53–2			0.1–0–4–0										5	6		11	166	5
v. Glamorgan (Cardiff)																					0	0
9–11 May	17–4–46–4		19–8–26–4	11–1–35–1		3–1–2–0		11–0–31–0									7	1	1	7	148	9A
v. Somerset (Taunton)	14.4–6–25–1	11–4–26–3	24–6–78–3					12–5–29–3										5		6	163	10
13–15 May	15–4–43–3	7–1–27–0	20–8–46–5					10–3–35–2									8	10		13	169	10
v. Leicestershire (Leicester)			20.1–2–49–5	9–1–48–1	4–1–13–0	12–2–26–2		17–3–56–1	15–4–33–1	2–0–17–0							11	3	4	2	256	10
23–25 May			43–20–72–1			19–6–31–3		10–4–31–0	17–3–73–3		22.5–8–36–2						9	17		3	269	10
v. Middlesex (Lord's)		14–0–62–2	22–1–73–4								12–2–44–0	11–3–27–1	9–2–14–0				2			7	222	8
30 May – 1 June																						
First Test Match (Edgbaston)		16–3–86–1	50–8–156–2			2–0–8–0	1–0–5–0				8–1–29–0	24–2–96–1	18–5–69–3				5	5	1	7	459	7
4–8 June																						
v. Nottinghamshire (Trent Bridge)	13.2–2–9–4	9–2–25–0						8–1–24–3	6–0–25–2				7–0–33–1						1	10	116	10
10–12 June	14–8–24–2	15–0–51–4						11–3–50–2	9.3–2–59–1				8–2–24–1				1	3	3	8	212	10
v. Northamptonshire	15–4–43–5	13–3–45–3									3–1–6–0	14–1–54–1	6.3–0–45–1						1	10	193	10
(Northampton) 13–15 June	22–2–74–5	13–6–25–1			2–0–10–0	6–1–9–0						12–2–52–2	7.2–2–37–2				5	1	6	13	213	10
Second Test Match (Lord's)	19–5–49–2	14–3–40–0	19.1–5–57–2								3–3–0–1	21–4–91–5					6	12		9	255	10
18–22 June	17.4–2–66–4	12–3–23–1	9–1–32–3								1–0–1–0	13–3–40–2					5	8		15	175	10
v. Oxbridge (Cambridge)			19.5–4–56–5	10–3–40–1	2–1–8–0	7–4–6–2					8–3–17–0		10–2–30–1				5	2	1	4	164	10
24–26 June			42–15–91–4		5–2–13–0	16–7–30–0		15–2–51–1			27–4–73–4		17–4–47–1	1–0–8–0			4	10		9	327	10
v. Hampshire (Southampton)	6.3–1–15–2	14–2–47–3	21–6–64–5								1–0–7–0	13–4–26–0						3		10	162	10
27–29 June	14.5–2–38–4	4–0–24–0	34–7–103–2								7–3–8–1	16–2–53–3					1	3		13	230	10
Third Test Match (Old Trafford)	36–4–128–5	21.4–1–100–4	10–1–50–0								1–1–0–0	32–6–96–1					8	8	2	35	390	10
2–7 July																						
v. Durham (Chester-le-Street)	17–4–67–1	6.1–0–35–1	8.5–1–59–0			1–0–7–0	4–0–15–1				4–0–28–0	14–2–48–0	15–2–65–1				6	11	1	12	341	4
14–16 July	17–2–65–3		6–1–35–0				7–0–28–0					17.1–5–22–5	8–2–39–1				1	8		11	198	9B
v. Derbyshire (Derby)	16.5–2–59–5		23–5–82–2			5–3–9–0						10–1–30–2	10–1–33–1					3	1	1	216	10
18–20 July	11–1–32–1		15–3–58–0			3–2–1–1					15–5–18–0	14–1–44–1	17–4–50–2				1	8	1	5	212	5
Fourth Test Match (Leeds)	36–12–80–1	16–3–48–1	29.5–6–60–3			2–2–0–0						30–3–117–5					1	14	1	23	320	10
23–27 July	17–4–36–0		13.4–3–27–2									12–2–28–2					5	3		4	99	4
v. Essex (Chelmsford)	35–6–102–4		13–0–21–1		1–0–5–0		2–0–4–0		23.4–4–69–2	2–1–8–0	13–2–45–1		17.2–2–76–1					16		12	357	9
1–3 August	23.5–8–48–4		33–15–57–3				4–0–15–2		14–4–37–1		4–2–13–0						10	8		12	188	10
Fifth Test Match (The Oval)	22.1–3–67–6	16–6–44–2	24–7–47–1									16–4–37–1					4	8	1	10	207	10
6–10 August	21–6–36–3	9–2–25–0	23–6–46–2			1–0–6–0						18–5–52–5					1	8		9	174	10
v. Gloucestershire (Bristol)	22–11–44–5	15.1–4–34–5	2–1–1–0						9–2–43–0									1		4	123	10
15–17 August	24–12–32–6	13–5–49–2	15.1–5–17–2		1–1–0–0				8–4–23–0									5			126	10
v. World XI (Scarborough)		22–4–73–1	16–5–51–1		5–0–17–0	22–1–87–1			5–1–17–0	9–1–48–0			9–1–59–2	1–0–5–1	5–2–17–2	1–0–3–0		8		13	385	8
26–28 August																						
Bowlers average	499.5–124–	292–58–	614.4–158–	65–9–	27–5–	103–29–	18.1–0–	94–21–	107.1–24–	13–2–	129.5–35–	287.1–50–	159.1–29–	2–0–	5–2–	1–0–						
	1330–82	966–36	1619–66	247–5	82–0	251–9	71–3	307–12	379–10	83–0	325–9	913–37	621–18	13–1	17–2	3–0						
	16.21	26.83	24.53	49.40	–	27.88	23.66	25.58	37.90	–	36.11	24.67	34.50	13.00	8.50	–						

A A.R. Butcher absent injured
B I.T. Botham absent hurt

CAMBRIDGE UNIVERSITY

BATTING

BATTING	v. Leicestershire (Cambridge) 14–16 April	v. Middlesex (Cambridge) 17–20 April	v. Essex (Cambridge) 25–28 April	v. Warwickshire (Cambridge) 12–14 May	v. Surrey (Cambridge) 15–18 May	v. Derbyshire (Cambridge) 16–18 June	v. Kent (Cambridge) 19–21 June	v. Nottinghamshire (Trent Bridge) 27–29 June	v. Oxford University (Lord's) 30 June – 2 July	M	Inns	NO	Runs	HS	Av
A.M. Hooper	– 0	48 4	5 30*	3 6	0 16	18 2	40 9	40 4	1 17	9	17	1	243	48	15.18
S.S.K. Das	– 9	24* 2	3 0							3	5	1	38	24*	9.50
J.P. Crawley	– 19	24* 46*	3 6	25 22	62 10	65 92	9 27	20 4	1 106*	9	17	3	541	106*	38.64
J.P. Arscott	– 0	– –	3 –	65* 7	47 79	18 –	58* 5	3 28	5 –	9	12	2	318	79	31.80
G.E. Thwaites	– 0									1	1	–	0	0	0.00
M.E.D. Jarrett	– 7	– –	0 –	27 8*	5 1	16 –	13 0	0 0	7* 22	9	13	2	106	27	9.63
R.M. Wight	– 12	– 27	13 –	17 48	4 3	15 19*	28 61	26 26	5 62*	9	15	2	366	62*	28.15
R.M. Pearson	– 1	– –	0 –	3* 2*	20* 33*	13 –	7 1*	4 4	– –	9	11	5	88	33*	14.66
S.W. Johnson	– 50	– –	3 0	33 4	0 8	14* –	10 45*	0 20	14 –	9	13	2	201	50	18.27
C.M. Pitcher	– 32*			0 0		3 –	0 0	12* 15*	– –	6	8	3	62	32*	12.40
M.B. Abington	– 5			– –	6 0	0 –	1 –	2 6	– –	7	7	–	20	6	2.85
P.M. Crawley		– 22*	39* –	0 11	1 45					4	6	2	118	45	29.50
T.R. Kemp		– –	0 –							2	1	–	0	0	0.00
R.H.J. Jenkins		– –	1 –							2	1	–	1	1	1.00
G.W. Jones				15 32	0 38	4 44	10 36	19 21	12 18	6	12	–	249	44	20.75
J.P. Carroll					3 11	9 18	0 92	6 29	7 –	5	9	–	175	92	19.44
Byes	1	8		11 4	3	3	2 1	8	3						
Leg-byes	9	3 5	1 5	8 8	5 2	14 2	1 5	7 2	3 4						
Wides		1	2		1	2		3 5	4						
No-balls	1	2 6	2	1 2	7 10	11 1	1 2	3	5 2						
Total	0 146	109 113	75 41	208 154	161 259	200 183	180 284	153 164	60 238						
Wickets	0 10	1 3	10 3	8 8	10 10	10 4	10 8	10 10	7 3						
Result	L	D	D	D	L	D	W	L	W						

FIELDING FIGURES

14 – J.P. Arscott (ct 9/st 5)
5 – J.P. Crawley
4 – S.W. Johnson and M.B. Abington
3 – R.M. Pearson and R.M. Wight
2 – M.E.D. Jarrett
1 – R.H.J. Jenkins, S.S.K. Das, T.R. Kemp, G.W. Jones, J.P.Carroll, A.M. Hooper, C.M. Pitcher (ct 0/st 1) and sub

BOWLING

BOWLING	S.W. Johnson	C.M. Pitcher	A.M. Hooper	M.B. Abington	R.M. Pearson	R.M. Wight	R.H.J. Jenkins	P.M. Crawley	T.R. Kemp	Byes	Leg-byes	Wides	No-balls	Total	Wkts
v. Leicestershire	11–2–30–0	8–0–53–0	1–0–5–0	25–5–97–1	18–5–69–1	7–1–19–0					6		3	279	2
(Cambridge) 14–16 April														0	0
v. Middlesex	10–3–24–0				21–4–67–0	11–3–26–1	8–1–24–0	15–3–36–2	11–1–51–0	1	9	1		238	3
(Cambridge) 17–20 April	7–0–18–0				8–0–23–0	10–4–25–1	8–1–43–1	1–0–14–0				1		123	2
v. Essex	17–2–56–2				26.2–4–73–3	21–1–62–1	10–3–46–0	16–7–34–0	8–0–35–1	4	5			315	8
(Cambridge) 25–28 April	10–1–27–1				17–4–49–0	5–1–22–1	6–0–24–1	5–0–29–0	10–1–42–0		2			195	3
v. Warwickshire	15–3–35–1	11–0–56–0		14–4–31–0	45.1–11–108–5	20–6–48–2		6–0–26–0		9	6	1		319	8
(Cambridge) 12–14 May	12–2–31–0			12–0–42–1	9–0–28–0	15–0–40–1				4	5	1		150	2
v. Surrey	12–1–51–0			11–0–54–1	33.2–3–113–0	30–2–117–3		13–2–37–0			9			381	5
(Cambridge) 15–18 May	5–1–17–0			2.4–0–32–0	8–1–26–0	10–1–40–1		10–1–60–1			4	3		179	2
v. Derbyshire	15–5–40–0	16–1–57–0	1.2–0–11–1	23–5–83–2	30–3–84–0	21–6–61–1				7	5	2		348	4
(Cambridge) 16–18 June	6–1–34–1	6–0–26–0		14–4–33–3	20–6–43–1	5–0–12–0				5	5			158	5
v. Kent	7–2–26–1	20–6–73–0	3–0–12–1	14–1–52–0	19.3–3–69–0	17–2–65–3					3			300	5
(Cambridge) 19–21 June	4–0–14–1	12–1–33–0		9–1–40–1	18–3–67–3	0.3–0–2–1					4			160	6
v. Nottinghamshire	3–0–20–0	20–5–45–1	7–4–19–0	16–2–49–0	32.3–5–93–2	18–4–63–1					11		2	300	4
(Trent Bridge) 27–29 June	6–0–34–0	10–2–35–1	3–1–11–0	2–0–8–0	10–1–41–2	7–0–48–0					2	1	1	179	3
v. Oxford University	18–4–62–3	17–5–36–1	5–2–5–1	2–1–2–1	14–4–37–1	11–5–14–0				15	11	6		182	7
(Lord's) 30 June – 2 July	6–0–22–0	11–0–31–0		2–0–7–0	8–0–39–0	5–0–13–1					3	1		115	1
Bowlers average	164–27– 541–10 54.10	131–20– 445–3 148.33	20.2–7– 63–3 21.00	146.4–23– 530–10 53.00	337.5–57– 1029–18 57.16	213.3–36– 677–18 37.61	32–5– 137–2 68.50	66–13– 236–3 78.66	29–2– 128–1 128.00						

BATTING

BATTING	v. Durham (Oxford) 14–16 April		v. Worcestershire (Oxford) 17–20 April		v. Nottinghamshire (Oxford) 7–9 May		v. Middlesex (Oxford) 12–14 May		v. Hampshire (Oxford) 15–18 May		v. Yorkshire (Oxford) 29 May – 1 June		v. Lancashire (Oxford) 2–4 June		v. Glamorgan (Oxford) 19–22 June		v. Cambridge University (Lord's) 30 June – 2 July		M	Inns	NO	Runs	HS	Av
R.R. Montgomerie	17	–	32	–	25	–	51	103*	10	31			36	45*	32	4	16	45*	8	13	3	447	103*	44.70
J.E.R. Gallian	53	–	112	–	18	–	37	5	28	3			13	8	18	12	1	66	8	13	–	374	112	28.76
A. Storie	23*	–	15	–	0	–	15	5	12	29			5	4			5	–	7	10	1	113	29	12.55
C.M. Gupte	8*	–	11	–	0	–	7	–	4	6									5	6	1	36	11	7.20
G.B.T. Lovell	–	–	7	–	0	–	6	11	14	20			19	41	64	110*	32	–	8	11	1	324	110*	32.40
S.N. Warley	–	–	4	–	35	–	11	10*	21	2			16	4*	4	10			7	10	2	117	35	14.62
D.J. Anderson	–	–	0	–	0	–	0*	–	9	1			0*	–	0	–	8*	–	8	8	3	18	9	3.60
R. Oliphant-Callum	–	–	19*	–	9	–													3	2	1	28	19*	28.00
M.P.W. Jeh	–	–	3	–	2	–	6	–	16	10*			0	–	0	6*	8	–	8	9	2	51	16	7.28
H.R. Davies	–	–	5	–	5*	–	7	0							6	0	39	–	6	7	1	62	39	10.33
B.S. Wood	–	–							3*	13							–	–	3	2	1	16	13	16.00
C.L. Keey			11	–	60	–	57*	64	0	15			5	9	11	6	33	–	7	11	1	271	64	27.10
C.J. Townsend							–	–	8	0			0	–	0*	–	–	–	5	4	1	8	8	2.66
H. Malik													4	–					1	1	–	4	4	4.00
R.H. MacDonald													1	–	4	–	8*	–	3	3	1	13	8*	6.50
D. Sandiford															20	1			1	2	–	21	20	10.50
Byes					1		3	4		7							15							
Leg-byes			7		2		6	4	5	8			4	5	3	1	11	3						
Wides					1		1	2		1			1		1	1	6	1						
No-balls	4		1		3		15	4	3	2					20	2								
Total	105		227		161		222	212	133	148			104	116	183	153	182	115						
Wickets	2		10		10		8	5	10	10			10	4	10	6	7	1						
Result	D		D		D		W		L		Ab.		D		D		L							

FIELDING FIGURES

7 – C.J. Townsend and G.B.T. Lovell
6 – J.E.R. Gallian
4 – A. Storie and D.J. Anderson
3 – R.R. Montgomerie
2 – M.P.W. Jeh and S.N. Warley
1 – R. Oliphant-Callum, C.L. Keey and C.M. Gupte

BOWLING

BOWLING	M.P.W. Jeh	B.S. Wood	J.E.R. Gallian	H.R. Davies	D.J. Anderson	C.M. Gupte	A. Storie	R.R. Montgomerie	R.H. MacDonald	H. Malik	Byes	Leg-byes	Wides	No-balls	Total	Wkts
v. Durham (Oxford) 14–16 April	20–4–74–0	12.3–0–39–0	15–1–64–2	13.3–2–62–0	5–0–25–0	2–0–16–0					2	4			286	2
v. Worcestershire (Oxford) 17–20 April	22–1–111–0		17–4–59–1	24–3–113–0	17.5–1–68–2		16–2–58–1				1	3	5	1	413	4
	14–5–44–3		4–1–4–0	12–1–52–2	5–2–20–1	3–0–22–0	6–1–17–1	2–2–0–0				3		2	162	7
v. Nottinghamshire (Oxford) 7–9 May	19–0–68–0		13–5–30–0	30–4–118–3	21–3–68–1		10–1–28–0				8	4	1	5	324	4
	9–3–13–0		7–0–27–0	11–0–38–0	7–2–16–0	3–1–6–0								2	100	0
v. Middlesex (Oxford) 12–14 May	17–2–70–3		20–5–41–1	15–1–74–0	24–8–77–1		8–1–25–0					3	2	4	290	5
	6–3–9–0		6–0–27–0	13–4–41–0	12–4–30–1	7–1–34–0						2	1	2	143	1
v. Hampshire (Oxford) 15–18 May	16–6–53–0	26–1–111–1	20–5–56–2		15–1–52–0	13–0–55–1						4	1	1	331	4
	13.5–2–38–1	16–6–29–2	10–3–22–1		7–3–19–1						1	2	2	3	111	5
v. Yorkshire (Oxford) 29 May–1 June																Ab.
v. Lancashire (Oxford) 2–4 June	22–1–102–2		17–4–47–1		16–7–29–0				20–5–66–0	14–2–61–0		9	7	11	314	3
	11–4–28–2		16–3–29–4		14–6–22–1				10–5–11–1	11–2–27–0	1	1		1	119	8
v. Glamorgan (Oxford) 19–22 June	17–3–45–0		19–3–48–2	23–3–101–1	17–1–56–1			5–0–9–0	24–4–53–1			5			317	5
	12–2–39–1		5–0–17–0	5–0–41–0				3–0–22–0	8–2–15–0		1	1		1	136	1
v. Cambridge University (Lord's) 30 June–2 July	8–1–15–2	4–0–19–1	8–4–10–2						5.4–3–13–2			3		5	60	7
	6–0–27–1	12.5–0–56–0	16–1–89–1		4–0–29–0				12–3–30–1		3	4	4	2	238	3
Bowlers average	212.5–37– 736–15 49.06	71.2–7– 254–4 63.50	193–39– 570–17 33.52	146.3–18– 640–6 106.66	164.5–38– 511–9 56.77	28–2– 133–1 133.00	40–5– 128–2 64.00	10–2– 31–0 –	79.4–22– 188–5 37.60	25–4– 88–0 –						

DERBYSHIRE CCC

BATTING

BATTING	v. Warwickshire (Edgbaston) 7–11 May	v. Worcestershire (Derby) 14–18 May	v. Lancashire (Blackpool) 20–22 May	v. Nottinghamshire (Derby) 23–26 May	v. Northamptonshire (Northampton) 29 May–1 June	v. Surrey (The Oval) 2–4 June	v. Durham (Chesterfield) 5–8 June	v. Yorkshire (Harrogate) 12–15 June	v. Cambridge University (Cambridge) 16–18 June	v. Warwickshire (Derby) 26–29 June	v. Gloucestershire (Derby) 30 June–2 July	v. Somerset (Taunton) 3–6 July	M	Inns	NO	Runs	HS	Av
K.J. Barnett	0 57	16 18	10 44	77 –	82* –	10 140*	16* –	16 1	– –				19	29	5	1270	160	52.91
P.D. Bowler	14 30	91 112	53 104*	155 –	90* –	40 31	15* –	60 1	75 –	7 –	– 77	– 147*	24	38	7	2044	241*	65.93
J.E. Morris	1 69	55 12	0 98	120 –	– –	36 –		8 0	73 –	74 –	– 50	– 109	23	33	–	1358	120	41.15
T.J.G. O'Gorman	0 0	0 9	27 42	29 –	– –	14 63*	– –	23 15	51* 12*	75 –	– 70*	– 1	24	37	8	1031	95	35.55
C.J. Adams	5 4	6 121	72 0	4 –		9 –	– –	25 6*	80 25*	39 –	– 29	– 0	23	33	6	1109	140*	41.07
K.M. Krikken	0 28	7 0	44 0*	29 –	– –	8 –	– –	0 0	55 1	10 –	– 6	– –	23	27	3	383	57*	15.95
D.G. Cork	13 72*	25 –			– –	44 –		47 7	– 47	0 –	– 1	– –	18	20	2	551	72*	30.61
I.R. Bishop	7 6	18 17		22* –	– –	32 –	– –	6 11		29 –	– 31	– –	20	21	2	388	90	20.42
A.E. Warner	1 13			8* –	– –	21 –	– –		– 55		– 2	– –	17	15	2	210	55	16.15
D.E. Malcolm	26 16	8* –	5 –	6* –	– –		– –	14* 8					15	14	4	144	26	14.40
O.H. Mortensen	9* 0		13* –		– –	4* –	– –		– –				15	13	10	47	13*	15.66
S.C. Goldsmith		17 100*	60* 6	9 –	– –		– –	10 13	– 3	40 –	– 0	– 15*	10	11	3	273	100*	34.12
R.W. Sladdin		1 27*	0 –			4 –		14 4	– 5	1* –		– –	13	16	2	131	39	9.35
M. Jean-Jacques			0 –	6 –									2	2	–	6	6	3.00
A.M. Brown							– –			17 –	– 10	– 0	7	8	–	144	27	18.00
S.J. Base										3 –	– 0*		2	2	1	3	3	3.00
F.A. Griffith													7	10	3	248	81	35.42
A.W. Richardson													1	1	–	5	5	5.00
T.A. Tweats													1	1	–	24	24	24.00
Byes	1 13		8 1	1		5 5		4	7 5	20								
Leg-byes	7 7	4 12	5 3	15	5	12 3		1 3	5 5	12	17	12						
Wides	10	2 2	1	1		1		1	2	2		4						
No-balls	1 2	1 3	3 2	24	3	10 1		2 1		14	10	13						
Total	85 327	251 433	300 301	500	180 0	249 244	31	227 74	348 158	343	0 303	0 301						
Wickets	10 10	10 7	9 5	9	0 0	10 1	0	10 10	4 5	10	0 9	0 4						
Result	L	D	W	D	L	D	D	L	D	W	D	W						
Points	4	4	23	8	1	6	0	3	–	24	4	18						

BATTING	v. Hampshire (Portsmouth) 14–16 July	v. Pakistanis (Derby) 18–20 July	v. Middlesex (Derby) 21–23 July	v. Worcestershire (Worcester) 24–27 July	v. Leicestershire (Ilkeston) 4–6 August	v. Sussex (Eastbourne) 7–10 August	v. Kent (Chesterfield) 14–17 August	v. Glamorgan (Chesterfield) 18–20 August	v. Somerset (Derby) 26–29 August	v. Nottinghamshire (Trent Bridge) 31 August – 3 September	v. Essex (Derby) 7–10 September	v. Glamorgan (Cardiff) 12–15 September	M	Inns	NO	Runs	HS	Av
K.J. Barnett			– –	1 36	47 117*	11 29	42 160	29 0	68 –	156* 37	25 12	– 19	19	29	5	1270	160	52.91
P.D. Bowler	241* –	28 79	9 46	50 100*	20 13	30 26	8 38	67 19*	66 –	28 61	4 4	– 5	24	38	7	2044	241*	65.93
J.E. Morris	7 –	49 0	82 –	67 –	50 107	68 0	17 55	1 0	0 –	0 43	6 55	– 46	23	33	–	1358	120	41.15
T.J. G. O'Gorman	95 –	46 42	68* 4*	33 4	16 0	10 0	32 62*	42 2*	0 –	5 27	64 7	– 41	24	37	8	1031	95	35.55
C.J. Adams	35 –	51 29*	112* –	18 140*	14 12*	3 1	8 0	– –	24 –	23 3	60 135	– 16	23	33	6	1109	140*	41.07
K.M. Krikken	– –	4 –	– –	3 –	8 –	24 20	39 9*	1 –	57* –	22 0	3 5		23	27	3	383	57*	15.95
D.G. Cork	65* –		– –	34 –	56 –	13 32	2 –		27 –	27 18	0 21		18	20	2	551	72*	30.61
I.R. Bishop	– –		– –	12 –	1 –	17 3	6 –	90 –	1 –	24 4	26* 25		20	21	2	388	90	20.42
A.E. Warner	– –	4 –	– –				26 –	7* –	8 –	2 4*	11 19	– 29	17	15	2	210	55	16.15
D.E. Malcolm	– –	0 –	– –	10 –			7 –	5 –	16* –		12 11		15	14	4	144	26	14.40
O.H. Mortensen	– –	0 –		0* –	0* –	12* 1*	0* –	– –			2 0*	– 6*	15	13	10	47	13*	15.66
S.C. Goldsmith													10	11	3	273	100*	34.12
R.W. Sladdin		0 0		7 –	0 –	21 0				8 –		– 39	13	16	2	131	39	9.35
M. Jean-Jacques													2	2	–	6	6	3.00
A.M. Brown	0 –	27 43	36 11										7	8	–	144	27	18.00
S.J. Base													2	2	1	3	3	3.00
F.A. Griffith		2* 4*			48 –	23 23		81 –	33 –	11 18*		– 5	7	10	3	248	81	35.42
A.W. Richardson												– 5	1	1	–	5	5	5.00
T.A. Tweats												– 24	1	1	–	24	24	24.00
Byes	10	1	1	1	1 1	4 4	4	1	1	7 2	1							
Leg-byes	8	3 8	10 3	2 1	2 4	7 2	14 2	5 2	2	12 4	5 6	8						
Wides	1	1 1			1	1	1	2			1	1						
No-balls	13	1 5	16 2	8 4	4	4 1	2 7	3	17	5 1	7 8							
Total	475	216 212	334 66	246 285	268 254	248 142	207 334	334 22	320 0	330 222	226 309	0 244						
Wickets	4	10 5	3 2	10 2	10 3	10 10	10 4	8 2	9 0	10 8	10 10	0 10						
Result	W	D	D	D	W	L	D	D	W	W	L	L						
Points	24	–	4	5	23	6	6	6	20	23	6	4						

FIELDING FIGURES

57 – K.M. Krikken (ct 52/st 5)
20 – C.J. Adams
12 – P.D. Bowler and D.G. Cork
11 – T.J.G. O'Gorman
7 – A.M. Brown
6 – I.R. Bishop, J.E. Morris, R.W. Sladdin, F.A. Griffith and sub
5 – K.J. Barnett
4 – D.E. Malcolm
3 – A.E. Warner, S.C. Goldsmith and O.H. Mortensen
2 – M. Jean-Jacques and S.J. Base
1 – T.A. Tweats

DERBYSHIRE CCC
BOWLING

	I.R. Bishop	D.E. Malcolm	O.H. Mortensen	D.G. Cork	A.E. Warner	C.J. Adams	S.C. Goldsmith	R.W. Sladdin	M. Jean-Jacques	T.J.G. O'Gorman	P.D. Bowler	K.J. Barnett	J.E. Morris	S.J. Base	A.M. Brown	F.A. Griffith	Byes	Leg-byes	Wides	No-balls	Total	Wkts
v. Warwickshire (Edgbaston) 7–11 May	17.2–7–32–3	21–1–83–4	21–6–39–1	19–5–45–2	14–4–23–0												4	9	1	7	235	10
	5–0–21–0	11–0–74–1	4–1–13–0	8–1–28–0	10–1–29–0	1–0–7–0											5	1	7		178	1
v. Worcestershire (Derby) 14–18 May	28–3–61–2	28–3–98–1		21–4–51–2			29–7–79–1	62–15–148–3									4	29		3	470	9
v. Lancashire (Blackpool) 20–22 May		16–1–64–0	21–6–46–2				18–2–64–1	27–4–92–0	17.4–5–46–4								4	11	1	4	327	7
		6–2–22–0	4–1–12–0			8–2–36–0	9–2–24–0	24–2–89–1	10–0–40–1	7–0–38–0	1–0–6–0						1	5	2	3	273	2
v. Nottinghamshire (Derby) 23–26 May	21–3–70–4	22–4–71–4			16–4–46–2		6–0–36–0		7–0–43–0			24–5–62–0					1	18	3	7	347	10
	4–2–3–0	6–0–25–0			3–0–11–0	13–0–39–0	15–4–51–0		1–0–6–0	17–0–83–1	14–3–48–0	21–0–67–0					3	6		4	342	1
v. Northamptonshire (Northampton) 29 May–1 June																					0	0
	8.3–0–34–1	7–1–48–1	8–0–19–0	6–0–50–0	7–2–27–0													3		10	181	2
v. Surrey (The Oval) 2–4 June	15–7–17–1		17–5–39–1	23.1–4–66–3	11–2–36–0			28–6–71–3				5–0–18–0					2	4	3	8	253	9
	5–3–13–0		8–1–10–0	5.2–1–9–3	4–0–11–0			5–1–18–0										8		1	69	3
v. Durham (Chesterfield) 5–8 June	6–1–17–0	6–1–29–1	8–0–29–1		4–1–11–0	8–0–60–1	13–1–82–0											13		2	241	3
v. Yorkshire (Harrogate) 12–15 June	18.5–6–37–5	21–7–44–0		21–6–63–1			5–1–9–1	45–13–119–2				8–2–28–0						5	1	19	305	10
v. Cambridge University (Cambridge) 16–18 June			16.4–5–35–2	16.2–3–41–1	19–2–52–1			29.2–15–58–6										14		11	200	10
				8–2–17–1		10–2–31–0	6–1–28–0	31–10–59–0		1.2–0–7–1	6–0–23–0		8–3–13–1				3	2	2	1	183	4
v. Warwickshire (Derby) 26–29 June	18.2–7–32–4			13–2–41–4										15–2–37–2				11		16	121	10
	12.2–2–29–3			13–0–63–1				14–6–45–1						13–6–35–5				2		15	174	10
v. Gloucestershire (Derby) 30 June–2 July	23–10–54–0			30.5–4–103–5	23–4–52–4		8–1–21–0							7–0–28–0			1	22	4	10	281	10
											3–0–20–0				3–0–9–0				1		29	0
v. Somerset (Taunton) 3–6 July	17–3–50–1			22–5–82–1	22–7–29–2		10–3–25–0	36–6–111–1										2	2	9	299	5
																					0	0
v. Hampshire (Portsmouth) 14–16 July	12–0–26–1	17–3–51–3	14–3–31–2	7.1–0–25–2	14–3–21–2													4		10	158	10
	16–7–34–7	17–2–80–0	10–3–24–1	8–1–28–0	8.3–3–10–2													6		4	182	10
v. Pakistanis (Derby) 18–20 July		16–2–62–3	15–6–24–2		13–6–19–1			18.5–3–67–3								11–6–23–1		2		1	197	10
v. Middlesex (Derby) 21–23 July	12–2–25–0	13–0–56–1		11–0–35–0	13–4–28–0	11–0–47–1						3–0–17–0					4	4		7	216	2
v. Worcestershire (Worcester) 24–27 July	19.1–1–39–2	18–3–51–3	12–4–31–0	17–1–59–1				33–15–62–3				2–0–11–0					5	8		14	266	9
	13–1–37–0	6–0–32–0	8–3–14–0	5–0–20–0				6–1–35–3			2–0–15–0						1	8	1	1	162	3
v. Leicestershire (Ilkeston) 4–6 August	18–1–52–1		12–5–17–1	18.1–2–48–3												11–2–33–4		10	2	6	160	10
	20–5–51–3		10.3–4–22–2	12–3–41–0				25–10–57–3								12–2–44–2		8	1	2	223	10
v. Sussex (Eastbourne) 7–10 August	19–7–35–2		16–4–34–2	26–3–52–2				19.2–3–66–3								15–4–40–1	2	1	1	7	230	10
	10–1–29–2		14.3–4–32–2	14–3–26–1				12–0–65–1									3	6		4	161	6
v. Kent (Chesterfield) 14–17 August	19–2–60–5	20–2–68–2	22–8–49–1	10.4–2–46–0	19–4–72–1														3	5	295	10
v. Glamorgan (Chesterfield) 18–20 August	14–4–22–1	18.2–6–45–5	20–2–47–1		18–5–29–2											6–2–22–1		5	3	6	170	10
	17–3–38–1	14–3–49–0	19–0–102–1		18–4–56–2							7.3–3–24–3				19–4–88–3		9	8	4	366	10
v. Somerset (Derby) 26–29 August																					0	0
	15–6–31–2	9–0–25–1		15–1–61–4	15–4–45–2											5–1–25–0	4	8	4	7	199	9A
v. Nottinghamshire (Trent Bridge) 31 August–3 September	15.2–6–24–3			18–6–36–5	14–6–24–0			30–14–55–1								7–6–8–0	4	15		2	166	10
	34–8–88–3			26–4–70–1	33–7–89–3			33–13–77–1								16–4–47–2	1	13	3	2	385	10
v. Essex (Derby) 7–10 September	11–4–18–6	7–1–25–1		8–1–29–1	9.4–4–15–2												4	5	5	1	96	10
	19–4–39–1	35–8–90–1	40–12–68–0	28–8–60–2	40.4–8–101–2	15–1–40–0						6–1–16–0					14	14	3	11	442	6
v. Glamorgan (Cardiff) 12–15 September			18–4–58–1		19–1–52–1			22–1–102–4				1.1–0–7–1				11–0–43–1	1	6		2	307	10B
																					0	0
Bowlers average	482.5–116– 1118–64 17.46	334.2–50– 1192–32 37.25	338.4–87– 795–23 34.56	430.4–72– 1295–46 28.15	367.5–86– 888–29 30.62	66–5– 260–2 130.00	119–22– 419–3 139.66	499.3–138– 1396–39 35.79	35.4–5– 135–5 27.00	28.2–0– 148–2 74.00	23–3– 92–0 –	77.4–11– 250–4 62.50	8–3– 13–1 13.00	35–8– 100–7 14.28	3–0– 9–0 –	113–31– 373–15 24.86						

A R.J. Turner retired hurt
B A.W. Richardson 13–2–38–2

DURHAM CCC

BATTING	v. Oxford University (Oxford) 14–16 April		v. Leicestershire (Durham) 25–29 April		v. Kent (Canterbury) 7–11 May		v. Glamorgan (Cardiff) 14–17 May		v. Northamptonshire (Stockton) 23–26 May		v. Hampshire (Southampton) 29 May–1 June		v. Somerset (Darlington) 2–4 June		v. Derbyshire (Chesterfield) 5–8 June		v. Essex (Hartlepool) 13–15 June		v. Sussex (Horsham) 19–22 June		v. Kent (Gateshead) 27–29 June		v. Gloucestershire (Stockton) 3–6 July		M	Inns	NO	Runs	HS	Av
J.D. Glendenen	117	–	16	18	28	57*	15	–	5	0	64	38	–	–	5	–	1	10					4	–	17	28	1	607	117	22.48
P.W.G. Parker	103	–	77	117	17	14	124	–	35	5	41	–	42	16*	75	–	55	0	44	11	72*	22	43	–	20	35	2	1331	124	40.33
D.M. Jones	36*	–	2	32	34	1	94	–	2	157	4	20*	21	78	93*	–	57	22	5	89*	6*	–	18	–	14	23	7	1179	157	73.68
P. Bainbridge	24*	–	19	9	11	61*	11	–	92*	5	6	–	45	14*	48*	–	60	6*							17	30	9	923	92*	43.95
I. Smith	–	–													–	–			17	–			12	–	12	16	1	435	110	29.00
C.W. Scott	–	–	0	1							3	–	57*	–	–	–	0	2	48	–	0	3*			18	24	5	433	57*	22.78
P.J. Berry	–	–	9	2	0	–											6	30							9	15	3	205	76	17.08
G.K. Brown	–	–																			16	48			4	6	–	136	48	22.66
D.A. Graveney	–	–	12	5	28	–	8*	–	5	5	33	–	13	–	–	–	5*	25*	27*	–	11	–			21	29	9	333	36	16.65
S.M. McEwan	–	–							22	0									0*	–					10	13	1	59	22	4.91
J. Wood	–	–									1	–			–	–	–	8	–	–	15	3	25*	–	8	6	1	80	28	16.00
W. Larkins			5	9	40	4	143	–	46	14	45	26	21	92	5	–			53	15	90	41	74	–	22	41	–	1536	143	37.46
I.T. Botham			12	105	8	–	40	–	18	3	51	–					55*	22					11	–	15	23	2	705	105	33.57
S.P. Hughes			3*	1	18	–	1	–	0	20	40	0*	6	–	–	–			9	–	1	–	–	–	20	25	5	224	42	11.20
S.J.E. Brown			0	2*	5*	–	–	–	19	5*	0*	–	5*	–			–	10			–	–	–	–	20	24	13	202	47*	18.36
A.R. Fothergill					23	–	8	–	1	15													11*	–	6	8	1	71	23	10.14
P.W. Henderson							46	–					8	–											5	7	–	119	46	17.00
M.P. Briers													12	–	–	–			2	62*	16	56*	15	–	16	28	4	460	62*	19.16
S. Hutton																	43	40	78	5	76	37			8	15	–	406	78	27.06
J.A. Daley																									2	4	1	190	88	63.33
Byes	2			2	1	4	13		4	4			4	1			1			1	7		1							
Leg-byes	4		6	14	22	3	9		6	11	16		6	11	13		8	1	16	3	10	6	6							
Wides			1				3		2	4	1			1			1				2		1							
No-balls			2	1	4	1	6		1	5	1	3	10		2		8	3	1	4	7		6							
Total	286		164	318	239	145	521		258	253	306	87	250	213	241		300	179	300	190	329	216	227							
Wickets	2		10	10	10	3	9		10	10	10	2	8	2	3		7	9†	8	3	8	5	7							
Result	D		L		D		W		L		D		W		D		L		L		D		D							
Points	–		3		6		24		5		8		23		0		8		5		8		0							

BATTING	v. Pakistanis (Chester-le-Street) 14–16 July		v. Nottinghamshire (Trent Bridge) 17–20 July		v. Leicestershire (Leicester) 21–23 July		v. Middlesex (Lord's) 24–27 July		v. Surrey (Durham) 31 July–3 August		v. Yorkshire (Durham) 4–6 August		v. Warwickshire (Edgbaston) 7–10 August		v. Glamorgan (Hartlepool) 14–17 August		v. Worcestershire (Worcester) 21–24 August		v. Hampshire (Darlington) 26–29 August		v. Somerset (Taunton) 7–10 September		v. Lancashire (Gateshead) 12–15 September		M	Inns	NO	Runs	HS	Av
J.D. Glendenen	33	36	13	0	6	5	9	0					0	8	0	0							76	43	17	28	1	607	117	22.48
P.W.G. Parker	0	10	6	7	22	10	4	42									1	94	68	6	16	10	70	52	20	35	2	1331	124	40.33
D.M. Jones	134*	105	15	154*																					14	23	7	1179	157	73.68
P. Bainbridge									39	9	14	21	11	71*	3	56	20	65*	84*	83	0	0	18	18	17	30	9	923	92*	43.95
I. Smith									29	74	6	8	4	–	23	0	44	–	68*	18	110	7	0	15	12	16	1	435	110	29.00
C.W. Scott			10	–	35*	33	3	2	0	35	25*	54	29	–	16	33	30	–	–	4	10*	–			18	24	5	433	57*	22.78
P.J. Berry	13*	8					76	14*	9	0	1	10			26	1*									9	15	3	205	76	17.08
G.K. Brown													7	16					10	39					4	6	–	136	48	22.66
D.A. Graveney					16	8*	4*	1	0	36	0	32*	2	–	6	1*	9	–	–	9*	29	3	0	0	21	29	9	333	36	16.65
S.M. McEwan	–	1	3	–	4	2			0	8	12	0					7	–	–	0					10	13	1	59	22	4.91
J. Wood																	28	–							8	6	1	80	28	16.00
W. Larkins	118	1	5	57	8	8	30	11	15	9	67	0	0	77	9	140	40	13	0	11	0	117	53	24	22	41	–	1536	143	37.46
I.T. Botham	–	–	7	–			16	20	36	48	29	13	44	28*	54	7					4	74			15	23	2	705	105	33.57
S.P. Hughes	–	2*	2	–	3	0	33	2			1	1	7*	–	4*	–			–	–	24	4	42	0	20	25	5	224	42	11.20
S.J.E. Brown	–	2	6*	–	0	4*	7	4	4*	47*			12	–	16	–	0*	–	–	3*	8	19*	6*	18	20	24	13	202	47*	18.36
A.R. Fothergill	–	13																					0	0	6	8	1	71	23	10.14
P.W. Henderson			7	–	31	27															0	0			5	7	–	119	46	17.00
M.P. Briers	13	0	53	30*	0	1	0	4	29	4	15	7	13	11	25	52	0	11*	5	2			15	7	16	28	4	460	62*	19.16
S. Hutton					13	5	33	1	0	42	31	0					2	–							8	15	–	406	78	27.06
J.A. Daley																					5	88	17	80*	2	4	1	190	88	63.33
Byes	6	1		1			2	2		5				14	4	7		8			4		1	7						
Leg-byes	11	8	7	11	5	10	9	6	16	11	4	2	7	8	7	11	2	3	6	10	2	10	10	3						
Wides	1						1			4				2	1	1			3	1										
No-balls	12	11	13	5	2	3	5	9	12	25	9	7		3	7	7	16	5	6	8	7	7	4	4						
Total	341	198	147	265	145	116	232	118	189	357	214	155	136	238	201	313	199	199	250	194	219	339	312	271						
Wickets	4	9≠	10	3	10	9[z]	10	10	10	10	10	10	10	4	10	7	10	2	4	8	10	9[x]	10	10						
Result	L		D		L		L		L		L		D		D		D		D		L		L							

FIELDING FIGURES

29 – C.W. Scott (ct 27/st 2)
16 – P.W.G. Parker and W. Larkins
13 – D.A. Graveney
11 – A.R. Fothergill (ct 11/st 1)
12 – D.M. Jones
8 – P. Bainbridge
7 – I.T. Botham, M.P. Briers andS.M. McEwan
6 – S.P. Hughes
5 – J.D. Glendenen and subs
4 – S.J.E. Brown and I. Smith
3 – G.K. Brown and S. Hutton
2 – J.A. Daley
1 – J. Wood and P.W. Henderson

† P. Bainbridge retired hurt
≠ I.T. Botham absent hurt
z D.A. Graveney retired hurt
x C.W. Scott absent hurt

DURHAM CCC

BOWLING

	J. Wood	S.M. McEwan	P. Bainbridge	I. Smith	P.J. Berry	D.A. Graveney	I.T. Botham	S.P. Hughes	S.J.E. Brown	D.M. Jones	P.W. Henderso	M.P. Briers	G.K. Brown	W. Larkins	P.W.G. Parker	S. Hutton	Byes	Leg-byes	Wides	No-balls	Total	Wkts
v. Oxford University (Oxford) 14–16 April	14–5–24–1	11–4–26–0	11–3–14–1	8–3–11–0	17–5–25–0	4–1–5–0														4	105	2
v. Leicestershire (Durham) 25–29 April					26–7–60–2	28–6–80–1	25–10–51–2	25–9–63–2	26–2–80–3									8		3	342	10
					12–4–44–1	12.2–2–37–1	5–2–7–1	9–3–17–0	3–0–10–0	7–0–20–0							2	5	4		142	3
v. Kent (Canterbury) 7–11 May			13–3–40–0		2–0–4–0	7–2–8–2	12–3–40–1	19–4–39–0	27–4–105–7								4	4			244	10
			3–0–35–0			16–6–43–0	7–3–5–1	14–0–63–0	19.2–2–94–2								4	9	1	1	253	3
v. Glamorgan (Cardiff) 14–17 May						2–2–0–0	8–0–35–0	22.5–5–51–3	22–6–70–3		17–4–61–3						3	4		3	224	10
						16–5–20–1	22–7–47–3	18–4–41–1	26.1–8–66–5	3–0–13–0							1	5			193	10
v. Northamptonshire (Stockton) 23–26 May		16–2–65–0	16–3–54–0			8–2–21–1	18–2–59–1	25–4–93–2	27–3–124–5									4	2		420	9
							5–0–41–1	3–0–38–0	1–0–5–1								5	6			95	2
v. Hampshire (Southampton) 29 May – 1 June	15.4–2–68–5					17–3–38–2	8–2–14–1	13–2–25–0	13–2–59–2									6	1		210	10
v. Somerset (Darlington) 2–4 June			20–4–45–2			15–4–30–0		20.5–2–50–1	19–3–71–4		19–1–59–3							15	4	2	270	10
			9–3–15–0			15–7–21–0		13.3–4–27–2	15–3–45–1		8–1–39–1	10–2–43–2					1	1	1	11	192	6
v. Derbyshire (Chesterfield) 5–8 June	5–0–23–0							6–0–8–0													31	0
v. Essex (Hartlepool) 12–15 June	22–2–86–2		24–7–46–1		5–0–39–1	19–3–65–2	14–2–67–0		9–0–51–2									6		1	360	10
	5–0–28–0		22–0–87–2		12–0–99–1	13–0–88–3											4	3			309	6
v. Sussex (Horsham) 19–22 June	11–0–47–3	10–3–24–0				3.1–0–15–0		8–0–30–0				7–2–29–0						6	1	3	151	4
	9–1–46–2	12–1–72–1				18–2–121–1		15–3–57–2				11–4–34–0					2	8			340	6
v. Kent (Gateshead) 27–29 June	24.4–3–92–4					22–2–93–3		30–6–114–2	23–4–76–1								2	15	2	7	392	10
	9–1–46–0					3.3–0–36–0		5–2–13–1	14–4–59–3			12.3–5–50–1	4–0–25–0					6	1	1	235	6
v. Gloucestershire (Stockton) 3–6 July	5–0–21–0			10–2–35–1			7–3–28–0	6–3–8–0	7–0–14–0	6.3–1–34–0		23–3–109–3					4	6		3	259	4
v. Pakistanis (Chester-le-Street) 14–16 July		23–8–52–3			8–0–40–1		19–2–73–2	14–2–37–0	17–2–67–1			9–0–37–0						2	1	4	308	7
		12–2–65–2			12–2–57–1			15–2–41–0	16–3–59–1	1.4–0–4–1		14–0–99–1						13	2	3	338	6
v. Nottinghamshire (Trent Bridge) 17–20 July		19–4–60–1					27–4–104–3	16–0–61–0	18–3–57–1		14–2–68–0	12–2–61–1					6	14	12		431	6
v. Leicestershire (Leicester) 21–23 July		17–4–44–1				15.2–6–22–3		20–5–41–2	20–2–84–2		13–1–56–2							9	2		256	10
														2–1–4–0	1.1–0–2–0						6	0
v. Middlesex (Lord's) 24–27 July					40–5–113–7		16–4–41–0	23–6–64–0	17–3–48–0			18–2–78–2					7	15			366	10
					18.3–1–78–3			5–0–30–0	13–2–44–0			1–0–2–0						5			159	3
v. Surrey (Durham) 31 July – 3 August		20–3–107–3	6–0–41–0			21.2–5–57–2	40–6–135–3		16–3–77–1			1–0–8–0					1	5	2		431	10
		9–1–40–2			9–1–15–0	4–0–20–0			7–0–31–0			1–0–3–0				0.1–0–4–0	1	2			116	3
v. Yorkshire (Durham) 4–6 August		5–2–10–1					21–2–72–4	15.4–8–25–5										1	1		108	1
		16–2–60–1				9–3–33–1	26–5–92–3	23.1–6–77–0									1				263	5
v. Warwickshire (Edgbaston) 7–10 August						18–3–79–2	15–2–61–0	22–0–88–1	16–1–77–1								2	9	2	1	316	4
v. Glamorgan (Hartlepool) 14–17 August					17–2–75–0	27–2–99–1	16–1–66–0	26–2–84–2	17.1–2–54–3								10	8	1		396	6
v. Worcestershire (Worcester) 21–24 August	14–3–53–0	21–1–70–0	7–2–12–1	8–2–26–2		30–16–49–2			15.2–1–69–1			1–0–7–0					1	7	2	5	294	6
v. Hampshire (Darlington) 26–29 August		27–6–75–2	14–4–46–1	3–0–9–0		5–1–13–0		28.3–7–80–1	20–4–72–2								1	7	11	2	303	6
		8–1–30–0	2–1–3–0					16–1–45–2	12–1–40–1			8–0–30–2	5–1–39–0		2–0–25–0		9	8	2		229	5
v. Somerset (Taunton) 7–10 September			14–5–31–1	21–6–70–2		12–1–46–0	11–2–45–0	32–5–112–4	22.1–3–115–2		23–5–110–1							5	4		534	10
									3–0–13–2		2–0–12–0											
v. Lancashire (Gateshead) 12–15 September			27.1–4–100–5	38–7–85–3		20–3–62–0		36–2–136–1	28–4–137–1			12–2–31–0					2	9	2	1	562	10
				2–0–6–0				3–1–14–0								0.1–0–4–0					24	0
Bowlers average	134.2–17– 534–17 31.41	226–44– 800–17 47.05	188.1–39– 569–14 40.64	90–20– 242–8 30.25	178.3–27– 649–17 38.17	380.4–87– 1201–28 42.89	322–62– 1083–26 41.65	548.3–98– 1672–34 49.17	509.1–75– 1973–58 34.01	18.1–1– 71–1 71.00	96–14– 405–10 40.50	140.3–22– 621–12 51.75	9–1– 64–0 –	2–1– 4–0 –	3.2–0– 31–0 –	0.1–0– 4–0 –						

ESSEX CCC

BATTING

BATTING	v. England 'A' (Lord's) 13–16 April		v. Cambridge University (Cambridge) 25–28 April		v. Leicestershire (Chelmsford) 7–11 May		v. Kent (Chelmsford) 14–18 May		v. Somerset (Taunton) 20–22 May		v. Glamorgan (Chelmsford) 2–4 June		v. Kent (Tunbridge Wells) 5–8 June		v. Durham (Hartlepool) 12–15 June		v. Yorkshire (Leeds) 16–18 June		v. Hampshire (Bournemouth) 19–22 June		v. Lancashire (Ilford) 26–29 June		v. Middlesex (Ilford) 30 June–2 July		v. Warwickshire (Edgbaston) 3–6 July		M	Inns	NO	Runs	HS	Av
G.A. Gooch	75	–			160	–	43	–							113	86					46	–					13	21	3	1466	160	81.44
P.J. Prichard	15	–	71	–	102	–			28	55	10	22	133	–	19	66	29	1	0	1	50	–	53	29	74	–	23	38	4	1485	136	43.67
M.E. Waugh	61	–			14*	–	120	–	19	33*	52	1	24	–	75	7	46	0	0	37	219*	–	38	94*	8	–	16	24	7	1314	219*	77.29
N. Hussain	0	–	7	10	33	–	77	–	43	–	25	7	75*	–			47	0	63	30	172*	–	9	16*	15	–	20	26	2	866	172*	37.65
N.V. Knight	5	–	62	104*	6*	–	0	–	1	47	70	11*	28*	–	21	32*	0	25	12	0	–	–	20	109	3	–	20	30	6	774	109	32.25
N. Shahid	0	–					132	–	5	–	96	–	–	–					16	48			9	–	28	–	15	21	1	561	132	28.05
M.A. Garnham	0	–	82*	–	–	–	43	–	0	–	30*	–	–	–	17	16	13	2	4	60*	–	–	8	–	–	–	24	28	4	569	82*	23.70
D.R. Pringle	102*	–			–	–	80	–							18	14*			10	51	–	–			17	–	13	13	4	507	112*	56.33
N.A. Foster	36	–									0	–	35	–	54	0	24	3	1	13	–	–			53	–	11	14	–	326	54	23.28
M.C. Ilott	12*	–			–	–	0*	–	13	–	–	–	–	–	7	–	5	22	11	7	–	–	3	–			23	22	4	164	28	9.11
J.H. Childs	–	–	–	–	–	–	0	–	8	–	–	–	–	–	4	–	16*	0	0*	12	–	–	–	–	–	–	22	17	8	110	43	12.22
J.P. Stephenson			15	5	91	–	6	–	113*	159*	3	60	18	–	23	81	9	0	18	20							21	37	5	1401	159*	43.78
J.J.B. Lewis			58	70																			31*	–	60*	–	13	20	4	746	133	46.62
A.G.J. Fraser			5	4*					2	–																	2	3	1	11	5	5.50
T.D. Topley			1	–			10	–	0	–	10*	0*											17	–	–	–	11	12	2	100	29	10.00
D.J.P. Boden			5	–																							1	1	–	5	5	5.00
P.M. Such			–	–	–	–									2*	–	15	2			–	–					15	13	3	113	35*	11.30
S.J.W. Andrew													–	–			5	14*					10*	–			10	12	4	38	14*	4.75
R.J. Rollins																											1	2	–	19	13	9.50
A.D. Brown																											1	–	–	–	–	–
Byes			4				4			4	5		8			4		2		4	14			4	10							
Leg-byes	7		5	2	14		3		7		3		14		6	3	6	2	3	9	8		4	3	4							
Wides							4		2	4	1		2				1	2		1												
No-balls	4				4		4		18	12	8	1	5		1		7	8	11	17	1		2		3							
Total	317		315	195	424		526		259	314	313	102	342	0	360	309	223	83	149	310	510		204	255	275	0						
Wickets	8		8	3	4		10		10	2	7	4	4	0	10	6	10	10	10	10	2		8	2	7	0						
Result	D		D		D		W		L		D		L		W		L		W		W		W		D							
Points	–		–		7		24		7		8		4		23		5		19		24		22		3							

FIELDING FIGURES

45 – M.A. Garnham (ct 42/st 3)
27 – M.E. Waugh
24 – N. Hussain
18 – P.J. Prichard
16 – N.V. Knight
12 – N.A. Foster
10 – J.P. Stephenson
8 – N. Shahid and T.D. Topley
7 – M.C. Ilott
6 – P.M. Such
5 – J.H. Childs and A.D. Brown (ct 4/st 1)
4 – J.J.B. Lewis and D.R. Pringle
2 – R.J. Rollins
1 – D.J.P. Boden, A.G.J. Fraser and sub

BATTING

BATTING	v. Gloucestershire (Southend) 14–16 July		v. Sussex (Southend) 17–20 July		v. Worcestershire (Kidderminster) 21–23 July		v. Leicestershire (Leicester) 24–27 July		v. Pakistanis (Chelmsford) 1–3 August		v. Northamptonshire (Chelmsford) 4–6 August		v. Nottinghamshire (Colchester) 14–17 August		v. Surrey (Colchester) 1–20 August		v. Sussex (Hove) 26–29 August		v. Hampshire (Chelmsford) 31 August–3 September		v. Derbyshire (Derby) 7–10 September		v. Gloucestershire (Bristol) 12–15 September		M	Inns	NO	Runs	HS	Av
G.A. Gooch	36	55	102	108*					141	4			28	–			77	46*	22	19	53	123*	28	101	13	21	3	1466	160	81.44
P.J. Prichard	8	47	68*	11	10	0*	2	106			46	23	136	–	26	–	18	24*	82	55*	1	12	30	22	23	38	4	1485	136	43.67
M.E. Waugh	74	125*	–	85*	138*	–	8	36																	16	24	7	1314	219*	77.29
N. Hussain			–	–	78	–	9	5	11	5	52	33	31	–	13	–	–	–							20	26	2	866	172*	37.65
N.V. Knight							8	11*			69	26	21	–	0	–			5	–	10	18	4	46	20	30	6	774	109	32.25
N. Shahid	17	10			27	–	9	4	86*	8	10	4									1	51	0	0	15	21	1	561	132	28.05
M.A. Garnham	32	3	–	–	0*	–	21	24	18	24	2	0			59	–	0	–	14	–	3	66	17	11	24	28	4	569	82*	23.70
D.R. Pringle			–	–									48	–	12	–	112*	–	14	–	1	28*			13	13	4	507	112*	56.33
N.A. Foster	26	40			–	–	13	28																	11	14	–	326	54	23.28
M.C. Ilott	5	–	–	–	–	–	1	0	1	8	13	6*	–	–	4	–	8	–	2	–	6*	–	28	2	23	22	4	164	28	9.11
J.H. Childs	2*	–	–	–			1*	11	3*	2*	1*	0	–	–	7	–	0*	–	43	–					22	17	8	110	43	12.22
J.P. Stephenson	5	22	123*	12	22	0*	0	42	45	27	64	37	74	–	9	–	15	3	6	83*	0	97	1	93	21	37	5	1401	159*	43.78
J.J.B. Lewis	34	21*			16	–			8	55	1	29	53*	–	66	–	133	–	43	4	4	5	2	53	13	20	4	746	133	46.62
A.G.J. Fraser																									2	3	1	11	5	5.50
T.D. Topley															7	–	4	–	16	–	1	–	5	29	11	12	2	100	29	10.00
D.J.P. Boden																									1	1	–	5	5	5.00
P.M. Such			–	–	–	–			7	6	0	0	–	–	12*	–	20	–	35*	–	1	–	9	4	15	13	3	113	35*	11.30
S.J.W. Andrew	0	–	–	–	–	–	0	0	3	6	0	0											0*	0*	10	12	4	38	14*	4.75
R.J. Rollins									6	13															1	2	–	19	13	9.50
A.D. Brown													–	–											1	–	–	–	–	–
Byes	1	3	1	8	2			4		10	11		3		1		5		2		4	14		1						
Leg-byes	2	4	4	1	1		2	2	16	8	4		13		2		5	5	5	3	5	14	4	15						
Wides	1							2					4		1			2	1		5	3		1						
No-balls	9	5	5	6	6		1	5	12	12			5		10		8		8	1	1	11		4						
Total	252	335	303	231	300	0	75	280	357	188	273	158	416		229		405	80	298	165	96	442	128	382						
Wickets	10	6	1	2	5	0	10	10	9	10	10	10	6		10		8	1	10	2	10	6	10	10						

ESSEX CCC

BOWLING

	N.A. Foster	D.R. Pringle	M.C. Ilott	M.E. Waugh	J.H. Childs	G.A. Gooch	T.D. Topley	D.J.P. Boden	A.G.J. Fraser	J.P. Stephenson	P.M. Such	N. Shahid	S.J.W. Andrew	P.J. Prichard	N. Hussain	Byes	Leg-byes	Wides	No-balls	Total	Wkts
v. England 'A' (Lords) 13–16 April	30–7–90–1	29–6–80–3	22–5–64–1	11–0–57–1	25–6–100–0	14–2–62–1										1	2	7	10	456	7
v. Cambridge University (Cambridge) 25–28 April							14–6–15–5	12–5–19–0	9.3–2–37–2	7–4–3–3							1	2	2	75	10
					1.3–1–0–1		3–1–11–1	4–1–23–0			2–1–2–1						5			41	3
v. Leicestershire (Chelmsford) 7–11 May		19–6–32–1	11–4–26–0	2.4–0–7–1	33–12–55–3					21–8–48–1	25–8–43–2					4	8		4	223	9A
		7–2–25–0	17–1–69–1	16–4–38–3	39–17–69–3					9–0–37–0	34–11–59–0					2	13			312	7
v. Kent (Chelmsford) 14–18 May		17–7–33–3	17.2–2–56–4	5–1–21–1	2–1–2–1		7–4–25–0			5–1–27–0							2		3	166	10
		19–5–52–1	23–8–41–1	12–3–61–1	35.2–17–69–5		15–3–41–1					1–1–0–0				4	6		1	274	9B
v. Somerset (Taunton) 20–22 May			30–12–76–4	12.2–3–46–2	11–5–13–1		23–5–73–2		8–3–23–1	11–2–32–0						5	7		18	275	10
			2.5–0–12–0	2.1–0–19–0	33.4–11–91–4		8–0–46–0		3–0–35–0	23–6–85–2						6	8		5	302	6
v. Glamorgan (Chelmsford) 2–4 June	18–5–57–2		20–6–59–1	5–0–30–0	27.4–8–82–6		13–4–57–1									1	3	2	1	289	10
v. Kent (Tunbridge Wells) 5–8 June																				0	0
	16–4–49–1		18.4–3–82–2	11–1–29–0	13–3–73–1					10–2–32–1			20–1–73–1			1	4	1	2	343	6
v. Durham (Hartlepool) 12–15 June	20–4–52–0	15–5–31–0	17–3–72–2		20–7–85–4					5.4–0–35–1	6–2–16–0					1	8	1	8	300	7
	20–8–49–4	10.2–1–50–3	11–2–43–1	6–0–27–1	3–0–9–0												1		3	179	9C
v. Yorkshire (Leeds) 16–18 June	13–4–34–2		19.4–7–72–2	6–1–28–1	26–11–53–2					19–5–41–2	9–2–31–0		22–5–97–1				5		1	361	10
v. Hampshire (Bournemouth) 19–22 June	13–5–32–0	18.3–2–57–2	22–4–63–1	3–0–12–0	26–4–87–3					16–2–49–2								2	12	300	8
	7–0–23–2	6–1–21–1	7.5–1–19–4		7–1–16–3												1			80	10
v. Lancashire (Ilford) 29–29 June	12–3–28–0		18–4–75–2		17.2–6–50–5						11–1–50–3						9	1		212	10
	14–4–46–3	10–3–31–3	9–2–30–0		19.3–5–63–2						19–3–69–2					8	14		1	261	10
v. Middlesex (Ilford) 30 June–2 July			17–3–75–2	10.4–1–44–1	16–2–26–1		32–10–67–4						15–3–49–2			6	6		11	273	10
				9–0–31–0	14–1–56–0		8–0–34–0					4–0–28–1	11–2–34–1				2		1	185	3
v. Warwickshire (Edgbaston) 3–6 July																				0	0
	21–6–56–3	13–5–23–2		9–2–27–1	14–2–40–1		8–1–38–0					1–0–4–0				5	11		6	204	7
v. Gloucestershire (Southend) 14–16 July	18–4–62–0		27.5–10–79–5	5–1–25–0	25–9–36–1	8–2–28–0				3–0–21–0		7–1–19–0	25–1–80–2			1	5	3	10	356	8
			9–0–45–0	1–0–4–0	19–3–60–1							6–0–31–2	15–1–40–1	3–0–46–0			4	2	2	230	4
v. Sussex (Southend) 17–20 July		19–1–75–1	20.5–3–92–1	4–0–21–2	38–8–101–4	7–1–14–0				5–1–18–0	27–10–55–0		8–1–38–0			1	14	2	6	429	9
		3–1–5–0	9–2–37–1		12.3–5–20–1						16–7–17–6		8–2–20–0				5		3	104	9D
v. Worcestershire (Kidderminster) 21–23 July	22–3–67–0		27–4–98–0	19–5–46–1						9–1–47–0	24–5–83–2		20–2–86–3			6	15	2	11	448	6
	9–1–19–2		7–2–23–0	4–0–14–1						4–3–4–0		2–1–7–0	7–2–24–1	5–0–54–0	4–0–38–1		3	1	2	186	5
v. Leicestershire (Leicester) 24–27 July	19–4–47–4		23–3–73–4	13.1–5–40–2									15–6–28–0				5	7	2	193	10
	4–1–13–0		17–5–34–2	17.4–4–44–3	2–0–6–0					18–4–68–1			24–8–54–4				11		3	230	10
v. Pakistanis (Chelmsford) 1–3 August			17–3–67–1		17–1–73–0					14–2–44–0	9.4–0–74–0	6–0–24–2	16–2–64–3			5	2	1	1	353	6
			11–0–56–0		10–0–51–2					4.1–0–34–1	7–0–44–0		2–0–6–0			4	1			196	3
v. Northamptonshire (Chelmsford) 4–6 August			12–3–61–0		49–13–121–2					7–1–21–0	36–7–114–5	7–0–31–2	17–1–59–0			9	28		1	444	9
v. Nottinghamshire (Colchester) 14–17 August		28–9–55–4	21–4–65–0		8–1–34–0	8–3–15–0				23–3–54–6	9–4–12–0					5	9	3	6	249	10
		3–1–5–0	5–1–15–0		27.5–10–59–4					2–1–6–0	30–15–39–6					4	1			196	3
v. Surrey (Colchester) 18–20 August		21–1–63–4	16–3–49–0		18–7–53–0		13–2–45–0			14–2–54–1	10.1–3–22–4						6		15	292	10
		2–1–3–0									2–0–7–0									10	0
v. Sussex (Hove) 26–29 August		20–5–7–0	21–5–60–5			2–0–4–1	17–4–46–3			3–1–9–0	6–1–12–1					1	2		8	204	10
		24–9–47–4	20.3–1–77–3		9–1–31–1	4–0–9–0	16–4–53–1			4–1–13–0	14–3–37–1					8	4		15	279	10
v. Hampshire (Chelmsford) 31 August–3 September		18.3–7–32–1	27–13–60–1		30–11–71–2	3–1–5–1	11–2–34–1				20–9–23–4					4	4	3		233	10
		20.3–8–42–3	16–4–44–2		35–17–67–3		2–0–7–0			3–2–5–1	29–13–46–1					8	10		6	229	10
v. Derbyshire (Derby) 7–10 September		19–2–63–5	16–2–54–2			12–4–32–0	12–3–31–2			7–0–35–0	2–1–5–0					1	5		7	226	10
		14–0–55–1	26–3–87–6			5–2–15–0	16–2–59–1			2–0–17–0	28–10–69–2	1–0–1–0					6	1	8	309	10
v. Gloucestershire (Bristol) 12–15 September			33–5–111–3			20–8–27–1	20.2–3–75–2			7–2–19–0	18–6–27–0		32–7–58–4			1	8	6	5	326	10
			10–2–43–0				2.2–0–22–0				14–1–55–0	5–1–22–2	8–1–39–1								
Bowlers average	256–63– 724–24 30.16	355.5–88– 950–42 22.61	675.3–145– 2264–64 35.37	184.4–31– 671–22 30.50	684.2–206– 1822–67 27.19	83–23– 211–4 52.75	240.4–54– 779–24 32.45	16–6– 42–0 –	20.3–5– 95–3 31.66	251.5–51– 854–22 38.81	411.5–126– 1015–40 25.37	40–4– 167–9 18.55	265–45– 849–24 35.37	8–0– 100–0 –	4–0– 38–1 38.00						

A J.J. Whitaker retired hurt
B N.R. Taylor retired hurt
C P. Bainbridge retired hurt
D P. Moores absent hurt

GLAMORGAN CCC

BATTING

	v. Middlesex (Lords) 25–29 April	v. Pakistanis (Cardi'ff) 9–11 May	v. Durham (Cardiff) 14–17 May	v. Warwickshire (Swansea) 20–22 May	v. Leicestershire (Swansea) 29 May–1 June	v. Essex (Chelmsford) 2–4 June	v. Lancashire (Colwyn Bay) 12–15 June	v. Worcestershire (Worcester) 16–18 June	v. Oxford University (Oxford) 19–22 June	v. Northamptonshire (Luton) 26–29 June	v. Surrey (Neath) 3–6 July	v. Hampshire (Portsmouth) 17–20 July	M	Inns	NO	Runs	HS	Av
S.P. James	22 94	– 27	2 5	26 35	– –	45 –	8 152*	6 11	111 –	0 0	105 19	30 73	24	39	4	1376	152*	39.31
H. Morris	146 40		46 0	36 28	– –	5 –	33 104	21 123		12 19	58 59	0 48	22	36	3	1546	146	46.84
P.A. Cottey	– 28*	– 12	24 112*	42* 9	– –	28 –		13 6	50 6		24 45	3 5	20	28	5	1076	141	46.78
M.P. Maynard	12* 40	– 28	88 15	62 0	– –	82 –	35 15*	12 14		8 0	6 66	73 0	23	36	4	1219	176	38.09
D.L. Hemp	0* 3	– 23							27 –			30 84*	12	17	2	326	84*	21.73
R.D.B. Croft	51 18	– 7	14 3	2* 8	– –	22 –	34 –	19* 40*	51* –	7 2	16* 15	2 1	24	34	10	650	60*	27.08
C.P. Metson	– 1	– 20	1 30	– 5*	– –	15 –	46* –	27 23		39* 6	14* 0	25 31*	23	28	6	437	46*	19.86
S.L. Watkin	– 0*	– 6	1 12	– 1	– –	10 –	0 –	8 41		16 3	– 0	7* –	22	24	4	153	41	7.65
S. Bastien	– –		1* 0	– –	– –	9* –	4 –	1 1			– 0*	4 –	10	10	3	21	9*	3.00
M. Frost	– –	– 0*							– –		– 0	4 –	8	5	2	4	4	1.33
D.J. Foster	– –								– –	15 6			8	4	1	40	17*	13.33
A.R. Butcher		– –					23 –			8 59*			3	3	1	90	59*	45.00
A. Dale		– 9	29 3	32 67*	– –	7 –	28 8	0 7	18 76*	18 29	8 1		22	33	5	1159	150*	41.39
S.R. Barwick		– 0	7 0	– –	– –	8 –	0 –	0 4		0 0			18	15	4	31	9*	2.81
I.V.A. Richards			1 7	127 –		51 –	68 –	18 33		49 13	0 27	21 19	14	23	–	722	127	31.39
C.S. Cowdrey					– –				50 –				2	1	–	50	50	50.00
M.C. Dobson									5* –				1	1	1	5	5*	–
J. Bishop									– 51*				1	1	1	51	51*	–
S. Kirnon									– –				1	–	–	–	–	–
S.D. Thomas													6	7	2	25	10	5.00
Byes	11 1	7	3 1	4 10		1	3 7	4	1	1		1 3						
Leg-byes	8 8	1	4 5	8 2		3	8 8	7 9	5 1	3 2	7 1	6 16						
Wides		1				2		2 1			2 1							
No-balls	5 4	7	3	7 2		1	6 4	16 22	1		10 14	2 4						
Total	255 237	0 148	224 193	346 167		289	296 298	150 339	317 136	176 139	250 248	208 284						
Wickets	3 6	0 9†	10 10	5 6		10	10 2	10 10	5 1	10 10	6 10	10 6						
Result	D	L	L	W	D	D	D	L	D	L	L	D						
Points	6	–	3	24	2	6	7	2	–	1	5	5						

BATTING

	v. Yorkshire (Cardiff) 21–23 July	v. Somerset (Abergavenny) 24–27 July	v. Kent (Swansea) 31 July–3 August	v. Sussex (Eastbourne) 4–6 August	v. Nottinghamshire (Trent Bridge) 7–10 August	v. Durham (Hartlepool) 14–17 August	v. Derbyshire (Chesterfield) 18–20 August	v. Gloucestershire (Swansea) 21–24 August	v. Warwickshire (Edgbaston) 26–29 August	v. Sussex (Cardiff) 31 August–3 September	v. Kent (Canterbury) 7–10 September	v. Derbyshire (Cardiff) 12–15 September	M	Inns	NO	Runs	HS	Av
S.P. James	80 26	29 8	91 29	42 20	45 8*	10 –	13 2	1* 14*	64 –	32 –	2 37	52 –	24	39	4	1376	152*	39.31
H. Morris	5 39	71 117	31 33	32 104*	17 –	126 –	12 52	2* 12*	0 –	80 –	2 17	16 –	22	36	3	1546	146	46.84
P.A. Cottey			37 65*	37 45	32 –	91 –	62 5	– –	67* –	58 –	29 141	0 –	20	288	5	1076	141	46.78
M.P. Maynard	30 36	0 57	36 113*	49 9	11 4*	22 –	13 176	– –	6 –	7 –	16 21	57 –	23	36	4	1219	176	38.09
D.L. Hemp	22 6	0 16	39 9	7 0	51 –			– –	7 –	2 –			12	17	2	326	84*	21.73
R.D.B. Croft	11* 25	19 37*	60* –	49 6*	0 –	29* –	3 7	– –	18 –	33 –	7 17	17 –	24	34	10	650	60*	27.08
C.P. Metson	0* 0	26 –	26 –	12 –	1 –	– –	14 4	– –	2 –	2 –	35 1	31 –	23	28	6	437	46*	19.86
S.L. Watkin	– 0	0 –	– –	6* –	2 –	– –	4 1		11 –	18* –	1 1	4 –	22	24	4	153	41	7.65
S. Bastien							1 0						10	10	3	21	9*	3.00
M. Frost	– 0*							– –	0 –				8	5	2	4	4	1.33
D.J. Foster		2 –	– –	– –	17* –	– –							8	4	1	40	17*	13.33
A.R. Butcher													3	3	1	90	59*	45.00
A. Dale	21 59*	67 45*	10 1	26 5	150* –	68 –	16 82	– –	127 –	18 –	48 50	26 –	22	33	5	1159	150*	41.39
S.R. Barwick	– 0	9* –	– –	– –	– –	– –		– –		0 –	2* 1*	0* –	18	15	4	31	9*	2.81
I.V.A. Richards	12 11	27 13				31 –	14 15				4 76	85 –	14	23	–	722	127	31.39
C.S. Cowdrey													2	1	–	50	50	50.00
M.C. Dobson													1	1	1	5	5*	–
J. Bishop													1	1	1	51	51*	–
S. Kirnon													1	–	–	–	–	–
S.D. Thomas							4* 1*	– –	0 –	8 –	2 0	10 –	6	7	2	25	10	5.00
Byes	4 6	4	8 4	5 4	2	10			5		4	1						
Leg-byes	11 8	8 6	13 1	7 3	1	8	5 9		8	3	2 13	6						
Wides		1	2	1		1	3 8			2	1 2							
No-balls	4 3	17 5	1	9 2	5		6 4	6	1	5	7 8	2						
Total	200 219	276 308	354 255	281 199	334 12	396	170 366	3 32	316 0	268	158 389	307 0						
Wickets	6 9	10 5	7 4	8 5	8 0	6	10 10	0 0	10 0	10	10 10	10 0						

FIELDING FIGURES

54 - C.P. Metson (ct 49/st 5)
20 - S.P. James
19 - M.P. Maynard
10 - R.D.B. Croft
18 - I.V.A. Richards
15 - H. Morris
9 - P.A. Cottey
8 - A. Dale and D.L. Hemp
6 - S.R. Barwick
5 - S.L. Watkin and C.S. Cowdrey
4 - I.R. Bishop
2 - M. Frost, S. Bastien and Sub
1 - D.J. Foster, A.R. Butcher, M.C. Dobson and S.D. Thomas
† - A.R. Butcher absent injured

BOWLING	S.L. Watkin	M. Frost	S. Bastien	D.J. Foster	R.D.B. Croft	S.R. Barwick	A. Dale	I.V.A. Richa	P.A. Cottey	H. Morris	S. Kirnon	M.C. Dobso	M.P. Mayna	S.D. Thomas	C.P. Metson	Byes	Leg-byes	Wides	No-balls	Total	Wkts
v. Middlesex (Lord's)	22.4–8–64–2	19–6–61–1	26–6–95–5	17–2–73–2	11–1–35–0												13	1	9	341	10
25–29 April	8–0–28–0	11–1–63–0	10–1–30–1	7–0–33–1	5–0–23–0												2		6	179	2
v. Pakistanis (Cardiff)	24–2–8–2	17–1–75–1			16–0–90–0	24–3–82–0	7–4–14–2									1	12		5	354	5
9–11 May																				0	0
v. Durham (Cardiff)	42–11–115–2		30–5–113–2		32.5–8–105–5	30–7–86–0	23–8–54–0	9–1–26–0								13	9	3	6	521	9
14–17 May																					
v. Warwickshire (Swansea)	16–5–38–2		15–5–44–0		37.5–5–103–6	18–5–54–2										1	8		3	248	10
20–22 May	16–3–34–1		9–3–17–1		24.5–6–66–8	19–6–42–0			3–2–2–0								11		1	172	10
v. Leicestershire (Swansea)	25.2–8–86–1		22–9–53–2		3–0–15–0	17–2–54–0	13–5–30–3										8	3		246	6
29 May–1 June																					
v. Essex (Chelmsford)	21–4–80–4		25–6–61–1		16–3–41–1	26–5–108–1	10–3–15–0									5	3	1	8	313	7
2–4 June	12–3–43–2		9–4–32–1		5–2–8–0	10–4–19–1													1	102	4
v. Lancashire (Colwyn Bay)	26–4–83–3		27–8–45–3		18–3–67–1	23.4–7–71–3	5–1–12–0									2	15		3	295	10
12–15 June	13–4–39–2		6.4–0–33–0		15–3–63–2	23–0–102–3										4	1	1		242	7
v. Worcestershire (Worcester)	21.1–5–58–2		20–2–92–0		37–5–137–3	35–9–91–0	6–3–16–0	3–1–8–0								1	4	1	5	407	5
16–18 June	10–4–18–0		8–1–26–0		4–0–19–0	13–8–14–2				0.5–0–2–0						3	1	1	1	83	2
v. Oxford University (Oxford)		15–3–51–2		15–0–73–4	11.3–3–24–2		7–3–15–1				8–3–14–1	3–1–3–0					3	1	20	183	10
19–22 June		11–1–43–1		5–2–10–1	19–7–28–1		9–2–21–2		1–0–1–0		6–2–7–0	15–6–42–1					1	1	2	153	6
v. Northamptonshire (Luton)	28–2–121–2			22.5–1–123–2	32–7–103–1	22–4–72–0	15–3–58–0									1	21		6	499	5
26–29 June																					
v. Surrey (Neath)	25–6–76–2	24–2–100–3	14.4–4–55–1		19–4–64–0		3–0–18–0									2	1	2	2	316	6
3–6 July	16–3–49–2	7–0–48–0	16–2–63–0		10–0–69–2												3	3	2	232	5
v. Hampshire (Portsmouth)	29.5–8–97–6	22–5–79–1	26–6–89–1		23–7–61–0											2	10	1	8	338	9
17–20 July	23–8–45–1	17–4–64–1	8.1–2–24–1		14–2–32–3											1	1	1	3	167	9
v. Yorkshire (Cardiff)	30–6–81–3	25–4–103–1			31–7–63–3	35–10–79–1	9–3–18–0										4		1	348	8
21–23 July	5–2–20–1				10–2–46–1	13–3–32–0										4		1		102	2
v. Somerset (Abergavenny)	10–4–12–0			22–5–92–1	29.2–4–94–3	21–10–23–1	8–2–25–0										4		7	250	5
24–27 July	10.5–3–32–2			4–0–16–0	17–0–89–1	20–2–61–2	11–1–35–1			4–0–55–0						2	3		2	293	8
v. Kent (Swansea)	14.1–1–78–2			11–1–79–1	12–1–78–2	14–1–37–0	5–1–20–0									4	4		3	300	6
31 July–3 August	8–0–27–0			3–0–27–0	25.5–4–112–6	21–4–101–3										1	5		1	273	10
v. Sussex (Eastbourne)	28.2–4–92–4			23–2–106–3	9–1–49–0	29–6–80–1	6–1–17–0						1–0–13–0				3		4	360	10
4–6 August	16–3–45–3			15–9–16–2	17–2–71–1	17.4–5–44–2			1–0–6–0								10			192	8
v. Nottinghamshire (Trent Bridge)	3–1–14–0				1–0–2–0	1–0–1–0														17	0
7–10 August	23–5–85–3			18–2–52–0	27–6–86–2	23.4–4–67–4	8–1–26–0										6			322	10
v. Durham (Hartlepool)	13–4–35–2			22.4–2–87–5		19–5–46–1	6–2–22–2									4	7	1	7	201	10
14–17 August	27–8–75–1			6–1–33–0	23–6–37–3	24–4–91–1	22–5–56–1						2–0–3–1			7	11	1	4	313	7
v. Derbyshire (Chesterfield)	35–7–89–2		33–9–82–0		14–1–37–0		13–3–40–1							29.2–7–80–5		1	5	2	3	334	8
18–20 August	3–1–9–2													2–0–12–0	1–1–0–0		1			22	2
v. Gloucestershire (Swansea)		16–2–68–1			42–11–79–3	38–13–59–3	3–0–10–0							14–2–38–1		7	11		8	272	8
21–24 August		4.1–0–21–0												4–1–10–0						31	0
v. Warwickshire (Edgbaston)																				0	0
26–29 August	13–0–47–1	10–0–57–1			7.4–1–50–1		8–1–30–1							9–0–66–0		1	5	1	2	256	4
v. Sussex (Cardiff)	16–0–59–2				3–0–6–0	17–9–29–1	1–0–1–1							13–3–46–3			5			146	7
31 August–3 September																					
v. Kent (Canterbury)	22.1–7–64–3				13–6–23–0	30–15–37–2	14–4–27–2							19–4–52–3		9	7	1	2	219	10
7–10 September	20–4–60–1				14–6–28–1	15–4–29–2	13–5–35–1							19–1–79–5		5	6		2	242	10
v. Derbyshire (Cardiff)																				0	0
12–15 September	13–0–48–0				7.3–0–49–6	3–0–16–0	9–1–29–2		2–0–17–0				4–0–56–0	4–0–21–1			8	1		244	10
Bowlers average	689.3–148– 2126–68 31.26	198.1–29– 833–13 64.07	305.3–73– 954–19 50.21	191.3–27– 820–22 37.27	657.1–124– 2152–68 31.64	602–155– 1627–36 45.19	234–62– 644–20 32.20	12–2– 34–0 –	7–2– 26–0 –	4.5–0– 57–0 –	14–5– 21–1 21.00	18–7– 45–1 45.00	7–0– 72–1 72.00	113.2–18– 404–18 22.44	1–1– 0–0 –						

GLOUCESTERSHIRE CCC

BATTING

	v. Somerset (Taunton) 25–28 April	v. Yorkshire (Leeds) 14–17 May	v. Worcestershire (Gloucester) 19–22 May	v. Somerset (Gloucester) 23–26 May	v. Worcestershire (Worcester) 29 May–1 June	v. Lancashire (Old Trafford) 5–8 June	v. Kent (Bristol) 16–18 June	v. Warwickshire (Bristol) 19–22 June	v. Surrey (Bristol) 26–29 June	v. Derbyshire (Derby) 30 June–2 July	v. Durham (Stockton) 3–6 July	v. Essex (Southend) 14–16 July	M	Inns	NO	Runs	HS	Av
G.D. Hodgson	1 –	124 7	3 17	14 14		0 50	32 75	4 32	68 37	50 –	35 –	147 46	21	36	1	1224	147	34.97
S.G. Hinks	34 –	31 15	17 26	18 60		16* 88*	50 6		8 6	7 –	10 –	10* –	10	16	3	402	88*	30.92
A.J. Wright	0 –	51 7	39 22	12 8		9* 5*	128 5	10 15	47 31	4 –	83* –	69 27	19	33	3	772	128	25.73
C.W.J. Athey	65 –	3 0	42 3	5 4		– –	11 33	43 19	57 0	39 –	56 –	10 94	20	32	–	1022	181	31.93
M.W. Alleyne	5 –	88* 16	36 1	0 5		– –	2 69	55 22	46 49	78* –	11 –	23 21	22	36	3	1065	93	32.27
J.T.C. Vaughan	34 –												11	18	4	473	99	33.78
R.C. Russell	13 –	29 48*	28 72*	58* 41					47 32			6 25*	17	30	9	929	75	44.23
T.H.C. Hancock	102 –	7 17					23* 22	0 11					10	17	1	436	102	27.25
M.C.J. Ball	54 –	1 7	4 6	2 0					53* 12				12	21	6	204	54	13.60
A.M. Babington	24 –						– 4	0 9	3* 0*	2 –	– –	6* –	9	11	4	75	24	10.71
M.J. Gerrard	0* –												4	4	1	6	4	2.00
C.A. Walsh		51 6	0 30*	4 0		– –	– 0	13 2	4 7			4 –	18	27	3	280	51	11.66
A.M. Smith		0 0	5* –	34 6		– –	– 4*	0* 51*		40 –	– –	18 –	12	14	5	169	51*	18.77
M. Davies		4 15	0 –	0 0		– –		1 0	1 0		– –	– –	19	23	10	145	32*	11.15
R.J. Scott			13 16	5 33*		– –	1 27	50 0	5 1	8 –	51* –	44 9*	19	31	3	751	73	26.82
R.I. Dawson						– –				1 –			6	8	–	88	29	11.00
R.C.J. Williams						– –	– 11*	11 6		5 18*	– –		5	5	2	51	18*	17.00
R.C. Williams										10 10*	– –		7	11	1	117	44	11.70
M.G.N. Windows													1	1	–	71	71	71.00
Byes		4	8	12		1	3 5	5 5	4	1	4	1						
Leg-byes	2	5 4	14 4	13 18		2 2	7 6	6 11	5 1	22	6	5 4						
Wides	1	1	1				1		1 1	4 1		3 2						
No-balls	9	12	4 5	12 2		2 2	6 4	1 1	3 1	10	3	10 2						
Total	344	411 142	206 210	177 203		29 148	263 272	199 184	352 178	281 29	259	356 230						
Wickets	10	10 10	10 7	10 10		1 1	6 9	10 10	9 10	10 0	4	8 4						
Result	D	W	W	L	Ab.	D	D	L	L	D	D	L						
Points	4	23	22	5	0	4	5	5	5	3	0	8						

BATTING

	v. Yorkshire (Cheltenham) 17–20 July	v. Hampshire (Cheltenham) 21–23 July	v. Sussex (Cheltenham) 24–27 July	v. Nottinghamshire (Worksop) 4–6 August	v. Middlesex (Lord's) 7–10 August	v. Pakistanis (Bristol) 15–17 August	v. Northamptonshire (Bristol) 18–20 August	v. Glamorgan (Swansea) 21–24 August	v. Kent (Canterbury) 26–29 August	v. Leicestershire (Bristol) 31 August–3 September	v. Essex (Bristol) 12–15 September	M	Inns	NO	Runs	HS	Av
G.D. Hodgson	2 –	56 4	82 0*	6 14	64 14	7 3		33 –	37 31	81 –	7 27	21	36	1	1224	147	34.97
S.G. Hinks												10	16	3	402	88*	30.92
A.J. Wright	24 –	8 17	0 21	3 20		5 13	30 21	30 –	4 4			19	33	3	772	128	25.73
C.W.J. Athey	2 –	25 4	22 181	133 13	41 9		4 42	49 –	12 0	1 –		20	32	–	1022	181	31.93
M.W. Alleyne	5 –	86 0	21 46	16 22	25 7	8 27	0 48	0 –	33 27	1 –	93 73*	22	36	3	1065	93	32.27
J.T.C. Vaughan	80 –	13* 1	8 19*	50 1	33* 0	3 20	99 13*		19 0	51 –	29 –	11	18	4	473	99	33.78
R.C. Russell	12 –	75 20*	41 57	0 0	25 43*	18 7	27 1	66* –	31 44*	40 –	16 7*	17	30	9	929	75	44.23
T.H.C. Hancock						11 29	82 9	9 –	14 1	74 –	25 0	10	17	1	436	102	27.25
M.C.J. Ball		2 0*	4 6*	4 8	0 8			0* 17*		9* –	7 –	12	21	6	204	54	13.60
A.M. Babington			15 –			8 4*						9	11	4	75	24	10.71
M.J. Gerrard									0 2	– –	4 –	4	4	1	6	4	2.00
C.A. Walsh	44 –	0 5	2 0	0 9	4 22		27 10*	0 –	1 9	– –	26* –	18	27	3	280	51	11.66
A.M. Smith	7 –	0* –				0 4						12	14	6	169	51*	18.77
M. Davies	32* –	– –	2* –	0* 1*	8* 5	22* 3	9* –	– 14*	2* 0	4* –	22 –	19	23	10	145	32*	11.15
R.J. Scott	27 –	41 42	1 5	65 0	44 21		41 2	45 –	10 41	24 –	6 73	19	31	3	751	73	26.82
R.I. Dawson	5 –				29 0	19 11	7 16					6	8	–	88	29	11.00
R.C.J. Williams												5	5	2	51	18*	17.00
R.C. Williams				44 7	9 0	17 0	0 6	14 –				7	11	1	117	44	11.70
M.G.N. Windows											71 –	1	1	–	71	71	71.00
Byes		10	3 1	4	7		4 5	7	2	3	1						
Leg-byes	7	8 1	14 3	10 6	22 1	1 5	11 3	11	9 3	9	8 6						
Wides			1 4		5 2		2			3	6						
No-balls	10	15 1	5 3	4 7	6 9	4	3	8	3	2	5 1						
Total	257	339 95	221 346	335 112	322 141	123 126	346 176	272 31	175 164	302 0	326 187						
Wickets	10	8 7	10 6	10 10	9 10	10 10	10 8	8 0	10 10	7 0	10 3						
Result	D	D	W	W	L	L	W	D	L	D	W						
Points	6	7	22	21	6	–	22	2	5	4	23						

FIELDING FIGURES

36 - R.C. Russell (ct 34/st 2)
23 - M.W. Alleyne
19 - C.W.J. Athey
13 - R.C.J. Williams (ct 9/st 4)
11 - A.J. Wright and J.T.C. Vaughan
10 - G.D. Hodgson and M. Davies
8 - T.H.C. Hancock
7 - R.J. Scott and C.A. Walsh
6 - M.C.J. Ball
3 - S.G. Hinks, A.M. Smith and A.M. Babington
2 - R.I. Dawson and Sub
1 - M.J. Gerrard and M.G.N. Windows

BOWLING	A.M. Babing	M.J. Gerrard	J.T.C. Vaugh	C.W.J. Athey	M.C.J. Ball	T.H.C. Hanc	M.W. Alley	C.A. Walsh	A.M. Smith	M. Davies	R.J. Scott	S.G. Hinks	G.D. Hodgs	A.J. Wright	R.C. Williar	Byes	Leg-byes	Wides	No-balls	Total	Wkts
v. Somerset (Taunton)	26–2–89–1	25–5–78–2	26–7–49–2	4–3–1–0	47–14–103–4	3.4–0–11–0	5–1–10–0										7		14	348	9
25–28 April																					
v. Yorkshire (Lord's)				9–3–11–0	18–4–58–1		3–1–21–0	26–4–77–4	16.3–3–40–2	17–4–58–3						4	3		8	272	10
14–17 May					8–3–11–0		5–1–18–1	20–7–27–7	15.1–3–37–1	11–3–35–1							6		11	134	10
v. Worcestershire (Gloucester)				6–0–20–0	17–3–52–0			16.3–4–30–2	16–2–55–2	30–8–75–4	14–4–33–2						5		11	290	10
19–22 May					15.5–2–47–4			20–9–34–2	16–5–36–2	16–10–19–2						3	6		5	145	10
v. Somerset (Gloucester)					11–5–29–1			22–6–55–5	18–1–53–3	39.4–17–68–1	13–3–45–0						7	2	9	257	10
23–26 May					5–0–17–0			12.4–2–30–5	12–2–25–2	16–4–31–2	7–0–31–1						6	1	3	140	10
v. Worcestershire (Worcester)																					Ab.
29 May–1 June																					
v. Lancashire (Old Trafford)				6–0–22–0			10–2–38–0	20–6–42–6	11–1–24–0	38–10–123–3	15–1–47–0						2		3	298	10
5–8 June				4–0–8–0			6–0–23–0				7–1–21–0	2.5–1–14–0					4		2	70	0
v. Kent (Bristol)	30–4–107–8			9–0–45–0		6–0–23–0	9–1–67–0	20–5–55–1	26–4–128–1		16–3–68–0					4	10		6	507	10
16–18 June								2–0–4–0					4–0–65–0	2–0–27–0						96	0
v. Warwickshire (Bristol)	14–2–45–1					2–0–4–1		19–4–52–3	6–1–36–0	37–6–102–3	6.3–1–9–2					1	4		8	253	10
19–22 June	9–0–31–0							23–7–60–4	4–2–3–0	31–7–72–3	13–4–27–2						12		4	205	9
v. Surrey (Bristol)	14–5–47–0				30.3–3–126–1			11–2–33–1		24–9–51–1	12–3–33–1					2	8		1	300	5
26–29 June	9–0–62–1				5–1–25–1			14–1–38–1		12–1–76–1	5.1–0–25–2					1	5	1	5	232	6
v. Derbyshire (Derby)																				0	0
30 June–2 July	16–3–50–1			8–0–24–1			3–1–14–0		20–1–81–3		17–0–71–2				8–0–46–1		17		10	303	9
v. Durham (Stockton)	13–0–64–0			2–0–8–0			5–0–28–2		9–0–43–1	14–0–73–4					3–1–4–0	1	6	1	6	227	7
3–6 July																					
v. Essex (Southend)	12–1–48–1			6–1–16–1			3–1–9–0	16–2–46–4	13–2–42–1	14.1–3–52–2	9–2–36–0					1	2	1	9	252	10
14–16 July	3–0–30–0			4–0–29–0			11–1–53–1	15–0–75–0	10–0–49–1	9.5–2–61–0	6–0–31–1					3	4		5	335	6
v. Yorkshire (Cheltenham)			13–1–43–0				12–3–29–3	28–4–8–3	21.4–5–68–3	21–4–65–0	24–4—70–1						9		13	364	10
17–20 July							3–2–4–1	5–0–21–1	3–0–4–0							1			3	30	2
v. Hampshire (Cheltenham)			4–1–6–0		20.3–3–79–2		4–2–13–0	22–8–33–6	7–1–16–1		6–1–17–0						3		5	167	10
21–23 July			6–2–18–0		26–6–93–2			27–10–57–3	8–2–24–0	9–1–30–0	9–2–42–1					7	3			274	8
v. Sussex (C heltenham)	15–0–55–1		6–1–25–0		17–1–86–1		5–2–25–1	17.2–6–39–4		16–3–47–3	12–3–38–0					5	4		2	324	10
24–27 July	1–0–14–0				25–2–101–5			6.5–2–19–0		20.3–1–84–3	5–0–19–1					4	1	1	1	242	9
v. Nottinghamshire (Worksop)			12–1–48–1		24.1–4–89–3			17–2–43–1		15–2–63–3	3–0–29–0				4–1–22–0		8		3	302	8
4–6 August			5–1–20–1		8–0–34–1		4–1–5–0	17.5–5–33–5		16–6–36–3							7	1		135	10
v. Middlesex (Lord's)			18.3–7–46–3		11–3–41–0		4–0–11–0	22–2–97–3		8–5–8–2	9–2–24–0				5–0–17–0	3	4	2	4	251	8
7–10 August			5–1–15–0				7–1–39–1	21–5–44–2		16–2–58–1	13–4–44–1						13	1		213	5
v. Pakistanis (Bristol)	16–3–61–2		18–3–63–2			7–2–34–1	5–2–13–0		10–0–39–0	26–4–100–0					18.3–5–44–3		3		4	357	8
15–17 August	10–1–50–1		6–1–26–1						7–0–32–1	5–1–24–1					11–0–47–0		5		2	184	4
v. Northamptonshire (Bristol)			14.4–5–38–2			9–0–43–2	4–0–8–0	22–8–38–0		12–3–34–1	6–0–32–0				14–2–56–1		2		10	251	6
18–20 August			8–1–25–2					17–4–50–2		9.3–0–51–3	8–0–54–1				10–0–48–0	1	3		8	232	10
v. Glamorgan (Swansea)								1–0–3–0							1–1–0–0					3	0
21–24 August								4–1–15–0		1–0–1–0					3–0–16–0				6	32	0
v. Kent (Canterbury)		9–2–39–1	14.3–3–35–2				12–4–26–1	23–6–50–5		2–0–8–0	7–0–30–1						1			189	10
26–29 August		14–2–47–0	25–5–75–2			6–2–21–0	2–0–23–0	25–5–69–4		34.4–6–119–3	5–1–21–1					5	3	1	2	383	10
v. Leicestershire (Bristol)																				0	0
31 August–3 September		4–1–11–0						4.1–1–13–0												24	0
v. Essex (Bristol)		16–6–51–2	6–2–15–0					18–5–38–7		2.3–0–7–1	5–0–13–0						4			128	10
12–15 September		25–4–71–2	15–2–41–0		33–7–81–2		16.1–6–25–3	32–5–69–1		37–21–30–2	15–0–49–0					1	15	1	4	382	10
	188–21–	93–20–	202.4–44–	58–7–	322–61–	33.4–4–	138.1–32–	587.2–138–	249.2–35–	560.5–143–	267.4–39–	2.5–1–	4–0–	2–0–	77.3–10–						
	753–17	297–7	588–18	184–2	1072–28	136–4	502–14	1469–92	835–24	1661–56	959–20	14–0	65–0	27–0	300–5						
Bowlers average	44.29	42.42	32.66	92.00	38.28	34.00	35.85	15.96	34.79	29.66	47.95	–	–	–	60.00						

HAMPSHIRE CCC

BATTING

	v. Sussex (Southampton) 25–29 April	v. Yorkshire (Leeds) 7–10 May	v. Oxford University (Oxford) 15–18 May	v. Surrey (Southampton) 19–22 May	v. Lancashire (Old Trafford) 23–26 May	v. Durham (Southampton) 29 May–1 June	v. Yorkshire (Basingstoke) 2–4 June	v. Warwickshire (Edgbaston) 12–15 June	v. Leicestershire (Leicester) 16–18 June	v. Essex (Bournemouth) 19–22 June	v. Pakistanis (Southampton) 27–29 June	v. Sussex (Arundel) 30 June–2 July	M	Inns	NO	Runs	HS	Av
V.P. Terry	141 –	0 –		131 –				38 22	99 69	9 12		13 –	11	17	2	766	141	51.06
T.C. Middleton	153 –	55 –	121 –	221 1*	73 138*	0 –	21 –	124 77	18 1	29 0	8 23	27 –	24	40	4	1780	221	49.44
R.A. Smith	107* –	0 –			34 –	25 –		49 15*			4 33		12	20	2	636	107*	35.33
D.I. Gower	55* –	68 –		3 –	74 71	0 –	155 –	22 28*	44* 80	41 21	55 15		17	28	5	1075	155	46.73
M.C.J. Nicholas	– –				26* 45	27 –	27 –	9 –	37* 46*	81 12	30 1	17 –	21	32	5	1003	95*	37.14
K.D. James	– –	116 –	0 45	35 1*	98 24	62 –	59 –	13 –	67 34	32 12	29 69	59 –	23	37	2	1149	116	32.82
M.D. Marshall	– –	46* –		10 –	13* –			0 –	– 8	36 2		12 –	19	25	5	513	70	25.65
A.N. Aymes	– –	4 –	19* 4	22* –	– 6	7 –	37* –	8 –					18	23	5	359	65	19.94
S.D. Udal	– –	0* –	– 16	24* –	– –	14* –	12 –	10 38	– 29	8* 3	7* 31*	9 –	23	29	10	400	44	21.05
K.J. Shine	– –	– –	– –		– –	5 –			– 1*		0 0		16	12	6	59	22*	9.83
C.A. Connor	– –	51 –		8 –	– –	0 –	0 –		– 0	– 4*		18* –	16	13	5	127	51	15.87
J.R. Ayling		24 –	121 –	14 –		6 –	0 –	4 –	– 1	28 5		15 –	18	26	1	593	121	23.72
J.R. Wood			33 0	38 –	14 13*	57 –	32 –				6 11	35 –	10	13	1	294	57	24.50
R.J. Parks			31* –						– 10	20* 4	0 13	33 –	7	10	3	169	33	24.14
R.J. Maru			– 27	2 –			0 –			2 4	10 11	13* –	8	11	3	119	27	14.87
R.S.M. Morris			– 11*										5	9	1	209	74	26.12
M.J. Thursfield			– –										1	–	–	–	–	–
P-J. Bakker							– –	1* –			0 6		6	7	1	69	22	11.50
R.M.F. Cox													3	3	–	26	13	8.66
I.J. Turner													6	7	1	31	16	5.16
Byes	1	1	1	4	4 11				11 5		1	4						
Leg-byes	3	13	4 2	16	6 7	6	8	9 2	3 10	1	3 3	9						
Wides	6	1	1 2	1		1			1	2		1						
No-balls	2	18	1 3	23	7 1			3	2	12	10 13	6						
Total	468 0	397	331 111	552 2	349 316	210	351	290 182	282 294	300 80	162 230	271 0						
Wickets	2 0	8	4 5	9 0	5 4	10	9	10 3	3 9	8 10	10 10	9 0						
Result	W	D	W	W	W	D	D	D	D	L	L	W						
Points	20	7	–	24	22	6	7	7	5	8	–	18						

FIELDING FIGURES

50 - A.N. Aymes (ct 47/st 3)
23 - R.J. Parks (ct 21/st 2)
16 - T.C. Middleton
13 - D.I. Gower
11 - M.D. Marshall
10 - K.D. James
9 - M.C.J. Nicholas and R.J. Maru
7 - V.P. Terry and R.S.M. Morris
6 - J.R. Wood
4 - J.R. Ayling and I.J. Turner
3 - S.D. Udal
1 - R.M.F. Cox
† M.D. Marshall retired hurt

BATTING

	v. Nottinghamshire (Southampton) 3–6 July	v. Derbyshire (Portsmouth) 14–16 July	v. Glamorgan (Portsmouth) 17–20 July	v. Gloucestershire (Cheltenham) 21–23 July	v. Worcestershire (Worcester) 4–6 August	v. Kent (Canterbury) 7–10 August	v. Northamptonshire (Bournemouth) 14–17 August	v. Middlesex (Bournemouth) 18–20 August	v. Somerset (Weston-super-Mare) 21–24 August	v. Durham (Darlington) 26–29 August	v. Essex (Chelmsford) 31 August–3 September	v. Worcestershire (Southampton) 12–15 September	M	Inns	NO	Runs	HS	Av
V.P. Terry	52 –	10 3	28* 0*		26 113								11	17	2	766	141	51.06
T.C. Middleton	71 –	35 30	17 28	64 47	12 20	52 17	11 23	14 –	27* 5	127* 12	17 2	9 50	24	40	4	1780	221	49.44
R.A. Smith		8 11	79 56				62 12			1 3	23 23	87 4	12	20	2	636	107*	35.33
D.I. Gower		54 48	11 9				24 13	17 –	14* 42*	38 39	30 4		17	28	5	1075	155	46.73
M.C.J. Nicholas	46 –	8 41	7 8	42 1	5 71	59 5	33 0	95 –	– –	0 95*	19 0	22 88*	21	32	5	1003	95*	37.14
K.D. James	8 –	17 0	39 26		17 29	4 0	74 2	33 –	2 12*	3 57	20 15	15 21	23	37	2	1149	116	32.82
M.D. Marshall	37* –	1 0	70 1	5 39	58 4*	17 6	30 3	37 –	– –		39 12	27* –	19	25	5	513	70	25.65
A.N. Aymes			31 18	9 1	7 –	15 12*	0 24	53 –	– –	0 4*	13 65	0 –	18	23	5	359	65	19.94
S.D. Udal	0* –	10* 7	13 0	4 –	21* –	38 0	2 0	16 –	– –		44 32	11* 1	23	29	10	400	44	21.05
K.J. Shine	– –	1 2	– –	7* 22*	– –		0 12*	– –		– –	4* 5*		16	12	6	50	22*	9.83
C.A. Connor	– –	0 4*				8* 2		24* –	– –	– –		8 –	16	13	5	127	51	15.87
J.R. Ayling	0 –			0 48	48 4	26 20	9 0	57 –		90 0	5 31	29 8*	18	26	1	593	121	23.72
J.R. Wood	7 –					44 4			– –				10	13	1	294	57	24.50
R.J. Parks	32* –	0 26											7	10	3	169	33	24.14
R.J. Maru				15 12*						23* –			8	11	3	119	27	14.87
R.S.M. Morris				4 64	49 3	4 0						0 74	5	9	1	209	74	26.12
M.J. Thursfield													1	–	–	–	–	–
P-J. Bakker			22 15	8 17					– –				6	7	1	69	22	11.50
R.M.F. Cox				1 13				12 –	– –				3	3	–	26	13	8.66
I.J. Turner					– –	5 0	2* 0			– –	8 16	0 –	6	7	1	31	16	5.16
Byes			2 1	7	2 1		1			1 9	4 8	4						
Leg-byes	2	4 6	10 1	3 3	6 4	6 2	8 5	6	1 2	7 8	4 10	14 3						
Wides			1 1		1		4	3		11 2	3	1						
No-balls	6	10 4	8 3	5	9 2	10 2	6	19	3 1	2	6	8 8						
Total	261 0	158 182	338 167	167 274	261 251	288 70	260 100	386	47 62	303 229	233 229	231 261						
Wickets	6 0	10 10	9 9	10 8	8 6	10 10	10 10	9	1 1	6 5	10 10	9† 5						

BOWLING

	M.D. Marshal	C.A. Connor	K.J. Shine	S.D. Udal	K.D. James	A.N. Aymes	T.C. Middle	J.R. Ayling	M.J. Thursf	R.J. Maru	R.A. Smith	P-J. Bakker	M.C.J. Nic	I.J. Turner	Byes	Leg-byes	Wides	No-balls	Total	Wkts
v. Sussex (Southampton)	5–0–16–0	6–3–4–1	5–2–6–0	8–1–8–0	3–0–16–0	7–0–75–1	6–0–44–0											4	169	2
25–29 April	10–1–44–1	9–2–25–1	6–1–20–0	23–12–50–8											1	9	1	6	149	10
v. Yorkshire (Leeds)	22.5–7–29–3	15–3–52–3	8–0–34–0	23–6–52–1	5–0–25–0			8–1–41–2							4	13		4	250	10
7–10 May	2–0–8–0	4–0–12–0	5–1–22–0	5–1–13–1	2–1–6–0			5–3–13–0										1	74	1
v. Oxford University (Oxford)			13–6–11–0	10.5–3–22–3	11–6–23–1			17–4–31–3	9–2–24–1	15–7–17–2						5		3	133	10
15–18 May			14–1–38–2	26.1–14–47–5	9–3–13–0			13–5–19–2	7–1–11–1	17–13–5–0					7	8	1	2	148	10
v. Surrey (Southampton)	19.3–6–58–6	13–3–38–1		10–3–40—0				5–1–15–1		13–5–31–1						2		17	184	10
19–22 May	26–9–72–2	30–7–77–2		30–8–73–2	6–0–20–0			16–3–58–1		26.4–9–56–3						13	2	16	369	10
v. Lancashire (Old Trafford)	10–1–48–0	15–1–91–0	16–3–58–5	18–5–61–1	13–2–42–0						1.5–0–15–0				5	2		9	322	6
23–26 May	5.1–2–8–1	11–0–44–1	16–3–47–8	17–5–41–0	7–0–28–0											3		6	171	10
v. Durham (Southampton)		27–10–58–5	24.4–3–99–2	12–2–38–0	18–7–45–2			13–2–50–1								16	1	1	306	10
29 May–1 June		12–1–34–1	5–1–18–0	4–0–18–0				2–0–17–1										3	87	2
v. Yorkshire (Basingstoke)		17–5–52–0		15–8–21–1	14–6–35–0			19.3–5–41–3		13–5–17–1		22–8–38–4				6			210	10
2–4 June		21–5–45–1		32–15–49–2	11–2–23–2			12–4–28–1		13–5–22–0		21–9–34–1	1–0–1–0		12	8		3	222	7
v. Warwickshire (Edgbaston)	23–4–59–3			25–11–56–2	14–4–23–1			20–6–37–3				15–6–30–0			5	6		6	216	9
12–15 June	17–3–42–1			20–5–78–3	6–2–12–0			10.5–2–28–1				8–1–24–3			11	3	1		198	8
v. Leicestershire (Leicester)	23–9–48–2	28–4–89–0	16–0–74–3	35–8–137–0	2–0–13–0			13–1–57–2							5	27		9	450	7
16–18 June		9–1–51–3	8–1–28–1				4–0–13–0	5–0–17–0					4.3–1–16–1		4	11		3	140	5
v. Essex (Bournemouth)	14.1–6–32–2	15–2–48–3		8–1–19–3	5–1–10–0			9–1–22–1		5–2–15–1						3		11	149	10
19–22 June	32–7–68–1	19–3–61–2		25.4–8–75–3	8–2–35–0			18–7–27–1		18–6–31–2					4	9	1	17	310	10
v. Pakistanis (Southampton)			17–2–80–0	18–4–76–0	14–4–40–1					15–1–91–0		25–5–78–0	3–0–30–0		2	9	6	6	406	1
27–29 June																				
v. Sussex (Arundel)																			0	0
30 June–2 July	16–3–44–3	9–2–22–0		19–8–33–1	10–4–14–1			6–2–8–1		15.4–10–8–4					4	8		2	141	10
v. Nottinghamshire (Southampton)																			0	0
3–6 July	13–1–55–2	12–0–56–1	8.4–1–41–0	7–0–42–0	7–1–24–1			7–0–36–1								8		8	262	5
v. Derbyshire (Portsmouth)	21–1–77–1	22–5–80–2	22–3–108–0	34–5–91–0	14–2–50–0						6–0–25–0		10–1–26–1		10	8	1	13	475	4
14–16 July																				
v. Glamorgan (Portsmouth)	19–6–37–1		16–3–36–4	12.1–4–35–1	13–3–29–2							19–5–64–2			1	6		2	208	10
17–20 July	18–5–54–1		11–0–60–1	25.1–5–89–4	4–0–24–0							9–1–38–0			3	16		4	284	6
v. Gloucestershire (Cheltenham)	26–11–47–1		24–4–79–2					18–3–49–4		26–6–62–1		28–7–84–0			10	8		15	339	8
21–23 July	2.5–0–20–0			4–0–36–4						2–0–38–1						1		1	95	7
v. Worcestershire (Worcester)	25–6–51–1		17–3–73–0	17–4–45–0	8–0–14–1			15–1–43–3						45–17–103–4		6	1		335	9
4–6 August	6–2–18–0		10–0–46–1	12–2–66–1				6–1–11–0						9.4–2–38–1				3	179	3
v. Kent (Canterbury)	19–4–47–1	14–2–63–1		1.1–0–9–0	12–4–41–0			10–1–30–3						12–3–51–1	5	6		15	252	6
7–10 August	4–1–18–0	4–0–20–0		7–0–23–0	2.3–1–19–1			5–0–26–0							3			1	109	1
v. Northamptonshire	23.3–8–49–4		13–2–75–2	20–3–60–1	8–1–43–0			20–6–65–0						14–4–34–1		12	1	6	338	8
(Bournemouth) 14–17 August			4–0–17–0	3.4–1–6–0															23	0
v. Middlesex (Bournemouth)	20–6–45–3	13–2–30–0	6–2–13–2	4–0–11–0				8.4–3–12–5								4	6	5	115	10
18–20 August	21–5–50–0	21–2–78–2	14.3–2–66–1	35.3–6–101–4	10–4–8–0			17–7–37–2							3	3	5	12	346	9
v. Somerset (Weston-super-Mare)	22–6–47–3	12–0–61–0		29–1–90–3	16–1–70–0							15–6–51–1	6–0–25–0		8	18		1	370	8
21–24 August																			0	0
v. Durham (Darlington)		16.2–2–55–1	12–3–48–0		8–3–29–1			10–3–24–2		20–4–42–0				13–2–46–0		6	3	6	250	4
26–29 August		12–1–55–0	17–2–68–6					11–3–35–1		5–2–9–1				6–2–17–0		10	1	8	194	8
v. Essex (Chelmsford)	24–7–40–1		5–0–25–0	24–2–91–1	3–0–7–0			15.2–0–44–3					1–0–3–0	38–12–81–5	2	5	1	8	298	10
31 August–3 September	11–3–33–0			10–0–40–0				9–3–34–0			0.2–0–1–0			14–5–54–2		3		1	165	2
v. Worcestershire (Southampton)	15–3–33–3	17–2–46–0		40–13–76–2	1–1–0–0			12–0–34–0						13–1–33–3		6	2	6	228	8
12–15 September	13–1–51–2	14–1–39–1		22–3–94–1										18–3–62–2	1	7		2	254	7
Bowlers average	529–134– 1348–49 27.51	417.2–69– 1386–32 43.31	333.5–49– 1290–40 32.25	692.2–177– 2012–58 34.68	264.3–65– 781–14 55.78	7–0– 75–1 75.00	10–0– 57–0 –	356.2–78– 989–48 20.60	16–3– 35–2 17.50	204.2–75– 444–17 28.72	8.1–0– 41–0 –	162–48– 441–11 40.09	25.3–2– 101–2 50.50	182.4–51– 519–19 27.31						

KENT CCC

BATTING

BATTING	v. Lancashire (Old Trafford) 25–28 April	v. Durham (Canterbury) 7–11 May	v. Essex (Chelmsford) 14–18 May	v. Yorkshire (Canterbury) 20–22 May	v. Sussex (Hove) 23–26 May	v. Worcestershire (Tunbridge Wells) 2–4 June	v. Essex (Tunbridge Wells) 5–8 June	v. Gloucestershire (Bristol) 16–18 June	v. Cambridge University (Cambridge) 19–21 June	v. Durham (Gateshead) 27–29 June	v. Nottinghamshire (Maidstone) 30 June–2 July	v. Lancashire (Maidstone) 3–6 July	M	Inns	NO	Runs	HS	Av
M.R. Benson	53 38	75 27	37 53	78 0	45 117	36 84*	– 67	10 –		46 5	131 –	1 –	21	35	2	1482	139	44.90
T.R. Ward	40 6	32 9	7 0	53 53	12 44	140* 59	– 11	12 –			3 26	4 55*	22	37	3	1648	153	48.47
N.R. Taylor	40 1	57 78*	4 42*	32 83*	47 61	67* 24	– 90	0 –		29 50*	40 –	34 –	21	35	7	1508	144	53.85
G.R. Cowdrey	1 27		3 82*	127 –	62 12	– 6*	– 57*	147 –		115 46	12 –	77 –	21	31	6	1291	147	51.64
M.V. Fleming	6 1	14 –	39 0	6 –	23 31		– 19	65 –		49 24	63 –	18 4*	21	32	2	797	100*	26.56
S.A. Marsh	78 37	20 –	0 1	125 –	17* 5	– –	– –	86 –	37* 43	24 0*	17 –	42 –	22	30	4	896	125	34.46
M.A. Ealham	0 33	32 –		6* –	1 2*	– –	– 5*	58 67*	25 1	0 2		1 54	17	27	5	452	67*	20.54
A.P. Igglesden	– –					– –	– –				5 –	2* –	16	13	5	67	16	8.37
M.J. McCague	– 1*	0 –	8* 4		– –			13 –		9 –	3 10*		16	18	5	120	25*	9.23
C. Penn	3* 0		9 0	– –	– –	– –			– 14*				7	5	2	26	14*	8.66
R.P. Davis	54* 24*	0* 9	5 3	– –				32* –	– 15	1 –	7 18*	10 –	18	24	11	312	54*	24.00
C.L. Hooper		1 115*	46 74	4 8*	121 43*	– 10	– 86	52 –		87 8	36 –	0 –	21	32	4	1329	131	47.46
J.I. Longley		5 –							110 –				3	4	–	169	110	42.25
R.M. Ellison		0 –	3 4	29* –	6* –	– –	– –	12 29*	64 1*	4* –	27* –	0 –	19	22	8	323	64	23.07
N.J. Llong						– –	– 0		25 18	2 92			4	5	–	137	92	27.40
D.P. Fulton									16 42				1	2	–	58	42	29.00
G.J. Kersey									20* 22				2	2	1	42	22	42.00
A. Tutt									– –				1	–	–	–	–	–
T.N. Wren									– –				1	–	–	–	–	–
Byes	5 9	4 4	4	4 2	13 1		1	4		2	1	1						
Leg-byes	13 6	4 9	2 6	2 6	2 16	1 4	4	10	3 4	15 6	7 1	2						
Wides	1	1		3		1	1			2 1		1						
No-balls	7 8	1	3 1	11 1	19 6	6 2	2	6		7 1	7							
Total	300 192	244 253	166 274	480 153	368 338	250 190	0 343	507 96	300 160	392 235	359 55	193 113						
Wickets	7 8	10 3	10 9†	7 2	7 6	1 3	0 6	10 0	5 6	10 6	10 1	10 1						
Result	D	D	L	D	W	D	W	D	L	D	W	D						
Points	7	5	3	7	22	4	17	6	–	6	20	1						

FIELDING FIGURES

52 – S.A. Marsh (ct 44/st 8)
25 – C.L. Hooper and T.R. Ward
15 – M.R. Benson
13 – M.V. Fleming and R.M. Ellison
12 – M.J. McCague
11 – R.P. Davis
10 – N.R. Taylor
8 – G.J. Kersey (ct 7/st 1)
6 – G.R. Cowdrey
4 – M.A. Ealham, A.P. Igglesden and N.J. Llong
3 – J.I. Longley
2 – D.P. Fulton, T.N.Wren and C. Penn
1 – sub

† N.R. Taylor retired hurt

BATTING

BATTING	v. Surrey (Guildford) 14–16 July	v. Somerset (Canterbury) 21–23 July	v. Glamorgan (Swansea) 31 July–3 August	v. Middlesex (Canterbury) 4–6 August	v. Hampshire (Canterbury) 7–10 August	v. Derbyshire (Chesterfield) 14–17 August	v. Leicestershire (Leicester) 18–20 August	v. Northamptonshire (Northampton) 21–24 August	v. Gloucestershire (Canterbury) 26–29 August	v. Glamorgan (Canterbury) 7–10 September	v. Warwickshire (Edgbaston) 12–15 September	M	Inns	NO	Runs	HS	Av
M.R. Benson	0 14		4 9	21 45	44 40*	39 –	139 –	23 0	6 10	22 41	122 –	21	35	2	1482	139	44.90
T.R. Ward	12 103	15 2	85 118	150 4	0 63	87 –	41 –	3 95*	42 41	15 53	153 –	22	37	3	1648	153	48.47
N.R. Taylor	7 4		42 7	3 30	39 2*	71 –	144 –	33 44*	39 96	74 16	78 –	21	35	7	1508	144	53.85
G.R. Cowdrey	29 3	36 44	27* 14	76* 60	10 –	2 –	37* –	30 –	22 4	0 35	88 –	21	31	6	1291	147	51.64
M.V. Fleming	23 5	47 4	28 12	21 35	100* –	15 –	58 –	4 –	5 67	0 0	11 –	21	32	2	797	100*	26.56
S.A. Marsh	3 17	35 8	1 0	6 52*		29 –	– –	65 –	5 70	60 6	7 –	22	30	4	896	125	34.46
M.A. Ealham	22 23	50 9	2* 4	4 1	9 –	10 –				1 30		17	27	5	452	67*	20.54
A.P. Igglesden	1* 0	11* –	– 16	6 –	– –	3 –	– –	3 –	5* 3*	10 2	– –	16	13	5	67	16	8.37
M.J. McCague	5 13	0 –		5 –	– –	11* –	– –	0 –	11 2	0 25*		16	18	5	120	25*	9.23
C. Penn											– –	7	5	2	26	14*	8.66
R.P. Davis		24 0*	– 34*	2 4*	23* –		– –	0 –	0 8	18* 18	3* –	18	24	11	312	54*	24.00
C.L. Hooper	4 131	10 48	100 11	65 0	1 –	1 –	62* –	3 –	41 56	0 3	102 –	21	32	4	1329	131	47.46
J.I. Longley		35 19										3	4	–	169	110	42.25
R.M. Ellison	0 11*	0 21	– 41			19 –	– –	21* –	12 15		4 –	19	22	8	323	64	23.07
N.J. Llong												4	5	–	137	92	27.40
D.P. Fulton												1	2	–	58	42	29.00
G.J. Kersey					– –							2	2	1	42	22	42.00
A. Tutt												1	–	–	–	–	–
T.N. Wren												1	–	–	–	–	–
Byes			4 1	3	5 3		7	5	5	9 5	16						
Leg-byes	4 2	4 5	4 5	2 2	6		5	2 2	1 3	7 6	16						
Wides				2		3	5	2	1	1							
No-balls	7 6	8	3 1	8 4	15 1	5	4	2	2	2 2	3						
Total	117 332	275 160	300 273	369 242	252 109	295	502	196 141	189 383	219 242	603						
Wickets	10 10	10 8	6 10	10 7	6 1	10	4	10 1	10 10	10 10	8						
Result	W	W	L	D	W	D	W	D	W	L	W						
Points	19	23	6	7	22	7	24	1	21	6	24						

BOWLING	A.P. Iggles	M.J. McCag	M.A. Ealha	C. Penn	R.P. Davis	M.V. Flem	G.R. Cowc	M.R. Bens	T.R. Ward	R.M. Ellisc	C.L. Hoop	S.A. Mars	N.J. Llong	T.N. Wrer	A. Tutt	Byes	Leg-byes	Wides	No-balls	Total	Wkts
v. Lancashire (Old Trafford)	34–5–85–4	24–4–82–0	24.3–4–81–4	18–4–72–0	19–5–58–1	4–1–7–1										1	11	1	7	397	10
25–28 April	7–2–20–1	5–0–20–0	6–0–33–1	10–2–23–0	8–2–33–0	7–1–35–1	6–2–15–1	2–0–18–1	1.5–0–10–0								6	2	8	213	5
v. Durham (Canterbury)		26–8–75–3	26–16–28–2			13–6–21–0				34.4–6–77–5	10–5–15–0					1	22		4	239	10
7–11 May		10–2–35–0			14–6–33–0	1–0–4–0				5–2–7–2	20–2–59–1					4	3		1	145	3
v. Essex (Chelmsford)		29–4–117–0		22–1–97–0	24–1–84–3	10–2–34–0				28–7–95–6	28–4–92–1					4	3	4	4	526	10
14–18 May																					
v. Yorkshire (Canterbury)			23–5–74–1	29–6–69–2	5–0–17–0	19–5–54–2				25–9–92–2	9–3–25–0					5	4	4	9	340	7
20–22 May			8–1–27–0	7–0–24–1	26–4–101–3	3–0–14–0				7–1–19–0	21–0–97–3					6	4		5	292	8
v. Sussex (Hove)		14–3–85–1	24–5–67–4	7–1–23–0		22–5–50–3				26–7–65–1	16.4–4–35–1						10	2	2	335	10
23–26 May		7–3–22–0	4–1–16–0				36–6–147–1		34–4–90–0	9–3–25–0	4–3–9–0	5–0–53–0					6	2	4	368	1
v. Worcestershire (Tunbridge Wells)	28–5–77–0		25.4–2–78–4	17–3–49–1						18–1–57–0	28–11–52–1		1–1–0–0				14	6	5	327	6
2–4 June	10–1–31–1			5–0–27–0						8–1–31–0	18–1–42–2		22–2–70–3			5	4		1	210	6
v. Essex (Tunbridge Wells)	4–0–13–0		27–4–76–1			24–3–67–3				27–4–93–0	9–0–32–0		5–1–39–0			8	14	2	5	342	4
5–8 June																				0	0
v. Gloucestershire (Bristol)		21–4–44–1	18–5–45–3		16–6–47–0					15–5–44–0	33.3–5–73–2					3	7		6	263	6
16–18 June			12–2–38–0		36–11–99–7					16–2–50–0	38–13–74–2					5	6	1	4	272	9
v. Cambridge University				10–4–17–0	21–6–49–4								15–3–50–3	13–3–38–2	10–3–23–0	2	1		1	180	10
(Cambridge) 19–21 June			13.4–1–50–1		25–3–91–3								12–0–53–1	11–1–54–3	9–2–30–0	1	5		2	284	8
v. Durham (Gateshead)		22–8–50–0	17–4–58–0		24.1–7–64–7	9–0–40–0				14–3–47–0	20–4–53–1					7	10	2	7	329	8
27–29 June		13.4–0–46–1	4–0–13–0		13–0–62–1	2–0–13–0				9–2–27–2	11–2–49–1						6			216	5
v. Nottinghamshire (Maidstone)	6–1–22–1	4–1–11–0			6–2–4–1	8–1–37–0				12–4–35–1							4		4	113	3
30 June–2 July	15–6–32–4	11–2–53–2			16–6–66–1					11–1–37–0	15.4–0–68–3						10		3	266	10
v. Lancashire (Maidstone)	3–1–4–0									2.1–0–6–0							1		1	11	0
3–6 July	21–5–62–3		19–3–42–0		27–3–70–1	10–2–24–1		1–0–7–0			9–1–31–1					4	2	1	8	242	6
v. Surrey (Guildford)	33–8–122–2	23.1–7–51–1	16–1–65–2							19–3–47–2	5–2–7–1						9	3	9	301	8
14–16 July	11.2–2–34–2	12–4–21–3	6–0–11–2							7–2–9–2							1			76	10
v. Somerset (Canterbury)	13–3–30–1	14–4–23–5	7–0–18–0		4–0–9–3					3–0–22–0	9.4–3–20–1					4	7	1	5	133	10
21–23 July	5–1–13–0	9–2–47–2	2–0–15–0		31.2–10–75–6	1–0–1–0					23–6–56–2					8	5		2	220	10
v. Glamorgan (Swansea)	28–4–96–2		19.2–4–76–2		39–10–69–3	5–1–15–0				9–1–31–0	23–6–46–0					8	13	2	1	354	7
31 July–3 August	8–0–31–0				27–9–54–1		2–0–39–0		1–0–2–0		22–5–51–3	3–0–73–0				4	1			255	4
v. Middlesex (Canterbury)	16–1–54–0	22–4–49–1	15–3–47–2		29.3–8–105–3	19–3–34–1					9–3–34–0						8	1	6	331	9
4–6 August	11–2–44–0	16–2–59–1	7–0–36–0		4–0–36–1	7–0–35–3					1–0–8–0						11	1	1	229	6
v. Hampshire (Canterbury)	25–8–55–3	12–1–37–1	23–4–49–2		28–5–75–2	8–1–27–0					13–1–39–2						6		10	288	10
7–10 August	6–2–13–0	12.2–5–26–8			12–6–29–1												2		2	70	10
v. Derbyshire (Chesterfield)	17–4–56–2	16.2–2–57–3	11–1–47–2							11–2–29–3						4	14		2	207	10
14–17 August	23–0–48–0	10–1–38–0	20–3–68–2			18–3–39–2	4–1–12–0		3–0–7–0	24–3–85–0	17–6–35–0						2	1	7	334	4
v. Leicestershire (Leicester)	8–1–27–0	14–1–52–7			20–7–40–3						17–6–43–0					5	14		9	181	10
18–20 August	16–4–41–5	14–1–63–2			14.1–3–25–2	1–0–1–0				5–0–19–0	21–9–24–1					4	6		5	183	10
v. Northamptonshire	16–3–39–1	10–2–20–0								6–0–24–1							2		1	85	2
(Northampton) 21–24 August	12–2–38–0	9–1–27–0			3–1–6–0	1–1–0–0				7–1–14–0	9–2–17–1					3	3		2	108	1
v. Gloucestershire (Canterbury)	22–6–45–2	20.5–3–42–5			9–3–15–1	2–0–9–0				21–4–55–2							9		3	175	10
26–29 August	14–1–51–0	21–4–44–5			27.4–9–61–5					1–0–3–0						2	3			164	10
v. Glamorgan (Canterbury)	16.2–2–45–5	11–1–46–1	9–1–27–1		1–0–7–0	12–2–31–3											2	1	7	158	10
7–10 September	31–7–78–2	24–2–88–0	20–1–58–1		15.1–4–46–3	29–6–63–4					10–2–39–0					4	13	2	8	389	10
v. Warwickshire (Edgbaston)	25–6–91–5			21–4–55–1	15–5–38–3	12–3–29–0				15–4–38–0	6.2–0–25–1					5	8	1	8	289	10
12–15 September	5–0–16–0			5–1–21–0	22–8–41–5	4–0–12–0				7–2–21–0	24–5–57–4					1	2		1		
Bowlers average	489.4–93– 1413–46 30.71	457.2–86– 1430–53 26.98	407.1–71– 1243–37 33.59	151–26– 477–5 95.40	582–150– 1609–74 21.74	251–46– 696–24 29.00	48–9– 213–2 106.50	3–0– 25–1 25.00	39.5–4– 109–0 –	401.5–80– 1204–29 41.51	499.5–114– 1307–35 37.34	8–0– 126–0 –	55–7– 212–7 30.28	24–4– 92–5 18.40	19–5– 53–0 –						

LANCASHIRE CCC

BATTING

BATTING	v. Kent (Old Trafford) 25–28 April		v. Middlesex (Lord's) 7–10 May		v. Leicestershire (Leicester) 14–18 May		v. Derbyshire (Blackpool) 20–22 May		v. Hampshire (Old Trafford) 23–26 May		v. Somerset (Old Trafford) 29 May–1 June		v. Oxford University (Oxford) 2–4 June		v. Gloucestershire (Old Trafford) 5–8 June		v. Glamorgan (Colwyn Bay) 12–15 June		v. Nottinghamshire (Trent Bridge) 16–18 June		v. Middlesex (Old Trafford) 19–22 June		v. Essex (Ilford) 26–29 June		M	Inns	NO	Runs	HS	Av
G.D. Mendis	12	8	17	1	31	–																			5	8	1	145	45	20.71
G. Fowler	0	66									56	–	106	15	28	39*	14	25	6	22	19	28	45	5	11	20	2	623	106	34.61
N.J. Speak	47	36	93	33	232	–	61	64	58	11	102	–			144	–	71	17	23	0	111	74*	1	35	22	36	3	1892	232	57.33
N.H. Fairbrother	24	30*	27	3	65	–							39*	6*	21	–									12	18	7	689	166*	62.63
G.D. Lloyd	132	20	2	17*	56	–	5	4*	102*	13	16	–	56*	23	6	–	1	52	2	37*	103*	34*	61	76	23	37	10	1389	132	51.44
M. Watkinson	34	7*			7	–	15	–	0	0	96	–	–	16	42	–	32	20			–	–	28	8	20	25	1	482	96	20.08
W.K. Hegg	38	–	63	–	28	–	59	–	80	1	6*	–			41	–	1	22*					9	3	18	24	7	618	80	36.35
P.A.J. DeFreitas	55*	–	69	–	29	–					0	–					72	0							11	12	1	322	72	29.27
P.J. Martin	18	30	0	–	3	–	–	–	4	2	14	–	–	–			9	24*	80	–	–	–	9*	1	22	24	6	492	133	27.33
D.K. Morrison	0	–	20	–	0	–	–	–	–	1	–	–			0	–	6*	–	30	–	–	–	1	12	14	12	1	113	30	10.27
A.A. Barnett	17	–	6*	–	2*	–	–	–	–	0*	–	–	–	9	0*	–	4	–	1*	–	–	–	6	1	22	17	10	70	17	10.00
M.A. Atherton			16	51*	17	–	18	140*	13	52	2	–	65	37*	4	25*	48	69	34	25	135	43	9	8	18	32	6	1453	199	55.88
I.D. Austin			16	–			115*	–	2*	1					1	–									8	10	2	230	115*	28.75
S.P. Titchard							29	54	47	73	7	–	21	0	6	–	17	7	25	15*	68*	–	11	74	14	24	3	668	74	31.80
R. Irani							5	–	–	8									7	–					5	6	–	68	22	11.33
J.D. Fitton													–	1											8	9	2	136	48*	19.42
J. Stanworth													–	9					21	–	–	–			5	2	–	30	21	15.00
S.D. Fletcher													–	0					23	–	–	–	22	15*	6	5	1	62	23	15.50
J.P. Crawley																									7	10	–	558	172	55.80
G. Chapple																									2	2	1	19	18	19.00
Byes	1		2				4	1	5		5			1			2	4	9	2	5	4		8						
Leg-byes	11	6	1	2	6		11	5	2	3	1		9	1	2	4	15	1	20	2	10	4	9	14						
Wides	1	2			2		1	2			1		7					1	2		1	1	1							
No-balls	7	8	11	6	7		4	3	9	6	7		11	1	3	2	3		9		4	2		1						
Total	397	213	343	113	485		327	273	322	171	313		314	119	298	70	295	242	292	103	456	190	212	261						
Wickets	10	5	10	3	10		7	2	6	10	7		3	8	10	0	10	7	10	3	3	2	10	10						
Result	D		D		W		L		L		D		D		D		D		D		D		L							
Points	7		5		24		8		6		8		–		3		7		7		5		2							

BATTING

BATTING	v. Kent (Maidstone) 3–6 July		v. Leicestershire (Southport) 14–16 July		v. Northamptonshire (Northampton) 17–20 July		v. Sussex (Hove) 21–23 July		v. Yorkshire (Leeds) 31 July–3 August		v. Surrey (Lytham) 4–6 August		v. Worcestershire (Old Trafford) 7–10 August		v. Warwickshire (Edgbaston) 18–20 August		v. Yorkshire (Old Trafford) 26–29 August		v. Sussex (Old Trafford) 7–10 September		v. Durham (Gateshead) 12–15 September		M	Inns	NO	Runs	HS	Av
G.D. Mendis															29	–					45	2*	5	8	1	145	45	20.71
G. Fowler	7*	52	62	12									16	–									11	20	2	623	106	34.61
N.J. Speak	–	16	13	39	49	5*	59	62	59	38*	95	20	71	–	52	–	42	–	18	21	20	–	22	36	3	1892	232	57.33
N.H. Fairbrother			51	7					166*	–	66*	16*	70*	–			67	–	11	20	0	–	12	18	7	689	166*	62.63
G.D. Lloyd	–	7	28	30	24	0*	96	0	56	–	2*	59	101	–	31	–	77*	–	56	2	2	–	23	37	10	1389	132	51.44
M. Watkinson	–	32	0	18	17	–			18	–	–	14	15	–	14	–	0	–	2	1	46	–	20	25	1	482	96	20.08
W.K. Hegg	–	29*	21	3	76*	–	5	6	33	–	–	20*	31*	–					0	27*	16	–	18	24	7	618	80	36.35
P.A.J. DeFreitas									0	–	–	17	–	–			44	–	0	14	22	–	11	12	1	322	72	29.27
P.J. Martin	–	11*	18	6	10	–	6	52*	4*	46	–	–	–	–	8	–	–	–	0	4	133	–	22	24	6	492	133	27.33
D.K. Morrison	–	–	14	2	27	–																	14	12	1	113	30	10.27
A.A. Barnett	–	–	5*	0*	11	–	–	0*	–	–	–	–	–	–			–	–	1*	0	7*	–	22	17	10	70	17	10.00
M.A. Atherton			86	11	15	12			14	53*					130	–	119	–	25	6	199	22*	18	32	6	1453	199	55.88
I.D. Austin					3	–			30	4					0	–					58	–	8	10	2	230	115*	28.75
S.P. Titchard	2*	71			27	5	54	0	0	32	23	–											14	24	3	668	74	31.80
R. Irani	–	9					22	17															5	6	–	68	22	11.33
J.D. Fitton			0	6			45	5			–	–	–	–	48*	–	22*	–	5	4			8	9	2	136	48*	19.42
J. Stanworth															–	–	–	–					5	2	–	30	21	15.00
S.D. Fletcher	–	–					–	2															6	5	1	62	23	15.50
J.P. Crawley					16	–	49	65			172	16	29	–	74	–	1	–	43	93			7	10	–	558	172	55.80
G. Chapple							1*	18							–	–							2	2	1	19	18	19.00
Byes		4	16	8	13		9	4			4		1		16		6		1	5	2							
Leg-byes	1	2	7	6	7		2		12	4	8	2	7		8		3		3	5	9							
Wides		1	1		2	1		1	1						4						2							
No-balls	1	8	9	2	1		1	6	6	5	6	3	8		1		3		9	5	1							
Total	11	242	280	150	298	23	349	238	399	182	376	167	349	0	415		384	0	174	207	562	24						
Wickets	0	6	10	10	10	2	8	9	8	3	3	5	5	0	8		6	0	10	10	10	0						
Result	D		L		D		D		L		W		D		W		D		L		W							
Points	4		7		6		6		5		20		4		24		4		2		24							

FIELDING FIGURES

39 – W.K. Hegg (ct 33/st 6)
21 – G.D. Lloyd
19 – M.A. Atherton
18 – N.J. Speakand P.J. Martin
10 – M. Watkinson
8 – N.H. Fairbrother, S.P. Titchard
7 – A.A. Barnett and G. Fowler
5 – J.P. Crawley and sub
4 – D.K. Morrison, R. Irani
2 – S.D. Fletcher and J. Stanworth (ct 7/st 1)
1 – J.D. Fitton and P.A.J. DeFreitas

LANCASHIRE CCC

BOWLING

	P.A.J. DeFreitas	P.J. Martin	D.K. Morrison	A.A. Barnett	M. Watkinson	I.D. Austin	M.A. Atherton	R. Irani	S.D. Fletcher	J.D. Fitton	G. Fowler	N.J. Speak	G.D. Lloyd	G. Chapple	J.P. Crawley	Byes	Leg-byes	Wides	No-balls	Total	Wkts
v. Kent (Old Trafford) 25–28 April	18–3–47–1	24–6–54–2	14–1–63–0	20–3–58–0	21–6–60–4											5	13		7	300	7
	13–2–34–1	11–1–26–2	13–3–41–3	12–4–29–0	18.5–5–47–2											9	6	1	8	192	8
v. Middlesex (Lord's) 7–10 May	35–1–125–2	29–3–92–1	19–3–70–1	29.5–2–111–2		22–6–59–1	5–1–22–0									4	10		3	493	8
v. Leicestershire (Leicester) 14–18 May	15–1–39–0	8–1–23–1	15–2–52–3	28.1–6–78–5	20–3–61–1											1	4		2	258	10
	13–1–32–2	7–2–23–1	10–1–39–3	11–1–74–3	1.4–0–5–1											8	1	1	4	182	10
v. Derbyshire (Blackpool) 20–22 May		22–5–40–2	21–3–59–1	21.3–6–83–1	19–1–75–3	10–3–30–2										8	5		3	300	9
		10–2–32–0	11–1–53–1	19–1–93–3	17.1–2–70–1	10–2–49–0										1	3	1	2	301	5
v. Hampshire (Old Trafford) 23–26 May		23–6–40–2	17–2–63–0	25–2–108–1	19–3–66–1	11–3–41–1		6–0–21–0								4	6		7	349	5
		8–5–8–0	7–1–30–0	26–4–96–2	24–1–90–1		17–0–74–1									11	7		1	316	4
v. Somerset (Old Trafford) 29 May–1 June	25.2–6–70–2	12.4–1–45–2	25–2–111–2	17.5–6–62–2	17–3–69–1											3	16	4	6	376	9
v. Oxford University (Oxford) 2–4 June		7.5–1–14–1		15.1–4–38–3	12–6–16–5				11–3–32–1								4	1		104	10
				8–1–35–0	18.4–6–44–2		8–5–6–1		7–4–14–1	5–1–12–0							5			116	4
v. Gloucestershire (Old Trafford) 5–8 June			0.3–0–1–0		3.3–0–18–1	3–1–8–0											2		2	29	1
			6–2–7–0	6–0–27–0	17–1–57–1	11–1–28–0	6–0–26–0									1	2		2	148	1
v. Glamorgan (Colwyn Bay) 12–15 June	19–2–59–3	15–3–45–1	17.2–5–55–4	22–1–80–1	17–3–42–1		4–3–4–0									3	8		6	296	10
	11–4–31–0	4.3–1–16–0	10–1–32–0	20–1–90–0	2–1–5–0		16–0–109–2									7	8		4	298	2
v. Nottinghamshire (Trent Bridge) 16–18 June		22–6–43–3	23.5–6–65–3	2–1–4–0				7–1–21–2	17–6–53–2								13	3		199	10
		24–6–72–2	29–5–84–1	17–1–81–0			5.1–0–35–0	9–4–31–0	13–2–69–0							14	6	1	9	392	5
v. Middlesex (Old Trafford) 19–22 June		20–7–67–3	15–2–43–0	12–1–58–0	26–5–85–0		3–0–14–0		8–0–33–0								6	1	10	306	3
		18–7–45–4	14–1–65–2	7–0–38–0	25–2–135–2				2–0–13–1							5	8			309	9
v. Essex (Ilford) 26–29 June		17–3–61–1	10–0–83–0	26–2–111–0	21.1–2–114–1		10–0–53–0		13–3–66–0							14	8		1	510	2
v. Kent (Maidstone) 3–6 July		21.2–9–67–4	18–4–48–6		14–2–52–0				8–1–23–0							1	2	1		193	10
											5–0–60–1	2–0–30–0	2–0–23–0							113	1
v. Leicestershire (Southport) 14–16 July		18–9–43–0	12–0–70–4	7–0–38–0	26–7–82–6					4–1–12–0						4	8	2	3	257	10
		9–2–22–1	11–6–20–1	21–4–57–3	17.1–4–55–3					9–2–16–2							11	2		181	10
v. Northamptonshire (Northampton) 17–20 July		16–3–38–0	12–1–44–1	24.5–2–82–5	36–6–136–2	10–1–36–0										2	7	2	6	345	8
		15–1–78–0	5–0–11–0	10–0–66–1	12–1–40–1	6–0–24–0											4			223	2
v. Sussex (Hove) 21–23 July		20–8–63–0		11–2–31–0				6–0–39–0	13–3–57–1	28.1–6–81–4				12–1–55–0		9	7		2	342	5
		5–0–15–0		12–2–33–1				5–0–25–1	9–1–49–0	7–1–18–0		4–0–36–0	6–0–22–0	4–1–7–0	10–0–90–1	7		2	302	3	
v. Yorkshire (Leeds) 31 July–3 August	14–2–47–0	13.5–3–41–0		25–5–51–2	31–7–116–1	9–0–34–0											11	1	2	300	3
	11–0–48–2	10–3–30–0		14–0–58–1	13–0–79–2	9.4–0–54–1										4	10	2	2	283	6
v. Surrey (Lytham) 4–6 August	8–1–20–0	7–1–27–0		22–1–86–1	17–5–40–0					27–5–67–1						4	9	1		253	2
	10–2–33–1	9–3–13–1		22–4–67–2	13.5–2–60–4					9–0–27–2						1	3		1	204	10
v. Worcestershire (Old Trafford) 7–10 August																				0	0
	17–5–40–2	11–4–23–0		14.5–3–40–2	28–11–54–2					12–2–30–2						4	6	3		197	8
v. Warwickshire (Edgbaston) 26–29 August		13–2–51–0			19–6–41–4	10.1–4–33–2				23–9–41–1				14–7–26–2		5	6			203	9A
		5–2–16–0			34.5–13–62–6	16–5–30–1				11–3–38–0				18–8–40–3		1			1	187	10
v. Yorkshire (Old Trafford) 26–29 August																				0	0
	5–0–26–0	9–2–26–1		4–3–6–1	13–4–29–1					11–4–31–0							3			121	3
v. Sussex (Old Trafford) 7–10 September	24–8–73–2	22–2–80–1		43.5–7–148–4	47–12–154–1					25–4–92–1						3	13		1	563	10
v. Durham (Gateshead) 12–15 September	26–7–94–3	19–5–62–0		11–1–30–0	24.1–7–63–5	22–11–52–1										1	10		4	312	10
	26.3–6–94–6	16–4–49–1		7–3–18–0	14–3–56–0	15–4–44–3										7	3		4	271	10
Bowlers average	290.5–51– 912–27 33.77	520.1–129– 1490–37 40.27	335.4–52– 1209–36 33.58	595–84– 2165–46 47.06	680–140– 2178–66 33.00	164.5–41– 522–12 43.50	74.1–9– 343–4 85.75	33–5– 137–3 45.66	101–23– 409–6 68.16	171.1–38– 465–13 35.76	5–0– 60–1 60.00	6–0– 66–0 –	8–0– 45–0 –	48–17– 128–5 26.60	10–0– 90–1 90.00						

A P.A. Smith absent ill

LEICESTERSHIRE CCC

BATTING

BATTING	v. Cambridge University (Cambridge) 14–16 April	v. Durham (Durham) 25–29 April	v. Essex (Chelmsford) 7–11 May	v. Lancashire (Leicester) 14–18 May	v. Middlesex (Leicester) 19–22 May	v. Pakistanis (Leicester) 23–25 May	v. Glamorgan (Swansea) 29 May–1 June	v. Northamptonshire (Northampton) 2–4 June	v. Middlesex (Lord's) 5–8 June	v. Sussex (Leicester) 12–15 June	v. Hampshire (Leicester) 16–18 June	v. Worcestershire (Leicester) 30 June–2 July	M	Inns	NO	Runs	HS	Av
T.J. Boon	51 –	110 6	26 82	139 5	0 0	13 1	69 –	4 14	14 12	24* –	3 5	– 97	24	41	3	1448	139	38.10
N.E. Briers	120 –	10 43	51 99	9 11	21 53	37 123	7 –	0 0	8 11	18 14*	63 10	– 122*	24	42	6	1372	123	38.11
J.J. Whitaker	73* –	2 35	33* –			35 21	0 –	18 27	1 0	74 –	21 27	– 8*	22	34	3	830	74	26.77
L. Potter	26* –	31 38*	70 27	10 2	4 8	0 11	65 –	19 26		0 –	96 25	– –	23	36	4	834	96	36.06
B.F. Smith	– –	100* –						0 1	24 67*	56 –	16 0	– –	15	20	3	441	100*	25.94
P.N. Hepworth	– –	8 –	4 13	28 2	29 5	38 4	2 –		17* 0				10	15	1	173	38	12.35
V.J. Wells	– –	42 9*	0 15	6 15	11 50*		34* –	14 6	9* 6*	28 –		– –	17	23	6	526	56	30.24
P. Whitticase	– –	11 –	0 14*	18* 2	6 0		9* –	2 0	– –				8	10	3	62	18*	8.85
A.D. Mullally	– –	1 –	0 –	8 10*	13* 4	5 1		3 10	– –	0 –	– –		19	23	6	118	21	6.94
G.J. Parsons	– –	10 –									20* –	– –	14	14	2	142	35	11.83
D.J. Millns	– –	6 –	22* 17*	0 21	1 8	0 1	– –	2* 5*	– –	1 –	– –	– –	19	19	9	144	33*	14.40
J.D.R. Benson			1 21	22 22	122 58	45 7	49 –	7 0	46 39	17 –	12 47*	– –	18	28	1	623	122	23.07
W.K.M. Benjamin			0 9	11 72	2 16		– –	3 10	– –	4* –	71 –	– –	20	25	3	453	72	20.59
M.I. Gidley				0 6	16 6								5	10	2	143	39	17.87
A. Roseberry						14 0							1	2	–	14	14	7.00
P.A. Nixon						49* 29				20 9*	107* 8*	– –	16	25	7	529	107*	29.38
R.P. Gofton						0 42*	– –						5	8	1	142	75	20.28
C.J. Hawkes													3	4	1	60	18	20.00
P.E. Robinson													1	2	–	19	19	9.50
Byes		2	4 2	1 8	4 1	11 9		9			5 4							
Leg-byes	6	8 5	8 13	4 1	7 3	3 17	8	2 3	1	4 1	27 11	3						
Wides		4		1	2 1	4	3		1									
No-balls	3	3	4	2 4	10 11	2 3		3 1	8 5	5	9 3	4						
Total	279 0	342 142	223 312	258 182	248 224	256 269	246	77 112	128 141	251 24	450 140	0 234						
Wickets	2 0	10 3	9† 7	10 10	10 10	10 10	6	10 10	5 5	9† 0	7 5	0 1						
Result	W	W	D	L	L	L	D	L	D	W	D	W						
Points	–	23	3	4	5	–	2	4	4	23	5	20						

BATTING	v. Yorkshire (Sheffield) 3–6 July	v. Lancashire (Southport) 14–16 July	v. Somerset (Leicester) 17–20 July	v. Durham (Leicester) 21–23 July	v. Essex (Leicester) 24–27 July	v. Warwickshire (Edgbaston) 31 July–3 August	v. Derbyshire (Ilkeston) 4–6 August	v. Surrey (The Oval) 14–17 August	v. Kent (Leicester) 18–20 August	v. Nottinghamshire (Leicester) 21–24 August	v. Gloucestershire (Bristol) 31 August–3 September	v. Northamptonshire (Leicester) 12–15 September	M	Inns	NOs	Runs	HS	Av
T.J. Boon	28 –	76 24	24 –	33 5*	58 52	13 8	18 45	48 32	25 72	13 7	– 14*	81 97	24	41	3	1448	139	38.10
N.E. Briers	6 –	8 46	1 –	93 1*	0 61	0 36	73* 27	6 5	2 19	70 66*	– 10*	12 0	24	42	6	1372	123	38.11
J.J. Whitaker	14 –	5 25	36 –	40 –	6 40	36 0	26 6	46 48	27 30	17 11	– –	13 29	22	34	3	830	74	26.77
L. Potter	5 –	21 24	17 –	8 –	0 27*	56 21	0 15	24 46*	0 15	7 30	– –	14 46	23	36	4	834	96	36.06
B.f. Smith	8 –	20 1	0 –	3 –	2 10	0 1		16 –				86 30*	15	20	3	441	100*	25.94
P.N. Hepworth							1 20	2 –					10	15	1	173	38	12.35
V.J. Wells	29* –	51 5	42 –	3 –	38 13			56 44			– –		17	23	6	526	56	30.24
P. Whitticase													8	10	3	672	18*	8.85
A.D. Mullally				2 –	14 2	0 21	2 0*	3* –	4 0*	1* –	– –	14 –	19	23	6	118	21	6.94
G.J. Parsons	– –	19 5	1 –			1* 7	5 12	1 –	9 4	35 –		13 –	14	14	2	142	35	11.83
D.J. Millns	– –	0 9*	0* –	8* –	33* 1						– –	9* –	19	19	9	144	33*	14.40
J.D.R. Benson	0 –			33 –	0 2	4 1	1 42			9 9	– –	0 7	18	28	1	623	122	213.07
W.K.M. Benjamin	– –	11 14	53 –	22 –	0 3	11* 8	4 6		39* 0	6 7	– –	71 –	20	25	3	453	72	20.59
M.I. Gidley						13 32*			25 4	39 2*			5	10	2	143	39	17.87
A. Roseberry													1	2	–	14	14	7.00
P.A. Nixon	31* –	12 3	68 –	0 –	28 5	22 0	5 28	5 3*	21 0	28 0	– –	30 18*	16	25	7	529	107*	29.38
R.P. Gofton							7 11	1 75	1 5				5	8	1	142	75	20.28
C.J. Hawkes		17* 12	18 –							13 –			3	4	1	60	18	20.00
P.E. Robinson									0 19				1	2	–	19	19	9.50
Byes		4	1			5		1	5 4			2						
Leg-byes	6	8 11	5	9	5 11	7 4	10 8	2 6	14 6	10 1		3 9						
Wides		2 2		2	7	1	2 1					1						
No-balls	5	3	4		2 3	1	6 2	6 7	9 5	4 1		6 1						
Total	132	257 181	270	256 6	193 230	169 140	160 223	216 267	181 183	252 134	0 24	352 240						
Wickets	6	10 10	10	10 0	10 10	9 10	10 10	10 5	10 10	10 6	0 0	10 5						
Result	D	W	D	W	W	L	L	W	L	D	D	L						
Points	0	23	6	23	21	1	5	22	1	7	3	6						

FIELDING FIGURES

45 – P.A. Nixon (ct 40/st 5)
30 – J.D.R. Benson
20 – P. Whitticase (ct 19/st 1)
15 – T.J. Boon and W.K.M. Benjamin
12 – J.J. Whitaker, D.J. Millns and N.E. Briers
10 – L. Potter
9 – B.F. Smith
7 – subs
6 – G.J. Parsons
5 – P.N. Hepworth
4 – A.D. Mullally
2 – R.P. Gofton, V.J. Wells and M.I. Gidley
1 – C.J. Hawkes
† J.J. Whitaker retired hurt
‡ T.J. Boon retired hurt

LEICESTERSHIRE CCC

BOWLING

	D.J. Millns	A.D. Mullally	G.J. Parsons	V.J. Wells	P.N. Hepworth	L. Potter	W.K.M. Benjamin	J.D.R. Benson	M.I. Gidley	T.J. Boon	R.P. Gofton	J.J. Whitaker	C.J. Hawkes	Byes	Leg-byes	Wides	No-balls	Total	Wkts
v. Cambridge University (Cambridge) 14–16 April																	0	0	
	10–4–27–3	8–3–11–1	8–4–12–3	8–3–13–0	12–5–52–1	7–1–21–2								1	9		1	146	10
v. Durham (Durham) 25–29 April	17–8–33–2	21.1–10–29–3	14–1–31–0	17–5–42–3		13–3–23–2									6	1	2	164	10
	21.3–4–69–5	24–9–53–1	12–3–28–0	29–13–57–3	8–0–45–0	26–10–50–1								2	14		1	318	10
v. Essex (Chelmsford) 7–11 May	13–2–61–1	13–2–54–1		27–7–72–1	13–3–66–0	19–3–70–0	17–1–66–0	9–1–21–1							14		4	424	4
v. Lancashire (Leicester) 14–18 May	28–7–123–4	26–3–86–1		10–4–34–1	8–0–29–2	11–1–47–0	23.3–4–76–2	4–0–14–0	19–6–70–0						6	2	7	485	10
v. Middlesex (Leicester) 19–22 May	35–5–123–2	25–3–55–0		24–10–38–2	24–5–85–1	19.5–4–52–3	30–5–74–2	1–0–10–0	1–0–3–0					8	19	1	5	467	10
					1.4–1–2–0					1–0–4–0								6	0
v. Pakistanis (Leicester) 23–25 May	17.2–0–66–2	23.2–4–80–2			17–2–55–1	9–1–33–0		8.4–2–33–2			27–4–107–1			6	13	2		393	8
	7–0–32–1	11–3–29–1			5–0–31–0						8.4–1–38–0				3			133	2
v. Glamorgan (Swansea) 29 May–1 June																			Ab.
v. Northamptonshire (Northampton) 2–4 June	13–4–25–1	7–1–24–2		13.1–3–26–4			20–8–33–3							4	5	2		117	10
	22–8–47–1	21.2–6–33–3		22–5–68–4			21–4–73–2							4	13		1	238	10
v. Middlesex (Lord's) 5–8 June	9–3–20–2	9–4–25–1		11.1–3–27–4			12–5–29–3								1			102	10
	13.3–2–77–1	14–3–46–0		12–4–33–1	12–0–62–0		8–3–23–0			2–0–18–0				3	3	1		265	2
v. Sussex (Leicester) 12–15 June	18–8–35–4	18–6–50–3		18–7–53–2			8–1–30–1							1	2	1		171	10
	13.4–7–19–3	13–4–22–1				5–0–9–2	16–3–50–3								3		1	103	10
v. Hampshire (Leicester) 16–18 June	14–4–38–0	19–3–59–1	14–4–39–0			35–11–85–1	20–6–47–1							11	3	1	2	282	3
	8–1–32–0	15–4–49–1	18–3–79–5			11–1–56–0	16–2–63–2							5	10			294	9
v. Worcestershire (Leicester) 30 June–2 July	30–6–87–6		17–6–15–0	10–6–14–0		9–4–17–2	20–5–50–1			4–0–17–0		3–0–23–0			9		8	232	9
																		0	0
v. Yorkshire (Sheffield) 3–6 July	6–1–23–1		5–1–10–0	6–3–7–1		8–3–19–0	6–3–13–0	8–1–24–2		10–1–70–0		2.3–0–30–0		5	6	1	4	207	5
v. Lancashire (Southport) 14–16 July	18–6–65–4		21–8–34–4	14–2–41–0		12–4–27–2	21–3–67–0						10–3–24–0	15	7	1	9	280	10
	7–0–46–2		9.5–4–25–4			7–2–18–0	6–0–29–0						10–3–18–4	8	6		2	150	10
v. Somerset (Leicester) 17–20 July	17.3–2–64–5		18–7–46–0	22–6–71–2		7–2–31–1	22–3–83–2						8–2–28–0		4			327	10
	9–3–15–1		4–0–8–1				9–1–22–1			3–0–32–2		2.2–0–29–1	1–0–1–0	1				108	6
v. Durham (Leicester) 21–23 July	16.1–2–41–5	14–3–39–4		5–1–10–0			13–5–50–1								5		2	145	10
	18.1–5–46–5	5–2–11–0		5–1–15–0			18–5–34–4								10		3	116	9A
v. Essex (Leicester) 24–27 July	7–1–23–3	5–3–2–2		5.4–2–16–2			6–2–32–3								2		1	75	10
	26–6–67–5	21.1–3–59–1		21–4–55–3		10–4–33–0	23–6–60–1							4	2	2	5	280	10
v. Warwickshire (Edgbaston) 31 July–3 August		34–8–119–5	27–5–110–2			24–3–85–0	15–5–39–0	3–0–13–0	17–3–56–0					6	5			433	7
v. Derbyshire (Ilkeston) 4–6 August		17–3–50–0	16–2–47–0			18–6–32–2	22.3–5–55–4				22–5–81–4			1	2	1	4	268	10
		15–3–54–1	13–2–41–1			4–0–31–0	11–1–60–0				13–3–63–1			1	4			254	3
v. Surrey (The Oval) 14–17 August		22–5–56–4	26.3–5–70–6	6–1–14–0	2–0–12–0	13–3–38–0					4–1–19–0			2	7	1	4	218	10
		8–4–18–1	21–4–93–3			18.3–2–73–4				3–3–0–2					9			193	10
v. Kent (Leicester) 18–20 August		33–6–121–0	23–4–84–1			10–1–39–0	27–2–125–2		18–2–68–1	2–0–13–0	7–1–40–0			7	5	5	4	502	4
v. Nottinghamshire (Leicester) 21–24 August		14.2–2–42–2	22–7–50–4				25–5–66–4								10		5	168	10
		14–2–51–0	11–5–20–0			9–0–23–0	20–3–54–2		25–9–51–1				13–3–51–1	4	7	2		261	4
v. Gloucestershire (Bristol) 31 August–3 September	20–5–80–1	12–2–37–0	11–6–13–3	15–3–45–0		12–3–28–1	12–2–35–2	10–2–27–0		4–0–21–0		0.1–0–4–0		3	9	3	2	302	7
																		0	0
v. Northamptonshire (Leicester) 12–15 September	21–2–90–3	24–5–75–0	21–10–54–1			22–5–50–2	8–4–19–1							6	9	3	1	303	7
	13–1–52–1	12–6–46–0	11–1–46–1			20.5–3–85–2	13–0–41–0							10	10	1	2	290	4
Bowlers average	468.5–107–1526–74 20.62	518.2–125–1485–42 35.35	343.2–92–955–39 24.48	301–93–751–33 22.75	102.4–16–439–5 87.80	360.1–80–1075–27 39.81	489–102–1498–47 31.87	43.4–6–142–5 28.40	80–20–248–2 124.00	29–4–175–4 43.75	81.4–15–348–6 58.00	8–0–86–1 86.00	42–11–122–5 24.40						

A D.A. Graveney retired hurt

MIDDLESEX CCC

BATTING	v. Cambridge University (Cambridge) 17–20 April		v. Glamorgan (Lord's) 25–29 April		v. Lancashire (Lord's) 7–10 May		v. Oxford University (Oxford) 12–14 May		v. Leicestershire (Leicester) 19–22 May		v. Surrey (Lord's) 23–26 May		v. Pakistanis (Lord's) 30 May–1 June		v. Nottinghamshire (Trent Bridge) 2–4 June		v. Leicestershire (Lord's) 5–8 June		v. Warwickshire (Coventry) 16–18 June		v. Lancashire (Old Trafford) 19–22 June		v. Somerset (Lord's) 26–29 June		v. Essex (Ilford) 30 June–2 July		M	Inns	NO	Runs	HS	Av
J.D. Carr	36	16	10	31	3	–	12	75*	12	–	52	–	21	–	47*	–	14	28*	7	–	7*	80	33*	13	102	–	25	39	7	1228	114	38.37
M.A. Roseberry	101	–	6	86	4	–	108*	–	51	–	63	–	111*	–	148	–	0	102	7	26	32	23	85	67	12	70*	25	41	5	2044	173	56.77
M.R. Ramprakash	49	48	30	6*	108	–					233	–	17	–					0	33*	69	63	68	18	33	4	16	27	2	1156	233	46.24
K.R. Brown	34*	53*	17	–	37	–	–	36	21	–	0	–	2	–	–	–	0	34*	0	–	38*	56	13	2	21	5*	25	37	7	776	106	25.86
P.N. Weekes	7*	5*	2	–			95	–	24	–	89*	–	1	–	–	–	0	–	39	–	–	3					17	21	7	589	95	38.50
D.W. Headley	–	–	17	–	40*	–	2	–	91	–	–	–	0	–	–	–	15	–			–	0	–	28*	10	–	17	14	3	270	91	24.54
P. Farbrace	–	–					51*	–																			2	1	1	51	51*	–
J.E. Emburey	–	–	57	–	78	–			102	–	16	–			–	–	7	–	2	–	–	26	7*	4*	15	–	23	27	6	554	102	26.38
N.G. Cowans	–	–																									1					–
J.M.S. Whittington	–	–																									1					–
S.A. Sylvester	–	–	0*	–	–	–							–	–													4	1	1	0	0*	–
M.W. Gatting			170	48*	103	–	–	–	86	–	0	–	20	–	65*	–	45	–	117	163*	126*	27	90	–	31	69	24	36	6	2000	170	66.66
N.F. Williams			0	–	32	–			14	–	–	–			–	–	1	–	2	–			–	17			17	17	3	186	46*	13.28
P.C.R. Tufnell			9	–	9*	–	–	–															–	–	3*	–	15	13	7	55	12	9.16
D.L. Haynes					62	–			2	2*	4	–			114	–	7	94	67	72	17	16	54	84	16	34	20	35	2	1513	177	45.84
J.C. Pooley							10	27*																			3	6	2	186	69	46.50
A.R.C. Fraser							3	–	23	–			27	–	–	–	9*	–	33	–	–	2*			1	–	18	20	7	218	33	16.76
C.W. Taylor							–	–	8*	4*	–	–	11*	–			3	–	0*	–	–	0*	–	–	6	–	18	14	7	75	14	10.71
R.J. Sims													3	–													1	1	–	3	3	3.00
P.H. Edmonds															–	–											1					–
R.L. Johnson																											1	1	–	1	1	1.00
Aftab Habib																											1	2	1	19	12	19.00
Byes	1				4				8		1		2		4			3	5			5			6							
Leg-byes	9		13	2	10		3	2	19		6				15		1	3	11	4	6	8	4		6	2						
Wides	1	1	1				2	1	1		1				1			1	10	1	1											
No-balls			9	6	3		4	2	5		21		7		7				4	1	10		1	1	11	1						
Total	238	123	341	179	493		290	143	467	6	486		222		401		102	265	304	299	306	309	355	234	273	185						
Wickets	3	2	10	2	8		5	1	10	0	7		8		2		10	2	10	2	3	9	5	6	10	3						
Result	D		D		D		L		W		D		D		D		D		W		D		D		L							
Points	–		5		7		–		23		8		–		8		2		21		5		7		6							

BATTING	v. Northamptonshire (Uxbridge) 14–16 July		v. Worcestershire (Uxbridge) 17–20 July		v. Derbyshire (Derby) 21–23 July		v. Durham (Lord's) 24–27 July		v. Kent (Canterbury) 4–6 August		v. Gloucestershire (Lord's) 7–10 August		v. Yorkshire (Uxbridge) 14–17 August		v. Hampshire (Bournemouth) 18–20 August		v. Sussex (Hove) 21–24 August		v. Northamptonshire (Northampton) 26–29 August		v. Warwickshire (Lord's) 8–11 September		v. Surrey (The Oval) 12–15 September		M	Inns	NO	Runs	HS	Av
J.D. Carr	0	72	64	9	9	–	1	–	42	15	15	66	36	1*	23	77*	51	–	2	0	0	32	114	–	25	39	7	1228	114	38.37
M.A. Roseberry	4	0	43	118	100*	–	173	81	27	17	1	1	11	18	26	52	32	32*	11	9	30	36	120	–	25	41	5	2044	173	56.77
M.R. Ramprakash	54	4	17	8									16	94			27	–	20	1	19	0	117	–	16	27	2	1156	233	46.24
K.R. Brown	0	39	3	50	–	–	17	18*	1	6	8	28	6	–	6	14	28	25*	17	2	25	106	8	–	25	37	7	776	106	25.86
P.N. Weekes					22*	–	5	–	46	3	36	4*	64*	48*	9	26							11	–	17	21	7	589	95	38.50
D.W. Headley	–	2							31	–	13*	–	–	–					1	20					17	14	3	270	91	24.54
P. Farbrace																									2	1	1	51	51*	–
J.E. Emburey	5*	50*	3	20	–	–	3	–	41	2*	29	–	9*	–	1	14	8	–	3	5	21	24	2	–	23	27	6	554	102	26.38
N.G. Cowans																									1					–
J.M.S. Whittington																									1					–
S.A. Sylvester																									4	1	1	0	0*	–
M.W. Gatting	24	18	0	66	–	–	90	37	26	102*	86	22	15	48	2	93	73	–	0	1	19	71	22	25*	24	36	6	2000	170	66.66
N.f. Williams			46*	3	–	–	0	–			11*	–	–	–	0	2	17*	–	10	19	1	11			17	17	3	186	46*	13.28
P.C.R. Tufnell	–	–	1	2	–	–	11*	–					–	–	12	0*	–	–	1	0*	0*	0	7*	–	15	13	7	55	12	9.16
D.L. Haynes	127*	61	0	1	70	–	26	18	32	68	18	22	83	6	12	44	177	–	19	16	40	28			20	35	2	1513	177	45.84
J.C. Pooley									69	3	21	56*													3	6	2	186	69	46.50
A.R.C. Fraser	–	1*	3	19*	–	–	4	–	1*	–					5	1	21*	–	1*	30	28	2	4	–	18	20	7	218	33	16.76
C.W. Taylor	–	–	13	8	–	–	14	–	–	–	–	–			4*	0	–	–			3	1*			18	14	7	75	14	10.71
R.J. Sims																									1	1	–	3	3	3.00
P.H. Edmonds																									1					–
R.L. Johnson																							1	–	1	1	–	1	1	1.00
Aftab Habib																							12	7*	1	2	1	19	12	19.00
Byes		4	1	4	4		7				3		4	10		3	1	5	4		3	4								
Leg-byes	4	2	2	9	4		15	5	8	11	4	13	1	8	4	3	10	1	3	2	9	9	8							
Wides			1						1	1	2	1	1		6	5					1	1								
No-balls	2		5	4	7				6	1	4		4	1	5	12			3		2	3	15							
Total	220	253	202	321	216		366	159	331	229	251	213	250	234	115	346	445	63	95	105	201	328	441	32						
Wickets	5	7	10	10	2		10	3	9	6	8	5	6	4	10	9	7	0	10	10	10	10	10	0						

FIELDING FIGURES

50 – K.R. Brown (ct 39/st 11)
41 – J.D. Carr
21 – J.E. Emburey
16 – M.W. Gatting
15 – P.N. Weekes
14 – M.A. Roseberry
8 – N.F. Williams
7 – M.R. Ramprakash and D.L. Haynes
5 – P. Farbrace and D.W. Headley
4 – C.W. Taylor
3 – A.R.C. Fraser
2 – P.C.R. Tufnell
1 – R.L. Johnson and sub

MIDDLESEX CCC

BOWLING

	N.G. Cowans	D.W. Headley	J.E. Emburey	S.A. Sylvester	J.M.S. Whittington	P.N. Weekes	M.A. Roseberry	N.F. Williams	P.C.R. Tufnell	C.W. Taylor	A.R.C. Fraser	J.D. Carr	D.L. Haynes	M.W. Gatting	P.H. Edmonds	M.R. Ramprakash	Byes	Leg-byes	Wides	No-balls	Total	Wkts
v. Cambridge University	7–3–9–0	9–0–50–0	4–2–5–1	8–4–20–0	7–2–14–0												8	3		2	109	1
(Cambridge) 17–20 April		18–5–32–1	2–2–0–0	19–5–34–2	12–0–30–0	11–3–12–0	2–2–0–0											5	1	6	113	3
v. Glamorgan (Lord's)		7–1–30–1	28–11–55–1	12–1–45–0		8–3–19–0		15.4–6–40–0	33–15–47–0								11	8		5	255	3
25–29 April		9–1–32–0	23.3–5–77–4	4–0–13–0				9–0–36–0	19–2–70–1								1	8		4	237	6
v. Lancashire (Lord's)		29.3–6–84–3	29–10–69–1	15–3–30–0				31–5–100–3	23–7–57–2								2	1		11	343	10
7–10 May		8–0–21–1	8–1–21–0	11–3–35–2				5.1–1–12–0	13–7–22–0									2		6	113	3
v. Oxvord University (Oxford)		18–1–65–1				24–4–52–1			28–11–42–1	15–6–29–1	16–8–16–3	6–1–9–1					3	6	1	15	222	8
12–14 May		12.3–1–38–3				3–0–24–0			17–1–64–0	7–2–22–1	18–6–56–1						4	4	2	4	212	5
v. Leicestershire (Leicester)		15–4–41–1	32.3–11–44–4			10–4–22–0		22–3–53–3		16–2–60–2	5–2–17–0						4	7	2	10	248	10
19–22 May		9–0–31–3	32.3–17–45–4			3–0–26–0		19–2–60–1		13–4–37–2	14–6–20–0		1–0–1–0				1	3	1	11	224	10
v. Surrey (Lord's)		15–4–46–3	28–11–50–2			16–3–35–1		14.3–4–31–4		12–7–19–0							2	5		8	188	10
23–26 May		22–12–31–2	42–21–47–1			14–7–23–0		20–2–72–2		18–5–50–4								4		7	227	9
v. Pakistanis (Lord's)		23–5–105–0		15–4–45–0		29–8–79–1	1–1–0–0			8–0–37–1	23–7–39–1	6–3–15–1						7		12	327	4
30 May–1 June											3.2–0–4–0			3–3–0–0				1			5	0
v. Nottinghamshire		6–0–19–0	25–4–55–4					17.2–3–59–2			10–3–29–0				28–10–48–4			1		8	211	10
(Trent Bridge) 2–4 June		5–2–8–0	8–3–12–0			4–2–5–0		4–0–11–0			6–2–15–0							2		3	53	0
v. Leicestershire (Lord's)		5–1–11–0	1–0–1–0					17–4–45–4		7–1–33–1	9–1–37–0							1		8	128	5
5–8 June		6–1–28–0	10–3–27–2					12–1–29–2		9–3–37–1	4–0–20–0								1	5	141	5
v. Warwickshire (Coventry)			13–6–29–1					16–1–65–0		20.5–3–72–1	16–7–52–0	12–7–17–1					4	12		4	251	3
16–18 June			11–3–23–5					6–1–24–0		12.3–1–50–4	7–0–25–0							4	2	1	126	10
v. Lancashire (Old Trafford)		19–1–72–1	29–4–77–0			29–2–95–1				25–3–98–1	28–4–73–0			3–0–26–0			5	10	1	4	456	3
19–22 June		1–1–0–0	7–2–25–1			5–0–16–1	7–0–70–0			7–0–23–0	5–1–14–0					7–0–34–0	4	4	1	2	190	2
v. Somerset (Lord's)		14–3–63–0	36–14–76–3					13–3–34–0	24.4–3–63–3	11–5–27–1								7	1	5	270	7
26–29 June		3–0–18–0	20–9–35–1				1–0–1–0	7–3–11–1	24–9–37–0	16–5–42–3										1	144	5
v. Essex (Ilford)		7–1–33–0	24–13–31–2						31.4–13–59–2	7–1–31–1	13–1–46–2							4		2	204	8
30 June–2 July			10–0–68–0						15–0–92–1	12–0–54–1	5–0–34–0						4	3			255	2
v. Northamptonshire (Uxbridge)		20–4–70–0	25–5–70–3						25.1–4–82–3	12–0–69–1	18–1–72–1							6		11	369	10
14–16 July			9.3–1–48–3						8–1–42–0	8–4–15–0	10–0–52–1						4	2		5	163	5
v. Worcestershire (Uxbridge)			34.3–5–98–3					14–2–43–1	33–11–70–3	15–2–75–2	12–4–35–0					3–1–7–0		18		19	346	10
17–20 July			11.5–4–17–2					2–0–10–0	11–4–24–4	7–2–25–1	6–0–28–1						4	10		3	118	8
v. Derbyshire (Derby)			21–5–53–1			2–1–4–0		19–1–71–2	15–4–39–0	17–1–72–0	19–4–68–0	4–3–4–0		3–0–12–0			1	10		16	334	3
21–23 July						7–2–14–0	2–2–0–0	7–5–9–0		12–4–23–0	11–4–13–1		1.4–0–4–1					3		2	66	2
v. Durham (Lord's)			44.2–12–94–4			2–0–5–0		8–1–16–0	34–5–83–5	6–4–3–0	10–1–20–1						2	9	1	5	232	10
24–27 July			12.3–2–43–5					5–0–20–0	14–1–26–3	7–2–16–2	4–3–5–0						2	6		9	118	10
v. Kent (Canterbury)		26–8–82–3	16–1–68–3							22–1–91–1	24–3–89–2	11–3–37–1						2		8	369	10
4–6 August		9–1–37–2	23–2–87–3			8–0–33–1				7–1–26–0	13–1–54–1						3	2	2	4	242	7
v. Gloucestershire (Lord's)		22–5–58–2	28–9–53–0			25–8–61–3		26–6–64–4		14–3–46–0		7–1–11–0					7	22	5	6	322	9
7–10 August		4–0–24–0	7–6–1–0					22.5–7–75–8		11–2–40–2								1	2	9	141	10
v. Yorkshire (Uxbridge)		18–3–52–3	27–5–83–2			4–1–11–1		17–6–46–0	37–8–92–4									2		16	286	10
14–17 August		5–1–14–0	19–6–63–2			5–0–20–0		6–1–10–0	23.5–6–71–2								8	8		5	194	4
v. Hampshire (Bournemouth)			40–11–105–5			2–0–8–0		20.2–3–85–2	23–4–59–0	12–2–47–1	20–3–76–1							6	3	19	386	9
18–20 August																						
v. Sussex (Hove)			20.4–4–57–2					16–6–31–1	16–3–30–0	12–2–46–0	6–0–17–0							6	1	5	187	3
21–24 August			4–3–2–0					13–4–25–1	1–0–4–0	6–0–28–0	6–3–17–0							3		8	79	1
v. Northamptonshire (Northampton)		20–2–63–1	10–2–26–1					18.1–2–49–5			26–4–59–3							6	1	16	203	10
26–29 August																						
v. Warwickshire (Lord's)			28–4–78–3					14–3–47–2	38–7–130–1	22–4–64–0	32.2–5–96–3	7–0–31–1					8	22	2	23	476	10
8–11 September			6–1–22–0						6–0–16–2	3–0–18–0	2–2–0–0							1	1	1	57	2
v. Surrey (The Oval)			14–3–25–0			6–0–26–1			14–4–21–0		10–1–40–1						2	2		3	141	3A
12–15 September			30–6–104–2			5–3–5–1			34–4–130–5		15–3–35–0						1	4	1	3	325	9
Bowlers average	7–3– 9–0 –	385–74– 1258–31 40.58	854.5–249– 2069–81 25.54	84–20– 222–4 55.50	19–2– 44–0 –	222–51– 595–12 49.58	13–5– 71–0 –	437–86– 1283–48 26.72	561.2–134– 1472–42 35.04	409.2–82– 1425–35 40.71	426.4–90– 1273–23 55.34	53–18– 124–5 24.80	2.4–0– 5–1 5.00	9–3– 38–0 –	28–10– 48–4 12.00	10–1– 41–0 –						

A R.L. Johnson 6–2–25–1
8–0–46–0

NORTHAMPTONSHIRE CCC

BATTING	v. Worcestershire (Worcester) 25–29 April		v. Surrey (Northampton) 7–11 May		v. Nottinghamshire (Northampton) 14–18 May		v. Durham (Stockton) 23–26 May		v. Derbyshire (Northampton) 29 May–1 June		v. Leicestershire (Northampton) 2–4 June		v. Pakistanis (Northampton) 13–15 June		v. Somerset (Bath) 16–18 June		v. Nottinghamshire (Trent Bridge) 19–22 June		v. Glamorgan (Luton) 26–29 June		v. Surrey (The Oval) 30 June–2 July		v. Sussex (Northampton) 3–6 July		M	Inns	NO	Runs	HS	Av
A. Fordham	32	16	192	38	88	16	18	39	–	15	14	31	2	15	3	71	8	119	137	–	39	10	0*	–	23	41	2	1710	192	43.84
N.A. Felton	21	0	22	23	64	1	20	–	–	58*	28	7	0	1	4	86	64	41	6	–	5	8	–	–	22	37	3	1076	103	31.64
R.J. Bailey	10	14*	30	28	5	40	34	8*	–	72	2	42	51	7	14	14	54	46	165	–	40	45*	–	–	23	39	7	1572	167*	49.12
A.J. Lamb	101	66			44	46	58	30	–	23*			38	18					109*	–	56	0	–	–	16	25	4	1406	209	66.95
D.J. Capel	22	26	6	41*	31	52	36	7*	–	–	7	24	4	0	17	18	4	35*	30	–	103	30	–	–	23	34	4	892	103	29.73
K.M. Curran	33	34			14	0	82	–	–	–	0	36	19	26	61	2	10	10*	0	–	31	3	–	–	21	30	1	730	82	25.17
R.G. Williams	12	3	14	–																					2	3		29	14	9.66
D. Ripley	60*	14*	49	–	22*	12	104	–	–	–	18	8	45*	64	107*	14	54	–	24*	–	16	0	–	–	22	31	10	891	107*	42.42
A.R. Roberts	5	0	6	–			0	–			16	24	4	41	15	6	62	–	–	–	0	0*			14	19	3	304	62	19.00
A. Walker	39	–																							1	1		39	39	39.00
J.P. Taylor	6	–	4	–	0	74*	–	–	–	–	11*	7*	7	1	21	9	21	–	–	–	–	–	–	–	23	19	8	188	74*	17.09
N.A. Stanley			16	7*																					1	2	1	23	16	23.00
M.N. Bowen			5	–																					2	1	–	5	5	5.00
C.E.L. Ambrose			1*	–	1	9	16*	–	–	–	5	10			20*	7	5*	–	–	–	2*	–	–	–	18	20	10	200	49*	20.00
M.B. Loye					0	0	46	–	–	–	0	31			34	10	13	14					0*	–	10	14	1	195	46	15.00
N.G.B. Cook					0	16							4	6*	–	10*	21*	–	–	–	–	–	–	–	17	11	6	118	37	23.06
A.L. Penberthy									–	–	5	0	8	9											10	14	1	164	33	12.61
R.M. Pearson																									1					–
R.J. Warren																									2	3	1	27	19	13.50
W.M. Noon																									1					–
J.N. Snape																									1					
Byes	5		2			3		5			4	4		5		10			1											
Leg-byes	3	4	13	3	2	7	4	6		3	5	13	1	1	9	6	10	6	21		9	1								
Wides							2				2			6	1															
No-balls	5	3	15	7	11	20				10		1	10	13	1	3		1	6		11	5								
Total	354	180	375	147	282	296	420	95	0	181	117	238	193	213	307	266	326	272	499		312	102	0							
Wickets	10	7	10	3	10	10	9	2	0	2	10	10	10	10	8	10	9	4	5		8	6	0							
Result	D		D		L		W		W		W		L		D		L		W		L		D							
Points	5		6		6		24		16		20		–		5		4		24		4		3							

BATTING	v. Middlesex (Uxbridge) 14–16 July		v. Lancashire (Northampton) 17–20 July		v. Warwickshire (Northampton) 21–23 July		v. Essex (Chelmsford) 4–6 August		v. Yorkshire (Northampton) 7–10 August		v. Hampshire (Bournemouth) 14–17 August		v. Gloucestershire (Bristol) 18–20 August		v. Kent (Northampton) 21–24 August		v. Middlesex (Northampton) 26–29 August		v. Yorkshire (Scarborough) 31 August–3 September		v. Leicestershire (Leicester) 12–15 September		M	Inns	NO	Runs	HS	Av
A. Fordham	28	14	122	81	1	75	65	–	1	40	22	14*	16	25	21	37	91	–	18	93	34	9	23	41	2	1710	192	43.84
N.A. Felton	52	57	66	38	3	2	51	–	103	15	1	9*	43	0	40	50*	19	–	19	49			22	37	3	1076	103	31.64
R.J. Bailey	39	18	25	76*	21	19	25	–	37	31	5	–	91	96	18*	13*	0	–	85	58	167*	27	23	39	7	1572	167*	49.12
A.J. Lamb	65	13	10	24*	209	107	83	–	6	5	160	–					13	–			0	122*	16	25	4	1406	209	66.95
D.J. Capel	14	0	59	–	12	7*	61	–	1	6	33	–	36	11	–	–	3	–	89	66	1	–	23	34	4	892	103	29.73
K.M. Curran	82	47*	5	–	9	–			8	14	12	–	16	23	–	–	4	–	50	0	47	52	21	30	1	730	82	25.17
R.G. Williams																							2	3	–	29	14	9.66
D. Ripley	16	3*	21	–	18	2*	3	–	18	24*	57	–	9*	25			6	–	49	5	24	–	22	31	10	891	107*	42.42
A.R. Roberts	31	–			39	–	16	–			20	–							17*	2*			14	19	3	304	62	19.00
A. Walker																							1	1		39	39	39.00
J.P. Taylor	1	–	–	–	2*	–	9	–	2*	–	–	–	–	5	–	–	0*	–	8*	0*	–	–	23	19	8	188	74*	17.09
N.A. Stanley																							1	2	1	23	16	23.00
M.N. Bowen															–	–							2	1	–	5	5	5.00
C.E.L. Ambrose	13	–	7*	–	5	–	49*	–	15	5*	9*	–	9*	5			7	–					18	20	10	200	49*	20.00
M.B. Loye															–	–			4	2	1	40	10	14	1	195	46	15.00
N.G.B. Cook	11*	–	–	–			11*	–	0	–	–	–	–	2*	–	–	37	–	–	–	–	–	17	11	6	118	37	23.06
A.L. Penberthy			13	–			33	–	16	22			–	23			0	–	0	8	10	17*	10	14	1	164	33	12.61
R.M. Pearson					–	–																	1					–
R.J. Warren													19	5	3*	–							2	3	1	27	19	13.50
W.M. Noon															–	–							1					–
J.N. Snape																					–	–	1					
Byes			2		3	4	9		4	4				1		3			5	7	6	10						
Leg-byes	6	4	7	4	8	1	28		6	5	12		2	3	2	3	6		5	5	9	10						
Wides		2	2			1					1						1				3	1						
No-balls	11	5	6		4		1		7	3	6		10	8	1	2	16		10	3	1	2						
Total	369	163	345	223	334	218	444		224	174	338	23	251	232	85	108	203		359	298	303	290						
Wickets	10	5	8	2	9	4	9		10	7	8	0	6	10	2	1	10		8	8	7	4						
Result	D		D		D		W		D		W		L		D		W		D		W							
Points	6		8		7		23		6		22		7		4		22		3		23							

FIELDING FIGURES

71 – D.J. Ripley (ct 66/st 5)
22 – R.J. Bailey
17 – N.A. Felton
16 – D.J. Capel
15 – A. Fordham
12 – A.J. Lamb
10 – K.M. Curran
9 – J.P. Taylor
7 – M.B. Loye
6 – A.L. Penberthy
5 – A.R. Roberts and C.E.L. Ambrose
3 – N.G.B. Cook
2 – W.M. Noon
1 – sub, R.M. Pearson and J.N. Snape

NORTHAMPTONSHIRE CCC

BOWLING

	J.P. Taylor	A. Walker	D.J. Capel	K.M. Curran	R.G. Williams	A.R. Roberts	C.E.L. Ambrose	M.N. Bowen	R.J. Bailey	N.G.B. Cook	N.A. Felton	A. Fordham	A.L. Penberthy	R.M. Pearson	D. Ripley	J.N. Snape	Byes	Leg-byes	Wides	No-balls	Total	Wkts
v. Worcestershire (Worcester)	35–11–80–2	29–8–66–1	26.1–8–61–5	33–10–82–1	12–1–41–1	1–0–4–0											4	7		1	345	10
25–29 April	17–2–54–1	16–6–24–1	9–4–12–0	15–4–33–0	19–4–42–3	35–8–101–4											4	12		2	282	9
v. Surrey (Northampton)	18–1–65–0		24–7–57–2			22–7–43–1	27–9–38–3	19–1–70–0										6		4	279	6
7–11 May	15–3–44–2		6–1–16–0			16–2–34–1	17–4–32–2		2–1–4–0								7	5	5	1	142	5
v. Nottinghamshire (Northampton)	23.2–1–94–2		18–4–63–0	21–3–64–3			28–9–80–2		1–0–4–0	9–4–17–1							2	18	1	2	342	9A
14–18 May	17.2–1–76–4		11–0–36–0	10–2–28–0			24–3–78–2		4–0–8–1								4	7	1	4	237	7
v. Durham (Stockton)	17–2–48–3		16–0–44–1	12.3–2–58–1		16–2–39–1	24–7–59–3										4	6	2	1	258	10
23–26 May	24–4–90–2		17–3–45–3	17–4–41–3		7–1–12–0	28–13–44–2		3–0–6–0								4	11	4	5	253	10
v. Derbyshire (Northampton)	4–2–11–0		1–1–0–0	1–1–0–0			5–1–16–0				12–1–84–0	11.2–0–64–0						5		3	180	0
29 May–1 June																					0	0
v. Leicestershire (Northampton)	8–3–12–1		3.3–0–12–3	8–2–17–3			13–2–34–2											2		3	77	10
2–4 June	11–2–53–3			6–2–20–4			7–2–27–3										9	3		1	112	10
v. Pakistanis (Northampton)	11–1–70–0		6–1–33–0	11–1–41–2		10–1–36–1				22–4–68–2			14–6–34–3				2	3			287	8
13–15 June	7–1–25–0			5–0–17–0		15–4–38–1				18–7–40–2							1	1			122	3
v. Somerset (Bath)	17–0–59–0		10.2–2–28–0	7–2–16–0		13–1–40–1	18–5–54–1			14–5–43–1							1	9		8	250	3
16–18 June	6–1–22–1		8–3–6–0	7–1–20–0		14–2–30–2	13–2–34–0		11–6–5–0	3–2–5–0	2–1–9–0	1–0–8–0					4	4	8		147	3
v. Nottinghamshire (Trent Bridge)	15–3–39–2		7–0–29–0	11–2–29–0		12–2–53–0	21–2–69–1		12–3–39–1	9–2–27–0							9	8	2		302	4
19–22 June	7–1–20–0		6–2–20–0	7–0–32–1		16–3–79–2	13.5–2–38–0		8–0–40–1	10–1–43–3							13	12		3	297	8
v. Glamorgan (Luton)	14–4–27–2		8–0–21–1	10–3–20–1		15.2–3–51–2	23–7–53–4										1	3			176	10
26–29 June	8.2–3–21–1		13–4–41–4	6.4–1–37–1		2–0–6–0	13–4–32–3											2			139	10
v. Surrey (The Oval)	14–2–52–2		5–0–16–0	10–1–41–0		5–0–20–0	11–1–21–0			4–1–12–0								2		1	164	2
30 June–2 July	10–1–42–1			1–0–8–0		6–0–63–0	12.5–2–45–0		2–1–5–1	15–0–83–3							1	5			252	5
v. Sussex (Northampton)	17–4–36–1		16–5–41–1	10–3–37–2			22.2–5–62–1		7–3–21–0	20–10–38–3							3	13	6	5	251	8
3–6 July																						
v. Middlesex (Uxbridge)	18–3–75–2		11–0–47–0	8–1–20–3			16.2–6–51–0			5–1–23–0								4		2	220	5
14–16 July	9–1–31–2		3–0–11–0	7–0–42–1		13–1–65–2	19.4–3–50–1		3–0–16–0	10–0–32–1							4	2			253	7
v. Lancashire (Northampton)	29–8–79–3		14–4–29–2	11–5–29–1			21–6–56–1			10–2–53–1			10–3–32–1				13	7	2	1	298	10
17–20 July	5–0–18–1						5.1–1–5–1												1		23	2
v. Warwickshire (Northampton)	14–3–42–2		7–2–21–1	4–1–11–0		25–4–91–1	17–6–37–1		4–0–8–0					27.4–2–90–2			11	5	1	1	316	7
21–23 July	4–0–18–0		11–0–42–2	5–0–26–0		5–0–33–0	13–2–38–3							8–0–40–0			8	1	5	1	206	5
v. Essex (Chelmsford)	9–2–45–0		3–0–12–0			18–6–59–1	16–4–27–3		16–4–34–1	30.4–6–63–3			9–2–18–1				11	4			273	10
4–6 August	6–2–16–0					20–5–35–1	11–5–25–1		17–5–41–1	18.4–8–34–7			5–2–7–0								158	10
v. Yorkshire (Northampton)	16–1–53–2		22–4–61–4	12.2–0–32–2			2.3–1–1–0		1–0–1–1	2–2–0–0			3–2–3–0				5	2		2	158	10
7–10 August	13–3–33–1		9–0–36–0	10–2–37–2			16–2–48–1		4–1–4–0	5–3–5–0							3	8		1	174	5
v. Hampshire (Bournemouth)	17–3–53–0		19–5–43–1	21.3–11–45–6			26–7–52–2		9–3–15–0	15–4–43–1							1	8	4		260	10
14–17 August	14–6–23–7		4–1–5–1	7–1–32–0			17–9–35–2			1–1–0–0								5		6	100	10
v. Gloucestershire (Bristol)	19–3–60–1		26–6–65–4	21–4–59–0			19–6–26–1		3–0–12–0	12–3–51–2			15–1–58–2				4	11	2	3	346	10
18–20 August	16–2–75–2		7–2–12–1	18–1–56–3			5–2–4–1		1–0–7–0	5–2–14–1							5	3			176	8
v. Kent (Northampton)	19–4–43–1		23–6–48–3	17–5–39–1				15–5–35–1	7–4–6–0	16–9–18–2							5	2	2	2	196	10
21–24 August	8–0–36–1			6–2–17–0				9–0–54–0		10–0–32–0								2			141	1
v. Middlesex (Northampton)	16–9–24–5		11–1–25–0	8.4–4–15–2			13–5–24–2										4	3		3	95	10
26–29 August	16–5–30–5		9–5–20–2	5–0–26–0			11–6–12–1		0.1–0–0–1	4–2–5–1			2–0–10–0					2			105	10
v. Yorkshire (Scarborough)	29–6–79–0		23–3–66–2	23–3–79–2		25–6–73–0			4–0–14–1	35.5–9–117–1			19–3–64–1				6	10	2	1	508	10
31 August–3 September	7–0–22–0			9–0–30–0		12–2–51–1			1–0–1–0	8–0–35–2			6–0–16–0		1–0–14–0		2			171	3	
v. Leicestershire (Leicester)	36.2–4–127–3		27–6–71–3	29–6–82–3						5–1–16–0			14–4–33–0			9–3–20–1		3		6	352	10
12–15 September	12–1–50–0		6–2–19–2	21–6–58–2						8–1–22–1			11–1–38–0			17–5–42–0	2	9	1	1	240	5
Bowlers average	648.2–119– 2072–68 30.47	45–14– 90–2 45.00	446–92– 1214–48 25.29	452.4–96– 1376–50 27.52	31–5– 83–4 20.75	323.2–60– 1056–22 48.00	549.2–151– 1307–50 26.14	43–6– 159–1 159.00	120.1–31– 291–9 32.33	325.1–90– 939–38 24.71	14–2– 93–0 –	12.2–0– 72–0 –	108–24– 313–8 39.12	35.4–2– 130–2 65.00	1–0– 14–0 –	26–8– 62–1 62.00						

A P.R. Pollard retired hurt

NOTTINGHAMSHIRE CCC

BATTING

BATTING	v. Warwickshire (Trent Bridge) 25–28 April	v. Oxford University (Oxford) 7–9 May	v. Northamptonshire (Northampton) 14–18 May	v. Sussex (Trent Bridge) 20–22 May	v. Derbyshire (Derby) 23–26 May	v. Middlesex (Trent Bridge) 2–4 June	v. Pakistanis (Trent Bridge) 10–12 June	v. Lancashire (Trent Bridge) 16–18 June	v. Northamptonshire (Trent Bridge) 19–22 June	v. Cambridge University (Trent Bridge) 27–29 June	v. Kent (Maidstone) 30 June–2 July	v. Hampshire (Southampton) 3–6 July	v. Worcestershire (Trent Bridge) 14–16 July	M	Inns	NO	Runs	HS	Av
B.C. Broad	27 104		38 40		29 117	28 31*	21 19	16 1	159* 31		4 3	– 8		14	27	3	1040	159*	43.33
P.R. Pollard	25 9	72 –	13* –					22 36	5 69		26 9	– 26	27 32	19	33	3	900	75	30.00
M.A. Crawley	0 64*	110* –	15 0	43 76	7 160*	0 17*	9 2	13 4	22* 26*	10 51*	– 102*	– 4*	115 23	25	44	9	1297	160*	37.05
P. Johnson	12 –	– –	3 95	26 42	75 –	4 –	6 60	19 62	44 11	5 60*	30 14	– 5	58 51*	18	28	4	1094	107*	45.58
D.W. Randall	9 17*		49 28	1 34	23 –	63 –	14 3	27 133*			3* 66	– 93	51 –	19	29	3	882	133*	33.92
C.C. Lewis	15 –		134* 22		14 –		12 47			10* 62			8 –	12	19	4	722	134*	48.13
C.L. Cairns	48 –		35 15	19 22	15 52*	14 –		25 102*	– 3	– 1	– 32	– 15*	62 –	21	30	6	984	107*	41.00
K.P. Evans	28 –		6 5	50 4	14 –	13 –	8 11	43 –	– 4		– 8	– –	55* –	19	24	4	438	104	21.90
B.N. French	24 –		3 4*	46 15*	29 –	6 –	11* 3	11 –	– 7		– 14	– –	0 –	17	20	4	260	55	16.25
E.E. Hemmings	52* –		23 12*											7	11	5	132	52*	22.00
R.A. Pick	52 –		0 –	12* 0	15* –	20* –	0 28	2 –	– 3*			– –		10	12	4	145	52	18.12
M. Newell		22 48*								5* –				2	3	2	75	48*	75.00
M. Saxelby		73 –		4 54										8	13	1	462	73	38.50
G.F. Archer		1 50*												7	13	3	475	117	47.50
G.W. Mike		28* –												5	6	2	130	61*	32.50
S. Bramhall		– –								– 1				8	10	3	114	37*	16.28
M.G. Field-Buss		– –		2 0*		9 –					– 1		0* –	8	7	2	27	13	5.40
K.E. Cooper		– –					0 2							2	2	–	2	2	1.00
J.A. Afford		– –		2 –	0 –	12 –	2 7*	1* –	– –	– –		– –	– –	18	17	6	42	12	3.81
R.T. Robinson				26 11	97 –	33 –	22 15	4 24	52 100		42* 1	– 95	8 64*	19	33	5	1547	189	55.25
W.A. Dessaur									1 15	148 –				2	3	–	164	148	54.66
J.R. Wileman										109 –				1	1	–	109	109	109.00
J.E. Hindson										– –				1					–
D.B. Pennett										– –	– 3			12	11	1	69	29	6.90
R.J. Chapman														1					–
Byes	7 3	8	2 4	15	1 3		1	14	9 13										
Leg-byes	9 5	4	18 7	7 12	18 6	1 2	3	13 6	8 12	11 2	4 10	8	8 3						
Wides	2	1	1 1	4	3		1 3	3 1	2	1			2						
No-balls	1	5 2	2 4	7 9	7 4	8 3	10 8	9	3	2 1	4 3	8	6 3						
Total	311 202	324 100	342 237	249 294	347 342	211 53	116 212	199 392	302 297	300 179	113 266	0 262	400 176						
Wickets	10 2	4 0	9† 7	10 8	10 1	10 0	10 10	10 5	4 8	4 3	3 10	0 5	8 2						
Result	W	D	W	D	D	D	L	D	W	W	L	W	L						
Points	23	–	24	5	5	2	–	4	23	–	2	18	6						

BATTING	v. Durham (Trent Bridge) 17–20 July	v. Surrey (The Oval) 21–23 July	v. Warwickshire (Edgbaston) 24–27 July	v. Gloucestershire (Worksop) 4–6 August	v. Glamorgan (Trent Bridge) 7–10 August	v. Essex (Colchester) 14–17 August	v. Yorkshire (Scarborough) 18–20 August	v. Leicestershire (Leicester) 21–24 August	v. Worcestershire (Worcester) 26–29 August	v. Derbyshire (Trent Bridge) 31 August – 3 September	v. Surrey (Trent Bridge) 7–10 September	v. Somerset (Taunton) 12–15 September	M	Inns	NO	Runs	HS	Av
B.C. Broad				41 1	7* 20	18 15	9 120	11 122					14	27	3	1040	159*	43.33
P.R. Pollard	23 –	10 74	37 0	32 1	10* 75	65 11	10 21*		41 –	44 28	0 0	5 42	19	33	3	900	75	30.00
M.A. Crawley	21 –	0 95	15 2	1 44	– 88	0 15	6 1	4 8	35 –	14 39	22 5	0 9	25	44	9	1297	160**	37.05
P. Johnson	20 –	107* 78	0 107*	98 2	– 0								18	28	4	1094	107*	45.58
D.W. Randall	22 –	– 25	9 –	0 30	– 43	1 1		21 20	66 –	6 24			19	29	3	882	133*	33.92
C.C. Lewis	107 –					2 35			70* –	8 82	52 26*	1 15	12	19	4	722	134*	48.13
C.L. Cairns	42 –	– 17*		107* 6	– 3	82* 26	69 61	17 –	58 –	9 13	5 9		21	30	6	984	107*	41.00
K.P. Evans	0* –	– 5*	0 –	7 2	– 5	3 13					104 –	27 23*	19	24	4	438	104	21.90
B.N. French	– –	– 0	7* –	4 2	– 55	13 6							17	20	4	260	55	16.25
E.E. Hemmings				0* 4*	– 13	5 0*	6 1	16 –					7	11	5	132	52*	22.00
R.A. Pick												7 6	10	12	4	145	52	18.12
M. Newell													2	3	2	75	48*	75.00
M. Saxelby			66 –					26 22*	17 –	57 0	43 10	26 64	8	13	1	462	73	38.50
G.F. Archer							27 29	21 52*	4 –	3 117	22 66	83* 0	7	13	3	475	117	47.50
G.W. Mike		– 18	61* –				0 23		0 –				5	6	2	130	61*	32.50
S. Bramhall							4 9	12* –	7 –	0* 16	37* –	22 6	8	10	3	114	37*	16.28
M.G. Field–Buss	– –	– –								2 13			8	7	2	27	13	5.40
K.E. Cooper													2	2	–	2	2	1.00
J.A. Afford					– 1*	0 0	3* –	9 –	0* –	0 5*	0 –	0 0	18	17	6	42	12	3.81
R.T. Robinson	164* –	73* 28	189 84	1 34	– 13	37 2	1 63	16 24			21 129*	74 0	19	33	5	1547	189	55.25
W.A. Dessaur													2	3	–	164	148	54.66
J.R. Wileman													1	1	–	109	109	109.00
J.E. Hindson													1					–
D.b. Pennett	– –	– –	– –	– 1			0 7*	0 –	5 –	2 29	12 –	4 6	12	11	1	69	29	6.90
R.J. Chapman			– –										1					–

FIELDING FIGURES

45 – B.N. French (ct 40/st 5)
21 – P.R. Pollard
20 – M.A. Crawley
19 – S. Bramhall (ct 16/st 3)
14 – R.T. Robinson
12 – K.P. Evans
11 – D.W. Randall
9 – C.C. Lewis
8 – C.L. Cairns and P. Johnson
7 – B.C. Broad
6 – G.F. Archer
5 – M.G. Field-Buss
4 – J.A. Afford and sub
3 – M. Newell and D.B. Pennett
2 – G.W. Mike, J.R. Wileman and E.E. Hemmings
1 – R.A. Pick, M. Saxelby and W.A. Dessaur

BATTING

	v. Durham (Trent Bridge) 17–20 July	v. Surrey (The Oval) 21–23 July	v. Warwickshire (Edgbaston) 24–27 July	v. Gloucestershire (Worksop) 4–6 August	v. Glamorgan (Trent Bridge) 7–10 August	v. Essex (Colchester) 14–17 August	v. Yorkshire (Scarborough) 18–20 August	v. Leicestershire (Leicester) 21–24 August	v. Worcestershire (Worcester) 26–29 August	v. Derbyshire (Trent Bridge) 31 August – 3 September	v. Surrey (Trent Bridge) 7–10 September	v. Somerset (Taunton) 12–15 September
Byes	6		8			5 4	1	4	2	4 1	3 1	2 4
Leg-byes	14	1 4	15 1	8 7	6	9 2	2 11	10 7	11	15 13	16 8	8 7
Wides			4 2	1		3	1	2		3		
No-balls	12	10 8	4 1	3		5	14 6	5	5	2 2	20 8	6 6
Total	431	201 352	415 197	302 135	17 322	249 130	152 353	168 261	321	166 385	357 262	265 188
Wickets	6	2 7	7 3	8 10	0 10	10 10	10 8	10 4	9	10 10	10 5	10 10
Result	D	W	W	L	L	L	D	D	D	L	W	L
Points	8	19	23	6	3	3	4	5	8	4	23	4

NOTTINGHAMSHIRE CCC

BOWLING

	C.C. Lewis	R.A. Pick	K.P. Evans	C.L. Cairns	E.E. Hemmings	M.A. Crawley	K.E. Cooper	G.W. Mike	J.A. Afford	M. Saxelby	M.G. Field-Buss	D.W. Randall	J.E. Hindson	D.B. Pennett	P. Johnson	P.R. Pollard	Byes	Leg-byes	Wides	No-balls	Total	Wkts
v. Warwickshire (Trent Bridge) 25–28 April	16–4–35–2	19.1–8–46–2	24–7–45–2	23–6–59–1	28–14–48–3	4–1–9–0											3	4	1	12	249	10
	26.1–9–54–2	15–5–33–3	17–5–40–1	17–5–53–2	34–12–65–1	4–0–11–0											2	5		16	263	10
v. Oxford University (Oxford) 7–9 May						4.4–1–18–3	26–9–41–4	22–8–38–2	13–4–20–0	6–2–22–0	10–5–19–1						1	2	1	3	161	10
v. Northamptonshire (Northampton) 14–18 May	22–3–59–2	15–2–76–1	16.2–6–27–5	19–2–87–0	3–1–11–0	7–3–20–2												2		11	282	10
	24–2–74–5	19–4–71–2	21–4–66–2	13.5–3–57–0	16–7–18–0												3	7		20	296	10
v. Sussex (Trent Bridge) 20–22 May		16–3–56–1	25–6–84–2	16–0–47–1		4–1–6–0			34.2–6–117–4		12–1–51–1							4		15	365	10
		6–0–28–0	12–3–40–2	12–1–55–0					18–6–68–6		3–0–15–0							2		9	208	8
v. Derbyshire (Derby) 23–26 May	26.3–3–88–4	15–3–57–0	23–4–90–0	27–4–109–2		14–2–59–1			25–7–81–1								1	15	1	24	500	9
v. Middlesex (Trent Bridge) 2–4 June		22–4–78–1	20–2–77–0	23–3–59–1		8–3–19–0			13–2–67–0		24–1–82–0						4	15	1	7	401	2
v. Pakistanis (Trent Bridge) 10–12 June	7–2–31–0	16–4–56–3	21.5–4–54–4				12–6–22–2												2	5	163	10
	12–2–43–0	4–0–22–0	15–5–36–1			6–1–21–0			14–2–36–1			0.2–0–0–0					4	5	2	6	167	2
v. Lancashire (Trent Bridge) 16–18 June		28–8–64–2		31.4–11–70–6		24–5–84–0			24–9–45–2								9	20	2	9	292	10
		10–1–39–2	9–1–27–0	7–1–25–0					7–0–8–1								2	2			103	3
v. Northamptonshire (Trent Bridge) 19–22 June		20–4–49–1	26–5–67–2	25–9–68–3		21–3–56–1			18–1–76–2									10			326	9
		12–1–38–0	12–0–45–0	9–0–51–1		5.5–0–38–3			15–1–94–1									6		1	272	5
v. Cambridge University (Trent Bridge) 27–29 June	9–5–10–0			10–4–14–1					13–3–34–2				20.5–9–42–5	16–2–38–1			8	7	3	3	153	10
	8–3–14–1			6–2–15–1		5–2–7–0			24–8–75–5				12.5–2–32–3	8–1–19–0				2	5		164	10
v. Kent (Maidstone) 30 June–2 July			33–5–117–2	28–7–75–5		5–0–29–0					9–0–65–2			13–2–65–1			1	7		7	359	10
			6.3–0–33–1											6–0–21–0				1			55	1
v. Hampshire (Southampton) 3–6 July		16–1–60–0	19–8–35–0	23–1–65–3		2–0–2–1			13–5–34–2						5–0–30–0	4–0–33–0		2		6	261	6
																					0	0
v. Worcestershire (Trent Bridge) 14–16 July	14–0–44–2		20–2–75–0	19–3–59–3		5.1–2–7–0			16–0–82–1		18–4–42–0						4	5	1	7	318	6
	15.5–2–51–2		7–2–31–0	13–1–52–2		1–1–0–0			13–0–64–1		12–2–50–0						5	9	2	4	262	5
v. Durham (Trent Bridge) 17–20 July	14–4–27–2		15.5–4–31–2	14–2–41–4										16–5–41–2				7		13	147	10
	15–2–40–0		15–2–63–0	20–4–93–3		4–2–2–0					11–0–34–0			5–1–21–0			1	11		5	265	3
v. Surrey (The Oval) 21–23 July			23–4–61–0	9–0–25–0		5–1–22–1		16–3–70–2			15–2–69–0			21–5–81–1				5	1	5	333	4
			14–1–49–0					7–1–52–1			15–0–71–4			8–0–45–2				2			219	7
v. Warwickshire (Edgbaston) 24–27 July			32–5–74–3			22–7–37–1		15–3–44–1						25.2–3–70–2				2	4	7	266	8A
			15.5–3–66–2			2–0–15–0		13–1–48–3						19–4–58–4				4	1	4	229	10
v. Gloucestershire (Worksop) 4–6 August			31–14–66–3	29–9–86–1	39.3–15–78–4	13–6–21–1								24–4–74–1				10		4	335	10
			12–4–13–3	9–1–38–1	13.2–5–30–4									7–3–21–1			4	6		7	112	10
v. Glamorgan (Trent Bridge) 7–10 August			22–7–48–3	19–1–82–2	29–8–79–1	5–1–17–0			31.3–6–105–2								2	1		5	334	8
												1–0–8–0									12	0B
v. Essex (Colchester) 14–17 August	35.5–8–97–2		16–3–51–0	14–2–53–0	41–14–122–1	8–2–26–1			16–3–51–2								3	13	4	5	416	6
v. Yorkshire (Scarborough) 18–20 August				34–5–106–2	23–9–51–1			15.2–1–60–1	15–4–56–2					30–5–117–3			1	13	1	17	404	9
v. Leicestershire (Leicester) 21–24 August				19–5–56–0	21–10–30–1	15–3–45–2			21–8–51–3					24–6–60–3				10		4	252	10
				2–0–11–0	12–0–70–2				10.3–1–35–4					3–0–17–0				1	1		134	6
v. Worcestershire (Worcester) 26–29 August	26.3–6–64–4			26–9–50–4				2–0–2–0	15–8–13–2					7–0–25–0			4	4	1	6	162	10
	6–5–4–0			6–1–24–1					1–1–0–0									4		1	32	1
v. Derbyshire (Trent Bridge) 31 August–3 September	21–2–64–1			19–2–77–1		2–0–5–0			37.4–15–70–3		29–13–60–2			18–5–35–2			7	12		5	330	10
	13–1–32–0			10–1–61–3					25.1–5–91–4		11–1–32–1						2	4		1	222	8
v. Surrey (Trent Bridge) 7–10 September	21–4–65–4		17.2–7–37–3	9–1–41–0					6–0–21–0					17–3–38–3				5	5	8	207	10
	32.4–4–90–6		25–3–79–1	31–4–110–2		9–4–11–1			31–15–54–0					14–2–50–0			7	10		8	411	10
v. Somerset (Taunton) 12–15 September	41–8–103–2	21–2–89–0	30–6–96–4			16–5–60–1			39–8–151–0					15–0–85–0			17	15	3	5	616	7
Bowlers average	406.3–79–1089–41 26.56	254.1–50–862–18 47.88	596.4–132–1723–48 35.89	592.3–110–1974–56 35.25	259.5–95–602–18 33.44	221.4–56–647–19 34.05	38–15–63–6 10.50	90.2–17–314–10 31.40	509.1–128–1599–51 31.35	6–2–22–0 –	169–29–590–11 53.63	1.2–0–8–0 –	33.4–11–74–8 9.25	296.2–51–981–26 37.73	5–0–30–0 –	4–0–33–0 –						

A R.J. Chapman 8–1–39–1
5–0–38–1

B R.T. Robinson 1–0–4–0

SOMERSET CCC

BATTING

BATTING	v. Gloucestershire (Taunton) 25–28 April		v. Sussex (Hove) 7–11 May		v. Pakistanis (Taunton) 13–15 May		v. Essex (Taunton) 20–22 May		v. Gloucestershire (Gloucester) 23–26 May		v. Lancashire (Old Trafford) 29 May–1 June		v. Durham (Darlington) 2–4 June		v. Yorkshire (Middlesbrough) 5–8 June		v. Northamptonshire (Bath) 16–18 June		v. Surrey (Bath) 19–22 June		v. Middlesex (Lord's) 26–29 June		v. Derbyshire (Taunton) 3–6 July		M	Inns	NO	Runs	HS	Av
A.N. Hayhurst	54	–	20	55	0	30	0	43	97	15	6	–	76	7	38	–	53	38	41	–	97	0	13	–	23	38	2	1197	102	33.25
G.T.J. Townsend	40	–			8	12																			7	13	1	272	49	22.66
R.J. Bartlett	4	–	41	72	2	23	46	27	0	13	43	–	21	4	56	–									8	13	–	352	72	27.07
R.J. Harden	13	–	36	6	40	26	72	68	0	56	9	–	24	35	7	–	33*	39	73	6*	30	58	166*	–	20	33	5	1387	187	49.53
C.J. Tavare	33	–	12	–			0	22	74	12	49	–	2	10			–	35*	14	–	53	2	59	–	21	32	2	1157	125	38.56
G.D. Rose	85	–	65	27	5	0	1	18	3	6	9	–	47	36	1	–	55*	–	41	–	0	27*	16	–	22	34	4	930	132	31.00
K.H. MacLeay	1	–	25	2	32	9									0	39*	5	19*	12	13*	0	50	2	–	12	19	3	427	74	26.68
N.D. Burns	20	–	35*	35*	44*	19	2	10*	4	8	73*	–	9	26*	2	–	–	–	27	–	7	5*	28*	–	22	33	12	772	73*	36.76
A. Payne	51*	–																							1	1	1	51	51*	–
A.R. Caddick	2	–	3	–	9	6*	9*	–			22	–	1*	–	37	–	–	–			–	–	–	–	20	19	6	261	54*	20.07
H.R.J. Trump	24*	–	2	–	11	1			3	3*			4	–	0	–	–	–	18*	–	–	–	–	–	18	18	6	154	28	14.00
N.A. Mallender			6	26*			7	–	24	6	7	–	7	–			–	–	14	–	13*	–			15	18	5	182	29*	14.00
A.C. Cottam			3	–					31	3					0	–			1*	–					6	8	1	43	31	6.14
K.A. Parsons					1	0																			1	2	–	1	1	0.50
A.P. van Troost					0	12	12	–	3*	8	–	–			1*	–							–	–	11	9	5	42	12	10.50
M.N. Lathwell							76	79	0	0	74	–	53	50	17	16*	86	0	114	1	22	1	2	–	19	33	1	1176	114	36.75
R.P. Snell							20	16*			55	–	5	10*			–	–	0	–	35*	–	–	–	16	20	4	436	81	27.25
R.P. Lefebvre																									3	4	–	70	36	17.50
R.J. Turner																									7	10	5	286	101*	57.20
N.A. Folland																									1	2	1	104	82*	104.00
Byes			2	6		8	5	6			3			1			1	4	4											
Leg-byes	7		11	10	5	10	7	8	7	6	16		15	1	2		9	4	6		7		2							
Wides			1	14					2	1	4		4	1				8			1		2							
No-balls	14		2		6	13	18	5	9	3	6		2	11	6	2	8		11		5	1	9							
Total	348		264	253	163	169	275	302	257	140	376		270	192	167	57	250	147	376	20	270	144	299	0						
Wickets	9		10	5	10	10	10	6	10	10	9		10	6	10	0	3	3	9	1	7	5	5	0						
Result	D		D		L		W		W		D		L		D		D		W		D		L							
Points	5		6		–		23		23		7		6		3		6		24		4		3							

BATTING

BATTING	v. Leicestershire (Leicester) 17–20 July		v. Kent (Canterbury) 21–23 July		v. Glamorgan (Abergavenny) 24–27 July		v. Sussex (Taunton) 31 July–2 August		v. Warwickshire (Taunton) 4–6 August		v. Worcestershire (Weston-super-Mare) 18–20 August		v. Hampshire (Weston-super-Mare) 21–24 August		v. Derbyshire (Derby) 26–29 August		v. Surrey (The Oval) 31 August–3 September		v. Durham (Taunton) 7–10 September		v. Nottinghamshire (Taunton) 12–15 September		M	Inns	NO	Runs	HS	Av
A.N. Hayhurst	5	5	14	11	70	24	86	15	0*	1*	23	36	82	–	–	0	5	14	102	8	13	–	23	38	2	1197	102	33.25
G.T.J. Townsend	49	0*	0	16	46	35	1	12	38	15													7	13	1	272	49	22.66
R.J. Bartlett																							8	13	–	352	72	27.07
R.J. Harden	6	47*	30	4	27	48	52	30	29*	–							0	4	126	–	187	–	20	33	5	1387	187	49.53
C.J. Tavare	69	8	0	14	23	14	99	55	44	0	3	18	115	–	–	2	24	43*	124	–	125	–	21	32	2	1157	125	38.56
G.D. Rose	59	19	0	1	13	50	25	32			51	11*	1	–	–	20	132	–	33	1*	40	–	22	34	4	930	132	31.00
K.H. Macleay									74	29	19	–	23	–	–	73							12	19	3	427	74	26.68
N.D. Burns	23	0*	42	33	36*	71*			13	68	5	6	0	–	–	1	27	–	54	8*	31	–	22	33	12	772	73*	36.76
A. Payne																							1	1	1	51	51*	–
A.R. Caddick			5*	17	–	0	0	–	7	14	54*	–	0*	–	–	3	37	–	35	–	–	–	20	19	6	261	54*	20.07
H.R.J. Trump	0	–	1	8*	–	8*	12*	–	8*	5	28	–					18	–			–	–	18	18	6	154	28	14.00
N.A. Mallender	0*	10					9	9*			7	–	7	–	–	0			1	–	29*	–	15	18	5	182	29*	14.00
A.C. Cottam									5	0							0	–					6	8	1	43	31	6.14
K.A. Parsons																							1	2	–	1	1	0.50
A.P. van Troost					–	–							–	–	–	0*	6*	–	0*	–			11	9	5	42	12	10.50
M.N. Lathwell	3	0	4	72			55	45	45	71	8	20	73	–	–	11	44	49	50	8	27	–	19	33	1	1176	114	36.75
R.P. Snell	81	18	20	23			2	11*	5	25	75	–	1	–	–	11			0	–	23	–	16	20	4	436	81	27.25
R.P. Lefebvre	28	–	0	6	–	36																	3	4	–	70	36	17.50
R.J. Turner					24*	0	0	11					41*	–	–	55*	45	9*	0	–	101*	–	7	10	5	286	101*	57.20
N.A. Folland											22	82*											1	2	1	104	82*	104.00
Byes		1	4	8		2	5	4	4	17	6		8			4	2				17							
Leg-byes	4		7	5	4	3	5		1	5	19	2	18			8	4	2	5		15							
Wides			1						1		1					4			4		3							
No-balls			5	2	7	2	5	8	4	14	7		1			7	8	3			5							
Total	327	108	133	220	250	293	356	232	278	264	328	175	370	0	0	199	352	124	534	25	616							
Wickets	10	6	10	10	5	8	10	7	8†	9	10	4	8	0	0	9‡	10	3	10	2	7							
Result	D		L		D		D		D		D		D		L		D		W		W							
Points	7		4		7		7		7		5		4		4		2		24		24							

FIELDING FIGURES

44 – N.D. Burns (ct 41/st 3)
15 – C.J. Tavare
14 – R.J. Harden, M.N. Lathwell and H.R.J. Trump
11 – G.D. Rose
7 – K.H. MacLeay
6 – A.N. Hayhurst, A.R. Caddick and R.J. Turner
5 – R.J. Bartlett and R.P. Snell
3 – A.P. van Troost, N.A. Mallender and R.P. Lefebvre
1 – N.A. Folland, A.C. Cottam and sub
† – A.N. Hayhurst, R.J. Harden retired hurt
‡ – R.J. Turner retired hurt

SOMERSET CCC

BOWLING

	A.R. Caddick	G.D. Rose	A. Payne	A.N. Hayhurst	H.R.J. Trump	K.H. MacLeay	N.A. Mallender	A.C. Cottam	A.P. van Troost	R.P. Snell	M.N. Lathwell	R.P. Lefebvre	R.J. Harden	C.J. Tavare	R.J. Turner	Byes	Leg-byes	Wides	No-balls	Total	Wkts
v. Gloucestershire (Taunton)	38–9–96–4	28.2–9–60–2	27–8–71–1	21–3–40–0	16–1–42–1	15–5–33–2											2	1	9	344	10
25–28 April																					
v. Sussex (Hove)	26.3–3–94–3	14–1–55–0		6–1–20–0	20–6–46–1		27–6–86–5	23–7–35–1								1	9		14	346	10
7–11 May																					
v. Pakistanis (Taunton)	20.2–3–73–6	18–7–58–3		5–2–4–1	5–1–26–0	8–1–25–0			12–3–40–0							8	6		6	240	10
13–15 May	9–1–48–1	1.1–0–13–1							8–0–31–3								1		5	93	5
v. Essex (Taunton)	16–1–45–0	10–0–43–0					16–2–63–2		13–4–48–6	14.1–3–53–2	1–1–0–0						7	2	18	259	10
20–22 May	11–2–57–0	16–1–61–1		9–1–38–0			14–2–41–1		13–0–64–0	2–0–16–0	9–2–33–0					4		4	12	314	2
v. Gloucestershire (Gloucester)		7–0–14–0			25–6–52–7		15–2–47–1	1.5–0–1–1	16–2–50–1								13		12	177	10
23–26 May		5–1–7–0			33.4–16–52–7		12–4–29–1	29–5–66–0	1–0–10–0		6–3–9–1					12	18		2	203	10
v. Lancashire (Old Trafford)	13–2–34–1	15–1–50–1		8–1–36–2			11–3–39–2		11–0–53–0	15–1–86–1	2–0–9–0					5	1	1	7	313	7
29 May–1 June																					
v. Durham (Darlington)	24–6–52–2	12–4–25–0		7–0–26–1	9.2–1–34–1		15–3–42–3			17–3–61–1						4	6		10	250	8
2–4 June	10–0–54–2	5–0–19–0		5–0–24–0	6–0–26–0		5–0–27–0			8–1–51–0						1	11	1		213	2
v. Yorkshire (Middlesbrough)	25–6–57–1	14–3–43–1		13–6–27–3	8–1–36–0	22–8–51–1		10–1–33–0	19–5–62–1								8		4	317	7
5–8 June																					
v. Northamptonshire (Bath)	24–5–78–2	11–4–22–2		2–1–1–0	14–6–31–1	9–0–48–1	17–2–48–1			19–3–70–0							9	1	1	307	8
16–18 June	15.4–1–56–4	5–2–15–0			27–7–75–3		13–1–43–2			14–1–53–0	1–0–8–0					10	6		3	266	10
v. Surrey (Bath)		7–2–21–1			15–4–35–1		14–4–29–5	5.2–1–8–1		14–6–17–2						3	3		7	116	10
19–22 June		21–9–34–2		5–2–9–1	25–9–52–0	7–3–8–1	22.2–7–51–3	12–5–32–1		32–8–73–2						6	11		3	276	10
v. Middlesex (Lord's)	23–3–64–0	11–2–44–0			34–4–103–3	9–4–22–1	17–3–47–0			19–3–71–1							4		1	355	5
26–29 June	12–0–54–0	4–0–37–1			4–0–26–0	6–1–28–1	8–0–47–1			14–3–29–3	1–0–13–0								1	234	6
v. Derbyshire (Taunton)																				0	0
3–6 July	13.5–0–55–2	6–1–28–0			6–1–36–0	6–0–27–0			9–0–77–0	12–0–66–2							12	4	13	301	4
v. Leicestershire (Leicester)		16.4–5–45–3		8–1–30–0	34–13–73–2		24–8–55–3			23–6–61–2						1	5		4	270	10
17–20 July																					
v. Kent (Canterbury)	24–5–105–4	7–3–14–0		4–1–5–0	19–5–53–1					19–3–61–1		13–5–33–2					4		8	275	10
21–23 July	16.3–1–52–6	10–2–30–1		3–0–5–0	10–1–53–0							7–1–15–1					5			160	8
v. Glamorgan (Abergavenny)	24–5–60–1	21–4–59–4		7–2–13–0	24–8–46–1				14–2–57–2			14–3–33–2					8	1	17	276	10
24–27 July	10–3–40–2	13–2–56–0		4–1–17–1	21–4–59–2				11–1–70–0			7–2–15–0	3–0–31–0	1–0–10–0		4	6		5	308	5
v. Sussex (Taunton)	22–3–73–3	13–1–56–1		7–2–15–0	14–0–67–0		17–6–45–2			12–2–52–1						1	1	1	1	310	7
31 July–2 August	10–0–36–1			6–0–24–0	8–2–32–0		7–0–22–1			9–0–35–1	3–1–4–0					5	1		1	159	4
v. Warwickshire (Taunton)	19–5–49–3				31–7–89–3	7–0–18–1		14–3–33–0		14–4–37–2	9–1–35–1					8	7		2	276	10
4–6 August	11–1–50–2				25–3–91–3	7–0–18–1		7–0–37–1		10–1–39–1						17	8			260	9
v. Worcestershire	13–1–32–1	7–2–18–0			26–8–62–2	7–3–6–0	18–4–35–1			15–3–49–0	10–2–32–1					5	11		12	250	5
(Weston-super-Mare) 18–20 August	13–4–25–0	6–2–4–1			12–2–44–0		9–2–17–1			4–0–13–0	8–2–23–0						4	1	1	130	2
v. Hampshire	8–4–4–0						8.3–2–17–1							1–0–14–0	1.1–0–11–0		1		3	47	1
(Weston-super-Mare) 21–24 August	8–3–19–1						6–1–21–0		1–0–1–0	4–0–19–0							2		1	62	1
v. Derbyshire (Derby)	16–0–77–5	12–0–55–1				12–3–27–0	10–0–44–0		11–1–46–2	9–1–44–1				1.2–0–9–0	1–0–15–0	1	2		17	320	9
26–29 August																				0	0
v. Surrey (The Oval)	31–4–134–0	25–5–93–0		6–2–19–0	40–6–143–3			14–3–35–1	28.4–2–104–6		2–0–17–0						12	5	2	557	10
31 August–3 September																					
v. Durham (Taunton)	14–1–62–4	4–1–16–0					13.4–2–65–5		4–0–31–0	9–2–39–1						4	2		7	219	10
7–10 September	24–9–53–4	19–2–75–0		8–0–31–0			13.1–3–26–1		4–0–22–0	22–3–81–3	12–2–41–1						10		7	339	9A
v. Nottinghamshire (Taunton)	20.5–4–69–3	15–3–48–1		8–4–23–0	24–7–47–3		16–4–50–2			9–3–18–0						2	8		6	265	10
12–15 September	22–4–61–3	13–4–32–1			22–5–53–4		13–3–31–1									4	7		6	188	10
Bowlers average	587.4–99– 1918–71 27.01	392.1–83– 1250–28 44.64	27–8– 71–1 71.00	142–30– 407–9 45.22	558–134– 1584–49 32.32	115–28– 311–9 34.55	361.4–74– 1067–45 23.71	116.1–25– 280–6 46.66	175.4–20– 766–21 36.47	339.1–60– 1194–27 44.22	64–14– 224–4 56.00	41–11– 96–5 19.20	3–0– 31–0 –	3.2–0– 33–0 –	2.1–0– 26–0 –						

A C.W. Scott, absent hurt

SURREY CCC

BATTING

BATTING	v. Yorkshire (The Oval) 25–29 April	v. Northamptonshire (Northampton) 7–11 May	v. Cambridge University (Cambridge) 15–18 May	v. Hampshire (Southampton) 19–22 May	v. Middlesex (Lord's) 23–26 May	v. Sussex (The Oval) 29 May–1 June	v. Derbyshire (The Oval) 2–4 June	v. Worcestershire (The Oval) 12–15 June	v. Somerset (Bath) 19–22 June	v. Gloucestershire (Bristol) 26–29 June	v. Northamptonshire (The Oval) 30 June–2 July	v. Glamorgan (Neath) 3–6 July	M	Inns	NO	Runs	HS	Av
D.J. Bicknell	0 10	99 20	49 –	23 71	28 2	3 –	4 14*	36 19	12 26	81 13	14* –	15 22	23	41	5	1225	120*	34.02
R.I. Alikhan	1 10		54 –										2	3	–	65	54	21.66
A.J. Stewart	15 29*	10 1	71 –		6 36	140 –		42 23*		6 41			14	25	3	837	140	38.04
G.P. Thorpe	21 –	64 42	114* –	16 50	28 0	53 –	70 14	28 69*	10 48	75 29	21 20	93 69*	23	40	4	1863	216	51.75
D.M. Ward	6 –	38* 4	11 112*	45 30	3 21	5 –	37 12*		5 20	0 82	30* 103*	138 18	18	30	6	879	138	36.62
M.A. Lynch	24 5*	20 1	61 –	21 32	51 42	71 –	8 –	107 9	30 22	24 33	69* 13	13 32	23	40	6	1465	107	43.08
N.M. Kendrick	31* –	– –	– 6*	6 26	8 55	24* –	15 –	51 38	3 2		– –		17	21	5	306	55	19.12
N.F. Sargeant	3 –	5 14*		0 9	2 17					– –	– 16	1 –	14	19	4	176	30	11.73
R.E. Bryson	4 –	– –	– –	4* 9	14 11*				28 15				11	13	2	257	76	23.36
A.J. Murphy	32 –									– –		– –	5	5	2	45	32	15.00
J.E. Benjamin	19 –	– –		5 1*	3* 8*	– –	4* –	9* –	0* 0		– –	– –	18	18	8	116	42	11.60
M.A. Feltham		33 42*	12* 33		13 21	24 –	43* –	0 –		38* 11*			13	19	6	437	50	33.61
M.P. Bicknell		0* –	– 21	4 88	17 3	6 –	37 1*	19* –	1 49*		– 30*	28* –	19	26	8	447	88	24.83
J. Boiling			– –			16* –	12 –	0 –	2 17	– –	– –	– 29	19	21	11	190	29	19.00
P.D. Atkins				7 1							27 48	11 49	7	14	–	382	99	27.28
J.D. Robinson				34 21				1 7	1 53	65* 6	– 16	10* 5*	9	17	5	307	65*	25.58
D.G.C. Ligertwood						28 –	0 19	0 1	11 4				4	7	–	63	28	9.00
A.D. Brown							6 0						11	16	1	740	175	49.33
M.A. Butcher										– 5*			2	2	1	52	47	52.00
I. Ward													1	1	–	0	0	0.00
Byes	4 7	7			2	1	2	2	3 6	2 1	1	2						
Leg-byes	4 1	6 5	9 4	2 13	5 4	14	4 8	4 2	3 11	8 5	2 5	1 3						
Wides	1	5	3	2		1	3			1		2 3						
No-balls	1	4 1		17 16	8 7	10	8 1	2 1	7 3	1 5	1	2 2						
Total	164 64	279 142	381 179	184 369	188 227	396	253 69	301 169	116 276	300 232	164 252	316 232						
Wickets	10 2	6 5	5 2	10 10	10 9	8	9 3	9 5	10 10	5 6	2 5	6 5						
Result	D	D	W	L	D	D	D	D	L	W	W	W						
Points	2	6	–	1	3	6	6	7	3	22	20	22						

FIELDING FIGURES

41 – N.F. Sargeant (ct 35/st 6)
24 – M.A. Lynch
19 – J.A. Boiling
18 – G.P. Thorpe
17 – A.J. Stewart
16 – N.M. Kendrick
8 – D.G.C. Ligertwood (ct 7/st 1) and J.D. Robinson
7 – M.P. Bicknell
6 – A.D. Brown
5 – J.E. Benjamin and D.J. Bicknell
3 – D.M. Ward and M.A. Feltham
2 – R.I. Alikhan, P.D. Atkins and sub
1 – I. Ward

BATTING	v. Kent (Guildford) 14–16 July	v. Warwickshire (Guildford) 17–20 July	v. Nottinghamshire (The Oval) 21–23 July	v. Durham (Durham) 31 July–3 August	v. Lancashire (Lytham) 4–6 August	v. Leicestershire (The Oval) 14–17 August	v. Essex (Colchester) 18–20 August	v. Yorkshire (Bradford) 21–24 August	v. Somerset (The Oval) 31 August–3 September	v. Nottinghamshire (Trent Bridge) 7–10 September	v. Middlesex (The Oval) 12–15 September	M	Inns	NO	Runs	HS	Av
D.J. Bicknell	44 29	1 4	60 –	8 49	120* 4	6 37	53 4*	16* 13	45 –	2 77	5 87	23	41	5	1225	120*	34.02
R.I. Alikhan												2	3	–	65	54	21.66
A.J. Stewart	3 10	67 4		42 1		1 20			76 –	5 85	51* 52	14	25	3	837	140	38.04
G.P. Thorpe	52 14	86 19	35 19	4 60*	66 28	30 44	13 –	– 79	216 –	6 100	45 13	23	40	4	1863	216	51.75
D.M. Ward	12* 2				– 11		29 –	– 18	25 –	18 1	9 34	18	30	6	879	138	36.62
M.A. Lynch	48 10	63 13	97* 1	11 1*	20* 17	106 58	102 –	– 43	39 –	29 70	24* 25	23	40	6	1465	107	43.08
N.M. Kendrick					– 0	11 0	2 –	– 18*	0 –	10 0	– 0*	17	21	5	306	55	19.12
N.F. Sargeant	29 0	– 18*	– 20*	30 –	– 2		4 6*	0 0				14	19	4	176	30	11.73
R.E. Bryson			– 14	48 –				– 8		76 2	– 24	11	13	2	257	76	23.36
A.J. Murphy	5* 0					0* 8						5	5	2	45	32	15.00
J.E. Benjamin	42 6	– –	– 5*	6* –	– 2	0 1	5 –		0 –			18	18	8	116	42	11.60
M.A. Feltham		22* 50	– 2				24 –	– 41	6 –	22 0		13	19	6	437	50	33.61
M.P. Bicknell	4 0	– 11*		21 –	– 58*	5 11	6 –	– 24	2 –	0 1		19	26	8	447	88	24.83
J. Boiling	11* 0*	17 3*	– –	18 –	– 5	13 0*	1* –	22* 10*	0* –	14* 0	– 0*	19	21	11	190	29	19.00
P.D. Atkins			99 18	60 2	33 10	13 4						7	14	–	382	99	27.28
J.D. Robinson	30 4	14* 4	9* 27									9	17	5	307	65*	25.58
D.G.C. Ligertwood												4	7	–	63	28	9.00
A.D. Brown		56 0	22 111	175 –	– 62	19 1	32 –	– 36	129 –	7 50*	– 34	11	16	1	740	175	49.33
M.A. Butcher											– 47	2	2	1	52	47	52.00
I. Ward											– 0	1	1	–	0	0	0.00
Byes		2		1 1	4 1	2				7	2 1						
Leg-byes	9 1	11 5	5 2	5 2	9 3	7 9	6	10	12	5 10	2 4						
Wides	3		1	2	1	1			5	5	1						
No-balls	9	2	5		1	4	15	1 6	2	8 8	3 3						
Total	301 76	341 131	333 219	431 116	253 204	218 193	292 10	39 306	557	207 411	141 325						
Wickets	8 10	6 7	4 7	10 3	2 10	10 10	10 0	1 9	10	10 10	3 9						
Result	L	D	L	W	L	L	D	W	D	L	D						

SURREY CCC

BOWLING	R.E. Bryson	J.E. Benjamin	A.J. Murphy	N.M. Kendrick	G.P. Thorpe	M.P. Bicknell	M.A. Feltham	J. Boiling	J.D. Robinson	M.A. Lynch	D.J. Bicknell	A.D. Brown	M.A. Butcher	A.J. Stewart	I. Ward	D.M. Ward	Byes	Leg-byes	Wides	No-balls	Total	Wkts
v. Yorkshire (The Oval) 25–29 April	38–9–120–0	44–13–107–3	41.4–9–121–1	35–10–89–4	9–2–44–0												3	11		25	495	9
v. Northamptonshire (Northampton) 7–11 May	20–0–98–0	24–5–72–2		21–7–48–1		29.2–3–92–3	13–4–50–2										2	13		15	375	10
	12–0–56–2	11–1–37–1				10–2–31–0	10–3–20–0											3		7	147	3
v. Cambridge University (Cambridge) 15–18 May	14–2–48–5			15–6–33–1		16–6–47–1	8–3–25–1	2.5–0–3–1										5	1	7	161	10
	14–3–43–1			23–4–70–2		15–3–42–3	8–1–29–1	31–13–70–3									3	2		10	259	10
v. Hampshire (Southampton) 19–22 May	35–4–119–3	34–1–104–0		45.5–9–164–6		38–9–109–0			9–2–27–0	3–1–9–0							4	16	1	23	552	9
										0.4–0–2–0											2	0
v. Middlesex (Lord's) 23–26 May	28–2–125–0	16–1–55–2		34–6–123–3		20–3–82–0	18.1–2–78–1			6–2–16–1							1	6	1	21	486	7
v. Sussex (The Oval) 29 May–1 June		24–4–69–0		18.2–6–56–1		15.4–0–47–4	18–2–71–0	11–3–50–0			0.2–0–4–0							3	1	9	300	6
v. Derbyshire (The Oval) 2–4 June		29–3–80–3		25–7–41–0		24–4–56–4	18–4–47–1	15–11–8–2									5	12		10	249	10
		9–0–33–0		8–3–18–0		7–0–31–0		12–4–16–1			9–0–86–0	8.3–0–52–0					5	3	1	1	244	1
v. Worcestershire (The Oval) 12–15 June		30–10–59–2		26–12–31–0		20–5–44–2	13–7–15–2	19–6–39–1										7		7	195	7
		15–5–40–1		24.4–8–60–4		10–1–42–1	8–0–39–0	10–1–34–1									4			3	219	7
v. Somerset (Bath) 19–22 June	14–2–63–0	20–2–82–1		21–7–80–2		22–2–58–2		20–9–61–1	6–1–22–3								4	6		11	376	9
		3–0–7–0							4–1–8–1	1.3–0–5–0											20	1
v. Gloucestershire (Bristol) 26–29 June			35–8–97–3				22–2–74–1	44–11–119–4	9–0–33–1				10–3–20–0				4	5	1	3	352	9
			18–5–41–2				10–2–38–0	24.2–4–84–6	7–4–14–2									1	1	1	178	10
v. Northamptonshire (The Oval) 30 June–2 July		22–3–83–0		16–6–44–1		30–5–107–6		21–4–49–1	6–0–20–0									9		11	312	8
		8.4–0–59–1				7–3–11–3		4–0–31–2										1		5	102	6
v. Glamorgan (Neath) 3–6 July		20–3–54–1	12.3–3–33–1			23–4–90–1		11–3–30–1	11.3–1–36–2									7	2	10	250	6
		17–1–75–1	17–3–54–2			15.3–2–43–5		10–3–32–1	7–1–43–1									1	1	14	248	10
v. Kent (Guildford) 14–16 July		15–3–29–5	11–0–37–1			16.2–3–47–4												4		7	117	10
		26–4–69–2	20–4–71–1			25.5–5–62–4		25–5–83–3	8–1–45–0									2		6	332	10
v. Warwickshire (Guildford) 17–20 July		23–1–95–2				25–5–79–2	25–6–74–1	14–2–77–0	7–0–39–1								4	4		13	372	6
		21–5–81–4				14–0–39–1	15–4–48–1	4–1–4–0	8–2–18–2								5	3		11	198	9
v. Nottinghamshire (The Oval) 21–23 July	12–0–43–0	14–2–39–1					12–1–63–0	6–2–18–0	11.1–1–36–0	1–0–1–0								1		10	201	2
	17–1–80–1	10–1–40–0					17–0–118–4	24–3–110–2										4		8	352	7
v. Durham (Durham) 31 July–3 August	11–0–80–2	15.3–9–30–6				15–4–39–1		5–0–24–1										16		12	189	10
	6–1–17–0	32.1–3–98–3			8–3–32–0	34–3–120–5		36–9–72–2				1–0–1–0		2–1–1–0			5	11	4	25	357	10
v. Lancashire (Lytham) 4–6 August		12–1–33–0		41–6–143–2		17–1–55–1		37–6–109–0		3–0–24–0							4	8		6	376	3
		5–0–19–0		16–5–46–4		3–0–17–0		14–3–55–1		1.5–0–20–0		1–0–8–0						2		3	167	5
v. Leicestershire (The Oval) 14–17 August		24–4–52–2	11–2–33–0	28.5–10–61–6		21–2–53–2		7–2–15–0										2		6	216	10
		17–0–67–1	12.3–0–44–0	25–5–60–2		18–2–48–2		8–2–41–0									1	6		7	267	5
v. Essex (Colchester) 18–20 August		18–4–58–1		26–10–43–2		25–7–53–4	14–2–39–0	23–9–33–3		1–1–0–0							1	2	1	10	229	10
v. Yorkshire (Bradford) 21–24 August	16–0–78–0			19–2–60–5		21–3–75–0	24–5–67–3	22–10–46–2									1	14		10	341	10
																					0	0
v. Somerset (The Oval) 31 August–3 September		23–5–54–0		43–13–90–1		31.1–11–68–3	24–5–75–4	30–9–55–2		2–0–4–0							2	4		8	352	10
				22–11–38–3		10–1–23–0	6–1–20–0	21–5–26–0		1–0–4–0		3.3–1–11–0						2		3	124	3
v. Nottinghamshire (Trent Bridge) 7–10 September	30–5–87–3			22–7–45–0		36–12–89–5	28–5–88–2	11–0–23–0				2–0–6–0					3	16		20	357	10
	21–2–82–1			21.3–7–64–1		14–5–24–2	15–2–47–1	10–1–36–0									1	8		8	262	5
v. Middlesex (The Oval) 12–15 September	45.4–10–117–5			18–3–60–0				59–15–126–4					34–7–95–1		8–0–35–0			8		15	441	10
					0.4–0–3–0									5–0–13–0		4–0–16–0					32	0
Bowlers average	333.4–41– 1256–23 54.60	582.2–94– 1780–45 39.55	178.4–34– 531–11 48.27	595.1–170– 1567–51 30.72	17.4–5– 79–0 –	628.5–116– 1823–71 25.67	326.1–61– 1125–25 45.00	591.1–156– 1579–45 35.08	93.4–14– 341–13 26.23	21–4– 85–1 85.00	9.2–0– 90–0 –	16–1– 78–0 –	44–10– 115–1 115.00	7–1– 14–0 –	8–0– 35–0 –	4–0– 16–0 –						

SUSSEX CCC

BATTING	v. Hampshire (Southampton) 25–29 April	v. Somerset (Hove) 7–11 May	v. Nottinghamshire (Trent Bridge) 20–22 May	v. Kent (Hove) 23–26 May	v. Surrey (The Oval) 29 May–1 June	v. Warwickshire (Hove) 2–4 June	v. Leicestershire (Leicester) 12–15 June	v. Durham (Horsham) 19–22 June	v. Worcestershire (Worcester) 26–29 June	v. Hampshire (Arundel) 30 June–2 July	v. Northamptonshire (Northampton) 3–6 July	M	Inns	NOs	Runs	HS	Av
D.M. Smith	61 8	47 –	1 20	9 35*	4 –	77 82	7 0	3 67	4 10	– 32	7 –	19	33	2	1076	213	34.70
K. Greenfield	10* 0									– 29	48 –	6	10	2	205	48	25.62
C.C. Remy	26 13											7	9	–	192	47	21.33
A.P. Wells	– 25	61 –	38 31	144 –	165* –	115 23	32 36	1 65	26 46	– 7	12 –	22	35	5	1465	165*	48.83
R. Hanley	– 1											1	1	–	1	1	1.00
P. Moores	– 29	0 –	15 29	47 –	20 –	0 4	46 35	26* 1	17 61*	– 0	39* –	21	30	5	851	109	34.04
F.D. Stephenson	– 29	133 –	8 15	17 –	1 –	14 6	0 0	– 30*	87* 29	– 4	19 –	18	25	4	680	133	32.38
B.T.P. Donelan	68* 14	0 –	33 5	15 –		25 3*	20 4	– 0*	31 0*	– 8		16	25	6	421	68*	22.15
A.C.S. Pigott	– 12	27 –			– –	3 1*	24* 11	– –	20 –	– 1*	27* –	17	19	7	191	27*	15.91
A.N. Jones	– 1		0* 9*	1 –	– –	14* –	17 0	– –			– –	10	9	4	56	17	11.20
A.G. Robson	– 0*	0* –	0 –	0* –				– –				5	4	3	0	0*	0.00
J.W. Hall		3 –	8 24	14 99	32 –	1 54	18 0	82* 0	59 13	– 27	18 –	20	34	5	1125	140*	38.79
M.P. Speight		0 –	166 41	27 –	12 –	5 38	2 0	28 49	17 4		42 –	20	33	2	1180	179	38.06
C.M. Wells		9 –										6	7	1	133	39	22.16
I.D.K. Salisbury		42 –	17 2*	11 –	– –		0 2*		0 –			17	18	2	177	42	11.06
N.J. Lenham			60 21	36 222*	0 –	12 2	1 11	1 118	9 14	– 12	9 –	20	34	2	1173	222*	36.65
J.A. North					53* –	9 9			0 1	– 6	3 –	5	7	1	81	53*	13.50
A.R. Hansford										– 1		1	1	–	1	1	1.00
E.S.H. Giddins												11	8	6	15	10*	7.50
Byes	1	1				23 2	1	2		4	3						
Leg-byes	9	9	4 2	10 6	3	13 22	2 3	6 8	4 10	8	13						
Wides	1			2 2	1	4 4	1	1	1		6						
No-balls	4 6	14	15 9	2 4	9		1	3	15 5	2	5						
Total	169 149	346	365 208	335 368	300	315 250	171 103	151 340	289 194	0 141	251						
Wickets	2 10	10	10 8	10 1	6	10 8	10 10	4 6	10 7	0 10	8						
Result	L	D	D	L	D	W	L	W	W	L	D						
Points	1	6	8	7	7	22	5	20	23	4	3						

FIELDING FIGURES

39 – P. Moores (ct 32/st 7)
24 – A.P. Wells
16 – M.P. Speight
15 – I.D.K. Salisbury
13 – D.M. Smith
10 – F.D. Stephenson
9 – N.J. Lenham
7 – J.W. Hall
5 – A.C.S. Pigott and K. Greenfield
3 – E.S.H. Giddins and sub
2 – B.T.P. Donelan
1 – A.G. Robson, A.N. Jones, C.C. Remy and C.M. Wells
† P. Moores absent hurt

BATTING	v. Essex (Southend) 17–20 July	v. Lancashire (Hove) 21–23 July	v. Gloucestershire (Cheltenham) 24–27 July	v. Somerset (Taunton) 31 July–2 August	v. Glamorgan (Eastbourne) 4–6 August	v. Derbyshire (Eastbourne) 7–10 August	v. Middlesex (Hove) 21–24 August	v. Essex (Hove) 26–29 August	v. Glamorgan (Cardiff) 31 August–3 September	v. Lancashire (Old Trafford) 7–10 September	v. Yorkshire (Hove) 12–15 September	M	Inns	NOs	Runs	HS	Av
D.M. Smith	213 10	105 32*	61 23	1 21	3 0		36 10	29 19		39 –		19	33	2	1076	213	34.70
K. Greenfield		14 33*				5 43					16 7	6	10	2	205	48	25.62
C.C. Remy		– –	42 16	1 21		47 8	– –		18 –			7	9	–	192	47	21.33
A.P. Wells	10 17	19 36	63 20	103 24	2 74*	20 7*	18* –	3 3	36 –	143 –	27 13*	22	35	5	1465	165*	48.83
R. Hanley												1	1	–	1	1	1.00
P. Moores	109 –		48 29	14* 10*	43 34	15 5	– –	73 2	6 –	74 –	20 –	21	30	5	851	109	34.04
F.D. Stephenson				0 –	80 30	8 44*		4 49	32* –	17 –	24 –	18	25	4	680	133	32.38
B.T.P. Donelan	34 6		0 28*		14 13	11 11			6* –	68 –	4 –	16	25	6	421	68*	22.15
A.C.S. Pigott	4 5*	– –	0 2	4* –	3 15	11* –	– –	11 10				17	19	7	191	27*	15.91
A.N. Jones	6* 8	– –										10	9	4	56	17	11.20
A.G. Robson												5	4	3	0	0*	0.00
J.W. Hall	9 19	140* 71	8 34	24 73*	16 1*		81 41*	15 17	13 –	14 –	90 7	20	34	5	1125	140*	38.79
M.P. Speight	2 7	39 119*	5 7	122 3	179 6	42 30	21* –	18 126	0 –	3 –	18 2	20	33	2	1180	179	38.06
C.M. Wells							– –	28 13	0 –	39 –	33 11*	6	7	1	133	39	22.16
I.D.K. Salisbury	4 0	– –	2 24	– –	9 0	20 –	– –	0 9	– –	10 –	25 –	17	18	2	177	42	11.06
N.J. Lenham	15 24	7 2	83 52	37 –	4 9	39 0	19 17*	12 4	30 –	136 –	135 20	20	34	2	1173	222*	36.65
J.A. North												5	7	1	81	53*	13.50
A.R. Hansford												1	1	–	1	1	1.00
E.S.H. Giddins	– 0	– –	1* –	– –	0* –	1 –	– –	0* 0*	– –	3* –	10* –	11	8	6	15	10*	7.50
Byes	1	9	5 4	1 5		2 3		1 8		3	4						
Leg-byes	14 5	7 7	4 1	1 1	3 10	1 6	6 3	2 4	5	13	9						
Wides	2		1	1		1	1										
No-balls	6 3	2 2	2 1	1 1	4	7 4	5 8	8 15		1	17 1						
Total	429 104	342 302	324 242	310 159	360 192	230 161	187 79	204 279	146	563	432 61						
Wickets	9 9†	5 3	10 9	7 4	10 8	10 6	3 1	10 10	7	10	10 4						
Result	L	D	L	D	D	W	D	L	D	W	W						
Points	4	7	8	8	7	22	2	3	3	24	23						

SUSSEX CCC

BOWLING

	F.D. Stephenson	A.G. Robson	A.N. Jones	A.C.S. Pigott	B.T.P. Donelan	K. Greenfield	I.D.K. Salisbury	C.M. Wells	A.P. Wells	J.W. Hall	D.M. Smith	N.J. Lenham	J.A. North	C.C. Remy	A.R. Hansford	E.S.H. Giddins	Byes	Leg-byes	Wides	No-balls	Total	Wkts
v. Hampshire (Southampton)	23–8–53–0	33–8–94–1	25–3–96–1	22.2–1–95–0	31–5–90–0	11–0–36–0											1	3	6	2	468	2
25–29 April																					0	0
v. Somerset (Hove)	20–6–30–1	18–7–37–4		17–3–39–1	13–1–43–1		29.1–10–73–3	16–2–29–0									2	11	1	2	264	10
7–11 May	8–1–18–0	9–3–26–1		13–3–28–1	19–7–55–0		34–6–106–3		2–1–4–0	1–1–0–0	1–1–0–0						6	10	14		253	5
v. Nottinghamshire	20–1–64–3	5–0–31–0	6–1–34–0		17–5–35–1		24.4–7–69–5					6–3–0						7	4	7	249	10
(Trent Bridge) 20–22 May	18.5–6–32–2	11–3–37–0	8–0–30–0		15–4–46–0		27–1–122–4										15	12		9	294	8
v. Kent (Hove)	12–3–40–0	17–2–76–2	16–1–76–3		12–2–58–2		22–2–102–0					1–0–1–0					13	2		19	368	7
23–26 May	19–1–91–3	10–0–55–0	7–0–64–1		7–0–40–0		10.2–0–71–2										1	16		6	338	6
v. Surrey (The Oval)	12–6–19–0		14–0–69–1	14–4–41–1			17–5–87–3		15–4–45–0			16–3–61–2	13.3–1–59–1				1	14	1	10	396	8
29 May–1 June																						
v. Warwickshire (Hove)	13.3–3–41–0		15–3–54–1	17.3–5–52–1	23–3–91–2				4–1–12–0			3–1–8–0	20–3–78–1					4			340	5
2–4 June			16–6–35–1	12–6–17–1	20–6–60–2					1–0–14–0	2–0–14–0	2–1–5–0	13–3–47–1				1	1	1	1	224	6A
v. Leicestershire (Leicester)	17–6–46–1		7–0–56–1	16.5–4–45–3	22–2–68–3		12–3–32–0											4		5	251	9B
12–15 June	3–2–4–0			2–0–5–0	2.1–1–6–0				2–1–8–0									1			24	0
v. Durham (Horsham)	25–8–65–4	10–1–20–0	13–0–63–0	15–3–34–3	32.4–4–102–1													16		1	300	8
19–22 June	1–1–0–0	6–0–29–0	9–0–72–1	11–2–38–2	8–0–47–0												1	3		4	190	3
v. Worcestershire (Worcester)	24.4–4–78–4			18–5–28–2			21–5–45–1					4–1–7–1	18–3–45–2				4	1		5	208	10
26–29 June	17.2–5–29–7			18–5–42–0	3–0–14–0		11–1–56–0						11–1–51–3					3		3	195	10
v. Hampshire (Arundel)	21–5–41–1			18–8–25–1	9–2–27–1	2–0–13–0						5–0–20–0	21–3–51–3		29–5–81–3		4	9	1	6	271	9
30 June–2 July																					0	0
v. Northamptonshire												0.1–0–0–0									0	0
(Northampton) 3–6 July																						
v. Essex (Southend)			5–0–29–0	10–3–48–0	10–1–60–0		15–3–71–1					17–1–48–0				9–1–42–0	1	4		5	303	1
17–20 July				6–0–27–0	13–0–90–1		17.3–1–89–1					3–0–16–0					8	1		6	231	2
v. Lancashire (Hove)			14–2–51–0	19.2–0–70–2		4–0–35–0	21–4–71–1					13–5–41–1		9–2–27–3		10–1–43–1	9	2		1	349	8
21–23 July			6.5–1–16–1	16–3–54–0			25–8–54–3					6–0–33–0		4–0–23–0		13.1–2–54–5	4		1	6	238	9
v. Gloucestershire (Cheltenham)				3–1–5–0	36.2–13–77–6		30–9–64–2					1–1–0–0		9–2–23–0		12–4–35–2	3	14	1	5	221	10
24–27 July				13–0–48–2	29–4–102–0		27–4–120–1							3–0–12–0		19.1–5–60–3	1	3	4	3	346	6
v. Somerset (Taunton)	22–4–92–3			13–2–52–1			24.2–9–61–5					7–3–18–0		14–1–60–0		15–2–63–1	5	5		5	356	10
31 July–2 August	19–1–76–1			14–5–29–1			34–17–68–3							5–1–9–0		15–2–46–2	4			8	232	7
v. Glamorgan (Eastbourne)	21–7–46–0			11–4–30–0	23–7–61–2		28.4–9–75–4					3–1–13–0				16–4–44–1	5	7		9	281	8
4–6 August	9–0–41–0			6–1–22–1	16–1–49–1		15–1–63–2									5–2–17–1	4	3	1	2	199	5
v. Derbyshire (Eastbourne)	19–2–49–2			12–2–46–2	8.5–2–23–1		30–11–67–2							8–2–19–1		13–4–33–2	4	7	1	4	248	10
7–10 August	13–3–36–1			3–0–4–0	7–2–27–1		12–1–26–3							4–0–11–0		13.5–5–32–5	4	2		1	142	10
v. Middlesex (Hove)				20–3–52–1			34–6–124–2	18–2–64–1				10–2–27–1		17–3–72–2		24–2–95–0	1	10			445	7
21–24 August									6–0–25–0		1–0–4–0	8–2–18–0		3.2–0–10–0			5	1			63	0
v. Essex (Hove)	28–3–88–2			22–1–87–1			45–15–106–1	11–1–33–0				2–1–2–1				24–3–79–2	5	5		8	405	8
26–29 August	7–1–33–0						3–0–13–0	5–1–22–1								1.4–0–7–0		5	2		80	1
v. Glamorgan (Cardiff)	17–2–43–0				8–3–21–2		26.1–5–79–4	24–12–26–3						20–1–70–0		8–2–26–0		3	2	5	268	10
31 August–3 September																						
v. Lancashire (Old Trafford)	14–3–50–1						14.5–6–29–6	12–1–47–2								9–0–44–1	1	3		9	174	10
7–10 September	9–0–51–2				8–3–15–1		18.5–5–54–5	11–1–43–2								5–0–34–0	5	5		5	207	10
v. Yorkshire (Hove)	15–0–62–1				7–3–16–0		19–7–54–7	14–4–42–1				7–2–14–0				12–4–38–1	4	2		6	232	10
12–15 September	19–1–57–1				4–4–0–0		30–9–84–5	8–2–17–0				6–1–21–0				23–9–65–4	4	11	1	8	259	10
Bowlers average	467.2–93– 1375–40 34.37	119–24– 405–8 50.62	161.5–17– 745–11 67.72	363–74– 1063–27 39.37	404–85– 1323–28 47.25	17–0– 84–0 –	678.3–170– 2135–79 27.02	119–26– 323–10 32.30	29–7– 94–0 –	2–1– 14–0 –	2–1– 18–0 –	120.1–28– 362–6 60.33	96.3–14– 331–11 30.09	96.2–12– 336–6 56.00	29–5– 81–3 27.00	247.5–52– 857–31 27.64						

A M.P. Speight 3–0–30–1
B T.J. Boon retired hurt

WARWICKSHIRE CCC

BATTING

BATTING	v. Nottinghamshire (Trent Bridge) 25–28 April	v. Derbyshire (Edgbaston) 7–11 May	v. Cambridge University (Cambridge) 12–14 May	v. Glamorgan (Swansea) 20–22 May	v. Worcestershire (Edgbaston) 23–26 May	v. Sussex (Hove) 2–4 June	v. Hampshire (Edgbaston) 12–15 June	v. Middlesex (Coventry) 16–18 June	v. Gloucestershire (Bristol) 19–22 June	v. Derbyshire (Derby) 26–29 June	v. Essex (Edgbaston) 3–6 July	v. Yorkshire (Sheffield) 14–16 July	M	Inns	NO	Runs	HS	Av
A.J. Moles	51 7	50 86*	17 50	66 13	4 16	122 28	95 2	55 18	5 4	1 1	– 14	34* 7	23	41	3	1359	122	35.76
J.D. Ratcliffe	34 4	50 45	7 46	9 1	11 22		8 0	35 0					7	14	–	272	50	19.42
T.A. Lloyd	10 41	10 34*	5 –	13 4	38 20	10 31	14 30	84* 43	23 22	1 4	– 26	– 19	23	39	2	919	84*	24.83
D.P. Ostler	0 102	0 –	9 44*		14 30	108 20	28 65	49 5	83 19	0 0	– 10	– 15	22	37	2	1225	192	35.00
M. Asif Din	40 35	28 –											2	3	–	103	40	34.33
R.G. Twose	55 17	37 –	44 –	26 31	43 13	7* 3	2 51	– 28	21 5	9 1	– 4	41* 66	23	38	3	1412	233	40.34
P.A. Smith	3 5	7 –	22 0*	25 26	30 0	4* 32*	33 23	– 7*	9 20	24 23	– 0*	– 5	19	27	5	416	45	18.90
K.J. Piper	18* 12					– –	0 0	– 8	0 26*	8 6	– 15	– 9*	19	25	8	345	72	20.29
P.A. Booth	8 10	10* –	14 –	1 0		10* –		– 0					8	11	4	78	22*	11.14
G.C. Small	1 7				19 12	– 31*	10* 10*	– 0	7 5	22* 22	– –	– –	17	17	6	181	31*	16.45
T.A. Munton	9 0*	6 –	– –	0 0	– 4*		4* –		0 5*	3 15			16	17	6	123	47	11.18
P.C.L. Holloway		16 –			102* 15								2	3	1	133	102*	66.50
A.A. Donald		0 –		4* 1*	33* 0	– –	4 1*	– 0	10* 2	9 16*	– –	– –	21	22	10	234	41	19.50
T.L. Penney			102* –						55 9	7 9	– 41	– 37	16	24	7	904	151	53.17
M. Burns			78 –	3 4									2	3	–	85	78	28.33
D.R. Brown			5* –										1	1	1	5	5*	–
D.A. Reeve				22 79	1 49	57 46	1 1	8* 10	27 72	10 60	– 54*	– 74	17	28	4	833	79	34.70
N.M.K. Smith				67 1		18 29					– 18	– 31*	12	20	2	454	67	25.22
M.A.V. Bell													3	5	2	10	5	3.33
Byes	3 2	4 5	9 4	1	1	1	5 11	4	1		5	4						
Leg-byes	4 5	9 1	6 5	8 11	7 4	4 1	6 3	12 4	4 12	11 2	11	7 6						
Wides	1	1 7	1 1		1	1	1	2										
No-balls	12 16	7		3 1	10 3	1	6	4 1	8 4	16 15	16	6 3						
Total	249 263	235 178	319 150	248 172	313 189	340 224	216 198	251 126	253 205	121 174	0 204	88 276						
Wickets	10 10	10 1	8 2	10 10	8 10	5 6	9 8	3 10	10 9	10 10	0 7	0 7						
Result	L	W	D	L	W	L	D	L	W	L	D W							
Points	6	22	–	4	24	8	5	7	23	3	3 18							

BATTING	v. Surrey (Guildford) 17–20 July	v. Northamptonshire (Northampton) 21–23 July	v. Nottinghamshire (Edgbaston) 24–27 July	v. Leicestershire (Edgbaston) 31 July–3 August	v. Somerset (Taunton) 4–6 August	v. Durham (Edgbaston) 7–10 August	v. Lancashire (Edgbaston) 18–20 August	v. Glamorgan (Edgbaston) 26–29 August	v. Worcestershire (Worcester) 31 August–3 September	v. Middlesex (Lord's) 8–11 September	v. Kent (Edgbaston) 12–15 September	M	Inns	NO	Runs	HS	Av
A.J. Moles	15 22	12 66	35 18	91 –	29 27	51 –	86 4	– 30	85* –	3 1	0 38	23	41	3	1359	122	35.76
J.D. Ratcliffe												7	14	–	272	50	19.42
T.A. Lloyd	4 31	5 3	47 13	1 –	50 4	60 –	16 1	– 53	21 –	40 4	76 8	23	39	2	919	84*	24.83
D.P. Ostler	192 31	29 14	21 2	29 –	22 25	45 –	0 56	– 60	20 –	0 13*	40 25	22	37	2	1225	192	35.00
M. Asif Din												2	3	–	103	40	34.33
R.G. Twose	55 14	49 78	30 32	233 –	7 45	65 –	53 0	– 51	20 –	84 36*	4 52	23	38	3	1412	233	40.34
P.A. Smith		3 –	16 1	0 –	40 45	– –	– 13	– –				19	27	5	416	45	18.90
K.J. Piper	2* 3	11* –	16* 62*	6 –	0 15	– –	0 18	– –	6 –	72 –	8 24*	19	25	8	345	72	20.29
P.A. Booth					3 22*				0* –			8	11	4	78	22*	11.14
G.C. Small	– 3	– –		12* –		– –		– –	– –	10 –	0* 10	17	17	6	181	31*	16.45
T.A. Munton	– 7*			– –		– –	6 11	– –	– –	0* –	47 6	16	17	6	123	47	11.18
P.C.L. Holloway												2	3	1	133	102*	66.50
A.A. Donald	– 32*	– –	25* 41	– –	0* 3	– –	13* 22	– –	– –	15 –	2 1	21	22	10	234	41	19.50
T.L. Penney	70* 5	100* 12*	40 1	50* –	80 38	37* –	0 40	– 13*	7 –	151 –	0 0	16	24	7	904	151	53.17
M. Burns												2	3	–	85	78	28.33
D.R. Brown												1	1	1	5	5*	–
D.A. Reeve	6 1	48 17	4 6			44* –		– 40*	38 –	7 –	51 0	17	28	4	833	79	34.70
N.M.K. Smith	7 30	41 1*	19 39	0 –	28 9		15 20			39 –	39 3	12	20	2	454	67	25.22
M.A.V. Bell			– 5		0 2*		3 0*					3	5	2	10	5	3.33
Byes	4 5	11 8		6	8 17	2	5 1	1	1	8	5 1						
Leg-byes	4 3	5 1	2 4	5	7 8	9	6	5	7	22 1	8 2						
Wides		1 5	4 1			2		1	4	2 1	1						
No-balls	13 11	1 1	7 4		2	1	1	2	1	23 1	8 1						
Total	372 198	316 206	266 229	433	276 260	316	203 187	0 256	210	476 57	289 171						
Wickets	6 9	7 5	8 10	7	10 9	4	9† 10	0 4	6	10 2	10 10						
Result	D	D	L	W	D	D	L	D	D	W	L						
Points	6	8	5	24	6	8	3	4	4	24	4						

FIELDING FIGURES

43 – K.J. Piper (ct 41 / st 2)
21 – D.P. Ostler
18 – A.J. Moles
16 – R.G. Twose
15 – D.A. Reeve
14 – A.A. Donald
8 – P.C.L. Holloway, M. Burns and T.A. Munton
6 – P.A. Smith and G.C. Small
5 – T.L. Penney, N.M.K. Smith and A. Lloyd
4 – J.D. Ratcliffe
1 – sub
† P.A. Smith absent ill

WARWICKSHIRE CCC

BOWLING

	T.A. Munton	G.C. Small	P.A. Smith	R.G. Twose	A.J. Moles	P.A. Booth	T.A. Lloyd	A.A. Donald	D.R. Brown	D.P. Ostler	N.M.K. Smith	D.A. Reeve	M.A.V. Bell	T.L. Penney	K.J. Piper	Byes	Leg-byes	Wides	No-balls	Total	Wkts
v. Nottinghamshire (Trent Bridge) 25–28 April	17–4–39–2	14–3–48–0	29.2–5–79–5	12–3–43–2	9–3–16–1	21–3–70–0										7	9	2	1	311	10
		1.2–0–9–0	10–1–44–1	16.4–2–41–1	2–0–11–0	27.5–3–81–0	2–1–8–0									3	5			202	2
v. Derbyshire (Edgbaston) 7–11 May	15.2–2–44–5		2–0–11–1					14–5–22–4								1	7		1	85	10
	39–14–87–0		27.1–5–91–6	3–0–16–0		24–13–39–2		26–5–74–1								13	7	10	2	327	10
v. Cambridge University (Cambridge) 12–14 May	13–5–12–1		9–2–28–0	10–5–13–2		30–9–64–3			19–7–43–2	4–0–29–0						11	8		1	208	8
	16.5–4–40–1			18–6–46–3	1–0–2–0	18–5–27–0			15–7–27–3							4	8		2	154	8
v. Glamorgan (Swansea) 20–22 May	24–8–44–0		19–5–52–1	6–2–22–2		32–4–129–2		12–3–51–0			5–1–28–0	2–0–8–0				4	8		7	346	5
	14–3–43–2					8–3–27–1		14–4–24–2			26–5–61–1					10	2		2	167	6
v. Worcestershire (Edgbaston) 23–26 May	18–4–40–3	15–6–35–2	15–3–55–3		5–2–8–0			17–2–60–2								7	3		4	208	10
	23–9–57–2	19–6–46–2	9–2–51–1					17.4–2–69–5								5	14		5	242	10
v. Sussex (Hove) 2–4 June		19–4–47–2	9–0–28–0			27.1–11–59–2	4–0–13–0	27–6–82–5			15–0–50–1					23	13	4		315	10
		4.3–2–5–0	18.3–1–88–2					5–0–32–1			20.5–2–101–4					2	22	4		250	8
v. Hampshire (Edgbaston) 12–15 June	27–8–55–1	18–1–56–0	18–2–63–5	10–4–21–0	4–0–12–0			17.4–5–46–3				10–2–28–0					9		3	290	10
	12–2–36–0	12–1–45–0		7–1–43–1				11–4–24–1				7–0–32–1					2			182	3
v. Middlesex (Coventry) 16–18 June		15.3–3–43–3	17–3–60–0	27–10–63–6	9–2–20–1	5–1–16–0		14–2–60–0				7–2–26–0				5	11	10	4	304	10
		5–1–19–0	8–0–34–1	11–1–37–0	5–1–25–0	13–1–95–1	7–1–26–0	5–2–14–0				12–0–45–0					4		1	299	2
v. Gloucestershire (Bristol) 19–22 June	23–5–53–2	16–4–43–1	2–0–13–0	5–1–7–1				21–8–44–5				12–4–28–1				5	6		1	199	10
	24–10–60–4	13–4–34–2	6–1–27–1					19–4–47–3				1–1–0–0				5	11		1	184	10
v. Derbyshire (Derby) 26–29 June	20–3–76–1	25–9–47–2	14–3–67–4	8–1–26–0				22–4–64–2				20–8–31–1				20	12	2	14	343	10
v. Essex (Edgbaston) 3–6 July		9–1–18–1	10–1–42–0	11–1–43–1			4–0–54–1	21–2–40–3			11–2–47–1	13–8–17–0				10	4		3	275	7
																				0	0
v. Yorkshire (Sheffield) 14–16 July		23–5–49–1	24–5–58–1	9.5–1–36–0			1–0–1–0	29–8–61–3			15–2–35–1	24–7–44–0				5	12	4	12	301	6
					4–0–27–0		5–0–34–0										1	1		62	0
v. Surrey (Guildford) 17–20 July	17–7–33–0	9–3–23–1					23.3–3–90–2	12–4–34–0			29–4–128–2	13–5–20–0				2	11		2	341	6
	13.1–3–42–1	10–3–24–0						15–3–49–6			9–3–11–0						5			131	7
v. Northamptonshire (Northampton) 21–23 July		16–0–50–2	19–4–67–1					19–4–63–2			26.2–3–88–1	18–3–55–2				3	8		4	334	9
		2–0–6–0	5–0–20–1	7–2–33–1			3–0–18–0	3–0–4–0		3–0–22–0	16–2–72–1	7–0–38–1				4	1	1		218	4
v. Nottinghamshire (Edgbaston) 24–27 July			22–2–101–1	12–1–33–0				27–8–82–3			20–5–63–0	17–5–35–0	26–8–78–3			8	15	4	4	415	7
				3–0–20–0	4–0–48–0					6–0–32–0		4–1–4–2		5–0–35–0	4.4–0–57–1		1	2	1	197	3
v. Leicestershire (Edgbaston) 31 July–3 August	24.1–14–46–5	13–5–37–2	13–3–43–0					16–7–27–2			5–3–4–0					5	7	1		169	9
	20–3–64–7	8–2–29–2						12.5–1–43–1									4		1	140	10
v. Somerset (Taunton) 4–6 August			13–2–53–1	6–1–23–1		24.4–6–85–2		22–7–41–2			15–3–51–2		5–0–20–0			4	1	1	4	278	8A
			8–0–26–0			14–4–29–4		21–3–68–2			9–3–35–0		25–2–84–3			17	5		14	264	9
v. Durham (Edgbaston) 7–10 August	22–7–45–1	13–3–41–2	3–1–6–0					16.1–6–37–7									7			136	10
	19–6–43–0	16–4–25–0	10–2–38–0	8–2–21–1				18–6–59–1				16–7–30–2				14	8	2	3	238	4
v. Lancashire (Edgbaston) 18–20 August	29–7–113–0		11–0–44–1	10–1–28–3				17–6–42–1			38–10–99–1		23.2–7–65–2			16	8	4	1	415	8
v. Glamorgan (Edgbaston) 26–29 August	17–7–51–0	12–4–30–1	22–4–73–5	11–3–44–2				23–8–64–1				10–2–41–1				5	8		1	316	10
																				0	0
v. Worcestershire (Worcester) 31 August–3 September	37–12–80–2	18–3–51–1		8–0–33–0		35–11–93–2		20–2–81–1				24–10–53–0				7	11	2	2	409	7
v. Middlesex (Lord's) 8–11 September	15–3–36–1	6–1–20–0					7.2–1–7–3	9–0–53–0			21–8–61–5	14–8–12–1				3	9	1	2	201	10
	22.4–3–71–2	22–3–74–3		3–0–11–0			7–2–19–0	18–5–36–5			21–4–84–0	10–4–20–0				4	9	1	3	328	10
v. Kent (Edgbaston) 12–15 September	28–1–131–1	13–2–49–0		27–2–91–1			5–0–25–0	14–3–50–0			30.2–3–160–4	26–3–65–2				16	16		3	603	8
Bowlers average	550.1–154– 1441–44 32.75	367.2–83– 1003–30 33.43	373–57– 1362–42 32.42	249.3–50– 794–28 28.35	43–8– 169–2 84.50	279.4–74– 814–19 42.84	68.5–8– 295–6 49.16	575.2–139– 1647–74 22.25	34–14– 70–5 14.00	13–0– 83–0 –	332.3–63– 1178–24 49.08	267–80– 632–13 48.61	79.2–17– 247–8 30.87	5–0– 35–0 –	4.4–0– 57–1 57.00						

A A.N. Hayhurst, R.J. Harden retired hurt

WORCESTERSHIRE CCC

BATTING

BATTING	v. Oxford University (Oxford) 17–20 April		v. Northamptonshire (Worcester) 25–29 April		v. Pakistanis (Worcester) 6–8 May		v. Derbyshire (Derby) 14–18 May		v. Gloucestershire (Gloucester) 19–22 May		v. Warwickshire (Edgbaston) 23–26 May		v. Gloucestershire (Worcester) 29 May–1 June		v. Kent (Tunbridge Wells) 2–4 June		v. Surrey (The Oval) 12–15 June		v. Glamorgan (Worcester) 16–18 June		v. Yorkshire (Worcester) 19–22 June		v. Sussex (Worcester) 26–29 June		M	Inns	NO	Runs	HS	Av
T.S. Curtis	76	1*	43	38	85	45	228*	–	0	32	40	54			140*	0	27	48	124	43*	197	31	15	1	23	41	5	1829	228*	50.80
A.C.H. Seymour	133	2	37	7	37	11	27	–	8	14	31	38			18	62	9	8	16	29	22	25			11	21	–	556	133	26.47
G.A. Hick	27	–	92	23	0	33	0	–			17	70					9	73					40	131	13	22	2	1239	213*	61.95
T.M. Moody	100*	–	21	33					118	18	54	1			13	100	1	22	12*	–					11	19	2	724	178	42.58
D.A. Leatherdale	67	24*	34	60	10	0	15	–	56	3	2	21			91	2	10	37*	66	4*	17	14	5	6	23	39	3	982	112	27.27
S.J. Rhodes	0*	6	18	45	46*	21*	21	–	8	9	1*	9			25	11*	0	0	46*	–	14	–	51	2	23	33	10	776	116*	33.73
S.R. Lampitt	–	3					14	–	26*	1	24	9			3	16	71*	19	66	–	8	4*	3	9	19	29	5	565	71*	23.54
P.J. Newport	–	4	30	10	–	–	42	–	0	4	2	1*			–	–	15	0	–	–	61	–	11	16*	22	25	6	467	75*	24.57
R.K. Illingworth	–	12	10	12	–	–	25	–			9	1			–	–	39*	5*	–	–	5*	–	2	4	20	20	6	294	43	21.00
N.V. Radford	–	66	23	17*	–	–	25*	–	0	12	0	0					–	–	–	–	–	–	2*	0	22	19	7	261	73*	21.75
G.R. Dilley	–	39	18	4*																					2	3	1	61	39	30.50
R.D. Stemp			7*	15					16	0*					–	–	–	–	–	–					11	6	4	70	16*	35.00
D.B. D'Oliveira					31	2	37	–	17	36	14	14													13	20	2	536	100	29.77
W.P.C. Weston					64*	32*	0	–	5	2													56	4	14	23	5	675	66*	37.50
C.M. Tolley					–	–									–	2*					11	–	7	16	13	10	4	89	27	14.83
G.R. Haynes															12	7			66	1	0	23*	6	0	9	13	2	288	66	26.18
P.A. Neale																					24	17			2	3	–	79	38	26.33
M.J. Weston																									2	3	3	26	17*	–
Byes	1		4	4	4	5	4			3	7	5				5		4	1	3	1	16	4							
Leg-byes	3	3	7	12	7	6	29		5	6	3	14			14	4	7		4	1	13	12	1	3						
Wides	5				3										6				1	1										
No-balls	1	2	1	2	16	11	3		11	5	4	5			5	1	7	3	5	1	13	2	5	3						
Total	413	162	345	282	303	166	470		270	145	208	242			327	210	195	219	407	83	386	144	208	195						
Wickets	4	7	10	9	5	5	9		10	10	10	10			6	6	7	7	5	2	9	4	10	10						
Result	D		D		W		D		L		L		Ab.		D		D		W		W		L							
Points	–		6		–		6		7		5		0		3		5		24		23		6							

BATTING	v. Leicestershire (Leicester) 30 June–2 July		v. Nottinghamshire (Trent Bridge) 14–16 July		v. Middlesex (Uxbridge) 17–20 July		v. Essex (Kidderminster) 21–23 July		v. Derbyshire (Worcester) 24–27 July		v. Hampshire (Worcester) 4–6 August		v. Lancashire (Old Trafford) 7–10 August		v. Somerset (Weston-super-Mare) 18–20 August		v. Durham (Worcester) 21–24 August		v. Nottinghamshire (Worcester) 26–29 August		v. Warwickshire (Worcester) 31 August–3 September		v. Hampshire (Southampton) 12–15 September		M	Inns	NO	Runs	HS	Av
T.S. Curtis	7	–	0	0	40	60	12	20	86	96	49	30	–	24	11	18	50	–	27	10*	7	–	11	3	23	41	5	1829	228*	50.80
A.C.H. Seymour																			22	0					11	21	–	556	133	26.47
G.A. Hick			213*	0	168	7					34	63	–	35					41	17*	146	–			13	22	2	1239	213*	61.95
T.M. Moody			5	0	9	9	178	–	26	4															11	19	2	724	178	42.58
D.A. Leatherdale	14	–	9	112	26	12	36	0	25	–	31	26	–	40	35	27	20	–	0	–	13	–	1	11	23	39	3	982	112	27.27
S.J. Rhodes	0	–	36	–	2	6	–	62*	1	–	4	–	–	16	18*	–	24*	–	6	–	116*	–	45	107	23	33	10	776	116*	33.73
S.R. Lampitt	2	–	16	14*	4	2*	26	63	2	–	42	–					4	–	9	–	14	–	22	69	19	29	5	565	71*	23.54
P.J. Newport	75*	–	15*	–	10	2*			15	–	60	–	–	5	–	–	25*	–	20	–	39	–	5	0	22	25	6	467	75*	24.57
R.K. Illingworth	7	–	–	–	30	1	–	–	19	–	31*	–	–	16*					1	–	22*	–	43	–	20	20	6	294	43	21.00
N.V. Radford	5	–	–	73*	0	1	–	–	14*	0	3*	–	–	–	–	–	–	–	5	–	–	–	–	15*	22	19	7	261	73*	21.75
G.R. Dilley																									2	3	1	61	39	30.50
R.D. Stemp	16*	–	–	–	16*	–			–	–					–	–	–	–							11	6	4	70	16*	35.00
D.B. D'Oliveira							100	8	16	1*	0	–	–	31	65	13*	81	–	0	–	25	–	43	2	13	20	2	536	100	29.77
W.P.C. Weston	27	–	7	43			22	26	35	50*	47	57*	–	9	12	66*	34	–			5	–	36	36	14	23	5	675	66*	37.50
C.M. Tolley					4	1	–	1*			27	–	–	4*	–	–	–	–	16*	–	–	–	–	–	13	10	4	89	27	14.83
G.R. Haynes	24	–					40*	–					–	4	64	–	41	–							9	13	2	288	66	26.18
P.A. Neale	38	–																							2	3	–	79	38	26.33
M.J. Weston															17*	–							8*	1*	2	3	3	26	17*	–
Byes			4	5		4	6		5	1				4	5		1		4		7			1						
Leg-byes	9		5	9	18	10	15	3	8	8	6			6	11	4	7		4	4	11		6	7						
Wides			1	2			2	1		1	1			3		1	2		1		2		2							
No-balls	8		7	4	19	3	11	2	14	1		3			12	1	5		6	1	2		6	2						
Total	232		318	262	346	118	448	186	266	162	335	179	0	197	250	130	294		162	32	409		228	254						
Wickets	9		6	5	10	8	6	5	9	3	9	3	0	8	5	2	6		10	1	7		8	7						
Result	L		W		D		D		D		D		D		D		D		D		D		D							
Points	2		22		7		6		7		6		2		7		7		5		5		6							

FIELDING FIGURES

49 – S.J. Rhodes (ct 44/st 5)
22 – G.A. Hick
16 – D.A. Leatherdale
15 – T.S. Curtis
13 – D.B. D'Oliveira
11 – T.M. Moody
9 – A.C.H. Seymour
8 – R.K. Illingworth
6 – S.R. Lampitt
5 – P.J. Newport and C.M. Tolley
4 – N.V. Radford and R.D. Stemp
3 – G.R. Haynes
2 – W.P.C. Weston
1 – M.J. Weston

WORCESTERSHIRE CCC

BOWLING

	G.R. Dilley	N.V. Radford	T.M. Moody	P.J. Newport	R.K. Illingworth	S.R. Lampitt	G.A. Hick	D.A. Leatherdale	R.D. Stemp	C.M. Tolley	W.P.C. Weston	D.B. D'Oliveira	T.S. Curtis	G.R. Haynes	M.J. Weston	Byes	Leg-byes	Wides	No-balls	Total	Wkts
v. Oxford University (Oxford)	14–4–23–0	16–5–38–1	5–1–14–0	16–3–39–2	45–11–79–4	13.3–5–18–2	7–3–9–1									7			1	227	10
17–20 April																					
v. Northamptonshire (Worcester)	11–3–34–0	33–9–82–1		37–9–102–5	25.1–5–66–2		4–2–12–0	5–2–13–0	12–3–37–1							5	3		5	354	10
25–29 April		6–1–28–1		9–0–39–1	19.4–7–43–4		3–3–0–0		15–2–66–1								4		3	180	7
v. Pakistanis (Worcester)		13–2–59–1		13–3–54–0	20–4–81–2		13–1–39–0			16–1–67–1	15–1–73–0						1		5	374	4
6–8 May		6–1–20–1		13.1–4–22–5						6–3–9–0	13–2–39–2					1	2	1	2	93	9A
v. Derbyshire (Derby)		22.4–4–67–5		16–3–43–1	33–18–48–1	21–5–60–2					10–4–28–0	1–0–1–0					4	2	1	251	10
14–18 May		28–6–88–6		26–7–68–1	43–14–87–0	22–3–66–0	10–4–25–0	3–0–10–0			8–0–24–0	12–4–36–0	3.2–0–17–0				12	2	3	433	7
v. Gloucestershire (Gloucester)		12–3–23–2	11–3–24–0	13–5–34–0		7–1–15–1			25.5–9–67–6			11–2–29–1					14	1	4	206	10
19–22 May		8.2–2–32–0		6–2–19–0		11–2–14–0			28–3–79–5			10–1–54–2				8	4		5	210	7
v. Warwickshire (Edgbaston)		17–0–71–0	21–5–50–4	25–8–69–2	12–3–21–0	23–3–80–2	4–1–15–0										7	1	10	313	8
23–26 May		4–1–26–0	9–2–24–2	22–3–45–5	5–0–20–0	17–2–51–3	7–3–18–0									1	4		3	189	10
v. Gloucestershire (Worcester)																					Ab.
29 May–1 June																					
v. Kent (Tunbridge Wells)			8–0–34–0	13–2–41–0	13–5–40–0	6–0–19–0			20.4–4–53–1	14–4–48–0				7–3–14–0			1		6	250	1
2–4 June			1–0–11–0	7–0–33–0	16–0–53–2	4–0–28–0			17–1–49–1	6–3–12–0							4	1	2	190	3
v. Surrey (The Oval)		22–5–74–1	12–2–32–2	24.1–10–56–3	16–2–58–1	17–2–54–2			8–0–21–0							2	4		2	301	9
12–15 June		11–3–25–1		9–2–23–1	8–2–58–2				14–1–61–1								2		1	169	5
v. Glamorgan (Worcester)		15–1–52–3		13–4–34–4		10–1–36–3								7–3–21–0			7	2	16	150	10
16–18 June		21–4–86–2		29.4–5–101–5	5–2–12–0	21–1–85–2			11–6–24–1					9–3–18–0		4	9	1	22	339	10
v. Yorkshire (Worcester)		19–4–41–4		18–4–44–1	19–12–23–2	12–1–34–1				17–4–52–1				6–0–30–0		5	5		18	234	9
19–22 June		22–2–86–3		23–5–69–4	9–2–10–1	9–0–35–2				5–3–2–0							5	2	8	207	10
v. Sussex (Worcester)		27–5–77–4		25–4–78–3	5–1–7–0	21–1–76–3				17–4–47–0							4		15	289	10
26–29 June		6–1–24–1		23–5–53–2	2–0–4–1	17–2–52–0				13–2–38–2				5–2–13–0			10	1	5	194	7
v. Leicestershire (Leicester)																				0	0
30 June–2 July		3–0–13–0		10–1–43–0	25–8–58–0	6–0–36–1			25.2–6–81–0								3		4	234	1
v. Nottinghamshire		15–2–45–0		22.4–4–67–2	35–6–103–3	21–3–70–2	9–3–37–0		19–5–70–1								8	2	6	400	8
(Trent Bridge) 14–16 July		6–1–17–0	3–0–25–0	4–1–15–1	14–3–47–0	3–0–17–0			9–1–35–1				2–0–17–0				3		3	176	2
v. Middlesex (Uxbridge)		12–1–56–1		18.4–2–59–4		11–2–33–2				19–3–51–3						1	2	1	5	202	10
17–20 July		20–3–48–5		10–1–26–1	27–7–66–0	3–0–13–0	24–9–50–1		29–6–95–2	6–2–10–1						4	9		4	321	10
v. Essex (Kidderminster)		11–1–50–2			17–3–66–0	13–1–42–0				16–2–62–0	11–0–29–0	14.1–1–48–2				2	1		6	300	5
21–23 July																					
v. Derbyshire (Worcester)		6–1–18–0		2–0–10–0	32.1–13–56–4	18–1–57–4			16–4–49–0		5–0–9–0	12–3–44–2				1	2		8	246	10
24–27 July		6–1–18–0	2–0–35–0		7–3–10–0	6–1–21–0		1–0–5–0	19–7–45–0			15–3–78–0	16.4–2–72–2				1		4	285	2
v. Hampshire (Worcester)		16–6–35–2		16–1–46–1	18–8–63–0	14–3–61–1	6.3–1–20–2			12–2–28–2						2	6	1	9	261	8
4–6 August		7–1–16–1		11–0–48–2	24–5–81–1		11–1–48–0			5–1–32–2		3–0–21–0				1	4		2	251	6
v. Lancashire (Old Trafford)		19–5–61–2		18–2–64–0	27–7–74–3		6–1–23–0			10–1–37–0	3–0–13–0	17–6–37–0		11.2–2–32–0		1	7		8	349	5
7–10 August																				0	0
v. Somerset (Weston-super-Mare)		26.2–8–48–2		26–7–70–2					40–14–112–5	10–4–25–1		14–4–24–0			7–0–24–0	6	19	1	7	328	10
18–20 August		4–0–30–0		6–1–16–1					15–1–60–2	5–1–17–0		12.2–1–50–1					2			175	4
v. Durham (Worcester)		21–3–60–5		15–1–62–1		9.3–2–35–2			9–6–14–0	12–4–26–1							2		16	199	10
21–24 August		7–0–21–1		12–4–41–0		6.3–0–38–0			4–1–36–0	4–1–16–0	6–1–17–0	7–2–19–1				8	3		5	199	2
v. Nottinghamshire (Worcester)		4–0–17–0		22–4–42–3	34–7–111–4	12–2–47–0	8–0–24–1			18–5–65–1		1–0–2–0				2	11		5	321	9
26–29 August																					
v. Warwickshire (Worcester)		14–3–47–0		13–5–22–1	39–12–56–2	6–0–18–0	12–5–32–3			6–2–14–0	2–1–4–0	2–0–9–0				1	7	4	1	210	6
31 August–3 September																					
v. Hampshire (Southampton)		18–4–39–2		19–5–51–3	22.3–9–39–3	13–0–23–0				7–1–30–0	1–0–1–0				12–3–34–1		14	1	8	231	9
12–15 September		8–0–32–0		12–3–22–1	18–6–40–0	6–0–23–0		1–0–5–0		15–3–38–3		22.1–2–84–1	2–0–10–0			4	3		8	261	5
Bowlers average	25–7– 57–0 –	532.2–99– 1670–60 27.83	72–13– 249–8 31.12	618.2–130– 1770–68 26.02	635.3–185– 1580–42 37.61	379.3–44– 1257–35 35.91	124.3–37– 352–8 44.00	10–2– 33–0 –	336.5–80– 1054–28 37.64	239–56– 726–18 40.33	74–9– 237–2 118.50	153.4–29– 536–10 53.60	24–2– 116–2 58.00	45.2–13– 128–0 –	19–3– 58–1 58.00						

A Asif Mujtaba absent hurt
B. M.D. Marshall

YORKSHIRE CCC

BATTING

Player	v. Surrey (The Oval) 25–29 April		v. Hampshire (Leeds) 7–10 May		v. Gloucestershire (Leeds) 14–17 May		v. Kent (Canterbury) 20–22 May		v. Oxford University (Oxford) 29 May–1 June		v. Hampshire (Basingstoke) 2–4 June		v. Somerset (Middlesbrough) 5–8 June		v. Derbyshire (Harrogate) 12–15 June		v. Essex (Leeds) 16–18 June		v. Worcestershire (Worcester) 19–22 June		v. Leicestershire (Sheffield) 3–6 July		v. Warwickshire (Sheffield) 14–16 July		M	Inns	NO	Runs	HS	Av
M.D. Moxon	141	–											117	–	64	–	7	–	47	17	7	–	34	28*	18	27	2	1314	183	52.56
A.A. Metcalfe	73	–	1	27*	4	10					39	38											26	–	11	17	1	422	73	26.37
S.A. Kellett	49	–	19	37	15	38	90	0			29	37	87	–	15	–	22	–	0	29	41	–	59	32*	22	36	1	1326	96	37.88
D. Byas	1	–	0	9*	29	11	51	82			24	4	0	–	12	–	55	–	16	7	22	–	52	–	20	30	4	784	100	30.15
P.W. Jarvis	62	–									9*	–									–	–	–	–	15	14	4	374	80	37.40
R.J. Blakey	12	–	72	–	66	24	28	95*			20	38	5	–	24	–	32	–	57	5	7	–	10	–	21	32	9	1065	125*	46.30
A.P. Grayson	57	–	10	–	0	6																			6	6	–	116	57	19.33
C.S. Pickles	49	–	21	–	0	2	3	17																	6	9	1	131	49	16.37
P. Carrick	6*	–	6*	–	7	3	0	3			18	4	26*	–	13*	–	19	–	3	0	–	–	13	–	19	25	5	261	46	13.05
J.D. Batty	0*	–			19	0*	–	–			1	–	–	–	0	–	49	–					–	–	18	15	4	155	49	14.09
D. Gough	6	–	2	–	22*	0	–	–			8	9*	4*	–	0	–	0	–	1	3	–	–			11	12	4	72	22*	9.00
S.R. Tendulkar			86	–	92	23	15	8			0	34	13	–	89	–	93	–	42	46	23	–			16	25	2	1070	100	46.52
P.J. Hartley			0	–	3	0	61*	4			46	0	15	–	10	–	8	–	7	1	17*	–	20*	–	20	23	3	353	69	17.65
M.A. Robinson			12	–									–	–	0	–	1*	–	0*	0	–	–	–	–	17	12	5	31	12	4.42
B. Parker							7	30																	1	2	–	37	30	18.50
C. White							63*	38			10	35*	38	–	53	–	69	–	31	79*	74*	–	54*	–	19	26	8	859	79*	47.72
S.M. Milburn																			2*	5					1	2	1	7	5	7.00
C.A. Chapman																									1	1	1	8	8*	–
Byes	3		4		4		5	6				12							5		5		5							
Leg-byes	11		13		3	6	4	4			6	8	8		5		5		5	5	6		12	1						
Wides							4								1					2	1		4	1						
No-balls	25		4	1	8	11	9	5				3	4		19		1		18	8	4		12							
Total	495		250	74	272	134	340	292			210	222	317		305		361		234	207	207		301	62						
Wickets	9		10	1	10	10	7	8			10	7	7		10		10		9	10	5		6	0						
Result	D		D		L		D		Ab.		D		D		W		W		L		D		L							
Points	8		5		5		6		–		3		7		22		23		5		0		2							

BATTING

Player	v. Gloucestershire (Cheltenham) 17–20 July		v. Glamorgan (Cardiff) 21–23 July		v. Lancashire (Leeds) 31 July–3 August		v. Durham (Durham) 4–6 August		v. Northamptonshire (Northampton) 7–10 August		v. Middlesex (Uxbridge) 14–17 August		v. Nottinghamshire (Scarborough) 18–20 August		v. Surrey (Bradford) 21–24 August		v. Lancashire (Old Trafford) 26–29 August		v. Northamptonshire (Scarborough) 31 August–3 September		v. Sussex (Hove) 12–15 September		M	Inns	NO	Runs	HS	Av
M.D. Moxon	183	14	103	–	90	25	25	44	8	1	5	18	25	–	48	–	–	21	77	101*	14	50	18	27	2	1314	183	52.56
A.A. Metcalfe											21	3	22	–	35	–	–	34	36	0	43	10	11	17	1	422	73	26.37
S.A. Kellett	50	7	1	1	91	89	6	30	9	41	25	16	30	–	78	–	–	39	96	29	53	36	22	36	1	1326	96	37.88
D. Byas	0	1*	10	68*	27	6	37	11	8	37*					70	–	–	–	100	–	10	24	20	30	4	784	100	30.15
P.W. Jarvis	30*	–	45	–	–	21*	0	–	16	12*	11	–	55	–	15	–	–	–	80	–	0	18	15	14	4	374	80	37.40
R.J. Blakey	1	–	125*	21*	22*	63	0	26*	11	6	46	43*	112*	–			–	0*	17	26*	23	28	21	32	9	1065	125*	46.30
A.P. Grayson															40	–	–	–	3	–			6	6	–	116	57	19.33
C.S. Pickles									20	19*					0	–							6	9	1	131	49	16.37
P. Carrick	20	–	0	–	–	1*	3	46	1	–	11	16	19	–							0	23	19	25	5	261	46	13.05
J.D. Batty	0	4*	–	–	–	–	5	–			37*	–	16	–	0	–	–	–	1	–	5	18	18	15	4	155	49	14.09
D. Gough									17*	–													11	12	4	72	22*	9.00
S.R. Tendulkar	45	–	18	7	56*	48	21	100	24	6	82	77*	22	–									16	25	2	1070	100	46.52
P.J. Hartley	9	–	6	–	–	–	0	–			1	–	69	–	19	–	–	–	34	–	0	23	20	23	3	353	69	17.65
M.A. Robinson	4	–	–	–	–	–	4*	–	0	–	2	–	–	–			–	–	2*	–	1	5*	17	12	5	31	12	4.42
B. Parker																							1	2	–	37	30	18.50
C. White	0	–	35	–	–	12	5	5*	35	40	27	–	2	–	3	–	–	24*	43	13	71*	0	19	26	8	859	79*	47.72
S.M. Milburn																							1	2	1	7	5	7.00
C.A. Chapman															8*	–							1	1	1	8	8*	–
Byes		1		4		4		1	5	3		8	1		1				6		4	4						
Leg-byes	9		4		11	10	1		2	8	2	8	13		14			3	10	2	2	11						
Wides				1	1	2	1						1						2			1						
No-balls	13	3	1		2	2			2	1	16	5	17		10				1		6	8						
Total	364	30	348	102	300	283	108	263	158	174	286	194	404		341	0	0	121	508	171	232	259						
Wickets	10	2	8	2	3	6	10	5	10	5	10	4	9		10	0	0	3	10	3	10	10						
Result	D		D		W		W		D		L		D		L		D		D		L							
Points	8		4		23		20		5		5		8		3		2		5		2							

FIELDING FIGURES

49 – R.J. Blakey (ct 44/st 5)
30 – D. Byas
23 – S.A. Kellett
14 – C. White
10 – S.R. Tendulkar
8 – M.D. Moxon
6 – P.J. Hartley and P. Carrick
4 – A.A. Metcalfe and M.A. Robinson
3 – J.D. Batty, A.P. Grayson and D. Gough
2 – C.S. Pickles and P.W. Jarvis
1 – B. Parker, C.A. Chapman and sub

YORKSHIRE CCC

BOWLING

	P.W. Jarvis	D. Gough	C.S. Pickles	P. Carrick	J.D. Batty	P.J. Hartley	M.A. Robinson	S.R. Tendulkar	S.M. Milburn	C. White	M.D. Moxon	A.P. Grayson	Byes	Leg-byes	Wides	No-balls	Total	Wkts
v. Surrey (The Oval)	3.1–0–14–1	18–6–43–4	15.5–5–28–1	26.5–7–60–4	4–0–11–0								4	4			164	10
25–29 April		4–0–16–0	8–2–16–1	6–2–6–0	12–5–18–1								7	1	1	1	64	2
v. Hampshire (Leeds)		25–4–90–0	20–4–66–1	29.1–6–75–3		33–12–85–3	16–0–56–1	7–1–11–0					1	13	1	18	397	8
7–10 May																		
v. Gloucestershire (Leeds)		21–5–76–0	12–4–36–2	51–19–88–3	26–5–102–0	24.2–3–65–2		15–4–35–2					4	5	1	12	411	10
14–17 May		15–5–35–1	1.5–0–2–2	21–5–44–2	4–1–9–0	19–3–48–5								4			142	10
v. Kent (Canterbury)		25–7–97–3	18–3–93–0	23–4–76–0	11–0–74–1	27–3–117–3		6–1–17–0					4	2	3	11	480	7
20–22 May		8–0–51–0	3–0–23–0			10–1–44–2		5–0–27–0					2	6		1	153	2
v. Oxford University (Oxford)																		Ab.
29 May–1 June																		
v. Hampshire (Basingstoke)	17–3–52–0	24–8–79–2		15–4–34–1	27.4–7–75–4	28–6–70–1		8–0–33–1						8			351	9
2–4 June																		
v. Somerset (Middlesbrough)		5–0–17–0		23–6–58–6	4–2–4–0	16–2–52–1	16–3–34–3							2		6	167	10
5–8 June		3–0–22–0			4–0–18–0		1–0–17–0									2	57	0
v. Derbyshire (Harrogate)		9–2–29–1		37.3–15–58–4	23–2–84–4	16–3–43–1	9–4–12–0							1	1	2	227	10
12–15 June		3–2–1–2		18–13–15–3	13.2–4–34–4	8–2–17–1							4	3		1	74	10
v. Essex (Leeds)		19.1–4–57–0		15–4–39–1	4–2–7–0	23.5–4–66–3	23.3–3–48–5							6	1	7	223	10
16–18 June		14–7–12–3		5–2–15–1		11–1–32–1	12–6–20–4						2	2	2	8	83	10
v. Worcestershire (Worcester)		23–1–99–3		29.1–11–52–1		25–9–82–2	27–5–70–3	4–1–8–0	17–2–61–0				1	13		13	386	9
19–22 June		5–0–32–0		9–2–16–2			6–1–14–1		11–0–54–1				16	12		2	144	4
v. Leicestershire (Sheffield)	15–8–32–4	12–2–41–2		8–2–11–0		9–0–29–0	2–0–5–0	1–0–8–0						6		5	132	6
3–6 July																		
v. Warwickshire (Sheffield)	7–3–16–0			11–2–20–0	5–2–9–0	8–3–9–0	8–1–27–0							7		6	88	0
14–16 July	16–1–50–2			28–6–69–1	14–2–45–0	16–3–47–1	16.3–1–55–3						4	6		3	276	7
v. Gloucestershire (Cheltenham)	18–4–65–2			18–6–50–2	5–1–10–0	23.1–4–66–5	19–3–59–1							7		10	257	10
17–20 July																		
v. Glamorgan (Cardiff)	15–5–48–0			32–16–51–2	14–4–30–1	17–6–27–2	12–3–29–0						4	11		4	200	6
21–23 July	10–1–42–2			12–2–49–0	17–3–59–3	7–2–30–1	7–1–25–1						6	8		3	219	9
v. Lancashire (Leeds)	20–4–77–3			44–11–129–4	9–0–52–0	18–2–58–0	19–4–71–1							12	1	6	399	8
31 July–3 August	10–4–12–0			6–3–8–0	11–3–29–0	14–1–38–2	9–0–41–1	2.3–0–28–0		3–0–22–0				4		5	182	3
v. Durham (Durham)	19–3–49–3			12–5–26–1	12–5–16–0	14–3–62–0	21.1–4–57–6							4		9	214	10
4–6 August	15–4–43–4			1–0–2–0		11–0–51–1	20.1–5–44–4	3–0–6–0			3–0–7–0			2		7	155	10
v. Northamptonshire	17–7–45–2	15–0–81–3	17.3–3–40–4	13–4–24–0			17–9–24–1						4	6		7	224	10
(Northampton) 7–10 August	12–1–54–1	7–0–32–1	11–2–41–3				16–2–38–2						4	5			174	7
v. Middlesex (Uxbridge)	18–4–42–0			25.3–9–59–1	16–2–49–0	23–6–64–2	16–2–31–3						4	1	1	4	250	6
14–17 August	11–2–49–1			12–0–59–2	9.1–0–44–0	7–0–33–0	6–0–31–0						10	8		1	234	4
v. Nottinghamshire (Scarborough)	10–2–21–0			8–1–28–0	5–1–12–3	15–3–40–3	12.1–2–36–3	6–1–13–1						2	1	14	152	10
18–20 August	28–4–91–2			38–14–60–2	32–10–75–2	19–4–62–2	18–5–44–0	5–2–9–0					1	11		6	353	8
v. Surrey (Bradford)	9–2–18–1		2–1–2–0			7–1–19–0										1	39	1
21–24 August	19.4–2–65–3		11–2–40–0		35–7–114–2	17–4–51–3						10–2–26–0		10		6	306	9
v. Lancashire (Old Trafford)	23–5–55–2				21–3–122–2	18–0–72–1	22–2–66–1					12–1–60–0	6	3		3	384	6
26–29 August																	0	0
v. Northamptonshire (Scarborough)	25–10–38–0				44–11–122–1	18–3–48–0	35.2–11–62–6					23–2–79–1	5	5		10	359	8
31 August–3 September	18.5–1–80–3				18–1–95–4	9–0–44–0	9–0–46–0					5–0–21–0	7	5		3	298	8
v. Sussex (Hove)	27–6–79–0			52–21–93–1	17–2–64–1	37.2–7–111–8	18–2–72–0						4	9		17	432	
12–15 September	10–3–27–4			1–0–1–0	8.5–2–25–0	2–0–8–0										1	61	4
	393.4–89–	255.1–53–	120.1–26–	630.1–202–	426–87–	550.4–101–	413.5–79–	62.3–10–	28–2–	3–0–	3–0–	50–5–						
	1164–40	910–25	387–14	1375–47	1408–33	1690–56	1134–50	195–4	115–1	22–0	7–0	186–1						
Bowlers average	29.10	36.40	27.64	29.25	42.66	30.17	22.68	48.75	115.00	–	–	186.00